20th-CENTURY
AMERICAN LITERATURE

GREAT WRITERS STUDENT LIBRARY

Editor: James Vinson
Associate Editor: D. L. Kirkpatrick

20th-CENTURY
AMERICAN LITERATURE

INTRODUCTION BY
WARREN FRENCH

M

First published 1980 by
THE MACMILLAN PRESS LIMITED
London and Basingstoke
Associated companies in New York, Dublin
Melbourne, Johannesburg and Madras

ISBN 0333 29334 1

CONTENTS

EDITOR'S NOTE

The entry for each writer consists of a biography, a complete list of his published books, a selected list of published bibliographies and critical studies on the writer, and a signed critical essay on his work.

In the biographies, details of education, military service, and marriage(s) are generally given before the usual chronological summary of the life of the writer; awards and honours are given last.

The Publications section is meant to include all book publications, though as a rule broadsheets, single sermons and lectures, minor pamphlets, exhibition catalogues, etc. are omitted. Under the heading Collections, we have listed the most recent collections of the complete works and those of individual genres (verse, plays, novels, stories, and letters); only those collections which have some editorial authority and were issued after the writer's death are listed; on-going editions are indicated by a dash after the date of publication; often a general selection from the writer's works or a selection from the works in the individual genres listed above is included.

Titles are given in modern spelling, though the essayists were allowed to use original spelling for titles and quotations; often the titles are "short." The date given is that of the first book publication, which often followed the first periodical or anthology publication by some time; we have listed the actual year of publication, often different from that given on the title-page. No attempt has been made to indicate which works were published anonymously or pseudonymously, or which works of fiction were published in more than one volume. We have listed plays which were produced but not published; librettos and musical plays are listed along with the other plays; no attempt has been made to list lost or unverified plays. Reprints of books (including facsimile editions) and revivals of plays are not listed unless a revision or change of title is involved. The most recent edited version of individual works is included if it supersedes the collected edition cited.

In the essays, short references to critical remarks refer to items cited in the Publications section or in the Reading List. Introductions, memoirs, editorial matter, etc. in works cited in the Publications section are not repeated in the Reading List.

INTRODUCTION

"In your rocking-chair, by your window, shall you dream such happiness as you may never feel." Thus ends Theodore Dreiser's *Sister Carrie,* the first outstanding American novel of the twentieth century, published in 1900, though largely ignored for the next ten years. Dreiser's description of Carrie's fate is uncannily prophetic of what awaits the protagonists of the major American literary works for the next eight decades that we can now recognize as the Age of Modernism. Dreiser brought to a reluctant United States a Modernist sensibility characterized by a feeling of isolation and alienation from an urbanized, mechanized society.

Dreiser was ahead of his time, however, even though he had conceived all of the novels that he would publish – including his Cowperwood trilogy about a corrupt businessman – by 1914. The "pre-Modernists," conventionally labeled "realists," gave up slowly and grudgingly the struggle to dominate American taste with the dogma that William Dean Howells had pronounced – that the writer "can no longer expect to be received on the ground of entertainment only; he assumes a higher function, something like that of a physician or priest," working within established society to adjust the individual to its institutions. While the Modernists were not content, either, only to entertain, they saw themselves as enemies of oppressive social institutions, presenting the individual's only hope as lying in flight.

1. The Age of Innocence, 1900–19

The beginning of the twentieth century was more than an arbitrary chronological dividing line in American literature. Few established writers of the previous century produced significant work after 1900; and the early death of Stephen Crane, who envisioned the individual transcendence of society in *The Red Badge of Courage* and his bitterly ironic poems, deprived us of a key transitional figure. Howells bravely attempted to maintain the status quo in *The Son of Royal Langbrith* (1904); but his subsequent work retreated to the midwest of his own childhood before the Civil War. Mark Twain's writings became so angry and bitter that readers shunned *What Is Man?* (1906) and *The Mysterious Stranger* (1916). Only Henry James produced triumphant curtain calls – *The Wings of the Dove* (1902), *The Golden Bowl* (1904), and *The Ambassadors* (1903), in which Lambert Strether's last eloquent speech – "That, you see, is my only logic. Not, out of the whole affair, to have got anything for myself" – definitively enunciates just as the voices of the pre-Modernists were fading into silence the altruistic principles their age failed to realize in practice.

Except for Booth Tarkington, who offered an indulgent criticism of the middle class in *The Magnificent Ambersons* (1918) and the Penrod stories, the novelists who flourished during the first years of the twentieth century were "muckrakers" concerned about the social breakdown resulting from persons in responsible positions seeking to get everything for themselves. These writers continued, however, to try to work within the Establishment, hoping that it might yet prove capable of reform. *The Thirteenth District* (1902) by Brand Whitlock, who became a reform mayor of Toledo, Ohio, was less successful than David Graham Phillips's exposure of New York City corruption in novels like *Susan Lenox: Her Fall and Rise* (1917). Winston Churchill (no kin to the British political leader) explored such problems against American historical backgrounds in novels like *The Crisis* (1901) and *Coniston* (1906).

By far the most popular and successful of the novelists who indicted American business ethics, however, was Upton Sinclair, whose *The Jungle* (1906) led to reform of the meat-packing industry. Although Sinclair continued to expose corruption for another thirty years and even ran for governor of California, he never equaled his early success until during World War II when he began a series of eleven novels about a kind of cosmopolitan superhero, Lanny Budd. Most critics, however, found the premise that altruistic and patriotic supermen could take over and redeem the international industrial/military complex old-fashioned.

The Modernist concept of escape began to dominate American writing with the fiction of Jack London. Though presumably a Socialist who predicted the return of a primitive Golden Age following a Fascist revolution in *The Iron Heel* (1908), London praised the Nietzschean superman in *The Sea-Wolf* (1904) and, in his most self-revelatory tale, *Martin Eden* (1909), portrayed a hero driven at last to suicide by the personal and political problems that he sought vainly to solve. George Cabot Lodge's even more bleakly cynical *The Genius of the Commonplace,* suppressed by the Howells consistory and only recently published, dramatizes the disillusionment as the century began of even Boston's traditionalist Brahmin society, as does also the posthumously published *Education of Henry Adams* (1918, privately printed in 1907) by the scholarly scion of one of the nation's most famous families. The collapse of the venerated role of the aristocrat as guardian of public morals finds its ultimate statement in philosopher George Santayana's novel *The Last Puritan* (1935).

The transition to Modernism was made most importantly but much less violently in the works of three distinguished women novelists who tempered their traditional conservatism with an awareness that the past was irretrievable in a changing world. Edith Wharton, one of the few American writers born into the wealthy international set, symbolically provided the name for the period that ended exactly with the appearance of her novel in *The Age of Innocence* (1920), which depicts the cost in human happiness of the rigid rules regulating New York's Victorian society. Earlier, in *The House of Mirth* (1905), she had shown the suicidal cost of attempting to play society's games. Most of her other fiction portrayed ironically international society, except for *Ethan Frome* (1911), which disposed of dreams of primitive virtue by showing how bad things could be in backwoods New England. Ellen Glasgow offered a similarly cheerless picture of another traditional society in her native Virginia.

More complex and most important is the fiction of Willa Cather, which seemed to offer fresh hope in two epic tributes to the passing frontier, *O Pioneers!* (1913) and *My Ántonia* (1918). Later, however, after she made the statement that her world fell apart in 1922 (the year of Eliot's *The Waste Land*), her fiction, especially *A Lost Lady* (1923) and *The Professor's House* (1925), reflected a bitter disillusionment with contemporary materialistic society. Her increasing desire to escape into memories of a more glorious past colors two of her finest works, *Death Comes for the Archbishop* (1927) and *Shadows on the Rock* (1931).

The Modernist sensibility also manifested itself in American poetry almost exactly at the turn of the century, when the genteel influence of New England's "fireside poets" was ebbing. About the only traditional poet active at the turn of the century likely to be anthologized today is William Vaughn Moody, whose "An Ode in Time of Hesitation" (1901) exactly captures in its title the bankruptcy of America's genteel dream in the face of a growing imperialism. Moody's Harvard friends, Trumbull Stickney and George Cabot Lodge, were already sounding in their poetry the notes of alienation and the rejection of American culture that would characterize Modernist expatriate writings; but both men died – like Stephen Crane – early in the century. Even Moody turned principally to drama before his death in 1910.

At first a dark new vision manifested itself in American poetry through the ironic regionalism of Edwin Arlington Robinson's *The Children of the Night* (1897) and Edgar Lee Masters's *Spoon River Anthology* (1915). Robert Frost's *A Boy's Will* (1913) and *North of Boston* (1914) exhibit a wider range of sympathies; but all are unprecedented psychological probings of determined and frustrated villagers and farmers from New England and the Midwest. Vachel Lindsay's attempt to promote "the higher vaudeville" through his "Gospel of Beauty," as exemplified by *General William Booth Enters into Heaven and Other Poems* (1913) also emphasized the use of small town figures and native legendry in a new "public poetry."

The triumph of an urban, cosmopolitan, elitist viewpoint was signaled, however, by the most important event in the development of twentieth-century American poetry, Harriet Monroe's founding in Chicago in 1912 of *Poetry: A Magazine of Verse,* which still remains the journal in which poets courting recognition wish to be published. An indifferent poet herself, Monroe helped re-establish the Whitman strain in American poetry by her early support of Carl Sandburg's Chicago songs; but her influence was more widely felt when she became allied with the international Imagist movement, led by Bostonian heiress Amy Lowell and her cohort and later bitter foe, Ezra Pound. Pound had removed to Europe in 1908 and had begun to develop an international reputation as a translator; but he was to loom largest when he turned to bitter social criticism after World War I.

The American drama made less progress than other native arts between 1900 and World War I. At the peak of its popularity during these years before it was seriously challenged by the cinema, the American theater was also at the nadir of its never previously very impressive artistic power. Turn of the century audiences favored exotic romantic works produced with elaborate naturalistic scenery, like David Belasco's *Madame Butterfly* (1900) and *The Girl of the Golden West* (1905), which live on as the basis for Puccini's operas. Genteel longings for a theater that combined high art with high seriousness were vainly focused upon William Vaughn Moody's idealistic appeals for human dignity in *The Great Divide* (1906) and *The Faith Healer* (1909) and Percy MacKaye's spectacular historical dramas like *The Scarecrow* (1908). Almost none of the hundreds of American dramas produced between 1900 and 1915 are revived today, even as period curiosities; the event that was to prove the equivalent for American drama of what the founding of *Poetry* magazine had been for American poetry was the establishment in 1915 of the Provincetown Players, which began in 1916 to produce the one-act plays of Eugene O'Neill, subsequently grouped as *The Long Voyage Home.*

Memorable American humor was also in short supply early in the century. Many of Mark Twain's later and bitter works were withheld from the public, while Finley Peter Dunne and George Ade did not repeat their initial successes with folksy humor in *Mr. Dooley in Peace and in War* (1898) and *Fables in Slang* (1900). Vaudeville and film clowns like W. C. Fields, Charlie Chaplin, and the Keystone Cops had taken over.

2. The Triumph of Modernism, 1919–29

Just as the decade of boom and bust really began with the end of World War I, so 1919 also marked the Modernist breakthrough in American fiction with the publication of Sherwood Anderson's *Winesburg, Ohio* and James Branch Cabell's *Jurgen.* These were joined the next year by Edith Wharton's *The Age of Innocence,* F. Scott Fitzgerald's *This Side of Paradise,* Eugene O'Neill's first full-length plays and the collected lyrics of Edna St. Vincent Millay. Above all 1920 brought Sinclair Lewis's *Main Street,* which lambasted the ugliness, complacency and vulgarity of the small Midwestern town and satirized the death of the pioneering spirit. These set the tone for the decade; sympathetic novels about rural America, like Rølvaag's immigrant epic, *Giants in the Earth* (1927), were rare.

Although Anderson's subsequent stories and Cabell's further legends of the mythical Poictesme were not widely read, Sinclair Lewis became the country's most famous novelist with *Babbitt* (1922), which provided the derogatory tag still attached to the kind of fatuous community booster it depicted; *Arrowsmith* (1925), about the persecution that drives a genuinely idealistic doctor into exile; *Elmer Gantry* (1927), about the hypocritical religious revivalists who save souls for the preacher's profit; and *Dodsworth* (1929), Lewis's first sympathetic international novel about a retired business man who goes abroad to find a decent life. These confirmations of the European intelligentsia's view of the parvenu excesses of the United States led to Lewis's becoming in 1930 the first American to win the Nobel Prize for literature.

None of Lewis's novels so well epitomizes, however, the reaction of a Modernist sensibility to a demoralized United States as F. Scott Fitzgerald's *The Great Gatsby* (1925), which presents Jay Gatsby, born James Gatz, who "springs from his Platonic conception of himself," as the possessor of "some heightened sensitivity to the promises of life," which in his innocence and ignorance, he puts at "the service of a vast, vulgar, and meretricious beauty," only to be destroyed by "what foul dust floated in the wake of his dreams." Although he became a legendary figure himself, Fitzgerald never matched *The Great Gatsby.* His novel about expatriate society, *Tender Is the Night,* never found its final form; and his tale of Hollywood, *The Last Tycoon,* is only a collection of brilliant fragments.

Fitzgerald's accomplishment in *Gatsby* was not quickly recognized because it was overshadowed in 1925 by the long-awaited publication of Dreiser's *An American Tragedy.* Though the novel does in a way epitomize the decadence of twentieth-century American society by portraying the inexorable way in which the appeal of quick material rewards ultimately destroys an attractive, impressionable, but not too bright youth, readers of a faster-paced age began to lose patience with Dreiser's lumbering style and heavy-handed moralizing.

Fitzgerald's reputation was also for years overshadowed by that of his sometime friend, often bitter foe and critic, the fellow expatriate Ernest Hemingway. Hemingway leaped to fame as the principal spokesman for the "lost generation" in his novels *The Sun Also Rises* (1926), about an aimless group of American expatriates in Europe after World War I, and *A Farewell to Arms* (1929), with its tragic message, set against the background of an Italian retreat during the war, that even the man who wishes to make "a separate peace" is at the mercy of a nature that man's puny dreams cannot control.

Like Hemingway, John Dos Passos began his literary career after serving as an ambulance driver in World War I and became subsequently involved in the Spanish Civil War. His *One Man's Initiation – 1917* (1919) and *Three Soldiers* (1921) rank with *A Farewell to Arms* as the classic American accounts of World War I. Dos Passos then went on to develop the technique of a montage novel in order to present first a cross-section of the chaos of New York City life in *Manhattan Transfer* (1925), and then an epic portrait of the decay of American life and values in the three novels constituting the *U.S.A.* trilogy – *The 42nd Parallel* (1930), *1919* (1932), and *The Big Money* (1936), which portrays the spectacular excesses leading to the stock market crash through a variety of factual and fictional materials.

The famous appellation "lost generation" for those morally disoriented by World War I has been attributed to Gertrude Stein's impatience with a Parisian auto mechanic. Whether or not she can be credited with the phrase, this redoubtable avant-garde writer, an expatriate since 1902, when she began to feel stifled by American conventionality, was the center of the American literary community in France between the World Wars. Her experimental works are also both thematically and formally at the very center of the Modernist tradition because of their attempt, on one hand, to adapt for literary purposes the techniques of the cubist painters like Picasso and, on the other, to portray the pointlessness and frustration of women's lives, from the clearly delineated portrayals of long-suffering women in *Three Lives* (1909) through the mazes of the massive *The Making of Americans* (1925) to the mysterious *Ida* (1941) and her opera librettos like *Four Saints in Three Acts* (1934, with music by Virgil Thomson). Despite the range and variety of her incessant experiments, however, Stein's reputation with the general public rested on *The Autobiography of Alice B. Toklas* (1933), her account of her life with her long-time companion.

Few other expatriates or experimentalists shared her fame. Djuna Barnes is known almost entirely for *Nightwood* (1936), a stream-of-consciousness novel about disturbed people; none of Glenway Wescott's other works enjoyed the popularity of his early *The Grandmothers* (1927), about a pioneering Wisconsin family as seen through the eyes of an expatriate descendant; and the lives of writers like Robert McAlmon, Harry and Caresse Crosby, and Charles Henri Ford remain better known than their works. Not all the uprooted went to Paris. The still mysterious B. Traven (Traven Torsvan?), wrote social protest novels like *The Death Ship* in Mexico for initial publication in Germany. Americans preferred, however, the exoticism of one of Gertrude Stein's friends, Thornton Wilder, whose *The Bridge of San Luis Rey* (1927), about an inscrutable tragedy in 18th century Peru, became one best-selling novel of permanent value.

Some writers like Maxwell Bodenheim (*Replenishing Jessica,* 1925) and Carl Van Vechten (*Peter Whiffle,* 1922) simply fled the midwest for Greenwich Village, where they joined poets like E. E. Cummings and Edna St. Vincent Millay in turning out highly stylized and wittily cynical works about the jazz age that are valued today principally as period pieces. Van Vechten, however, achieved a more enduring reputation through his association with the Harlem Renaissance, which he depicted with sympathetic realism in *Nigger Heaven* (1926).

This Harlem Renaissance of the 1920's provided the first serious opportunity for black writers to depict a developing black culture in a black community, in the hope of cultivating a black audience; but their contemporary audiences were largely sympathetic white patrons. Black writers had been producing notable novels since late in the nineteenth century; but the works of Charles W. Chesnutt, like *The Wife of His Youth* (1899), and James Weldon Johnson's *The Autobiography of an Ex-Colored Man* (1912) dealt principally with the problems of light-skinned blacks "passing" for whites to overcome the handicaps of racial prejudices. Encouraged, however, by the freedom of "jazz age" Harlem, blacks like sociologist-educator W. E. B. DuBois and Claude McKay began to produce distinguished novels about the problems of aspiring members of a black community that would be fragmented again by the Depression.

Most striking of these novels was the long-neglected but now much discussed *Cane* (1923) by Jean Toomer, a mysterious figure of uncertain origins who abandoned a promising career to devote himself to the teachings of philosopher Georgi Gurdjieff. A collage of stories, songs, and plays, *Cane* has often been the subject of pointless controversy over its form; what matters is that Toomer uses all the means at his disposal to dramatize the plight of blacks twice alienated both by race and the common neglect of artists in the twentieth century.

Although Langston Hughes has written one of the finest novels about black life, *Not Without Laughter* (1930), he is best known for his stories of a black folk-philosopher, Simple, and the poetry in which he experimented with the use of black folk song and jazz rhythms. Countée Cullen also experimented with lyrical forms in *The Ballad of the Brown Girl* (1927) and *The Black Christ* (1929), but he used traditional English forms and, as Gerald Moore explains, "attacked the whole notion of an American-Negro school of poetry and urged the importance of the Anglo-American poetic tradition upon his fellow black writers."

Cullen's attitude was closely in tune with the most respected poets of the decade who viewed their dissolute period with dismay. Ezra Pound launched the attack in 1920 with his "Mauberley" poems. The opening stanza of *Hugh Selwyn Mauberley* epitomizes the Modernist poet's state of mind: "For three years, out of key with his time,/He strove to resuscitate the dead art/Of poetry; to maintain 'The sublime'/In the old sense. Wrong from the start –." Pound's increasing displeasure took the form of a long series of "Cantos," collages of miscellaneous erudition drawn from cultures of all times and all places mixed with the rantings against modern economic and political systems that became the substance also of his increasingly frequent prose polemics. While a small cult of ultra-elitists has admired these works hysterically, most readers have found them too cryptic, dogmatic, or offensive. Pound ultimately became much more a political symbol than a poetic force when, after making propaganda broadcasts for Italy's fascist government during World War II, he was arrested for treason and confined for some years in an insane asylum.

Pound's place in the poetic hierachy was early usurped, however unintentionally, by his major discovery, T. S. Eliot, an American expatriate in London, whose *The Waste Land* (1922) became the most quoted and imitated poem of the century – the high-water mark of the Modernist era. It is entirely possible to take at face value the statement attributed to Eliot that to him the poem was "only the relief of a personal and wholly insignificant grouse against life" and yet to maintain as I have in *The Twenties* that it is "the embodiment of a world-view widely characteristic of thoughtful and sensitive individuals during the 1920s." Eliot's personal protest happened to give voice to the feelings of the sensitive persons of a generally gross age.

Yet, despite the idolization of Eliot, there were vigorous dissenters from his view. Chief among these were Hart Crane and William Carlos Williams, who could only begin to win proper recognition when Eliot's influence began to wane after World War II. As Donald Pease points out, Hart Crane felt that it was Eliot who had to be transcended in creating *The Bridge* (1930), his "epic of modern consciousness." Although scholars still debate the "unity" of Crane's mystical epic with some finding it only a chaos of fragments like the age it mirrors, others find its vast structure a coherent reinvigoration of the lapsed tradition of Walt Whitman (whom Eliot greatly mistrusted).

Williams even more indignantly protested that "Eliot returned us to the classroom just at the moment when I felt that we were on the point of escape ... to a new art form ... rooted in the locality which should give it fruit." As Robert K. Johnson points out, Williams put forward, against Eliot's increasingly metaphysical concerns, a creed based on the beauty contained in physical reality that is best illustrated by his own epic of the commonplace, *Paterson* (1946–58), based on impressions of his home city in New Jersey.

Another dissenting voice took an even bleaker view than Eliot's of the contemporary world and the entire human experience. Also going against the grain of an age that cultivated principally the brief lyric by writing long blank verse narratives about the forbidding California coast near Big Sur, where he lived, Robinson Jeffers in works like *Tamar* (1924) and *Roan Stallion* (1925) shocked readers with his misanthropic legends of violent, amoral people bent on courses leading to self-destruction.

Although Jeffers considered protest only a bubble "in the molten mass," some surfaced in Greenwich Village in the typographically eccentric satires of E. E. Cummings like "Poem, or Beauty Hurts Mr. Vinal" and "Next to Of Course God America I," which are still unmatched vignettes of empty-headed pomposity. One other New York writer who managed to maintain a unique stability in the midst of madness was Marianne Moore, editor of the revived *The Dial* (1926–29), who persisted throughout the years in viewing poets as "liberators of the imagination."

A once enormously admired poem that has been virtually forgotten over a half century is Stephen Vincent Benét's *John Brown's Body* (1928), an epic account of the Civil War from a Union point of view. Americans have lost their taste for historical epics, for the fate of Benét's work was shared by Archibald MacLeish's narration of Cortez's conquest of Mexico, *Conquistador* (1932), though MacLeish's shorter "Ars Poetica" has continued to be regarded, perhaps wrongly, as a statement of the Modernist aesthetic, just as his much anthologized "You, Andrew Marvell" sums up a cyclical theory of destiny.

The United States developed a drama of truly international importance for the first time in the 1920's in the plays of Eugene O'Neill, whose first full-length offering in New York, *Beyond the Horizon* (1920), carried off the Pulitzer Prize. O'Neill won two more Pulitzer Prizes during the decade for *Anna Christie* (1921) and *Strange Interlude* (1928) and presented four other major productions in New York during the decade. While all his plays are Modernist statements of the need of individuals to escape the deadly constraints of monotonous lives or oppressive institutions, they are written in two strikingly different styles. While some are sombre dramas of personal frustration in the prevailing naturalistic mode of the period (*Beyond the Horizon, Desire under the Elms*), others are practically the only important American examples of the European Expressionist drama that sought to suggest interior states of mind through stylized sets and actions (*The Emperor Jones, The Hairy Ape, The Great God Brown*). In his greatest triumph during his lifetime, the nine-act *Strange Interlude*, he combined naturalistic action with expressionist revelation through a double set of speeches that allow the audience to hear both what the characters are saying and what they are thinking.

Most of even the other Pulitzer prize-winning plays of the decade pale beside O'Neill's work. The few foreshadowings of a generally brilliant decade ahead included Sidney Howard's *The Silver Cord* (1926), an archetypal picture of a mother fixation, and the only other important American expressionist play besides O'Neill's, Elmer Rice's *The Adding Machine* (1923), a devastating picture of dehumanization. Audiences enjoyed especially, however, two rollicking farces that caught the bumptious pseudo-sophisticated tone of the decade, Maxwell Anderson and Laurence Stallings's *What Price Glory?* (1924) and Ben Hecht and Charles MacArthur's *The Front Page* (1926). But the biggest hit of all was Anne Nichols's ethnic farce, *Abie's Irish Rose* (1922).

American humor generally made a great comeback during years of careless laughter. H. L. Mencken had been delighting the "smart set" with his iconoclastic attacks on the "booboisie" and defenses of American authors like Theodore Dreiser since 1914; but he and the outrageous drama critic George Jean Nathan scored their greatest successes after founding *The American Mercury* in 1924. Its cynical wit was soon overshadowed by that of *The New Yorker,* founded in 1925 by editor Harold Ross, "not for the old lady in Dubuque." The magazine attracted the sophisticated funsters who became members of the Algonquin Round Table (named for the hotel where they met for lunch) – James Thurber, poet and short-story writer Dorothy Parker, essayist E. B. White, monologuist Robert Benchley, popular book reviewer Alexander Woollcott. They did not have the New York scene to themselves, however, for even more popular were the ironically comic short stories of Ring Lardner (*The Big Town,* 1921) and the poems that Don Marquis attributed to a newspaper-office cockroach madly in love with a fickle cat (*Archy and Mehitable,* 1927).

3. Alienation Vindicated – Depression and World War, 1929–45

If American writings of the 1920's were not equalled in brilliance by those of the 1930's, they were surpassed in profundity by the outpouring of moving responses to the human condition inspired by the international depression and the rise to power of the authoritarian regimes that precipitated World War II.

Apparently traumatized by the end of the world they had known, few established American novelists matched their earlier accomplishments after 1929. Sinclair Lewis's satirical portraits of pretentious Americans began to resemble comic strips. Only *It Can't Happen Here* (1935), a warning about the possibility of a fascist takeover by popular demagogues in the United States, and *Kingsblood Royal* (1947), an early attack on anti-Negro prejudice outside the South, won great attention, but even these were overstated, two-dimensional tracts. After publishing *U.S.A.,* John Dos Passos became embittered by his experiences with both sides in the Spanish Civil War and became increasingly a right-wing isolationist stressing the American values of the founding fathers. The Spanish Civil War, however, brought Ernest Hemingway out of a long slump to find a new voice in praising the individual whose dreams exceed the squalid possibilities of the world about him in *For Whom the Bell Tolls* (1940) and again in his very popular fable, *The Old Man and the Sea* (1952).

The most enduring novelists of the 1930's, however, were those who found their inspirations rooted in their localities, as William Carlos Williams had hoped poets would. After making a false start with the stylized history of a pirate (*Cup of Gold,* 1929), John Steinbeck found his locality in the rural valleys of central California in the mystical *To a God Unknown* (1933) and the ironic story-cycle *The Pastures of Heaven* (1932). After revealing a gift for humorous allegory in *Tortilla Flat* (1935) and naturalistic tragedy (*Of Mice and Men,* 1937), he published what both public and critics have acclaimed as the greatest work of American social protest since *Uncle Tom's Cabin, The Grapes of Wrath* (1938), a novel about the sufferings of the dispossessed "Okies" from the Dust Bowl on Highway 66 and in an unfriendly California, in which his hitherto morbidly Modernist irony gives way to a transcendent faith in the ultimate triumph of simple people. Also noteworthy are his story-cycle of a boy's coming of age after the passing of the frontier in a diminished America, *The Red Pony* (1937), and his denunciation of middle-class smugness and praise of "outcasts" in his tribute to his friend Ed Ricketts, *Cannery Row* (1945).

The long depressed South, however, was the region that would really experience a Renaissance while long-favored lands sank into lethargy. Beginning in 1929 with *Look Homeward, Angel,* Thomas Wolfe turned the memories of his childhood in Asheville, North Carolina, and his adult journeyings throughout this country and in Europe into epic fiction, especially in *Of Time and the River* (1935). Erskine Caldwell devastatingly satirized the rednecks of the Southern backwoods in *Tobacco Road* (1932) and *God's Little Acre* (1933), while Elizabeth Madox Roberts paid tribute to the heroically sacrificial life of the pioneers in Kentucky in *The Great Meadow* (1930). The most important southern writer of this period, however, a figure of international stature, was William Faulkner.

After an unpromising start in two "jazz age" novels influenced by Sherwood Anderson, Faulkner found his "little postage stamp of territory" in Yoknapatawpha County, modeled on the region where he lived in the red clay hills of northeast Mississippi. In *Sartoris* (1929), he relates a late chapter in the history of the aristocratic family that becomes the foil for the upstart, white trash Snopeses, whose tale is told in the trilogy *The Hamlet* (1940), *The Town* (1957), and *The Mansion* (1959). Other novels and short stories, including his four supreme achievements – *The Sound and the Fury* (1929), *As I Lay Dying* (1930), *Light in August* (1932) and *Absalom, Absalom!* (1936) – fill in the story, pieces of which have been brilliantly arranged into a chronological history by Malcolm Cowley in *The Portable Faulkner*. The typical Modernist concept that underlies the whole cycle of the human loss of innocence that accompanies the destruction of the wilderness comes into sharpest focus in two companion stories of the *Go Down, Moses* cycle (1942) – "The Bear," in which the isolated Ike McCaslin protests greedy man's destruction of his bond with nature, and "Delta Autumn," in which a dying Ike thinks to himself, "No wonder the ruined woods I used to know don't cry for retribution.... The people who have destroyed it will accomplish its revenge."

Perhaps inspired by Faulkner's example, James Agee paid what remains the most sympathetic tribute to the hard life of Southern poor whites in *Let Us Now Praise Famous Men* (1941), and Southern fiction flourished as never before. Four women novelists made especially distinguished contributions to the movement. Caroline Gordon was directly associated with the influential Southern agrarian poets and in novels from *Penhally* (1931) to *The Malefactors* (1956) a most outspoken critic of the region's departure from its traditional culture, as was her husband, Allen Tate, in his one novel, *The Fathers* (1938). More impressive, however, were Katherine Anne Porter's tales of her native Texas, like *Noon Wine* (1937), and of Mexico. Late in the period the changing life in small Southern rural communities became the subjects of stories by Carson McCullers and Eudora Welty. McCullers published her first novel, *The Heart Is a Lonely Hunter* in 1940, and Welty's fantastic novelette *The Robber Bridegroom* appeared in 1942. McCullers, however, quickly reached the peak of her career with her third novel, *The Member of the Wedding* (1946) and her play version of it (1950), while Welty did not produce her most ambitious work, *Losing Battles*, until 1970. The most popular novel ever to come out of the South, however, was Margaret Mitchell's mammoth *Gone with the Wind* (1936), a mythical evocation of life in the plantation South during the Civil War that was made into what has remained the country's favorite motion picture.

The fiction that bulked largest, however, in the United States during the depression years was the work of the "tough guy" proletarian writers. The most prolific of these, James T. Farrell was never able to equal the success of his first naturalistic stories about growing up on Chicago's South Side, the *Studs Lonigan* trilogy (1932–35), and many other prolific writers of the time like Josephine Herbst have been largely forgotten. Edward Dahlberg proved an exception when he developed a belated reputation for the autobiographical *Because I Was Flesh* (1964). James M. Cain, however, won a wide following for his tales of the seedy elements of society in glamorous Southern California like *The Postman Always Rings Twice* (1934) and *Double Indemnity* (1943).

The grimmest work about decadent movieland, however, was Nathanael West's hal--lucinatory prediction of the destruction of Los Angeles, *The Day of the Locust* (1939), which followed his other powerful indictments of the American myth of the self-made man (*A Cool Million*, 1934) and the Christ complex developed by an advice-to-the-lovelorn columnist (*Miss Lonelyhearts*, 1933). Another cynical attack on the shoddiness of American middle-class values was John O'Hara's *Appointment in Samarra* (1934). The most outrageous novels about the period, however, were Henry Miller's *Tropic of Cancer* (1934) and *Tropic of Capricorn* (1939), curious melanges of turgid philosophizing and explicit pornography that were banned from this country for decades until they were the subject of a court battle in the 1960's.

An even more telling indictment of social injustices was Richard Wright's *Native Son* (1940), an account of the corruption and destruction of an ambitious but ill-educated Chicago black boy, modeled after Dreiser's *An American Tragedy*. Wright was the first black novelist to win major critical and public recognition for both his novel and his harrowing autobiography, *Black Boy* (1945).

The poets who dominated the American academies beginning in the mid-1930's came, like Wright, from the South; but they represented not its belligerent black fugitives, but conservative white "fugitives" from the twentieth century's urban society. The group at Vanderbilt University who had styled themselves the "Fugitives" attracted national attention when they identified themselves as Agrarians and called for a return to traditional values in an essay collection, *I'll Take My Stand* (1930). Although the reputation of their leader, Donald Davidson, arch-foe of TVA, has declined, three of the group have heavily influenced American literary culture generally. Allen Tate's "Ode to the Confederate Dead" has overshadowed his more ambitious efforts to give a peculiarly Southern cast to T. S. Eliot's concept of the value of traditional orthodoxy. John Crowe Ransom has won distinction as a poet, but is best known as the theorist in *The World's Body* (1938) of the "New Criticism" that dominated American universities from the late 1930's to the 1960's. The most prominent of the group, however, has been Robert Penn Warren, who has won distinction not only as a poet, for works like *Brother to Dragons* (1953), but as a novelist, especially for *All the King's Men* (1946), a cautionary tale about a Southern demagogue resembling Louisiana's Huey Long, and particularly – along with his Yale colleague Cleanth Brooks – as the principal popularizer of New Criticism techniques in the uniquely influential *Understanding Poetry* (1938).

Despite this Southern offensive, the center of poetic activity began to shift back during the 1930's to New England, where Robert Frost – his important writing behind him – was just beginning to make his impact as a lecturer and embodiment of Yankee tradition. The most telling satirical poetry of the decade was Archibald MacLeish's *Frescoes for Mr. Rockefeller's City*, inspired by the controversy over Mexican muralist Diego Rivera's designs for the Rockefellers' Art Deco Radio City. The caustic "Empire Builders," which tells of the "making of America in five panels" by Harriman, Commodore Vanderbilt, J. P. Morgan, Andrew Mellon, and Bruce Barton, concludes with the observation that there is "nothing to see of America but land." MacLeish's subsequent pioneering in radio dramas like *The Fall of the City* (1937) set a model not yet equalled for this aborted form.

MacLeish's polemics have been overshadowed, however, by those of the theorist of the "Supreme Fiction," the Hartford, Connecticut, insurance executive Wallace Stevens. Stevens's complex and subtle work defies brief synthesis. Perhaps one can only be as cryptic as Stevens himself in "Notes Toward a Supreme Fiction" (1942) by specifying that the three requirements for its achievement are that "It must be abstract," "It must change," and "It must give pleasure." To suggest how such contradictory demands may be reconciled, one turns back to Stevens's early "Sunday Morning," in which the narrator specifies, "We live in an old chaos of the sun," and then leap forward to the very late "Final Soliloquy of the Interior Paramour," whose narrator tells us that "The world imagined is the ultimate good" – a world like that of "the single artificer of the world in which she sang" in "The Idea of Order at Key West," who "knew that there never was a world for her/Except the one she sang and, singing, made." It is impossible to go beyond this point in celebrating the rejection of the world of received opinion for the one that the artist creates. If American literature appears static since 1945, it is because the Modernist frame of reference had been by then established; and no important breakthrough has been made in another direction.

Within this framework, however, the drama achieved an unparalleled effectiveness. O'Neill no longer dominated the stage. After capping his great decade with a trilogy audaciously transplanting the sole surviving Greek trilogy, Aeschylus's *Oresteia*, to nineteenth-century New England in *Mourning Becomes Electra* (1931), O'Neill withdrew from the scene after his one nostalgic comedy, *Ah, Wilderness!* (1933), not to be heard from again until the long, cheerless drama of the triumph of dreams over life, *The Iceman Cometh*, reached Broadway in 1946.

An unprecedented number of other dramatists, however, commanded attention. Most honored at the time was Maxwell Anderson for his commercial success with a blank-verse play, *Winterset* (1935), inspired by the notorious Sacco-Vanzetti case that had outraged many American artists. Even more popular at the time were Robert E. Sherwood's serio-comic responses to the Fascist march to European war in *Idiot's Delight* (1936) and *There Shall Be No Night* (1940). Politics also influenced the radical critique of the depravity of American bourgeois society in Clifford Odets's *Awake and Sing!* (1935) and *Golden Boy* (1937) and especially in Lillian Hellman's bitter and controversial *The Children's Hour* (1934), *The Little Foxes* (1939) and the anti-Nazi *Watch on the Rhine* (1941). Comparable pieces were offered by the subsidized Federal Theater Project, which also provided the start for Orson Welles's Mercury Theater.

An antidote to the grim exposures of the failure of the American dream like Sidney Kingsley's *Dead End* (1935) and John Steinbeck's *Of Mice and Men* (1937) were the comic collaborations of George S. Kaufman and Moss Hart, especially *You Can't Take It With You* (1936), which championed individualist rejection of pressures toward social conformity in a way that delighted depression-weary Americans. William Saroyan also achieved his one enduring success with *The Time of Your Life* (1939), a zany reversal of O'Neill's tragedies about defeated dreamers. The most heartening plays of the period – and even perhaps of the world's theater – were Thornton Wilder's two internationally acclaimed meditations on the value of every moment of human experience and of the struggle to preserve the often threatened race in *Our Town* (1938) and *The Skin of Our Teeth* (1942). These were also important experimental efforts to break away from the dominant naturalistic tradition of the proscenium-arch stage in theatrical production.

4. The Harvest of Modernism, 1946–57

Relatively few new writers published their first works during World War II. Mary McCarthy and John Cheever published short-story collections and Wright Morris, Saul Bellow, and Jean Stafford, novels; but wartime paper shortages and the absence in military service and other war work of promising young writers precluded the development of a new generation of fictionists influenced by the war until 1946.

Gore Vidal, who was to become one of our most prolific writers, was the first soldier-author to break into print with *Williwaw* (1946), a fictional account of his experiences on the little-known Alaskan front; but he was to become most famous for one of the first American novels to broach the forbidden subject of homosexuality (*The City and the Pillar,* 1948) and for the outrageously campy *Myra Breckinridge* (1968). His works were overshadowed, however, by Norman Mailer's *The Naked and the Dead* (1948), an episodic novel, influenced by John Dos Passos's *U.S.A.,* about one Army squad's role in the taking of a Pacific island from the Japanese. Mailer made his dozen men, however, representative of a cross-section of American life and their story a powerful indictment of the power in this country and its army of the very fascism that we expended our resources and lives to defeat. The novelist subsequently became, in less celebrated works, culminating in the hallucinatory account of the moral disintegration of the country, *Why Are We in Vietnam?* (1967), a controversial critic of American political life, before abandoning fiction for the journalistic "non-fiction novel."

Another large-scale novel also attacked the depravities of the American military establishment – James Jones's *From Here to Eternity* (1951) – but other forms of decadence began to command even more attention. In a novel (*Other Voices, Other Rooms,* 1948) and short stories (*A Tree of Night,* 1949), Truman Capote presented a South even more degenerate than Faulkner's before also turning to the "non-fiction novel" to present in *In Cold Blood* (1966) a minutely detailed account of the senseless murder of a family by two drifters. An even more appallingly grotesque picture of the South emerged in the novels (*Wise Blood,* 1952, and *The Violent Bear It Away,* 1960) and the short stories (*A Good Man Is Hard to Find,*

1955) of Flannery O'Connor. Less Gothic in its excesses, but equally critical of the hypocrisy of decadent Southern aristocrats was *Lie Down in Darkness* (1951) by William Styron.

The South had no monopoly on decadence, however. Two of the most shocking novels of the post-war period to still tender-minded Americans seeking to preserve a few ideals were Paul Bowles's tale of Morocco, *The Sheltering Sky* (1949), and John Hawkes's surrealist account of occupied Germany, *The Cannibal* (1949). Certainly not coincidentally, the years following the war saw the development of a cult of admirers for the earlier writings of H. P. Lovecraft, who in horror fantasies principally published in the pulp magazine *Weird Tales* had created a mythology about the once dispossessed minions of the god Cthulu attempting to take over our planet by subversion.

It was the still inconceivable decadence of the Nazi holocaust in Europe, too, that in part accounted for the rise after the war of a group of Jewish-American novelists keenly aware of their people's ancient traditions and recent persecutions. Saul Bellow, the most remarkable of the group and the Nobel Prize winner in 1976, began to publish during the war, but first gained international recognition for *The Adventures of Augie March* (1953), a picaresque account of the *wanderjahren* of a young opportunist from the Chicago slums. Bellow's cryptic *Henderson the Rain King* (1959) has attracted much speculation; but his most powerful work is *Herzog* (1964), the self-revelation of a typically alienated, overly ambitious modern man who is at last able to make peace with himself (even if the world thinks him mad) through his imaginary conversations with the living and the dead.

The most impressive of Bernard Malamud's novels remains *The Assistant* (1957), in which the novelist most directly deals with racial and religious problems through the touching account of the relationship between an aggressive young Italian and his employer, a poor Jewish grocer. Growing to be even more respected, however, are the many works, originally written in Yiddish, by Isaac Bashevis Singer, particularly stories of life before World War I in the *shtetls* in Czarist Russia from which the ancient Jewish communities were driven. (Malamud also deals with a gruesome incident involving the Jews in Russia in *The Fixer*, 1966.) The most troubling tale to involve recollections of a direct involvement with the Nazi persecution, however, is Edward Lewis Wallant's *The Pawnbroker* (1961).

Another oppressed group, the Blacks, also began to win greater recognition for their fiction after World War II. Although Richard Wright's later works, written in exile in France and heavily influenced by existentialist philosophy, were disappointing, Ralph Ellison's *Invisible Man* (1952), a brilliant *bildungsroman* about the transformation of a naive, ambitious Southern black boy into a sophisticated fugitive living off a society that he rejects as a result of his disillusioning experiences with both whites and other blacks, conservatives and reformers, business men and religious revivalists, transcends any racial bounds to stand beside James Joyce's *A Portrait of the Artist as a Young Man* as a prototypical account of the creation of a Modernist sensibility. More limited in scope but deeply revealing of the sufferings of a sensitive young black are James Baldwin's *Go Tell It on the Mountain* (1953) and the related non-fictional *The Fire Next Time* (1963), based on recollections of the indignities and illuminations experienced while growing up in Harlem.

The most popular novel of this period, especially with young readers, however, concerns the indignities and illuminations also experienced by a boy growing up during the same years as Baldwin a few miles south of Harlem in the upper-middle-class high-rise apartment district of Manhattan, J. D. Salinger's *The Catcher in the Rye* (1951). Although Salinger had been publishing short stories since 1941, he first attracted attention with a short story in the *New Yorker*, "A Perfect Day for Bananafish," about the suicide of Seymour Glass, who with his six siblings was to be the subject of most of the only thirteen other stories that Salinger has allowed to be published in book form. He received almost hysterical adulation for his one novel, a colloquial monologue about the traumatic experiences of a seventeen-year-old boy seeking to maintain an innocence doomed to adulteration in the corrupted world of New York at Christmas.

Despite the popular triumph of this culmination of "waste land" thinking in *The Catcher in the Rye* and the Glass family stories, the Modernist sensibility remained under attack from some able traditionalists who sought the rejuvenation of nineteenth-century moral codes. J. P. Marquand had begun a sentimental satirization of a vanished culture in *The Late George Apley* (1937) and *Wickford Point* (1939). James Gould Cozzens was writing at the same time, but did not attract great attention until his *Guard of Honor* (1948), about problems of command in a Florida training camp, was cited by the conservative forces of the *New York Times Book Review* as the best American novel about World War II, its sober judgments providing a counter to Norman Mailer's violent excesses. Even as late as 1957, Cozzens's mammoth *By Love Possessed* was hailed as a kind of nine-day's-wonder by critics alienated by Modernism, but its reputation faded quickly. The novels of socialite-lawyer Louis Auchincloss, like *The Rector of Justin* (1964), however, have continued to be well received; and even as late as 1977 a rabid attack on Modernist decadence, especially Southern, attracted interest in Walker Percy's austere *Lancelot*. John Steinbeck in his later works, especially his most ambitious novel, *East of Eden* (1952), also argued for a return to traditional values; but these writings failed to match the artistry of his earlier stories. A serious call for a rediscovery of the principal of "sacrality" in life also underlies the delicately-wrought fictions of Walter Van Tilburg Clark, beginning with his effort to create a new kind of "Western" in *The Ox-Bow Incident* (1940).

Traditional values exerted, for a time at least, a greater force than they did in fiction after World War II in the poetry of Robert Lowell, the only poet to emerge during those years whose place in American literary history seems, even after two decades, indisputably fixed. Critical consensus is wanting. Gay Wilson Allen, Walter B. Rideout and James K. Robinson's bulky anthology *American Poetry* (1965) includes of the poets who became prominent then only Lowell, Theodore Roethke, Karl Shapiro, Randall Jarrell, John Berryman and Richard Wilbur; and they are widely separated both by birthdates and dates of first publication from Allen Tate and James Dickey on either side of them. But this list is overselective. While other anthologies omit some of this half dozen (except Lowell) and propose a bewildering variety of substitutes, a substantial number include Robert Duncan, Richard Eberhart, Howard Nemerov, Charles Olson, and Kenneth Patchen.

Of the dozen that must be seriously considered, two – Jarrell and Shapiro – began their careers with poems about their participation in the War, a paltry number in view of the millions of American servicemen. Even this link was soon broken: Shapiro became increasingly contentious as he adopted prosy stances as "bourgeois poet" and "Jewish poet"; Jarrell withdrew to an academic life, writing, like many of his contemporaries, several works for children. Berryman and Roethke also became college teachers, but led increasingly troubled lives that led to suicides. Richard Wilbur, a model of style and sanity among his contemporaries, has devoted himself increasingly to witty translations from the French. Eberhart, another of the hardiest, has become a grand old man at Dartmouth College. Nemerov has written, besides his introspective poems, several competent novels. Patchen also wrote novels, but they proved too extreme for most American readers, and, after a long and painful illness, he died in obscurity, celebrated only by the youngsters of the Beat Generation, with which Robert Duncan was briefly associated. Duncan has consistently shunned the spotlight, however, something that cannot be said of Charles Olson, who, as founder of the influential Black Mountain group and theorist for "projectivist verse," has sought more than any other recent poet to develop a school based on his own often adumbrated theories that some anthologists find more important than his "Maximus of Gloucester" poems.

A most curious feature of the treatment of the years under consideration by anthologists is the entire neglect of women poets. One responsible anthology of American literature does include, along with selections from the work of only four of the men mentioned, extensive selections from the work of Elizabeth Bishop and Gwendolyn Brooks, the first black woman poet of distinction in this century.

While it is apparent that there is no agreement about what may have been poetically significant during these years beyond Lowell's "confessional" poetry, one thing that is clear is that the long narrative poem, which had been going out of fashion since the end of the nineteenth century, had been almost totally replaced by short, highly personal, and often cryptic lyrics like John Berryman's "Dream Songs." Yet curiously the only earlier poet who added substantially to his reputation during these years was William Carlos Williams, whose long narrative evocation of his home town, *Paterson*, appeared in five sections between 1946 and 1958.

The situation in post-World War II American drama was as clear-cut as it was fuzzy in poetry. Our stage was dominated not by just two playwrights, but by two plays. Not even O'Neill's works have created as much speculation and controversy as Tennessee Williams's *A Streetcar Named Desire* (1947) and Arthur Miller's *Death of a Salesman* (1949), which are often paired in discussions of whether "tragedy" is possible in modern secular terms. Both Williams's Blanche DuBois and Miller's Willy Loman dream such happiness as they will never feel. They are models of the Modernist vision, for both have made complete shambles of their real worlds in their frantic pursuits of impossible dreams.

In an important sense, *Streetcar* is Williams's only play (despite the popularity of the earlier *The Glass Menagerie*), for all of his steadily less successful works have dealt with the inability of a sensitive individual to adjust to the demands of a crass, materialistic world, especially its sexual demands on the spiritualized idealist. Miller's work has been much more varied, since most of his frustrated heroes have been victims of society rather than of their own fantasies. Only in *After the Fall* (1964), based on Miller's troubled marriage to his second wife, the film star Marilyn Monroe, has his work become as richly personal as O'Neill's and Williams's. Williams's quarrel with the world is, of course, haunted by problems of sexual orientation, while Miller's grows from his ambiguous feelings about an economic system that he deplores, but that has rewarded him well.

A third playwright, William Inge, enjoyed popularity as long as he avoided or sublimated his personal sexual problems in plays like *Picnic* (1953); but when he confronted problems of homosexuality directly in his later plays, audiences rejected them, leading to a despondency that resulted in his suicide.

The ghost of Eugene O'Neill returned also to promote him to an even higher place than he had hitherto occupied in the hierarchy of world dramatists, not through his long study of the hopeless state of alcoholic dreamers, *The Iceman Cometh* (1946), but through the posthumous *Long Day's Journey into Night* (1956), in which by facing squarely at last the love-hate relationships within his own family, he made his greatest contribution to the theater. O'Neill's characters in this play, which he withheld during his lifetime, are doomed by neither external social nor cosmic forces, but by their own lack of self-knowledge and self-criticism; as such they make the play, like Eliot's *The Waste Land* and Ralph Ellison's *Invisible Man*, not "a personal grouse," but a synecdoche for a culture seemingly irreversibly set on a course that will lead to its own destruction.

As the drama, like the novel, became increasingly despairing and preoccupied with decadence, humor as an art form declined in the United States. Even the *New Yorker* became less funny and more threatening, though it did sponsor the dazzling word play of S. J. Perelman. Even most of his short comic sketches, however, contemptuously belittled the present or evoked, as in "Cloudland Revisited," the superficialities of an innocent past.

5. Modernist Decadence, 1957–79

The year 1959 is remarkable in that it saw the first important publications of fiction by an unusually large group destined to become some of our most prominent writers, a larger group than would appear in any subsequent year for at least the next two decades. These modern scriptures were preceded by two prophetic novels that subsequently became idols of cult worship.

William Gaddis's *The Recognitions* (1955) is a monstrously long tale with many bizarre characters and plot lines that has attracted a small band of avid readers. Jack Kerouac's *On the Road* (1957), which circulated for years in manuscript until it became the best known unpublished novel in the country, is an epic of the frenzied cross-country travels of the progenitors of the "Beat Generation." Gaddis has subsequently published only one more big, puzzling novel, *JR* (1975), and remains himself a mysterious figure. Kerouac published many more books during the decade after *On the Road* (many of them written during his earlier days of obscurity), before his sudden death – apparently from the ravages of too high living – in 1969. Dissimilar as the novels are, they share important characteristics. Both are rambling works that ignore and even mock traditional forms, and both feature characters who live unplanned lives, often involving hysterical fantasies and deceptive behavior. They depict a world in which individuals lack any frame of reference but their own self-indulgent delusions.

This is the world also of the novelists who began to achieve recognition in 1959. The world of William Burroughs's *Naked Lunch* is, in fact, the most chaotic that a drugged vision could convey to paper at all. While the worlds of James Purdy (*Malcolm*), Philip Roth (*Goodbye, Columbus*), and John Updike (*The Poorhouse Fair*) are tersely mapped in better disciplined fables, they all deal with characters caught up in their own fantasies and only spasmodically in touch with the external realities of their situations (if indeed *Malcolm* has a geographical reality at all). The same comments can be applied to the works of a number of other contemporaries. John Barth had published *The Floating Opera* in 1956 (though not in its original form until 1967), but his reputation was established by a historical fantasy (*The Sot-Weed Factor*, 1960) and an allegorical tour-de-force about a computerized culture (*Giles Goat-Boy*, 1966). Donald Barthelme's short stores in *Come Bank, Dr. Caligari* (1964) and his "novel" *Snow White* (1967) presented figures from folklore and contemporary media against artificial backgrounds reminiscent of the Pop Art painting of the period. Joseph Heller's anti-war *Catch-22* (1962) dealt with characters whose private fantasies made more sense than the public world that oppressed them. Thomas Pynchon's *V.* (1963) seemed, like Vladimir Nabokov's *Lolita* (1955) and *Pale Fire* (1962), elaborate and masterfully inventive word games that shuffled the same deck of cards as *Alice in Wonderland* to suggest the ultimate unreality of all human action.

These tendencies had begun to manifest themselves as early as 1952 in the relatively thin apprentice works of the man who was eventually to have the last word in such matters, Kurt Vonnegut, Jr. Although *Player Piano* seemed only a kind of comic strip spinoff from the increasingly popular science fiction that had begun to win serious critical attention, Vonnegut's work became increasingly serious in its portraits of paranoid self-destruction (*Mother Night,* 1961) and universal destruction (*Cat's Cradle,* 1963). *Slaughterhouse-Five* (1969) combined the historical horror of the fire raid on Dresden during World War II with science-fiction fantasy to suggest that the only possible hope for humanity lay beyond our own corrupted planet; but Vonnegut returned to the confines of this planet to deliver in *Breakfast of Champions* (1973) a damning indictment of every facet of American society, in which existence becomes tolerable only when the author-narrator withdraws into his own head "where the big show is" and ultimately "sets at liberty" all his literary characters.

Vonnegut's erasing of the line that reputedly exists between external and internal realities completes the withdrawal begun in American literature by Sister Carrie's passive dreaming in her rocking chair; but his action is only the most flamboyant execution of a step already taken by Nabokov, Barth, and Purdy, among others. Some critics have recently tended to regard these writers as "post-Modernist"; but I think that the use of this terminology is premature. While some critics have suggested that the Modernist Age ended as early as 1930 or as late as 1960, the characters in our most respected recent fiction have not behaved fundamentally differently from Henry Fleming and Sister Carrie; they have only been more blatant and extreme in their alienation. The fables that critics sometimes described as "post-Modernist" are still concerned with the complete and irrevocable divorce of the utterly disillusioned individual from an irredeemably corrupt and demoralized society. Such a movement is not in a new direction; it is rather a milling about at the end of a road that goes no further. So far, no American novelist has mapped out any new direction that the individual might take, except possibly for Tom Robbins, who in *Another Roadside Attraction*

(1975) and *Even Cowgirls Get the Blues* (1976) plays, as yet somewhat clumsily, with the concept of "the replacement of societal with individual rituals."

Having reached an impasse through which they cannot apparently break, the novelists have reacted in a variety of ways. Only J. D. Salinger has retreated into total silence, though William Gaddis, William Styron, and Joseph Heller rarely deliver new books. Even John Barth, probably the one of the group with the shrewdest idea of what has happened and where he is, has written nothing of significance since the aptly named *Lost in the Funhouse* (1968).

Some have taken to repeating themselves with the usual diminishing returns. Donald Barthelme and John Updike have not advanced beyond their first celebrated writings. Even Kurt Vonnegut, Jr., seems to have – predictably – nowhere to go since "liberating" his characters. Others have, however, more profitably, backtracked from the extreme positions that they reached while trying to cultivate an audience and have turned again to more conventional fictions to expose the decadence and disease that they find particularly offensive in their society. Unlikely as it seems not even all the criticisms of American culture that twentieth-century writers have produced have exhausted the subject, although we must not be surprised to find, either, that the diminishing audience of humanists for any kind of serious literature has become increasingly inhospitable to those they should most cherish as they have abandoned as useless the attack on distant robber barons and power brokers and struck closer to home in the very resorts of the middle-class liberals.

Most successful of these back-trackers has been James Purdy, whose early surrealist fantasies about a mad elite, culminating in *I Am Elijah Thrush* (1972), have given way to gruesome indictments, in *The House of the Solitary Maggot* (1974) and *Narrow Rooms* (1978), of selfish, loveless parents who have brought a deteriorating culture to the brink of moral catastrophe. Philip Roth has also won new laurels for broadening the scope of his inquiry in a maliciously satirical trio – *Portnoy's Complaint* (1969), *Our Gang* (1971) and *The Great American Novel* (1973). Even more excitement and controversy have been generated, however, by William Styron's exploration of two matters that still most gnaw at the American conscience – slavery and racial warfare in *The Confessions of Nat Turner* (1967) and the Nazi extermination of the Jews in *Sophie's Choice* (1979).

The continued absence of any critical consensus about the achievement of American poets has really not been a bad thing. At least poetry has escaped one of the dilemmas of the Modernist years by being unprofitable enough to escape the attention of the commercial conglomerates that have sought to control the money-making media. With rare exceptions, poetry has not proved financially rewarding to either poets or publishers since World War II, so that the poets have generally had to retreat into college teaching to make a living. One damaging result of this practice has been the development of a new elitism, with college writers' workshops, like the famous one presided over by Paul Engle at the University of Iowa, attempting to dictate taste and thereby further narrowing both audiences and appropriate subjects for lyric verse.

While there have probably never been so many technically competent poets at work as at present, only Allen Ginsberg, a non-academic, with a single poem, *Howl* (1956), has made a striking impression on the general public. The importance of *Howl* is that, as James E. Miller, Jr., has pointed out, it has established Ginsberg, one of the charter members of the Beat Generation, as the last spokesman for a national audience in the tradition of Whitman, Hart Crane, and Carl Sandburg. Ginsberg was one of six poets who participated at a legendary reading at San Francisco's Six Gallery in the autumn of 1955 that launched the brief San Francisco Renaissance, the last literary movement with large public support, especially among dissident youths who have since become increasingly politicized. *Howl* became notorious through the efforts of the police and customs officials to suppress it; but it is the only Beat poem, to attain enduring popularity. Of Ginsberg's fellow readers at the Six Gallery – older sponsor Kenneth Rexroth, Michael McClure, Philip Lamantia, Philip Whalen, and Gary Snyder – only Snyder remains almost universally respected for his deeply sensitive nature poetry inspired by his years of study of oriental religions. The movement itself as a newsworthy phenomenon was exhausted by 1960, but the attack on conventional respectability that it launched has continued to affect drastically American life-styles.

A question that continues to divide critics is whether even *Howl* is a classic or obscene trash, as traditionalists maintain. The issue has polarized opinion particularly because of the failure of any subsequent work to attract anything like comparable attention. The heart of the problem is that the opening line of the poem, "I saw the best minds of my generation destroyed by madness, starving hysterical naked ...," sums up histrionically the fundamental reason for the Modernist rejection of materialist culture, so that the poem leaves little room except for others to imitate it or to refute it convincingly, as none has so far succeeded in doing.

Like contemporary novelists, some poets have escaped the problem of finding no new roads to take by backtracking to investigate specific trouble spots in our culture not fully explored previously by a poetic consciousness. Robert Creeley has a devoted following for the brief lyric epiphanies that are his development of Olson's "objectivist" theories. Robert Bly has become an idol of sensitive youthful dissidents through his roles as flamboyant reader-lecturer, translator-editor, and leader of the artistic protest against the Vietnam war. More spectacularly, James Dickey has brought into poetry the *macho* tactics of Jack London and Norman Mailer. Although he is usually considered a better poet than prose writer, his novel *Deliverance* (1970) best embodies through its confusions the ambiguous feelings of those who seek to return to the purity of the primitive wilderness only to find that it is both corrupted and vanishing. The only woman poet to challenge Dickey's hold on the imagination is Sylvia Plath, whose brief life ended in suicide even before the appearance of her most remarkable works. Like Dickey she complemented confessional poetry (*Ariel*, 1965) with a self-revelatory novel, *The Bell Jar* (1961). Another poet who died tragically young (but accidentally), Frank O'Hara, has become a legendary hero of the gay activist movement for the frank revelation of his homosexual sensibility.

Beyond this group, there are many admirable poets admired by splinter groups. *American Poetry* includes the work of Denise Levertov, W. D. Snodgrass, and W. S. Merwin. Richard Poirier's anthology, however, omits all of them and includes James Merrill, John Ashbery, and LeRoi Jones (now transformed into the black activist Amiri Baraka). But where, others would ask, are the equally deserving A. R. Ammons, Adrienne Rich, Louis Simpson, and William Stafford.

Yet this collapse of critical consensus is not at all bad, for it suggests that in an age of increasing homogenization, poets have succeeded in maintaining their individuality and integrity, despite enormous financial and psychic sacrifices. Were there more general agreement about the value of their work, its ultimate value as a humanistic protest against the dehumanizing reductivism of a statistically oriented culture would be less great.

The year 1959 is as important for the American drama as the American novel, for it saw the first off-Broadway performances of the work of the only recent playwright who can be placed beside O'Neill, Miller, and Williams. Like O'Neill, Edward Albee first reached the American public through electrifying one-act plays, *The Zoo Story* (1959) and *The American Dream* (1961), which managed to live up to its pretentious title by stripping the façade of respectable success from the stereotyped American family of grandmother, daddy, mommy, and handsome but catatonically oriented son. Immediately debate arose as to whether Albee could follow up his success with a full-length play; but these doubts were quickly put to rest with *Who's Afraid of Virginia Woolf?* (1962), the Walpurgis night exorcism of the decadent dreams of an American academic couple, which remains the last really outstanding addition to the American repertory, despite Albee's fascinating experimentation in *Tiny Alice* (1964) and the display of his command of conventional dramaturgy in *A Delicate Balance* (1966). Like the contemporary novelists, aspiring dramatists face the problem of where to go beyond the dead end of the Modernist sensibility that has been reached in the international "absurdist" drama of Samuel Beckett's *Endgame* and Eugene Ionesco's *Rhinoceros*.

Black drama has also not lived up to the promising start that it made in the 1960's. LeRoi Jones/Amiri Baraka scored a spectacular success with *Dutchman* (1964), a two-character play about the confrontation between a black man and a white woman on a New York subway; but *The Toilet* (1962) and *The Slave* (1964) proved too gross even for off-Broadway's blasé audiences. Lorraine Hansberry, however, did enjoy a heartening public and critical success with her first full-length play, *A Raisin in the Sun* (1959), a 1930's-type inspirational drama about a Chicago black family's aspirations to own its own home; but her attempts to follow up this triumph before her early death proved unavailing.

A number of other playwrights, principally writing for the off-Broadway theater, have similarly failed to follow up promising starts. Sam Shepard has persisted, however, and has scored successes with *The Tooth of Crime* (1972) and *Action* (1974). The most promising sign for the future, however, is the career of Arthur Kopit, who, after making a brilliant start with an absurdist farce, *Oh Dad, Poor Dad* (1960), faltered with plays like *Indians* (1969), but has recently been strikingly successful with *Wings* (1978), a one-character monologue about a woman's heroic effort to regain control of her faculties after suffering a stroke.

By far the most financially successful recent American playwright, however, is Neil Simon, whose work returns to the 1930's tradition of the well-made farce; but even his work has become increasingly serious, as have the farcical films of Woody Allen, the most admired comedian of these decadent years. Writers can find little to be funny about as American life has become increasingly what it was for Dreiser's Sister Carrie back at the beginning of the century – an unattainable dream. With four-fifths of the century passed, the problem of twentieth-century American writers remains that of Robert Frost's "Oven Bird": "What to make of a diminished thing?"

READING LIST

1. Bibliographies, handbooks, etc.

Dictionary of American Biography, 20 vols. and index, 1928–37; supplement, 1944, 1958, 1973; concise edition, 1964.

Hart, James D., *The Oxford Companion to American Literature*, 1941; 5th edition, 1975.

Spiller, Robert E., and others, *Literary History of the United States: Bibliography*, 1946; 4th edition, 1974.

Leary, Lewis, editor, *Articles on American Literature 1900–1950*, 1954; *1950–1967*, 1971; *1968–1975*, 1979.

Blanck, Jacob, *Bibliography of American Literature*, 1955—

Jones, Howard Mumford, and Richard M. Ludwig, editors, *Guide to American Literature and Its Backgrounds since 1890*, 1959; revised edition, 1972.

Woodress, James, editor, *Dissertations in American Literature*, 1962.

Woodress, James, editor, *American Literary Scholarship*, 1963— (annual review).

Bufkin, E. C., *The Twentieth-Century Novel in English: A Checklist*, 1967.

Rubin, Louis D., Jr., *A Bibliographical Guide to the Study of Southern Literature*, 1969.

Murphy, Rosalie, and James Vinson, editors, *Contemporary Poets of the English Language*, 1970; revised edition, by Vinson, as *Contemporary Poets*, 1975, 1980.

Long, E. Hudson, *American Drama from Its Beginnings to the Present*, 1970.

Nevius, Blake, *The American Novel: Sinclair Lewis to the Present*, 1970.

Nilon, Charles, *Bibliography of Bibliographies of American Literature*, 1970.

Turner, Darwin T., *Afro-American Writers*, 1970.

Gerstenberger, Donna, and George Hendrick, *The American Novel: A Checklist of Criticism of Novels Written since 1789*, 2 vols., 1970.

Havelice, Patricia P., *Index to American Author Bibliographies*, 1971.

Vinson, James, editor, *Contemporary Novelists,* 1972; revised edition, 1976.
Vinson, James, editor, *Contemporary Dramatists,* 1973; revised edition, 1977.
Woodress, James, editor, *American Fiction 1900–1950: A Guide to Information Sources,* 1975.
Leary, Lewis, *American Literature: A Study and Research Guide,* 1976.
Rubin, Louis D., Jr., *A Biographical Guide to the Study of Southern Literature,* 1979.

2. General Histories

Geismar, Maxwell, *Rebels and Ancestors: The American Novel 1890–1915,* 1953; *The Last of the Provincials: The American Novel 1915–1925,* 1947; *Writers in Crisis: The American Novel Between Two Wars,* 1942; *American Moderns: A Mid-Century View of Contemporary Fiction,* 1958.
Kazin, Alfred, *On Native Grounds,* 1942.
Spiller, Robert E., and others, *Literary History of the United States,* 1946; 4th edition, 1974.
Jones, Howard Mumford, *The Theory of American Literature,* 1948; revised edition, 1965.
Cowie, Alexander, *The Rise of the American Novel,* 1948.
Hoffman, Frederick J., *The Modern Novel 1900–1950,* 1951.
West, Ray B., *The Short Story in America 1900–1950,* 1952.
Cunliffe, Marcus, *The Literature of the United States,* 1954; 3rd edition, 1967.
Spiller, Robert E., *The Cycle of American Literature,* 1955; revised edition, 1967.
Thorp, Willard, *American Writing in the Twentieth Century,* 1960.
Pearce, Roy Harvey, *The Continuity of American Poetry,* 1961.
Allen, Walter, *The Modern Novel in Britain and the United States,* 1963.
Peden, William, *The American Short Story,* 1964; *The American Short Story 1940–1975,* 1975.
Meserve, Walter, *An Outline History of American Drama,* 1965.
Waggoner, Hyatt, *American Poets from the Puritans to the Present,* 1968.
Nye, Russel B., *The Unembarrassed Muse: The Popular Arts in America,* 1970.
Rexroth, Kenneth, *American Poetry in the Twentieth Century,* 1971.
Stauffer, Donald Barlow, *A Short History of American Poetry,* 1974.
Bogard, Travis, and others, *American Drama,* 1977.

3. Topics, themes, short periods, etc.

Cowley, Malcolm, *After the Genteel Tradition: American Writers since 1910,* 1937.
Beach, Joseph Warren, *American Fiction 1920–1941,* 1941.
Cowley, Malcolm, *Exile's Return,* 1951.
Feidelson, Charles, *Symbolism and American Literature,* 1953.
Hoffman, Frederick J., *The Twenties: American Writing in the Postwar Decade,* 1955; revised edition, 1962.
Rideout, Walter B., *The Radical Novel in the United States 1900–1954,* 1956.
Walcutt, Charles Child, *American Literary Naturalism: A Divided Stream,* 1956.
Bone, Robert A., *The Negro Novel in America,* 1958; revised edition, 1965.
Fiedler, Leslie, *Love and Death in the American Novel,* 1960.
Aaron, Daniel, *Writers on the Left: Episodes in American Literary Communism,* 1961.
Hassan, Ihab, *Radical Innocence: Studies in the Contemporary American Novel,* 1961.
Parkinson, Thomas, editor, *A Casebook on the Beat,* 1961.
Weales, Gerald, *American Drama since World War II,* 1962; *The Jumping-Off Place: American Drama in the 1960's,* 1969.
Guttman, Allen, *The Wound in the Heart* (American writers on the Spanish Civil War), 1962.
Malin, Irving, *New American Gothic,* 1962.
Eisinger, Chester, *Fiction of the Forties,* 1963.
Phillips, Robert, *The Confessional Poets,* 1963.
Bradbury, John M., *Renaissance in the South: A Critical History of the Literature 1920–1960,* 1963.

Rabkin, Gerald, *Drama and Commitment: Politics in the American Theatre of the 1930's,* 1964.

Klein, Marcus, *After Alienation: American Novels in Mid-Century,* 1964.

Millgate, Michael, *American Social Fiction: James to Cozzens,* 1964.

Widmer, Kingsley, *The Literary Rebel,* 1965.

Tanner, Tony, *The Reign of Wonder: Naivety and Reality in American Literature,* 1965.

Malin, Irving, *Jews and Americans,* 1965.

Mills, Ralph J., Jr., *Contemporary American Poetry,* 1965.

Galloway, David, *The Absurd Hero in American Fiction,* 1966; revised edition, 1971.

Cooperman, Stanley, *World War I and the American Novel,* 1967.

French, Warren, *The Social Novel at the End of an Era,* 1967.

French, Warren, editor, *The Twenties [Thirties, Forties, Fifties]: Fiction, Poetry, Drama,* 4 vols., 1967–75.

Bigsby, C. W. E., *Confrontation and Commitment: A Study of the Contemporary American Drama 1959–1966,* 1967.

Madden, David, editor, *Tough Guy Writers of the Thirties,* 1968; *Proletarian Writers of the Thirties,* 1968.

Bigsby, C. W. E., editor, *The Black American Writer,* 2 vols., 1969.

Howard, Richard, *Alone with America: Essays on the Art of Poetry in the United States since 1950,* 1969.

Madden, David, editor, *American Dreams, American Nightmares,* 1970.

Bryant, Jerry H., *The Open Decision: The Contemporary American Novel and Its Intellectual Background,* 1970.

Glicksberg, Charles J., *The Sexual Revolution in Modern American Literature,* 1971.

Guttman, Allen, *The Jewish Writer in America: Assimilation and the Crisis of Identity,* 1971.

Huggins, Nathan, *Harlem Renaissance,* 1971.

Kenner, Hugh, *The Pound Generation,* 1971.

Bradbury, Malcolm, and David Palmer, editors, *The American Novel and the Nineteen Twenties,* 1971.

Handy, William, *Modern Fiction: A Formalist Approach,* 1971.

Tanner, Tony, *City of Words: American Fiction 1950–1970,* 1971.

Valgemae, Mardi, *Accelerated Grimace: Expressionism in the American Drama of the 1920's,* 1972.

Olderman, Raymond M., *Beyond the Waste Land: The American Novel in the Nineteen Sixties,* 1972.

Tuttleton, James W., *The Novel of Manners in America,* 1972.

Sutton, Walter, *American Free Verse: The Modern Revolution in Poetry,* 1973.

Allen, Donald M., and Warren Tallman, *The Poetics of the New American Poetry,* 1973.

Hassan, Ihab, *Contemporary American Literature 1945–1972,* 1973.

Kazin, Alfred, *Bright Book of Life: American Novelists and Storytellers from Hemingway to Mailer,* 1973.

Lehan, Richard, *A Dangerous Crossing: French Literary Existentialism and the Modern American Novel,* 1973.

Kenner, Hugh, *A Homemade World: The American Modernist Writers,* 1975.

Gelpi, Albert, *The Tenth Muse: The Psyche of the American Poet,* 1975.

Helterman, Jeffrey, and Richard Layman, editors, *American Novelists since World War II,* 1978.

4. Anthologies of primary works

Mantle, Burns, and Garrison P. Sherwood, editors, *The Best Plays of 1899–1909,* 1944; *The Best Plays of 1909–1919,* 1933; and annual volumes, edited by Mantle and others, from 1920 to the present.

Blair, Walter, editor, *Native American Humor,* 1937; revised edition, 1960.

Hall, Donald, Robert Pack, and Louis Simpson, editors, *New Poets of England and America,* 1957; second selection, edited by Hall and Pack, 1962.

Miller, Jordan Y., editor, *American Dramatic Literature,* 1961.

Rideout, Walter B., Gay Wilson Allen, and James K. Robinson, editors, *American Poetry,* 1965.

Jones, LeRoi, and Larry Neal, editors, *Black Fire: An Anthology of Afro-American Writing,* 1968.

Schorer, Mark, Irving Howe, and Larzer Ziff, editors, *The Literature of America,* 3 vols., 1970.

Angoff, Charles, and Meyer Levin, editors, *The Rise of Jewish Literature,* 1971.

ADE, George. American. Born in Kentland, Indiana, 9 February 1866. Educated at local schools, and Purdue University, Lafayette, Indiana, 1883–87 (Editor, *Purdue*), B.S. 1887. Reporter, Lafayette *Morning News*, 1888, and Lafayette *Call*, 1888–90; worked for the Chicago *Morning News*, later *News-Record*, then the *Record*, 1890–1900: from 1893 collaborated with cartoonist John T. McCutcheon on a daily illustrated column about Chicago life; settled on a farm near Brook, Indiana, 1904. Delegate, Republican National Convention, 1908; Trustee, Purdue University, 1908–15, and promoted the Ross-Ade Stadium at Purdue, 1923–24; Grand Consul, Sigma Chi fraternity, 1909; Director of Publicity, Indiana State Council of Defense, 1917–18; Member, Indiana Commission for the Chicago World's Fair, 1933. L.H.D.: Purdue University, 1926; LL.D.: Indiana University, Bloomington, 1927. Member, National Institute of Arts and Letters, 1908. *Died 16 May 1944.*

PUBLICATIONS

Collections

The America of Ade: Fables, Short Stories, Essays, edited by Jean Shepherd.   1960.
Letters, edited by Terence Tobin.   1973.

Fiction

Artie.   1896.
Pink Marsh.   1897.
Doc' Horne.   1899.
Fables in Slang.   1900.
More Fables.   1900.
Forty Modern Fables.   1901.
The Girl Proposition.   1902.
People You Know.   1903.
Circus Day.   1903.
Handsome Cyril.   1903.
Clarence Allen.   1903.
In Babel.   1903.
Rollo Johnson.   1904.
Breaking into Society.   1904.
True Bills.   1904.
In Pastures New.   1906.
The Slim Princess.   1907.
I Knew Him When— .   1910.
Hoosier Hand Book.   1911.
Knocking the Neighbors.   1912.
Ade's Fables.   1914.
Hand-Made Fables.   1920.
Single Blessedness and Other Observations.   1922.
Stay with Me Flagons.   1922.
Bang! Bang!   1928.

Plays

The Back-Stair Investigation (produced 1897).

The Night of the Fourth (produced 1901).
The Sultan of Sulu, music by Alfred G. Wathall (produced 1902).   1903.
The County Chairman (produced 1903).   1924.
Peggy from Paris, music by William Loraine (produced 1903).
Bird Center: Cap Fry's Birthday Party (produced 1904).
The Sho-Gun, music by Gustav Luders (produced 1904).
The College Widow (produced 1904).   1924.
Just Out of College (produced 1905).   1924.
The Bad Samaritan (produced 1905).
Marse Covington (produced 1906).   1918.
Artie (produced 1907).
Father and the Boys (produced 1908).   1924.
Mrs. Peckham's Carouse (produced 1908).
The Fair Co-ed, music by Gustav Luders (produced 1909).
The City Chap (produced 1910).
U.S. Minister Bedloe (produced 1910).
The Old Town (produced 1910).
The Mayor and the Manicure (produced 1912).   1923.
Nettie (produced 1914).   1923.
Speaking to Father.   1923.
The Persecuted Wife, in *Liberty,* 4 July 1925.
The Willing Performer, in *The Country Gentleman,* February 1928.
Aunt Fanny from Chautauqua.   1949.

Screenplays: many short films, and the following: *Our Leading Citizen,* with Waldemar Young, 1922; *Back Home and Broke,* with J. Clarkson Miller, 1922; *Woman-Proof,* with Tom Geraghty, 1923; *The Confidence Man,* with others, 1924.

Verse

Verses and Jingles.   1911.

Other

The Old-Time Saloon (essays).   1931.
Revived Remarks on Mark Twain, edited by George Hiram Brownell.   1936.
One Afternoon with Mark Twain.   1939.

Editor, *An Invitation to You and Your Folks, from Jim and Some More of the Home Folks.*   1916.

Bibliography: *A Bibliography of Ade* by Dorothy R. Russo, 1947.

Reading List: *Ade, Warmhearted Satirist* by Fred C. Kelly, 1947; *Ade* by Lee Coyle, 1964; "Ade: The City Uncle" by Edmund Wilson, in *The Bit Between My Teeth,* 1965.

*   *   *

Born in a small Indiana town in 1866, George Ade grew up fascinated with the talk around main-street shops and country stores. While attending Purdue College (later University) he became an avid theater-goer, rarely missing a minstrel show or musical comedy at the

Lafayette Opera House. Not surprisingly, transcribing speech and writing plays became his lucrative livelihood. Following a stint as a hometown newspaper man, Ade went up to Chicago in 1890 to join his friend, the cartoonist John T. McCutcheon, on the *Chicago Morning News*.

In 1893 these two collaborated on a daily illustrated column, "All Roads Lead to the World's Fair," a potpourri of interviews and observations centered on the Columbian Exposition. After the Fair closed, their column continued as "Stories of the Streets and of the Town." Taking all Chicago as their province, Ade and McCutcheon described urban life and common speech in hundreds of vivid sketches. Stylistically, Ade experimented in the "Stories" with straight narrative, light verse, dramatic dialogue, and various ethnic dialects. The pieces were popular enough to be saved and sold in eight paperback collections between 1894 and 1900. Ade also extracted three recurring characters, stitched their scattered appearances into sustained narratives, and published the results as *Artie*, *Pink Marsh*, and *Doc' Horne*. The title characters were, respectively, a brash street-wise office worker, a black shoeshine boy in a basement barbershop, and a genial yarn-spinner living at the Alfalfa European Hotel. Not coherent enough to be considered novels, these books remain important as pioneering realistic transcriptions of urban vernacular voices – particularly Artie's colorful slang and Pink's northern Negro dialect.

Ade's best work is in his "Fables in Slang," the first of which appeared in the "Streets and Towns" column in 1897 after Ade had asked himself, "why not retain the archaic form and the stilted manner of composition [of the fable] and, for purposes of novelty, permit the language to be 'fly,' modern, undignified, quite up to the moment?" (Fred C. Kelly, *George Ade*, p. 136). The fables became a regular Saturday feature, and were soon syndicated and collected into book form. Nine additional collections followed, the last in 1920. Most of Ade's fables were gently satiric exempla of pretension and folly, set in Mid-Western small towns or in Chicago, and capped by incongruous, undercutting moral tag lines. They follow his earlier work in reproducing familiar character types and common street talk. His master stroke was the use of capital letters for comic and ironic emphasis of the tendency of such talk toward platitudes and slang. (For example: "One morning a Modern Solomon, who had been chosen to preside as Judge in a divorce Mill, climbed to his Perch and unbuttoned his Vest for the Wearisome Grind.") The fables brought to literary visibility a host of ordinary people: the bombastic preacher and the travelling salesman, college students, bohemian writers and fast-talking vaudevillians, and numbers of country folk lost in the city. They are valuable as a microcosm of Mid-Western, middle-class life at the turn of the century. More important, Ade's use of the vernacular instead of genteel-academic English provided a shot of vitality to the language, and helped make it more flexible for the next generation of American writers.

During his most productive decade, 1900–10, Ade also wrote over a dozen plays. Three were very successful on Broadway: *The Sultan of Sulu*, a musical-comedy satire on American assumption of the "white man's burden" in the South Pacific; *The County Chairman*, a comedy-drama about politics in the rural Mid-West; and his best play, *The College Widow*, which introduced college life and football to the American stage.

—Charles Fanning

AGEE, James.   American.   Born in Knoxville, Tennessee, 27 November 1909. Educated at Phillips Exeter Acadmy, New Hampshire; Harvard University, Cambridge, Massachusetts, 1928–32, B.A. 1932. Settled in New York City, 1932; staff writer for the Luce publications *Fortune* and *Time*, 1932–48; Film Reviewer for *Time*, 1941–48; Film Critic, *The Nation*, 1943–48. Recipient: National Institute of Arts and Letters award, 1949; Pulitzer Prize, 1958. *Died 16 May 1955.*

PUBLICATIONS

Collections

Collected Poems, edited by Robert Fitzgerald.   1968.
Collected Short Prose, edited by Robert Fitzgerald.   1968.

Fiction

The Morning Watch.   1951.
A Death in the Family.   1957.
Four Early Stories, edited by Elena Harap.   1964.

Plays

Agee on Film: Five Film Scripts (includes *The Blue Hotel, The African Queen, The Bride Comes to Yellow Sky, The Night of the Hunter, Noa Noa).*   1960.

Screenplays: *The Quiet One* (documentary), 1949; *The African Queen,* with John Huston, 1951; *The Bride Comes to Yellow Sky* (in *Face to Face),* 1953; *White Man* (documentary), 1953; *The Night of the Hunter,* 1955.

Verse

Permit Me Voyage.   1934.

Other

Let Us Now Praise Famous Men: Three Tenant Families, photographs by Walker Evans.   1941.
Agee on Film: Reviews and Comments.   1958.
Letters to Father Flye.   1962; revised edition, 1971.
A Way of Seeing: Photographs of New York, photographs by Helen Levitt.   1965.

Reading List: *Agee* by Peter H. Ohlin, 1966; *Remembering Agee* edited by David Madden, 1974; *The Restless Journey of Agee* by Genevieve Moreau, 1977.

*   *   *

In 1941 James Agee and the photographer Walker Evans published *Let Us Now Praise Famous Men.* A long, journalistic piece that would become the central fixture of Agee's critical fame, the book was the result of eight months that he and Evans had spent in Alabama sympathetically chronicling in prose and photographs the daily lives of sharecropper families in the deep South.

Prior to the appearance of *Let Us Now Praise Famous Men,* Agee had published a book of poetry, *Permit Me Voyage,* as well as many magazine articles – most of them anonymously – as a member of the staff of *Fortune.* He had also begun writing film criticism for *Time,* an activity which he continued for *The Nation* and which signaled the beginnings of a deep involvement with cinema, not only as an out-spoken critic of the medium but also as a writer of highly detailed screenplays.

Let Us Now Praise Famous Men and his film work aside, Agee is best remembered for his novels, *The Morning Watch* and *A Death in the Family*, which was published two years after his death and for which he was posthumously awarded the Pulitzer Prize. Largely autobiographical, both novels reveal the influence in Agee's life and work of two elemental facts of his childhood: the death of his father when Agee was six years old, and the religious piety of his mother, a piety with which he would constantly struggle. *The Morning Watch*, for instance, is the story of a young student at a religious school who grows away from orthodoxy toward self-awareness and, eventually, alienation. And in *A Death in the Family* the young protagonist's father has been killed in an automobile accident – as Agee's own father had been killed – leaving the boy and his family to cope with his absence, even as had the Agee family.

Many critics have felt that Agee failed to reach the artistic achievement that was his birthright. Never one to settle on a particular genre, they point out, he chose instead to do all: poetry, journalism, fiction, criticism, screenplays. And never one to care for his own health, he lived, as film director John Huston wrote, as though "body destruction was implicit in his make-up." Still, James Agee achieved much in his forty-five years, and his premature death meant, finally, that his greatest fame would have to come posthumously.

—Bruce A. Lohof

AIKEN, Conrad (Potter). American. Born in Savannah, Georgia, 5 August 1889. Educated at Middlesex School, Concord, Massachusetts; Harvard University, Cambridge, Massachusetts (President, *Harvard Advocate*), 1907–12, A.B. 1912. Married 1) Jessie McDonald in 1912 (divorced, 1929), one son, two daughters; 2) Clarice Lorenz, 1930 (divorced, 1937); 3) Mary Hoover, 1937. Contributing Editor, *The Dial*, New York, 1916–19; American Correspondent, *Athenaeum*, London, 1919–25, and *London Mercury*, 1921–22; London Correspondent, *The New Yorker*, 1933–36. Instructor, Harvard University, 1927–28. Fellow, 1948, and Consultant in Poetry, 1950–52, Library of Congress, Washington, D.C. Recipient: Pulitzer Prize, 1930; Shelley Memorial Prize, 1930; Guggenheim Fellowship, 1934; Bryher Award, 1952; National Book Award, 1954; Bollingen Prize, 1956; Academy of American Poets Fellowship, 1957; National Institute of Arts and Letters Gold Medal, 1958; Huntington Hartford Foundation Award, 1961; Brandeis University Creative Arts Award, 1966; National Medal for Literature, 1969. Member, American Academy of Arts and Letters, 1957. *Died 17 August 1973.*

PUBLICATIONS

Collections

Selected Letters, edited by Joseph Killorin. 1978.

Verse

Earth Triumphant and Other Tales in Verse.   1914.
The Jig of Forslin: A Symphony.   1916.
Turns and Movies and Other Tales in Verse.   1916.
Nocturne of Remembered Spring and Other Poems.   1917.
The Charnal Rose, Senlin: A Biography, and Other Poems.   1918.
The House of Dust: A Symphony.   1920.
Punch: The Immortal Liar.   1921.
The Pilgrimage of Festus.   1923.
Priapus and the Pool and Other Poems.   1925.
(Poems), edited by Louis Untermeyer.   1927.
Prelude.   1929.
Selected Poems.   1929.
John Deth, A Metaphysical Legend, and Other Poems.   1930.
Preludes for Memnon.   1931.
The Coming Forth by Day of Osiris Jones.   1931.
Landscape West of Eden.   1934.
Time in the Rock: Preludes to Definition.   1936.
And in the Human Heart.   1940.
Brownstone Eclogues and Other Poems.   1942.
The Soldier.   1944.
The Kid.   1947.
The Divine Pilgrim.   1949.
Skylight One: Fifteen Poems.   1949.
Collected Poems.   1953.
A Letter from Li Po and Other Poems.   1955.
The Flute Player.   1956.
Sheepfold Hill: 15 Poems.   1958.
Selected Poems.   1961.
The Morning Song of Lord Zero: Poems Old and New.   1963.
A Seizure of Limericks.   1964.
Thee.   1967.
The Clerk's Journal: An Undergraduate Poem, Together with a Brief Memoir of Dean
    LeBaron Russell Briggs, T. S. Eliot, and Harvard, in 1911.   1971.
Collected Poems 1916–1970.   1971.

Play

Mr. Arcularis (produced 1949).   1957.

Fiction

Bring! Bring! and Other Stories.   1925.
Blue Voyage.   1927.
Costumes by Eros.   1928.
Gehenna.   1930.
Great Circle.   1933.
Among the Lost People (stories).   1934.
King Coffin.   1935.
A Heart for the Gods of Mexico.   1939.
Conversation; or, Pilgrims' Progress.   1940; as The Conversation, 1948.

The Short Stories.   1950.
The Collected Short Stories.   1960.
The Collected Novels.   1964.

Other

Scepticisms: Notes on Contemporary Poetry.   1919.
Ushant: An Essay (autobiography).   1952.
A Reviewer's ABC: Collected Criticism from 1916 to the Present, edited by Rufus A. Blanshand.   1958; as *Collected Criticism,* 1968.
Cats and Bats and Things with Wings (juvenile).   1965.
Tom, Sue, and the Clock (juvenile).   1966.

Editor, *Modern American Poets.*   1922; as *Twentieth Century American Poetry,* 1944; revised edition, 1963.
Editor, *Selected Poems of Emily Dickinson.*   1924.
Editor, *American Poetry, 1671–1928: A Comprehensive Anthology.*   1929; as *A Comprehensive Anthology of American Poetry,* 1944.
Editor, with William Rose Benét, *An Anthology of Famous English and American Poetry.*   1945.

Reading List: *Aiken: A Life of His Art* by Jay Martin, 1962; *Aiken* by Frederick J. Hoffman, 1962; *Aiken* by Reuel Denney, 1964.

*   *   *

Characteristically, Conrad Aiken himself raises the essential critical problem in a note he wrote in 1917: "It is difficult to place Conrad Aiken in the poetic firmament, so difficult that one sometimes wonders whether he deserves a place there at all" (*Collected Criticism*). The problem is further complicated by the fact that Aiken was not only a poet, but also a respected novelist and critic. The list of his admirers is persuasive: R. P. Blackmur, Allen Tate, Malcolm Lowry all find in him one of the central voices of his age. Yet to the contemporary reader such claims are likely to seem excessive.

About the scope of his ambition there can be no doubt. Five long, complicated novels; many lengthy poetic sequences, or "symphonies," dealing with themes as varied, and as large, as the history of America (*The Kid*), the importance of his Puritan heritage ("Mayflower"), the problems of the self encountering the realities of love and death (*Preludes for Memnon* and *The Coming Forth by Day of Osiris Jones*): all testify to the courageous attempt to convey a rich, complex life in a wide-ranging, always technically experimental, art.

The centre of this art lies in the difficultly maintained balance between aesthetic purity and formal perfection on the one hand, and the menacing chaos of terrifying experience on the other. It is tempting to relate this to Aiken's very early experience as a child when he discovered the bodies of his parents after a mutual suicide pact: this moment is placed at the centre of his long autobiographical essay *Ushant*. This deeply buried memory may also have encouraged Aiken's passionate interest in Freud. The five novels show this interest everywhere: the hero of *Blue Voyage*, Demarest, is on a voyage of self-discovery through journey, quest, and dream. This novel, like *Great Circle* – which Freud himself admired – is an elaborate metaphor for the author's psychic search, the exploration of his own consciousness. At their best, the novels find a language for disturbing, hidden states of the psyche: the combination of thriller form and psychoanalytic imagery in *King Coffin* is uniquely memorable. But too often the novels slip into vagueness and imprecision. As

Frederick J. Hoffman has observed, their separate parts fail *quite* to cohere. The lack of adequate characterisation, and the over-literariness of the enterprise, are at odds with our valid expectations of prose fiction. It is significant, then, that Aiken's "autobiography,". *Ushant*, should seem to so many of his critics his finest achievement in prose. Here, Aiken as writer, and his literary friends, including Eliot and Pound, are at the centre of a "fictionalised" account of the author's life. Apart from its other intrinsic interests, this quite extraordinary, unclassifiable work is justified, almost alone, by the majestic sweep and lyrical seductiveness of Aiken's rhetoric.

It is this majestic rhetoric that one also recognises in the poetry: Malcolm Lowry referred to Aiken as "the truest and most direct descendant of our own great Elizabethans" (*Wake, 11*, 1952). This quality is immediately apparent in *Preludes for Memnon*:

> What dignity can death bestow on us,
> Who kiss beneath a street lamp, or hold hands
> Half hidden in a taxi, or replete
> With coffee, figs and Barsac make our way
> To a dark bedroom in a wormworn house?

The combination here of the common and quotidian – street lamp, taxi, coffee – with noble, "Elizabethan" cadences, is the characteristic Aiken manner. It is a manner that frequently skirts parody and pastiche, but equally often rises to a rich, solemn verbal music. In poem after poem in his enormous output, Aiken sustains a long, flowing musical line, celebrating, as in "Landscape West of Eden," the capacity of language to order the chaos of the unaccomodated self. What one misses, however, in too much of this poetry, and what contributes to a certain lack of *energy* in the verse, is any intense verbal particularity, or, often, the sense of real feeling significantly expressed. In *Time in the Rock*, one of his most ambitious pieces, there is little sense of any real pressure or urgency behind the words; they have a tendency, as it were, to slip off the edge of the page as we read; nothing seems to make it all *cohere*.

His more objective, "dramatic" poems, like *The Kid* and "Mayflower," with their incorporation of historical and legendary material and their evocations of New England landscape and geography, are perhaps more valuable, in the end, than his lyrical self-communings. The contemporary reader is also likely to be more drawn to the lighter side of Aiken: in a poem like "Blues for Ruby Matrix" the rhetoric remains, but allied now to a delightful sexiness and tenderness.

Whatever the mode, however, there is always in Aiken, even if only residually, that sense of horror, of terror, and of death – "The sombre note that gives the chord its power," as he puts it in "Palimpsest" – that gives the best poetry its capacity to hurt and wound us. When, in *Preludes for Memnon*, he defines the role of the poet, Aiken finds a definition that takes full note of this fundamental ground-bass of his own work: the poet is one who

> by imagination [apes]
> God, the supreme poet of despair ...
> Knowing the rank intolerable taste of death,
> And walking dead on the still living earth.

—Neil Corcoran

ALBEE, Edward (Franklin, III).   American.   Born in Washington, D.C., 12 March 1928. Educated at Lawrenceville School; Valley Forge Military Academy, Pennsylvania; Choate School, Connecticut, graduated 1946; Trinity College, Hartford, Connecticut, 1946–47. Served in the United States Army. Worked as a radio writer, WNYC, office boy, Warwick and Legler, record salesman, Bloomingdale's, book salesman, G. Schirmer, counterman, Manhattan Towers Hotel, messenger, Western Union, 1955–58, all in New York. Producer, with Richard Barr and Clinton Wilder, New Playwrights Unit Workshop, later Albarwild Theatre Arts, and Albar Productions, New York; also a stage director. Founder, William Flanagan Center for Creative Persons, Montauk, Long Island, New York, 1971. United States Cultural Exchange Visitor to Russia. Recipient: Berlin Festival Award, 1959, 1961; Vernon Rice Award, 1960; Obie Award, 1960; Argentine Critics Award, 1961; Lola D'Annunzio Award, 1961; New York Drama Critics Circle Award, 1964; Outer Circle Award, 1964; Antoinette Perry Award, 1964; Margo Jones Award, 1965; Pulitzer Prize, 1967, 1975. Litt.D.: Trinity College, 1974. Member, National Institute of Arts and Letters, 1966. Lives in Montauk, New York.

PUBLICATIONS

Plays

> *The Zoo Story* (produced 1959).   In *The Zoo Story, The Death of Bessie Smith, The Sandbox*, 1960.
> *The Sandbox* (produced 1960).   In *The Zoo Story, The Death of Bessie Smith, The Sandbox*, 1960.
> *The Death of Bessie Smith* (produced 1960).   In *The Zoo Story, The Death of Bessie Smith, The Sandbox*, 1960.
> *The Zoo Story, The Death of Bessie Smith, The Sandbox: Three Plays.*   1960; as *The Zoo Story and Other Plays*, 1962.
> *Fam and Yam* (produced 1960).   1961.
> *The American Dream* (produced 1961).   1961.
> *Bartleby*, with James Hinton, Jr., music by William Flanagan, from the story by Melville (produced 1961).
> *Who's Afraid of Virginia Woolf?* (produced 1962).   1962.
> *The Ballad of the Sad Café*, from the story by Carson McCullers (produced 1963).   1963.
> *Tiny Alice* (produced 1964).   1965.
> *Malcolm*, from the novel by James Purdy (produced 1966).   1966.
> *A Delicate Balance* (produced 1966).   1966.
> *Breakfast at Tiffany's*, music by Bob Merrill, from the story by Truman Capote (produced 1966).
> *Everything in the Garden*, from the play by Giles Cooper (produced 1967).   1968.
> *Box and Quotations from Chairman Mao Tse-Tung: Two Inter-Related Plays* (as *Box-Mao-Box*, produced 1968; as *Box and Quotations from Chairman Mao Tse-Tung*, produced 1968).   1969.
> *All Over* (produced 1971).   1971.
> *Seascape* (produced 1975).   1975.
> *Listening* (broadcast 1976; produced 1977).   In *Two Plays*, 1977.
> *Counting the Ways* (produced 1976).   In *Two Plays*, 1977.
> *Two Plays.*   1977.
> *The Lady from Dubuque.*   1978.

Radio Play: *Listening*, 1976.

Bibliography: *Albee at Home and Abroad: A Bibliography, 1958–June 1968* by Richard E. Amacher and Margaret Rule, 1970.

Reading List: *Albee* by Ruby Cohn, 1969; *Albee* by Richard E. Amacher, 1969; *Albee* by C. W. E. Bigsby, 1969, and *Albee: A Collection of Critical Essays* edited by Bigsby, 1975; *Albee* by Ronald Hayman, 1971; *From Tension to Tonic: The Plays of Albee* by Anne Paolucci, 1972; *Albee: The Poet of Loss* by Anita M. Stenz, 1978.

*   *   *

At age fifty, after two decades of playwriting, Edward Albee remains the most controversial playwright of the United States. Critics are divided as to whether he is a realist or absurdist. Critics and public are divided as to the quality of his writing after *Who's Afraid of Virginia Woolf?* Actors and directors are divided as to whether he is wise to direct his own plays. Never one to soar above the battle, Albee wittily attacks his attackers. More importantly, he continues to write plays in his own restless search for new dramatic forms.

The Zoo Story, completed in 1958 when he was thirty years old, played in New York City on the same bill as Beckett's *Krapp's Last Tape*, and Albee was immediately pigeonholed as absurdist. Rather than dramatize a metaphysical impasse, however, Albee creates a protagonist who is a martyr to brotherly love and cultural vigor. In arousing smug Peter to enact a zoo story, Jerry strikes hard at complacent conformity, and Albee strikes hard at conventional theater.

Albee's next few plays in the next few years are more traditionally satiric. *The Death of Bessie Smith* lacerates white racism; *The American Dream* and *The Sandbox* ridicule American materialism and mindlessness. *Fam and Yam*, a slight piece which Albee continues to direct, confronts an old established playwright with a bright young novice.

For all the energetic idiom of *The Zoo Story* and the satiric verve of his other short plays, Albee remained a fringe playwright until his very full evening of theater, *Who's Afraid of Virginia Woolf?* The play has been misunderstood as a marital problem play, a campus satire, or veiled homosexuality, but, even misunderstood, its verbal pyrotechnics attracted audiences. Slowly, its symbolic import has seeped through an apparently realistic surface. George and Martha, ostensibly an American academic couple but related by name to the father (and mother) of the United States, have based their union on the illusion of a child. On the eve of the child's twenty-first birthday, the fantasy parents return home from a campus party. Drinking heavily, the older couple uses a younger couple for "flagellation." As in O'Neill's *Long Day's Journey into Night* alcohol proves confessional and penitential for all four characters. In the play's third act "Exorcism" George kills their imaginary son. The middle-aged couple, alone at daybreak, has to learn to live with naked reality.

A direct challenge to O'Neill's *The Iceman Cometh*, *Who's Afraid of Virginia Woolf?* is a noteworthy contribution to American dramatic preoccupation with illusion, in the lineage of Williams's *Streetcar Named Desire* and Miller's *Death of a Salesman*. In this big four O'Neill and Williams are the romantics, Miller and Albee the realists, and yet *Virginia Woolf* reveals hints of nostalgia for illusion. Moreover, with time, the play's verbal vitriol seems diluted, clarifying the theatricalization of a crisis in Western culture.

All Albee's subsequent plays hinge on this theme, for which he finds new forms. He continues the corruscating dialogue of *Virginia Woolf* into the first scene of *Tiny Alice* but then shifts to slower rhythms of mystery – both murder and metaphysics. As in *Zoo Story* and *Virginia Woolf*, the protagonist of *Tiny Alice* seeks the reality beneath the surface, and the surface glitters theatrically with such devices as a model castle, a Cardinal who keeps caged cardinal-birds, a beautiful woman disguised as an old crone, an operatic staircase, and visual reminders of the Pietà and Crucifixion. Brother Julian claims to be "dedicated to the reality of things, rather than the appearance." Abandoned on his wedding day by his bride Alice and her entourage, literally shot into reality, Julian finally lies in cruciform posture, clinging to illusion as he really dies.

A Delicate Balance returns to a more realistic surface; as in *Virginia Woolf* a love relationship in one couple is explored through the impact of another couple. In Friday's Act I terrorized friends seek refuge with Tobias and Agnes; in Saturday's Act II Tobias welcomes them, but his daughter Julia reacts hysterically. In Sunday's Act III the friends know they are not welcome, know that they would not have welcomed, and they leave. The passion leads not to resurrection but restitution of a delicate family balance.

After two related and exploratory plays, *Box-Mao-Box*, Albee returns in *All Over* to the upper middle-class American milieu that he stylizes deftly. He brings to the center of this play a theme at the periphery of his other plays – the existential impact of death. In spite of the title, "all" is not quite "over," for a once powerful man is dying behind a stage screen. Waiting for his death are his wife, mistress, best friend, son, and daughter, whose mannered conversation traces the man's presence everywhere or "all over." Death precariously joins these people, only to sunder them again, as each is suffused in his/her own unhappiness.

Between *A Delicate Balance* and *All Over*, upper middle-class plays in credible settings, Albee wrote "two inter-related" and experimental plays, *Box* and *Quotations from Chairman Mao Tse-Tung*. In *Box*, "a parenthesis around *Mao*," a brightly lit cube usurps the whole stage while the audience hears nearby an associational monologue of a middle-aged woman. Apparently rambling, the speech is carefully structured: "When art hurts. That is what to remember." *Quotations* theatricalizes art hurting. Within the cube appears a steamship deck with four characters on it – a silent minister, Chairman Mao speaking only in the titular quotations, a shabby old woman speaking only doggerel verse of Will Carleton, and a middle-class, middle-aged, long-winded lady whose discourse further develops the themes of art and suffering. Skillfully and movingly counterpointed, the three voices dramatize the frailty of art – how it is nourished by suffering and how it suffers.

After the jejune lapse of *Seascape* Albee created another two short experimental plays, *Listening* and *Counting the Ways*. *Listening*, "a chamber play" translated from radio, resembles a chamber quartet in its blend of four voices – a recorded voice announcing the twenty scenes, a fifty-year old man, a fifty-year old woman, and a twenty-five year old "girl." Grouped about a fountain pool, the three visible characters engage in non-linear dialogue through which certain themes recur, particularly the girl's charge: "You don't listen.... Pay attention, rather, is what you don't do." Though the characters seem to speak in a limbo beyond life, the play is climaxed by a shocking suicide and a last reiteration of the girl's charge countered by the fifty-year old woman: "*I* listen." Less resonant but nevertheless witty and inventive is the two-character *Counting the Ways*, "A Vaudeville" in twenty-one scenes varying the moods of a love affair as Bergman does that of a marriage.

The corpus of Albee's work shows more stylistic variety and closer attention to the nuances of language than the work of any American playwright, living or dead. Rarely facile, never clumsy, recently mannered, Albee continues to dramatize deep themes in distinctive theatrical forms.

—Ruby Cohn

ALGREN, Nelson. American. Born in Detroit, Michigan, 28 March 1909. Educated at the University of Illinois, Urbana, 1928–31, B.S. in journalism 1931. Served in the United States Army Medical Corps, 1942–45. Married in 1936 (divorced, 1940); married Betty Ann Jones in 1965 (divorced, 1967). Worked as a salesman, migratory worker, carnival shill, and part-owner of a gas station, 1931–35; for the Works Progress Administration (WPA),

1936–40; for the Venereal Disease Program of the Chicago Board of Health, 1941–42. Editor, with Jack Conroy, *The New Anvil*, Chicago, 1939–41. Teacher of creative writing, University of Iowa, Iowa City, 1967, and University of Florida, Gainesville, 1974. Recipient: National Institute of Arts and Letters grant, 1947; Newberry Library Fellowship, 1947; National Book Award, 1950; American Academy of Arts and Letters Award of Merit, 1974. Lives in Chicago.

PUBLICATIONS

Fiction

Somebody in Boots. 1935; as *The Jungle*, n.d.
Never Come Morning. 1942.
The Neon Wilderness (stories). 1946.
The Man with the Golden Arm. 1949.
A Walk on the Wild Side. 1956.
The Last Carousel (stories). 1973.

Other

Chicago: City on the Make. 1951.
Who Lost an American? Being a Guide to the Seamier Sides of New York City, Inner London, Paris, Dublin, Barcelona, Seville, Almeria, Istanbul, Crete and Chicago, Illinois. 1963.
Conversations with Algren, with H. E. F. Donohue. 1964.
Notes from a Sea-Diary: Hemingway All the Way. 1965.

Editor, *Algren's Own Book of Lonesome Monsters.* 1962.

Bibliography: *Algren: A Checklist* by Kenneth G. McCollum, 1973.

Reading List: *Algren* by Martha Heasley Cox and R. W. Chatterton, 1975.

*   *   *

Four novels, some fifty short stories, numerous sketches, essays, poems, travel books, book reviews and other literary criticism produced over a period of more than forty years assure Nelson Algren a place in American literature. Chicago, where Algren lived for much of his life, is the setting for most of his work. Characters, themes, symbols, and imagery, as well as the Chicago settings, recur throughout his canon as he becomes the spokesman for the derelicts, professional tramps, prostitutes, addicts, convicts, prize-fighters, and baseball players who inhabit his city jungle, "The Neon Wilderness," as he titled one of his collection of short stories. While most of Algren's characters speak the dialogue of the gutter, his style varies from staccato reporting to the richly poetic passages that have gained him the title "the poet of the Chicago slums." His books contain much offbeat information revealed with satire, irony, humor, and farce.

His first novel, *Somebody in Boots*, is a "Depression novel," a chronicle of poverty and failure dedicated to "those innumerable thousands: the homeless boys of America." His second, *Never Come Morning*, is a story of rape and murder with a doomed Chicago Polish boxer as its hero. His best known work, however, is his third novel *The Man with the Golden Arm*, which won him the first National Book Award. In this book, written two decades before drug addiction became a national dilemma, Algren fictionalized the world of the drug addict with as yet unsurpassed authority and impact.

His last novel, *A Walk on the Wild Side*, the result of an attempt to rework *Somebody in Boots*, is Algren's favorite work as well as that of most of his later critics. Though Algren once maintained that no one has understood *A Walk on the Wild Side* – a book, he says, of a kind never before written, "an American fantasy – a poem written to an American beat as truly as *Huckleberry Finn*" – the novel is now acclaimed for its prophetic qualities and for its influence on later novels and films, particularly the novel and film *Midnight Cowboy* and the film *Easy Rider*.

—Martha Heasley Cox

AMMONS, A(rchie) R(andolph). American. Born in Whiteville, North Carolina, 18 February 1926. Educated at Wake Forest College, North Carolina, B.A. 1949; University of California, Berkeley, 1950–52. Served in the United States Naval Reserve, 1944–46. Married Phyllis Plumbo in 1949; one child. Principal, Hatteras Elementary School, North Carolina, 1949–50; Executive Vice-President, Friedrich and Dimmock Inc., Mellville, New Jersey, 1952–62. Since 1964, Member of the Faculty, Associate Professor, 1969–71, since 1971, Professor of English, and since 1973, Goldwin Smith Professor of English, Cornell University, Ithaca, New York. Visiting Professor, Wake Forest University, 1974–75. Poetry Editor, *Nation*, New York, 1963. Recipient: Bread Loaf Writers Conference Scholarship, 1961; Guggenheim Fellowship, 1966; American Academy of Arts and Letters Travelling Fellowship, 1967; National Endowment for the Arts grant, 1969; National Book Award, 1973; Bollingen Prize, 1975; National Institute of Arts and Letters award, 1977. D.Litt.: Wake Forest University, 1972; University of North Carolina, Chapel Hill, 1973. Lives in Ithaca, New York.

PUBLICATIONS

Verse

Ommateum, with Doxology. 1955.
Expressions of Sea Level. 1964.
Corsons Inlet. 1965.
Tape for the Turn of the Year. 1965.
Northfield Poems. 1966.
Selected Poems. 1968.
Uplands. 1970.
Briefings: Poems Small and Easy. 1971.
Collected Poems 1951–1971. 1972.

Reading List: "Ammons Issue" of *Diacritics*, 1974.

*   *   *

A.R. Ammons is one of the most prolific poets of his generation, amassing to date some dozen books of verse that have won him the National Book Award in 1973, for his *Collected Poems 1951–1971*, and the Bollingen Award for *Sphere: The Form of a Motion*. The earliest poems, searching boldly for a center of self from which to project his persona, achieve their best effect from his recklessly strewn imagery and the pressure of his imagination to find the edges and furthest barriers of experience. The excellent *Selected Poems* of 1968, a winnowing of all the early work, dramatizes this search with varied, often profoundly moving language.

Ammons's attention ranges from intricately detailed portraits of the landscape of upper New York state, to travels throughout the southwestern United States, and memories of his childhood growing up on a farm in North Carolina, where he is fresh and original as a lyric poet. His reminiscence of the partly mute woman who raised him as a child, "Nelly Myers," is a minor classic of the modern elegy, with its lilting rhythms and its quiet, loving tribute to her wisdom and imperfections.

Much of Ammons's poetry depends upon a texture of rapid, rambling speech that precipitates a poem within its often lush formations. The edge of his poem is not silence but the banter and commentary in which it lies embedded. This pointedly risky strategy of creating a lyric can, when it is not in control, produce tracts and harangues that run tediously on devoid of any poetry. When inspired, however, the language gives way to a charged form of words partly submerged in the verbal undergrowth. His poems are like forms half perceived lying in high grass.

His verbal felicity has, however, occasioned more dry commentary than inspired lyricism. In an experiment with writing on adding machine tape, which imposed a narrow frame on the poet, Ammons wrote a seemingly endless discourse on the minutiae of his life during the winter of 1964–65, published as *Tape for the Turn of the Year*. As a professor teaching at Cornell University and living in Ithaca, New York, the persona lacks adventure and change, and the poet's journal suffers from the uneventful pace of his days. In succeeding volumes, *Northfield Poems* and *Uplands,* the style is noticeably more clipped and abrupt, approaching Imagist concision. The poet is clearly inspired by natural phenomena, particularly in the latter volume where his attention to mountain scenery is keenly alert. In *Briefings* he continues to experiment with short, sudden articulations of feeling and momentary perceptions. But in *Sphere* the style changes again into a long sequential discourse patterned by sections of four triplets where language is only partly sculpted. *The Snow Poems* returns to the mode of shorter poems and is a large collection devoted to the poet's favourite landscape, the snow-laden terrain of the northeast.

Throughout this large canon, Ammons continues to search for a final center of self irreducible of ambiguity. In his natural landscapes he has sought the recesses of the mystery of his own nature. But in chronicling his middle years and the details of his life from day to day, he provides the fullest account of the frustrations and triumphs of the middle class American reluctant to accept his professional life as the whole of his existence.

—Paul Christensen

ANDERSON, Maxwell.   American.   Born in Atlantic, Pennsylvania, 15 December 1888; grew up in North Dakota. Educated at Jamestown High School, North Dakota, graduated 1908; University of North Dakota, Grand Forks, 1908–11, B.A. 1911; Stanford University, California, 1913–14, M.A. 1914. Married 1) Margaret C. Haskett in 1911 (died, 1931), three sons; 2) Gertrude Maynard in 1933 (died, 1953), one daughter; 3) Gilda Oakleaf in 1954. Teacher, Minnewaukan High School, North Dakota, 1911–13, and Polytechnic High School, San Francisco, 1914–17; Professor and Head of the English Department, Whittier College, California, 1917–18; Staff Member, *New Republic* magazine, New York, 1918–19, New York *Evening Globe*, 1919–21, and New York *World*, 1921–24; Founder-Editor, with Frank Ernest Hill, *Measure* magazine, New York, 1921; Founder, with Robert E. Sherwood, Elmer Rice, S. N. Behrman, Sidney Howard, and John F. Wharton, Playwrights Company, 1938. Recipient: Pulitzer Prize, 1933; New York Drama Critics Circle Award, 1936, 1937; American Academy of Arts and Letters Gold Medal, 1954. *Died 28 February 1959.*

PUBLICATIONS

Collections

Dramatist in America: Letters 1912–1958, edited by Laurence G. Avery.   1977.

Plays

White Desert (produced 1923).
What Price Glory?, with Laurence Stallings (produced 1924).   In *Three American Plays*, 1926.
First Flight, with Laurence Stallings (produced 1925).   In *Three American Plays*, 1926.
The Buccaneer, with Laurence Stallings (produced 1925).   In *Three American Plays*, 1926.
The Feud.   1925.
Outside Looking In, from the novel *Beggars of Life* by Jim Tully (produced 1925).   With *Gods of the Lightning*, 1929.
Forfeits (produced 1926).
Saturday's Children (produced 1927).   1926.
Gypsy (produced 1929).   Shortened version in *The Best Plays of 1928–29*, edited by Burns Mantle, 1929.
Gods of the Lightning, with Harold Hickerson (produced 1928).   1929.
Elizabeth the Queen (produced 1930).   1930.
Night over Taos (produced 1932).   1932.
Sea-Wife (produced 1932).
Both Your Houses (produced 1933).   1933.
Mary of Scotland (produced 1933).   1934.
Valley Forge (produced 1934).   1934.
Winterset (produced 1935).   1935.
The Masque of Kings (produced 1937).   1936.
The Wingless Victory (produced 1936).   1936.
High Tor (produced 1937).   1937.
The Feast of Ortolans (broadcast 1937; produced 1938).   1938.
The Star-Wagon (produced 1937).   1937.
Knickerbocker Holiday, music by Kurt Weill (produced 1938).   1938.
Second Overture (produced 1940).   1938.

Key Largo (produced 1939). 1939.

Journey to Jerusalem (produced 1940). 1940.

The Miracle of the Danube (broadcast 1941). In *The Free Company Presents*, edited by James Boyd, 1941.

Candle in the Wind (produced 1941). 1941.

The Eve of St. Mark (produced 1942). 1942.

Your Navy, in *This Is War!* 1942.

Letter to Jackie, in *The Best One-Act Plays of 1943*, edited by Margaret Mayorga. 1944.

Storm Operation (produced 1944). 1944.

Joan of Lorraine (produced 1946). 1947.

Truckline Cafe (produced 1946).

Anne of the Thousand Days (produced 1948). 1948.

Joan of Arc (screenplay, with Andrew Solt). 1948.

Lost in the Stars, music by Kurt Weill, from the novel *Cry the Beloved Country* by Alan Paton (produced 1949). 1950.

Barefoot in Athens (produced 1951). 1951.

The Bad Seed, from the novel by William March (produced 1954). 1955.

A Christmas Carol, music by Bernard Heermann, from the story by Dickens (televised 1954). 1955.

The Masque of Pedagogues, in *North Dakota Quarterly*, Spring 1957.

The Day the Money Stopped, from the novel by Brendan Gill (produced 1958).

The Golden Six (produced 1958).

Radio Plays: *The Feast of Ortolans*, 1937; *The Bastion Saint-Gervais*, 1938; *The Miracle of the Danube*, 1941; *The Greeks Remember Marathon*, 1944.

Television Play: *A Christmas Carol*, 1955.

Screenplays: *All Quiet on the Western Front*, with others, 1930; *We Live Again*, with others, 1934; *So Red the Rose*, 1935; *Joan of Arc*, with Andrew Solt, 1948; *The Wrong Man*, with Angus MacPhail, 1957.

Verse

You Who Have Dreams. 1925.

Notes on a Dream, edited by Laurence G. Avery. 1971.

Other

The Essence of Tragedy and Other Footnotes and Papers. 1939.

The Bases of Artistic Creation: Essays, with Rhys Carpenter and Roy Harris, 1942.

Off Broadway: Essays about the Theatre. 1947.

Bibliography: *A Catalogue of the Anderson Collection* by Laurence G. Avery, 1968; *Anderson and S. N. Behrman: A Reference Guide* by William Klink, 1977.

Reading List: *Anderson: The Man and His Plays* by Barrett H. Clark, 1933; *Anderson: The Playwright as Prophet* by Mabel Driscoll Bailey, 1957; *Life among the Playwright's Producing Company* by John F. Wharton, 1974; *Anderson* by Alfred S. Shivers, 1976.

*   *   *

Maxwell Anderson became a playwright by accident, but once committed to a career in the theater, he set out to base his work on carefully wrought principles of composition. His dramatic theories were based on the practices of ancient Greece and the Elizabethan period, and he was fiercely dedicated to the ideal of the theater as the democratic cultural institution. He reintroduced the idea of poetic tragedy and attracted large audiences to his historical verse plays though there are few striking passages of poetry in his work.

For Anderson the theater was both a spiritual experience and a commercial medium. While he agreed with Aristotle that the audience should be led by the playwright to experience strong emotions, he was sure that the proper mark of success was ticket sales. He accepted the maxim that no playwright deserves or will get posthumous adulation who has not attracted an enthusiastic audience during his lifetime. He attacked the New York critics for short-circuiting the gleaning process with their first-night reviews, but was personally willing to accept the audience's spontaneous judgment. He rejected the notion of government subsidization because he thought it would interfere with the natural selection process and resisted the lure of off-Broadway production on the grounds that only the more rigorous Broadway circuit was an ample test. Anderson successfully countered the commercial forces of Broadway for more than a quarter of a century and dominated American theater in the 1930's.

Anderson believed in theater of ideas. In an essay called "Keeping the Faith" he enunciated as rule number one the necessity of having a central idea or conviction which cannot be excised without killing the play. His *Joan of Lorraine* dramatizes the process of making concessions to the realities of play production while trying to protect the central core of the play's integrity. Though his convictions changed markedly during his career, his use of the stage to express them did not. He attacked big government, defended democracy, preached pacifism, and urged commitment to war. As his ideas about war, for instance, changed from the cynicism of *What Price Glory?* (written with Laurence Stallings) to the patriotic fervor of *The Eve of St. Mark* and *Storm Operation*, he presented each new certainty with as much strength as the one before.

Anderson's overriding theme is the spiritual victory of humanity. In his essay "Off Broadway" he defined theater as "a religious institution devoted entirely to the exaltation of the spirit of man." He tried through the disillusionment of the 1920's, the depression of the 1930's, and the global war of the 1940's to present the triumphant human spirit. He has been accused of being a pessimist, but his view is essentially that of an optimistic humanist. He emphasized the importance of individual choice and the necessity of commitment. King McCloud of *Key Largo*, for instance, having failed to make a stand in the last days of the Spanish Civil War, finds it hard to stop running. His spirit triumphs only when he finds something for which he is willing to die. Mio of *Winterset*, emotionally crippled by lust for revenge, becomes a complete person only when he accepts love.

In many plays Anderson used the lives of historical characters to illumine broad questions of power and choice. He wrote plays about Christ, Socrates, Elizabeth I, Mary Stuart, George Washington, and Peter Stuyvesant. A comparison of *Elizabeth the Queen* with *Masque of Kings* illustrates the major problem in Anderson's method of historical tragedy. He is able to delineate Elizabeth's choice to have her lover Essex beheaded as a triumph of wise government over personal weakness, but Rudolph's suicide will not fit into such a neat pattern. As a result the third act of *Masque of Kings* takes a different direction from the one we might reasonably expect after the recognition scene of Act II, and the ending is weak and inappropriate.

The high seriousness of his subject matter is often a mistake. It is unfortunate that he did not leaven his work with comedy more often. In *High Tor* and *Knickerbocker Holiday* (music by Kurt Weill) he demonstrated a rich gift for humor. *Both Your Houses*, a play about Congressional corruption, makes excellent use of satire and was highly praised by critics.

Anderson's deficiences as a playwright seem to be related to conflicts between his intellectual approach to form and his spontaneous ideas for content. He wanted to emphasize the primacy of individual choice, for instance, but Aristotelian tragedy, which he chose to emulate, best communicates the powerful forces that neutralize free will. He wanted to write plays constructed around a second act recognition scene followed by spiritual triumph in physical defeat, but some of the historical characters he chose do not fit this pattern. He wanted to show the triumph of the human spirit, but one of his most successful plays, *The Bad Seed*, demonstrates the victory of congenital evil. He wanted to treat universal themes, but in plays such as *Gods of the Lightning* and *Wingless Victory* he got bogged down in heavy social commentary.

Anderson has been criticized for lack of innovation, and that is a fair criticism. His approach and subject matter are quite traditional. Echoes of *Medea* are clear in the plot of *Wingless Victory*, and the parallels between *Winterset* and *Romeo and Juliet* are obvious. His concern is less with striking out into new territories than with re-vitalizing the old. The actors in *Elizabeth the Queen* actually use Shakespeare's lines, for instance, but the effect is to illuminate the Queen's character and judgment.

Anderson was a prolific writer whose work attracted audiences and made money; by his own criteria he was a success. In comparison with his fellow writers in the American theater he must also be rated a success; only O'Neill outshone him in his time. Anderson did not always overcome the problems posed by his own methods, but he did illuminate the mazes of power, freedom, and faith he set out to explore. For over a quarter of a century, especially with works such as *Elizabeth the Queen*, *High Tor*, and *Winterset*, he dramatized the human condition in some striking scenes and created some high moments in American theater.

—Barbara M. Perkins

ANDERSON, Sherwood (Berton). American. Born in Camden, Ohio, 13 September 1876. Educated at a high school in Clyde, Ohio; Wittenberg Academy, Springfield, Ohio, 1899–1900. Served in the United States Army in Cuba during the Spanish-American War, 1898–99. Married 1) Cornelia Pratt Lane in 1904 (divorced, 1916), two sons and one daughter; 2) Tennessee Claflin Mitchell in 1916 (divorced, 1924); 3) Elizabeth Prall in 1924 (divorced, 1932); 4) Eleanor Copenhaver in 1933. Worked in a produce warehouse in Chicago, 1896–97; Advertising Copywriter, Long-Critchfield Company, Chicago, 1900–05; President, United Factories Company, Cleveland, 1906, and Anderson Manufacturing Company, paint manufacturers, Elyria, Ohio, 1907–12; free-lance copywriter, then full-time writer, Chicago, 1913–23; visited France and England, 1921; lived in New Orleans, 1923–24; settled on a farm near Marion, Virginia, 1925: Publisher of the *Smyth County News* and *Marion Democrat* from 1927; travelled extensively in the United States in the mid 1930's reporting on depression life. Member, National Institute of Arts and Letters, 1937. *Died 8 March 1941.*

PUBLICATIONS

Collections

Anderson Reader, edited by Paul Rosenfeld. 1947.
Letters, edited by Howard Mumford Jones and Walter B. Rideout. 1953.
Short Stories, edited by Maxwell Geismar. 1962.

Fiction

Windy McPherson's Son. 1916.
Marching Men. 1917; edited by Ray Lewis White, 1972.
Winesburg, Ohio: A Group of Tales of Ohio Small Town Life. 1919.
Poor White. 1920.
The Triumph of the Egg and Other Stories. 1921.
Many Marriages. 1923.
Horses and Men (stories). 1923.
Dark Laughter. 1925.
Alice, and The Lost Novel (stories). 1929.
Beyond Desire. 1932.
Death in the Woods and Other Stories. 1933.
Kit Brandon: A Portrait. 1936.

Plays

Winesburg (produced 1934). In *Winesburg and Others*, 1937.
Mother (produced ?). In *Winesburg and Others*, 1937.
Winesburg and Others (includes *The Triumph of the Egg*, dramatized by Raymond O'Neil; *Mother, They Married Later*). 1937.
Textiles, in *Contemporary One-Act Plays*, edited by William Kozlenko. 1938.
Above Suspicion (broadcast 1941). In *The Free Company Presents*, edited by James Boyd, 1941.

Radio Play: *Above Suspicion*, 1941.

Other

Mid-American Chants. 1918.
A Story Teller's Story. 1924; edited by Ray Lewis White, 1968.
The Modern Writer. 1925.
Notebook. 1926.
Tar: A Midwest Childhood. 1926; edited by Ray Lewis White, 1969.
A New Testament. 1927.
Hello Towns! 1929.
Nearer the Grass Roots. 1929.
The American County Fair. 1930.
Perhaps Women. 1931.
No Swank. 1934.
Puzzled America. 1935.
A Writer's Conception of Realism. 1939.
Home Town. 1940.
Memoirs. 1942; edited by Ray Lewis White, 1969.
Return to Winesburg (essays), edited by Ray Lewis White. 1967.
The Buck Fever Papers, edited by Welford Dunaway Taylor. 1971.
France and Anderson: Paris Notebook 1921, edited by Michael Fanning. 1976.

Bibliography: *Anderson: A Bibliography* by Eugene P. Sheehy and Kenneth A. Lohf, 1960; *Merrill Checklist of Anderson* by Ray Lewis White, 1969.

Reading List: *Anderson: His Life and Work* by James E. Schevill, 1951; *Anderson* by Irving Howe, 1951; *Anderson* by Brom Weber, 1964; *Anderson* by Rex Burbank, 1964; *The Achievement of Anderson: Essays in Criticism* edited by Ray Lewis White, 1966; *Anderson: An Introduction and Interpretation* by David D. Anderson, 1967; *The Road to Winesburg: A Mosaic of the Imaginative Life of Anderson* by William A. Sutton, 1972; *Anderson: A Collection of Critical Essays* edited by Walter B. Rideout, 1974; *Anderson* by Welford Dunaway Taylor, 1977.

*   *   *

In an interview for the *Paris Review* (Spring 1956), William Faulkner stated that Sherwood Anderson was "the father of my generation of American writers and the tradition of American writing which our successors will carry on." Anderson's importance in literary history is accurately summed up in Faulkner's statement, for Anderson is a seminal figure whose prose style has had a significant impact on the direction of American literature in the twentieth century. As a boy from a small town in Ohio Anderson fell under the spell of Twain's *Huckleberry Finn* with its innocent narrator and non-literary, vernacular style. Later, as an aspiring writer in Chicago and New York, he became fascinated with Gertrude Stein's attempt to use language as a plastic medium, the way an artist uses paints. These influences on Anderson resulted in the development of a simple, concrete style close to the rhythms of American speech, a style which left an indelible imprint on the prose of Hemingway and his followers.

Anderson also developed a number of characteristically American themes in his fiction. The celebration of youth and innocence is one of those distinguishing features of American writing, and Anderson, raised in the middle west before the turn of the century, celebrates small-town life in the days of the horse and buggy. A boy's wonder and innocent joy in rural life, his love of horses and the open countryside, his admiration for the craftsmen of the village are all part of a nostalgic vein running through Anderson's writing. But Anderson, raised in poverty, was intimate with another side of American life, one which he eventually termed "grotesque." As a young man he observed the people of his town caught in a struggle for material wealth and cowed by a repressive Puritan ethic and consequently wrote with great feeling about people like his parents whose lives were made wretched by their society's values. Anderson is very sensitive in his fiction to movement, to the restlessness of the individual and to the movements of peoples within the ever-changing fabric of society. He documents America's transition from a rural to an industrial society, and in several books he represents Americans, working in factories, as trapped in a form of living death. He saw the great masses of working Americans as alienated from creative work, and he pondered the artist's role in reawakening his countrymen to more meaningful forms of life.

Anderson's influence and reputation, however, outweigh his actual achievement as a writer. He published seven novels, but critics are not agreed that any one of the novels is wholly successful. The first, *Windy McPherson's Son*, which at the outset effectively recreates something of Anderson's own youth, particularly his relation to his father, becomes a rambling, incoherent narrative about a man's quest for a family and meaningful work. *Marching Men* is an ideological novel with a cranky and finally incoherent vision of men marching for the betterment of humankind. *Poor White*, which dramatizes the industrialization of America, is usually considered the best of the novels, but the charges of diffuseness and unnecessary repetition are not without some justification. Critics generally feel Anderson's worst novel is *Many Marriages*, the story of a man on the point of giving up his business and family in order to escape what has become for him a living death. Anderson himself walked out on his family and a successful career in order to become a writer, which explains perhaps his own fondness for *Many Marriages*. The other novels, *Dark Laughter*, *Beyond Desire*, and *Kit Brandon* all contain interesting variations on the theme of the individual's quest for a more vital existence, but none of these books succeeds completely in terms of characterization and especially plot. More valuable and interesting are Anderson's autobiographical writings, *A Story Teller's Story*, *Tar: A Midwest Childhood*, and the posthumous *Memoirs*, all of which fictionalize to a degree the actual events of Anderson's life and reveal the contrary and powerful impulses of the writer's imagination.

Anderson's success as a fiction writer, however, is undisputed in the short story form, and all the collections he published contain at least one or two first rate pieces. Stories such as "I Want to Know Why," "I'm a Fool," and "The Man Who Became a Woman" in which Anderson employs an innocent narrator and a simple, direct style have a unified purpose and effect that is lacking in all the longer fictions. These are initiation stories wherein a youth, usually an innocent boy from the country who loves horses, is awakened to fear, sexual guilt, and a knowledge of his own limitations. "Death in the Woods" is another short masterpiece; it describes a peasant woman's work-burdened existence with a simplicity and sureness of craft that have made critics compare it with the best of Turgenev's stories.

But the book for which Anderson will always be best known is *Winesburg, Ohio*, a cycle of stories about lonely people in a small midwestern town. Anderson originally titled it "The Book of the Grotesque" and in these stories he portrays with both compassion and clinical accuracy the secret lives of people who have been irreparably thwarted and frustrated in different ways. The narrator explains by means of a dream vision that the characters have become grotesque because they have chosen to believe in a single truth. Whether they believe in love, virginity, or godliness, the truth becomes a lie because such a narrow view distorts reality and tragically cuts people off from each other. The grotesques, caught up in their obsessive beliefs, are unable to communicate their ideas and feelings to each other. For example, a farmer consumed with the idea of being a Biblical patriarch so confuses and terrifies his only grandson in a ritual of sacrifice that the boy runs away forever. A young man, obsessed with the idea that he is "queer," hopelessly different from other people, breaks into a frantic dance and physically strikes out at his one sympathetic listener. A shy woman, who has waited many years for the return of her lover, one night in desperation runs naked across her front lawn in the rain. Appearing in several stories is the young newspaper reporter, George Willard, to whom some of the grotesques tell their story. George's mother, one of the aliens of the town, finds an ultimate release from her frustration and loneliness through death, but before she dies she prays that some day her son will "express something" for them both, that he will redeem their lives through art. The mother gives the book a tragic cast, for her prayer cannot be answered. The artists in *Winesburg, Ohio* are ineffectual figures, often persons the least capable of expressing themselves. George Willard at the end of the book leaves Winesburg and we can assume he has written the stories we have read, but he has not been able to "save" his people because the underlying insight in his book is that each man lives by a truth and no one can fully understand or express that truth for someone else.

Anderson once assessed himself as "the minor author of a minor masterpiece," and one recognizes here an author's startlingly accurate self-assessment. But what the author's statement does not comprehend is the powerful influence Anderson had on other writers like Hemingway and Faulkner and on the course of American literature as a whole.

—David Stouck

ASHBERY, John (Lawrence).   American.   Born in Rochester, New York, 28 July 1927. Educated at Deerfield Academy, Massachusetts; Harvard University, Cambridge, Massachusetts (Member of the Editorial Board, *The Harvard Advocate*), B.A. in English 1949; Columbia University, New York, M.A. in English 1951; New York University, 1957–58. Copywriter, Oxford University Press, New York, 1951–54, and McGraw-Hill

Book Company, New York, 1954–55. Art Critic, European Edition of the *New York Herald Tribune*, Paris, 1960–65, and *Art International*, Lugano, Switzerland, 1961–64; Editor, *Locus Solus* magazine, Lans-en-Vercors, France, 1960–62; Editor, *Art and Literature*, Paris, 1963–64; Paris Correspondent, 1964–65, and Executive Editor, 1965–72, *Art News*, New York. Since 1974, Professor of English, Brooklyn College of the City University of New York. Since 1976, Poetry Editor, *Partisan Review*, New Brunswick, New Jersey. Recipient: Fulbright Fellowship, 1955, 1956; Yale Series of Younger Poets Award, 1956; Poets Foundation grant, 1960, 1964; Ingram Merrill Foundation grant, 1962, 1972; Guggenheim Fellowship, 1967, 1973; National Endowment for the Arts grant, 1968, 1969; National Institute of Arts and Letters award, 1969; Shelley Memorial Award, 1973; Modern Poetry Association Frank O'Hara Prize, 1974; National Book Critics Circle Award, 1976; Pulitzer Prize, 1976; National Book Award, 1976. Lives in New York City.

PUBLICATIONS

Verse

Turandot and Other Poems.   1953.
Some Trees.   1956.
The Poems.   1960.
The Tennis Court Oath.   1962.
Rivers and Mountains.   1966.
Selected Poems.   1967.
Sunrise in Suburbia.   1968.
Three Madrigals.   1968.
Fragment.   1969.
The Double Dream of Spring.   1970.
The New Spirit.   1970.
Three Poems.   1972.
The Vermont Notebook, with Joe Brainard.   1975.
Fragment, Clepsydre, Poèmes Francais.   1975.
Self-Portrait in a Convex Mirror.   1975.
Houseboat Days.   1977.

Plays

The Heroes (produced 1952).   In *Three Plays*, 1978.
The Compromise (produced 1956).   In *Three Plays*, 1978.
Three Plays (includes *The Heroes, The Compromise, The Philosopher*).   1978.

Fiction

A Nest of Ninnies, with James Schuyler.   1969.

Other

Editor, with others, *American Literary Anthology 1*.   1968.
Editor, *Penguin Modern Poets 24*.   1973.

Editor, *Muck Arbour,* by Bruce Marcus.   1974.

Translator, *Melville,* by Jean-Jacques Mayoux.   1960.
Translator, *Alberto Giacometti,* by Jacques Dupin.   1963.

Bibliography: *Ashbery: A Comprehensive Bibliography Including the Art Criticism, and with Selected Notes from Unpublished Material* by David K. S. Kermani, 1976.

Reading List: *Alone with America* by Richard Howard, 1969; *American Free Verse: The Modern Revolution in Poetry* by Walter Sutton, 1973; "Ashbery: The Charity of Hard Moments" by Harold Bloom, in *Salmagundi,* Spring-Summer 1973.

*   *   *

John Ashbery was originally associated with the New York school of poets, whose central figure is Frank O'Hara, and whose poetic style is noted for its painterly emphasis on setting, luxurious detailing, and leisurely meditative argument. This group closely identified itself with the abstract expressionist painters and with the Museum of Modern Art; some of these poets wrote for *Art News.* Ashbery was directly connected with all three spheres, and from the painters learned a curious collage-like style of poetry made of bits and pieces of lyric phrasing. This mode of speech, lacking transition between leaps of thought and reflection, early marked Ashbery as difficult, if not impenetrable. As he remarked in a later poem,

> I know that I braid too much my own
> Snapped-off perceptions of things as they come to me.
> They are private and always will be.

The root of Ashbery's lyric style may be traced back to the Symbolists, and to the allusive poems of T. S. Eliot, whose echo is frequently heard in Ashbery's work. At his best, Ashbery can give uncanny immediacy to his language; his stance of uncertainty before life draws him to the appearance of the phenomenal world which he contemplates in a delicate, sinewy language.

Some Trees is Ashbery's first work of note, and contains one of his most anthologized poems, "The Instruction Manual." His second major book of poems, *The Tennis Court Oath,* in particular emphasizes the style of pastiche. Beginning with *Rivers and Mountains,* Ashbery introduced his specialty, the long discursive meditation running to many pages in which the effort is made to piece together the fragments of experience into a sensible whole. "The Skaters" makes up half of the book. The meditative style is pursued most fully in *Three Poems,* prose poems that are linked like the moments of dialectical reason, in which the speaker struggles to reveal the metaphysical and spiritual basis of his existence.

Much of the poetry of these books is suffused with a restrained melancholy. Ashbery is articulating the post-existential awareness, in which existence is an accepted but utterly unknowable dimension. That stance is succinctly phrased in "Poems in Three Parts":

> One must bear in mind one thing.
> It isn't necessary to know what that thing is.
> All things are palpable, none are known.

No faith or hope can fully support the speaker, and he is recurrently plunged into self-analysis to discover the purpose of his life. *Self-Portrait in a Convex Mirror* continues this self-analysis and metaphysical exploration, particularly in the brilliant long title poem and in "Grand Galop." In his recent books, there is a perceptible effort to take up subjects beyond the self, but the poems are still deeply absorbed with the absence of a philosophical and religious context in which to value or understand life. Ashbery's innovative and sophisticated humor is clear in *The Double Dream of Spring,* particularly in such surreal high jinks as his "Variations, Calypso and Fugue on a Theme of Ella Wheeler Wilcox."

—Paul Christensen

ATHERTON, Gertrude (Franklin, née Horn). American. Born in San Francisco, California, 30 October 1857. Educated in private schools in California and Kentucky. Married George H. Bowen Atherton in 1876 (died, 1887). After her husband's death travelled extensively and lived in Europe; in later life returned to San Francisco. Trustee, San Francisco Public Library; Member, San Francisco Art Commission. President, American National Academy of Literature, 1934; Chairman of Letters, League of American Pen Women, 1939; President, Northern California Section of P.E.N. Recipient: International Academy of Letters and Sciences of Italy Gold Medal. D.Litt.: Mills College, Oakland, California, 1935; LL.D.: University of California, Berkeley, 1937. Chevalier, Legion of Honor, 1925; Honorary Member, Institut Littéraire et Artistique de France. *Died 14 June 1948.*

PUBLICATIONS

Fiction

> *What Dreams May Come.* 1888.
> *Hermia Suydam.* 1889; as *Hermia, An American Woman,* 1889.
> *Los Cerritos: A Romance of the Modern Time.* 1890.
> *A Question of Time.* 1891.
> *The Doomswoman.* 1893.
> *Before the Gringo Came.* 1894; revised edition, as *The Splendid Idle Forties: Stories of Old California,* 1902.
> *A Whirl Asunder.* 1895.
> *His Fortunate Grace.* 1897.
> *Patience Sparhawk and Her Times.* 1897.
> *American Wives and English Husbands.* 1898; revised edition, as *Transplanted,* 1919.
> *The Californians.* 1898; revised edition, 1935.
> *The Valiant Runaways.* 1898.
> *A Daughter of the Vine.* 1899.
> *Senator North.* 1900.
> *The Aristocrats, Being the Impressions of the Lady Helen Pole During Her Sojourn in the Great North Woods.* 1901.
> *The Conqueror, Being the True and Romantic Story of Alexander Hamilton.* 1902.
> *Heart of Hyacinth.* 1903.

Mrs. Pendleton's Four-in-Hand. 1903.
Rulers of Kings. 1904.
The Bell in the Fog and Other Stories. 1905.
The Travelling Thirds. 1905.
Rezánov. 1906.
Ancestors. 1907.
The Gorgeous Isle: A Romance: Scene, Nevis, B.W.I., 1842. 1908.
Tower of Ivory. 1910.
Julia France and Her Times. 1912.
Perch of the Devil. 1914.
Mrs. Balfame. 1916.
The White Morning: A Novel of the Power of the German Women in Wartime. 1918.
The Avalanche: A Mystery Story. 1919.
The Sisters-in-Law: A Novel of Our Time. 1921.
Sleeping Fires. 1922; as *Dormant Fires*, 1922.
Black Oxen. 1923.
The Crystal Cup. 1925.
The Immortal Marriage. 1927.
The Jealous Gods: A Processional Novel of the Fifth Century B.C. (Concerning One Alcibiades). 1928; as *Vengeful Gods*, 1928.
Dido, Queen of Hearts. 1929.
The Sophisticates. 1931.
The Foghorn: Stories. 1934.
Golden Peacock. 1936.
Rezánov and Doña Concha. 1937.
The House of Lee. 1940.
The Horn of Life. 1942.

Play

Screenplay: *Don't Neglect Your Wife*, with Louis Sherwin, 1921.

Other

California: An Intimate History. 1914.
Life in the War Zone. 1916.
The Living Present (essays). 1917.
Adventures of a Novelist (autobiography). 1932.
Can Women Be Gentlemen? (essays). 1938.
Golden Gate Country. 1945.
My San Francisco: A Wayward Biography. 1946.

Editor, *A Few of Hamilton's Letters, Including His Description of the Great West Indian Hurricane of 1772.* 1903.

Bibliography: "A Checklist of the Writings of and about Atherton" by Charlotte S. McClure, in *American Literary Realism 1870–1910*, Spring 1976.

Reading List: *Atherton* by Joseph H. Jackson, 1940.

*   *   *

Gertrude Atherton was a popular and prolific writer, publishing nearly forty novels, several volumes of short stories, three collections of essays, a history of California, two books about San Francisco, a selection of Alexander Hamilton's letters, and numerous uncollected articles. Although her novels lack great artistic merit, they are significant for the literary historian because they helped to free American literature from the shackles of Victorian prudery. From the beginning of her career, Atherton rejected the Victorian myths about woman's moral superiority and sexual imbecility. Her heroines are sensual, egotistical, and intellectually ambitious. They seek an identity based on their own needs and talents rather than on the attributes society ascribed to women. Her treatment of female sexuality in particular gained her considerable critical attention both in America and in England; liberal critics singled her out for her "fearless treatment of the problems of sex," while conservatives screamed that she exalted "the morals of the barn-yard into a social ideal" and accelerated "the corruption of private life and the destruction of the family relation."

Atherton's California fiction is of particular interest to the cultural historian, focussing, as it does, on the effects of the "gringo" coming to power at the expense of the Mexican aristocracy. Her best novel, *The Californians*, effectively analyzes the conflict between the heritages of Hispanic indolence and pride and Yankee shrewdness and pragmatism. In this novel, Atherton's conception of her heroine is firmly rooted in her knowledge of the patriarchal, restrictive Spanish tradition as well as the shallow ambiance of San Francisco society. However, in many of her other California novels, Atherton romanticizes her subject matter. As Kevin Starr points out in *Americans and the California Dream*, Atherton speaks for the California elite which, on the one hand, mourned the loss of the Arcadian existence of the Hispanic settlers, but, on the other hand, repudiated that existence as inimical to the progress of the state.

In most of her fiction, Atherton sensationalized and romanticized her subject matter. Thus, the heroine of *Patience Sparhawk and Her Times* is wrongly convicted of her husband's murder, the heroine of *Black Oxen* is a rejuvenated fifty-eight year old woman who falls in love with a man in his thirties, and the heroine of *The Immortal Marriage* is Aspasia, whom Atherton presents not as a prostitute, but as Pericles' beloved wife, supremely beautiful and intelligent enough to provoke admiration from men such as Sophocles and Socrates. Despite Atherton's artistic shortcomings, her lifelong concern with the contribution of women to civilization as well as her fictional observation of fifty years of America's social history suggests that her work deserves further examination by literary and cultural historians.

—Sybil B. Weir

AUCHINCLOSS, Louis (Stanton). American. Born in Lawrence, New York, 27 September 1917. Educated at Groton School, Connecticut, graduated 1935; Yale University, New Haven, Connecticut, 1935–38; University of Virginia Law School, Charlottesville, LL.B. 1941; admitted to the New York Bar, 1941. Served in the United States Naval Reserve, 1941–45: Lieutenant. Married Adele Lawrence in 1957; three sons. Associate Lawyer, Sullivan and Cromwell, New York, 1941–51. Associate, 1954–58, and since 1958 Partner, Hawkins, Delafield and Wood, New York. Since 1966, President of the Museum of the City of New York. Trustee, Josiah Macy Jr. Foundation, New York; Member of the Executive Committee, Association of the Bar of New York City; Member of the Administrative Committee, Dumbarton Oaks Research Library and Collection, Washington, D.C. Litt.D.: New York University, 1974. Member, National Institute of Arts and Letters. Lives in New York City.

PUBLICATIONS

Fiction

The Indifferent Children. 1947.
The Injustice Collectors (stories). 1950.
Sybil. 1952.
A Law for the Lion. 1953.
The Romantic Egoists: A Reflection in Eight Minutes. 1954.
The Great World and Timothy Colt. 1956.
Venus in Sparta. 1958.
Pursuit of the Prodigal. 1959.
The House of Five Talents. 1960.
Portrait in Brownstone. 1962.
Powers of Attorney (stories). 1963.
The Rector of Justin. 1964.
The Embezzler. 1966.
Tales of Manhattan. 1967.
A World of Profit. 1968.
Second Chance (stories). 1970.
I Come as a Thief. 1972.
The Partners. 1974.
The Winthrop Covenant. 1976.
The Dark Lady. 1977.
The Country Cousin. 1978.

Play

The Club Bedroom (produced 1967).

Other

Edith Wharton. 1961.
Reflections of a Jacobite. 1961.
Ellen Glasgow. 1964.
Pioneers and Caretakers: A Study of 9 American Women Novelists. 1965.
Motiveless Malignity (on Shakespeare). 1969.
Henry Adams. 1971.
Edith Wharton: A Woman in Her Time. 1971.
Richelieu. 1972.
A Writer's Capital (autobiography). 1974.
Reading Henry James. 1975.

Editor, An Edith Wharton Reader. 1965.
Editor, Fables of Wit and Elegance. 1972.

Bibliography: Auchincloss and His Critics: A Bibliographical Record by Jackson R. Bryer, 1977.

*   *   *

Louis Auchincloss is a successor to Edith Wharton as a chronicler of the New York aristocracy. In this role he necessarily imbues his novels with an elegiac tone as he observes the passing beauties of the city and the fading power of the white Anglo-Saxon Protestants of old family and old money who can no longer sustain their position of dominance. His principal subject is thus the manners and morals, the money and marriages, the families and houses, the schools and games, the language and arts of the New York aristocracy as he traces its rise, observes its present crisis, and meditates its possible fall and disappearance. The point of vantage from which he often observes the aristocracy is that of the lawyer who serves and frequently belongs to this class.

The idea of good family stands in an uneasy relation to money in Auchincloss's fiction. Auchincloss dramatizes the dilemma of the American aristocracy by showing that it is necessary to possess money to belong to this class but fatal to one's standing within the class to pursue money. People who have connections with those who are still in trade cannot themselves fully qualify as gentlemen, as the opportunistic Mr. Dale in *The Great World and Timothy Colt* shows. On the other hand, Auchincloss is clearly critical of those aristocrats like Bertie Millinder or Percy Prime who do nothing constructive and are engaged simply in the spending of money. Auchincloss recognizes that the family is the most important of aristocratic institutions and that its place in its class is guaranteed by the conservation of its resources. This task of preserving the family wealth falls to the lawyers, and his fiction is rich in the complexities, both moral and financial, of fiduciary responsibility; *Venus in Sparta* is a novel in point.

Auchincloss fully exploits the conflict between the marriage arranged for the good of the family, often by strong women, and romantic or sexual impulses that are destructive of purely social goals, as *Portrait in Brownstone* illustrates. Sex and love are enemies to the organicism of conservative societies, in which the will of the individual is vested in the whole. Auchincloss observes the workings of this organic notion in the structure of family and marriage as well as in institutions like the school and the club. Such institutions preserve a way of life and protect those who live by it from those on the outside who do not.

Auchincloss's fiction does more than present us with a mere record of the institutions that support the American aristocracy. The dramatic interest in his novels and whatever larger importance may be accorded them lies in his recognition that the entire class is in jeopardy and that individual aristocrats are often failures. Sometimes Auchincloss sees problems arising within the context of aristocracy itself, as when individual will or desire comes in conflict with the organicism; perhaps Reese Parmalee, in *Pursuit of the Prodigal*, makes the most significant rebellion of all Auchincloss's characters, but he is rejecting a decadent aristocracy and not aristocracy itself. But the real failures are those aristocrats who suffer, as so many of Auchincloss's male characters do, from a sense of inadequacy and insecurity that leads them to self-destructiveness. They are not strong and tough-fibred, as so many of the women are; they seem too fastidious and over-civilized, and they are failing the idea of society and their class. *A World of Profit* is the most explicit recognition of this failure.

Auchincloss has made his record of the New York aristocracy in a style which is clear and simple, occasionally elegant and brilliant, and sometimes self-consciously allusive. He has a gift for comedy of manners, which he has not sufficiently cultivated, and a fine model in Oscar Wilde. Yet among his faults as a novelist, especially evident because of the particular genre he has chosen, is a failure to give the reader a richness of detail. Furthermore, he sometimes loses control of his novels and permits action to overwhelm theme. The most serious criticism to be made of his work is that while he does indeed pose moral dilemmas for his characters, he too easily resolves their problems for them. He has given us, on balance, a full enough record of upper class life in New York, but he has fallen short of the most penetrating and meaningful kinds of social insight that the best of the novelists of manners offer.

—Chester E. Eisinger

BALDWIN, James (Arthur). American. Born in New York City, 2 August 1924. Educated at Public School 139, Harlem, New York, and DeWitt Clinton High School, Bronx, New York. Lived in Europe, mainly in Paris, 1948–56. Member, Actors Studio, New York; National Advisory Board of CORE (Congress on Racial Equality); and National Committee for a Sane Nuclear Policy. Recipient: Saxton Fellowship, 1945; Rosenwald Fellowship, 1948; Guggenheim Fellowship, 1954; National Institute of Arts and Letters grant, 1956; Ford Fellowship, 1958; National Conference of Christians and Jews Brotherhood Award, 1962; George Polk Award, 1963; Foreign Drama Critics Award, 1964. D.Litt.: University of British Columbia, Vancouver, 1964. Member, National Institute of Arts and Letters, 1964. Lives in New York City.

PUBLICATIONS

Fiction

Go Tell It on the Mountain. 1953.
Giovanni's Room. 1956.
Another Country. 1962.
Going to Meet the Man (stories). 1965.
Tell Me How Long the Train's Been Gone. 1968.
If Beale Street Could Talk. 1974.

Plays

The Amen Corner (produced 1955). 1965.
Blues for Mr. Charlie (produced 1964). 1964
One Day, When I Was Lost: A Scenario Based on "The Autobiography of Malcolm X." 1972.
A Deed from the King of Spain (produced 1974).

Screenplay: The Inheritance, 1973.

Other

Notes of a Native Son. 1955.
Nobody Knows My Name: More Notes of a Native Son. 1961.
The Fire Next Time. 1963.
Nothing Personal, with Richard Avedon. 1964.
A Rap on Race, with Margaret Mead. 1971.
No Name in the Street. 1971.
A Dialogue: James Baldwin and Nikki Giovanni. 1973.
Little Man, Little Man (juvenile). 1976.
The Devil Finds Work: An Essay. 1976.

Bibliography: "James Baldwin: A Checklist, 1947–1962" by Kathleen A. Kindt, and "James Baldwin: A Bibliography, 1947–1962" by Russell G. Fischer, both in Bulletin of Bibliography, January–April 1965; "James Baldwin: A Checklist, 1963–67" by Fred L. Standley, in Bulletin of Bibliography, May–August 1968.

Reading List: *The Furious Passage of Baldwin* by Ferm M. Eckman, 1966; *Baldwin: A Critical Study* by Stanley Macebuh, 1973; *Baldwin: A Collection of Critical Essays* edited by Keneth Kinnamon, 1974; *Baldwin: A Critical Evaluation* edited by Therman B. O'Daniel, 1977.

*   *   *

James Baldwin's major theme has always been identity or its denial. He develops the complex personal and social dimensions of this theme in four main subjects: church, self, city, and race. The result is a substantial body of writing in fiction, drama, and the personal essay characterized by intense feeling, stylistic eloquence, and social urgency.

As Baldwin was making his first adolescent efforts to write, he was simultaneously preaching in store-front churches in Harlem. Of brief duration, his religious vocation both satisfied his need to prove his worth to his father and complicated his intellectual development. Seeming to simplify personal problems, his religious commitment actually generated tensions that were to make Baldwin an eloquent critic of Christianity, especially its pernicious social effects, as well as a witness of its emotional power and richness. The enduring fictional achievement of Baldwin's involvement with the church is his brilliant first novel, *Go Tell It on the Mountain*. By means of a carefully crafted tripartite structure, rich characterizations, and a distinctive stylistic voice, Baldwin tells the story not only of John Grimes, a Harlem youth undergoing a personal and religious crisis, but also of his stepfather, Gabriel; his stepfather's sister, Florence; and his mother, Elizabeth. With historical scope as well as personal immediacy, the author shows how sex, race, and religion affect the lives of these worshippers in The Temple of the Fire Baptized. Religious experience is conveyed to the reader with overwhelming emotional power, but he is also forced to recognize how it erodes social reality or even, in the case of Gabriel, becomes a means of oppression. The critique of the church is carried further in the play *The Amen Corner*, in which a fanatical woman preacher substitutes her small church for the love of her husband. Narrowly fulfilling, but in the final analysis life-denying, religion must be abandoned, Baldwin implies, if the self is to be realized.

Many of Baldwin's best early essays and stories – "Autobiographical Notes," "Notes of a Native Son," "Stranger in the Village," "The Discovery of What It Means to Be an American," "Previous Condition," "The Rockpile," "The Outing" – concern his search for self. His second novel, *Giovanni's Room*, explores the theme mainly as it relates to love and sexuality. David, an American expatriate in France, must choose between his mistress Hella and his lover Giovanni. By rejecting Giovanni, David denies his true homosexual self and his deepest feeling for another person in favor of socially sanctioned heterosexuality. As Baldwin develops it, the choice is also between America and Europe, conformity and freedom, safety and the risks necessary to realize love. In search of psychological security, David instead precipitates chaos and tragedy for himself, Hella, and Giovanni.

Both *Go Tell It on the Mountain* and *Giovanni's Room* express social concerns, but their emphasis is on psychological conflict. In his third novel, *Another Country*, Baldwin gives greater attention to the city itself as both the arena and the cause of personal problems. The New York setting of this novel, seething with hatred, corruption, and moral disarray, dooms the characters who inhabit its inhuman confines. The most obvious victim is Rufus Scott, a disconsolate black jazz musician who commits suicide at the end of the long first chapter, but the other seven major characters also suffer as they struggle to assuage their guilt and satisfy their craving for love in the unloving urban environment. Some of these concerns appear in the splendid earlier story, "Sonny's Blues" (1957), where, however, racial suffering in the northern city is controlled, expressed, and thus to some degree transcended through music. In his recent novel *If Beale Street Could Talk*, Baldwin again tries to transcend the hostility of urban life, this time through a story of young love, but his effort is vitiated by sentimentality and problems of fictional technique.

With few exceptions, most of Baldwin's books have dealt in one way or another with race and racism. From youthful disengagement he has moved through commitment to interracial efforts to achieve civil rights to black nationalism to bitter prophecies of racial vengeance on the white West. *The Fire Next Time* is an eloquent statement of militant intergrationism, but the play *Blues for Mister Charlie* expresses a deeper racial outrage and a diminished but not entirely abandoned hope for improvement. The social pathology revealed in this drama of race relations in the South derives from psychosexual origins much more than from political or economic causes. The shift from the nonviolent mode of resistance to racism to the advocacy of violence as the appropriate means of black self-defense begins in the play, and receives a stronger endorsement in the idealized portrait of Christopher, a fierce young black nationalist, in the novel *Tell Me How Long the Train's Been Gone*. The protagonist of this novel, a middle-aged actor named Leo Proudhammer, is an autobiographical character whose experience Baldwin sentimentalizes tiresomely, but in the autobiographical material of the tough-minded *No Name in the Street* the author avoids self-pity. Shifting back and forth between private experience and the public history of the violence-wracked sixties, Baldwin offers in this work a sad and embittered testimony on race and racism. Quite different in its restrained tone and deliberately flat rhetoric from the hortatory *The Fire Next Time*, it is equally impressive.

By comparison Baldwin's recent books – a film scenario, film criticism, transcripts of conversations, a children's book – are minor efforts. He may yet produce the genuinely major novel for which stylistic resources, his capacity for feeling, and his thematic breadth equip him. In any event, as a master of the personal essay, as racial commentator, and as a gifted if uneven novelist and short story writer, James Baldwin has been one of the indispensable writers of the third quarter of the twentieth century.

—Keneth Kinnamon

BARAKA, Amiri.   See JONES, LeRoi.

BARNES, Djuna (Chappell).   American.   Born in Cornwall-on-Hudson, New York, 12 June 1892. Privately educated; studied art at the Pratt Institute, Brooklyn, New York, and the Art Students' League, New York. Journalist and illustrator, 1913–31; full-time writer since 1931; also an artist: exhibited at Art of This Century Gallery, New York, 1946. Has lived in Paris and London. Trustee, New York Committee, Dag Hammarskjöld Foundation. Member, National Institute of Arts and Letters. Lives in New York City.

PUBLICATIONS

Fiction

The Book of Repulsive Women (stories).   1915.

A Book (stories, verse, and plays).   1923; augmented edition, as *A Night among the Horses*, 1929; shortened version, stories only, as *Spillway*, 1962.
Ryder.   1928.
Nightwood.   1936.
Vagaries Malicieux: Two Stories.   1974.

Plays

Three from the Earth (produced 1919).   In *A Book*, 1923.
Kurzy of the Sea (produced 1919).
An Irish Triangle (produced 1919).   In *Playboy*, 1921.
To the Dogs, in *A Book*.   1923.
The Dove (produced 1926).   In *A Book*, 1923.
She Tells Her Daughter, in *Smart Set*,   1923.
The Antiphon (produced 1961).   1958.

Other

Ladies Almanack: Showing Their Signs and Their Tides; Their Moon and Their Changes; The Seasons as It Is with Them; Their Eclipses and Equinoxes; As Well as a Full Record of Diurnal and Nocturnal Distempers Written and Illustrated by a Lady of Fashion.   1928.
Selected Works.   1962.

Bibliography: *Barnes: A Bibliography* by Douglas Messerli,   1976.

Reading List: *The Art of Barnes: Duality and Damnation* by Louis F. Kannenstine, 1977.

*   *   *

Djuna Barnes, a woman of striking beauty, was one of the original members of the Theater Guild and acted in New York in plays by Tolstoi and Paul Claudel in the early 1920's. By the late 1930's the publication of her novel *Nightwood*, with an enthusiastic introduction by T. S. Eliot, had led to her being considered the most important woman novelist living in Paris. In the fiction of Anaïs Nin she appears frequently as "Djuna," and David Gascoyne's poem "Noctambules" carries the dedication "Hommage à Djuna Barnes." When her play *The Antiphon* was published, Edwin Muir declared that it was "one of the greatest things written in our times." Yet, despite such high praise, her books have become collectors' items rather than popular successes.

Nightwood is about the obsession of two American women for each other in the 1920's. Their Paris is not the Paris of Scott Fitzgerald, but that of Romaine Brooks, Natalie Clifford Barney, and the circle of "Amazonians" which surrounded them. Norah Flood, one of the protagonists of the novel, arranges publicity from time to time for Denckman Circus, and she also runs a *salon*. Some thirty years before, Dr. Matthew O'Connor assisted at her birth; now living in Paris, he has given way to his homosexual-transvestite urges. He is called one night from a cafe to a nearby hotel to attend Robin Vote, a boyish young woman who has had a collapse. The doctor takes along with him his drinking companion, Baron Felix Volkbein, who falls in love with Robin and subsequently marries her. In due course Robin bears him a son, but she cannot stand the course of marriage and starts an affair with Norah. A passionate and tempestuous sequence of events follows and Robin's promiscuity nearly unhinges Norah's mind. Her old friend the doctor sits with her through the night boozing and pouring forth great streams of disconnected thoughts of life, literature, and the vagaries of the human condition. Had the novel been adapted for radio, the role of the doctor was one that Dylan Thomas aspired to play.

The Antiphon, written in blank verse, recalls a Jacobean closet drama:

> You have such sons
> Would mate the pennies on a dead man's eyes
> To breed the sexton's fee.

But the setting is modern and takes place in England during the second World War. Augusta Burley betrays her aristocratic lineage by marrying a coarse, uncultivated Mormon from Salem, by whom she has three sons and a daughter. Now a widow, she arranges a reunion at Burley Hall for the whole family. Yet nothing is what it seems. For as two of the brothers and their sister await their third brother, he enjoys himself at their expense disguised as "a coachman." Recriminations and suppressed violence cause the two identified sons to plan a matricide, while their sister acts as inquisitor to her mother for marrying her father. Finally incensed by the desertion of her two sons, the mother turns on her daughter to kill her and brings about her own death at the same time. The original production of this powerful play – by the Royal Dramatic Theatre of Stockholm in 1961 – was in a translation by Dag Hammarskjöld.

Djuna Barnes has also illustrated books and written poems, short stories, and other plays.

Ladies Almanack, which she brought out anonymously in Paris, created a minor *succès de scandale* in the 1920's. A number of lesbians are gently mocked – among them Radclyffe Hall (Lady Buck-and-Balk), Natalie Clifford Barney (Evangeline Musset), and Lady Una Troubridge (Tilly-Tweed-in-Blood).

—Neville Braybrooke

BARRY, Philip. American. Born in Rochester, New York, 18 June 1896. Educated in public schools in Rochester; Yale University, New Haven, Connecticut (Editor, *Yale Review*), A.B. 1919; studied with George Pierce Baker at Harvard University, Cambridge, Massachusetts, 1919–22. Worked in the Code Department of the U.S. Embassy, London, 1918–19. Married Ellen Semple in 1922; two sons. Professional playwright from 1922; wrote for M.G.M., Hollywood, from 1934; lived in France, 1938–39. Member, National Institute of Arts and Letters. *Died 3 December 1949.*

PUBLICATIONS

Collections

States of Grace: Eight Plays, edited by Brendan Gill.   1975.

Plays

A Punch for Judy (produced 1921).   1922.
You and I (produced 1922).   1923.
God Bless Our Home.   1924.
The Youngest (produced 1924).   1925.
In a Garden (produced 1925).   1926.
White Wings (produced 1926).   1927; revised version, music by Douglas Moore
  (produced 1935).
John (produced 1927).   1929.
Paris Bound (produced 1927).   1929.
Cock Robin, with Elmer Rice (produced 1928).   1929.
Holiday (produced 1928).   1929.
Hotel Universe (produced 1930).   1930.
Tomorrow and Tomorrow (produced 1931).   1931.
The Animal Kingdom (produced 1932).   1932.
The Joyous Season (produced 1934).   1934.
Bright Star (produced 1935).
Spring Dance, from a play by Eleanor Golden and Eloise Barrangon (produced
  1936).   1936.
Here Come the Clowns (produced 1938).   1939.
The Philadelphia Story (produced 1939).   1939.
Liberty Jones (produced 1941).   1941.
Without Love (produced 1943).   1943.
Foolish Notion (produced 1945).   Abridged version in The Best Plays of 1944–45, edited
  by Burns Mantle, 1945.
Second Threshold, completed by Robert E. Sherwood (produced 1951).   1951.

Fiction

War in Heaven.   1938.

Reading List: The Drama of Barry by Gerald Hamm, 1948; Barry by Joseph Roppolo, 1965.

*   *   *

   American theater has never been particularly congenial to that honorable but somewhat amorphous genre high comedy. Philip Barry is one of the very few American playwrights who is a celebrated practitioner of the form. In plays like Paris Bound, The Animal Kingdom, Without Love, and – most famously – Holiday and The Philadelphia Story, he places articulate and well-to-do people in well-appointed homes and forces them to face domestic crises – usually a marriage in danger – with an equanimity that might be called courage and a wit which demands – but does not always get – audiences willing to listen for the precise meaning of lines which will direct them to the seriousness which lies at the heart of all the plays. That Barry is not simply an elegant entertainer can be seen in the variety of work in his canon – in which the successful comedies share space with a satirical extravaganza (White Wings), a Biblical play more concerned with theology than anecdote (John), a mood play in which characters find spiritual regeneration through psychodrama (Hotel Universe), a parable of good and evil among vaudevillians (Here Come the Clowns, based on Barry's own novel War in Heaven), a symbolic political drama (Liberty Jones), and a mixture of the real and the imaginary (Foolish Notion).
   The comedies tend to be more effective than the overtly earnest plays, in which art

sometimes loses out to exposition. But the important thing about Barry as a serious playwright is that, light or heavy, his work is informed by a major theme. Most of his plays, from *You and I* to *Second Threshold*, deal with man's need to be faithful to himself and his possibilities, personal and professional. The Barry protagonists have to escape the rigidities dictated by family (*The Youngest*), convention (*The Animal Kingdom*), society (*Holiday*). Sometimes, as with John and Herodias in *John*, the characters are trapped by their own preconceptions, and the luckier among them learn to live by discovering that, however benign their intentions, they too are manipulators (Nancy in *The Youngest*, Linda in *Holiday*) or by accepting their own imperfect, human condition (Tracy Lord in *The Philadelphia Story*). Barry's central concern is supported by recurrent minor themes – marriage as a bond of love, not a legal or religious ritual; work as a self-fulfilling activity, not a social imposition – and by the implicit religious assumptions that mark him even at his most secular. That *Holiday* and *The Philadelphia Story* are likely to remain Barry's most popular plays should not hide the fact that a number of the others – particularly the neglected *In a Garden* – deserve a place in the working American repertory.

—Gerald Weales

BARTH, John (Simmons). American. Born in Cambridge, Maryland, 27 May 1930. Educated at the Juilliard School of Music, New York; Johns Hopkins University, Baltimore, A.B. 1951, M.A. 1952. Married 1) Anne Strickland in 1951, one daughter and two sons; 2) Shelley Rosenberg in 1970. Junior Instructor in English, Johns Hopkins University, 1951–53; Instructor to Associate Professor of English, Pennsylvania State University, University Park, 1953–65; Professor of English, State University of New York at Buffalo, 1965–73. Since 1973, Professor of English and Creative Writing, Johns Hopkins University. Recipient: Brandeis University Creative Arts Award, 1965; Rockefeller grant, 1965; National Institute of Arts and Letters grant, 1966; National Book Award, 1973. Litt.D.: University of Maryland, College Park, 1969. Lives in Baltimore.

PUBLICATIONS

Fiction

The Floating Opera.   1956; revised edition, 1967.
The End of the Road.   1958; revised edition, 1967.
The Sot-Weed Factor.   1960; revised edition, 1967.
Giles Goat-Boy; or, The Revised New Syllabus.   1966.
Lost in the Funhouse: Fiction for Print, Tape, Live Voice (stories).   1968.
Chimera (stories).   1972.

Bibliography: *Barth: A Descriptive Primary and Annotated Secondary Bibliography* by Joseph Weixlmann, 1975.

Reading List: *Barth* by Gerhard Joseph, 1969; *Barth: The Comic Sublimity of Paradox* by Jac Tharpe, 1974; *Barth: An Introduction* by David Morrell, 1977

*   *   *

Highly susceptible to the sport of metaphysical games and passionately attracted to the conundrums of self-consciousness, John Barth has moved steadily away from the objective and realistic toward myth and unashamed fable. His first two novels, *The Floating Opera* and *The End of the Road* – novels which he has claimed to be twin explorations of the comic and tragic aspects of philosophical nihilism – fall well within the conventions of realism. But his next novel, *The Sot-Weed Factor*, takes an entirely different direction. It is framed on a gigantic scale of multiple plots, disguises, coincidences, intrigues, and deceptions, and it is written in an exuberant and constantly inventive pastiche of 17th-century prose style. Mingling history, legend, fiction, and outrageous lie in a bawdy, funny, and learned parody of the initiation-and-quest novel, *The Sot-Weed Factor* purports to chronicle the life and career of Ebenezer Cooke, Poet-Laureate of Maryland. Partly a reinterpretation of the primal fall from innocence, and partly a re-examination of the rich ambiguities in the archetypal American experience, it is both a dazzling *tour de force* and a major contribution to the novel of fabulation.

Barth is even more ambitious in scope and substance in *Giles Goat-Boy*. In this gargantuan spoof, he attempts to fuse myth, allegory, satire, parody, and the conventions of science-fiction to produce a comically revised New Testament which will expose the fictive sources of all myths while leaving a new one in their place. Although the novel inevitably falls short of its excessive aims, its relative failure – it goes on too long and its plot becomes mechanical – is still a significant and startling achievement. In *Lost in the Fun House* and *Chimera*, he has withdrawn into an increasingly abstract and cerebral style, deliberately focusing on the naked process of story-telling itself as a subject – if not a substitute – for telling stories. The results are curiously mixed: over-clever, strained, whimsical, desperate, terrifying, boring, and funny. Whether these works represent a temporary exhaustion of Barth's imaginative energies or are, instead, a necessary and courageous phase in his development as a major writer, there is little doubt that his literary intelligence and mastery of language place him in the forefront of his generation of writers.

—Earl Rovit

BARTHELME, Donald.   American.   Born in Philadelphia, Pennsylvania, 7 April 1931. Served in the United States Army. Married to Birgit Barthelme; one daughter. Museum Director, Houston, in the mid-1950's. Visiting Professor, Boston University, 1973, and City College of New York, 1974–75. Formerly, Managing Editor, *Location* magazine, New York. Recipient: Guggenheim Fellowship, 1966; National Book Award, 1972; National Institute of Arts and Letters Morton Dauwen Zabel Award, 1972. Lives in New York City.

PUBLICATIONS

Fiction

 Come Back, Dr. Caligari (stories).   1964.
 Snow White.   1967.
 Unspeakable Practices, Unnatural Acts (stories).   1968.
 City Life (stories).   1971.
 Sadness (stories).   1972.

Guilty Pleasures (stories).   1974.
The Dead Father.   1975.
Amateurs (stories).   1976.

Other

The Slightly Irregular Fire Engine; or, The Hithering Dithering Djinn (juvenile).   1972.

*   *   *

Since the American publication of two volumes of fictions by Argentinian Jorge Luis Borges in 1962, an interest in short, highly self-conscious, directly philosophical fiction has become apparent in the United States. Donald Barthelme is perhaps the best exemplar of this strain of fiction. His best work to date has been in the short story (for lack of a more expansive term), particularly in the sub-strain "metafiction," a term coined by William Gass. Like Borges, the Americans John Barth, Gass, and Robert Coover, and the Italian Italo Calvino, Barthelme has little interest in mimetic fiction which works from the bedrock of the "real" world. Instead of protracted social or psychological studies, he busies himself with very short, often truncated and discontinuous, literary pieces that depend on other literary works, philosophy, film, pop culture, and high art for their fictional matrices. There is throughout his work a suspicion of received morality or attitude, indeed of any unself-conscious and sustained human construct – including fiction. Thus his works are brief, constantly shifting in tone and style, reliant as much on the juxtaposition and reverberation of image and language in modern poetry and on the open randomness and "objectness" of the collage and much modern art as on traditional fictional technique.

Barthelme's first work, *Come Back, Dr. Caligari*, was very well-reviewed, but one notes the bewilderment of critics who searched for "meaning" in his work. His best works have been collections of short fiction; of these, *City Life* and *Sadness* are most sustained in imagination and execution.

While Barthelme has little interest in miming reality, he does have a recurrent interest in modern consciousness, particularly as manifested in urban Americans. He issues elegant fictional reports on the state of consciousness in "The City," and, indeed, the daily sorrowful, maddening minutiae of city life – tattered marriages, the loss of innocence, the failure of love, the absurd hope of social or political "progress," the torrent of stimulation by the media – comprise the stuff of his reports. "The City" is dangerous and confusing, and is finally a configuration of human consciousness: "It heaves and palpitates. It is multi-dimensional and has a mayor. To describe it takes many hundreds of thousands of words. Our muck is only a part of a much greater muck – the nation state – which is itself the creation of that muck of mucks, human consciousness" ("City Life").

Indeed, the human urban condition is Barthelme's major subject, and like his city, his vision can certainly appear bleak and pessimistic. Endlessly self-conscious (his narrators offer clues as to the significance of their tales), satiric and parodic (Barthelme's liberated *Snow White* is hilarious), a mournful connoisseur of the many flavors of metaphysical *malaise* and *angst* of our time (a character "pickets" the human condition in an early story: "THE HUMAN CONDITION: WHY DOES IT HAVE TO BE THAT WAY?"), he can often seem depressing and negative. Yet his wit and humor are a delight, and his stylistic command is among the most deft of writers in English in our time.

Barthelme demands a creative reader, and he offers his own best apologia in writing on the work of Samuel Beckett: "His pessimism is the premise necessary to a marvelous pedantic high-wire performance, the wire itself supporting a comic turn of endless virtuosity. No one who writes as well as Beckett can be said to be doing anything but celebrating life."

—Jack Hicks

BAUM, L(yman) Frank. American. Born in Chittenango, New York, 15 May 1856. Educated at schools in Syracuse, New York, and Peekskill Military Academy, New York. Married Maud Gage in 1882; four sons. Reporter, New York *World*, 1873–75; Founding Editor, *New Era*, Bradford, Pennsylvania, 1876; actor (as Louis F. Baum and George Brooks), theatre manager, and producer, New York and on tour; poultry farmer in the 1880's; salesman, Baum's Castorine axle grease, 1886–88; Owner, Baum's Bazaar general store, Aberdeen, Dakota Territory, 1888–90; Editor, *Saturday Pioneer*, Aberdeen, 1890–91; Reporter, Chicago *Post*, and Buyer, Siegel Cooper and Company, Chicago, and Salesman, Pitkin and Brooks, Chicago, 1891–97; Founder, National Association of Window Trimmers, 1897, and Founding Editor and Publisher, *The Show Window* magazine, Chicago, 1897–1902; Founding Director, Oz Film Manufacturing Company, Los Angeles, 1914. *Died 6 May 1919.*

PUBLICATIONS

Fiction

A New Wonderland. 1900: as *The Surprising Adventures of the Magical Monarch of Mo,* 1903.
The Wonderful Wizard of Oz.. 1900; as *The New Wizard of Oz,* 1903.
Dot and Tot of Merryland. 1901.
The Master Key: An Electrical Fairy Tale. 1901.
The Life and Adventures of Santa Claus. 1902.
The Enchanted Island of Yew. 1903.
The Marvelous Land of Oz. 1904.
Queen Zixi of Ix. 1905.
The Woggle-Bug Book. 1905.
The Fate of a Crown. 1905.
Daughters of Destiny. 1906.
John Dough and the Cherub. 1906.
Annabel. 1906.
Sam Steele's Adventures on Land and Sea. 1906; as *The Boy Fortune Hunters in Alaska,* 1908.
Aunt Jane's Nieces. 1906.
Aunt Jane's Nieces Abroad. 1906.
Twinkle Tales. 6 vols., 1906; as *Twinkle and Chubbins,* 1911.
Tamawaca Folks. 1907.
Ozma of Oz. 1907; as *Princess Ozma of Oz,* 1942.
Sam Steele's Adventures in Panama. 1907; as *The Boy Fortune Hunters in Panama,* 1908.
Policeman Bluejay. 1907; as *Babes in Birdland,* 1911.
The Last Egyptian. 1908.
Dorothy and the Wizard in Oz. 1908.
The Boy Fortune Hunters in Egypt. 1908.
Aunt Jane's Nieces at Millville. 1908.
The Road to Oz. 1909.
The Boy Fortune Hunters in China. 1909.
Aunt Jane's Nieces at Work. 1909.
The Emerald City of Oz. 1910.
The Boy Fortune Hunters in Yucatan. 1910.
Aunt Jane's Nieces in Society. 1910.

The Sea Fairies.   1911.
The Daring Twins.   1911.
The Boy Fortune Hunters in the South Seas.   1911.
Aunt Jane's Nieces and Uncle John.   1911.
The Flying Girl.   1911.
Sky Island.   1912.
Phoebe Daring.   1912.
Aunt Jane's Nieces on Vacation.   1912.
The Flying Girl and Her Chum.   1912.
The Patchwork Girl of Oz.   1913.
The Little Wizard Series.   6 vols., 1913; as *Little Wizard Stories of Oz,* 1914.
Aunt Jane's Nieces on the Ranch.   1913.
Tik-Tok of Oz.   1914.
Aunt Jane's Nieces Out West.   1914.
The Scarecrow of Oz.   1915.
Aunt Jane's Nieces in the Red Cross.   1915.
Rinkitink in Oz.   1916.
The Snuggle Tales.   6 vols., 1916–17; as *Oz-Man Tales,* 6 vols,. 1920.
Mary Louise.   1916.
Mary Louise in the Country.   1916.
The Lost Princess of Oz.   1917.
Mary Louise Solves a Mystery.   1917.
The Tin Woodman of Oz.   1918.
Mary Louise and the Liberty Girls.   1918.
Mary Louise Adopts a Soldier.   1919.
The Magic of Oz.   1919.
Glinda of Oz.   1920.
Jaglon and the Tiger Fairies.   1953.
A Kidnapped Santa Claus.   1961.

Plays

The Maid of Arran, music and lyrics by Baum, from the novel *A Princess of Thule* by
   William Black (produced 1882).
Matches (produced 1882).
Kilmourne; or, O'Connor's Dream (produced 1883).
The Wizard of Oz, music by Paul Tietjens, lyrics by Baum, from the story by Baum
   (produced 1902); revised version, as *There Is Something New under the Sun*
   (produced 1903).
The Woggle-Bug, music by Frederic Chapin, from the story *The Marvelous Land of Oz*
   by Baum (produced 1905).
The Tik-Tok Man of Oz, music by Louis F. Gottschalk, from the story by Baum
   (produced 1913).
Stagecraft: The Adventures of a Strictly Moral Man, music by Louis F. Gottschalk
   (produced 1914).
The Uplift of Lucifer; or, Raising Hell, music by Louis F. Gottschalk (produced
   1915).   Edited by Manuel Weltman, 1963.
The Uplifters' Minstrels, music by Byron Gay (produced 1916).
The Orpheus Road Company, music by Louis F. Gottschalk (produced 1917).

Screenplays: *The Fairylogue and Radio-Plays,* 1908–09; *The Patchwork Girl of Oz,*
1914, *The Babes in the Wood,* 1914; *The Last Egyptian,* 1914; *The New Wizard of Oz,*
1915.

Verse

> *By the Candelabra's Glare.* 1898.
> *Father Goose, His Book.* 1899.
> *The Army Alphabet.* 1900.
> *The Navy Alphabet.* 1900.
> *The Songs of Father Goose*, music by Alberta N. Hall. 1900.
> *Father Goose's Year Book: Quaint Quacks and Feathery Shafts for Mature Children.* 1907.

Other

> *The Book of the Hamburgs: A Brief Treatise upon the Mating, Rearing, and Management of the Different Varieties of Hamburgs.* 1886.
> *Mother Goose in Prose.* 1897.
> *The Art of Decorating Dry Goods Windows and Interiors.* 1900.
> *American Fairy Tales.* 1901; augmented edition, 1908.
> *Baum's Juvenile Speaker* (miscellany). 1910; as *Baum's Own Book for Children*, 1912.
> *Our Landlandy* (newspaper columns). 1941.

Bibliography: *Bibliographia Oziana* by Peter E. Hanff and Douglas G. Greene, 1976.

Reading List: *The Wizard of Oz and Who He Was* edited by Russel Nye and Martin Gardner, 1957; *To Please a Child: A Biography of Baum* by Frank Joslyn Baum and Russell P. MacFall, 1961; *The Annotated Wizard of Oz* edited by Michael Patrick Hearn, 1973 (includes bibliography); *Wonderful Wizard Marvelous Land* by Raylyn Moore, 1974.

*　　*　　*

L. Frank Baum's *The Wonderful Wizard of Oz*, illustrated by W. W. Denslow, is his masterpiece. It made him famous and, with its 13 sequels, has established him as a classic writer of children's stories.

The Wonderful Wizard of Oz was a novelty in children's books at the time it was published, lacking the didactic, moralizing, and stilted tone so common. Its characters spoke the American vernacular; its plot was simple but intriguing and well-structured. Moreover, Baum created five characters worthy to stand with Lewis Carroll's. Dorothy and the Wizard, and the three non-human characters (the Tin Woodman, the Scarecrow, and the Cowardly Lion), are all archetypes yet sharply distinguished individuals. The quest of the Scarecrow for brains, the Woodman for a heart, and the Lion for courage, qualities they already possessed but did not know how to use, is the stuff of which classics are made. All have become literary figures as instantly recognizable as Alice and Peter Pan.

The Wizard was also Baum's most successful, though not his best, example of what he called the American or modernized fairy tale. Responding to ideas expressed by Hamlin Garland and others, he intended to write fantasies which would be distinct from the European and New England tradition. They would recognize the existence and importance of the industry, technology, and social concepts of the dawning 20th century. He did incorporate mechanical gadgets (particularly electricity, which fascinated him) into his works – *The Master Key: An Electrical Fairy Tale* is the best example – and dealt with such modern concepts as Populism. But in general his ambition to create a new genre was only partly successful. Though the visitors to Oz were American, the country itself was as foreign as James Branch Cabell's Poictesme or Swift's Lilliput. Furthermore, he often used such traditional fairy tale paraphernalia as witches, gnomes, talking animals, and wishing caps.

What many consider his best book, *Queen Zixi of Ix*, is entirely derived from European children's literature, though it contains many imaginative novelties.

Baum tired of his Oz series. But just as public demand kept Doyle writing his Sherlock Holmes stories when he would have preferred to concentrate on his more "serious" works, so it kept Baum at his Oz tales, though he did write many other children's books, few of them fantasies. Though written "to please a child" (Baum's phrase), the Oz books have also been popular with adults, who recognize subtleties which escaped them as children. *The Wonderful Wizard of Oz* is still popular, and now seems to have passed the judgment of time.

—Philip José Farmer

BEHRMAN, S(amuel) N(athaniel). American. Born in Worcester, Massachusetts, 9 June 1893. Educated at Clark College, now Clark University, Worcester, 1912–14; Harvard University, Cambridge, Massachusetts, B.A. 1916 (Phi Beta Kappa); Columbia University, New York, M.A. 1918. Married Elza Heifetz in 1936; one son, two step-children. Book Reviewer for the *New Republic*, New York, and the *New York Times*; Columnist, *The New Yorker*. Founder, with Robert E. Sherwood, Elmer Rice, Maxwell Anderson, Sidney Howard, and John F. Wharton, Playwrights Company, 1938. Trustee, Clark University. Recipient: American Academy of Arts and Letters grant, 1943; New York Drama Critics Circle Award, 1944; Brandeis University Creative Arts Award, 1962. LL.D.: Clark University, 1949. Member, National Institute of Arts and Letters, and American Academy of Arts and Sciences. *Died 9 September 1973.*

PUBLICATIONS

Plays

Bedside Manners: A Comedy of Convalescence with J. Kenyon Nicholson (produced 1923). 1924.
A Night's Work, with J. Kenyon Nicholson (produced 1924). 1926.
The Man Who Forgot, with Owen Davis (produced 1926).
The Second Man (produced 1927). 1927.
Love Is Like That, with J. Kenyon Nicholson (produced 1927).
Serena Blandish, from the novel by Enid Bagnold (produced 1929). In Three Plays, 1934.
Meteor (produced 1929). 1930.
Brief Moment (produced 1931). 1931.
Biography (produced 1932). 1933.
Love Story (produced 1934).
Three Plays: Serena Blandish, Meteor, The Second Man. 1934.
Rain from Heaven (produced 1935). 1935.
End of Summer (produced 1936). 1936.

Amphitryon 38, with Roger Gellert, from a play by Jean Giraudoux (produced 1937). 1938.
Wine of Choice (produced 1938). 1938.
No Time for Comedy (produced 1939). 1939.
The Talley Method (produced 1941). 1941.
The Pirate, from a work by Ludwig Fulda (produced 1942). 1943.
Jacobowsky and the Colonel, with Franz Werfel (produced 1944). 1944.
Dunnigan's Daughter (produced 1945). 1946.
Jane, from a story by W. Somerset Maugham (produced 1946; as *The Foreign Language,* produced 1951). 1952.
I Know My Love, from a play by Marcel Achard (produced 1949). 1952.
Let Me Hear the Melody (produced 1951).
Fanny, with Joshua Logan, music by Harold Rome, from a trilogy by Marcel Pagnol (produced 1954). 1955.
Four Plays: The Second Man, Biography, Rain from Heaven, End of Summer. 1955.
The Cold Wind and the Warm (produced 1958). 1959.
The Beauty Part (produced 1962).
Lord Pengo: A Period Comedy, based on his book *Duveen* (produced 1962). 1963.
But for Whom Charlie (produced 1964). 1964.

Screenplays: *Liliom,* with Sonya Levien, 1930; *Lightnin',* with Sonya Levien, 1930; *The Sea Wolf,* with Ralph Block, 1930; *The Brat,* with others, 1931; *Surrender,* with Sonya Levien, 1931; *Daddy Long Legs,* with Sonya Levien, 1931; *Rebecca of Sunnybrook Farm,* with Sonya Levien, 1932; *Tess of the Storm Country,* with others, 1932; *Brief Moment,* 1933; *Queen Christina,* 1933; *Cavalcade,* 1933; *Hallelujah, I'm a Bum,* 1933; *My Lips Betray,* 1933; *Biography of a Bachelor Girl,* 1934; *As Husbands Go,* with Sonya Levien, 1934; *The Scarlet Pimpernel,* with others, 1934; *A Tale of Two Cities,* with W. P. Lipscomb, 1935; *Conquest,* with others, 1937; *Parnell,* with John Van Druten, 1937; *The Cowboy and the Lady,* with Sonya Levien, 1938; *No Time for Comedy,* 1940; *Waterloo Bridge,* with others, 1940; *Two-Faced Woman,* with others, 1941; *Quo Vadis,* with others, 1951; *Me and the Colonel,* with George Froeschel, 1958; *Fanny,* with Joshua Logan, 1961.

Fiction

The Burning-Glass. 1968.

Other

Duveen. 1952.
The Worcester Account (*New Yorker* sketches). 1954.
Portrait of Max: An Intimate Memoir of Sir Max Beerbohm. 1960; as *Conversation with Max,* 1960.
The Suspended Drawing Room. 1965.
People in a Diary: A Memoir. 1972; as *Tribulations and Laughter: A Memoir,* 1972.

Bibliography: *Maxwell Anderson and Behrman: A Reference Guide* by William Klink, 1977.

Reading List: "Behrman: The Quandary of the Comic Spirit" by Charles Kaplan, in *College English 9,* 1950.

*   *   *

It is now 50 years since S. N. Behrman's *The Second Man* was produced by the Theatre Guild and made him famous. Even by the 1950's the material was old-hat, and writers of comedies of manners (even better ones, such as Philip Barry) are now quite out of date. Behrman's work after the 1930's was fairly unimportant, largely adaptations. His sophisticated comedy belongs to an earlier generation. A recent revival of *The Second Man* looked very old-fashioned. It, of course, lacked the Lunts, who created roles in it (and Noël Coward and Raymond Massey, who played it in London), and it needed them.

In his time Behrman also had the assistance of stars like Greta Garbo, Ina Claire, Katherine Cornell, and Laurence Olivier. He, like the blasé and aphoristic writer Clark Storey in *The Second Man*, said "(*Seriously*) Life is sad. I know it's sad. But I think it's gallant to pretend that it isn't." In the 1930's this approach made him an American Noël Coward and gave him "perhaps the most considerable reputation" among young playwrights (A. H. Quinn). But soon proletarian and "socially significant drama" was to render inoperable the approach of the heroine of *Biography*, which was to laugh at injustice because nothing could be done about it, and the hero of *No Time for Comedy*, who chose to write light comedy instead of propagandist melodrama. The depression and World War II wiped out Behrman's impassive, indifferent, intellectual sophisticates who gracefully soared above reality. In *Rain from Heaven*, even though it revolves around Fascists and German refugees, the sophisticates are still doing arabesques on the thin ice of political problems.

Behrman wrote a number of screenplays, including such movies as *Queen Christina* and *Anna Karenina*, both with Garbo, *Waterloo Bridge*, and *Quo Vadis*. For the *New Yorker* he wrote the sketches that became *Duveen* (about the art dealer who became Lord Millbank) and *The Worcester Account* (about his boyhood in Worcester, Massachusetts). These, I think, surpass his original comedies of manners, his adaptation of Giraudoux (*Amphytrion 38*) or his collaboration with Franz Werfel (*Jacobowsky and the Colonel*), his dramatization of stories by Enid Bagnold (*Serena Blandish*) and W. Somerset Maugham (*Jane*), all his theatre work, and his cinema writing. It is unfortunate that he did not find time in his 80 years to write a work for the stage about the sort of people who enliven *The Worcester Account*. His cosmopolitan intellectuals may be well observed for a "Brief Moment" (as a 1931 play of his was called), but they are seen by a stranger, however clever. The people of Providence Street in Worcester, Behrman knew.

—Leonard R. N. Ashley

BELASCO, David.   American.   Born in San Francisco, California, 25 July 1853; moved with his family to Victoria, British Columbia, 1858. Educated at a monastery in Victoria, 1858–62; in various schools in San Francisco, where his family returned in 1865; Lincoln College, California, 1875. Married Cecilia Loverich in 1873; two daughters. Worked as an actor in repertory, touring California; acted at Piper's Opera House in Virginia City, where he was employed briefly by Dion Boucicault as a secretary, 1873; Stage Manager, Maguire's Theatre, San Francisco, 1874; Assistant to the Manager, 1875–78, and Stage Manager, 1878–82, Lucky Baldwin's Academy of Music, San Francisco; began writing for the stage in the late 1870's; Lighting Manager, then Stage Manager, Madison Square Theatre, New York, 1882–86; Manager, with David Frohman, Lyceum Theatre, New York, 1886–90; Independent Actor/Manager, New York, 1890–1906; Owner, Stuyvesant Theatre, later Belasco Theatre, New York, 1906 until his death. Produced over 350 plays for Broadway and stock companies. *Died 14 May 1931.*

PUBLICATIONS

Collections

The Plays of Henry C. DeMille and Belasco (includes *The Senator's Wife, Lord Chumley, The Charity Ball, Men and Women*), edited by Robert Hamilton Ball.   1941.

The Heart of Maryland and Other Plays (includes *The Stranglers of Paris, La Belle Russe, The Girl I Left Behind Me, Naughty Anthony*), edited by Glenn Hughes and George Savage.   1941.

Plays

The Doll Master (produced 1874–75?).

Sylvia's Lovers (produced 1875?).

The Creole, from a play by Adolphe Belot (produced 1876–77?).

Olivia, from the novel *The Vicar of Wakefield* by Goldsmith (produced 1878).

Proof Positive (produced 1878).

Within an Inch of His Life, with James A. Herne, from a play by Emile Gaboriau (produced 1879).   Edited by Arthur Hobson Quinn, in *The Early Plays of Herne*, 1940.

A Fast Family, from a play by Sardou (produced 1879).

The Millionaire's Daughter (produced 1879).

Marriage by Moonlight, with James A. Herne, from the play *Camilla's Husband* by Watt Philips (produced 1879).

Drink, from a novel by Zola (produced 1879).

Hearts of Oak, with James A. Herne (as *Chums*, produced 1879; as *Hearts of Oak*, produced 1879).   Edited by Mrs. James A. Herne, in *Shore Acres and Other Plays*, by Herne, 1928.

Paul Arniff; or, The Love of a Serf (produced 1880).

True to the Core, from the play by A. R. Slous (produced 1880).

La Belle Russe, from the plays *Forget-Me-Not* and *New Magdalen* (produced 1881).   1914; in *The Heart of Maryland and Other Plays*, 1941.

The Stranglers of Paris, from a novel by Adolphe Belot (produced 1881).   In *The Heart of Maryland and Other Plays*, 1941.

The Curse of Cain, with Peter Robinson (produced 1882).

American Born, from the play *British Born* (produced 1882).

Valerie, from a play by Sardou (produced 1886).

The Highest Bidder, from the play *Trade* by John Maddison Morton and Robert Reece (produced 1887).

Baron Rudolph, with Bronson Howard, revised version (produced 1887).   Edited by Allan H. Halline, in *The Banker's Daughter and Other Plays*, by Howard, 1941.

Pawn Ticket 210, with Clay M. Greene (produced 1887).

The Senator's Wife, with Henry C. DeMille (as *The Wife*, produced 1887; as *The Senator's Wife*, produced 1892).   In *The Plays of DeMille and Belasco*, 1941.

Lord Chumley, with Henry C. DeMille (produced 1888).   In *The Plays of DeMille and Belasco*, 1941.

The Charity Ball, with Henry C. DeMille (produced 1889).   In *The Plays of DeMille and Belasco*, 1941.

The Marquis, from a play by Sardou (produced 1889).

Men and Women, with Henry C. DeMille (produced 1890).   In *The Plays of DeMille and Belasco*, 1941.

Miss Helyett, from a play by Maxime Boucheron (produced 1891).

The Girl I Left Behind Me; or, The Country Ball, with Franklin Fyles (produced 1893).   In *The Heart of Maryland and Other Plays*, 1941.

The Younger Son, from a play by O. Vischer (produced 1893).

The Heart of Maryland (produced 1895).   In *The Heart of Maryland and Other Plays*, 1941.

Under the Polar Star, with Clay M. Greene (produced 1896).

Zaza, from a play by Pierre Berton and Charles Simon (produced 1898).

Naughty Anthony (produced 1899).   In *The Heart of Maryland and Other Plays*, 1941.

Madame Butterfly, from the story by John Luther Long (produced 1900).   In *Six Plays*, 1928.

Du Barry (produced 1901).   In *Six Plays*, 1928.

The Darling of the Gods, with John Luther Long (produced 1902).   In *Six Plays*, 1928.

Sweet Kitty Bellairs, from the novel *The Bath Comedy* by Agnes and Egerton Castle (produced 1903).

Adrea, with John Luther Long (produced 1904).   In *Six Plays*, 1928.

The Girl of the Golden West (produced 1905).   In *Six Plays*, 1928.

The Rose of the Rancho, from the play *Juanita* by Richard Walton Tully (produced 1906).   1936.

A Grand Army Man, with Pauline Phelps and Marion Short (produced 1907).

The Lily, from a play by Pierre Wolff and Gaston Leroux (produced 1909).

The Return of Peter Grimm (produced 1911).   In *Six Plays*, 1928.

The Governor's Lady, with Alice Bradley (produced 1912).

The Secret, from a work by Henri Bernstein (produced 1913).

Van Der Decken: A Legendary Play of the Sea (produced 1915).

The Son-Daughter, with George Scarborough (produced 1919).

Timothy Shaft, with W. J. Hurlbut (produced 1921).

Kiki, from the play by André Picard (produced 1921).

The Merchant of Venice, from the play by Shakespeare (produced 1922).   1922.

The Comedian, from a play by Sacha Guitry (produced 1923).

Laugh, Clown, Laugh!, with Tom Cushing, from a play by Fausto Martini (produced 1923).

Salvage.   1925.

Fanny, with Willard Mack (produced 1926).

Mima, from a play by Molnar (produced 1928).

Six Plays (includes *Madame Butterfly*, *Du Barry*, *The Darling of the Gods*, *Adrea*, *The Girl of The Golden West*, *The Return of Peter Grimm*).   1928.

Other

My Life's Story.   2 vols., 1915.

The Theatre Through Its Stage Door, edited by Louis V. Defoe.   1919.

A Souvenir of Shakespeare's Merchant of Venice.   1923.

Plays Produced under the Stage Direction of David Belasco.   1925.

Editor, with Charles A. Byrne, *Fairy Tales Told by Seven Travellers at the Red Lion Inn*.   1906.

Reading List: *The Life of Belasco* by William Winter, 2 vols., 1918; *The Life and Work of Belasco, The Bishop of Broadway* by Craig Timberlake, 1954; *Belasco: Naturalism in the American Theatre* by Lise-Lone Marker, 1974.

*   *   *

The parents of David Belasco came to San Francisco from England during the Gold Rush, and his early theatrical experience was gained entirely in the American and Canadian west. Humphrey Abraham Belasco was a harlequin turned shopkeeper, and his son at the age of eleven played the Duke of York to Charles Kean's Richard III. At twelve, he wrote and produced his first melodrama. He supered, prompted, played Hamlet, Uncle Tom, and Armand on tour, and in 1876 was secretary to Dion Boucicault, whose "sensation dramas" heavily influenced the would-be playwright.

While stage manager at Baldwin's Academy of Music, Belasco began to experiment with spectacle and stage lighting as well as adapting and collaborating on several plays, one of which, La Belle Russe was a success in New York. Its derivative plot involves a woman's impersonation of her virtuous twin sister, even to the sister's titled husband. Here Belasco began treating "strong," sometimes demonic, always sexual female characters and tense situations. The sketchy good twin also foreshadows Belasco's virtuous, suffering heroines such as Adrea and Cho-Cho-San.

In 1882 Belasco came east, where he was at times associated with the Frohmans, and in the late 1880's collaborated with Henry C. DeMille on four very popular but immemorable plays. Belasco's real success as a playwright began with The Heart of Maryland in 1895, in which Mrs. Leslie Carter swung on the clapper of a bell to save her soldier-sweetheart, Belasco having been inspired by the Civil War and "Curfew Shall Not Ring Tonight!" Mrs. Carter, the star of a scandalous divorce trial, was taught to act by Belasco, who later wrote Zaza, Du Barry, and Adrea for her. Too high in voice and too low in stature to be effective on stage himself, he acted through the players he coached and in his own off-stage character as the silver-haired, clerical-collared "Bishop of Broadway."

In 1900 Belasco collaborated with John Luther Long on Madame Butterfly, from which Puccini derived his opera, and when the same composer set Belasco's The Girl of the Golden West, the playwright directed Caruso and the Metropolitan Opera cast for its 1910 premiere. Belasco's later work was largely as director and deviser of scenic effects, and the plays he dealt with were inconsequential except for his productions of Sacha Guitry's Deburau, The Merchant of Venice with David Warfield as Shylock, and Molnar's Mima – unsuccessful but stupendous.

It is doubtful that David Belasco did anything which could be called truly original, but he improved all he touched and he touched almost everything in the theatre of his day. A master of the exciting plot, he developed from the physical sensationalism of Boucicault to the emotional sensationalism of Sardou. In The Girl I Left Behind Me, for example, he used elements of Boucicault's Defense of Lucknow for a situation which John Ford would adapt for his film Stage Coach. Belasco heroines such as Du Barry, Minnie, and Yo-San face Tosca's dilemma of proscribed lover and lascivious authority, while Adrea with its blind princess, wicked sister, exotic kingdom, disloyal lover, and tower of death recalls the extravagant costume dramas Sardou created for Sarah Bernhardt. Yet Belasco could also devise plays of quiet sentiment such as The Return of Peter Grimm with its affectionate ghost ex machina (and its only partly-acknowledged debt to the young Cecil B. DeMille). As Belasco explained in The Theatre Through Its Stage Door, his plays appealed because he tried "to tug at the hearts of my audience." He also made those heart-strings zing with excitement, part of which arose from his extraordinary scenic effects.

Dion Boucicault had blown up steamboats on stage; David Belasco created battlefields. Later, working in the tradition of realistic mise en scène introduced by Tom Robertson, Belasco used a real switchboard and telephone booths in his production of William C. DeMille's The Woman and re-created the interior of a Childs' Restaurant on stage in The Governor's Lady by Alice Bradley. The theatres which he built (the Belasco and the Stuyvesant) contained the most sophisticated stage equipment of their day, and he experimented endlessly with electricity, first used by W. S. Gilbert at the Savoy Theatre.

Belasco believed that color and light could "communicate to audiences the underlying symbolism of a play." Cho-Cho-San's pathetic vigil was accompanied by fourteen minutes of mood lighting in which twilight darkened to night, stars appeared, lamps were lighted and flickered out one by one, and dawn broke. The River of Souls in *The Darling of the Gods* was composed of shadowy spirits "floating across and disappearing," an anticipation of back projection. For *The Girl of the Golden West*, Belasco spent three months designing a sunset, only to reject it – "It was a good sunset, but it was not Californian."

Although Belasco's meticulous realism is no longer fashionable, it is still significant in the *verismo* operas which Puccini based on his plays and productions. Moreover, like his predecessors Robertson and Gilbert, Belasco played a part in turning the stage from a star-dominated playhouse to a director's theatre. Finally, the exciting motifs which he developed or adapted are still part of the vocabulary of American melodrama.

—Jane W. Stedman

BELLOW, Saul.   American.   Born in Lachine, Quebec, Canada, 10 June 1915; grew up in Montreal; moved with his family to Chicago, 1924. Educated at the University of Chicago, 1933–35; Northwestern University, Evanston, Illinois. 1935–37, B.S. (honors) in sociology and anthropology 1937; did graduate work in anthropology at the University of Wisconsin, Madison, 1937. Served in the United States Merchant Marine, 1944–45. Married 1) Anita Goshkin in 1937 (divorced), one son; 2) Alexandra Tschacbasov in 1956 (divorced), one son; 3) Susan Glassman in 1961, one son. Teacher, Pestalozzi-Froebel Teachers College, Chicago, 1938–42; Member of the Editorial Department, "Great Books" Project, *Encyclopaedia Britannica*, Chicago, 1943–46; Instructor, 1946, and Assistant Professor English, 1948–49, University of Minnesota, Minneapolis; Visiting Lecturer, New York University, 1950–52; Creative Writing Fellow, Princeton University, New Jersey, 1952–53; Member of the English faculty, Bard College, Annandale-on-Hudson, New York, 1953–54; Associate Professor of English, University of Minnesota, 1954–59; Visiting Professor of English, University of Puerto Rico, Rio Piedras, 1961. Since 1962, Professor, Committee on Social Thought, University of Chicago. Co-Founding Editor, *The Noble Savage*, Cleveland, 1960–62. Fellow, Academy for Policy Study, 1966; Fellow, Branford College, Yale University, New Haven, Connecticut. Recipient: Guggenheim Fellowship, 1948, 1955; National Institute of Arts and Letters grant, 1952; National Book Award, 1954, 1965, 1971; Ford Foundation grant, 1959, 1960; Friends of Literature award, 1960; James L. Dow Award, 1964; Prix International de Littérature, France, 1965; Jewish Heritage Award, 1968; Nobel Prize for Literature, 1976; Pulitzer Prize, 1976; American Academy of Arts and Letters Gold Medal, 1977. D. Litt.: Northwestern University, 1962; Bard College, 1963. Member, National Institute of Arts and Letters. Lives in Chicago.

PUBLICATIONS

Fiction

Dangling Man.   1944.
The Victim.   1947.
The Adventures of Augie March.   1953.
Seize the Day, with Three Short Stories and a One-Act Play.   1956.
Henderson the Rain King.   1959.

Herzog. 1964.
Mosby's Memoirs and Other Stories.   1968.
Mr. Sammler's Planet.   1970.
Humboldt's Gift.   1975.

Plays

The Wrecker (televised, 1964).   In *Seize the Day ...,* 1956.
The Last Analysis (produced 1964).   1965.
Under the Weather (includes *Out from Under, A Wen, Orange Soufflé*) (produced 1966;
    as *The Bellow Plays,* produced 1966).   *A Wen* and *Orange Soufflé* in *Traverse Plays,*
    1967.

Other

Dessins, by Jess Reichek; text by Bellow and C. Zervos.   1960.
*Like You're Nobody: The Letters of Louis Gallo to Bellow, 1961–62, Plus Oedipus-
    Schmoedipus, The Story That Started It All.*   1966.
The Future of the Moon.   1970.
The Portable Bellow, edited by Gabriel Josipovici.   1974.
To Jerusalem and Back: A Personal Account.   1976.

Editor, *Great Jewish Short Stories.*   1963.

Translator, with others, *Gimpel the Fool and Other Stories,* by Isaac Bashevis
    Singer.   1957.

Bibliography: *Bellow: A Comprehensive Bibliography* by B. A. Sokoloff and Mark E. Posner,
1973; *Bellow, His Works and His Critics: An Annotated International Bibliography* by
Marianne Nault, 1977.

Reading List: *Bellow* by Tony Tanner, 1965; *Bellow* by Earl Rovit, 1967, and *Bellow: A
Collection of Critical Essays* edited by Rovit, 1974; *Bellow: A Critical Essay* by Robert
Detweiler, 1967; *The Novels of Bellow: An Introduction* by Keith Michael Opdahl, 1967;
Bellow and the Critics edited by Irving Malin, 1967, and *Bellow's Fiction* by Malin, 1969;
Bellow: In Defense of Man by John Jacob Clayton, 1968; *Bellow* by Robert R. Dutton, 1971;
Bellow's Enigmatic Laughter by Sarah Blacher Cohen, 1974; *Whence the Power? The Artistry
and Humanity of Bellow* by M. Gilbert Porter, 1974.

*   *   *

Since 1976, when he received the Nobel Prize for Literature, Saul Bellow has been assured
an important position in American literature. This position was not new for the Chicago
writer. For the past twenty years, at least since the publication of his popular *Adventures of
Augie March,* Bellow has been heralded as the major spokesman of realism in America, as the
most articulate voice for humanism in America, as the most sophisticated comedian of the
modern predicament, and even as the one on whose shoulders has fallen the mantle of genius
previously worn by William Faulkner. No matter how exaggerated these evaluations might
seem, Bellow is surely one of the major American novelists of the past twenty years.

It is as a novelist that he assumes his important position. However, Bellow also writes
essays, short stories, and plays. Most of his non-fiction is a clarification of his view of the

duties of novelist and human being. For Bellow fiction should be basically realistic; it should not obscure the human condition, but should delve deeply into the psychological idiosyncrasies that explain an individual act. *To Jerusalem and Back* relates a visit to Israel less for the purpose of providing an answer to the Middle East question than for the fascinating personalized portraits of individuals. It is not sociology, but psychology.

Most of the short pieces that appear in journals are sections of novels in progress, but some of these short pieces have remained as short stories, the best of which have been collected in *Mosby's Memoirs and Other Stories*. Perhaps the best of these tales in relation to his major work is "The Old System," a short story that approaches one of Bellow's significant themes: the conflict between modern Jewish man and his ageless ties to a Jewish past. The plays of Saul Bellow, especially the one-act sketches, barely hint at the power of his novels. *The Last Analysis*, a full-length work, is his best attempt in this genre. The fragmentation, confusion, and discomfort of modern life color the play as much as they do the novels.

Bellow's first novel, *Dangling Man*, is a diary of a young man awaiting induction into the army during World War II. Joseph quits his job, planning to relax and read before being subjected to the rigors of army life. Instead, the period becomes one of inaction and meaninglessness. Joseph begins to question the value of his friendships, the meaning of his family, and finally even the goodness of life. After months of stultification, existence seems absurd; relief comes in the promise of the regimentation of military life. Joseph no longer awaits induction; he enlists.

The Victim is similar to the previous novel in atmosphere and tone, but dissimilar in form. Asa Leventhal is plagued by family responsibilities, human responsibilities, and anti-Semitism. He is the victim. But in his treatment, or rather his acceptance, of his major tormentor, Kirby Allbee, Asa victimizes his tormentor and himself. The bleak picture of human irrationality, death, and sorrow is broken only by the end of an unbearably hot summer, the return of Asa's wife, and the philosophy of humanism that is spoken by the Yiddishist Schlossberg. These reprieves assure Asa's escape.

The Adventures of Augie March was the novel that thrust Bellow before the American public as a major writer. An exuberant picaresque tale of a Chicago boy, born to a retarded mother, *Augie March* bespeaks an American innocence and joy in existence that Bellow seemed shy of in his first novels. This joyousness is not, however, unadulterated. Augie is a Jewish bastard who must learn to fend for himself in the confused and constantly changing world that was America in the 1940's: he encounters abortion, political manipulation, the black-market, and sexual perversion. In the face of all of this, Augie can still laugh.

Seize the Day, a novella, tells of a middle-aged Wilky Adler forced to recognize the aimlessness of his life. Always a failure in his father's eyes, Wilky tries to establish an independent identity by attaining what his father most admires – wealth. Wilky is, of course, an abysmal failure, though he learns the valuelessness of money. His epiphany is of his shared humanity with all man. The beauty of humanity is not revealed in the predatory stalking for materialistic gain, but rather in the prayer over the corpse of a stranger.

Henderson the Rain King is a fantasy of a trip to an Africa of the spirit. Here in the continent that saw the first man evolve, Eugene Henderson tries to return to essentials. Henderson leaves America as a man who feels his soul gnawed at by a demanding voice crying "I want! I want!" By the time he returns from Africa, after encountering the primitive power that is in a lion and in an African tribal king, he assumes the status of human being, with all its grace and goodness. His desires to do good for others, his love for his family and wife, are directed now so that he can accept the joy of existence. Suffering is no longer his only means of definition.

In *Herzog*, Bellow created a character that caught the consciousness of the American intellectual of the 1960's. Moses Elkanah Herzog, on the brink of divorce (for the second time) and professional suicide, begins to develop his naturally reflective nature to the point of insanity. He writes letters, letters to his friends, to his family, to famous people both dead and alive, even notes to himself. These attempts to come to terms with his changing self-image center especially on his feeling for his Jewish past. During his adult life, Moses has been a

Jew totally assimilated into the Christian intellectual world; he has learned the history of the Christian West; he has accepted the precepts of the Christian philosophers and theologians; and he has taken a Christian wife. Suddenly, this life begins to disintegrate. Before Herzog can attain any equanimity he must learn how to balance his present individuality with his past tradition.

In *Mr. Sammler's Planet*, the conflict between past and present is again a concern of the novelist, but with many added ambiguities. Arthur Sammler, representative of the Old World, survivor of the Holocaust, is divorced from his Jewish past. He is one who admires and studies the Christian ideals of the West. In America, his benefactor and nephew, Elya Bruner, a gynecologist who got rich by doing illegal abortions for the Mafia, is the representative of the Old World patterns. He is the one who, despite his flaws, follows the ideals of humanism that was the backbone of the East European *shtetl*. Only at the end of the novel can Sammler articulate the beauty that he sees in his nephew. In most of the novel, Sammler is suffering life in New York, dodging nymphomaniacs, pickpockets, exhibitionists, violent madmen, and schizophrenics. In the face of such disruption of morals, his own delicacy is not the answer; Elya's goodness is the only philosophy that provides order.

Humboldt's Gift relates the growth of a dilettante writer, Charlie Citrine, who must learn the true value of his mad mentor, Von Humboldt Fleischer (a personalized portrait of the poet Delmore Schwartz). As a young man, Charlie worships the charismatic Humboldt. Moving East to follow his god, Charlie becomes a friend and colleague of the poet. Only after Charlie's success on Broadway do the two writers part – Humboldt accusing Charlie of stealing his personality for the hero of his play. This big, funny, and poignant novel centers on the young man's reflections on Humboldt and on his true value as an artist and mentor. Through flashbacks Citrine reveals the despair and paranoia that destroy his idol. The persistence of Humboldt's spiritual presence in Charlie's later life, long after the poet's death, bespeaks the importance of Humboldt to Charlie.

The gift that the mentor leaves is really twofold. The most obvious gift is the absurd play that will probably become a great success as a film. But more importantly, Humboldt serves as an exemplum for Charlie's own life. The reflection of later years gradually reveals that Humboldt is indeed mad; he was a genius who was driven insane and finally killed by his own unwritten poems. He was one who misused his talents. After this realization, Charlie is able to accept the memory of Humboldt. The reburial of the poet's body is a significant rite of passage for Charlie. No longer is he possessed by his mentor's personality.

The variety and power of Bellow's novels assure him a place in American literature. When Bellow resists the term "Jewish writer," it is because his art is not a chauvinistic and narrow one. But as readers we must not be misled by his resistance to this term: he is most assuredly a writer whose style, characters, form, and humor derive in large part from his Jewish past.

—Barbara Gitenstein

BEMELMANS, Ludwig. American. Born in Meran, Austria, now Merano, Italy, 27 April 1898; emigrated to the United States in 1914; naturalized, 1918. Educated at schools in Regensburg and Rothenburg, Bavaria. Served in the United States Army during World War I. Married Madeline Freund in 1935; one daughter. Worked as a hotel clerk and restaurant proprietor in New York City; writer for *The New Yorker*; also an artist: works exhibited in principal galleries in the United States and abroad. Recipient: American Library Association Caldecott Medal, 1954. *Died 1 October 1962.*

PUBLICATIONS

Fiction

I Love You, I Love You, I Love You (stories).   1942.
Now I Lay Me Down to Sleep.   1943.
The Blue Danube.   1945.
Dirty Eddie.   1947.
The Eye of God.   1947; as *The Snow Mountain*, 1950.
The Woman of My Life.   1957.
Are You Hungry, Are You Cold.   1960.
The Street Where the Heart Lies.   1963.

Other

Hansi (juvenile).   1934
The Golden Basket (juvenile).   1936.
The Castle Number Nine (juvenile).   1937.
My War with the United States.   1937.
Life Class.   1938.
Quito Express (juvenile).   1938.
Madeline (juvenile).   1938.
Small Beer.   1939.
Fifi (juvenile).   1940.
At Your Service: The Way of Life in a Hotel.   1941.
Hotel Splendide.   1941.
The Donkey Inside.   1941.
Rosebud (juvenile).   1942.
Hotel Bemelmans.   1946.
A Tale of Two Glimps (juvenile).   1947.
The Best of Times: An Account of Europe Revisited.   1948.
Sunshine (juvenile).   1950.
How to Travel Incognito.   1952.
The Happy Place (juvenile).   1952.
Madeline's Rescue (juvenile).   1953.
Father, Dear Father (autobiography).   1953.
The High World (juvenile).   1954.
Parsley (juvenile).   1955.
To the One I Love the Best.   1955.
The World of Bemelmans.   1955.
Madeline and the Bad Hat (juvenile).   1956.
My Life in Art.   1958.
Madeline and the Gypsies (juvenile).   1959.
Welcome Home! (juvenile).   1960.
How to Have Europe All to Yourself.   1960.
Italian Holiday.   1961.
Madeline in London (juvenile).   1961.
Marina (juvenile).   1962.
On Board Noah's Ark.   1962.
La Bonne Table (writings and drawings), edited by Donald and Eleanor Friede. 1964.

Editor, *Holiday in France.*   1957.

*   *   *

William McFee once wrote of Ludwig Bemelmans, the writer, stage designer, illustrator and painter, that he was "one of those fortunate writers who have all the reviewers ranged on one side, rooting for him." I must at the outset confess myself one of that number. Whether chronicling the adventures of Madeline, the irrepressible little French *gamine*, or reporting his own adventures as "El Señor Bnelemaas" in Ecuador (*The Donkey Inside*) or as a waiter (in *Hotel Splendide*), he is delightful. He always wanted to be a painter (despite his family's belief that all artists are "hunger candidates") and only wrote because he had insomnia, but in his acerb and risible little essays, even more than in his drawings, every line is precisely *right*.

To him happen all the most fabulous things. He meets "Mr. Sigsag" of the Hotel Splendide and a host of other charming eccentrics. Just for him a war breaks out (*My War with the United States*) to galvanize a gallery of characters into action. He encounters a little girl who contrives to make her schoolmates livid with jealousy by having an appendix operation. For him tables and chairs have something droll about them. For him people do the most ludicrous things. The world ("I regard it as a curiousity") is funny and he has only to report it (*I Love You, I Love You, I Love You*). He claimed he had no imagination.

Bemelmans is always satirical, but at his best when his unquenchable good humor is given free play, as in the novel *Now I Lay Me Down to Sleep* or the collection of *New Yorker* essays *Small Beer*. It is hard not to gush when mentioning his works. But his delightful humor disarms criticism.

—Leonard R. N. Ashley

BENCHLEY, Robert (Charles).   American.   Born in Worcester, Massachusetts, 15 September 1889. Educated at Worcester High School, 1904–07; Phillips Exeter Academy, New Hampshire, 1907–08; Harvard University, Cambridge, Massachusetts (member of the Board of Editors of *Lampoon*), 1908–12, B.A. 1913. Married Gertrude Darling in 1914; two sons, including the writer Nathaniel Benchley. Worked for the Boston Museum of Fine Art, 1912, and for Curtis Publishing Company, 1912–14 (Editor of the house journal *Obiter Dicta*); did welfare work in Boston and New York, 1914; worked in advertising, then as a reporter for the New York *Tribune* and *Tribune* magazine, 1916–17; Drama Critic, *Vanity Fair*, New York, 1917; journalist and office worker in Washington, D.C., 1918; Managing Editor of *Vanity Fair*, 1919–20; Columnist, New York *World*, 1920–21; Drama Critic, 1920–24, and Editor, 1924–29, *Life* magazine, New York; Columnist, 1925–40, and Drama Critic, 1929–40, *The New Yorker*; Columnist for King Features Syndicate, 1933–36. Also an actor: stage debut, 1923; also wrote and starred in 48 motion pictures, 1928–45; radio broadcaster from 1938. Recipient: Academy Award, for short film, 1935. *Died 21 November 1945.*

PUBLICATIONS

Essays and Sketches

Of All Things!   1921.
Love Conquers All.   1922.
Pluck and Luck.   1925.

The Early Worm. 1927.
The Bridges of Binding. 1928.
20,000 Leagues under the Sea; or, David Copperfield. 1928.
The Treasurer's Report and Other Aspects of Community Singing. 1930.
No Poems; or, Around the World Backwards and Sideways. 1932.
From Bed to Worse; or, Comforting Thoughts about the Bison. 1934.
Why Does Nobody Collect Me? 1935.
My Ten Years in a Quandary and How They Grew. 1936.
After 1903 — What? 1938.
Inside Benchley (selection). 1942.
Benchley Beside Himself. 1943.
One Minute Please. 1945.
Benchley – or Else! 1947.
Chips off the Old Benchley. 1949.
The "Reel" Benchley, edited by George Hornby. 1950.
The Bedside Manner; or, No More Nightmares. 1952.
The Benchley Roundup, edited by Nathaniel Benchley. 1954.
Benchley Lost and Found: 39 Fugitive Pieces. 1970.

Reading List: *Benchley: A Biography* by Nathaniel Benchley, 1955; *Benchley* by Norris W. Yates, 1968.

*   *   *

After the customary false starts, forays into advertising and personnel work, Robert Benchley, like most of the American humorists of his generation, found his way to journalism. He began as a reporter for the New York *Tribune* in 1916, and within a few years became editor, columnist, or occasional contributor to *Collier's, Vanity Fair*, the New York *World, Life, The Bookman*, and *The New Yorker*. Aside from his comic writing, his most sustained work in the magazines was as a drama reviewer, primarily for *Life* and *The New Yorker*, and as a press critic, in which capacity he used a pseudonym, Guy Fawkes, and initiated "The Wayward Press" department in *The New Yorker*. His first book, *Of All Things!*, was published in 1921 and between that time and his death in 1945, some dozen more volumes appeared, all of them collections of pieces written for magazines or newspapers. Some of the later ones, like *Benchley Beside Himself*, cannibalize earlier collections.

In a letter to his mother written in 1922, E. B. White called *Of All Things!* "about as funny as anything there is on the market today," and, in a letter to Walter Blair in 1964, he admitted that he imitated Benchley in his early work. That writers like White and James Thurber, who so early found their own authentic voices, were influenced by Benchley is evidence not simply of the pervasiveness of his subject matter – the little indignities of daily life which have always beset humorists – but of the quality of his prose. Benchley could, like Frank Sullivan, rise to complete nonsense, but most of the time he wrote simple, deceptively rational sentences in which a judicious choice of adjective or a demanding parenthesis could turn the sentence, the whole piece, a conventional way of thinking inside out.

Benchley early developed a firm comic personality, created a character who sometimes appears in the pieces, is more often the voice that creates them. His persona became a Benchley after-image, through the Gluyas Williams illustrations for his books and the bumbling character he played in movie shorts and in feature films. As he emerges in Benchley's writing, the character is more than the conventional little man so loved by humorists, cartoonists, and politicians. He is both vain and ponderous, using his own self-esteem as the banana peel on which to slip; he is easily embarrassed, but he will snarl – a bit tentatively – if he is cornered by too preposterous an assault from social usage. His ordinary antagonists are things like pigeons, roadmaps, ocean liners, Christmas, but there are hints of darker enemies, as in "My Trouble" in which he asks, "Do all boys of 46 stop breathing when they go to bed?" This disquieting undertone emerges infrequently in Benchley's work; for the most part, his confused and confusing other self is satisfied to worry a pomposity or a platitude to death and in the process leave the reader laughing.

—Gerald Weales

BENÉT, Stephen Vincent.   American.   Born in Bethlehem, Pennsylvania, 22 July 1898; brother of the poet William Rose Benét, *q.v.* Educated at Summerville Academy; Yale University, New Haven, Connecticut (Chairman, *Yale Literary Magazine*, 1919), A.B. 1919, M.A. 1920; the Sorbonne, Paris. Married Rosemary Carr in 1921; one son, two daughters. During the Depression and war years became an active lecturer and radio propagandist for the liberal cause. Editor, Yale Series of Younger Poets. Recipient: Poetry Society of America Prize, 1921; Guggenheim Fellowship, 1926; Pulitzer Prize, 1929, 1944; O. Henry Award, 1932, 1937, 1940; Shelley Memorial Award, 1933; National Institute of Arts and Letters Gold Medal, 1943. D.Litt.: Middlebury College, Vermont, 1936. Vice-President, National Institute of Arts and Letters. *Died 13 March 1943.*

PUBLICATIONS

Collections

> *Selected Poetry and Prose,* edited by Basil Davenport.   1960.
> *Selected Letters,* edited by Charles A. Fenton.   1960.

Verse

> *The Drug-Shop; or, Endymion in Edmonstoun.*   1917.
> *Young Adventure.*   1918.
> *Heavens and Earth.*   1920.
> *The Ballad of William Sycamore 1790–1880.*   1923.
> *King David.*   1923.
> *Tiger Joy.*   1925.
> *John Brown's Body.*   1928.
> *Ballads and Poems 1915–1930.*   1931.
> *A Book of Americans,* with Rosemary Benét.   1933.
> *Burning City.*   1936.
> *The Ballad of the Duke's Mercy.*   1939.
> *Nightmare at Noon.*   1940.
> *Listen to the People: Independence Day 1941.*   1941.
> *Western Star.*   1943.

The Last Circle: Stories and Poems.   1946.

Plays

Five Men and Pompey: A Series of Dramatic Portraits.   1915.
The Headless Horseman, music by Douglas Moore (broadcast 1937).   1937.
The Devil and Daniel Webster, music by Douglas Moore, from the story by Benét (produced 1938).   1939.
Elementals (broadcast 1940–41). In *Best Broadcasts of 1940–41,* edited by Max Wylie, 1942.
Freedom's a Hard Bought Thing (broadcast 1941).   In *The Free Company Presents,* edited by James Boyd, 1941.
Nightmare at Noon, in *The Treasury Star Parade,* edited by William A. Bacher.   1942.
A Child Is Born (broadcast 1942).   1942.
They Burned the Books (broadcast 1942).   1942.
All That Money Can Buy (screenplay), with Dan Totheroh, in *Twenty Best Film Plays,* edited by John Gassner and Dudley Nichols.   1943.
We Stand United and Other Radio Scripts (includes *A Child Is Born, The Undefended Border, Dear Adolf, Listen to the People, Thanksgiving Day – 1941, They Burned the Books, A Time to Reap, Toward the Century of Modern Man, Your Army*).   1945.

Screenplays: *Cheers for Miss Bishop,* with Adelaide Heilbron and Sheridan Gibney, 1941; *All That Money Can Buy,* with Dan Totheroh, 1941.

Radio Plays: *The Headless Horseman,* 1937; *The Undefended Border,* 1940; *We Stand United,* 1940; *Elementals,* 1940–41; *Listen to the People,* 1941; *Thanksgiving Day – 1941,* 1941; *Freedom's a Hard Bought Thing,* 1941; *Nightmare at Noon; A Child Is Born,* 1942; *Dear Adolf,* 1942; *They Burned the Books,* 1942; *A Time to Reap,* 1942; *Toward the Century of Modern Man,* 1942; *Your Army,* 1944.

Fiction

The Beginning of Wisdom.   1921.
Young People's Pride.   1922.
Jean Huguenot.   1923.
Spanish Bayonet.   1926.
The Barefoot Saint (stories).   1929.
The Litter of Rose Leaves (stories).   1930.
James Shore's Daughter.   1934.
Thirteen O'Clock: Stories of Several Worlds.   1937.
The Devil and Daniel Webster.   1937.
Johnny Pye and the Fool-Killer (stories).   1938.
Tales Before Midnight.   1939.
Short Stories: A Selection.   1942.
O'Halloran's Luck and Other Short Stories.   1944.

Other

A Summons to the Free.   1941.
Selected Works.   2 vols., 1942.
America.   1944.

Benét on Writing: A Great Writer's Letter of Advice to a Young Beginner, edited by George Abbe. 1964.

Editor, with others, *The Yale Book of Student Verse 1910–1919.* 1919.

Bibliography: "Benét: A Bibliography" by Gladys Louise Maddocks, in *Bulletin of Bibliography 20,* 1951–52.

Reading List: *Benét* by William Rose Benét, 1943; *Benét: The Life and Times of an American Man of Letters* by Charles A. Fenton, 1958; *Benét* by Parry Stroud, 1962.

*   *   *

Stephen Vincent Benét occupies a curiously equivocal position in American letters. One of America's best known and rewarded poets and storytellers, he has at the same time been virtually ignored in academic discussions of major 20th-century writers, and seldom anthologized. In light of the greater critical success enjoyed by his student friends at Yale – Thornton Wilder, Archibald MacLeish, and Philip Barry, themselves often unremarked among "major" writers – Benét's reputation seems thin indeed.

Benét's permanent place in the history of American fiction is nevertheless assured by the fact that among his many volumes of prose and verse there are several minor classics that are widely read and admired. His early light and ironic verse, such as "For City Spring" and "Evening and Morning," and such frolicking ballads as "Captain Kidd," "Thomas Jefferson," "The Mountain Whippoorwill," and "The Ballad of William Sycamore" are highly regarded. His long narrative poem about the Civil War, *John Brown's Body,* dramatized by Charles Laughton in 1953 and called by Henry Steele Commager "not only the best poem about the Civil War, and the best narrative, but also the best history," won Benét his first Pulitzer Prize. Benét's best known short story, "The Devil and Daniel Webster," which combines the author's flare for fantasy and old folktale traditions, shares an equally prominent place in the tall-tale genre of American story-telling. Finally, *Western Star,* another long narrative poem about the heroic pioneering of America, begun in 1934 and incomplete at his death, won for Benét a second Pulitzer prize in 1944.

Among the notes for the continuation of *Western Star* found after Benét's death, the following quatrain was saved:

> Now for my country that it still may live,
> All that I have, all that I am I'll give.
> It is not much beside the gift of the brave
> And yet accept it since tis all I have.

What Benét had – an unbounded, 19th-century faith in the promises of American democracy, and an expansive, Whitmanesque love for what seemed the nation's special attributes, diversity, amplitude, self-sufficiency, frankness, innocence – he poured into every poem, story, and novel he wrote. He praised New York as the communal achievement of the spirit of man, and America because there every man could most freely become what God meant him to be. "Out of your fever and your moving on," he said in the "Prelude" to *Western Star,* "Americans, Americans, Americans ... I make my song."

Both in sentiment and in style, Benét's work attempts to embody the very democratic virtues it is about. Like Sandburg, Hart Crane, and Vachel Lindsay, he uses the zesty tempos, conversational rhythms, and laconic vernacular to capture the spirit of greatness in the strength and simplicity of the nation's common people. In his book of fifty-six verses about famous American men and women, great and small, *A Book of Americans,* Benét says of the greatest and humblest of American native sons:

Lincoln was a long man
He liked out of doors.
He liked the wind blowing
And the talk in country stores.

Just as *John Brown's Body* projects Benét's sensitive feeling for half a dozen countrysides, racial strains, and political attitudes, so this book stands in praise of the nation's heroic ability to reconcile its opposites among that "varied lot" who "each by deed and speech/Adorned our history."

Despite the warmth, genuineness, and impish charm with which Benét celebrates the country's democratic potential, his failure to win wider critical respectability is clearly attributable to the fact that his breadth of sympathy and deep-rooted patriotism seem parochial and old-fashioned to today's audiences, and that even his best work, viewed along side the more realistic and richly inventive fiction of such contemporaries as Crane, Joyce, Proust, and Eliot, appears lacking in depth, subtlety, and originality. The pastoral rebellion of the earth against machines, against the "Age of Steam," which pervades so many of his poems, and his use of conventional verse forms and technical devices that have made him dear to school teachers, seem, in the words of one critic, "all too clear and all too facile." It is significant that Benét's writing has been praised more for its lively evocation of American history than for its aesthetic value.

—Lawrence R. Broer

BENÉT, William Rose.   American.   Born in New York City, 2 February 1886; brother of the poet Stephen Vincent Benét, *q.v.* Educated at Albany Academy, New York; Yale University, New Haven, Connecticut (Chairman, *Yale Courant*; Editor, *Yale Record*). Served in the United States Army Air Force in Europe, 1918: Second Lieutenant. Married 1) Teresa Frances Thompson in 1921 (died), one son, two daughters; 2) the poet Elinor Wylie, *q.v.*, in 1923 (died, 1928); 3) Lora Baxter; 4) the writer Marjorie Flack in 1943. Journalist: Reader, 1911–14, and Assistant Editor, 1914–18, *Century* magazine; Assistant Editor, *Nation's Business*, 1918–19; Associate Editor, *New York Evening Post* "Literary Review," 1920–24; Founder, with Christopher Morley, 1924, Associate Editor, 1924–29, and Contributing Editor after 1929, *Saturday Evening Post*; Editor, Brewer and Warren, publishers, 1929–30. Recipient: Pulitzer Prize, 1942. Secretary, National Institute of Arts and Letters. *Died 4 May 1950.*

PUBLICATIONS

Verse

Merchants from Cathay.   1913.
The Falconer of God and Other Poems.   1914.
The Great White Wall.   1916.
The Burglar of the Zodiac and Other Poems.   1918.
Perpetual Light: A Memorial.   1919.

Moons of Grandeur.   1920.
Man Possessed: Selected Poems.   1927.
Sagacity.   1929.
Rip Tide: A Novel in Verse.   1932.
Starry Harness.   1933.
Golden Fleece.   1935.
Harlem and Other Poems.   1935.
A Baker's Dozen of Emblems.   1935.
With Wings as Eagles: Poems and Ballads of the Air.   1940.
The Dust Which Is God: A Novel in Verse.   1941.
Adolphus; or, The Adopted Dolphin and the Pirate's Daughter (juvenile), with Marjorie
   Flack.   1941.
Day of Deliverance.   1944.
The Stairway of Surprise.   1947.
Timothy's Angels (juvenile).   1947.
Poetry Package, with Christopher Morley.   1949.
The Spirit of the Scene.   1951.

Play

Day's End, in *The Best One-Act Plays of 1939,* edited by Margaret Mayorga.   1939.

Fiction

The First Person Singular.   1922.

Other

Saturday Papers: Essays, with Henry Seidel Canby and Amy Loveman.   1921.
The Flying King of Kurio (juvenile).   1926.
Wild Goslings: A Selection of Fugitive Pieces.   1927.
Stephen Vincent Benét: My Brother Steve.   1943.

Editor, *Poems for Youth: An American Anthology.*   1925.
Editor, with John Drinkwater and Henry Seidel Canby, *Twentieth-Century
   Poetry.*   1929.
Editor, *Collected Poems, Collected Prose,* by Elinor Wylie.   2 vols., 1932–33.
Editor, *Fifty Poets: An American Auto-Anthology.*   1933.
Editor, *Guide to Daily Reading.*   1934.
Editor, *The Pocket University.*   13 vols., 1934.
Editor, with others, *Adventures in English Literature.*   1936.
Editor, *Mother Goose: A Comprehensive Collection of the Rhymes.*   1936.
Editor, *From Robert to Elizabeth Barrett Browning* (letters).   1936.
Editor, with Norman Holmes Pearson, *The Oxford Anthology of American
   Literature.*   1938.
Editor, with Adolph Gillis, *Poems for Modern Youth.*   1938.
Editor, *Supplement to Great Poems of the English Language,* edited by Wallace Alvin
   Briggs.   1941.
Editor, with Conrad Aiken, *An Anthology of Famous English and American
   Poetry.*   1945.
Editor, with Norman Cousins, *The Poetry of Freedom.*   1945.

Editor, *The Reader's Encyclopedia.* 1948.

Translator, with Teresa Frances, *The East I Know,* by Paul Claudel. 1914.

*   *   *

William Rose Benét has perhaps been more remarked upon in recent American literary history as the "older brother" of the writer Stephen Vincent Benét, and as husband of the poet Elinor Wylie, than as an accomplished poet in his own right. Serious attention to his verse has also been diverted by his prominence as a reviewer, critic, and anthologist, and by his numerous activities as a promoter of the arts. But despite this dispersion of energies, Benét managed to publish many volumes of verse whose value has not properly been acknowledged.

The obvious unevenness of Benét's creative output is hinted at by the fact that Rolfe Humphries rates him no better than a mere "journeyman of letters," while Marguerite Wilkinson says he was a "builder [whose] strongest rhythms have the certitude of an arch...." Certainly Benét's weakest poems are unapologetically romantic and lacking in intensity. When he announces his poetic intentions in his most celebrated work, *The Dust Which Is God,* as "I will be plain at least," he does more than alert us to what he hopes will be a poetic voice free of bombast and ornamentation; unwittingly, he indicts a good number of poems whose over-statedness results in an absence of colour or emotional vitality. "Throw wide/The gates of the heart," he counsels in his poem "Study of Man," "Taking your part/In percipient life ... Ever extend/Your boundaries, and be/Inwardly free!"

Such direct statement issues from the poet's almost passionate reverence for the freedom and dignity of man, and for the ample spirit of God and nature, which he finds so abundantly manifest in his native America, as in "Men on Strike":

> The Country of the Free! Yes, a great land.
> Thank God that I have known it East to West
> And North to South, and still I love it best
> Of all the various world the seas command.

From the point of view of the wise primitivist, Benét celebrates the democratic virtues of common men, and envisions portents of disaster in the encroachments of the machine age. In "The Stricken Average," he writes:

> Little of brilliance did they write or say.
> They bore the battle of living, and were gay.
> Little of wealth or fame they left behind.
> They were merely honorable, brave, and kind.

He yearns for that "pristine creation/Unsullied by our civilization," ("Young Girl") whose elemental harmonies are forever threatened by factories, corporations, "towers of glass and steel" ("Shadow of the Mountain Man").

Such romantic attitudes were bound to lessen the appeal of Benét's work in an age whose best literary efforts were in direct opposition to such simple and sentimental verse. Yet there are indisputable qualities in Benét's best work, perhaps most forcibly realized in *The Dust Which Is God,* which in 1942 won him a Pulitzer Prize. An autobiographical verse narrative, it demonstrates a remarkable range of interests and intellect, and admirable versatility in the use of changing forms and rhythms to capture the diverse and sprawling nature of his subject – the birth and growth of the country, which he treats as synonymous with his own life. The poetry here reveals a lively and sophisticated grasp of cultural ideas, and often achieves a rich synthesis of opposites: classical and modern, noble and banal, holy and sensual, lyrical and prosaic. At their best, these "vignette illustrations" project for us a poetic talent of greater potential stature than that of the author's more celebrated brother – more original, more sensuous, and more varied and universal in scope.

—Lawrence R. Broer

BERRYMAN, John. American. Born in McAlester, Oklahoma, 25 October 1914. Educated at South Kent School, Connecticut; Columbia University, New York, A.B. 1936 (Phi Beta Kappa); Clare College, Cambridge (Kellett Fellow, 1936–37; Oldham Shakespeare Scholar, 1937), B.A. 1938; Princeton University, New Jersey (Creative Writing Fellow), 1943–44. Married 1) Eileen Patricia Mulligan in 1942 (divorced, 1953); 2) Ann Levine in 1956 (divorced, 1959); 3) Kathleen Donahue in 1961; three children. Instructor in English, Wayne State University, Detroit, 1939, and Princeton University, 1940–43; Briggs-Copeland Instructor in English Composition, Harvard University, Cambridge, Massachusetts, 1945–49; Lecturer in English, University of Washington, Seattle, 1950; Elliston Lecturer in Poetry, University of Cincinnati, 1951–52; Member of the English Department, rising to the rank of Professor, University of Minnesota, Minneapolis, 1954–72. Recipient: Rockefeller grant, 1944, 1946; Shelley Memorial Award, 1949; National Institute of Arts and Letters grant, 1950; Hodder Fellowship, Princeton University, 1950; Guggenheim Fellowship, 1952, 1966; Harriet Monroe Award, 1957; Brandeis University Creative Arts Award, 1959; Loines Award, 1964; Pulitzer Prize, 1965; Academy of American Poets Fellowship, 1966; National Endowment for the Arts grant, 1967; Bollingen Prize, 1968; National Book Award, 1969. D.Let.: Drake University, Des Moines, Iowa, 1971. Member, National Institute of Arts and Letters, American Academy of Arts and Sciences, and Academy of American Poets. *Died* (by suicide) *7 January 1972.*

PUBLICATIONS

Verse

Five Young American Poets, with others. 1940.
Poems. 1942.
The Dispossessed. 1948.
Homage to Mistress Bradstreet. 1956; as *Homage to Mistress Bradstreet and Other Poems,* 1959.
His Thought Made Pockets and the Plane Buckt. 1958.
77 Dream Songs. 1964.
Berryman's Sonnets. 1967.
Short Poems. 1967.
His Toy, His Dream, His Rest: 308 Dream Songs. 1968.
The Dream Songs. 1969.
Love and Fame. 1970; revised edition, 1972.
Selected Poems 1938–1968. 1972.
Delusions, Etc. 1972.
Henry's Fate and Other Poems, edited by John Haffenden. 1977.

Fiction

Recovery.   1973.

Other

Stephen Crane (biography).   1950.
The Freedom of the Poet (miscellany).   1976.

Editor, with Ralph Ross and Allen Tate, *The Arts of Reading* (anthology).   1960.
Editor, *The Unfortunate Traveller; or, The Life of Jack Wilton*, by Thomas Nashe.   1960.

Bibliography: *Berryman: A Descriptive Bibliography* by Ernest C. Stefanik, Jr., 1974; *Berryman: A Reference Guide* by Gary Q. Arpin, 1976.

Reading List: *Berryman* by William J. Martz, 1969; *Berryman* by James M. Linebarger, 1974; *The Poetry of Berryman* by Gary Q. Arpin, 1977; *Berryman: An Introduction to the Poetry* by Joel Conarroe, 1977.

*   *   *

John Berryman spent his childhood on a farm in Oklahoma under the sombre and difficult aegis of a father whose improvidence finally led to his suicide, an event which haunted and disturbed the poet for the rest of his life. From these dark beginnings, he leapt into the brighter world of his education, first at a private school in Connecticut, and then at Columbia University, where his immense energies and brilliance were manifested. A scholarship to Cambridge University led to his studies in Shakespeare and the English Renaissance, the stylistic exuberance of which was to influence his own discordant, richly embellished mode of verse. At Princeton University, he began a frenzied pace of writing that led to his first full-length collection of short poems, *The Dispossessed*. He had also completed much of the cycle of poems later published as *Berryman's Sonnets*. In both volumes Berryman is a mature craftsman of traditional forms and meters, which he renewed with his energetic speech.

Berryman's major work begins with *Homage to Mistress Bradstreet*, which includes poems from *The Dispossessed*. The title poem, a sequence of 57 eight-line stanzas, evokes the life and hardships of this American poet through an original strategy of merging the narrator's voice with his subject's, in which all the details of her sickness, frailty, and harsh family life are rendered with powerful immediacy. The poet's speech slips into the Colonial tongue and out again into a flinty modern colloquialism with masterful control. Berryman etches the character of Bradstreet and holds her up as an instance of the artist's eternal struggle against adversity:

> Headstones stagger under great draughts of time
> after heads pass out, and their world must reel
> speechless, blind in the end
> about its chilling star: thrift tuft,
> whin cushion – nothing. Already with the wounded flying
> dark air fills, I am a closet of secrets dying,
> races murder, foxholes hold men,
> reactor piles wage slow upon the wet brain rime.

Included in *Homage* is the series "The Nervous Songs," where he again inhabits other strained minds and articulates their emotions. They are important, however, chiefly for their form; each poem is cast in three six-line stanzas, the form employed throughout his greatest work, *The Dream Songs*.

The persona of the *Dream Songs* is variously referred to as Henry, Pussy-Cat, and Mr. Bones, and the poems evoke his daily inner life as he struggles through the routines of teaching, drying-out from chronic alcoholism, and writing ambitious books of poems. His deepest dilemma is with his own identity, which fits him in the middle of every extreme of life: he is middle-aged, of the middle-class, and of middling talent. Against all these middlings he struggles to find an edge, by occasionally daubing burnt cork on his face, by heavy drinking, and by hard working, but each time falls back into the slough of his middleness depressed and exhausted:

> He lay in the middle of the world, and twicht.
> More Sparine for Pelides,
> human (half) & down here as he is,
> with probably insulting mail to open
> and certainly unworthy words to hear
> and his unforgivable memory.

Or again, "Henry felt baffled, in the middle of the thing," which is a refrain of his efforts and sufferings.

The desire to transcend his undefined existence wears down into defeat in later sections of this sequence, until "Henry hates the world. What the world to Henry/did will not bear thought." The despair deepens into rejection: "This world is gradually becoming a place/ where I do not care to be any more." He broods upon death in all its forms and nightmare possibilities, including the frequent lamentations for other poets who have died recently, and who seem to share his dark view of the world:

> I'm cross with God who has wrecked this generation.
> First he seized Ted [Roethke], then Richard [Blackmur], Randall [Jarrell], and now
> > Delmore [Schwartz].
> In between he gorged on Sylvia Plath.
> That was a first rate haul. He left alive
> fools I could number like a kitchen knife
> but Lowell he did not touch.

In a later, grimmer juncture of the *Songs*, Henry remarks bitterly, "The world grows more disgusting dawn by dawn." The poems then take up a plot of sorts with a residence in Ireland, followed by a return to the United States and the long attempt to recover from alcoholism, a turn that also involves Henry in religious conversion.

The whole work, including the posthumous additions, *Henry's Fate*, amounts to a vast mosaic of pieces of Henry's life and character, without transforming such pieces into a unified vision. The work is discordant throughout, in its language and in its jagged progression of themes and motifs. It is essentially a long and despairing examination of a poet's alienation from the post-war world, in which his brilliance and cultural inheritance appear to have no place or value. The grave, devoted artist founders and ultimately destroys himself, lamenting throughout the cursed and crooked fate of his fellow poets. This tragedy is lifted above self-pity and sentimentality by the essential good character of Henry, whose complicated interiors give us a Hamlet for this age.

Berryman's later works, *Love and Fame*, *Delusions, Etc.*, and the novel *Recovery*, turn away from the *Dream Songs* to treat more directly of the poet's life. *Love and Fame* is unabashed autobiography of the poet's education and rise to prominence, delivered in a flat, narrative style unlike his earlier verse. In *Delusions, Etc.* his religious turning is expressed in a section of liturgical poems where Berryman is again the effortless master of sonorous lyrics. *Recovery*, unfinished at the poet's death, exposes the torment of the alcoholic and eloquently pleads for understanding of this disease from which the poet suffered much of his life.

—Paul Christensen

BISHOP, Elizabeth. American. Born in Worcester, Massachusetts, 8 February 1911. Educated at Vassar College, Poughkeepsie, New York, A.B. 1934. Lived in Brazil for 16 years. Consultant in Poetry, Library of Congress, Washington, D.C., 1949–50. Poet-in-Residence, University of Washington, Seattle, 1966, 1973. Since 1970, Lecturer in English, Harvard University, Cambridge, Massachusetts. Recipient: Guggenheim Fellowship, 1947; National Institute of Arts and Letters grant, 1951; Shelley Memorial Award, 1953; Pulitzer Prize, 1956; Amy Lowell Traveling Fellowship, 1957; Chapelbrook Fellowship, 1962; Academy of American Poets Fellowship, 1964; Rockefeller Fellowship, 1967; Ingram Merrill Foundation grant, 1969; National Book Award, 1970; Harriet Monroe Prize, 1974. LL.D.: Smith College, Northampton, Massachusetts, 1968; Rutgers University, New Brunswick, New Jersey, 1972; Brown University, Providence, Rhode Island, 1972. Chancellor, Academy of American Poets, 1966; Member, American Academy of Arts and Letters, 1976. Order of Rio Branco (Brazil), 1971.

PUBLICATIONS

Verse

    North and South. 1946.
    Poems: North and South – A Cold Spring. 1955.
    Poems. 1956.
    Questions of Travel. 1965.
    Selected Poems. 1967.
    The Ballad of the Burglar of Babylon (juvenile). 1968.
    The Complete Poems. 1969.
    Geography III. 1977.

Other

    Brazil, with the Editors of Life. 1962.

    Editor and Translator, *Anthology of Contemporary Brazilian Poetry,* vol. 1. 1972.

    Translator, *The Diary of Helena Morley.* 1957.

Reading List: *Bishop* by Anne Stevenson, 1966.

*   *   *

Elizabeth Bishop's autobiographical "In the Village," a story which moves towards poetry and was included at the center of *Questions of Travel*, shows how the sounds and sights and textures of a Nova Scotia village enable a child to come to terms with the sound of the scream which signified her mother's madness and, ultimately, with human isolation, loss, mortality; the child's capacity for meticulous attention serves not merely as a method of escaping from intolerable pain, but also as an opening from the prison of the self and its wounds to a rejoicing in both human creativity and the things and events of an ordinary day. The story, with its nod of homage to Chekhov, provides an accurate anticipation of the peculiar virtues of Elizabeth Bishop's poetry: her fantastic powers of observation, her impeccable ear, and her precise and often haunting sense of tone.

Her first volume, *North and South*, was a rigorous selection from earlier work. Although some of its poems are set in New York or Paris or New England or have no localized geographical setting, a number of the best ones are firmly placed in Nova Scotia or Florida. *A Cold Spring* continued the emphasis on place: a farm in Maryland, Nova Scotia again, Washington, D.C., Key West and New York, and, with "Arrival at Santos," Brazil, which was to be her home for a number of years. The poems in *Questions of Travel* are divided into two groups: "Brazil" and "Elsewhere." (Another result of her residence in Brazil was her beautiful translation of *The Diary of Helena Morley*.) *The Complete Poems* included new original poems set in Brazil as well as translation from Carlos Drummond de Andrade and João Cabral de Melo Neto.

The title and some of the directions of *Geography III* were anticipated in the final line of "The Map," the first poem in her first volume: "More delicate than the historian's are the map-maker's colors." The map-maker (not the tourist) who comes truly to know differing peoples and their places for himself can see with fresh and multiple perspectives, and his discriminations may well be finer than the historian's if his powers of observation are intense, his sympathies wide, his moral judgments delicate, and his imagination that of a poet.

Miss Bishop's geography is also of the imagination and the soul. Her poems treat their readers with unusual consideration. With the beginning of each poem we know that we *are* somewhere interesting (whether in a real or a surreal or a dream world), and we hear immediately a recognizable human voice: the poems make absorbing sense on a simple or naturalistic level. She is interested in, and asks our respectful attention for, everything that she puts into her poems; ultimate and "large" significances come only (and naturally) out of our experience of the whole.

The consideration is real, and one of its chief instruments is an unusual purity of diction. On a number of occasions one may be surprised to discover an image or detail or even a quoted phrase from the poetry of George Herbert. She found Herbert's example thoroughly congruent with one of the things she admired most about modernist poetry of the early twentieth century: the rejection of familiar public rhetoric and the consciously poetic for a language closer to that of a conversation between literate friends. Miss Bishop has consistently sustained her own high version of that standard: no inversions and no inflations, no Ciceronian periods, no elevated "poetic diction." Her indebtedness to Marianne Moore's imaginative precision is handsomely acknowledged in "Invitation to Miss Marianne Moore" (the poem also owes something to Pablo Neruda). Her uses of other writers are markedly individual: her few epigrams are from Bunyan, Hopkins, and Sir Kenneth Clark; the poignant "Crusoe in England" owes as much to Charles Darwin as to Defoe.

Also like Herbert, Miss Bishop seems to have sought a unique form for almost every poem. Her range extends from prose poems such as "Rainy Season; Sub-Tropics" and "12 O'Clock News" through relatively "free" and blank verse and unrhymed Horatian forms to strict quatrains and elaborately "counter-pointed" stanzas, a double sonnet ("The Prodigal," one of her best poems), sestinas and a villanelle, including along the way the lengthening triplets of "Roosters," derived from Crashaw's "Wishes to his (supposed) Mistress," "Visits to St. Elizabeths," modelled on "The House that Jack Built," a true ballad, "The Burglar of Babylon," and the songs that she wrote for Billie Holiday. Whatever the forms, they provide opportunities rather than limitations, and their art is self-effacing: the lines of "Sestina" end with the words *house, grandmother, child, stove, almanac,* and *tears.* Her use of assonance and slant-rhymes and variable line-lengths and rhyme patterns promises a useful freedom. Her example suggested to Robert Lowell the "way of breaking through the shell of my old manner" indicated by "Skunk Hour."

Miss Bishop has remained remarkably independent of schools or movements, religious, political, or literary. One modern practice that has proved fruitful for her is that of the collage, in which the artist discovers his subject and his form in ordinary or unexpected materials and objects. ("Objects and Apparitions," Bishop's translation of Octavio Paz's poem for Joseph Cornell, suggests the relation between collage and all art – as do her poems on the pictures of her great-uncle George.) Although the fictional speakers of her poems are often moving or witty (the Trollope of the Journals, a Brazilian friend in "Manuelzinho," Crusoe, a giant snail, a very small alien who reports on the writer's desk as a foreign landscape – all remarkable observers), in most of the poems the poet speaks in a voice recognizably her own. That the poems remain deeply personal rather than confessional may owe something to how firmly they are rooted in the "found": "Trouvée" in the flattened white hen on West 4th Street, "The Man-Moth" in a newspaper misprint for *mammoth,* "The Burglar of Babylon" in the fact that on the hills of Rio the rich and poor live their melodramas and lives within sight and sound of each other, "The Moose" in the Nova Scotia busride, "In the Waiting Room" in the events of late afternoon, "the fifth/of February, 1918." Almost every poem of Elizabeth Bishop's represents a human discovery both of the world and of an angle of vision. It is only superficially paradoxical that such creative novelty returns us, like "The Prodigal," to a familiar place and life: "But it took him a long time/finally to make his mind up to go home."

—Joseph H. Summers

BISHOP, John Peale.   American.   Born in Charles Town, West Virginia, 21 May 1892. Educated at high school in Hagerstown, Maryland; Mercersburg Academy, Pennsylvania; Princeton University, New Jersey, 1913–17 (Managing Editor, *Nassau Literary Magazine*), Litt.B. 1917 (Phi Beta Kappa). Served in the United States Army Infantry, 1917–19: First Lieutenant; Director of the Publications Program, 1941–42, and Special Consultant, 1943, Office of the Coordinator of Inter-American Affairs, Washington, D.C. Married Margaret Grosvenor Hutchins in 1922; three sons. Managing Editor, *Vanity Fair*, New York, 1920–22; free-lance writer from 1922; lived in Paris and Sorrento, 1922–24, New York, 1924–26, France, 1927–33, Louisiana and Connecticut, 1933–37, and in South Chatham, Massachusetts, 1937–44. *Died 4 April 1944.*

PUBLICATIONS

Collections

Collected Poems, edited by Allen Tate.   1948; *Selected Poems,* 1960.
Collected Essays, edited by Edmund Wilson.   1948.

Verse

> *Green Fruit.* 1917.
> *The Undertaker's Garland* (poems and stories), with Edmund Wilson. 1922.
> *Now with His Love.* 1933.
> *Minute Particulars.* 1935.
> *Selected Poems.* 1941.

Fiction

> *Many Thousands Gone* (stories). 1931.
> *Act of Darkness.* 1935.

Other

> Editor, with Allen Tate, *American Harvest: Twenty Years of Creative Writing in the United States.* 1942.

Bibliography: "Bishop: A Checklist" by J. Max Patrick and Robert W. Stallman, in *Princeton University Library Chronicle 7*, 1946.

Reading List: *A Southern Vanguard: The Bishop Memorial Volume* edited by Allen Tate, 1947; "The Achievement of Bishop" by Joseph Frank, in *The Widening Gyre*, 1963; *Bishop* by Robert L. White, 1966; "Bishop and the Other Thirties" by Leslie Fiedler, in *Commentary 43*, 1967; "Bishop" by Allen Tate, in *Essays of Four Decades*, 1968.

*　　*　　*

John Peale Bishop seems to owe his posthumous reputation to Allen Tate and Edmund Wilson, whose editing of the *Collected Poems* and *Collected Essays* in 1948 brought his most important work to the attention of a small audience. These books have long been out of print, but he continues to attract critics as different as Joseph Frank and Leslie Fiedler, and no account of American literary life between the two World Wars is complete without his name. He was at Princeton with Wilson and F. Scott Fitzgerald and consequently has associations with the milieu popularized by Fitzgerald's early novels; indeed he is the original for a character in *This Side of Paradise*. During the 1930's, especially after his return to America, he was thought of as a Southerner, partly because of his friendship with Tate. His two works of prose fiction are set in the "lost" part of West Virginia where he spent his boyhood and certainly have something in common with the Southern tradition of Faulkner, Caroline Gordon, and the others.

Bishop, however, must be thought of mainly as a poet, and it is the verse of his last decade that is most impressive. His regional allegiances count for very little here, though his residence on Cape Cod after 1938 was surely responsible for such late poems as "A Subject of Sea Change" and the group called "The Statues." These meditations on the sea and the destiny of civilizations carry forward the strongly pictorial qualities of such earlier poems as "The Return." Eventually one should see Bishop as an American poet who is descended from a great tradition of European humanism, and his criticism of the American scene is conducted from this point of view. One of his finest poems, "The Burning Wheel," sets the American pioneers beside the figure of Aeneas:

They, too, the stalwart conquerors of space,
Each on his shoulders wore a wise delirium
Of memory and age: ghostly embrace
Of fathers slanted toward a western tomb.

A hundred and a hundred years they stayed
Aloft, until they were as light as autumn
Shells of locusts. Where then were they laid?
And in what wilderness oblivion?

This refined yet deeply felt humanism is perhaps not characteristic of American writers, and Bishop was a writer on a small scale, but his best work in poetry and criticism survives very well.

—Ashley Brown

BLY, Robert (Elwood). American. Born in Madison, Minnesota, 23 December 1926. Educated at St. Olaf College, Northfield, Minnesota, 1946–47; Harvard University, Cambridge, Massachusetts, B.A. (magna cum laude) 1950; University of Iowa, Iowa City, M.A. 1956. Served in the United States Navy, 1944–46. Married Carolyn McLean in 1955; four children. Since 1958, Founding-Editor, *The Fifties* magazine (later *The Sixties* and *The Seventies*) and The Fifties Press (later The Sixties and The Seventies Press), Madison, Minnesota. Recipient: Fulbright Fellowship, 1956; Amy Lowell Traveling Fellowship, 1964; Guggenheim Fellowship, 1964, 1972; National Institute of Arts and Letters grant, 1965; Rockefeller Fellowship, 1967; National Book Award, 1968. Lives in Madison, Minnesota.

PUBLICATIONS

Verse

Silence in the Snowy Fields. 1962.
The Lion's Tail and Eyes: Poems Written Out of Laziness and Silence, with James Wright and William Duffy. 1962.
The Light Around the Body. 1967.
Chrysanthemums. 1967.
Ducks. 1968.
The Morning Glory: Another Thing That Will Never Be My Friend: Twelve Prose Poems. 1969; revised edition, 1970.
The Teeth-Mother Naked at Last. 1970.
Poems for Tennessee, with William Stafford and William Matthews. 1971.
Jumping Out of Bed. 1973.
Sleepers Joining Hands. 1973.

Point Reyes Poems. 1974.
The Hockey Poem. 1974.
Old Man Rubbing His Eyes. 1975.
This Body Is Made of Camphor and Gopherwood. 1977.

Other

Editor, with David Ray, *A Poetry Reading Against the Vietnam War.* 1966.
Editor, *The Sea and the Honeycomb: A Book of Tiny Poems.* 1966.
Editor, *Forty Poems Touching on Recent American History.* 1970.
Editor, *Selected Poems,* by David Ignatow. 1975.
Editor, *Leaping Poetry: An Idea with Poems and Translations.* 1975.

Translator, *Reptiles and Amphibians of the World,* by Hans Hvass. 1960.
Translator, with James Wright, *Twenty Poems of Georg Trakl.* 1961.
Translator, *The Story of Gösta Berling,* by Selma Lagerlöf. 1962.
Translator, with James Wright and John Knoepfle, *Twenty Poems of César Vallejo.* 1962.
Translator, with Eric Sellin and Thomas Buckman, *Three Poems,* by Thomas Tranströmer. 1966.
Translator, *Hunger,* by Knut Hamsun. 1967.
Translator, with Christina Paulston, *I Do Best Alone at Night,* by Gunnar Ekelöf. 1967.
Translator, with Christina Paulston, *Late Arrival on Earth: Selected Poems of Gunnar Ekelöf.* 1967.
Translator, with others, *Selected Poems* by Yvan Goll. 1968.
Translator, with James Wright, *Twenty Poems of Pablo Neruda.* 1968.
Translator, *Forty Poems of Juan Ramón Jiménez.* 1969.
Translator, *Ten Poems,* by Issa Kobayashi. 1969.
Translator, with James Wright and John Knoepfle, *Neruda and Vallejo: Selected Poems.* 1971.
Translator, *Twenty Poems of Tomas Tranströmer.* 1971.
Translator, *The Fish in the Sea Is Not Thirsty: Versions of Kabir.* 1971.
Translator, *Night Vision,* by Tomas Tranströmer. 1971.
Translator, *Lorca and Jiménez: Selected Poems.* 1973.
Translator, *Basho.* 1974.
Translator, *Ten Sonnets to Orpheus,* by Rilke. 1974.
Translator, *Friends, You Drank Some Darkness: Three Swedish Poets, Henry Martinson, Gunnar Ekelöf, Tomas Tranströmer.* 1975.
Translator, *Try to Live to See This: Versions of Kabir.* 1976.
Translator, *The Kabir Book.* 1977.
Translator, *The Voices,* by Rilke. 1977.

Bibliography: "Bly Checklist" by Sandy Dorbin, in *Schist 1,* Fall 1973.

Reading List: *Alone with America* by Richard Howard, 1969; "Bly Alive in Darkness" by Anthony Libby, in *Iowa Review,* Summer 1972.

*   *   *

The spirited presence of Robert Bly is felt throughout the realms of modern poetry and literary criticism; he emerged from the early 1960's as one of the more stubbornly independent and critical poets of his generation, bold to state his positions against war and commercial monopoly, spread of federal government, and crassness in literature wherever a forum was open to him. He was a dominating spokesman for the anti-war circles during the course of the Vietnam War, staging readings around the United States and compiling (with David Ray) the extraordinary poetic protests in the anthology, *A Poetry Reading Against the Vietnam War*. Throughout his career, he has been a cranky but refreshing influence on American thought and culture for the very grandeur of his positions and the force he has given to his artistic individuality.

Although his output of poetry has been relatively small in an era of prolific poets, his books follow a distinctive course of deepening conviction and widening of conceptions. *Silence in the Snowy Fields*, his first book, is a slender collection of smooth, mildly surreal evocations of his life in Minnesota and of the landscape, with its harsh winters and huddled townships. Bly's brief poems animate natural settings with a secret, wilful life-force, as in this final stanza from "Snowfall in the Afternoon":

> The barn is full of corn, and moving toward us now,
> Like a hulk blown toward us in a storm at sea:
> All the sailors on deck have been blind for many years.

Silence in the Snowy Fields has an immediacy of the poet's personal life that reflects the inward shift of poetry during the late 1950's and early 1960's, a direction that Bly then actively retreated from, claiming poetry deserved a larger frame of experience than the poet's own circumstances and private dilemmas.

The Light Around the Body moves into the political and social arena, with poems against corporate power and profiteering, presidential politics, and the Vietnam War. Here the poems are charged with greater flight of imagination and a more intensely surreal mode of discourse. The poems wildly juxtapose the familiar with the bizarre, in "A Dream of Suffocation" – "Accountants hover over the earth like helicopters,/Dropping bits of paper engraved with Hegel's name" – and "War and Silence" –

> Filaments of death grow out.
> The sheriff cuts off his black legs
> And nails them to a tree

To explain his poetic and to give it context, Bly edited a volume of poems entitled *Leaping Poetry* in which he argued that consciousness had now expanded to a new faculty of the brain where spiritual and supralogical awareness is stored. His commentary is wonderfully speculative and vivid, but bluffly assertive of its premise. Building on this provocative thesis, he commented in an essay, "I Came Out of the Mother Naked," part of his volume *Sleepers Joining Hands*, that society is now returning to a matriarchal order, where sensuousness of thought and synthetic reason are replacing the patriarchal emphasis on rationality and analytic thinking. *The Kabir Book*, Bly's translations of the 15th-century Indian poet, are an effort to present the work of a figure who both "leaps" in his poetry and illustrates the kind of thinking Bly has argued for recently.

Bly continues to read poetry on the university circuit and to translate Scandinavian literature as his livelihood, but even in these facets of his life he has rooted his new convictions. His readings are now made dramatic with masks, singing, and extemporaneous lectures on the new mind he feels is emerging throughout the West.

—Paul Christensen

BODENHEIM, Maxwell. American. Born in Hermanville, Mississippi, 26 May 1892. Self-educated; studied law and art in Chicago. Joined the Army, 1909: jailed for desertion and discharged, 1911. Married 1) Minna Schein in 1918 (divorced, 1938), one son; 2) Grace Finan in 1939 (died, 1950); 3) Ruth Fagan in 1951. Travelled in the Southwest, 1911–12; lived in Chicago, 1914; settled in New York City, 1915; writer for the *Literary Times*, Chicago, 1923–24; worked for the Federal Writers Project, 1939–40 (fired for being a communist). *Died 7 February 1954.*

PUBLICATIONS

Fiction

> *Blackguard.* 1923.
> *Crazy Man.* 1924.
> *Cutie, A Warm Mamma,* with Ben Hecht. 1924.
> *Replenishing Jessica.* 1925.
> *Ninth Avenue.* 1926.
> *Georgie May.* 1928.
> *Sixty Seconds.* 1929.
> *A Virtuous Girl.* 1930.
> *Naked on Roller Skates.* 1930.
> *Duke Herring.* 1931.
> *6 A.M.* 1932.
> *Run, Sheep, Run.* 1932.
> *New York Madness.* 1933.
> *Slow Vision.* 1934.

Plays

> *Knot Holes* (produced 1917).
> *The Gentle Furniture Shop* (produced 1917). In *Drama 10,* 1920

Verse

> *Minna and Myself.* 1918.
> *Advice.* 1920.
> *Introducing Irony: A Book of Poetic Short Stories and Poems.* 1922.
> *Against This Age.* 1923.
> *The Sardonic Arm.* 1923.
> *Returning to Emotion.* 1927.
> *The King of Spain.* 1928.
> *Bringing Jazz!* 1930.
> *Lights in the Valley.* 1942.
> *Selected Poems 1914–44.* 1946.

Other

> *My Life and Loves in Greenwich Village.* 1954.

Reading List: *Bodenheim* by Jack B. Moore, 1970.

*   *   *

Maxwell Bodenheim's slow but steady and determined pursuit of self-destruction, and the frequently giddy capers he cut while parading (at first) and then lurching around New York's literary scene, have almost completely obscured his solid if inconsistent achievements as a writer. Easily forgotten, because buried under an avalanche of anecdotes, novels, and plays by other writers about his escapades during the Jazz Age and Great Depression years, is the undoubted evidence that he was sometimes a very powerful, often an innovative, and nearly always a fascinating poet-novelist of the world that ultimately passed him by.

Bodenheim's social and literary criticism is perhaps the least well known aspect of his literary career. Ezra Pound wanted to have published Bodenheim's "whole blooming book" on aesthetics although (or perhaps because) Pound claimed only he and a few other writers would understand it. In fact only a few chapters of the book were ever printed, and these were published separately as essays. As a reviewer for many of the leading journals of the 1920's, he championed the work of such contemporaries as Conrad Aiken, Wallace Stevens, and William Carlos Williams; lambasted what he considered the sham pastoralism in modern fiction where "young men lie upon their backs in cornfields and feel oppressed by their bodies"; and tilted with the very popular and he felt often fake Freudianism of his times for trumpeting that "sex underlies all human motives and is the basis of all creations." He also sought out new writers. When he was one of the editors of the avant-garde little magazine *Others* he went out of his way to praise and secure publication for the very young Hart Crane.

From 1923 to 1934 he published some dozen novels, which, together with the poetry he wrote around the same period, refute the idea that he crippled himself as a writer simply through dissipating his resources in sordid adventures. He was by no means a major novelist, for his works lack artistic control. Too often he used the form as a way to settle personal scores, or, worse, did not attend strictly enough to technical details of his craft. He sometimes seemed more intent upon setting down striking phrases than in constructing a coherent and compelling story. But most of the novels display solid and significant attainments: the touching comic (and autobiographic) portrait of the young artist in *Blackguard*; the sad, sordid decline of the prostitute Georgie May; the urban nightmare of *Ninth Avenue*; the parade of numbed derelicts that sleepwalk through *Slow Vision*, his Depression novel.

Bodenheim's artistic reputation rests most solidly upon his poetry, and his ultimate failure to become a first-rate poet is probably the saddest element of his professional career. Bodenheim was early considered one of the most promising writers taking part in the American literary renaissance of the 1910's: Harriet Monroe and Margaret Anderson, editors of the two most influential literary magazines of the day, both strove to be the first to announce the arrival of his genius. Conrad Aiken and William Carlos Williams were only two of the many writers who, though sometimes appalled by his antics, highly praised his poetry. Among his chief virtues as a poet were his ability to compose beautiful and exotic images and to weave them harmoniously into the texture of a unified poem, such as "Death." He could also write harshly and effectively about the ugliness of modern city life, as in "Summer Evening: New York Subway Station." His jazz poems, such as those in *Bringing Jazz!*, were interesting experiments in a form one critic said had been successfully employed only by one other poet – T. S. Eliot.

Bodenheim's artistic death, which long preceded his physical death, was lamentable, for he never came close to attaining the greatness his early promise and ability seemed to predict. Yet he accomplished far more than his relatively obscure reputation today would suggest.

—Jack B. Moore

BOGAN, Louise.   American.   Born in Livermore Falls, Maine, 11 August 1897. Educated at Mount St. Mary's Academy, Manchester, New Hampshire, 1907–09; Girls' Latin School, Boston, 1910–15; Boston University, 1915–16. Married 1) Curt Alexander, 1916 (died, 1920), one daughter; 2) Raymond Holden in 1925 (divorced, 1937). Poetry Editor of *The New Yorker*, 1931–70. Visiting Professor, University of Washington, Seattle, 1948; University of Chicago, 1949; University of Arkansas, 1952; Salzburg Seminar in American Studies, 1958; Brandeis University, Waltham, Massachusetts, 1964–65. Recipient: Guggenheim Fellowship, 1933, 1937; Harriet Monroe Poetry Award, 1948; National Institute of Arts and Letters grant, 1951; Bollingen Prize, 1955; Academy of American Poets Fellowship, 1959; Brandeis University Creative Arts Award, 1961; National Endowment for the Arts grant, 1967. Library of Congress Chair in Poetry, 1945–46. L.H.D.: Western College for Women, Oxford, Ohio, 1956; Litt.D.: Colby College, Waterville, Maine, 1960. Member, American Academy of Arts and Letters. *Died 4 February 1970.*

PUBLICATIONS

Collections

What the Woman Lived: Selected Letters 1920–1970, edited by Ruth Limmer.   1973.

Verse

Body of This Death.   1923.
Dark Summer.   1929.
The Sleeping Fury.   1937.
Poems and New Poems.   1941.
Collected Poems 1923–1953.   1954.
The Blue Estuaries: Poems 1923–1968.   1968.

Other

Works in the Humanities Published in Great Britain 1939–1946: A Select List.   1950.
Achievement in American Poetry 1900–1950.   1951.
Selected Criticism: Prose, Poetry.   1955.
A Poet's Alphabet: Reflections on the Literary Art and Vocation, edited by Robert Phelps and Ruth Limmer.   1970.

Editor, with William Jay Smith, *The Golden Journey: Poems for Young People.*   1965.

Translator, with W. H. Auden and Elizabeth Mayer, *The Sorrows of Young Werther, and Novella*, by Goethe.   1971.

Reading List: "Bogan and Léonie Adams" by Elder Olson, in *Chicago Review 8*, Fall 1954.

*   *   *

Louise Bogan's collected poems, *The Blue Estuaries*, make up a slender volume that brings together work published from 1923 to 1968. She rarely wrote poems longer than a page, and all her earlier published books are brief and cut to the bone. She was a relentless reviser of her work and a slow, cautious craftsman who refused publishers' urgings to increase her output.

Although she was keenly aware of the revolutions in poetic technique throughout her life, her poems adhered to rhyme and set meter and treated the themes of love, regret, death, memory, landscape meditation in subtly alliterative language. Her style shows the influence of Emily Dickinson and perhaps the wit of Metaphysical poetry, but the essential charm of her best work is the quiet, feminine perception she expresses in her strict, tightly framed forms, as in "Second Song," an early poem:

> I said out of sleeping:
> Passion, farewell.
> Take from my keeping
> Bauble and shell.
>
> Black salt, black provender.
> Tender your store
> To a new pensioner,
> To me no more.

Although she relaxes into a certain lyric frankness of feeling in her later work, her style of spare restraint remains consistent throughout her work. In several of her poems a more strident feminine consciousness flares, as in "Women," with its sardonic portrayal of woman caught in her stereotype of the put-upon mate:

> Their love is an eager meaninglessness
> Too tense, or too lax.
>
> They hear in every whisper that speaks to them
> A shout and a cry.
> As like as not, when they take life over their door-sills
> They should let it go by.

Bogan regarded the poem as a deliberate and highly worked distillation of thought, and was perhaps too strict with her own imagination. The fire and wit of her mind are muted in most of her poetry but luxuriously displayed in her brilliant correspondence, collected in *What the Woman Lived*, where her sarcasm and acute critical nature are shared with a circle of notable literary figures of her time, including Edmund Wilson, Morton Dauwen Zabel, Rolfe Humphries, and Theodore Roethke.

Like her poetry, her critical writing eschewed partisanship and fashion in favor of a classical standard of moderation, balance, and form. As the poetry critic for *The New Yorker*, she was well known for her honest and abrasive judgments of the work of even her close friends, and her essays of these years, published in *A Poet's Alphabet*, endure in their accuracy and acumen. A brief treatise on modern poetry, *Achievement in American Poetry 1900–1950*, though merely a sketch of the main trends of these years, argues a provocative thesis that female poets of the late 19th century were chiefly responsible for revitalizing poetry with their sensuous, daring imaginations.

—Paul Christensen

BOWLES, Paul (Frederick).   American.   Born in New York City, 30 December 1910. Educated at the University of Virginia, Charlottesville, 1928–29; studied music with Aaron Copland in New York and Berlin, 1930–32, and with Virgil Thomson in Paris, 1933–34. Married the writer Jane Sydney Auer (i.e., Jane Bowles) in 1938 (died, 1973). Music Critic, *New York Herald Tribune,* 1942–46; also composer. Recipient: Guggenheim Fellowship, 1941; National Institute of Arts and Letters grant, 1950; Rockefeller grant, 1959; Translation Center grant, 1975. Since 1952 has lived in Tangier.

PUBLICATIONS

Fiction

The Sheltering Sky.   1949.
The Delicate Prey and Other Stories.   1950.
A Little Stone: Stories.   1950.
Let It Come Down.   1952.
The Spider's House.   1955.
· *The Hours after Noon.*   1959.
A Hundred Camels in the Courtyard (stories).   1962.
Up above the World.   1966.
The Time of Friendship (stories).   1967.
Pages from Cold Point and Other Stories.   1968.
Three Tales.   1975.

Play

Senso, with Tennessee Williams, in *Two Screenplays,* by Luigi Visconti.   1970.

Screenplay: *Senso (The Wanton Countess,* English dialogue), with Tennessee Williams, 1949.

Verse

Scenes.   1968.
The Thicket of Spring: Poems 1926–1969.   1972.

Other

Yallah (travel).   1956.
Their Heads Are Green (travel).   1963; as *Their Heads Are Green and Their Hands Are Blue,* 1963.
Without Stopping: An Autobiography.   1972.

Editor, with Mohammed Mrabet, and Translator, *The Boy Who Set the Fire and Other Stories.*   1973.

Translator, *No Exit,* by Jean-Paul Sartre.   1946.
Translator, *The Lost Trail of the Sahara,* by Roger Frison-Roche.   ·1962.

Translator, *A Life Full of Holes*, by Driss ben Hamed Charhadi.   1964.
Translator, *Love with a Few Hairs*, by Mohammed Mrabet.   1967.
Translator, *The Lemon*, by Mohammed Mrabet.   1969.
Translator, *Mhashish*, by Mohammed Mrabet.   1969.
Translator, *For Bread Alone*, by Mohamed Choukri.   1974.
Translator, *Jean Genet in Tangier*, by Mohamed Choukri.   1974.
Translator, *Look and Move On*, by Mohammed Mrabet.   1975.
Translator, *Harmless Poisons, Blameless Sins*, by Mohammed Mrabet.   1976.

Reading List: "Bowles and the Natural Man" by Oliver Evans, in *Recent American Fiction*, 1963; *Bowles: The Illumination of North Africa* by Lawrence D. Stewart, 1974.

*   *   *

A prolific writer of music, Paul Bowles did not commit himself seriously to writing fiction until after the Second World War, when he was in his mid-thirties and living in New York after many years spent in North Africa. He has described the period as "the Atomic Age" (*The Sheltering Sky*), and his characters are appropriate to a period of fear and desolation – most are empty, deracinated, and hopeless, the hollow men of T. S. Eliot, as Chester Eisinger has described them (*Fiction of the Forties*, 1965).

His first novel, *The Sheltering Sky*, may be taken as typical of most of his fiction. In it, three young Americans, a married couple and a male friend, have left fashionable New York for adventure in North Africa. There, they move steadily into the Sahara, leaving their morality, sense of purpose, and identities further behind them as they move from town to town. They become separated: Porter Moresby dies of typhoid after a horrifying vision of blood and excrement; his wife, Kit, a neurotic socialite, eventually loses her sanity after living with Arabs. Only their companion, Tunner, survives, left with the task of escorting the remnant of the woman he loves back to civilization. Some critics would agree with the reaction of Doubleday, the publishers who commissioned but then rejected the novel on the grounds that it lacked coherence and purpose. It is a charge that could be brought against several of his stories, which seem full of gratuitous violence and emptiness, as well as his second novel, *Let It Come Down*, which follows the steady degeneration of a single American, Dyar, in North Africa – he too moves steadily away from civilization and morality and toward murder and violence, ending with nothing but confirmation of his basic nature.

But what such a critical response ignores is the virility and vigour of the native life that is so central to Bowles's writing, which needs his apathetic Europeans and Americans to make a contrast with his vision of authenticity. Every native in his fiction is as much an individual as each European and American is not. His third novel, *The Spider's House*, is probably more successful than the first two because it gives considerable weight to such a native – Amar, the Moroccan youth who shares the story with a couple of Americans. Details and rituals of native life come into the foreground and the novel is given a liveliness and colour that is rather lacking in the others. His fourth novel, *Up above the World*, although set in Central America, is another disintegration into violence and death, and there is probably more satisfaction to be gained from Bowles's recent translations of stories told by pre-literate Moroccan story-tellers, in which the patterns of native life are once more dominant.

—Patrick Evans

BOYD, James. American. Born in Harrisburg, Pennsylvania, 2 July 1888. Educated at Hill School, Pottstown, Pennsylvania, 1901–06; Princeton University, New Jersey 1906–10, B.A. 1910; Trinity College, Cambridge, 1910–12. Served in the New York Infantry, 1916, as a Red Cross volunteer, 1917, and in the United States Army Ambulance Service, in Italy and France, 1917–19: Lieutenant. Married Katharine Lamont in 1917; two sons and one daughter. Staff writer and cartoonist, Harrisburg *Patriot*, 1910; teacher of English and French at the Harrisburg Academy, 1912–14; Member of the editorial staff of *Country Life in America*, 1916; settled on a family farm in Southern Pines, North Carolina, 1919: Owner and Editor, *Southern Pines Pilot*, 1941–44. Founder and first National Chairman, Free Company of Players, 1941. Member, National Institute of Arts and Letters, 1937; Society of American Historians, 1939. *Died 25 February 1944.*

PUBLICATIONS

Fiction

　Drums. 1925.
　Marching On. 1927.
　Long Hunt. 1930.
　Roll River. 1933.
　Bitter Creek. 1939.
　Old Pines and Other Stories. 1952.

Play

　One More Free Man (broadcast 1941). In *The Free Company Presents*, 1941.

Verse

　Eighteen Poems. 1944.

Other

　Mr. Hugh David MacWhirr Looks after His $1.00 Investment in the Pilot Newspaper (sketches). 1943.

　Editor, *The Free Company Presents: A Collection of Plays about the Meaning of America.* 1941.

Reading List: *Boyd* by David E. Whisnant, 1972.

*　　*　　*

In the 1920's James Boyd was in the forefront of those who set about revitalizing and reconditioning the American historical novel, which had lapsed into romantic clichés and suspect authenticity. His deliberate apprenticeship in professional writing consisted of a series of experimental short stories testing his ability to master such techniques as dialogue, mood, and setting. Though his research for sketching in the Revolutionary milieu of *Drums* was facilitated by the availability of archival depositories then being developed and enlarged, he went a step further by uncovering period documents on his own and by visiting the scenes about which he would write. His authoritative historicity was never questioned. But Boyd's principal contribution to the historical novel was an emphasis on a "psychological realism" overlying the romantic conventions and accuracy of detail. For example, in *Drums*, Boyd's most highly acclaimed work, the ambivalent loyalties of the backwoodsman Johnny Fraser during the dislocations of the American Revolution, and his slow development from an acceptance of British rule in the Colonies to his realization that change is inevitable, are never subsidiary to events, which instead are used to support the demands of characterization and motivation. From the hinterlands of North Carolina to the famed battle between the *Serapis* and John Paul Jones's *Bonhomme Richard*, the incidents of history are mere background to the novelist's multi-dimensional portrait of his hero.

In *Marching On*, it is from the point of view of the Confederate infantryman James Fraser, descendant of Johnny Fraser, that the Civil War is seen as "a rich man's war but a poor man's fight." In addition to such climactic chapters as that narrating James's participation in the Battle of Antietam, the novel provides social commentary in depicting and contrasting the lower segments of Southern life, Fraser's middle class, and the landed aristocrats. Often criticized is Boyd's yielding to romantic practice in allowing his hero at war's end to marry the planter's daughter. *Long Hunt*, though it required as much research in gathering historical minutiae as did Boyd's first two books, is more properly defined as a frontier novel of the 1790's when settlers moved from North Carolina across the mountains into Indian territory and on to the Mississippi River. *Roll River* was a change in pace. In it Boyd wrote from personal observation of the shifting values among four generations of a proud, wealthy family in the city of Midian (the author's native Harrisburg, Pennsylvania). *Bitter Creek* is a cowboy "western" to which Boyd, as in the other books, applied his gift for psychological analysis.

His biographer wrote that Boyd saw man as "first of all a creature of history whose problems had to be understood in historical depth." His books, especially the two war novels which profited from his battlefield experience in World War I, were so highly regarded as exemplary of the "new" American historical novels that their other virtues have been for the most part overlooked by readers and critics alike.

—Richard Walser

BOYLE, Kay. American. Born in St. Paul, Minnesota, 19 February 1903. Studied violin at the Cincinnati Conservatory of Music, and agriculture at the Ohio Mechanics Institute, 1917–19. Married 1) Richard Brault in 1923 (divorced), one daughter; 2) Laurence Vail in 1931 (divorced, 1943), three daughters; 3) Baron Joseph von Franckenstein (died, 1963), one daughter and one son. Lived in Europe for 30 years before and after the Second World War. Foreign Correspondent, *The New Yorker*, 1946–54. Lecturer, New School for Social Research, New York, 1962; Fellow, Wesleyan University, Middletown, Connecticut, 1963; Professor of English, San Francisco State College, 1963–72; Director, New York Writers Conference, Wagner College, New York, 1964; Fellow, Radcliffe Institute for Independent Study, Cambridge, Massachusetts, 1965; Writer-in-Residence, Hollins College, Virginia, 1970–71. Recipient: Guggenheim Fellowship, 1934, 1961; O. Henry Award, 1935, 1941; California Literary Medal Award, 1971. D. Litt.: Columbia College, Chicago, 1971. Member, National Institute of Arts and Letters, 1958. Lives in New York City.

PUBLICATIONS

Fiction

Short Stories.   1929.
Wedding Day and Other Stories.   1930.
Plagued by the Nightingale.   1931.
Year Before Last.   1932.
The First Lover and Other Stories.   1933.
Gentlemen, I Address You Privately.   1933.
My Next Bride.   1934.
The White Horses of Vienna and Other Stories.   1936.
Death of a Man.   1936.
Monday Night.   1938.
The Crazy Hunter: Three Short Novels.   1940; as *The Crazy Hunter and Other Stories,* 1940.
Primer for Combat.   1942.
Avalanche.   1944.
Thirty Stories.   1946.
A Frenchman Must Die.   1946.
1939.   1948.
His Human Majesty.   1949.
The Smoking Mountain: Stories of Post-War Germany.   1951.
The Seagull on the Step.   1955.
Three Short Novels.   1958.
Generation Without Farewell.   1960.
Nothing Ever Breaks Except the Heart.   1966.
The Underground Woman.   1975.

Verse

A Statement.   1932.
A Glad Day.   1938.
American Citizen: Naturalized in Leadville, Colorado.   1944.
Collected Poems.   1962.
Testament for My Students.   1970.

Other

The Youngest Camel (juvenile).   1939; revised edition, 1959.
Breaking the Silence: Why a Mother Tells Her Son about the Nazi Era.   1962.
Pinky: The Cat Who Liked to Sleep (juvenile).   1966.
Pinky in Persia (juvenile).   1968.
Being Geniuses Together, with Robert McAlmon.   1968.
The Long Walk at San Francisco State and Other Essays.   1970.
Four Visions of America, with others.   1977.

Editor, with Laurence Vail and Nina Conarain, *365 Days.*   1936.
Editor, *The Autobiography of Emanuel Carnevali.*   1967.
Editor, *Enough of Dying! An Anthology of Peace Writings.*   1972.

Translator, *Don Juan*, by Joseph Delteil. 1931.
Translator, *Mr. Knife, Miss Fork*, by René Crevel. 1931.
Translator, *The Devil in the Flesh*, by Raymond Radiguet. 1932.

Acted as ghost-writer for the books *Relations and Complications, Being the Recollections of H. H. the Dayang Muda of Sarawak*, by Gladys Palmer Brooke, 1929, and *Yellow Dusk*, by Bettina Bedwell, 1937.

Reading List: "Boyle" by Richard C. Carpenter, in *College English 15*, November 1953; "Boyle's Fiction" by Harry T. Moore, in *Kenyon Review*, Spring 1960.

                    *   *   *

What is most memorable in Kay Boyle's fiction are specific scenes – the sight of the sea tide building and crashing through the mouth of a river; a young man, sick with tuberculosis, leaning over a basin to vomit blood; a bus-driver arguing recklessly with his passengers while the bus careens along a cliff road; a run-over dog pulling itself forward, as its spilled-out entrails drag and turn white in the dust; Americans and Germans waiting over real fox holes in a German forest, ready to club the young foxes as they come out, and underground, moving through the tunnels, now near, now distant, the sound of the yelping pack and pursuing dog.

Miss Boyle's concern here is to heighten our responses to these events. She asks us not only to respond to the vivid and extreme sensations which they present, but to see them in sharp moral and aesthetic terms, as beautiful or dangerous or agonizingly brutal.

It is this intense kind of involvement that Miss Boyle asks from us generally. She offers very little neutral ground on which we may look at these scenes on our own. The youthful idealists, who play a major role in her novels, will give us, I think, the right emotional cues for appreciating her work. Inexperienced in the ways of the world, their feelings are open and unmitigated; they do not quite believe in evil and yet they are deeply troubled by pain and injustice. Bridget, Victoria John, Mary Farrant, Milly Roberts – young Americans whose destinies are connected with Europe – are such figures. If the fictional situation would seem to echo James, there are major differences in its development, for Kay Boyle's morality is active rather than introspective.

Indeed, whether her heroes be young Americans in Europe or former German soldiers, they express themselves in concrete acts. What her heroes have in common is the courage to act – it is the only thing people ever remember, one character says. But action is, of course, no guarantee of success. Involved in every human venture, it would seem, are elements that bring about its destruction. Those elements may be physical in nature – not malevolent but merely indifferent – stupid accident, or man's incapacity to make a social world that is supportive and helpful.

Thus, in *Plagued by the Nightingale*, the closely-bound world of a French family becomes so destructive that three daughters and a son wait desperately for an escape. Only Charlotte, the fourth daughter, loves her richly domestic life and her place within the family; and only Charlotte is deprived of it by death. In *Year Before Last*, Martin, a young poet, dying of tuberculosis, and Eve, his aunt, are bound together by their dedication to art. Yet the emotion that shapes their lives is Eve's cruel jealousy of Hanah, whom Martin loves and who would shield him from the agonies of poverty and illness. In *My Next Bride*, the artist, Sorrel, uses the common funds of the art colony to buy a magnificent and expensive automobile. In this shallow attempt to escape poverty and ugliness, he betrays the destitute craftsmen who work for him, as well as the artistic creed he has professed to live by.

Miss Boyle's novels have, I think, a potentially tragic feeling. The qualities she projects in her strongest characters – courage to act as a counter to failure, energy rather than hopeless despair – offer this possibility. Very often, it seems wasted, for although Miss Boyle insists upon courageous action, the possible choices she sees in such action are limited. Also, perhaps equally harmful, these choices do not necessarily grow out of the fictional situation; they seem fixed from the beginning. It is for this reason, perhaps, that her characters sometimes take unreal positions – in *Avalanche*, the mountain men are total in their dedication to a good cause, the German agent, total in his dedication to a bad one; in *The Seagull on the Step*, the doctor commits melodramatic villanies, the teacher-reformer, heroic deeds; in *Generation Without Farewell*, the American colonel is brutal and gross, his wife and daughter are gentle and sensitive. Such extreme divisions in realistic novels are unconvincing.

What gives her work strength is but her understanding that our human connections lie finally in our limitations, most of all in our common mortality. From the beginning, she has had this kind of knowledge.

At moments we see it expressed with startling clarity. In her first novel, Charlotte's family is hastily called to her bedside. Those who have waited through the day – Charlotte's young children, her sisters – make their way through the dark, wet fall night, to Charlotte's house, up the great stairs and to her room. There, they wait in silence until the door is opened, and the children walk "calmly into the roar of Charlotte's death." In her most recent novel of post-war Germany, a power shovel in downtown Frankfurt accidentally unearths an underground air raid shelter and releases a single survivor, entombed there since the war. As the mad, tattered figure runs wildly across the upturned ground, bewildered by his resurrection, any ideals we may hold about nationality, military success, moral justification, diminish into nothingness. Only a sense of our common inhumanity persists.

—Jacqueline Hoefer

BRADFORD, Roark. American. Born in Lauderdale County, Tennessee, 21 August 1896. Educated in local schools. Served in the Artillery Reserve of the United States Army, 1917–20: Lieutenant; United States Navy Reserve, assigned to the Bureau of Aeronautics Training Literature Division, Navy Department, Washington, D.C., 1942–45. Married Mary Rose Himler; one son. Reporter, Atlanta *Georgian*, 1920–22, *Telegraph*, Macon, Georgia, 1923, and the *Daily Advertiser*, Lafayette, Louisiana, 1923; Night City Editor, later Sunday Editor, *Times Picayune*, New Orleans, 1924–26; full-time writer from 1929. Recipient: O. Henry Award, 1927. Member, National Institute of Arts and Letters. *Died 13 November 1948.*

PUBLICATIONS

Fiction

Ol' Man Adam an' His Chillun. 1928.
This Side of Jordan. 1929.
Ol' King David and the Philistine Boys. 1930.
John Henry. 1931.

Kingdom Coming. 1933.
Let the Band Play Dixie and Other Stories. 1934.
The Three-Headed Angel. 1937.

Plays

How Come Christmas: A Modern Morality. 1930.
John Henry, music by Jacques Wolfe, from the story by Bradford. 1939.

Other

The Green Roller (miscellany). 1949.

* * *

To read the stories and novels of Roark Bradford is to enter into a world separated from us by time, space, and especially by temperament. In his depiction of the life on southern plantations, the white man's world fades into the background, becoming no more nor less important than the plowing of fields or the picking of cotton. Bradford wrote of the southern black out of a deep respect and love, which, coupled with his uncanny gift for imitating dialectical speech, makes his writing altogether unique in a white man.

Bradford turned to writing full-time in 1927, concerning himself not with philosophical or moral evalutions of the Negro's life, but rather with the reality of his situation, and the problems of coping with it. His prose, like his characters, is simple and direct, even childlike, but never sentimental. Death can come quickly and unromantically to them, and when it does, they face it with the deep faith that was a part of the author himself, up until his death in 1948.

Above all, "Brad" was a storyteller. His work vibrates with the strong, simple rhythms of speech, whether in his realistic novels or in his modern myths like *John Henry*: "The night John Henry was born the moon was copper-colored and the sky was black.... Forked lightning cleaved the air and the earth trembled like a leaf. The panthers squalled in the brake like a baby and the Mississippi ran upstream a thousand miles."

Bradford won the O. Henry prize in 1927 with his second published short story, "Child of God." His retelling of Biblical stories, *Ol' Man Adam and His Chillun,* was adapted for the stage by Marc Connelly, and became the highly successful play *The Green Pastures.*

—Walter Bode

BROMFIELD, Louis. American. Born in Mansfield, Ohio, 27 December 1896. Educated at Cornell University Agricultural College, Ithaca, New York, 1914–15; School of Journalism, Columbia University, New York, 1916, honorary war degree 1920. Served in the American Ambulance Corps, with the 34th and 168th divisions of the French Army, 1917–19: Croix de Guerre. Married Mary Appleton Wood in 1921 (died, 1952); three daughters. Reporter, City News Service and Associated Press, New York, 1920–22; Editor and/or Critic for *Musical America, The Bookman,* and *Time,* also worked as an assistant to a theatrical producer and as Advertising Manager of Putnam's, publishers, all New York, 1922–25; lived in Senlis, France, 1925–38; settled on a farm in Richland County, Ohio,

1939, and lived there until his death. President, Emergency Committee for the American Wounded in Spain,1938. Director, United States Chamber of Commerce. Recipient: Pulitzer Prize, 1927. LL.D: Marshall College, Huntington, West Virginia; Parsons College, Fairfield, Iowa; Litt.D.: Ohio Northern University, Ada. Chevalier, Legion of Honor, 1939. Member, National Institute of Arts and Letters. *Died 18 March 1956.*

PUBLICATIONS

Fiction

The Green Bay Tree. 1924.
Possession. 1925; as *Lilli Barr,* 1926.
Early Autumn. 1926.
A Good Woman. 1927.
The Strange Case of Miss Annie Spragg. 1928.
Awake and Rehearse (stories). 1929.
Tabloid News (stories). 1930.
Twenty-Four Hours. 1930.
A Modern Hero. 1932.
The Farm. 1933.
Here Today and Gone Tomorrow: Four Short Novels. 1934.
The Man Who Had Everything. 1935.
It Had to Happen. 1936.
The Rains Came: A Novel of Modern India. 1937.
It Takes All Kinds (omnibus). 1939.
Night in Bombay. 1940.
Wild Is the River. 1941.
Until the Day Break. 1942.
Mrs. Parkington. 1943.
Bitter Lotus. 1944.
What Became of Anna Bolton. 1944.
The World We Live In: Stories. 1944.
Colorado. 1947.
Kenny. 1947.
McLeod's Folly. 1948.
The Wild Country. 1948.
Mr. Smith. 1951.

Plays

The House of Women, from his novel *The Green Bay Tree* (produced 1927).
DeLuxe, with John Gearnon (produced 1934).
Times Have Changed (produced 1935).

Screenplay: *Brigham Young – Frontiersman,* with Lamar Trotti, 1940.

Other

The Work of Robert Nathan. 1927.

England, A Dying Oligarchy.   1939.
Pleasant Valley.   1945.
A Few Brass Tacks.   1946.
Malabar Farm.   1948.
Out of the Earth.   1950.
The Wealth of the Soil.   1952.
A New Pattern for a Tired World.   1954.
From My Experience: The Pleasures and Miseries of Life on a Farm.   1955.
Animals and Other People.   1955.
Walt Disney's Vanishing Prairie.   1956(?).

Reading List: *Bromfield and His Books* by Morrison Brown, 1956; *Bromfield* by David D. Anderson, 1964.

*   *   *

One of the most promising young American novelists of the 1920's, Louis Bromfield fell into critical disfavor in the early 1930's, a condition that prevailed until his death in 1956, in spite of a continued prodigious production of novels and short stories and a remarkable popular success. To assess his contributions to American literature is not difficult; the many literary shortcomings that prevented the fulfillment of his early literary promise are sufficient to keep him out of the first rank of American novelists. But at the same time he deserves a better literary fate than he has received: his effective style, his character portrayal, and his narrative technique are consistently strong, and his interpretations of American life are effective and intelligent.

The themes with which he dealt are significant: the decline of American individualism and agrarian democracy and the growth of industrialism; the unique role of the strong woman in American life; the egalitarian philosophy that permits a young person to rise above his origins. In his use of them in his work he came close to the essence of American life as thoughtful Americans know it. That he did not go on to chronicle the rise of an industrial democracy, as the Marxist critics of the 1930's demanded, but attempted instead to return to the past, contributed to the demise of his reputation, but it resulted in some of his best works, those in which he develops his major themes effectively as he reiterates the values upon which the country was built and emphasizes the need to return to those values in an increasingly materialistic age.

Among his substantial literary contributions must be included his four panel novels, *The Green Bay Tree, Possession, Early Autumn,* and *A Good Woman,* which document in human terms the impact of sweeping social changes and perverted values in the early years of this century. These novels also illustrate his literary talents: a forthright, literate style; character portrayal that is human and intense; and a strong narrative technique. To these novels must be added *The Farm,* his best single work, *Twenty-Four Hours,* a remarkably controlled work in spite of its lapses, and *The Rains Came,* the most dramatic and philosophically unified of his work. Of his later work, *Mrs. Parkington* is an intensely human portrait of a magnificent American woman, and *The Wild Country* comes close to a definitive expression of the American Midwestern experience in transition from frontier to civilization.

One must recognize, too, his contributions to the literature of nature, folklore, and agriculture. Most of the best of his folklore and nature writing is included in *Animals and Other People,* while *Pleasant Valley* and *Malabar Farm* indicate what technical writing may achieve when it is lively, imaginative, and literate.

Unfortunately, Bromfield still suffers from the fact that he has received little objective criticism. The unfair criticisms of the early 1930's have discouraged later critics from looking at his work clearly and coherently. He wrote too well too easily, and his early critical and commercial successes proved ultimately to be adverse. But in almost all of his work he wrote well and he constructed human, memorable characters and situations. These are not common abilities in any age.

—David D. Anderson

BROOKS, Gwendolyn.   American.   Born in Topeka, Kansas, 17 June 1917. Educated at Wilson Junior College, Chicago, graduated 1936. Married Henry L. Blakely in 1939; one son, one daughter. Publicity Director, National Association for the Advancement of Colored People Youth Council, Chicago, in the 1930's. Taught at Northeastern Illinois State College, Chicago, Columbia College, Chicago, Elmhurst College, Illinois, and the University of Wisconsin, Madison; Distinguished Professor of the Arts, City College of the City University of New York, 1971. Editor, *The Black Position* magazine; Member, Illinois Arts Council. Recipient: Guggenheim Fellowship, 1946, 1947; National Institute of Arts and Letters grant, 1946; Pulitzer Prize, 1950; Friends of Literature Award, 1964; Monsen Award, 1964; Anisfield-Wolf Award, 1968; Black Academy Award, 1971; Shelley Memorial Award, 1976. L.H.D.: Columbia College, 1964; D. Litt.: Lake Forest College, Illinois, 1965; Brown University, Providence, Rhode Island, 1974. Poet Laureate of Illinois, 1969. Member, National Institute of Arts and Letters, 1976. Lives in Chicago.

PUBLICATIONS

Verse

A Street in Bronzeville.   1945.
Annie Allen.   1949.
Bronzeville Boys and Girls.   1956.
The Bean Eaters (verse for children).   1960.
Selected Poems.   1963.
In the Time of Detachment, In the Time of Cold.   1965.
In the Mecca.   1968.
For Illinois 1968: A Sesquicentennial Poem.   1968.
Riot.   1969.
Family Pictures.   1970.
Aloneness.   1971.
Beckonings.   1975.

Fiction

Maud Martha.   1953.

Other

A Portion of That Field, with others.   1967.
The World of Gwendolyn Brooks (miscellany).   1971.
Report from Part One: An Autobiography.   1972.
The Tiger Who Wore White Gloves; or, You Are What You Are (juvenile).   1974.

Editor, *A Broadside Treasury.*   1971.
Editor, *Jump Bad: A New Chicago Anthology.*   1971.

*   *   *

Gwendolyn Brooks solves the critical question of whether to judge black poetry in America by standards different from those applied to white poetry: she simply writes so powerfully and universally out of the black American milieu that the question does not arise. Her poems may sometimes be bitter, angry, or threatening, but always they are poems and never mere propaganda. She may personally feel caught between racial allegiance and the need for social action on the one hand and purer and higher art on the other, but in her work the distinction dissolves.

Indeed, *In the Mecca,* published in 1968, and especially the poems published since, reflect the conversion from deep racial pride to a harsher militancy that she experienced under the tutelage of a group of young blacks at a meeting at Fisk University in 1967. Thus she speaks in "Young Africans" (from *Family Pictures*) of "our black revival, our black vinegar,/our hands and our hot blood," and warns in the acerbic *Riot,* "Cabot! John! You are a desperate man,/and the desperate die expensively today." But nearly always she finds the tight poetic structure, the *things* in which to embody the idea, so that the reader comes away with that sense of surprise and delight at the insight – in addition to any other emotion – that means that the work was a poem, and that the poem was a fine one.

Gwendolyn Brooks has devoted much of her time since the late 1960's to helping young black Americans, and especially writers. But she speaks out of the American consciousness and to the American conscience, and it is the color-blind America that has rightly given her a Pulitzer Prize, the Poet Laureateship of the State of Illinois, and other testaments to her great lyrical voice.

—Alan R. Shucard

BROWN, Sterling (Allen).   American.   Born in Washington, D.C., 1 May 1901. Educated at public schools in Washington, D.C.; Williams College, Williamstown, Massachusetts, A.B. 1925 (Phi Beta Kappa); Harvard University, Cambridge, Massachusetts, A.M. 1930. Married Daisy Turnbull in 1919. Teacher, Virginia Seminary and College, Lynchburg, 1923–26, Lincoln University, Jefferson City, Missouri, 1926–28, and Fisk University, Nashville, Tennessee, 1929. Since 1929, Professor of English, Howard University, Washington, D.C. Visiting Professor, New York University, New School for Social Research, New York, Sarah Lawrence College, Bronxville, New York, and Vassar College, Poughkeepsie, New York. Literary Editor, *Opportunity* magazine, in the 1930's; Editor of *Negro Affairs* for the Federal Writers' Project, 1936–39. Recipient: Guggenheim Fellowship, 1937. Lives in Washington, D.C.

PUBLICATIONS

Verse

   Southern Road.   1932.
   The Last Ride of Wild Bill and Eleven Narrative Poems.   1975.

Other

   Outline for the Study of the Poetry of American Negroes (study guide for James Weldon
       Johnson's *The Book of American Negro Poetry*).   1931.
   The Negro in American Fiction.   1937.
   Negro Poetry and Drama.   1937.

   Editor, with Arthur P. Davis and Ulysses Lee, *The Negro Caravan.*   1941.

*   *   *

Essentially a traditional song-maker and story teller, Sterling Brown has witnessed cross-currents of American literature, and chooses in his poetry to depict blacks and the clash of their roles with those of whites in the variegated society of the American South, particularly in the time caught between two world wars.

His poetry has been collected in anthologies as early as James Weldon Johnson's *The Book of American Negro Poetry* (1922), and, like Johnson himself and Langston Hughes, he set about disrupting the patently false and banal image of the docile American Negro with his charming *patois*, artificially stylized and mimicked by the whites in the minstrel shows still popular in the 1920's and 1930's. Johnson says in his preface of Hughes and Brown that they "*do* use a dialect, but it is not the dialect of the comic minstrel tradition or the sentimental plantation tradition; it is the common, racy, living, authentic speech of the Negro in certain phases of real life."

Brown uses original Afro-American ballads such as "Casey Jones," "John Henry," and "Staggolee" as counterpoint for his modern ones, but the portent of his ironic wit should not be underestimated, for it is actually a tool to shape an ironic, infernal vision of American life as Hades: "The Place was Dixie I took for Hell," says Slim in "Slim in Hell." The American Negro is heralded not as Black Orpheus but as modern tragic hero Mose, a leader of *all* people while futilely attempting to save his own: "A soft song, filled with a misery/Older than Mose will be." In "Sharecropper" he is broken as Christ was broken; his landlord "shot him in the side" to put him out of his misery; he is lost and wild as Odysseus in "Odyssey of a Big Boy"; and found again:

> Man wanta live
> Man want find himself
> Man gotta learn
> How to go it alone.

Though minimal in quantity, Brown's poetry is epic in conception; his ballad, blues, and jazz forms are the vehicles for creative insight into themes of American life.

—Carol Lee Saffioti

BUCK, Pearl S(ydenstricker).   American.   Born in Hillsboro, West Virginia, 26 June 1892; daughter of Presbyterian missionaries in China. Educated at boarding school in Shanghai, China, 1907–09; Randolph-Macon Women's College, Lynchburg, Virginia, B.A. 1914 (Phi Beta Kappa); Cornell University, Ithaca, New York, M.A. 1926. Married 1) the missionary John Lossing Buck in 1917 (divorced, 1935), one daughter; 2) the publisher Richard J. Walsh in 1935 (died, 1960); eight adopted children. Taught psychology at Randolph-Macon Women's College, 1914; taught English at the University of Nanking, 1921–31, Southeastern University, Nanking, 1925–27, and Chung Yang University, Nanking, 1928–31; returned to the United States, 1935; Co-Editor, *Asia* magazine, New York, 1941–46; Founder and Director, East and West Association, 1941–51; Founder, Welcome House, an adoption agency, 1949, and the Pearl S. Buck Foundation, 1964; Member of the Board of Directors, Weather Engineering Corporation of America, Manchester, New Hampshire, 1966. Recipient: Pulitzer Prize, 1932; Howells Medal, 1935; Nobel Prize for Literature, 1938; National Conference of Christians and Jews Brotherhood Award, 1955; President's Commission on Employment of the Physically Handicapped Citation, 1958; Women's National Book Association Skinner Award, 1960; ELA Award in Literature, 1969. M.A.: Yale University, New Haven, Connecticut, 1933; D.Litt.: University of West Virginia, Morgantown, 1940; St. Lawrence University, Canton, New York, 1942; Delaware Valley College, Doylestown, Pennsylvania, 1965; LL.D.: Howard University, Washington, D.C., 1942; Muhlenberg College, Allentown, Pennsylvania, 1966; L.H.D.: Lincoln University, Pennsylvania, 1953; Woman's Medical College of Philadelphia, 1954; University of Pittsburgh, 1960; Bethany College, West Virginia, 1963; Hahnemann Medical College, Philadelphia, 1966; Rutgers University, New Brunswick, New Jersey, 1969; D.Mus.: Combs College of Music, Philadelphia, 1962; D.H.: West Virginia State College, Institute, 1963. Member, American Academy of Arts and Letters. *Died 6 March 1973.*

PUBLICATIONS

Fiction

    East Wind: West Wind.   1930.
    The Good Earth.   1931.
    Sons.   1932.
    The First Wife and Other Stories.   1933.
    The Mother.   1934.
    A House Divided.   1935.
    This Proud Heart.   1938.
    The Patriot.   1939.
    Other Gods: An American Legend.   1940.
    Today and Forever: Stories of China.   1941.
    China Sky.   1942.
    Dragon Seed.   1942.
    The Promise.   1943.
    China Flight.   1945.
    The Townsman.   1945.
    Portrait of a Marriage.   1945.
    Pavilion of Women.   1946.
    The Angry Wife.   1947.
    Far and Near: Stories of Japan, China, and America.   1948.
    Peony.   1948; as *The Bondmaid,* 1949.
    Kinfolk.   1949.

The Long Love. 1949.
God's Men. 1950.
The Hidden Flower. 1952.
Satan Never Sleeps. 1952.
Bright Procession. 1952.
Come, My Beloved. 1953.
Voices in the House. 1953.
Imperial Women. 1954.
Letter from Peking. 1957.
Command the Morning. 1959.
Fourteen Stories. 1961; as *With a Delicate Air and Other Stories,* 1962.
Hearts Come Home and Other Stories. 1962.
The Living Reed. 1963.
Stories of China. 1964.
Death in the Castle. 1965.
The Time Is Noon. 1967.
The New Year. 1968.
The Good Deed and Other Stories of Asia, Past and Present. 1969.
The Three Daughters of Madame Liang. 1969.
Mandala. 1970.
The Goddess Abides. 1972.
All under Heaven. 1973.
The Rainbow. 1974.
Book of Christmas (stories). 1974.
East and West (stories). 1975.
Secrets of the Heart. 1976.
The Lovers and Other Stories. 1977.

Plays

Flight into China (produced 1939).
Sun Yat Sen: A Play, Preceded by a Lecture by Dr. Hu-Shih. 1944(?).
China to America (radio play), in *Free World Theatre,* edited by Arch Oboler and Stephen Longstreet. 1944.
Will This Earth Hold? (radio play), in *Radio Drama in Action,* edited by Erik Barnouw. 1945.
The First Wife (produced 1945).
A Desert Incident (produced 1959).
Christine, with Charles K. Peck, Jr., music by Sammy Fain, from the book *My Indian Family* by Hilda Wernher (produced 1960).
The Guide, from the novel by R. K. Narayan (produced 1965).

Screenplays: *The Big Wave,* 1962, and *The Guide,* 1965, both with Ted Danielewski.

Verse

Words of Love. 1974.

Other

The Young Revolutionist (juvenile). 1932.

Is There a Case for Foreign Missions? 1932.
East and West and the Novel: Sources of the Early Chinese Novel. 1932.
The Exile (biography). 1936.
Fighting Angel: Portrait of a Soul (biography). 1936.
Stories for Little Children. 1940.
When Fun Begins (juvenile). 1941
Of Men and Women. 1941.
American Unity and Asia. 1942; as *Asia and Democracy*, 1943.
The Chinese Children Next Door (juvenile). 1942.
The Water Buffalo Children (juvenile). 1943.
What America Means to Me. 1943.
The Dragon Fish (juvenile). 1944.
Talk about Russia, with Masha Scott. 1945.
Tell the People · Talks with James Yen about the Mass Education Movement. 1945.
Yu Lan: Flying Boy of China (juvenile). 1945.
How It Happens: Talk about the German People, 1914–1933, with Erna von Pustau. 1947.
The Big Wave (juvenile). 1947.
American Argument, with Eslanda Goode Robeson. 1949.
One Bright Day (juvenile). 1950; as *One Bright Day and Other Stories for Children*, 1952.
The Child Who Never Grew. 1950.
The Man Who Changed China: The Story of Sun Yat Sen (juvenile). 1953.
My Several Worlds (autobiography). 1954.
The Beech Tree (juvenile). 1954.
Johnny Jack and His Beginnings (juvenile). 1954.
Christmas Miniature (juvenile). 1957; as *The Christmas Mouse*, 1958.
Friend to Friend, with Carlos P. Romulo. 1958.
The Delights of Learning. 1960.
The Christmas Ghost (juvenile). 1960.
A Bridge for Passing (autobiography). 1962.
The Joy of Children. 1964.
Welcome Child (juvenile). 1964.
The Gifts They Bring: Our Debts to the Mentally Retarded, with Gweneth T. Zarfoss. 1965.
Children for Adoption. 1965.
The Big Fight (juvenile). 1965.
The People of Japan. 1966.
For Spacious Skies: Journey in Dialogue, with Theodore F. Harris. 1966.
The Little Fox in the Middle (juvenile). 1966.
My Mother's House, with others. 1966.
To My Daughters, With Love. 1967.
Matthew, Mark, Luke, and John (juvenile). 1967.
The People of China. 1968.
The Kennedy Women: A Personal Appraisal. 1970.
China as I See It, edited by Theodore F. Harris. 1970.
The Story Bible. 1971.
The Chinese Storyteller (juvenile). 1971.
China Past and Present. 1972.
A Community Success Story: The Founding of the Pearl Buck Center. 1972.
Oriental Cookbook. 1972.
A Gift for the Children (juvenile). 1973.
Mrs. Sterling's Problem (juvenile). 1973.

Editor, *China in Black and White: An Album of Woodcuts by Contemporary Chinese Artists.*   1945.
Editor, *Fairy Tales of the Orient.*   1965.

Translator, *All Men Are Brothers,* by Shui Hu Chan.   2 vols., 1933.

Reading List: *Buck* by Paul A. Doyle, 1965; *Buck: A Biography* by Theodore F. Harris, 2 vols., 1969–71.

*   *   *

The amount and variety of Pearl S. Buck's writing and the strong correlation between her writing and her life make critical analysis complex. She admired the work of such naturalists as Zola and Dreiser and often emphasized the power of nature and culture, but she was never sordid nor pessimistic, and her realistic details of places, events, and people are organized around such romantic tenets as individuality, the nobility of common people, the corrupting influence of wealth and cities, and the universal interest in "love." Her years in China, her missionary connections, her exposure to many marital situations, and her humanitarian projects furnished both the material and the themes of her stories. And while her masterpiece, *The Good Earth,* and the biographies of her parents, *The Exile* and *Fighting Angel,* are almost universally rated as classics, much of the rest of her work is of uneven artistic merit.

The Good Earth achieves a perfect blending of appropriate diction, informative detail, epic structure, and universal themes. Such semi-biblical lines as "I am with child," and such "Chinese" lines as "There is this woman of mine," are held together with such thematic lines as: "He had no articulate thought of anything; there was only this perfect sympathy of movement, of turning this earth of theirs over and over to the sun, this earth which formed their home and fed their bodies and made their gods." Occasionally there are poetic lines as delicate as a Chinese painting: "A small soft wind blew gently from the east, a wind mild and murmurous and full of rain." While she used a similar style in her other Chinese books, she both modernized and Americanized the language when appropriate.

The Good Earth is the "epic" of a "rags-to-riches" farmer-hero of Old China, practicing his native customs but experiencing the universal drama of birth and death, prosperity and famine, work and sex, tradition and change. The plot is structured by Wang's relationship to three wives – and to his land. The "good" wives sympathize with his love of the land; the "bad" wife hates the land. Like nearly all of Miss Buck's male characters, Wang is inept in human relations, controlled by forces he never understands, yet capable of resisting social pressure and remaining loyal to personal qualities of honesty and kindness. In contrast, nearly all of her female characters are wiser, or craftier, than the men they are destined to serve – an "autobiographical" point of view especially apparent in *This Proud Heart, Pavilion of Women, Peony,* and *Letter from Peking.*

Throughout her writing she portrays religion, slavery, economic tyranny, war, and government as capable of being manipulated by individuals. And although she occasionally generalizes about settings or classes, her character development is consistent, the variety of her "solutions" credible. Certainly her informative handling of cultural conflicts has served her overriding purposes, freedom and reconciliation.

—Esther Marian Greenwell Smith

BULLINS, Ed. American. Born in Philadelphia, Pennsylvania, 2 July 1935. Educated in Philadelphia public schools; William Penn Business Institute, Philadelphia; Los Angeles City College; San Francisco State College. Served in the United States Navy. Playwright-in-Residence, 1967–71, and since 1967, Associate Director, The New Lafayette Theatre, Harlem, New York. Editor, *Black Theatre* agazine, Harlem, 1969–74. Recipient: Rockefeller grant, 1968; Vernon Rice Award, 1968; American Place grant, 1968; Obie Award, 1971; Guggenheim grant, 1971; National Endowment for the Arts grant, 1974; New York Drama Critics Circle Award, 1975, 1977. D.L.: Columbia College, Chicago, 1976. Lives in Brooklyn, New York.

PUBLICATIONS

Plays

Clara's Ole Man (produced 1965). In *Five Plays*, 1969.
How Do You Do: A Nonsense Drama (produced 1969). 1965.
Dialect Determinism (produced 1965). In *Spontaneous Combustion: Eight New American Plays*, edited by Rochelle Owens, 1972.
In New England Winter (produced 1967). In *New Plays from the Black Theatre*, edited by Bullins, 1969.
In the Wine Time (produced 1968). In *Five Plays*, 1969.
A Son, Come Home (produced 1968). In *Five Plays*, 1969.
The Electronic Nigger (produced 1968). In *Five Plays*, 1969.
Goin' a Buffalo: A Tragifantasy (produced 1968). In *Five Plays*, 1969.
The Gentleman Caller (produced 1969). In *Illuminations 5*, 1968.
Five Plays. 1969; as *The Electronic Nigger and Other Plays*, 1970.
The Game of Adam and Eve, with Shirley Tarbell (produced 1969).
It Has No Choice (produced 1969).
The Corner (produced 1969). In *Black Drama Anthology*, edited by Woodie King and Ron Milner, 1972.
Street Sounds (produced 1970).
The Fabulous Miss Marie (produced 1970). In *The New Lafayette Theatre Presents*, edited by Bullins, 1974.
It Bees Dat Way (produced 1970). In *Four Dynamite Plays*, 1971.
The Pig Pen (produced 1970). In *Four Dynamite Plays*, 1971.
Death List (produced 1970). In *Four Dynamite Plays*, 1971.
State Office Building Curse, in *The Drama Review*, September 1970.
The Duplex: A Black Love Fable in Four Movements (produced 1970). 1971.
The Devil Catchers (produced 1971).
Night of the Beast (screenplay), in *Four Dynamite Plays*, 1971.
Four Dynamite Plays (includes *It Bees Dat Way, Death List, The Pig Pen, Night of the Beast*). 1971.
The Psychic Pretenders (produced 1972).
You Gonna Let Me Take You Out Tonight, Baby (produced 1972).
House Party, music by Pat Patrick, lyrics by Bullins (produced 1973).
The Taking of Miss Janie (produced 1975).
The Mystery of Phyllis Wheatley (produced 1976).
Jo Anne!!! (produced 1976).
Home Boy, music by Aaron Bell, lyrics by Bullins (produced 1976).
Michael (produced 1978).

Screenplays: *Night of the Beast*, 1971; *The Ritual Masters*, 1972.

Fiction

The Hungered One: Early Writings (stories).   1971.
The Reluctant Rapist.   1973.

Verse

To Raise the Dead and Foretell the Future.   1971.

Other

Editor, *New Plays from the Black Theatre.*   1969.
Editor, *The New Lafayette Theatre Presents: Plays with Aesthetic Comments by 6 Black Playwrights.*   1974.

Bibliography: in *Black Image on the American Stage* by James V. Hatch, 1970.

Reading List: "The Polished Reality: Aesthetics and the Black Writer" in *Contact Magazine,* 1962; "The Theatre of Reality" in *Black World,* 1966; "Up from Politics" in *Performance,* 1972.

*   *   *

Ed Bullins is the most original and prolific playwright of the American Black Theatre movement. To quote him: "To make an open secret more public: in the area of playwrighting, Ed Bullins, at this moment in time, is almost without peer in America – black, white or imported." Written in 1973, the statement exaggerates little. Included in a volume *The Theme Is Blackness,* Bullins's title polemically reduces his actual thematic range; he dramatizes many relationships of black people – family, friendship, business, the business of crime. From urban black ghettos Bullins draws characters who speak with humor, obscenity, and sophistication. Whereas Langston Hughes had to strain to capture underworld idiom in Harlem, Bullins modulates a language that ignores the black as the white middle-class.

As ambitious as O'Neill, Bullins has embarked on a Twentieth Century Cycle of twenty plays, to depict the lives of certain Afro-Americans between 1900 and 1999. Five of these plays have been completed to date (1977), very loosely tracing the experiences of the Dawson – it would be inaccurate to call them a family, since the men found households, abandon them, disappear, reappear. Even incomplete, the cycle stresses the necessarily fragmentary nature of relationships of black urban males in twentieth-century America. Each of the plays focuses on a complete action, free in dramatic form, often embellished with song and dance, rich in rhythmic speech and terse imagery which Bullins crafts so beautifully. Indefatigable, Bullins has also written agit-prop Dynamite Plays, in which his anti-white rage is indistinguishable from that of LeRoi Jones. Other extra-cycle plays resemble Chekhov in their evocation of a dying class, e.g., *Clara's Ole Man* and *Goin' a Buffalo.* Like Chekhov, Bullins dramatizes the foibles of his people, endearing them to us through a poignant humor.

—Ruby Cohn

BURROUGHS, Edgar Rice. American. Born in Chicago, Illinois, 1 September 1875. Educated at the Harvard School, Chicago, 1888–91; Phillips Academy, Andover, Massachusetts, 1891–92; Michigan Military Academy, Orchard Lake, 1892–95. Served in the United States 7th Cavalry, 1896–97; Illinois Reserve Militia, 1918–19. Married 1) Emma Centennia Hulbert in 1900 (divorced, 1934), two sons and one daughter; 2) Florence Dearholt in 1935 (divorced, 1942). Instructor and Assistant Commandant, Michigan Military Academy, 1895–96; owner of a stationery store, Pocatello, Idaho, 1898; worked in his father's American Battery Company, Chicago, 1899–1903; joined his brother's Sweetser-Burroughs Mining Company, Idaho, 1903–04; railroad policeman, Oregon Short Line Railroad Company, Salt Lake City, 1904; Manager of the Stenographic Department, Sears, Roebuck and Company, Chicago, 1906–08; Partner, Burroughs and Dentzer, advertising contractors, Chicago, 1908–09; Office Manager, Physicians Co-Operative Association, Chicago, 1909; Partner, Stace-Burroughs Company, salesmanship firm, Chicago, 1909; worked for Champlain Yardley Company, stationers, Chicago, 1910–11; Manager, System Service Bureau, Chicago, 1912–13; free-lance writer after 1913: formed Edgar Rice Burroughs Inc., publishers, 1913; Burroughs-Tarzan Enterprises, 1934–39, and Burroughs-Tarzan Pictures, 1934–37; lived in California after 1919; Mayor of Malibu Beach, 1933; also United Press Correspondent in the Pacific during World War II, and Columnist ("Laugh It Off"), *Honolulu Advertiser*, 1941–42, 1945. *Died 19 March 1950.*

PUBLICATIONS

Fiction

Tarzan of the Apes. 1914.
The Return of Tarzan. 1915.
The Beasts of Tarzan. 1916.
The Son of Tarzan. 1917.
A Princess of Mars. 1917.
Tarzan and the Jewels of Opar. 1918.
The Gods of Mars. 1918.
Jungle Tales of Tarzan. 1919.
The Warlord of Mars. 1919.
Tarzan the Untamed (stories). 1920.
Thuvia, Maid of Mars. 1920.
Tarzan the Terrible. 1921.
The Mucker (stories). 1921; as *The Mucker* and *The Man Without a Soul* 2 vols., 1922.
The Chessmen of Mars. 1922.
At the Earth's Core. 1922.
Tarzan and the Golden Lion. 1923.
The Girl from Hollywood. 1923.
Pellucidar. 1923.
Tarzan and the Ant Men. 1924.
The Land That Time Forgot (stories). 1924.
The Bandit of Hell's Bend. 1925.
The Eternal Lover (stories). 1925; as *The Eternal Savage*, 1963.
The Cave Girl (stories). 1925.
The Mad King (stories). 1926.
The Moon Maid (stories). 1926; as *The Moon Men*, 1962.
The Tarzan Twins (juvenile). 1927.
The Outlaw of Torn. 1927.

The War Chief. 1927.
Tarzan, Lord of the Jungle. 1928.
The Master Mind of Mars. 1928.
Tarzan and the Lost Empire. 1929.
The Monster Men. 1929.
Tarzan at the Earth's Core. 1930.
Tanar of Pellucidar. 1930.
Tarzan the Invincible. 1931.
A Fighting Man of Mars. 1931.
Tarzan Triumphant. 1932.
Jungle Girl. 1932; as *The Land of Hidden Men*, 1963.
Tarzan and the City of Gold. 1933.
Apache Devil. 1933.
Tarzan and the Lion-Man. 1934.
Pirates of Venus. 1934.
Tarzan and the Leopard Man. 1935.
Lost on Venus. 1935.
Tarzan and the Tarzan Twins with Jad-Bal-Ja, The Golden Lion (juvenile).   1936.
Tarzan's Quest. 1936.
Swords of Mars. 1936.
The Oakdale Affair; The Rider. 1937.
Back to the Stone Age. 1937.
Tarzan and the Forbidden City. 1938.
The Lad and the Lion. 1938.
Tarzan the Magnificent (stories).   1939.
Carson of Venus. 1939.
The Deputy Sheriff of Comanche County. 1940.
Synthetic Men of Mars. 1940.
Land of Terror. 1944.
Escape on Venus (stories).   1946.
Tarzan and the Foreign Legion. 1947.
Llana of Gathol (stories).   1948.
Beyond Thirty (story).   1955.
The Man-Eater (story).   1955.
The Lost Continent (stories).   1963.
Savage Pellucidar (stories).   1963.
Escape on Venus (stories).   1964.
Tales of Three Planets.   1964.
John Carter of Mars (stories).   1964.
Beyond the Farthest Star.   1964.
Tarzan and the Castaways (stories).   1964.
Tarzan and the Madman.   1964.
The Girl from Farris's.   1965.
The Efficiency Expert.   1966.
I Am a Barbarian.   1967.
Pirate Blood.   1970.

Other

Official Guide of the Tarzan Clans of America.   1939.

Reading List: *Explorers of the Infinite* by Sam Moskowitz, 1963; *Burroughs, Master of*

Adventure by Richard A. Lupoff, 1965; *Burroughs, The Man Who Created Tarzan* by Irwin Porges, 1975 (includes bibliography).

* * *

When almost 36 years old, with a wife and three children, disappointed in his military and various business careers, Edgar Rice Burroughs decided to try fiction-writing. His first sale, later printed in hardcovers as *A Princess of Mars*, was serialized in *All-Story Magazine* in 1912. The first of a series still immensely popular, the novel illustrates most of the strengths and weaknesses of his works. Fast-paced, colorful, and often strikingly imaginative, it stimulates the sense of wonder, especially of children and juveniles. The one-dimensional characters are either evil or good, and the use of coincidence is abused. Though his "Barsoomian" cultures are vividly presented, they are not developed in depth. The historical novel that he next wrote, *The Outlaw of Torn*, and his "realistic" stories, notably those of crime and corruption in Chicago and Hollywood, illustrate his failure to be convincing at anything other than fantasy. Tales set on Mars, in darkest Africa, or in earth's centre, worlds which neither he nor his readers knew much about, were never-never lands that he could deal with.

Burroughs is best known as the creator of Tarzan, son of an English nobleman, Lord Greystoke, raised from the age of one in the African jungle by language-using great apes. Critics have maintained that Burroughs wrote *Tarzan of the Apes* to demonstrate his belief in the superiority of heredity over environment, and especially of the superior heredity of the British nobility. In one sense they are correct. Tarzan's human genes gave him an intelligence superior to the apes'; they gave him an innate curiosity and drive which would have taken him out of any ghetto or other underprivileged community he had been born into. But in the final analysis it was the environment which molded Tarzan's character. Raised as a feral child, he is a classic example of the outsider, one who has an objective view of human society because he has not imbibed its irrationalities along with his mother's milk. Through Tarzan's eyes, Burroughs satirizes Homo sapiens, as he did through some of his other heroes, notably Carson Napier of the "Venus" series.

However, Burroughs's ape-man is more than a Voltairean observer or noble savage. Though he regards pre-literates as superior in their way of life to civilized peoples, he is never quite human. He is, when in the jungle, free of the mundane, drab, wearing, and often tragic restrictions of tribal or civilized life. It is his being a law unto himself and his extreme closeness to nature which have been part of his appeal. But Burroughs, though unconsciously, also gave him most of the attributes of the pre-literate and classical hero of fairy tale, legend, and mythology, including the Trickster. He is the last of the Golden Age heroes, a literary character who reflects the archetypal images and feelings of the unconscious mind noted by Carl Jung and Joseph Campbell.

Like Arthur Conan Doyle, Burroughs had the gift of writing adventure stories with an indefinable quality that made them endure while thousands of similar novels dropped into oblivion. Like Doyle he created a classical fictional character of whom he wearied. The later Tarzan novels, in fact all of his works written in the latter part of his career, show a flagging invention, repetitiveness of plot and incident, excess of coincidences and improbabilities, and failure to develop fully promising themes.

He never thought of himself as anything but a commercial writer of romances. His works betray the biases, conservatisms, and timidities of his social class and times, and his style is old-fashioned. With the exception of Tarzan and a few others, his characters are cardboard. His genius was in the creation of the archetypal feral Tarzan and the writing of many pseudo-scientific romances which have enthralled generations of young readers, many of whom have remained loyal to him through their middle age.

—Philip José Farmer

BURROUGHS, William S(eward).   American.   Born in St. Louis, Missouri, 5 February 1914. Educated at Los Alamos Ranch School, New Mexico; Harvard University, Cambridge, Massachusetts, A.B. in anthropology 1936; studied medicine at the University of Vienna, and at Mexico City College, 1948–50. Served in the United States Army, 1942. Married Jean Vollmer in 1945 (died); one son. Has worked as a journalist, private detective, and bartender; now a full-time writer. Heroin addict, 1944–57. Recipient: National Institute of Arts and Letters award, 1975. Lived for many years in Tangier; now lives in New York City.

PUBLICATIONS

Fiction

> *Junkie: Confessions of an Unredeemed Drug Addict,* with *Narcotic Agent,* by Maurice Helbront. 1953.
> *The Naked Lunch.* 1959; as *Naked Lunch,* 1962.
> *The Soft Machine.* 1961.
> *The Ticket That Exploded.* 1962; revised edition, 1963.
> *Dead Fingers Talk.* 1963.
> *Nova Express.* 1964.
> *Speed.* 1970.
> *The Wild Boys: A Book of the Dead.* 1971.
> *Port of Saints.* 1973.
> *Exterminator!* 1974.
> *Short Novels.* 1978.
> *Ah Pook Is Here and Other Texts.* 1978.

Plays

> *The Last Words of Dutch Schultz: A Fiction in the Form of a Film Script.* 1970.
>
> Screenplay: *Towers Open Fire,* 1963.

Verse

> *Minutes to Go: Poems,* with others. 1968.

Other

> *The Exterminator,* with Brion Gysin. 1960.
> *The Yage Letters,* with Allen Ginsberg. 1963.
> *Roosevelt after Inauguration.* 1964.
> *Valentine's Day Reading.* 1965.
> *Time.* 1965.
> *Health Bulletin: APO–33.* 1965.
> *APO–33 Bulletin: A Metabolic Regulator: A Report on the Synthesis of the Amorphine Formula,* edited by Mary Beach and Claude Pelieu. 1966.
> *So Who Owns Death TV?,* with Claude Pelieu and Carl Weissner. 1967.
> *The Dead Star.* 1969.

Ali's Smile. 1969.

Fernseh-Tuberkulose, with Claude Pelieu and Carl Weissner. 1969.

Entretiens avec Burroughs, by Daniel Odier. 1969; translated as *The Job: Interviews with Burroughs,* 1970; revised edition, 1974.

The Third Mind. 1970.

The Braille Film: With a Counterscript by Burroughs, by Carl Weissner. 1970.

Electronic Revolution 1970–71. 1971.

Brion Gysin Let the Mice In, with Brion Gysin and Ian Somerville, edited by Somerville. 1973.

The Electronic Generation. 1973.

White Subway, edited by James Pennington. 1974.

Smack: Two Tape Transcripts, with Eric Mottram. 1975.

Sidetripping, with Charles Gatewood. 1975.

The Book of Breeething. 1976.

Lasers. 1976.

The Third Mind, with Brion Gysin. 1978.

Bibliography: *A Descriptive Catalogue of the Burroughs Archives,* edited by Miles Associates, 1973; *Burroughs: An Annotated Bibliography of His Works and Criticism* by Michael B. Goodman, 1975.

Reading List: *Burroughs: The Algebra of Need* by Eric Mottram, 1971.

* * *

There are two fields of experience central to the life and work of William Burroughs. They mark points at which criticism of his work must begin, and around which controversy has swirled. Scion of the Burroughs Machine family, he has travelled for most of his adult life (only recently settling in New York), during which he became addicted to heroin in 1944, remaining so across three continents and fourteen years. His addiction and cure (the last and presumably final in 1957) have provided the controlling metaphor for an *oeuvre* of cosmic dimensions.

The second area of concern is, like Burroughs's opiate addiction, an extended series of drug experiences. In 1953, he journeyed to the Peruvian Amazon expressly for the purpose of taking *yage,* a mescaline-like natural hallucinogen used sacramentally by the Indians of the region. These and subsequent psychedelic experiences provided not only primary materials for *Naked Lunch, The Soft Machine* and *The Ticket That Exploded,* but served to expand and intensify his vision beyond the relative solipsism of "junk."

For Burroughs's most fervent admirers he has become a cult figure: an international underworld traveller, a gifted teacher, a universal personage reborn, at least partially, from innumerable deaths, returned to speak and write of his experiences. For this group, his life is an example and his writing is a report, a formal statement of an entire life-style. He is a beatific figure, the madman-saint, like de Sade, Artaud, Céline and his contemporary Genet. His life is a message, as Alan Ansen writes unabashedly: "In the case of Burroughs, the writing is only a by-product, however brilliant, of a force. What I am writing is not only a paean to a writer; it is also a variant of hagiography." His detractors are equally enthusiastic: George Garrett speaks for John Wain, George Steiner, Anaïs Nin, and others when he complains: "Do we have to become connoisseurs of vomit? Is the world doing so badly a job at tearing itself apart that it needs the aid of gifted writers to finish it off?"

The indelible image of the heroin addict is presented in Burroughs's first work, *Junkie* – the addict slumped nodding in his chair or out on the street, waiting, making his ruins public. The rhetoric of this small book has the economy and force of needle and spoon, and its initial sociological value is as reportage, in the lucid pictures of the addict world. But more, in the linking of the heroin addict with the metaphysical condition of the "enslaved" condition of modern man, it establishes the single radical image from which Burroughs's "new mythology for the space age" develops.

The Naked Lunch is Burroughs's most famous work. Admitted for publication to the United States after several famous obscenity trials, "composed" with aid from his friends Allen Ginsberg and Jack Kerouac, the novel is a series of fantastic episodes arranged in collage form, the whole being held together by a mantic and comic narrative voice that turns matters inevitably to the theme of human control. *Naked Lunch* becomes increasingly disjointed and surrealistic in technique, and it displays the misogynist/homosexual concerns and the satiric comic vision that have become his signatures.

Subsequent longer works, especially *The Soft Machine* and *The Ticket That Exploded*, have ranged from anthropological pre-history to the uncertain future of dystopian science fiction, but share a predilection for radical linquistic and textual experiment: the "cut-up," the "fold in," and similar dislocations. As revealed in *The Job: Interviews with William Burroughs* (Daniel Odier), Burroughs's recent interests have been less in fiction than in the possibilities for human growth – evidenced especially in his fascination with out-of-body experience and psychobiology. His most recent fiction, *Exterminator!* and *The Wild Boys*, is more accessible than much of his previous work, but no less unsettling. John Tytell, for one, suggests that *The Wild Boys* is Burroughs's best work since *The Naked Lunch*.

The piercing of flesh by the needle, the body by the phallus, the rending of language and – finally – the physical cosmos itself, these are transformations. William Burroughs's endless, cranky linguistic experiments – with cut-ups, fold-ins, the shattering of images, sentences and words, with nightclub routines and carnival "drums" and surreal war and sex fantasies – flawed and confusing as they can be, I see as an attempt to use The Word itself to negate its own power, to lay bare the multiple prisons of corporeal existence, the passage of time, the deceits of language, the illusions of individual consciousness, the endless charades of mass social and political existence.

—Jack Hicks

CABELL, James Branch. American. Born in Richmond, Virginia, 14 April 1879. Educated at the College of William and Mary, Williamsburg, Virginia, A.B. 1898. Married 1) Priscilla Bradley Shepherd in 1939 (died, 1949), one son; 2) Margaret Waller Freeman in 1950. Instructor in Greek and French at the College of William and Mary while an undergraduate, 1896–97; worked in the pressroom of the Richmond, Virginia *Times*, 1898; member of staff of the New York *Herald*, 1899–1901, and the Richmond *News*, 1901; engaged in genealogical research in America and Europe, 1901–11; coal miner in West Virginia, 1911–13; Genealogist for the Virginia Society of Colonial Wars, 1916–28, and the Virginia Sons of the American Revolution, 1917–24; Editor, Virginia War History Commission, 1919–26; silent editor, *The Reviewer*, Richmond, 1921; one of the editors of *The American Spectator*, 1932–35. President, Virginia Writers Association, 1918–21. Member, National Institute of Arts and Letters. *Died 5 May 1958.*

PUBLICATIONS

Collections

The Letters, edited by Edward Wagenknecht. 1975.

Fiction

The Eagle's Shadow.   1904; revised edition, 1923.
The Line of Love (stories).   1905; revised edition, 1921.
Gallantry (stories).   1907; revised edition, 1922.
Chivalry (stories).   1909.
The Cords of Vanity.   1909; revised edition, 1920.
The Soul of Melicent.   1913; revised edition, as Domnei, 1920.
The Rivet in Grandfather's Neck.   1915.
The Certain Hour (stories).   1916.
The Cream of the Jest.   1917; revised edition, 1923.
Beyond Life.   1919.
Jurgen.   1919.
Figures of Earth.   1921.
The High Place.   1923.
The Silver Stallion.   1926.
The Music from Behind the Moon (stories).   1926.
Something about Eve.   1927.
The Works (revised editions).   18 vols., 1927–30.
The White Robe (stories).   1928.
The Way of Ecben.   1929.
Smirt: An Urbane Nightmare.   1934.
Smith: A Sylvan Interlude.   1935.
Smire: An Acceptance in the Third Person.   1937.
The King Was in His Counting House.   1938.
Hamlet Had an Uncle.   1940.
The First Gentleman of America.   1942.
There Were Two Pirates.   1946.
The Witch-Woman (includes The Music from Behind the Moon, The Way of Ecben, The
   White Robe).   1948.
The Devil's Own Dear Son.   1949.

Play

The Jewel Merchants.   1921.

Verse

From the Hidden Way.   1916; revised edition, 1924.
Ballades from the Hidden Way.   1928.
Sonnets from Antan.   1929.

Other

Branchiana (genealogy).   1907.
Branch of Abingdon.   1911.
The Majors and Their Marriages.   1915.
The Judging of Jurgen.   1920.
Jurgen and the Censor.   1920.
Taboo: A Legend Retold from the Dirghic of Saevius Nicanor.   1921.
Joseph Hergesheimer.   1921.

The Lineage of Lichfield: An Essay in Eugenics.   1922.
Straws and Prayer-Books.   1924.
Some of Us: An Essay in Epitaphs.   1930.
Townsend of Lichfield.   1930.
Between Dawn and Sunrise: Selections, edited by John Macy.   1930.
These Restless Heads: A Trilogy of Romantics.   1932.
Special Delivery: A Packet of Replies.   1933.
Ladies and Gentlemen: A Parcel of Reconsiderations.   1934.
Preface to the Past.   1936.
The Nightmare Has Triplets: An Author's Note on Smire.   1937.
On Ellen Glasgow.   1938.
The St. John: A Parade of Diversities.   1943.
Let Me Lie.   1947.
Quiet, Please.   1952.
As I Remember It: Some Epilogues in Recollection.   1955.
Between Friends: Letters of Cabell and Others, edited by Padraic Colum and Margaret
    Freeman Cabell.   1962.

Bibliography: *Cabell: A Complete Bibliography* by James N. Hall, 1974.

Reading List: *No Place on Earth: Ellen Glasgow, Cabell, and Richmond-in-Virginia* by Louis
D. Rubin, Jr., 1959; *Cabell* by Joe Lee Davis, 1962; *Jesting Moses: A Study in Cabellian
Comedy* by Arvin R. Wells, 1962; *Cabell: The Dream and the Reality* by Desmond Tarrant,
1967; *Cabell: Three Essays* by Carl Van Doren, H. L. Mencken, and Hugh Walpole, 1967.

*   *   *

Reckoned in the top echelon of American writers throughout the 1920's, James Branch
Cabell has never regained the prestige he then knew. But even during the decade of his
greatest fame, Cabell was outside the mainstream. While his contemporaries found
increasing fascination with life in their period and used the standard of critical realism to treat
the immediate, Cabell's preference was for romance and myth. He defined his preference
brilliantly in *Beyond Life* and reiterated it in essays and romances throughout his long career.
He avowed "the auctorial virtues of distinction and clarity, of beauty and symmetry, of
tenderness and truth and urbanity."

Cabell's tastes, like his ancestry, were aristocratic and mannered. The elegant prose style he
perfected was appropriate to his Virginia roots and his subject matter. It is ironic that so
cultivated a writer with a specialized appeal became so popular. One important reason was
that Cabell was almost the only sign of hope H. L. Mencken could find that the culture of the
post-Civil War South was not to be damned totally, and Mencken made very loud noises
about Cabell's work. More important was Cabell's novel *Jurgen,* the tale of a medieval
pawnbroker in Cabell's mythical kingdom of Poictesme. Jurgen was ever willing to do the
gentlemanly thing, and word got around that Cabell's book was lascivious. It was suppressed
in 1920, but Cabell's cause rallied the foes of censorship, ensuring booming sales. The novel,
which certainly has its Rabelaisian touches, was exonerated in 1922.

Jurgen is a part of Cabell's most ambitious and most important work, the eighteen-volume
"Biography of the Life of Manuel." Dom Manuel is the founder of Poictesme, and his
followers and offspring (legitimate and otherwise) inherit his legend and face the same
tensions between the dream (the dynamic illusion) and the frustrating reality of everyday life.
The most brilliant of the Romances besides *Jurgen* are *Figures of Earth, The Silver Stallion,
The High Place,* and *Something about Eve.* Cabell revised his earlier Romances of Virginia as
later volumes of the Biography because they, too, were illustrative of the attitudes of

Chivalry, Gallantry, and Poetry treated in the more famous books. Virginia and Poictesme have much in common.

After the completion of the Biography, Cabell published for a time under the name Branch Cabell, to symbolize the completion of his grand design and perhaps in recognition of the end of the era of his greatest fame. During the years of the Great Depression and World War II, Cabell tenaciously followed his own ideals and eschewed the contemporary. A trilogy of high satire (*Smirt, Smith, Smire*) treated the dream life of the writer, mirroring the dream experience more fully than anything Cabell had written previously. Another trilogy dealt with murder, conquest, and intrigue in Hamlet's Denmark, the family circle of Cosimo dei Medici, and the Virginia of Nemattanon, an Indian Prince during the time of the Spanish conquests. A final trilogy explored Florida's legendary past.

Cabell then focused attention on his own life with several volumes of reminiscences and assessments of his career and those of many of his contemporaries. He viewed his progress with humor and detachment. His professed goal was to write beautifully of beautiful happenings. Although he can certainly sting his readers with a sense of reality, it seems clear that writing gave him great joy. He wrote mainly for himself, he tells us, but he did so with such humor and insight that he insures himself a loyal group of enthusiasts.

—Joseph M. Flora

CAIN, James M(allahan). American. Born in Annapolis, Maryland, 1 July 18⁵ Educated at Washington College, Chestertown, Maryland, A.B. 1910, A.M. 1917. Served ɛ a private in the 79th Division of the American Expeditionary Forces, 1918–19; Editor of the *Lorraine Cross*, the official newspaper of the 79th Division, 1919. Married 1) Mary Rebekah Clough in 1920 (divorced); 2) Elina Sjosted Tyszecka in 1927 (divorced); 3) Aileen Pringle in 1944 (divorced); 4) Florence Macbeth Whitwell in 1947 (died). Staff Member, *Baltimore American*, 1917–18; Reporter, *Baltimore Sun*, 1919–23; Professor of Journalism, St. John's College, Annapolis, Maryland, 1923–24; Editorial Writer, *New York World*, 1924–31; full-time writer from 1931; screenwriter, in Hollywood, 1932–48. Recipient: Mystery Writers of America Grand Master Award, 1969. *Died 27 October 1977.*

PUBLICATIONS

Fiction

The Postman Always Rings Twice. 1934.
Serenade. 1937.
Mildred Pierce. 1941.
Love's Lovely Counterfeit. 1942.
Three of a Kind: Career in C Major, The Embezzler, Double Indemnity. 1943.
Past All Dishonor. 1946.
The Butterfly. 1947.
The Sinful Woman. 1947.
The Moth. 1948.
Jealous Woman. 1950.

The Root of His Evil.   1951.
Galatea.   1953.
Mignon.   1962.
The Magician's Wife.   1965.
Rainbow's End.   1975.
The Institute.   1976.

Plays

Hero; Hemp; Red, White, and Blue; Trial by Jury; Theological Interlude; Citizenship; Will of the People (short plays), in *American Mercury* 6 to 29, 1926–29.
The Postman Always Rings Twice, from his own novel (produced 1936).
Algiers (screenplay), with John Howard Lawson, in *Foremost Films of 1938,* edited by Frank Vreeland.   1939.

Screenplays: *Algiers,* with John Howard Lawson, 1938; *Stand Up and Fight,* with others, 1939; *When Tomorrow Comes,* with Dwight Taylor, 1939; *Gypsy Wildcat,* with others, 1944; *Everybody Does It,* with Nunnally Johnson, 1949.

Other

Our Government.   1930.

Editor, *For Men Only: A Collection of Short Stories.*   1944.

Reading List: "Man under Sentence of Death: The Novels of Cain" by Joyce Carol Oates, in *Tough Guy Writers of the Thirties* edited by David Madden, 1967; *Cain* by David Madden 1970.

*   *   *

James M. Cain is the twenty-minute egg of the hard-boiled school. The tough-guy novel made a lasting impact on "serious" American and European fiction; for instance, Albert Camus admitted that *The Postman Always Rings Twice* was a model for *The Stranger.*

Cain has said that he has always had only one story to tell: a love story. "I write of the wish that comes true, for some reason a terrifying concept ... I think my stories have some quality of the opening of a forbidden box." The act of forcing the wish to come true isolates Cain's obsessed lovers from society and places them on what he calls a "love-rack."

If Cain's "heels and harpies" are to consummate and prolong their sexual passion, they must commit a crime. Frank Chambers and Cora in *The Postman* must murder Cora's husband; in *Serenade,* Juana must slaughter Winston Hawes, a homosexual symphony conductor, to ensure the sexual salvation of her lover, Howard Sharp, an opera singer; sex and money are the motives in Walter's and Phyllis's murder of her husband in *Double Indemnity;* in *The Butterfly,* when his apparently incestuous lust for his daughter Kady is threatened, Jess Tyler, a West Virginia farmer, shoots Moke Blue.

In his novels dealing with criminal love, even in his romances *Career in C Major* and *Galatea* and his historical novels *Past All Dishonor* and *Mignon,* Cain effectively dramatizes profound insights into the American character and scene and into the way American dreams degenerate into nightmares. In his novels of character, *Mildred Pierce* and *The Moth,* set in the depression years, his scrutiny is most direct. Physically and often intellectually aggressive, Cain's audacious American male is an inside-dopester equipped with great know-how in many areas (even food, music, and the art of biography); but self-dramatizing inclinations, a suppressed sentimentality, and a misconceived American romanticism and optimism often defeat him. The female is realistic, ruthless, materialistic, and sensitive to minor social taboos even while violating major laws. A deadly pair, they are more often destroyed by their own sexual and materialistic overreaching than by the police. In their total commitment to each other, severing all ties to other people, Cain's lovers experience a blazing, self-consuming flash of self-deceptive purity and hideous innocence.

Without style and technique, Cain's rich and fascinating subject matter, energized by imagination and controlled by formula, would lack sustaining power. A few characters and a simple plot with a first-person narrator – that is the magic combination of a Cain "natural," producing a style like the "metal of an automatic," a pace like "a motorcycle," and a sense of immediacy that hypnotizes the reader. The first person narration enables Cain to use basic technical devices with special skill and appropriateness. His distinctive dialog is especially powerful when it is all of a piece with the cold objectivity and immediacy of the arrogant, commanding first-person voice. Cain, whose conscious intention is to "cast a spell on the beholder," has stated that he developed "the habit of needling a story at the least hint of a breakdown," striving for a "rising coefficient of intensity."

Cain would never use the term "existential," but as a consequence of his primary intention to tell a story superbly well, he has created an objective, disinterested, often pessimistic view of life that is simultaneously terrifying and starkly beautiful.

—David Madden

CALDWELL, Erskine (Preston). American. Born in Moreland, Georgia, 17 December 1903. Educated at Erskine College, Due West, South Carolina, 1920–21; University of Virginia, Charlottesville, 1922, 1925–26; University of Pennsylvania, Philadelphia, 1924. Married 1) Helen Lannigan in 1925 (divorced), two sons and one daughter; 2) the photographer Margaret Bourke-White in 1939 (divorced, 1942); 3) June Johnson in 1942, one son; 4) Virginia Moffett in 1957. Reporter, *Atlanta Journal*, Georgia, 1925; screenwriter in Hollywood, 1930–34, 1942–43; Foreign Correspondent in Mexico, Spain, Czechoslovakia, Russia, and China, 1938–41; Editor, American Folkways series, 1941–55. Member, National Institute of Arts and Letters. Lives in Dunedin, Florida.

PUBLICATIONS

Fiction

The Bastard. 1930.
Poor Fool. 1930.
American Earth (stories). 1931; as *A Swell-Looking Girl*, 1959.
Mama's Little Girl (story). 1932.
Tobacco Road. 1932.
Message for Genevieve (story). 1933.
God's Little Acre. 1933.
We Are the Living: Brief Stories. 1933.

Journeyman.   1935; revised edition, 1938.
Kneel to the Rising Sun and Other Stories.   1935.
The Sacrilege of Alan Kent (story).   1936.
Southways: Stories.   1938.
Trouble in July.   1940.
Jackpot: The Short Stories.   1940.
All Night Long: A Novel of Guerrilla Warfare in Russia.   1942.
Georgia Boy (stories).   1943.
Stories by Caldwell: 24 Representative Stories, edited by Henry Seidel Canby.   1944.
Tragic Ground.   1944.
A House in the Uplands.   1946.
The Caldwell Caravan: Novels and Stories.   1946.
The Sure Hand of God.   1947.
This Very Earth.   1948.
Place Called Estherville.   1949.
Episode in Palmetto.   1950.
A Lamp for Nightfall.   1952.
The Courting of Susie Brown.   1952.
The Complete Stories.   1953.
Love and Money.   1954.
Gretta.   1955.
Gulf Coast Stories.   1956.
Certain Women (stories).   1957.
Claudelle Inglish.   1958.
When You Think of Me (stories).   1959.
Men and Women: 22 Stories.   1961.
Jenny by Nature.   1961.
Close to Home.   1962.
The Last Night of Summer.   1963.
Miss Mama Aimee.   1967.
Summertime Island.   1968.
The Weather Shelter.   1969.
The Earnshaw Neighborhood.   1971.
Annette.   1973.

Plays

Screenplays: *A Nation Dances,* 1943; *Volcano,* 1953.

Other

Tenant Farmer.   1935.
Some American People.   1935.
You Have Seen Their Faces, with Margaret Bourke-White.   1937.
North of the Danube, with Margaret Bourke-White.   1939.
Say! Is This the U.S.A.?, with Margaret Bourke-White.   1941.
All-Out on the Road to Smolensk.   1942; as *Moscow under Fire: A Wartime Diary, 1941,* 1942.
Russia at War, with Margaret Bourke-White.   1942.
The Humorous Side of Caldwell, edited by Robert Cantwell.   1951.
Call It Experience: The Years of Learning How to Write.   1951.
Molly Cottontail (juvenile).   1958.

Around about America. 1964.
In Search of Bisco. 1965.
The Deer at Our House (juvenile). 1966.
In the Shadow of the Steeple. 1967. ˙
Deep South: Memory and Observation (includes *In the Shadow of the Steeple*). 1968.
Writing in America. 1968.
Afternoons in Mid-America. 1976.

Reading List: *The Southern Poor-White from Lubberland to Tobacco Road* by Shields McIlwaine, 1939; *Caldwell* by James Korges, 1969.

*   *   *

The degenerate side of life that Erskine Caldwell exploited so successfully in 1932 in *Tobacco Road* extends back some two hundred years in Southern life, suggesting some kinship between his work and that of the frontier humorists. A hallmark of Caldwell's exploitation of Southern folk and folkways is his use of what Shields McIlwaine calls "idiotic gravity," emanating from characters who are in dead earnest in their sometimes misguided, if not perverted, commitment.

Caldwell's humorous approach to the seaminess and poverty of Southern life, whether in *Tobacco Road*, *God's Little Acre*, or *Georgia Boy*, accounts for his avoidance of the melodramatic and banal. As Robert Cantwell has suggested (*Georgia Review*, 1957), Caldwell's comic treatment of materials makes the poverty of his characters "unforgettable."

In terms of literary tradition, it is Caldwell's Chaucerian treatment of sex that places his novels in the mainstream of the *fabliau*, McIlwaine noting that the author's poor whites like Ty Ty Walden (*God's Little Acre*) and Jeeter Lester (*Tobacco Road*) enjoy the "game of sex without self consciousness." Cantwell, moreover, points out that Caldwell's sexual scenes normally have witnesses – visitors, Negroes peering over fences, etc. – thus suggesting an initiation process. Caldwell's frank treatment of sex marks in the 1930's a major shift in popular literature. After the success of *Tobacco Road* – especially in resisting suppression – similar works by later writers became a staple of commercial fiction. But, with the exception of *Trouble in July* (1940), few of Caldwell's own novels after *God's Little Acre* add to his stature as a creative artist.

In an equally important sense the Caldwell canon owes much to the tradition of naturalism in American writing. Thus Caldwell's characters – oppressed by barren land, mill life, heredity, or other circumstances beyond their control – fail to perceive any solution in flight. The author, moreover, creates with some consistency character after character who is a victim of his heredity and/or environment. Jeeter Lester (*Tobacco Road*), for example, is but the inevitable outcome of one hundred years of family degeneration and disintegration, whereas Ty Ty Walden's degeneracy (*God's Little Acre*) is owed to a "perverted idealism" (McIlwaine).

Current criticism of Caldwell's work, however, places it in the American Gothic vein. The author's use of deformed and sometimes mentally deficient and perverted characters defines his purpose. In *Tobacco Road* one is confronted by a grandmother consumed by pellagra, in *God's Little Acre* by Pluto's obesity, and in *Tragic Ground* by Bubber's permanent grin. Whereas eighteenth and nineteenth-century Gothicists exploited setting and the supernatural as vehicles, both Caldwell and Faulkner turned Southern sociology and misshapen personalities into effective Gothic pronouncements concerning the quality of modern life.

The Complete Stories reveals the author's true métier: Southern settings, disenfranchised

Blacks and poor whites, a depression background. "Candy-Man Beechum," his most frequently anthologized story, presents the artist at his best: passionate in his commitment to social values, primitive in his rhythmic articulation, and genuine in the sense of uncontrolled fate that he evokes.

—George C. Longest

CALISHER, Hortense. American. Born in New York City, 20 December 1911. Educated at Barnard College, New York, A.B. 1932. Married Curtis Harnack in 1959; two children by a previous marriage. Adjunct Professor of English, Barnard College, 1956–57; Visiting Professor, University of Iowa, Iowa City, 1957, 1959–60, Stanford University, California, 1958, Sarah Lawrence College, Bronxville, New York, 1962, and Brandeis University, Waltham, Massachusetts, 1963–64; Adjunct Professor of English, Columbia University, New York, 1968–70; Clark Lecturer, Scripps College, Claremont, California, 1969; Visiting Professor, State University of New York at Buffalo, 1971–72, and Bennington College, Vermont, 1977–78. Recipient: Guggenheim Fellowship, 1952, 1955; Department of State American Specialists grant, 1958; National Institute of Arts and Letters grant, 1967; National Endowment for the Arts Award, 1967. Member, National Institute of Arts and Letters, 1977.

PUBLICATIONS

Fiction

> *In the Absence of Angels: Stories.* 1952.
> *False Entry.* 1962.
> *Tale for the Mirror: A Novella and Other Stories.* 1963.
> *Textures of Life.* 1963.
> *Extreme Magic: A Novella and Other Stories.* 1964.
> *Journal from Ellipsia.* 1965.
> *The Railway Police, and The Last Trolley Ride* (two novellas). 1966.
> *The New Yorkers.* 1969.
> *Queenie.* 1971.
> *Standard Dreaming.* 1972.
> *Eagle Eye.* 1973.
> *The Collected Stories.* 1975.
> *On Keeping Women.* 1977.

Other

> *Herself* (memoir). 1972.

*   *   *

Hortense Calisher may be too demanding to find a wide audience, despite her remarkable perceptions and formidable talent. She marks an elliptical narrative with subtle, verbal humor and penetrating examinations of the heart. The patient reader is always richly rewarded.

Her shorter fiction is probably more successful than her full-length novels. The mandarin precision in the telling is better sustained in "an apocalypse, served in a very small cup," in Calisher's own definition of a story. Her range is astonishing: as serious as children confronting death by way of professional mourners; as levitous as a dinner party at which the women suddenly decide to remove their blouses. In *Extreme Magic* two people suffering from the intensity of emotional scars find solace in each other's pain and memory, singled out for the implication in the title of this novella. In another, *The Railway Police* – which is, perhaps, Calisher's most powerful work – a woman abandons the artificial identity represented by her collection of elaborate wigs in order to face the world with a bald skull.

Textures of Life, an early novel, represents Calisher at her most accessible: a conventional, even romantic plot salvaged from the ordinary by a vast intelligence and compassion. *False Entry* and *The New Yorkers*, loosely connected novels of rich complexity in both plot and narrative, contain brilliant set pieces – the Ku Klux Klan section in the former, the childhood story of a Hungarian immigrant in the latter – but are probably too prolix for most readers. *Journal from Ellipsia*, which "only the uninitiate still call science fiction," has an interplanetary Gulliver as heroine and sometime narrator. *Queenie*, a verbal *tour de force*, is Calisher's sexual fable in answer to Portnoy, by way of Colette and a 1970's bawdy of immaculate taste.

Calisher's autobiography, *Herself*, discloses less about Calisher than about her view of art, including, in "Pushing Around the Pantheon," an entertaining and enlightening discussion of sexuality in literature in relation to the masculine and feminine roles tradition has imposed on writers. "The magic is in her writing," Marya Mannes has written, "the marvel is in her range."

—Bruce Kellner

CAPOTE, Truman. American. Born in New Orleans, Louisiana, 30 September 1924. Educated at Trinity School and St. John's Academy, New York; Greenwich High School, Connecticut. Worked in the Art Department, also wrote for "Talk of the Town," *The New Yorker* magazine; now a full-time writer. Recipient: O. Henry Award, 1946, 1948, 1951; National Institute of Arts and Letters grant, 1959; Edgar Allan Poe Award, 1966; Emmy Award, for television adaptation, 1967. Member, National Institute of Arts and Letters. Lives in New York City.

PUBLICATIONS

Fiction

Other Voices, Other Rooms. 1948.
A Tree of Night and Other Stories. 1949.
The Grass Harp. 1951.
Breakfast at Tiffany's: A Short Novel and 3 Stories. 1958.
A Christmas Memory. 1966.

Plays

The Grass Harp (produced 1952).   1952.
House of Flowers, music by Harold Arlen (produced 1954).   1968.
The Thanksgiving Visitor.   1968.
Trilogy: An Experiment in Multimedia, with Eleanor Perry.   1969.

Screenplays: *Beat the Devil*, with John Huston 1953; *Indiscretion of an American Wife*, with others, 1954; *The Innocents*, with William Archibald and John Mortimer, 1961; *Trilogy*, with Eleanor Perry, 1969.

Other

Local Color.   1950.
The Muses Are Heard: An Account.   1956.
Observations, with Richard Avedon.   1959.
Selected Writings, edited by Mark Schorer.   1963.
In Cold Blood: A True Account of a Multiple Murder and Its Consequences.   1966.
The Dogs Bark: Public People and Private Places.   1973.
Then It All Came Down: Criminal Justice Today Discussed by Police, Criminals, and Correction Officers, with Comments by Capote.   1976.

Reading List: *The Worlds of Capote* by William L. Nance, 1970.

*   *   *

Few contemporary writers project a public image as compelling or as enduring as that of Truman Capote. John W. Aldridge in *After the Lost Generation*, for example, compared the popular image of Capote to that of Hemingway and Byron, noting that the author's publishers exploited him in order to reinforce the reader's "impression of fragile aestheticism" evident in his works. Certainly Capote's personal idiosyncrasies and the superficial effects of the style and atmosphere of his work have done much to enhance his popular following.

Although the art of Truman Capote speaks directly to his own day and age, the best of it is rooted in nineteenth-century American literary traditions reflected in Hawthorne and James. Like Hawthorne, for example, his work focuses upon the dichotomy of good and evil, light and dark. Capote's craft, moreover, is that of the romance as defined by James. Dream symbolism adds to the gothic impact of the author's resonance.

Recent critics have tended to divide Capote's works into two fictional modes, the nocturnal and the daylight, or the dark and the light. The light Capote fiction tends to take place in a public world (*The Grass Harp*) and reveals an often aggressive social order. The daylight fiction, moreover, is keynoted by a realistic, colloquial, often funny, first-person narrative (*Breakfast at Tiffany's*). The nocturnal, by contrast, is manifest in the dreamlike, detached, inverted, third-person narrative focusing on an inner complex world, often approaching the surreal as in *Other Voices, Other Rooms*.

Because of the romance tradition implicit in his work, Capote's characters are rooted in gothic narcissism. As an instance of that narcissism, a major Capote theme is the discovery of one's *real* identity. In the author's use of the supernatural, a character often confronts his alter ego, as in *Other Voices, Other Rooms*. The tree house in *The Grass Harp* becomes a place for wish fulfilment, a refuge for fighting off the hypocrisy of the social order. Even Holly Golightly's rebellion in *Breakfast at Tiffany's* suggests a degree of self-love. The more recent

In Cold Blood emphasizes the nocturnal motif, the use of the modern Gothic, and the skillful manipulation of narcissus. This last book, an experiment with what has been called the non-fiction novel, is an excellent example of Capote's skillful penetration of the nightmarish enigma of evil, suggesting again his kinship to Hawthorne, Melville, and James.

—George C. Longest

CATHER, Willa (Sibert). American. Born in Back Creek Valley, near Winchester, Virginia, 7 December 1873; moved with her family to a farm near Red Cloud, Nebraska, 1883. Educated at Red Cloud High School, graduated 1890; preparatory school in Lincoln, Nebraska, 1891; University of Nebraska, Lincoln, 1891–95, B.A. 1895. Member of the editorial staff, *Home Monthly,* Pittsburgh, 1896; Telegraph Editor and Drama Critic, *Pittsburgh Leader,* 1897–1901; Latin and English Teacher, Central High School, Pittsburgh, 1901–03; English Teacher, Allegheny High School, Pittsburgh, 1903–06; Editor, *McClure's Magazine,* New York, 1906–12; full-time writer from 1912. Recipient: Pulitzer Prize, 1923; Howells Medal, 1930; Prix Femina Américaine, 1933; National Institute of Arts and Letters Gold Medal, 1944. Litt.D.: University of Nebraska, 1917; University of Michigan, Ann Arbor, 1922; Columbia University, New York, 1928; Yale University, New Haven, Connecticut, 1929; Princeton University, New Jersey, 1931; D.L.: Creighton University, Omaha, Nebraska, 1928; University of California, Berkeley, 1931. Member, American Academy of Arts and Letters. *Died 24 April 1947.*

PUBLICATIONS

Fiction

The Troll Garden (stories). 1905.
Alexander's Bridge. 1912.
O Pioneers! 1913.
The Song of the Lark. 1915.
My Antonia. 1918.
Youth and the Bright Medusa. 1920.
One of Ours. 1922.
A Lost Lady. 1923.
The Professor's House. 1925.
My Mortal Enemy. 1926.
Death Comes for the Archbishop. 1927.
Shadows on the Rock. 1931.
The Fear That Walks by Noonday (stories). 1931.
Obscure Destinies (stories). 1932.
Lucy Gayheart. 1935.
Novels and Stories. 13 vols., 1937–41.

Sapphira and the Slave Girl.   1940.
The Old Beauty and Others.   1948.
Early Stories, edited by Mildred R. Bennett.   1957.
Collected Short Fiction 1892–1912, edited by Virginia Faulkner.   1965.
Uncle Valentine and Other Stories: Uncollected Fiction 1915–29, edited by Bernice
    Slote.   1973.

Verse

April Twilights.   1903.
April Twilights and Other Poems.   1923; revised edition, 1933; edited by Bernice Slote,
    1962.

Other

My Autobiography, by S. S. McClure.   1914 (ghost-written by Cather).
Not Under Forty.   1936.
On Writing: Critical Studies on Writing as an Art.   1949.
Writings from Cather's Campus Years, edited by James R. Shively.   1950.
Cather in Europe: Her Own Story of the First Journey, edited by George N.
    Kates.   1956.
The Kingdom of Art: Cather's First Principles and Critical Principles 1893–1896, edited
    by Bernice Slote.   1966.
The World and the Parish: Cather's Articles and Reviews 1893–1902, edited by William
    M. Curtin.   2 vols., 1970.

Editor, *The Life of Mary Baker G. Eddy, and the History of Christian Science,* by
    Georgine Milmine.   1909.
Editor, *The Best Stories of Sarah Orne Jewett.*   2 vols., 1925.

Bibliography: *Cather: A Checklist of Her Published Writing* by JoAnna Lothrop, 1975.

Reading List: *Cather: A Critical Introduction* by David Daiches, 1951; *Cather: A Critical
Biography* by E. K. Brown, completed by Leon Edel, 1953; *The World of Cather* by Mildred
R. Bennett, 1961; *Cather* by Dorothy Van Ghent, 1964; *Cather and Her Critics* edited by
James Schroeter, 1967; *Cather: Her Life and Art* by James Woodress, 1970; *Cather: A
Pictorial Memoir* by Bernice Slote, 1973; *Cather's Imagination* by David Stouck, 1975;
Cather by Philip L. Gerber, 1975.

*   *   *

Willa Cather, who now can be ranked as one of the most important American woman
writers of the first half of this century, is best known for her novels and stories depicting the
early years of Nebraska. Her range is considerably broader, however, and also includes
notable work laid in the American Southwest, Quebec, and Virginia. Her reputation is based
on an extraordinary ability to capture the sense of place and a meticulous craftsmanship that
combines a very clear prose style with effective use of myth and symbol. In an age when
authors were increasingly able to exploit their literary talents in the market-place Cather
displayed an awesome dedication to her art. She wrote slowly and carefully, consistently
refused to allow her works to be anthologized, dramatized, or sold in paperback editions, and

when she died she had produced twelve novels and at least 55 stories of consistently high quality.

Cather served a long literary apprenticeship before she was able to cut loose from journalism and devote her time exclusively to writing. Her ideas and values, however, were formed early, as the recently published volumes of her early newspaper writings show. During her early years of journalism and teaching she wrote mostly short fiction, producing 45 stories before 1912, when she resigned from her editorship of *McClure's Magazine*. These stories, which show a slowly maturing talent, explore themes and subjects that she later employed in her novels. Her first book, however, was *April Twilights*, a volume of verse published while she was teaching high school in Pittsburgh. Her first fiction was a collection of stories, *The Troll Garden*. These stories deal in various ways with the artist and society and show a strong Jamesian influence. They also make use of western material, particularly "A Sculptor's Funeral" and "A Wagner Matinee," but the tone of these last is more akin to the revolt-from-the-village strain in early 20th-century American literature than Cather's later work celebrating the land in novels like *O Pioneers!* and *My Ántonia*.

In 1911 Cather took a leave from *McClure's* and wrote "The Bohemian Girl," a long story that uses for the first time in a nostalgic and affirmative manner the memories of her early years on a Nebraska farm and in the prairie village of Red Cloud. She blends a realistic use of detail with a romantic sensibility in a very successful story that encouraged her to plunge into full-length novels of the same genre. Even before writing "The Bohemian Girl," however, she had published her first novel, *Alexander's Bridge*, but, despite the fact that it is a well-written work of considerable interest, she later deprecated the book and regarded it as a false start. The novel is very Jamesian, takes place in Boston and London, and concerns a bridge-builder whose bridge, like his character, contains a fatal flaw. The story ends with the collapse of the bridge and the death of the protagonist.

O Pioneers!, *The Song of the Lark*, *My Ántonia*, *One of Ours*, and *A Lost Lady* are laid entirely or in part in Nebraska, and form the basis for Cather's identification with that part of the United States. It is important to note that she began using this material nearly two decades after she had left Nebraska to live in the East. By then the youthful experience was ripe and ready for artistic employment. In a 1925 introduction to the stories of Sarah Orne Jewett, who had been her friend and a literary influence, she quoted from a letter from Jewett: "The thing that teases the mind over and over for years, and at last gets itself put down rightly on paper – whether little or great, it belongs to literature." This was a literary principle in which Cather thoroughly believed, and it places Cather closer to Wordsworth with his view of poetry as "emotion recollected in tranquility" than it does to the realists or naturalists of the late 19th and early 20th centuries like Howells, Garland, or Dreiser, who "worked up" their materials.

O Pioneers! is the story of Alexandra Bergson, a Swedish immigrant who tames the wild land in the pioneer days of Nebraska. Alexandra's life is a success story told with a loving affirmation of the beauty of the land and the value of the pioneer struggle. The novel is not all light, however, as two of Alexandra's brothers turn out to be mean-spirited materialists and her beloved younger brother dies at the hand of a Czech farmer whose wife he has fallen in love with. *The Song of the Lark* combines Cather's memories of her young life in Red Cloud with her great interest in music and in particular the Wagnerian soprano Olive Fremstad, who had grown up in an immigrant family in Minnesota. Thus the youth of the singer is Cather's own youth and the career of the artist is a fictionalized biography of Olive Fremstad. *My Ántonia*, regarded by many readers as Cather's best novel, creates a memorable character in a Bohemian immigrant heroine who had her prototype in a childhood friend. This story is told retrospectively by a male narrator whose experience growing up on a farm and in the town of Black Hawk (Red Cloud) parallels Cather's own life. Again the same sense of place is evoked memorably, and the land and its pioneer settlers are presented with a haunting nostalgia. The book is episodic in character, which is typical of Cather, and contains stories within stories. The novel is carefully constructed, however, and given an organic form that suits the material.

One of Ours is less successful, though the early parts of the novel laid in Nebraska create a vivid picture of life on a Nebraska farm and in a college town like Lincoln where Cather attended the university. The story was suggested by the life of her cousin who was killed in France during the First World War. Ironically, this novel won a Pulitzer Prize and brought Cather handsome royalties for the first time. She returned to an all-Nebraska setting in *A Lost Lady*, and again evoked childhood memories in the creation of Captain and Mrs. Forrester, the chief characters. The setting is again a fictionalized Red Cloud, and the story of the lost lady, who is a sort of Nebraskan Emma Bovary, is told from the perspective of a boy growing up in the small town. This novel demonstrates the literary technique that Cather explains in her essay "The Novel Démeublé." It is a work of about 50,000 words in which all the excess detail is stripped away. "The higher processes of art are all processes of simplification," she wrote. She also was fond of quoting Dumas *père*, who once had said that to make a drama all "a man needed [was] one passion, and four walls."

The Professor's House is a different sort of novel from the Nebraska stories. It's the tale of a middle-aged professor of history who loses the will to live and barely escapes death. Although he had won an important literary prize and apparently had everything to live for, he is profoundly depressed by the materialism of his family and his culture. There is a good deal of autobiography in this novel, for Cather, too, felt that for her "the world broke in two in 1922 or thereabouts." There is a long tale inserted in the middle of this novel, "Tom Outland's Story," that evokes the ancient civilization of the Mesa Verde Indians in sharp contrast to the 1920's and also reflects Cather's growing interest in the Southwest.

Her most significant use of the Southwest came two years later in *Death Comes for the Archbishop*, the novel that she thought her best. It creates in episodic form the life of Jean Latour, the first bishop of New Mexico. She long had been fascinated by the story of the Catholic church in the Southwest, and had begun visiting the area as early as 1912. When she ran across a letter collection that gave her a clear account of the real Bishop Lamy's career in New Mexico in the 19th century, she found her story and produced a distinguished historical novel. Much of the detail is fiction and it is romanticized, but the material does not do violence to history or to the historical characters it recreates. The work represents Cather at the peak of her creative powers.

Two more historical novels followed, *Shadows on the Rock* and *Sapphira and the Slave Girl*, and Cather after 1927 seemed to take refuge in writing about the past. *Shadows* is a story of Quebec at the end of the 17th century, a novel that is dramatically thin but pictorially rich. *Sapphira*, the only novel Cather ever wrote about her native Virginia, takes place in the Shenandoah Valley before the Civil War and deals with an incident of family history, her grandmother's successful efforts to help a slave escape to Canada.

—James Woodress

CHANDLER, Raymond (Thornton). American. Born in Chicago, Illinois, 23 July 1888; moved to England with his mother; naturalized British subject, 1907; again became an American citizen, 1956. Educated in a local school in Upper Norwood, London; Dulwich College, London, 1900–05; studied in France and Germany, 1905–07. Served in the Canadian Army, 1917–18, and in the Royal Air Force, 1918–19. Married Pearl Cecily Hurlburt in 1924 (died, 1954). Worked in the supply and accounting departments of the Admiralty, London, 1907; Reporter for the *Daily Express*, London, and the *Western Gazette*, Bristol, 1908–12; returned to the United States, 1912; worked in St. Louis, then on a ranch and in a sporting goods firm in California; accountant and bookkeeper at the Los Angeles

Creamery, 1912–17; worked in a bank in San Francisco, 1919; worked for the *Daily Express*, Los Angeles, 1919; Bookkeeper, then Auditor, Dabney Oil Syndicate, Los Angeles, 1922–32; full-time writer from 1933. President, Mystery Writers of America, 1959. Recipient: Edgar Allan Poe Award, 1946, 1955. *Died 26 March 1959.*

PUBLICATIONS

Fiction

The Big Sleep. 1939.
Farewell, My Lovely. 1940.
The High Window. 1942.
The Lady in the Lake. 1943.
Five Murderers (stories). 1944.
Five Sinister Characters (stories). 1945.
Finger Man and Other Stories. 1946.
The Little Sister. 1949.
The Simple Art of Murder (stories). 1950.
The Long Goodbye. 1953.
Playback. 1958.
Killer in the Rain (stories). 1964.

Plays

Double Indemnity, with Billy Wilder, in *Best Film Plays 1945*, edited by John Gassner and Dudley Nichols. 1946.
The Blue Dahlia (screenplay). 1976.

Screenplays: *And Now Tomorrow*, with Frank Partos, 1944; *Double Indemnity*, with Billy Wilder, 1944; *The Unseen*, with Hagar Wilde and Ken Englund, 1945; *The Blue Dahlia*, 1946; *Strangers on a Train*, with Czenzi Ormonde and Whitfield Cook, 1951.

Other

Chandler Speaking, edited by Dorothy Gardiner and Kathrine Sorley Walker. 1962.
Chandler Before Marlowe: Chandler's Early Prose and Poetry 1908–1912, edited by Matthew J. Bruccoli. 1973.
The Notebooks of Chandler, and English Summer: A Gothic Romance, edited by Frank MacShane. 1976.

Bibliography: *Chandler: A Checklist* by Matthew J. Bruccoli, 1968.

Reading List: *Down These Mean Streets a Man Must Go* by Philip Durham, 1963; *Chandler on Screen* by Stephen Pendo, 1976; *The Life of Chandler* by Frank MacShane, 1976.

*   *   *

Raymond Chandler first attempted a literary career in London in his early twenties, when he unsuccessfully tried to establish himself as a poet and critic. Twenty years later, after losing his important job with an oil company because of his drinking, he tried again, writing stories for pulp magazines, notably *Black Mask*. This time he was immediately successful, and, along with Dashiell Hammett, became the principal champion of the "hard-boiled" school of detective fiction.

Chandler was scornful of the English school of detective fiction which, as he said in a famous remark, was an "affair of the upper classes, the week-end house party and the vicar's rose garden." He believed that crime fiction should deal with real criminals and should employ the language actually used by murderers and policemen. Chandler used what he called the "objective method" which assures authenticity. At the same time, his work has a strong emotional center that is capable of illuminating "an utterly unexpected range of sensitivity."

In 1939, he published *The Big Sleep*, his first novel. In quick succession he published *Farewell, My Lovely*, *The High Window*, and *The Lady in the Lake*, reworking material from his earlier stories. Chandler's novels are narrated by the central character, Philip Marlowe, an idealistic and romantic detective who is also tough and cynical. The books are dramatic and funny: Chandler's prose is formal but his vocabulary is full of the slang of his characters. The prose is a mirror of the political and financial corruption that lies under the bland surface of California life. Chandler was the first to give Los Angeles a literary identity.

During the 1940's and early 1950's, Chandler wrote movie scripts in Hollywood, notably *Double Indemnity* (with Billy Wilder), *The Blue Dahlia*, and *Strangers on a Train*. Chandler disliked Hollywood, but earned enough money to retire with his wife, Cissy, to La Jolla, where he returned to fiction, writing *The Little Sister* and his most ambitious novel, *The Long Goodbye*. This book is a conscious effort to stretch the conventions of the detective novel so as to convert it into a general work of fiction. It brings crime fiction to the highest level it has attained in modern times. Chandler also wrote an essay, "The Simple Art of Murder," which places his work in the context of other crime novelists. It attempts to justify his blend of idealism and realism and may be considered his literary testament. He also wrote incisively about Hollywood.

Following the death of his wife, Chandler spent much time in England, where he became a celebrity, acknowledged as a master of contemporary fiction. Nevertheless, he was lonely and withdrawn, and succeeded in writing only one further novel, *Playback*. Since his death his stature has continued to grow, and he is now generally considered to be among the most important American novelists of his time.

—Frank MacShane

CHAYEFSKY, Paddy. American. Born Sidney Chayefsky in the Bronx, New York, 29 January 1923. Educated at DeWitt Clinton High School, Bronx, graduated 1939; City College of New York, B.S. 1943. Served as a Private First Class in the United States Army, 1943–45: Purple Heart. Married Susan Sackler in 1949; one son. President, Sudan Productions, New York, 1956, and Carnegie Productions, New York, 1957. Since 1959, President of S.P.D. Productions; since 1967, President of Sidney Productions; since 1971, President of Simcha Productions – all New York. Since 1962, Member of the Council of the

Dramatists Guild. Recipient: Screen Writers Guild Best Screenplay Award, 1954, 1971; Academy Award, 1955, 1972; New York Film Critics Award, 1956, 1971; Cannes Film Festival Award, 1955; Brussels, Venice and Edinburgh film festivals awards, 1958. Lives in New York City.

PUBLICATIONS

Plays

> *Printer's Measure* (televised 1953). In *Television Plays*, 1955.
> *Middle of the Night* (televised 1954; revised version, produced 1956). 1957.
> *Televison Plays* (includes *The Bachelor Party, The Big Deal, Holiday Song, Marty, The Mother,* and *Printer's Measure*). 1955.
> *The Bachelor Party* (screenplay). 1957.
> *The Goddess* (screenplay; stage version produced 1971). 1958.
> *The Tenth Man* (produced 1959). 1960.
> *Gideon* (produced 1961). 1962.
> *The Passion of Josef D* (produced 1964). 1964.
> *The Latent Heterosexual* (produced 1968). 1967.

> Screenplays: *As Young as You Feel,* with Lamar Trotti, 1951; *Marty,* 1955; *The Bachelor Party,* 1957; *The Goddess,* 1958; *Middle of the Night,* 1959; *The Americanization of Emily,* with Alan Jay Lerner, 1964; *Paint Your Wagon,* 1969; *The Hospital,* 1971; *Network,* 1975.

> Television Plays: *Holiday Song,* 1952; *The Reluctant Citizen,* 1953; *Printer's Measure,* 1953; *Marty,* 1953; *The Big Deal,* 1953; *The Bachelor Party,* 1953; *The Sixth Year,* 1953; *Catch My Boy on Sunday,* 1953; *The Mother,* 1954; *Middle of the Night,* 1954; *The Catered Affair,* 1955.

Fiction

> *Altered States.* 1978.

*   *   *

Paddy Chayefsky was nurtured in television. There, he says, he learned to concentrate on "small moments in people's lives" and no more than "four people at the same time. TV drama cannot expand in breadth, so it must expand in depth." His first TV drama, *Holiday Song,* was set in a synagogue and based on a *Reader's Digest* story. The next year he was even more successful with *Marty*: the *New Yorker* described it as the story of "a shy, portly, and homely butcher of thirty-four, whose chief problem in life is to find a girl" (calling the plot "not only simple but even outlandish"). But Chayefsky, as he said, was "determined to shatter the shallow and destructive illusions ... that love is simply a matter of physical attraction."

Harriet Van Horne, TV critic for the *New York World Telegram and Sun,* thought Chayefsky "as important to television drama in the 1950's as was Ibsen to the stage in the 1890's. He has broken new ground, introduced a new realism, and resolutely turned his back on some of the old, constricting conventions" (27 July 1955). The famous "tape-recorder" ear for dialogue helped a great deal to make Chayefsky's reputation, but it was nothing new. It was Bronx Odets without quite so much pretension, and was familiar from Arthur Laurents's *Home of the Brave* (1946). Walter Kerr commented in his pointed *How Not to Write a Play* (1955): "He is on the side of the angels; so am I. He is going to develop his argument along certain lines; I know them. He is going to complete his charge to the jury in a burst of warm rhetoric; I can recite it in my sleep."

More recently, in films like *Hospital* and *Network*, Chayefsky has adopted still another device which connects him with television, the commercial, and indeed the television commercial. The larger screen has enabled him, in several ways, to turn up the volume.

The still minor art of television drama derived much benefit from this minor playwright. That he works long and hard and deftly with inarticulate characters and semi-hysterical situations is interesting. But what increasingly emerges is that he has really very little to say.

—Leonard R. N. Ashley

CHEEVER, John. American. Born in Quincy, Massachusetts, 27 May 1912. Educated at the Thayer Academy. Served in the United States Army in World War II. Married Mary M. Winternitz in 1941; one daughter and two sons. Taught at Barnard College, New York, 1956–57; Visiting Professor of Creative Writing, Boston University, 1974–75. Recipient: Guggenheim Fellowship, 1951; Benjamin Franklin Award, 1955; O. Henry Award, 1956, 1964; National Institute of Arts and Letters grant, 1956; National Book Award, 1958; Howells Medal, 1965. Member, National Institute of Arts and Letters. Lives in Ossining, New York.

PUBLICATIONS

Fiction

The Way Some People Live: A Book of Stories. 1943.
The Enormous Radio and Other Stories. 1953.
The Wapshot Chronicle. 1957.
The Housebreaker of Shady Hill and Other Stories. 1958.
Some People, Places, and Things That Will Not Appear in My Next Novel. 1961.
The Brigadier and the Golf Widow (stories). 1964.
The Wapshot Scandal. 1964.
Bullet Park. 1969.
The World of Apples (stories). 1973.
Falconer. 1977.
The Stories. 1978.

Reading List: *Cheever* by Samuel Coale, 1977.

*   *   *

John Cheever has made his mark as a chronicler of a modern American sensibility that is well-educated, disoriented, and generally bitter toward the situations, sexual and cultural, in which it finds itself. That sensibility is usually represented as able to look back on an earlier generation in which moral codes were fixed and confident; that fixity and confidence almost constitute a romantic backdrop against which the frustrations of current life play out their inconclusive courses. These courses are often presented in short stories which combine the irony of sheer event with Cheever's own comments on what is happening – happening to persons who endure the events rather than understand them. For example, one story, "The Swimmer" (in *The Brigadier and the Golf Widow*), illustrates the texture and scope of many a Cheever tale. A man decides, for reasons that he does not clearly understand, to reach his home by swimming through all the private pools that extend toward his own home and pool. In the course of his feat, no more sensible than climbing the Himalayas, the swimmer has contact, ironic for Cheever and his readers, with several aspects of the swimmer's society. And at the end, the swimmer arrives at his own pool, only to find his own house empty; there is no explanation of this shocking conclusion. The man's dismay is but an intensification of the pressures that set him on his way.

Novels allow Cheever to explore at greater length destinies no more controlled and intelligible than the afternoon efforts of the swimmer. Two closely related novels, *The Wapshot Chronicle* and *The Wapshot Scandal*, represent the decline of a "good family" in a small New England community; the modest certainties of an older generation ravel out in the adventures of two sons as they wander from job to job and from one sexual relation to another. Stories loosely connected with the fates of the two young men ornament the novels and illustrate the impact of conspicuous wealth, American go-getting, scientific research, and the soft life that lies in wait for most Cheever characters. *Bullet Park* presents these themes with more rigor as they apply to two men, Hammer and Nailles. In Nailles appears a man who is fairly content with the disintegrating Zion where he finds himself. In Hammer, Cheever offers a man whose wealth and success create in him only a nameless bitterness. It is a bitterness that leads Hammer to an envy of the complacent Nailles, whose unconsidered contentment he tries to destroy; Hammer attempts to crucify Nailles' son.

Is this the end of the road? *Falconer* seems to say "Not necessarily." Farragut, the hero of this novel, has one of the bitterest experiences that Cheever has contrived. The man is a drug addict who has been sent to prison for the murder of his brother. In a highly unified narrative, Farragut experiences the heartless pressures of the prison system, goes through the routine inhumanity, homosexuality, and sheer boredom of prison life – and has enough energy left to contrive his escape into a world whose qualities are not necessarily superior to the concentrated hell of the prison. Farragut's will to persist, to continue in a life made up of the absurdities that society and fate and Cheever contrive, sums up the counsel that Cheever offers. It is a counsel offered with a skill that is ingenious and deft; it is a counsel immersed in an auctorial consciousness that is condescending rather than sympathetic.

—Harold H. Watts

CHURCHILL, Winston. American. Born in St. Louis, Missouri, 10 November 1871. Educated at Smith Academy, St. Louis, 1879–88; United States Naval Academy, Annapolis, Maryland, 1890–94; naval cadet on the cruiser *San Francisco*, New York Navy Yard, 1894. Married Mabel Harlakenden Hall in 1895 (died, 1945); one daughter and two sons. Editor, *Army and Navy Journal*, New York, 1894; Managing Editor, *Cosmopolitan* magazine, New York, 1895; full-time writer from 1895; served as Republican Member of the New

Hampshire Legislature for Cornish, 1903–05, and as Delegate for New Hampshire, Republican National Convention, Chicago, 1904; Progressive Party Candidate for the New Hampshire governorship, 1912; toured European battle fronts, and wrote for *Scribner's* magazine, New York, 1917–18. President, Authors League of America, 1913. *Died 12 March 1947.*

PUBLICATIONS

Fiction

The Celebrity: An Episode. 1898.
Richard Carvel. 1899.
The Crisis. 1901.
Mr. Keegan's Elopement (stories). 1903.
The Crossing. 1904.
Coniston. 1906.
Mr. Crewe's Career. 1908.
A Modern Chronicle. 1910.
The Inside of the Cup. 1913.
A Far Country. 1915.
The Dwelling-Place of Light. 1917.
The Faith of Frances Craniford (story). 1917.

Plays

The Title-Mart (produced 1905). 1905.
Dr. Jonathan. 1919.

Other

A Traveller in War-Time, with an Essay on the American Contribution and the Democratic Idea. 1918.
The Green Bay Tree. 1920.
The Uncharted Way: The Psychology of the Gospel Doctrine. 1940.

Reading List: *The Romantic Compromise in the Novels of Churchill* by Charles C. Walcutt, 1951; *Churchill* by Warren I. Titus, 1963.

*   *   *

Winston Churchill was a gifted storyteller who became very popular with well-researched but episodic romances concerning the American Revolution in *Richard Carvel*, the Civil War in *The Crisis*, and the settlement of Tennessee and Kentucky in *The Crossing*. Drawing upon his personal experience as a legislator and candidate for gubernatorial nomination in New Hampshire, Churchill then became a more serious social critic in *Coniston*, a novel about political bossism. The boss, Jethro Bass (based on a real political figure, Ruel Durkee), is a complex mixture of good and evil who in part manipulates the system, and is in part a product of it. He is probably Churchill's best developed and most human character. *Mr.*

Crewe's Career does not so much concern the bumbling political efforts of the amateur politician Humphrey Crewe (said by Churchill to be a self-satire) as it concerns the corrupting influence of the railroad and other industries on the state legislature and the courts. Churchill mars these two novels by resolving the conflicts with a marriage between a daughter and a son of the opposing major figures. Although this device was supposed to show how the dynamism of industry could be combined with the idealism of politics, it actually leaves the essential differences of the two views unsettled, and reflects Churchill's mild "Progressive" approach in these novels (he was a friend and admirer of Roosevelt's).

Churchill first evidenced in his fiction a concern for religion in *The Inside of the Cup*, a novel which concerns a clergyman of an unspecified persuasion (Churchill was an active Episcopal layman) who comes to see the necessity for preaching a social gospel rather than a purely "spiritual" one. Although he meets resistance from a slum-landlord in his congregation, the minister makes many converts to his position and remains in the good graces of his church. The novel is therefore less hard-hitting than, say, Sheldon's *In His Steps*. *A Far Country* deals even more forcefully with the conflict Churchill saw between Christianity and capitalism and with society's ill-treatment of unwed mothers. Churchill lent his pen to the propaganda effort during the First World War, but immediately afterward returned in *Dr. Jonathan* to call for more social justice and a more equitable distribution of wealth.

Churchill's popularity had been declining gradually since he forsook the historical romance, but in 1920 he found himself almost without an audience. He then devoted twenty years to research in psychology and theology before publishing a non-fiction reinterpretation of the world and of the Bible, *The Uncharted Way*. Churchill did not think his analysis of history as the conflict between the "moral" self and the "technical" self, the generous and selfish side of each man, would be immediately understood, but looked to future generations for vindication.

—William Higgins

CLARK, Walter Van Tilburg. American. Born in East Orland, Maine, 3 August 1909. Educated at the University of Nevada, Reno, B.A. 1931, M.A. 1932; University of Vermont, Burlington, M.A. 1934. Married Barbara Frances Morse in 1933 (died), one son and one daughter. Taught in high schools in Cazenovia and Rye, New York, 1936–45; Associate Professor of English, University of Montana, Missoula, 1953–56; Professor of English and Creative Writing, San Francisco State College, 1956–62; Fellow in Fiction, Center for Advanced Studies, Wesleyan University, Middletown, Connecticut, 1960–61; Writer-in-Residence, University of Nevada, 1962–71. Recipient: O. Henry Award, 1945. D.Litt.: Colgate University, Hamilton, New York, 1958; University of Nevada, 1969. Died 11 November 1971.

PUBLICATIONS

Fiction

The Ox-Bow Incident. 1940.

The City of Trembling Leaves. 1945; as *Tim Hazard*, 1951.
The Track of the Cat. 1949.
The Watchful Gods and Other Stories. 1950.

Verse

Christmas Comes to Hjalsen, Reno. 1930.
Ten Women in Gale's House and Shorter Poems. 1932.

Other

Editor, *The Journals of Alfred Doten, 1849–1903.* 3 vols., 1974.

Bibliography: "Clark: A Bibliography" by Richard Etulain, in *South Dakota Review*, Autumn 1965.

Reading List: *Clark* by Max Westbrook, 1969; *Clark* by Lawrence L. Lee, 1973.

*   *   *

The place of Walter Van Tilburg Clark in literary history rests on two of his three novels, *The Ox-Bow Incident* and *The Track of the Cat*. If that perch is narrow, it is also firm, not merely because both were made into memorable motion pictures, but, more importantly, because both are sensitive psychological studies of great impact.

Taken as a parable of fascism at the time of its writing, *The Ox-Bow Incident*, set in the American West, is a powerful examination of leadership and mob violence. Against a dry-tinder backdrop of lassitude reminiscent of the setting of Faulkner's "dry September," the men of Bridger's Wells need only an act of violence and the imposition of a strong will to be ignited into a flaming mob. The point is that violence triumphs by default; that a single-minded person can take charge and use the vast energy latent in boredom and resentment for evil as long as no one will take steps sufficient to stop him.

Four years after his jejune second novel, *The City of Trembling Leaves*, Clark published his second successful novel, *The Track of the Cat*. Much more self-consciously artistic than *The Ox-Bow Incident*, the novel uses as its focus a mountain lion that becomes, literally and symbolically, the *bête noire* of the men who are tracking it. In the death of the two men, there is penetrating insight into human character: one, the overbearing realist, cannot cope with the mythic dimensions of the cat and falls from a cliff in fear of it; the other, the arch romantic, forgets the cat's deadly reality and is struck down.

Clark's problem as a novelist resides in his inability to proportion characters appropriately to plot. He invests no one in *The Track of the Cat*, for example, with stature commensurate with the great task of hunting the real and mythic beast. His characters are sometimes sententious. But in his two fine western novels, he largely overcomes the problem by sheer narrative force and by showing his audience some revealing habits of the human animal.

—Alan R. Shucard

COHAN, George M(ichael).   American.   Born in Providence, Rhode Island, 3 July 1878; son of the vaudevillians Jerry and Helen Cohan. Briefly attended two elementary schools in Providence; received no formal education after age 8. Married 1) Ethelia Fowler (the actress Ethel Levey) in 1899, one daughter; 2) Agnes Nolan in 1907, two daughters and one son. Travelled with his parents as a child, and made his stage debut with them in 1887; thereafter regularly appeared with his parents and sister as The Four Cohans; appeared as an actor in *Peck's Bad Boy*, in New York, 1890; toured America, with The Four Cohans, throughout the 1890's, and was appearing with them in leading vaudeville houses in New York and Chicago by the turn of the century; produced first musical for the New York stage, starring The Four Cohans and his wife, in 1901; formed producing partnership with Sam Harris, 1904, and wrote, presented, and starred in number of musical hits on Broadway; presented plays, with Harris, at the New Gaiety Theatre, New York, 1908–10, and at the George M. Cohan Theatre, New York, 1910–20; lived in semi-retirement after 1920, occasionally appearing on the New York stage. Produced 150 plays, and wrote more than 500 songs. Recipient: United States Congress gold medal, 1940. *Died 5 November 1942.*

PUBLICATIONS

Plays

The Governor's Son (produced 1901).   Songs published 1901(?).
Running for Office (produced 1903); revised version, as *The Honeymooners* (produced 1907).
Little Johnny Jones (produced 1904).
Popularity (produced 1906).
Forty-Five Minutes from Broadway (produced 1906).
George Washington, Jr. (produced 1906).
Fifty Miles from Boston (produced 1907).
The Talk of New York (produced 1907).
The American Idea (produced 1908).   1909.
The Yankee Prince (produced 1908).
The Man Who Owns Broadway (produced 1909).   Songs published 1909(?).
Get-Rich-Quick Wallingford, from a story by George Randolph Chester (produced 1910).
The Little Millionaire (produced 1911).   1911.
Broadway Jones (produced 1912).   1923; revised version, music by the author, as *The Two of Us* (as *Billie*, produced 1928), 1928.
Seven Keys to Baldpate, from the novel by Earl Derr Biggers (produced 1913).   1914.
The Miracle Man, from a story by Frank L. Packard (produced 1914).
Hello, Broadway!, music by the author (produced 1914).
What Advertising Brings, with L. Grant (produced 1915).
Hit-the-Trail Holliday (produced 1915).   1916.
The Cohan Revue 1916 (produced 1916).
Honest John O'Brien (produced 1916).
The Cohan Revue 1918 (produced 1918).
The Voice of McConnell (produced 1918).
The Fireman's Picnic.   1918.
A Prince There Was, from the novel *Enchanted Hearts* by Darragh Aldrich (produced 1918).   1927.
The Royal Vagabond, with Stephen Ivor-Szinny and William Cary Duncan, music by Anselm Goetzl (produced 1919).   1919.

The Farrell Case: A One Act Mystery (produced 1919).
Madeleine and the Movies (produced 1922).
Little Nelly Kelly (produced 1922).
The Song and Dance Man (produced 1923).
The Rise of Rosie O'Reilly (produced 1923).   Songs published 1923(?).
American Born (produced 1925).
The Home-Towners (produced 1926).
The Baby Cyclone (produced 1927).   1929.
The Merry Malones (produced 1927).
Whispering Friends (produced 1928).
Gambling (produced 1929).
Friendship (produced 1931).
Confidential Service.   1932.
Pigeons and People (produced 1933).   1941.
Dear Old Darling (produced 1935).
Fulton of Oak Falls, from a story by Parker Fennelly (produced 1936).
The Return of the Vagabond (produced 1940).   1940.

Verse

Songs of Yesteryear.   1924.

Other

Twenty Years on Broadway, and the Years It Took to Get There.   1925.

*   *   *

Cohan the dramatist? Surely not. Cohan the Yankee Doodle Dandy, the song and dance man, the song writer (not only "Yankee Doodle Dandy" but also "Mary's a Grand Old Name" and "Give My Regards to Broadway"). But Cohan the playwright is as unknown today as Cohan the vaudevillean and Cohan the movie star. The only play of his that is still remembered is probably *Seven Keys to Baldpate*, a comedy-thriller filmed five times.

In his own time, however, Cohan was significant not only as an actor but as a playwright. As Alan S. Downer puts it (in *Fifty Years of American Drama*, 1951), "Out of the variety houses and into the legitimate theatre came George M. Cohan, the apostle of rampant Americanism. With a sharp ear for the colloquial speech of New York ... , with his single-minded devotion to the color combination in Old Glory, he created a wise-cracking, quick-footed, dashing young hero who could instantaneously declare and prove his superiority to all lesser mortals, 'reubens' or 'limeys' or both." From his success derive plays such as those of Winchell Smith and George Kelly, the tough talk of the 1930's films, the snappy wisecracks of Kaufman and Dorothy Parker.

The best of the plays are probably *Little Johnny Jones*, *Forty-Five Minutes from Broadway*, *Get-Rich-Quick Wallingford*, *Seven Keys to Baldpate*, *The Miracle Man*, and *Gambling*. Cohan learned his craft in the 1880's and 1890's and seldom went beyond what he learned. He used theatrical tricks in many of the plays, shocked the audience by putting Billy Sunday on the stage in *Hit-the-Trail Holliday*, kept the title character offstage in *The Miracle Man*, had no intermission in *Pigeons and People*, revealed the identity of the robber in the first act of *Confidential Service*, always with an eye on theatrical effect. His one rule was to "wow them." When he died, he had long outlasted his time as a personality and writer.

— Leonard R. N. Ashley

CONNELLY, Marc(us Cook). American. Born in McKeesport, Pennsylvania, 13 December 1890. Educated at Trinity Hall, Washington, Pennsylvania, 1902–07. Married Madeline Hurlock in 1930 (divorced, 1935). Reporter and Drama Critic for the Pittsburgh *Press* and *Gazette-Times,* 1908–15; moved to New York, 1915: free-lance writer and actor, 1915–33; Reporter, New York *Morning Telegraph,* 1918–21; associated with *The New Yorker* in the 1920's; wrote screenplays and directed in Hollywood, 1933–44; Professor of Playwriting, Yale University Drama School, New Haven, Connecticut, 1947–52. United States Commissioner to UNESCO, 1951; Adviser, Equity Theatre Library, 1960. Since 1920, Member of the Council of the Dramatists Guild; Member, Executive Committee, United States National Committe for UNESCO. Recipient: Pulitzer Prize, 1930; O. Henry Award, for short story, 1930. Litt.D.: Bowdoin College, Brunswick, Maine, 1952; Baldwin-Wallace College, Berea, Ohio, 1962. Past President, Authors League of America; President, National Institute of Arts and Letters, 1953–56. Lives in New York City.

PUBLICATIONS

Plays

> *$2.50* (produced 1913).
> *The Lady of Luzon* (lyrics only; produced 1914).
> *Follow the Girl* (lyrics only, uncredited; produced 1915).
> *The Amber Express,* music by Zoel Joseph Parenteau (produced 1916).
> *Dulcy,* with George S. Kaufman (produced 1921). 1921.
> *Erminie,* revised version of the play by Henry Paulton (produced 1921).
> *To the Ladies!,* with George S. Kaufman (produced 1922). 1923.
> *No, Sirree!,* with George S. Kaufman (produced 1922).
> *The 49ers,* with George S. Kaufman (produced 1922).
> *West of Pittsburgh,* with George S. Kaufman (produced 1922; revised version, as *The Deep Tangled Wildwood,* produced 1923).
> *Merton of the Movies,* with George S. Kaufman, from the story by Harry Leon Wilson (produced 1922). 1925.
> *A Christmas Carol,* with George S. Kaufman, from the story by Dickens, in *Bookman,* December 1922.
> *Helen of Troy, N.Y.,* with George S. Kaufman, music and lyrics by Harry Ruby and Bert Kalmar (produced 1923).
> *Beggar on Horseback,* with George S. Kaufman, music by Deems Taylor, from a play by Paul Apel (produced 1924). 1925.
> *Be Yourself,* with George S. Kaufman (produced 1924).
> *The Wisdom Tooth: A Fantastic Comedy* (produced 1925). 1927.
> *The Wild Man of Borneo,* with Herman J. Mankiewicz (produced 1927).
> *How's the King?* (produced 1927).
> *The Green Pastures: A Fable Suggested by Roark Bradford's Southern Sketches "Ol' Man Adam an' His Chillun"* (produced 1930). 1929.
> *The Survey* (skit), in *New Yorker,* 1934.
> *The Farmer Takes A Wife,* with Frank B. Elser, adaptation of the novel *Rome Haul* by Walter D. Edmonds (produced 1934). Abridgement in *Best Plays of 1934–1935,* edited by Burns Mantle, 1935.
> *Little David: An Unproduced Scene from "The Green Pastures."* 1937.
> *Everywhere I Roam,* with Arnold Sundgaard (produced 1938).
> *The Traveler.* 1939.

The Mole on Lincoln's Cheek (broadcast 1941). In *The Free Company Presents,* edited by James Boyd, 1941.

The Flowers of Virtue (produced 1942).

The Good Earth, with others, in *Twenty Best Film Plays,* edited by John Gassner and Dudley Nichols. 1943.

A Story for Strangers (produced 1948).

Hunter's Moon (produced 1958).

The Portable Yenberry (produced 1962).

Screenplays: *Whispers,* 1920; *Exit Smiling,* with others, 1926; *The Bridegroom, The Burglar, The Suitor,* and *The Uncle* (film shorts), 1929; *The Unemployed Ghost* (film short), 1931; *The Cradle Song,* 1933; *The Little Duchess* (film short), 1934; *The Green Pastures,* 1936; *The Farmer Takes a Wife,* 1937; *Captains Courageous,* 1937; *The Good Earth,* with others, 1937; *I Married a Witch,* 1942; *Reunion (Reunion in France),* 1942; *The Imposter* (additional dialogue), 1944; *Fabiola* (English dialogue), 1951; *Crowded Paradise* (additional scenes), 1956.

Radio Play: *The Mole on Lincoln's Cheek,* 1941.

Fiction

A Souvenir from Qam. 1965.

Other

Voices Off-Stage: A Book of Memoirs. 1968.

Reading List: *Connelly* by Paul T. Nolan, 1969.

* * *

Born to parents who had both had stage careers, Marc Connelly early became dedicated to the theatre. As a young child, he says in his memoirs, he got the "feeling that going to the theater is like going to an unusual church, where the spirit is nourished in mystical ways, and pure magic may occur at any moment." Connelly has spent his life as a man of the theatre seeking to produce that pure magic – as actor, director, and playwright.

Convinced that there was much to be enjoyed in life, Connelly as a young man fell in naturally with the famed "Round Table" of the 1920's at New York's Algonquin Hotel. His first New York stage venture had been the lyrics for the musical *The Amber Express* (1916), but success did not come until the collaborations with George S. Kaufman. In 1921 their *Dulcy,* a mixture of gentle satire and fun, helped to set the standard for the Broadway comedy of the 1920's. hey collaborated on six other plays. Their *Merton of the Movies,* based on the story by Harry Leon Wilson, inaugurated an era of Broadway satires on Hollywood. The play's success was marked by Hollywood's turning it into a movie.

The most important play of the Kaufman-Connelly collaboration was *Beggar on Horseback,* a masterpiece of American expressionism and a fitting symbol of the *joie de vivre* the collaborators consistently sought to bring to the stage. The play is based on Paul Apel's *Hans Sonnestössers Höllenfahrt,* but it is no slavish copy of the German play – the expressionism has been completely Americanized in technique and in its satiric ends. Framed by scenes of comic realism, the visual and audial effects of the expressionism, helped by cinematic techniques, are more varied than those of Elmer Rice's *The Adding Machine* (1923).

After the success of *Beggar on Horseback*, the collaborators decided to pursue their careers apart. Connelly wrote musicals and plays (most successfully *The Wisdom Tooth*) and wrote short stories for *The New Yorker* (he was on the editorial board of the struggling new magazine), but it was not until he read Roark Bradford's *Ol' Man Adam an' His Chillun* that he wrote the play that insured his unique position in twentieth-century drama. In Bradford's rendering of Old Testament stories from the viewpoint of uneducated Louisiana Negroes, Connelly immediately perceived the basis of a drama where pure magic might nourish the human spirit. The result was *The Green Pastures*, a work which, while it contained much of the fun of Bradford, gave it a greater dignity and a greater vision. Connelly's Lawd is a growing protagonist; his play's action concerns man's search for God and God's search for man. Connelly enhanced his episodically structured play through the use of Negro spirituals, suggesting other aspects of the folk longings. By framing the play with a children's Sunday School, Connelly conveyed the value of his material: unless one becomes as a little child, the play's vision would be beyond him. Broadway had long been without a religious play, and an all-Negro cast was also unusual. Connelly had difficulty getting backing for the play, but the production (directed by himself) proved the sceptics wrong. The play ran for five years, totalling 1642 performances.

Connelly was in Hollywood often in the 1930's, writing screenplays (some of the best of the period) and directing. (He would later act in *Our Town* and in other plays.) While he wrote some scripts and other plays, none has matched his earlier successes. He published *A Souvenir from Qam*, his only novel, in 1965. He reminisced about his many years on the stage and in the movies in *Voices Off-Stage*, which gives brief glimpses of famous contemporaries but is most valuable in its story of *The Green Pastures*.

—Joseph M. Flora

COZZENS, James Gould. American. Born in Chicago, Illinois, 19 August 1903. Educated at the Kent School, Connecticut, graduated 1922; Harvard University, Cambridge, Massachusetts, 1922–24. Served in the United States Army Air Force, 1942–45: Major. Married Bernice Beaumgarten in 1927. Schoolteacher, Santa Clara, Cuba, 1925; lived in Europe, 1926–27; Associate Editor, *Fortune* magazine, New York, 1938. Recipient: O. Henry Award, 1936; Pulitzer Prize, 1949; Howells Medal, 1960. Litt.D.: Harvard University, 1952. Member, National Institute of Arts and Letters. *Died 9 August 1978.*

PUBLICATIONS

Fiction

Confusion. 1924.
Michael Scarlett: A History. 1925.

Cock Pit.   1928.
The Son of Perdition.   1929.
S.S. San Pedro: A Tale of the Sea.   1931.
The Last Adam.   1933; as *A Cure of Flesh.*   1933.
Castaway.   1934.
Men and Brethren.   1936.
Ask Me Tomorrow; or, The Pleasant Comedy of Young Fortunatus.   1940.
The Just and the Unjust.   1942.
Guard of Honor.   1948.
By Love Possessed.   1957.
Children and Others (stories).   1964.
Morning Noon and Night.   1968.
A Flower in Her Hair (stories).   1975.

Other

A Rope for Dr. Webster (essay).   1976.

Bibliography: *Cozzens: An Annotated Checklist* by Pierre Michel, 1972; *Cozzens: A Checklist* by James Meriwether, 1973.

Reading List: *Cozzens* by Granville Hicks, 1958; *The Novels of Cozzens* by Frederick Bracher, 1959; *Cozzens: Novelist of Intellect* by Harry John Mooney, Jr., 1963; *Cozzens* by D. E. S. Maxwell, 1964; *Cozzens* by Pierre Michel, 1974.

*   *   *

James Gould Cozzens is a writer whose work offers, with a quiet persistence, an account of American life that is not really duplicated elsewhere. After tentative starts in novels which were modish at the times of their appearance, Cozzens found a stride that carried him off in a more personal direction. The early novel *Confusion* played off the refinement of Europe against the crudity of America, as many novelists of the time were doing. The somewhat later novel, *The Last Adam*, stridently celebrated the lusty and primitive energy of the hero as if he were cousin to the gamekeeper in *Lady Chatterley's Lover*.

But these novels – and *The Last Adam* is excellent in its own right – were apprentice exercises: a cutting-away of underbrush that kept Cozzens from reaching his own territory. This territory is kept strictly to in novels like *The Just and the Unjust* and *By Love Possessed*. It is only apparently departed from in *Men and Brethren*, Cozzens's "clerical" novel with a big-city setting, and *Guard of Honor*, a "war" novel with an army base for its background. Cozzens's domination of his territory has not been difficult; few other American writers have wanted to enter it. Of those who seem to, it is Louis Auchincloss who comes closest to Cozzens; both Auchincloss and Cozzens depict the lives of a privileged minority. But Auchincloss's characters are both more wealthy and more powerful than Cozzens's, "big city" and mobile. In contrast, Cozzens's "right people" are provincial and fixed in their habitations and their careers.

The typical Cozzens heroes, most fully displayed in *The Just and the Unjust* and *By Love Possessed* but represented elsewhere, are the latest members of families that have enjoyed privilege, education, and position for several generations in American towns of medium size. The heroes are at the center of the web of custom and law which continues to hold together the communities they serve, often as lawyers and always as thoughtful and responsible citizens. Both men have fathers who speak of the order they supported in *their* days; the fathers encourage their sons to continue the quiet battle of preserving a way of life that is already old, shadowed by elms and dominated by court-house domes and the law-courts beneath those domes. It is a way of life best enjoyed by people of substance and privilege – a way both misunderstood and resented by those who are "outside the law": Poles, Irish Catholics, and blacks. For these persons, whose drunkenness and violence often take them into the lawyers's offices, the lawyers (and Cozzens the novelist) offer sympathy and comprehension but hardly acceptance; the clients' disorder is part of a more general confusion which is always threatening not just the privileged but the entire community.

This confusion – as most of Cozzens's narratives suggest – can be held back by law and custom; it will not cease. So, in face of the disorder in "alien" behavior and the outbreaks of lust and malice in their own beings, the Cozzens heroes fight and learn while they fight. Their battles are related by Cozzens in such a way that all events, all human deliberations, are bathed in a rationality that is calm and unmilitant; absent from the novels is the self-righteousness of many a novelist whose orientation is liberal. Cozzens has faith in what he says, but the faith is not excessive. Absent also are the transcendental hopes of novelists who have heard a gospel. Cozzens and his heroes are committed to a kind of dubiety, a dubiety both provincial and shrewd. It is a world in which expectations of happiness are both clear and quite modest.

Cozzens's analysis of human motive is sharp. Cozzens and his most perceptive characters – he is not easily to be separated from them – are armed with generations of common sense and desultory talk rather than with the Freudian or Jungian strategies that are useful to many of Cozzens's contemporaries. Cozzens is – differences being allowed for – the Anthony Trollope of the recent American day, judging the life he knows with sharp intelligence rather than dismissing it with contempt or violence.

—Harold H. Watts

CRANE, (Harold) Hart. American. Born in Garrettsville, Ohio, 21 July 1899; spent his childhood in Cleveland. Educated in local schools. Assistant Editor, *The Pagan*, 1918; worked in a shipyard in Cleveland, and as a reporter in New York, 1918; Advertising Solicitor, *The Little Review*, 1919; worked for his father in a drug store in Akron, Ohio, 1919–20, and in a Cleveland warehouse, 1920; worked in Washington, D. C. briefly, 1920, and in Cleveland, 1920–21; Copywriter, Cleveland advertising agencies, 1922–23; moved to New York, 1923: clerk, then copywriter, in an advertising agency, 1923; clerk in a publishing firm, 1924–25; patronized by Otto Kahn, 1925; travelled in Europe, 1928, Mexico, 1931–32. Recipient: Guggenheim Fellowship, 1931. Drowned himself on the voyage back from Mexico. *Died 27 April 1932.*

PUBLICATIONS

Collections

Letters 1916–1932, edited by Brom Weber.   1952.
Complete Poems and Selected Letters and Prose, edited by Brom Weber.   1966.

Verse

White Buildings: Poems. 1926.
The Bridge. 1930.
Ten Unpublished Poems. 1972.

Other

Twenty-One Letters to George Bryan, edited by Joseph Katz and others. 1968.
Letters of Crane and His Family, edited by Thomas S. W. Lewis. 1974.
Crane and Yvor Winters: Their Literary Correspondence, edited by Thomas
Parkinson. 1978.

Bibliography: *Crane: A Descriptive Bibliography* by Joseph Schwartz and Robert C. Schweik,
1972.

Reading List: *Crane: A Biographical and Critical Study* by Brom Weber, 1948; *Crane: An
Introduction and Interpretation,* 1963, and *Smithereened Apart: A Critique of Crane,* 1977,
both by Samuel Hazo; *Crane* by Vincent Quinn, 1963; *Crane* by Monroe K. Spears, 1965;
The Poetry of Crane by R. W. B. Lewis, 1967; *The Crane Voyages* by Hunce Voelcker, 1967;
Crane: An Introduction to the Poetry by Herbert A. Leibowitz, 1968; *Voyager: A Life of Crane*
by John Unterecker, 1969; *Crane: The Patterns of His Poetry* by M. D. Uroff, 1974; *Crane's
The Bridge: A Description of Its Life* by Richard P. Sugg, 1977.

*   *   *

As with some other American writers, it is difficult to give a final and objective estimate of
Hart Crane's place as a poet. He is important, on more than one count, for what he set out to
do, but critics have differed widely as to his actual achievement. Furthermore, there is the
legend, as we may call it, of his life. We are presented with the picture of a man driven by
compulsive and self-destructive urges, both alcoholic and sexual, culminating in a spectacular
suicide. Hart Crane himself identified with such doomed and outcast figures as Christopher
Marlowe and Arthur Rimbaud, and it is easy to make him into the romantic scapegoat of
American civilisation. On the other hand, a critic like Ivor Winters can too readily move from
a moral disapproval of the undisciplined life to a total dismissal of the work.

The Bridge is Crane's longest and clearly his most important poem. In form it is modelled
on Eliot's *The Waste Land,* and it is generally agreed that Crane intended his own poem as a
kind of riposte, giving a positive rather than a negative view of the modern metropolitan city.
In *The Waste Land,* and in Joyce's *Ulysses,* the protaganist moves about the city – London or
Dublin – which becomes a symbolic landscape, crowded with mythical and heroic
archetypes. Past splendours contrast with modern squalor. *The Bridge* follows the same plan.
The setting is New York. The protagonist wakes in the morning, passes over Brooklyn
Bridge, wanders about the city and returns in the evening by the subway under the River
Hudson. Hart Crane tries to create a mythology for America out of scraps of literature,
history, and tradition. Columbus, Rip Van Winkle and the Wright brothers appear, as well as
Whitman, Poe, Emily Dickinson, and Isadora Duncan. In the section entitled "Powhatan's
Daughter" Pocahontas represents the American earth itself and its Red Indian past: "Lie to
us. Dance us back our tribal dawn." In "The Tunnel," through the suffocating atmosphere of
a rush hour subway, Crane encounters the ghost of Edgar Allan Poe:

And why do I often meet your visage here,
Your eyes like agate lanterns – on and on
Below the toothpaste and the dandruff ads?
– And did their riding eyes right through your side,
And did their eyes like unwashed platters ride?
And Death, aloft, – gigantically down
Probing through you – toward me, O evermore!

In this remarkable passage, Crane shows that he is aware that the American dream of materialistic, technological progress has its reverse side of neurotic nightmare, and that Poe represents this nightmare. But it is Brooklyn Bridge itself which is the unifying symbol of the poem. The bridge unites the two halves of the city, and by the railroad that it carries unites the city with the country and thus its present with its past. As a feat of engineering it denotes human achievement, and in its clean functional beauty the union of aesthetics and technics.

We may thus consider Crane, as does Harold Bloom, as standing in the succession of Romantic, myth making, and visionary poets. He is one of the explorers of what Charles Williams called "the Image of the City." But as an urban poet he differs sharply from his British and American successors of the 1930's in that his poetry is almost devoid of social and political comment. He has indeed been reproached by left-wing critics for his unreflecting celebration of the American capitalist system. Indeed, the sudden collapse of that system in the Slump was one of the factors contributing to his despair and his suicide.

Crane may also be considered, at least in part, as the most notable representative in the English speaking world of the Futurist movement of the 1920's. The term "Futurism" was coined by the Italian Marinetti, a figure more notable for self-publicity than literary genius. But his claim that art should celebrate the achievements and imitate the rhythms of a machine civilisation influenced poets better than himself. These included Apollinaire in France and Mayakovsky in Russia. The latter, like Crane, found his new faith inadequate to sustain him and ended in suicide. But Crane, as we have seen, did not regard the traditions of the past as irrelevant. He suffered, however, from a certain paucity in his own cultural background: it really does seem that he thought the phrase "Panus angelicus" which he quotes in the "Cape Hatteras" section of The Bridge meant "angelic Pan" and could be applied to Walt Whitman. And some may feel that the only religious tradition he seems to have been acquainted with, his mother's Christian Science, lacked a richness compared with the theological currents which fertilised the work of Eliot and Joyce.

Although Whitman's popularist rhetoric represents one of Crane's stances, his free verse is not in the least Whitmanesque. Like that of Eliot, it is based on an extension of principles already found in the blank verse of Shakespeare's contemporaries. But while Eliot's is founded upon that of Webster and his generation, that of Crane is to be related to the practice of Marlowe, with its strongly stressed iambic rhythm and its terminal pause. As in Marlowe there is an element of bombast in Crane, and a certain degree of rhythmical monotony. At his best he sweeps us along by the sheer energy of his writing, in spite of the frequent difficulty of grasping the exact sense of what he is saying. Crane is undeniably often very obscure. But his much quoted letter to Harriet Monroe, defending his poem "At Melville's Tomb," shows that he was very much intellectually in control. The poem consists in fact of a series of compressed conceits, rather different from the extended metaphysical conceits of Donne and his school. At times it is difficult to translate these into completely logical terms. These lines (from "Voyages") are difficult – "In all the argosy of your bright hair, I dreamed/Nothing so flagless as this piracy" – yet their haunting quality is manifest. As a visual poet Crane is remote from Pound and the Imagists; instead of a clear pictorial impression of a scene or object we get a kind of kaleidoscope of sense impressions. His style might best be described as manneristic, and in this respect his affinities are less with his contemporaries and immediate predecessors than with certain poets who came into prominence a decade later, such as George Barker and Dylan Thomas. Crane has indeed been claimed as an influence on the latter poet, but this is difficult to determine.

When Crane moved from the early short poems of *White Buildings* to the elaborately planned *The Bridge* he was attempting to encompass something in the nature of an epic style. What he in fact achieved might more properly be described as quasi-Pindaric or dithyrambic lyric. This dithyrambic quality is even more marked in "For the Marriage of Faustus and Helen." This sequence of three poems continues some of the themes of *The Bridge*. Faustus's evocation of the shade of Helen is, of course, one of the most memorable moments in Marlowe's *Doctor Faustus*; and Marlowe, as we have seen, was one of Crane's heroes. The marriage of Faust and Helen, in the second part of Goethe's *Faust*, was a symbol of the union of the modern and the antique spirits. Crane may have taken his cue from this, since the theme of these three poems is the union of American technological civilization with the traditional idea of beauty. Crane here forces language almost to the breaking point as he strives to evoke Helen first from a vision of the metropolitan city, second (it would seem) from a scene of jazz revelry at the summit of a skyscraper, and third from the airman's conquest of distance:

> Capped arbiter of beauty in this street
> That narrows darkly into motor dawn, –
> You, here beside me, delicate ambassador
> Of intricate slain numbers that arise
> In whispers, naked of steel;
>   religious gunman!
> Who faithfully, yourself, will fall too soon,
> And in other ways than as the wind settles
> On the sixteen thrifty bridges of the city:
> Let us unbind our throats of fear and pity.

In contrast to this, the series of poems entitled "Voyages" represent Crane's return to a purer and more personal lyricism. These may in the end constitute his most enduring, though not his most ambitious achievement. In these poems Crane imagines himself united with one of his lovers, a merchant seaman, as he voyages through imaginary seascapes. The verse of these poems has a new kind of music, and they are less rhetorically accentuated. Hart Crane now uses enjambment with effect, especially a characteristic trick of ending a line with a grammatically unimportant word as in the second line of the following quotation:

> O minstrel galleons of Carib fire,
> Bequeath us to no earthly shore until
> Is answered in the vortex of our grave
> The seal's wide spindrift gaze toward paradise.

Crane's final days were spent in Mexico. He had gone there on a grant from the Guggenheim Foundation, with a project to compose a long poem on the Spanish Conquest of Mexico. This historical theme, almost too highly charged with imaginative potential, has more than once proved a trap for poets. What Hart Crane might have made of it we can only conjecture. In fact his Mexican days were a disaster, and, before he committed suicide by drowning on his return voyage to the U.S.A., he knew that he had no work on the project to show and in the light of the changed economic situation it was unlikely his grant would be renewed. Nevertheless, some of the last poems, such as "The Idiot" and "Bacardi Spreads the Eagle's Wings," give a compassionate view of the poor and outcast which hints at a grasp of reality previously somewhat wanting in Hart Crane's poetry.

—John Heath-Stubbs

CREELEY, Robert (White). American. Born in Arlington, Massachusetts, 21 May 1926. Educated at Holderness School, Plymouth, New Hampshire; Harvard University, Cambridge, Massachusetts, 1943–46; Black Mountain College, North Carolina, B.A. 1955; University of New Mexico, M.A. 1960. Served with the American Field Service in India and Burma, 1944–45. Married 1) Ann McKinnon in 1946 (divorced, 1955), two sons, one daughter; 2) Bobbie Louise Hall in 1957, three daughters. Taught on a finca in Guatemala for two years; Instructor, Black Mountain College, Spring 1954, Fall 1955; Visiting Lecturer, 1961–62, and Lecturer, 1963–66, 1968–69, University of New Mexico; Lecturer, University of British Columbia, Vancouver, 1962–63. Visiting Professor, 1966–67, and since 1967 Professor of English, State University of New York at Buffalo. Visiting Professor of Creative Writing, San Francisco State College, 1970–71. Operated the Divers Press, Palma, Majorca, 1953–55; Editor, *Black Mountain Review*, North Carolina, 1954–57, and associated with *Wake, Golden Goose, Origin, Fragmente, Vou, Contact, CIV/n*, and *Merlin* magazines in the early 1950's, and other magazines subsequently. Recipient: D. H. Lawrence Fellowship, 1960; Guggenheim Fellowship, 1964, 1971; Rockefeller Fellowship, 1965. Lives in Bolinas, California.

PUBLICATIONS

Verse

Le Fou. 1952.
The Kind of Act of. 1953.
The Immoral Proposition. 1953.
A Snarling Garland of Xmas Verses. 1954.
All That Is Lovely in Men. 1955.
Ferrini and Others, with others. 1955.
If You. 1956.
The Whip. 1957.
A Form of Women. 1959.
For Love: Poems 1950–1960. 1962.
Words. 1965.
About Women. 1966.
Poems 1950–1965. 1966.
A Sight. 1967.
Words. 1967.
Robert Creeley Reads (with recording). 1967.
The Finger. 1968.
5 Numbers. 1968.
The Charm: Early and Uncollected Poems. 1968.
Numbers. 1968.
Divisions and Other Early Poems. 1968.
Pieces. 1968.
Hero. 1969.
A Wall. 1969.
Mary's Fancy. 1970.
In London. 1970.
The Finger: Poems 1966–1969. 1970.
As Now It Would Be Snow. 1970.
America. 1970.
Christmas: May 10, 1970. 1970.

> *St. Martin's*.   1971.
> *Sea*.   1971.
> *1.2.3.4.5.6.7.8.9.0*.   1971.
> *A Day Book* (includes prose).   1972.
> *For My Mother*.   1973.
> *Kitchen*.   1973.
> *Sitting Here*.   1974.
> *Thirty Things*.   1974.
> *Selected Poems*.   1976.
> *Away*.   1976.
> *Hello − A Journal February 23-May 3, 1976*.   1978.

Play

> *Listen* (produced 1972).   1972.

Fiction

> *The Gold Diggers*.   1954.
> *The Island*.   1963.
> *Mister Blue*.   1964.
> *The Gold Diggers and Other Stories*.   1965.
> *Mabel*.   1976.
> *Presences*.   1976.

Other

> *An American Sense* (essay).   1965(?).
> *Contexts of Poetry*.   1968.
> *A Quick Graph: Collected Notes and Essays*.   1970.
> *A Day Book*.   1970.
> *A Sense of Measure* (essays).   1973.
> *Contexts of Poetry: Interviews 1961–1971*, edited by Donald Allen.   1973.
>
> Editor, *Mayan Letters*, by Charles Olson.   1953.
> Editor, with Donald Allen, *New American Story*.   1965.
> Editor, *Selected Writings*, by Charles Olson.   1966.
> Editor, with Donald Allen, *The New Writing in the U.S.A.*   1967.
> Editor, *Whitman*.   1973.

Bibliography: *Creeley: An Inventory 1945–1970* by Mary Novik,   1974.

Reading List: *Three Essays on Creeley* by Warren Tallman, 1973; *Measures: Creeley's Poetry* by Ann Mandel, 1974; *Creeley's Poetry: A Critical Introduction* by Cynthia Edelberg, 1978.

*   *   *

In his 1967 Berlin lecture, "I'm Given to Write Poems," Robert Creeley acknowledged his indebtedness to William Carlos Williams for teaching him the use of an American speech in poetry and for the emotional perception he has achieved, as well as his debt to Charles Olson for "the *freedom* I have as a poet." This freedom lies not in the lyric itself, which is tightly restrained from committing verbal excess, but in the flow of the thought which ranges freely over a complex psychological interior. Creeley's best poems contain remarkable articulation of shades and hues of mood, often achieved by the subtle word play of the discourse. The poems, brief seizures of attention, are a chronicle of his two marriages, in which the self undergoes remorseless scrutiny and analysis. The larger canon of these miniature self-portraits reveals a life of emotional isolation as a man attempts both to possess and submit to women who are repelled by his profound vulnerability.

The early poems, collected in *For Love: Poems 1950–1960*, are intensely formal in their compactness and closure. Many tend toward epigram in their brevity and pithy advice. A typical instance is "The Warning":

> For Love – I would
> split open your head and put
> a candle in
> behind the eyes.
>
> Love is dead in us
> if we forget
> the virtue of an amulet
> and quick surprise.

But the best of the short poems define the self from an oblique but penetrating angle of insight, as in the three couplets of "The End":

> When I know what people think of me
> I am plunged into my loneliness. The grey
>
> hat bought earlier sickens.
> I have no purpose no longer distinguishable.
>
> A feeling like being choked
> enters my throat.

Creeley's marital theme is expressed in the majority of poems in *For Love*, but "The Whip," "A Form of Women," "The Way," "A Marriage," and "Ballad of the Despairing Husband" capture its dilemmas with deep poignance. Other poems in this large collection depict the female as not only a sexual partner, but as a force or element to sustain male consciousness. "The Door," among the longest and most ambitious of these poems, explores the female in her divine and archetypal aspect.

In recent years, Creeley has dissolved the formalism of his verse in order to create verse fields in book-length serial compositions, in the manner of Charles Olson and Robert Duncan. He has abandoned the structural neatness of his earlier verse, but the more fluid compositions of *Words, Pieces*, and *A Day Book* tend to be lax and to include much trivial detail of his daily life.

His prose work follows the themes of his verse. The novel *The Island* deals with his marriage to his first wife. Creeley's prose is unique in modern fiction: his use of detail is extraordinarily delicate and precise, producing an uncanny perceptiveness in his narrators. Self-absorption in *The Island* is all the more compelling as the narrator dismantles his own thinking process to inspect the deterioration jealousy causes in him. Although a highly provocative writer of prose, his poetry has had a more pervasive influence.

In his criticism *A Quick Graph*, and in interviews, collected in *Contexts of Poetry*, he has proved an astute chronicler of modern poetry, particularly on the work and influence of Charles Olson, with whom he launched the movement now known as Black Mountain poetry.

—Paul Christensen

CROTHERS, Rachel. American. Born in Bloomington, Illinois, 12 December 1878. Educated at Illinois State Normal School, Bloomington, graduated 1892; Wheatcroft School of Acting, New York, 1893. Acted with an amateur dramatic society in Bloomington; with Felix Morris's Company; directed and staged all her own plays. Founder and First President, American Theatre Wing. Recipient: Megrue Prize, 1933; Chi Omega National Achievement Award, 1939. *Died in 1958.*

PUBLICATIONS

Plays

Nora (produced 1903).
The Point of View (produced 1904).
Criss Cross.   1904.
The Rector.   1905.
The Three of Us (produced 1906).   1916.
The Coming of Mrs. Patrick (produced 1907).
Myself, Bettina (produced 1908).
Kiddie.   1909.
A Man's World (produced 1910).   1915.
He and She (as *The Herfords*, produced 1912; as *He and She*, produced 1920).   1932.
Young Wisdom (produced 1914).   1913.
Ourselves (produced 1913).
The Heart of Paddy Whack (produced 1914).   1925.
Old Lady 31, from the novel by Louise Forsslund (produced 1916).   In *Mary the Third* ..., 1923.
Mother Carey's Chickens, with Kate Douglas Wiggin, from the novel by Wiggin (produced 1917).   1925.
Once upon a Time (produced 1918).   1925.
39 East (produced 1919).   In *Expressing Willie* ..., 1924.
Everyday (produced 1921).   1930.
Nice People (produced 1921).   In *Expressing Willie* ..., 1924.
Mary the Third (produced 1923).   In *Mary the Third* ..., 1923.
Mary the Third, Old Lady 31, A Little Journey: Three Plays.   1923.
Expressing Willie (produced 1924).   In *Expressing Willie* ..., 1924.

Expressing Willie, Nice People, 39 East: Three Plays.   1924.
Six One-Act Plays (includes *The Importance of Being Clothed, The Importance of Being Nice, The Importance of Being Married, The Importance of Being a Woman, What They Think, Peggy*).   1925.
A Lady's Virtue (produced 1925).   1925.
Venus (produced 1927).   1927.
Let Us Be Gay (produced 1929).   1929.
As Husbands Go (produced 1931).   1931.
Caught Wet (produced 1931).   1932.
When Ladies Meet (produced 1932).   1932.
The Valiant One.   1937.
Susan and God (produced 1937).   1938.

*   *   *

Rachel Crothers was that rarity, a total woman of the theatre. Not since the Duke of Saxe-Meiningen and André Antoine in the last quarter of the 19th century had such a complexity of personal supervision over an entire theatrical production been seen. She was even more commanding than these two estimable and influential gentlemen since this complete control was exercised over her *own* plays which were generally directed, and occasionally even acted in, by her. Most extraordinary was the fact that it was a woman who had such a multi-leveled theatrical success and over so long a period of time. Altogether, the career of Rachel Crothers was unparalleled.

As a writer, she was a playwright and a playwright only, and the singlemindedness of her literary style also became the singlemindedness of her essential theme, that of woman emerging from the oppressions of society. Her "problem comedies" – which were notable for their witty and natural dialogue – dealt with such themes as career versus marriage (*He and She*), the "liberated" girl of the 1920's (*Nice People*), the generation gap (*Mary the Third*), divorce (*Let Us Be Gay*), adultery (*When Ladies Meet*), and emotional-cum-spiritual restlessness (*Susan and God*).

Miss Crothers was critically and popularly acclaimed as America's foremost woman playwright for over thirty years. Always concerned with human dignity, Miss Crothers organized war relief committees in both world wars. This patriotism carried into her work, for, in addition to her depiction of her theme of the feminine view of life in many variations, she was a very endemically American playwright. Speaking of her play on love firmly rooted in Yankee soil (*Old Lady 31*), a *New York Times* article of 9 February 1919 compared her to Booth Tarkington, saying "Rachel Crothers must be admitted to the small and select group of those who tend to reveal America to the Americans."

In her time she was enormously successful, and perhaps the wholesomeness of her approach and the sound common sense and decency of spirit underlying all her plays (which stand up theatrically because of their timely situations and excellent dialogue) are the essential reasons behind this resounding success. Her interest in the "balanced or everyday life" was epitomized in her work: it is her plea for "sanity in all art," as she herself termed it, which her plays so ably exemplify.

—Zoë Coralnik Kaplan

CULLEN, Countée. American. Born Countée L. Porter in New York City, 30 May 1903; adopted by Reverend and Mrs. Cullen, 1918. Educated at De Witt Clinton High School, New York; New York University, B.A. 1925 (Phi Beta Kappa); Harvard University, Cambridge, Massachusetts, M.A. in English 1926. Married 1) Yolande Du Bois in 1928 (divorced, 1930); 2) Ida Mae Roberson in 1940. Assistant Editor, *Opportunity*, magazine of the National Urban League, 1927; French teacher, Frederick Douglass Junior High School, New York, 1934–46. Recipient: Guggenheim Fellowship, 1929. *Died 9 January 1946.*

PUBLICATIONS

Collections

On These I Stand: An Anthology of the Best Poems of Cullen.   1947.

Verse

Color. 1925.
Copper Sun. 1927.
The Ballad of the Brown Girl: An Old Ballad Retold.   1927.
The Black Christ and Other Poems. 1929.
The Medea and Some Poems. 1935.
The Lost Zoo (A Rhyme for the Young, But Not Too Young).   1940.

Plays

St. Louis Woman, with Arna Bontemps (produced 1946).
The Third Fourth of July, with Owen Dodson, in *Theatre Arts,* August 1946.

Fiction

One Way to Heaven. 1932.
My Lives and How I Lost Them (juvenile).   1942.

Other

Editor, *Caroling Dusk: An Anthology of Verse by Negro Poets.*   1927.

Bibliography: *Cullen: A Bio-Bibliography of Cullen* by Margaret Perry,   1971.

Reading List: *Roots of Negro Racial Consciousness: Three Harlem Renaissance Authors* by Stephen H. Bronz, 1964; *Cullen and the Negro Renaissance* by Blanche E. Ferguson, 1966; *In a Minor Chord* (on Cullen, Hurston, and Toomer) by Darwin T. Turner, 1971; *A Many-Colored Coat of Dreams: The Poetry of Cullen* by Houston A. Baker, Jr., 1974.

*   *   *

Countée Cullen, a Negro American, was a lyricist who found his inspiration among the 19th-century Romantic poets, especially John Keats. As Cullen himself said in 1928, "good poetry is a lofty thought beautifully expressed" (*St. Louis Argus*, 3 February 1928). Even though Cullen wrote poetry that was racially inspired, he was, first of all, a poet consciously in search of beauty.

Cullen was described frequently as being the least race-conscious among the early modern Negro poets who achieved fame in the 1920's during the period labelled "The Harlem Renaissance." Cullen suffered in his efforts to pay homage to Beauty and his race, and critics were divided about the effect of this conflict of universal vs. black experience (few then, including Cullen, speculated on aesthetic value from a strictly black point of view). When Cullen's first book, *Color*, appeared, one reviewer wrote, "Countée Cullen is a supreme master of Beauty" (*International Book Review*, March 1926). What a reader of Cullen's poetry must understand, however, is that Cullen was trying to place all of his poetry on the same level of achievement, rather than have his "racial" poetry (e.g., "Heritage," "Shroud of Color") judged by one set of standards and his "non-racial" poetry (e.g., "Wisdom Cometh with the Years," "To John Keats, Poet. At Spring Time") judged upon another, more universal, academic set.

As a black man, Cullen was not insensitive to the genre of music and sound indigenous to black Africa. The influence on Cullen's poetry, in most cases, is extremely subtle. Indeed, there is an interesting combination of black sensuousness and Romantic language in such lines as "Her walk is like the replica/Of some barbaric dance/Wherein the soul of Africa/Is winged with arrogance" ("A Song of Praise"). In his poetry, Cullen was consistently absorbed by the themes of love (both its joy and sorrow), beauty, and the evanescence of life as well as racial sorrow and racial problems; and he also revealed a romantic evocation of the African heritage he shared with his fellow poets in Harlem.

In his one novel, *One Way to Heaven*, Cullen displayed a deft skill at characterization and symbolism. His novel was, in Cullen's words, a "two-toned picture" of the upper and lower classes of blacks in Harlem during the 1920's.

Countée Cullen never achieved the heights many felt he was destined to reach when the reading public was exposed to his famous poem "Heritage" in March 1925. But he may have been restrained by the poignant last lines of this particular poem — "Yet do I marvel at this curious thing/To make a poet black and bid him sing!"

—Margaret Perry

CUMMINGS, E(dward) E(stlin). American. Born in Cambridge, Massachusetts, 14 October 1894. Educated at a private school in Cambridge; Cambridge High and Latin School; Harvard University, Cambridge, 1911–16 (Co-Founder, Harvard Poetry Society, 1915), B.A. (magna cum laude), 1915, M.A. 1916. Served in the Norton Harjes Ambulance Corps, 1917; prisoner of war, 1917–18. Married 1) Marion Morehouse; 2) Anne Barton. Worked at P. F. Collier and Company, mail order books, New York, 1916–17; lived in Paris, 1921–23; writer for *Vanity Fair*, New York, 1925–27. Artist: paintings included several times in group shows at the Society of Independent Artists, Paris; one-man shows include Painters and Sculptors Gallery, New York, 1932; American British Art Center, New York, 1944, 1949; Rochester Memorial Art Gallery, New York, 1945, 1950, 1954, 1957. Charles Eliot Norton Professor of Poetry, Harvard University, 1952–53. Recipient: Guggenheim Fellowship, 1933; Shelley Memorial Award, 1945; Academy of American Poets Fellowship, 1950; Harriet Monroe Poetry Award, 1950; National Book Award, 1955; Bollingen Prize, 1958. *Died 3 September 1962.*

PUBLICATIONS

Collections

Three Plays and a Ballet, edited by George Firmage.   1967.
Complete Poems.   1968.
Poems 1905–1962, edited by George Firmage.   1973.

Verse

Tulips and Chimneys.   1923; complete edition, 1937; edited by George Firmage, 1976.
Puella Mea.   1923.
XLI.   1925.
&.   1925.
Is 5.   1926.
Christmas Tree.   1928.
(No Title).   1930.
VV (Viva: Seventy New Poems).   1931.
No Thanks.   1935; edited by George Firmage, 1978.
1/20 (One Over Twenty).   1936.
Collected Poems.   1938.
Fifty Poems.   1940.
1 × 1.   1944.
Xaipe.   1950.
Poems 1923–1954.   1954.
95 Poems.   1958.
100 Selected Poems.   1959.
Selected Poems 1923–1958.   1960.
73 Poems.   1963.

Plays

Him.   1927.
Tom: A Ballet.   1935.
Anthropos; or, The Future of Art.   1945.
Santa Claus: A Morality.   1946.

Fiction

The Enormous Room.   1922; edited by George Firmage, 1978.

Other

CIOPW (drawings and paintings).   1931.
Eimi (travel).   1933.
i: Six Nonlectures.   1953.
Cummings: A Miscellany, edited by George Firmage.   1958; revised edition, 1965.
Adventures in Verse, photographs by Marion Morehouse.   1962.
Fairy Tales (juvenile).   1965.

Selected Letters, edited by F. W. Dupee and George Stade. 1969.

Translator, *The Red Front,* by Louis Aragon. 1933.

Bibliography: *Cummings: A Bibliography* by George Firmage, 1960.

Reading List: *The Magic-Maker: Cummings* by Charles Norman, 1958, revised edition, 1964; *Cummings: The Art of His Poetry,* 1960, and *Cummings: The Growth of a Writer,* 1964, both by Norman Friedman; *Cummings and the Critics* edited by Stanley V. Baum, 1962; *Cummings* by Barry Marks, 1964; *The Poetry and Prose of Cummings* by Robert E. Wegner, 1965; *Cummings* by Eve Triem, 1969; *Cummings: A Collection of Critical Essays* edited by Norman Friedman, 1972; *Cummings: A Remembrance of Miracles* by Bethany K. Dumas, 1973.

* * *

Edward Estlin Cummings, better known in lower case as e. e. cummings, is a major poet of the modern period, who grew up in a comfortable, liberal household in Cambridge, Massachusetts, where ingenuity was energetically cultivated. The neighborhood of the Irving Street home was populated by Harvard faculty; his father had taught at Harvard before becoming a Unitarian minister of considerable renown in Boston. Cummings's parents had been introduced to each other by the distinguished psychologist William James, also a neighbor. Summers were spent on the family farm in New Hampshire, where the young Cummings spent his hours musing in a study his father had built him; another was situated in a tree behind their Cambridge house. Both father and mother encouraged the gifted youth to paint and write, and, by their excessive indulgence, perhaps nurtured his diffident character. At Harvard, Cummings distinguished himself and graduated with honors in Greek and English studies, and delivered a commencement address entitled "The New Art," his survey of Cubism, new music, the writings of Gertrude Stein and Amy Lowell, all of which he defended with insight and daring before his proper Bostonian audience. It was an early declaration of Cummings's bold taste and artistic direction.

At Harvard, Cummings wrote and published poems in the undergraduate reviews, but most of them were conventional and uninspired, except for a brief collection of poems issued in a privately printed anthology, *Eight Harvard Poets* (1917). After a brief stint of work in a mail-order publishing house, the first and only regular employment in his career, Cummings quit and volunteered for service in the Norton Harjes Ambulance Corps in France. Soon after he and a friend, William Slater Brown, were interrogated by security police regarding Brown's correspondence with a German professor at Columbia University, and both were incarcerated in a French concentration camp. Cummings was freed after three months, but only after his father had written to President Wilson requesting special attention to his son's internment. From that experience, Cummings wrote *The Enormous Room,* a World War I classic, at the insistence of his father who viewed the incident as a sinister act of an ally. The long autobiographical account sparkles with reportorial details, insight, and comic invention, and asserts a theme of anti-authoritarianism throughout.

Cummings submitted his first book of poems to the publisher of *The Enormous Room,* Boni, but was refused there and at other houses. The large manuscript, entitled *Tulips and Chimneys,* contained 152 poems ranging from a long, rambling epithalamion and other derivative exercises to short, pithy works of explosive energy and significant innovation. As a last resort, Cummings's old classmate John Dos Passos found a publisher for a shortened version of 60 poems in 1923. Two years later 41 more poems were issued as *XLI,* and

Cummings printed the remaining poems with some additions in &. In 1937, the original manuscript was issued in its entirety under its first title and now stands as one of the great classics of Modernist poetry.

For lyric energy, imagination, and verve, few books of poems compare with it. Even Cummings's later books do not have the vigor of this first work. Among the poems in the collection are "All in green went my love riding," "In Just," "O sweet spontaneous," "Buffalo Bill's/defunct." The work is astounding for its variety of voice, tone, technique, and theme, and the content ranges widely from outrageous satire to jazzy lyrics, from naive rhymes to sexually explicit portraits. Cummings caught the irreverent, slapdash tonality of the jazz age in his sprawling, sensuous lyrics. The old decorums were exploded and replaced by a humor Cummings had absorbed from vaudeville shows, burlesque houses, and music halls of the day.

But there is more to these experiments than we might suspect. The young Cummings was fascinated with the asyntactic language of Stein and the grotesque, paralogical imagery of Amy Lowell, and in the dismantled shapes of Cubist paintings, all of which seemed to liberate the artist from traditional logic. The new art made spontaneous perception the basis of expression. This was equally the force of jazz itself: the soloist departed from the melodic pattern to perform his own spontaneous variations according to his mood. Cummings attacked the conventional lyric with the lesson of these other arts. He took the formal lyric apart and redistributed each of its components: punctuation becomes a series of arbitrary signals he sometimes uses even as words. The function of nouns, pronouns, adverbs, and adjectives could all be interchanged in verbal flights. The barrel shape of the standard lyric could simply be blown open, as though the staves had all been unhooped. Language drips, spills, dribbles, runs over the frame in one of Cummings's Cubist-style poems. The genius in the experiment is that Cummings caught upon a series of innovations that seemed to Americanize the European-born lyric poem: in his irreverent care, the poem had become a display of verbal energy and exuberance, a vehicle of melting-pot humor and extravagance, a youthfully arrogant jazz variation of an old standard form. The modern lyric has continued to sprawl whimsically down the page ever since Cummings first scattered it in *Tulips and Chimneys*.

Cummings's innovations in other forms and media are less sure and significant, but he is nonetheless a refreshing influence. In the play form, he was drawn to over-subtle psychological comedy, as in *Him*, but he was far ahead of his time in his absurdist dialogue and surreal sets and costumes. Cummings was also a prolific graphic artist who worked in most media. Some of this work was published in *CIOPW*. Cummings strained the immediacy of prose with his massive account of a visit to Russia entitled *Eimi*, in which he assails the Marxist state and the regimented condition of Soviet citizens. The book offended the American left at home, which dominated the publishing field during the first years of the depression, and for several years Cummings published little work. A volume entitled *No Thanks*, the title directed at publishers who had rejected the manuscript, appeared in 1935, followed three years later by his first *Collected Poems*.

The many books of poems that succeeded *Tulips and Chimneys* sustained the nervous energy of his first experiments, but Cummings did not advance in new techniques so much as refine and consolidate his discoveries from the first book. As Norman Friedman points out, Cummings experimented with different aspects of his style in the years after 1923. In the 1930's, in *VV (ViVa)* and *No Thanks*, Cummings sought the limits of typographical experiment, extending to the curious strategy known as *tmesis*, or, the breaking up and mingling of words to achieve intense immediacy. The dismantled language of his poems focused attention on the individual word and its component letters, and often gave expressiveness to the word through its spatial arrangement. A famous poem of his later years, "l(a," is an arrangement of letters that plummet abruptly down the page, emblematic of a falling leaf and of autumn.

Over the span of his career, Cummings moved slowly away from the simple delight in love, in the seasons, in nature and simplicity, to more urgent and didactic poems that finally came to preach the virtues of naive existence, as in *Xaipe* and *95 Poems*. His argument against science, with he sometimes equated with "death," may have turned him too much against the modern world and toward pastoral themes. As a result, he is a poet of a large canon of work that is marked by much repetition of theme and perspective, but his status as a major poet is secure; one has only to "look" at an anthology of new poems to see his pervasive influence.

—Paul Christensen

DAHLBERG, Edward.   American.   Born in Boston, Massachusetts, 22 July 1900; grew up in Kansas City and Cleveland. Educated at the University of California, Berkeley, 1922–23; Columbia University, New York, 1923–25, B.S. in philosophy 1925. Served in World War I. Married 1) Winifred Donlea in 1942; 2) Julia Lawlor in 1967; two children. Writer from 1926; lived in London and Paris, 1926–28; taught at Boston University, 1947; Lecturer in the School of General Education, New York University, 1961–62; Cockefair Professor, 1964–65, and Professor of Language and Literature, 1966, University of Missouri at Kansas City; taught at Columbia University, 1968. Recipient: Longview Foundation Award, 1961; National Institute of Arts and Letters award, 1961; Rockefeller grant, 1965; Ariadne Foundation award, 1970; Cultural Council Foundation award, 1971. Member, National Institute of Arts and Letters, 1968. *Died 27 February 1977.*

PUBLICATIONS

Fiction

> *Bottom Dogs.*   1929.
> *From Flushing to Calvary.*   1932.
> *Kentucky Blue Grass Henry Smith* (story).   1932.
> *Those Who Perish.*   1934.
> *Because I Was Flesh.*   1964.
> *The Olive of Minerva; or, The Comedy of a Cuckold.*   1976.
> *Bottom Dogs, From Flushing to Calvary, Those Who Perish, and Other Unpublished and Uncollected Works.*   1976.

Verse

> *Cipango's Hinder Door.*   1965.

Other

> *Do These Bones Live.*   1941; revised edition, as *Can These Bones Live*, 1960.

Sing, O Barren. 1947.
The Flea of Sodom. 1950.
The Sorrows of Priapus. 1957.
Truth Is More Sacred: A Critical Exchange on Modern Literature, with Herbert Read. 1961.
Alms for Oblivion: Essays. 1964.
Reasons of the Heart: Maxims. 1965.
The Dahlberg Reader. 1967.
Epitaphs of Our Times: The Letters of Dahlberg. 1967.
The Leafless American. 1967.
The Carnal Myth: A Search into Classical Sensuality. 1968.
The Confessions of Dahlberg. 1971.
The Gold of Ophir: Travels, Myths and Legends in the New World. 1972.

Bibliography: *A Bibliography of Dahlberg* by Harold Billings, 1971.

Reading List: *Dahlberg: American Ishmael of Letters* edited by Harold Billings, 1968; *Dahlberg: A Tribute* edited by Jonathan Williams, 1970; *Dahlberg* by Fred Moramarco, 1972.

*   *   *

Edward Dahlberg was the illegitimate son of a lady barber whose hardships and endurance were to be a central subject in his work.

His first book, *Bottom Dogs*, was published with a preface by D. H. Lawrence. Based on his own experience of poverty, it shows the influence of his left-wing political leanings. His next two novels, *From Flushing to Calvary* and *Those Who Perish*, were reportorial pieces of social realism, the first affected by the hardships of the depression, the second by anti-Nazi sentiments, the result of a trip to Germany. For a while, Dahlberg was associated with the Communist Party, but he abandoned politics for aesthetic reasons. He then entered a long period of silence broken only by occasional works of literary criticism such as *Do These Bones Live* and *Sing, O Barren* that examine the heritage of Poe, Thoreau, Melville and other writers, as well as the sexlessness of American literature. Dahlberg's years of study and rumination bore fruit in *Because I Was Flesh*, an autobiography in fictional form. The book is a rewriting of *Bottom Dogs*, but the events and characters are related to literary and mythical antecedents. The prose is aphoristic and affected by classical and Biblical overtones. *Because I Was Flesh* is Dahlberg's most universal book and is already considered a masterpiece of contemporary prose.

In 1965 Dahlberg returned to America after living abroad for many years, mainly in Spain and Ireland. In the last decade of his life, Dahlberg made up for his long silence by publishing on average of a book a year – poems, a collection of aphorisms, essays, fiction, a selection of letters and a literary autobiography entitled *The Confessions of Edward Dahlberg*. Writing in a style reminiscent of Sir Thomas Browne, Dahlberg was a literary Jeremiah, attacking materialism and lamenting the loneliness of human existence. He was also a steadfast foe of modernism, opposed to the work of Faulkner, Hemingway, Pound, Eliot, and Joyce. He felt kinship with Anderson, Dreiser, and William Carlos Williams.

Dahlberg's writing is extremely individualistic, purposefully unfashionable. He thought our age desiccated; he wanted flesh and blood in life as well as literature. He influenced many of his contemporaries but remained an isolated nay-sayer.

—Frank MacShane

DAVIDSON, Donald (Grady).   American.   Born in Campbellsville, Tennessee, 18 August 1893. Educated at Branham and Hughes School, 1905–09; Vanderbilt University, Nashville, B.A. 1917, M.A. 1922. Served in the 324th Infantry, 81st Division, of the United States Army, in France, 1917–19: First Lieutenant. Married Theresa Sherrer in 1918; one daughter. Teacher in schools in Cedar Hill and Mooresville, Tennessee, 1910–14, and Pulaski, Tennessee, 1916–17, and at Kentucky Wesleyan College, Winchester, 1919–20; Instructor in English, 1920, Professor, 1927–64, and Professor Emeritus, 1964–68, Vanderbilt University; also, Member of the Faculty, Bread Loaf School of English, Middlebuty College, Vermont, Summers 1931–68. Co-Founder, *Fugitive* magazine, Nashville, 1922; Literary Editor and Columnist ("Spyglass"), *Nashville Tennessean*, 1924–30. Member, Advisory Board, *Modern Age* and *The Intercollegiate Review*. Chairman, Tennessee Federation for Constitutional Government, 1955–59. Litt.D.: Cumberland University, 1946; Washington and Lee University, Lexington, Virginia, 1948; L.H.D.: Middlebury College, 1965. *Died 25 April 1968.*

PUBLICATIONS

Verse

> *Avalon*, with *Armageddon* by John Crowe Ransom and *A Fragment* by William Alexander Percy.   1923.
> *An Outland Piper.*   1924.
> *The Tall Men.*   1927.
> *Lee in the Mountains and Other Poems.*   1938.
> *The Long Street.*   1961.
> *Poems 1922–1961.*   1966.

Play

> *Singin' Billy*, music by Charles Faulkner Bryan (produced 1952).

Other

> *The Attack on Leviathan: Regionalism and Nationalism in the United States.*   1938.
> *American Composition and Rhetoric.*   1939; revised edition, with Ivar Lou Myhr, 1947, 1959.
> *The Tennessee.*   2 vols., 1946–48.
> *Twenty Lessons in Reading and Writing Prose.*   1955.
> *Still Rebels, Still Yankees, and Other Essays.*   1957.
> *Southern Writers in the Modern World.*   1958.
> *Concise American Composition and Rhetoric.*   1964.
> *The Spyglass: Views and Reviews 1924–1930*, edited by John T. Fain. 1963.
> *It Happened to Them: Character Studies of New Testament Men and Women.*   1965.
> *The Literary Correspondence of Davidson and Allen Tate*, edited by John T. Fain and T. D. Young.   1974.

> Editor, *British Poetry of the Eighteen-Nineties.*   1937.
> Editor, with Sidney E. Glenn, *Readings for Composition.*   1942; revised edition, 1957.
> Editor, *Selected Essays and Other Writings of John Donald Wade.*   1966.

Reading List: *The Fugitive Group,* 1957, and *The Southern Critics,* 1971, both by Louise Cowan; *The Fugitive Poets* edited by William Pratt, 1965; *Davidson: An Essay and a Bibliography* by T. D. Young and M. Thomas Inge, 1965; *Davidson* by T. D. Young, 1971.

*   *   *

An original member of the group of poets who published *The Fugitive,* Davidson published some of his first poems in that journal. From 1924 to 1930 he was literary editor of the *Nashville Tennessean* and produced what one critic has called the "best literary page ever published in the South." He contributed to both agrarian symposia, *I'll Take My Stand* (1930) and *Who Owns America?* (1938), and is widely known and respected as poet, essayist, editor, historian, and critic.

As poet Davidson's reputation must stand on *The Tall Men,* "Lee in the Mountains" (1934), and a half dozen poems from *The Long Street. The Tall Men,* a book-length narrative, is organized around a young man's search for a meaningful tradition, a heritage of heroism and humanism. The exploration of Davidson's protagonist, a modern southern American, is not a vague, nostalgic meandering into a far distant past. Instead, his excruciating self-analysis is an attempt "to name and set apart from time/One sudden face" and to understand his present situation by discovering how he is related to the history and history makers of his own section of the country. He finally becomes aware not only of his traditional heritage but of the forces that would destroy it. "Lee in the Mountains," Davidson's most widely anthologized poem, presents Davidson's art at its best. In its epic dignity, its purity of form, its dramatic presentation of theme, it demonstrates as no other poem of his does the totality of his vision and the range of his imagination. The force and clarity of his presentation in this and many other of his poems give him a place almost unique among the poets of his generation. For Davidson, however, prose was the dominant means of expression throughout his career. As literary critic and social and political philosopher he offered cogent and convincing arguments in a prose that was lucid, smooth, and supple. As a prose stylist Davidson has few peers in contemporary American literature.

—T. D. Young

DELL, Floyd.   American.   Born in Barry, Illinois, 28 June 1887. Educated in schools in Barry and Quincy, Illinois, and Davenport High School, Iowa. Served in the United States Army, 1918. Married 1) Margery Curry in 1909 (separated, 1913); 2) Berta-Maria Gage in 1919, two sons. Reporter, Davenport *Times,* 1905; Editor, *Tri-City Workers' Magazine,* Davenport, 1906; Reporter, Davenport *Democrat,* 1906, and Chicago *Evening Post,* 1909, and Assistant Editor, 1909–10, Associate Editor, 1910–11, and Editor, 1911–13, of the *Evening Post's Friday Literary Review;* settled in New York, 1913: Associate Editor, *The Masses,* 1914–17, and on editorial board of its successor, *The Liberator,* 1918–21; tried for sedition for his pacifist writings, 1917; full-time writer from 1921; Editor for the WPA (Works Progress Administration), Washington, D.C., 1935–47. *Died 23 July 1969.*

Fiction

Moon-Calf.   1920.
The Briary-Bush.   1921.
Janet March.   1923; revised edition, 1927.
This Mad Ideal.   1925.
Runaway.   1925.
Love in Greenwich Village (stories and poems).   1926.
An Old Man's Folly.   1926.
An Unmarried Father.   1927; as *Little Accident*, 1930.
Souvenir.   1929.
Love Without Money.   1931.
Diana Stair.   1932.
The Golden Spike.   1934.

Plays

Human Nature (as *A Five Minute Problem Play*, produced 1913).   In *King Arthur's Socks* ..., 1922.
The Chaste Adventures of Joseph (produced 1914).   In *King Arthur's Socks* ..., 1922.
Ibsen Revisited (produced 1914).   In *King Arthur's Socks* ..., 1922.
Enigma (produced 1915).   In *King Arthur's Socks* ..., 1922.
Legend (as *My Lady's Mirror*, produced 1915).   In *King Arthur's Socks* ..., 1922.
The Rim of the World (produced 1915).   In *King Arthur's Socks* ..., 1922.
King Arthur's Socks (produced 1916).   In *King Arthur's Socks* ..., 1922.
The Angel Intrudes (produced 1917).   1918.
A Long Time Ago (produced 1917).   In *King Arthur's Socks* ..., 1922.
Sweet-and-Twenty (produced 1918).   1921.
Poor Harold! (produced 1920).   In *King Arthur's Socks* ..., 1922.
King Arthur's Socks and Other Village Plays.   1922.
A Little Accident, with Thomas Mitchell, from the novel *An Unmarried Father* by Dell (produced 1928).
Cloudy with Showers, with Thomas Mitchell (produced 1931).

Other

Women as World Builders: Studies in Modern Feminism.   1913.
Were You Ever a Child?   1919.
Looking at Life.   1924.
Intellectual Vagabondage: An Apology for the Intelligentsia.   1926.
The Outline of Marriage.   1926.
Upton Sinclair: A Study in Social Protest.   1927.
Love in the Machine Age: A Psychological Study of the Transition from Patriarchal Society.   1930.
Homecoming: An Autobiography.   1933.
Children and the Machine Age.   1934.

Editor, *Poems*, by Wilfred Scawen Blunt.   1923.
Editor, *Poems of Robert Herrick.*   1924.

Editor, *Poems and Prose of William Blake*. 1925.
Editor, with Paul Jordan-Smith, *The Anatomy of Melancholy*, by Robert Burton.   1927.
Editor, *Daughter of the Revolution and Other Stories*, by John Reed.   1927.

Reading List: *Dell* by John D. Hart, 1971.

*   *   *

In a writing career running from 1908 to 1935, Floyd Dell published over twenty books and roughly one thousand periodical pieces. They, like his life, fall into several distinct periods and reflect his connection with many of the important literary movements and intellectual concerns in the United States during the first quarter of the century.

In his Chicago period (1908–13), his output consisted chiefly of book reviews and essays for the *Friday Literary Review* of the *Chicago Evening Post*, which during his editorship found itself at the heart of what has come to be known as the "Chicago renaissance." His brisk and often highly personal discussions for the *Review* championed the "new" literature, introduced the work of many continental novelists, and surveyed current books on socialism and sex; one of his series of articles, "Modern Women," taking up the views of ten feminists, became his first book, *Women as World Builders*.

His Greenwich Village years (1913–20, chronicled nostalgically in prose sketches, short stories, and poetry in *Love in Greenwich Village*) coincided with a period of intense creative and intellectual activity there, and he became one of the leading figures both through his participation in the little theatre movement – several of his short plays gently satirizing the intellectual concerns of the Villagers were collected as *King Arthur's Socks and Other Village Plays* – and his writings as an editor of the socialistic journals *The Masses* and its successor, *The Liberator*. The books that resulted from this writing reflect the dualism both of Dell and of these magazines, which were concerned with art as well as politics and were often as conservative in the former as they were radical in the latter. *Looking at Life* draws together forty short pieces, largely unconnected with socialism; they display an acute intelligence playing lightly and entertainingly, but seldom profoundly, over a wide range of subjects. *Were You Ever a Child?*, based on a series in *The Liberator*, is a plea for educational reform, popularizing the ideas of John Dewey and other educational theorists and presenting them with humor and playfulness (and often in dialogue form). *Intellectual Vagabondage*, based on another series written for *The Liberator* (but after Dell left the Village), is the most important of the three, and is Dell's most ambitious effort at interpreting literature from a social and economic standpoint; with characteristic lightness of touch he traces the historical role of the intelligentsia and then, more significantly, sets forth the "spiritual autobiography" of his own generation, depicting, among other things, the idealistic revolt of youth against the restraints of a commercial world.

This perennial theme of Dell's runs through the novels that he produced during what may be regarded as his third period, the years when he lived at Croton-on-the-Hudson, New York (1920–35). His first – and most famous and best – novel, *Moon-Calf*, draws heavily on his own pre-Chicago years and describes with great sensitivity the intellectual development of a young dreamer and poet; with it he made the analysis of moon-calves, and their adjustment to reality, his own special province. In ten succeeding novels he continued to explore the predicaments of youthful idealists, who in the end find happiness by accepting conventions; like his other writings, these novels are facile and exhibit a keen sense of irony and humour, but they do not fulfill the promise suggested by *Moon-Calf*. The interest in psychological and social problems manifested in the novels reaches its climax in Dell's substantial study of adolescent adjustment, *Love in the Machine Age*, a well-written exposition of the thesis that the neuroses of the modern world are the result of outmoded but still operative patriarchal conventions.

For psychological insight, however, readers are likely to prefer his autobiography,

Homecoming, especially the first half dealing with the years covered fictionally in *Moon-Calf*. As the title implies, the movement of the book and of his life is toward the stability finally found in marriage and a home; but he never lost the ability to write perceptively of youthful rebellion, and the book contains some of his best work. The dust jacket calls it "not Floyd Dell's autobiography but your own," a remark that points to Dell's importance as a representative figure. He will be best remembered as an intelligent and articulate commentator on the characteristic concerns of a sizable segment of his literary generation.

—G. T. Tanselle

DICKEY, James (Lafayette). American. Born in Atlanta, Georgia, 2 February 1923. Educated at Clemson College, South Carolina, 1942; Vanderbilt University, Nashville, Tennessee, B.A. (magna cum laude) 1949 (Phi Beta Kappa), M.A. 1950. Served in the United States Army Air Force during World War II, and in the Air Force during the Korean War. Married 1) Maxine Syerson in 1948 (died, 1976), two sons; 2) Deborah Dobson in 1976. Taught at Rice University, Houston, 1950, 1952–54, and University of Florida, Gainesville, 1955–56; Poet-in-Residence, Reed College, Portland, Oregon, 1963–64, San Fernando Valley State College, Northridge, California, 1964–66, and the University of Wisconsin, Madison, 1966. Consultant in Poetry, Library of Congress, Washington, D.C., 1966–68. Since 1969, Professor of English and Writer-in-Residence, University of South Carolina. Recipient: Vachel Lindsay Prize, 1959; Longview Foundation Award, 1960; Guggenheim Fellowship, 1961; Melville Cane Award, 1966; National Book Award, 1966; National Institute of Arts and Letters grant, 1966. Lives in South Carolina.

PUBLICATIONS

Verse

Into the Stone and Other Poems. 1960.
Drowning with Others. 1962.
Helmets. 1964.
Two Poems of the Air. 1964.
Buckdancer's Choice. 1965.
Poems 1957–1967. 1967.
The Achievement of James Dickey: A Comprehensive Selection of His Poems, edited by Laurence Lieberman. 1968.
The Eye-Beaters, Blood, Victory, Madness, Buckhead, and Mercy. 1970.
The Zodiac. 1976.

Plays

Screenplay: *Deliverance*, 1972.

Television Play: *The Call of the Wild*, from the novel by Jack London, 1976.

Fiction

Deliverance. 1970.

Other

The Suspect in Poetry. 1964.
A Private Brinksmanship. 1965.
Spinning the Crystal Ball: Some Guesses at the Future of American Poetry. 1967.
Babel to Byzantium: Poets and Poetry Now. 1968.
Self-Interviews, edited by Barbara and James Reiss. 1970.
Sorties (essays). 1971.
Exchanges ..., Being in the Form of a Dialogue with Joseph Trumbull Stickney. 1971.
Jericho: The South Beheld. 1974.
God's Images: The Bible – A New Vision. 1977.
Tucky the Hunter (juvenile). 1978.

Translator, *Stolen Apples,* by Evgenii Evtushenko. 1971.

Bibliography: *Dickey, The Critic as Poet: An Annotated Bibliography* by Eileen Glancy, 1971; *Dickey: A Checklist* by Franklin Ashley, 1972.

Reading List: *Dickey: The Expansive Imagination* edited by Richard J. Calhoun, 1973.

*   *   *

James Dickey emerged as an important American poet and as a still underrated literary critic through an astonishing period of creative productivity from 1957 to 1967. He was regarded so much as a poet without imitators and without specific social or political concerns that his important contributions to post-modernism, both as poet and critic, were not adequately recognized. But Dickey should be seen as a post-modernist romantic – because of his desire to make imaginative contact with natural forces which have been lost to modern man, because of his romantic faith in the power of his imagination, and because of the expansive, affirmative character of most of his poems.

Dickey has always violated the modernist practice of impersonality in poetry, for there has always been a close correspondence between the chronology of his poems and his life. In his earliest poems he drew from such autobiographical data as the death (before Dickey was born) of his brother Eugene and his experiences as a fighter pilot in two destructive wars, as well as from his love for hunting, archery, and the southern landscape. Many of these poems feature encounters leading to vividly imagined exchanges of identity between the living and the dead, between men and "unthinking" nature, for the purpose of understanding through the imagination what reason alone cannot comprehend.

Dickey early declared himself as an affirmative poet, with an acknowledged affinity for the poetry of his friend and mentor, Theodore Roethke; but his affirmations were from the knowing perspective of a grateful survivor of two wars. His poems have always portrayed those who were *not* survivors and affirmed the risk inherent in an exchange of identity. In his later poems, especially in *The Eye-Beaters*, Dickey's persona is a middle-aged survivor of the destructive forces of nature. In addition, Dickey has exhibited a fascination with fantasy, with what he has called his "country surrealism," blurring distinctions between reality and dreams, or even hallucinations. His intention has been to produce a poetry that releases the unconscious and the irrational, with results that are both life affirmative and life threatening.

Two poems that might serve as transitions from his earlier to his later themes are "Power and Light" and "Falling," both from *Poems 1957–1967*. There is a shift of emphasis from a celebration of "more life" through the imaginative comprehension of nature to the necessity of confronting destructive forces and of finding spiritual resources for that confrontation. Dickey's formal interests have likewise shifted from regular towards more irregular forms, from the directness of "the simple declarative sentence" to the intimations of open and "big forms," and to such devices a split space punctuation within lines – effective in a tour de force like "Falling," but less effective in more recent poems.

Dickey is by birth and residence a southern poet, with academic credentials from the stronghold of agrarianism, Vanderbilt University. Yet he makes it clear that he is no "latter-day Agrarian." Still, like John Crowe Ransom, who feared the loss of "the world's body," and Allen Tate, who feared the loss of "complete knowledge" of man and his universe in an era dominated by science, Dickey has his own version of agrarian fears of technology and urbanization. He is "much more interested in a man's relationship to the God-made world, or the universe made, than to the man-made. . . . The relationship of the human being to the great natural cycles of birth and death, the seasons, the growing up of seasons out of dead leaves, the generations of animals and of men, all on the heraldic wheel of existence is very beautiful to me" (*Self-Interviews*).

In the 1970's Dickey's production of poetry has lessened with a developing interest in the novel, television and movie scripts, and a form of literary criticism, the self-interview. His successful novel, *Deliverance*, shares with his poetry a concern with the cycle of entry into "unthinking nature," followed by a return to the world, perhaps having become while in nature "another thing." The return to the human realm is just as important as the entry into the natural. He has most recently been engaged in writing prose-poem celebrations of the southern landscape (*Jericho*), and poetic "imitations" of the poems of a drunken, Dutch sailor-poet of the 1940's (*The Zodiac*) and of the King James version of the Bible (*God's Images*).

—Richard J. Calhoun

DOOLITTLE, Hilda ("H. D."). American. Born in Bethlehem, Pennsylvania, 10 September 1886. Educated at Gordon School, and Friends' Central School, 1902–04, both in Philadelphia; Bryn Mawr College, Pennsylvania, 1904–06. Married the writer Richard Aldington in 1913 (divorced, 1937); one daughter. Lived in Europe after 1911. Closely associated with the Imagist movement after 1913: took over editorship of *Egoist* magazine from her husband, 1916–17. Recipient: Brandeis University Creative Arts Award, 1959; American Academy of Arts and Letters Award of Merit Medal, 1960. *Died 28 September 1961*.

PUBLICATIONS

Verse

Sea Garden.   1916.
Choruses from the Iphigenia in Aulis by Euripides.   1916.
The Tribute, and Circe.   1917.

Choruses from the Iphigenia in Aulis and the Hippolytus by Euripides.   1919.
Hymen.   1921.
Helidora and Other Poems.   1924.
Collected Poems.   1925.
The Usual Star.   1928.
Red Roses for Bronze.   1929; revised edition, 1931.
What Do I Love.   1943(?).
The Walls Do Not Fall.   1944.
Tribute to the Angels.   1945.
The Flowering of the Rod.   1946.
By Avon River.   1949.
Selected Poems.   1957.
Helen in Egypt.   1961.
Hermetic Definition.   1972.

Plays

Hippolytus Temporizes.   1927.
Ion, by Euripides.   1937.

Fiction

Palimpsest.   1926, revised edition, 1968.
Hedylus.   1928.
Kora and Ka.   1930.
Nights.   1935.
The Hedgehog (juvenile).   1936.
Bid Me to Live: A Madrigal.   1960.

Other

Tribute to Freud, with Unpublished Letters by Freud to the Author.   1956, revised
    edition, 1974.

Reading List: *The Classical World of H. D.* by Thomas Burnett Swann, 1962; *Doolittle – H. D.* by Vincent Quinn, 1967; "Doolittle Issue" of *Contemporary Literature 10,* 1969.

*   *   *

Hilda Doolittle, whose works were published under the initials H. D., was an American poet of considerable significance. Her work itself is precise, careful, sharp, and compressed; it gives one the sense that the poet is excluding much more than she expresses. Natural objects (e.g., "Oread," "Pear Tree") are presented in lines that are free of conventional poetic rhythms and that are yet as carefully shaped as a piece of Greek statuary. So the immediate pleasure of much of H. D.'s work is a response to an object that is created by a few carefully chosen phrases: phrases that exist in the presence of easy and facile language that has been excluded. As painters say, the "negative space" – the area around a represented object – is as important as the object itself.

Miss Doolittle's work has an air of being isolated, of being simply her considered and purified record of what has stirred her senses and her emotions: the natural world with, for human context, the ancient Greek world as Miss Doolittle remembers it. Birds fly through air that is radiantly Greek, love intensifies its expression in the presence of Helen and Lais, and the mysteries of life and death bring into view satyrs and not Christian saints.

But Miss Doolittle's work did not actually proceed in isolation; she was closely associated with the Imagist movement from 1913 onwards. Ezra Pound, John Gould Fletcher, Amy Lowell, and others thought of their poetic effort as a realization of Walt Whitman's demand for new words that would bring poetry closer to the object it was "rendering" and free poetic expression from the abstractions and the overt moral purposes which had made much nineteenth-century poetry vague and imprecise. Poetry – and this was a main drive of Imagist theory – was a medium in which could appear the poet's direct apprehension of physical entities and the poet's immediate reaction to those entities. In pursuit of object and emotion, the poet should be free to discard both conventional rhythms and shop-worn poetic diction. Much of Miss Doolittle's poetry achieves these aims. Thus, the emotion in many a poem is coerced, to be recreated in the mind of the reader, by the carefully selected physical details – details which pass before the reader following a syntax that is simple and uninvolved and expressed in words that are familiar and unmysterious. But the poems, in the long run, are not free of general impressions or even abstractions although they state very few. The impressions and abstractions must vary from reader to reader, but they concern the beneficence that reaches the human mind through the senses; it is a beneficence unsullied by ancient dogma and more recent social purpose. Poets like Shelley and Tennyson did not hesitate to offer "gospels." If there is some sort of message in much of Miss Doolittle's work, it is very nearly fused with the external world she duplicates.

A modification of these effects appears in a late work like *The Walls Do Not Fall*. This work, using the techniques of the writer's previous verse, moves beyond the innocent and "natural" invocations of Greek health – health which is also of the physical world. But the destructions of World War II make the Greek health an insufficient corrective to modern chaos. *The Walls Do Not Fall* becomes quite specific about the sources of human health. Those sources find expression not only in halcyon flight and the play of light on the Aegean Sea. They can be traced in the essence of all great religions, and it is particularly the work of Egyptian gods that allows us to see the physical world achieving completion in myths and rituals. In such a body of faith as the Egyptian are myth and "Vision" coming into a focus of great human relevance. H. D. sees the Egyptian Amen and the later "Christos" as identical. They and other august entities are the symbols if not the ultimate élan of the eternal cycles of excellence and health which modern insanity – in its pursuit of power and inferior sorts of knowledge – has ignored.

This concluding attitude in the work of H. D. may strike some readers as going beyond the confines of the early Imagism. The attitude can also be regarded as an effort to defend and exploit the initial stance of Imagist simplicity and directness. These are opposing judgments. At any rate, in her late work Miss Doolittle's implications intensify and complicate themselves. But the modes of expression do not change. Perhaps their persistence indicates an essential continuity in the entire body of Miss Doolittle's poetry.

—Harold H. Watts

DOS PASSOS, John (Roderigo).   American.   Born in Chicago, Illinois, 14 January 1896. Educated at Choate School, Wallingford, Connecticut, 1907–11; Harvard University, Cambridge, Massachusetts (Editor, *Harvard Monthly*), 1912–16, B.A. (cum laude) 1916;

studied in Castille, 1916–17. Served with the Norton-Harjes Ambulance Unit in France, 1917, and on Red Cross Ambulance duty in Italy, 1918; served in the United States Medical Corps, 1918–19. Married 1) Katharine F. Smith in 1929 (died, 1947); 2) Elizabeth Hamlin Holdridge in 1950, one daughter. Writer from 1918; lived in Spain and Portugal, 1919; travelled in the Near East with the Near East Relief Organization, 1921; settled in New York, 1922; travelled in Spain, 1923; Co-Founder, *New Masses*, New York, 1926, and contributor until the early 1930's; Founder, New Playwrights Theatre, New York, 1927–28; visited the U.S.S.R., 1928; moved to Provincetown, Massachusetts, 1930; Contributor to *Common Sense*, 1932; screenwriter, in Hollywood, 1934; War Correspondent in the Pacific, and at Nuremburg, 1945, and in South America, 1948, for *Life* magazine, New York. Treasurer, National Committee for the Defense of Political Prisoners, 1931; Chairman, National Committee to Aid Striking Miners, 1931; Treasurer, Campaign for Political Refugees, 1940. Artist: one-man show of sketches, New York, 1937. Recipient: Guggenheim Fellowship, 1939, 1940, 1942; National Institute of Arts and Letters Gold Medal Award, 1957. Member, American Academy of Arts and Letters. *Died 28 September 1970.*

PUBLICATIONS

Fiction

One Man's Initiation – 1917.   1919; as *First Encounter,* 1945.
Three Soldiers.   1921.
Streets of Night.   1923.
Manhattan Transfer.   1925.
The 42nd Parallel.   1930; *1919,* 1932; *The Big Money,* 1936; complete version, as *U.S.A.,* 1938.
Adventures of a Young Man.   1939; *Number One,* 1943; *The Grand Design,* 1949; complete version, as *District of Columbia,* 1952.
Most Likely to Succeed.   1954.
The Great Days.   1958.
Mid-Century: A Contemporary Chronicle.   1961.
Century's End.   1975.

Plays

The Garbage Man: A Parade with Shouting (as *The Moon Is a Gong,* produced 1925; as *The Garbage Man,* produced 1926).   1926.
Airways, Inc. (produced 1927).   1928.
Fortune Heights (produced 1933).   In *Three Plays,* 1934.
USA: A Dramatic Revue, with Paul Shyre.   1963.

Verse

A Pushcart at the Curb.   1922.

Other

Rosinante to the Road Again.   1922.

Orient Express. 1927.
Facing the Chair: The Story of the Americanization of Two Foreignborn Workmen (on
    Sacco and Vanzetti). 1927.
In All Countries. 1934.
The Villages Are the Heart of Spain. 1937.
Journeys Between Wars. 1938.
The Ground We Stand On: Some Examples from the History of a Political Creed. 1941.
State of the Nation. 1944.
Tour of Duty. 1946.
The Prospect Before Us. 1950.
Life's Picture History of World War II. 1950.
Chosen Country. 1951.
The Head and Heart of Thomas Jefferson. 1954.
The Theme Is Freedom. 1956.
The Men Who Made the Nation. 1957.
Prospects of a Golden Age. 1959.
Mr. Wilson's War. 1962.
Brazil on the Move. 1963.
Thomas Jefferson: The Making of a President (juvenile). 1964.
Occasions and Protests: Essays 1936–1964. 1964.
The Shackles of Power 1801–1826: Three Jeffersonian Decades. 1966.
The Best Times: An Informal Memoir. 1966.
The Portugal Story: Three Decades of Exploration and Discovery. 1969.
Easter Island: Island of Enigmas. 1971.
The Fourteenth Chronicle: Letters and Diaries, edited by Townsend Ludington. 1973.

Editor, *The Living Thoughts of Tom Paine.* 1940.

Translator, *Metropolis,* by Manuel Maples Arce. 1929.
Translator, *Panama,* by Blaise Cendrars. 1931.

Reading List: *Dos Passos* by John H. Wrenn, 1961; *Dos Passos* by Robert Gorham Davis,
1962; *The Fiction of Dos Passos* by John D. Brantley, 1968; *Dos Passos: A Collection of
Critical Essays* edited by Andrew Hook, 1974; *Dos Passos* by George J. Becker, 1974; *Dos
Passos and the Fiction of Despair* by Iain Colley, 1978.

*   *   *

John Dos Passos was involved in many of the episodes that have played an important part
in twentieth-century literary history; not surprisingly, these had an important effect on his
writing. After a lonely childhood living in Europe and then being a bookish student among
advocates of the strenuous life at the Choate School in Wallingford, Connecticut, he went
through Harvard University with a number of the writers who became part of the artistic
renaissance that started during the period just before World War I. T. S. Eliot was still at
Harvard while he was there; E. E. Cummings, Robert Hillyer, and Stewart Mitchell were
among his close friends. He drove an ambulance during World War I, then roamed the
Continent afterward and passed frequently through the Paris expatriate scene, though he was
never truly a part of it. He was a friend of writers like Scott Fitzgerald, Upton Sinclair, Van
Wyck Brooks, and a close friend of Archibald MacLeish, Edmund Wilson, and – for a while
– Ernest Hemingway, among others. He became deeply involved in political radicalism
during the 1920's but was never the activist that his writings made him seem; he interviewed
and wrote about the Italian anarchists Sacco and Vanzetti, who had been found guilty of
murder on dubious evidence; he worked as a director of a left-wing, experimental drama

group, the New Playwrights, in the late 1920's; he traveled to Russia in 1928; he visited the Harlan County, Kentucky, coal mines with Theodore Dreiser in 1931; he experienced the "big money" briefly as a screen writer in Hollywood in 1934; and he went to Spain many times, returning in 1937 with Hemingway to report on the Civil War. During World War II he wrote about the domestic scene, visited the Pacific, and reported on Europe and the war-crimes trials in Germany after the war. In the 1940's and subsequently he took an interest in capitalism – this time viewing it favorably – in Jeffersonian liberalism, and in the development of Latin America.

Although his reputation is not what it was in 1938 when Jean-Paul Sartre declared, "I regard Dos Passos as the greatest writer of our time," his works of fiction, which he came to call chronicles, and his non-fiction continue to be read widely. He is one of the two or three most important political novelists the United States has produced, and certain of his books – in particular *Three Soldiers, Manhattan Transfer*, and the three volumes of *U.S.A.* – are landmarks in the nation's literary history. *Three Soldiers* was the first of the significant novels to come from a United States writer's experiences during World War I. *Manhattan Transfer* represents Dos Passos's innovative application to literature of the artistic theories and techniques which emerged during the decades before and after the turn of the century, when a veritable revolution in the arts occurred in Europe and then in the United States. This chronicle of the city incorporates impressionism, expressionism, montage, simultaneity, reportage, and other techniques of "the new" in the arts and is important also for its themes of alienation and loss, as well as for its satiric treatment of the urban scene.

The three volumes of *U.S.A.* are Dos Passos's attempt to employ his techniques of art to chronicle United States civilization from 1900 to the beginning of the Great Depression in 1929. While he was writing *U.S.A.* from 1927 to 1936, he was far to the left politically, although he began turning toward the center by 1934. The trilogy, a panorama of the nation's life from his political perspective, is deeply satiric about business and the materialistic society it had created. The period he was chronicling, he wrote the critic Malcolm Cowley, was a time when the country moved from "competitive" to "monopoly" capitalism.

From being a political leftist, Dos Passos moved toward the right after believing himself personally betrayed by the Communists, a feeling culminating with the execution – he claimed at the hands of the Communists – of his close friend José Robles in Spain in 1937. Betrayal by the Communists became the fate of the hero in his next novel, the distinctly anti-left *Adventures of a Young Man*. Dos Passos's own adventure with the left was over by then; his subsequent chronicles, which dealt with the years until his death, were increasingly strident satires, most of them about the modern liberalism and government bureaucracy that he saw to be the heritage of Franklin Roosevelt's New Deal Administration. A single exception is *Chosen Country* where, through the adventures of an autobiographical hero, Jay Pignatelli, Dos Passos told of his gradual allegiance to the United States and his romance with his first wife, Katharine Smith.

But Dos Passos was not only a novelist. He wrote numerous books of reportage describing his world travels and analyzing the life and politics of his own and other nations. After 1937, he began also to write histories, repeatedly considering the origins of the United States in books such as *The Ground We Stand On, Men Who Made the Nation, Prospects of a Golden Age*, and *Shackles of Power: Three Jeffersonian Decades*. He became fascinated by Thomas Jefferson, who was, in fact, a sort of hero for him; he wrote a biography – *The Head and Heart of Thomas Jefferson* – as well as several other studies of the man and his era. In addition to all these works he wrote a volume of poetry, several plays, and many articles about politics, drama, and art, among other subjects.

In the early 1950's he sympathized with Senator Joseph McCarthy's efforts to ferret Communists out of the government, but did not support McCarthy's methods. In 1964 he applauded Senator Barry Goldwater for the Presidency; yet Dos Passos's conservatism was never the simplistic matter his critics took it to be. Committed to a right-wing support of the United States by 1958, nevertheless he could write to the historian Arthur Schlesinger, Jr.: "It seems to me that there is a myth of the war [World War II] and our position vis-à-vis the rest of the world which has been swallowing us up in an alarming way. Actually, we are disliked and feared by the rest of the world just as Napoleon, and England and Germany have been. At the same time, we have worked up a self-justificatory fantasy about the nobility of our actions and aims." Always critical rather than doctrinaire, Dos Passos wanted to remain independent, something of the anarchist, in his works supporting individual freedoms against bureaucracies and monoliths wherever he saw them while portraying the swirl of life in his chosen country. Granting Dos Passos his political perspectives, the reader can get from his works a remarkably broad chronicle of the twentieth-century United States.

—Townsend Ludington

DREISER, Theodore (Herman Albert). American.   Born in Terre Haute, Indiana, 27 August 1871; lived with his family in various Indiana towns; settled in Warsaw, Indiana, 1884. Educated in public schools in Warsaw, Terre Haute, Sullivan, and Evansville, Indiana; Indiana University, Bloomington, 1889–90. Married 1) Sara Osborne White in 1898 (separated, 1909; died, 1942); 2) Helen Patges Richardson in 1944. Worked in a restaurant, and for a hardware company, in Chicago, 1887–89; real estate clerk and collection agent, Chicago, 1890–92; Reporter for the Chicago *Globe*, 1892; Dramatic Editor, St. Louis *Globe-Democrat*, 1892–93; settled in New York, 1895: Editor, *Ev'ry Month*, 1895–96, *Smith's Magazine*, 1905–06, and *Broadway Magazine*, 1906–07; Editor-in-Chief, Butterick Publications, New York, and Editor of Butterick's *Delineator*, 1907–10; Editor, *Bohemian* magazine, 1909–10; full-time writer from 1911; lived in Hollywood, 1919–23; Co-Editor, *American Spectator* magazine, 1932–34; applied for membership in the Communist Party, 1945. Chairman, National Committee for the Defense of Political Prisoners, 1931. Recipient: American Academy of Arts and Letters Award of Merit, 1944. *Died 28 December 1945.*

PUBLICATIONS

Collections

    Letters: A Selection, edited by Robert H. Elias.   3 vols., 1959.
    A Dreiser Reader, edited by James T. Farrell.   1962.
    Selected Poems, edited by Robert P. Saalback.   1969.

Fiction

    Sister Carrie.   1900; edited by Donald Pizer, 1970.
    Jennie Gerhardt.   1911.
    The Financier.   1912.
    The Titan.   1914.
    The "Genius."   1915.
    Free and Other Stories.   1918.
    Twelve Men.   1919.
    An American Tragedy.   1925.

Chains: Lesser Novels and Stories.   1927.
A Gallery of Women.   1929.
Fine Furniture (stories).   1930.
The Bulwark.   1946.
The Stoic.   1947.

Plays

Laughing Gas (produced 1916).   In *Plays*, 1916.
Plays of the Natural and the Supernatural (includes *The Girl in the Coffin, The Blue
    Sphere, Laughing Gas, In the Dark, The Spring Recital, The Light in the Window, The
    Old Ragpicker).*   1916; augmented edition (includes *Phantasmagoria* and *The Count
    of Progress*), 1926; (includes *The Dream*), 1927; as *Plays, Natural and Supernatural*
    (includes *The Anaesthetic Revelation*), 1930.
The Girl in the Coffin (produced 1917).   In *Plays*, 1916.
The Old Ragpicker (produced 1918).   In *Plays*, 1916.
The Hand of the Potter (produced 1921).   1919.

Verse

Moods, Cadenced and Declaimed.   1926; revised edition, 1928; as *Moods Philosophic
    and Emotional, Cadenced and Declaimed,* 1935.
The Aspirant.   1929.
Epitaph.   1930.

Other

A Traveler at Forty.   1913.
A Hoosier Holiday.   1916.
Life, Art, and America.   1917.
Hey Rub-a-Dub-Dub: A Book of the Mystery and Wonder and Terror of Life.   1920.
A Book about Myself.   1922; as *Newspaper Days*, 1931; *Dawn: A History of Myself,*
    1931; complete version, as *Autobiography*, 2 vols., 1965.
The Color of a Great City (on New York City).   1923.
Dreiser Looks at Russia.   1928; shortened version, as *Dreiser's Russia*, 1928.
My City.   1929.
The Carnegie Works at Pittsburgh.   1929.
Tragic America.   1931.
Tom Mooney.   1933.
America Is Worth Saving.   1941.
Letters to Louise, edited by Louise Campbell.   1959.
Notes on Life, edited by Marguerite Tjader and John J. McAleer.   1974.
A Selection of Uncollected Prose, edited by Donald Pizer.   1977.

Editor, *The Living Thoughts of Thoreau.*   1939.

Bibliography: *Dreiser: A Primary and Secondary Bibliography* by Donald Pizer, 1975.

Reading List: *Dreiser, Apostle of Nature* by Robert H. Elias, 1949, revised edition, 1970;
Dreiser by Philip L. Gerber, 1964; *Dreiser* by W. A. Swanberg, 1965; *Two Dreisers* by Ellen

Moers, 1969; *Dreiser: A Collection of Critical Essays* edited by John Lydenberg, 1971; *Dreiser* by Richard D. Lehan, 1971; *Dreiser* by James Lundquist, 1974; *The Novels of Dreiser: A Critical Study* by Donald Pizer, 1976.

* * *

The first major writer to emerge from America's "melting pot" population (his father was a German-Catholic weaver), Theodore Dreiser almost single-handedly created and made respectable a socially oriented fiction that surprisingly complements the romance tradition of Hawthorne and Melville, while expanding the narrowly focused realism of Howells and James. His achievement is vast, paradoxical, and, considering the conditions of his birth and the poverty of his youth, highly unlikely. Personally ungainly, erratically educated, and possessing an unusually shoddy conception of aesthetics, he succeeds through a combination of passionate integrity and a brutal determination to exhaust his material completely. For the first time in American fiction he introduced on an epic scale a literary effort in which the social environment was given a detailed attention equal to, if not greater than, that which was focused on the individual protagonist. His heroes are neither orphans set adrift in a bewildering chaotic world, nor are they archetypal symbols occupying spaces in a moral or allegorical diagram. Instead they are begotten out of concrete family relationships within particular socio-economic situations. And although Dreiser's characters are never the mere pawns of their social and biological circumstances, still they can only be understood in terms of those circumstances. Sex and money have ever been the twin thematic strands out of which novels are built, but Dreiser is the first American novelist to scrutinize these concerns with a consistently unashamed and unaverted gaze. His reluctance to apply moralistic judgments and the spacious compassion with which he views the behavior of his characters infuse his fiction with a vitality and a sense of wonder that transcend by far the mechanical operations of the naturalistic formulas that are sometimes invoked to explain – or explain away – his work.

Partly influenced by Herbert Spencer's interpretation of evolution and excited by the honesty he found in the novels of Balzac, Tolstoy, Zola, and Hardy, Dreiser is, of course, far less intellectual than his intellectual influences. Nearer to the bone he drew upon the chequered adventures of his own large family and his personal experiences as an ill-favored ambitious young man struggling to make good in the big blustering city. With the successes and failures of his brothers and sisters in mind, he had no need of philosophical theory to perceive the sharp disparity between the sanctimonious cant of the pulpit and the popular press and the actual practices of life in the booming economy of the last years of the 19th century. And, perhaps most important, his capacity to project himself autobiographically into such different personalities as Carrie Meeber, Hurstwood, Drouet, Jennie Gerhardt, Frank Cowperwood, and Clyde Griffiths makes his novels both impersonal and personal – wide-scale renderings of American life as viewed from a detached brooding perspective and intimately felt transcriptions of the loneliness, frustration, and burning desire to succeed that torment the sensibilities of the American temperament.

His first novel, *Sister Carrie*, already shows Dreiser in full possession of his powers. The pilgrimage of the eighteen year-old country girl to Chicago and then later to stardom on the New York stage follows the hackneyed scenario of the sentimental fiction (the Horatio Alger-Cinderella fairy tale) that Dreiser knew well as an editor for Butterick publications. But Dreiser does more than simply refuse to disapprove of his amoral heroine; he transforms these stock melodramatic materials into a dispassionate dissection of the factors that conjoin for success and failure in a society where "making" and "being" good are sometimes in radical disalignment. Carrie's rise, Drouet's complacent survival, and Hurstwood's fall are complementary elements in the turbulence of a collective life-force surging and ebbing in accord with its own laws of movement. Man may attempt to resist or try to ride along with the current, but, in terms of his most profoundly cherished ideals, he is alien to the purposes of life and doomed to recurrent and ultimate dissatisfaction.

Sister Carrie introduces the themes that were to preoccupy Dreiser throughout his career and also displays his novelistic techniques in full maturity. Although he has been frequently condemned by critics as a wretched stylist, it might be more accurate to suggest that he simply had no personal style at all. Instead, he absorbed the highly detailed, prolix, occasionally ornate but usually lucid magazine-style of the Mauve Decade and employed it as an impersonal instrument in the fashioning of his fiction. In Dreiser's case, his personal style may be more fruitfully sought in his characteristic use of structure. He built his novels in large narrative blocks, each of them composed of simple sequences of action; these he relates unhurriedly, setting minutely observed detail upon detail like a workman laying bricks. These narrative sequences succeed one another in ponderous waves of relentless motion suggesting a sense of the irrevocable passage of time, a cumulative weight of authenticity, and a rhythm of inevitability. With the writing of *Sister Carrie*, Dreiser's development as a novelist was complete. In his subsequent novels he might intensify, broaden, or polish aspects of his ideas and craftsmanship, but his work would remain within the same methodology and frame of bemused compassion that constitute his signature in *Sister Carrie*.

After *Jennie Gerhardt* – a curiously neglected novel that turns *Sister Carrie* inside-out, as it were, and presents in its title character the nearest approach to a saint that Dreiser ever made – he produced his study of an American "robber baron" in *The Financier* and *The Titan*. Modeling his protagonist, Frank Cowperwood, on the millionaire Charles T. Yerkes, Dreiser's intention is to show the obverse side of the Darwinian coin – the ruthless Superman, cooly aware of the amoral rules of the game, who stakes his formidable energies in a singleminded drive for power. Utterly persuasive in its grasp of the political and financial minutiae of stock transfers and bond issues, Dreiser's treatment of Cowperwood's career is easily the authoritative – if caricatured – portrait of the American businessman, relentless in his pursuit of wealth and power, but destined to the same frustration as the weak and victimized whom he manipulates.

The last of Dreiser's major novels and perhaps his single most impressive work is *An American Tragedy*. Here Dreiser is at the very peak of his ability, identifying closely with his protagonist, Clyde Griffiths, even as he broods with Olympian resignation over the wretched banality of Clyde's life. Dreiser reveals that life with magisterial authority, piece by painstaking piece, from Clyde's beginnings as a small embarrassed boy walking the city streets with his missionary parents to his final state execution for murder. More like a massive monument that turns in slow-motion before the reader than a literary portrait, *An American Tragedy* patiently and inexorably amasses evidence to show how a weak malleable personality can be so thoroughly molded by his circumstances and by the shallow values of his culture as to become virtually negligible as a generative force in himself. By the end of the novel, the reader so fully understands the elements that have created Clyde that the character himself almost recedes into the landscape of the novel as merely one more passive factor. And although – or because – every relevant fact in his life has been clearly illumined, the reader can no more determine to what extent Clyde is a murderer and to what extent a victim than can Clyde himself.

Dreiser not only wrote long novels, but he was prolific in many genres. Of the poetry, short stories, plays, and non-fiction as well as other novels in his bibliography, we might cite as of special interest *A Book About Myself* and *Dawn*, two volumes of memoirs, *Hey, Rub-A-Dub-Dub!*, a characteristic volume of essays, and *The "Genius"*, his least successful but most nakedly autobiographical novel. Dreiser's stature in American letters is huge, stubborn, and undeniable. As the 19-century Russian novelists are supposed to have climbed out from under Gogol's overcoat, so one might suggest that Dreiser must bear a similar paternal responsibility for the fiction of the 1920's (Anderson, Faulkner, Fitzgerald, Hemingway, Lewis, Wolfe), the 1930's (Farrell, Steinbeck, Wright), and even the 1940's (Bellow, Mailer). There is a sense in which his achievement may seem crude, I suppose, but it required something stronger than gentility to clear a continent in which his successors could pursue their visions of truth unimpeded by the barriers of hypocrisy, reticence, and prudential caution. The momentum of history was in this direction, of course, but yet some of the richness and power of the modern American novel is due to Dreiser's sweeping redefinition of the novelist's task.

—Earl Rovit

DU BOIS, W(illiam) E(dward) B(urghardt). Ghanaian. Born in Great Barrington, Massachusetts, 23 February 1868; emigrated to Ghana, 1961; naturalized, 1963. Educated in Great Barrington public schools; Fisk University, Nashville (Editor, *Fisk Herald*), A.B. 1888; Harvard University, Cambridge Massachusetts, A.B. 1890, A.M. 1891, Ph.D. 1895. Married 1) Nina Gomer in 1896 (died, 1950), one son and one daughter; 2) Shirley Graham in 1951. Professor of Greek and Latin, Wilberforce University, Ohio, 1894–96; Assistant Instructor of Sociology, University of Pennsylvania, Philadelphia, 1896–97; Professor of Economics and History, Atlanta University, 1897–1910; Editor, *The Moon Illustrated Weekly*, Memphis, 1906, and *The Horizon*, Washington, D.C., 1907–10; a Founder of the National Association for the Advancement of Colored People, 1910, and Director of Publicity and Research for the NAACP and Editor of the NAACP's magazine *Crisis*, New York, 1910–34; Editor, with A. G. Dill, *The Brownies' Book*, 1920–22; Columnist ("A Forum of Fact and Opinion"), *Pittsburgh Courier*, 1936–38, and ("As the Crow Flies"), *Amsterdam News,* 1939–44; Editor, *Phylon*, Atlanta, 1940–44; Director of the Department of Special Research, NAACP, New York, 1944–48; Columnist ("The Winds of Time"), *Chicago Defender*, 1945–48, and *People's Voice*, 1947–48. Founder, Pan-African Congress, 1900, and the Niagara Movement, 1904; Vice-Chairman, Council on African Affairs, 1949–54. Recipient: Spingarn Medal, 1920; International Peace Prize, 1952. Knight Commander, Liberian Order of African Redemption. Fellow, American Association for the Advancement of Science; Member, National Institute of Arts and Letters. *Died 27 August 1963.*

PUBLICATIONS

Collections

The Seventh Son: The Thoughts and Writings of Du Bois, edited by Julius Lester.   2 vols., 1971.
Correspondence, edited by Herbert Aptheker.   3 vols., 1973–78.

Fiction

The Quest of the Silver Fleece.   1911.
Dark Princess: A Romance.   1928.
The Black Flame: The Ordeal of Mansart.   1957; *Mansart Builds a School,* 1959; *Worlds of Color,* 1961.

Play

The Star of Ethiopia (pageant, produced ?).   1913.

Verse

Selected Poems.   1965.

Other

Suppression of African Slave-Trade to the United States of America 1638–1870.   1896.
The Philadelphia Negro: A Social Study, with *A Report on Domestic Service* by Isabel Eaton.   1899.
Possibilities of the Negro: The Advance Guard of Race.   1903.
Souls of Black Folk: Essays and Sketches.   1903; revised edition, 1953.
Of the Wings of Atlanta.   1904.
The Black Vote of Philadelphia.   1905.
The Negro South and North.   1905.
The Negro in the South, with Booker T. Washington.   1907.
John Brown (biography).   1909.
The Social Evolution of the Black South.   1911.
Disfranchisement.   1912.
The Negro.   1915.
Darkwater: Voices from Within the Veil.   1920.
The Gift of Black Folk: Negroes in the Making of America.   1924.
Africa: Its Geography, People, and Products.   1930.
Africa: Its Place in Modern History.   1930.
Black Reconstruction in America: An Essay.   1935.
A Pageant in Seven Decades 1868–1938.   1938.
Black Folk Then and Now: An Essay in the History and Sociology of the Negro Race.   1939.
The Revelation of Saint Orgne, The Damned.   1939.
Dusk of Dawn: An Essay Toward an Autobiography of a Race Concept.   1940.
Encyclopedia of the Negro: Preparatory Volume.   1945; revised edition, 1946.
Color and Democracy: Colonies and Peace.   1945.
An Appeal to the World.   1947.
The World and Africa.   1947; revised edition, 1965.
In Battle for Peace: The Story of My 83rd Birthday.   1952.
The Story of Benjamin Franklin.   1956.
Africa in Battle Against Colonialism, Racialism, Imperialism.   1960.
An ABC of Color.   1963.
Autobiography.   1968.
The Black North in 1901: A Social Study.   1969.
Du Bois Speaks: Speeches and Addresses 1890–1963, edited by Philip Foner.   2 vols., 1970.
The Emerging Thought of Du Bois (*Crisis* articles), edited by Henry Lee Moon.   1972.
The Education of Black People: Ten Critiques 1906–1960, edited by Herbert Aptheker.   1973.
Book Reviews.   1977.
Du Bois on Sociology and the Black Community, edited by Dan S. Green and Edwin D. Driver.   1978.

Editor, *Atlanta University Publications* (pamphlets published in 1898–1913).   2 vols., 1968–69.

Bibliography: *Annotated Bibliography of the Published Writings of Du Bois* by Herbert Aptheker, 1973.

Reading List: *Du Bois: A Profile* edited by Rayford W. Logan, 1971; *The Art and Imagination of Du Bois* by Arnold Rampersand, 1976.

*   *   *

At the age of 35, in 1903, W. E. B. Du Bois took intellectual leadership of those within the Afro-American world who preferred liberal idealism to compensatory realism. Du Bois was prepared for his role by rigorous training in the traditional liberal arts as well as the newer empirical social sciences. But it was confidence and the moral absolute of truth and a poetic imagination that were to prove the sources of his effectiveness.

Souls of Black Folk, the book in which Du Bois publicly announced his differences with Booker T. Washington, is constructed from first-hand observation, historical research, and reasoned analysis. Its power, however, derives from the images of divided consciousness (souls), a culturally united black nation (folk), and the veil behind which black remained nearly invisible. In a time when Jim Crow shaped perception as much as policy, Du Bois's metaphors represented intellectual liberation, giving blacks a profoundly dignified way of conceiving their own lives and history. The cultural nationalism of *Souls of Black Folk* had been implicit in the earlier study *The Philadelphia Negro*, where Du Bois documented class structure and shared institutions. It reappeared as motivation for the Utopian vision of agricultural cooperatives in *Quest of the Silver Fleece* and the romantic narrative of world-wide organization for colored people in *The Dark Princess*.

Du Bois's well-known commitment to the idea of leadership by a talented tenth has its counterpart in the learned rhetoric of his essays and the grandiose design of his novels. It is no wonder that writing as a critic in *Crisis* he was unsympathetic to the experimentation and modern realism of the younger generation in the Negro Renaissance. Still, he made his own characteristic contribution to the "new Negro." His book *The Negro*, anticipating anti-colonial conferences organized after the First World War, corrected popular impressions that American blacks were without roots by celebrating the African past. Then *Black Reconstruction*, written out of Du Bois's new enthusiasm for Marxism in the 1930's, recovered the significance of black people in the history of the South. Despite limitations of style, these historical re-evaluations initiated a scholarly revisionism comparable to the re-direction of thought in the book *Souls of Black Folk*.

Nearing the end of his life, Du Bois published his most comprehensive treatment of America, *The Black Flame*, a trilogy binding into one narrative an historical account of the years corresponding roughly to his own life and a fictional account of Manuel Mansart. That the plots are meant to inter-relate goes without saying. More to the point is the observation that Du Bois's career, capped by the trilogy, was his most important dialectical demonstration. Seeking to write as truthfully as possible, he became not only a scribe of history but its maker.

—John M. Reilly

DUNCAN, Robert (Edward).   American.   Born in Oakland, California, 7 January 1919. Educated at the University of California, Berkeley, 1936–38, 1948–50. Editor, *The Experimental Review*, Berkeley, 1938–40, and *The Berkeley Miscellany*, 1948–49. Lived in

Majorca, 1955–56; taught at Black Mountain College, North Carolina, 1956; Assistant Director of the Poetry Center (Ford grant), 1956–57, and Lecturer in the Poetry Workshop, 1965, San Francisco State College. Recipient: Guggenheim Fellowship, 1963; National Endowment for the Arts grant, 1966 (two grants). Lives in San Fransisco.

PUBLICATIONS

Verse

Heavenly City, Earthly City. 1947.
Poems 1948–1949. 1950.
Medieval Scenes. 1950.
Caesar's Gate: Poems 1949–1950. 1955; revised edition, 1972.
Letters. 1958.
Selected Poems. 1959.
The Opening of the Field. 1960.
Roots and Branches: Poems. 1964.
Writing, Writing: A Composition Book of Madison 1953, Stein Imitations. 1964.
A Book of Resemblances: Poems 1950–1953. 1966.
Of the War: Passages 22–27. 1966.
The Years As Catches: First Poems 1939–1946. 1966.
Fragments of a Disordered Devotion. 1966.
Epilogos. 1967.
Bending the Bow. 1968.
Names of People. 1968.
The First Decade: Selected Poems 1940–1950. 1968.
Derivations: Selected Poems 1950–1956. 1968.
Play Time, Pseudo Stein, 1942: A Story, and A Fairy Play. 1969.
Achilles' Song. 1969.
Poetic Disturbances. 1970.
Tribunals: Passages 31–35. 1970.
Ground Work No. 1. 1971.
In Memoriam Wallace Stevens. 1972.
Poems from the Margins of Thom Gunn's "Moly." 1972.
A Seventeenth Century Suite in Homage to the Metaphysical Genius in English Poetry 1590–1690. 1973.
An Ode and Arcadia, with Jack Spicer. 1974.
Dante. 1974.

Plays

Faust Foutu (produced 1955). 1958; complete edition, as Faust Foutu: An Entertainment in Four Parts, 1960.
Medea at Kolchis: The Maiden Head (produced 1956). 1965.

Other

The Artist's View. 1952.
On Poetry (radio interview with Eugene Vance). 1964.

As Testimony: The Poem and the Scene. 1964.
The Sweetness and Greatness of Dante's "Divine Comedy," 1265–1965. 1965.
Six Prose Pieces. 1966.
The Cat and the Blackbird (juvenile). 1967.
The Truth and Life of Myth: An Essay in Essential Autobiography. 1968.
65 Drawings: A Selection of 65 Drawings from One Drawing-Book: 1952–1956. 1970.
An Interview with George Bowering and Robert Hogg, April 19, 1969. 1971.

Reading List: Robert Duncan Issue of *Origin*, June 1963, of *Audit 4*, 1967, and of *Maps 6*, 1974; *Godawful Streets of Man* by Warren Tallman, 1976.

*   *   *

The poet, Robert Duncan has said, is akin to the paranoiac: everything seems to belong to the plot. Raised in a Theosophist environment, in much of his work Duncan seeks, like the paranoiac but without his fear, for something that does *not* belong to the coherent cosmic plot. Duncan, therefore (as he expounds it most clearly in the sections of the incomplete "The H. D. Book"), lives in a world in which "things strive to speak," where the poet seeks to read "the language of things," where "the poet must attend not to what he means to say but to what what he says means" (*Caterpillar 7*). The poet is, then, subject not to "inspiration" so much as he is to "possession," where he may be had by an idea, and poetry is – in Duncan's language – an Office: the text the poet writes is part of a larger text: the Poem, and the office of poet is subsumed in the larger Office, of Poet.
    It is thus perhaps to be expected that Duncan, of all poets associated with Black Mountain College and with post-Modernism, should be the American writer most closely associated with the great tradition of English poetry and of mystical poetry, while at the same time he is the one who seems most consistently and perversely to be at odds with the traditions and conventions of English poetry. Such apparent perversity arises in part from Duncan's insistence, drawn from Heraclitus that "an unapparent connexion is stronger than an apparent": it derives also, in part, from "the strongest drive of my life, that things have not come to the conclusions I saw around me, and this involved the conclusions that I saw shaping in my own thought and actions" (*Caterpillar 8/9*). Thus "A Poem Beginning with a Line by Pindar" (1958) is a combination of traditional devices, forms, and sources with the unexpected and unconventional. The synecdoche of "the light foot *hears*," quoted from Pindar's First Pythian Ode, involves the breaking of things "normal" in the language; this in turn suggests a range of possible meanings for "*light*" foot." The poem, an extended meditation and discovery on – among other things – the notion of Adulthood, proposes a world in which the Real is found, not in a landscape, but "in an obscurity" – hidden, that is to say, from normal, familiar, conventional (or mortal) sight. In two essays central to his work, "Ideas of the Meaning of Form" (*Kulchur 4*) and "Man's Fulfillment in Order and Strife" (*Caterpillar 8/9*), Duncan insists that "to the conventional mind" form is "what can be impo ed," and, in all of his writing, conventional syntax and language are a part of conventional form, and man is a creature of language. In section Two of the "Pindar" poem the language, individual words and syllables, breaks down, loses its articulation, becomes almost nonsense. The breakdown is triggered by the word "stroke" which – initially of a brush, painting, or of a pen, writing – becomes a medical stroke (Eisenhower's?), and the poem, which at that point seems to be struggling to a halt, moves into a firm political rhetoric which reveals adulthood as a condition of nations as well as of individuals, and the condition itself as a process. Reading the poem, we witness the testimony of the poet discovering the world as it reveals itself to him through language. Meaning, in such poems as this, is to be

found in the play of possible meanings, rather than in the conventionally ordered exposition of rational or reasonable thought. Duncan's insistence "not to reach a conclusion but to keep our exposure to what we do not know" has led to *Passages*, a series of rhetorical poems which, resting on the Julian motto "The even is bounded, but the uneven is without bounds," explores all possible voices as its testimony to What Is.

—Peter Quartermain

EBERHART, Richard (Ghormley).   Born in Austin, Minnesota, 5 April 1904. Educated at the University of Minnesota, Minneapolis, 1922–23; Dartmouth College, Hanover, New Hampshire, B.A. 1926; St. John's College, Cambridge, B.A. 1929, M.A. 1933; Harvard University, Cambridge, Massachusetts, 1932–33. Served in the United States Naval Reserve, 1942–46: Lieutenant Commander. Married Helen Butcher in 1941; has two children. Worked as floorwalker, and as deckboy on tramp ships; tutor to the son of King Prajadhipok of Siam, 1930–31; English Teacher, St. Mark's School, Southboro, Massachusetts, 1933–41, and Cambridge School, Kendal Green, Massachusetts, 1941–42; Assistant Manager to the Vice-President, Butcher Polish Company, Boston, 1946–52 (Honorary Vice-President, 1952, and Member of the Board of Directors, 1958); Visiting Professor, University of Washington, Seattle, 1952–53, 1967, 1972; Professor of English, University of Connecticut, Storrs, 1953–54; Visiting Professor, Wheaton College, Norton, Massachusetts, 1954–55; Resident Fellow and Gauss Lecturer, Princeton University, New Jersey, 1955–56; Distinguished Visiting Professor, University of Florida, Gainesville, Winters 1974, 1977, 1978. Professor of English and Poet-in-Residence, 1956–68, Class of 1925 Professor, 1968–70 and since 1970 Professor Emeritus, Dartmouth College. Elliston Lecturer, University of Cincinnati, 1961. Founder, 1950, and First President, Poets' Theatre, Cambridge, Massachusetts; Member, 1955, and since 1964, Director, Yaddo Corporation; Member, Advisory Committee on the Arts, John F. Kennedy Memorial Theatre, Washington, D.C. Consultant in Poetry, 1959–61, and Honorary Consultant in American Letters, 1963–69, Library of Congress, Washington, D.C. Recipient: New England Poetry Club Golden Rose, 1950; Shelley Memorial Award, 1952; Harriet Monroe Poetry Award, 1955; National Institute of Arts and Letters grant, 1955; Bollingen Prize, 1962; Pulitzer Prize, 1966; Academy of American Poets Fellowship, 1969; National Book Award, 1977. D.Litt.: Dartmouth College, 1954; Skidmore College, Saratoga, New York, 1966; College of Wooster, Ohio, 1969; Colgate University, Hamilton, New York, 1974. Since 1972, Honorary President, Poetry Society of America. Member, National Institute of Arts and Letters, 1960, and American Academy of Arts and Sciences, 1967. Lives in New Hampshire.

PUBLICATIONS

Verse

A Bravery of Earth.   1930.
Reading the Spirit.   1936.
Song and Idea.   1940.

Poems, New and Selected. 1944.
Burr Oaks. 1947.
Brotherhood of Men. 1949.
An Herb Basket. 1950.
Selected Poems. 1951.
Undercliff: Poems 1946–1953. 1953.
Great Praises. 1957.
The Oak: A Poem. 1957.
Collected Poems 1930–1960, Including 51 New Poems. 1960.
The Quarry: New Poems. 1964.
The Vastness and Indifference of the World. 1965.
Fishing for Snakes. 1965.
Selected Poems 1930–1965. 1965.
Thirty One Sonnets. 1967.
Shifts of Being: Poems. 1968.
The Achievement of Richard Eberhart: A Comprehensive Selection of His Poems, edited
   by Bernard F. Engle. 1968.
Three Poems. 1968.
Fields of Grace. 1972.
Two Poems. 1975.
Collected Poems 1930–1976. 1976.
Selected Poems. 1978.

Plays

The Apparition (produced 1951). In *Collected Verse Plays,* 1962.
The Visionary Farms (produced 1952). In *Collected Verse Plays,* 1962.
Triptych (produced 1955). In *Collected Verse Plays,* 1962.
The Mad Musician, and Devils and Angels (produced 1962). In *Collected Verse Plays,*
   1962.
Collected Verse Plays (includes *Preamble I* and *II*). 1962.
The Bride from Mantua, from a play by Lope de Vega (produced 1964).

Other

Editor, with Selden Rodman, *War and the Poet: An Anthology of Poetry Expressing
   Man's Attitude to War from Ancient Times to the Present.* 1945.
Editor, *Dartmouth Poems.* 12 vols., 1958–71.

Reading List: *Eberhart* by Ralph J. Mills, Jr., 1966; *Eberhart: The Progress of an American
Poet* by Joel H. Roache, 1971; *Eberhart* by Bernard F. Engle, 1972.

*   *   *

Even Richard Eberhart's most ardent admirers admit the striking unevenness of his work
– stirring and exquisite poems published with others marred by sentimentality, pedantic
diction, and banal abstractions. That his work might indeed be so uneven derives from
Eberhart's vision of what poetry is, as well as his method of composition: "Poetry is
dynamic, Protean," he writes. "In the rigors of composition ... the poet's mind is a filament,
informed with the irrational vitality of energy as it was discovered in our time in quantum
mechanics. The quanta may shoot off any way." Eberhart rewrites little. His is an

inspirational poetry; through it, he discovers life's significances. "You breathe in maybe God," and at those moments, "the poet writes with a whole clarity."

Unlike many of his contemporaries during the 1930's Eberhart never worked for the hard, spare line; he created no personae. He wrote a personal poetry, much in the vein of the Romantics, especially Blake, Wordsworth, and Whitman, a poetry concerned with understanding and transcending concrete experience. Regardless of the inevitable problems such an aesthetic might invite, there remains a large body of inspired and original verse wherein Eberhart is able to "aggravate" perception into life. Eberhart's best work results from his success in transforming keenly felt sense perceptions, through the language of the experience itself, into meaning – moral, metaphysical, mystical, even religious. His most significant work retains the urgency and radiance of the felt experience, as it simultaneously transforms it into the significant; Eberhart is epiphanic much like Gerard Manley Hopkins. "The poet," he states, "makes the world anew; something grows out of the old, which he locks in words."

In Eberhart's first volume, *A Bravery of Earth*, he writes about the three types of "awareness" one must accomplish in order to gain maturity – mortality, mentality, and men's actions. These goals have been reflected throughout Eberhart's career. However, particular subjects have also persisted – the poet's sheer wonder in nature, the fierce exhilaration inspired by "lyric" and "lovely" nature, within which is "God" "incarnate," as in "This Fevers Me":

> This fevers me, this sun on green,
> On grass glowing, this young spring.
> The secret hallowing is come,
> Regenerate sudden incarnation,
> Mystery made visible
> In growth, yet subtly veiled in all,
> Ununderstandable in grass,
> In flowers, and in the human heart,
> This lyric mortal loveliness,
> The earth breathing, and the sun.

Such an intimate involvement with physical nature, nevertheless, involves the poet in its cycles of growth and decay, and Eberhart, always aware of his own mortality, searches for intimations of immortality. Some of his poems address death as a creative force, in its recurrent cycles:

> When I can hold a stone within my hand
> And feel time make it sand and soil, and see
> The roots of living things grow in this land,
> Pushing between my fingers flower and tree,
> Then I shall be as wise as death,
> For death has done this and he will
> Do this to me, and blow this breath
> To fire my clay, when I am still.

Eberhart's compassion extends toward all living things which share a common fate. In a poem like "For a Lamb," after describing the lamb as "putrid," "on the slant hill," and "propped with daisies," the poet speaks of the fundamental continuity of life in nature:

> Where's the lamb? whose tender plaint
> Said all for the mute breezes.
> Say he's in the wind somewhere,
> Say, there's a lamb in the daisies.

"The Groundhog," one of Eberhart's best known poems, evokes another sort of wild, extravagant transcendence in the face of physical decay. The poet now experiences an exhilaration not through an awareness of nature's eternal, recurrent cycles, but rather through his creative articulation of the fact of decay. Returning year after year to the dead groundhog, he wishes for its absorption within nature's processes, but instead he witnesses its transformation from simple decay − "I saw a groundhog lying dead./Dead lay he" − to something artistically beautiful, its few bones "bleaching in the sunlight/Beautiful as architecture." He moves from a sense of "naked frailty" to "strange love," "a fever," a "passion of the blood." Elsewhere Eberhart has said: "Poetry is a spell against death," and he concludes "The Groundhog" with:

> I stood there in the whirling summer,
> My hand capped a withered heart,
> And thought of China and of Greece,
> Of Alexander in his tent;
> Of Montaigne and his tower,
> Of Saint Theresa in her wild lament.

Eberhart comes to identify with the mighty figures of the past who transcended the ravages of time through the very energy of their creative living, and through the legacy of historical memory and art. The poet has transcended through the creation of his poem.

Eberhart writes about a variety of experiences associated with death. In "Imagining How It Would Be to Be Dead" and "When Golden Flies upon My Carcass Come," he tries to apprehend his own death. Death may also be the moment of revelation and transcendence, of "worldless Ecstasy/Of mystery." But death may also be "merely death" − "This is a very ordinary experience./A name may be glorious but death is death" ("I Walked over the Grave of Henry James"). In "The Cancer Cells," he expresses an aesthetic glee in the artistic design of malignant cells: "They looked like art itself .../I think Leonardo would have in his disinterest/enjoyed them precisely with a sharp pencil."

Poems like "If I Could Only Live at the Pitch That Is Near Madness" represent another theme through Eberhart's poetry − his desire to retain the intensity of childhood, "the incomparable light," "when everything is as it was in my childhood/Violent, vivid, and of infinite possibility." But Eberhart accepts, indeed embraces, the "moral answer," that awareness that one cannot leave the world of men and maturity; and, as he returns "into a realm of complexity," there is a sense of new wonder and exaltation, as of joyful paternity, in his acceptance of the responsibilities of adulthood. One must not just feel experience; one must understand and articulate it.

Also recurrent are the variety of images of man's fallen state, his cruelty to his fellow man, the varieties of human suffering that grow out of social, political, and family strife. One is under obligation, implies Eberhart in his famous "Am I My Neighbor's Keeper?," to care for his fellow man. Perhaps best known among this group is his "The Fury of Aerial Bombardment," one of his many poems concerned with the inhumanity of war, where the poet ultimately wonders what sort of God would permit the barbarism of war: "You would feel that after so many centuries/God would give man to relent."

Throughout his fifty years of writing, Eberhart has emphasized the importance of man's creating a credo, a transcending vision, through personal and concrete experience. As intensely aware of man's existential condition as many of his contemporaries, Eberhart focuses on life and its creative possibilities. (In his acceptance speech of the National Book Award 1977, he lamented the suicides of some of his contemporaries and said, "Poets should not die for poetry but live for it.") Eberhart has focused upon concrete and everyday experience as the avenue toward transcendence, even if just momentary. For him, words, poetry itself, leads to "joy" and "ecstasy": "The only triumph is some elegance of style."

But each man is a poet, in a sense, for each man is, in his everyday life, the creator of any meaning his life will have. Each man must "make ... [his] own myth." Nature remains benignly indifferent. As James Cotter expressed it, in reviewing Eberhart's *Collected Poems 1930–1976* (*America*, 18 September 1976), the owl's cry tells man nothing unless one goes "somewhere beyond realism," and learns to "listen to the tune of the spiritual. Nature does not love or heed us. We are the lovers of nature."

—Lois Gordon

ELIOT, T(homas) S(tearns).   English.   Born in St. Louis, Missouri, U.S.A., 26 September 1888; naturalized, 1927. Educated at Smith Academy, St. Louis, 1898–1905; Milton Academy, Massachusetts, 1905–06; Harvard University, Cambridge, Massachusetts (Editor, *Harvard Advocate*, 1909–10; Sheldon Fellowship, for study in Munich, 1914), 1906–10, 1911–14, B.A. 1909, M.A. 1910; the Sorbonne, Paris, 1910–11; Merton College, Oxford, 1914–15. Married 1) Vivienne Haigh-Wood in 1915 (died, 1947); 2) Esmé Valerie Fletcher, 1957. Teacher, High Wycombe Grammar School, Buckinghamshire, and Highgate School, London, 1915–17; Clerk, Lloyds Bank, London, 1917–25; Editor, later Director, Faber and Gwyer, later Faber and Faber, publishers, London, 1926–65. Assistant Editor, *The Egoist*, London, 1917–19; Founding Editor, *The Criterion*, London, 1922–39. Clark Lecturer, Trinity College, Cambridge, 1926; Charles Eliot Norton Professor of Poetry, Harvard University, 1932–33; Page-Barbour Lecturer, University of Virginia, Charlottesville, 1933; Theodore Spencer Memorial Lecturer, Harvard University, 1950. President, Classical Association, 1941, Virgil Society, 1943, and Books Across the Sea, 1943–46. Resident, Institute for Advanced Study, Princeton University, New Jersey, 1950; Honorary Fellow, Merton College, Oxford, and Magdalene College, Cambridge. Recipient: Nobel Prize for Literature, 1948; New York Drama Critics Circle Award, 1950; Hanseatic Goethe Prize, 1954; Dante Gold Medal, Florence, 1959; Order of Merit, Bonn, 1959; American Academy of Arts and Sciences Emerson-Thoreau Medal, 1960. Litt.D.: Columbia University, New York, 1933; Cambridge University, 1938; University of Bristol, 1938; University of Leeds, 1939; Harvard University, 1947; Princeton University, 1947; Yale University, New Haven, Connecticut, 1947; Washington University, St. Louis, 1953; University of Rome, 1958; University of Sheffield, 1959; LL.D.: University of Edinburgh, 1937; University of St. Andrews, 1953; D.Litt.: Oxford University, 1948; D.Lit.: University of London, 1950; Docteur-ès-Lettres, University of Aix-Marseille, 1959; University of Rennes, 1959; D.Phil.: University of Munich, 1959. Officer, Legion of Honor; Honorary Member, American Academy of Arts and Letters; Foreign Member, Accademia dei Lincei, Rome, and Akademie der Schönen Künste. Order of Merit, 1948. *Died 4 January 1965.*

PUBLICATIONS

Collections

Selected Prose, edited by Frank Kermode.   1975.

Verse

Prufrock and Other Observations.   1917.

Poems. 1919.
Ara Vos Prec. 1920; as *Poems,* 1920.
The Waste Land. 1922; *A Facsimile and Transcripts of the Original Drafts Including the Annotations of Ezra Pound,* edited by Valerie Eliot, 1971.
Poems 1909–1925. 1925.
Ash-Wednesday. 1930.
Sweeney Agonistes: Fragments of an Aristophanic Melodrama. 1932.
Collected Poems 1909–1935. 1936.
Old Possum's Book of Practical Cats. 1939.
The Waste Land and Other Poems. 1940.
East Coker. 1940.
Later Poems 1925–1935. 1941.
The Dry Salvages. 1941.
Little Gidding. 1942.
Four Quartets. 1943.
A Practical Possum. 1947.
Selected Poems. 1948.
The Undergraduate Poems of T. S. Eliot. 1949.
Poems Written in Early Youth, edited by John Hayward. 1950.
Collected Poems 1909–1962. 1963.

Plays

The Rock: A Pageant Play (produced 1934). 1934.
Murder in the Cathedral (produced 1935). 1935; revised version, as *The Film of Murder in the Cathedral,* 1952.
The Family Reunion (produced 1939). 1939.
The Cocktail Party (produced 1949). 1950; revised edition, 1950.
The Confidential Clerk (produced 1953). 1954.
The Elder Statesman (produced 1958). 1959.
Collected Plays: Murder in the Cathedral, The Family Reunion, The Cocktail Party, The Confidential Clerk, The Elder Statesman. 1962; as *The Complete Plays,* 1969.

Other

Ezra Pound: His Metric and Poetry. 1917.
The Sacred Wood: Essays on Poetry and Criticism. 1920.
Homage to John Dryden: Three Essays on Poetry in the Seventeenth Century. 1924.
For Lancelot Andrewes: Essays on Style and Order. 1928.
Dante. 1929.
Thoughts after Lambeth. 1931.
Selected Essays 1917–1932. 1932; revised edition, 1950.
John Dryden: The Poet, The Dramatist, The Critic. 1932.
The Use of Poetry and the Use of Criticism: Studies in the Relation of Criticism to Poetry in England. 1933.
After Strange Gods: A Primer of Modern Heresy. 1934.
Elizabethan Essays. 1934; as *Elizabethan Dramatists,* 1963.
Essays Ancient and Modern. 1936.
The Idea of a Christian Society. 1939.
Points of View, edited by John Hayward. 1941.
Reunion by Destruction: Reflections on a Scheme for Church Unity in South India Addressed to the Laity. 1943.

Notes Towards the Definition of Culture. 1948.
The Complete Poems and Plays. 1952.
Selected Prose, edited by John Hayward. 1953.
On Poetry and Poets. 1957.
George Herbert. 1962.
Knowledge and Experience in the Philosophy of F. H. Bradley (doctoral dissertation). 1964.
To Criticize the Critic and Other Writings. 1965.
The Literary Criticism of Eliot: New Essays, edited by David Newton de-Molina. 1977.

Editor, *Selected Poems,* by Ezra Pound. 1928; revised edition, 1949.
Editor, *A Choice of Kipling's Verse.* 1941.
Editor, *Introducing James Joyce.* 1942.
Editor, *Literary Essays of Ezra Pound.* 1954.
Editor, *The Criterion 1922–1939.* 18 vols., 1967.

Translator, *Anabasis: A Poem* by St.-John Perse. 1930; revised edition, 1938, 1949, 1959.

Bibliography: *Eliot: A Bibliography* by Donald Gallup, 1952, revised edition, 1969; *The Merrill Checklist of Eliot* by B. Gunter, 1970.

Reading List: *The Achievement of Eliot: An Essay on the Nature of Poetry* by F. O. Matthiessen, 1935, revised edition, 1947, with additional material by C. L. Barber, 1958; *Four Quartets Rehearsed* by R. Preston, 1946; *Eliot: The Design of His Poetry* by Elizabeth Drew, 1949; *The Art of Eliot* by Helen Gardner, 1949; *The Poetry of Eliot* by D. E. S. Maxwell, 1952; *Eliot's Poetry and Plays: A Study in Sources and Meaning* by Grover Smith, 1956, revised edition, 1975; *The Invisible Poet: Eliot* by Hugh Kenner 1959; *Eliot: A Collection of Critical Essays* edited by Hugh Kenner, 1962; *Eliot's Dramatic Theory and Practice* by Carol H. Smith, 1963; *Eliot* by Northrop Frye, 1963; *Eliot: Movements and Patterns* by Leonard Unger, 1966; *Eliot* by Bernard Bergonzi, 1972; *Eliot in His Time: Essays on the Occasion of the Fiftieth Anniversary of The Waste Land* edited by A. Walton Litz, 1973; *Eliot: The Longer Poems* by Derek Traversi, 1976.

*   *   *

T. S. Eliot's influence was predominant in English poetry in the period between the two World Wars. His first small volume of poems, *Prufrock and Other Observations* appeared in 1917. The title is significant. Eliot's earliest verse is composed of *observations*, detached, ironic, and alternately disillusioned and nostalgic in tone. The prevailing influence is that of French poetry, and in particular of Jules Laforgue; the mood is one of reaction against the comfortable certainties of "Georgian" poetry, the projection of a world which presented itself to the poet and his generation as disconcerting, uncertain, and very possibly heading for destruction.

The longest poem in the volume, "The Love Song of J. Alfred Prufrock," shows these qualities, but goes beyond them. The speaker is a kind of modern Hamlet, a man who after a life passed in devotion to the trivial has awakened to a sense of his own futility and to that of the world around him. He feels that some decisive act of commitment is needed to break the meaningless flow of events which his life offers. The question, however, is whether he really dares to reverse the entire course of his existence by a decision the nature of which eludes him:

And indeed there will be time
To wonder, "Do I dare?" and, "Do I dare?"
Time to turn back and descend the stair,
With a bald spot in the middle of my hair ...
Do I dare
Disturb the universe?

The answer, for Prufrock, is negative. Dominated by his fear of life, misunderstood when he tries to express his sense of a possible revelation, Prufrock concludes "No! I am not Prince Hamlet, nor was meant to be," refuses to accept the role which life for a moment seemed to have thrust upon him, and returns to the stagnation which his vision of reality imposes.

After a second small volume, published in 1919, which shows, more especially in its most impressive poem, "Gerontion," a notable deepening into tragedy, the publication in 1922 of *The Waste Land* burst upon its readers with the effect of a literary revolution. Many of its first readers found the poem arid and incomprehensible, though it was in fact neither. The poet tells us that he is working through "a heap of broken images." He does this because it is a world of dissociated fragments that he is describing; but his aim, like that of any artist, is not merely an evocation of chaos. The poem is built on the interweaving of two great themes: the broken pieces of the present, as it presents itself to a disillusioned contemporary understanding, and the significant continuity of tradition. These two strains begin apart, like two separate themes in a musical composition, but the poem is animated by the hope, the *method*, that at the end they will converge into some kind of unity. Some critics, reading it in the light of Eliot's later development, have tried to find in the poem a specifically "religious" content, which however is not there. At best, there is a suggestion at the close that such a content, were it available, might provide a way out of the "waste land" situation, that the life-giving rain *may* be on the point of relieving the intolerable drought; but the poet cannot honestly propose such a resolution and the step which might have affirmed it is never rendered actual.

For some years after 1922, Eliot wrote little poetry and the greater part of his effort went into critical prose, much of it published in *The Criterion*, the literary quarterly which he edited until 1939. Eliot's criticism, which profoundly affected the literary taste of his generation, contributed to the revaluation of certain writers – the lesser Elizabethan dramatists, Donne, Marvell, Dryden – and, more controversially, to the depreciation of others, such as Milton (concerning whom, however, Eliot later modified his views) and some of the Romantic poets. It was the work of a poet whose interest in other writers was largely conditioned by the search for solutions to the problems raised by his own art; and, as such, it was marked by the idiosyncracies which constitute at once its strength and its limitation.

In 1928, in his preface to the collection of essays *For Lancelot Andrewes*, Eliot declared himself Anglo-Catholic in religion, royalist in politics, classicist in literature: a typically enigmatic statement which indicated the direction he was to give to the work of his later years. 1930 saw the publication of *Ash-Wednesday*, his first considerable poem of explicitly Christian inspiration: a work at once religious in content and modern in inspiration, personal yet without concession to sentiment. The main theme is an acceptance of conversion as a necessary and irretrievable act. The answer to the question posed by Prufrock – "Do I dare/ Disturb the universe?" – is seen, in the translation of the first line of the Italian poet Guido Cavalcanti's ballad, "Because I do not hope to turn again," as an embarkation, dangerous but decisive, upon the adventure of faith.

The consequences of this development were explored in the last and in some respects the most ambitious of Eliot's poetic efforts: the sequence of poems initiated in 1935 and finally published, in 1943, under the title of *Four Quartets*. The series opens, in *Burnt Norton*, with an exploration of the *possible* significance of certain moments which seem to penetrate, briefly and elusively, a reality beyond that of normal temporal experience. "To be conscious," the poem suggests, "is not to be in time": only to balance that possibility with the counter-assertion that "Only through time time is conquered." The first step towards an understanding of the problems raised in the *Quartets* is a recognition that time, though inseparable from our human experience, is not the whole of it. If we consider time as an ultimate reality, our spiritual intuitions are turned into an illusion: whereas if we seek to deny the reality of time, our experience becomes impossible. The two elements – the temporal and the timeless – need to be woven together in an embracing pattern of experience which is, in fact, the end to which the entire sequence points.

The later "quartets" build upon this provisional foundation in the light of the poet's experience as artist and human being. The impulse to create in words reflects another, still more fundamental, impulse which prompts men to seek *form*, coherence, and meaning in the broken intuitions which their experience offers them. The nature of the search is such that it can never be complete in time. The true value of our actions only begins to emerge when we abstract ourselves from the temporal sequence – "time before and time after" – in which they were realized; and the final sense of our experience only reveals itself when the pattern is completed, at the moment of death. This moment, indeed, is not properly speaking a single final point, but a reality which covers the whole course of our existence.

These reflections lead the poet, in the last two poems of the series, *The Dry Salvages* and *Little Gidding*, to acceptance and even to a certain optimism. The end of the journey becomes the key to its beginning, and this in turn an invitation to confidence: "Not fare well,/But fare forward, voyagers." The doctrine of detachment explored in the second poem, *East Coker*, becomes an "expanding" one of "love beyond desire." The conclusion stresses the continuity between the "birth" and "death" which are simultaneously present in each moment, in each individual life, and in the history of the human race. It is true, as the closing section of *Little Gidding* puts it, that "we die with the dying"; but it is equally true, as they also go on to say, that "we are born with the dead." We die, in other words, as part of the tragedy which the fact of our humanity implies, but we are born again when, having understood the temporal process in its true light, we are ready to accept our present position within a still-living and continually unfolding tradition.

Eliot's poetic output was relatively small and intensely concentrated: a fact which at once confirms its value and constitutes, in some sense, a limiting factor. It should be mentioned that in his later years he devoted himself to the writing of verse plays, in an attempt to create a contemporary mode of poetic drama. The earlier plays, *Murder in the Cathedral* and *The Family Reunion*, which are also the best, take up the themes which were being explored at the same time in his poetry and develop them in ways that are often interesting. *The Cocktail Party*, though still a skilful work, shows some decline in conception and execution, and the later plays – *The Confidential Clerk* and *The Elder Statesman* – can safely be said to add little to Eliot's achievement.

—Derek A. Traversi

ELLISON, Ralph (Waldo).   American.   Born in Oklahoma City, Oklahoma, 1 March 1914. Educated at a high school in Oklahoma City, and at Tuskegee Institute, Alabama, 1933–36. Served in the United States Merchant Marine, 1943–45. Married Fanny McConnell in 1946. Writer from 1936; Lecturer, Salzburg Seminar in American Studies, 1954; Instructor of Russian and American Literature, Bard College, Annandale-on-Hudson, New York, 1958–61; Alexander White Visiting Professor, University of Chicago, 1961; Visiting Professor of Writing, Rutgers University, New Brunswick, New Jersey, 1962–64; Whittall Lecturer, Library of Congress, Washington, D.C., 1964; Ewing Lecturer, University of

California at Los Angeles, 1964; Visiting Fellow in American Studies, Yale University, New Haven, Connecticut, 1966. Since 1970, Albert Schweitzer Professor in the Humanities, New York University. Chairman, Literary Grants Committee, National Institute of Arts and Letters, 1964–67; Member, National Council on the Arts, 1965–67; Member, Carnegie Commission on Educational Television, 1966–67; Member of the Editorial Board, *American Scholar*, Washington, D.C., 1966–69; Honorary Consultant in American Letters, Library of Congress, Washington, D.C., 1966–72. Trustee, John F. Kennedy Center of the Performing Arts, Washington, D.C., New School for Social Research, New York, Bennington College, Vermont, Educational Broadcasting Corporation, and the Colonial Williamsburg Foundation. Recipient: Rosenwald Fellowship, 1945; National Book Award, 1953; National Newspaper Publishers Association Russwarm Award, 1953; National Academy of Arts and Letters Prix de Rome, 1955, 1956; United States Medal of Freedom, 1969. Ph.D. in Humane Letters: Tuskegee Institute, 1963; Litt.D.: Rutgers University, 1966; University of Michigan, Ann Arbor, 1967; Williams College, Williamstown, Massachusetts, 1970; Long Island University, New York, 1971; College of William and Mary, Williamsburg, Virginia, 1972; Wake Forest College, Winston-Salem, North Carolina, 1974; Harvard University, Cambridge, Massachusetts, 1974; L.H.D.: Grinnell College, Iowa, 1967; Adelphi University, Garden City, New York, 1971; University of Maryland, College Park, 1974. Chevalier de l'Ordre des Arts et Lettres, France, 1970. Member, American Academy of Arts and Letters, 1975. Lives in New York City.

PUBLICATIONS

Fiction

Invisible Man.   1952.

Other

Shadow and Act (essays).   1964.

Bibliography: "A Bibliography of Ellison's Published Writings" by Bernard Benoit and Michel Fabre, in *Studies in Black Literature 2*, 1971; *The Blinking Eye: Ellison and His American, French, German, and Italian Critics* by Jacqueline Covo, 1974.

Reading List: *Five Black Writers* edited by Donald B. Gibson, 1970; "Ellison Issue" of *C.L.A. Journal 13*, 1970; *Twentieth-Century Interpretations of "Invisible Man"* edited by John M. Reilly, 1970; *The Merrill Studies in "Invisible Man"* edited by Ronald Gottesman, 1971; *Ellison: A Collection of Critical Essays* edited by John Hersey, 1973.

*   *   *

A bookish as well as a musical child, Ralph Ellison began to read some of the classics of modern literature, including *The Waste Land*, while a student at Tuskegee. His literary education was accelerated after he met Richard Wright in 1937. In addition to providing an example of commitment to social and racial justice, Wright helped to persuade Ellison to direct his creative energies to writing, encouraging him to turn to "those works in which writing was discussed as a craft ... to Henry James' prefaces, to Conrad, to Joseph Warren Beach and to the letters of Dostoievsky" (*Shadow and Act*). Despite some later disavowals,

Ellison was deeply influenced by Wright's own fiction as well as by his literary tutelage. Such early short stories as "Slick Gonna Learn" and "Mister Toussan'," for example, reveal how carefully Ellison had read Wright's *Uncle Tom's Children*.

When one looks at *Invisible Man*, however, one sees that Ellison's creative consciousness encompasses a vast range of the world's literature. Such modern giants as Eliot, Joyce, Malraux, Hemingway, Pound, Stein, and Faulkner are clearly part of his literary inheritance, but so are the writers of the Harlem Renaissance; the Continental (especially Dostoevsky), British, and American (especially Melville and Twain) masters of nineteenth-century fiction; and his namesake Emerson and other Transcendentalists. Some critics have argued for *The Odyssey* or *The Aeneid* as major influences on Ellison's novel. However allusive, Ellison is also profoundly original, putting his sophisticated technique and literary education to the service of his vision of the racial and human condition in America.

Invisible Man concerns the quest of an unnamed young black man for personal identity and racial community as he travels from South to North, from innocence to experience, from self-deception to knowledge, from a spurious visibility to an existential invisibility. These journeys take place in the immediate context of the late depression, but, as they unfold, their implications extend backward in time to the Reconstruction, slavery, and the founding of the Republic, and outward from the protagonist's self to the social situation of black America and to the very nature of the democratic experiment.

Framed by a prologue and an epilogue set in an underground chamber to which the protagonist has retreated from the chaos of life above ground, the narrative proper begins in the Deep South with his initiation rite into the social order of white supremacy as he graduates from high school and prepares to matriculate at a black college closely resembling Tuskegee Institute, where he hopes to learn to become a black leader. There the idyllic setting and his personal ambition are disrupted by his naivety, by a northern white capitalist's ambiguous "philanthropy," and by the ruthless self-aggrandizement of Dr. Bledsoe, the black president of the institution. Expelled from college and from the South, the protagonist travels to New York to seek employment in a white-collar position. Unsuccessful in that effort, he undergoes a still more disastrous experience as an industrial worker in the Liberty Paint plant. After these repeated failures in his personal pursuit of success, the protagonist becomes involved with the Brotherhood, a radical political organization paralleling the Communist Party. Here, he hopes, he can achieve self-realization while contributing to social amelioration. But political radicalism fails him – and his race – just as completely as southern segregation and northern employment, and for similar reasons of personal and racial exploitation. When his very physical existence is threatened in a Harlem race riot, he goes underground for sanctuary and reassessment. Ending in the epilogue where it began in the prologue, the narrative completes its circular ("boomerang") structure. Whatever one thinks of the rather forced optimism concerning a possible resurrection and return to the world above ground, the success of which may be viewed as problematical given his repeated rebuffs, the protagonist has at last and at least achieved for himself and for the reader the kind of self-actualization that knowledge of self and society can bring. To that extent he is no longer an invisible man.

Ellison's other published book, *Shadow and Act*, is a prose miscellany deriving some unity from its tripartite arrangement: "The Seer and the Seen" – topics in literature (especially his own career) and folklore; "Sound and the Mainstream" – topics in music, especially the blues and jazz; and "The Shadow and the Act" – black American social and cultural conditions in the context of national patterns. This organization emphasizes the lifelong interests of the author: books, music, and race.

Ellison's long second novel on religion and politics, published excerpts from which indicate high quality, has been in progress for more than two decades. It is clear that Ellison's reputation as a novelist will rest not on an ample *oeuvre* but on the brilliance, verbal dexterity, and mythic and social dimensions of one or two books.

—Keneth Kinnamon

FARRELL, James T(homas).   American.   Born in Chicago, Illinois, 27 February 1904. Educated at DePaul University, Chicago, 1924–25; University of Chicago, 1926–29; New York University, 1941. Married 1) Dorothy Butler in 1931 (divorced); 2) Hortense Alden (divorced, 1955), one son; 3) remarried Dorothy Butler in 1955 (separated, 1958). Writer from 1930; Adjunct Professor, St. Peter's College, Jersey City, New Jersey, 1964–65; Writer-in-Residence, Richmond College, Virginia, 1969–70, and Glassboro State College, New Jersey, 1973. Served as Chairman, National Board, Workers Defense League. Recipient: Guggenheim Fellowship, 1936; Messing Award, 1973. D.Litt.: Miami University, Oxford, Ohio, 1968; Columbia College, Chicago, 1974. Member, National Institute of Arts and Letters. Lives in New York City.

PUBLICATIONS

Fiction

> *Young Lonigan: A Boyhood in Chicago Streets.*   1932; *The Young Manhood of Studs Lonigan,* 1934; *Judgment Day,* 1935; complete version, as *Studs Lonigan,* 1935.
> *Gas-House McGinty.*   1933.
> *Calico Shoes and Other Stories.*   1934; as *Seventeen and Other Stories,* 1959.
> *Guillotine Party and Other Stories.*   1935.
> Danny O'Neill pentalogy: *A World I Never Made.*   1936; *No Star Is Lost,* 1938; *Father and Son,* 1940 (as *A Father and His Son,* 1943); *My Days of Anger,* 1943; *The Face of Time,* 1953.
> *Can All This Grandeur Perish? and Other Stories.*   1937.
> *The Short Stories.*   1937; as *Fellow Countrymen: Collected Stories,* 1937.
> *Tommy Gallagher's Crusade.*   1939.
> *Ellen Rogers.*   1941.
> *$1000 a Week and Other Stories.*   1942.
> *Fifteen Selected Stories.*   1943.
> *To Whom It May Concern and Other Stories.*   1944.
> *When Boyhood Dreams Come True.*   1946.
> *More Fellow Countrymen.*   1946.
> Bernard Carr trilogy: *Bernard Clare.*   1946 (as *Bernard Clayre,* 1948; as *Bernard Carr,* 1952); *The Road Between,* 1949; *Yet Other Waters,* 1952.
> *The Life Adventurous and Other Stories.*   1947.
> *A Misunderstanding* (story).   1949.
> *An American Dream Girl* (stories).   1950.
> *This Man and This Woman.*   1951.
> *French Girls Are Vicious and Other Stories.*   1955.
> *An Omnibus of Short Stories.*   1956.
> *A Dangerous Woman and Other Stories.*   1957.
> *Saturday Night and Other Stories.*   1958.
> *The Girls at the Sphinx* (stories).   1959.
> *Looking 'em Over* (stories).   1960.
> *Side Street and Other Stories.*   1961.
> *Boarding House Blues.*   1961.
> *Sound of a City.*   1962.
> A Universe of Time:
>> *The Silence of History.*   1963.
>> *What Time Collects.*   1964.
>> *When Time Was Born.*   1966.

Lonely for the Future. 1966.
A Brand New Life. 1968.
Judith. 1969.
Invisible Swords. 1971.
Judith and Other Stories. 1973.
The Dunne Family. 1976.
The Death of Nora Ryan. 1978.
Olive and Mary Anne (stories). 1978.
New Year's Eve/1929. 1967.
Childhood Is Not Forever and Other Stories. 1969.

Verse

The Collected Poems. 1965.

Other

A Note on Literary Criticism. 1936.
The League of Frightened Philistines and Other Papers. 1945.
The Fate of Writing in America. 1946.
Literature and Morality. 1947.
The Name Is Fogarty: Private Papers on Public Matters. 1950.
Reflections at Fifty and Other Essays. 1954.
My Baseball Diary: A Famed Author Recalls the Wonderful World of Baseball, Yesterday and Today. 1957.
It Has Come to Pass (on Israel). 1958.
Dialogue with John Dewey, with others. 1959.
Selected Essays, edited by Luna Wolf. 1964.

Editor, *Prejudices: A Selection,* by H. L. Mencken. 1958.
Editor, *A Dreiser Reader.* 1962.

Bibliography: *A Bibliography of Farrell's Writings 1921–1957* by Edgar M. Branch, 1959, supplements in *American Book Collector 11,* 1961, and *17,* 1967.

Reading List: *Farrell* by Edgar M. Branch, 1971.

*   *   *

The son and grandson of Irish Catholic working-class laborers, James T. Farrell was raised in a South-Side Chicago neighborhood that became the source for much of his remarkable body of work, which constitutes the greatest sustained production in twentieth-century America of uncompromisingly realistic fiction. Filling, to date, some fifty volumes, this corpus includes four large fictional cycles, three of which are further connected as progressive explorations of their main characters' varying responses to an urban ethnic environment similar to Farrell's. Published between 1932 and 1953, these three related groups are the Studs Lonigan trilogy, the O'Neill-O'Flaherty pentalogy, and the Bernard Carr trilogy.

Begun with Farrell's first novel, *Young Lonigan,* the first group traces the downward drift to death at twenty-nine of its weak-willed, misguided protagonist. A normally inquisitive boy, Studs shows signs of intelligence, even imagination, in early scenes. And yet he assumes the facile and corrupting "tough guy" values of the Chicago street-corner society to which he is drawn after graduation from eighth grade. As a partial explanation of the boy's failure of judgment, the trilogy chronicles the breakdown in the twentieth-century city of the previously directing institutions of family, school, and church, and Studs's origin in a well-fixed, middle-class family makes the indictment of urban "spiritual poverty" (Farrell's phrase) all the more severe. The result is a powerful narrative, terrifying in its seemingly inexorable progress to *Judgment Day*, an American tragedy in the Dreiserian mold.

In the O'Neill-O'Flaherty novels, Farrell uses his own family history much more directly. The main figure is Danny O'Neill, a slightly younger contemporary of Studs Lonigan who takes an opposite road – out of Chicago and toward understanding and control of his own life. More intelligent than Studs, Danny is driven by a persistent dream of accomplishment that crystallizes into the desire to be a writer. On the other hand, he also sometimes slips into aimless idling and drinking, and his economic and family situations are potentially dangerous to his normal development. The O'Neills are so poor that some of the children, including Danny, have had to be raised by his mother's parents, the O'Flahertys. This arrangement alienates Danny but provides the pentalogy with a large number of major characters, including his grandfather, Tom O'Flaherty, an aging immigrant teamster, fully evoked in *The Face of Time*, and his grandmother, an archetypal Irish-American matriarch, strong-willed and fiercely maternal, who dominates the early novels of the series. Danny's father, Jim O'Neill, works his way from teamster to shipping clerk, only to be dealt a cruel, decisive blow by a series of paralyzing strokes. His hysterical, hyper-religious wife, Lizz, is no help to him, and in *Father and Son* Jim faces inutility, boredom, and approaching death – but with lonely courage and dignity that make him one of the most memorable characters in Farrell's fiction. Painful attempts at closeness between "father and son," Danny's high school graduation, and Jim's death bring the novel to its climax. In *My Days of Anger*, Danny begins to find his way, through attendance at the University of Chicago, great gulps of reading, and a final decision in 1927 to leave Chicago for New York and a writing career.

Instead of the tight, fatalistic narrative drive of the Lonigan trilogy, the five O'Neill-O'Flaherty novels are diffused and episodic; and in this looser structure is embodied a broader, more open and optimistic, but still unsentimentalized view of urban society. Moreover, in his complex creation of the interrelated lives of the O'Neills and O'Flahertys, Farrell has provided the most thoroughly realized second-generation-immigrant community in American literature.

The Bernard Carr trilogy, published between 1946 and 1952, continues the action of the O'Neill novels in dealing with the young manhood of a working-class Chicago Irishman with literary ambitions who has fled to New York in search of experience and perspective. His ambition is akin to that of Joyce's Stephen Dedalus, with whom Farrell's O'Neill/Carr figure has much in common. In these novels of education, Bernard Carr learns to reject the Catholic Church, his own naive appropriation of Nietzsche, and the Communist Party, all of which he comes to find as threatening to his artistic integrity. His emergence as a successful writer rounds out the Lonigan-O'Neill-Carr connected cycles. The Carr trilogy lacks the rootedness in place and community of the previous Chicago-based novels, but it compensates by providing a vivid rendering of the lives of New York left-wing intellectuals in the 1930's, with particular attention given to their passionate engagement with the question of the relationship between the artist and society.

In addition to his large cycles and a few isolated novels, Farrell has published about two hundred and fifty short stories and novelettes, in which his presentation of twentieth-century life has become even more inclusive. Many stories concern the protagonists of his novels (there are fifty about Danny O'Neill alone); others place new characters in familiar Chicago or New York settings, and still others are set in Europe, especially Paris. True to Farrell's realistic aesthetic, the stories are strong on character revelation and spurn machinations of plot.

Farrell's critical writings also fill several volumes, from *A Note on Literary Criticism* to *Selected Essays*; these contain useful explanations of the relationship between his life and his work, appreciations of writers who have been important to him, including Dreiser, Joyce, and Sherwood Anderson, and declarations of his position as a realist who writes "as part of an attempt to explore the nature of experience."

In 1963 Farrell published *The Silence of History*, his sixteenth novel, and the first of *A Universe of Time*, his fourth and continuing fictional cycle, which, in his heroic projection, will run to thirty volumes. Integrated by the central recurrent character of Eddie Ryan, another Chicago writer, born, like his creator, in 1904, the *Universe* cycle embodies a reassessment of Farrell's life-long concern with the experience of the artist in the modern world, as well as a continuation of the "lifework" that he has defined, in an introduction to the new cycle's sixth unit, *Judith*, as "a panoramic story of our days and years, a story which would continue through as many books as I would be able to write."

Farrell is first and foremost an American realist: fiercely and scrupulously honest, immune to sentimentality, and, in the earlier novels especially, pioneering in his commitment to giving serious literary consideration to the common life in an urban-immigrant-ethnic community. In his later fiction he has gone beyond Chicago and the Irish to explore more widely his most important themes, the possibilities in modern life for self-knowledge, growth, and creativity. His great strengths as a novelist have always been the development of convincing characters, the firm placement of these characters in a detailed, realistic urban setting, and the ability to conceive and carry through monumental fictional cycles. In this vein, Farrell's fullest and most compassionate creation remains Chicago's Irish Catholic South-Side, which emerges in his fiction as a realized world, as whole and coherent as Faulkner's Mississippi.

—Charles Fanning

FAULKNER, William. American. Born William Cuthbert Falkner in New Albany, Mississippi, 25 September 1897; moved with his family to Oxford, Mississippi, 1902. Educated at local schools in Oxford, and at the University of Mississippi, 1919–20. Served in the Royal Canadian Air Force, 1918. Married Estelle Oldham Franklin in 1929; one daughter. Worked in the University Post Office, Oxford, 1921–24; lived in New Orleans briefly, and wrote for the New Orleans *Times-Picayune*, then lived in Paris, and travelled in Italy, Switzerland, and England, 1925; returned to Oxford, 1926: thereafter a full-time writer; screenwriter for Metro-Goldwyn-Mayer, 1932–33, 20th Century Fox, 1935–37, and Warner Brothers, 1942–45; Writer-in-Residence, University of Virginia, Charlottesville, 1957, and part of each year thereafter until his death. Recipient: O. Henry Award, 1939, 1949; Nobel Prize for Literature, 1950; Howells Medal, 1950; National Book Award, 1951, 1955; Pulitzer Prize, 1955, 1963; American Academy of Arts and Letters Gold Medal, 1962. Member, National Institute of Arts and Letters, 1939. *Died 6 July 1962.*

PUBLICATIONS

Collections

The Portable Faulkner, edited by Malcolm Cowley.   1946.
The Faulkner Reader, edited by Saxe Commins.   1954.

Selected Letters, edited by Joseph Blotner. 1977.

Fiction

Soldiers' Pay. 1926.
Mosquitoes. 1927.
Sartoris. 1929; early version, as *Flags in the Dust*, 1973.
The Sound and the Fury. 1929.
As I Lay Dying. 1930.
Sanctuary. 1931.
These Thirteen: Stories. 1931.
Idyll in the Desert. 1931.
Light in August. 1932.
Miss Zilphia Gant. 1932.
Doctor Martino and Other Stories. 1934.
Pylon. 1935.
Absalom, Absalom! 1936.
The Unvanquished. 1938.
The Wild Palms (includes *Old Man*). 1939.
The Hamlet. 1940; excerpt, as *The Long Hot Summer*, 1958.
Go Down, Moses and Other Stories. 1942.
Intruder in the Dust. 1948.
Knight's Gambit (stories). 1949.
Collected Stories. 1950.
Notes on a Horsethief. 1951.
Requiem for a Nun. 1951.
Mirrors of Chartres Street. 1953.
A Fable. 1954.
Big Woods (stories). 1955.
Jealousy and Episode: Two Stories. 1955.
The Town. 1957.
The Mansion. 1959.
The Reivers: A Reminiscence. 1962.
Selected Short Stories. 1962.

Plays

The Big Sleep (screenplay), with Leigh Brackett and Jules Furthman, in *Film Scripts One*, edited by George P. Garrett, O. B. Harrison, Jr., and Jane Gelfmann. 1971.

Screenplays: *Today We Live*, 1933; *The Road to Glory*, with Joel Sayre, 1936; *Slave Ship*, with others, 1937; *Air Force* (uncredited), with Dudley Nichols, 1943; *To Have and Have Not*, with Jules Furthman, 1945; *The Big Sleep*, with Jules Furthman and Leigh Brackett, 1946; *Land of the Pharaohs*, with Harry Kurnitz and Harold Jack Bloom, 1955.

Verse

The Marble Faun. 1924.
This Earth. 1932.
A Green Bough. 1933.

Other

Salmagundi.   1932.

New Orleans Sketches, edited by Ichiro Nishizaki.   1955; revised edition, edited by Carvel Collins, 1958.

Faulkner's County.   1955.

On Truth and Freedom: Remarks Made During His Manila Visit.   1955(?).

Faulkner at Nagano, edited by Robert A. Jelliffe.   1956.

Faulkner in the University: Class Conferences at the University of Virginia 1957–58, edited by Frederick L. Gwynn and Joseph Blotner.   1959.

Early Prose and Poetry, edited by Carvel Collins.   1962.

University Pieces, edited by Carvel Collins.   1962.

Faulkner at West Point, edited by Joseph L. Fant.   1964.

The Faulkner-Cowley File: Letters and Memories 1944–1962, edited by Malcolm Cowley.   1966.

Essays, Speeches, and Public Letters, edited by James B. Meriwether.   1966.

Lion in the Garden: Interviews 1926–1962, edited by James B. Meriwether and Michael Millgate.   1968.

Bibliography: *Faulkner: A Check List,* 1957, and *The Literary Career of Faulkner,* 1961, both by James B. Meriwether; "Criticism of Faulkner: A Selected Checklist" by Maurice Beebe, in *Modern Fiction Studies 13,* 1967; *Faulkner, Man Working 1919–1962* by Linton R Massey, 1968.

Reading List: *Faulkner: A Critical Study* by Irving Howe, 1952; *The Tangled Fire of Faulkner* by William Van O'Connor, 1954; *Faulkner: The Yoknapatawpha Country,* 1963, and *Toward Yoknapatawpha and Beyond,* 1978, both by Cleanth Brooks; *The Novels of Faulkner* by Olga W. Vickery, 1959, revised edition, 1964; *Faulkner's People* (handbook) by Robert W. Kirk and Marvin Klotz, 1963; *Faulkner: A Collection of Critical Essays* edited by Robert Penn Warren, 1966; *The Achievement of Faulkner* by Michael Millgate, 1966; *Faulkner's Narrative* by Joseph W. Reed, Jr., 1973; *Faulkner: A Biography* by Joseph Blotner, 2 vols., 1974; *Faulkner: The Critical Heritage* edited by John Bassett, 1975; *A Glossary of Faulkner's South* by Calvin S. Brown, 1976.

*   *   *

William Faulkner often said that he regarded poetry as the most difficult genre and himself as a "failed poet." Although he wrote prose quite early, he devoted most of his energy as a beginning writer to verse, imitating Housman and Swinburne, translating French Symbolist poets, and coming under the spell of Pound and Eliot. *The Marble Faun,* however, was a cycle of pastoral poems, and one of the keys to both the complexity and power of his mature prose is the carryover of poetic techniques and pastoral imagery into his realistic fiction. In his Waste Land novel, *Soldiers' Pay,* he struck the contemporary note of postwar disillusionment, but in his third, *Sartoris,* he set his scene in Mississippi and began to mine the resources of his native region. Conventional in technique, this novel drew upon his own family, especially Colonel William C. Falkner, in the creation of Colonel John Sartoris and his troubled descendants. Placed in opposition to them were the Snopeses, a family of landless whites who had proliferated near Faulkner's fictional town of Jefferson. In their craft, rapacity, and savagery, they represented the negative aspects of the rise of the new man in the New South but also perennial facets of human nature castigated by literature's classic moralists and satirists.

By the time Faulkner began his next novel he had not only read Joyce and imitated Eliot, he had also composed highly experimental drama and prose tales. All of this exploration and maturation, together with frustration he felt at repeated rejections of the manuscript of *Sartoris*, combined to produce in his new work a novel of extraordinary power and poetic sensibility. In *The Sound and the Fury* he told the story of the tragic Compson family from four different points of view, employing complex patterns of image and symbol and exploiting the stream of consciousness technique quite as much as Joyce had done. This novel, showing him suddenly at the height of his powers, would later be studied and explicated almost as much as Joyce's *Ulysses*.

In his next two works he employed the Chickasaw name he had chosen for his apocryphal county: Yoknapatawpha. One of these, *Sanctuary*, seemed *grand guignol* to some readers, updated Greek tragedy to others. Its violence and atrocities in a gangland setting, combined with ribald humor and poetic sensibility, constituted a virtuoso performance which gained Faulkner the mass attention which had eluded him. But books such as *As I Lay Dying* repelled many readers, not only because their poor Southern whites seemed strange and often violent, but also because of the technical complexity with which Faulkner presented them, employing fifty-nine separate interior monologues to tell the story of the Bundrens and their disaster-plagued journey undertaken to bury their mother in her family plot.

In novels such as *Light in August* Faulkner continued his exploration of the range of human possibility, not only "the human heart in conflict with itself," but also man in conflict with society, as in the case of Joe Christmas, who does not know whether he is white or black and cannot come to terms with life in either of these worlds. Here Faulkner continued his probing into the psychologies of his characters, their lives deeply determined by their past. Increasingly he employed flashbacks, shifts in chronology, and poetic renderings of perception combined with vivid factual narration and scrupulous use of dialects both black and white.

Now clearly a master of prose fiction, Faulkner published his second and last book of verse, *A Green Bough*, comprising poems written over a decade or more. Embodying several different styles, they showed his versatility but justified his earlier judgment that he was primarily a fiction writer and not a poet. One critic, however, would aptly call him an epic poet in prose.

When *Absalom, Absalom!* appeared (the novel which would challenge *The Sound and the Fury* for pre-eminence), it revealed not only the further exploration of Yoknapatawpha County and its people but also Faulkner's use of the mystery story genre in his attempts to understand history. In part a narrative of the Civil War, it went beyond the regional and the particular to constants in human experience. Like *The Sound and the Fury*, it left some questions unanswered in a kind of aesthetic expression of a principle of indeterminacy in human life and the capacity of literature to represent that life. Continuing his work in shorter fiction, Faulkner depicted his county in the days before the white man came in a sequence of Indian stories which showed his imaginative grasp of another people's culture. Other short stories were later reworked, deepened, and augmented to form novels: *The Unvanquished*, a further tale of the Sartoris family and the South; *The Hamlet*, an account of country people and particularly the Snopeses, whose rise would be further chronicled in *The Town* and *The Mansion*; and *Go Down, Moses*, a narrative of the relations between black and white in Yoknapatawpha County.

A striking quality in his fiction was the interrelationships from book to book, as though the whole panorama of his creation was there in his mind at once, with people, places, and events to be summoned up at will, at times even seeming to obsess him, demanding his creative efforts whether he willed it or not. Nearly twenty years after *Sanctuary* he brought back the ill-starred Temple Drake in a work which explored her partial atonement and that of her husband for their sins in *Sanctuary*. Begun as a play, *Requiem for a Nun* refused to coalesce for Faulkner, and so he turned to narrative prose, introducing each act with a long prologue which set this new drama of passion and murder against the history of Yoknapatawpha County, beginning in the dawn of time and coming up to the present.

Faulkner did not, however, limit himself to settings in Yoknapatawpha, as *A Fable*, set in France during the Great War, testified. More than ten years in the writing, this book was the only one, Faulkner would say, that he had ever written from an idea: what would happen if Christ were to return, giving man his last chance not only for salvation but for survival? His retelling of the story of Christ's Passion and Death during the false armistice on the Western Front was in its way his most explicit statement of his own humanistic faith, using conventional Christian lore as a metaphor. The novel was an ambitious if not wholly successful attempt at a kind of summary statement.

But it was in the Yoknapatawpha novels that his genius found its fullest expression. *The Town* and *The Mansion* completed his chronicle of the rise of the Snopeses and the decline of the Sartoris class, reflecting social changes in the South over the better part of a century yet at the same time remaining faithful to such patterns in other times and other societies. Though these novels had in them something of the same quality of family chronicle as had the earlier *Sartoris*, he continued his technical experimentation, passing the narration from one major character to another and intervening in an omniscient narrative voice when his strategy demanded it. In this latter part of his career, a volume of detective stories and a volume of hunting stories testified to his continuing vigor and versatility. One book, *Intruder in the Dust*, had begun as a detective story, turned into a novel, and evolved as well into a study of racial prejudice and conflict in the South and the process by which a young white boy came to see the humanity of the innocent Negro whom he helped to save from lynching. Faulkner's last book, a kind of valedictory, was a retrospective and often mellow novel, a story of a boy's initiation which was amusing and touching by turns. *The Reivers* showed him once more as master of this domain he had created and exploited as no one had done since Balzac.

Thus it is that he can be called the greatest of modern American novelists. To his strongest admirers he is the greatest of American novelists, a claim that rests upon his prodigious creativity and productivity, his extraordinary mastery of literary techniques, and a breadth of characterization and insight into the human condition which made Yoknapatawpha County a paradigm for the larger world beyond its forests and rivers.

—Joseph Blotner

FEARING, Kenneth (Flexner). American. Born in Oak Park, Illinois, 28 July 1902. Educated at public schools in Oak Park; University of Wisconsin, Madison, B.A. 1924. Married 1) Rachel Meltzer in 1933, one son; 2) Nan Lurie in 1945 (divorced, 1958). Free-lance writer in New York City from 1924: contributor to various poetry magazines. Recipient: Guggenheim Fellowship, 1936, 1939; National Institute of Arts and Letters award, 1945. *Died 26 June 1961.*

PUBLICATIONS

Verse

Angel Arms. 1929.
Poems. 1935.
Dead Reckoning. 1938.

Collected Poems.   1940.
Afternoon of a Pawnbroker and Other Poems.   1943.
Stranger at Coney Island and Other Poems.   1948.
New and Selected Poems.   1956.

Fiction

The Hospital.   1939.
Dagger of the Mind.   1941.
Clark Gifford's Body.   1942.
The Big Clock.   1946.
Loneliest Girl in the World.   1951.
The Generous Heart.   1954.
The Crozart Story.   1960.

Reading List: "The Meaning of Fearing's Poetry" by M. L. Rosenthal, in *Poetry*, July 1944.

*   *   *

Poet, novelist, and editor, Kenneth Fearing is associated with the literature of disillusionment which was written in America during the 1930's and 1940's when technological achievements and social institutions appeared incapable of remedying the profound evils of economic depression. Severely affected by the suffering which he encountered in his environment, Fearing became disillusioned with capitalistic systems of government and industry, espousing instead a Marxist belief in the inherent goodness of the common man, whom he hoped would unite with one another and lead the world into a new era of utopian humanism.

Into this crusade for social justice, Fearing enlisted his talents as a writer. His poetry earned him the admiration of his contemporaries and a lasting position of respect in modern literature. The deft ironic tone which characterizes much of Fearing's poetry and which undercuts the optimism of the Whitmanesque lines in which he wrote is admirably suited to capturing his anger and bitterness at the disregard of institutions for the liberties of the individual, and his sympathy and pity for those people who were trapped by social circumstance in sterile urban environments where they were forced by industrial and political taskmasters to lead mechanical lives of quiet desperation.

But if the economic and social conditions of the 1930's provided Fearing with the subject matter for his poetry, they also limited the scope of his poetic growth. In many respects, Fearing's hatreds and fears shackle his imagination to themes and obsessions which do not sustain repeated or extended treatment. As a result, the reader who indulges in more than one volume of Fearing's poems receives the impression that while the setting and characters of his poems may vary from volume to volume the ideas which they embody remain the same. In his best poems, however, Fearing captures the anxieties, hopes, and frustrations of his generation in a manner which reflects both sensitivity and talent, and *Dead Reckoning* and *Afternoon of a Pawnbroker and Other Poems* are deserving of serious critical analysis.

As a novelist, Fearing specialized in pulp thrillers into which he interjected social commentary. His first novel, *The Hospital*, is replete with scandals and intrigues which expose the machinations behind the workings of the medical profession. Equally shocking and equally involved are *Clark Gifford's Body*, a murder mystery which explores the possibility of revolution in America, and *The Generous Heart*, a novel which depicts the graft and greed involved in the misappropriation of funds by a charitable organization. Another novel, *The Big Clock*, proved so popular that it became the subject of a film. Ostensibly about a murder, *The Big Clock* also analyzes the ruthlessness of journalistic rivalry and muckraking.

—James A. Levernier

FERBER, Edna.   American.   Born in Kalamazoo, Michigan, 15 August 1887. Educated at Ryan High School, Appleton, Wisconsin. Reporter for the Appleton *Daily Crescent* and, subsequently, for the *Milwaukee Journal* and *Chicago Tribune*, 1904–10; full-time writer from 1910; settled in New York; served as a War Correspondent for the United States Army Air Force during World War II. Recipient: Pulitzer Prize, 1924. Litt.D.: Columbia University, New York; Adelphi College, Garden City, New York. Member, National Institute of Arts and Letters. *Died 16 April 1968.*

PUBLICATIONS

Fiction

>   *Dawn O'Hara, The Girl Who Laughed.*   1911.
>   *Buttered Side Down* (stories).   1912.
>   *Roast Beef, Medium: The Business Adventures of Emma McChesney and Her Son, Jock.*   1914.
>   *Personality Plus: Some Experiences of Emma McChesney and Her Son, Jock.*   1914.
>   *Emma McChesney & Co.*   1915.
>   *Fanny Herself.*   1917.
>   *Cheerful, By Request* (stories).   1918.
>   *Half Portions* (stories).   1920.
>   *The Girls.*   1921.
>   *Gigolo* (stories).   1922; as *Among Those Present*, 1923.
>   *So Big.*   1924.
>   *Show Boat.*   1926.
>   *Mother Knows Best.*   1927.
>   *Cimarron.*   1930; revised edition, 1942.
>   *American Beauty.*   1931.
>   *They Brought Their Women* (stories).   1933.
>   *Come and Get It.*   1935.
>   *Nobody's in Town.*   1938.
>   *No Room at the Inn* (stories).   1941.
>   *Saratoga Trunk.*   1941.
>   *Great Son.*   1945.
>   *One Basket: 31 Stories.*   1947.
>   *Giant.*   1952.
>   *Ice Palace.*   1958.

Plays

Our Mrs. McChesney, with George V. Hobart (produced 1905).
$1200 a Year, with Newman Levy.   1920.
Minick, with George S. Kaufman, from the story "Old Man Minick" by Ferber
    (produced 1924).   1925.
The Eldest: A Drama of American Life.   1925.
The Royal Family, with George S. Kaufman (produced 1927).   1928; as *Theatre Royal*
    (produced 1935), 1936.
Dinner at Eight with George S. Kaufman (produced 1932).   1932.
Stage Door, with George S. Kaufman (produced 1936).   1936.
The Land Is Bright, with George S. Kaufman (produced 1941).   1946.
Bravo!, with George S. Kaufman (produced 1948).   1949.

Screenplay: *A Gay Old Dog*, 1919.

Other

A Peculiar Treasure (autobiography).   1939.
A Kind of Magic (autobiography).   1963.

Reading List: *Ferber: A Biography* by Julie Goldsmith Gilbert, 1978.

*   *   *

Although many of Edna Ferber's novels were very big best sellers, she acquired among some critics the reputation of being more than an entertainer. Grant Overton, for instance, called her a social critic. It is primarily as a social historian, however, that she made her critical reputation. William Allen White said of her books that there is "no better picture of America in the first three decades of this century." And it is this aspect of her work – appearing to tell the unvarnished truth about American life – that has most appealed to her serious readers.

Whatever the final judgment about Edna Ferber's work, there is no doubt that her finger was always on the pulse of what many American readers felt or wanted to feel about American life. She had the journalist's gift of "working up" her subject with a minimum of research and often no first-hand experience, though doubtless her earliest books about shrewd, hard-driving working girls came out of her own early career. Books like *Dawn O'Hara*, *Roast Beef, Medium*, and *Emma McChesney & Co.* helped establish her reputation as a writer who knew the facts about American life. She won the Pulitzer Prize in 1924 for *So Big*, a novel dealing with farm life, a subject, she confessed, about which she knew nothing first-hand. Later books were written after quick trips to the locale to get the feel of the territory and gather a few facts.

Cimarron purported to deal with the opening of the Oklahoma Territory and the discovery of oil, *Saratoga Trunk* with the career of a 19th century self-made millionaire (whose exciting life story newspaper reporters refused to believe). *Giant* dealt with the fabulous excesses of the Texas new-rich. But all of these books (regarded by many reviewers as telling the "truth" about American life) and Edna Ferber's two dozen or so other books are all movie-like romances about the lure of money and big-time success, presented with a clever blend of voyeuristic fascination and a satirical undercutting which permits the reader to luxuriate in the fantasy but at the same time feel superior to it.

In addition to romances about working girls, farmers, Oklahoma roustabouts, Indians, and self-made millionaires, Edna Ferber also published several collections of short stories, two autobiographical volumes, and several plays (most written in collaboration with George S. Kaufman). A number of her novels have also been turned into successful stage musicals and motion pictures, *Show Boat* and *Saratoga Trunk* being perhaps the best known. Edna Ferber's popularity and the critical attention she has received suggest that when the definitive study of popular taste in America is written her novels, plays, and short stories will have to be reckoned with.

—W. J. Stuckey

FISHER, Vardis (Alvero).   American.   Born in Annis, Idaho, 31 March 1895. Educated at Rigby High School, Idaho, graduated 1915; University of Utah, Salt Lake City, B.A. 1920; University of Chicago, A.M. 1922, Ph.D. (magna cum laude) 1925. Served in the United States Army Artillery Corps, 1918. Married 1) Leona McMurtrey in 1917 (died, 1924), two sons; 2) Margaret Trusler in 1928 (divorced, 1939), one son; 3) Opal Laurel Holmes in 1940. Assistant Professor of English at the University of Utah, 1925–28, and New York University, 1928–31; full-time writer from 1931; taught at Montana State University, Bozeman, Summer 1932, 1933; Director, Idaho Writers' Project and Historical Records Project of the Works Progress Administration, 1935–39; Syndicated Columnist ("Vardis Fisher Says") in Idaho newspapers, 1941–68. *Died 9 July 1968.*

PUBLICATIONS

Fiction

    Toilers of the Hills.   1928.
    Dark Bridwell.   1931.
    In Tragic Life.   1932; as *I See No Sin*, 1934; as *The Wild Ones*, 1958.
    Passions Spin the Plot.   1934.
    We Are Betrayed.   1935.
    No Villain Need Be.   1936.
    April: A Fable of Love.   1937.
    Odyssey of a Hero.   1937.
    Forgive Us Our Virtues: A Comedy of Evasions.   1938.
    Children of God.   1939.
    City of Illusion.   1941.
    The Mothers.   1943.
    Darkness and the Deep.   1943.
    The Golden Rooms.   1944.
    Intimations of Eve.   1946.
    Adam and the Serpent.   1947.
    The Divine Passion.   1948.
    The Valley of Vision.   1951.
    The Island of the Innocent.   1952.
    Jesus Came Again: A Parable.   1956.
    A Goat for Azazel.   1956.

Pemmican: A Novel of the Hudson's Bay Company. 1956.
Peace Like a River. 1957.
My Holy Satan: A Novel of Christian Twilight. 1958.
Tale of Valor: A Novel of the Lewis and Clark Expedition. 1958.
Love and Death: The Complete Stories. 1959.
Orphans in Gethsemane. 1960.
Mountain Man. 1965.

Verse

Sonnets to an Imaginary Madonna. 1927.

Other

The Neurotic Nightingale. 1935.
The Caxton Printers in Idaho: A Short History. 1944.
God or Caesar? The Writing of Fiction for Beginners. 1953.
Suicide or Murder? The Strange Death of Governor Meriwether Lewis. 1962.
Thomas Wolfe as I Knew Him and Other Essays. 1963.
Gold Rushes and Mining Camps of the Early American West, with Opal Laurel
    Holmes. 1968.

Editor, *Idaho: A Guide in Word and Picture.* 1937.
Editor, *The Idaho Encyclopedia.* 1938.
Editor, *Idaho Lore.* 1939.

Bibliography: "Fisher: A Bibliography" by George Kellogg, in *Western American Literature,*
Spring 1970.

Reading List: "Fisher Issue" of *American Book Collector,* September 1963; *Fisher* by Joseph
M. Flora, 1965; *Fisher: The Frontier and Regional Works* by Wayne Chatterton, 1972; "The
Primitive World of Fisher: The Idaho Novels" by John R. Milton, in *Midwest Quarterly,*
Summer 1976.

*   *   *

Vardis Fisher is usually placed with the naturalists in American literature and among the
strident voices of protest in the 1930's. While his greatest fame came in the depression years –
climaxed with the Harper Prize in 1939 for *Children of God* – he was a prolific writer whose
work spanned four decades. He wore no labels easily and relished defying definition. Not
interested in literary trends, he stuck doggedly to the goals he set himself. He survived
numerous battles with publishers and lived to see a modest but genuine revival of interest in
his work.
    Fisher's youth in an isolated area along the Snake River in Idaho was lonely and terrifying.
Alfred Kazin called him America's last authentic novelist of the frontier. More importantly,
Fisher was the first to write significant novels of the Rocky Mountain West. His passionate,
sometimes violent and ambiguous, response to his mountain country produced his best work.
His first published novel, *Toilers of the Hills,* gave a poignant rendering of pioneer efforts to
farm the difficult Antelope Hills bordering the South Fork of the Snake. The sense of place
and people was even stronger in his second novel, *Dark Bridwell* – his most satisfying work
of fiction. Fisher seemed on the way to founding a Western counterpart to Faulkner's

Yoknapatawpha County, for he was also writing short stories and poems about the people of the Antelope Hills. Vridar Hunter, the protagonist of *In Tragic Life*, had already appeared as a minor character in *Dark Bridwell*; and Dock Hunter, the farmer of *Toilers*, is Vridar's uncle.

But Vridar was not simply a character who had played a part in the earlier novel. As his name indicates, he was also an autobiographical figure. *In Tragic Life* renders Fisher's first eighteen, largely agonized, years forcefully. The book became the first volume of an autobiographical tetralogy – and as the other volumes appeared Antelope became less significant. It became clear that Fisher was intent on exploring his own agonies more than a region. His first wife had committed suicide while he was a graduate student, and there were major psychological problems he had to work out. The confessional aspect of his work is large. Vridar made an unusual hero, for Fisher was often castigating him. Hence, the tetralogy becomes increasingly intellectual and loaded with indictments of a world Vridar never made – the final volume being decidedly a novel of ideas.

Not overly concerned with critical objections to his tetralogy, Fisher felt that his autobiographical searches had not led him to understand Vridar as he would have liked. Even as he finished the tetralogy, Fisher made plans for his *Testament of Man* novels – a series to be based on extended research into man's evolutionary development, particularly his ideas about divinity. Beginning with *Darkness and the Deep*, when man is little more than an ape and possessed only the simplest speech, Fisher traces man's "progress" until he eventually retells Vridar's story as the final volume in the series of twelve. The most successful books are the first two and the final one. The later volumes become increasingly discursive and the presentation of research as experience less successfully integrated.

Still, Fisher has an important place among the American writers of historical novels. The impetus behind his famous *Children of God* was a search into his most immediate religious heritage – Mormonism. He focuses directly on the lives of Joseph Smith and Brigham Young for the major part of his long novel. His intention was to be as accurate as possible. The success of *Children of God* led Fisher to pursue other aspects of the Western American past, with the goal of accurate rendering a prime consideration. He also wrote non-fictional works about the West as well as about writing.

Fisher's final novel, *Mountain Man*, is vastly different from his other historical novels of the West. Although based on an actual mountain man, "Liver-eating" Johnson, the novel is markedly different from Fisher's more factual novels like *Children of God* or *The Mothers*. It is patterned on music and highlights the romantic spirit more carefully hidden in his other work.

—Joseph M. Flora

FITZGERALD, F(rancis) Scott (Key). American. Born in St. Paul, Minnesota, 24 September 1896. Educated at the St. Paul Academy, 1908–11; Newman School, Hackensack, New Jersey, 1911–13; Princeton University, New Jersey, 1913–17. Served in the United States Army, 1917–19: 2nd Lieutenant. Married Zelda Sayre in 1920; one daughter. Advertising Copywriter for Barron Collier Agency, New York, 1919–20; full-time writer from 1920; lived in Europe, 1924–26, 1929–31; screenwriter for Metro-Goldwyn-Mayer, 1937–38. *Died 21 December 1940.*

PUBLICATIONS

Collections

The Bodley Head Fitzgerald, edited by Malcolm Cowley and J. B. Priestley.   6 vols.,
   1958–63.
The Fitzgerald Reader, edited by Arthur Mizener.   1963.
Letters, edited by Andrew Turnbull.   1963; excerpts, as *Letters to His Daughter,* 1965.

Fiction

This Side of Paradise.   1920.
Flappers and Philosophers (stories).   1920.
The Beautiful and Damned.   1922.
Tales of the Jazz Age.   1922.
John Jackson's Arcady, edited by Lilian Holmes Stack.   1924.
The Great Gatsby.   1925; *A Facsimile of the Manuscript* edited by Matthew J. Bruccoli,
   1973; *Apparatus* edited by Matthew J. Bruccoli, 1974.
All the Sad Young Men (stories).   1926.
Tender Is the Night: A Romance.   1934; revised edition, 1951.
Taps at Reveille (stories).   1935.
*The Last Tycoon: An Unfinished Novel, Together with The Great Gatsby and Selected
   Writings.*   1941.
The Mystery of the Raymond Mortgage (story).   1960.
The Pat Hobby Stories.   1962.
The Apprentice Fiction of Fitzgerald, edited by John Kuehl.   1965.
Dearly Beloved.   1969.
Bits of Paradise: 21 Uncollected Stories, with Zelda Fitzgerald, edited by Matthew J.
   Bruccoli and Scottie Fitzgerald Smith.   1973.
The Basil and Josephine Stories, edited by Jackson R. Bryer and John Kuehl.   1973.

Plays

Fie! Fie! Fi-Fi! (plot and lyrics only), book by Walker M. Ellis, music by D. D. Griffin,
   A. L. Booth, and P. B. Dickey (produced 1914).   1914.
The Evil Eye (lyrics only), book by Edmund Wilson, music by P. B. Dickey and F.
   Warburton Guilbert (produced 1915).   1915.
Safety First (lyrics only), book by J.F. Bohmfalk and J. Biggs, Jr., music by P. B. Dickey,
   F. Warburton Guilbert, and E. Harris (produced 1916).   1916.
The Vegetable; or, From President to Postman (produced 1923).   1923.
Screenplay for Three Comrades, edited by Matthew J. Bruccoli.   1978.

Screenplays: *A Yank at Oxford,* with others, 1938; *Three Comrades,* with Edward E.
Paramore, 1938.

Radio Play: *Let's Go Out and Play,* 1935.

Other

The Crack-Up, with Other Uncollected Pieces, Note-Books, and Unpublished Letters,
   edited by Edmund Wilson.   1945.

Afternoon of an Author: A Selection of Uncollected Stories and Essays, edited by Arthur Mizener. 1957.

Thoughtbook, edited by John Kuehl. 1965.

Fitzgerald in His Own Time: A Miscellany, edited by Matthew J. Bruccoli and Jackson R. Bryer. 1971.

Dear Scott/Dear Max: The Fitzgerald-Perkins Correspondence, edited by John Kuehl and Jackson R. Bryer. 1971.

As Ever, Scott Fitz–: Letters Between Fitzgerald and His Literary Agent Howard Ober 1919–1940, edited by Matthew J. Bruccoli. 1972.

Ledger. 1972.

The Cruise of the Rolling Junk (travel). 1976.

The Notebooks, edited by Matthew J. Bruccoli. 1978.

Bibliography: *Fitzgerald: A Descriptive Bibliography* by Matthew J. Bruccoli, 1972.

Reading List: *The Far Side of Paradise* (biography), by Arthur Mizener, 1951, revised edition, 1965; *The Fictional Technique of Fitzgerald* by James E. Miller, 1957, revised edition, as *Fitzgerald: His Art and His Technique,* 1964; *Beloved Infidel,* 1958, and *The Real Fitzgerald: Thirty-Five Years Later,* 1976, both by Sheila Graham; *Fitzgerald,* by Kenneth Eble, 1963; *Fitzgerald: A Collection of Critical Essays* edited by Arthur Mizener, 1963; *Fitzgerald and His Contemporaries* by William F. Goldhurst, 1963; *Fitzgerald: A Critical Portrait* by Henry Dan Piper, 1965; *Fitzgerald and the Craft of Fiction* by Richard D. Lehan, 1966; *Fitzgerald: The Last Laocoön* by Robert Sklar, 1967; *Fitzgerald: An Introduction and Interpretation* by Milton Hindus, 1968; *Fitzgerald* by Andrew Turnbull, 1975.

*   *   *

Like so many modern American writers, F. Scott Fitzgerald created a public image of himself as a representative figure of his times, which may have been a part of the promotional campaign to sell his fiction. It worked for a while, with such success that any effort to evoke the Jazz Age or the Roaring Twenties is inevitably accompanied by a reference to or a photograph of Fitzgerald. But the public memory is fickle, and after he and Zelda had left the big stage and the gossip columnists no longer had their reckless antics to report, people forgot that he was once considered a writer of great promise and talent, and few realised that he had produced a body of work that bids well to bring him status as a writer for all times.

When Fitzgerald appeared on the literary scene in 1920 with *This Side of Paradise*, a semi-autobiographical guide to life at Princeton and the story of a sensitive young man who is trying to find his place in society, the critics were taken with its sophisticated style, its use of the social milieu, its honest treatment of emotional experience, and its somewhat bold portrayal of the younger generation. His readers, then, looked for even better writing in the following five years, but few would agree that he fulfilled his promise. Neither of the two collections of intriguing, skillful, but often uneven short stories, *Flappers and Philosophers* and *Tales of the Jazz Age*, nor the weak play *The Vegetable* seemed to satisfy their expectations. His second novel, *The Beautiful and Damned*, was looked to more eagerly and was more widely reviewed than any other work by the author. The hero, Fitzgerald said in a letter to his publisher, was intended as "one of those many with the tastes and weaknesses of an artist but with no actual creative inspiration," and the novel related how he and his beautiful young wife were "wrecked on the shoals of dissipation." The use of autobiographical details again occasioned some speculation and caused the book to sell well, but many critics found it an unsuccessful effort at a somber tragedy of a typical American sensibility and thought that it lacked organization or focus. Some recent critics, however, have felt it to be a better novel than contemporary readers realized.

Whatever faults one may find in Fitzgerald's early work, with the publication of *The Great*

Gatsby he fulfilled his highest promise and gave to American literature one of its masterworks. On the surface, of course, *The Great Gatsby* is much a part of its age as a brilliant dramatization of the social and economic corruptions of the jazz age, marked by Prohibition, gangsterism, blasé flappers, and uprootedness. American morality was marked by questionable business ethics, commercial criteria for success, and ultraconservatism in social and political thinking. Historians like Charles Beard were insisting that materialistic and economic factors rather than idealistic motives had determined the course of American history. Through character and theme, Fitzgerald dealt in one way or another with all of these historic factors with such a sensitivity that one can even intuit in the text slight prophetic reverberations of the stock market crash of 1929 and the Great Depression in the offing.

Beyond these surface concerns, the novel deals symbolically with the failure of the American dream of success, which in Fitzgerald's time was still best-known through the Horatio Alger novels. Like Benjamin Franklin before him, Horatio Alger expounded, by way of his dime novels, the possibility of rising from rags to riches through industry, ambition, self-reliance, honesty, and temperance. In this myth, and the frontier tradition of self-reliance, lies the genesis of what impels Gatsby. Behind his simple and touching study and work schedule in the copy of *Hopalong Cassidy* cherished by his father lies the childhood dreams of a Franklin or a Thomas Edison, the lectures on self-improvement of a Russell Conwell or a Dale Carnegie, the lessons on bodily development of a Charles Atlas, and the tradition that every American boy could make a million dollars or become President. But what an ironic reversal! By imitating the great American moralists, Gatsby rises to be a rich and powerful criminal.

A second significant thematic concern of the novel relates to its symbolic use of the Mid-West as a contrast with the East. In his nostalgic reverie on the Mid-West near the end of the novel, Nick Carraway concludes, "I see now that this has been a story of the West, after all – Tom and Gatsby, Daisy, Jordan, and I, were all Westerners, and perhaps we possessed some deficiency in common which made us subtly unadaptable to Eastern life." This last line is ironic, because Nick left his Minnesota home originally because it "seemed like the ragged edge of the universe," but by the end of the novel it is the place to which he returns to regain a sense of balance and moral equilibrium. Fitzgerald is playing with the traditional American dichotomy between the East as a model of European sophistication and corruption and the West as a repository of the fundamental decencies and virtues derived from contact with the American soil, the new Garden of Eden.

A figure who lurks in the background of the novel is Dan Cody, whose name suggests the mythic traditions surrounding Daniel Boone and Buffalo Bill Cody. Cody had helped settle the nation and made a fortune besides, and therefore he represents the energies that sparked the Western frontier movement. But as Frederick Jackson Turner had reminded everyone in 1893, the frontier had been closed and no longer carried the significance it once had as the source of sudden wealth and the place of refuge for those seeking a second chance. By the time Gatsby met him, Dan Cody had degenerated into a senile old man subject to the advances of opportunists and gold-diggers. Gatsby takes him as his ideal, nevertheless, and, like the romantic that he is, he refuses to let historic circumstance stand in his way. Rather than wrest his fortune from the raw earth, he pioneers eastward and conquers the urban wilderness through adapting its devious means to the romantic end of recapturing the past. But history cannot be repeated, and the historic promise that Gatsby learned from Cody was, Nick notes, "already behind him, somewhere back in that vast obscurity beyond the city, where the dark fields of the republic rolled on under the night."

Jay Gatsby, then, is the ultimate American arch-romantic. Because he lacked the wealth and timing, he missed the girl on whom he had focused what Nick calls his "heightened sensitivity to the promises of life." After obtaining the wealth through corrupt means, he returns five years later to fulfill his "incorruptible dream" by attempting to repeat the one golden moment of his life when he possessed that "elusive rhythm," that "fragment of lost words" which we all seek to recall in this mundane existence from a former life, time or world. Not since Don Quixote's pursuit of Dulcinea has literature seen such a noble, heartbreaking, and impossible quest.

Adopting a modified first-person narrative form from Conrad, Fitzgerald unfolds Gatsby's tragedy for us through the eyes of the narrator, Nick Carraway. What we learn through Nick is that pure will power divorced from rationality and decency leads to destruction, and that a merely selfish dream or notion is insufficient to justify the enormous amount of energy and life expended by Gatsby. It is a lesson that this nation would not learn for almost another fifty years, and a suggestion that Fitzgerald's prophetic vision saw farther into the future than the Depression years. When Gatsby is viewed against the moral decadence and cowardly conduct of the Buchanans – "You're worth the whole damn bunch put together," Nick tells him – his unassailable romanticism makes him appear heroic. As an individual, then, who dreams higher than he can achieve, whose reach exceeds his grasp, Gatsby is at the heart of the tragic condition and thus shares certain characteristics with Oedipus, Hamlet, and other tragic heroes of Western literature. Unlike Arthur Miller's modern tragic figure, Willy Loman, Gatsby doesn't evoke mere pity and disgust at the end, as he faithfully waits for a phone call that will never come.

Aside from its concern with social and moral questions of continuing consequence, *The Great Gatsby* is one of the most carefully constructed and precisely written novels in American literature. The subtle complexity of the language; the calculated use of colors, references, and connotations; the striking configurations of verbal patterns and repetitions – all lead the reader to read and reread sentences time and time again to catch the multi-level nuances of meaning. The style is poetic and repays the application of the techniques of studied explication.

Because of the disarray of his personal life, his dwindling financial resources, and his increasing self-doubts as a writer, Fitzgerald was unable to bring his artistry to such a perfect pitch again. His numerous short stories written primarily for pay (some of which were collected in *All the Sad Young Men* and *Taps at Reveille* and his indifferent work for Hollywood only occasionally encouraged his best talents. His next novel, *Tender Is the Night*, which came nine years after *Gatsby*, used European locales and his experiences with his wife's mental illness, another foray into autobiographical materials. What some critics felt was an unresolved problem in structure and a failure to provide clear character motivation caused many to overlook its impressive sweep of characters and its admirable effort to deal with significant psychological and social themes. After his death, the fragments of a novel, *The Last Tycoon*, were found, many pages of which suggest that Fitzgerald was regaining control of his creative skills at the last. Despite his lapses and occasional self-indulgence, the high quality of his best work, and most certainly the striking achievement in *The Great Gatsby*, has brought his achievement the success which eluded his grasp during his own lifetime.

—M. Thomas Inge

FLETCHER, John Gould. American. Born in Little Rock, Arkansas, 3 January 1886. Educated at high school in Little Rock, 1899–1902; Phillips Academy, Andover, Massachusetts, 1902–03; Harvard University, Cambridge, Massachusetts, 1903–07. Married 1) Florence Emily Arbuthnot in 1916; 2) Charlie May Simon in 1936. Lived in England, 1908–14, 1916–33: one of the founders of the Imagist group of poets; returned to the United States and settled in Arkansas, 1933: associated with the Agrarian group of writers. Recipient: Pulitzer Prize, 1939. LL.D.: University of Arkansas, Fayetteville, 1933. Member, National Institute of Arts and Letters. *Died 10 May 1950.*

PUBLICATIONS

Verse

> The Book of Nature 1910–1912. 1913.
> The Dominant City. 1913.
> Fire and Wine. 1913.
> Fool's Gold. 1913.
> Visions of the Evening. 1913.
> Irradiations: Sand and Spray. 1915.
> Goblins and Pagodas. 1916.
> Japanese Prints. 1918.
> The Tree of Life. 1918.
> Breakers and Granite. 1921.
> Preludes and Symphonies. 1922.
> Parables. 1925.
> Branches of Adam. 1926.
> The Black Rock. 1928.
> XXIV Elegies. 1935.
> The Epic of Arkansas. 1936.
> Selected Poems. 1938.
> South Star. 1941.
> The Burning Mountain. 1946.

Other

> La Poésie d'André Fontainas. 1919.
> Some Contemporary American Poets. 1920.
> Paul Gauguin: His Life and Art. 1921.
> John Smith – Also Pocahontas. 1928.
> The Crisis of the Film. 1929.
> The Two Frontiers: A Study in Historical Psychology (on Russia and America). 1930;
>   as Europe's Two Frontiers, 1930.
> Life Is My Song (autobiography). 1937.
> Arkansas. 1947.

Editor, Edgar Allan Poe. 1926.

Translator, The Dance over Fire and Water, by Elie Favre. 1926.
Translator, The Reveries of a Solitary, by Rousseau. 1927.

Reading List: Fletcher by Edna B. Stephens, 1967 (includes bibliography); Fletcher and Imagism by Edmund S. de Chasca, 1978.

*   *   *

Although most often linked with the Imagist movement because of his early association with Amy Lowell, John Gould Fletcher belongs to no one "school" of poetry; his work covers a wide range of styles and themes. But in all of his work an emphasis upon the visual is a reflection not only of his interest in art but of his early experience with Imagist philosophy. In 1908, at the age of twenty-two, Fletcher left America for Europe, and spent the next twenty-five years moving between the two continents. In 1913, having published, at his own expense, five volumes of poetry, he went to Paris where he came under the influence of Impressionist art, new music, and Ezra Pound. But it was with Amy Lowell that he aligned himself, joining her Imagist circle in 1914; Lowell included some of Fletcher's poems in her anthologies, he dedicated some of his work to her, and together they formulated a poetic style of "polyphonic prose."

Of Fletcher's many works, the most famous are his "symphonies"; these are expressions of mood symbolized by a distinct color, one for each symphony. They are all divided into movements (the poems of *Sand and Spray* are even given tempo markings), each reflecting another aspect of the color stressed in the imagery of the poem. The result is an effective synaesthetic blend of verbal, visual, and musical elements. In "White Symphony," for instance, mood is reflected in white peonies "like rockets in the twilight," the "white snow-water of my dreams," and a "white-laden" snowy landscape. Fletcher retains the idea of symphonic form in later poems as well. Orientalism, so influential upon the Imagists, also had a profound effect upon Fletcher; Chinese philosophy and Japanese poetry (especially *haiku*) were important to the writing of the symphonies, and Fletcher's viewing of Oriental art exhibited in America in 1914 and 1915 is reflected in *Goblins and Pagodas* and *Japanese Prints*. The subjects of the latter volume are not necessarily Japanese, as Fletcher notes in his preface, "but all illustrate something of the charm I have found in Japanese poetry and art." Here he seeks "to universalize our emotions," to show "that the universe is just as much in the shape of a hand as it is in armies, politicians, astronomy, or the exhortations of gospel-mongers; that style and technique rest on the thing conveyed and not the means of conveyance." This emphasis upon the concrete remains constant throughout all of Fletcher's poetry, which, in general, is fairly traditional in form.

In the 1920's, traveling through the American South, Fletcher met the writers of the agrarian "Fugitive" movement, in whom he had been interested for several years. Although he did not embrace the Fugitives' belief in purely intellectual poetry, he did share their concept of Southern agrarian culture as a bastion against modern industrialism. His contribution to the 1929 Fugitive symposium was a discussion of "Education, Past and Present" (published in 1930 in *I'll Take My Stand*), in which he stressed the importance of encouraging folk education to help the South maintain its distinct culture. In 1933, Fletcher returned to his native Little Rock, and from that point he can be considered a Southern regional writer.

—Jane S. Gabin

FRANK, Waldo (David).   American.   Born in Long Branch, New Jersey, 25 August 1889. Educated at De Witt Clinton High School, New York, 1902–06; Les Chamettes Pensionnat, Lausanne, Switzerland, 1906–07; Yale University, New Haven, Connecticut, B.A. and M.A. 1911. Married 1) Margaret Naumberg in 1916 (divorced, 1926), one son; 2) Alma Magoon in 1927 (divorced, 1943), two daughters; 3) Jean Klempner in 1943, two sons. Theatre Critic, *Courier-Journal*, New Haven, 1910–11; Reporter, *New York Evening Post*, 1911–12, and *New York Times*, 1912; lived abroad, 1913–14; Founding Editor, *Seven Arts*, New York, 1916; conscientious objector during World War I; member of staff of the *Ellsworth County*

Leader, Kansas, 1919; Contributing Editor, *New Republic*, New York, 1925–40, and *New Masses*, New York, 1926; Lecturer, New School for Social Research, New York, 1927; Honorary Professor, Central University of Ecuador, 1949. Chairman, Independent Miners' Relief Committee, 1932; First Chairman, League of American Writers, 1935. Litt.D.: Universidad Nacional de San Marcos, Lima, Peru, 1929. Member, National Institute of Arts and Letters, 1952. *Died 9 January 1967.*

PUBLICATIONS

Fiction

> *The Unwelcome Man.* 1917.
> *The Dark Mother.* 1920.
> *Rahab.* 1922.
> *City Block.* 1922.
> *Holiday.* 1923.
> *Chalk Face.* 1924.
> *The Death and Birth of David Markand.* 1934.
> *The Bridegroom Cometh.* 1938.
> *Summer Never Ends.* 1941.
> *Island in the Atlantic.* 1946.
> *Invaders.* 1948.
> *Not Heaven.* 1953.

Play

> *New Year's Eve.* 1929.

Other

> *The Art of the Vieux Colombier: A Contribution of France to the Contemporary Stage.* 1918.
> *Our America.* 1919; as *The New America*, 1922.
> *Salvos: An Informal Book about Books and Plays.* 1924.
> *Time Exposure, By Search-Light.* 1926.
> *Virgin Spain: Scenes from the Spiritual Drama of a Great People.* 1926; revised edition, 1942.
> *Five Arts,* with others. 1929.
> *The Re-Discovery of America: An Introduction to a Philosophy of American Life.* 1929.
> *America Hispana: A Portrait and a Prospect.* 1931.
> *Dawn in Russia: The Record of a Journey.* 1932.
> *In the American Jungle 1925–1936.* 1937.
> *Chart for Rough Water: Our Role in a New World.* 1940.
> *South American Journey.* 1943.
> *The Jew in Our Day.* 1944.
> *Birth of a World: Bolívar in Terms of His Peoples.* 1951.
> *Bridgehead: The Drama of Israel.* 1957.
> *The Rediscovery of Man: A Memoir and a Methodology of Modern Life.* 1958.
> *Cuba, Prophetic Island.* 1961.

Editor, *Tales from the Argentine,* translated by Anita Brenner.   1930.
Editor, *The Collected Poems of Hart Crane.*   1933; revised edition, as *The Complete Poems,* 1958.
Editor, with others, *America and Alfred Stieglitz: A Collective Portrait.*   1934.

Translator, *Lucienne,* by Jules Romains.   1925.

Reading List: *The Novels of Frank* by William R. Bittner, 1958; *The Shared Vision of Frank and Hart Crane* by Robert L. Perry, 1966; *Frank* by Paul J. Carter, 1967.

*   *   *

Although Waldo Frank produced a large and varied body of work in prose – history, fiction, essays – he considered himself a poet. In his memoirs, he refers to himself as a poet, describes his novels as lyrical, and says that *Virgin Spain* represents a subjective, lyrical expression of the author. The memoirs provide a useful introduction to the man and to the genesis and the attitudes informing some of his important books.

Surprisingly, his important books are history, not fiction or essays. Frank's essays were written for periodicals, and consist principally of commentary on literature, the theatre, the current American scene, and the position of the Jew in the modern world. Occasionally they are listed as criticism, but Frank lacked the tools of criticism. He also lacked wit and humor, as is painfully evident in a collection of brief "Profiles," first published in *The New Yorker.* Like his history and fiction, his essays offer a poet's vision and use of language. In the best, in the introduction to Hart Crane's poems, for example, this vision enlarges the reader's understanding. It tends to vitiate much of his other writing, especially his fiction.

At the heart of Frank's work is his vision of a social and personal Whole – variously termed Cosmos or Being or The Great Tradition – achieved in western Europe in the middle ages by the church, through the teaching of Jesus. In succeeding ages, according to Frank, this very teaching – that the Kingdom of God is within man – gave rise to an ego which, particularly in America, replaced the Ptolemaic universe with a secular, mechanistic multiverse. The chaos of the multiverse is but a stage, however, in man's history, which must culminate in the Whole once more, the knowledge that God, the universal, is within man, whose life therefore has purpose and direction.

The timeless, spaceless nature of this vision of the Whole precludes the development of character and situation in Frank's fiction, as he himself asserts. Consequently, his short stories are made up essentially of moments of epiphany, and his novels contain inert ideological and symbolic material. Like a poet, he attempts to re-create language, using nouns as verbs and adjectives as nouns. These usages and his poetic descriptions unhappily abound to the point of embarrassment in his writing.

On account of his vision, his histories of North and South America, Russia, and Spain must be accepted on his terms, as works of art. His considerable research gives substance to some that otherwise would amount to little more than poetic travel books. As history, *Birth of a World* is his best, undoubtedly in part because it was commissioned by the Venezuelan Government and because Bolívar, not Frank, is at the center of the narrative. Most important for the reader's comprehension and intelligent assessment of Frank's work is *The Rediscovery of America.* For it presents his vision, interpreting religion and history from a poet's perspectives, with a poet's insights.

—Robert F. Richards

FROST, Robert (Lee).   American.   Born in San Francisco, California, 26 March 1874. Educated at Lawrence, Massachusetts, High School, graduated 1892; Dartmouth College, Hanover, New Hampshire, 1892; Harvard University, Cambridge, Massachusetts, 1897–99. Married Elinor Miriam White in 1895; one son, three daughters. Mill worker and teacher, Lawrence, 1892–97; farmer, Derry, New Hampshire, 1900–12; English Teacher, Pinkerton Academy, Derry, 1905–11; conducted course in psychology, State Normal School, Plymouth, New Hampshire, 1911–12; sold the farm, and lived in England, 1912–15; returned to America and settled on a farm near Franconia, New Hampshire, 1915; Poet-in-Residence, Amherst College, Massachusetts, 1916–20; subsequently Visiting Lecturer at Wesleyan University, Middletown, Connecticut; University of Michigan, Ann Arbor, 1921–23, 1925–26; Dartmouth College; Yale University, New Haven, Connecticut; and Harvard University. A Founder, Bread Loaf School, Middlebury College, Vermont, 1920. Poetry Consultant to the Library of Congress, Washington, D.C., 1958. Recipient: Pulitzer Prize, 1924, 1931, 1937, 1943; New England Poetry Club Golden Rose, 1928; Loines Award, 1931; American Academy of Arts and Letters Gold Medal, 1939; Academy of American Poets Fellowship, 1953; Sarah Josepha Hale Award, 1956; Emerson-Thoreau Medal, 1959; U.S. Senate Citation of Honor, 1960; Poetry Society of America Gold Medal, 1962; MacDowell Medal, 1962; Bollingen Prize, 1963. Litt.D.: Cambridge University, 1957; D.Litt.: Oxford University, 1957. Member, American Academy of Arts and Letters. *Died 29 January 1963.*

PUBLICATIONS

Collections

    The Poetry, edited by Edward Connery Lathem.   1969.
    Selected Letters, edited by Lawrance Thompson.   1964.
    Selected Prose, edited by Hyde Cox and Edward Connery Lathem.   1966.

Verse

    Twilight.   1894.
    A Boy's Will.   1913.
    North of Boston.   1914.
    Mountain Interval.   1916.
    Selected Poems.   1923.
    New Hampshire: A Poem with Notes and Grace Notes.   1923.
    West-Running Brook.   1928.
    The Lovely Shall Be Choosers.   1929.
    Collected Poems.   1930; revised edition, 1939.
    The Lone Striker.   1933.
    Three Poems.   1935.
    The Gold Hesperides.   1935.
    From Snow to Snow.   1936.
    A Further Range.   1936.
    Selected Poems.   1936.
    A Considerable Speck.   1939.
    A Witness Tree.   1942.
    Come In and Other Poems, edited by Louis Untermeyer.   1943; revised edition, as *The Road Not Taken,* 1951.

> *A Masque of Reason.* 1945.
> *The Courage to Be New.* 1946.
> *Poems.* 1946.
> *Steeple Bush.* 1947.
> *A Masque of Mercy.* 1947.
> *Complete Poems.* 1949.
> *Hard Not to Be King.* 1951.
> *Aforesaid.* 1954.
> *Selected Poems.* 1955.
> *Dedication: The Gift Outright.* 1961.
> *In the Clearing.* 1962.
> *One Favored Acorn.* 1969.

Plays

> *A Way Out* (produced 1919?). 1929.
> *The Cow's in the Corn.* 1929.

Other

> *Two Letters.* 1931.
> *Frost and John Bartlett: The Record of a Friendship,* edited by Margaret Bartlett
>   Anderson. 1963.
> *Letters to Louis Untermeyer.* 1963.
> *Frost: Farm-Poultryman,* edited by Edward Connery Lathem and Lawrance
>   Thompson. 1963.
> *Frost: Life and Talks-Walking,* edited by Louis Mertins. 1965.
> *Frost and the Lawrence, Massachusetts "High School Bulletin": The Beginning of a*
>   *Literary Career,* edited by Edward Connery Lathem and Lawrance
>   Thompson. 1966.
> *Interviews with Frost,* edited by Edward Connery Lathem. 1967.
> *Family Letters of Robert and Elinor Frost,* edited by Arnold Grade. 1972.
> *Frost on Writing,* edited by Elaine Barry. 1973.
> *A Time to Talk,* edited by Robert Francis. 1973.

Bibliography: *A Descriptive Catalogue of Books and Manuscripts in the Clifton Waller Barrett Library, University of Virginia* by Joan St. C. Crane, 1974; *The Critical Reception of Frost: An Annotated Bibliography of Secondary Comment* by Peter VanEgmond, 1974.

Reading List: *Frost: A Collection of Critical Essays* edited by James M. Cox, 1962; *An Introduction to Frost* by Elizabeth Isaacs, 1962; *The Major Themes of Frost* by Radcliffe Squires, 1963; *The Poetry of Frost: Constellations of Intention* by Reuben Brower, 1963; *Frost* by Elizabeth Jennings, 1964; *Frost* by James Doyle, 1965; *Frost* by Philip L. Gerber, 1966; *Frost: The Early Years,* 1966, *The Years of Triumph,* 1970, and *The Later Years,* 1977, by Lawrance Thompson and R. H. Winnick; *Frost* by Elaine Barry, 1973; *Frost: The Work of Knowing* by Richard Poirier, 1977.

*   *   *

In 1959, at a dinner celebrating Robert Frost's eighty-fifth birthday, Lionel Trilling gave an after-dinner address that was later incorporated in "A Speech on Robert Frost: A Cultural

Episode." Trilling announced his antipathy for those poems by Frost which expressed a "distaste for the life of the city" and for "the demand that is made upon intellect to deal with whatever are the causes of complexity, uncertainty, anxiety." Then Trilling specified poems he did admire, poems that led him to define Frost as a "terrifying poet" who depicted a "terrifying universe." The speech confused Frost (who was not sure whether he had been attacked or praised), outraged many of his friends, and caused quite a furor.

It would seem ludicrous that as late as at the time of Frost's eighty-fifth birthday there could be so much confusion concerning what constituted Frost's basic point of view. Yet several factors make this situation plausible. For one thing, although such critics as John Crowe Ransom and Randall Jarrell praised Frost's poetry, his work gained comparatively little critical attention in the decades when the practitioners of the New Criticism reigned supreme. Further complications were caused by many of the critics who did laud his work. These admirers touted precisely the glib, sentimental, shallow poems by Frost that Trilling disliked. The main source of the confusion, however, was Robert Frost himself. Because Frost hungered so insatiably for popularity and esteem, he meticulously created a "folksy" public image of himself that his audiences would be entranced by. He never read any of his somber poems in public. He saw to it that his unattractive traits – his obsessive need to win at everything, his violent temper, his delight in back-biting, his race prejudices – remained totally unknown to the public. With equal skill, he hid his family misfortunes – his sister's insanity, his severe marital problems, his son's suicide, a daughter's insanity.

It is no wonder, then, that although Frost began writing in the late 1800's, we are still only beginning to formulate an intelligent evaluation of his poetry. Yet, despite all the obfuscations, such an evaluation is well worth pursuing, for Frost's best poems – and there are many of them – are of a very high quality. Frost was a consummate craftsman. He mastered a variety of forms; he wrote excellent sonnets, heroic couplets, and blank verse poems. His rime patterns are deftly wrought. He was even more adroit in matters of meter and rhythm. He proved repeatedly that there is no reason to believe that traditional rhythmical patterns inevitably lead to monotony.

What ultimately makes Frost's best poems valuable, however, is their dynamic view of our daily life. Frost believed that we live in a God-directed universe, but despite all his religious meditations Frost found God's ways absolutely inscrutable. At his most grim, as represented in "Design," Frost not only acknowledges the presence of the appalling in physical reality, but wonders if there is any cosmic design at all. It is certain in any case, as "Nothing Gold Can Stay" states, that no purity can abide in physical reality. What is pure is almost immediately contaminated. Nature is lovely at times, yet its very loveliness can prove fatally alluring, as the speaker in "Stopping by Woods on a Snowy Evening" testifies. Nor can we imitate the animal world and rely on our instincts; "The White-Tailed Hornet" reports that nature's creatures, acting on pure instinct, often blunder ridiculously.

Man experiences no clarifying visions. "The Fear" insists that we live surrounded by a literal and metaphorical darkness which harbors the hostile and the terrifyingly ambiguous. Weariness and loneliness define the archetypal human being who narrates "Acquainted with the Night." Isolation and poverty can crush a person physically, mentally, and spiritually, as they do characters in "A Servant to Servants" and "The Hill Wife." Moreover, man is badgered by his suppressed desires – the point of "The Sound of the Trees." Yet "The Flood" states that man cannot always control his destructive urges.

Frost also makes it clear that people cannot easily offer each other solace. The difficulty of understanding another human being is sometimes insurmountable. In "Home Burial," a husband and wife attempt to cope with the death of their child in two different ways. Neither can understand the other's attitude or behavior; neither can in any way help the other.

In his recent essay " 'The Death of the Hired Man': Modernism and Transcendence," Warren French pinpoints why Frost's poetry is especially valuable today. French remarks that, aware of modern man's grim situation, Frost – unlike the pre-Modernists – did not proclaim the need for every individual to retreat at all costs to the safety of society; nor did Frost adopt or advocate the lifestyle lauded by Modernist writers – the deliberate withdrawal on the part of the individual from society. Instead, Frost concentrated on what marks him – in French's term – as a "post-Modernist." He struggled to discover what positive course is possible for a man who wants to maintain his individuality without exiling himself from society.

The affirmative albeit starkly limited goal Frost strove for and suggested to others is best indicated by his statement that his poems offer "a momentary stay against confusion." A series of momentary stays, created by the individual, is all man can hope for. As Lawrance Thompson wrote in his introduction to Frost's *Selected Letters*, Frost "bluntly rejected all the conventional stays which dogmatists call permanent"; they are too inflexible to contend successfully with physical reality's ever-shifting conditions. Frost was equally uninterested in trying to transcend the physical – material – world. He thought that the label "materialist" was used too quickly as a pejorative term. He said that it was "wrong to call anybody a materialist simply because he tried to say spirit in terms of matter, as if that were a sin." Nor did Frost fall back on the Romantic belief that man is basically good. He spurned the view that because man and nature are God's creations, they can do no wrong.

According to Frost, in order to achieve a momentary stay against confusion the first thing man needs is courage. A character in *A Masque of Mercy* says, "The saddest thing in life/Is that the best thing in it should be courage." Man must also try to maintain his equilibrium. Again and again, as in "The Vantage Point," "Goodbye and Keep Cold," and "To Earthward," Frost underscores the need to have the right perspective on all things, including oneself. Men should focus on the facts – and not daydream. In "Mowing," he declares that "The fact is the sweetest dream that labor knows." "Labor" is another key word. In "Two Tramps in Mud Time," he states that we should work and that our work should be motivated simultaneously by "love" and "need."

In some ways, nature can be supportive. "The Onset" and "The Need of Being Versed in Country Things" remind us that many things on earth are cyclical; this means that although evil comes to us, it will not last. So, too, nature is a revitalizing force, and sometimes awesomely beautiful, as described in "Iris by Night." It can also startle us out of a black mood created by too much self-centeredness – the development recorded in "Dust of Snow." It should also be remembered, as "Our Hold on the Planet" points out, that nature is at least "one fraction of one per cent" in "favor of man" – otherwise we would never have been able to thrive on earth.

Finally, Frost specifically advises us to preserve our individual integrity, but to link ourselves to society. Frost's emphasis on the value of society (often symbolized by the home) is coupled with his emphasis on the value of love. Love can be tenderly lyrical, as described in "Meeting and Passing." "Putting In the Seed" proclaims that love can be dynamically fertile. Love can alter reality – the point in "Never Again Would Birds' Song Be the Same." Love, breeding forgiveness and acceptance, provides a home against adversity. This is what Mary, in "The Death of the Hired Man," knows to be so, and what her husband Warren comes to realize. They decide to nurse Silas, their old hired man, but also to allow him his self-respect. Perhaps the finest example of Frost's stress on the importance of a viable balance between the individual and society is "The Silken Tent." Here, the woman described is a vibrant individual, yet held – willingly – by "countless ties of love and thought/To everything on earth."

—Robert K. Johnson

GADDIS, William. American. Born in New York City in 1922. Educated at Harvard University, Cambridge, Massachusetts. Recipient: National Institute of Arts and Letters grant, 1963; National Endowment for the Arts grant, 1966, 1974; National Book Award, 1976.

PUBLICATIONS

Fiction

The Recognitions. 1955.
JR. 1975.

* * *

William Gaddis's *The Recognitions* and *JR* are both huge works, and the reputation they have earned for Gaddis testifies to the intrinsic interest of these difficult novels. The reputation also testifies to a widespread impatience with old fashions of narrative and a thirst for other ways of presenting experience. Among these "other ways" – ways that can also be observed in John Barth, Thomas Pynchon, Richard Brautigan, and others – are the modes of transmuting reality, perhaps of getting at its essence by stringent rearrangement, which the reader meets in *The Recognitions* and *JR*.

JR is, as a story, an account of the fraudulent manipulation of stocks by a sixth-grader in a Long Island school for delinquents. The boy (JR) uses adults as agents and exploits for his own benefit the fatuities and self-deceptions of the great American world of trade and "development." An amusing anecdote. But Gaddis opens it out to deal with all that takes place in the universe that is composed of stock flotation, management of industry, manipulation of bequests, and even in the arts, which are not independent of the commercial textures that surround them. In these tossing seas, the little craft of the boy JR often vanishes from view to reappear a hundred pages later.

All this is presented in a way that leaves a realistic copying of the world to one side. Interminable conversations, by telephone or face-to-face, blend with other conversations, and one learns by osmosis rather than by explicit statement which characters are speaking on a certain page. Moreover, many characters are endowed with knowledge they would not have in "real life"; obscure Christian heresies or reference to Eliot's *Waste Land* occasionally sum up what a fumbling speaker is trying to say. To some readers, the result of all this is just confusion; others will find *JR* an often comic and revealing view of a world in which conventional pieties, familial and sexual, conform to the laws of trade. From this point of view, the novel is a confident innovation that refines a reader's awareness and encourages his detachment from what the bulk of mankind regard as important.

The earlier novel, *The Recognitions*, also views a great variety of persons and settings, but under the sign of religion rather than money. Persons try to see the sum of human meaning expressed by the various religions of the world and express some of these meanings in works of art and, even, in personal involvements. If Gaddis himself has an attitude toward the motley adventures and aspirations he reports, it is perhaps indicated by several references to Frazer's *Golden Bough*, where the effort of a scholar's mind to free itself from delusion is displayed. But such a firm center to *The Recognitions* becomes dim as endless inconsequence and violence mingle, undoing the "noble" hope of this character or that one. Scenes of great comic power alternate with interminable discussion.

In both the novels there is an odor of spoilt culture. Money, religion, and even sex are played off against each other and become the subjects of contemptuous regard. The two books are an ambitious report on the dubious achievements of the human imagination. To none of these achievements does Gaddis commit himself, either by the design of his fiction or by sympathy with what he relates.

—Harold H. Watts

GALE, Zona.   American.   Born in Portage, Wisconsin, 26 August 1874.   Educated in Portage public schools, and at the University of Wisconsin, Madison, 1891–95, B.L. 1895, M.L. 1899. Married William L. Breese in 1928; one adopted daughter. Reporter for the Milwaukee *Evening Wisconsin*, 1895–96, the *Milwaukee Journal*, 1896–1901, and the New York *Evening World*, 1901–03; returned to Portage, 1904; thereafter a full-time writer. Member, Wisconsin Library Commission, 1920–32; Member of the Board of Regents, 1923–29, and of the Board of Visitors, 1936–38, University of Wisconsin; Delegate from Wisconsin, International Congress of Women, Chicago, 1933. Recipient: Butterick Prize, 1911; Pulitzer Prize, for drama, 1921. D.Litt.: Ripon College, Wisconsin, 1922; University of Wisconsin, 1929; Rollins College, Winter Park, Florida, 1930. Honorary Member, Phi Beta Kappa, Western Reserve University, Cleveland, 1925. *Died 27 December 1938.*

PUBLICATIONS

Fiction

   Romance Island.   1906.
   The Loves of Pelleas and Etarre (stories).   1907.
   Friendship Village (stories).   1908.
   Friendship Village Love Stories.   1909.
   Mothers to Men.   1911.
   Christmas: A Story.   1912.
   Neighborhood Stories.   1914.
   Heart's Kindred.   1915.
   A Daughter of the Morning.   1917.
   Birth.   1918.
   Peace in Friendship Village (stories).   1919.
   Miss Lulu Bett.   1920; edited by Lella B. Kelsey, 1928.
   Faint Perfume.   1923.
   Preface to a Life.   1926.
   Yellow Gentians and Blue (stories).   1927.
   Borgia.   1929.
   Bridal Pond (stories).   1930.
   Papa La Fleur.   1933.
   Old-Fashioned Tales.   1933.
   Light Woman.   1937.
   Magna.   1939.

Plays

   The Neighbours (produced 1912).   1926.
   Miss Lulu Bett, from her own novel (produced 1920).   1921.
   Uncle Jimmy.   1922.
   Mister Pitt (produced 1925).   1925.
   Evening Clothes.   1932.
   Faint Perfume, from her own novel.   1934.
   The Clouds.   1936.

Verse

   The Secret Way.   1921.

Other

Civic Improvement in Little Towns.   1913.
When I Was a Little Girl. 1913.
What Women Won in Wisconsin.   1922.
Portage, Wisconsin, and Other Essays.   1928.
Frank Miller of Mission Inn.   1938.

Bibliography: "Gale" by Harold P. Simonson, in *American Literary Realism 3,* 1968.

Reading List: *Still Small Voice: The Biography of Gale* by August Derleth, 1940; *Gale* by Harold P. Simonson, 1962.

*   *   *

"There is no contemporary author," wrote Joseph Wood Krutch in 1929, "whose evolution is more interesting than that of Zona Gale." Although she lived most of her life in the village of her birth – Portage, Wisconsin – and wrote largely in the village vein that attracted the talents of so many other writers of her generation, she was nevertheless a child of her age who responded to the astonishing variety of its pressures.

After four years in New York, during which she wrote *Romance Island* and *The Loves of Pelleas and Etarre,* two novels of saccharine sentimentality, Gale returned to Portage to write a series of novels and tales, including *Friendship Village, Friendship Village Love Stories, Neighborhood Stories,* and *Peace in Friendship Village.* Unlike the meanness of Lewis's Gopher Prairie, the grotesquery of Anderson's Winesburg, or the enervation of Garland's Middle Border, Gale's Friendship Village, though not so sentimentally drawn as her earlier Romance Island, was an idyllic and hospitable town dedicated to children, family, and community.

However, her pastoral rendering of Friendship Village obscured her growing concerns with the issues and movements of her day – pacifism, women's rights, prohibition, civil liberties, progressivism, and others – even as it did her labors in their behalf: writing pamphlets and delivering speeches, campaigning for the progressive La Follettes of her native Wisconsin, joining the ill-fated protest against the execution of Sacco and Vanzetti. In truth, Gale's increasingly realistic image of the world found its way even into the Friendship Village tales, which by the decade's end had begun to compromise the idyll with an occasional suggestion of reform. More important, her growing politicization was signaled in three novels of social relevance, all written during the Friendship Village period: *Heart's Kindred,* a pacifist piece; *A Daughter of the Morning,* a portrait of the working woman's plight; and what is perhaps her best work, *Birth.* In the last of these three, readers found a vision of small-town Americana whose acerbity approaches that of the better-known realist writers of her time. Indeed, *Birth,* along with *Miss Lulu Bett,* an equally acerbic novel of village life for which, after dramatization, Gale was awarded the Pulitzer Prize, nearly established their author as an authentic if minor realist writer.

Zona Gale soon moved on, however. Prompted on a personal level by thdeath of her doting mother and more generally by the rise of a variety of New Thought movements in which she took interest, Gale moved from realism to spiritualism and the occult, a vantage point from which she wrote a number of short stories and also *Preface to a Life,* a novel whose major character, though living on some higher astral plane, is understood by his fellow villagers to be insane.

Her talent having been a modest one, Zona Gale has fallen into the obscurity which most critics agree she deserves. Still, she was in tune with many of the social currents of her day. And had her powers of imagination been greater, had her artistic control been stronger, her contribution to American letters might well have been of a higher rank.

—Bruce A. Lohof

GARDNER, Erle Stanley. Pseudonyms: A. A. Fair, Carleton Kendrake, and Charles J. Kenny. American. Born in Malden, Massachusetts, 17 July 1889; as a child lived with his family in mining camps in California, Oregon, and the Klondike. Educated at Palo Alto High School, California; studied law in the offices of various California lawyers: admitted to the California bar, 1911. Married 1) Natalie Talbert in 1912 (died, 1968), one daughter; 2) Agnes Jean Bethell in 1968. Lawyer in Oxnard, California, 1911–16, and in Ventura, California, 1916–33; also, President, Consolidated Sales Company, San Francisco, 1918–21; began to write in 1921; visited China, 1931; full-time writer from 1933. Served as President of the Ventura County Bar Association; Co-Founder, "Court of Last Resort," *Argosy* magazine. Recipient: Mystery Writers of America Grand Master Award, 1961. Honorary alumnus: Kansas City University, 1955; D.L.: McGeorge College of Law, Sacramento, California, 1956. *Died 11 March 1970.*

PUBLICATIONS

Fiction

The Case of the Velvet Claws. 1933.
The Case of the Sulky Girl. 1933.
The Case of the Curious Bride. 1934.
The Case of the Howling Dog. 1934.
The Case of the Lucky Legs. 1934.
The Case of the Counterfeit Eye. 1935.
The Case of the Caretaker's Cat. 1935.
The Clue of the Forgotten Murder. 1935.
This Is Murder. 1935.
The Case of the Sleepwalker's Niece. 1936.
The Case of the Stuttering Bishop. 1937.
The Case of the Dangerous Dowager. 1937.
The Case of the Lame Canary. 1937.
The D.A. Calls It Murder. 1937.
Murder up My Sleeve. 1937.
The Case of the Shoplifter's Shoe. 1938.
The Case of the Substitute Face. 1938.
The D.A. Holds a Candle. 1938.
The Case of the Perjured Parrot. 1939.
The Case of the Rolling Bones. 1939.
The D.A. Draws a Circle. 1939.

The Bigger They Come.   1939; as *Lam to the Slaughter,* 1939.
The Case of the Baited Hook.   1940.
Gold Comes in Bricks.   1940.
Turn on the Heat.   1940.
The Case of the Silent Partner.   1940.
The D.A. Goes to Trial.   1940.
The Case of the Haunted Husband.   1941.
The Case of the Turning Tide.   1941.
The Case of the Empty Tin.   1941.
Double or Quits.   1941.
Spill the Jackpot!   1941.
Bats Fly at Dusk.   1942.
Owls Don't Blink.   1942.
The Case of the Careless Kitten.   1942.
The Case of the Drowning Duck.   1942.
The D.A. Cooks a Goose.   1942.
The Case of the Buried Clock.   1943.
The Case of the Drowsy Mosquito.   1943.
The Case of the Smoking Chimney.   1943.
Cats Prowl at Night.   1943.
Give 'em the Ax.   1944; as *An Axe to Grind.*   1951.
The D.A. Calls a Turn.   1944.
The Case of the Crooked Candle.   1944.
The Case of the Black-Eyed Blonde.   1944.
The Case of the Half-Wakened Wife.   1945.
The Case of the Golddigger's Purse.   1945.
The Case of the Borrowed Brunette.   1946.
The Case of the Backward Mule.   1946.
The D.A. Breaks the Seal.   1946.
Crows Don't Count.   1946.
Fools Die on Friday.   1947.
The Case of the Fan-Dancer's Horse.   1947.
The Case of the Lazy Lover.   1947.
Two Clues: The Clue of the Runaway Blonde, The Clue of the Hungry Horse.   1947.
The D.A. Takes a Chance.   1948.
The Case of the Vagabond Virgin.   1948.
The Case of the Lonely Heiress.   1948.
The Case of the Dubious Bridegroom.   1949.
The D.A. Breaks an Egg.   1949.
Bedrooms Have Windows.   1949.
The Case of the Cautious Coquette.   1949.
The Case of the Musical Cow.   1950.
The Case of the Negligent Nymph.   1950.
The Case of the One-Eyed Witness.   1951.
The Case of the Angry Mourner.   1951.
The Case of the Fiery Fingers.   1951.
The Case of the Moth-Eaten Mink.   1952.
The Case of the Grinning Gorilla.   1952.
Top of the Heap.   1952.
Some Women Won't Wait.   1953.
The Case of the Green-Eyed Sister.   1953.
The Case of the Hesitant Hostess.   1953.
The Case of the Runaway Corpse.   1954.
The Case of the Fugitive Nurse.   1954.

The Case of the Restless Redhead.   1954.
The Case of the Glamorous Ghost.   1955.
The Case of the Sun Bather's Diary.   1955.
The Case of the Nervous Accomplice.   1955.
The Case of the Terrified Typist.   1956.
The Case of the Gilded Lily.   1956.
The Case of the Demure Defendant.   1956.
Beware the Curves.   1956.
Some Slips Don't Show.   1957.
You Can Die Laughing.   1957.
The Case of the Daring Decoy.   1957.
The Case of the Lucky Loser.   1957.
The Case of the Screaming Woman.   1957.
The Case of the Long-Legged Models.   1958.
The Case of the Foot-Loose Doll.   1958.
The Case of the Calendar Girl.   1958.
The Count of Nine.   1958.
Pass the Gravy.   1959.
The Case of the Waylaid Wolf.   1960.
The Case of the Singing Skirt.   1959.
The Case of the Mythical Monkeys.   1959.
The Case of the Deadly Toy.   1959.
The Case of the Shapely Shadow.   1960.
The Case of the Duplicate Daughter.   1960.
Kept Women Can't Quit.   1960.
Bachelors Get Lonely.   1961.
Shills Can't Cash Chips.   1961; as *Stop at the Red Light,* 1962.
The Case of the Bigamous Spouse.   1961.
The Case of the Spurious Spinster.   1961.
The Case of the Reluctant Model.   1961.
The Case of the Blonde Bonanza.   1962.
The Case of the Ice-Cold Hands.   1962.
Try Anything Once.   1962.
Fish or Cut Bait.   1963.
The Case of the Amorous Aunt.   1963.
The Case of the Mischievous Doll.   1963.
The Case of the Stepdaughter's Secret.   1963.
The Case of the Phantom Fortune.   1964.
Up for Grabs.   1964.
The Case of the Horrified Heirs.   1964.
The Case of the Daring Divorcee.   1964.
The Case of the Crimson Kiss (stories).   1964; augmented edition, 1971.
The Case of the Beautiful Beggar.   1965.
Cut Thin to Win.   1965.
The Case of the Troubled Trustee.   1965.
Widows Wear Weeds.   1966.
The Case of the Worried Waitress.   1966.
The Case of the Queenly Contestant.   1967.
Traps Need New Bait.   1967.
The Case of the Careless Cupid.   1968.
The Case of the Murderer's Bride and Other Stories, edited by Ellery Queen.   1969.
The Case of the Fabulous Fake.   1969.
All Grass Isn't Green.   1970.
The Case of the Crying Swallow (stories).   1971.

The Case of the Fenced-In Woman.   1972.
The Case of the Irate Witness (stories).   1972.
The Case of the Postponed Murder.   1973.

Other

The Land of Shorter Shadows.   1948.
The Court of Last Resort.   1952.
Neighborhood Frontiers.   1954.
Hunting the Desert Whale.   1960.
Hovering over Baja.   1961.
The Hidden Heart of Baja.   1962.
The Desert Is Yours.   1963.
The World of Water.   1965.
Hunting Lost Mines by Helicopter.   1965.
Off the Beaten Track in Baja.   1967.
Gypsy Days on the Delta.   1967.
Mexico's Magic Square.   1968.
Host with the Big Hat (on Mexico).   1969.
Drifting Down the Delta.   1969.
Cops on Campus and Crime in the Street.   1970.

Bibliography: *Gardner: A Checklist* by E. H. Mundell, 1968.

Reading List: *The Case of Gardner* by Alva Johnston, 1947; *Gardner: The Case of the Real Perry Mason* (includes bibliography) by Dorothy B. Hughes, 1978.

*   *   *

Erle Stanley Gardner spent much of his childhood traveling with his mining-engineer father through the remote regions of California, Oregon, and the Klondike. In his teens he not only boxed for money but promoted a number of unlicensed matches. Soon after entering college he was, by his own account, expelled for slugging a professor. But in the practice of law he found the form of combat he seemed born to master. He was admitted to the California bar in 1911 and opened an office in Oxnard, where he represented the Chinese community and gained a reputation for flamboyant trial tactics. In one case, for instance, he had dozens of Chinese merchants exchange identities so that he could discredit a policeman's identification of a client. In the early 1920's he began to write western and mystery stories for magazines, and eventually he was turning out and selling the equivalent of a short novel every three nights while still lawyering during the business day. With the sale of his first novel in 1933 he gave up the practice of law and devoted himself to full-time writing, or more precisely to dictating. Thanks to the popularity of his series characters – lawyer-detective Perry Mason, his loyal secretary Della Street, his private detective Paul Drake, and the foxy trio of Sergeant Holcomb, Lieutenant Tragg and District Attorney Hamilton Burger – Gardner became one of the wealthiest mystery writers of all time.

The 82 Mason adventures from *The Case of the Velvet Claws* (1933) to the posthumously published *The Case of the Postponed Murder* (1973) contain few of the literary graces. Characterization and description are perfunctory and often reduced to a few lines that are repeated in similar situations book after book. Indeed virtually every word not within quotation marks could be deleted and little would be lost. For what vivifies these novels is the sheer readability, the breakneck pacing, the involved plots, the fireworks displays of courtroom tactics (many based on gimmicks Gardner used in his own law practice), and the dialogue, where each line is a jab in a complex form of oral combat.

The first nine Masons are steeped in the hardboiled tradition of *Black Mask* magazine, their taut understated realism leavened with raw wit, sentimentality, and a positive zest for the dog-eat-dog milieu of the free enterprise system during its worst depression. The Mason of these novels is a tiger in the social-Darwinian jungle, totally self-reliant, asking no favors, despising the weaklings who want society to care for them, willing to take any risk for a client no matter how unfairly the client plays the game with him. Asked what he does for a living, he replies: "I fight!" or "I am a paid gladiator." He will bribe policemen for information, loosen a hostile witness' tongue by pretending to frame him for a murder, twist the evidence to get a guilty client acquitted and manipulate estate funds to prevent a guilty non-client from obtaining money for his defense. Besides *Velvet Claws*, perhaps the best early Mason novels are *The Case of the Howling Dog* and *The Case of the Curious Bride* (both 1934).

From the late 1930's to the late 1950's the main influence on Gardner was not *Black Mask* but the *Saturday Evening Post*, which serialized most of the Mason novels before book publication. In these novels the tough-guy notes are muted, "love interest" plays a stronger role, and Mason is less willing to play fast and loose with the law. Still the oral combat remains breathlessly exciting, the pace never slackens and the plots are as labyrinthine as before, most of them centering on various sharp-witted and greedy people battling over control of capital. Mason, of course, is Gardner's alter ego throughout the series, but in several novels of the second period another author-surrogate arrives on the scene in the person of a philosophical old desert rat or prospector who delights in living alone in the wilderness, discrediting by his example the greed of the urban wealth – and power-hunters. Among the best cases of this period are *Lazy Lover*; *Hesitant Hostess*, which deals with Mason's breaking down a single prosecution witness; and *Lucky Loser* and *Foot-Loose Doll* with their spectacularly complex plots.

Gardner worked without credit as script supervisor for the long-running *Perry Mason* television series (1957–66), starring Raymond Burr, and within a few years television's restrictive influence had infiltrated the new Mason novels. The lawyer evolved into a ponderous bureaucrat mindful of the law's nicetices, just as Burr played him, and the plots became chaotic and the courtroom sequences mediocre, as happened all too often in the TV scripts. But by the mid-1960's the libertarian decisions of the Supreme Court under Chief Justice Earl Warren had already undermined a basic premise of the Mason novels, namely that defendants menaced by the sneaky tactics of police and prosecutors needed a pyrotechnician like Mason in their corner. Once the Court ruled that such tactics required reversal of convictions gained thereby, Mason had lost his *raison d'être*.

Several other detective series sprang from Gardner's dictating machine during his peak years. The 29 novels he wrote under the by-line of A.A. Fair about diminutive private eye Donald Lam and his huge irascible partner Bertha Cool are often preferred over the Masons because of their fusion of corkscrew plots with fresh writing, characterizations, and humor. The high spots of the series are *The Bigger They Come* and *Beware the Curves*. And in his nine books about small-town district attorney Doug Selby Gardner reversed the polarities of the Mason series, making the prosecutor his hero and the defense lawyer the oft-confounded trickster. But most of Gardner's reputation stems from Perry Mason, and his best novels in both this and his other series offer abundant evidence of his natural storytelling talent, which is likely to retain its appeal as long as people read at all.

—Francis M. Nevins, Jr.

GINSBERG, Allen.   American. Born in Newark, New Jersey, 3 June 1926. Educated at Paterson High School, New Jersey; Columbia University, New York, B.A. 1948. Served in the Military Sea Transport Service. Associated with the Beat movement and the San Francisco Renaissance in the 1950's. Widely travelled: has participated in many poetry readings and demonstrations. Lived in the Far East, 1962–63. Since 1971, Director, Committee on Poetry Foundation, New York; Director, Kerouac School of Poetics, Naropa Institute, Boulder, Colorado. Recipient: Guggenheim Fellowship, 1965; National Endowment for the Arts grant, 1966; National Institute of Arts and Letters grant, 1969; National Book Award, 1974. Member, National Insitute of Arts and Letters, 1973. Lives in New York City.

PUBLICATIONS

Verse

> *Howl and Other Poems.*   1956; revised edition of *Howl*, as *Howl for Carl Solomon*, 1971.
> *Empty Mirror: Early Poems.*   1961.
> *Kaddish and Other Poems, 1958–1960.*   1961.
> *Reality Sandwiches, 1953–60.*   1963.
> *T.V. Baby Poems.*   1967.
> *Wales – A Visitation, July 29, 1967.*   1968.
> *Scrap Leaves, Tasty Scribbles.*   1968.
> *Planet News, 1961–1967.*   1968.
> *Airplane Dreams: Compositions from Journals.*   1968.
> *Ankor-Wat.*   1969.
> *Iron Horse.*   1972.
> *The Fall of America: Poems of These States 1965–1971.*   1972.
> *The Gates of Wrath: Rhymed Poems 1948–1952.*   1972.
> *Bixby Canyon Ocean Path Word Breeze.*   1972.
> *New Year Blues.*   1972.
> *Sad Dust Glories.*   1975.
> *First Blues: Rags, Ballads, and Harmonium Songs, 1971–1974.*   1975.
> *Mind Breaths: Poems 1972–1977.*   1977.

Plays

> *Don't Go Away Mad,* in *Pardon Me, Sir, But Is My Eye Hurting Your Elbow?,* edited by Bob Booker and George Foster.   1968.
> *Kaddish* (produced 1972).   1973.

Other

> *The Yage Letters,* with William S. Burroughs.   1963.
> *Indian Journals: March 1962–May 1963: Notebooks, Diary, Blank Pages, Writings.*   1970.
> *Improvised Poetics.*   1972.
> *Allen Verbatim: Lectures on Poetry, Politics, Consciousness,* edited by Gordon Ball.   1974.

The Visions of the Great Remembrancer (on Jack Kerouac).   1974.
Chicago Trial Testimony.   1975.
As Ever: The Collected Correspondence of Ginsberg and Neal Cassady.   1977.
Journals: Early Fifties–Early Sixties, edited by Gordon Ball.   1977.

Bibliography: *A Bibliography of the Works of Ginsberg* by George Dowden, 1970.

Reading List: *Howl of the Censor* by J. W. Ehrlich, 1961; *Ginsberg* by Thomas F. Merrill, 1969; *Ginsberg in America* by Jane Kramer, 1969, as *Paterfamilias,* 1970; *Scenes along the Road* edited by Ann Charters, 1971; *Ginsberg in the '60's* by Eric Mottram, 1972.

*   *   *

Like Whitman, his forebear, Allen Ginsberg is a prolific poet who writes too much: some of his work is, like Whitman's, unfocused, emotionally scattered, and prone to large abstractions unrelated to any concrete particularity. And, like Whitman, Ginsberg insists that any subject is a fit one for poetry. And so, like Whitman, he has been attacked for his vulgarity, for his failure to be "proper" or dignified; yet at the same time, like both Whitman and Blake (from whom he has learned much), he appeals to the young, to those who do not think that poetry and the business of daily life are essentially grave matters whose languages have to be separated from one another. Ginsberg is a World-Poet, like Neruda and Yevtushenko, and like Gibran, Tagore, Whitman, and Blake in previous times. And, like each of these, he has written a quantity of slight but interesting occasional verse, of which "Portland Coloseum" (in *Planet News*), about a Beatles concert, is representative.

In *Improvised Poetics* Ginsberg talks about writing this poem. "I changed things," he said, "like *Hands waving* LIKE *myriad snakes of thought* to *Hands waving myriad/snakes of thought*. Ah ... *The million children* OF *the thousand worlds,* so I just changed *The million children,/the thousand worlds.*" These apparently minor revisions are significant: Ginsberg talks about his "paragraphal" mode of composition and explains, "when I'd get three or four [phrases] that made an apposition I'd start a new paragraph." In taking out "a lot of syntactical fat" and thus "putting two short lines together that had just images in them," Ginsberg prunes the lines of prepositions which express relationship and embraces the technique of juxtaposition, learned from Pound. The danger of such technique is that the poem can degenerate into a mere list (although, as Emerson remarked in *The Poet*, "bare lists of words are found suggestive to an imaginative and excited mind"). The value of such appositional language is that it can *imply* cause-and-effect relationships, but it does not state them: cause and effect are not to be assumed in or about the world of event; it is a world of immediacy. That is to say, the reader is moved into a world of event, a place *where things happen*, for (to quote Emerson again) "the quality of the imagination is to flow, and not to freeze." Ginsberg's reader can, therefore, often be overwhelmed by a rush of sensory, social, political and/or intellectual data to very good effect, as in poems like *Howl* or *Kaddish.*

The concern of the poet is for registering the precise nature of the occurrence (his thought, his feeling, the particularities from which they arise) in the here and now. So Ginsberg, like other modernists, finds crucial the accuracy of the poem as notation of the spoken voice or as notation of the processes of thought. The notation is exact: in *Airplane Dreams* the lines of the long poem "New York to San Fran" are, in Ginsberg's words, "hung out on the page a little to the right.... A little bit like diagramming a sentence, you know, the old syntactical diagrammatic method of making a little platform and you put the subject and object on it and hang adjectives and adverbial clauses down" (*Improvised Poetics*). Here is a short sequence from "Portland Coloseum":

> The million children
> the thousand worlds
> bounce in their seats, bash
> each other's sides, press
> legs together nervous
> Scream again & claphand

Like Olson's, Ginsberg's line-breaks serve an emphatic, syntactic purpose, in which the slight hesitancy at the end of the line provides for unexpected semantic conjunctions and emphases, while at the same time they direct the reader's voice into the (in this case slightly nervous) rhythm and rhetorical inflection of the verse.

Such a line, the unit of thought or the unit of speech, reinforces the air of spontaneous improvisation characteristic of much of Ginsberg's work. The publication of *Howl* in 1956, brought Ginsberg to prominence and gave wide currency to the notion that poetry might be a spontaneous art, requiring little or no skill or revision. Deceptively simple in appearance, *Howl* rests on an extensive apprenticeship in rhymed verse (some of which has been published in *The Gates of Wrath*) and in conscious craftsmanship. As Ginsberg wrote to Richard Eberhart, the "general ground plan" of the poem, "quite symmetrical, surprisingly," structures the three sections of the poem round three main devices: the fixed base of "who" and a long line; the repetition and variation of the fixed base "Moloch"; and the "fixed base/reply/fixed base/longer reply" of the final section. Such writing is not always done, of course, in a single extended burst of composition (the result of a fairly extended gestation): Ginsberg's compositions are often leisurely and deliberative, and very often, in revising a poem, Ginsberg in effect composes a completely new one. "Sunflower Sutra," for example, is a revised version of "In Back of the Real." It is fundamentally a different poem that came about as the result of "re-seeing" the same event. With its long lines, its introduction of a second person into the poem, and its focus on the *perceiver* of the flower, "Sunflower Sutra" is both less general and more immediate in its effect. At the same time it is, as is much of Ginsberg's work, more a celebration and affirmation of the individual, of the personal, and of nature than a denunciation of the world of man. Ginsberg's great strengths as poet are to be found in such visionary poems as this, with its long and carefully controlled lines juxtaposed against shorter lines, leading the poem to a crescendo which is not rhetorical only but quite literally *physical*: Ginsberg's long interest in yoga and in the breath as a measure in verse has led him to speculate on the correlations in Sanskrit poetry between prosody and human physiology, and has led him to attempt similar correlations in his own work. At the same time, the unabashed frankness of his words and the declarative nature of much of his writing have made the work accessible to the casual reader, and have thus given Ginsberg a wide following.

—Peter Quartermain

GLASGOW, Ellen (Anderson Gholson).   American.   Born in Richmond, Virginia, 22 April 1874, and lived there for all of her life. Educated at home, and in private schools in Richmond; began to lose her hearing at age 16, and eventually went deaf. Writer from 1896. President, Richmond Society for the Prevention of Cruelty to Animals. Recipient: Howells Medal, 1941; Pulitzer Prize, 1942. D.Litt.: University of North Carolina, Chapel Hill, 1930;

D.L.: University of Richmond, 1938; Duke University, Durham, North Carolina, 1938; College of William and Mary, Williamsburg, Virginia, 1939. Member, American Academy of Arts and Letters, 1938. *Died 21 November 1945.*

PUBLICATIONS

Collections

Letters, edited by Blair Rouse. 1958.
Collected Stories, edited by Richard K. Meeker. 1963.

Fiction

The Descendent. 1897.
Phases of an Inferior Planet. 1898.
The Voice of the People. 1900; edited by William L. Godshalk, 1972.
The Battle-Ground. 1902.
The Deliverance. 1904.
The Wheel of Life. 1906.
The Ancient Law. 1908.
The Romance of a Plain Man. 1909.
The Miller of Old Church. 1911.
Virginia. 1913.
Life and Gabriella. 1916.
The Builders. 1919.
One Man in His Time. 1922.
The Shadowy Third and Other Stories. 1923; as *Dare's Gift and Other Stories*, 1924.
Barren Ground. 1925.
The Romantic Comedians. 1926.
They Stooped to Folly: A Comedy of Morals. 1929.
The Sheltered Life. 1932.
Vein of Iron. 1935.
In This Our Life. 1941.
Beyond Defeat: An Epilogue to an Era, edited by Luther Y. Gore. 1966.

Verse

The Freeman and Other Poems. 1902.

Other

Works. 8 vols., 1929–33; revised edition, 12 vols., 1938.
A Certain Measure: An Interpretation of Prose Fiction. 1943.
The Woman Within (autobiography). 1954.

Bibliography: *Glasgow: A Bibliography* by William L. Kelley, edited by Oliver L. Steele, 1964.

Reading List: *Glasgow and the Ironic Art of Fiction* by Frederick P. W. McDowell, 1960; *Glasgow* by Blair Rouse, 1962; *Glasgow* by Louis Auchincloss, 1964; *Glasgow's American Dream* by Joan Foster Santas, 1966; *Three Modes of Modern Southern Fiction: Glasgow, Faulkner, and Wolfe* by C. Hugh Holman, 1966; *Without Shelter: The Early Career of Glasgow* by J. R. Raper, 1971; *Glasgow's Development as a Novelist* by Marion K. Richards, 1971; *Glasgow and the Woman Within* by E. S. Godbold, 1972.

* * *

Ellen Glasgow was the first clear voice in the movement that became known as the American Southern Renascence. She was the first writer to apply the principles of critical realism and a detached and ironic point of view to the people, the region, and the problems of the American South. Beginning with her first novel, *The Descendent*, in 1897, and ending with *Beyond Defeat*, posthumously published in 1966, she produced twenty novels in which with varying degrees of success she brought to Virginia and the South what she felt it most needed, "blood and irony." In addition to these novels, she published a volume of critical introductions to a collected edition of her novels, *A Certain Measure*; a volume of undistinguished verse, *The Freeman and Other Poems*; and a collection of mediocre short stories, *The Shadowy Third*.

Her first two novels, both laid in New York, point to her later work only in attempting a clear-eyed realism and in having southern characters. But beginning in 1900, with *The Voice of the People*, and continuing through *The Battle-Ground*, *The Deliverance*, *The Romance of a Plain Man*, *The Miller of Old Church*, *Virginia*, and *Life and Gabriella*, Ellen Glasgow constructed a fictional social history of the Commonwealth of Virginia from the Civil War to the First World War, placing a particular emphasis upon the transition from a ruling aristocracy to the rise of the middle class to political and economic power. In this series of novels, she traced the petrifaction of the aristocratic ideals of pre-war Virginia and recorded through the lives of fictional characters the major social revolution which the rise of the middle class produced. These novels are historical only in the sense that all historical novels deal with issues of manners, politics, and economic forces in an earlier age, for they do not deal with historical personages or actual events. She treated social history with detachment, irony, and a self-consciously witty style. In 1925 she published *Barren Ground*, a novel of a lower-middle-class country woman, Dorinda Oakley, in her struggle with self, circumstance, and the soil. In this novel Ellen Glasgow reached the highest expression of her historical view, although there are no historical events as such in the novel. *Barren Ground* is a grim story, reminiscent of the works of Thomas Hardy, whom she greatly admired. It recounts, she declared, events that could happen "wherever the spirit of fortitude has triumphed over the sense of futility." She also said that it demonstrated that "one may learn to live, one may even learn to live gallantly without delight." Though she was acquainted with modern scientific, social, and anthropological views of man and society, her fundamental view of life remained shaped, as this statement suggests, by a firm but non-theological Calvinistic determinism.

Barren Ground not only summed up the first period in her active career, a period which had seen, in addition to the works named, the publication of four minor novels and her short stories and poetry; it also launched the most productive and artistically successful period in her career. In 1926 she published *The Romantic Comedians*, an almost perfectly constructed novel of manners, laid in Queenborough, her name for her native city of Richmond. The novel, centered in the marriage of an old man to a young girl, is a witty and amusing attack upon the social customs of the surviving Virginia aristocracy. She followed *The Romantic Comedians* with *They Stooped to Folly*, another comedy of manners laid in Queenborough, which plays amusing variations on the idea of the ruined woman through three generations of a Virginia family. *The Sheltered Life*, a tragi-comedy which concludes the Queenborough trilogy, ranks with *Barren Ground* as one of her two best works. *The Sheltered Life* is particularly noteworthy for its treatment of time and memory. "The Deep Past," a section of the novel consisting of the recollections of a very old man, is her finest single piece of work. Two other novels published during her life-time portray the growing darkness of her view of life. *Vein of Iron* is a grim picture of life in the Virginia mountains, a story which she called "a drama of mortal conflict with fate." *In This Our Life*, a Pulitzer Prize winner, is a despairing view of modern life in Queenborough, a book which, she said, shows "that character is an end in itself." *Beyond Defeat*, written as a sequel to it, strongly supports this view.

Ellen Glasgow was a committed realist with a tragic view of human potentialities. Her world view was strongly shaped by a sense of imperfection and failure in all human efforts. Supremely the novelist and fictional historian of her native Virginia, she maintained toward the places in which she lived and the people whom she loved an ironic detachment largely the result of her witty and polished and consciously fashioned style. A half-dozen of her novels, including *Virginia*, *Barren Ground*, the Queenborough trilogy, and *Vein of Iron* are works of considerable distinction. In her own time, she enjoyed both popular and critical respect. Since her death she has received little attention, but she deserves to be better known and more widely read.

—C. Hugh Holman

GLASPELL, Susan (Keating).   American. Born in Davenport, Iowa, 1 July 1882. Educated at Drake University, Des Moines, Iowa, 1897–99, Ph.B. 1899; did graduate work at the University of Chicago, 1903. Married 1) the writer George Cram Cook in 1913 (died, 1923); 2) the writer Norman Matson in 1925 (divorced 1931). State House and Legislative Reporter, *Daily News* and *The Capital*, Des Moines, 1899–1901; returned to Davenport, 1901, to concentrate on writing: supported himself by writing stories for *Harper's*, the *American*, and other magazines; moved to Provincetown, Massachusetts, 1911; with her husband helped found the Provincetown Players, 1915, and wrote for the company, in Provincetown and New York, 1916–22; lived in Greece, 1922–24. Recipient: Pulitzer Prize, 1931. *Died 27 July 1948.*

PUBLICATIONS

Plays

Suppressed Desires, with George Cram Cook (produced 1915).   1916.
Trifles (produced 1916).   1916.
The People (produced 1917).   1918.
Close the Book (produced 1917).   With *The People*, 1918.
The Outside (produced 1917).   In *Plays*, 1920.
Woman's Honor (produced 1918).   In *Plays*, 1920.
Tickless Time, with George Cram Cook (produced 1918).   In *Plays*, 1920.
Bernice (produced 1919).   In *Plays*, 1920.
Plays.   1920; as *Trifles and Other Short Plays*, 1926.

Inheritors (produced 1921).   1921.
The Verge (produced 1921).   1922.
Chains of Dew (produced 1922).
The Comic Artist, with Norman Matson (produced 1928).   1927.
Alison's House (produced 1930).   1930.

Fiction

The Glory of the Conquered.   1909.
The Visioning.   1911.
Lifted Masks: Stories.   1912.
Fidelity.   1915.
A Jury of Her Peers (stories).   1927.
Brook Evans.   1928; as *The Right to Love*, 1930.
The Fugitive's Return.   1929.
Ambrose Holt and Family.   1931.
The Morning Is near Us.   1939.
Cherished and Shared of Old.   1940.
Norma Ashe.   1942.
Judd Rankin's Daughter.   1945; as *Prodigal Giver*, 1946.

Other

The Road to the Temple (on George Cram Cook).   1927.

Editor, *Greek Coins* (verse), by George Cram Cook.   1925.

Reading List: *Glaspell* by Arthur E. Waterman, 1966.

*   *   *

When the Provincetown Players opened a subscription theatre in Greenwich Village in 1916, their two major playwrights were Eugene O'Neill and Susan Glaspell. With her husband, George Cram "Jig" Cook, Glaspell was a founder of the Provincetown Players and, before his dissatisfaction with the direction the theatre was taking and their departure for Greece in 1922, she was a substantial contributor to the success of the group. Although she lacked O'Neill's theatricality, at this time, she was much closer to O'Neill in his concern for intense, meaningful drama than any of their contemporaries.

An intelligent and perceptive person, confident in her art and the values she found meaningful, she was most impressive in her thoughtful and theatrically effective one-act plays. *Suppressed Desires* (written with Cook) is a clever satire on the idea of complete freedom in self-expression. *Trifles* combines mystery with a penetrating understanding of a woman's character in a single tense scene. Other one-act plays performed by the Provincetown Players were *The People*, *The Outside*, and *Woman's Honor*.

Her full-length plays, all of which reveal a liberal woman's approach with force and dignity, never quite reached the quality she seemed destined to produce. *Bernice*, although too conversational and contrived, shows the power and thoughtful ingenuity of a loving wife to effect a dramatic and sustaining change upon her husband after her death. One of her most popular plays from this period is *Inheritors*, which dramatizes the problems of a mid-western college in carrying on the liberal ideas of its founder over the conservatism of its present Board of Trustees. It is mainly in *The Verge* that Glaspell approached the emotional struggles that determined O'Neill's playwriting. Searching for an understanding of herself, the heroine is on the "verge" both of insanity and that answer which eludes her. In language and idea the play suggests a power which was never completely dramatized.

After her husband's death in Greece, Glaspell wrote a moving and interesting biography-autobiography of their work together in theatre and his last years – *The Road to the Temple.* She also produced a number of short stories and novels which did little for her reputation as a writer. Her single outstanding work of this later period was the Pulitzer Prize-winning *Alison's House*, a thought-provoking and beautifully expressed play based on Emily Dickinson's life. Her major contribution to American drama and theatre, however, rests almost entirely on those years of the Provincetown Players, an extremely important time in the growth of American drama.

—Walter J. Meserve

GOLD, Michael. American. Born Irving Granich in New York City, 12 April 1894; changed his name when he began writing. Educated in local schools until age 13. Married. Worked as a night porter, clerk, and driver for an express company, 1907–11; carpenter's helper, section gang laborer, shipping clerk, and factory hand, 1911–15; settled in Boston, 1915, and lived there for several years; returned to New York, and worked as a copy reader for the New York *Call*; joined the Communist Party after the Russian Revolution, and was thereafter associated with various radical publications: Assistant Editor, *Masses*; Founder and Editor, *Liberator*, 1920–22; Founder, with Hugo Gellert, *New Masses*, 1926, and Editor until 1948; also contributed to the *Daily Worker*; in later years, Contributing Editor, *Masses and Mainstream*. Died 14 May 1967.

PUBLICATIONS

Collections

A Literary Anthology, edited by Michael Folsom. 1972.

Fiction

The Damned Agitator and Other Stories. 1926.
Jews Without Money. 1930.

Plays

Hoboken Blues (produced 1928).
Fiesta (produced 1929).
Money. 1930.
Battle Hymn, with Michael Blankfort (produced 1936). 1936.

Other

Life of John Brown.   1924.
120 Million.   1929.
Charlie Chaplin's Parade (juvenile).   1930.
Change the World!   1937.
The Hollow Men.   1941.

Editor, with others, *Proletarian Literature in the United States: An Anthology.*   1935.

*   *   *

Michael Gold's passion for the flowering of a truly proletarian culture was the direct outcome of the life he had known in the ghetto. "When I hope it is the tenement hoping ...," he reminisced in his celebrated essay, "Towards Proletarian Art," "I am all that the tenement group poured into me during those early years of my spiritual travail." His semi-autobiographical novel, *Jews Without Money*, which vividly and poignantly evoked the squalid and suffocating reality of his boyhood world, with its stench and filth, hoodlums and prostitutes, bugs, sweatshops, and swarming immigrants, was in itself intended as a model of the kind of art he was keen to see in vogue in the United States. A proletarian movement in art could take root, he felt, only if there was a spontaneous resurgence of creativity among workers at all levels – when "in every American factory there is a dramatic group ... when mechanics paint in their leisure, and farmers write sonnets." It was, therefore, necessary that preference in art be given to the sufferings of the hungry and persecuted masses over the "precious silly little agonies" of bourgeois writers. Workers, he maintained, must employ "swift action, clear form, the direct line, cinema in words" to create an art imbued with social purpose and bristling with the complex nuances of their lives. *The New Masses*, which he helped to start in 1926 with the express aim of publishing and popularising the contributions of working men and women, did succeed, to a limited extent, in providing a forum of artistic expression to obscure worker-poets such as H. H. Lewis and Martin Russak, but the experiment could not be sustained and continued for long. His plays, *Hoboken Blues*, describing with intimate nearness the Harlem poor in the jazz-age, and *Fiesta*, dealing with the life of the peons and patricians of Mexico countryside, though not successful commercially, at least attested to his earnestness in providing a scathing critique of a literary culture desperately struggling to arrive at a meaningful comprehension of its aims and values.

Gold, never a stickler for stylistic perfection, staked his trust in the absolute sovereignty of the "message" of art, and, in spite of his well-known fondness for Shakespeare and Schiller, often insisted that the artists of the working-class had nothing to learn from the great literature of the bourgeois past. If in his poetry he resorted to the direct statement – with a view to dramatising the predicament of "Vanzetti in the Death House" or celebrating the raw pleasures of ordinary life in "Bucket of Blood" – he generally inclined, Whitmanlike, toward lyricism and prophetic bursts of eloquence in his prose to invoke the grandeur of the Marxist apocalypse awaiting the decay of the old economic order: "For out of our death shall arise glories, and out of the final corruption of this old civilization we have loved shall spring the new race – the supermen." His political sympathies notwithstanding, he could display real glimmerings of objectivity and candour in his literary criticism. His admiration for Upton Sinclair, for instance, was always tempered by his awareness that Sinclair's vision was limited by a fuzzy and unrealistic idealising of the working class and an inbred puritanism that grudged "the poor little jug of wine and hopeful song of the worker." Likewise, his criticism of Hemingway's "colourful if sterile world ... completely divorced from the experience of the great majority of mankind" never overlooked the great American writer's stylistic and narrative accomplishments.

Though faded in appearance, Gold's writings today serve as a powerful reminder of the often forgotten truth that artistic possibilities can be discovered even in the most neglected sections of society and that it is mostly the writers "corrupted by all the money floating everywhere" that find it "unfashionable to believe in human progress ... to work for a better world."

—Chirantan Kulshrestha

GOODMAN, Paul. American. Born in New York City, 9 September 1911. Educated at the City College of New York, B.A. 1931; University of Chicago, Ph.D. 1940 (received, 1954). Married twice; two daughters and one son. Reader for Metro-Goldwyn-Mayer, 1931; Instructor, University of Chicago, 1939–40; Teacher of Latin, physics, history, and mathematics, Manumit School of Progressive Education, Pawling, New York, 1942; also taught at New York University, 1948, Black Mountain College, North Carolina, 1950, and Sarah Lawrence College, Bronxville, New York, 1961; Knapp Professor, University of Wisconsin, Madison, 1964; taught at the Experimental College of San Francisco State College, 1966, and at the University of Hawaii, Honolulu, 1969, 1971. Editor, *Complex* magazine, New York; Film Editor, *Partisan Review*, New Brunswick, New Jersey; Television Critic, *New Republic*, Washington, D.C.; Editor, *Liberation* magazine, New York, 1962–70. Recipient: American Council of Learned Societies Fellowship, 1940; National Institute of Arts and Letters grant, 1953. Fellow, New York Institute for Gestalt Therapy, 1953, and Institute of Policy Studies, Washington, D.C., 1965. *Died 3 August 1972.*

PUBLICATIONS

Collections

> *Collected Poems*, edited by Taylor Stoehr. 1973.
> *Collected Stories and Sketches.* vol. 1 (of 4), 1978.

Fiction

> *The Grand Piano; or, The Almanac of Alienation.* 1942.
> *The Facts of Life* (stories). 1945.
> *The State of Nature.* 1946.
> *The Break-Up of Our Camp and Other Stories.* 1949.
> *The Dead of Spring.* 1950.
> *Parents' Day.* 1951.
> *The Empire City.* 1959.
> *Our Visit to Niagara* (stories). 1960.
> *Making Do.* 1963.
> *Adam and His Works: Collected Stories.* 1968.
> *Don Juan; or, The Continuum of the Libido.* 1977.

Plays

The Tower of Babel, in *New Directions in Poetry and Prose*.   1940.
2 Noh Plays (produced 1950).   In *Stop-Light*, 1941.
Stop-Light (5 Noh plays: *Dusk: A Noh Play, The Birthday, The Three Disciples, The Cyclist, The Stop Light*).   1941.
The Witch of En-Dor, in *New Directions 1944*.   1944.
Theory of Tragedy, in *Quarterly Review of Literature 5*, 1950.
Faustina (produced 1952).   In *Three Plays*, 1965.
Abraham (cycle of Abraham plays: produced 1953).   *Abraham and Isaac* in *Cambridge Review*, November 1955.
The Young Disciple (produced 1955).   In *Three Plays*, 1965.
Little Hero (produced 1957).   In *Tragedy and Comedy: 4 Cubist Plays*, 1970.
The Cave at Machpelah (produced 1959).   In *Commentary*, June 1958.
Three Plays.   1965.
Jonah (produced 1966).   In *Three Plays*, 1965.
Tragedy and Comedy: 4 Cubist Plays (includes *Structure of Tragedy, After Aeschylus; Structure of Tragedy, After Sophocles; Structure of Pathos, After Euripides; Little Hero, After Molière*).   1970.

Verse

Ten Lyric Poems.   1934.
12 Ethical Sonnets.   1935.
15 Poems with Time Expressions.   1936.
Homecoming and Departure.   1937.
Childish Jokes: Crying Backstage.   1938.
A Warning at My Leisure.   1939.
Pieces of Three, with Meyer Liben and Edouard Roditi.   1942.
Five Young American Poets, with others.   1945.
The Copernican Revolution.   1946.
Day and Other Poems.   1954.
Red Jacket.   1956.
Berg Goodman Mezey.   1957.
The Well of Bethlehem.   1959.
The Lordly Hudson (Collected Poems).   1963.
Hawkweed.   1967.
North Percy.   1968.
Homespun of Oatmeal Gray.   1970.
Two Sentences.   1970.

Other

Art and Social Nature (essays).   1946.
Kafka's Prayer.   1947.
Communitas: Means of Livelihood and Ways of Life, with Percival Goodman.   1947; revised edition, 1960.
Gestalt Therapy: Excitement and Growth in the Human Personality, with Frederick Perls and Ralph Hefferline.   1951.
The Structure of Literature.   1954.
Censorship and Pornography on the Stage, and Are Writers Shirking Their Political Duty?   1959.

Growing Up Absurd: Problems of Youth in the Organized Society.   1960.
The Community of Scholars.   1962.
Utopian Essays and Practical Proposals.   1962.
Drawing the Line.   1962.
The Society I Live in Is Mine.   1963.
Compulsory Mis-Education.   1964; revised edition, 1971.
People or Personnel: Decentralizing and the Mixed System.   1965.
Mass Education in Science.   1966.
Five Years: Thoughts During a Useless Time.   1966.
Like a Conquered Province: The Moral Ambiguity of America.   1967.
The Open Look.   1969.
New Reformation: Notes of a Neolithic Conservative.   1970.
Speaking and Language: Defence of Poetry.   1971.
Little Prayers and Finite Experience.   1972.
Drawing the Line: Political Essays, edited by Taylor Stoehr.   1977.
Nature Heals: Psychological Essays, edited by Taylor Stoehr.   1977.
Creator Spirit, Come: Literary Essays, edited by Taylor Stoehr.   1977.

Editor, *Seeds of Liberation.*   1965.

*   *   *

Towards the end of his life Paul Goodman became a cult figure among young, disaffected Americans. His writings were in favour of sexual liberation (he was avowedly, bi-sexual) and freedom from planners' control, and they passionately protested against American involvement in Vietnam – these were all causes that could be and were embraced by a large number of students and their sympathisers. Goodman became suddenly famous, his books went into paperback, he led marches, received many offers to speak on and off campus; and in a sense he wore himself out trying to make the armies of the night into an efficient fighting force against corporation America.

Cult figures rise and fall. But Goodman is a far more substantial figure than his momentary status might make him appear. I would guess that comparatively few of those who began buying his books in the 1960's managed to work their way through them. And this is not because the books are poor, or badly written, but because Goodman is a tough-minded thinker, a man of real intellectual distinction, who refuses to be caught out in simplistic postures, and who never pandered to popular demands that he should become a generation's guru. In short, Goodman is in no way to be blamed for the odd, upward turn of his reputation during those last hopeful, bewildering, and finally sad years of his life. (The sadness was caused by a series of heart attacks and more grievously by the death of his beloved son, Matty, about which he writes in a series of moving poems in his volume of poetry *Homespun of Oatmeal Gray*.)

Perhaps the single work that did most to endear him to the young was *Growing Up Absurd*, which he subtitled "Problems of youth in the organised society." Yet this is not a glib tract for the times: on the contrary, it clearly grew out of Goodman's lifelong dedication to his own particular brand of intellectual anarchism, his deeply-held and passionately-argued for belief that the life of the individual was being more and more threatened by the state. Goodman is really a descendant of John Stuart Mill and Walt Whitman: he longs to invite his soul to loaf, but he fears that the time for loafing may well be past. The themes of *Growing Up Absurd* are also presented in fictional form in many of his stories, in *The Empire City*, and, particularly, in *Making Do*.

Behind *Growing Up Absurd* is a quite magnificent study of the American city as it is and as it might be, *Communitas*, written with his brother Percival. Wonderfully well-written, rigorous in method, in argument, and in detailed application, *Communitas* seems to me a deeply sane and wise book. And the same may be said for most of the essays in *Utopian*

Essays and Practical Proposals. Goodman is indeed an extraordinarily good essayist, better, I would say, than Orwell; he is also a minor poet of some distinction (his posthumous *Little Prayers and Finite Experience* is an interesting experiment in intercutting small lyrical prayers-in-verse with longer prose meditations); and also, though not so successfully, a writer of fiction. Reviewing *Growing Up Absurd*, Webster Schott pointed out that Goodman is "a rational Utopian who has most of the analytical apparatus and theoretical formulations of modern sociology, psychology, historiography and aesthetics at his finger tips."

This almost terrifying breadth and depth – along with his warm and loving heart – help give Goodman his distinction.

—John Lucas

GORDON, Caroline.   American.   Born in Trenton, Kentucky, 6 October 1895. Educated at Bethany College, West Virginia, A.B. 1916. Married Allen Tate, *q.v.*, in 1924 (divorced, 1954); one daughter. Reporter, *Chattanooga News*, Tennessee, 1920–24; Lecturer in English, University of North Carolina Woman's College, Greensboro, 1938–39; Lecturer in Creative Writing, School of General Studies, Columbia University, New York, from 1946; Visiting Professor of English, University of Washington, Seattle, 1953; Writer-in-Residence, University of Kansas, Lawrence, 1956, and University of California at Davis, 1962–63. Recipient: Guggenheim Fellowship, 1932; O. Henry Award, 1934; National Institute of Arts and Letters grant, 1950; National Endowment for the Arts grant, 1966, D.Litt.: Bethany College, 1946; St. Mary's College, Notre Dame, Indiana, 1964. Lives in Princeton, New Jersey.

PUBLICATIONS

Fiction

>*Penhally.*   1931.
>*Aleck Maury, Sportsman.*   1934; as *The Pastimes of Aleck Maury: The Life of a True Sportsman*, 1935.
>*None Shall Look Back.*   1937.
>*The Garden of Adonis.*   1937.
>*Green Centuries.*   1941.
>*The Women on the Porch.*   1944.
>*The Forest of the South* (stories).   1945.
>*The Strange Children.*   1951.
>*The Malefactors.*   1956.
>*Old Red and Other Stories.*   1963.
>*The Glory of Hera.*   1972.

Other

>*How to Read a Novel.*   1957.

A Good Soldier: A Key to the Novels of Ford Madox Ford. 1963.

Editor, with Allen Tate, *The House of Fiction: An Anthology of the Short Story.* 1950; revised edition, 1960.

Bibliography: *Flannery O'Connor and Gordon: A Reference Guide* by Robert E. Golden and Mary C. Sullivan, 1977.

Reading List: *Gordon* by Frederick P. W. McDowell, 1966; *Gordon* by W. J. Stuckey, 1972.

*   *   *

Caroline Gordon is rightly grouped with writers of the so-called Southern Literary Renaissance, but is sometimes inappropriately called a regionalist. Most of her novels and short stories are set in her native Kentucky and in other nearby regions of the South, but her fiction strives toward the kind of universality achieved by the writers she most admires: Flaubert, Henry James, and James Joyce. She is an artist of the "dramatic" school, that is, she attempts to efface herself as author and allow her fiction to speak for itself. In addition to her nine novels and two short story collections, *Forest of the South* and *Old Red and Other Stories,* Caroline Gordon has written a critical book, *How to Read a Novel,* in which she sets down the theoretical basis for her own fiction. With Allen Tate she is also editor of *The House of Fiction,* a widely used anthology of the short story with critical commentary on the craft and teaching of the short story form.

Gordon is a novelist, however, not a critic. Her life-long theme has been the quest for heroic paradigms, a search that has lead her back to pioneer Kentucky (*Green Centuries*), to the pre-Civil War South (*Penhally*), to the War itself (*None Shall Look Back*) and, in modern times, to a Southern plantation in the 1930's (*Garden of Adonis*) ruined by drouth and the depression. Gordon's heros are men or women who, on principle or out of commitment to a cause, stand up for what they believe to be right. This quest, as her fictions moved toward the 20th century, necessarily involved her with the widespread modern preference for the anti-hero and its attendant cultural implications, particularly with the view that meaningful action is impossible to an intellectually aware individual. In *The Women on the Porch,* set in New York and Kentucky, she takes as her hero a deracinated intellectual-poet and "saves" him from emotional detachment through a final reconciliation with his estranged wife, a resolution that points toward the next stage in Gordon's development. In *Strange Children,* narrated by a young girl, the hero – also an intellectual – comes to the realization that what is missing from his life is religious faith. *The Malefactors* carries this resolution a step farther: the hero, Thomas Claiborne, cures his emotional paralysis by entering the Catholic Church. In *The Glory of Hera,* Miss Gordon returns once more to the past, finding her hero and her heroic paradigm in Hercules of Greek myth; she sets forth his story with all the sharpness of detail and dramatic enactment that characterized her earlier work.

The fiction of Caroline Gordon has much in common with the major fiction of the modern period, particularly with Hemingway's tightly controlled, dramatic, impersonal symbolic novels and stories, and it reflects the same attachment to the natural world and traditional values to be found in southern writers generally and Faulkner in particular. The chief difference, perhaps, between the work of Caroline Gordon and that of her contemporaries is in her lack of moral ambiguity. Her fiction is less a discovery of acceptable shades of meaning than a bodying forth in enigmatic form of timeless moral truths.

—W. J. Stuckey

GREEN, Paul (Eliot). American. Born in Lillington, North Carolina, 17 March 1894. Educated at Buies Creek Academy, North Carolina, graduated 1914; University of North Carolina, Chapel Hill, A.B. 1921, graduate study 1921–22; Cornell University, Ithaca, New York, 1922–23. Served in the United States Army Engineers, 1917–19: Lieutenant. Married Elizabeth Atkinson Lay in 1922; four children. Lecturer, then Associate Professor of Philosophy, 1923–39, Professor of Dramatic Arts, 1939–44, and Professor of Radio, Television, and Motion Pictures, 1962–63, University of North Carolina. Editor, *The Reviewer* magazine, Chapel Hill, 1925. President, National Folk Festival, 1934–35; President, National Theatre Conference, 1940–42; President, North Carolina State Literary and Historical Association, 1942–43; Member of the United States Executive Committee, and Member of the National Commission, UNESCO, 1950–53, and United States Delegate to the UNESCO Conference, Paris, 1951; Director, American National Theatre Company, 1959–61; Delegate to the International Conference on the Performing Arts, Athens, 1962. Recipient: Pulitzer Prize, 1927; Guggenheim Fellowship, 1928, 1929; Clare M. Senie Drama Study Award, 1939; Freedoms Foundation George Washington Medal, 1951, 1956, 1966; Susanne M. Davis Award, 1966. Litt.D.: Western Reserve University, Cleveland, 1941; Davidson College, North Carolina, 1948; University of North Carolina, 1956; Berea College, Kentucky, 1957; University of Louisville, Kentucky, 1957; Campbell College, Buies Creek, North Carolina, 1969; Moravian College, Bethlehem, Pennsylvania, 1976; D.F.A.: North Carolina School of the Arts, Winston-Salem, 1976. Member, National Institute of Arts and Letters, 1941. Lives in Chapel Hill, North Carolina.

PUBLICATIONS

Plays

> *Surrender to the Enemy* (produced 1917).
> *The Last of the Lowries* (produced 1920). In *The Lord's Will and Other Carolina Plays*, 1925.
> *The Long Night*, in *Carolina Magazine*, 1920.
> *Granny Boling*, in *Drama*, August–September 1921.
> *Old Wash Lucas (The Miser)* (produced 1921). In *The Lord's Will and Other Carolina Plays*, 1925.
> *The Old Man of Edenton* (produced 1921). In *The Lord's Will and Other Carolina Plays*, 1925.
> *The Lord's Will* (produced 1922). In *The Lord's Will and Other Carolina Plays*, 1925.
> *Blackbeard*, with Elizabeth Lay Green (produced 1922). In *The Lord's Will and Other Carolina Plays*, 1925.
> *White Dresses* (produced 1923). In *Lonesome Road*, 1926.
> *Wrack P'int* (produced 1923).
> *Sam Tucker*, in *Poet Lore*, Summer 1923; revised version, as *Your Fiery Furnace*, in *Lonesome Road*, 1926.
> *Fixin's*, with Erma Green (produced 1924). 1934.
> *The No 'Count Boy* (produced 1925). In *The Lord's Will and Other Carolina Plays*, 1925; revised (white) version, 1953.
> *In Aunt Mahaly's Cabin: A Negro Melodrama* (produced 1925). 1925.
> *The Lord's Will and Other Carolina Plays*. 1925.
> *Quare Medicine* (produced 1925). In *In the Valley and Other Carolina Plays*, 1928.
> *The Man Who Died at Twelve O'Clock* (produced 1925). 1927.
> *In Abraham's Bosom* (produced 1926). In *The Field God, and In Abraham's Bosom*, 1927.

Lonesome Road: Six Plays for the Negro Theatre (includes *In Abraham's Bosom*, one-act version; *White Dresses; The Hot Iron; The Prayer Meeting; The End of the Row; Your Fiery Furnace*). 1926.

The Hot Iron, in *Lonesome Road*. 1926; revised version, as *Lay This Body Down* (produced 1972), in *Wings for to Fly*, 1959.

The Field God (produced 1927). In *The Field God, and In Abraham's Bosom*, 1927.

The Field God, and In Abraham's Bosom. 1927.

Bread and Butter Come to Supper. 1928; as *Chair Endowed* (produced 1954).

In the Valley and Other Carolina Plays (includes *Quare Medicine, Supper for the Dead, Saturday Night, The Man Who Died at Twelve O'Clock, In Aunt Mahaly's Cabin, The No 'Count Boy, The Man on the House, The Picnic, Unto Such Glory, The Goodbye*). 1928.

Supper for the Dead (produced 1954). In *In the Valley and Other Carolina Plays*, 1928.

Unto Such Glory (produced 1936). In *In the Valley and Other Carolina Plays*, 1928.

The Goodbye (produced 1954). In *In the Valley and Other Carolina Plays*, 1928.

Blue Thunder; or, The Man Who Married a Snake, in *One Act Plays for Stage and Study*. 1928.

Old Christmas. 1928.

The House of Connelly (produced 1931). In *The House of Connelly and Other Plays*, 1931; revised version (produced 1959), in *Five Plays of the South*, 1963.

The House of Connelly and Other Plays. 1931.

Potter's Field (produced 1934). In *The House of Connelly and Other Plays*, 1931; revised version, as *Roll Sweet Chariot: A Symphonic Play of the Negro People*, music by Dolphe Martin (produced 1934), 1935.

Tread the Green Grass, music by Lamar Stringfield (produced 1932). In *The House of Connelly and Other Plays*, 1931.

Shroud My Body Down (produced 1934). 1935; revised version, as *The Honeycomb*, 1972.

The Enchanted Maze: The Story of a Modern Student in Dramatic Form (produced 1935). 1939.

Hymn to the Rising Sun (produced 1936). 1936.

Johnny Johnson: The Biography of a Common Man, music by Kurt Weill (produced 1936). 1937; revised version, 1972.

The Southern Cross (produced 1936). 1938.

The Lost Colony (produced 1937). 1937; revised version, 1939, 1946, 1954, 1962.

Alma Mater, in *The Best One-Act Plays of 1938*, edited by Margaret Mayorga. 1938.

Out of the South: The Life of a People in Dramatic Form (includes *The House of Connelly, The Field God, In Abraham's Bosom, Potter's Field, Johnny Johnson, The Lost Colony, The No 'Count Boy, Saturday Night, Quare Medicine, The Hot Iron, Unto Such Glory, Supper for the Dead, The Man Who Died at Twelve O'Clock, White Dresses, Hymn to the Rising Sun*). 1939.

The Critical Year: A One-Act Sketch of American History and the Beginning of the Constitution. 1939.

Franklin and the King. 1939.

The Highland Call: A Symphonic Play of American History (produced 1939). 1941.

Native Son (The Biography of a Young American), with Richard Wright, from the novel by Wright (produced 1941). 1941.

A Start in Life (broadcast 1941). In *The Free Company Presents*, edited by James Boyd, 1941; as *Fine Wagon*, in *Wings for to Fly*, 1959.

The Common Glory: A Symphonic Drama of American History (produced 1947). 1948; revised version, 1975.

Faith of Our Fathers (produced 1950).

Peer Gynt, from the play by Ibsen (produced 1951). 1951.

The Seventeenth Star (produced 1953).

Serenata, with Josefina Niggli (produced 1953).
Carmen, from the libretto by H. Meilhac and L. Halévy, music by Bizet (produced 1954).
Salvation on a String (includes *The Goodbye, Chair Endowed, Supper for the Dead, The No 'Count Boy)* (produced 1954).
Wilderness Road: A Symphonic Outdoor Drama (produced 1955; revised version, produced 1972). 1956.
The Founders: A Symphonic Outdoor Drama (produced 1957). 1957.
The Confederacy: A Symphonic Outdoor Drama Based on the Life of General Robert E. Lee (produced 1958). 1959.
The Stephen Foster Story: A Symphonic Drama Based on the Life and Music of the Composer (produced 1959). 1960.
Wings for to Fly: Three Plays of Negro Life, Mostly for the Ear But Also for the Eye (includes *The Thirsting Heart, Lay This Body Down, Fine Wagon).* 1959.
The Thirsting Heart (produced 1971). In *Wings for to Fly,* 1959.
Five Plays of the South (includes *The House of Connelly, In Abraham's Bosom, Johnny Johnson, Hymn to the Rising Sun, White Dresses).* 1963.
Cross and Sword: A Symphonic Drama of the Spanish Settlement of Florida (produced 1965). 1966.
The Sheltering Plaid. 1965.
Texas: A Symphonic Outdoor Drama of American Life (produced 1966). 1967.
Sing All a Green Willow (produced 1969).
Trumpet in the Land (produced 1970). 1972.
Drumbeats in Georgia: A Symphonic Drama of the Founding of Georgia by James Edward Oglethorpe (produced 1973).
Louisiana Cavalier: A Symphonic Drama of the 18th Century French and Spanish Struggle for the Settling of Louisiana (produced 1976).
We the People: A Symphonic Drama of George Washington and the Establishment of the United States Government (produced 1976).

Screenplays: *Cabin in the Cotton,* 1932; *State Fair,* 1933; *Dr. Bull,* 1933; *Voltaire,* 1933; *The Rosary,* 1933; *Carolina,* 1934; *David Harum,* 1934; *Time Out of Mind,* 1947; *Roseanna McCoy,* 1949; *Broken Soil,* 1949; *Red Shoes Run Faster,* 1949.

Radio Play: *A Start in Life,* 1941.

Fiction

Wide Fields (stories). 1928.
The Laughing Pioneer: A Sketch of Country Life. 1932.
This Body the Earth. 1935.
Salvation on a String and Other Tales of the South. 1946.
Dog on the Sun: A Volume of Stories. 1949.
Words and Ways: Stories and Incidents from My Cape Fear Valley Folklore Collection. 1968.
Home to My Valley (stories). 1970.
Land of Nod and Other Stories: A Volume of Black Stories. 1976.

Verse

The Lost Colony Song-Book. 1938.
The Highland Call Song-Book. 1941.
Song in the Wilderness. 1947.

The Common Glory Song-Book. 1951.
Texas Song-Book. 1967.
Texas Forever. 1967.

Other

Contemporary American Literature: A Study of Fourteen Outstanding American Writers,
     with Elizabeth Lay Green. 1925; revised edition, 1927.
The Hawthorn Tree: Some Papers and Letters on Life and the Theatre. 1943.
Forever Growing: Some Notes on a Credo for Teachers. 1945.
Dramatic Heritage (essays). 1953.
Drama and the Weather: Some Notes and Papers on Life and the Theatre. 1958.
Plough and Furrow: Some Essays and Papers on Life and the Theatre. 1963.

Reading List: *Green* by Barrett H. Clark, 1928; *Green of Chapel Hill* by Agatha Boyd Adams,
1951; *Green* by Walter S. Lazenby, 1970; *Green* by Vincent S. Kenny, 1971.

*   *   *

Paul Green's career as a playwright can be divided conveniently into four overlapping
periods. Utilizing the history, dialect, superstitions, customs, and beliefs of both white and
black inhabitants of his native region in eastern North Carolina, he began by writing short
realistic folkplays, comedies as well as tragedies. Noticeable from the outset was a
compassion for society's expendibles, those cast-offs who, though victims of social injustice,
held within them the dreams and hopes common to all mankind. The full-length *In
Abraham's Bosom*, its protagonist a luckless black schoolteacher, was an extended treatment
of a one-act play. It was followed on Broadway by *The Field God*, dealing with the oppressive
religious orthodoxy among back-country whites.
     Tread the Green Grass, a deliberate experiment, turned from realism toward a mythic non-
realistic folk drama, but retained the kind of rustic characters who were now his special
province. Green's stylized blend of pantomime, dance, ritual, dream sequences, puppetlike
movements, fantasy and legend, with music an integral part of the play as with the Greeks,
expanded, he believed, the accepted concepts of time and space on the stage. For those plays
by him synthesizing the theatrical arts – plays like *Roll Sweet Chariot* (earlier title, *Potter's
Field*), *Shroud My Body Down*, and *Sing All a Green Willow* – Green coined the term
"symphonic drama," intending apparently to devise an American *Gesamtkunstwerk*.
     Meanwhile he did not abandon the commercial theater. *The House of Connelly*, a
dramatization of the fluctuating conditions among aristocrats and "poor whites" in the post-
Civil War South, conformed to Broadway standards of what a well-made play should be. The
anti-war musical *Johnny Johnson* was a collaborative effort with Kurt Weill, and *Native Son*
an adaptation of Richard Wright's tragic story of a black misfit in Chicago. For the New York
stage he provided an English version of *Peer Gynt*, and for an opera theater in Colorado a
translation of Carmen.
     The fourth phase began in 1937 with *The Lost Colony*, an "outdoor symphonic drama"
produced on the very spot where Sir Walter Ralegh's colonists landed in 1587. Applying the
elements of his experimental plays, and superimposing upon an event in history a tightly
drawn plot, Green was finally permitted, on the huge open-air stage, the freedom of sweeping
folk dances, large choruses, and broad movements of men, women, and children. The
throngs of unsophisticated ticket-buyers who attended *The Lost Colony* inspired him to
establish away from Broadway a "theater of the people." In 1947 came *The Common Glory*
for Virginia, then *Faith of Our Fathers* (Washington, D.C.), and other plays like *Wilderness
Road* (Kentucky), *Cross and Sword* (Florida), *Texas*, and *Trumpets in the Land* (Ohio). Four

decades after *The Lost Colony*, Green and his followers had used his "formula" for more than sixty similar works, spread out from the Atlantic coastline to California and Alaska. Never satisfied with his last versions, Green constantly revised the annual summertime repetitions of his outdoor plays.

—Richard Walser

GREGORY, Horace (Victor).   American.   Born in Milwaukee, Wisconsin, 10 April 1898. Educated at the Milwaukee School of Fine Arts, Summers 1913–16; German-English Academy, Milwaukee, 1914–19; University of Wisconsin, Madison, 1919–23, B.A. 1923. Married the poet Marya Zaturenska in 1925; two children. Free-lance writer, New York and London, 1923–34; Member of the English Department, 1934–60, and since 1960, Professor Emeritus, Sarah Lawrence College, Bronxville, New York. Lecturer, New School for Social Research, New York, 1955–56. Associate Editor, *Tiger's Eye* magazine, New York. Recipient: Levinson Award, 1936; Russell Loines Award, 1942; Guggenheim Fellowship, 1951; Academy of American Poets Fellowship, 1961; Bollingen Prize, 1965; Horace Gregory Foundation Award, 1969. Member, National Institute of Arts and Letters, 1964. Lives in Rockland County, New York.

PUBLICATIONS

Verse

Chelsea Rooming House.   1930; as *Rooming House*, 1932.
No Retreat.   1933.
A Wreath for Margery.   1933.
Chorus for Survival.   1935.
Poems 1930–1940.   1941.
Selected Poems.   1951.
Medusa in Gramercy Park.   1961.
Alphabet for Joanna (juvenile).   1963.
Collected Poems.   1964.
Another Look.   1976.

Other

Pilgrim of the Apocalypse: A Critical Study of D. H. Lawrence.   1933; revised edition, 1957.
The Shield of Achilles: Essays on Beliefs in Poetry.   1944.
A History of American Poetry 1900–1940, with Marya Zaturenska.   1946.
Amy Lowell: Portrait of the Poet in Her Time.   1958.

The World of James McNeill Whistler.   1959.
The Dying Gladiators and Other Essays.   1961.
Dorothy Richardson: An Adventure in Self-Discovery.   1967.
The House on Jefferson Street: A Cycle of Memories.   1971.
Spirit of Time and Place: The Collected Essays.   1973.

Editor, with Eleanor Clark, *New Letters in America.*   1937.
Editor, *Critical Remarks on the Metaphysical Poets,* by Samuel Johnson.   1943.
Editor, *The Triumph of Life: Poems of Consolation for the English-Speaking World.*   1945.
Editor, *The Portable Sherwood Anderson.*   1949.
Editor, *Selected Poetry,* by Robert Browning.   1956.
Editor, with Marya Zaturenska, *The Mentor Book of Religious Verse.*   1957.
Editor, with Marya Zaturenska, *The Crystal Cabinet: An Invitation to Poetry.*   1962.
Editor, with others, *Riverside Poetry 4: An Anthology of Student Verse.*   1962.
Editor, *Evangeline and Selected Tales and Poems of Longfellow.*   1964.
Editor, *Selected Poems,* by E. E. Cummings.   1965.
Editor, with Marya Zaturenska, *The Silver Swan: Poems of Romance and Mystery.*   1966.
Editor, *Selected Poems of Lord Byron.*   1969.

Translator, *The Poems of Catullus.*   1931.
Translator, *Poems,* by Catullus.   1956.
Translator, *The Metamorphoses,* by Ovid.   1958.
Translator, *Love Poems of Ovid.*   1964.

Reading List: "Gregory Issue" of *Modern Poetry Studies,* May 1973.

*   *   *

Horace Gregory is perhaps best known as the translator of Catullus and Ovid. But he has also published critical studies on Amy Lowell, D. H. Lawrence, James McNeill Whistler and others, as well as collaborating with his wife, the poet Marya Zaturenska, on *A History of American Poetry 1900–1940.*

Elizabeth Drew has written that his "emotional range is perhaps the most comprehensive among modern poets," and Louis Untermeyer wrote that Gregory "does not share Eliot's disillusions or Crane's disorganization," a statement that is unfair to all three poets. However, poems like "Valediction to My Contemporaries" compare interestingly with Hart Crane's "The Bridge" in their language, their idealism, their purposes; and many of Gregory's efforts to recapture in monologues the pathos and cacophony of life in the modern city remind one of Eliot. In the final analysis, however, authenticity and integrity may not be enough; subtleties of syntax, powers of condensation, originality of imagery, distinguish Eliot and Crane from those who wrote with comparable verve.

Gregory is academic, ordered, descriptive, even-paced; he might be quite properly compared with MacLeish for his intellectual ambition, rhetorical power, and sense of American history. Most of his poems are based on classical subjects in one way or another, though he often juxtaposes classical imagery with modernistic impressions; he also has many poems about paintings, European scenes, and – like MacLeish – his country's cultural history. His well-known poem on Emerson recapitulates Emerson's life in an investigation of the intellectual's role ("To know too well, to think too long") in a land where action and immortality are even more akin than rhetoric and relevance. Gregory, like MacLeish, bears a heavy weight of idealism at all times, perhaps more than his country's history can support. Because the idealism is more muted in his Chelsea rooming house poems, they are perhaps more appealing than his poems with more epic ambitions. In poems like "McAlpin Garfinkel, Poet" and "Time and Isidore Lefkowitz", Gregory seems to have absorbed the influence of Edwin Arlington Robinson and to have looked forward to the work of poets like Kenneth Fearing:

> Look at Isidore Lefkowitz,
> biting his nails, telling how
> he seduces Beautiful French Canadian
> Five and Ten Cent Store Girls,
> beautiful, by God, and how they cry
> and moan, wrapping their arms
> and legs around him
> when he leaves them....

In an age when we have come to think of poems as the swiftly captured sound of madness, Gregory's work stands as a celebration of order, with the glimpsed backstreet life crying out to have a part of that order and the consideration due to it.

> How can I unlearn
> the arts of love within a single hour:
> How can I close my eyes before a mirror,
> believe I am not wanted, that hands, lips, breast
> are merely deeper shadows behind the door
> where all is dark?

—David Ray

GREY, Zane.   American.   Born Pearl Zane Gray in Zanesville, Ohio, 31 January 1872. Educated at Moore High School, Zanesville; University of Pennsylvania, Philadelphia, D.D.S. 1896. Married Lena Elise Roth in 1905; two sons and one daughter. Practised dentistry in New York City, 1896–1904; thereafter a full-time writer; traveled in the West, 1907–18; settled in California, 1918. *Died 23 October 1939.*

PUBLICATIONS

Fiction

Betty Zane. 1903.
The Spirit of the Border. 1906.
The Last of the Plainsmen. 1908.
The Last Trail. 1909.
The Short Stop. 1909.
The Heritage of the Desert. 1910.
The Young Forester. 1910.
The Young Pitcher. 1911.
The Young Lion Hunter. 1911.

Riders of the Purple Sage.   1912.
Ken Ward in the Jungle.   1912.
Desert Gold.   1913.
The Light of Western Stars.   1914.
The Lone Star Ranger.   1915.
The Rainbow Trail.   1915.
The Border Legion.   1916.
Wildfire.   1917.
The U.P. Trail.   1918.
The Desert of Wheat.   1919.
The Man of the Forest.   1920.
The Red-Headed Outfield and Other Stories.   1920.
The Mysterious Rider.   1921.
To the Last Man.   1922.
The Day of the Beast.   1922.
Wanderer of the Wasteland.   1923.
Tappan's Burro and Other Stories.   1923.
The Call of the Canyon.   1924.
Roping Lions in the Grand Canyon.   1924.
The Thundering Herd.   1925.
The Deer Stalker.   1925.
The Vanishing American.   1925.
Under the Tonto Rim.   1926.
Forlorn River.   1927.
Nevada.   1928.
Wild Horse Mesa.   1928.
Don: The Story of a Dog.   1928.
Rogue River Feud.   1929.
Fighting Caravans.   1929.
The Wolf Tracker.   1930.
The Shepherd of Guadaloupe.   1930.
Sunset Pass.   1931.
Arizona Ames.   1932.
Robber's Roost.   1932.
The Drift Fence.   1933.
The Hash Knife Outfit.   1933.
The Code of the West.   1934.
Thunder Mountain.   1935.
The Trail Driver.   1936.
The Lost Wagon Train.   1936.
King of the Royal Mounted [and the Northern Treasure, in the Far North, Gets His Man,
   Policing the Far North, and the Great Jewel Mystery, and the Ghost Guns of Roaring
   River].   7 vols., 1936–46.
West of the Pecos.   1937.
Tex Thorne Comes Out of the West.   1937.
Majesty's Rancho.   1938.
Raiders of the Spanish Peaks.   1938.
Western Union.   1939.
Knights of the Range.   1939.
30,000 on the Hoof.   1940.
Twin Sombreros.   1941.
Stairs of Sand.   1943.
The Wilderness Trek.   1944.
Shadow of the Trail.   1946.

Valley of Wild Horses. 1947.
The Maverick Queen. 1950.
The Dude Ranger. 1951.
Captives of the Desert. 1952.
Wyoming. 1953.
Lost Pueblo. 1954.
Black Mesa. 1955.
Stranger from the Tonto. 1956.
The Fugitive Trail. 1957.
The Arizona Clan. 1958.
Horse Heaven Hill. 1959.
The Ranger and Other Stories. 1960.
Blue Feather and Other Stories. 1961.
Boulder Dam. 1963.
Zane Grey, Outdoorsman: Best Hunting and Fishing Stories, edited by George
    Reiger. 1972.

Other

Last of the Great Scouts (Buffalo Bill), with Helen Cody Wetmore. 1918.
Tales of Fishes [Lonely Trails, Southern Rivers, Fishing Virgin Seas, the Angler's
    Eldorado, Swordfish and Tuna, Fresh Water Fishing, Tahitian Waters]. 8 vols.,
    1919–31.
Book of Camps and Trails. 1931.
An American Angler in Australia. 1937.
Adventures in Fishing, edited by Ed Zern. 1952.

Reading List: Grey by Carlton Jackson, 1973; Grey by Ann Ronald, 1975.

*   *   *

Zane Grey's literary career typifies the American Horatio Alger success story, and Grey
helped to perpetuate the Horatio Alger myth, using striking settings in the American West.
Grey struggled for several years in New York City and near Lackawaxen, Pennsylvania,
writing essays on fishing and a trilogy based on the Zane family history in the settlement of
the Ohio Valley. But Grey received little encouragement, save from his wife, and gathered
rejection slips until he found his subject in the American West as a result of a visit to Arizona
at the request of C. J. "Buffalo" Jones, a business entrepreneur.

Grey's own taste in literature was for the romantic, and he realized that the West was still
close enough to frontier conditions for him to use it as a splendid testing ground of a man's
worth. Owen Wister had discovered the cowboy as romantic hero with The Virginian (1902),
and Grey was quick to capitalize on Wister's discovery. He paid his debt to Wister by using
the subtitle of Wister's famous novel as the title for his first book about the West, The Last of
the Plainsmen.

That book was largely a narrative of travel and was followed by his first proper novel of
the West, The Heritage of the Desert. The success in sales was moderate, but in the story of
the rise to manhood of an Eastern misfit, John Hare, Grey had found those elements of
adventure, suspense, and history that were to make him the most popular writer of his time.
Riders of the Purple Sage, his next Western, was to insure that Grey's struggles to establish
himself as a writer were at an end. From then on he easily outdistanced other American
writers in sales and popular, although not critical, appreciation.

Grey was bothered by the reaction of critics to his work. There is, however, much of the formula in Grey. He is often melodramatic and sentimental, and his style is stilted or awkward. But his fiction has emphasized the importance of the West to the American psyche, and embodied values in American life that those given critical acclaim frequently scoffed at or ignored. Grey was concerned about changing mores in American society. His *The Call of the Canyon*, for example, is contemporary in its concern for the plight of the returned soldier and in its objection to the "new woman." Grey's views, obviously, reflected a large segment of popular opinion in the 1920's, when he was frequently at or near the top of the best-seller lists.

While Grey also wrote many books for boys and books about the outdoors, he will continue to be known for his Western fiction. His energies were so great that new Grey titles were published for years after his death. His work is perennially popular.

—Joseph M. Flora

GUTHRIE, Ramon. American. Born in New York City, 14 January 1896. Educated at Mt. Hermon, 1912–14; University of Toulouse, Docteur en Droit, 1922; the Sorbonne, Paris, 1919, 1922–23. Served in the American Field Service, 1916–17; United States Army Air Corps, 1917–19; Office of Strategic Services, 1943–45; Silver Star. Married Marguerite Maurey in 1922. Assistant Professor of Romance Languages, University of Arizona, Tucson, 1924–26; Professor of French, 1930–63, and Professor Emeritus, 1963–73, Dartmouth College, Hanover, New Hampshire. Recipient: National Endowment for the Arts grant, 1969, 1971; Marjorie Peabody Waite Award, 1970. M.A., 1939, and D.Litt., 1971, Dartmouth College. *Died 22 November 1973.*

PUBLICATIONS

Verse

> *Trobar Clus.* 1923.
> *A World Too Old.* 1927.
> *The Legend of Ermengarde.* 1929.
> *Scherzo, From a Poem to be Entitled "The Proud City."* 1933.
> *Graffiti.* 1959.
> *Asbestos Phoenix.* 1968.
> *Maximum Security Ward, 1964–1970.* 1970.

Novels

> *Marcabrun: The Chronicle of a Foundling Who Spoke Evil of Women and of Love and Who Followed Unawed the Paths of Arrogance Until They Led to Madness, and of His Dealings with Women and of Ribald Words, the Which Brought Him Repute as a Great Rascal and as a Great Singer.* 1926.
> *Parachute.* 1928.

Other

Editor, with George E. Diller, *French Literature and Thought since the Revolution.* 1942.
Editor, with George E. Diller, *Prose and Poetry of Modern France.* 1964.

Translator, *The Revolutionary Spirit in France and America,* by Bernard Faÿ. 1927.
Translator, *The Other Kingdom,* by David Rousset. 1947.
Translator, *The Republic of Silence,* edited by A. J. Liebling. 1947.

Reading List: *Guthrie Kaleidoscope,* 1963 (includes bibliography by Alan Cooke); "La Poésie de Guthrie" by L. Véza, in *Etudes Anglaises,* January–March 1967.

*   *   *

Ramon Guthrie's last and most important work, *Maximum Security Ward,* appeared when he was seventy-four. Indeed, although he was a contemporary of Cummings and Crane, most of his significant work belongs to the late 1950's and 1960's and is collected in *Graffiti, Asbestos Phoenix,* and *Maximum Security Ward.* All three books contain striking poems, but the cumulative force of the last, which derives from its dramatic center, is by far Guthrie's most sustained success. The speaker, a critically ill and suffering old man, uses all the resources of his imagination, memory, intellect, and humor to overcome his bewildering isolation and disappointment in himself and his fellow human beings. The book is a particularly valuable addition to the genre of the modern lyric sequence.

The best introduction to the poet and his style comes in the first of the forty-nine poems of *Maximum Security Ward*:

> So name her Vivian. I, scarecrow Merlin –
> our Broceliande this frantic bramble of
> glass and plastic tubes and stainless steel –
> could count off such illusions as I have
> on a quarter of my thumbs.

Here are all the hallmarks of Guthrie's mature verse: the passionate immediacy of the speaking voice; the subtle internal rhymes and skilful assonance, alliteration, and colliteration (the use of related consonants); the unpretentious, humorous, colloquial tone combined with a scholarly range of reference and romantic wistfulness; and the recurrent reference to French art and literature, particularly medieval romance, as a psychological touchstone.

Guthrie was bilingual and a Francophile, and his intimate knowledge of France is reflected in his poetry. He lived, studied, and wrote in France during most of the 1920's and sporadically thereafter and knew the expatriate community of artists well. He served in France in two wars, married a Frenchwoman, and taught French literature throughout his academic career. His earliest important literary influences were French, and Proust was his philosophical mentor. But he was an eminently American poet, writing out of the traditions of American verse and at times satirizing his country's hypocrisies and cruelties – particularly her role in Vietnam – for the good of the body politic. Of course, his great subject in *Maximum Security Ward* is supranational: the meaning of the whole human enterprise – what it is to be fully human psychologically, socially, politically – and the role of any artist, whether writer, painter, musician, or sculptor, in uncovering what is essentially a sacred meaning.

A good amateur painter, Guthrie had a visual imagination that matched and reinforced his great love for the texture of language and that enhanced the exquisitely tactile sensuousness of some of his most evocative passages:

this smooth knoll of your shoulder,
this cwm of flank, this moss-delineated quite
un-Platonic cave....

Everywhere about is landscape as far as foot can feel
lamps exude their light on flagstones
there are quaint quiet trains in
corridors of pure perspective

Guthrie's poems are filled with concrete, memorable phrases and imagery; he moves skilfully from tone to tone, from the most jarring to the most lyrical; wit, intelligence, and a deep sympathy and humanity inform his work. It is a pity it is not better known.

—Sally M. Gall

HAMMETT, (Samuel) Dashiell. American. Born in St. Mary's County, Maryland, 27 May 1894. Educated at the Baltimore Polytechnic Institute to age 13. Served as a sergeant with the Motor Ambulance Corps of the Unites States Army in World War I, 1918–19, and with the United States Army Signal Corps in World War II, 1942–45. Married Josephine Annas Dolan in 1920 (divorced, 1937); two daughters. Worked as a clerk, stevedore, advertising manager, and as a private detective for the Pinkerton Agency, 1908–22; full-time writer from 1922; Instructor, Jefferson School of Social Science, New York, 1946–47. President, Civil Rights Congress of New York, 1946–47; Member, Advisory Board, *Soviet Russia Today*; President, League of American Writers. *Died 10 January 1961.*

PUBLICATIONS

Collections

   The Big Knockover: Selected Stories and Short Novels, edited by Lillian
   Hellman. 1966; as *The Hammett Story Omnibus,* 1966.

Fiction

   $106,000 Blood Money. 1927; as *Blood Money,* 1943.
   The Dain Curse. 1929.
   Red Harvest. 1929.
   The Maltese Falcon. 1930.
   The Glass Key. 1931.
   Secret Agent X-9 (comic strip), illustrated by Alex Raymond. 1934.
   The Thin Man. 1934.
   The Adventures of Sam Spade and Other Stories. 1944.

The Continental Op.   1945.
The Return of the Continental Op.   1945.
A Man Called Spade and Other Stories.   1945(?).
Hammett Homicides, edited by Ellery Queen.   1946
Dead Yellow Women, edited by Ellery Queen.   1947.
Nightmare Town, edited by Ellery Queen.   1948.
The Creeping Siamese, edited by Ellery Queen.   1950.
Woman in the Dark: More Adventures of the Continental Op, edited by Ellery
    Queen.   1951.
A Man Called Thin, and Other Stories, edited by Ellery Queen.   1962.

Plays

Watch on the Rhine (screenplay), with Lillian Hellman, in *Best Film Plays of 1943–44*,
    edited by John Gassner and Dudley Nichols.   1945.

Screenplays: *After the Thin Man*, with Frances Goodrich and Albert Hackett, 1937;
Another Thin Man, with Frances Goodrich and Albert Hackett, 1939; *Watch on the
Rhine*, with Lillian Hellman, 1943.

Other

Editor, *Creeps by Night: Chills and Thrills.*   1931.
Editor, *Modern Tales of Horror.*   1932.
Editor, *The Red Brain and Other Thrillers.*   1961; as *Breakdown and Other Thrillers*,
    1968.

Bibliography: *A List of the Original Appearances of Hammett's Magazine Work* by E. H.
Mundell, 1968.

Reading List: "The Black Mask School" by Philip Durham and "The Poetics of the Private-
Eye: The Novels of Hammett" by Robert I. Edenbaum, both in *Tough Guy Writers of the
Thirties* edited by David Madden, 1968; *Hammett: A Casebook* edited by William F. Nolan,
1969; *Unfinished Woman*, 1969, *Pentimento*, 1974, and *Scoundrel Time*, 1976, all by Lillian
Hellman; Introduction by Steven Marcus to *The Continental Op*, 1974.

*   *   *

In the same year (1923) that he began publishing his stories of the Continental Op in *Black
Mask*, the monthly pulp magazine founded by H. L. Mencken and George Jean Nathan,
Dashiell Hammett contributed to their more sophisticated *Smart Set* a collection of terse
observations about his career as a Pinkerton agent under a title echoing the writings of his
former employer: "From the Memoirs of a Private Detective." In form these "memoirs" play
against familiar conventions of detective literature. A wry remark such as "I know a forger
who left his wife because she had learned to smoke cigarettes while he was serving a term in
prison" diminishes the categorical morality of crime literature, and other comments on the
inadequacy of fingerprints as clues or the number of unsolved cases in a detective's files
disparage all accounts of infallible detective procedures. Since the stories of the Continental
Op, Ned Beaumont, Sam Spade, and Nick Charles similarly transgress familiar conventions,
it is not hard to see why readers, like Raymond Chandler in his famous essay "The Simple

Art of Murder," consider Hammett to have added realism to a form grown effete by its emphasis on the myths of ratiocinative detection.

Hammett is notable for the versimilitude in his use of criminal argot and the description of underworld life, but that cannot be confused with imitation of *the real world*. And his use of American vernacular speech in the first person narrations of the Continental Op or Nick Charles and the density of action and dialogue in the futile quest for the Maltese falcon or the political crimes of *The Glass Key* should be seen as the requirement of the contract between author and reader of fiction that there be a specific world within the fiction. The extraordinarily complicated, and unlikely, plotting even in the novelettes about the Op, are as incongruent with the reader's known world as the private detectives are unlike their real-life counterparts who occupy themselves with tawdry divorce cases or employee theft.

What, then, is Hammett's achievement, if it is not in mimetic narrative? The answer seems to be that he supplants the mystery puzzle and idealized heroes of earlier detective fiction with themes that codify a modern sense of urban disorder. He achieves this, first of all, by creation of a milieu of pervasive corruption. In his novels – all but *The Thin Man* originally serialized in *Black Mask* – and short stories the socially reputable are as criminal as the gangsters with whom they often collaborate. The action of plot necessarily follows. Everyone becomes involved in crime, while the force of violence is the common expression of will for those who recognize no law but their own domination, and for the detective because his reason is insufficient alone. When the systems of our social and political myths cannot account for the feel of confusion and menace in urban life, the caricature of a naturalistic world in Hammett's fiction becomes a plausible image.

Similarly, Hammett's stylized representation of hard-boiled detectives offers an appropriate common-sense theme of behavior. Sam Spade repressing sentiment, Ned Beaumont acting on motives that are unclear even to himself, the Continental Op just doing his job, and Nick Charles affecting sophistication are all masked figures. Behind the tough and cool face they maintain before their world, as though there were no such thing as subjective psychology, we sense a vulnerability that becomes justification for wariness and a disposition to violence. We are intrigued by the thought that Hammett's detectives are what Huck Finn would have become when he found the Territory where he hoped to escape civilization dotted with cities, and in adulthood converted his sense of complicity in events beyond his control into a principle of behavior.

—John M. Reilly

HANSBERRY, Lorraine (Vivian).   American.   Born in Chicago, Illinois, 19 May 1930. Educated at the Art Institute, Chicago; University of Wisconsin, Madison, 1948. Married Robert Barron Nemiroff in 1953 (divorced, 1964). Worked as a journalist and editor. Recipient: New York Drama Critics Circle Award, 1959. *Died 12 January 1965.*

PUBLICATIONS

Collections

> *Les Blancs: The Collected Last Plays* (includes *Les Blancs, The Drinking Gourd, What Use are Flowers?*), edited by Robert Nemiroff. 1972.

Plays

A Raisin in the Sun (produced 1959).   1959.
The Sign in Sidney Brustein's Window (produced 1964).   1965.
To Be Young, Gifted, and Black: A Portrait of Hansberry in Her Own Words, adapted by
   Robert Nemiroff (produced 1969).   1971.
Les Blancs, edited by Robert Nemiroff (produced 1970).   In *Les Blancs* (collection),
   1972.

Screenplay: *A Raisin in the Sun*, 1961.

Other

The Movement: Documentary of a Struggle for Equality.   1964; as *A Matter of Colour:
   Documentary of the Struggles for Racial Equality in the USA*, 1965.
To Be Young, Gifted, and Black: Hansberry in Her Own Words, adapted by Robert
   Nemiroff.   1969.

*   *   *

The importance of Lorraine Hansberry as an American dramatist rests with two plays, *A
Raisin in the Sun* and *The Sign in Sidney Brustein's Window*, both produced during her
tragically short life of thirty-four years. The first, by all measurements, was a major success.
The second was a commercial failure, meeting only limited critical support. There were two
posthumous productions, the effective but somewhat pasted-up collection presented as *To Be
Young, Gifted, and Black* and *Les Blancs*, more or less complete but obviously still
unfinished.

Lorraine Hansberry is an important, though minor, figure in American drama if for no
more than the fact that she wrote an outstanding play of substantial popular and critical
success as a Black writer contributing to an essentially white-oriented commercial theatre
during a period when the Black identity in American letters was at a very delicate stage. It
was a period when a strong pull existed between those Blacks who would prefer to stand on
their achievements as artists, irrespective of race, and those who would prefer to take a stand,
artistic as well as social or political, because of the very fact of their blackness. It is clear, as
one encounters the opinions of critics who evaluate Lorraine Hansberry as a Black writer,
that a dichotomy exists. While she herself was completely uncontroversial – she was indeed
no LeRoi Jones nor Dick Gregory – and avoided the pointedly racial-political involvements
associated with Black writers of her era, there is some controversy as to whether or not her
two major plays were merely outstanding, relatively conventional, dramatic works of a fine
young American playwright of promising talent who happened to be black, or were the
works of a dedicated Black playwright treating subjects directly involved in the causes
espoused by the writers overtly conscious of their race.

A Raisin in the Sun at first glance would suggest that Hansberry is squarely in the camp of
those Black writers choosing to place onstage the social issue of the ghetto-trapped family.
The specifications are there from the exasperated young Black male, fumbling and frustrated
in The Man's world, to the matriarch holding the fatherless family together. But Lorraine
Hansberry has actually composed a solid, almost conventional "well-made" play, centering
upon a theme which could have at one time as easily been Irish, Jewish, or Oriental, but
which happens, given the time it was written and the knowledge of its creator, to be Black.
True, the plight of the Youngers, a serious and prevalent American theme, exists almost
entirely *because* they are black, but the confrontations, save for that with the rather pitiful
Linder, who brings the outside forces briefly into the Youngers' living room, remain offstage

or are postponed until after the curtain falls. Audience interest in the Youngers is in their human, not their racial, qualities.

The Sign in Sidney Brustein's Window is a sensitive comedy far removed in subject and intent from *Raisin*. The world of a white Jewish flat in Greenwich Village, visited by attractive, if not always "normal" characters and centered upon a strictly local political campaign, is not the usual subject associated with a Black writer intent on attacks against the social injustices of a racist society. Hansberry attacks petty individual prejudices, those against Black or sexual deviant, as well as personal selfishness which can be fatal to those one ought to love.

It is impossible to know where Lorraine Hansberry might have gone. Perhaps she would have become "radicalized," or perhaps she was already more radicalized than we recognize. It hardly matters. Judgment of her two important plays shows that she was a writer of singular promise, a very important voice in an uncertain historical and social period.

—Jordan Y. Miller

HART, Moss. American. Born in New York City, 24 October 1904. Educated in New York public schools. Married the actress Kitty Carlisle in 1946; one son and one daughter. Worked with the Thalian Players, New York, then as a floor walker in a clothing store, and directed little theatre groups in Brooklyn and Newark, New Jersey; full-time playwright from 1930, often in collaboration with George S. Kaufman; later also produced and directed for the Broadway stage. Recipient: Megrue Prize, 1930; Pulitzer Prize, with George S. Kaufman, 1937; New York Drama Critics Circle Award, for direction, 1955; Antoinette Perry Award, for direction, 1957. *Died 20 December 1961.*

PUBLICATIONS

Plays

The Hold-Up Man (produced 1923).
Jonica, with Dorothy Heyward, music by Joseph Meyer, lyrics by William Moll (produced 1930).
No Retreat (produced 1930).
Once in a Lifetime, with George S. Kaufman (produced 1930).   1930.
Face the Music, music by Irving Berlin (produced 1932).
As Thousands Cheer, with Irving Berlin, music and lyrics by Edward Heyman and Richard Myers (produced 1933).
The Great Waltz, from a play by Ernst Marischka and others, music by Johann Strauss (produced 1934).
Merrily We Roll Along, with George S. Kaufman (produced 1934).   1934.
The Paperhanger, with George S. Kaufman.   1935(?).
Jubilee, music by Cole Porter (produced 1935).
The Show Is On (revue), with others (produced 1936).
You Can't Take It with You, with George S. Kaufman (produced 1936).   1937.
I'd Rather Be Right, with George S. Kaufman, music by Richard Rodgers, lyrics by Lorenz Hart (produced 1937).   1937.

The Fabulous Invalid, with George S. Kaufman (produced 1938).   1938.
The American Way, with George S. Kaufman, music by Oscar Levant (produced 1939).   1939.
The Man Who Came to Dinner, with George S. Kaufman (produced 1939).   1940.
George Washington Slept Here, with George S. Kaufman (produced 1940).   1940.
Lady in the Dark, music by Kurt Weill, lyrics by Ira Gershwin (produced 1941).   1941.
Winged Victory (produced 1943).   1943.
Christopher Blake (produced 1946).   1947.
Light Up the Sky (produced 1948).   1949.
The Climate of Eden, from the novel *Shadows Move among Them* by Edgar Mittelholzer (produced 1952).   1953.

Screenplays: *Winged Victory,* 1944; *Gentleman's Agreement,* 1947; *Hans Christian Andersen,* with Myles Connolly, 1952; *A Star Is Born,* 1954; *Prince of Players,* 1954.

Other

Act One (autobiography).   1959.

*   *   *

Moss Hart's first play, *The Hold-Up Man,* written at 19, folded in Chicago, but his *Once in a Lifetime* caught Sam Harris's eye, he was given George S. Kaufman as a collaborator (a story wittily told in Hart's autobiography, *Act One*), and the rest is history. Their play *Once in a Lifetime* was a success and the team continued with *Merrily We Roll Along,* the classic *You Can't Take It With You, The Man Who Came to Dinner,* and *George Washington Slept Here.*
Then Hart, never secure alone, sought other collaborators and produced important work. Having written *Face the Music* and *As Thousands Cheer* with Irving Berlin, *Jubilee* with Cole Porter, and *I'd Rather Be Right* with Kaufman and Rodgers and Lorenz Hart, he carried on his musical success in 1941 with Kurt Weill and Ira Gershwin: *Lady in the Dark.* This was probably the highlight of his own musical work though he directed such hits by others as Irving Berlin's *Miss Liberty* (1949) and the Lerner and Loewe blockbusters *My Fair Lady* (1956) and *Camelot* (1960). In 1943 he created a "spectacle in two acts and seventeen scenes" for the USAF called *Winged Victory,* starring 300 servicemen, including Red Buttons and Lee J. Cobb. "The Army Emergency Relief Fund needs the money," was Lewis Nichols' review in *The Times,* but he patriotically if not critically added that it was "a wonderful show." After World War II Hart gave us *Christopher Blake* (1946) – which can be forgotten. *Light Up the Sky,* however, is one of my favorite plays about theatre folk – slick, sentimental, simplistic, and very funny. It is a delightful expansion of real life. In *The Climate of Eden,* "Eden" turns out to be the British Guiana mission of Gregory Hawke's uncle, and there our hero, feeling guilty for his wife's death, is obsessed with various problems. More interesting are Hart's films such as *Gentleman's Agreement* and *A Star Is Born.*
Moss Hart was always the innovative sort of theatre man who could call for four revolving stages where no one had ever used more than two before – and the dependent sort of theatre man that leaned on collaborators but also got four times as much out of them, and himself, as had ever been obtained before. He was also the sort who could submit *Once in a Lifetime* to six managers (all of whom accepted it) and then sell it to Sam Harris with the understanding that Kaufman would collaborate.
That collaboration produced one of the best comedies of the American theatre, *The Man Who Came to Dinner.* Of course, "real life" made them a gift of the inimitable Alexander Woollcott, but *they* knew what to do with him. It also takes a crack at Noël Coward, one of the Marx Brothers, the Lizzie Borden story (which is rather ineptly worked in), and the Middle West, would-be writers, fussy nurses, "the most chic actress on the New York or

London stage," etc. The plot (largely Hart's?) is carpentry, but the wisecracks (mostly Kaufman's) are pure gold. Add Monty Woolley (who, said Richard Severo in *The New York Herald Tribune* of 7 May 1963, "wore his beard with the aplomb of a Madison Ave. Santa Claus," brought from Yale some "class" Kaufman and Hart always lacked, and "reduced the nurse ... to the potency of a pound of wet Kleenex") and the audience was limp with laughter. Without him the play is inevitably much less, but is still runs beautifully.

—Leonard R. N. Ashley

HAWKES, John (Clendennin Burne, Jr.). American. Born in Stamford, Connecticut, 17 August 1925. Educated at Trinity School, 1940–41; Pawling High School, 1941–43; Harvard University, Cambridge, Massachusetts, 1943–49, A.B. 1949. Served as an ambulance driver with the American Field Service in Italy and Germany, 1944–45. Married Sophie Goode Tazewell in 1947; three sons and one daughter. Assistant to the Production Manager, Harvard University Press, 1949–55; Visiting Lecturer, 1955–56, and Instructor in English, 1956–58, Harvard University. Assistant Professor, 1958–62, Associate Professor, 1962–67, Professor of English, 1967–73, and since 1973 University Professor, Brown University, Providence, Rhode Island. Special Guest, Aspen Institute for Humanistic Studies, Colorado, 1962; member of the staff of the Utah Writers Conference, summer 1962, and Bread Loaf Writers Conference, Vermont, summer 1963; Visiting Professor of Creative Writing, Stanford University, California, 1966–67; Visiting Distinguished Professor of Creative Writing, City College of the City University of New York, 1971–72. Member, Panel on Educational Innovation, Washington, D.C., 1966–67. Recipient: National Institute of Arts and Letters grant, 1962; Guggenheim Fellowship, 1962; Ford Fellowship, for drama, 1964; Rockefeller Fellowship, 1968; Prix du Meilleur Livre Etranger, 1973. Lives in Providence, Rhode Island.

PUBLICATIONS

Fiction

> *The Cannibal.* 1949.
> *The Beetle Leg.* 1951.
> *The Goose on the Grave, and The Owl: Two Short Novels.* 1954.
> *The Lime Twig.* 1961.
> *Second Skin.* 1964.
> *Lunar Landscapes: Stories and Short Novels 1949–1963.* 1969.
> *The Blood Oranges.* 1971.
> *Death, Sleep, and the Traveler.* 1974.
> *Travesty.* 1976.

Plays

The Wax Museum (produced 1966).   In *The Innocent Party*, 1966.
The Questions (produced 1966).   In *The Innocent Party*, 1966.
The Innocent Party: Four Short Plays.   1966.
The Undertaker (produced 1967).   In *The Innocent Party*, 1966.
The Innocent Party (produced 1968).   In *The Innocent Party*, 1966.

Other

Editor, with others, *The Personal Voice: A Contemporary Prose Reader.*   1964.
Editor, with others, *The American Literary Anthology 1: The 1st Annual Collection of the Best from the Literary Magazines.*   1968.

Bibliography: *Three Comtemporary Novelists: An Annotated Bibliography* by Robert M. Scotto, 1977; *Hawkes: An Annotated Bibliography* by Carol A. Hryciw, 1977.

Reading List: *The Fabulators* by Robert Scholes, 1967; *City of Words* by Tony Tanner, 1971; *Comic Terror: The Novels of Hawkes* by Donald J. Greiner, 1973; *Hawkes and the Craft of Conflict* by John Kuehl, 1975.

*   *   *

American letters has not, on the whole, been particularly receptive to the cultivation of truly esoteric talents, probably because some appeal to a general audience is almost morally as well as commercially compulsory in American culture. John Hawkes, however, comes close to being a writer whose intransigent dedication to a special conception of art provides the exception to this rule. But if he has colonized for himself a separate place in contemporary fiction, he has done so not through the promulgation of an exotic or cultist philosophy, nor through the projection of a public personality that cuts against the grain of conventional mores, but pre-eminently as a prose stylist. In his first full-length novel, *The Cannibal*, he staked out the literary area which he would make uniquely his own: the creation of an uncompromising verbal artifice that aims at rendering sensuously and in the modern idiom the melodramatic atmosphere of traditional Gothic materials in a manner designed to implicate the reader in ambivalent sado-masochistic responses. That is, Hawkes has deliberately conceived of his fiction as a premeditated assault against a victimized reader. The establishment of a powerful tension between the outrageously unacceptable behavior of the plot and characters and the equally undeniable visceral reactions of the individual reader results in that impasse of aesthetic distortion that is usually assumed to be within the provenance of "the grotesque." And in Hawkes's work the largest part of the burden in achieving this goal is entrusted to his style – a lean, elusive, visual-kinetic succession of images that alternately beguiles, frustrates, and shocks the reader's expectations.

Set in a fantastic post-World War II Occupied Germany, *The Cannibal* ignores conventional time-sequences, character development, and cause-effect probabilities to describe the triumphant uprising of the defeated nation in the persons of a crippled handful of mutated life-forms tortuously emerging from the debris of their own corruption. Belying its own stoic bitterness, the novel moves casually back and forth through time, dispassionately issuing a series of vividly etched vignettes of murder, betrayal, cannibalism, and destructive perversions of love. And although the work occasionally suggests the experimentalism of Dada and Surrealism, its rigorous stylistic attachment to the matter-of-fact conventions of realism forces it on the reader with the imperative of a personal nightmare.

After *The Cannibal*, Hawkes experimented with a bleak parody of the Western (*The Beetle*

Leg) and a grim excursion in archaism (*The Goose on the Grave*) before producing the masterful *The Lime Twig*. Partly indebted to *Brighton Rock* and the post-war British movies, and partly a sardonic parody of the detective novel, *The Lime Twig* depicts brilliantly the ironic confluence of banal bourgeois fantasies (Hencher, Margaret and Michael Banks) and a ruthless underworld gang that brings those fantasies to terrible realization as it endeavors to make a fortune on a horse-race. Hawkes's uncanny evocation of the seedy atmosphere of the British demi-monde and his persuasive characterization of the twisted loneliness of Hencher and the semi-voluntary brutalization of the Bankses give this novel a quality of sadistic and yet poetic grotesquerie remarkable in its integrity to its own cruel aesthetic purposes.

With *Second Skin* Hawkes inaugurates a new direction in narrative focus, restricting himself to the consciousness of the first-person point of view (the Skipper's), throwing some doubt on the reliability of that point of view, and adding an element of playfulness to the chronicle of the horrible events (rape, sodomy, suicide) that mark the Skipper's journey toward ambiguous self-understanding. And in the trilogy of novels that has followed (*Blood Oranges, Death, Sleep, and the Traveler,* and *Travesty*), this use of an increasingly unreliable narrator and a playfulness that sometimes borders on the frivolous have become even more marked. But if the last three or four novels show a falling-off from the concentrated purity of Hawkes's earlier excursions in seductive horror, his prose style has remained as sensuous, supple, and shocking as it was in the beginning. He remains well outside the mainstream of contemporary fiction, but he has settled a small but solid island of stylistic rigor which stands as a kind of navigational guide for his contemporaries and those who are voyaging after him.

—Earl Rovit

HAYDEN, Robert (Earl). American. Born in Detroit, Michigan, 4 August 1913. Educated at Wayne State University, Detroit, A.B.: University of Michigan. Ann Arbor (Hopwood Award, 1938, 1942), M.A. 1944. Married; one daughter. Teaching Fellow, University of Michigan, 1944–46; Member of the English Department, Fisk University, Nashville, Tennessee, 1946–68. Visiting Professor, 1968, and since 1969, Professor of English, University of Michigan. Bingham Professor, University of Louisville, Kentucky, Spring 1969; Visiting Poet, University of Washington, Seattle, Summer 1969, University of Connecticut, Storrs, 1971, and Denison University, Granville, Ohio, 1971; Staff Member, Breadloaf Writers Conference, Middlebury, Vermont, 1972. Member, and Poetry Editor, *World Order*, Baha'i Faith. Recipient: Rosenwald Fellowship, 1947; Ford Foundation grant, 1954; World Festival of Negro Arts Poetry Prize, Dakar, Senegal, 1966; Russell Loines Award, 1970; American Academy of Poets Fellowship, 1971. Lives in Ann Arbor, Michigan.

PUBLICATIONS

Verse

Heart-Shape in the Dust. 1940.
The Lion and the Archer, with Myron O'Higgins. 1948.
Figures of Time. 1955.

A Ballad of Remembrance.   1962.
Selected Poems.   1966.
Words in the Mourning Time.   1970.
The Night-Blooming Cereus.   1972.
Angle of Ascent: New and Selected Poems.   1975.

Other

How I Write 1, with Judson Philips and Lawson Carter.   1972.
Nine Black American Doctors (juvenile), with Jacqueline Harris.   1976.

Editor, *Kaleidoscope: Poems by American Negro Poets.*   1967.
Editor, with David J. Burrows and Frederick R. Lapides, *Afro-American Literature: An Introduction.*   1971.

*   *   *

Much in the manner of Countée Cullen, the Harlem Renaissance poet, though more comfortable experimenting with free forms of verse, Robert Hayden has steadfastly claimed refusal to write racial poetry but quite consistently been at his poetic best precisely when he has used the material of the black American experience in his work. He warned in *Kaleidoscope* against placing the black writer in "a kind of literary ghetto," where he would be "not considered a writer but a species of race-relations man, the leader of a cause, the voice of protest." It must be said that even when Hayden employs racial material and themes, he usually molds them into interesting and often exquisite universal shapes that make him far more than a mere "race-relations man." If there is a criticism to be levelled at him, it would be that he is occasionally too academic (indeed, he has spent much of his life in academe), occasionally lapsing into preciousness (e.g., in "Veracruz": "Thus reality/bedizened in the warring colors/of a dream ...").

Mostly, however, Hayden composes with notable power and beauty. For example, his evocation, in "The Ballad of Nat Turner," of the nineteenth-century leader of a slave uprising is perhaps the most succinct and spiritually true in all of imaginative literature. Such poems as "The Diver" capture the essence of the moment or act (in this case the descent of a sea diver from the sinking "through easeful azure" to the time when "somehow began the measured rise") with the felicitous marriage of sound and sense that is quintessential poetry.

—Alan R. Shucard

HECHT, Ben. American. Born in New York City, 28 February 1894; moved with his family to Chicago, then to Racine, Wisconsin. Educated at Racine High School. Married 1) Marie Armstrong in 1915 (divorced, 1925), one daughter; 2) Rose Caylor in 1925. Journalist, *Chicago Journal,* 1910–14; Reporter, 1914–18, Correspondent in Berlin, 1918–19, and Columnist, 1919–23, *Chicago News*; Founding Editor and Publisher, *Chicago Literary Times,* 1923–25; thereafter a full-time writer for the stage, and for motion pictures from

1933; formed a production company with Charles MacArthur, 1934; Columnist ("1001 Afternoons in Manhattan") *PM* newspaper, Long Island, New York, 1940–41. Active Zionist from 1946: Co-Chairman, American League for a Free Palestine. Recipient: Academy Award, 1928, 1936. *Died 18 April 1964.*

PUBLICATIONS

Plays

The Wonder Hat: A Harlequinade, with Kenneth Sawyer Goodman (produced 1916). 1920.
The Hero of Santa Maria, with Kenneth Sawyer Goodman (produced 1916–17?). 1920.
The Master Poisoner, with Maxwell Bodenheim, in *Minna and Myself,* by Bodenheim. 1918.
The Hand of Siva, with Kenneth Sawyer Goodman. 1920.
The Egoist (produced 1922).
The Wonder Hat and Other One-Act Plays (includes *The Two Lamps, An Idyll of the Shops, The Hand of Siva, The Hero of Santa Maria*), with Kenneth Sawyer Goodman. 1925.
The Stork, from a play by Laszlo Fodor (produced 1925).
Christmas Eve: A Morality Play. 1928.
The Front Page, with Charles MacArthur (produced 1928). 1928.
Twentieth Century, with Charles MacArthur (produced 1932). 1932.
The Great Magoo, with Gene Fowler (produced 1932). 1933.
Jumbo, with Charles MacArthur, music by Richard Rodgers, lyrics by Lorenz Hart (produced 1935). 1935.
To Quito and Back (produced 1937). 1937.
Ladies and Gentlemen, with Charles MacArthur, from a play by Ladislas Bush-Fekete (produced 1939). 1941.
Fun to Be Free: A Patriotic Pageant, with Charles MacArthur (produced 1941). 1941.
Lily of the Valley (produced 1942).
We Will Never Die (produced 1943). 1943.
Wuthering Heights (screenplay), with Charles MacArthur, in *Twenty Best Film Plays,* edited by John Gassner and Dudley Nichols. 1943.
A Tribute to Gallantry, in *The Best One-Act Plays of 1943,* edited by Margaret Mayorga. 1943.
Miracle of the Pullman (broadcast 1944). In *The Best One-Act Plays of 1944,* edited by Margaret Mayorga, 1945.
Swan Song, with Charles MacArthur, from a story by Ramon Romero and Harriett Hinsdale (produced 1946). In *Stage Works of MacArthur,* 1974.
A Flag Is Born, music by Kurt Weill (produced 1946).
Spellbound (screenplay), with Angus MacPhail, in *Best Film Plays 1945,* edited by John Gassner and Dudley Nichols. 1946.
Hazel Flagg, music by Jule Styne, lyrics by Bob Hilliard, from a story by James Street and the screenplay *Nothing Sacred* (produced 1953). 1953.
Winkelberg (produced 1958). 1958.

Screenplays: *Underworld,* with others, 1927; *The Big Noise,* with George Marion, Jr., and Tom J. Geraghty, 1928; *The Unholy Night,* with others, 1929; *Roadhouse Nights,* with Garrett Fort, 1930; *The Great Gabbo,* with Hugh Herbert, 1930; *The Front Page,* with Charles MacArthur, 1931; *Scarface, Shame of the Nation*, 1932; *Design for Living*, 1933; *Hallelujah, I'm a Bum*, 1933; *Topaze*, 1933; *Viva Villa!*, 1934; *Twentieth Century*, with Charles MacArthur, 1934; *Crime Without Passion*, with Charles MacArthur, 1934; *The Scoundrel*, with Charles MacArthur, 1935; *Barbary Coast*, with Charles MacArthur, 1935; *The Florentine Dagger*, 1935; *Once in a Blue Moon*, with Charles MacArthur, 1935; *Soak the Rich*, with Charles MacArthur, 1936; *Nothing Sacred*, 1937; *Goldwyn Follies*, with others, 1938; *Gunga Din*, with others, 1939; *Lady of the Tropics*, 1939; *Wuthering Heights*, with Charles MacArthur, 1939; *It's a Wonderful World*, with Herman J. Mankiewicz, 1939; *Let Freedom Ring*, 1939; *Until I Die*, with Charles MacArthur, 1940; *Angels over Broadway*, 1940; *Comrade X*, with Charles Lederer and Walter Reisch, 1940; *Lydia*, with others, 1941; *Tales of Manhattan*, with others, 1942; *The Black Swan*, with Seton I. Miller, 1942; *China Girl*, with Melville Crossman, 1942; *Spellbound*, with Angus MacPhail, 1945; *Specter of the Rose*, 1946; *Notorious*, 1946; *Her Husband's Affairs*, with Charles Lederer, 1947; *Kiss of Death*, with Charles Lederer and Eleazar Lipsky, 1947; *Ride the Pink Horse*, with Charles Lederer, 1947; *The Miracle of the Bells*, with Quentin Reynolds, 1948; *Whirlpool*, with Andrew Solt, 1950; *Where the Sidewalk Ends*, with others, 1950; *Actors and Sin*, 1952; *The Indian Fighter*, with Frank Davis and Ben Kadish, 1955; *Ulysses*, with others, 1955; *Miracle in the Rain*, 1956; *The Iron Petticoat*, 1956; *Legend of the Lost*, with Robert Presnell, Jr., 1957; *A Farewell to Arms*, 1957; *Queen of Outer Space*, with Charles Beaumont, 1958; *Mutiny on the Bounty* (uncredited), with others, 1962; *Circus World*, with others, 1964; *Casino Royale* (uncredited), with others, 1967.

Radio Play: *Miracle of the Pullman*, 1944.

Fiction

Erik Dorn. 1921.
Fantazius Mallare: A Mysterious Oath. 1922.
A Thousand and One Afternoons in Chicago (stories). 1922.
Gargoyles. 1922.
The Florentine Dagger. 1923.
Humpty Dumpty. 1924.
The Kingdom of Evil: A Continuation of the Journal of Fantazius Mallare. 1924.
Cutie, A Warm Mamma, with Maxwell Bodenheim. 1924.
Broken Necks, Containing More 1001 Afternoons (stories). 1926.
Count Bruga. 1926.
A Jew in Love. 1931.
The Champion from Far Away (stories). 1931.
Actor's Blood (stories). 1936.
A Book of Miracles (stories). 1939.
1001 Afternoons in New York. 1941.
Miracle in the Rain. 1943.
I Hate Actors! 1944; as *Hollywood Mystery!*, 1946.
The Collected Stories. 1945.
Concerning a Woman of Sin and Other Stories. 1947.
The Cat That Jumped Out of the Story (juvenile). 1947.
The Sensualists. 1959.
In the Midst of Death. 1964.

Other

A Guide for the Bedevilled. 1944.

A Child of the Century (autobiography).   1954.
Charlie: The Improbable Life and Times of Charles MacArthur.   1957.
A Treasury of Ben Hecht.   1959.
Perfidy.   1961.
Gaily, Gaily (autobiography).   1963.
Letters from Bohemia.   1964.

*   *   *

Ben Hecht began his writing career before the "audience renaissance," a term he used in a 1963 Theatre Arts article for the evolution of "play lovers" into "play decipherers," a process which undermined the status of the theatre as "our most ancient bridgehead of lucidity." Hecht's earliest literary values, influenced by his career in journalism, taught him that "whatever confusions possessed the other arts, the art of the theatre remained basically that of a Western Union telegram – terse and informative." These principles were to govern most of his dramatic output, and partially explain why such a disciplined, intelligent, and prolific writer has only intermittently attracted critical attention.

The journalist's attention to incident and detail, the "katatonic armor" that shields him in daily contact with the extremes and eccentricities of life, and the pragmatism of shaping these into a "story" are all prominent factors in his plays. Hecht's most famous collaboration with Charles MacArthur, The Front Page, has often been dismissed as a romantic melodrama about journalism; however, it also generates a poignant dilemma between individual values and public significance, articulated with a vigorous realism that was all but unique on Broadway in 1928. To Quito and Back, considered by many to be the best play that Hecht wrote alone, also introduces a journalist as a secondary character to sift out a situation in Ecuador similar to that of the Spanish Civil War. However, the diversity of content and style in Hecht's drama is almost as great as in his screenplays. His early one-act plays (written 1914–18) show experimentation with various types of stylisation then fashionable in "art theatres," a tendency which declines after the death of his first collaborator, the more experienced playwright Kenneth Sawyer Goodman, in 1918. Working with MacArthur, Hecht produced the Hollywood satire Twentieth Century, the musical extravaganza Jumbo, and the murder melodrama Swan Song; with Gene Fowler, he wrote the "dramatic cartoon" The Great Magoo; with Kurt Weill, he collaborated in the pageant of Jewish history A Flag Is Born, which gave a starring part to the young Marlon Brando and netted nearly one million dollars for the Zionist cause in 1946. Several of Hecht's later plays are also graveyard dramas: Lily of the Valley is a purgatorial allegory, and his last play, Winkelberg, is a work of expressionistic nostalgia. This stylistic eclecticism of Hecht's drama is reflected in the range of collaborators with whom he proved compatible, but his claim to a place in American dramatic history must rest on his tough, anecdotal realism.

Antedating Hecht's "audience renaissance" was the "Chicago literary renaissance" to which he was a central contributor, and which provided the context of Winkelberg. Criticism of the "clever saccharinity" of the Chicago school is substantiated by a reading of his earliest prose fiction, from Erik Dorn to Gargoyles. Hecht's foundation editorship of the Chicago Literary Times (which he also printed, published, managed, proofed, and helped distribute) was a watershed in his career, and it was a much less pretentious Hecht who emerged to write The Front Page; his original purpose in that play was to reflect his "intellectual disdain of and superiority to the Newspaper," but a much more honest, frontal attitude to his writing developed, resulting in his finest novel, A Jew in Love, as well as the best of his short stories.

Ironically, it was only late in his career that Hecht found a commitment that would have given cohesive solidity to his central output. Jews and journalists abound in his early novels and plays, but it is only in his later autobiographical writings that he deliberately anatomises his own identity as an American Jew. However, the growth of this commitment during World War II resulted in one of his finest books: *A Guide for the Bedevilled* confronts anti-Semitism with a sense of stylistic strategy and a passionate urbanity that recall the best prose writing of Bernard Shaw.

—Howard McNaughton

HELLER, Joseph. American. Born in Brooklyn, New York, 1 May 1923. Educated at New York University, B.A. 1948; Columbia University, New York, M.A. 1949; Oxford University (Fulbright Scholar), 1949–50. Served in the United States Army Air Force in World War II: Lieutenant. Married Shirley Held in 1945; one son and one daughter. Instructor in English, Pennsylvania State University, University Park, 1950–52; Advertising Writer, *Time* magazine, New York, 1952–56, and *Look* magazine, New York, 1956–58; Promotion Manager, *McCall's* magazine, New York, 1958–61; full-time writer from 1961. Recipient: National Institute of Arts and Letters grant, 1963. Member, National Institute of Arts and Letters, 1977.

PUBLICATIONS

Fiction

  Catch-22. 1961.
  Something Happened. 1974.

Plays

  We Bombed in New Haven (produced 1967). 1968.
  Catch-22, from his own novel. 1971.
  Clevinger's Trial, adaptation of chapter 8 of his novel *Catch-22* (produced 1974). 1973.

  Screenplays: *Sex and the Single Girl,* with David R. Schwartz, 1964; *Casino Royale* (uncredited), with others, 1967; *Dirty Dingus Magee,* with others, 1970.

Bibliography: *Three Contemporary Novelists: An Annotated Bibliography* by Robert M. Scotto, 1977.

Reading List: "Heller's *Catch-22*" by Burr Dodd, in *Approaches to the Novel* edited by John Colmer, 1967; "The Sanity of *Catch-22*" by Robert Protherough, in *The Human World*, May 1971; *Critical Essays on Catch-22* edited by James Nagel, 1974; "*Something Happened*: A New Direction" by George J. Searles, in *Critique 18*, 1977.

*   *   *

Joseph Heller's fame rests firmly on a single novel, *Catch-22*. His play, *We Bombed in New Haven*, which dramatizes similar material, is a failure, while his second novel, *Something Happened*, with its unattractive hero and deliberately pedestrian style, lacks the originality and linguistic vitality of its predecessor.

Catch-22 is not, as has often been supposed, just another anti-war novel in the Remarque, Frederick Manning, Norman Mailer tradition. Its theme is altogether more comprehensive. Heller invents a series of lunatic incidents to show that the comic formula "Catch-22" applies not only to the insanity of war but to love, business, and even religion. Thus early in the novel the hero, Yossarian, a flyer in World War Two, discovers that in war a man cannot plead madness to escape from further missions because, as Doc Daneeka says, "anyone who wants to get out of combat missions isn't really crazy." Later he finds that the same catch prevents him from marrying the girl he loves. "You won't marry me because I'm crazy, and you say I'm crazy because I want to marry you? Is that right?" The same circular formula extends beyond love and war to big business and even religion. Through the unscrupulous Milo Minderbinder, it touches the roots of capitalist enterprise, revealing that behind the compulsive acquisitiveness of capitalism lies a completely amoral destructive force, blind in its operation and totally unconcerned with human consequences. At the highest level the formula "Catch-22" seems to apply to God's laws as well as to man's; or, rather, men project their own irrationality on God. Heller's comprehensive indictment of society achieves its amazing breadth through his suggestion that a single unifying mental structure underlies the human predicament. We are caught. Although we may enjoy an illusion of freedom, as soon as we reach out to grasp it we become more firmly enslaved.

In order to enforce this dilemma Heller carefully manipulates patterns of logic and language to lay bare two opposite structures of behaviour and belief. On the one hand there is the system of irrational conformity represented by the generals. On the other hand there is the system of rational revolt typified by the rebels Yossarian and Orr. Each group regards the other an insane and often a single word may express the contrasting mental structures. An equally ingenious manipulation of time schemes serves to create a sense of an absurd universe and to embody comprehensive criticism of society. Yossarian's visits to hospital establish some framework of clock-time, but the main narrative sequence is not chronological but psychological. All events are described as if they were equally present in the hero's mind. The fact that it is impossible to reconcile the time schemes that apply to Yossarian's and Minderbinder's experiences and the fact that their paths cross at significant moments reinforce the contrast between Yossarian's unsuccessful rebellion against authority and Minderbinder's unprincipled triumph. When the narrative comes spiralling round to the last account of Snowden's death alongside Yossarian, Minderbinder's message in place of the stolen morphine tablets, "What is good for M & M Enterprises is good for the country" (a parody of an American President's phrase about General Motors), brings home the inhuman consequences of blind, selfish commercialism. This harrowing memory provides the ultimate justification for Yossarian's decision to desert to neutral Sweden.

Catch-22 is a bawdy, gimmicky novel that owes much of its popular success to its attacks on authority, its deliberate shock tactics, its inspired moments of farce, its gallery of comic characters, and its fashionable invitation to opt out of the system. Yet it stands up to rigorous analysis surprisingly well. Indeed it only yields up its full meaning when the intricacies of the time schemes and the inversions of language and logic have been fully grasped. It offers a model proof that the secret of truth-telling lies in form-making just as *Something Happened* proves that the choice of a dull hero and a dull style may produce a dull book

—John Colmer

HELLMAN, Lillian (Florence). American. Born in New Orleans, Louisiana, 20 June
1907. Educated at New York University, 1923–25; Columbia University, New York, 1926.
Married the writer Arthur Kober in 1925 (divorced, 1932). Reader, Horace Liveright,
publishers, New York, 1924–25; Reviewer, New York *Herald Tribune*, 1925–28; Theatrical
Play Reader, 1927–30; Reader, MGM, 1930–32. Taught at Yale University, New Haven,
Connecticut, 1966; and at Harvard University, Cambridge, Massachusetts; Massachusetts
Institute of Technology, Cambridge; and the University of California, Berkeley. Recipient:
New York Drama Critics Circle Award, 1941, 1960; Brandeis University Creative Arts
Award, 1960; National Institute of Arts and Letters Gold Medal, 1964; Paul Robeson
Award, 1976. M.A.: Tufts College, Medford, Massachusetts, 1940; LL.D.: Wheaton College,
Norton, Massachusetts, 1961; Rutgers University, New Brunswick, New Jersey, 1963;
Brandeis University, Waltham, Massachusetts, 1965; Yale University, 1974; Smith College,
Northampton, Massachusetts, 1974; New York University, 1974; Franklin and Marshall
College, Lancaster, Pennsylvania, 1975; Columbia University, 1976. Member, National
Institute of Arts and Letters; American Academy of Arts and Sciences. Lives in New York
City.

PUBLICATIONS

Plays

The Children's Hour (produced 1934). 1934.
Days to Come (produced 1936). 1936.
The Little Foxes (produced 1939). 1939.
Watch on the Rhine (produced 1941). 1941.
The North Star: A Motion Picture about Some Russian People. 1943.
The Searching Wind (produced 1944). 1944.
Watch on the Rhine (screenplay), with Dashiell Hammett, in *Best Film Plays of 1943–44*,
    edited by John Gassner and Dudley Nichols. 1945.
Another Part of the Forest (produced 1946). 1947.
Montserrat, from a play by Emmanuel Roblès (produced 1949) 1950.
Regina, music by Marc Blitzstein (produced 1949).
The Autumn Garden (produced 1951). 1951.
The Lark, from a play by Jean Anouilh (produced 1955). 1955.
Candide, music by Leonard Bernstein, lyrics by Richard Wilbur, John LaTouche and
    Dorothy Parker, from the novel by Voltaire (produced 1956). 1957.
Toys in the Attic (produced 1960). 1960.
My Mother, My Father and Me, from the novel *How Much?* by Burt Blechman (produced
    1963). 1963.
The Collected Plays. 1972.

Screenplays: *The Dark Angel*, with Mordaunt Shairp, 1935; *These Three*, 1936; *Dead
End*, 1937; *The Little Foxes*, with others, 1941; *Watch on the Rhine*, with Dashiell
Hammett, 1943; *The North Star*, 1943; *The Searching Wind*, 1946; *The Children's
Hour*, with John Michael Hayes, 1961; *The Chase*, 1966.

Other

An Unfinished Woman: A Memoir. 1969.
"Pentimento": A Book of Portraits. 1973.

Scoundrel Time. 1976.

Editor, *Selected Letters*, by Chekhov, translated by Sidonie Lederer. 1955.
Editor, *The Big Knockover: Selected Stories and Short Novels*, by Dashiell
Hammett. 1966; as *The Dashiell Hammett Story Omnibus*, 1966.

Reading List: *Hellman, Playwright* by Richard Moody, 1971; *The Dramatic Works of
Hellman* by Lorena R. Holmin, 1973; *Hellman* by Doris V. Falk, 1978.

*   *   *

Lillian Hellman is one of America's major dramatists. She entered a male-dominated field
when she was nearly thirty and wrote some dozen plays in three decades. Her early model
was Ibsen, and she shared his love of tightly knit plots and emphasis on sociological and
psychological forces. Her best plays, like Ibsen's, are those in which a powerful character cuts
loose and transcends the limitations of the play's rigid symmetry and plot contrivance. Along
with Clifford Odets, the other significant writing talent of the 1930's, Hellman showed a keen
interest in Marxist theory and explored the relationship between the nuclear family and
capitalism. Hellman, more than Odets, held ambiguous views of man and society. Her
antagonists are not wholly the products of environment but seem at times innately malicious.
The quest for power fascinated the author and her characters became famous for their
ruthlessness and cunning. Most of her plays verge on melodrama but are admired for their
energetic protagonists and swift-moving plots.

In her first play, *The Children's Hour*, Hellman showed how the capricious wielding of
power could ruin innocent people. Two young women at a girl's school are falsely accused of
having a lesbian relationship by a disturbed child. They are brought to trial by outraged
parents and eventually lose their case – and their school. One of the teachers commits suicide
and, too late, the child's treachery is discovered. The homosexual motif, though discreetly
handled, accounted for the play's notoriety in 1934; but the abuse of power by an arrogant
elite is its enduring theme.

Usurping power is also the motivating force in Hellman's best-known play, *The Little
Foxes*, at once a political statement and a complex study of family dynamics. The rapacious
Hubbard family represents a new brand of Southern capitalist who subordinates all traditions
and human values to the goal of acquiring wealth and property. The strength of the play lies
in Hellman's implicit comparison of the Hubbard siblings' rivalries with the competitiveness
of Americans in the free enterprise system. The role of Regina Hubbard, who withholds her
dying husband's heart medicine and who outwits her equally greedy brothers in a major
business coup, has become a favorite vehicle for American actresses.

At the beginning of World War II Hellman wrote *Watch on the Rhine* and *The Searching
Wind* which both dealt with the fascist menace. The former play contains some witty repartee
and suspenseful moments; but its solutions to the international crisis are simplistic, and it is
better described as an adventure story than a thesis play.

When the war ended, Hellman returned to the easy-to-hate Hubbard family in *Another
Part of the Forest*. Unfortunately the exaggerated spitefulness and hysteria of the characters
and the unrelieved high-tension atmosphere of this play become nearly ludicrous. The
concept of personal manipulation had become an obsession with the author, and a correlation
seemed to have developed between her studies of social and societal exploitation and her own
excessive control over plot characterization and stage effects. Perhaps the playwright realized
this, because in her last plays she turned from Ibsen to Chekhov for inspiration. Both *The
Autumn Garden* and *Toys in the Attic* recall the mood and ambiguous moral judgments of the
great Russian dramatist. Neither of these plays has a truly pernicious villain, and most of the
characters seem to be suffering from a Chekhovian paralysis of will. The atmosphere is
deterministic and the plots are truer to life. What has changed is that all bids for personal

power prove self-defeating – the predatory are caught in traps of their own making and hardly struggle before acknowledging defeat. Nevertheless these plays also include sharp, amusing verbal exchanges and the famous blackmail scenes associated with Hellman. Blackmail, present in all of her plays, is Hellman's favorite metaphor for personal manipulation; but in the later works she uses blackmail and other devices with greater subtlety, and presents a somewhat blurred but more convincing vision of stumbling modern man and his society.

Hellman's dramatic mode, based on her adherence to continental models, is bound to an earlier era. Most of her experiments with film-writing proved frustrating. Her best recent works have been autobiographical sketches. In *An Unfinished Woman*, *Penitmento*, and *Scoundrel Time* she reveals her penetrating intelligence but tacitly acknowledges that her insights and talents are presently better suited to the historical memoir.

—Kimball King

HEMINGWAY, Ernest. American. Born in Oak Park, Illinois, 21 July 1899. Educated at Oak Park High School, graduated 1917. Served as a Red Cross Ambulance driver in Italy, 1918; also served on the western front with the Italian Arditi: wounded in action: Medaglia d'Argento al Valore Militare; Croce di Guerra; involved in anti-submarine patrol duty off the coast of Cuba, 1942–44. Married 1) Hadley Richardson in 1921 (divorced, 1927), one son: 2) Pauline Pfeiffer in 1927 (divorced, 1940), two sons; 3) the writer Martha Gellhorn in 1940 (divorced, 1946); 4) Mary Welsh in 1946. Reporter, *Kansas City Star*, 1917; Reporter, then Foreign Correspondent, Toronto *Star* and *Star Weekly*, 1920–24; covered the Greco-Turkish War, 1922; settled in Paris, 1921, and became associated with the expatriate community, including Gertrude Stein and Ezra Pound; Correspondent in Paris for the Hearst newspapers, 1924–27; full-time writer from 1927; settled in Key West, Florida, 1928, later moved to Cuba, then to Idaho; War Correspondent for the North American Newspaper Alliance, in Spain, 1937–38; War Correspondent for *Collier's* in Europe, 1944–45. Recipient: Pulitzer Prize, 1953; Nobel Prize for Literature, 1954; American Academy of Arts and Letters Award of Merit, 1954. *Died* (by suicide) *2 July 1961*.

PUBLICATIONS

Collections

A Hemingway Selection, edited by Denniś Pepper. 1972.

Fiction

Three Stories and Ten Poems. 1923.
In Our Time: Stories. 1924; revised edition, 1925.

The Torrents of Spring: A Romantic Novel in Honor of the Passing of a Great Race. 1926.
The Sun Also Rises. 1926; as *Fiesta,* 1927.
Men Without Women (stories). 1927.
A Farewell to Arms. 1929.
God Rest You Merry Gentlemen (stories). 1933.
Winner Take Nothing (stories). 1933.
To Have and Have Not. 1937.
The Fifth Column and the First Forty-Nine Stories (includes play). 1938.
For Whom the Bell Tolls. 1940.
The Portable Hemingway, edited by Malcolm Cowley. 1944.
The Essential Hemingway. 1947.
Across the River and into the Trees. 1950.
The Old Man and the Sea. 1952.
Hemingway in Michigan (stories), edited by Constance Cappel Montgomery. 1966.
The Fifth Column and Four Stories of the Spanish Civil War. 1969.
Islands in the Stream. 1970.
The Nick Adams Stories, edited by Philip Young. 1972.
A Divine Gesture: A Fable. 1974.

Plays

Today Is Friday. 1926.
The Spanish Earth (screenplay). 1938.
The Fifth Column (produced 1940). In *The Fifth Column ...,* 1938.

Screenplay: *The Spanish Earth* (documentary). 1937.

Verse

Collected Poems. 1960.

Other

Death in the Afternoon. 1932.
Green Hills of Africa. 1935.
The Hemingway Reader, edited by Charles Poore. 1953.
The Wild Years (newspaper articles), edited by Gene Z. Hanrahan. 1962.
A Moveable Feast (autobiography). 1964.
By-Line: Selected Articles and Dispatches of Four Decades, edited by William White. 1967.
Cub Reporter: "Kansas City Star" Stories, edited by Matthew J. Bruccoli. 1970.

Editor, *Men at War: The Best War Stories of All Time.* 1942.

Bibliography: *Hemingway: A Comprehensive Bibliography* by Audre Hanneman, 1967, and supplement, 1975; *Hemingway: A Reference Guide* by Linda Wagner, 1977.

Reading List: *Hemingway: The Writer as Artist* by Carlos Baker, 1952, revised edition, 1972; *Hemingway* by Philip Young, 1952, revised edition, as *Hemingway: A Reconsideration,* 1966;

Hemingway and His Critics: An International Anthology edited by Carlos Baker, 1961; *Hemingway: A Collection of Critical Essays* edited by Robert P. Weeks, 1962; *Hemingway* by Earl Rovit, 1963; *Hemingway: An Introduction and Interpretation* by Sheridan Baker, 1967; *Hemingway and the Pursuit of Heroism* by Leo Gurko, 1968; *Hemingway: The Inward Terrain* by Richard B. Hovey, 1968; *Hemingway's Heroes* by Delbert E. Wylder, 1969; *Hemingway and His World* by Anthony Burgess, 1978.

* * *

When Ernest Hemingway was awarded the Nobel Prize for Literature the Swedish Academy commented on the central themes of his work. Courage and compassion in a world of violence and death were seen as the distinguishing marks of "one of the great writers of our time ... who, honestly and undauntedly, reproduces the genuine features of the hard countenance of the age." These comments sum up perceptively the characteristic preoccupations of Hemingway's fiction and of the heroic code of behaviour which it explores. But they do less than justice to another aspect of his writing. Hemingway was also a deliberate and careful artist, for whom every book was, in his own words, "a new beginning" in which the writer "should always try for something that has never been done."

Hemingway started his working life as a newspaper reporter, an excellent training in writing graphic declaratory prose. Covering crime stories was one introduction to a violent world, service with a Red Cross ambulance unit in Italy another. Severely wounded just before his nineteenth birthday, he received further emotional wounds when rejected by an American nurse with whom he fell in love. These experiences epitomise themes he was to explore in his short stories and novels, in prose which he deliberately stripped bare of adjectival colouring and rhetorical flourishes.

His first books, *Three Stories and Ten Poems* and *In Our Time*, were slim volumes which attracted coterie attention. The second of them consisted of twelve stark vignettes – scenes of war, bull-fighting, murder – which in a later edition were interleaved between lengthier short stories in which the Hemingway hero, and the heroic code of grace under pressure, first appear. Seven of the stories are episodes in the experience of a young man whose sensitivity has been violated in various ways, physically, emotionally, and spiritually. One day, he knows, his traumata will be healed; but this will take time, courage, and an effort of will. In the meantime he holds on stoically.

The Torrents of Spring, an uncharacteristic burlesque, is unimportant except as an indication of Hemingway's considerable skill as a comic satirist: it foreshadows the very funny ironical humour in, for instance, passages of *Death in the Afternoon* and *A Moveable Feast. In Our Time*, however, is the matrix from which the rest of his fiction is cast, both the later volumes of short stories and the succession of brilliantly finished, though occasionally flawed, novels.

The Sun Also Rises established Hemingway beyond question as a significant new novelist. Narrated in the first person, it deals with the predicament of the hero, emasculated by an unlucky war wound, in his frustrated love for an Englishwoman whom time and misfortune have driven into alcoholism, nymphomania, and self-destructive irresponsibility. Charting the mores of Paris cafe society playboys and would-be artists, Hemingway for some readers obscured the moral seriousness of his novel through the brilliance of his writing, especially in the scenes at the fiesta in Pamplona. But the message is there. The hero has learnt to accept his plight with honesty and courage; and even the heroine, though morally ruined, is honest with herself and in her own fashion also honourable. The hero's own moral strength allows him to treat her with compassion.

In his next novel Hemingway settled for third person narration. A romantic tragedy of love and war, *A Farewell to Arms* shows considerable technical development. Formally constructed in five acts, it is closely knit by complex sub-structures beneath the surface of the story. Symbols of weather and topography unobstrusively counterpoint the action, while contrasts of profane and sacred love are made both overtly and covertly in the evolving relationship between the hero and the novel's innocent tragic heroine. In this novel, too, Hemingway tried to communicate directly his own experience of being wounded by trench-mortar fire, in a cardinal passage which supports his occasionally expressed view that writing is a kind of self-therapy.

Hemingway's views on fiction, which incidentally show how closely he had studied the English, French, and Russian novelists, are for the most part woven into his classic study of bull-fighting, *Death in the Afternoon*. In brief, his aim was to write simply and directly about directly received experience. The more precisely a writer can express the essential impact of experience, the more precisely he will impress that experience on his readers. His task is to set down "the sequence of motion and fact which made the emotion," which "with luck and if you stated it purely enough" should remain valid always. By concentrating on describing his characters in action a writer should be able to communicate unwritten emotional reverberations, whereas to write as an omniscient commentator is to spoil his fiction by adding what is structurally unnecessary and undesirable. In a famous comparison, Hemingway likens the artist's work to the tip of an iceberg, whose dignity of movement is due to only one-eighth of it being above water. It is an austere approach to the writer's craft, but one whose discipline gives Hemingway's work unmistakable authority and strength.

While many writers in the early 1930's were as much concerned with political as with literary preoccupations, Hemingway fed his experience and his literary production by big-game hunting, fishing, and shooting. This is the period of some of his best short stories, including "The Snows of Kilimanjaro," technically superb in its accumulated moves from reality to illusory vision. His novel *To Have and Have Not* is less satisfying. An attempt to portray characters under economic stress in the depression, it was cobbled together from two earlier short stories and was written hastily between visits to Spain during the Civil War. This also is the period of *The Fifth Column*, an undistinguished venture into the theatre.

The Spanish Civil War, however, provided Hemingway with the theme of another outstanding novel, *For Whom the Bell Tolls*, in which again he extended his techniques. The story is built around twin themes, the dynamiting of a bridge by a guerilla group and the love affair of an American partisan and a girl in the group. The action is restricted to some seventy hours, the location to a single valley, the personae to a handful; but by dipping into the stream of the hero's thoughts about his former life and by having various characters recount their memories, Hemingway works beyond these confines to create an ample but tightly organised novel of epic dimensions. There is an optimistic shift, too, in the heroic code, in that the Hero is now in command of himself and meets death alone but fearless. Contemporary judgments of this novel were often politically coloured, ranging from allegations that Hemingway had "largely sloughed off his Stalinism" to accusations of Fascist sympathies: today these reflect clearly Hemingway's sypathetic treatment of the complexity of political and human predicaments. Of the novel's literary quality there has never been any doubt.

His next two novels, *Across the River and into the Trees* and *The Old Man and the Sea*, take the heroic code further. The latter's message that a man can be destroyed but not defeated carries a suggestion of Christian salvation. Though *Across the River and into the Trees* contains some of Hemingway's intensest writing (e.g., the description of the duck-shoot with which the novel opens), it is flawed by occasional obtrusions of the author's own personality and by his as yet incomplete mastery of new modes of symbolism operating at multiple levels. These are under perfect control in *The Old Man and the Sea*, a work of flawless craftsmanship that can be read literally, or as an allegory of human life, or of the Crucifixion, or of the artist's struggle to dominate his material.

The posthumous publication of the long, uneven *Islands in the Stream*, unrevised by his skilled hand, neither adds to nor detracts from the reputation of a dedicated and sensitive artist, one of the greatest and most influential prose writers of the twentieth century.

—Stewart F. Sanderson

HENRY, O. Pseudonym for William Sydney, or Sidney, Porter. American. Born in Greensboro, North Carolina, 11 September 1862. Educated in a private school in Greensboro to age 15; apprentice pharmacist in Greensboro, 1877–81: licensed by the North Carolina Pharmaceutical Association, 1881. Married 1) Athol Estes in 1887 (died, 1897), one son and one daughter; 2) Sara Lindsay Coleman in 1907. Moved to Texas, 1882, and worked on a ranch in LaSalle County, 1882–84; bookkeeper in Austin, 1884–86; contributed to the *Detroit Free Press*, 1887; Draftsman, Texas Land Office, Austin, 1887–91; Teller, First National Bank, Austin, 1891–94; Founder/Editor, *The Iconoclast*, later the *Rolling Stone* magazine, Houston, 1894–95; Columnist ("Tales of the Town," later "Some Postscripts"), *Houston Post*, 1895–96; accused of embezzling funds from his previous employers, First National Bank, Austin, 1896; fled to Honduras; returned to Austin because of wife's illness, 1897: jailed for embezzling in the Federal Penitentiary, Columbus, Ohio, 1898–1901: while in prison began publishing stories as O. Henry; moved to New York, 1902; thereafter a full-time writer; regular contributor to the New York *Sunday World*, 1903–05. O. Henry Memorial Award established by the Society of Arts and Sciences, 1918. *Died 5 June 1910.*

PUBLICATIONS

Collections

    The Complete Works. 1937.
    Stories, edited by Harry Hansen. 1965.

Fiction (stories)

    Cabbages and Kings. 1904.
    The Four Million. 1906.
    The Trimmed Lamp. 1907.
    Heart of the West. 1907.
    The Voice of the City. 1908.
    The Gentle Grafter. 1908.
    Roads of Destiny. 1909.
    Options. 1909.
    Strictly Business: More Stories of the Four Million. 1910.
    Whirligigs. 1910.
    Let Me Feel Your Pulse. 1910.
    Sixes and Sevens. 1911.
    Rolling Stones. 1912.
    Waifs and Strays. 1917.

Other

    Letters to Lithopolos from O. Henry to Mabel Wagnalls. 1922.
    Postscripts (from *Houston Post*), edited by Florence Stratton. 1923.
    O. Henry Encore: Stories and Illustrations (from *Houston Post*), edited by Mary Sunlock Harrell. 1939.

Bibliography: *A Bibliography of O. Henry* by Paul S. Clarkson, 1938.

Reading List: *Henry Biography* by C. Alphonso Smith, 1916; *The Caliph of Bagdad* by Robert H. Davis and Arthur B. Maurice, 1931; *Henry: The Man and His Work*, 1949, and *Henry, American Regionalist*, 1969, both by Eugene Hudson Long; *The Heart of Henry* by Dale Kramer, 1954; *Alias O. Henry: A Biography* by Gerald Langford, 1957; *Henry from Polecat Creek* by Ethel Stephen Arnett, 1962; *Henry* by Eugene Current-Garcia, 1965; *Henry: The Legendary Life* by Richard O'Connor, 1970.

*   *   *

William Sydney Porter's first story to appear in a national magazine was published in September 1898 while he was in prison, and it was in prison that he began writing in earnest. Following his release, Porter moved to New York where he wrote prodigiously; during 1904 and 1905 he is said to have produced a story a week for the New York *World*. Fame and notoriety, which he shunned, came to him quickly, as did money, which he spent lavishly and usually unwisely. *Cabbages and Kings*, his first collection of stories, established him as an author to be taken seriously. By 1908, with the publication of *The Voice of the City*, he was hailed as having "breathed new life into the short story; the stigma of the genre is wearing off, and for its rehabilitation ... [Porter] is responsible"; and in 1914, in a symposium conducted by the New York *Times*, "A Municipal Report" was voted "the greatest American short story ever written."

By 1920, ten years after his death, five million volumes of Porter's stories had been sold, but the current of critical opinion had turned against them and their author: not uncharacteristic is H. L. Mencken's pronouncement that "in the whole canon of O. Henry's work you will not find a single recognizable human character." A just estimate of Porter's fiction lies somewhere between such extremes. O. Henry brought verve, excitement, and humor to the genre. Enormously interested in people, he is capable of swift and compassionate insights into the average person, and his sympathy for the under-dog, the little man or woman dwarfed in the maze of comtemporary life, to a degree accounted for his enormous popularity. He was a good reporter with a keen eye for the significant detail, and he had a feeling for setting unmatched by most of his contemporaries. His brisk openings and the engrossing narrative pace of even his least successful stories are perhaps the major reasons for his instant appeal. Perhaps most important of all, he influenced an entire generation of writers and helped provide an enthusiastic audience for their work.

Porter's faults are as conspicuous as his assets – contrivance, sentimentality, repetition, and melodrama; his trick endings, particularly, seemed patently dated in the context of the new realism of the Twenties. He wrote rapidly – "once I begin a yarn I must finish it without stopping or it kinda goes dead on me" – and revised seldom. Haunted by memories of the past, increasingly engulfed in alcohol, Porter had no illusions about his literary shortcomings. "I'm a failure," he wrote to a friend. "My stories? No, they don't satisfy me. It depresses me to have people point me out as 'a celebrated author.' It seems such a big label for such picayune goods."

Porter's work, as one of his contemporaries commented, never did justice to his talents. Perhaps the soundest estimate of his contribution has been made by one of the most important English fiction writers of the twentieth century, H. E. Bates. However one belittles O. Henry, Bates comments in *The Modern Short Story*, "he still emerges, by his huge achievement and the immense popularity of his particular method, as an astonishingly persistent influence on the short story of almost every decade since his day."

—William Peden

HERGESHEIMER, Joseph. American. Born in Philadelphia, Pennsylvania, 15 February 1880. Educated at a Quaker school in Germantown, Philadelphia; studied painting at the Pennsylvania Academy of Fine Arts, Philadelphia. Married Dorothy Hemphill in 1907. Settled in Virginia, and began to write, 1900; subsequently moved to West Chester, Pennsylvania, and later to Stone Harbor, New Jersey. *Died 25 April 1954.*

PUBLICATIONS

Fiction

> *The Lay Anthony.* 1914.
> *Mountain Blood.* 1915.
> *The Three Black Pennys.* 1917.
> *Gold and Iron.* 1918.
> *The Happy End* (stories). 1919.
> *Linda Condon.* 1919.
> *Java Head.* 1919.
> *Cytherea.* 1922.
> *The Bright Shawl.* 1922.
> *Balisand.* 1924.
> *Tol'able David* (stories). 1923.
> *Merry Dale.* 1924.
> *Tampico.* 1926.
> *Quiet Cities* (stories). 1928.
> *Triall by Armes* (stories). 1929.
> *The Party Dress.* 1930.
> *The Limestone Tree.* 1931.
> *Love in the United States, and The Big Shot.* 1932.
> *Tropical Winter* (stories). 1933.
> *The Foolscap Rose.* 1934.

Play

> Screenplay: *Flower of Night*, with Willis Goldbeck, 1925.

Other

> *Hugh Walpole: An Appreciation.* 1919.
> *San Cristóbal de la Habana.* 1920.
> *The Presbyterian Child* (autobiography). 1923.
> *From an Old House* (autobiography). 1925.
> *Swords and Roses.* 1929.
> *Sheridan: A Military Narrative.* 1931.
> *Berlin.* 1932.

Bibliography: "Hergesheimer: A Selected Bibliography 1913–45" by James J. Napier, in *Bulletin of Bibliography 24*, 1963–64.

Reading List: *Hergesheimer: The Man and His Books* by Llewellyn Jones, 1920; *Hergesheimer* by James Branch Cabell, 1921; *The Fiction of Hergesheimer* by Ronald E. Martin, 1965; *Ingenue among the Lions: Letters of Emily Clark to Hergesheimer*, 1965.

*   *   *

James Branch Cabell called Joseph Hergesheimer "the most insistently superficial of writers" and meant it as a compliment; half a century later the remark speaks unintentionally for his detractors. Writing from "aspiration hopelessly in advance of accomplishment," as Hergesheimer described his endeavors, he was reputed one of America's foremost novelists; today he is almost forgotten, and many readers would think deservedly so. After several quasi-historical novels, Hergesheimer turned to his immediate milieu – the American 1920's – and made the subject glossily his own. Later, his attempts at *belles lettres* – travel books and descriptions of old houses in fancy prose – blurred into his fiction, and flesh and blood disappeared into the architecture.

Of his early books, *Java Head* is an excellent adventure story of clipper ships and miscegenation in eighteenth-century Salem, with a Manchu princess as catalyst. *The Three Black Pennys* is an underrated novel about a Pennsylvania coal mining family, tracing an emotional decline from the eldest, sober and hard-working, to the youngest, a dilettante; finely written, even moving, it is undeserving of its present neglect.

The later novels "flash and glitter like so many fricaseed rainbows," according to George Jean Nathan. *Linda Condon* and *Cytherea* trace the hedonism of the twenties – prohibition, permanent waves, "extraordinary qualities of superlative jewels and superfine textures" – with ironic detachment. In *The Party Dress*, however, written at the end of the decade, Hergesheimer detailed the mystique of golf – not only the shots in a game but the look of the greens and the quality of the clubs – in deadly earnest, and he lavished as much attention on his characters' houses, clothing, table manners, including the silver and crystal, as he did on their love affairs. Later historical novels, *Balisand* and *The Limestone Tree*, for example, had not even the glamour of the twenties to enliven them.

Alfred Kazin spotted the quintessential Hergesheimer passage in *Cytherea*: "'I want to be outraged!' Her low ringing cry seemed suppressed, deadened as though the damasked and florid gilt and rosewood, now inexpressibly shocked, had combined to muffle the expression, the agony, of her body." Kazin called Hergesheimer's passion "vulgar"; Wilson Follett called it an "aristocratic distinction" although "a distinctly un-American trait."

Readers in an audio-visual age may grow impatient with Hergesheimer's tales of beautiful women and wise men stifled by sybaritic description; but many of the novels accurately reflect their own time, however meretricious that time was. Hergesheimer still has much to say, by the fact of his reputation during the twenties, to a later period preoccupied with pop culture.

—Bruce Kellner

HEYWARD, DuBose. American. Born in Charleston, South Carolina, 31 August 1885. Educated in local schools until age 14. Married the playwright Dorothy Hartzell Kuhns in 1923; one daughter. Worked from 1899 in a hardware store, as a clerk with a Charleston steamboat line, and as a checker in a cotton shed; later formed an insurance business with a friend; Founder, with Hervey Allen, The Poetry Society of South Carolina, 1920, and subsequently lectured and read his works for the Society throughout the South; gave up the insurance business to become a full-time writer, 1924. Recipient: Pulitzer Prize, for drama, 1927. Litt.D.: University of North Carolina, Chapel Hill, 1928; College of Charleston, 1929. Honorary Member, Phi Beta Kappa; Member, National Institue of Arts and Letters. Lived in Charleston all his life. *Died 16 June 1940.*

PUBLICATIONS

Fiction

Porgy. 1925.
Angel. 1926.
The Half Pint Flask (story).   1929.
Mamba's Daughters. 1929.
Peter Ashley. 1932.
Lost Morning. 1936.
Star Spangled Virgin. 1939.

Plays

Porgy, with Dorothy Heyward, from the novel by DuBose Heyward (produced 1927).   1928.
Brass Ankle (produced 1931).   1931.
Porgy and Bess, with Ira Gershwin, music by George Gershwin (produced 1935).   1935.
Mamba's Daughters, with Dorothy Heyward, from the novel by DuBose Heyward (produced 1939).   1939.

Verse

Carolina Chansons: Legends of the Low Country, with Hervey Allen.   1922.
Skylines and Horizons.   1924.
Jasbo Brown and Selected Poems.   1931.

Other

Fort Sumter, with Herbert Ravenal Sass.   1938.
The Country Bunny and the Little Gold Shoes (juvenile).   1939.

Editor, with others, *Year Book of the Poetry Society of South Carolina, 1921–24.*   4 vols., 1921–24.

Reading List: *Heyward, The Man Who Wrote Porgy* by Frank Durham, 1965.

*   *   *

Novelist, storywriter, playwright, and poet, DuBose Heyward was a sensitive romantic artist whose earnest but realistic humanitarianism, sympathetic understanding of the Negro, and lyrical evocations of the landscape, folklore, and legends of his region made him a fore-runner of the Southern literary movement which the Poetry Society of South Carolina, under his leadership, helped to initiate among writers' groups and little magazines in the 1920's. His poetry, dealing mainly with the grim battle for survival on the mountains, nostalgic descriptions of low country life, and the mystery and vitality of the Negro personality, brought him early recognition and served as a crucible for experimenting with the settings, themes, incidents, and tones he was to exploit later in his fiction and drama. It is not hard to see how crucially his novel *Angel* and short-story "Brute" — to think of two instances — depend on poems such as "A Mountain Woman" and "A Yoke of Steers" for their vivid scenic particulars, characterization, and treatment of the innate strength and resilience of the human spirit engaged in a fierce and near-impossible struggle with a hostile environment.

Porgy, Heyward's most popular and accomplished novel, makes full use of his poetic and narrative gifts. Heyward subtly intertwines the developing stages of his narrative with the cycle of seasons to provide symbolic elevation to his story of a beggar-murderer whose futile search for stability and peace eventually leads to the recognition that the inexorable pressure of a contrary, even malevolent, fate can be withstood, if not substantially minimised, by an attitude of acceptance. In *Mamba's Daughters*, a more ambitious though less competently executed novel, a variant of the same theme is employed in recounting the trials of three generations of a Negro family in their upward climb toward social security and prosperity.

But, to Heyward, the Negro was more than a symbol of resistance against overwhelming odds: he was, in most events, conceived as an emissary from an enchanting world of exotic customs and beliefs, possessing an inimitable primitive aura and energy that are vulnerable to the forces of modernization. This view of the Negro is given eloquent expression in "The Half-Pint Flask," a haunting story about the erosion of rational and scientific attitudes in the face of time-honoured superstitions. Approaching the same issue in an altered context in *Star Spangled Virgin*, Heyward makes use of entertaining but biting satire to expose the inadequacy of all reformist measures that ignore the intractable rhythms and perceptions of Negro life. Such views are also symptomatic of his whole-hearted agreement with a primary assumption of Southern writing that art belongs more to the realm of the heart than of the head.

An uneven writer whose later performance, despite occasional enthusiastic responses, never really measured up to the expectations aroused by his early promise, Heyward wrote at his best when he employed dramatic contrivances such as violence and natural calamities to lend pace to the narrative. His treatment of ideas in art generally tended to be feeble and often regressed to the level of dull pontification. *Porgy* is the single work for which he is likely to be remembered, for it has become, in Frank Durham's words, "a part of native folklore, its characters and their romantic story having gradually so embedded themselves into the group consciousness that the name of their creator is almost forgotten. Not many authors have gained such enduring, if increasingly anonymous, immortality."

—Chirantan Kulshrestha

HOWARD, Sidney (Coe). American. Born in Oakland, California, 26 June 1891. Educated at the University of California, Berkeley, B.A. 1915; studied with George Pierce Baker at Harvard University, Cambridge, Massachusetts, 1915–16. Served in the American Ambulance Corps, and later in the United States Army Air Corps, in World War I: Captain. Married 1) the actress Clare Jenness Eames in 1922 (divorced, 1930), one daughter; 2) Leopoldine Blaine Damrosch in 1931, one daughter and one son. Member of the Editorial

Staff, 1919–22, and Literary Editor, 1922, *Life* magazine, New York; Special Investigator and Feature Writer, *New Republic* and *Hearst's International Magazine*, New York, 1923; full-time playwright from 1923; Founder, with Robert E. Sherwood, Elmer Rice, Maxwell Anderson, S. N. Behrman, and John F. Wharton, Playwrights Company, 1938. Member, Board of Directors, American Civil Liberties Union; President, American Dramatists Guild. Recipient: Pulitzer Prize, 1925. Litt.D.: Washington and Jefferson College, Washington, Pennsylvania, 1935. Member, American Academy of Arts and Letters. *Died 23 August 1939.*

PUBLICATIONS

Plays

Swords (produced 1921).   1921.
Casanova, from a play by Lorenzo de Azertis (produced 1923).   1924.
Lexington (produced 1925).   1924.
They Knew What They Wanted (produced 1924).   1925.
Bewitched, with Edward Sheldon (produced 1924).
Lucky Sam McCarver (produced 1925).   1926.
Ned McCobb's Daughter (produced 1926).   1926.
The Silver Cord (produced 1926).   1927.
Salvation, with Charles MacArthur (produced 1928).   In Stage Works of MacArthur, 1974.
Olympia, from a play by Molnar (produced 1928).   1928.
Half Gods (produced 1929).   1930.
Lute Song, with Will Irwin (as Pi-Pa-Ki, produced 1930); revised version, as Lute Song, music by Raymond Scott, lyrics by Bernard Hanighen (produced 1946).   1955.
The Late Christopher Bean, from a play by René Fauchois (produced 1932).   1933.
Alien Corn (produced 1933).   1933.
Ode to Liberty, from a play by Michel Duran (produced 1934).
Dodsworth, from the novel by Sinclair Lewis (produced 1934).   1934.
Yellow Jack, with Paul de Kruif, from a work by de Kruif (produced 1934).   1934.
Paths of Glory, from the novel by Humphrey Cobb (produced 1935).   1935.
The Ghost of Yankee Doodle (produced 1937).   1938.
Madam, Will You Walk? (produced 1953).   1955.

Screenplays: *Bulldog Drummond*, with Wallace Smith, 1929; *Condemned*, 1929; *A Lady to Love*, 1930; *Free Love*, 1930; *Raffles*, 1930; *Arrowsmith*, 1931; *One Heavenly Night*, 1931; *The Greeks Had a Word for It*, 1932; *Dodsworth*, 1936; *Gone with the Wind*, 1939; *Raffles*, with John Van Druten, 1939.

Fiction

Three Flights Up (stories).   1924.

Other

The Labor Spy: A Survey of Industrial Espionage.   1921; revised edition, 1924.
Professional Patriots, with John Hearley, edited by Norman Hapgood.   1927.

*   *   *

The first major writer of social drama after American drama approached the age of maturity following World War I, Howard mixed melodrama and comedy with the established mode of realism in literature to reflect a dominant social idea of the 1920's – *They Knew What They Wanted*. As the title of one of his best plays, it presented the positive individualism of his generation which other playwrights (Philip Barry, S. N. Behrman, Maxwell Anderson, Paul Green) soon emphasized. In contrast to some of his outstanding contemporaries, Howard was not an innovator in dramatic form nor a particularly profound writer. He readily admitted such shortcomings, if indeed, they were that. Instead, he was a substantial playwright of considerable theatrical skill and imagination who stepped into the ongoing stream of social drama in America and produced at least two major plays in that genre.

They Knew What They Wanted is a modern version of the Paolo-Francesca love story but with a modern twist that none of those who told the story from Dante to Wagner would have accepted. But Howard's intelligently expedient people, battling the exigencies of the modern world, know what they want, and his hero, Tony, can become, as Frank Loesser's musical adaptation made him, "The Most Happy Fella." In *The Silver Cord* Howard took advantage of ideas propounded by Strindberg and Freud. With a diabolic cunning worthy of Strindberg's Laura, Howard's protagonist fights for the control of her sons in an emotion-packed drama that remains one of America's best thesis plays. Emotion and spectacle are always major aspects of a Howard play. He wrote about people, frequently with a strong sense of irony, and all of his plays held at least one spectacular scene which he handled with a craftsmanship critics have admired. The best include *Lucky Sam McCarver*, *Ned McCobb's Daughter*, and *The Late Christopher Bean*; he also adapted Sinclair Lewis's *Dodsworth* to the stage.

During a life cut short by a farm accident in 1939 Howard wrote some twenty plays, most of them either adaptations or collaborations. But his reputation in American drama rests solidly upon the plays he wrote by himself, the best of which appeared during the 1920's. He seemed unable to relate successfully to the social atmosphere of the Depression years which followed.

—Walter J. Meserve

HUGHES, (James) Langston. American. Born in Joplin, Missouri, 1 February 1902. Educated at Central High School, Cleveland, 1916–20; Columbia University, New York, 1921–22; Lincoln University, Pennsylvania (Witter Bynner Award, 1926), B.A. 1929. During World War II, Member of the Music and Writers war boards. Seaman, 1923–25; busboy, Wardman Park Hotel, Washington, D.C., 1925; Madrid Correspondent, Baltimore *Afro-American*, 1937; Columnist, Chicago *Defender*, 1943–67, and New York *Post*, 1962–67. Founder of the Harlem Suitcase Theatre, New York, 1938, New Negro Theatre, Los Angeles, 1939, and Skyloft Players, Chicago, 1941. Visiting Professor in Creative Writing, Atlanta University, Gerogia, 1947; Poet-in-Residence, University of Chicago Laboratory School, 1949. Recipient: Harmon Gold Medal for Literature, 1931; Rosenwald Fellowship, 1931, 1940; Guggenheim Fellowship, 1935; National Institute of Arts and Letters grant, 1946; Anisfield-Wolfe Award, 1953; Spingarn Medal, 1960. D.Litt.: Lincoln University, 1943; Howard University, Washington, D.C., 1963; Western Reserve University, Cleveland, 1964. Member, National Institute of Arts and Letters, 1961, and American Academy of Arts and Sciences. *Died 22 May 1967.*

PUBLICATIONS

Verse

The Weary Blues. 1926.
Fine Clothes to the Jew. 1927.
Dear Lovely Death. 1931.
The Negro Mother and Other Dramatic Recitations. 1931.
The Dream-Keeper and Other Poems. 1932.
Scottsboro Limited: Four Poems and a Play in Verse. 1932.
A New Song. 1938.
Shakespeare in Harlem. 1942.
Jim Crow's Last Stand. 1943.
Lament for Dark Peoples and Other Poems, edited by H. Driessen. 1944.
Fields of Wonder. 1947.
One-Way Ticket. 1949.
Montage of a Dream Deferred. 1951.
Selected Poems. 1959.
Ask Your Mama: 12 Moods for Jazz. 1961.
The Panther and the Lash: Poems of Our Times. 1967.
Don't You Turn Back: Poems (juvenile), edited by Lee Bennett Hopkins. 1969.

Plays

The Gold Piece, in *The Brownies' Book*, July 1921.
Mulatto (produced 1935; original version produced 1939). In *Five Plays*, 1963.
Little Ham (produced 1935). In *Five Plays*, 1963.
Troubled Island (produced 1935; revised version, music by William Grant Still, produced 1949). 1949.
When the Jack Hollers, with Arna Bontemps (produced 1936).
Joy to My Soul (produced 1937).
Soul Gone Home (produced 1937?). In *Five Plays*, 1963.
Don't You Want to Be Free?, music by Carroll Tate (produced 1937). In *One Act Play Magazine*, October 1938.
Front Porch (produced 1938).
The Sun Do Move (produced 1942).
Freedom's Plow (broadcast, 1943). 1943.
Pvt. Jim Crow (radio script), in *Negro Story*, May-June 1945.
Booker T. Washington at Atlanta (broadcast, 1945). In *Radio Drama in Action*, edited by Eric Barnouw, 1945.
Street Scene (lyrics only), book by Elmer Rice, music by Kurt Weill (produced 1947). 1947.
The Barrier, music by Jan Meyerowitz (produced 1950).
Just Around the Corner (lyrics only), book by Abby Mann and Bernard Drew, music by Joe Sherman (produced 1951).
Simply Heavenly, music by David Martin (produced 1957). 1959.
Esther, music by Jan Meyerowitz (produced 1957).
Shakespeare in Harlem, with James Weldon Johnson (produced 1959).
Port Town, music by Jan Meyerowitz (produced 1960).
The Ballad of the Brown King, music by Margaret Bonds (produced 1960).
Black Nativity (produced 1961).
Gospel Glow (produced 1962).

Tambourines to Glory, music by Jobe Huntley, from the novel by Hughes (produced 1963). In *Five Plays,* 1963.
Five Plays (includes *Mulatto, Soul Gone Home, Little Ham, Simply Heavenly, Tambourines to Glory*), edited by Webster Smalley. 1963.
Jericho-Jim Crow (produced 1963).
The Prodigal Son (produced 1965).

Screenplay: *Way Down South,* with Clarence Muse, 1939.

Radio scripts: *Jubilee,* with Arna Bontemps, 1941; *Brothers,* 1942; *Freedom's Plow,* 1943; *John Henry Hammers It Out,* with Peter Lyons, 1943; *In the Service of My Country,* 1944; *The Man Who Went to War,* 1944 (UK); *Booker T. Washington at Atlanta,* 1945; *Swing Time at the Savoy,* with Noble Sissle, 1949.

Television scripts: *The Big Sea,* 1965; *It's a Mighty World,* 1965; *Strollin' Twenties,* 1966.

Fiction

Not Without Laughter. 1930.
The Ways of White Folks (stories). 1934.
Simple Speaks His Mind. 1950.
Laughing to Keep from Crying (stories). 1952.
Simple Takes a Wife. 1953.
Simple Stakes a Claim. 1957.
Tambourines to Glory. 1958.
The Best of Simple. 1961.
Something in Common and Other Stories. 1963.
Simple's Uncle Sam. 1965.

Other

Popo and Fifina: Children of Haiti (juvenile), with Arna Bontemps. 1932.
The Big Sea: An Autobiography. 1940.
The First Book of Negroes (juvenile). 1952.
The First Book of Rhythms (juvenile). 1954.
Famous American Negroes (juvenile). 1954.
The Sweet Flypaper of Life, with Roy De Carava (on Harlem). 1955.
Famous Negro Music-Makers (juvenile). 1955.
The First Book of Jazz (juvenile). 1955; revised edition, 1962.
A Pictorial History of the Negro in America, with Milton Meltzer. 1956; revised edition, 1963.
I Wonder As I Wander: An Autobiographical Journey. 1956.
The First Book of the West Indies (juvenile). 1956; as *The First Book of the Caribbean,* 1965.
The Langston Hughes Reader. 1958.
Famous Negro Heroes of America (juvenile). 1958.
The First Book of Africa (juvenile). 1960; revised edition, 1964.
Fight for Freedom: The Story of the NAACP. 1962.
Black Magic: A Pictorial History of the Negro in American Entertainment, with Milton Meltzer. 1967.
Black Misery. 1969.

Good Morning, Revolution: Uncollected Social Protest Writings, edited by Faith Berry. 1973.

Editor, *Four Lincoln University Poets.* 1930.
Editor, with Arna Bontemps, *The Poetry of the Negro 1746–1949: An Anthology.* 1949; revised edition, 1970.
Editor, with Waring Guney and Bruce M. Wright, *Lincoln University Poets.* 1954.
Editor, with Arna Bontemps, *The Book of Negro Folklore.* 1958.
Editor, *An African Treasury: Articles, Essays, Stories, Poems by Black Africans.* 1960.
Editor, *Poems from Black Africa.* 1963.
Editor, *New Negro Poets: USA.* 1964.
Editor, *The Book of Negro Humor.* 1966.
Editor, *La Poésie Negro-Américaine* (bilingual edition). 1966.
Editor, *Anthologie Africaine et Malgache.* 1966.
Editor, *The Best Short Stories by Negro Writers: An Anthology from 1899 to the Present.* 1967.

Translator, with Mercer Cook, *Masters of the Dew*, by Jacques Roumain. 1947.
Translator, with Ben Frederic Carruthers, *Cuba Libre*, by Nicolás Guillén. 1948.
Translator, *Gypsy Ballads*, by Federico García Lorca. 1951.
Translator, *Selected Poems of Gabriela Mistral.* 1957.

Bibliography: *A Bio-Bibliography of Hughes, 1920–1967* by Donald C. Dickinson, 1967, revised edition, 1972.

Reading List: *Hughes* by James A. Emanuel, 1967; *Hughes: A Biography* by Milton Meltzer, 1968; *Hughes, Black Genius: A Critical Evaluation* edited by Therman B. O'Daniel, 1971 (includes bibliography); *Hughes: An Introduction to the Poetry* by Onwuchekwa Jemie, 1977; *Hughes: The Poet and His Critics* by Richard K. Barksdale, 1977.

*   *   *

As impressive as Langston Hughes is for his versatility and productivity, his claim to enduring literary importance rests chiefly on his poetry and his Simple sketches. In his poetry his sure lyric touch, his poignant insight into the urban black folk soul rendered with remarkable fidelity to a variety of black idioms, his negative capability of subordinating his own personality so as to convey a vivid impression of scene or incident or mood or character, and his willingness to experiment are his richest endowments, though one also often finds in his verse the comic sense (often ironic or bittersweet), the broad democratic faith, and the total understanding of character which so irradiate the Simple tales.

Although Hughes wrote some verse without specific racial reference, the three major categories of his poetry comprise poems related to black music, poems of racial protest, and poems of racial affirmation. These categories naturally overlap, but it is convenient to discuss them separately. For the entire course of his literary career, Hughes was fascinated by black music: blues, jazz in its several varieties, and gospel. The classic blues stanzaic form, consisting of a statement of a problem or situation in the first line repeated in the second (often with a slight variation) followed by a third line resolving, interpreting, or commenting on the first two, appears frequently in Hughes, as in the following from "Red Sun Blues":

> Gray skies, gray skies, won't you let the sun shine through?
> Gray skies, gray skies, won't you let that sun shine through?
> My baby's left me, I don't know what to do.

Elsewhere, as in the title poem of *The Weary Blues*, Hughes uses the blues and bluesmen as subject in a poem which may incorporate blues stanzas but has its own larger structure. His poems deriving from jazz are more complicated in their experimentation. Taken together, they provide a kind of poetic graph of developments in jazz from the Harlem cabaret life of the exuberant 1920's, through the boogie-woogie of the 1930's and the bebop of the 1940's, to the progressive jazz of the 1950's. From such early examples as "Jazzonia" and "The Cat and the Saxophone" to the ambitious later works *Montage of a Dream Deferred* and *Ask Your Mama*, Hughes used the varieties of jazz as both subject and style, designing the last-named work for musical accompaniment and often reading his poetry on tour to a jazz background. Though less prominently than blues and jazz, spirituals and gospel music figure also in Hughes's poetry (for example, the "Feet of Jesus" section in *Selected Poems*), as well as in his numerous song-plays.

As a poet of racial protest Hughes was less strident than some other well-known black writers, but not necessarily less trenchant or effective. Such poems as "I, Too" and "Let America Be America Again" express a wistful longing for racial equality. Others, such as "Brass Spittoons" and "Ballad of the Landlord" develop miniature dramas of the hardships and injustices of black life in a racist society. Some of the later poems included in the "Words on Fire" section of *The Panther and the Lash* sound notes of rising militancy. Surely among Hughes's best poems in this category are "American Heartbreak," whose laconic understatement achieves a sense of bitter finality, and "Song for a Dark Girl," a starkly tragic and strangely beautiful lyric about a girl's response to the lynching of her lover. Whether wistful, dramatic, angry, or tragic in mood, Hughes was always alive throughout his career to the oppression of his people.

He was equally sensitive to the dignity with which they endured or resisted that oppression. "Mother to Son" and "The Negro Mother" are among his many poems celebrating the black quest for freedom and social justice. Hughes was one of the first writers to use "soul" in a special racial sense, as in his very early poem "The Negro Speaks of Rivers." Color itself delights the poet in the carefully crafted "Dream Variation" and the delicious "Harlem Sweeties." And his comic vision to be developed in such loving detail in the Simple sketches is prefigured in "Sylvester's Dying Bed" and the Madam Alberta K. Johnson poems. Lowlife and working class blacks, shunned by bourgeois spokesmen of the Harlem Renaissance, often receive special tribute in Hughes's poems of racial affirmation.

Hughes's interest in fiction developed later than his instinct for poetry. The novels *Not Without Laughter* and *Tambourines to Glory* are highly readable if somewhat weak in structure. The best of his sixty-six published short stories are proficient in technique and perceptive in their treatment of a variety of human situations. The most striking achievement in fiction is the creation of Jesse B. Semple. As Richard K. Barksdale has noted, Simple "had just the right blend of qualities to be Black America's new spokesman – just enough urban humor, cynicism, and sardonic levity and just enough down-home simplicity, mother-wit, innocence, and naiveté" (*Black Writers of America*, edited by Richard Barksdale and Keneth Kinnamon). The marvelous talk elicited from this fully realized black working man by the middle-class, intellectual narrator of the sketches constitutes one of the most valuable treasures of American literary humor.

In drama Hughes is perhaps more important for the extent of his activity and the stimulus he gave to black theater than for the intrinsic artistic merit of his own plays. As translator, anthologist, historian, and biographer he played a major role in popularizing Afro-American, Afro-Caribbean, and African subjects. As devoted friend and sponsor of generations of aspiring writers he was at the center of black literary activity for more than four decades. Together with his own accomplishments as poet and humorist, these efforts constitute a total contribution to literature matched by that of few writers in this century.

—Keneth Kinnamon

HUNEKER, James (Gibbons). American. Born in Philadelphia, Pennsylvania, 31 January 1860. Educated at Roth's Military Academy, Philadelphia, subsequently studied law; studied piano in Paris with Georges Mathias, and in New York City with Rafael Joseffy. Teacher of piano at the National Conservatory, New York, 1886–98; Art Critic for the New York *Sun*, 1900–12; Music Critic for the New York *Times*, 1912–19, and the *Sun*, 1919–21. *Died 9 February 1921.*

PUBLICATIONS

Collections

  Letters and *Intimate Letters*, edited by Josephine Huneker.   2 vols., 1922–24.
  Essays, edited by H. L. Mencken.   1929.

Fiction

  Melomaniacs (stories).   1902.
  Visionaries (stories).   1905.
  Painted Veils.   1921.

Other

  Mezzotints in Modern Music.   1899.
  Chopin: The Man and His Music.   1900.
  Overtones: A Book of Temperaments.   1904.
  Iconoclasts: A Book of Dramatists.   1905.
  Egoists: A Book of Supermen.   1909.
  Promenades of an Impressionist.   1910.
  Franz Liszt.   1911.
  The Pathos of Distance: A Book of a Thousand and One Moments.   1913.
  Old Fogy: His Musical Opinions and Grotesques.   1913.
  New Cosmopolis: A Book of Images.   1915.
  Ivory, Apes, and Peacocks.   1915.
  Unicorns.   1917.
  *The Philharmonic Society of New York and Its Seventy-Fifth Anniversary: A
    Retrospect.*   1917(?).
  The Steinway Collection of Paintings by American Artists.   1919.
  Bedouins; Mary Garden (essays and stories).   1920.
  Steeplejack (autobiography).   2 vols., 1920.
  Variations.   1921.

  Music editions: *Forty Piano Compositions* by Chopin, 1902; *Forty Songs* by Brahms, 1903; *The Greater Chopin*, 1908; *Forty Songs* by Strauss, 1910; *Forty Songs* by Tchaikovsky, 1912; *Romantic Preludes and Studies for Piano,* 1919.

Bibliography: in *Bibliography of American Literature* by Jacob Blanck, 1963.

Reading List: *Huneker* by Benjamin DeCasseres, 1925; *Huneker, Critic of the Seven Arts* by Arnold T. Schwab, 1963.

* * *

James Huneker is probably America's most versatile critic. Beginning in the late 1880's as a music critic, he acquired an international reputation in the next fifteen years, especially for his writings on Chopin, Liszt, and Richard Strauss. The musical associations of Baudelaire, Gautier, Huysmans, George Moore, and others led him to their non-musical books and thus into literary criticism, of which his best book was *Egoists*. His deep interest in the new psychology quickly attuned him to the work of Ibsen, Strindberg, Shaw, Maeterlinck, Hauptmann, and Sudermann, and his *Iconoclasts* was the most brilliant study of these playwrights to appear in America.

Best known for popularizing contemporary or near-contemporary Continental writers, Huneker also singled out the best American novelists of his day – James, Howells, Wharton, Norris, Dreiser – and called attention to Whitman, Poe, Dickinson, and Robinson at a time when these poets were either vilified or ignored by many other critics. But his talent in detecting the most enduring of early twentieth-century American artists was most notably reflected, perhaps, in his praise of painters such as Bellows, Davies, Henri, Luks, Marin, Maurer, Prendergast, Shinn, and Sloan.

As a critic, Huneker was probably most comfortable, technically, in music (he had studied and taught piano) and least secure, despite his perspicacity, in art. Fond of anecdotes, puns, and parodies, he produced essays admired for their wit, humor, urbanity, and range. His tendency to dart from topic to topic, idea to idea, name to name, paying little attention to connecting links and logical development, sometimes made him seem superficial or irritating to those who valued clear, sustained reasoning above the picturesque phrase and the evocative association. But the staccato manner and the incessant allusions sprang from a mind richly loaded with gleanings from life and literature and quick with intuitive perception and sympathy. Not hesitating to pass judgment, in an undogmatic way, on artists of his own day, he was usually right: few of his swans turned out to be geese.

In his short stories – collected in *Melomaniacs, Visionaries*, and *Bedouins* – and in his one novel, *Painted Veils*, Huneker displayed the wide reading, powerful curiosity about the artist as a human being, the fascination with sexual or sensory abnormality, and the colorful, epigrammatic style reflected in his criticism. If the stories smack a bit too much of the grotesqueries of Hoffman and Poe, they achieve some originality in Huneker's attempt to penetrate and portray the emotional life of the musician. In coming to grips with sexual themes, he was clearly ahead of his time in his fiction as well as his criticism. His plots reveal his flair for the humorously bizarre, and touches of comic description accompany his lively imagination. If his skill in execution – especially in characterization and dialogue – had matched his inventive facility, Huneker might have become the outstanding writer of fiction he always wanted to be.

—Arnold T. Schwab

HURSTON, Zora Neale. American. Born in Eatonville, Florida, 7 January 1903. Educated at a primary school in Eatonville; Morgan Academy of Morgan College, Baltimore, graduated 1921; Howard University, Washington, D.C., 1924–26; Barnard College, New York, 1926–28, B.A. 1928. Researcher in American folklore (Rosenwald Foundation grant),

1928–32; writer from 1932; researcher in Haiti and the British West Indies (Guggenheim Fellowship), 1936–38; subsequently Professor of Drama, North Carolina College for Negroes. Recipient: Anisfield Wolf Award, 1943; Howard University Alumni Award, 1943. Litt.D.: Morgan State College, Baltimore, 1939. *Died 28 January 1960.*

PUBLICATIONS

Fiction

> *Jonah's Gourd Vine.* 1934.
> *Their Eyes Were Watching God.* 1937.
> *Moses, Man of the Mountain.* 1939.
> *Seraph on the Suwanee.* 1948.

Play

> *The First One,* in *Ebony and Topaz: A Collectanea,* edited by Charles S. Johnson. 1927.

Other

> *Mules and Men.* 1935.
> *Tell My Horse.* 1938; as *Voodoo Gods: An Inquiry into Native Myths and Magic in Jamaica and Haiti.* 1939.
> *Dust Tracks on a Road: An Autobiography.* 1942.

> Editor, *Caribbean Melodies.* 1947.

Reading List: *In A Minor Chord* (on Hurston, Cullen and Toomer) by Darwin T. Turner, 1971; *Hurston: A Literary Biography* by Robert E. Hemenway, 1977.

*   *   *

The leading fact about Zora Neale Hurston is her identification with black folklore. She spent her childhood in the black town of Eatonville, Florida. As a student in anthropology, she recorded the oral literature of the black South and Caribbean, and her best writing employs the intangible artifacts of traditional culture. Yet the preoccupation with folk life had ambivalence. As Robert E. Hemenway has shown, she experienced conflict between her role as a scientific observer of culture and the need to express her feelings as an intuitive participant. She never denied the value of science, but eventually art alone claimed her talents.

Art, however, had its own ambivalence. For, while the substance of Hurston's work derived from spontaneous folk life, she was, of course, a deliberate literary writer. *Mules and Men* represents an early effort to resolve the consequent aesthetic problem. In it Hurston adapts folklore to the requirements of written literature by creating a persona and framing folktales in the context of a return home. This structure provides readers with a sense of entry into the community. One feels a privileged listener, but it must be remembered that one actually hears Hurston's selectively condensed version of the tales. Several years later, in

Moses, Man of the Mountain, Hurston's confidence in her ability to reshape folk matter permitted her to assume the role openly. Taking as her premise the traditional parallel between the children of Israel and enslaved Africans she synthesizes legends and images to establish Moses as a humanized Afro-American.

Still more literary ways of using folk life appear in *Jonah's Gourd Vine* and *Their Eyes Were Watching God*. The first book presents as its central figure a preacher endowed with magnificent command of poetic language who thereby typifies the creativity of folk culture. At the same time he is morally flawed by a sexual drive that continually brings him low. Possibly through this flaw Hurston meant to create a tragic figure, but there can be no doubt that with the preacher's wife she touched the theme of her most distinguished book. *Their Eyes Were Watching God*, a novel about Janie Crawford's disappointing marriages and exhilirating love affair with the ebullient Tea Cake fully merges author and folk subject. The theme of a woman struggling to realize herself was inevitable for a female artist as independent as Hurston. That Janie becomes free within the culture of the black South, however, represents both a social and an aesthetic resolution. The social resolution appears as preference for black cultural values despite shortcomings, the aesthetic resolution as the assimilation of folk to the consciousness of a modern artist.

—John M. Reilly

INGE, William (Motter). American. Born in Independence, Kansas, 3 May 1913. Educated at the University of Kansas, Lawrence, A.B. 1935; Peabody Teachers College, Nashville, Tennessee, M.A. 1936; Yale University, New Haven, Connecticut, Summer 1940. Taught at Columbus High School, Kansas, 1937–38, and Stephens College, Columbia, Missouri, 1938–43; Art Critic, St. Louis *Star-Times*, 1943–46; taught at Washington University, St. Louis, 1946–49, University of North Carolina, Chapel Hill, 1969, and the University of California at Irvine, 1970. Recipient: George Jean Nathan Award, 1951; Pulitzer Prize, 1953; New York Drama Critics Circle Award, 1953; Donaldson Award, 1953; Academy Award, 1962. *Died 10 June 1973.*

PUBLICATIONS

Plays

> *The Dark at the Top of the Stairs* (as *Farther Off from Heaven*, produced 1947; revised version, as *The Dark at the Top of the Stairs*, produced 1957). 1958.
> *Come Back, Little Sheba* (produced 1950). 1950.
> *Picnic: A Summer Romance* (produced 1953). 1953; revised version, as *Summer Brave* (produced 1962), in *Summer Brave and Eleven Short Plays*, 1962.
> *Bus Stop* (produced 1955). 1955.
> *Glory in the Flower* (produced 1959). In *24 Favorite One-Act Plays*, edited by Bennett Cerf and Van H. Cartmell, 1958.
> *The Tiny Closet* (produced 1959). In *Summer Brave and Eleven Short Plays*, 1962.
> *A Loss of Roses* (produced 1959). 1960.

Splendor in the Grass: A Screenplay. 1961.
Natural Affection (produced 1962). 1963.
Summer Brave and Eleven Short Plays (includes *To Bobolink, For Her Spirit; A Social Event; The Boy in the Basement; The Tiny Closet; Memory of Summer; The Rainy Afternoon; The Mall; An Incident at the Standish Arms; People in the Wind; Bus Riley's Back in Town; The Strains of Triumph).* 1962.
Where's Daddy? (as *Family Things Etc.*, produced 1965; as *Where's Daddy?*, produced 1966). 1966.
The Disposal (as *Don't Go Gentle*, produced 1967–68?; as *The Last Pad*, produced 1972). In *Best Short Plays of the World Theatre 1958–1967*, edited by Stanley Richards, 1968; revised version, as *The Disposal*, music by Anthony Caldarella, lyrics by Judith Gero (produced 1973).
Two Short Plays: The Call, and A Murder. 1968.
Midwestern Manic, in *Best Short Plays 1969*, edited by Stanley Richards. 1969.
Caesarian Operation (produced 1972).
Overnight (produced 1974).
Love Death Plays: Dialogue for Two Men, Midwestern Music, The Love Death, Venus and Adonis, The Wake, The Star (produced 1975).

Screenplays: *Splendor in the Grass*, 1961; *All Fall Down*, 1962.

Television Play: *On the Outskirts of Town*, 1964–65?

Fiction

Good Luck, Miss Wyckoff. 1971.
My Son Is a Splendid Driver. 1972.

Reading List: *Inge* by Robert B. Shuman, 1965.

*   *   *

William Inge remains an interesting phenomenon in American drama. His impact upon critic and public alike demands that he be included in any serious consideration of the post-war theatre, but in subject matter and in style he was so counter to the patterns of his contemporaries as to seem from quite another generation. Leaving behind a minimal impression upon the development of recent American drama, his name rapidly fading, he was nonetheless a major figure for almost a decade and wrote some of the most appealing dramatic pieces of the fifteen post-war years.

William Inge's place in American drama is limited to four plays: *Come Back, Little Sheba, Picnic, Bus Stop,* and *The Dark at the Top of the Stairs.* His first, *Farther Off from Heaven,* produced by Margo Jones in Dallas, got to New York only in a much-revised version. *A Loss of Roses* failed completely, as did *Natural Affection* and *Family Things, Etc.* His screenplays brought no added fame, and his prose fiction is limited in appeal.

While Tennessee Williams, Arthur Miller, and Eugene O'Neill dwelt upon the tragic nature of their often inauspicious characters, Inge chose to emphasize his characters' fundamentally pathetic and frequently comic nature. The tragic fates are nowhere in evidence. Inge's appeal lies in a compassionate understanding of and a great sensitivity toward his petty little people, as he conveys successfully to his audiences the universally amusing and simultaneously agonizing quality of ordinary human nature under very ordinary circumstances. Furthermore, at a time when his major contemporaries favored impressionistic stagings, stylized settings, politico-historical themes, and regional emphases,

Inge remained consistently a writer of straightforward, single-set plays of Ibsenesque realism. His characters, straight from the unprepossessing streets and towns of the vast mid-section of contemporary America, moved within settings, both geographical and theatrical, remarkable for their unobtrusive, innocuous nature. Inge is one of the most regional of dramatists, but he is emphatically not a "regionalist"; that is, his chosen locale is so lacking in specific regional association and importance, and hence influence upon his characters, as to be virtually neutral. The importance of the surroundings into which Inge places his characters lies precisely in their lack of any importance at all.

Nor does Inge permit the many individual problems of his characters to become the central "problem" of the plays as a whole. His first success, *Come Back, Little Sheba*, is a fine case in point. For instance, we learn a great deal about A.A. and alcoholism, but it is not a play *about* alcoholism. Sexual restraints, taboos, and frustrations, past and present, cause serious personal problems for Doc and Lola, but the play is in no way *about* sex. The air of pessimistic hopelessness surrounding the Delaneys may be the strongest theme, but the play refuses to dwell upon the subject and, in fact, displays a considerable awareness of the positive aspect of human resilience *and* ultimate hope. *Come Back, Little Sheba* is, then, a play which sends out strong shock waves from all of these problems, permitting none of them to dominate the action. The audience finds itself attracted to these wholly undistinguished people in this undistinguished small town by bonds of mutual sympathy and understanding, together with an appreciation of Inge's outstanding ability to demonstrate what human love, patience, and endurance really mean to virtually all of us. Much has been lost by Doc and Lola in the course of the action, but much has been gained in return. Everybody, at the final curtain, is back at the beginning, more or less, and that, in the end, is far more the way of the world than otherwise. Inge's characters, here and elsewhere, will move no mountains in their lifetimes, but they are, as one critic has said, the salt of the earth, their importance lying almost entirely in the fact of their being human.

Picnic, as one opening night critic observed, is still "basic Inge." The sensation of the season, the play won a Pulitzer Prize and remains probably Inge's most famous play. Adding a few characters and moving them from kitchen to back yard, Inge proved that his formula for the dramatic impact of *Sheba* had been no fluke. "Affectionate, understanding, interesting, engagingly funny, emotionally touching, with fascinating characters" were the critical terms that greeted the play's portrayal of what happens on a Labor Day weekend in a Kansas back yard among a group of almost embarrassingly stock stage figures from clucking-hen mother to sexually frustrated old-maid schoolteacher. Highly emotional things happen in *Picnic*, as they do in *Sheba*, caused mainly by the intrusion of the handsome semi-clad drifter who causes a general loosening of assorted libidos, culminating in fornication, drunkenness, and elopement. But none of these things in themselves, any more than in *Sheba*, is the point. What matters is Inge's highly skilled and absolutely convincing portrayal of the driving human forces of underlying desires, frustrations, fears, and joys of these routinely bland people in an equally bland environment.

In *Bus Stop* Inge falls back on a device that worked for Shakespeare on Prospero's island, for Melville aboard the *Pequod*, and for James Jones in his pre-Pearl Harbor army. Into Grace's microcosmic lunchroom, driven by the unalterable force of a prairie blizzard, the playwright sends a group of individuals as stereotyped and undistinguished as anything he or many another artist has attempted. What emerges, for all that, is a wholly delightful human comedy with an underlying drama of deep human pathos. The pursuit and capture of the pitifully floozy "chantoosie" by the frantically infatuated, rambunctious but innocent cowboy is superbly comic, beautifully controlled. Simultaneously, the parallel affair of the decadent professor and the naive waitress, while ever on the edge of the pit of gratuitous sensation, carries the more serious theme with touching effectiveness. Before he is through with us, Inge has made us care a great deal about Bo, Cherie, Lyman, Elma, and Virgil. Normally we, as well as the rest of the world, would take little note of them, but Inge has shown us that they are highly important people to themselves and in many ways to each other. Cherie, hopelessly tarnished, artistically a fiasco, has stood her ground with dignity while vigorously defending her womanly honor against the onrushing Bo. He, in turn, literally forced to bow before her, has learned, to his wondering astonishment, that women are not calves to be bulldogged, hogtied, and subdued. Elma has come dangerously close to the total destruction of her innocence, but that very innocence has given the aging sensualist pause enough to permit both of them, for the time, to escape. By the time Inge returns all on stage to equilibrium and sends his bus on its journey, we have encountered a touching human experience of lasting impressiveness.

In his final and least noteworthy "success," *The Dark at the Top of the Stairs*, Inge unfortunately surrenders to artificialities of plot, less than subtle symbolism, gratuitous violence, and remarkably unconvincing characters. There is much of the "basic Inge" to be seen and, upon occasion, praised, but the strong human appeal of the first three plays is lost amid generally unsatisfactory handling of marital problems, racial prejudices, and parent–child relationships. We may still understand some of the reasons for Rubin Flood's infidelity and Sonny's mamma's boy behavior, as well as little Sammy's suicide, but, on the whole, there is too much of the trite and unimaginative to be as convincing as we would like.

The ultimate appeal of William Inge seems to lie in his ability to transform the lives and behavior of drab people in drab surroundings into a significant drama of human experience. Taking us inside and outside the houses most of us pass every day down the block and around the corner, he reveals some rather profound human truths, and he grips us in fascination as he does so.

—Jordan Y. Miller

JACKSON, Shirley. American. Born in San Francisco, California, 14 December 1919. Educated at Syracuse University, New York, B.A. 1940. Married the writer Stanley Edgar Hyman in 1940; two daughters and two sons. Recipient: Edgar Allan Poe Award, 1961. *Died 8 August 1965.*

PUBLICATIONS

Collections

The Magic of Jackson, edited by Stanley Edgar Hyman.   1966.

Fiction

The Road Through the Wall.   1948; as *The Other Side of the Street,* 1956.
The Lottery; or, The Adventures of James Harris (stories).   1949.
Hangsaman.   1951.
The Bird's Nest.   1954; as *Lizzie,* 1957.
The Sundial.   1958.

The Haunting of Hill House. 1959.
We Have Always Lived in the Castle. 1962.

Plays

The Lottery, from her own story, in *Best Television Plays 1950–51,* edited by William I.
Kauffman. 1952.
The Bad Children: A Play in One Act for Bad Children. 1959.

Other

Life among the Savages. 1953.
The Witchcraft of Salem Village (juvenile). 1956.
Raising Demons. 1957.
Special Delivery: A Useful Book for Brand-New Mothers. 1960; as *And Baby Makes Three,* 1960.
9 Magic Wishes (juvenile). 1963.
Famous Sally (juvenile). 1966.
Come Along with Me: Part of a Novel, Sixteen Stories, and Three Lectures, edited by
Stanley Edgar Hyman. 1968.

Reading List: *Jackson* by Lenemaja Friedman, 1975.

*   *   *

Throughout her work Shirley Jackson focuses on incongruities in an everyday setting,
whether for comic or sinister effect. This is as true of her "disrespectful memoir" of her
children, *Life among the Savages,* and its equally hilarious sequel, *Raising Demons,* as of the
dark psychological explorations of her novels and short stories. In her later fiction she wrote
about extraordinary characters and situations, but these were always located in an everyday
setting, whose juxtaposition provided her staple ingredient of incongruity.

Much of Jackson's work is concerned with an attempt to gain, or regain, an identity. *The
Bird's Nest* concerns a mentally disturbed girl who has four different voices and identities. It
is triumphantly structured, but, like the earlier *Hangsaman,* the positive note on which it ends
fail to remove our doubts about the future of its main character. In *The Sundial* Jackson
focuses on an eccentric group of characters in the Halloran family house, where, directed by
a dead relative, they await the end of the world in the belief that they alone will be saved.
Allegorical relationships emerge between the characters, and the narrative, characteristically
both comic and macabre, develops baroque motifs of sundial and maze.

Like *The Sundial* and her famous spine-chiller *The Haunting of Hill House* (with its
"clashing disharmonies"), *We Have Always Lived in the Castle* centres on a house. Even
more than in *The Sundial* the reader is induced to identify with its inhabitants – eccentric or
criminal though they may be – against "them" in the world outside. Eighteen-year-old
"Merricat" describes her life with her sister Constance after the latter's aquittal from a charge
of poisoning the rest of the family – a charge of which the local people believe her to be
guilty. The destructive invasion of the world outside parallels the set-piece of the peaceable
invasion of the locals invited to the final barbeque in *The Sundial.* The portrayal of the sisters'
loving relationship, albeit in macabre circumstances, makes *We Have Always Lived in the
Castle* the most remarkable of Jackson's books.

A few of Jackson's short stories delight the incongruous for its own sake; however, most
of her stories, including the title story of *The Lottery* (which caused a sensation on its

publication in the *New Yorker* in 1948), are informed by a genuine sense of evil. The stories generally centre on an isolated female, often the inadequate victim of a daemon lover (such as James Harris in *The Lottery*). These characters are lost in the concrete jungle of the Kafkaesque city or are on long-distance journeys "to the end of the night." This theme is habitually announced by laughter, lines from songs and poems, or nursery rhymes, transmuted to sinister leitmotivs.

To portray the fragmented personality Jackson resorted to a kind of zany verbal logic and semantic irony. Yet though there are passages in her work reminiscent of Borges, she kept any experimental tendency in her writing subordinated to the demands of story-telling, her prime considerations as the lectures in *Come Along with Me* make clear.

—Val Warner

JARRELL, Randall.   American.   Born in Nashville, Tennessee, 6 May 1914. Educated at Vanderbilt University, Nashville, B.S. in psychology 1936 (Phi Beta Kappa), M.A. in English 1939. Served as a celestial navigation tower operator in the United States Army Air Corps, 1942–46. Married Mary Eloise von Schrader in 1952. Instructor in English, Kenyon College, Gambier, Ohio, 1937–39, University of Texas, Austin, 1939–42, and Sarah Lawrence College, Bronxville, New York, 1946–47; Associate Professor, 1947–58, and Professor of English, 1958–65, Women's College of the University of North Carolina (later, University of North Carolina at Greensboro). Lecturer, Salzburg Seminar in American Civilization, 1948; Visiting Fellow in Creative Writing, Princeton University, New Jersey, 1951–52; Fellow, Indiana School of Letters, Bloomington, Summer 1952; Visiting Professor of English, University of Illinois, Urbana, 1953; Elliston Lecturer, University of Cincinnati, Ohio, 1958; Phi Beta Kappa Visiting Scholar, 1964–65. Acting Literary Editor, *The Nation*, New York, 1946–47; Poetry Critic, *Partisan Review*, New Brunswick, New Jersey, 1949–53, and *Yale Review*, New Haven, Connecticut, 1955–57; Member of the Editorial Board, *American Scholar*, Washington, D.C., 1957–65. Consultant in Poetry, Library of Congress, Washington, D.C., 1956–58. Recipient: Guggenheim Fellowship, 1946; National Institute of Arts and Letters grant, 1951; National Book Award, 1961; Oliver Max Gardner Award, University of North Carolina, 1962; American Association of University Women Juvenile Award, 1964; Ingram Merrill Award, 1965. D.H.L.: Bard College, Annandale-on-Hudson, New York, 1962. Member, National Institute of Arts and Letters; Chancellor, Academy of American Poets, 1956. *Died 14 October 1965.*

PUBLICATIONS

Collections

The Complete Poems.   1969.
The Achievement of Jarrell: A Comprehensive Selection of His Poems, edited by Frederick J. Hoffman.   1970.

Verse

> Five Young American Poets, with others.   1940.
> Blood for a Stranger.   1942.
> Little Friend, Little Friend.   1945.
> Losses.   1948.
> The Seven-League Crutches.   1951.
> Selected Poems.   1955.
> Uncollected Poems.   1958.
> The Woman at the Washington Zoo: Poems and Translations.   1960.
> Selected Poems.   1964.
> The Lost World: New Poems.   1965.
> Jerome: The Biography of a Poem.   1971.

Play

> The Three Sisters, from a play by Chekhov (produced 1964).   1969.

Fiction

> Pictures from an Institution: A Comedy.   1954.

Other

> Poetry and the Age (essays).   1953.
> A Sad Heart at the Supermarket: Essays and Fables.   1962.
> The Gingerbread Rabbit (juvenile).   1964.
> The Bat-Poet (juvenile).   1964.
> The Animal Family (juvenile).   1965.
> The Third Book of Criticism (essays).   1969.
> Fly by Night (juvenile).   1976.
> A Bat Is Born (juvenile).   1977.
> Kipling, Auden & Co.   1979.

> Editor, The Anchor Book of Stories.   1958.
> Editor, The Best Short Stories of Kipling.   1961; as In the Vernacular: The English in
>   India and The English in England, 2 vols., 1963.
> Editor, Six Russian Short Novels.   1963.

> Translator, with Moses Hadas, The Ghetto and the Jews of Rome, by Ferdinand
>   Gregorovius.   1948.
> Translator, The Rabbit Catcher and Other Fairy Tales of Ludwig Bechstein.   1962.
> Translator, The Golden Bird and Other Fairy Tales, by the Brothers Grimm.   1962.
> Translator, Snow White and the Seven Dwarfs: A Tale from the Brothers Grimm.   1972.
> Translator, The Juniper Tree and Other Tales, by the Brothers Grimm.   1973.
> Translator, Goethe's Faust: Part One.   1974; Part Two, 1978.

Bibliography: Jarrell: A Bibliography by Charles M. Adams, 1958, supplement in Analects 1, Spring 1961; "A Checklist of Criticism on Jarrell 1941–70" by D. J. Gilliken, in Bulletin of the New York Public Library, April 1971.

Reading List: *Jarrell 1914–1965* edited by Robert Lowell, Peter Taylor, and Robert Penn Warren, 1967; *The Poetry of Jarrell* by Suzanne Ferguson, 1971; *Jarrell* by M. L. Rosenthal, 1972.

*   *   *

Shortly after his death, the elegant, brilliant, and quixotic Randall Jarrell was eulogized by Karl Shapiro as the greatest poet-critic since T. S. Eliot. At a memorial service at Yale, such men as Robert Lowell, Robert Penn Warren, and Richard Eberhart came to honor their dead friend as a master among men of their craft. Robert Lowell called him "the most heartbreaking English poet of his generation." Celebrated as well was Jarrell's literary criticism, for in work like *Poetry and the Age*, he had altered dominant critical trends and tastes. He had brought Walt Whitman into prominence, and had imparted new light on Frost, Stevens, Williams, and Marianne Moore, among others; he had attacked the New Critics, and he had affirmed the relevance of art to life. Not unlike Ezra Pound, Jarrell was one of those truly committed critics who, although a poet himself, had helped the writers around him to define twentieth century art.

As Walter Rideout in his essay in *Poets in Progress* (edited by Edward Hungerford, 1962) has noted, when Jarrell published his *Selected Poems* in 1955, he grouped them in such a way as to obscure the rather marked delineations in central subject matter that had distinguished volume from volume. The style of his first book, however, *Blood for a Stranger*, is noticeably derivative, and shows the influence of Allen Tate, John Crowe Ransom, and particularly W. H. Auden in its experiments with villanelles, sestinas, and unusual rhyming patterns, as well as in its intellectual brilliance and metaphysical questionings. The volume cries out against a world politically heaving itself toward catastrophe. Jarrell's tone is one of existential loneliness and despair.

Little Friend, Little Friend and *Losses* are less formal; Jarrell establishes a more direct and characteristic tone; the poet seems, in fact, personally more attracted to death. Jarrell's ambiguous view of humanity, man as murderer and victim, innocent and guilty, ultimately like the child facing the "capricious infinite" parental power, found its perfect expression in these war poems. But Jarrell's war poems treat the human condition, their central image, man as soldier/prisoner. Jarrell dramatizes man's guilt and suffering upon a stage of world-wide struggle. *Losses* treats all sorts of prisoners – children, black Americans, DP's at Haifa, Jews in concentration camps – and focuses upon how each is a victim within "the necessities that governed every act." Even the enemy contains the child, who, called upon to commit a terrible violence, is himself an innocent. Utilizing the perspective of the child, Jarrell makes the outcome of war the product of innocence:

> The other murderers troop in yawning;
> Three of them play Pitch, one sleeps, and one
> Lies counting missions, lies there sweating
> Till even his heart beats: One; One; One.
> O *murderers*! ... Still, this is how it's done.

Reality is defined as nightmare, "experience" before and after life, the dream. In "The Death of the Ball Turret Gunner," he writes: "From my mother's sleep I fell into the State/... I woke to black flak and the nightmare fighters." Jarrell supports no conventional political position, no "program for chance." Instead, the man-child is "a ticket/Someone bought and lost on, a stray animal/... Bewildered .../What have you understood, to die?" His compassion extends even to the enemy; the powerful also suffer: "Who will teach the Makers how to die?" he writes.

Jarrell's great and fertile period concluded with *The Seven-League Crutches*. The early works focused upon lost childhood and innocence, the terrible shock of awareness of adult hypocrisy and social disintegration. Jarrell now moves away from more public concerns to private life; his poems are more relaxed. Although the theme of illness remains in the poems about children, his work is more psychological, more dream-filled. One senses now, in addition, "a way out," in the face of "Necessity": "Man you must learn to live/though you want nothing but to die." Stoical, compassionate, and even at times capable of a bittersweet humor, some of Jarrell's most mature work now appears. Man may perhaps even transcend Necessity through the imaginative life, the creation and perception of art.

After this Jarrell turned to fairy tale and became preoccupied with children's stories, with German Romanticism. The fairy tale offered him the innocent's victory over the potent and evil forces of the universe. In "The Märchen" (Grimm's Tales), he wrote, for example:

> We felled our islands there, at last, with iron.
> The sunlight fell to them, according to our wish,
> And we believed, till nightfall, in that wish;
> And we believed, till nightfall, in our lives.

The title poem of *The Woman at the Washington Zoo*, a return to Jarrell's more formal style of the 1940's, crystallizes the poet's concern with aging and loneliness. The woman cries out for relief, for transformation again, from her empty life: "the world goes by my cage and never sees me." She cries: "You know what I was,/You see what I am: change me, change me!"

In *The Lost World*, published after a nervous breakdown, many of his recurrent themes appear: loneliness, lovelessness, age, lost youth, the world's hypocrisy, and, as Robert Lowell put it, childhood, "above all childhood!" *The Lost World* fails to exhibit the brilliance, power, elegance, and diversity that characterize his earlier work. More importantly, there is about it too much of a confessional quality; the poems are awkward and read like revelations on the analyst's couch. The speaker appears filled with a sense of guilt and helplessness. He tries to forgive, especially, his parents, but he is unsuccessful. In "The Piano Player," for example, he confesses: "I go over, hold my hands out, play I play – /If only, somehow, I had learned to live!" His childhood football hero, Daddy Lipscomb, admits: "I've been scared/Most of my life. You wouldn't think so to look at me./It gets so bad I cry myself to sleep." Many of these poems contain a female persona, a woman sometimes unfaithful to her lover, often cruel to people and animals to the point of murder, but, most frequently, unmitigatingly unkind to her child. Although one senses Jarrell's attempt to understand and forgive these people, the poet remains in despair: "I identify myself, as always/With something that there's something wrong with."

One feels a debt toward Jarrell for his enormous encouragement and advice to the poets of his time. But one must regard him as well as an important poet with a brilliant intelligence, elegance, and humor. Jarrell's uniqueness remains in his special combination of sophistication with undiminished yearnings for childhood, that bittersweet faith that through art, or dreams, or fairy tales, one could regain childhood innocence and joy and negate the inevitable processes of aging, isolation, and death.

—Lois Gordon

JEFFERS, (John) Robinson. American. Born in Pittsburgh, Pennsylvania, 10 January 1887. Tutored by his father; attended schools in Switzerland and Germany; University of Western Pennsylvania, Pittsburgh, 1902; Occidental College, Los Angeles, California, 1903–05, graduated 1905; University of Zurich; University of Southern California, Los Angeles, M.A.; School of Medicine, University of Southern California; studied forestry at the

University of Washington, Seattle. Married Una Call Kuster in 1913. Turned to writing after inheriting a modest income, 1912; after 1924 lived in seclusion in a house he built on the California coast near Carmel. Recipient: Academy of American Poets Fellowship, 1958; Shelley Memorial Award, 1961. D.Litt.: Occidental College, 1937. Member, National Institute of Arts and Letters. *Died in January 1962.*

PUBLICATIONS

Collections

    Selected Poems.   1965.
    Selected Letters 1897–1962, edited by Ann N. Ridgeway.   1968.

Verse

    Flagons and Apples.   1912.
    Californians.   1916.
    Tamar and Other Poems.   1924.
    Roan Stallion, Tamar, and Other Poems.   1925.
    The Women at Point Sur.   1927.
    Poems.   1928.
    An Artist.   1928.
    Cawdor and Other Poems.   1928.
    Dear Judas and Other Poems.   1929.
    Stars.   1930.
    Apology for Bad Dreams.   1930.
    Descent to the Dead: Poems Written in Ireland and Great Britain.   1931.
    Thurso's Landing and Other Poems.   1932.
    Give Your Heart to the Hawks and Other Poems.   1933.
    Solstice and Other Poems.   1935.
    The Beaks of Eagles.   1936.
    Such Counsels You Gave to Me and Other Poems.   1937.
    The Selected Poetry.   1938.
    Be Angry at the Sun.   1941.
    The Double Axe and Other Poems.   1948.
    Hungerfield and Other Poems.   1954.
    The Beginning and the End and Other Poems.   1963.

Plays

    Medea, from a play by Euripides (produced 1947).   1946.
    The Cretan Women, from a play by Euripides (produced 1954?).   In *From the Modern Repertory 3,* edited by Eric Bentley, 1956.

Other

    Poetry, Gongorism, and a Thousand Years.   1949.
    Themes in My Poems.   1956.

Bibliography: *The Critical Reception of Jeffers: A Bibliographical Study* by Alex Vardamis, 1972.

Reading List: *The Loyalties of Jeffers* by Radcliffe Squires, 1956; *Jeffers* by Frederic I. Carpenter, 1962; *The Stone Mason of Tor House: The Life and Work of Jeffers* by Melba B. Bennett, 1966; *Jeffers: Fragments of an Older Fury* by Brother Antoninus (William Everson), 1968; *Jeffers, Poet of Inhumanism* by Arthur B. Coffin, 1971; *Jeffers* by Robert Brophy, 1973.

*   *   *

In 1925 *Roan Stallion, Tamar, and Other Poems* established Robinson Jeffers as one of the major poets of his generation. But beginning in 1927 with *The Women at Point Sur* his repeated use of forbidden themes alienated many readers, and in 1941 his opposition to American participation in World War II all but destroyed his reputation. Since his death in 1962 a better perspective has been achieved, and now he is recognized as one of the most powerful – if also most controversial – of modern poets.

Most of his volumes include one or more long narrative poems, together with many shorter lyrics. And these longer poems all deal, either implicitly or explicitly, with the materials of myth. His *Medea*, for instance, is a free adaptation of the play of Euripides, but *Solstice* attempts to domesticate the violent Greek myth in a realistic California setting. His most successful narrative poems, such as "Roan Stallion" which describes a woman's passionate adoration of a horse, use mythical materials most unobtrusively. But the aura of myth and the forbidden passions which the old myths described, such as incest, parricide, and the love of man for beast, all trouble the narrative poetry of Jeffers.

Besides these myths, his poetry gives vivid expression to an extraordinary sense of place. The wild coast of the country south of Carmel, where he lived all his creative life, provides both actual setting and the conviction of immediate reality for all his poems, both narrative and lyric. But most significant of all is the symbolic nature of this actual country. Here is "Continent's End," both in fact and in idea, "the long migrations' end," where human civilization now faces "the final Pacific" and looks Westward toward its first beginnings in "mother Asia."

In his poetry this realistic sense of place combines with a consciousness of the symbolic significance of this place and a remembrance of the prehistoric origins of civilization suggested by the ancient myths. At its best this poetry realizes a vision of human history unique in its temporal scope and its imaginative power. It is small wonder if it sometimes fails to unify these disparate elements and to realize this all-inclusive vision.

The volume which first established Jeffers's reputation probably remains his best, and the three narrative poems which it includes illustrate the various combinations of narrative realism with mythical symbolism which his later poetry developed. "Roan Stallion" is most completely realistic, and perhaps for this reason has remained the favorite of traditional minded readers. "Tamar" is most extreme, both in plot and in technique, although the strange story of incest plays itself out in a California setting. "The Tower Beyond Tragedy" retells the story of the Oresteia in its original Greek setting, but with modern characterization.

The heroine of "Roan Stallion" is named "California," and both name and plot recall the Greek myth of Europa. But the god-like stallion remains simply an animal, and the woman's adoration for him remains psychological. Meanwhile the mythical dimensions of the naturalistic story are emphasized by poetic suggestion:

The fire threw up figures
And symbols meanwhile, racial myths formed and
dissolved in it, the phantom rulers of humanity
That without being are yet more real than what
they are born of, and without shape, shape that
which makes them.

"Tamar" is a very different poem, perhaps unique in literature. Its incestuous heroine rejects all the inhibitions of civilization, but her seemingly realistic actions are motivated by passages of dream, vision, and racial memory until the modern story seems to reenact the earliest creation myths of the incestuous union of Coelus and Terra, of gods and men. The heroine's absolute rejection of morality is paralleled only by that of the later *Women at Point Sur*. But here the repeated use of dream and vision transforms the realistic story into the realm of timeless myth.

"The Tower Beyond Tragedy" narrates the plot of the Oresteia in realistic terms, but focuses on the character of Cassandra and her predictions of doom. Midway through the poem these enlarge into an all-embracing prophecy of the ultimate destruction of future empires, ending with "a mightier to be cursed and a higher for malediction," America. The poem concludes with the refusal of Orestes to inherit Mycenae, or imperial power, and an eloquent poetic statement of his philosophy of total detachment in a "tower beyond tragedy."

This denunciation of imperial power and this celebration of human detachment is also the theme of many of Jeffers' best shorter poems, such as "Shine, Perishing Republic" and "Continent's End." Other lyrics celebrate simply the beauty of nature, such as "Night" and "Boats in a Fog." Perhaps the best of his short poems is "To the Stone Cutters," which treats the ancient theme of mutability.

After the *Roan Stallion* volume, *The Women at Point Sur* narrated a story of the total rejection of traditional morality by a renegade Christian minister. But this longest of Jeffers' poems was also most realistic, so that the mythical and instinctual incest of "Tamar" became calculated and explicit. Actually the poem recalls the story of Euripides' *Bacchae*, which Jeffers also used in his short poem "The Humanist's Tragedy," but the longer poem abandoned all reference to myth and symbol. Although most contemporary readers rejected it, Jeffers' chief modern disciple, William Everson (Brother Antoninus), has praised it highly in *Fragments of an Older Fury*.

In *Dear Judas* Jeffers retold the gospel story with new characterization, as he had retold the Oresteia in "The Tower Beyond Tragedy." The striking originality of his conception and the soaring poetry with which he clothed it make the poem memorable. But his rejection of Christian orthodoxy seemed blasphemous to many readers. "The Loving Shepherdess," a companion narrative poem, created a character of such beauty that her story seems unique among Jeffers' dark tragedies.

In the 1930's Jeffers turned to a series of more realistic long poems with contemporary California settings, without mythical overtones. "Cawdor," "Thurso's Landing," and "Give Your Heart to the Hawks" all take place in "Jeffers Country" south of Carmel, and all develop their tragic stories effectively. Only some names and passages of poetic commentary suggest larger themes. Near the end of "Thurso's Landing" the poet comments:

> The platform is like a rough plank theatre-stage
> Built on the brow of the promontory: as if our blood had labored all around the
>   earth from Asia
> To play its mystery before strict judges at last, the final ocean and sky, to prove our
>   nature
> More shining than that of the other animals. It is rather ignoble in its quiet times,
>   mean in its pleasures,
> Slavish in the mass; but at stricken moments it can shine terribly against the dark
>   magnificence of things.

After 1935 Jeffers published new volumes every few years, but only a few of the narrative poems achieved excellence. "At the Birth of an Age" develops incidents from the Niblung Saga, but the poetry overshadows the story, and the mythical and philosophic elements which it illustrates find powerful expression. The second narrative poem in *The Double Axe*, entitled "The Inhumanist," creates a hermit-hero who gives expression to Jeffers' philosophy both in speech and in action. Finally, "Hungerfield" creates a brief modern myth recalling that of Herakles.

Many readers prefer Jeffers' shorter poems to his long narratives. His "Apology for Bad Dreams" offers both illustration and explanation of the violent imagery and pessimistic philosophy which characterize all his poetry. A later poem, "The Bloody Sire," gives perfect expression to this philosophy of violence, ending: "Who would remember Helen's face/ Lacking the terrible halo of spears?"

Much of the difficulty of his poetry stems from his insistence upon the philosophy of "Inhumanism," which he attempted to define in his later writing. His opposition both to human self-importance and to the classical tradition of humanism emphasized instead the modern search for objective truth. In contrast to T. S. Eliot's traditional classicism, Jeffers celebrated the values of science and discovery.

—Frederic I. Carpenter

JOHNSON, James Weldon. American. Born in Jacksonville, Florida, 17 June 1871. Educated at Atlanta University, A.B. 1894, A.M. 1904; also studied at Columbia University, New York, for three years. Married Grace Nail in 1910. Principal, Stanton Central Grammar School for Negroes, Jacksonville; helped found *Daily American*, Jacksonville; admitted to the Florida Bar, and practised in Jacksonville, 1897–1901; moved to New York, to collaborate with his brother, the composer J. Rosamond Johnson, in writing popular songs and light opera, 1901–06; United States Consul in Puerto Cabello, Venezuela, 1906–09, and Corinto, Nicaragua, 1909–12; Executive Secretary, National Association for the Advancement of Colored People, 1916–30; Spence Professor of Creative Literature, Fisk University, Nashville, Tennessee, 1930–38; Visiting Professor of Creative Literature, New York University, 1934. Columnist, New York *Age*. Director, American Fund for Public Service; Trustee, Atlanta University. Recipient: Spingarn Medal, 1925; Du Bois Prize for Negro Literature, 1933. Litt.D.: Talladega College, Alabama, 1917; Howard University, Washington, D.C., 1923. Member, Academy of Political Science. *Died 26 June 1938.*

PUBLICATIONS

Verse

Fifty Years and Other Poems. 1917.
God's Trombones: Seven Negro Sermons in Verse. 1927.
Saint Peter Relates an Incident of the Resurrection Day. 1930.
Saint Peter Relates an Incident: Selected Poems. 1935.

Plays

Goyescas; or, The Rival Lovers, from a play by Fernando Periquet, music by Enrique Granados (produced 1915). 1915.
Shakespeare in Harlem, with Langston Hughes (produced 1959).

Fiction

The Autobiography of an Ex-Colored Man.   1912.

Other

The Changing Status of Negro Labor.   1918.
Africa in the World Democracy, with Horace M. Kallen.   1919.
Self-Determining Hayti.   N.d.
Lynching: America's National Disgrace.   1924.
The Race Problem and Peace.   1924.
Fundamentalism Versus Spiritualism: A Layman's Viewpoint.   1925.
Native African Races and Culture.   1927.
Legal Aspects of the Negro Problem.   N.d.
Black Manhattan.   1930.
The Shining Life.   1932.
Along This Way (autobiography).   1933.
Negro Americans, What Now?   1934.

Editor, *The Book of American Negro Poetry.*   1922; revised edition, 1931.
Editor, *The Book of American Negro Spirituals.*   1925; *Second Book,* 1926.

Reading List: *Roots of Negro Racial Consciousness: Three Harlem Renaissance Authors* (on Countée Cullen, Claude McKay, and Johnson) by Stephen H. Bronz, 1964; *Johnson, Black Leader, Black Voice* by Eugene D. Levy, 1973 (includes bibliography).

*   *   *

James Weldon Johnson's literary output is slight but it is a solid achievement and one that proves crucial when viewed in the perspective of an Afro-American aspiring to authorship in the United States in the early twentieth century. In *God's Trombones: Seven Negro Sermons in Verse* Johnson achieves a considerable success in melding Afro-American folk and Euro-American sophisticated modes of expression to gain the kind of artistic synthesis he hoped would assist in confirming the right to full citizenship for peoples of African descent in the United States, by virtue of a demonstrated capacity (which their detractors would argue they did not possess) to contribute significantly to the formation of a national culture. This task of recuperation becomes a theme in Johnson's influential picaresque novel now regarded as a classic, *The Autobiography of an Ex-Colored Man,* first published anonymously in 1912. The novel's "tragic mulatto" protagonist is a trained musician who earns his way as an inspired ragtime pianist. He professes, however ironically (and it is to Johnson's skillful manipulation of irony that the novel owes the greater part of its success), to bring "glory and honour to the Negro race." This he intends to achieve through compositions in the European classical tradition incorporating elements of Afro-American folk music, the projected field research for which, however, never gets done. Further insight into Johnson's recuperative aims is available in the important Prefaces to the two editions of his equally influential and classic anthology, *The Book of American Negro Poetry.* In these he compares the Afro-American poet's need to achieve a distinct mode of expression rooted in and supportive of Afro-American life ("a form that will express the racial spirit by symbols from within"; rather than from without), to that recognized by the Irish poet-playwright J. M. Synge which led to the assimilation of indigenous folk material into his works.

Johnson's accidental death cut short his efforts but his poems in *God's Trombones* record a significant step in the direction he envisioned. This work has continued to serve as an inspiration and a model for Afro-American writers. Stylistically inspired by the folk preaching Johnson observed in Afro-American churches, the poems assume the form and essential rhythm of the sermons and prayers he heard. As such they score a marked stylistic departure from the prevailing Anglo-American poetic tradition of the day. Also, they constitute a corrective to the artificial and, as Johnson saw it, denigrating folk speech of the stereotype-fostering dialect mode that had been grafted onto that tradition, including its use in Johnson's own early dialect poetry. On the Euro-American side, the poems in *God's Trombones* are biblical-Whitmanesque, gaining an appeal at once sophisticated and folk oriented. Similarly, *The Autobiography of an Ex-Colored Man* delineates the artistic defusing of the various stereotypes Afro-American writers were coming to recognize as an obligatory function of their works. Toward that end, Johnson imbues his protagonist with the superficialities of the "tragic mulatto" stereotype but protrays him with psychological verisimilitude and with irony, thus enabling the stereotypical aspect to achieve a virtual self-destruction. He thus carries forward a tradition of corrective aesthetics pioneered by his predecessors, the Afro-American writers Charles W. Chesnutt and, to a lesser degree, Paul Laurence Dunbar.

—Alvin Aubert

JONES, James.   American.   Born in Robinson, Illinois, 6 November 1921. Educated at the University of Hawaii, Honolulu, 1942; New York University, 1945. Served in the United States Army, 1939–44: Bronze Star; Purple Heart. Married Gloria Mosolino in 1957; one son and one daughter. Recipient: National Book Award, 1952. *Died 9 May 1977.*

PUBLICATIONS

Fiction

> *From Here to Eternity.*   1951.
> *Some Came Running.*   1957
> *The Pistol.*   1959.
> *The Thin Red Line.*   1962.
> *Go to the Widow-Maker.*   1967.
> *The Ice-Cream Headache and Other Stories.*   1968.
> *The Merry Month of May.*   1971.
> *A Touch of Danger.*   1973.
> *Whistle: A Work-in-Progress.*   1974; complete version, 1978.

Other

> *Viet Journal.*   1974.
> *WWII: A Chronicle of Soldiering,* with Art Weithas.   1975.

Bibliography: *Jones: A Checklist* by John R. Hopkins, 1974.

*   *   *

Generally regarded as the most successful "war-novelist" to emerge from World War II, James Jones, at his best, writes the way a good combat infantryman serves out a campaign. His prose is direct, muscular, prepared to take advantage of tactical opportunities, efficient, cynical without being pessimistic, and cannily aware of the ambiguous areas where fear mingles with bravery, and self-interest and self-sacrifice shade together. One of the few modern writers to depict the character of man-as-warrior sympathetically and without romantic illusions, Jones will probably be remembered for *From Here to Eternity*, *The Thin Red Line*, and his acute nonfictional study, *WWII: A Chronicle of Soldiering*.

In *From Here to Eternity*, Jones found a story perfectly adequate to his thematic interests: the heroic struggle of the warrior-individual trying to maintain his sense of self against the pressures of the very system that provides him with his cherished identity. Prewitt, the doomed protagonist, becomes an indelible figure in the gallery of American fictional soldiers that runs from Crane's Henry Fleming through Hemingway's Frederic Henry to Joseph Heller's Yossarian. Unlike the others, however, Prewitt is a soldier by choice and devotion; he is neither a rebel against, nor a victim of, the institution in which he finds his fullest realization. Jones's non-military fiction – including *Some Came Running*, *Go to the Widow-Maker*, and *The Merry Month of May* – tends to lack the controlled narrative focus of his war novels; characteristically, the prose is much looser, the action moves toward the melodramatic and sensational, and the novels suffer from a combination of verbosity and sentimentality.

—Earl Rovit

JONES, (Everett) LeRoi. Pseudonym: Amiri Baraka. American. Born in Newark, New Jersey, 7 October 1934. Educated at the Central Avenue School, and Barringer High School, Newark; Howard University, Washington, D.C. Served in the United States Air Force, 1954–56. Married 1) Hettie Cohen in 1958 (divorced, 1965), two daughters; 2) Sylvia Robinson (Bibi Amina Baraka) in 1966, five children. Taught at the New School for Social Research, 1961–64; State University of New York at Buffalo, Summer 1964; Columbia University, 1964; Visiting Professor, San Francisco State College, 1966–67. Founder, *Yugen* magazine and Totem Press, New York, 1958; Editor, with Diane di Prima, *Floating Bear* magazine, New York, 1961–63. Founding Director, Black Arts Repertory Theatre, Harlem, New York, 1964–66. Since 1966, Founding Director, Spirit House, Newark. Involved in Newark politics: Member of the United Brothers, 1967, and Committee for Unified Newark, 1968. Member of the International Coordinating Committee, Congress of African Peoples; Chairman, Congress of Afrikan People; Secretary-General, National Black Political Assembly. Recipient: Whitney Fellowship, 1961; Obie Award, 1964; Guggenheim Fellowship, 1965; Dakar Festival Prize, 1966; National Endowment for the Arts grant, 1966. Member, Black Academy of Arts and Letters. Lives in Newark, New Jersey.

PUBLICATIONS

Plays

A Good Girl is Hard to Find (produced 1958).
Dante (produced 1961; as *The 8th Ditch*, produced 1964). In *The System of Dante's Hell*, 1965.

The Toilet (produced 1962).   In *The Baptism and The Toilet,* 1967.
Dutchman (produced 1964).   In *Dutchman and The Slave,* 1964.
The Slave (produced 1964).   In *Dutchman and The Slave,* 1964.
Dutchman, and The Slave.   1964.
The Baptism (produced 1964).   In *The Baptism and The Toilet,* 1967.
Jello (produced 1965).   1970.
Experimental Death Unit No. 1 (produced 1965).   In *Four Black Revolutionary Plays,* 1969.
A Black Mass (produced 1966).   In *Four Black Revolutionary Plays,* 1969.
The Baptism and The Toilet.   1967.
Arm Yrself or Harm Yrself (produced 1967).   1967.
Slave Ship: A Historical Pageant (produced 1967).   1967.
Madheart (produced 1967).   In *Four Black Revolutionary Plays,* 1969.
Home on the Range (produced 1968).   In *Drama Review,* Summer 1968.
Police, in *Drama Review,* Summer 1968.
The Death of Malcolm X, in *New Plays from the Black Theatre,* edited by Ed Bullins.   1969.
Great Goodness of Life (A Coon Show) (produced 1969).   In *Four Black Revolutionary Plays,* 1969.
Four Black Revolutionary Plays.   1969.
Junkies Are Full of (SHHH ...), and Bloodrites (produced 1970).   In *Black Drama Anthology,* edited by Woodie King and Ron Milner, 1971.
BA-RA-KA, in *Spontaneous Combustion: Eight New American Plays,* edited by Rochelle Owens.   1972.
A Recent Killing (produced 1973).
Sidnee Poet Heroical (produced 1975).
S-1 (produced 1976).   In *The Motion of History and Other Plays,* 1978.
The Motion of History (produced 1977).   In *The Motion of History and Other Plays,* 1978.
The Motion of History and Other Plays (includes *S-1* and *Slave Ship*).   1978.

Other plays: *Columbia the Gem of the Ocean; Resurrection of Life.*

Screenplays: *Dutchman,* 1967; *A Fable,* 1971.

Fiction

The System of Dante's Hell.   1965.
Tales.   1967.

Verse

Preface to a Twenty Volume Suicide Note.   1961.
The Dead Lecturer.   1964.
Black Art.   1966.
Black Magic: Poetry 1961–1967.   1969.
It's Nation Time.   1970.
In Our Terribleness: Some Elements of Meaning in Black Style, with Billy Abernathy.   1970.
Spirit Reach.   1972.
Afrikan Revolution.   1973.
Hard Facts.   1976.

Other

Cuba Libre. 1961.
Blues People: Negro Music in White America. 1963.
Home: Social Essays. 1966.
Black Music. 1968.
A Black Value System. 1970.
Raise Race Rays Raze: Essays since 1965. 1971.
Strategy and Tactics of a Pan-African Nationalist Party. 1971.
The Creation of the New Ark. 1975.

Editor, *Four Young Lady Poets*. 1962.
Editor, *The Moderns: New Fiction in America*. 1964.
Editor, with Larry Neal, *Black Fire: An Anthology of Afro-American Writing*. 1968.
Editor, *African Congress: A Documentary of the First Modern Pan-African Congress*. 1972.
Editor, with Diane di Prima, *The Floating Bear: A Newsletter, Numbers 1–37*. 1974.

Bibliography: *Jones (Imamu Amiri Baraka): A Checklist of Works by and about Him* by Letitia Dace, 1971.

Reading List: *From LeRoi Jones to Amiri Baraka: The Literary Works* by Theodore R. Hudson, 1973; *Baraka: The Renegade and the Mask* by Kimberly W. Benston, 1976; *Baraka/Jones: The Quest for a "Populist Modernism"* by Werner Sollors, 1978.

*   *   *

LeRoi Jones – now known as Amiri Baraka – says he has "always tried to be a revolutionary." That is the consistent quality in a twenty-year career which has included writing in every literary genre and representing contradictory points of view.

The rebel in Jones led him in his youth to prefer running with the ghetto gangs to remaining in his respectable middle-class home. At Howard University, which he found distastefully bourgeois, it led him to quit college after his junior year to join the Air Force. In New York in the late 1950's, it prompted him to become a Greenwich Village bohemian and a disciple of Allen Ginsberg and Jack Kerouac, to turn out lyric poetry and surreal fiction expressing the romantic *angst* and waggish frivolity which permitted publication under titles such as *The System of Dante's Hell* and *Preface to a Twenty Volume Suicide Note*: "My wife is left-handed./which implies a fierce de-/termination. ITS WEIRD BABY./The way some folks are always trying to be/different. A sin & a shame."

Jones in the late 1950's and early 1960's possessed a boundless energy and an extraordinarily diverse talent. He was still speaking to white people and writing for a racially mixed audience. He founded periodicals with two white women, the magazine *Yugen* with his wife Hettie Cohen and the newsletter *The Floating Bear* – its title derived from an A. A. Milne Winnie the Pooh story – with the poet Diane di Prima. His saturation in the western literary tradition (William Carlos Williams, Whitman, Eliot, Yeats, Pound, and the Black Mountain poets) was clearly discernible in his poetry and novel. At that time Jones did not write specifically ethnic literature. Indeed, he alleged in 1959 that "Negro writing" can at best be folklore, for what is written out of racial consciousness cannot achieve literary status. In 1961 his poetry muses "Africa/is a foreign place. You are/as any other sad man here/american."

Yet even in the early work techniques analogous to black music – jazz and the blues – are evident, and Jones was also writing music criticism and essays expressing an increasingly inflammatory political consciousness. He was becoming politicized as early as 1960, when he visited Cuba and wrote the essay *Cuba Libre* in praise of Castro and that island's revolution. His verse became edgy, uneasy with his white life, and his essays and plays began to express an urgency which was turning, by 1964, to racial militancy.

Although a portion of his novel and the play *The Toilet* had been produced earlier, 1964 was the year that Baraka really won attention as a playwright. In March *The Eighth Ditch* (his *Dante* play) opened and was quickly closed by police on grounds of obscenity. Within a week *The Baptism*, an equally startling play, this one a religious satire which drew charges of both obscenity and blasphemy, jarred and amused its spectators. The very next day *Dutchman* opened, and later that year a double bill of *The Toilet* and *The Slave* further solidified Baraka's reputation. (A full-length play, *A Recent Killing*, which was written in this year but not produced until a decade later, dramatizes an inter-racial cooperation in which Jones was already losing faith.)

These plays are blistering in their dramatization of raw racial tensions on a realistic level, but they also function on an allegorical plane. *Dutchman*, in particular, is generally acknowledged to be his finest achievement. The Flying Dutchman constitutes one of the more obvious symbolic references in this play about a woman picking up a man on a New York City subway, but critical opinion has been divided over whether white Lula or black Clay embodies the legendary captain who is doomed to roam until his final peace can be purchased by a lover willing to die with him. Perhaps it is white racism, as exemplified by the murderous Lula, that won't die, or possibly the swallowing of pride and suppression of rage which the superficially assimilated Clay practices represents what Jones had in mind. Whatever the parallel, a double death does not occur, so the spectre of racism is not exorcised.

Dutchman can also be interpreted as a modernization of the Adam and Eve story in which Lula – who keeps eating and offering apples – is a corrupter of the innocent, natural man of Africa and the cause of his expulsion from the paradise of the American dream. Other religious parables which have been discerned include that of Clay as Christ and Lula as Satan (with the young man at the end representing the resurrection) and the idea that Clay is being baptized in hell-fire. *Dutchman* can therefore be viewed as a reference to disguise and the voluntary assumption of roles. Lula is an author creating a series of characters for herself. When Clay stops concealing his blackness behind white clothes, intellectual interests, and a courteous demeanor, Lula rewards his self-assertion with murder.

Equally playable and nearly equally subject to glosses (sometimes more arcane than illuminating), *The Toilet* and *The Slave* take somewhat different approaches to racial conflict. The earlier play, *The Toilet*, depicts interracial relations in a fashion which Jones later came to regard as more sentimental than realistic, for the black gang leader really loves the white boy who is beaten up in the lavatory, and he returns to comfort Karolis when the bullies have left. A major factor in the play's appeal is Jones's embodiment in his protagonist of a universal conflict between the gentle, nurturing, reflective aspect of the character (the "Ray" side of us) and the belligerent, aloof, authoritative aspect (the "Foots" side). The split in this particular temperament, of course, sets up a conflict between the assimilationist with aspirations to white goals (Ray, the good student who is attracted to Karolis) and the true black man (Foots, the natural leader).

Although *The Toilet* is milder than *Dutchman*, *The Slave* finds its protagonist has progressed beyond the birth of militance, which Clay barely reaches, to full leadership in a race war. Walker has left the insurgents just long enough to visit a white couple, his ex-wife and her new husband, the latter a college professor who represents the western culture to which Walker has bidden farewell. That he would pay such a call at all suggests that Walker is still something of a slave to the white liberal heritage, and the old slave whom Walker becomes in a long monologue reinforces that notion. Still, Walker is wiping out, literally, the old associations, and he, like Jones himself at this time of his life, sets a new, independent course.

Jones's drama had been by and large realistic and by and large addressed to a white or racially mixed audience. But the radical changes in his life – his departure in 1965 for Harlem and soon thereafter for the Newark ghetto, his divorce (subsequent to the prophetic *The Slave*) from the white wife (who now felt she was the enemy) and his remarriage to a black woman, his conversion to the Kawaida sect of Muslim and his adoption of an African name, Amiri (prince) Baraka (blessedness), preceded for a time by the religious title Imamu (spiritual leader) – all reflect an ideological transformation which had a profound effect upon all his writing. The essays grew violent, the poetry took on the dialect of black speech, and the plays increasingly spoke only to blacks and were presented in segregated theatres. Realism was generally rejected in favor of a technique sometimes expressionistic and sometimes a montage of brief episodes, cinematic juxtapositions.

The first plays of this black militant period, including *Experimental Death Unit No. 1*, *Jello*, *A Black Mass*, and *Madheart*, explicitly proclaim the superiority of black to white, of black revolutionist to assimilationist, and of male to female. *Jello* is also a quite funny parody of Jack Benny's radio show in which Rochester stops serving Benny and starts asserting his new-found black manhood, and *A Black Mass* is a lyrical evocation of a misguided black man's creation of the white race. While some later black nationalist plays by Baraka – *Arm Yrself or Harm Yrself*, for instance – are simple didactic dramas with lines which preach the point, others make considerable use of nonverbal techniques and are theatrical in ways Antonin Artaud would have appreciated. *Slave Ship*, for instance, forces its spectators to feel they themselves are manacled in the hold of that ship, and it employs Swahili and moans and groans quite as much as English dialogue. The play's spectacle of human suffering is marvelously powerful drama. Some other plays of the late 1960's are cinematic or surreal, and some experiment with language in ways outside the tradition of mainstream American drama.

A recent resurgence of the polemical in Baraka's dramaturgy has followed another political change. The creator of and foremost writer in the black arts movement by 1973 had become a Communist leader and had rejected his nationalist rage and rancor toward whites as racist. Therefore, *S-1* and *The Motion of History* employ agit-prop techniques, in the former to attack the proposed Senate Bill 1, the Federal Criminal Code reform bill which opponents feel would abridge freedom of speech and assembly, and in the latter to urge the solidarity of blacks and whites in a revolution to overthrow their oppressors. *The Motion of History* dramatizes instances from the past four centuries in which the ruling class has pitted poor blacks and whites against each other so as to obscure their common interests in ending exploitation. This play even ridicules the black militant, who is represented as a mindless robot chanting "the white man is the devil."

In 1961, LeRoi Jones was president of the Fair Play for Cuba Committee. He strayed far afield from such politics, but has returned now to a Marxist-Leninist-Maoist stance. Whatever his particular affiliation, he continues to be one of the foremost of contemporary committed writers.

—Tish Dace

KAUFMAN, George S(imon). American. Born in Pittsburgh, Pennsylvania, 16 November 1889. Educated at Liberty School, New Castle School, and Central High School, Pittsburgh, graduated 1907; Western University of Pennsylvania Law School, 1907. Married 1) Beatrice Bakrow in 1917 (died, 1945), one adopted daughter; 2) the writer Leueen MacGrath in 1949 (divorced, 1957). Worked as a surveyor, clerk in the Allegheny County

Tax Office, and stenographer in the Pittsburgh Coal Company; travelling salesman for the Columbia Ribbon Company, Paterson, New Jersey; Jornalist: Columnist, *Washington Times*, 1912–13; Drama Critic, New York *Tribune*, 1914–15; Columnist, New York *Evening Mail*, 1915; Drama Critic, *New York Times*, 1917–30. Writer for the stage from 1918, often in collaboration; stage director from 1928. Chairman of the Board, Dramatists' Guild 1927. Recipient: Megrue Prize, 1931; Pulitzer Prize, 1932, 1937. *Died 2 June 1961.*

PUBLICATIONS

Plays

Among Those Present, with Larry Evans and Walter C. Percival (produced 1918; as *Someone in the House*, produced 1918).

Jacques Duval, with Hans Mueller (produced 1919).

Dulcy, with Marc Connelly (produced 1921).   1921.

To the Ladies!, with Marc Connelly (produced 1922).   1923.

No, Sirree!, with Marc Connelly (produced 1922).

A Christmas Carol, with Marc Connelly, from the story by Dickens, in *Bookman*, December 1922.

The 49ers, with Marc Connelly (produced 1922).

West of Pittsburgh, with Marc Connelly (produced 1922); revised version, as *The Deep Tangled Wildwood* (produced 1923).

Merton of the Movies, with Marc Connelly, from the story by Harry Leon Wilson (produced 1922).   1925.

Helen of Troy, N.Y., with Marc Connelly, music and lyrics by Harry Ruby and Bert Kalmar (produced 1923).

Beggar on Horseback, with Marc Connelly, music by Deems Taylor, from a play by Paul Apel (produced 1924).   1925.

Sketches, in *'Round the Town* (produced 1924).

Be Yourself, with Marc Connelly (produced 1924).

Minick, with Edna Ferber, from the story "Old Man Minick" by Ferber (produced 1924).   1925.

The Butter and Egg Man (produced 1925).   1925.

The Cocoanuts, music by Irving Berlin (produced 1925).   1925.

If Men Played Cards Like Women Do.   1926.

The Good Fellow, with Herman J. Mankiewicz (produced 1926).   1931.

The Royal Family, with Edna Ferber (produced 1927).   1928; as *Theatre Royal* (produced 1935), 1936.

Animal Crackers, with Morrie Ryskind, music and lyrics by Harry Ruby and Bert Kalmar (produced 1928).

The Still Alarm (sketch), in *The Little Show* (produced 1929).   1930.

June Moon, with Ring Lardner, from the story "Some Like Them Cold" by Lardner (produced 1929).   1931.

The Channel Road, with Alexander Woollcott (produced 1929).

Strike Up the Band, book by Morrie Ryskind from a libretto by Kaufman, music by George Gershwin, lyrics by Ira Gershwin (produced 1930).

Once in a Lifetime, with Moss Hart (produced 1930).   1930.

The Band Wagon, with Howard Dietz, music by Arthur Schwartz (produced 1931).

Eldorado, with Laurence Stallings (produced 1931).

Of Thee I Sing, with Morrie Ryskind, music by George Gershwin, lyrics by Ira Gershwin (produced 1931).   1932.

Dinner at Eight, with Edna Ferber (produced 1932). 1932.
Let 'em Eat Cake, with Morrie Ryskind, music by George Gershwin, lyrics by Ira Gershwin (produced 1933). 1933.
The Dark Tower, with Alexander Woollcott (produced 1933). 1934.
Merrily We Roll Along, with Moss Hart (produced 1934). 1934.
Bring on the Girls, with Morrie Ryskind (produced 1934).
Prom Night. 1934.
Cheating the Kidnappers. 1935.
The Paperhanger, with Moss Hart. 1935(?).
First Lady, with Katharine Dayton (produced 1935). 1935.
Stage Door, with Edna Ferber (produced 1936). 1939.
You Can't Take It with You, with Moss Hart (produced 1936). 1937.
I'd Rather Be Right, with Moss Hart, music by Richard Rodgers, lyrics by Lorenz Hart (produced 1937). 1937.
The Fabulous Invalid, with Moss Hart (produced 1938). 1938.
The American Way, with Moss Hart, music by Oscar Levant (produced 1939). 1939.
The Man Who Came to Dinner, with Moss Hart (produced 1939). 1939.
George Washington Slept Here, with Moss Hart (produced 1940). 1940.
The Land Is Bright, with Edna Ferber (produced 1941). 1946.
Six Plays, with Moss Hart. 1942.
The Late George Apley, with John P. Marquand, from the novel by Marquand (produced 1944). 1946.
Hollywood Pinafore (produced 1945).
Park Avenue, with Nunnally Johnson, music by Arthur Schwartz, lyrics by Ira Gershwin (produced 1946).
Bravo!, with Edna Ferber (produced 1948). 1949.
The Small Hours, with Leueen MacGrath (produced 1951). 1951.
Fancy Meeting You Again, with Leueen MacGrath (produced 1952). 1952.
The Solid Gold Cadillac, with Howard Teichmann (produced 1953). 1954.
Silk Stockings, with Leueen MacGrath and Abe Burrows, music by Cole Porter, suggested by Melchior Lengyel (produced 1955). 1955.
Amicable Parting, with Leueen MacGrath (produced 1957). 1957.

Screenplays: *Business Is Business,* with Dorothy Parker, 1925; *If Men Played Cards As Women Do,* 1929; *Roman Scandals,* with others, 1933; *A Night at the Opera,* with Morrie Ryskind, 1935; *Star Spangled Rhythm,* with others, 1943.

Reading List: *Kaufman: An Intimate Portrait,* by Howard Teichmann, 1972; *Kaufman and His Friends* by Scott Meredith, 1974, abridged version, as *Kaufman and the Algonquin Round Table,* 1977.

*   *   *

George S. Kaufman was a devastating wit and a serious satirist who worked, almost always in collaboration, on successful plays, musicals, and films. He was especially effective with Moss Hart, a productive blend of talents much studied and much admired: "Their most distinguished works, *You Can't Take It with You* and *The Man Who Came to Dinner,* reveal Kaufman and Hart," says Milton Levin (in *The Reader's Encyclopedia of World Drama*), "as the best satirists in American drama."

Kaufman's first play was with the team of Larry Evans and Walter Percival. Then he and Marc Connelly (another newspaperman from Pennsylvania active in New York) entered on a series of collaborations: *Dulcy, To the Ladies, Merton of the Movies, The Deep Tangled Wildwood,* and *Beggar on Horseback.* Of these only *The Deep Tangled Wildwood* (a satire "upon the Winchell-Smith type of play") was a failure. *Merton of the Movies*, the story of a movie-struck clerk who achieves success because he, unconsciously, burlesques serious roles, was a delight. The dream sequence of *Beggar on Horseback* (a penniless composer, Neil McRae, is given a sedative and has nightmares about having to work in a "widget" factory and then a Consolidated Art Factory, where he has to write music for songs like: "You've broken my heart like you broke my heart/So why should you break it again?") was considered "a fine expression of the resentment of the artist" for those who are "contemptuous of those who show originality" (A. H. Quinn). *Beggar on Horseback* is considered a milestone in American expressionism. The team broke up and Kaufman wrote his one unaided work, *The Butter and Egg Man* (1925), and Connelly tried an original also, *The Wisdom Tooth* (1926). Neither was much good, for Kaufman's farce and Connelly's fantasy did not seem to work separately.

"I have always been smart enough to attach myself to the most promising lad that came along in the theater," said Kaufman, and he joined forces with a number of burgeoning, bright talents. With Edna Ferber he wrote *Minick, The Royal Family, Dinner at Eight, Stage Door*, and *The Land is Bright*. With Herman J. Mankiewicz, another journalist and wit, he wrote *The Good Fellow*, which flopped (Mankiewicz went on to success as a screenwriter, probably writing most of *Citizen Kane*, though that is still argued), but the same year Kaufman had a hit with Ring Lardner, that "wonderful man" with such a great ear for American speech, in an hilarious take-off of Tin-Pan Alley, *June Moon*. About the same time Kaufman began to work with one of the madcap writers behind the Marx Brothers, the too-little-acknowledged zany genius, Morrie Ryskind. With Ryskind Kaufman entered the world of Broadway musicals, starting with *Animal Crackers*. Their collaboration was later to produce *Of Thee I Sing* (with the Gershwins; Pulitzer Prize 1932) and *Let 'em Eat Cake* (with the Gershwins), satires of politics and revolutionaries. With Alexander Woollcott, Kaufman wrote *The Channel Road* and, not much better, *The Dark Tower*. With Katharine Dayton he did a comedy of Washington politics and social life, *First Lady*. In the 1930's he was at his best with Moss Hart. *Once in a Lifetime* was a facile but funny satire on Hollywood. *Merrily We Roll Along* cleverly told its story backwards, taking the middle-aged failure back to the promise of his youth. *I'd Rather Be Right* took its title from a Henry Clay speech of 1850 ("I would rather be right than be President"), but attacked the administration of Franklin Delano Roosevelt. *You Can't Take It with You* well deserved its Pultizer Prize for 1936, for the crazy Sycamore family creates one of the fastest, most furious, funniest farces ever and manages to effect a sweet, sentimental ending as well. The musicals *Strike Up the Band* and *The Band Wagon* (with Howard Dietz) were fun – but *The Man Who Came to Dinner*, with Hart, was fabulous. At the center of the chaos stands (or sits, in a wheelchair) Sheridan Whiteside, described by Monty Woolley in the film biography of Cole Porter as "an intolerable ass." As Woolley played him on stage and screen, this caricature of Alexander Woollcott was irresistible and, though the play is cluttered with other matters (such as cartoons of Noël Coward, one of the Marx Brothers, and a Lizzie Borden character), he delightfully dominates the action as he dominates the poor family who were unlucky enough to have him break a hip on their premises. The play contains some of the best single lines in American comedy.

The Man Who Came to Dinner may be the highspot of Kaufman's career. *George Washington Slept Here* was accurately reviewed as "George Kaufman slipped here" and later work such as *The Late George Apley* (with novelist J. P. Marquand) and *The Solid Gold Cadillac* (with Howard Teichmann) were a part of Kaufman's long career as a play doctor, though much of their success was no doubt due to his expertise. He also worked with other play doctors (such as Abe Burrows) and with Nunnally Johnson, Leueen MacGrath, and others.

Kaufman gained various strengths from various collaborators – farce, fantasy, satire, structure – but, to put it briefly, he can best be understood if one thinks of him as a Jewish comedian. He was a leader among the "Broadway intellectuals" (with Hart, Dorothy Parker, S. N. Behrman, George Jean Nathan) and a master of the wisecrack. His is the *echt* Jewish humor that plays with language (as in Goodman Ace); often sees the world as *ash und porukh* (ashes and dust) but will hang on to see what happens ("You might as well live" – Dorothy Parker); deals in insult; sometimes takes off into nonsense, intoxicated by words (S. J. Perelman), and sometimes into sentimentality (Sam Levine), attracted to nostalgia for better times; is repelled by pretension and more than a little attracted to cyncism (though not at Kaufman's time going as far as the Shock Schlock of Lenny Bruce) and always loves to tinker with logic until it explodes (you had best read Leo Rosten's *The Joys of Yiddish* rather than Freud on humor). In *World of Our Fathers* (1977), Irving Howe dissects this Jewish humor which chooses laughter as the alternative to tears and often uses satire as both a defensive and an offensive weapon. Professor Howe quotes Gilbert Seldes, who claimed that the Jewish entertainers' "daemonic" approach was traceable to "their fine carelessness about our superstitions of politeness and gentility ... contempt for artificial notions of propriety."

Kaufman was businessman enough to know that an all-out assault on The Establishment would not pay off. His pose was that of the hero of *The Butter and Egg Man*, the naïf in the big city. His targets were the obvious, safe ones that are best suited to musical comedy and farce. When he tried something "positive," like *The American Way* (a patriotic panorama), he was at his weakest. A wisecrack has to be a *zinger*, not a compliment. He never let himself get bitter: *that* was the kind of satire, as he said, which "closes on Saturday night." He wasn't a *kvetch* or a nag or a moralist, just a very funny wisecracking wit, one of the best.

—Leonard R. N. Ashley

KELLY, George (Edward).   American.   Born in Philadelphia, Pennsylvania, 16 January 1887. Educated privately. Actor as a young man: debut, 1908; subsequently played in touring companies and vaudeville; playwright from 1916. Recipient: Pulitzer Prize, 1926; Brandeis University Creative Arts Award, 1959. D.F.A.: LaSalle College, Philadelphia, 1962. *Died 18 June 1974.*

PUBLICATIONS

Plays

> *Mrs. Ritter Appears* (produced 1917); revised version, as *The Torchbearers: A Satirical Comedy* (produced 1922).   1923; revised version of Act III, as *Mrs. Ritter Appears*, 1964.
> *Poor Aubrey* (produced 1922).   In *The Flattering Word and Other One-Act Plays*, 1925; revised version, as *The Show-Off: A Transcript of Life* (produced 1924), 1924.
> *Mrs. Wellington's Surprise* (produced 1922).
> *Finders-Keepers.*   1923.
> *The Flattering Word and Other One-Act Plays* (includes *Smarty's Party, The Weak Spot, Poor Aubrey*).   1925.
> *Craig's Wife* (produced 1925).   1926.
> *Daisy Mayme* (produced 1926).   1927.
> *One of Those Things*, in *One-Act Plays for Stage and Study, Third Series*.   1927.
> *Behold the Bridegroom* (produced 1927).   1928.
> *A La Carte* (sketches and lyrics only; produced 1927).

Maggie the Magnificent (produced 1929).
Philip Goes Forth (produced 1931). 1931.
Reflected Glory (produced 1936). 1937.
The Deep Mrs. Sykes (produced 1945). 1946.
The Fatal Weakness (produced 1946). 1947.

Screenplay: *Old Hutch*, 1936.

Bibliography: "Kelly: An Eclectic Bibliography" by Paul A. Doyle, in *Bulletin of Bibliography*, September-December 1965.

Reading List: *Kelly* by Foster Hirsch, 1975.

*   *   *

George Kelly had a lot of brothers and sisters and he followed his older brother Walter ("The Virginia Judge" of vaudeville) into the theatre. In those days it was not quite so unusual a place to find a moralist, even an anti-romantic, deeply-puritanical one.

Kelly played juveniles in the Keith and Orpheum circuits and began to write playlets, sketches really, such as *One of Those Things*, *Finders-Keepers*, *The Flattering Word*, and *Poor Aubrey*. They were light little satires on character flaws such as vanity and bragging. People who overstepped the accepted moral code were given their comeuppance, like the adventuress who outsmarts herself in *Smarty's Party*. They were popular enough: really trenchant satire (as George S. Kaufman remarked) "closes on Saturday night," but audiences like to see obvious targets hit skilfully and wittily.

But then Kelly expanded *Poor Aubrey* into the full-length play of *The Show-Off*, in which Aubrey Piper's bragging and bluffing are exposed and his lies and pretensions exploded. It was Kelly's first success, for *The Torchbearers*, a rather gentle send-up of the pretensions of Little Theatres with even littler talents in them, did not catch on at first, though it later was to achieve some recognition.

Kelly achieved the height of his career (and the Pulitzer Prize) with *Craig's Wife*. The vanity of *Flattering Word* and the manipulator defeated of *Smarty's Party* combine in the well-constructed but rather grimly determined story of a woman whose concern with appearances and control of her sterile environment give "Good Housekeeping" a bad name. But character study is confused with the problem play and Kelly is no Ibsen. Mrs. Craig (mordantly played by Chrystal Herne) was unforgettable but essentially just revealed, not developed. A revival of the play in the 1970's made the theatrical success of a half century before look too theatrical and the character of Mrs. Craig too static and that of her long-suffering husband too trivial.

After *Craig's Wife*, Kelly was on the slide. He had four failures in a row: *Daisy Mayme* was talky; *Behold the Bridegroom* was worse, preachy; *Maggie the Magnificent* and *Philip Goes Forth* convinced the dramatist to give up Broadway, though he returned with *Reflected Glory*, and *The Deep Mrs. Sykes*.

After the poor reception of *The Fatal Weakness* in 1946, he seemed to recognize his own fatal weaknesses as a playwright – getting in the way of the characters, imposing himself and his views on the situation and using the stage as a soapbox without the brilliance of Shaw or the cleverness of Brecht – and retired. Today he is known as the author of *Craig's Wife* and *The Torchbearers*.

—Leonard R. N. Ashley

KEROUAC, Jack. American. Born Jean Louis Lebris de Kerouac in Lowell, Massachusetts, 12 March 1922. Educated at Horace Mann School, New York; Columbia University, New York, 1940–41, 1942. Served in the United States Merchant Marine, and Navy, during World War II. Married in 1944 (annulled), and 1950 (divorced); married Stella Sampas in 1966; one daughter. Sports Reporter for the Lowell *Sun*, 1942; became a writer after the war, supporting himself by various odd jobs; worked as brakeman with the Southern Pacific Railroad, San Francisco, 1952–53; travelled throughout the United States and Mexico, 1953–56; fire lookout for the United States Agricultural Service in Washington state, 1956; full-time writer from 1957. *Died 21 October 1969.*

PUBLICATIONS

Fiction

The Town and the City. 1950.
On the Road. 1957; edited by Scott Donaldson, 1978.
The Subterraneans. 1958.
The Dharma Bums. 1958.
Doctor Sax: Faust Part Three. 1959.
Maggie Cassidy. 1960.
Excerpts from "Visions of Cody." 1959; complete version, 1972.
Tristessa. 1960.
Book of Dreams. 1960.
Big Sur. 1962.
Visions of Gerard. 1963.
Desolation Angels. 1965.
Satori in Paris. 1966.
Vanity of Duluoz: An Adventurous Education 1935–46. 1968.
Pic. 1971.
Two Early Stories. 1973.

Play

Pull My Daisy (screenplay). 1961.

Screenplay: *Pull My Daisy,* 1959.

Verse

Mexico City Blues. 1959.
Hymn – God Pray for Me. 1959.
Rimbaud. 1960.
The Scripture of the Golden Eternity. 1960; revised edition, 1970.
Poem. 1962.
A Pun for Al Gelpi. 1966.
Hugo Weber. 1967.
Scattered Poems. 1971.
Trip, Trap: Haiku along the Road from San Francisco to New York, 1959, with Albert Saijo and Lew Welch. 1973.

Heaven and Other Poems, edited by Donald Allen.   1977.

Other

Lonesome Traveler, drawings by Larry Rivers.   1960.

Bibliography: *A Bibliography of Works by Kerouac* by Ann Charters, 1967; revised edition, 1975.

Reading List: *No Pie in the Sky: The Hobo as American Culture Hero in the Works of Jack London, John Dos Passos, and Kerouac* by Frederick Feied, 1964; *Kerouac: A Biography*, by Ann Charters, 1973; *Jack's Book: An Oral Biography* by Barry Gifford and Lawrence Lee, 1978.

*   *   *

Along with Gary Snyder, Allen Ginsberg, William Burroughs, Neal Cassady, and their compatriots, Jack Kerouac was an unlikely cultural hero. Each, in his own very different way, was a thread in the vast social ethnic called the United States. Kerouac was rooted more than most in a traditional American *mythos*. Raised in a working-class Catholic family in Lowell, Massachusetts, given to normal boyhood fantasies of early greatness as a football star (he very nearly recognized them in his brief stay at Columbia University), he later became the leading prose writer of the Beat Movement. His group and its substantial youthful following sparked a cultural renaissance in mid-century United States – in literature, music, painting, and the larger realms of society and politics – that will not soon be forgotten.

Kerouac's favourite early nickname was "memory babe," suggestive of his own prodigious memory and the accompanying later desire to preserve, in a weakly fictionalized pickle, the experiences of childhood and youth in Lowell, his days on the road in the heart of America, and particularly his friends and exploits along the way. From his first and most conventional work, *The Town and the City*, he sought to preserve in their essences: himself (as Peter Martin, Sal Paradise, and Jack Duluoz), Snyder (as Japhy Ryder), Ginsberg (as Carlo Marx and Irwin Garden), Burroughs (as Old Bull Lee and Bull Hubbard), and Neal Cassady (as Dean Moriarity and Cody Pomeray). He had hoped, in later life, to collect his works – uniformly bound as multi-volumes of a single gigantic work, with real names and places restored.

Kerouac, the man and the writer, represented a revitalization of the romantic spirit in America. He idealized a return to a more essential and authentic life and intense existence in the present, be it in the streets of his fictional Lowell (*The Town and the City, Doctor Sax*), along the streams and firetrails of his fictional Oregon (*The Dharma Bums*), in the *barrios* of his fictional California and Mexico (*On the Road, Big Sur, Mexico City Blues*), or in subterranean clubs of New York, Denver, San Francisco, and points along the way. His biographers, particularly Ann Charters and Charles Marcus, document his own fierce and often troubled individualism, recurrent optimism, and reverence for sentient life, and the tragedy of his later years – virtually alone in Florida and finally Lowell.

Jack Kerouac's work depicted both the ideals of the "hot" beats – those like Neal Cassady who burned their lives as filaments in a quest for "IT!," "kicks," pure ecstatic existence in what Norman Mailer calls "the enormous present" – and the "cool" beats – Gary Snyder and kindred spirits who sought a return to essence in the more Eastern detached, ascetic realms of Zen and allied philosophies. A keynote of his fiction and poetry is the notion that the act of creating literature is in itself a performance, an authentic act testifying to intensely-felt experience. (We should recall the great popularity of poetry as a *declaimed* form, a *song* as well as a text, often combined with jazz, during the Beat years.) Thus Kerouac's work rarely responds well to the techniques of close textual reading. He claimed to have written *On the Road* "at white heat" in several weeks on an unbroken roll of teletype paper; his later work is rarely revised, very loose in form, episodic and lyrical at best, improvised like the jazz the Beats so admired, given to humor and nostalgia and the crests and valleys of romantic fiction.

Like many of his fellow Beats (a predominantly masculine group), Kerouac was widely lauded and damned – in his own day and in the present. Like Burroughs and Cassady and Ginsberg, Kerouac lived his life as a kind of work of art, an action painting, a jazz riff. Their experiments in sexuality, with drugs, with the many and often frightening potentialities of psychic and social order and disorder, their bold and often naive desires to re-awaken dormant chords in American life and writing – these have rarely been met with balanced opinions. And Kerouac, as the central figure of the most well-defined literary movement in twentieth-century America, like most truly revolutionary figures, found no final peace in his life and will not soon rest easily in mass thought or literary history.

—Jack Hicks

KINGSLEY, Sidney.   American.   Born Sidney Kieschner in New York City, 22 October 1906. Educated at Townsend Harris Hall, New York, 1920–24; Cornell University, Ithaca, New York (state scholarship), 1924–28, B.A. 1928. Served in the United States Army, 1941–43: Lieutenant. Married the actress Madge Evans in 1939. Worked as an actor in the Tremont Stock Company, Bronx, New York, 1928; thereafter worked as a play-reader and scenario-writer for Columbia Pictures; full-time writer and stage director from 1934. Past President, Dramatists Guild. Recipient: Pulitzer Prize, 1934; New York Theatre Club Medal, 1934, 1936, 1943; New York Drama Critics Circle Award, 1943, 1951; New York Newspaper Guild Front Page Award, 1943, and Page One Citation, 1949; Edgar Allan Poe Award, 1949; Donaldson Award, 1951; American Academy of Arts and Letters Award of Merit Medal, 1951. Lives in New Jersey.

PUBLICATIONS

Plays

Men in White (produced 1933).   1933.
Dead End (produced 1935).   1936.
Ten Million Ghosts (produced 1936).
The World We Make, from the novel *The Outward Room* by Millen Brand (produced 1939).   1939.
The Patriots (produced 1943).   1943.
Detective Story (produced 1949).   1949.
Darkness at Noon, from the novel by Arthur Koestler (produced 1951).   1951.
Lunatics and Lovers (produced 1954).   Condensed version in *Theater 1955*, 1955.
Night Life (produced 1962).   1966.

Screenplay: *Homecoming*, with Paul Osborn and Jan Lustig, 1948.

*   *   *

Sidney Kingsley was one of "the young radicals our colleges are said to be full of nowadays" (as S. N. Berhman put it in *End of Summer*). His agit-prop approach to theatre was a bit less strident than that of some other proletarian dramatists, but sufficient to endear him to the famous Group Theater, whose financial life he saved early in its career with the success of his first play, *Men in White*.

The story of the Group Theater is brilliantly told by Harold Clurman in *The Fervent Years*. The story of *Men in White* is accurately told by John Mason Brown (*Two on the Aisle*, 1938): it "is a piffling script, mildewed in its hokum, childishly sketchy in its characterization, and so commonplace in its every written word that it in no way justifies its own unpleasantness." Moreover, "the finished result, as Arthur Hopkins once observed when Mr. [David] Belasco converted his stage into a Child's Restaurant, is *only remarkable because it is not real*." Very just; but just also to add that Kingsley's approach has since been copied, in its dab-hand dramaturgy and somewhat fuzzy concern with ethical standards, in Paddy Chayefsky's *Hospital* and *Network* and in many television soap operas and feature films.

Also seminal was *Dead End*, establishing for the cinema many of the clichés of slum-life sociology, "a raucous tone-poem of the modern city" (Brooks Atkinson), a shaky melodrama set down in a handsome set (by Norman Bel Geddes) with a pier-head jutting right into the orchestra pit. The contrived plot brings the Dead End kids and other poor folk into contact with some rich East Siders in New York: the façade of the wealthy apartment house is under repair, which brings the rich people round to the back and right on stage. Unfortunately for Kingsley, he does not seem to remember poverty without sentimentality and, at least before the considerable success of *Dead End*, seems never to have met anyone rich. His sociology is superficial and his dramaturgy profoundly pedestrian.

Ten Million Ghosts is a confused discussion of munitions magnates. Kingsley was well out of his intellectual depth. *The World We Make* was not much better, although for once in the 1930's the emphasis is upon character rather than upon "The System" and environment. *The Patriots* is about a decade in the life of Thomas Jefferson. In none of these plays did Kingsley have the advantages he had in *Dead End*. He desperately needed stars and set designers and a whole team to "make something" of his scripts. He once half perceived this when he said: "When two people have a baby, the baby is a bit of a surprise. In the theater we have a marriage of many people. I can't really tell how the baby will come out."

Kingsley was once a leading Broadway playwright. He became known to a wider audience through such films as *Men in White*, *Dead End*, and *Detective Story*. He was at his best whenever he had help: the committed cast of *Men in White*, the street arabs and street scene of *Dead End*, Millen Brand's novel *The Outward Room* as a basis for *The World We Make*, Madge Evans to help with *The Patriots*, Arthur Koestler's novel behind *Darkness at Noon*. *Crowell's Handbook of Contemporary Drama* (1971) give as fair an estimate as any: "In most of his work Kingsley relies on a sense of atmosphere generated by realistic re-creation of a particular world – hospitals, slums, police stations, prisons – a vivid milieu that supplies much of the vivid impact of the play and also constitutes its limitation. The plays are frequently melodramatic in plot and sketchy in characterization; timely issues have made them at first appear more substantial than they later are seen to be."

—Leonard R. N. Ashley

KOPIT, Arthur (Lee).   American.   Born in New York City, 10 May 1937. Educated at Lawrence High School, New York, graduated 1955; Harvard University, Cambridge, Massachusetts, B.A. (cum laude) 1959 (Phi Beta Kappa). Married Leslie Ann Garis.

Recipient: Vernon Rice Award, 1962; Outer Circle Award, 1962; Guggenheim Fellowship, 1967; Rockefeller grant, 1968; National Institute of Arts and Letters award, 1971; National Endowment for the Arts grant, 1974; Wesleyan University Center for the Humanities Fellowship, 1974. Lives in Connecticut.

PUBLICATIONS

Plays

The Questioning of Nick (produced 1957).   In *The Day the Whores Came Out to Play Tennis and Other Plays*, 1965.
Gemini (produced 1957).
Don Juan in Texas, with Wally Lawrence (produced 1957).
On the Runway of Life, You Never Know What's Coming Off Next (produced 1957).
Across the River and into the Jungle (produced 1958).
To Dwell in a Place of Strangers, Act I published in *Harvard Advocate*, May 1958.
Aubade (produced 1959).
Sing to Me Through Open Windows (produced 1959; revised version, produced 1965).   In *The Day the Whores Came Out to Play Tennis and Other Plays*, 1965.
Oh Dad, Poor Dad, Mama's Hung You in the Closet and I'm Feelin' So Sad: A Pseudoclassical Tragifarce in a Bastard French Tradition (produced 1960).   1960.
Mhil'daim (produced 1963).
Asylum; or, What the Gentlemen Are Up To, and And As for the Ladies (produced 1963; *And As for the Ladies* produced, as *Chamber Music*, 1971).   *Chamber Music* in *The Day the Whores Came Out to Play Tennis and Other Plays*, 1965.
The Conquest of Everest (produced 1964).   In *The Day the Whores Came Out to Play Tennis and Other Plays*, 1965.
The Hero (produced 1964).   In *The Day the Whores Came Out to Play Tennis and Other Plays*, 1965.
The Day the Whores Came Out to Play Tennis (produced 1965).   In *The Day the Whores Came Out to Play Tennis and Other Plays*, 1965.
The Day the Whores Came Out to Play Tennis and Other Plays. 1965; as *Chamber Music and Other Plays*, 1969.
Indians (produced 1968). 1969.
An Incident in the Park, in *Pardon Me, Sir, But Is My Eye Hurting Your Elbow?*, edited by Bob Booker and George Foster.   1968.
What's Happened to the Thorne's House (produced 1972).
Louisiana Territory; or, Lewis and Clark – Lost and Found (produced 1975).
Secrets of the Rich (produced 1976).   1978.
Wings (produced 1978).   1978.

*   *   *

A brilliant satirist with a highly developed sense of the theatrical, Arthur Kopit has been concerned from the time of his earliest plays with America's continuing need to create myth and mythic heroes in order to justify its barbaric cruelty and unlimited greediness. He is deeply disturbed by the power of these myths to shape its actions, to destroy its people's ability to make moral judgements, and to transform its real heroes into garish, bewildered caricatures of human beings.

In his first play, *The Questioning of Nick*, Kopit develops the crude prototype of his later mythic heroes. Nick Carmonatti, a high school basketball player "named in *Sport* as one of the five hun'red leading basketball prospects in the whole country," is so overpowered by the illusion of his importance that he not only admits that he accepted a bribe to throw a game but also brags that he was the only player good enough to be offered one.

In such early farces as *Don Juan in Texas* and *Across the River and into the Jungle*, as well as in *The Conquest of Everest* and *The Day the Whores Came Out to Play Tennis*, Kopit creates outrageously funny characters – "eighteen bare assed" whores who invade the staid atmosphere of the Cherry Valley Country Club; a soap salesman who is mistaken for Billy the Kid; two American barefooted tourists in Florida garb who climb Everest without realizing what they've accomplished, who eat sandwiches and drink cokes, and who then rejoin their tour for dinner. Through these characters he ridicules such minor American flaws as stuffiness, cowardice, provincialism, and prudishness.

In his more serious works, the ridicule is underscored with a strong sense of menace. *Chamber Music*, for example, features eight hilarious madwomen, each of whom believes she is a well-known historical figure. These women convince themselves that they are in danger of being attacked by the inmates of the men's ward. Then, using logic appropriate to the asylum, they decide to protect themselves by a show of strength, by a sign of their ferocity. So they kill Amelia Earhart, one of their own, and are satisfied that they have thus protected themselves from danger. *Oh Dad, Poor Dad*, Kopit's most vicious satire, again combines the ludicrous and the terrifying. Focusing on the myth of Supermom, Kopit creates Madame Rosepettle, a woman who hangs the stuffed corpse of her husband in her closet, locks her adult son Jonathan in her apartment, keeps a piranha in her living room, and grows Venus's-flytraps on her balcony. When Jonathan rebels – kills the piranha, the Venus's-flytraps, and his seductive babysitter, who is herself a potential supermom – Madame Rosepettle is shocked into a state of bewilderment. She cannot understand the meaning of his action.

Kopit carries the bewildered mythic hero a step further in his best work, *Indians*, where the genocide practiced against the American Indians is used as the metaphor for the American violence in Vietnam. William Cody's frantic struggle to live up to the myth of Buffalo Bill and his futile attempt to regain his own identity, once the barbaric cruelty of the conquest of the West and the bizarre sham of the Wild West Show threaten to destroy all sense of his humanity, epitomize for Kopit the continuing struggle of contemporary America. Thus, he demonstrates most powerfully here what he has already said in his earlier plays and what he reiterates in his most recent works: America has created the wrong kinds of heroes in order to justify the wrong kinds of actions, and it is trapped by its need to perpetuate the myth of its glorious past.

—Helen Houser Popovich

KOSINSKI, Jerzy (Nikodem). American. Born in Lodz, Poland, 14 June 1933; emigrated to the United States, 1957; naturalized, 1965. Educated at the University of Lodz, 1950–55, M.A. in history 1953, M.A. in political science 1955; Columbia University, New York, 1958–64; New School for Social Research, New York, 1962–65. Married Mary Hayward Weir in 1962 (died, 1968). Aspirant (Associate Professor), Polish Academy of Sciences, Warsaw, 1955–57; Fellow, Center for Advanced Studies, Wesleyan University, Middletown, Connecticut, 1968–69; Senior Fellow, Council for the Humanities, and Visiting Lecturer in English Prose, Princetown University, New Jersey, 1969–70; Professor of English Prose and Criticism, School of Drama, and Resident Fellow, Davenport College, Yale University, New Haven, Connecticut, 1970–72. President, American P.E.N. Club, 1973.

Member of the Executive Board, National Writers Club; Director, International League for the Rights of Man. Recipient: Polish Academy of Sciences grant, 1955; Ford Fellowship, 1958; Prix du Meilleur Livre Etranger, France, 1966; Guggenheim Fellowship, 1967; National Book Award, 1969; American Academy of Arts and Letters grant, 1970; John Golden Fellowship in Playwriting, 1970. Lives in New York City.

PUBLICATIONS

Fiction

The Painted Bird.   1965; revised edition, 1970.
Steps.   1968.
Being There.   1971.
The Devil Tree.   1973.
Cockpit.   1975.
Blind Date.   1977.

Other

The Future Is Ours, Comrade.   1960.
No Third Path.   1962.
Notes of the Author on "The Painted Bird" 1965.   1965.
The Art of the Self: Essays à propos "Steps."   1968.
The Time of Life: The Time of Art (essays; in Dutch).   1970.

*   *   *

In Jerzy Kosinski's first novel, *The Painted Bird*, there is an incident that sums up not only the thrust of the novel in which it appears; the incident points to the core of the great variety of experiences that appear in Kosinski's later novels. A peasant catches a raven, paints it with brilliant colors, and releases it to return to its fellows. But the other birds will not accept it and tear it to pieces. This image is a metaphor which expresses the experience of the narrator in the novel, a child of dark aspect ("gypsy" or "Jewish" by turns) who wanders through Poland, deprived of his parents and depending on the ungentle mercies of the peasants he encounters; the peasants, blond and stupid, regard the child as full of evil magic. And the "painted" child learns to survive by duplicity; he endures a solitude that he has not chosen; the only morality he knows is that of survival.

It is a morality which, with appropriate alterations, the central figures of the other novels sense; just so do they define and experience their existences. Such a morality is tested – admired from several angles – in *Steps*, a collection of narrative fragments and mostly unlocalized amorous dialogues. Much of this material is linked with the education and migration to a foreign country of a young man who is, like the child in *The Painted Bird*, on the run, exploited and exploiting wherever he goes. To him every new acquaintance is both an affront and an opportunity.

For a change of pace, the hero of *Being There* is no person displaced by war; rather, he is an orphan without identity, unable to read, skillful only as a gardener. But when he leaves the Eden where he has learned his only skills, his oddity and peculiar vulnerability arouse wonder and respect, rather than antipathy as in *The Painted Bird*. His trivial remarks about gardening are taken as profound and enigmatic insights by those he encounters; business men, TV reporters, and others surround him with an aura of ultimate authority. In *The Devil*

Tree, a young man named Jonathan James Whalen wanders through another landscape of solitude, this one created by his great inherited wealth. There is practically nothing that he cannot purchase and manipulate, and the absolute control he can exercise separates him from other persons as fully as does, for example, the "gypsy" aspect of the child in *The Painted Bird*. Whatever can be purchased can also be thrown away; this is the core of Whalen's experience.

The wanderings presented in *Cockpit* are those of a secret agent named Tarden. Born in a Communist country, he soon learns what *his* precious endowment is: intelligence and guile that surpass the intelligence and guile of all other persons. Every person he meets is a predestined victim whom Tarden can mislead and abuse, all with the intent of showing that Tarden is one "painted bird" whom his hostile peers cannot destroy.

Each of Kosinski's novels is a demonstration of one variety of solipsism. Community of any kind is a figment that misleads inferior imaginations. Each of Kosinski's novels dissolves such illusions. Innocence, wealth, and guile are alternate strategies, but they have a common goal. All confirm that each human being is alone, and those who have a degree of wisdom recognize their solitude and enforce it.

—Harold H. Watts

KUNITZ, Stanley (Jasspon). American. Born in Worcester, Massachusetts, 29 July 1905. Educated at Harvard University, Cambridge, Massachusetts (Garrison Medal, 1926), A.B. (summa cum laude) 1926 (Phi Beta Kappa), A.M. 1927. Served in the United States Army, 1943–45: Staff Sergeant. Married 1) Helen Pearce in 1930 (divorced, 1937), one daughter; 2) Eleanor Evans in 1939 (divorced, 1958); 3) Elise Asher in 1958. Editor, *Wilson Library Bulletin*, New York, 1928–43; Member of the Faculty, Bennington College, Vermont, 1946–59; Professor of English, State University of New York at Potsdam, 1949–50, and Summers 1949–53; Lecturer, and Director of the Poetry Workshop, New School for Social Research, New York, 1950–57; Visiting Professor of Poetry, University of Washington, Seattle, 1955–56; Visiting Professor of English, Queens College, Flushing, New York, 1956–57, and Brandeis University, Waltham, Massachusetts, 1958–59; Director, YM-YWHA Poetry Workshop, New York, 1958–62; Danforth Visiting Lecturer, various American colleges, 1961–63; Fellow, 1969, and Visiting Professor of Poetry, 1970, Yale University, New Haven, Connecticut. Lecturer, 1963–67, and since 1967 Adjunct Professor of Writing, Graduate School of the Arts, Columbia University, New York. Since 1968, Chairman, Writing Department, Fine Arts Work Center, Provincetown, Massachusetts; since 1969, Editor, Yale Series of Younger Poets, Yale University Press. Formerly, Cultural Exchange Lecturer, U.S.S.R. and Poland. Consultant in Poetry, Library of Congress, Washington, D.C., 1974–76. Recipient: Guggenheim Fellowship, 1945; Amy Lowell Traveling Fellowship, 1953; Harriet Monroe Award, 1958; Pulitzer Prize, 1959; Ford Foundation grant, 1959; National Institute of Arts and Letters grant, 1959; Brandeis University Creative Arts Award, 1964; Academy of American Poets Fellowship, 1968; American Academy of Arts and Letters Award of Merit, 1975; Translation Center grant, 1975. Litt.D.: Clark University, Worcester, Massachusetts, 1961. Member, American Academy of Arts and Letters; Chancellor, Academy of American Poets, 1970. Lives in New York City.

PUBLICATIONS

Verse

Intellectual Things. 1930.
Passport to the War: A Selection of Poems. 1944.
Selected Poems 1928–1958. 1958.
The Testing-Tree. 1971.
The Terrible Threshold: Selected Poems, 1940–1970. 1974.

Other

A Kind of Order, A Kind of Folly: Essays and Conversations. 1975.

Editor, *Living Authors: A Book of Biographies.* 1931.
Editor, with Howard Haycraft and Wilbur C. Hadden, *Authors Today and Yesterday: A Companion Volume to "Living Authors".* 1933.
Editor, with others, *The Junior Book of Authors.* 1934; revised edition, 1961.
Editor, with Howard Haycraft, *British Authors of the Nineteenth Century.* 1936.
Editor, with Howard Haycraft, *American Authors, 1600–1900: A Biographical Dictionary of American Literature.* 1938.
Editor, with Howard Haycraft, *Twentieth Century Authors: A Biographical Dictionary of Modern Literature.* 1942; *First Supplement,* with Vineta Colby, 1955.
Editor, with Howard Haycraft, *British Authors Before 1800: A Biographical Dictionary.* 1952.
Editor, *Poems,* by John Keats. 1964.
Editor, with Vineta Colby, *European Authors, 1000–1900: A Biographical Dictionary of European Literature.* 1967.
Editor and Translator, with Max Hayward, *Poems of Akhmatova.* 1973.

Translator, with others, *Antiworlds and the Fifth Ace,* by Andrei Voznesensky. 1967.
Translator, with others, *Stolen Apples,* by Yevgeny Yevtushenko. 1972.
Translator, with others, *Story under Full Sail,* by Andrei Voznesensky. 1974.

Reading List: "The Poetry of Kunitz" by James Hagstrum, in *Poets in Progress,* edited by Edward Hungerford, 1962; *The Comtemporary Poet as Artist and Critic* edited by Anthony Ostroff, 1964; "Man with a Leaf in His Head" by Stanley Moss, in *The Nation,* 20 September 1971.

*   *   *

Stanley Kunitz's *Selected Poems 1928–1958* offers us a good standard of the classic forms and modes of American poetry that largely governed poets of these three decades. Kunitz has more often fought the form imposed on his sometimes extravagant lyrical language than given in to it, and where this creative conflict between a restless content and a rigid, enveloping form is sustained the result has unusual vigor and freshness. The effect is of loosely woven statements held under intense pressure of symmetry and repeated rhythm, as in this nervous, jaggedly expressed love lyric, "Green Ways":

Let me not say it, let me not reveal
How like a god my heart begins to climb
The trellis of the crystal
In the rose-green moon;
Let me not say it, let me leave untold
This legend, while the nights snow emerald.

Let me not say it, let me not confess
How in the leaflight of my green-celled world
In self's pre-history
The blind moulds kiss;
Let me not say it, let me but endure
This ritual like feather and like star.

Let me proclaim it – human be my lot! –
How from my pit of green horse-bones
I turn, in a wilderness of sweat,
To the moon-breasted sibylline,
And lift this garland, Danger, from her throat
To blaze it in the foundries of the night.

But "Green Ways" is the balance that Kunitz has not always been able to strike in his poetry; here passion and form give way to each other, but in some of his work the feeling has been too thoroughly subdued by order and conscious craft, creating a lyric that is too dry and rehearsed in its utterance. But even in the severest of his poems, the reader is aware of the intensity of the poet's mind, the irrepressible energy of his imagination.

Often called the poet's poet, a term he has tended to dismiss more vigorously in later years, Kunitz has himself defended the unruly side of the poetic medium. As editor of the Yale Younger Poets Series, Kunitz has been enthusiastic in his advocacy of a poetry of process and impulsive strategies. In his occasional and critical prose, he has also tended to favor the ungoverned muse: in his essay "A Kind of Order" he says: "With young writers I make a nuisance of myself talking about order, for the good reason that order is teachable; but in my bones I know that only the troubled spirits among them, those who recognize the disorder without and within, have a chance to become poets."

In the strictest balance, however, Kunitz's *Selected Poems* conveys, even it its most rigid formulations of lyric, a stubbornly individual mind that has known all the extremes of feeling and mood. "Night-Piece," "The Man Upstairs" with its Eliotic strain of irony and wit, the poems gathered under the section "The Terrible Threshold" and much else in this collection are provocative and vital.

—Paul Christensen

LA FARGE, Oliver (Hazard Perry). American. Born in New York City, 19 December 1901. Educated at the Groton School, Connecticut, graduated 1920; Harvard University, Cambridge, Massachusetts (Editor, *Harvard Lampoon*; President, *Advocate*; Class Poet), 1920–24, graduated 1924, then did graduate work in anthropology (Hemenway Fellow), M.A. 1929. Served in the United States Army, 1942–46: Lieutenant-Colonel; Legion of

Merit, 1946. Married 1) Wanden E. Mathews in 1929 (divorced), one son and one daughter; 2) Consuelo Otille C. de Baca in 1939, one son. Anthropologist: involved in expeditions for the Peabody Museum, Harvard, in Arizona, 1921, 1922, 1924; Assistant in Ethnology, Department of Middle American Research, Tulane University, New Orleans, 1925–26; involved in research expeditions to Mexico and Guatemala, 1926–28; Research Associate in Ethnology, Columbia University, New York, 1931; Director of the Columbia University expedition to Guatemala, 1932; thereafter a full-time writer and historian. President, Association on American Indian Affairs, 1932–41, 1948. Recipient: Pulitzer Prize, 1930; O. Henry Prize, 1931; Guggenheim Fellowship, 1941. A.M.: Brown University, Providence, Rhode Island, 1932. Fellow, American Association for the Advancement of Science, 1938, American Anthropological Association, 1947, and American Academy of Arts and Sciences, 1953. Member, National Institute of Arts and Letters, 1957. *Died 2 August 1963.*

PUBLICATIONS

Fiction

Laughing Boy. 1929.
Sparks Fly Upward. 1931.
Long Pennant. 1933.
All the Young Men (stories). 1935.
The Enemy Gods. 1937.
The Copper Pot. 1942.
A Pause in the Desert (stories). 1957.
The Door in the Wall (stories). 1965.

Other

Tribes and Temples: A Record of the Expedition to Middle America Conducted in 1925, with Frans Blom. 2 vols., 1926–27.
The Year Bearer's People, with Douglas Byers. 1931.
As Long as the Grass Shall Grow. 1940.
War below Zero: The Battle for Greenland, with B. Balchen and C. Ford. 1944.
Raw Material (autobiography). 1945.
Santa Eulalia: The Religion of the Cuchumatán Indian Town. 1947.
The Eagle in the Egg. 1949.
Cochise of Arizona: The Pipe of Peace Is Broken (juvenile). 1953.
Mother Ditch. 1954.
A Pictorial History of the American Indian. 1956.
Behind the Mountains. 1956.
Santa Fe: The Autobiography of a Southwestern Town, with Arthur N. Morgan. 1959.
American Indian. 1960.
The Man with the Calabash Pipe (essays), edited by Winfield Townley Scott. 1966.

Editor, with Jay Bryan Nash, *The New Day for the Indians.* 1938.
Editor, *The Changing Indian.* 1940.

Translator, *A Man's Place,* by Ramón Sender. 1940.

*   *   *

Of the more than twenty books by Oliver La Farge, nearly half are scientific or historical, and a third are fiction. Yet he is generally known as the author of but one book, his first novel, *Laughing Boy*.

It is not surprising that his histories are virtually unknown. Of those concerning Indians, his most important is *A Pictorial History of the American Indian*, which offers a wealth of material about the various tribes to a public aware of the minority question. Other histories, however – about World War II, the city of Santa Fe, the events of La Farge's own life – are too specialized to be of general interest.

For a similar reason, his scientific work is all but unknown. Not only has the subsequent accumulation of knowledge dwarfed his contributions to ethnology, but as he notes in his personal history, *Raw Material*, the details that absorb the scientist are unlikely to interest more than a handful of fellow scientists. The accounts of expeditions to Central America in which he took part – *Tribes and Temples, The Year Bearer's People, Santa Eulalia* – are highly readable, but too narrowly concerned with the Indian to interest the public for which they were intended.

On the other hand, his second novel, *Sparks Fly Upward*, using the same Indian material, was a best seller. This and *The Enemy Gods*, dealing with the Navajos in the Southwest, reveal the plight of the Indian caught between two cultures. The theme is also explored in a collection of short stories, *All the Young Men*.

With his fifth novel, *The Copper Pot*, La Farge attempted to avoid being typecast as a writer about Indians. This story of an artist in New Orleans is more an affectionate memoir, however, than a novel. Two short story collections, *A Pause in the Desert* and *The Door in the Wall*, use other than Indian material, as does *The Long Pennant*, a novel about the aftermath of piracy by a New England vessel.

Yet it is La Farge's knowledgeable use of Indian material that distinguishes his fiction. A symbiotic relationship exists between the scientific and the creative in his work, the former providing it with substance and originality. Although a first-rate story teller, he exhibits no particularly original turn of mind. He breaks no new ground in his use of language or fictional techniques. As he makes plain in his newspaper columns, collected in *The Man with the Calabash Pipe*, he wished to preserve traditional values, in language and elsewhere – an attitude reflected in his lifelong involvement with the Indian.

This attitude and his unique material are most happily met in his two finest novels, *Laughing Boy* and *The Enemy Gods*. The latter is considered superior, presenting more information and dealing with weightier problems. Yet it is unremittingly melancholy and gray compared with *Laughing Boy*, whose young lovers in an Indian Eden are likely to continue to make it the book by which Oliver La Farge will be known.

—Robert F. Richards

LARDNER, Ring(old Wilmer). American. Born in Niles, Michigan, 6 March 1885. Educated at Niles High School, graduated 1901; Armour Institute of Technology, now Illinois Institute of Technology, Chicago, 1901–02. Married Ellis Abbott in 1911; four sons. Worked as a freight clerk and bookkeeper in Niles, 1902–05; Reporter, *South Bend Times*, Indiana, 1905–07; Sportswriter for *Inter Ocean*, Chicago, 1907, *Chicago Examiner*, 1908, and the *Chicago Tribune*, 1909–10; Editor, *Sporting News*, St. Louis, 1910–11; Sportswriter, *Boston American*, 1911, *Chicago American*, 1911–12, and *Chicago Examiner*, 1912–13; Columnist ("In the Wake of the News"), *Chicago Tribune*, 1913–19; moved to Long Island, New York, 1919; thereafter a writer for the Bell Syndicate; later wrote radio reviews for *The New Yorker*. Died 25 September 1933.

PUBLICATIONS

Collections

The Lardner Reader, edited by Maxwell Geismar.   1963.

Fiction

You Know Me Al: A Busher's Letters.   1916.
Gullible's Travels (stories).   1917.
Own Your Own Home.   1919.
The Real Dope.   1919.
The Big Town.   1921.
How to Write Short Stories (with Samples).   1924.
The Love Nest and Other Stories.   1926.
Round Up: The Stories.   1929; as Collected Short Stories, 1941.
First and Last.   1934.
Some Champions: Sketches and Fiction, edited by Matthew J. Bruccoli and Richard
   Layman.   1976.

Plays

Zanzibar, music and lyrics by Harry Schmidt (produced 1903).   1903.
Elmer the Great (produced 1928).
June Moon, with George S. Kaufman (produced 1929).   1930.

Screenplay: The New Klondike, with Tom Geraghty, 1926.

Verse

Bib Ballads.   1915.

Other

My Four Weeks in France.   1918.
Treat 'Em Rough: Letters from Jack the Kaiser Killer.   1918.
Regular Fellows I Have Met.   1919.
The Young Immigrunts.   1920.
Symptoms of Being 35.   1921.
Say It with Oil: A Few Remarks about Wives, with Say It with Bricks: A Few Remarks
   about Husbands, by Nina Wilcox Putnam.   1923.
What of It?   1925.
The Story of a Wonder Man.   1927.
Lose with a Smile.   1933.
Ring Around Max: The Correspondence of Lardner and Max Perkins, edited by Clifford
   M. Caruthers.   1973.

Editor, with Edward G. Heeman, March 6th, 1914: The Home Coming of Charles A.
   Comisky, John J. McGraw, James J. Callahan.   1914.

Bibliography: *Lardner: A Descriptive Bibliography* by Matthew J. Bruccoli and Richard Layman, 1977.

Reading List: *Lardner* by Donald Elder, 1956; *Lardner* by Walton R. Patrick, 1963; *Lardner* by Otto A. Friedrich, 1965; *Ring: A Biography of Lardner* by Jonathan Yardley, 1977.

*   *   *

Ring Lardner wrote in the tradition of a long line of American popular journalists and humourists who exploited slang and the illiteracies of vernacular speech for comic ends. In doing so, he transmuted what was initially a stock comic device into something much more, an instrument of satire. At the same time, he was, however unwittingly, one of those writers, of whom Mark Twain is the great exemplar, whose sensitivity to the value of the spoken word helped to liberate American prose from the artificial diction that marked so much nineteenth-century writing.

Beginning as a sports writer on an Indiana paper, in 1913 he took over the "In the Wake of the News" column in the *Chicago Tribune*. The Jack Keefe letters were meanwhile appearing in magazines, purporting to be written by an oafish, semi-literate baseball player who through his own words all-unconsciously exposes himself in all his obnoxiousness. Published as an epistolary novel, *You Know Me Al*, they brought him the attention of a wider public, and *How to Write Short Stories*, the title of which has been seen as typical of his inability to believe that he was a serious writer, brought critical acclaim. Edmund Wilson, for example, commenting on the discrepancy between the matter of the book and the jokey way in which it was presented, wrote, "what one finds in *How to Write Short Stories* is a series of studies of American types almost equal in importance to those of Sherwood Anderson and Sinclair Lewis."

Among the stories appearing in the volume were "Some Like Them Cold," an exchange of letters wonderfully funny in their dead-pan way between an aspiring popular song-writer on the make in New York City and a girl he has met by chance in the LaSalle Street railway station in Chicago, and "The Golden Honeymoon," in which an elderly middle-class American, from Trenton, New Jersey, father-in-law of "John H. Kramer, the real estate man," recounts the holiday he and his wife spent in Florida to celebrate their golden wedding.

These stories illustrate two things. The first is that Lardner, as Wilson pointed out in his *Dial* review, had "an unexcelled, a perhaps unrivalled, mastery" of the American language, that he knew equally well the language of the popular-song writer and the "whole vocabulary of adolescent clichés of the middle-aged man from New Jersey," and that he understood the difference between the spoken language of these types and the language they used for writing. The other thing is that, as all his critics have pointed out, Lardner's is nothing if not a reductive art. His characters expose themselves unerringly in their speech and letters in all the grossness of their complacency and self-regard. No element of affection or compassion is allowed to creep into their delineation. It measures the difference between Lardner's art and Sinclair Lewis's on the one hand and Sherwood Anderson's on the other.

In other words, Lardner was essentially a satirist, and increasingly since his death he has been seen as one of the major American satirists. In this respect he has, perhaps, been over-rated. In his 1924 review Edmund Wilson, who had put Lardner forward as in some sense a latter-day Mark Twain, asked: "Will Ring Lardner then, go on to his *Huckleberry Finn* or has he already told all he knows?" The appearance of *The Love Nest and Other Stories* two years later, though it contained the merciless "Haircut," showed in effect that he had already told us all he knew. Admirable as his satire is, it seems time once again to emphasise the part he played in the liberation of American prose by bringing back into it the rhythms of native speech.

—Walter Allen

LAURENTS, Arthur. American. Born in Brooklyn, New York, 14 July 1918. Educated at Cornell University, Ithaca, New York, B.A. 1937. Served in the United States Army, rising to the rank of Sergeant, 1940–45: Radio Playwright, 1943–45 (Citation, Secretary of War, 1945). Director, Dramatists Play Service, New York, 1961–66. Since 1955, Member of the Council of the Dramatists Guild. Recipient: National Institute of Arts and Letters grant, 1946; Sidney Howard Memorial Award, 1946; Antoinette Perry Award, 1967. Lives on Long Island, New York.

PUBLICATIONS

Plays

> *Now Playing Tomorrow* (broadcast 1939).   In *Short Plays for Stage and Radio,* edited by Carless Jones, 1939.
> *Western Electric Communicade* (broadcast 1944).   In *The Best One-Act Plays of 1944,* edited by Margaret Mayorga, 1944.
> *The Last Day of the War* (broadcast 1945).   In *Radio Drama in Action,* edited by Erik Barnouw, 1945.
> *The Face* (broadcast 1945). · In *The Best One-Act Plays of 1945,* edited by Margaret Mayorga, 1945.
> *Home of the Brave* (produced 1945; as *The Way Back,* produced 1946).   1946.
> *Heartsong* (produced 1947).
> *The Bird Cage* (produced 1950).   1950.
> *The Time of the Cuckoo* (produced 1952).   1953.
> *A Clearing in the Woods* (produced 1957).   1957.
> *West Side Story,* music by Leonard Bernstein (produced 1957).   1958.
> *Gypsy,* music by Jule Styne, lyrics by Stephen Sondheim, from a book by Gypsy Rose Lee (produced 1959).   1960.
> *Invitation to a March* (produced 1960).   1961.
> *Anyone Can Whistle,* music by Stephen Sondheim (produced 1964).   1965.
> *Do I Hear a Waltz?,* music by Richard Rodgers, lyrics by Stephen Sondheim (produced 1965).   1966.
> *Hallelujah, Baby!,* music and lyrics by Jule Styne, Betty Comden and Adolph Green (produced 1967).   1967.
> *The Enclave* (produced 1973).   1974.

Screenplays: *The Snake Pit*, with Frank Partos and Millen Brand, 1948; *Rope*, with Hume Cronyn, 1948; *Anna Lucasta*, with Philip Yordan, 1949; *Caught*, 1949; *Anastasia*, 1956; *Bonjour Tristesse*, 1958; *The Way We Were*, 1973; *The Turning Point*, 1977.

Radio Plays: *Now Playing Tomorrow*, 1939; *Hollywood Playhouse, Dr. Christian, The Thin Man, Manhattan at Midnight*, and other series, 1939–40; *The Last Day of the War, The Face, Western Electric Communicade*, 1944, and other plays for *The Man Behind the Gun, Army Service Force Presents* and *Assignment Home* series, 1943–45; *This Is Your FBI* series, 1945.

Fiction

The Way We Were. 1972.

* * *

Brooklyn-born, Hollywood-bred, Arthur Laurents is best known for his work in the two most successful American art forms, the Broadway musical and the Hollywood film.

His films include *Caught* and *The Snake Pit* and versions of two of his stage plays, *Home of the Brave* and *Time of the Cuckoo* (filmed as *Summertime*). All tend to prove Samuel Beckett's thesis: "We are all born mad. Some remain so." Psychology, especially self-realization, is Laurents's major interest and it runs through all of his serious work, even getting into musicals.

His musicals are *West Side Story* (*Romeo and Juliet* updated), *Gypsy* (based on the life of stripper Gypsy Rose Lee), *Do I Hear a Waltz?* and *Hallelujah, Baby!* These musicals show all the inventiveness and commercial savvy one would expect from a writer whose work ranges from adapting Marcel Maurette's TV play *Anastasia* for Ingrid Bergman's return to the screen to a modern version of the Sleeping Beauty legend in which the heroine refuses to tread boring conventional paths and takes off with a plumber (*Invitation to a March*). Laurents attempted to make Broadway musicals in some way more serious. He didn't always succeed. As Walter Kerr put it in *Thirty Plays Hath November*, "if a musical is going to be as serious as *Do I Hear a Waltz?* it has got to be more serious than *Do I Hear a Waltz?* ... Half measures taken toward sobriety tend to leave us all halfhearted, torn between an elusive passion on the one hand and a lost playfulness on the other." Shall we settle for the *ersatz*, typically Broadway idea of the serious (especially in diversions such as *A Chorus Line*) and not strive for reality?

Laurents's plays do make a serious effort at seriousness: in a sense they are religious, if psychology is the New Religion. In *The Bird Cage* downtrodden employees of a dictatorial employer fly their nightclub cage. We sense Symbolism and are tempted to ask, like the psychoanalyst greeted with a "hello" in the street: What Does That *Mean*? In *A Clearing in the Woods* a woman yearns "to rise in the air just a little, to climb, to reach a branch, even the lowest" and this bird learns to accept herself as "an imperfect human being," thus escaping the cage of her past. If Tom Driver is right (in *Romantic Quest and Modern Theory*, 1970) that in *West Side Story* "adult authority does not exist ... [and] there is more 'order' in the improvised life of the young than in public institutions," can it be that Laurents, for all his interest in psychology, is telling us in *A Clearing in the Woods* that we should avoid all the psychiatrists who want to adjust us, and achieve "mental health" just by learning to be happy with our craziness, accepting ourselves as "imperfect human beings"? In *Home of the Brave* (which Kenneth Tynan found pat but promising), an Army shrink copes with Coney, a soldier who learns that though he is Jewish he is just another "imperfect human being" like Mingo and everyone else who is secretly glad that it was The Other Guy who got killed, regardless of race, color, or creed. In *Time of the Cuckoo* the uptight New England spinster

Leona Samish has to work out for herself the appropriate reactions to a brief encounter in Venice with a dashing (but married) Italian. Predictably, "those louses/Go back to their spouses" (as *Diamonds Are a Girl's Best Friend* teaches) and Ms. Samish realizes, reviewing her Puritan Code, that he wasn't such a nice man, after all. This psychologizing may not be as broad as a barn door, nor so deep as a well, but it will serve in the theatre, where Thornton Wilder once got away with summing up all of Freud in a single sentence: "We're all just as wicked as we can be." Well, not wicked, imperfect.

In 1960, Henry Hewes introducing *Famous American Plays of the 1940's* wrote about Laurents:

> In form it is the sort of play that has become an increasingly popular stereotype for American drama. Someone in trouble reviews the reasons for his trouble to find something he has not been facing up to. Because Mr. Laurents introduced the psychiatrist himself and had the answer up his sleeve all the time, some critics found the play too clinical. However, *Home of the Brave* contains the driving theme which seems to motivate most of this young writer's work. It is the acceptance of our imperfections in a society where everyone expects the ideal.

That is a nice, comforting thought! And we can go to movies and musicals and enjoy ourselves and rest very content with our human, albeit imperfect, selves.

—Leonard R. N. Ashley

LAWSON, John Howard. American. Born in New York City, 25 September 1894. Educated at Yonkers High School, New York; Cutler School, New York, graduated 1910; Williams College, Williamstown, Massachusetts, 1910–14, B.A. 1914. Served in the American Ambulance Service in France and Italy during World War I. Married 1) Kathryn Drain in 1919 (divorced, 1923), one son; 2) Susan Edmond in 1925, one son and one daughter. Cable Editor, Reuters Press, New York, 1914–15; lived in Paris for two years after the war; a Director, New Playwrights Theatre, New York, 1927–28; film writer in Hollywood, 1928–47. Member of the Council of the Authors League of America, 1930–40; Founding President, 1933–34, and Member of the Executive Board, 1933–40, Screen Writers Guild. One of the "Hollywood Ten": served a one-year sentence for contempt of the House Un-American Activities Committee, 1950–51. *Died 11 August 1977.*

PUBLICATIONS

Plays

    Servant-Master-Lover (produced 1916).
    Standards (produced 1916).
    Roger Bloomer (produced 1923). 1923.
    Processional: A Jazz Symphony of American Life (produced 1925). 1925.
    Nirvana (produced 1926).
    Loudspeaker (produced 1927). 1927.
    The International (produced 1928). 1928.
    Success Story (produced 1932). 1932.

The Pure in Heart (produced 1934).   In *With a Reckless Preface,* 1934.
Gentlewoman (produced 1934).   In *With a Reckless Preface,* 1934.
With a Reckless Preface: Two Plays.   1934.
Marching Song (produced 1937).   1937.
Algiers (screenplay), with James M. Cain, in *Foremost Films of 1938,* edited by Frank
    Vreeland.   1939.
Parlor Magic (produced 1963).

Screenplays: *Dream of Love,* with others, 1928; *The Pagan,* with Dorothy Farnum,
1929; *Dynamite,* with Jeanie Macpherson and Gladys Unger, 1929; *The Sea Bat,* with
others, 1930; *Our Blushing Brides,* with Bess Meredyth and Helen Mainard, 1930; *The
Ship from Shanghai,* 1930; *Bachelor Apartment,* 1931; *Success at Any Price,* with
others, 1934; *Blockade,* 1938; *Algiers,* with James M. Cain, 1938; *They Shall Have
Music,* with Irmgard Von Cube, 1939; *Four Sons,* with Milton Sperling, 1940;
Earthbound, with Samuel C. Engel, 1940; *Sahara,* with others, 1943; *Action in the
North Atlantic,* with others, 1943; *Counter-Attack,* 1945; *Smashup – The Story of a
Woman,* with others, 1947.

Other

Theory and Technique of Playwriting.   1936; revised edition, as *Theory and Technique
    of Playwriting and Screenwriting,* 1949.
*The Hidden Heritage: A Rediscovery of the Ideas and Forces That Link the Thought of
    Our Time with the Culture of the Past.*   1950.
Film in the Battle of Ideas.   1953.
*Film: The Creative Process: The Search for an Audio-Visual Language and
    Structure.*   1964; revised edition, 1967.

*   *   *

John Howard Lawson was one of the "Hollywood Ten" who went to jail rather than tell
the House Un-American Activities Committee about their Marxist views. HUAC need not
have asked. They could have read his plays or seen his movies. Whether he belonged to the
Communist Party or not is basically none of our business. That his work is imbued with
Marxism and that he is characteristic of a period in which (as the Garment Workers' musical
Pins and Needles put it) many sang "Sing Me a Song of Social Significance," is abundantly
clear. In his time, it gave him strength. Now it makes all but a few of his film works look
impossibly dated.
  Servant-Master-Lover, Standards, and *Roger Bloomer* gave him his start, and with
Processional his left-wing sympathies were expressed in the story of "the West Virginia coal
fields during a strike" told in "this new technique ... essentially vaudevillesque in character."
The theory is adumbrated in a Preface (more of his interesting ideas appear in prefactory
material to *The Pure in Heart* and *Gentlewoman* and in the excellent textbook *Theory and
Technique of Playwriting*) and illustrated in a series of scenes which recall the Living
Newspaper of the depression, the propaganda techniques of agitprop, and other attempts at
"an immediate emotional response across the footlights." All the force and all the faults of the
left-wing theatre tracts of the 1920's and 1930's, "the fervent years" (as Harold Clurman calls
them), are here: the party-line dogmatism and narrow vision; the confusion of tragedy and
pathos; the axe-to-grind earnestness, where comedy (and everything else that relates to a
sense of proportion) perishes; and so on, down to the stereotyped characters: Cohen the
Jewish comedian, Rastus the minstrel clown, the hard-boiled Sheriff, the city-slicker
newspaperman Phillpots, the woman called Mrs. Euphemia Stewart Flimmins, even a Man
in a Silk Hat.

George Abbott played Dynamite Jim in *Processional*, but only in the last act did he soar for a moment above what Stark Young called "antagonisms, bad taste and crass thinking." The critics thought it basically an amateur play "conceived with varying degrees of taste, intelligence, insight and imagination." When it is good it is very, very good – Stark Young risked "streaked with genius" – and when it is bad it's as foolish as Odets without his primitive charm. It is not that the characters are unrealistic – "Mr. Lawson," reported Watson and Pressey in *Contemporary Drama,* "says that he can find vaudeville characters on every street corner, whereas the so-called realistic characters he sees on the stage he never meets in life" – but that the politics distort the truth.

Processional was produced by the Theatre Guild and ran 96 performances in 1925 and 81 more when The Federal Theatre revived it in 1937. Today it would not run any more than would *Nirvana, Loudspeaker, The International* (a musical), *Success Story, Marching Song,* or other Lawson efforts. "All great art and literature," boomed Shaw, "is propaganda," but that does not mean that all propaganda is great art.

Some of Lawson's films have survived better. Very typical are, say, *Blockade* and *Smashup.* The cinema was more congenial to Lawson's talents, though *Theory and Technique of Playwriting* amply demonstrates that, as Théophile Gautier said of drama critics and eunuchs in harems, those who see it done every night may know all about it but be quite unable to do it themselves.

—Leonard R. N. Ashley

LEVERTOV, Denise. American. Born in Ilford, Essex, England, 24 October 1923; emigrated to the United States, 1948; naturalized, 1955. Educated privately. Married the writer Mitchell Goodman in 1947; one son. Poetry Editor, *The Nation,* New York, 1961; taught at the YM-YWHA Poetry Center, New York, 1964; Honorary Scholar, Radcliffe Institute for Independent Study, Cambridge, Massachusetts, 1964–66; Visiting Lecturer, City College of New York, 1965; Drew University, Madison, New Jersey, 1965; Vassar College, Poughkeepsie, New York, 1966–67, and University of California, Berkeley, 1969; Visiting Professor, Massachusetts Institute of Technology, Cambridge, 1969–70; Artist-in-Residence, Kirkland College, 1970–71; Elliston Lecturer, University of Cincinnati, Spring 1973. Visiting Professor, 1973–74, 1974–75, and since 1975 Professor, Tufts University, Medford, Massachusetts. Recipient: Longview Award, 1961; Guggenheim Fellowship, 1962; National Institute of Arts and Letters grant, 1966, 1968; Lenore Marshall Prize, 1976. D.Litt.: Colby College, Waterville, Maine, 1970; University of Cincinnati, 1973. Lives in New York City.

PUBLICATIONS

Verse

The Double Image. 1946.
Here and Now. 1957.

Overland to the Islands. 1958.
5 Poems. 1958.
With Eyes at the Back of Our Heads. 1959.
The Jacob's Ladder. 1961.
O Taste and See: New Poems. 1964.
City Psalm. 1964.
Psalm Concerning the Castle. 1966.
The Sorrow Dance. 1967.
Three Poems. 1968.
A Tree Telling of Orpheus. 1968.
The Cold Spring and Other Poems. 1968.
A Marigold from North Vietnam. 1968.
Embroideries. 1969.
Relearning the Alphabet. 1970.
Summer Poems 1969. 1970.
A New Year's Garland for My Students, MIT 1969–70. 1970.
To Stay Alive. 1971.
Footprints. 1972.
The Freeing of the Dust. 1975.

Fiction

In the Night: A Story. 1968.

Other

The Poet in the World (essays). 1973.
Conversation in Moscow. 1973.

Editor, *Out of the War Shadow: An Anthology of Current Poetry.* 1967.
Editor and Translator, with Edward C. Dimock, Jr., *In Praise of Krishna: Songs from the Bengali.* 1967.

Translator, *Selected Poems of Guillevic.* 1969.

Bibliography: *A Bibliography of Levertov* by Robert A. Wilson, 1972.

Reading List: *Levertov* by Linda Wagner, 1967.

*   *   *

By her own admission, Denise Levertov began writing as a "British Romantic with almost Victorian background" and has since become one of the powerful probing voices of contemporary American poetry. Her outspoken advocacy of women's liberation, her opposition to the Vietnam War, her adherence generally to the values of the political left came about through the gradual transformations of awareness since publishing *Here and Now* in 1957.

Raised and educated in a literary household in England, she published a first book of poems, *The Double Image*, in 1946. In 1948 she emigrated to the United States with her American husband, the novelist Mitchell Goodman, whose friendship with Robert Creeley led to her association with the Black Mountain movement and the journal *Origin*, which began publishing her work. Her early poems show the influence of Williams and Olson in their diction and form, but by the middle of the 1950's, Robert Duncan encouraged her to experiment more boldly with mythic perception of her identity and circumstances. She has since explained her own poetic in the essay "Organic Form," which distinguishes between a free verse of disjointed statements and organic poetry, where "form," all facets of technique, is "a revelation of content." But her poems retain traditional verse conventions, and she has occasionally attacked the improvisatory mode of other poets.

In her first substantial work, *With Eyes at the Back of Our Heads*, her poems moved to frank self-disclosures, in an effort to grasp a personal identity underlying sexual stereotype. In "The Goddess," one of the finest poems of the volume, she dramatizes her awakening to an inner nature after her expulsion from "Lie Castle," where she has been flung

> across the room, and
> room after room (hitting the walls, re-
> bounding — to the last
> sticky wall — wrenching away from it
> pulling hair out!)
> til it lay
> outside the outer walls!
>
> There in the cold air
> lying still where her hand had thrown me,
> I tasted the mud that splattered my lips
> the seeds of a forest were in it,
> asleep and growing! I tasted
> her power!

O Taste and See pursues the implications of "The Goddess" by boldly reaching into the feminine psyche to discover its raw vitality, as in this startling image of appetite:

> In the black of desire
> we rock and grunt, grunt and
> shine

Beginning with *Relearning the Alphabet*, she has moved beyond purely personal issues to larger political concerns, war resistance, women's liberation, poverty and oppression in the Third World. The poems of *To Stay Alive* and *Footprints*, many taking a longer, serial form, follow her increasingly activist participation in various resistance movements of the last two decades.

—Paul Christensen

LEWIS, (Harry) Sinclair.   American.   Born in Sauk Center, Minnesota, 7 February 1885. Educated at Sauk Center High School; Oberlin Academy, Ohio, 1902–03; Yale University, New Haven, Connecticut (Editor, *Yale Literary Magazine*), 1903–06, 1907–08, A.B. 1908. Married 1) Grace Livingston Hegger in 1914 (divorced, 1925), one son; 2) the columnist Dorothy Thompson in 1928 (divorced, 1942), one son. Worked as a janitor in Upton Sinclair's socialist community at Helicon Hall, Englewood, New Jersey, 1906–07; Assistant Editor, *Transatlantic Tales*, New York, 1907; successively, reporter on a newspaper in

Waterloo, Iowa, promoter for a charity organization in New York, secretary to Alice MacGowan and Grace MacGowan Cook in Carmel, California, writer for the Associated Press and the *Bulletin* in San Francisco, Assistant Editor of the *Volta Review* in Washington, D.C., and, in New York, manuscript reader for the publishers Frederick A. Stokes, Assistant Editor of *Adventure*, Editor for the Publishers' Newspaper Syndicate, and Editor for the George H. Doran Company, 1908–16; full-time writer from 1916; reported the Viennese Revolution for the New York *Evening Post* and Philadelphia *Ledger*, 1918. Recipient: Pulitzer Prize, 1926 (refused); Nobel Prize for Literature, 1930. Litt.D.: Yale University, 1936. Member, American Academy of Arts and Letters, 1938. Lived in Vermont and, in later years, in Europe. *Died 10 January 1951.*

PUBLICATIONS

Collections

> *The Man from Main Street: Selected Essays and Other Writings 1904–1950,* edited by Harry E. Maule and Melville H. Cane. 1953.

Fiction

> *Hike and the Aeroplane* (juvenile). 1912.
> *Our Mr. Wrenn.* 1914.
> *The Trail of the Hawk.* 1915.
> *The Job.* 1917.
> *The Innocents.* 1917.
> *Free Air.* 1919.
> *Main Street.* 1920.
> *Babbitt.* 1922.
> *Arrowsmith.* 1925; as *Martin Arrowsmith*, 1925; edited by Barbara G. Spayd, 1933.
> *Mantrap.* 1926.
> *Elmer Gantry.* 1927.
> *The Man Who Knew Coolidge.* 1928.
> *Dodsworth.* 1929.
> *Ann Vickers.* 1933.
> *Work of Art.* 1934.
> *Selected Short Stories.* 1935.
> *It Can't Happen Here.* 1935.
> *The Prodigal Parents.* 1938.
> *Bethel Merriday.* 1940.
> *Gideon Planish.* 1943.
> *Cass Timberlane.* 1945.
> *Kingsblood Royal.* 1947.
> *The God-Seeker.* 1949.
> *World So Wide.* 1951.

Plays

> *Hobohemia* (produced 1919).
> *Jayhawker,* with Lloyd Lewis (produced 1934). 1935.

It Can't Happen Here, from his own novel (produced 1936).   1938.
Storm in the West (screenplay), with Dore Schary.   1963.

Other

John Dos Passos' "Manhattan Transfer."   1926.
Cheap and Contented Labor: The Picture of a Southern Mill Town in 1929.   1929.
From Main Street to Stockholm: Letters of Lewis 1919–1930, edited by Harrison Smith.
1952.

Bibliography: *A Lewis Checklist* by James Lundquist, 1970.

Reading List: *Lewis: An American Life,* 1961 (includes bibliography), and *Lewis,* 1963, both
by Mark Schorer; *Lewis* by Sheldon Norman Grebstein, 1962; *Dorothy and Red* by Vincent
Sheean, 1963; *The Art of Lewis* by D. J. Dooley, 1967; *The Quixotic Vision of Lewis* by
Martin Light, 1974.

*   *   *

Sinclair Lewis, the first American Nobel Laureate in Literature, was recognized with
justice by the Nobel Prize committee for the accuracy and the detail with which he portrayed
American life. He applied the concepts of critical realism as they had been developed in the
nineteenth century to the subject of the American midwest, and, using a gift for satiric
caricature and a remarkable skill at mimicry, created a vivid picture of middle-class America
and its values, ideals, and assumptions in the early twentieth century. He portrayed with
devastating satiric power and sardonic force the lack of beauty, dignity, and value in
America's materialistic culture. Lewis, although he was hailed in his own day as the
spokesman of a new literary movement, was actually a culmination of the movement of
critical realism which had begun in the decades immediately after the Civil War. He came as
the summarizing expression of moods and methods typical of the midwestern "revolt from
the village" that had produced such writers as Hamlin Garland, E. W. Howe, and Edgar Lee
Masters. Like many other midwest writers, Lewis moved from the West to the East – in his
case from Minnesota to Connecticut and New York – and then used the land of his childhood
as his chief subject and often his principal target.

Between 1914 and 1920 he published five novels, the best being *The Job* and *Free Air,* and
a number of short stories in popular periodicals. Critical hindsight now shows us that these
early works, although clearly in the tradition of the popular fiction of their time, also
adumbrated in theme, treatment, and character the major work which was to come. In 1920
he published *Main Street,* a corruscating picture of the dullness, drabness, conformity, and
materialism of a small, midwestern town. With it his career was brilliantly launched to the
acclaim of the nation and the world. He followed it with *Babbitt,* a portrayal of a petit-
bourgeois businessman in a middle-sized midwestern city, a weak man who vainly attempts
to break out of the pattern of conformity which shapes his days and to understand himself
and achieve his own freedom. This plot pattern was to be recurrent in most of Lewis's work.
Babbitt, perhaps his most satisfactory single work, was the first of a long series of novels each
of which examined a specific business or profession. After publishing it, he started collecting
material for a novel on the labor movement, but that book was never written. *Arrowsmith,*
written with the aid of the biologist Paul DeKruif, and in its own time regarded by many as
his finest single piece of work, studied the profession of medicine and contrasted it with the
idealized view of scientific research. Lewis pointed his satiric guns at the Protestant ministry
in *Elmer Gantry,* a howling comedy of extravagant and slashing satire; and he
sympathetically portrayed the American businessman abroad and satirized the cultural

pretensions of his wife in *Dodsworth*. This novel begins Lewis's significant shift from the harsh treatment of his middle-class American subjects to a steadily growing sympathy for them.

In 1930, he received the Nobel Prize for literature and in his acceptance speech attacked Howells, whose critical movement he was himself the product of, and praised a group of young writers, such as Thomas Wolfe and Ernest Hemingway, who were soon to be important in advancing novelistic innovations that quickly dated his own work. In the 1920's Lewis had defined America, or at least important aspects of it, for itself and had produced vital, lively, original, and important satiric portraits of America's middle-class failings. The Nobel Prize came as the crowning accolade on one of the major accomplishments in the social novel which any American has ever achieved. But it came when that accomplishment was virtually complete. For following 1930, Lewis's career seems almost to be a search for subject matter.

In *Ann Vickers*, a book much influenced by his admiration for and exasperation with his second wife, the famous journalist Dorothy Thompson, Lewis examined the career woman, but with clearly mixed feelings. He examined the hotel industry in *Work of Art*, the first of his "major" works which was, as Mark Schorer declared, "completely without distinction." *It Can't Happen Here* re-established an important position for him with the American public. This study of the potentiality for American fascism seemed to be a political warning that spoke directly and responsibly to major issues in American life. Today, however, it seems thin and surprisingly conservative. That Lewis was indeed becoming increasingly conservative despite his attacks upon fascism was evident in *Prodigal Parents*, a book about radical and irresponsible children, in which he draws what is almost a comic strip view of communism. Its protagonist, Fred Cornplow, whom Lewis admires, is essentially the same middle-class businessman he had earlier satirized as Babbitt and the denizens of *Main Street*. *Bethel Merriday* is the story of the education of a young actress in summer stock and touring companies. It is embarrassingly sentimental. *Gideon Planish* is an attack on organized philanthrophy. More like *Elmer Gantry* than any book Lewis had written since 1927, it is angry and intemperate, an example of slashing satire and violent comedy; yet it is so overdrawn that it seems almost a parody of Lewis's earlier work. *Cass Timberlane* is an account of American marriage. *Kingsblood Royal* takes up the issue of race in a mechanical and unconvincing parable. *The God-Seeker* is a historical novel laid in Minnesota in the days of its early settlement. Although it can be considered the first novel in an unfinished panel of labor books, it is too much like costume romance to be taken seriously. In *World So Wide*, published posthumously in 1951, the year of his death, Lewis returns to the theme of the American in Europe in a book which is virtually a rewriting of *Dodsworth*, though now the satiric edge is gone, and the European culture that he once supported has become the target of his attack. The characters in this last sad work seemed, as Malcolm Cowley said, "survivors from a vanished world."

Sinclair Lewis's work fall easily into three periods – the early apprenticeship work, followed by the great accomplishment of the 1920's in which in five novels he gives a vigorous and emphatic picture of his world, followed by a long, sad, groping toward suitable subjects. Few American writers have had a greater impact on their world than Lewis during his ten great years, 1920–29. As Mark Schorer said, "He gave us a vigorous, perhaps unique thrust into the imagination of ourselves." But after this great success he was increasingly removed from the materials which were his primary subject matter, and he wrote out of memory rather than direct experience, so that his later novels were increasingly the memorials to a world and an age that was past. He was a very good social novelist but not a truly great writer. Nevertheless, it was appropriate that the first American Nobel Laureate in Literature should have been a man intimately committed to using literature to portray his fellow countrymen and to instruct them through satiric portraiture.

—C. Hugh Holman

LINDSAY, (Nicholas) Vachel. American. Born in Springfield, Illinois, 10 November 1879. Educated at Hiram College, Ohio, 1897–1900; studied for the ministry; studied art at the Chicago Art Institute, 1901, and New York Art School, 1905. Married Elizabeth Conner in 1925; one son, one daughter. Pen and ink designer, 1900–10; lecturer on the history of art, 1905–10; also travelled through the U.S. living by reciting his poems, 1906–12; after 1912 became known for his verses and was thereafter in demand as lecturer and reader. Taught at Gulf Park College, Mississippi, 1923–24. Litt.D.: Hiram College, 1930. Member, National Institute of Arts and Letters. *Died* (by suicide) *5 December 1931.*

PUBLICATIONS

Collections

> *Selected Poems,* edited by Mark Harris.   1963.

Verse

> *The Tramp's Excuse and Other Poems.*   1909.
> *Rhymes to Be Traded for Bread.*   1912.
> *General William Booth Enters into Heaven and Other Poems.*   1913.
> *The Congo and Other Poems.*   1914.
> *The Chinese Nightingale and Other Poems.*   1917.
> *The Golden Whales of California and Other Rhymes in the American Language.*   1920.
> *The Daniel Jazz and Other Poems.*   1920.
> *Going-to-the-Sun.*   1923.
> *Collected Poems.*   1923; revised edition, 1925.
> *Going-to-the-Stars.*   1926.
> *The Candle in the Cabin: A Weaving Together of Script and Singing.*   1926.
> *Johnny Appleseed and Other Poems* (juvenile).   1928.
> *Every Soul Is a Circus.*   1929.
> *Selected Poems,* edited by Hazelton Spencer.   1931.

Other

> *The Village Magazine.*   1910.
> *Adventures While Preaching the Gospel of Beauty.*   1914.
> *The Art of the Moving Picture.*   1915; revised edition, 1922.
> *A Handy Guide for Beggars, Especially Those of the Poetic Fraternity.*   1916.
> *The Golden Book of Springfield, Being a Review of a Book That Will Appear in 2018.*   1920.
> *The Litany of Washington Street* (miscellany).   1929.
> *Letters to A. Joseph Armstrong,* edited by Armstrong.   1940.

Reading List: *Lindsay: A Poet in America* by Edgar Lee Masters, 1935; *The West-Going Heart: A Life of Lindsay* by Eleanor Ruggles, 1959; *Lindsay* by Raymond Purkey, 1968; *Lindsay: Fieldworker for the American Dream* by Ann Massa, 1970.

*   *   *

Vachel Lindsay was a man out of phase with his time. He was also a writer who had the misfortune to be judged solely on the basis of his poetry, even though he produced a sizeable corpus of prose, work which he felt to be ultimately more important than his poetry. While it is true that he has recently begun to receive the critical appreciation and intepretation he deserves, it is equally true that he is still considered by many to be a writer (and reciter) of verse – a 20th-century troubadour who toured the country reciting his poems to hugely enthusiastic audiences, a propagandist for America whose exhortations were clothed in bombast, naivety, sentimentality, and theatrics, a phenomenon whose time had already come and gone. His role as social critic was unrecognized and such prose works as *Adventures While Preaching the Gospel of Beauty*, *The Art of the Moving Picture*, *A Handy Guide for Beggars*, and *The Golden Book of Springfield* were virtually ignored.

Lindsay's early books of verse, *General William Booth Enters into Heaven and Other Poems* and *The Congo and Other Poems*, established his reputation as a herald of the New Poetry. They mark a dramatic break with the genteel, derivative verse that then dominated the American literary scene, while marking a continuity with the Whitmanesque mode. His best poems ring with genuine music and vibrate with energy, and Lindsay's theatrical recitation of them established his reputation as an entertainer. But the latter reputation eclipsed the former and clung to him throughout the remainder of his life. His problem was two-fold: his superb qualities as an entertainer and the public's refusal to accept his definition of the role of the poet.

Lindsay felt poetry should serve the masses; that art for art's sake had no place on the American scene; that elitism in poetry was a negative and destructive force; and that Americans had to be awakened to the fact that they were allowing their country's true destiny to slip away. Lindsay considered his poetry to be the best means by which he could jolt the people into an awareness of what was happening; when they were made aware of it they would then fall in line behind him and join his efforts to recapture and restore to America its original promise.

But Lindsay's vision of America was not the vision of the American majority. Moreover, his pessimism and fundamentalist viewpoint (both of America's problems and of the solutions to them) were anathema to political, social, and literary arbiters of the day. And finally, since Lindsay believed poetry to be a social as opposed to artistic instrument (content should take precedence over style), he was not part of the imagist movement which influenced the course of 20th-century American poetry from his day to the present.

Lindsay never recovered from the realization that the people wanted only entertainment from him and that his crusade for "religion, equality and beauty," his "gospel," was doomed. He died by his own hand, a bitter and psychotic man, "Staking his last strength and his final fight/That cost him all, to set the old world right" ("Litany of the Heroes").

—Catherine Seelye

LOCKRIDGE, Ross. American. Born in Bloomington, Indiana, 25 April 1914. Educated at Indiana University, Bloomington, B.A. in English 1935; did post-graduate work at Harvard University, Cambridge, Massachusetts, 1940–41. Married Vernice Baker in 1937; four children. Instructor in English at Indiana University, 1936–40, and at Simmons College, Boston, 1941–47. *Died* (by suicide) *6 March 1948.*

PUBLICATIONS

Fiction

Raintree County. 1948.

Reading List: *Ross and Tom: Two American Tragedies* by John Leggett, 1974.

*　　*　　*

Ross Lockridge's one published work, the sprawling thousand-page novel *Raintree County*, was a huge popular and critical success in 1948. Praised as "a novel of rare stature," the first American epic since *Moby-Dick*, then increasingly disparaged as "an amalgam of undigested Wolfe, murky Faulkner, and watery Whitman," it is now rarely read or mentioned. Periodically literary historians try to restore it to prominence, even eminence, but with lean results, perhaps because the novel's sunny optimism, frontier humor, and abiding faith in the American dream are not congenial to contemporary readers. On all its many layers, *Raintree County* is an exuberant Fourth of July festival of Americana.

On the Fourth of July, 1892, in the small town of Waycross, Indiana, the townspeople join together for a holiday of celebration, oratory, reminiscence, as observed by John Wickliff Shawnessy, a 53-year-old schoolteacher reunited with his boyhood friends – a sleek senator, an ailing railroad tycoon, a wry journalist. Flash-backs re-create their common past, which eventuates in montage: structurally, events in John's life contrast with national events (his wedding is counterpointed with John Brown's execution, the birth of his son with the firing on Fort Sumter), and stylistically each event is viewed in the contrasting styles of fictitious newspaper accounts, old diaries and letters, blustering gossips and salty frontiersmen. The montages build into a panoramic view of American history and a critique of the 19th-century corrosion of the Declaration of Independence. The omniscient, disillusioned, but still hopeful narrator implies that the second American Revolution was the Civil War, epic atonement for slavery, and that the third was the Rail Strike of 1877, epic industrialism and enslavement of the poor. The urbane, witty journalist (a fine comic character) is the hero's Darwinian alter ego, cosmopolitan theoretician of the American experiences that Hoosier Johnny must undergo and struggle to understand – such as soldiering against the South, watching the first trains arrive in the Mid-West. The hero himself, a Jeffersonian idealist, is also America's fledgling poet, the modern Johnny Appleseed restoring the national earth with his words, his ideals, and his faith. Ringed with comic Bunyanesque characters and somber Lincolnesque tragedies, Johnny is in many ways the uncorruptible soul of epic America, and his life documents the century's "contest for my soul." On multiple levels of historical and literary allusion, each level complete with its contrapuntal movements of personal and national life, Lockridge weaves a kaleidoscopic epic, striving to be myth, that owes obvious debts to Joyce, Melville, Whitman. Lockridge's America is "mancreated," "greatchested," "buntinghung." Though the symbolism is sometimes muddled, and the sentiment sometimes saccharine, Lockridge's gigantesque conception and his technical virtuosity were perhaps unparalleled in America until Pynchon's *Gravity's Rainbow*. There is ample reason to consider *Raintree County* an important novel for its era and a substantial achievement.

—Jan Hokenson

LONDON, Jack (John Griffith London).   American.   Born in San Francisco, California, 12 January 1876. Educated at a grammar school in Oakland, California; Oakland High School, 1895–96; University of California, Berkeley, 1896–97. Married 1) Bessie Maddern in 1900 (separated, 1903; divorced, 1905), two daughters; 2) Charmian Kittredge in 1905. Worked in a cannery in Oakland, 1890; sailor on the *Sophie Sutherland*, sailing to Japan and Siberia, 1893; returned to Oakland, wrote for the local paper, and held various odd jobs, 1893–94; tramped the United States and Canada, 1894–96: arrested for vagrancy in Niagara Falls, New York; joined the gold rush to the Klondike, 1897–98, then returned to Oakland and became a full-time writer; visited London, 1902; War Correspondent in the Russo-Japanese War for the *San Francisco Examiner*, 1904; settled on a ranch in Sonoma County, California, 1906, and lived there for the rest of his life; attempted to sail round the world on a 45-foot yacht, 1907–09; War Correspondent in Mexico, 1914. *Died 22 November 1916.*

PUBLICATIONS

Collections

> *Short Stories,* edited by Maxwell Geismar.   1960.
> *(Works),* edited by I. O. Evans.   18 vols., 1962–68.
> *The Bodley Head London,* edited by Arthur Calder-Marshall.   4 vols., 1963–66.

Fiction

> *The Son of the Wolf: Tales of the Far North.*   1900; as *An Odyssey of the North,* 1915.
> *The God of His Fathers and Other Stories.*   1901; as *The God of His Fathers: Tales of the Klondike,* 1902.
> *Children of the Frost* (stories).   1902.
> *The Cruise of the Dazzler.*   1902.
> *A Daughter of the Snows.*   1902.
> *The Kempton-Wace Letters,* with Anna Strumsky.   1903.
> *The Call of the Wild.*   1903.
> *The Sea-Wolf.*   1904.
> *The Faith of Men and Other Stories.*   1904.
> *Tales of the Fish Patrol.*   1905.
> *The Game.*   1905.
> *White Fang.*   1906.
> *Moon-Face and Other Stories.*   1906.
> *Love of Life and Other Stories.*   1907.
> *Before Adam.*   1907.
> *The Road* (stories).   1907.
> *The Iron Heel.*   1908.
> *Martin Eden.*   1909.
> *Burning Daylight.*   1910.
> *Lost Face* (stories).   1910.
> *When God Laughs and Other Stories.*   1911.
> *South Sea Tales.*   1911.
> *Adventure.*   1911.
> *The Strength of the Strong* (story).   1911.
> *The House of Pride and Other Tales of Hawaii.*   1912.
> *A Son of the Sun* (stories).   1912; as *The Adventures of Captain Grief,* 1954.

Smoke Bellew (stories).   1912; as *Smoke and Shorty*, 1920.
The Night-Born, and Also The Madness of John Horned, When the World Was Young, The Benefit of the Doubt, Winged Blackmail, Bunches of Knuckles, War, Under the Deck Awnings, To Kill a Man, The Mexican.   1913.
The Abysmal Brute.   1913.
John Barleycorn.   1913; as *John Barleycorn; or, Alcoholic Memoirs*, 1914.
The Valley of the Moon.   1913.
The Mutiny of the Elsinore.   1914.
The Strength of the Strong (collection).   1914.
The Scarlet Plague.   1915.
The Jacket (The Star Rover).   1915.
The Little Lady of the Big House.   1916.
The Turtles of Tasman (stories).   1916.
The Human Drift.   1917.
Jerry of the Islands.   1917.
Michael, Brother of Jerry.   1917.
Hearts of Three.   1918.
The Red One (stories).   1918.
On the Makaloa Mat.   1919; as *Island Tales*, 1920.
Dutch Courage and Other Stories.   1922.
The Assassination Bureau Ltd., completed by Robert L. Fish.   1963.
Stories of Hawaii, edited by A. Grove Day.   1965.

Plays

Scorn of Woman.   1906.
Theft.   1910.
The Acorn-Planters: A California Forest Play.   1916.
Daughters of the Rich, edited by James E. Sisson.   1971.

Other

The People of the Abyss.   1903.
War of the Classes.   1905.
London: A Sketch of His Life and Work.   1905.
Revolution.   1909.
Revolution and Other Essays.   1910.
The Cruise of the Snark.   1911.
London by Himself.   1913.
Letters from Jack London, Containing an Unpublished Correspondence Between London and Sinclair Lewis, edited by King Hendricks and Irving Shepard.   1965.

Bibliography: *London: A Bibliography* by Hensley C. Woodbridge, John London, and George H. Tweney, 1966, supplement by Woodbridge, 1973; in *Bibliography of American Literature* by Jacob Blanck, 1969.

Reading List: *Sailor on Horseback: The Biography of London* by Irving Stone, 1938; *London: A Biography* by Richard O'Connor, 1964; *London, American Rebel* by Philip S. Foner, 1964; *London* by Earle Labor, 1974; *London: The Man, The Writer, The Rebel* by Robert Barltrop, 1977; *Jack: A Biography* by Andrew Sinclair, 1977.

*   *   *

Jack London was a talented writer so caught up in certain myths that they were part of what destroyed him. The illegitimate son of an impoverished spiritualist, Flora Wellman, he early learned self-reliance. Although he attended high school and, briefly, college, he was largely self-educated. London's university was the world he experienced and subsequently wrote about: San Francisco Bay, first as an oyster pirate and then as a member of the State Fish Patrol; the Pacific, the Orient, and the Bering Sea as an able seaman on a schooner hunting seals; the nation, across which he tramped as a vagabond; Alaska, where he prospected for gold; and California, where eventually he was a wealthy landowner burdened by the problems of maintaining a large ranch. London saw himself as an exemplar of the rags-to-riches story, an Anglo-Saxon superman who succeeded because of his superior intelligence and physical prowess, who took pride in his individualism, yet sympathized with the masses and believed that some form of socialism was the cure for the inequities of capitalist society.

To assert that his deprived childhood and his personal adventures were central to his development is not to deny that he was profoundly influenced by what he read as a young man. Early in his adolescence he delved into the seminal thinkers of the nineteenth century; his biographer Andrew Sinclair writes that during a winter in the Alaskan Klondike London absorbed "the books that became the bedrock of his thought and writing, underlying even the socialism which was his faith." Among London's readings that winter were the works of Darwin, Thomas Huxley, Spencer, and Kipling. "Charles Darwin and Herbert Spencer, messiahs of the new creed, became his intellectual mentors, along with Frederick Nietzsche and Karl Marx," Charles Child Walcutt wrote in a pamphlet about London, declaring that the author's struggles came to seem to himself "an epitome of the Darwinian Struggle for Existence, his success an example of the Spencerian Survival of the Fittest." Natural laws governed everything, London decided, so his problem became to reconcile the unimportance of the individual in a Darwinian universe and the Marxist certainty of social revolution with his equal certainty that he had the force and intelligence to rise above his fellow men.

His writing constantly reflects these contradictory beliefs, sometimes emphasizing one, sometimes another. In a succession of essays, short stories, novels, plays, travel books, and autobiographical tracts – during his forty years of life he wrote more than fifty books, too many for them all to be good – he portrayed the immutable laws of nature and man's need for community, while at the same time creating heroic figures who dominated both people and environment. As London's success grew, he heeded his socialist beliefs less, ultimately in his fiction painting what he liked to think were self-portraits of supermen defying the forces of nature and the demands of capitalism or of the masses. At his best London was able to hold these contradictions in balance; and technically his work, as H. L. Mencken wrote in *Prejudices: First Series*, contained "all the elements of sound fiction: clear thinking, a sense of character, the dramatic instinct, and, above all, the adept putting together of words – words charming and slyly significant, words arranged, in the French phrase, for the respiration and the ear." But finally his techniques could not sustain work that had lost its thematic equilibrium. He was an individualist, not a socialist. His lip service to socialism, wrote Walcutt, was "a protest against his early poverty"; London, he added, never dwelled on what might be the benefits of socialism.

London's heroes and heroines are individualists who survive the challenges of nature and society if they are strong enough, or are defeated if they are not – or, one might add, if London was pained by his socialist conscience. Thus in what is perhaps his best and best known story, *The Call of the Wild*, the powerful dog Buck, snatched from an easy life and submitted to brutal treatment and a harsh environment in the Klondike, survives because he is the superior individual. Buck, returned to the world of his ancestors, eventually runs with a pack of wolves, but he is at their head, where his intelligence and strength have put him. Wolf Larsen, the superman figure of *The Sea-Wolf*, both attracts and repels the beautiful, fragile poetess Maud Brewster and the effete Humphrey Van Weyden, whom Larsen rescues aboard his ship, the *Ghost*. Antagonized by Larsen, the two escape to an island, only to have him reappear aboard the wrecked *Ghost*. The arrogant individualist Larsen eventually dies, but it is his strength and skill that are admirable; the other two survive because they become strong like Wolf, yet lack his utter egotism. London would later assert that his point had been that a Wolf Larsen could not survive in modern society; but clearly he empathized with the arch-individualist, and Van Weyden's victory comes only after he has assimilated Larsen's qualities.

Another of London's heroes, Martin Eden, would die because of his individualism, but his death by suicide seems gratuitous, not, as London claimed, the result of Eden's believing in nothing and not accepting the socialism the author professed to favor. London could not portray a socialist state even before he abandoned socialism, which he did in his fiction when – as in the novels *Burning Daylight, The Valley of the Moon*, and *The Little Lady of the Big House* – he blatantly espoused Aryan supermen and escape from the urban masses. His socialist novel *The Iron Heel* takes the form of a text discovered long after socialism has triumphed. What the novel describes, however, is not a socialist utopia, but the violent rise of a repressive totalitarian state opposed by small cadres of insurgents led by a blond superman, Ernest Everhard. By 1914, when London reported for *Collier's* magazine on the revolution in Mexico, he "no longer spoke as the compassionate revolutionary," notes Andrew Sinclair, "but as the racist and jingoist supporter of the American oil interests – a man of property, a man used to servants, who was echoing the views of other men used to property and servants."

London died in 1916, by then severely ill and depressed by the recognition that he could not live out the myths he portrayed in his fiction. Still, he had not failed; his best work is vivid and dramatic; and his hyperbole, if annoying, nevertheless tells the reader much about United States culture.

—Townsend Ludington

LOVECRAFT, H(oward) P(hillips). American. Born in Providence, Rhode Island, 20 August 1890, and lived there for the rest of his life. Educated in local schools. Married the writer Sonia Greene in 1924 (divorced, 1929). Writer from 1908, supporting himself by ghost writing and working as a revisionist; regular contributor to *Weird Tales* from 1923. *Died 15 March 1937.*

PUBLICATIONS

Collections

Collected Poems. 1963.
Selected Letters 1911–1931, edited by August Derleth and Donald Wandrei. 3 vols., 1965–71.

Fiction

The Shadow over Innsmouth. 1936.
The Outsider and Others, edited by August Derleth and Donald Wandrei. 1939.

The Survivor and Others, with August Derleth.   1957.
Dreams and Fancies.   1962.
Dagon and Other Macabre Tales.   1965.
The Dark Brotherhood.   1966.

Other

Beyond the Wall of Sleep (miscellany), edited by August Derleth and Donald
   Wandrei.   1943.
Marginalia, edited by August Derleth and Donald Wandrei.   1944.
Something about Cats and Other Pieces, edited by August Derleth.   1949.
The Shuttered Room and Other Pieces, with others, edited by August Derleth.   1959.

Bibliography: *The New Lovecraft Bibliography* by Jack Chalker, 1962, revised edition, as
Mirage on Lovecraft, 1965.

Reading List: *H. P. L.: A Memoir,* 1945, and *Some Notes on Lovecraft,* 1959, both by August
Derleth; "Lovecraft Issue" of *Fresco,* Spring 1958; *Lovecraft: A Biography* by L. Sprague de
Camp, 1975; *The Lovecraft Companion* by Philip A. Shreffler, 1977.

*   *   *

H. P. Lovecraft's reputation depends not so much on any particular one of the sixty-odd
fantastic stories that he published, mostly in the pulp magazine *Weird Tales,* but rather on the
way in which most of these stories contribute to what has become known since the author's
death as the "Cthulhu Mythos." Although the stories are not consistent with each other and
although Lovecraft never codified his cosmology (he was a visionary, not a blueprint-maker),
the basic construct of the Mythos is that, in the days before mankind, this planet was
inhabited by a group of fish-like beings called the "Old Ones," who worshipped Cthulhu,
represented in "The Call of Cthulhu" as a gigantic, gelatinous form. Apparently because their
culture decayed, the "Old Ones" were driven from the earth by man; but they were not
destroyed. Led by the apparently immortal Yog-Sothoth, they retreated to the remote, dark
planet Yogguth, where they still conspire to regain control of the earth. Sometimes, as in
"The Whisperer in Darkness," they contemplate an attack on a decadent mankind; but more
often, as in Lovecraft's longest work, "The Case of Charles Dexter Ward," they seek, through
unspeakable rites of black magic, to mate with human beings through the connivance of
dissolute human collaborators.
   The generally suppressed knowledge of the Cthulhuites has been hinted at only in the
forbidden *Necronomicon* of the mad Arab Abdul Alhazred, one Latin copy of which is
preserved at Miskatonic University in Arkham, a mouldering New England seaport that is
the setting of many of Lovecraft's tales. When the plots of the "Old Ones" are foiled, the
earthly invaders or fishy-looking halfbreeds dissolve leaving behind only a pool of noxious-
smelling, jelly-like material. Those who are willfully or inadvertently involved in the
conspiracies – like those in "The Dunwich Horror" and "The Color Out of Space" – usually
face madness and inevitable destruction. The Mythos, despite vagueness and inconsistencies,
is a remarkable fictional manifestation of the mentality that has produced many conspiratorial
theories about local and extra-terrestrial threats to human societies. At first Lovecraft had
difficulty finding readers, but he found his advocate to the world in 1926 when he attracted
the attention of August Derleth. Derleth expanded and regularized the mythos, kept it in
print, and even invited others to contribute to it; and Lovecraft attracted a small but fanatical
band of cultists in the United States and abroad, especially in France.
   Ordinary critical standards are irrelevant to such an enterprise. Lovecraft's fables were

often awkwardly plotted and obscurely worded, but so are many "scriptures." Critics complained that he did not write novels, but, like Poe, his visions were best suited to shorter forms. Although many find his fantasies preposterous, he did create one of the most remarkable imaginative constructs of the twentieth century – an original myth that arises from a child's enormous fascination with sex and his repressive fear of it. Lovecraft's uniqueness lies in his ability to preserve – if perhaps only through dreams – and to articulate in adulthood the fantasies that provide a child's internal defense against inscrutable threats.

—Warren French

LOWELL, Amy (Lawrence).   American.   Born in Brookline, Massachusetts, 9 February 1874. Educated privately. Travelled a good deal abroad; associated with the Imagists in London, 1913, and thereafter promoted their work in America. Lecturer, Brooklyn Institute of Arts and Sciences, 1917–18. Recipient: Pulitzer Prize, 1926. Litt.D.: Baylor University, Waco, Texas, 1920. *Died 12 May 1925.*

PUBLICATIONS

Collections

The Complete Poetical Works.   1955.
A Shard of Silence: Selected Poems, edited by Glenn Richard Ruihley, 1957.

Verse

A Dome of Many-Coloured Glass.   1912.
Sword Blades and Poppy Seed.   1914.
Men, Women, and Ghosts.   1916.
Can Grande's Castle.   1918.
Pictures of the Floating World.   1919.
Legends.   1921.
Fir-Flower Tablets: Poems Translated from the Chinese by Florence Ayscough, English Versions by Lowell.   1921.
A Critical Fable.   1922.
What's O'Clock, edited by Ada Dwyer Russell.   1925.
East Wind, edited by Ada Dwyer Russell.   1926.
The Madonna of Carthagena.   1927.
Ballads for Sale, edited by Ada Dwyer Russell.   1927.

Play

Weeping Pierrot and Laughing Pierrot, music by Jean Hubert, from a work by Edmond Rostand.   1914.

Fiction

> *Dream Drops; or, Stories from Fairy Land,* with Elizabeth Lowell and Katherine
> Bigelow Lowell. 1887.

Other

> *Six French Poets: Studies in Contemporary Literature.*   1915.
> *Tendencies in Modern American Poetry.*   1917.
> *John Keats.*   2 vols., 1925.
> *Poetry and Poets: Essays,* edited by Ferris Greenslet.   1930.
> *Florence Ayscough and Lowell: Correspondence of a Friendship,* edited by Harley
> Farnsworth MacNair.   1946.

Reading List: *Lowell: A Critical Appreciation* by Bryher, 1918; *Lowell: A Chronicle, with Extracts from Her Correspondence* by S. Foster Damon, 1935; *Lowell: Portrait of the Poet in Her Time* by Horace Gregory, 1958; *Lowell* by Frank C. Flint, 1969; *The Thorn of a Rose: Lowell Reconsidered* by Glenn Richard Ruihley, 1975.

*   *   *

Even more than is commonly the case with rebel poets and personalities, Amy Lowell was subjected to heavy-handed abuse as well as uncritical admiration in her own life-time, there was little or no understanding of the nature of her work, and, following her untimely death in 1925, a shift in poetic fashions all but obliterated the memory of her unusual achievements. The reasons for that eclipse lie both in the poet and in her audience. Lowell was one of the most prolific and most uneven poets ever to appear in America. Because so much of her poetry was bad, it was easy to judge her harshly. Moreover, her best and most characteristic poetry was very puzzling to conventional readers and remains so to this day. The language of these poems is chiefly pictorial, with the result that she was dismissed as a writer who touched only the physical surfaces of the world and so failed to illuminate any of its deeper meanings. As for the defects in her audience, the misreading of the poet was due to the ignorance and superficiality of the literary journalists of her day. After her death, the misunderstanding was perpetuated by the "new critics" who scorned writers who fell outside the pale of the poetry of wit and cultural memory promoted by T. S. Eliot and Ezra Pound. Though Lowell, at her best, is a writer of extraordinary verve, freshness, and beauty of expression, she was little better understood fifty years after her death than she was in 1912 when she published her first book of poems, *A Dome of Many-Coloured Glass*.

This book was rightly criticized for its feebleness and conventionality of expression; but it has one merit unnoticed by the interpreters of her poetry. The poems are written in a late Romantic style of direct statement and they chart with unusual thoroughness all of the facets of her idealistic and mystical thought. After 1912, as suggested above, Miss Lowell expressed herself imagistically. To a poet concerned with extrarational areas of experience, the new style was a great advance over the confines of logical statement, but it also led to the failures of communication which have persisted to the present day. Fortunately, we can study the poems published in *A Dome* and so know precisely the content of her thought and the beliefs she had adopted, as a substitute for Christianity, to explain her own insights into reality.

The most important of these concerns the existence of a transcendent power that permeates the world and accounts for the divinity that the poet sensed in all created things. In her poem "Before the Altar," a lonely and penniless worshipper offers his life and being as sacrifice to this Power, which she also celebrates in "The Poet," another early poem. Moved by the awesome splendors of creation, the poet is urged, she says, to forsake the ordinary pleasures of life to pursue the ideality symbolized by the "airy cloudland palaces" of sunset. Such a man, she says, "spurns life's human friendships to profess/Life's loneliness of dreaming ecstasy." In much of Lowell's most admirable imagistic poetry, this mystical conception of reality is rendered by means of her "numinous landscape" or scene, as in the poems "Ombre Chinoise" or "Reflections" where the physical objects concerned are presented with a kind of divine nimbus.

The realm of ideality envisioned in these four poems is sometimes perceived as a solution to the painful incompletions of life. This is the second major theme in Lowell's poetry, and the incompletion is most tragic in the case of the denial of love. Such denial is a spiritual *malaise*, in her view, because she identifies love not with sex but with inner emotional development. "Patterns," which is this author's most famous poem, dramatizes the withering of spirit resultant on the death of the heroine's lover. The poem is highly voluptuous and insists strongly on the physical beauties of lover and lady and the formal, spring-time garden where the poem is set, but the heroine's decision to live a loveless, celibate life calls attention to the deeper meaning of the relationship.

The spirituality that is implicit in romantic attachments includes recognition of an element of divinity in the beloved. The achievement of love as sacred rite is a third principal theme in Lowell's writings and it occurs in many of her most striking poems, beginning with a loose effusion in *A Dome* but ending with the sublimity of "In Excelsis" and her six sonnets written to Eleonora Duse. The loved one as sacred presence or, at the least, a part of an all-encompassing Divinity is consistent with the poet's preoccupation with a transcendent reality and completes the circle of her themes by returning her thought to its starting place. In terms of individual poems, Lowell's treatment of these themes is so varied and intermixed with nearly all the other issues of life that only a long survey can do them justice. But it is important to note that Lowell approached life *as a mystic* at a profound, intuitive level, and the imagistic mode in which she cast her poems was the one best suited to her gifts and the visionary character of her poetry. As poet her contribution is a revivification of the human sense of the beauties and mysteries of existence.

In addition to the solitary, contemplative role of poet that she adopted for herself, Lowell fulfilled another dynamic "political" role in the far-reaching effort she made to obtain public acceptance of the "new poetry" that appeared in America in 1912. The role she played was political in that the new poetry, seemingly odd and irregular in its form, challenged nearly all established social norms and ideals. Through her critical writings as well as her countless public appearances as lecturer and reader, Lowell assumed leadership of this movement and was responsible for a large measure of its success in creating a new poetic taste and awareness in America.

—Glenn Richard Ruihley

LOWELL, Robert (Traill Spence, Jr.).   American.   Born in Boston, Massachusetts, 1 March 1917. Educated at St. Mark's School, Southboro, Massachusetts; Harvard University, Cambridge, Massachusetts, 1935–37; Kenyon College, Gambier, Ohio, 1938–40, A.B. (summa cum laude) 1940 (Phi Beta Kappa). Conscientious objector during World War II: served prison sentence, 1943–44. Married 1) Jean Stafford, *q.v.*, in 1940 (divorced, 1948); 2) the writer Elizabeth Hardwick in 1949 (divorced, 1972), one son; 3) the writer Caroline Blackwood in 1972, one son. Editorial Assistant, Sheed and Ward, publishers, New York, 1941–42; taught at the University of Iowa, Iowa City, 1949–50, 1952–53; Salzburg Seminar on American Studies, 1952; Boston University; New School for Social Research, New York;

Harvard University; Professor of Literature, University of Essex, Wivenhoe, Colchester, 1970–72. Consultant in Poetry, Library of Congress, Washington, D.C., 1947–48; Visiting Fellow, All Souls College, Oxford, 1970. Recipient: Pulitzer Prize, 1947; National Institute of Arts and Letters grant, 1947; Guggenheim Fellowship, 1947, 1974; Harriet Monroe Poetry Award, 1952; Guinness Prize, 1959; National Book Award, 1960; Bollingen Poetry Translation Award, 1962; New England Poetry Club Golden Rose, 1964; Ford Foundation grant, for drama, 1964; Obie Award, for drama, 1965; Sarah Josepha Hale Award, 1966; Copernicus Award, 1974; National Medal for Literature, 1977. Member, American Academy of Arts and Letters. *Died 12 September 1977.*

PUBLICATIONS

Verse

Land of Unlikeness. 1944.
Lord Weary's Castle. 1946.
Poems 1938–1949. 1950.
The Mills of the Kavanaughs. 1951.
Life Studies. 1959; augmented edition, 1959, 1968.
Imitations. 1961.
For the Union Dead. 1964.
Selected Poems. 1965.
The Achievement of Lowell: A Comprehensive Selection of His Poems, edited by William J. Martz. 1966.
Near the Ocean. 1967.
The Voyage and Other Versions of Poems by Baudelaire. 1968.
Notebook 1967–1968. 1969; augmented edition, as *Notebook,* 1970.
For Lizzie and Harriet. 1973.
History. 1973.
The Dolphin. 1973.
Poems: A Selection, edited by Jonathan Raban. 1974.
Selected Poems. 1976.
Day by Day. 1977.

Plays

Phaedra, from the play by Racine (produced 1961). In *Phaedra and Figaro,* 1961.
The Old Glory (Benito Cereno and My Kinsman, Major Molineux) (produced 1964). 1964; expanded version, including *Endecott and the Red Cross* (produced 1968), 1966.
Prometheus Bound, from a play by Aeschylus (produced 1967). 1969.

Other

Editor, with Peter Taylor and Robert Penn Warren, *Randall Jarrell 1914–1965.* 1967.

Reading List: *Lowell: The First Twenty Years* by Hugh B. Staples, 1962; *The Poetic Themes of Lowell* by Jerome Mazzaro, 1965; *Lowell: A Collection of Critical Essays* edited by Thomas

Parkinson, 1968; *The Public Poetry of Lowell* by Patrick Cosgrave, 1970; *Lowell: A Portrait of the Artist in His Time* edited by Michael London and Robert Boyars, 1970 (includes bibliography by Jerome Mazzaro); *Lowell* by Richard J. Fein, 1970; *Critics on Lowell: Readings in Literary Criticism* edited by Jonathan Price, 1972; *The Poetic Art of Lowell* by Marjorie G. Perloff, 1973; *Pity the Monsters: The Political Vision of Lowell* by Alan Williamson, 1974; *Lowell* by John Crick, 1974.

*   *   *

Robert Lowell has been described as "a poet of restlessness without repose" (John Crick). His career is the history of violent changes in subject matter, and in manner, which often annoyed and confused his critics. Even now, after his death, there is little general agreement about his stature. But perhaps, even in this, Lowell is a *representative* figure: the last thirty years (Lowell's publishing history runs from 1944 to 1977) have witnessed a fragmentation of culture that denies us the sorts of certainty about the status that it was once possible to accord to Eliot, or to Yeats. This period will never, one suspects, be accepted as "The Age of Lowell." Individual poets seem no longer capable of this sort of centrality of significance.

But if any poet in this period has – perhaps sometimes with too earnest a deliberateness – lived through, proved upon his pulses, the central concerns, preoccupations, and pains of his time, it is Lowell. The career may, conveniently, be seen in three parts: the early poetry of Lowell's Catholicism that embraces *Land of Unlikeness*, *Lord Weary's Castle*, and *The Mills of the Kavanaughs*; the mid-period poetry of personal breakdown and political concern that includes *Life Studies*, *For the Union Dead*, and *Near the Ocean*; and the final period that saw the various attempts to create a larger, freer form through the subsequent stages of *Notebook*, *History*, *For Lizzie and Harriet*, and *The Dolphin*, a period concluding with the sustained elegiac note of *Day by Day*.

On the face of it, the three phases of the career seem to have little in common, apart from certain stylistic tics – most notably, and often irritatingly, Lowell's penchant for the triple adjective and the attention-seeking oxymoron. Some insight into an underlying continuity in Lowell's "one life, one writing" may be provided by remarking on his exceptional insistence on revising himself in public. One of the most upsetting aspects of *Notebook*, for many of its reviewers, was the shock of coming across familiar Lowell lines either in very different contexts, or procrusteanly racked into the uniform regularity of the book's "sonnets." Lowell's apparently cavalier freedom with his own published work suggests not so much a desire to do a little better what he has done brilliantly before, but rather a deep-seated impatience with his own enormous talent and with poetry itself. In the poem "Tired Iron" in *The Dolphin*, there is an almost Beckettian dismissal of the work, even as he is engaged on it – "I can't go on with this, the measure is gone." It is possible to see in Lowell, as in some of the greatest artists of the second half of the twentieth century, a radical dissatisfaction with art itself, with its consolations, its sense of order, its morality. What gives Lowell's dissatisfaction its unique savour is his refusal of the obvious alternative of a bleak nihilism in favour of a worried, guilty commitment to a traditional New England liberalism. The oddity of Robert Lowell's sensibility is perhaps suggested in a shorthand way by pointing to the poems in *Notebook* and *History* dedicated to Eugene McCarthy and Robert Kennedy: an existential absurdist clinging precariously to sanity celebrates the pragmatic politics of liberal capitalism.

Dissatisfaction, restlessness, unease: these are the signatures of Lowell's work. The early formalist poetry nominally takes its cue from Allen Tate and the Southern Fugitives. In fact, the formal majesty of the poems is everywhere disturbed by a raucous alliterative bellowing; the Catholicism is everywhere collapsed into savage heresy and blasphemy:

> O Mother, I implore
> Your scorched, blue thunderbreasts of love to pour
> Buckets of blessings on my burning head.

If this is rhetoric, it is a rhetoric of desperation. Even in the more tender poems – "The Quaker Graveyard in Nantucket" and "Mother Marie Therese" – Lowell's sonic boom threatens his formal perfection. His dissatisfaction compels him almost to wring the neck of his magnificent rhetoric. Such dissatisfactions led to a long silence during "the tranquillized Fifties," a silence during which the dissatisfactions of his personal life involved periods in mental hospitals. The silence was broken only at the end of the decade by the publication of *Life Studies*, a book in an entirely different mode and manner; Lowell was now so dissatisfied with his earlier work that he attempted almost its polar opposite, a poetry close to Chekhovian prose. This is the one work of Lowell's about which almost all critics agree: it was *the* book of its time, following, with total assurance, a direction more hesitantly beginning to be taken by some of his contemporaries, profoundly influential in its discovery of a new sort of personal voice. It signals, in "Beyond the Alps," Lowell's break with Catholicism, and it proceeds to worry out, "confessionally," the psychic disturbances and extremities of his harrowing personal experience. This is a poetry resolutely committed to walking naked; but the voice is moving and desperate and rises to a unique and instantly recognisable "Lowellian" pathos:

> A car radio bleats,
> 'Love, O careless Love ...' I hear
> my ill-spirit sob in each blood cell,
> as if my hand were at its throat ...
> I myself am hell,
> nobody's here —.

But, unlike that of some poets who crawled in under the mantle of "confessional" poetry, Lowell's writing refuses the temptations of an easy solipsism. Christopher Ricks, in a *New Statesman* review of *For the Union Dead* (26 March 1965), maintained that "The singular strength of Robert Lowell's poetry has always been a matter of his power to enforce a sense of context." The work after *Life Studies* evidences a desire to speak, out of personal pain and catastrophe, about society and politics, and about literature, religion, and history, the sustaining "outer contexts" of our lives. Restlessly moving away from the "prose" style of *Life Studies*, Lowell wrote, in the central poems of *Near the Ocean* – especially, perhaps, in "Waking Early Sunday Morning" – the greatest elegies for a generation that suffered the Vietnam war and the threat of nuclear extinction, and he wrote them, with his casually characteristic refusal of the obvious, in a finely judged, perfectly achieved neo-classical form that recalls that other poet of the barbarities of which a "civilised" society is capable, Andrew Marvell:

> Pity the planet, all joy gone
> from this sweet volcanic cone;
> peace to our children when they fall
> in small war on the heels of small
> war – until the end of time
> to police the earth, a ghost
> orbiting forever lost
> in our monotonous sublime.

In *For the Union Dead*, the forms are again free, though the relatively uncluttered simplicity of these poems belies a carefully crafted subtlety of association, allusion, and symbolism. These haunted, nostalgic poems begin in a consideration of the joys and pains of personal relationship but extend themselves into the troubles of political life. The volume's title-poem relates private and public breakdown in a muted poetry of understatement, working by implication and suggestion. The poem's final stanza is as devastating as anything in Lowell, but the devastation comes across quietly, hesitantly, thrown off almost parenthetically compared to the aggressive climaxes of the poems in *Lord Weary's Castle*:

> The Aquarium is gone. Everywhere,
> giant finned cars nose forward like fish;
> a savage servility
> slides by on grease.

The ability to relate his own trouble to the trouble of his times is the impulse behind *Notebook*. This, and the works that grew out of it, are the most ambitious of Lowell's writing: he is attempting a large, inclusive form, a form for all occasions, in the manner of Pound's *Cantos*, of Berryman's *Dream Songs*. In the poems in the sequence – all irregular fourteen-liners – that deal with "history," there is too often the feeling of formal monotony, rhythmic inertia, a tired, mechanical repetitiveness. The lack of a real voice, and the absence of anything but the most straightforward chronology to serve as "plot," render *History* a generally wearying experience. The failure derives, perhaps, from Lowell's refusal to admit that a sonnet sequence, or its equivalent, is really capable of handling only limited types of material. The larger successes of *For Lizzie and Harriet* and *The Dolphin* are perhaps the result of their being more traditionally plotted around the themes and occasions of personal love and marriage. The idea of writing "history" as a sequence of sonnets has an almost wilful perversity about it, as though Shakespeare had decided to put the material of the history plays, as well as the story of his "two loves," into a sonnet sequence.

But such perversity, and the overall failure of a single book, are perhaps the inevitable price of an heroic refusal to repeat himself, a nervous, restless desire to define and re-define the protean self. "We are words," Lowell insists in a poem in *History* addressed to Berryman, "John, we used the language as if we made it." The claim is large; it is characteristic of Lowell's proud ambition that he should make it for himself; but in the formal variety, the technical ingenuity, and the inventiveness of his poems – and of his translations and plays – he comes, at the very least, close to justifying it.

—Neil Corcoran

LYTLE, Andrew (Nelson). American. Born in Murfreesboro, Tennessee, 26 December 1902. Educated at Sewanee Military Academy, Tennessee; Exeter College, Oxford, 1920; Vanderbilt University, Nashville, B.A. 1925; Yale University School of Drama, New Haven, Connecticut, 1927–29. Married Edna Langdon Barker in 1938 (died, 1963); three daughters. Writer from 1930; Professor of History, Southwestern College, Memphis, Tennessee, 1936; Professor of History, University of the South, Sewanee, Tennessee, and Managing Editor of the *Sewanee Review*, 1942–43; Lecturer, 1946–48, and Acting Head, 1947–48, University of Iowa School of Writing, Iowa City; Lecturer in Creative Writing, University of Florida, Gainesville, 1948–61; Lecturer in English, 1961–67, and Professor of English, 1968–73, University of the South, Sewanee, and Editor of the *Sewanee Review*, 1961–73. Recipient: Guggenheim Fellowship, 1940, 1941, 1960; National Endowment for the Arts grant, 1966. Litt.D.: Kenyon College, Gambier, Ohio, 1965; University of Florida, 1970; University of the South, 1973. Lives in Monteagle, Tennessee.

PUBLICATIONS

Fiction

The Long Night.   1936.
At the Moon's Inn.   1941.
A Name for Evil.   1947.
The Velvet Horn.   1957.
A Novel, A Novella and Four Stories.   1958.

Other

Bedford Forrest and His Critter Company (biography).   1931; revised edition, 1960.
The Hero with the Private Parts: Essays (literary criticism).   1966.
A Wake for the Living: A Family Chronicle.   1975.

Editor, Craft and Vision: The Best Fiction from "The Sewanee Review."   1971.

Reading List: "Lytle Issue" of Mississippi Quarterly, Fall 1970; The Form Discovered: Essays on the Achievement of Lytle edited by M. E. Bradford, 1973.

*   *   *

Andrew Lytle's family on both sides was prominent in Middle Tennessee, and in fact Murfreesboro, the town where he was born, was founded on land given by his ancestor. His family chronicle, A Wake for the Living, traces the course of their history for almost two centuries. Lytle's movement into the writing of fiction was gradual. His undergraduate years at Vanderbilt University coincided with the heyday of the Fugitive group, and the friendships he formed with these poets led him into his own literary career. His main interest during the 1920's, however, was theater; he studied playwriting at the Yale School of Drama, and in New York he had a brief career as an actor.

Even before he left New York he had begun the research on his first book, Bedford Forrest and His Critter Company. He thus followed his friends Allen Tate and Robert Penn Warren, whose first prose works were likewise Civil War biographies. In 1930 these men and nine of their friends, led by their former teacher John Crowe Ransom, published I'll Take My Stand. This famous symposium inaugurated the Agrarian movement, to which Lytle was passionately committed. He was indeed about the only Agrarian who actually practiced farming during the 1930's, and for a few years he attempted to combine this with the literary profession. His great interest in the history of his region led to his first novel, The Long Night, a tragedy of revenge set against the background of the Civil War.

Although Lytle is usually identified with Tennessee, where three of his four novels are set, he is keenly aware of the larger clash of cultures. At the Moon's Inn brings the Spanish explorer De Soto to his fate in North America as he attempts to overcome the vast wilderness through an act of will. The short novel "Alchemy" likewise has Pizarro confronting the Inca world of Peru. In the foreword to A Novel, A Novella, and Four Stories Lytle comments that "The westward movement of Europeans, beginning with Columbus, not only shattered the narrow physical boundaries of Christendom but, like all extension, weakened it by reducing a union composite of spiritual and temporal parts to the predominance of material ends." This statement might serve as the theme that links all of Lytle's books. His third novel, A Name for

Evil, is about a modern Southerner who brings ruin upon himself and his family in an abortive effort to restore the past; the fictional convention here is the ghost story. *The Velvet Horn*, which is set in the Cumberland Mountains soon after the Civil War, involves a boy's initiation into manhood and an extraordinary tangle of family relationships. It is the richest of Lytle's books and one of the masterpieces of Southern fiction.

—Ashley Brown

MacARTHUR, Charles. American. Born in Scranton, Pennsylvania, 5 November 1895. Educated at the Wilson Memorial Academy, Nyack, New York. Served as a trooper in the 1st Illinois Cavalry, Mexican Border, 1916; Private in the 149th Field Artillery of the United States Army, 1917–19; Assistant to the Chief of the Chemical Warfare Service, Washington, D.C., with rank of Lieutenant Colonel, 1942–45. Married 1) Carol Frink (divorced); 2) the actress Helen Hayes in 1928, one daughter and one son, the actor James MacArthur. Reporter, City News Bureau, Chicago, 1914, *Herald and Examiner*, Chicago, 1915–16, and the *Chicago Tribune*, 1916–17; worked on the New York *American*, 1921–23; Special Writer, *Hearst's International Magazine*, New York, 1924; full-time writer and producer from 1929; screen writer and director from 1930; formed a production company with Ben Hecht, 1934. *Died 21 April 1956.*

PUBLICATIONS

Collections

> *The Stage Works* (includes *Lulu Belle; Salvation; The Front Page; Twentieth Century; Ladies and Gentlemen; Swan Song; Johnny on a Spot; Stag at Bay*, with Nunnally Johnson), edited by Arthur Dorlag and John Irvine. 1974.

Plays

> *My Lulu Belle*, with Edward Sheldon (as *Lulu Belle*, produced 1926). 1925; in *Stage Works*, 1974.
> *Salvation*, with Sidney Howard (produced 1928). In *Stage works*, 1974.
> *The Front Page*, with Ben Hecht (produced 1928). 1928; in *Stage Works*, 1974.
> *Twentieth Century*, with Ben Hecht (produced 1932). 1932; in *Stage Works*, 1974.
> *Jumbo*, with Ben Hecht, music by Richard Rodgers, lyrics by Lorenz Hart (produced 1935). 1935.
> *Ladies and Gentlemen*, with Ben Hecht, from a play by Ladislas Bush-Fekete (produced 1939). 1941; in *Stage Works*, 1974.
> *Fun to Be Free: A Patriotic Pageant*, with Ben Hecht (produced 1941). 1941.
> *Johnny on a Spot*, from a story by Parke Levy and Alan Lipscott (produced 1942). In *Stage Works*, 1974.

Wuthering Heights (screenplay), with Ben Hecht, in *Twenty Best Film Plays*, edited by John Gassner and Dudley Nichols. 1943.
Swan Song, with Ben Hecht, from a story by Ramon Romero and Harriett Hinsdale (produced 1946). In *Stage Works*, 1974.
Stag at Bay, with Nunnally Johnson (produced 1976). In *Stage Works*, 1974.

Screenplays: *Billy the Kid*, with Wanda Tuckock and Laurence Stallings, 1930; *The King of Jazz*, with others, 1930; *Paid*, with Lucien Hubbard, 1930; *Way for a Sailor*, with others, 1930; *The Girl Said No*, with Sarah Y. Mason and A. P. Younger, 1930; *New Adventures of Get-Rich-Quick Wallingford*, 1931; *The Sin of Madelon Claudet*, 1931; *The Front Page*, with Ben Hecht, 1931; *Rasputin and the Empress*, 1933; *Twentieth Century*, with Ben Hecht, 1934; *Crime Without Passion*, with Ben Hecht, 1934; *The Scoundrel*, with Ben Hecht, 1935; *Barbary Coast*, with Ben Hecht, 1935; *Once in a Blue Moon*, with Ben Hecht, 1936; *Soak the Rich*, with Ben Hecht, 1936; *Wuthering Heights*, with Ben Hecht, 1939; *Gunga Din*, with others, 1939; *I Take This Woman*, with James Kevin McGuinness, 1940; *Until I Die*, with Ben Hecht, 1940; *The Senator Was Indiscreet*, with Edwin Lanham, 1947.

Other

A Bug's-Eye View of the War. 1919.
War Bugs. 1928.

Reading List: *Charlie: The Improbable Life and Times of MacArthur* by Ben Hecht, 1957.

*   *   *

The young Charles MacArthur was a reporter for the City News Bureau, the *Herald and Examiner*, and the *Tribune* in Chicago, worked on the *New York American*, and contributed to Hearst's *International Magazine* and other journals. From their Chicago journalism experience, but chiefly from Jed Harris traditions of Broadway melodrama, MacArthur and Ben Hecht created the famous play, *The Front Page*. The *New York Times* (15 August 1928) liked this sensational and sentimental, if somewhat raucous and callous hymn to the antics of the working press. It said the play opened the season "noisily": "By superimposing a breathless melodrama upon a good newspaper play the authors and directors [actually George S. Kaufman] of 'The Front Page' ... have packed an evening with loud, rapid, coarse and unfailing entertainment ... have told a racy story with all the tang of front-page journalism ... [and] convey the rowdy comedy of the pressroom, the whirr of excitement, of nerves on edge ... in the hurly-burly of a big newspaper yarn."

MacArthur's unaided work (such as the forced farce of *Johnny on a Spot*) was undistinguished, but in collaboration he did well. In collaboration he also wrote *Lulu Belle* (with Edward Sheldon), *Salvation* (with Sidney Howard), and *Twentieth Century* (with Ben Hecht, 1932). All were solid Broadway vehicles. With Hecht he also wrote the spectacular *Jumbo, Ladies and Gentlemen, Swan Song*, and several film scripts.

MacArthur married as his second wife Helen Hayes, later to be queen of the legitimate stage, but professionally after 1928 he was more or less married to the movies. He began with several scripts in 1930, but hit the jackpot with a vehicle for Helen Hayes, *The Sin of Madelon Claudet*. Later films include *Rasputin and the Empress* (with the Barrymores), *Crime Without Passion* (writer, producer, director), *The Scoundrel, Gunga Din*, and *Wuthering Heights*. When he died he was working with Anita Loos on a vehicle for Miss Hayes. He was by then one of Hollywood's most respected writers.

His service with the Rainbow Division in France in World War I led to *A Bug's-Eye View of the War* and *War Bugs*. It is too bad he did not do more humorous prose. He brought together a nice combination of sentiment and wit and a touch of irony with a raucous sense of fun and irreverence. All these elements are at their best in *The Front Page*. Brooks Atkinson (in his introduction to *Sixteen Famous American Plays*, 1946) wrote that *"The Front Page* is to journalism what *What Price Glory?* is to the marines – rudely realistic style but romantic in its loyalties, and also audaciously profane." Actually, the "baldest profanity and most slatternly jesting as has ever been heard on the public stage" (as the *New York Times* had it in 1928) today sounds rather tame – and the play is not as realist as it seemed then. But some reporters still at least attempt to sound like MacArthur-Hecht characters (for nature imitates art), and *The Front Page* still has life in it, while *Five Star Final, Press Time, The Squeaker, Freedom of the Press,* and *Kiss the Boys Goodbye* and a host of other newspaper plays are long dead.

—Leonard R. N. Ashley

MacKAYE, Percy (Wallace).   American.   Born in New York City, 16 March 1875; son of the dramatist Steele MacKaye. Educated at Harvard University, Cambridge, Massachusetts, A.B. 1897; studied at the University of Leipzig, 1898–1900. Married Marion Homer Morse in 1898 (died, 1939), two daughters and one son. Teacher, Craigie School for Boys, New York, 1900–04; full-time writer from 1904; Fellow in Poetry, Miami University, Ohio, 1920–24; Advisory Editor, *Folk-Say* journal, from 1929; Teacher of poetry and folk backgrounds, Rollins College, Winter Park, Florida, 1929–31; Visiting Professor of the creative aspects of drama, Sweet Briar College, Virginia, 1932–33; Director, White Top Mountain Folk Festival, Virginia, 1933; engaged in research into folklore in the Appalachian Mountains, 1933–35, and in Switzerland and the British Isles, 1936–37. Founder Member, Phi Beta Kappa Associates, 1941; President, Pan American Poets League of North America, 1943; Founder, Marion Morse-Percy MacKaye Collection at Harvard University Library, 1943. Recipient: Shelley Memorial Award, 1943; Academy of American Poets Fellowship, 1948. M.A.: Dartmouth College, Hanover, New Hampshire, 1914; Litt.D.: Miami University, 1924. Member, National Institute of Arts and Letters. *Died 31 August 1956.*

PUBLICATIONS

Plays

    Kinfolk of Robin Hood (as *Inhabitants of Carlysle,* produced 1901).   1924.
    The Canterbury Pilgrims (produced 1903).   1903; revised version, music by Reginald DeKoven, 1916.
    Fenris the Wolf.   1905.
    St. Gaudens Masque-Prologue (produced 1905).   1910.
    Jeanne d'Arc (produced 1906).   1906.
    Sappho and Phaon (produced 1907).   1907.
    Mater: An American Study in Comedy (produced 1908).   1908.
    The Scarecrow, from the story "Feathertop" by Hawthorne (produced 1908).   1908.
    A Garland to Sylvia: A Dramatic Reverie.   1910.

Anti-Matrimony (produced 1910).   1910.

Hannele, with Mary Safford, from a play by Gerhart Hauptmann (produced 1910).

A Masque of Labor.   1912.

Tomorrow (produced 1913).   1912.

Yankee Fantasies (includes *Chuck, Gettysburg, The Antick, The Cat-Boat, Sam Average*).   1912.

Chuck (produced 1912).   In *Yankee Fantasies*, 1912.

Sam Average (produced 1912).   In *Yankee Fantasies*, 1912.

Gettysburg (produced 1912).   In *Yankee Fantasies*, 1912.

The Antick (produced 1915).   In *Yankee Fantasies*, 1912.

Sanctuary: A Bird Masque (produced 1913).   1914.

A Thousand Years Ago: A Romance of the Orient (produced 1913).   1914.

St. Louis: A Civic Pageant, with Thomas Wood Stevens (produced 1914).   1914.

The Immigrants, music by Frederick Converse.   1915.

The New Citizenship: A Civic Ritual (produced 1916).   1915.

Caliban, By the Yellow Sands (produced 1916).   1916.

The Evergreen Tree (produced 1917).   1917.

Sinbad the Sailor.   1917.

The Roll Call: A Masque of the Red Cross (produced 1918).   1918.

The Will of Song: A Dramatic Service of Community Singing, music by Harry Barnhart (produced 1919).   1919.

Washington, The Man Who Made Us (produced 1920).   1919; shortened versions published, as *George Washington*, 1920, *Washington and Betsy Ross*, 1927, and *Young Washington at Mt. Vernon*, 1927.

Rip Van Winkle, music by Reginald DeKoven (produced 1920).   1919.

The Pilgrim and the Book.   1920.

This Fine-Pretty World (produced 1923).   1924.

Kentucky Mountain Fantasies (includes *Napoleon Crossing the Rockies, The Funeralizing of Crickneck, Timber*).   1928; revised edition, 1932.

The Sphinx.   1929.

Wakefield: A Folk-Masque of America, music by John Tasker Howard (produced 1932).   1932.

The Mystery of Hamlet, Prince of Denmark; or, What We Will: A Tetralogy (produced 1949).   1950.

Fiction

Tall Tales of the Kentucky Mountains.   1926.
Weathergoose Woo!   1929.

Verse

Johnny Crimson: A Legend of Hollis Hall.   1895.
Ode on the Centenary of Abraham Lincoln.   1909.
Poems.   1909; as *The Sistine Eve and Other Poems*, 1915.
Uriel and Other Poems.   1912.
The Present Hour.   1914.
Dogtown Common.   1921.
The Skippers of Nancy Gloucester.   1924.
April Fire.   1925.
Winged Victory.   1927.
The Gobbler of God: A Poem of the Southern Appalachians.   1928.

Songs of a Day. 1929.
William Vaughn Moody, Twenty Years After. 1930.
Moments en Voyage: Nine Poems for the Harvard Class of 1897. 1932.
In Another Land, with Albert Steffen. 1937.
The Far Familiar. 1938.
Poem-Leaflets in Remembrance of Marion Morse MacKaye. 1939.
My Lady Dear, Arise! Songs and Sonnets in Remembrance of Marion Morse MacKaye. 1940.
What Is She? A Sonnet of Sonnets to Marion Morse. 1943.
Rememberings 1895–1945: Four Poems. 1945.
The Sequestered Shrine. 1950.
Discoveries and Inventions: Victories of the American Spirit. 1950.

Other

The Playhouse and the Play, and Other Addresses Concerning the Theatre and Democracy in America. 1909.
The Civic Theatre in Relation to the Redemption of Leisure. 1912.
The New Citizenship. 1915.
A Substitute for War. 1915.
Poems and Plays. 2 vols., 1916.
Epoch: The Life of Steele MacKaye. 2 vols., 1927.
American Theatre-Poets. 1935.
Poesia Religio. 1940.
Poog's Pasture: The Mythology of a Child: A Vista of Autobiography. 1951.
Poog and the Caboose Man: The Mythology of a Child: A Vista of Autobiography. 1952.

Editor, *Letters to Harriet,* by William Vaughn Moody. 1935.
Editor, *An Arrant Knave and Other Plays,* by Steele MacKaye. 1941.

Translator, *The Canterbury Tales of Chaucer: A Modern Rendering into Prose of the Prologue and Ten Tales.* 1904.
Translator, with John S. P. Tatlock, *The Modern Reader's Chaucer: Complete Poetical Works Now First Put into Modern English.* 1912; selection as *Canterbury Tales,* edited by Carl W. Ziegler, 1923.

Reading List: *MacKaye: A Sketch of His Life with Bibliography of His Works,* 1922; *Dipped in Sky* by Frank A. Doggett, 1930; *Annals of an Era: Percy MacKaye and the MacKaye Family* edited by E. O. Grover, 1932.

*   *   *

As the son of Steele MacKaye, Percy MacKaye might have been expected to show an interest in experimental drama. And he did, beginning with his graduation speech from Harvard in 1897 entitled "The Need of Imagination in the Drama of Today." Early in his career he added his efforts to the work of a small group of poetic dramatists – William Vaughn Moody, Josephine Peabody Marks, George Cabot Lodge – who were attempting to offset the excess of Realism on the American stage with something of the artistry which Yeats and Maeterlinck were creating abroad. MacKaye's poetic dramas, however – *The Canterbury Pilgrims, Jeanne d'Arc, Sappho and Phaon* – were minor contributions to the genre.

It was with pageant drama and community theatre that MacKaye trod most successfully in the steps of his father, generally celebrating America's heritage on the grand scale his father envisioned. As a crusader for community theatre he wrote several books and numerous articles – *The Playhouse and the Play*, *The Civic Theatre*. One of his most successful pageants – allegorical masques is a more accurate descriptive term: he called his work "poetry for the masses; the drama of democracy" – was *St. Louis: A Civic Pageant* which had a cast of 7,500 and attracted over half a million people to its five performances. *Caliban, By the Yellow Sands*, produced on the 300th anniversary of Shakespeare's death, was an elaborate pageant using various scenes from Shakespeare's plays to humanize Caliban, to suggest, as MacKaye explained, "the slow education of mankind through the influences of cooperative art." His other pageants included *The Roll Call*, requested by the American Red Cross, and *Wakefield*, in which he attempted to dramatize the effect of "the Folk-Spirit of America" on American freedom.

For the historian of American drama one of MacKaye's particular contributions is his definitive two-volume biography of his father, *Epoch*, a man Percy worshipped and with whom he shared the dream of creating drama for the people. As a poet and a dramatist, MacKaye's best and most enduring work was his dramatization of Nathaniel Hawthorne's "Feathertop" which he called *The Scarecrow*. Created before the audience's eyes with a display of imagination and theatrical skill, the scarecrow comes to life as Lord Ravensbane and achieves a considerable sense of humanity before it succumbs to the wiles of mankind and its own artificial construction. It is a fine example of MacKaye's commentary on the "need of imagination" and still retains its theatrical magic for modern audiences.

—Walter J. Meserve

MacLEISH, Archibald.   American.   Born in Glencoe, Illinois, 7 May 1892. Educated at the Hotchkiss School, Lakeville, Connecticut; Yale University, New Haven, Connecticut, A.B. 1915; Harvard University, Cambridge, Massachusetts, LL.B. 1919. Served in the United States Army, 1917–19: Captain. Married Ada Hitchcock in 1916; three children. Lecturer in Government, Harvard University, 1919–21; Attorney, Choate Hall and Stewart, Boston, 1920–23; Editor, *Fortune* magazine, New York, 1929–38; Curator of the Niemann Foundation, Harvard University, 1938; Librarian of Congress, Washington, D.C., 1939–44; Director, United States Office of Facts and Figures, 1941–42, Assistant Director of the Office of War Information, 1942–43, and Assistant Secretary of State, 1944–45, Washington, D.C. Chairman of the United States Delegation to the UNESCO drafting conference, London, 1945, and Member of the Executive Board, UNESCO, 1946. Rede Lecturer, Cambridge University, 1942; Boylston Professor of Rhetoric and Oratory, Harvard University, 1949–62; Simpson Lecturer, Amherst College, Massachusetts, 1964–67. Recipient: Shelley Memorial Award, 1932; Pulitzer Prize, 1933, 1953, for drama, 1959; New England Poetry Club Golden Rose, 1934; Bollingen Prize, 1952; National Book Award, 1953; Sarah Josepha Hale Award, 1958; Antoinette Perry Award, 1959; National Association of Independent Schools Award, 1959; Academy of American Poets Fellowship, 1965; Academy Award, 1966; National Medal for Literature, 1978. M.A.: Tufts University, Medford, Massachusetts, 1932; Litt.D.: Wesleyan University, Middletown, Connecticut, 1938; Colby College, Waterville, Maine, 1938; Yale University, 1939; University of Pennsylvania, Philadelphia, 1941; University of Illinois, Urbana, 1947; Rockford College, Illinois, 1952; Columbia University, New York, 1954; Harvard University, 1955; Carleton College, Northfield, Minnesota, 1956; Princeton University, New Jersey, 1965; University of Massachusetts, Amherst, 1969; York University, Toronto, 1971; LL.D.: Dartmouth College, Hanover, New Hampshire, 1940; Johns Hopkins University, Baltimore, 1941; University of California, Berkeley, 1943;

Queen's University, Kingston, Ontario, 1948; University of Puerto Rico, Rio Piedras, 1953; Amherst College, Massachusetts, 1963; D.C.L.: Union College, Schenectady, New York, 1941; L.H.D.: Williams College, Williamstown, Massachusetts, 1942; University of Washington, Seattle, 1948. Commander, Legion of Honor; Commander, El Sol del Peru. President, American Academy of Arts and Letters, 1953–56. Lives in Massachusetts.

PUBLICATIONS

Verse

> *Songs for a Summer's Day (A Sonnet-Cycle).*   1915.
> *Tower of Ivory.*   1917.
> *The Happy Marriage and Other Poems.*   1924.
> *The Pot of Earth.*   1925.
> *Streets in the Moon.*   1926.
> *The Hamlet of A. MacLeish.*   1928.
> *Einstein.*   1929.
> *New Found Land: Fourteen Poems.*   1930.
> *Before March.*   1932.
> *Conquistador.*   1932.
> *Frescoes for Mr. Rockefeller's City.*   1933.
> *Poems 1924–1933.*   1933; as *Poems*, 1935.
> *Public Speech: Poems.*   1936.
> *Land of the Free – U.S.A.*   1938.
> *America Was Promises.*   1939.
> *Actfive and Other Poems.*   1948.
> *Collected Poems 1917–1952.*   1952.
> *Songs for Eve.*   1954.
> *Collected Poems.*   1963.
> *"The Wild Old Wicked Man" and Other Poems.*   1968.
> *The Human Season: Selected Poems 1926–1972.*   1972.
> *New and Collected Poems 1917–1976.*   1976.

Plays

> *Nobodaddy.*   1926.
> *Union Pacific* (ballet scenario; produced 1934).   In *The Book of Ballets*, 1939.
> *Panic: A Play in Verse* (produced 1935).   1935.
> *The Fall of the City: A Verse Play for Radio* (broadcast, 1937).   1937.
> *Air Raid: A Verse Play for Radio* (broadcast, 1938).   1938.
> *The States Talking* (broadcast, 1941).   In *The Free Company Presents*, edited by James Boyd, 1941.
> *The American Story: Ten Radio Scripts* (includes *The Admiral; The American Gods; The American Name; Not Bacon's Bones; Between the Silence and the Surf; Discovered; The Many Dead; The Names for the Rivers; Ripe Strawberries and Gooseberries and Sweet Single Roses; Socorro, When Your Sons Forget)* (broadcast, 1944).   1944.
> *The Trojan Horse* (broadcast, 1952).   1952.
> *This Music Crept by Me upon the Waters* (broadcast, 1953).   1953.
> *J.B.: A Play in Verse* (produced 1958).   1958.
> *The Secret of Freedom* (televised, 1959).   In *Three Short Plays*, 1961.

Three Short Plays: The Secret of Freedom, Air Raid, The Fall of the City.   1961.
Our Lives, Our Fortunes, and Our Sacred Honor (as *The American Bell*, music by David
   Amram, produced 1962).   In *Think*, July–August 1961.
Herakles: A Play in Verse (produced 1965).   1967.
An Evening's Journey to Conway, Massachusetts: An Outdoor Play (produced
   1967).   1967.
Scratch, suggested by *The Devil and Daniel Webster* by Stephen Vincent Benét
   (produced 1971).   1971.
The Great American Fourth of July Parade (produced 1975).   1975.

Screenplays: *Grandma Moses*, 1950; *The Eleanor Roosevelt Story*, 1965.

Radio Plays: *The Fall of the City*, 1937; *King Lear*, from the play by Shakespeare, 1937;
Air Raid, 1938; *The States Talking*, 1941; *The American Story* series, 1944; *The Son of
Man*, 1947; *The Trojan Horse*, 1952; *This Music Crept by Me upon the Waters*, 1953.

Television Play: *The Secret of Freedom*, 1959.

Other

Housing America, by the Editors of *Fortune*.   1932.
Jews in America, by the Editors of *Fortune*.   1936.
Background of War, by the Editors of *Fortune*.   1937.
The Irresponsibles: A Declaration.   1940.
The Next Harvard, As Seen by MacLeish   1941.
A Time to Speak: The Selected Prose.   1941.
The American Cause.   1941.
A Time to Act: Selected Addresses.   1943.
*Poetry and Opinion: The Pisan Cantos of Ezra Pound: A Dialogue on the Role of
   Poetry.*   1950.
*Freedom Is the Right to Choose: An Inquiry into the Battle for the American
   Future.*   1951.
Poetry and Journalism.   1958.
Poetry and Experience.   1961.
The Dialogues of MacLeish and Mark Van Doren, edited by Warren V. Busch.   1964.
The Eleanor Roosevelt Story.   1965.
A Continuing Journey.   1968.
The Great American Frustration.   1968.
Riders of the Earth: Essays and Reminiscences.   1978.

Editor, *Law and Politics*, by Felix Frankfurter.   1962.

Bibliography: *A Catalogue of the First Editions of MacLeish* by Arthur Mizener, 1938;
MacLeish: A Checklist by Edward J. Mullahy, 1973.

Reading List: *MacLeish* by Signi Lenea Falk, 1965; *MacLeish* by Grover C. Smith, 1971.

*   *   *

By 1940, Archibald MacLeish had written numerous books of poems, and was a well-
known writer. He was also the target of adverse criticism. MacLeish's early work is too

derivative. It abounds with the distracting influence of Eliot and Pound, among others. MacLeish writes on the same subjects as Eliot and Pound and from exactly their point of view. MacLeish's early long poems proved very weak. His most famous one is *Conquistador*, which won him the first of three Pulitzer Prizes. It is a verbose, unqualified glorification of Spain's slaughter and enslavement of Mexican Natives, and is, at best, unthinkingly adolescent. Other works in this period are marred by the confusing about-face MacLeish executes concerning the role of the poet. In his "Invocation to the Social Muse," MacLeish criticizes those who would urge the poet to concentrate on social issues. These issues, however, soon become central to his own work. MacLeish proceeds to sermonize, harangue – and produce much poor poetry, especially in *Public Speech* and his plays for radio.

Yet, despite the inferior work written in these decades, MacLeish was beginning to compile an outstanding body of lyric poetry. Some of the short poems in *Streets in the Moon* and *New Found Land* hold up very well. "L'an trentiesme de mon eage" is a superior presentation on the subject of the lost generation. Other fine peoms include "Eleven," "Immortal Autumn," and "Memorial Rain." "Ars poetica" develops the stimulating idea that "A poem should not mean/But be." Perhaps the best of all is "The End of the World," a dramatization of the belief that the universe is basically meaningless. *Poems 1924–1933* brought together such superior lyrics as "Pony Rock," "Unfinished History," and "Lines for an Interment."

What became increasingly apparent in the 1940's and thereafter is that MacLeish's primary strength as a writer resides in the lyric form. In fact, MacLeish has done most of his best work after the age of fifty.

Even some of MacLeish's later plays and long poems, two genres he never really excels at, rise above the mediocre. The full-length play *J.B.*, despite its bland poetry and tepid main character, effectively dramatizes the tragedies that engulf J.B. and offers a frequently rousing debate between Mr. Zuss (representing orthodox religion) and Nickles (representing a pragmatic outlook). MacLeish's one-act play *This Music Crept by Me upon the Waters* is also successful. The main characters, Peter and Elizabeth, are interesting; the plot builds in suspense; and the poetry and the theme (a preference for the present over the past) are powerful. *Actfive* is MacLeish's best long poem. The first section, which delineates modern man's basic predicament, is quite absorbing.

Still, it is MacLeish's lyric poetry that will be remembered the longest. Starting with the poems collected in 1948, the number of excellent lyrics mounts steadily. For this reason, the critical neglect MacLeish has suffered in recent years is unjust. These later lyrics center on three sometimes overlapping subjects. One presents MacLeish's increasing awareness of the mystery that permeates human experience. Earlier in his life, he wrote several poems that spoke confidently, if not cockily about setting out on explorations; now he writes "Voyage West," a sensitive expression of the uncertainty involved in a journey. Significantly, "Poet's Laughter" and "Crossing" are full of questions, while "The Old Man to the Lizard" and "Hotel Breakfast" end with questions, not answers. MacLeish sums up his sense of the mysterious in "Autobiography" when he says, "What do I know of the mystery of the universe?/Only the mystery."

MacLeish has also written several tender eulogies and epitaphs. Two such poems about his mother are "The Burial" and "For the Anniversary of My Mother's Death." A pair of even finer poems, "Poet" and "Hemingway," have Ernest Hemingway for their subject. Other outstanding poems in this vein include "Edwin Muir," "Cummings," and "The Danger in the Air."

Finally, MacLeish has written a host of fine poems about old age. The difficulty of creativity when one is no longer young is described in "They Come No More, Those Words, Those Finches." Tiredness is poignantly depicted in "Walking" and "Dozing on the Lawn." "Ship's Log" records the narrowing awareness of the old. Here, MacLeish states: "Mostly I have relinquished and forgotten/Or grown accustomed, which is a way of forgetting." Yet " 'The Wild Old Wicked Man' " presents an old person's wisdom and passion. In the two poems concerning "The Old Gray Couple," he offers the reader a moving portrait of the final, deepest stage of human love. Lastly, using Odysseus as narrator, MacLeish chooses human love (symbolized by his aging wife) and mortal life over love for the abstract (symbolized by the goddess Calypso) and the metaphysical in his lovely poem "Calypso's Island." This poem declares, "I long for the cold, salt,/Restless, contending sea and for the island/Where the grass dies and the seasons alter."

—Robert K. Johnson

MAILER, Norman.   American.   Born in Long Branch, New Jersey, 31 January 1923. Educated at Harvard University, Cambridge, Massachusetts, S.B. in aeronautical engineering 1943; did postgraduate work at the Sorbonne, Paris, 1944. Served in the United States Army Infantry, 1944–46. Married 1) Beatrice Silverman in 1944 (divorced, 1951), one daughter; 2) Adele Morales in 1954 (divorced, 1962), two daughters; 3) Lady Jeanne Campbell in 1962 (divorced, 1963), one daughter; 4) Beverly Bentley in 1963 (divorced, 1971), two sons; 5) Carol Stevens in 1971, one daughter. Co-Editor, *Dissent*, New York, 1953–63; Co-Founding Editor, *Village Voice*, New York, 1954; Columnist, *Esquire* magazine, New York, 1962–63; Independent Candidate for Mayor of New York City, 1968; film director. Recipient: National Institute of Arts and Letters grant, 1960; Pulitzer Prize, for non-fiction, 1969; National Book Award, for non-fiction, 1969; Edward MacDowell Medal, 1973; National Art Club's Gold Medal for Literature, 1976. Member, National Institute of Arts and Letters. Lives in Brooklyn, New York.

PUBLICATIONS

Fiction

The Naked and the Dead.   1948.
Barbary Shore.   1951.
The Deer Park.   1955.
Advertisements for Myself (includes essays and verse).   1959.
An American Dream.   1965.
The Short Fiction.   1967.
Why Are We in Vietnam?   1967.
A Transit to Narcissus, edited by Howard Fertig.   1978.

Plays

The Deer Park (produced 1967).   1967.
Maidstone: A Mystery (screenplay).   1971.

Screenplays: *Wild 90,* 1967; *Beyond the Law,* 1967; *Maidstone,* 1968.

Verse

Deaths for the Ladies and Other Disasters.   1962.

Other

The White Negro.   1959.
The Presidential Papers.   1963.
Cannibals and Christians.   1966.
The Bullfight.   1967.
The Armies of the Night: History as a Novel, The Novel as History.   1968.
Miami and the Siege of Chicago: An Informal History of the Republican and Democratic Conventions of 1968.   1969.
The Idol and the Octopus: Political Writings on the Kennedy and Johnson Administrations.   1968.
Of a Fire on the Moon.   1970.
The Prisoner of Sex.   1971.
The Long Patrol: 25 Years of Writing from the Works of Mailer, edited by Robert Lucid.   1971.
Existential Errands.   1972.
St. George and the Godfather.   1972.
Marilyn.   1973.
The Faith of Graffiti, with Mervyn Kurlansky and Jon Naar.   1974; as *Watching My Name Go By,* 1975.
The Fight.   1975.
Some Honorable Men: Political Conventions 1960–1972.   1976.
Genius and Lust: A Journey Through the Major Writings of Henry Miller, with Henry Miller.   1976.

Bibliography: *Mailer: A Comprehensive Bibliography* by Laura Adams, 1974.

Reading List: *Mailer* by Richard J. Foster, 1968; *The Structured Vision of Mailer* by Barry H. Leeds, 1969; *Mailer: The Man and His Work* edited by Robert Lucid, 1970; *Mailer* by Richard Poirier, 1972; *Mailer: A Critical Study* by Jean Radford, 1974; *Down Mailer's Way* by Robert Solotaroff, 1974; *Existential Battles: The Growth of Mailer* by Laura Adams, 1975; *Mailer* by Philip Bufithis, 1978.

*   *   *

Even in the ferment of the American literary scene since 1950 few novelists have provoked – from deans of criticism as from common readers – the ferment of praise and attack that greets every new work by Norman Mailer. A definitive assessment of Mailer cannot yet be written, both because each work must be considered part of the whole, the *oeuvre* that Mailer is still extending and defining in his own terms, and because many people (not excluding Mailer), consider his present writings preparation for, indeed perhaps part of, the greatest American novel of his generation. His objective has not changed since 1959, when he wrote that he "will settle for nothing less than making a revolution in the consciousness of our time." The young James Joyce couched such hyperbole in the third person, but Mailer is obstreperously the artist as "I." It is typical of Mailer's caustic, profoundly ironic aggrandizement of himself as artist, America's seer and clown, to have added, "I could be wrong, and if I am, then I'm the fool who will pay the bill" (*Advertisements for Myself*). Even Mailer's fiercest detractors agree that he has by now more than met his own challenge, and the question is whether he has yet to write, or has already written, his great work.

Provisionally Mailer's canon can be described in four stages: an apprenticeship from 1948–58 including his first three novels; a difficult transition from 1959–64 in public self-criticism; the mastery of prose fiction culminating in the works of 1965–67; and the period since 1968 which, to appropriate his subtitle to *Armies of the Night*, consists in his explorations of "History as a Novel, the Novel as History."

The Naked and the Dead is the work of a young social realist indebted to Dos Passos: on a Pacific island in World War II an American platoon (an ethnic composite) is sent on a hopeless mission by a disdainful general for personal reasons of vindictiveness, and under the immediate command of a brutal illiterate sergeant, proletarian homologue of the fascistic general; deftly Mailer evokes the past lives and the present ordeals of the platoon, the intense, but purposeless valor of little men enmeshed in tycoons' wars. Thereafter Mailer turned away from naturalist techniques and from focus on character to develop the allegorical tendencies that underlay his first study of Americans at war. Just as the island was a metaphor for America, so in *Barbary Shore* a madcap urban boardinghouse is context for the allegorical collisions of national political and social forces; artistically unsuccessful, because the tight political framework is overwhelmed by unaccountable fears and inconsistencies in the characters, *Barbary Shore* remains the experimental keystone of all Mailer's later use of metaphorical structures. In *The Deer Park* he drew back into more traditional modes, for the realistic account of a young writer's apprenticeship in a film colony among embattled Hollywood idealists and nihilists, victims and agents of both America's cinema-induced fantasies and the McCarthy Committee; confused in crucial ways, *The Deer Park* initiates Mailer's supple use of clashing rhetorical styles and introduces Marion Faye, a theologian of evil who prefigures major issues in the later fiction. The *warfare*, the political then increasingly moral and aesthetic combat between opposing aspects of American culture (nature and technology, creativity and waste, Christian humanism and capitalist lust), shapes the form and tone of all three novels, their dualistic structures and their still discordant mix of stridency and sentiment. The three novels concern extinction of spirit and creative energy by the capitalist system, as its antagonists confront their own terrors, at the limits of sanity, in opposing it. Chronologically Mailer structures his novels less and less on the dualities inherent in the American political system and more on those in the self as participant in the system.

Advertisements for Myself burst the constraints that had kept Mailer's work so anxious, both daring and tentative, through most of the 1950's. The volume is a collection of all his work to date (in entirety or excerpt) and, through meticulous prefaces, his assessment of himself as creator of it. He publicly adopts the first person as the "voice" of his work (most later third-person work will feature his character "Mailer," a novelist), he works out his aesthetic as America's artist, he fixes his political position as (vestigial Marxist) Existentialist "moral anarchism," he announces his program for himself, and – as in all subsequent works – he attempts to divine the future from the present state of culture, literature, and himself. *Advertisements* is the fulcrum, the self-scrutiny enabling Mailer to move away from mentors (Hemingway, the naturalists, Malraux) to fiction uniquely his own. Three short pieces inform that transition. "The Man Who Studied Yoga" gently mocks Sam Slovoda, defeated writer and middle-class conformist, and marks a terminus, Mailer's last calm moment before his fiery (some say foul-mouthed barroom brawling) rebellion against such passive death. "The White Negro" posits creative self-assertion, announcing "Mailer" the Hipster of literature: Hip (modulated in the 1960's to Protest and in the 1970's to Aquarius) fascinates him as active, anarchic opposition to the WASP fascism that threatens to appropriate human freedom and even dignity; Hip entails obscenity, which Mailer values as active assault on hypocrisy and thus as the linguistic essence of street-based democracy, and *machismo*, Mailer's prized – and much maligned – assertion of the masculine. His story "The Time of Her Time" is both a mock-epic battle of the sexes and a serious refusal to deny instinct as the price of civilization, even if that means virtually raping a Freudian co-ed. The Advertisements led Mailer to excesses (many since modified), but the important base is "Mailer" the novelist addressing the dichotomies in the culture and in himself, the artist as antagonist of his own cultural and literary past and as its interpreter, hero of the creative effort – denied by the forces of corporate power – to interpret, indeed to shape history.

An American Dream and *Why Are We in Vietnam?* are masterful dramatizations of his cultural and artistic argument, in consummate styles. In the first novel middle-aged Rojack, radical intellectual married to a tycoon's daughter, murders her and then, for 32 hours, tries to locate in himself as in the world the "fine divide" between madness and sanity. He tries to poise himself between the daily world of newspaper lies, CIA, police, and the nightmare world of psychotic imaginings, death, hallucination (thus *in* the schizophrenia that is the heart of the American dream, as in the rapidly shifting, telescoped languages of these milieux), only to find that they are contemporaneous and coextensive, that there is no safe parapet overlooking the incoherence, neither in the city nor in himself. In the second novel D.J., 18-year-old son of a Dallas millionaire, recounts (as if in the electronically broadcast chatter of a Texas disc jockey) going bear hunting with his Pa in Alaska and welcoming that greatest of American puberty rites with a slavering satisfaction. Vietnam is mentioned only in the last sentence, in searing fillip to this horrific allegory of the greater atrocity that is the character of the nation. The novel is a comic masterwork forcing the reader to poise on Mailer's fine edge between laughter and dread, where the ghastly implications of the title corrode the Huckleberry Finn humor. The hyped style is in the end a devaluation of language (always an ironic operation in Mailer), the media blasting the human mind. In the two novels, in complex metaphors and a rhetorical virtuosity as rich as Faulkner's, Mailer dismantles the American self-image, dramatizing the dualisms that entrap his villainous hero and his heroic villain.

All Mailer's fiction played character against context, dialectically observing character as both creator-of and created-by the event in which he is participant. Moving in the late 1960's from fiction to real people and events, Mailer developed that technique into a methodology for exploring the "fine divide" between history and the novel. Bringing to journalism both the techniques of fiction-writing and the subjective moral seriousness of the novelist, Mailer now writes about extraordinary spectacles in American public life. He does so as "Mailer," "the Historian" or "the Novelist," interchangeably, both participant and observer, citizen and artist. One such report won rebel Mailer respectability, the Pulitzer Prize for "Non-Fiction," but the aesthetic status of his "Reports" is still far from decided; certain readers (such as John Hollowell in *Fact & Fiction*) hail Mailer as progenitor of the new "non-fiction novel," and others term Mailer's late work a renegade form of autobiography. With great deftness of historical and literary allusion, "the Reporter" describes his thoughts and feelings in the midst of political or other public extravaganzas, which he sees as epic battles of forces in the American psyche, manifesting to public view elements of the national character which otherwise remain concealed. *The Armies of the Night* (perhaps the best among these works) chronicles the anti-war march on the Pentagon; "Superman Comes to the Supermarket," "In the Red Light," *Miami and the Siege of Chicago, St. George and the Godfather* describe the political conventions of 1960–72; *Of a Fire on the Moon* details the moonshot and queries the possibility of personal heroism in a technocracy; *The Fight* and *The Faith of Graffiti* concern two famous prize fighters and a host of famous ghetto street artists, personal combat and personal name as public spectacle. Richard Poirier in *Norman Mailer* (the finest critical study to date) explains the significance of "Mailer": "We are invited to see him in these books within intricately related fields of force, and then to watch him act simultaneously as participant, witness, and writer, who evokes in the clashes of his style a 'war' among the various elements that constitute the life of the country and of the self." In cunning interplay between history and memoir, "Mailer" the novelist blunders through events, dissecting their significance and pondering the ambivalences in his own response as participant-observer, until "Mailer" effectively constitutes the narrative field as the archetypally American duality of dream and dread, angel and swine.

There are now signs that Mailer has exhausted his reporter's mode. Distaste and new experimentation began before *St. George and the Godfather*, a disaffected testament whose patent dualisms bored even Mailer. There is no doubt that to "Mailer," quintessential American sensibility, Watergate was a horror; in the 1976 preface to *Some Honorable Men* he chides, too severely, his old belief in history as the product of forces visible to the skilled observer ("So we are obliged to recognize that much of what we looked on as history is, in fact, not much related to the facts"), and therefore redoubles his insistence that the world of fiction be brought to bear on the facts of journalism. His recent work focuses on the multiple selves warring within the public individual, notably Marilyn Monroe and Henry Miller, embodiments of the worlds of sex and aestheticism that continue to absorb him. One sign of his turning away from public spectacle was the shift of voice in *Graffiti* to "Aesthetic Investigator"; the text is a brief, deeply disturbed investigation of correlatives between street kids' graffiti and the modern artist's disappearance from the work of art (Rauschenberg erasing De Kooning and selling the signed erasure) as a last defiance against the corporate take-over of art. The aesthetics of defiance are also a subject of *Marilyn* concerning cinema and of *Genius and Lust* concerning autobiographical fiction.

Now under contract to complete a major novel "large in scope" by 1981, Mailer is writing his first fictional work in many years. In the 1976 preface to the political writings he notes, "How much America becomes the character, no, the protagonist of that novel no genius is large enough to write," adding, not so typically, "Shakespeare would grow modest before America." The new novel may not prove to be the masterwork expected, nor so immodest as once predicted, but it is certain to be praised and attacked on grounds of greatness.

—Jan Hokenson

MALAMUD, Bernard. American. Born in Brooklyn, New York, 26 April 1914. Educated at Erasmus Hall, New York; City College of New York, 1932–36, B.A. 1936; Columbia University, New York, 1937–38, M.A. 1942. Married Ann de Chiara in 1945; one son and one daughter. Teacher, New York high schools, evenings 1940–49; Instructor to Associate Professor of English, Oregon State University, Corvallis, 1949–61. Since 1961, Member of the Division of Language and Literature, Bennington College, Vermont. Visiting Lecturer, Harvard University, Cambridge, Massachusetts, 1966–68. Recipient: Rosenthal Award, 1958; Daroff Memorial Award, 1958; Ford Fellowship, 1959, 1960; National Book Award, 1959, 1967; Pulitzer Prize, 1967; O. Henry Award, 1969, 1973. Member, National Institute of Arts and Letters, 1964; American Academy of Arts and Sciences, 1967.

PUBLICATIONS

Fiction

The Natural. 1952.
The Assistant. 1957.
The Magic Barrel (stories). 1958.
A New Life. 1961.
Idiots First (stories). 1963.
The Fixer. 1966.
Pictures of Fidelman: An Exhibition. 1969.
The Tenants. 1971.
Rembrandt's Hat (stories). 1973.

Other

A Malamud Reader, edited by Philip Rahv.   1967.

Bibliography: *Malamud: An Annotated Checklist* by R. N. Kosofsky, 1969.

Reading List: *Malamud* by Sidney Richman, 1966; *Malamud: A Collection of Critical Essays* edited by Joyce and Leslie Field, 1974; *Art and Idea in the Novels of Malamud* by Robert Ducharme, 1974; *Malamud and the Trial by Love* by Sandy Cohen, 1974.

*   *   *

Bernard Malamud, one of the most popular contemporary writers of Jewish-American fiction, contributes significantly to the growth in ethnic consciousness in American letters. He raises serious questions about the American dream and the American tradition. The luckless and bungling heroes who populate his fiction are twentieth-century replies to the supernatural powers of Natty Bumpo, the heroic stature of Captain Ahab, and the moral development of Isabel Archer.

Malamud's short stories and novels derive from two essential aspects of his past: his Jewish upbringing and his secular education. The Jewish past provides Malamud with much surface detail (setting, dialect) and with the ironic tone and biting humor of much of his fiction. Also Malamud is a careful student of the Western Christian literary tradition which often provides him with symbol sets and literary parallels. It even colors his theme of redemption through suffering to the extent that his characters appear more as Christian martyrs than as Yiddish-speaking immigrants.

His first novel, *The Natural,* is his most ingenious adaptation of Christian legend. A story of the baseball hero, Roy Hobbs, it is a conflation of the American myth of the sports hero, specifically the baseball hero, and the medieval legends of the Fisher King and the Grail. A natural athlete, Roy is plagued by false goddesses and unworthy goals. In the end, when promised the opportunity to redeem the dry land, the unsuccessful team, Roy fails morally. He helps fix the game.

The Assistant, also a novel of striving after new gods, is one of Malamud's most oppressive: it is, however, not a story of hopelessness. Frank Alpine, a Gentile who participates in the robbery of Morris Bober's grocery and rapes Helen Bober, learns to repent for his earlier self. An admirer of St. Francis, Frank is redeemed through his suffering – he becomes a Jew like his former employer Morris Bober. One of the most effective aspects of this novel is the vividly evoked setting. The Bobers are living a life of poverty and desperation. Into this darkened vision beam the lights of Frank's love for Helen and his gradual salvation through the laws of self-sacrifice.

A New Life, a barely disguised *roman à clef* of Malamud's years at Oregon State University, chronicles the growth of Sam Levin from loser to father. He arrives at a first teaching position; he is approaching thirty, anxious to please, yet filled with aspirations. Only after he gets to Cascadia College does he discover that the school is not a liberal arts school but a technical institute. This is only the first of a series of disappointments and reversals in his original plan. In his first year, he has an affair with the wife of the chairman of the English department and is forced to leave Cascadia and the profession of teaching. He takes with him a pregnant woman whom he no longer loves, her two adopted children, and a mature vision of the responsibility of the individual.

In *The Fixer,* Malamud turns from the American landscape to the Russian countryside. The plot of the novel is based on the Mendel Belis case of the early twentieth century. But the character Yakov Bok is a production of the imagination of Malamud. A simple, irreligious Jew, Yakov attempts to escape the *shtetl,* Jewishness, and an unfaithful wife by slipping out of the Pale of Settlement. He is discovered living in a Christian area and accused to the ritual murder of a Gentile boy. The development of his Jewish and humanitarian consciousness is a direct result of his torture in the Russian prison. His victory over disease, death, and insanity is more than a physical one and more than an individual one.

In *Pictures of Fidelman*, a picaresque novel, Arthur Fidelman travels to Italy, first to study art, then to paint, finally simply to become human. Three of the episodes collected in this novel had been previously published as short stories. By collecting them into a single volume and adding new episodes, Malamud rounds out the bungling and lost character that is Fidelman. In this foreign setting, an American innocent, like many American innocents before him, learns what Europe has to offer. But, more than that, he learns what his own inadequacies are.

The Tenants, an experimental novel, suggests some of the complexities of the relationship between blacks and Jews in mid-twentieth-century America. Malamud's ambivalence about this relationship is apparent in the three suggested endings to the novel. Added to the problems of black-white interaction are the deprived atmosphere of the setting (an abandoned tenement house) and the jealousy of competitors (both main characters are novelists). As the conflict intensifies between Harry Lesser and Willie Spearmint, Malamud develops social, sexual, political, and even aesthetic implications of their argument. In the end, they represent also the struggle between the formalist writer and the Marxist writer.

The tales in Malamud's collections run the gamut from sheer fantasy to painful realism. These short stories are most often peopled by the Jews of Malamud's experience – immigrants and second generation Americans. Even in the most fantastic of the tales, the quality of the Yiddish past filters through the fiction, either in the turn of a phrase or in the detail of a setting or biographical background or in a thematic concern with the holiness of intellectuality.

In the best examples of his short fiction the main characters share more with the Yiddish past than do the main characters of his novels. Whether that hero be an unfeeling *yeshive* student ("Magic Barrel"), a father protecting an idiot son ("Idiots First"), a modern-day Job confronted by a black Jewish angel ("Angel Levine"), a talking bird ("The Jewbird"), a guilty son duped by a fake miracle rabbi ("The Silver Crown"), a frightened American in Russia accosted by a censored writer ("Man in the Drawer"), or a talking horse ("The Talking Horse"), each of these individuals is clearly indebted to the Jewish past in the Diaspora. Each is specifically indebted to the feelings of ambivalent chosenness that is the position of the Jew in Europe since the first century.

—Barbara Gitenstein

MARQUAND, John P(hillips). American. Born in Wilmington, Delaware, 10 November 1893. Educated at Newburyport High School, Massachusetts; Harvard University, Cambridge, Massachusetts, 1912–15, A.B. 1915. Served with the Massachusetts National Guard in the Mexican Border Service, 1916; student, Camp Plattsburg, 1917; commissioned 1st Lieutenant in the Field Artillery, and served with the 4th Brigade of the American Expeditionary Forces in France, 1917–18; Special Consultant to the Secretary of War, Washington, D.C., 1944–45; War Correspondent for the United States Navy, 1945. Married 1) Christina Davenport Sedgwick in 1922 (divorced, 1935), one son and one daughter; 2) Adelaide Hooker in 1937 (divorced, 1958), two sons and one daughter. Assistant Magazine Editor, *Boston Transcript*, 1915–17; with the Sunday Magazine Department, *New York Tribune*, 1919–20; advertising copywriter for the J. Walter Thompson Company, New York, 1920–21; full-time writer from 1921. Member, Board of Overseers, Harvard

University; Member, Editorial Board, Book-of-the-Month Club, New York. Litt.D.:
University of Maine, Orono, 1941; University of Rochester, New York, 1944: Yale
University, New Haven, Connecticut, 1950; D.H.L.: Bates College, Lewiston, Maine, 1954.
Member, National Institute of Arts and Letters. *Died 16 July 1960.*

PUBLICATIONS

Fiction

The Unspeakable Gentleman. 1922.
Four of a Kind (stories). 1923.
The Black Cargo. 1925.
Do Tell Me, Doctor Johnson. 1928.
Warning Hill. 1930.
Haven's End (stories). 1933.
Ming Yellow. 1935.
No Hero. 1935.
Thank You, Mr. Moto. 1936.
The Late George Apley: A Novel in the Form of a Memoir. 1937.
Think Fast, Mr. Moto. 1937.
Mr. Moto Is So Sorry. 1938.
Wickford Point. 1939.
Mr. Moto Takes a Hand. 1940.
Don't Ask Questions. 1941.
H.M. Pulham, Esquire. 1941.
Last Laugh, Mr. Moto. 1942.
So Little Time. 1943.
Repent in Haste. 1945.
B.F.'s Daughter. 1946; as *Polly Fulton,* 1947.
Point of No Return. 1949.
It's Loaded, Mr. Bauer. 1949.
Melville Goodwin, USA. 1951.
Sincerely, Willis Wayde. 1955.
North of Grand Central (omnibus). 1956.
Mr. Moto's Three Aces (omnibus). 1956.
Stopover: Tokyo. 1957.
Life at Happy Knoll (stories). 1957.
Women and Thomas Harrow. 1958.

Play

The Late George Apley, with George S. Kaufman, from the novel by Marquand
(produced 1944). 1946.

Other

Prince and Boatswain: Sea Tales from the Recollections of Rear-Admiral Charles Clark,
with James Morris Morgan. 1915.
Lord Timothy Dexter of Newburyport, Mass. 1925.

Federalist Newburyport; or, Can Historical Fiction Remove a Fly from Amber?   1952.
Thirty Years (miscellany).   1954.
Timothy Dexter Revisited.   1960.

Reading List: *Marquand* by John J. Gross, 1963; *Marquand* by C. Hugh Holman, 1965; *The Late J. P. Marquand* by Stephen Birmingham, 1972.

*   *   *

John P. Marquand was a popular professional writer who whetted the skills of realistic and gently satiric writing to a very fine edge in several popular novels and scores of short stories in the mass circulation magazines before, in 1937, he set out to employ these skills with affectionate irony and gentle satire to the society of affluent upper-middle-class America in its seats of influence and power. For the twenty years that followed he was not only a practiced portrayer of American life but also one of the most popular novelists that America has produced.

The Late George Apley, which in 1937 broke the pattern of Marquand's popular fiction, is a parody of "collected letters with commentary" of distinguished people. It is a satiric picture of a very proper Bostonian and the ways in which the constraints of his society kept him in line and made him a good but stuffy and frustrated man. It received the Pulitzer Prize and launched Marquand's career as an important American social novelist. It was the first of three novels in which Marquand explored in contrasting panels aspects of the life of Boston. *Wickford Point* is the story of a decaying family loosely bound to the Transcendentalists, a comic picture of the diminishment of greatness and the sadness of the Indian summer of the spirit, and *H. M. Pulham, Esquire* is a self-portrait by a contemporary Bostonian, a post-World War I businessman, and the account of his ineffectual revolt against his class and its customs. These three novels form a triptych of New England life and utilize a variety of satiric skills, largely resulting from ironic points of view and the extensive use of the device of narrative flashback.

Like Sinclair Lewis, whom he greatly admired, Marquand moved on, after his complex portrait of Boston, to other cities and other professions in his growing list of studies of American life. *So Little Time* explores the vulgarly opulent world of West Coast movie-makers. It is laid during World War II, and suggests the inexorable passage of time. His other wartime novel, *B.F.'s Daughter*, deals with big business and the Washington bureaucracy, and is only a limited success. (A short novel *Repent in Haste* also deals with the war, but it is very slight.) *Point of No Return* is, after *The Late George Apley*, Marquand's best novel. It is the story of a banker who explores his New England small-town roots in an effort to find bases for a decision he must make, only to discover that all the decisions had already been made without his being aware of it, and that he has passed "the point of no return," a conclusion that most Marquand protagonists reach after painfully reviewing their lives. In addition to many amusing social caricatures, the book contains a serious examination of the sociology of New England towns, and to some degree of New York City. It and the Boston trilogy are Marquand's works which seem most likely to survive.

Melville Goodwin, USA is a portrayal of a General seen through the admiring eyes of a popular journalist. The journalist is a devastating portrait of the shallowness of the view of man held by the popular media, but, at the time the book was published, few critics recognised that it was an ironic novel that cut both ways, and they made the mistake of assuming that Marquand approved of the military officer and his decisions. It represents, after *The Late George Apley*, Marquand's most complex use of narrative point of view for satire, and indicates that his use of technical devices and his skill as a satiric novelist continued to grow through much of his long career. *Sincerely, Willis Wayde* is that Marquand novel most obviously like the Sinclair Lewis of the 1920's. It is a devastating portrait of a big business promoter, a man utterly without character. In 1958 Marquand published what he declared in advance would be his last novel, *Women and Thomas Harrow*, the story of a very successful playwright and his three marriages. This novel is a kind of self-consciously ironic *Tempest* to John P. Marquand's career.

Marquand is particularly notable for the double vision through which he could be in his world and still see it and himself from the vantage point of a detached on-looker. The result was that his portraits of American citizens, their frustrations, the extent to which their lives had already been determined by a structure of social decisions made by others without their awareness, and the sort of quiet desperation in which they lived out their days was particularly powerful. The reader who sees himself in some of his more absurd actions and postures in Marquand's novels has the feeling that he is also seeing Marquand as well. Like Sinclair Lewis he is the chronicler of men who make ineffectual revolts, of men who lack the stature of character and mind to be in any significant sense heroes; thus his ultimate view is comic. He examined the social conditions of American lives with irony and grace, and his "badgered American male" captures in his recurrent problems and poses not only how we behave, but also how hollow our lives often are at the core. He speaks both to our social-historical sense and to an unslaked spiritual thirst which our aridity creates. He never was capable of poetic soaring, but to his own age, at least, he spoke with ease and skill, with irony and wit, but, above all, with the authority of unsentimental knowledge.

—C. Hugh Holman

MARQUIS, Don(ald Robert Perry).   American.   Born in Walnut, Illinois, 29 July 1878. Educated at Walnut High School until age 15; worked at various jobs, then studied at the Corcoran Art School, Washington, D.C., 1899–1900. Married 1) Reina Melcher in 1909 (died, 1923), one son and one daughter; 2) the actress Marjorie Vonnegut in 1926. Worked as a clerk in the United States Customs Bureau, Washington, D.C., and as a reporter for the *Washington Times*, 1900–02; moved to Atlanta, Georgia: Associate Editor, *Atlanta News*, 1902–04; Editorial Writer, *Atlanta Journal*, 1904–07; Assistant Editor, to Joel Chandler Harris, on *Uncle Remus's Magazine*, Atlanta, 1907–09; moved to New York City, 1909; worked as a reporter on the New York *American* and the *Brooklyn Daily Eagle*, 1909–12; member of the editorial staff, 1912, and Columnist ("The Sun Dial"), 1912–20, New York *Evening Sun*; Columnist ("The Lantern"), *New York Tribune*, 1920–22; full-time writer from 1922. Recipient: Mark Twain Medal. Member, National Institute of Arts and Letters, 1923. *Died 29 December 1937.*

PUBLICATIONS

Collections

The Best of Marquis, edited by Christopher Morley.   1939.

Fiction

Danny's Own Story.   1912.

The Cruise of the Jasper B. 1916.
Carter and Other People (stories). 1921.
Pandora Lifts the Lid, with Christopher Morley. 1924.
When the Turtles Sing and Other Unusual Tales. 1928.
A Variety of People (stories). 1929.
Off the Arm. 1930.
Chapters for the Orthodox (stories). 1934.
Sun Dial Time (stories). 1936.
Sons of the Puritans. 1939.

Plays

The Old Soak (produced 1922). 1924.
The Dark Hours: Five Scenes from a History (produced 1932). 1924.
Words and Thoughts. 1924.
Out of the Sea (produced 1927). 1927.
Master of the Revels. 1934.

Verse

Dreams and Dust. 1915.
Noah an' Jonah an' Cap'n John Smith. 1921.
Poems and Portraits. 1922.
Sonnets to a Red-Haired Lady (from a Gentleman with a Blue Beard) and Famous Love Affairs. 1922.
The Awakening and Other Poems. 1924.
Archy and Mehitabel. 1927.
Love Sonnets of a Cave Man and Other Verses. 1928.
An Ode to Hollywood. 1929.
Archys Life of Mehitabel. 1933.
Archy Does His Part. 1935.

Other

Hermione and Her Little Group of Serious Thinkers. 1916.
Prefaces. 1919.
The Old Soak, and Hail and Farewell. 1921.
The Revolt of the Oyster. 1922.
Mr. Hawley Breaks into Song. 1923.
The Old Soak's History of the World with Occasional Glances at Baycliff, L.I., and Paris, France. 1924.
The Almost Perfect State (essays). 1927.
Her Foot Is on the Brass Rail. 1935.

Reading List: *O Rare Don Marquis: A Biography* by Edward Anthony, 1962.

*   *   *

Don Marquis is remembered as a humorist, but he wrote both humorous and serious plays, poetry, and fiction. His last novel, *Sons of the Puritans*, is serious. Although unfinished, this autobiographical narrative about a boy who grows to manhood in a small midwestern town presents greater depth of feeling and complexity of character and situation than Marquis's earlier, lighter novels. Like most of his work, it is well written and interesting. Like his other serious short work, however, it possibly suffers from Marquis's constant depression over having to do hack work to survive.

His serious poetry in particular sounds like the well written, graceful verse of other poets on the same well-worn themes. Yet his first collection of serious poems, *Dreams and Dust*, served a purpose; for the effect of much of his later comic verse – *Love Sonnets of a Cave Man*, for example – depends upon his sure knowledge of such themes in just such terms. Even his parodies of free verse, over the name of "Archy the Cockroach," occasionally contain poems that are comic largely on account of their sprightly elegant meter and rhyme.

Marquis is remembered chiefly for his creation of Archy, whose ideas and adventures first filled his newspaper columns and then were collected in books. Other columns, collected in *The Almost Perfect State*, deal lightly, humorously, sometimes seriously, with Marquis's notions concerning that State. Still other columns resulted in books about "The Old Soak," who became the central character in Marquis's only successful play.

The Old Soak, Archy the Cockroach, and Mehitabel the Cat reveal Marquis's comic capabilities at their best. As Archy, Marquis views life from the underside, that is, the side from which it appears ridiculous and therefore not to be taken seriously. So the incongruities, discrepancies, paradoxes, involved in this view – whether of man's morality and politics, Mehitabel's social and artistic pretensions, or any other matter – strike the reader as comic. Further, Archy's literary efforts make him ridiculous in turn, both because he is a cockroach and because he has the quite human soul of a free verse poet. For his broken typographic lines, without punctuation or capital letters, could not have been written by a cockroach and should not have been written by a poet. The comic effect is increased by the mockery of free verse and its maker.

Similarly, the Old Soak can not be taken seriously. His views of history, the Good Book, and prohibition, together with his misspellings and malapropisms, expose his ignorance and turn him into a figure of fun. For good reason, the play about him succeeded, banal as it is, whereas Marquis's more serious plays – mainly derived from legend and history – failed. Marquis's strength lies not in development of character, but in "characters," not in suspenseful action, but in absurd situations. These express his real gift, rare and rewarding in literature, the truly comic angle of vision.

—Robert F. Richards

MASTERS, Edgar Lee.   American.   Born in Garnett, Kansas, 23 August 1868; brought up in Lewistown, Illinois. Educated at schools in Lewistown; Knox College, Galesburg, Illinois, 1889; studied law in his father's law office; admitted to the Illinois Bar, 1891. Married 1) Helen M. Jenkins in 1898 (divorced, 1925), three children; 2) Ellen Coyne in 1926. Practised law in Chicago, 1891–1921, when he retired and moved to New York, to devote himself to writing. Recipient: Twain Medal, 1927; Academy of American Poets Fellowship, 1946. *Died 5 March 1950.*

Publications

Collections

Selected Poems, edited by Denys Thompson.   1972.

Verse

A Book of Verses. 1898.
The Blood of the Prophets.   1905.
Songs and Sonnets. 2 vols., 1910–12.
Spoon River Anthology. 1915; revised edition, 1916.
The Great Valley. 1916.
Songs and Satires. 1916.
Toward the Gulf. 1918.
Starved Rock. 1919.
Domesday Book 1920.
The Open Sea. 1921.
The New Spoon River. 1924.
Selected Poems. 1925.
The Fate of the Jury: An Epilogue to Domesday Book.   1929.
Lichee Nuts. 1930.
The Serpent in the Wilderness. 1933.
Invisible Landscapes. 1935.
The Golden Fleece of California. 1936.
Poems of People. 1936.
The New World. 1937.
More People. 1939.
Illinois Poems. 1941.
Along the Illinois. 1942.
Harmony of Deeper Music: Posthumous Poems, edited by Frank K. Robinson.   1976.

Plays

Maximilian. 1902.
Althea. 1907.
The Trifler. 1908.
The Leaves of the Tree. 1909.
Eileen. 1910.
The Locket. 1910.
The Bread of Idleness. 1911.
Lee: A Dramatic Poem. 1926.
Jack Kelso: A Dramatic Poem. 1928.
Gettysburg, Manila, Acoma. 1930.
Godbey: A Dramatic Poem. 1931.
Dramatic Duologues (includes *Henry VIII and Ann Boleyn, Andrew Jackson and Peggy Eaton, Aaron Burr and Madam Jumel, Rabelais and the Queen of Whims*).   1934.
Richmond: A Dramatic Poem. 1934.

Fiction

Mitch Miller. 1920.
Children of the Market Place. 1922.
Skeeters Kirby. 1923.
The Nuptial Flight. 1923.
Mirage. 1924.
Kit O'Brien. 1927.
The Tide of Time. 1937.

Other

The New Star Chamber and Other Essays.   1904.
Levy Mayer and the New Industrial Era: A Biography.   1927.
Lincoln, The Man.   1931.
The Tale of Chicago.   1933.
Vachel Lindsay: A Poet in America.   1935.
Across Spoon River: An Autobiography.   1936.
Whitman.   1937.
Mark Twain: A Portrait.   1938.
The Sangamon (on the Sangamon River).   1942.

Editor, *The Living Thoughts of Emerson.*   1940.

Bibliography: *Masters: Catalogue and Checklist* by Frank K. Robinson, 1970.

Reading List: *The Chicago Renaissance in American Letters* by Bernard Duffey, 1954; *The Vermont Background of Masters* by Kimball Flaccus, 1955; in *America's Literary Revolt* by Michael Yatron, 1959; *Spoon River Revisited* by Lois Hartley, 1963; *Masters: The Spoon River Poet and His Critics* by John T. Flanagan, 1974.

*   *   *

One of the ancient Greek poets has written: "No man knows happiness; all men/Learn misery who live beneath the sun," thereby anticipating the spirit of Edgar Lee Masters's *Spoon River Anthology*. Though the book was brilliantly successful, the road to it was a long and arduous one. Seventeen years earlier Masters's first book of poems was an ignominious failure. The next few books were also unsuccessful. By this date the poet was a well-known lawyer, a robust man about town in Chicago who had made an unsuitable marriage but never allowed matrimony to interfere with his libertine instincts. The contrast between the poems, classic in form and hackneyed in thought, and their lusty author led one literary friend of Masters, the editor of *Reedy's Mirror*, to nudge him in the direction of a more original subject-matter. In any case, at the age of forty-five, Masters had failed at poetry, the one great passion of his life, and in his personal life. His one transcendent gift, fascination with human nature and insight into its workings, had found expression only in his legal career where he had espoused the cause of lower-class victims of capitalist greed.

This was the situation in May 1914, when the poet's mother arrived to visit him. According to Masters, this lady was witty, acutely observant, and "full of divinations" into the lives of the townspeople they had known in Petersburg and Lewistown, Illinois. Mother and son reviewed these lives, reviving emotions and interests that had long been dormant in the poet's mind. The result was the sudden eruption of his latent gifts as chronicler of a whole community of inter-related lives. Between May and December, though under heavy pressure from his legal duties, Masters composed the 214 epitaphs that were published that year in *Reedy's Mirror*. Other than the memory of his neighbors, the chief sources of inspiration were the polished epigrams of the *Greek Anthology* and the stimulus of the American free verse revolt that had just burst on a startled, genteel reading public. These three sources, along with the sobering reflections on human mortality induced by his mother's visit, produced "the most read and talked of volume of poetry that has ever been written in America."

Five years after the publication of *Spoon River*, Masters retired from the law and devoted himself to the writing of thirty or more books of poetry, novels, biographies, and Illinois history and geography. Though he showed a dogged determination to succeed, he never caught fire again. His first great achievement was his last and the remaining thirty-five years of his life were an embarrassing anticlimax as his first forty-five were a despairing preparation. Masters's own life, which he includes in his book under the name Webster Ford, was one of the most curious and ironical of the tales he tells there.

The anthology, as expanded and republished in 1916, contains a short prologue, "The Hill," and 243 individual epitaphs. The verses, of a marvelous concision and vitality, relate only the most essential features of the speakers' lives. Each soul, speaking for himself from the grave, bares his innermost nature and the secrets of his life, his own self-portrait being qualified by the words of those with whom his fate was interlocked, so that nineteen separate story lines are developed. Each epitaph has its own tone and style; each speaker treats the climactic experiences or insights of his life. Depending on the character of the speaker, the language varies from mystical utterance downwards to sonorous rhetoric and racy colloquialism. The criticism that the style is prosy and flat, made by Floyd Dell and others when the book first appeared, is traceable to the lack of conventional prettiness in meter and rhyme. Though rarely "pretty," many of the poems are written in a highly imaginative metaphoric style, all are freshly conceived on the basis of a unifying rhetorical design with ample use of every form of verbal patterning, many are haunting, and some contain images of real beauty.

Without the power of its language, *Spoon River* would never have aroused its readers as it did. But its essence is in its portraiture. As few other authors have done, and no other author, perhaps, in the compass of a single book, Masters produced a "summation" and "universal depiction of life." Every variety of human nature is represented: celebrants at life's feast and neurasthenics, rowdies and lovers, pious Christians and atheists, rapists and whores, society women and laundresses, scientists and factory hands, clairvoyants, preachers, and a stable boy who sees the face of God. One of the largest groups is the philosophers. Masters was a zealous scholar and had read widely in several languages. Along with the anti-Christian and libertarian elements in his make-up, there was also the social idealist, the cosmic optimist, and the mystic that he counted as his essential self. The epitaphs of the philosophers are usually limited to one strand of thought from which one may infer their life and character, and their reflections are framed in such a way that they are as dramatic as the life histories.

Two criticisms of Masters should be considered here. The first is that the poet is preoccupied with sex, and much of the anthology is sordid and obscene. This charge, originating with Amy Lowell and others, is curious because there are only a dozen poems that are chiefly concerned with sex, none of these is salacious, and they tend to show that the wages of sin are death. The basis of the complaint lies in the candor with which Masters treats sex wherever it appears in life. Readers had been conditioned to literature in which the subject-matter was not actual life but a given writer's conception of it so that much of the earth and roots had been removed – as well as the uppermost reaches of branches that were beyond the interests of a workaday world. One of the novelties of Masters's treatment was to eliminate authorial censorship and to allow his characters, based as they were on real-life persons, to speak honestly of their lives. Though this was not his intention, the result was the first exposé of village life, which set a new pattern for literature, while the poet's views are said to have influenced subsequent writing between the two world wars.

According to the second objection, the poet falsified the American mid-western town by presenting an overly sensationalistic and pessimistic account of its life. It is true that the incidence of crime and sudden death is greater than one would normally find, but Masters was not writing a sociological report. The epitaphs taken together form a highly patterned comical tragedy that represents life as it works on the human imagination. At some moment all of these disasters actually happen to someone, but the book, as Alice Henderson remarked, is also steeped in a "flaming idealism." There are many heroes and noble souls, and the final impression that it makes is of the dignity, stoic courage, and resilience of humanity in its hapless "fool's errand" to the grave. In writing these portraits, Masters creates the bond of understanding and sympathy with a many-faced humanity that motivated his own legal work for luckless victims of circumstances.

—Glenn Richard Ruihley

McCARTHY, Mary (Therese).   American.   Born in Seattle, Washington, 21 June 1912. Educated at Forest Ridge Convent, Seattle; Annie Wright Seminary, Tacoma, Washington; Vassar College, Poughkeepsie, New York, A.B. 1933 (Phi Beta Kappa). Married 1) Harold Johnsrud in 1933; 2) Edmund Wilson, *q.v.*, in 1938, one son; 3) Bowden Broadwater in 1946; 4) James Raymond West in 1961. Editor, Covici Friede, publishers, New York, 1936–38; Editor, 1937–38, and Drama Critic, 1937–62, *Partisan Review*, New Brunswick, New Jersey; Instructor, Bard College, Annandale-on-Hudson, New York, 1945–46, and Sarah Lawrence College, Bronxville, New York, 1948. Recipient: Guggenheim Fellowship, 1949, 1959; National Institute of Arts and Letters grant, 1957. D.Litt.: Syracuse University, New York, 1973; University of Hull, Yorkshire, 1974. Lives in Paris.

PUBLICATIONS

Fiction

>   *The Company She Keeps.*   1942.
>   *The Oasis.*   1949; as *A Source of Embarrassment*, 1950.
>   *Cast a Cold Eye* (stories).   1950.
>   *The Groves of Academe.*   1952.
>   *A Charmed Life.*   1955.
>   *The Group.*   1963.
>   *Birds of America.*   1971.

Other

>   *Sights and Spectacles, 1937–56.*   1956; as *Sights and Spectacles: Theatre Chronicles, 1937–58*, 1959; augmented edition, as *McCarthy's Theatre Chronicles, 1937–62*, 1963.
>   *Venice Observed: Comments on Venetian Civilization.*   1956.
>   *Memories of a Catholic Girlhood.*   1957.
>   *The Stones of Florence.*   1959.
>   *On the Contrary* (essays).   1961.
>   *Vietnam.*   1967.
>   *Hanoi.*   1968.
>   *The Writing on the Wall* (essays).   1970.

Medina. 1972.
The Mask of State: Watergate Portraits. 1974.
The Seventeenth Degree. 1974.

Translator, *The Iliad; or, The Poem of Force,* by Simone Weil. 1948.
Translator, *On the Iliad,* by Rachel Bespaloff. 1948.

Bibliography: *McCarthy: A Bibliography* by Sherli Goldman, 1968.

Reading List: *McCarthy* by Barbara McKenzie, 1966; *The Company She Kept* by Doris Grumbach, 1967; *McCarthy* by Irvin Stock, 1968.

*   *   *

Mary McCarthy belongs to that set of modern American authors who appear at first to be circumscribed by the time in which they write. Her first novel, *The Company She Keeps*, is the most charming and vigorous of her novels in spite of being almost too conscious of the political and social milieu of Greenwich Village. *The Company She Keeps* is light reading, but, in terms of plot, a daring experiment. It contains six chapters, each differing from the other in time and place, with one personality to hold the stories together. The strength of the personality, of the viewing eye, and the consistency of outlook which that eye provides, form the only cohesion to the "novel." It has about it the feel of the early experiments with surrealist fiction and at the same time the freshness and youthful vitality one sees in the early stories of Fitzgerald. McCarthy has captured, through details, the spirit of her generation just as surely. In the historical-social context, one learns more from writers like McCarthy and Fitzgerald than one can from our more literary authors. *The Company She Keeps* also offers a fascinating glimpse of McCarthy's powers as a journalist. Her critical essays are collected in *On the Contrary* and *The Writing on the Wall*. Her *Theatre Chronicles*, also begun early, offer the same strong command and vigor along with a truly original understanding and analysis of the theatre. Her essay on *Macbeth* in *The Writing on the Wall* is a perfect example of the way McCarthy's critical eye catches out similarities and modern relevancy that are startling and revealing to the reader. Her essays show what kind of professor she must have been: funny, inventive, clever, determined to catch at the sparkling threads of every idea. With *The Groves of Academe*, she created a small scandal with a biting portrait of a college President struggling with the politics of his English Department. *The Groves of Academe* and her fourth novel, *A Charmed Life*, are probably meant to be allegories – the former of Senator McCarthy's communist hunts, and the latter of a moral and philosophical sort where generalizations are drawn out of a small community that are meant to apply to all of us. *A Charmed Life* is a magnificent book – unlimited by time or distracting political concepts, it concerns what happens to people who retire from the world, to devote themselves to something, in this case Art. It is a gentle but shocking reminder to modern man that he cannot hide from the world out of sensibility or devotion to an unworldly goal; life remains dangerous. The characters in this novel come to life more thoroughly than the eight heroines of *The Group*, her most famous novel. *The Group* was a great success when it appeared: its vision of life affected an entire generation. Her own autobiography, *Memories of a Catholic Girlhood*, is a beautiful, classic, searching piece of writing. Along with *A Charmed Life*, *Memories* is the best showcase for her prose.

Mary McCarthy has always walked a very delicate line between her knowledge that the modern novel is plotless and between her love for the world and its myriad details. *The Company She Keeps* is a very carefully plotted novel, but it does not follow a time-line; *The Groves of Academe* has a traditional novelistic conception but, lacking the freewheeling movement of *Company*, is less successful; *A Charmed Life* is positioned insecurely but brilliantly on the line between the Dickensian novel of action and detail and the plotless modern impressionistic novel: it is a written play where the dramatic conflict is between clashing ideas and philosophies; *The Group* returns to a novel form that is more disjointed but richer of plot. Her last novel, *Birds of America*, is an interesting idea that somehow has not taken form, but it is sweet, funny, and very clever.

—Brady Nordland

McCULLERS, (Lula) Carson (née Smith). American. Born in Columbus, Georgia, 19 February 1917. Educated at Columbia University, New York; New York University, 1935–36. Married Reeves McCullers in 1937 (divorced, 1940); remarried Reeves McCullers in 1945 (died, 1953). Recipient: Guggenheim Fellowship, 1943; National Institute of Arts and Letters grant, 1943; New York Drama Critics Circle Award, 1950; Donaldson Award, for drama, 1950. Member, National Institute of Arts and Letters. *Died 29 September 1967.*

PUBLICATIONS

Fiction

> *The Heart Is a Lonely Hunter.* 1940.
> *Reflections in a Golden Eye.* 1941.
> *The Member of the Wedding.* 1946.
> *The Ballad of the Sad Cafe: The Novels and Stories.* 1951.
> *Seven* (stories). 1954.
> *Clock Without Hands.* 1961.

Plays

> *The Twisted Trinity*, music by David Diamond. 1946.
> *The Member of the Wedding*, from her own novel (produced 1950). 1957.
> *The Square Root of Wonderful* (produced 1957). 1958.

Other

> *Sweet as a Pickle and Clean as a Pig* (juvenile). 1964.
> *The Mortgaged Heart* (uncollected writings), edited by Margarita G. Smith. 1971.

Bibliography: *Katherine Anne Porter and McCullers: A Reference Guide* by Robert F. Kiernan, 1976.

Reading List: *The Ballad of McCullers* by Oliver Evans, 1966, as *McCullers: Her Life and Work*, 1968; *McCullers* by Lawrence S. Graver, 1969; *The Lonely Hunter: A Biography of McCullers* by Virginia Spencer Carr, 1975; *McCullers* by Richard M. Cook, 1975.

*   *   *

Carson McCullers, though a person whom nearly all her friends found charming, was through much of her life an invalid, suffering from melancholia and loneliness. In spite of a remarkably full production for a comparatively short life, she only occasionally gathered energy to write with the perfection of style and structure she demanded of herself the narratives – in their essence long *nouvelles* rather than short novels – on which (though the dramatisation of her story *The Member of the Wedding* was very successful) her reputation rests. Her early novel *Reflections in a Golden Eye*, which made her famous, is set in an army post in peacetime, whose dullness and ordinariness she emphasises. But nothing is really dull and ordinary in McCullers's works, and there is mounting horror from the moment when the bewildered heroine's frustrated and slightly mad husband puts a tiny live kitten into a freezing post box till the moment when the heroine (who has had a love affair with a common soldier for whom her husband has a sadistic hatred) is seen sick in hospital having, in desperation, sheared off her nipples. The heroine, like many of McCullers's heroines, is simple, generous, and childlike, and it is a mark of McCullers's fine talent and charity that she does not force us to condemn anyone, even the husband. The horror of life is something coolly and charitably accepted by her, like its frustration, even like its innocence and fulfilment. She is a most moving and disturbing writer precisely because it seems not her purpose to move or disturb, or to make the reader share pain as he often does, but to present events and characters with coolness and precision.

The tone is in fact often near that of comedy (McCullers is always an amusing writer), even when the material verges on the tragic. *The Ballad of the Sad Cafe* has a grotesquerie, for instance, that makes one both cry and laugh. In a dull little southern town, a gruff young woman, grotesquely tall, with a kind heart which she conceals even from herself, runs a little cafe which gradually becomes a refuge for all the eccentric, lonely, and absurd characters in the town, and thus unconsciously has its own distinction. The awkward, clumsy heroine takes them all in, and is generous about credit, for they are not so very different – are mostly less odd, in fact – than herself. Unfortunately, she is susceptible to love, and falls in love with a malicious dwarf. He is ready enough to exploit her generosity, but hates everybody, and comes to hate the heroine with special intensity when he realises that she loves him. If anybody could at all attract him it would be a man with the normal height, the athletic bearing, the easy self-confidence, which he himself as a little monster so singularly lacks. And such men, of course, will treat him with contempt. There is almost a philosophy in this short novel, the philosophy that some people at least are drawn to love those who cannot love them, and that unwanted love can arouse not pity but resentment and malice.

The Member of the Wedding is a gentler book, about a girl in adolescence excited by a wedding in her family and vaguely ambitious to become "a member of the wedding," an organic part of it, in a way that is not physically or psychologically possible. Fortunately, in this story the heroine's troubles are responded to with love and understanding. But the novel makes us realise that both the attractiveness and the misfortunes of McCullers's heroines spring from an essential innocence in their nature.

Her later writing tended more towards comedy and revealed even more vividly her detailed, half-mocking, half-loving, knowledge of the *mores* of the American south. She was not a great writer, but a very good and original one, with the classic virtues. To turn to her from the wordy rhetorical improvisations of a major figure, William Faulkner, is to become refreshingly aware that McCullers's grace and economy are a model of how prose ought to be written. It is like turning from Dostoevsky to Turgenev.

—G. S. Fraser

McKAY, Claude. Jamaican. Born Festus Claudius McKay in Sunny Ville, Clarendon Parish, Jamaica, 15 September 1889. Educated at grammar school in Jamaica; Tuskegee Institute, Alabama, 1912; Kansas State College, Manhattan, 1912–14. Married Eulalie Imelda Edwards in 1914 (separated, 1914), one daughter. Policeman in Jamaica; migrated to New York City, did various jobs and opened a restaurant, 1914; Staff Member, *Workers' Dreadnought* communist newspaper, London, 1920; Staff Member, 1921–22, and Co-Editor, with Michael Gold, 1922, *The Liberator*, New York; visited Russia, 1922–23, and lived in Europe and Tangier, 1923–34, then returned to the United States: writer for the WPA (Works Progress Administration) in the late 1930's. Recipient: Harmon Prize, 1929. *Died 22 May 1948.*

PUBLICATIONS

Collections

Selected Poems. 1953.
The Passion of McKay: Selected Prose and Poetry 1912–1948, edited by Wayne Cooper. 1973.

Verse

Constab Ballads. 1912.
Songs from Jamaica. 1912; with Constab Ballads, as The Dialect Poetry, 1972.
Songs of Jamaica. 1912.
Spring in New Hampshire and Other Poems. 1920.
Harlem Shadows. 1922.

Fiction

Home to Harlem. 1928.
Banjo: A Story Without a Plot. 1929.
Gingertown (stories). 1932.
Banana Bottom. 1933.

Other

Negry v Amerike (Negroes in America). 1923.
A Long Way from Home (autobiography). 1937.
Harlem: Negro Metropolis. 1940.

Bibliography: "McKay" by Manuel D. Lopez, in *Bulletin of Bibliography*, October–December 1972.

Reading List: *Roots of Negro Racial Consciousness: Three Harlem Renaissance Authors* by Stephen H. Bronz, 1964; *The West Indian Novel and Its Background* by Kenneth Ramchand, 1970; *McKay: The Black Poet at War* by Addison Gayle, Jr., 1972.

* * *

Claude McKay attempted throughout his career to resolve the complexities surrounding the black man's paradoxical situation in the West. A widely travelled man, he lived for twelve years (1922–1934) in Great Britain, Russia, Germany, France, Spain and Morocco. It is during these years that a new wave of Afro-American writing, now widely known as the Harlem Renaissance, spread across the American continent. McKay is generally credited with having inspired the Renaissance with his militant poem "If We Must Die" (1919) when the nation was gripped with the Great Red Scare and racial riots in the Northern cities. Later, however, the self-exiled McKay developed an ambivalent relationship with the New Negroes of the 1920's; he did not share the "social uplift" philosophy of Alian Locke and W. E. B. DuBois although he had affinities as writer with Jean Toomer, Langston Hughes and Zora Neale Hurston. McKay is also considered a pioneer in the development of West Indian fiction, though he never returned to the land of his birth, Jamaica, having left it at age 23. Today, many regard his fiction as his most valuable contribution, but McKay also published four collections of poems, an autobiography, many essays, and a sociological study of Harlem.

It is as a poet that McKay first won attention in both the West Indies and the United States. In 1912, before he went to Kansas as an agriculture student (hoping to become the prophet of scientific farming on his return home!), he had published two volumes of dialect verse, *Songs of Jamaica* and *Constab Ballads*, and won himself a reputation as "the Jamaican Bobby Burns." Soon, he was drawn towards the intricacies of the American colour caste and he decided to cast his lot with working-class Afro-Americans. McKay was both stimulated and angered by the American environment – "Although she feeds me bread of bitterness/... I love this cultured hell that tests my youth!" ("America"). His background in the Jamaican society where the blacks formed a majority often gave him an edge as poet-observer over black American artists whose careers were sometimes wrecked by a debilitating bitterness. In his poems of personal love and racial protest, McKay gave strong expression to joy and anger, pride and stoicism. "If We Must Die," although not his best poem, won him great popularity because it powerfully evoked, in lines charged with emotion, the militant mood of Afro-American communities over the treatment meted out to black soldiers returning from World War I. The poem achieved a kind of universality in spite of its trite diction, as was well-demonstrated when Winston Churchill related it to the Allied cause by reading it to the House of Commons during World War II.

McKay's influence on later black poetry is measured better by the power of his sentiment than by any innovations in form, style or diction. McKay empathises with the sufferings of working-class blacks in the many poems of *Harlem Shadows*, but he succeeds best when he focusses on an individual's tragedy to protest against the forces of oppression. This is evident in poems such as "The Harlem Dancer," where a young female dancer is surrounded by a crowd of "wine-flushed, bold-eyed boys" which has no inkling of her soulful pride. In "Baptism," he expresses a Victorian stoicism that asserts the individual's victory through the harshest of tests. McKay often tried his hand at the sonnet form, using irregular rhyme and metre to achieve his own poetic ends. "One Year After," dealing with inter-racial love in a two-sonnet sequence, anticipates contemporary black attitudes in attributing the failure of a black-white relationship not to society's pressures but to the lover's black pride: "Not once in all our days of poignant love/Did I a single instant give to thee/My undivided being wholly free." McKay also wrote many poems about love and sex that had little to do with racial conflict and in some of these (e.g., "Flower of Love" and "A Red Flower") – as often in his fiction, especially in *Home to Harlem* – he creates erotic effects through suggestive portrayals of sexual pleasure. And yet, McKay's link to the more recent black literature is based primarily on his protest poems and his three novels.

McKay wrote both short stories and novels. *Gingertown*, his only collection of short stories, is important mainly as a source of clues and parallels to his development as novelist-thinker. The three novels – *Home to Harlem*, *Banjo*, and *Banana Bottom* – together form a thematic trilogy exploring the Western black man's special situation against the Manichean opposition between "instinct" and "intellect." *Home to Harlem* and *Banjo*, both essentially plotless novels, raise issues relating to the black's alleged primitivism, and its possible uses in an age when the fear of standardization was obsessive. The two protagonists – Jake and Banjo respectively – are rollicking roustabouts, taking life and women as they come. Their life of instinctive simplicity is, however, not without a Hemingway-like code. If they would not scab against a fellow worker, they would not be gullible enough to join a union either. As lovers, they do not permit themselves to become pimps or demean themselves to satisfy their women's masochistic desires. In the sexual metaphor that is McKay's lens in all the three novels, sexual deviations and perversions symbolize the pernicious influence of white values on black lives. In *Banana Bottom*, there is a tentative resolution of these conflicts in the character of Bita Plant who (like McKay himself) cannot allow self-hatred to reject native traditions completely even as she continues to find uses in her life for Western thought. Bita is, in some ways, a dramatization of the tangled thought on the significance of race and heritage in modern life that McKay had filtered through the character of Ray, who appears in both *Home to Harlem* and *Banjo*.

There is no hint in either his autobiography, *A Long Way from Home*, or his sociological study, *Harlem · Negro Metropolis*, of McKay's conversion in 1944 to Roman Catholicism, an astonishing turnabout by any standards. McKay's autobiography is unusual in not giving any details of his personal life, although useful as a mirror to his independence in the midst of stimulating encounters with issues, places, and people (including Frank Harris, H. G. Wells, Isadora Duncan, Sinclair Lewis). The section on his Russian visit is particularly valuable in determining a phase of his uneasy relationship with the leftist movement, from the days of his association with Max Eastman and *The Liberator* to the anti-Communist sentiments of his final years. *Harlem: Negro Metropolis* offers a scathing view of Harlem's community life and the obsessive fight of its leaders against segregation. The reviewers criticized the book justifiably for its frequent failures in objectivity. Although McKay never became an apologist for capitalist imperialism, he did try in his last years to vindicate his conversion to Catholicism in his essay "On Becoming a Roman Catholic" and in many letters to his life-long friend, Max Eastman. One cannot, however, help feeling that a tired McKay surrendered his difficult search for the positive meanings of black life by giving in to the traditional discipline of the Roman Church. As he himself put it in a letter (16 October 1944) to Eastman: "It seems to me that to have a religion is very much like falling in love with a woman. You love her for her ... Beauty, which cannot be defined."

—Amritjit Singh

MENCKEN, H(enry) L(ouis). American. Born in Baltimore, Maryland, 12 September 1880, and lived there for the rest of his life. Educated at Knapp's Institute, Baltimore, and the Baltimore Polytechnic Institute. Married Sara Powell Haardt in 1930 (died, 1935). Reporter, *Baltimore Morning Herald*, 1899–1903; City Editor, 1903–05, and Chief Editor, 1905–06, *Baltimore Evening Herald*; member of the editorial staff of the *Baltimore Sun* and *Evening Sun*, 1906–41: Columnist ("The Free Lance"), 1910–16; War Correspondent in Germany, 1916–18; Literary Critic, 1908–23, and Editor, with George Jean Nathan, 1914–23, *Smart Set*, New York; Literary Adviser to Alfred A. Knopf, publishers, New York, from 1917; Contributing Editor, *The Nation*, New York, 1931–32; Co-Founder, with Nathan, 1923, and Editor, 1924–33, *American Mercury*, New York. Recipient: American Academy of Arts and Letters Gold Medal, 1950. *Died 29 January 1956.*

PUBLICATIONS

Collections

>Letters, edited by Guy J. Forgue. 1961.
>The American Scene: A Reader, edited by Huntington Cairns. 1965.

Fiction

>Christmas Story. 1946.

Plays

>The Artist (produced 1927). 1912.
>Heliogabalus: A Buffoonery, with George Jean Nathan. 1920.

Verse

>Ventures into Verse. 1903.

Other

>George Bernard Shaw: His Plays. 1905.
>The Philosophy of Friedrich Nietzsche. 1908.
>What You Ought to Know about Your Baby, with Leonard Keene Hirshberg. 1910.
>Men Versus the Man: A Conversation Between Robert Rives La Monte, Socialist, and Mencken, Individualist. 1910.
>Europe after 8:15, with George Jean Nathan and Willard Huntington Wright (travel). 1914.
>A Little Book in C Major. 1916.
>A Book of Burlesques. 1916.
>A Book of Prefaces. 1917.
>Pistols for Two, with George Jean Nathan. 1917.
>Damn! A Book of Calumny. 1918.
>In Defense of Women. 1918; revised edition, 1922.
>The American Language. 1919; revised edition, 1921, 1923, 1936; supplement, 1945, 1948.
>Prejudices, First Series. 1919; Second Series, 1920; Third Series, 1922; Fourth Series, 1924; Fifth Series, 1926; Sixth Series, 1927; Selected Prejudices, 1927; edited by James T. Farrell, as Prejudices: A Selection, 1958.
>The American Credo, with George Jean Nathan. 1920.
>Notes on Democracy. 1926.
>Treatise on the Gods. 1930; revised edition, 1946.
>Making a President: A Footnote to the Saga of Democracy. 1932.
>Treatise on Right and Wrong. 1934.
>Happy Days 1880–1892 (autobiography). 1940.
>Newspaper Days 1899–1906 (autobiography). 1941.
>A New Dictionary of Quotations on Historical Principles. 1942.
>Heathen Days 1890–1936 (autobiography). 1943.

A Mencken Chrestomathy. 1949.
The Vintage Mencken, edited by Alistair Cooke. 1955.
Minority Report: Mencken's Notebooks. 1956.
A Carnival of Buncombe (essays), edited by Malcolm Moos. 1956; as *On Politics,* 1960.
The Bathtub Hoax and Other Blasts and Bravos from the Chicago Tribune, edited by Robert McHugh. 1958.
Mencken on Music: A Selection of His Writings on Music, Together with an Account of Mencken's Musical Life and a History of the Saturday Night Club, edited by Louis Cheslock. 1961.
Smart Set Criticism, edited by William H. Nolte. 1968.
New Letters, edited by Carl Bode. 1976.

Editor, *A Doll's House, Little Eyolf,* by Ibsen. 2 vols., 1909.
Editor, *The Gist of Nietzsche.* 1910.
Editor, *The Free Lance Books.* 5 vols., 1919–21.
Editor, *Americana.* 1925.
Editor, *Essays,* by James Gibbons Huneker. 1929.
Editor, *The American Democrat,* by James Fenimore Cooper. 1931.
Editor, *Southern Album,* by Sara Haardt. 1936.
Editor, *The Sunpapers of Baltimore.* 1937.

Translator, *The Antichrist,* by Nietzsche. 1920.

Bibliography: *Mencken: The Bibliography* by Betty Adler, 1961.

Reading List: *Mencken: A Portrait from Memory* by Charles Angoff, 1956; *Mencken: Literary Critic* by William H. Nolte, 1966; *Mencken* by Philip Wagner, 1966; *The Constant Circle: Mencken and His Friends* by Sara Mayfield, 1968; *Mencken* by Carl Bode, 1969; *Serpent in Eden: Mencken and the South* by Fred C. Hobson, Jr., 1974; *Mencken: A Study of His Thought* by Charles A. Fecher, 1978; *Mencken: Critic of American Life* by George H. Douglas, 1978.

*   *   *

H. L. Mencken's reputation was etched by the acidic wit that characterized his commentary on the American culture of his day. Trained as a newspaperman, Mencken reached the height of his powers in the 1920's when, as an associate of the *Sun* papers in Baltimore and an editor first of *The Smart Set* and then of *The American Mercury,* he became one the nation's most influential critics.

A prodigious writer, he published some twenty-five books – not to mention literally thousands of articles, essays, stories, editorials, book reviews – during the course of his career, beginning curiously with the now-forgotten *Ventures into Verse* in 1903 and moving in 1905 and 1908 respectively to the more representative *George Bernard Shaw: His Plays* and *The Philosophy of Friedrich Nietzsche.* Throughout, however, his style and his messages were those found in *Prejudices,* his most representative work, a six-volume collection of opinion published between 1919 and 1927. The messages were intensely iconoclastic: American culture had become stultified by its rigid adherence to a peculiarly "Puritan" form of Christian morality, and the quality of American politics – and, indeed, of American life – was being compromised by a foolish but persistent belief in egalitarianism. These messages and their many corollaries he published again and again, employing a style which became his particular signature, a style whose ingredients were the acerbic allusion, the caustic joke, the unusual word, the irreverent comparison. However, a story like "The Girl from Red Lion,

P.A." is essentially a good-natured look at an ignorant country girl, with more than a hint of compassion.

With the advent of the 1930's depression, the popularity of Mencken's social commentary waned. In 1919, however, he had published *The American Language*, a book which he revised and supplemented at various times until 1948. In *The American Language* Mencken sought, as he said in his sub-title, to inquire "into the development of English in the United States." The volume was quickly accepted by linguists, and continues today as a standard reference work in the field. Indeed, it may well account for Mencken's fame long after his other work has become dated and been forgotten.

—Bruce A. Lohof

MERRILL, James (Ingram). American. Born in New York City, 3 March 1926. Educated at Lawrenceville School; Amherst College, Massachusetts, B.A. 1947. Served in the United States Army, 1944–45. Recipient: National Book Award, 1967; Bollingen Prize, 1973. Member, National Institute of Arts and Letters, 1971. Lives in Connecticut.

PUBLICATIONS

Verse

Jim's Book: A Collection of Poems and Short Stories.   1942.
The Black Swan.   1946.
First Poems.   1951.
Short Stories.   1954.
The Country of a Thousand Years of Peace and Other Poems.   1959; revised edition, 1970.
Selected Poems.   1961.
Water Street.   1962.
The Thousand and Second Night.   1963.
Violent Pastoral.   1965.
Nights and Days.   1966.
The Fire Screen.   1969.
Two Poems.   1972.
Braving the Elements.   1972.
The Yellow Pages: 59 Poems.   1974.
Yannina.   1973.
Divine Comedies.   1976.

Plays

The Bait (produced 1953). In Artists' Theatre: Four Plays, edited by Herbert Machiz, 1960.

The Immortal Husband (produced 1955). In *Playbook: Plays for a New Theatre*, 1956.

Fiction

The Seraglio. 1957.
The (Diblos) Notebook. 1965.

Reading List: *Alone with America* by Richard Howard, 1969; "Feux d'Artifice" by Stephen Yenser, in *Poetry*, June 1973.

*   *   *

James Merrill's books of poems are like the rings of a tree: each extends beyond the content, expression, outlook, and craft of the previous work. Merrill has patiently, even doggedly, pursued his craft, giving each poem, however short or terse or ephemeral, a certain lapidary sheen and hardness. Merrill's complete output of verse, fiction, and plays is characterized by an absorption with technique and difficulty.

But his earliest poems are overworked with rhyme scheme, metric pattern, enamelled diction. Merrill came onto the literary scene during the vogue of revived metaphysical poetry, verse wrought in a traditional manner with high polish and much verbal flourishing under formal restraint. Such is the poetry of his first major book, *The Country of a Thousand Years of Peace*, with its elegant experiences, its widely cultivated tastes, its voice of leisured travel and gracious living – the poetry, in other words, of an American aristocrat. *Water Street* continues this elegant discourse on the vicissitudes of life, love, travel, the perennially chilly rooms and beds of his daily life.

But with *The Fire Screen* a new dimension to the persona comes into view: his life in Greece, where the warm sun, the old culture, the intimacy of life release a deeper self-awareness into his poems. Instead of the isolated, inward existence of New England, here the speaker is thrust into a more primal and assertive culture where his passions and convictions are awakened. There are also poems of return to the northeastern United States, lyrics of resignation and quiet regrets. In the American edition is the too-long verse narrative "The Summer People," with its heavy-handed irony; Robert Lowell said more about the vacation culture in his one page poem "Skunk Hour." *Braving the Elements* is both freer in its verse forms and more open and intimate in its content. Instead of the choppy quality of his earlier, too tightly wrought lines, there is now a smooth, conversational rhythm in his three or four line stanza structures. "Days of 1935," "18 West 11th Street" (which laments the death of young anti-war radicals), and "Days of 1971" are open, intimate revelations of the poet's mind.

Merrill's progress is toward a compromise between rigid formalism and the open poem, where craft would continue to discipline the choice and assembly of language but where the content would be free to take its own course. That balance is reached in the long sequence "The Book of Ephraim" in *Divine Comedies*. The twenty-six alphabetically ordered parts are interwoven through a leisurely plot where the poet and his lover communicate with the spirit of Ephraim through the Ouija board, whose insight and wit make life seem a mere changing room in a vast spiritual universe. In discovering this broader realm, Merrill is dazzling as a conversational poet. Ephraim's reckless honesty about the other side enables the speaker to unravel a complex plot of lives and after-lives, including his own father's, in a humorous, novel-like progression of poems. The verse never impedes the narrative; it enhances it with its exuberance of puns, amazing condensations of ideas and observations, feats of beautiful lyric sound.

The success of this sequence makes clear Merrill's earlier difficulties with orthodox convention: his verve and spontaneity of imagination, his life as a contemporary, were too straitened by the demands of closed forms of verse. Merrill has seized upon the cut-and-paste, leaping perceptual technique of today's poets without relinquishing his skill to craft the diction of his now fluid poems.

—Paul Christensen

MERWIN, W(illiam) S(tanley). American. Born in New York City, 30 September 1927. Educated at Princeton University, New Jersey, A.B. in English 1947. Married Diana Whalley in 1954. Tutor to Robert Graves's son, Majorca, 1950; Playwright-in-Residence, Poet's Theatre, Cambridge, Massachusetts, 1956–57; Poetry Editor, *The Nation*, New York, 1962; Associate, Theatre de la Cité, Lyons, France, 1964–65. Recipient: National Institute of Arts and Letters grant, 1957; Arts Council of Great Britain bursary, 1957; Rabinowitz Research Fellowship, 1961; Ford Foundation grant, 1964; Chapelbrook Award, 1966; National Endowment for the Arts grant, 1968; P.E.N. Translation Prize, 1969; Rockefeller Foundation grant, 1969; Pulitzer Prize, 1971; Academy of American Poets Fellowship, 1973; Shelley Memorial Award, 1974.

PUBLICATIONS

Verse

A Mask for Janus.   1952.
The Dancing Bears.   1954.
Green with Beasts.   1956.
The Drunk in the Furnace.   1960.
The Moving Target.   1963.
The Lice.   1967.
Three Poems.   1968.
Animae.   1969.
The Carrier of Ladders.   1970.
Signs, with A. D. Moore.   1971.
Chinese Figures: Second Series.   1971.
Japanese Figures.   1971.
Asian Figures.   1972.
Writings to an Unfinished Accompaniment.   1973.
The Compass Flower.   1977.

Plays

Darkling Child, with Dido Milroy (produced 1956).
Favor Island (produced 1957).
Eufemia, from the play by Lope de Rueda, in *Tulane Drama Review*, December 1958.
The Cid, from a play by Corneille (produced 1960).   In *The Classic Theatre*, edited by Eric Bentley, 1961.

The Gilded West (produced 1961).
Turcaret, from the play by Alain Lesage, in *The Classic Theatre,* edited by Eric Bentley, 1961.
The False Confession, from a play by Marivaux (produced, 1963). In *The Classic Theatre,* edited by Eric Bentley, 1961.
Yerma, from the play by Garcia Lorca (produced 1966).
Iphigenia at Aulis, with George E. Dimock, Jr., from a play by Euripides. 1978.

Other

A New Right Arm (essay). N.d.
Selected Translations, 1948–1968. 1968.
The Miner's Pale Children. 1970.
Houses and Travellers: A Book of Prose. 1977.

Editor, *West Wind: Supplement of American Poetry.* 1961.
Editor, with J. Moussaieff Masson, *Classical Sanskrit Love Poetry.* 1977

Translator, *The Poem of the Cid.* 1959.
Translator, *The Satires of Perseus.* 1961.
Translator, *Some Spanish Ballads.* 1961; as *Spanish Ballads,* 1961.
Translator, *The Life of Lazarillo de Tormes: His Fortunes and Adversities.* 1962.
Translator, *The Song of Roland,* in *Medieval Epics.* 1963.
Translator, *Transparence of the World: Poems of Jean Follain.* 1969.
Translator, *Products of the Perfected Civilization: Selected Writings,* by Sebastian Chamfort. 1969.
Translator, *Voices: Selected Writings of Antonio Porchia.* 1969.
Translator, *Twenty Love Poems and a Song of Despair,* by Pablo Neruda. 1969.
Translator, with others, *Selected Poems: A Bilingual Edition,* by Pablo Neruda, edited by Nathaniel Tarn. 1969.
Translator, with Clarence Brown, *Selected Poems of Osip Mandelstam.* 1973.
Translator, *Vertical Poetry,* by Robert Juarrox. 1977.

Bibliography: in "Seven Princeton Poets," in *Princeton Library Chronicle,* Autumn 1963.

Reading List: "Merwin Issue" of *Hollins Critic,* June 1968.

*   *   *

W. S. Merwin's writing career erupted suddenly in 1952 with the publication of *A Mask for Janus.* Both it and *The Dancing Bears* are books of traditional poetry, stressing short, consciously crafted lines that move with densely worded statement. *Dancing Bears,* slightly freer in form and showing more confidence in composition, is dry and bookish, but Merwin has exercised his skill in these earliest volumes, and his intelligence and promise are evident throughout.

In *Green with Beasts* and *The Drunk in the Furnace* Merwin is in greater control of his imagination, and the experience in his lyrics is suddenly intense and compelling. The mythic content of *Green with Beasts* anticipates the bold explorations of subjectivity of later volumes. But sheer variety of tone and diction, clarity of image, leaps of thought and perception give *Green with Beasts* surges of power. *The Drunk in the Furnace* retreats slightly from the daring pursuit of the earlier volume, but the ordinary world is rediscovered here, especially in the title poem, in which the poet discovers a man living contentedly in an abandoned furnace. The landscape of these mature works is charged with magic and the fabulous, and the drunk rattling his bottle of liquor against the iron walls of his home is typical of the uncanny world in which Merwin has rooted his lyric.

By 1960, Merwin appears to have exhausted his interest in traditional English poetry, for in translating certain Spanish poets he discovered surrealist techniques that continue to affect his unique, wistfully lyrical style. The problem with *The Moving Target*, however, is the emphasis given to a disembodied voice whose lyric statements arise from unstated situations and have little or no core of argument. There is a sameness to this poetry as each poem passes into the other with its silky array of words touching briefly on the particulars of life.

In his most recent volumes, Merwin has written what appears to be the stages of a spiritual progress. Each volume is intent to mine a deeper layer of the subjective mind, to test the limits of perception where it borders on fantasy and archetypal thought, to let merge the states of dream and waking. *The Lice* is composed in the soft, remote language of surrealist lyrics and offers a distant reflection of the turbulence of the 1960's, without indictment or direct reference to actual events. A sense of political terror and unrest pervades these sombre poems. *The Carrier of Ladders* broods on absence of meaning, on death, on spiritual transcendence of the objective and alien landscape. In *Writings to an Unfinished Accompaniment*, Merwin comes to an end of the disjunctive, loosely imagistic poem. A noticeable change of attention takes over in *The Compass Flower* where the quotidian is suddenly fresh and vital, and his poems come to crisp focus on objects of immediate experience.

—Paul Christensen

MILLAY, Edna St. Vincent. American. Born in Rockland, Maine, 22 February 1892. Educated at schools in Rockland and Camden, Maine; Barnard College, New York; Vassar College, Poughkeepsie, New York, graduated 1917. Married Eugen Jan Boissevain in 1923. Worked as a free-lance writer in New York City; also associated with the Provincetown Players. Recipient: Pulitzer Prize, 1923. Litt.D.: Tufts University, Medford, Massachusetts; Colby College, Waterville, Maine; University of Wisconsin, Madison; L.H.D.: New York University. Member, American Academy of Arts and Letters. *Died 19 October 1950.*

PUBLICATIONS

Collections

    Letters, edited by Allan Ross Macdougall.   1952.
    Collected Poems, edited by Norma Millay.   1956.

Verse

    Renascence and Other Poems.   1917.
    A Few Figs from Thistles.   1920.

Second April. 1921.
The Ballad of the Harp-Weaver. 1922.
The Harp-Weaver and Other Poems. 1923; as *Poems,* 1923.
(*Poems*), edited by Hughes Mearns. 1927.
The Buck in the Snow and Other Poems. 1928.
Poems Selected for Young People. 1929.
Fatal Interview: Sonnets. 1931.
Wine from These Grapes. 1934.
Conversation at Midnight. 1937.
Huntsman, What Quarry? 1939.
Make Bright the Arrows: 1940 Notebook. 1940.
Collected Sonnets. 1941.
The Murder of Lidice. 1942.
Collected Lyrics. 1943.
Mine the Harvest: A Collection of New Poems, edited by Norma Millay. 1954.

Plays

Aria da Capo (produced 1921). 1921.
The Lamp and the Bell (produced 1921). 1921.
Two Slatterns and a King: A Moral Interlude (produced 1921). 1921.
The King's Henchman, music by Deems Taylor (produced 1927). 1927.
The Princess Marries the Page. 1932.

Other

Distressing Dialogues. 1924.
Fear. 1927(?).

Translator, with George Dillon, *Flowers of Evil,* by Baudelaire. 1936.

Bibliography: *A Bibliography of the Works of Millay* by Karl Yost, 1937.

Reading List: *The Indigo Bunting: A Memoir of Millay* by Vincent Sheean, 1957; *Restless Spirit: The Life of Millay* by Miriam Gurko, 1962; *Millay* by Norman A. Brittin, 1967; *Millay* by James Gray, 1967; *The Poet and Her Book: A Biography of Millay* by Jean Gould, 1969.

*   *   *

If it is true that "You cannot touch a flower without disturbing a star," then the whole firmament must have been tremulous at the birth of Edna St. Vincent Millay. A woman of pronounced and strongly held convictions, she was catapulted to fame in 1920 by her book *A Few Figs from Thistles,* and became the prototype of the "new, emancipated women." The unheard of freedom which this lady demanded – freedom in love, freedom of thought in matters of morality and religion, equal rank with the male, and, above all, the freedom to act out her own individuality unhampered by outworn social codes – was one that was needed to counteract the deadening effects of Victorian proprieties. The rebellion that Millay promoted opened many new paths for the adventuresome human spirit and she is not to be blamed if the new freedoms are often abused. As she noted in one of her finest sonnets, "What rider spurs him," civilization is a contest fought in the dark against tremendous obstacles and requiring a continuous forward motion to counteract the destructive and stultifying tendencies in human nature. It is curious that Millay, the proponent of new, creative designs for life, clothed her verse in traditional forms and language, while T. S. Eliot, who harked to the past and worshipped authority as the solution to the world's ills, developed a new language and style for poetry. His contribution was also a forward motion for poetry, but the great admiration for this poet among academicians served for many years to minimize the recognition of the achievements of lyrical poets such as Millay.

More, perhaps, than any other poet in English, Millay's stance vis-à-vis the universe was one of a human being almost totally absorbed in her own human situation, whose reactions to that situation, including, of course, the condition of the whole human race, are nearly always of an immediate, personal character. She does not stand outside herself but reports all the tumults of existence as they reverberate in her own being. Since she was a personality more than life-size and was gifted with "a high sense of drama," her personalist approach created poetry of great vitality and conviction. On the other hand, being caught in the cage of personal, individual existence becomes suffocating, and, in her case, largely excluded awareness of the strange Otherness of things, the transcendent order of reality that we call the Divine.

Such as it was, however, Millay's outlook produced a large body of lyrical works of the highest distinction and expressiveness. It is easy to understand Louis Untermeyer's hyperbolic statement in 1923 that "Renascence," written when Millay was nineteen years old, was "possibly the most astonishing performance of this generation." Sentiments of great verve and freshness are given classic expression in a style that is always concise and musical. As James Gray says, the content of her poetry is equally attractive since it consists of her own version of the ageless contest between life and death, in both the physical and spiritual senses, the raptures and failures of love, and the ever-present struggle between the processes of decay and rebirth. There are times, as suggested above, when the reader may feel oppressed by the weight of her tortured self-absorption, but this is the price that must be paid for the sharply etched and poignant account of her soul's turnings.

—Glenn Richard Ruihley

MILLER, Arthur. American. Born in New York City, 17 October 1915. Educated at the University of Michigan, Ann Arbor (Hopwood Award, 1936, 1937), 1934–38, A.B. 1938. Married 1) Mary Slattery in 1940 (divorced, 1956), one son and one daughter; 2) the actress Marilyn Monroe in 1956 (divorced, 1961) ; 3) Ingeborg Morath in 1962, one daughter. Member of the Federal Theatre Project, 1938. Wrote for the CBS and NBC Radio Workshops. International President, P.E.N., London and New York, 1965–69. Recipient: Theatre Guild Award, 1938; New York Drama Critics Circle Award, 1947, 1949; Antoinette Perry Award, 1947, 1949, 1953; Pulitzer Prize, 1949; National Association of Independent Schools Award, 1954; American Academy of Arts and Letters Gold Medal, 1959; Brandeis University Creative Arts Award, 1969. D.H.L.: University of Michigan, 1956. Member, American Academy of Arts and Letters, 1971.

PUBLICATIONS

Plays

Honors at Dawn (produced 1936).
No Villains (They Too Arise) (produced 1937).
The Pussycat and the Expert Plumber Who Was a Man and *William Ireland's
  Confession*, in *100 Non-Royalty Radio Plays*, edited by William Kozlenko.   1941.
The Man Who Had All the Luck (produced 1944).   In *Cross-Section 1944*, edited by
  Edwin Seaver, 1944.
That They May Win (produced 1944).   In *Best One-Act Plays of 1944*, edited by
  Margaret Mayorga, 1945.
Grandpa and the Statue, in *Radio Drama in Action*, edited by Erik Barnouw.   1945.
The Story of Gus, in *Radio's Best Plays*, edited by Joseph Liss.   1947.
The Guardsman, radio adaptation of a play by Ferenc Molnar, in *Theatre Guild on the
  Air*, edited by H. William Fitelson.   1947.
Three Men on a Horse, radio adaptation of the play by George Abbott and John Cecil
  Holm, in *Theatre Guild on the Air*, edited by H. William Fitelson.   1947.
All My Sons (produced 1947).   1947.
Death of a Salesman: Certain Private Conversations in Two Acts and a Requiem
  (produced 1949).   1949.
An Enemy of the People, from a play by Ibsen (produced 1950).   1951.
The Crucible (produced 1953).   1953.
A View from the Bridge, and A Memory of Two Mondays: Two One-Act Plays (produced
  1955).   1955; revised version of *A View from the Bridge* (produced 1956), 1956.
Collected Plays (includes *All My Sons, Death of a Salesman, The Crucible, A Memory of
  Two Mondays, A View from the Bridge*).   1957.
After the Fall (produced 1964).   1964.
Incident at Vichy (produced 1964).   1965.
The Price (produced 1968).   1968.
Fame, and The Reason Why (produced 1970).   *Fame* in *Yale Literary Magazine*, March
  1971.
The Creation of the World and Other Business (produced 1972).   1973.
Up from Paradise (produced 1974).
The Archbishop's Ceiling (produced 1976).

Screenplay: *The Misfits*, 1961.

Radio Plays: *The Pussycat and the Expert Plumber Who Was a Man, William Ireland's
Confession, Grandpa and the Statue*, and *The Story of Gus*, in early 1940's.

Fiction

Focus.   1945.
The Misfits (screenplay in novel form).   1961.
I Don't Need You Any More: Stories.   1967.

Other

Situation Normal.   1944.
Jane's Blanket (juvenile).   1963.

In Russia, photographs by Inge Morath. 1969.
The Portable Miller, edited by Harold Clurman. 1971.
In the Country, photographs by Inge Morath. 1977.
The Theatre Essays of Miller, edited by Robert A. Martin. 1978.

Bibliography: "Miller: The Dimension of His Art: A Checklist of His Published Works," in *The Serif*, June 1967, and *Miller Criticism (1930–1967)*, 1969, both by Tetsumaro Hayashi.

Reading List: *Miller*, 1961, and *Miller: A Study of His Plays*, 1979, both by Dennis Welland; *Miller* by Robert G. Hogan, 1964; *Miller: The Burning Glass* by Sheila Huftel, 1965; *Miller* by Leonard Moss, 1967 (includes bibliography); *Miller, Dramatist* by Edward Murray, 1967; *Miller: A Collection of Critical Essays* edited by Robert W. Corrigan, 1969; *Miller: Portrait of a Playwright* by Benjamin Nelson, 1970; *Miller* by Ronald Hayman, 1970.

*   *   *

In "On Social Plays," the introduction to the 1955 edition of *A View from the Bridge*, Arthur Miller expressed his dissatisfaction with the subjective play so popular on Broadway in the 1950's. At the same time, he rejected the customary definition of the social play ("an arraignment of society's evils") and identified his own work as "the drama of the whole man," an inextricable mixture of the social and the psychological. The emphasis on one side or the other varied over the years and his conception of the nature of man underwent a change in the 1960's, but his 1955 sense of his work is a useful description of the whole career of Arthur Miller as a social playwright.

In his student plays, his wartime one-acters, his early radio plays, even his first Broadway offering, *The Man Who Had All the Luck*, Miller can be seen working his way toward the theme that was to dominate his early plays. From *All My Sons* through *A View from the Bridge*, Miller places his protagonist in a setting in which society functions as a creator of images, and the hero-victim is destroyed because, as he says in the essay quoted above, "the individual is doomed to frustration when once he gains a consciousness of his own identity." Ironically, the destruction comes whether a man accepts or rejects the role that society asks or demands that he play. Joe Keller, in *All My Sons*, is a good man, a loving husband and father, a successful business man who believes that his responsibility ends "at the building line"; when his son teaches him that neither the welfare of his family nor the self-protective impulse of conventional business ethics can excuse a shipment of faulty airplane parts, he commits suicide. Willy Loman, in *Death of a Salesman*, embraces the American dream, assumes that success is not only possible, but inevitable, and, faced with his failure, kills himself; the irony of the final suicide and the strength of the play is that Willy goes to his death, his dream still intact, convinced that the elusive success will be visited on his son, Biff, a man already crippled by society's neatly packaged ideas. In *The Crucible*, the victim becomes a romantic hero. John Proctor, guilty of adultery, confuses his accusing wife with an accusing society and admits to practicing witchcraft, but, finally unwilling to sign his name, he rejects society's demand for ritual confession, regains his identity, and dies, purely, in an act of defiance. Eddie Carbone, in *A View from the Bridge*, dies crying out for his name, too, but he wants a lie, the pretense that he has not violated the neighborhood ethic; like Joe Keller and Willy Loman, he accepts his society, but he breaks its rules when his desire for his niece and his attraction to her sweetheart threaten him with labels more frightening than informer. The explicit assumption of all these plays is that, win or lose, in contemporary society you can't win; the implicit assumption is that the individual is at his strongest, philosophically and dramatically, when the tensions between self and society are made manifest by a revealing crisis. The artistic result of the twin assumptions is a group of remarkably effective plays, reflecting Miller's theatrical skill as clearly as they do his moral concerns. In the best of them, *Death of a Salesman*, Miller's social-psychological mix has given birth, in Willy Loman, to one of the richest characters in American drama.

Between 1956, when the revised version of *A View from the Bridge* appeared, and 1964, Miller was inactive in the theater. During those years he published a number of short stories, later collected in *I Don't Need You Any More*, including "The Misfits," which was the basis for the short novel and screenplay, written for his wife Marilyn Monroe. The most startling thing about the work is that in it Miller seems to be accepting the concept of the curative power of love in a way that recalls the prevailing cliché of Broadway in the 1950's; he had already given the idea explicit statement in two essays published a few years before the story-novel-film – the introduction to *Collected Plays* and "Bridge to a Savage World" (*Esquire*, October 1958).

When Miller returned to the theater with *After the Fall* and *Incident at Vichy*, he had put aside the momentary softness of *The Misfits*, but he had also discarded the concept of man as an admirable loser which marked his earlier plays. "The first problem," he wrote in "Our Guilt for the World's Evil" (*New York Times Magazine*, 3 January 1965), "is ... to discover our own relationship to evil, its reflection of ourselves." Quentin in *Fall* learns to live and Von Berg in *Vichy* to die by the process of self-discovery already familiar in Miller's work, but identity is no longer individual. Miller, like the Salem of *The Crucible*, is now forcing an image of guilt on his characters. Finally in 1972, with *The Creation of the World and Other Business*, Miller makes obvious what has already been stated in the title *After the Fall*, that his post-1964 subject is original sin translated into the psychological commonplace that makes everyone responsible for "the World's Evil." Miller does not try to dramatize the corollary, that when everyone is guilty no one is, but it is possible – or so the autobiographical elements in *After the Fall* suggest – that the idea is working on the author if not within the play. One result of Miller's new concept of man is that the later plays have a schematic look to them; the characters lack the vitality of Miller's early protagonists and often appear to be simply figures in an exemplum. *The Price* is the only one of the later plays that escapes the look of drama as demonstration. Ideologically one with the other post-1964 plays, it returns to the domestic setting familiar with Miller as far back as the time of his student work *They Too Arise*. Whether it is the inherent drama of two brothers at odds or the presence of the old furniture dealer, Miller's only successful comic figure, *The Price* escapes Significance with a capital S and finds theatrical validity. In his most recent work, *The Archbishop's Ceiling*, Miller seems to have moved away from the ideological concerns that marked his drama from *After the Fall* to *Creation of the World*, but the play is more intellectual than dramatic and the characters are more complex in conception than in presentation.

Since Miller is a playwright of ideas, it is perhaps fitting that I have largely stuck to his themes in discussing his work, stopping occasionally to suggest that the ideational content of a play can interfere with the dramatic action or dehumanize character. These strictures are valid only to the extent that Miller is a realistic playwright in the American tradition, a dramatist who wants to create psychologically valid characters with whom audiences can identify directly. That is Miller's tradition, although he is one of a number of postwar American playwrights who recognize that that kind of character can exist outside a conventional realistic play. *Death of a Salesman* and *After the Fall* are examples of domesticated American Expressionism in which realistic scenes are played in an anti-realistic context. *The Crucible* is a romantic history play with a consciously artificial language, and Alfieri's stilted speeches in *A View from the Bridge*, which turn into free verse in the original version, are an attempt to impose the label *tragedy* on the play. *The Creation of the World* is an unhappy mixture of philosophical drama and Jewish low comedy. *Incident at Vichy* is a roundtable discussion and *The Price* is a debate of sorts with exits and entrances so artificially conceived that Miller surely means them to be seen as devices. The playwright's nearest approaches to traditional realism are *All My Sons* and the affectionate short play *A Memory of Two Mondays*.

Aside from his plays, Miller's work includes not only the short stories and screenplay mentioned above, but a novel, *Focus*; a report on Americans in training during World War

II, *Situation Normal*; a children's book, *Jane's Blanket*; two volumes in which his text shares space with photographs by his wife Inge Morath, *In Russia* and *In the Country*; and a great many articles and essays, most of them about the theater. The chief value of these works lies less in their specific generic virtues than in those analogies – in theme, in method – that heighten our appreciation of the plays. After all, Arthur Miller is pre-eminently a playwright, one of the best the American theater has produced.

—Gerald Weales

MILLER, Henry (Valentine). American. Born in Yorkville, New York City, 26 December 1891. Attended the City College of New York, 1909. Married 1) Beatrice Sylvas Wickens in 1917 (divorced, 1924); 2) June Edith Smith in 1924 (divorced, 1934); 3) Martha Lepska in 1944 (divorced, 1952); 4) Eve McClure in 1953 (divorced); 5) Hoki Tokuda in 1967; one son and two daughters. Has held many jobs: with the Atlas Portland Cement Company, New York, 1909; Reporter, Washington, D.C., 1917; with the Bureau of Economic Research, New York, 1919; Employment Manager, Western Union Telegraph Company, 1920–24; lived in Europe, 1930–39: Proofreader, *Chicago Tribune* Paris edition, 1932; teacher at the Lycée Carnot, Dijon, 1932; Psychoanalyst, 1936; Editor, with Lawrence Durrell and Alfred Perlès, *The Booster*, later *Delta*, Paris, 1937–38; Continental Editor, *Volontes*, Paris, 1938–39; European Editor, *Phoenix*, Woodstock, New York, 1938–39; returned to the United States in 1940; settled in California, 1942. Also an artist: has exhibited water colors in New York, 1927, London, 1944, and Los Angeles, 1966. Recipient: Formentor Prize Committee Citation, 1961. Member, National Institute of Arts and Letters, 1957.

PUBLICATIONS

Fiction

> *Tropic of Cancer.* 1934.
> *Black Spring.* 1936.
> *Tropic of Capricorn.* 1939.
> *The Rosy Crucifixion: Sexus.* 1949; *Plexus*, 1953; *Nexus*, 1960.
> *Quiet Days in Clichy.* 1956.

Plays

> *Scenario: A Film with Sound.* 1937.
> *Just Wild about Harry: A Melo-Melo in 7 Scenes* (produced 1963). 1963.

Other

What Are You Going to Do About Alf?   1935.
Aller Retour New York.   1935.
Money and How It Gets That Way.   1938.
Max and the White Phagocytes.   1938.
The Cosmological Eye.   1939.
Hamlet, with Michael Fraenkel.   2 vols., 1939–41.
The World of Sex.   1940; revised edition, 1957.
Wisdom of the Heart.   1941.
The Colossus of Maroussi; or, The Spirit of Greece.   1941.
The Angel Is My Watermark.   1944.
Sunday after the War.   1944.
The Plight of the Creative Artist in the United States of America.   1944.
Semblance of a Devoted Past.   1944; unexpurgated edition, with *To Paint Is to Love Again,* 1968.
Echolalia: Reproductions of Water Colors by Miller.   1945.
Why Abstract?, with Hilaire Hiler and W. Saroyan.   1945.
Miller Miscellanea.   1945.
The Air-Conditioned Nightmare.   1945; vol. 2, *Remember to Remember,* 1947.
Obscenity and the Law of Reflection.   1945.
Maurizius Forever.   1946; abridged edition, as *Reflections on the Maurizius Case,* 1974.
Patchen: Man of Anger and Light, with A Letter to God by Kenneth Patchen.   1947.
Of, By and About Miller: A Collection of Pieces by Miller, Herbert Read, and Others.   1947.
Portrait of General Grant.   1947.
Varda: The Master Builder.   1947.
The Smile at the Foot of the Ladder.   1948.
The Waters Reglitterized (includes reproductions of pictures by Miller).   1950.
The Books in My Life.   1952.
Nights of Love and Laughter.   1955.
A Devil in Paradise: The Story of Conrad Mourand, Born Paris, 7 or 7:15pm, January 17, 1887, Died Paris, 10:30pm, August 31, 1954.   1956.
Argument about Astrology.   1956.
The Time of the Assassins: A Study of Rimbaud.   1956.
Big Sur and the Oranges of Hieronymus Bosch.   1957.
The Red Notebook.   1959.
Art and Outrage: A Correspondence about Miller Between Alfred Perlès and Lawrence Durrell, with an Intermission by Miller.   1959.
A Miller Reader, edited by Lawrence Durrell.   1959; as *The Best of Miller,* 1960.
The Intimate Miller.   1959.
To Paint Is To Love Again (includes reproductions of pictures by Miller).   1960.
Stand Still like the Hummingbird.   1962.
Watercolors, Drawings and His Essay "The Angel Is My Watermark."   1962.
Lawrence Durrell and Miller: A Private Correspondence, edited by George Wickes.   1963.
Books Tangent to Circle: Reviews.   1963.
Greece.   1964.
Miller on Writing.   1964.
Letters to Anaïs Nin.   1965.
Selected Prose.   2 vols., 1965.
Order and Chaos chez Hans Reichel.   1966.
Writer and Critic: A Correspondence, with W. A. Gordon.   1968.

Collector's Quest: Correspondence, 1947–1965, with J. R. Child.   1968.
Insomnia; or, The Devil at Large.   1970.
My Life and Times, edited by Bradley Smith.   1971.
Journey to an Antique Land.   1972.
Reflections on the Death of Mishima.   1972.
On Turning Eighty.   1972.
Miller in Conversation with Georges Belmont.   1972.
The Immortal Bard (on John Cowper Powys).   1973.
First Impressions of Greece.   1973.
This Is Henry – Henry Miller from Brooklyn, by Robert Snyder.   1974.
Letters of Miller and Wallace Fowlie 1943–1972.   1975.
The Nightmare Notebook.   1975.
Genius and Lust: A Journey Through the Major Writings of Miller, with Norman Mailer.   1976.
Four Visions of America, with others.   1977.
Miller's Book of Friends (memoirs).   1976; vol. 2, *My Bike and Other Friends*, 1978.
Miller: Years of Trial and Triumph 1962–1964: The Correspondence of Miller and Elmer Gertz, edited by Gertz and Felice Flanery Lewis.   1978.

Bibliography: *Miller: A Chronology and Bibliography* by Bern Porter, 1945; *Bibliography of Miller* edited by Thomas H. Moore, 1961; *A Bibliography of Miller, 1945–1961* by Maxine Renken, 1962.

Reading List: *Miller* by Kingsley Widmer, 1963; *Miller* by Frédéric Temple, 1965; *The Mind and Art of Miller* by W. A. Gordon, 1967; *The Literature of Silence · Miller and Beckett* by Ihab Hassan, 1968; *Miller · Three Decades of Criticism* edited by Edward B. Mitchell, 1971.

*   *   *

Henry Miller's name became known to a wider public than that of a fashionable, rather trendy literary *élite* largely as an unexpected result of the Allied Forces in Paris after 1944. The soldiers and the civilians who accompanied them discovered his books – *Tropic of Cancer, Black Spring, Tropic of Capricorn* – most of which had been refused publication in the Anglo-Saxon countries because of their blatantly sexual matter. But they were available in Paris published by Girodias's Obelisk Press, and were eagerly seized on by Americans and Britons, many of whom succeeded in smuggling their finds into their home countries. Later on, many of these books were published in England and America.

Too often they were large, inchoate, rambling works with an autobiographical thread. They passed rapidly, like a rushing, uncontrolled stream, from the rhapsodic to the sordid to the pornographic. Miller's freedom of language and subject had a deep influence on the thousands of writers who benefitted from the literary emancipation from censorship. Miller himself may have been influenced by much of the *erotica* of the ages. But he was influenced also by such American writers as Whitman and Robinson Jeffers, by the back-to-nature animists such as Thoreau and D. H. Lawrence (about whom he wrote an unpublished study), and by all the European writers who in one way or another contributed to such movements as Dadaism and Surrealism. He praises such not always well-known writers as Céline, Cingria, Blaise Cendrars, Milosz, Knut Hamsun, and Rimbaud, whose *Season in Hell* he translated. He has a sort of American-Irish dislike of Britons, except for Durrell and John Cowper Powys (whose novels he claims to understand, but whose real virtue was that he had written *In Defence of Sensuality*, and sensuality was a habit to which Miller always gave a high priority).

Miller as a writer is for freedom in every possible sense, an indecent Shelley, a Tom Paine with the lid off. He expresses, too, a semi-mystical belief that everything links with everything else and that the Creator will arrange that "If there is a genuine need it will be met." Miller, indeed, has himself had amazing luck in becoming a highly saleable writer. He always suffered from logorrhea – and, when he realized that he could earn real money by writing, from appalling over-production. He can be funny in a boisterous sort of way; he is a *farceur*; he can even convince one from time to time that he is genuinely perceptive, though the conviction seldom lasts long. He had a gift for assimilating trendy names and attitudes; Zen, Hokusai, the Essenes, Restif de la Bretonne, astrology, the occult, Milarepa the Tibetan monk. But paradoxically he can still react salutarily against the fashionable, against the claims, for example, of American medicine and the endless, self-defeating "don'ts" of urban Western societies – don't over-eat, don't walk if you can run, don't listen to the radio or watch television, don't get vaccinated or inoculated, don't get frightened if you are over or under weight. And, he concludes: "The great hoax which we are perpetuating every day of our lives is that we are making life easier, more comfortable, more enjoyable, more profitable. We are doing just the contrary. We are making life stale, flat and unprofitable every day in every way...." His attitude is far from new. It is certainly as old as the time of the Romantic poets. Nor does it advance our perceptions to keep on saying these things. Miller is not a great writer, and he can *en masse* be a great bore.

His best literary work, written with skill and *brio*, is *The Colossus of Maroussi*, for it carries to us the whole flavour of Athens in the months immediately preceding the Second World War, and the sense of the Greek-ness of Greeks. In general his early works are much the best for he was then really trying. *The Tropic of Cancer* is a gay, racy account of his life as a poor, often hungry, always lustful, writer in the Paris suburbs, just as *Sexus* (part of *The Rosy Crucifixion* trilogy) does give a picture of the lower middle class, working class, and prostitutes' life in New York in the years before the first World War. There are some rather fine passages in these books – "Easter came in like a frozen hare – but it was fairly warm in bed." Nor can one deny that he achieves at least novelty in his descriptions, sometimes quite comic, of sexual organs and of varieties of the sexual act. But the characters in his long autobiographical reminiscences are seldom visualised, except occasionally as extreme oddities when we see them like comic caricatures. There is little consideration of motives and less of psychology. The men and women move and act but we know only that it is because of the prime, crude instincts – sexual and the desire for food of which Miller makes a great deal.

Miller has been a copious letter writer all his life and an entertaining one. The correspondence between him and Durrell makes excellent reading, and there are vast stores of Miller letters in the archives of the University of California at Los Angeles.

—Kenneth Young

MITCHELL, Margaret (Munnerlyn).   American.   Born in Atlanta, Georgia, in 1900, and lived there for the rest of her life. Educated at the Washington Seminary, Atlanta, 1914–18; Smith College, Northampton, Massachusetts, 1918–19. Married John R. Marsh in 1925. Feature Writer and Reporter, *Atlanta Journal*, 1922–26. Recipient: Pulitzer Prize, 1937; Bohnenberger Memorial Award, 1938; New York Southern Society Gold Medal, 1938. M.A.: Smith College, 1939. *Died 16 August 1949.*

PUBLICATIONS

Fiction

Gone with the Wind. 1936.

Other

"Gone with the Wind" Letters 1936–1949, edited by Richard Harwell. 1976.

*   *   *

Margaret Mitchell wrote only one novel, *Gone with the Wind,* but it proved to be the most popular novel of her generation. At the time of her death in 1949, 3,800,000 copies were in print, and it continues to attract a large number of readers. *Gone with the Wind* was also made into a motion picture that at the time broke all attendance records and has since been revived more than once.

The continuing popularity of *Gone with the Wind* is not hard to account for. The tempestuous love affair of Scarlet O'Hara and Rhett Butler is in the great popular tradition. The Civil War background, the pathos of the South's defeat, the poverty and suffering (with its clear parallels to the 1930's depression) and eventual economic triumph of Scarlet, so cheering to readers with little to feel cheerful about, and then the "realistic" ending with its bitter-sweet parting of Rhett and Scarlet, contained more excitement than a dozen lesser novels. When one adds to the plethora of homely details about Southern life, the humor, the dozens of colorful minor characters all presented in competent if somewhat florid prose, one understands how even a writer as discriminating as F. Scott Fitzgerald would be impressed with what Margaret Mitchell had been able to pull off.

Literary critics also found things to admire in *Gone with the Wind*; some even felt it deserved the Pulitzer prize it won in 1937 by nosing out George Santayana's *The Last Puritan.* In *Cavalcade of the American Novel,* Edward Wagenknecht praised it for undercutting the "futilitarianism" and "deflation of values" that had been so smart in the 1920's. One can see how a political message could be extracted from Scarlet O'Hara's willingness to do anything (exploit convict labor, seduce her sister's fiancé) to get the money to save the family plantation. Even more significant, however, is the contrast afforded between Margaret Mitchell's vision of Southern history and William Faulkner's, particularly Mitchell's pragmatism and Faulkner's traditionalism. If one considers Faulkner's Flem Snopes one side of the moral coin, on the other side of which is Scarlet O'Hara, Margaret Mitchell's pragmatic history takes on an even deeper significance.

—W. J. Stuckey

MOODY, William Vaughn. American. Born in Spencer, Indiana, 8 July 1869; grew up in New Albany, Indiana. Educated at New Albany High School; Harvard University, Cambridge, Massachusetts (an editor of the *Harvard Monthly*), 1889–94, B.A. 1893, M.A. 1894. Married Harriet Tilden Brainard in 1909. Taught in a high school in Spencer, 1885–89; Instructor in English, Harvard University and Radcliffe College, Cambridge, Massachusetts,

1894–95; Instructor in English and Rhetoric, 1895–99, and Assistant Professor of English, 1901–07, University of Chicago; full-time writer, 1907 until his death. Litt.D.: Yale University, New Haven, Connecticut, 1908. Member, American Academy of Arts and Letters, 1908. *Died 17 October 1910.*

PUBLICATIONS

Collections

Selected Poems, edited by Robert Morss Lovett.   1931.

Plays

The Masque of Judgment: A Masque-Drama.   1900.
The Fire-Bringer.   1904.
The Great Divide (as *A Sabine Woman,* produced 1906; as *The Great Divide,* produced 1906).   1909.
The Faith Healer.   1909.

Verse

Poems.   1901; as *Gloucester Moors and Other Poems,* 1909.

Other

A History of English Literature, with Robert Morss Lovett.   1902; revised edition, 1918; simplified edition, as *A First View of English Literature,* 1905; as *A First View of English and American Literature,* 1909.
Poems and Plays, edited by John M. Manly.   2 vols., 1912.
Some Letters, edited by Daniel Gregory Mason.   1913.
Letters to Harriet, edited by Percy MacKaye.   1935.

Editor, *The Pilgrim's Progress,* by Bunyan.   1897.
Editor, *The Rime of the Ancient Mariner by Coleridge and The Vision of Sir Launfal by Lowell.*   1898.
Editor, *The Lady of the Lake,* by Scott.   1899.
Editor, with Wilfred Wesley Cressy, *The Iliad of Homer,* books 1, 6, 22, 24.   1899.
Editor, *The Complete Poetical Works of Milton.*   1899.
Editor, with George Cabot Lodge and John Ellerton Lodge, *The Poems of Trumbull Stickney.*   1905.
Editor, *Selections from De Quincey.*   1909.

Reading List: *Moody: A Study* by David D. Henry, 1934; *Moody* by Martin Halpern, 1964; *Estranging Dawn: The Life and Works of Moody* by Maurice F. Brown, 1973.

*   *   *

After William Vaughn Moody's early death, Edwin Arlington Robinson, his close friend and literary ally, wrote Harriet Moody, "Thank God he lived to do his work – or enough of it to place him among the immortals." While that assessment now seems exaggerated, Moody's work, as a scholar, poet, and dramatist, is sufficient to give him a firm place in literary history. As the author of *The Great Divide*, he is considered the first playwright to provide the American stage with a serious, realistic, modern drama, thus ushering in the new age in American theatre. Critics have speculated that had he lived to realize his full potential, his only rival would have been Eugene O'Neill.

Martin Halpern, in his critical biography of Moody, has suggested that his literary career falls into two periods: from 1890 until the publication of *The Masque of Judgment* and *Poems*, in 1900 and 1901 respectively, his primary interest was poetry; from then until his final illness debilitated him in 1909 he worked consciously as a practicing dramatist. Although *The Masque of Judgment* is the first part of a projected dramatic trilogy, it is a closet drama in verse. And while two of the four plays he wrote during the last decade of his life are also verse dramas, they were intended for the stage.

Moody's poems have few admirers today, largely because they seem imitative of the English romantics in inflated diction and archaic subject matter. Some of his poems are innovative, however, notably his poems that involve social commentary or those that are conscious attempts to use the vernacular. "On a Soldier Fallen in the Philippines," for instance, is an ironic attack on American foreign policy. Perhaps his most celebrated poem today is "The Menagerie," a comic soliloquy in which the inebriated speaker speculates on how the animals in the zoo regard the putative fulfillment of the evolutionary process, man. The psychologically honest "The Daguerreotype," a tribute to his mother, and the ambiguous "I Am the Woman" are two disparate treatments of the symbolic and psychic implications of the feminine principle, an interest that informs "The Death of Eve." Generally his poems, like his poetic trilogy, are full of high seriousness, frequently devolving upon theological, especially eschatological, matters.

Moody's two prose plays successfully combine realistic and symbolic dramatic techniques. Originally produced as *A Sabine Woman* in Chicago, *The Great Divide* was a commercial as well as a critical success, playing for two years in New York. The play deals with the conflicting cultures of the eastern and western United States, symbolized by the abduction and eventual marriage of a woman from Massachusetts to a rough but honest man from Arizona. The less well-received *Faith Healer* deals with the conflict between human and spiritual passions; the conflict is resolved when the protagonist discovers that his religious work is effective only when he has accepted human love.

Although *The Fire-Bringer*, Moody's verse play based on the Prometheus legend, and the fragment, *The Death of Eve*, were not produced commercially, critics have found them to be more artistically interesting than the prose plays. Moody was able to complete only one act of *The Death of Eve*, but the poem by the same title and his recorded plans for the play suggest that with it he might have achieved his dream of making verse drama a viable theatrical experience. Even so, his contribution to American drama and poetry is considerable.

—Nancy C. Joyner

MOORE, Marianne (Craig).   American.   Born in Kirkwood, Missouri, 15 November 1887. Educated at the Metzger Institute, Carlisle, Pennsylvania; Bryn Mawr College, Pennsylvania, B.A. 1909; Carlisle Commercial College, Pennsylvania, 1910. Head of the

Commercial Studies Department, United States Indian School, Carlisle, 1911–15; worked as a private tutor and secretary in New York City, 1919–21, and as a Branch Librarian for the New York Public Library system, 1921–25; Acting Editor, *The Dial*, 1926 until it ceased publication, 1929. Visiting Lecturer, Bryn Mawr College, 1953; Ewing Lecturer, University of California, Berkeley, 1956. Recipient: Hartsock Memorial Prize, 1935; Shelley Memorial Award, 1941; Harriet Monroe Poetry Award, 1944; Guggenheim Fellowship, 1945; National Institute of Arts and Letters grant, 1946, and Gold Medal, 1953; Pulitzer Prize, 1952; National Book Award, 1952; Bollingen Prize, 1953; Poetry Society of America Gold Medal, 1960, 1967; Brandeis University Creative Arts Award, 1963; Academy of American Poets Fellowship, 1965; MacDowell Medal, 1967; National Medal for Literature, 1968. Litt.D.: Wilson College, Chambersburg, Pennsylvania, 1949; Mount Holyoke College, South Hadley, Massachusetts, 1950; University of Rochester, New York, 1951; L.H.D.: Rutgers University, New Brunswick, New Jersey, 1955; Smith College, Northampton, Massachusetts, 1955; Pratt Institute, Brooklyn, New York, 1959; D.Litt.: New York University, 1967; Washington University, St. Louis, Missouri, 1967; Harvard University, Cambridge, Massachusetts, 1969. Member, American Academy of Arts and Letters, 1955. *Died 5 February 1972.*

PUBLICATIONS

Verse

Poems. 1921.
Observations. 1924.
Selected Poems. 1935.
The Pangolin and Other Verse. 1936.
What Are Years? 1941.
Nevertheless. 1944.
Collected Poems. 1951.
Like a Bulwark. 1956.
O to Be a Dragon. 1959.
Eight Poems. 1962.
The Arctic Ox. 1964.
Tell Me, Tell Me: Granite, Steel, and Other Topics. 1966.
The Complete Poems. 1967.
Unfinished Poems. 1972.

Play

The Absentee, from a story by Maria Edgeworth. 1962.

Other

Predilections. 1955.
Idiosyncracy and Technique: Two Lectures. 1958.
Letters from and to the Ford Motor Company, with David Wallace. 1958.
A Moore Reader. 1961.
Dress and Kindred Subjects. 1965.
Poetry and Criticism. 1965.

Editor, with W. H. Auden and Karl Shapiro, *Riverside Poetry 1953: Poems by Students in Colleges and Universities in New York City.*   1953.

Translator, with Elizabeth Mayer, *Rock Crystal: A Christmas Tale,* by Adalbert Stifter.   1945.
Translator, *The Fables of La Fontaine.*   1954; *Selected Fables,* 1955.
Translator, *Puss in Boots, The Sleeping Beauty, and Cinderella: A Retelling of Three Classic Fairy Tales,* by Charles Perrault.   1963.

Bibliography: *Moore: A Descriptive Bibliography* by Craig S. Abbott, 1977.

Reading List: *The Achievement of Moore: A Biography, 1907–1957* by Eugene P. Sheehy and Kenneth A. Lohf, 1958; *Moore* by Bernard F. Engel, 1964; *Moore* by Jean Garrigue, 1965; *Moore: An Introduction to the Poetry* by George W. Nitchie, 1969; *Moore* by Sister M. Thérèse, 1969; *Moore: A Collection of Critical Essays* edited by Charles Tomlinson, 1970; *Moore: The Cage and the Animal* by Donald Hall, 1970; *Moore: Poet of Affection* by Pamela White Hadas, 1977.

*   *   *

Marianne Moore seems the best poet of her sex to have written in the United States during this century. Her poetry is richer and more inclusive than that of H. D. or of Elizabeth Bishop, to name two who resemble her in their fastidious interest in natural history – Miss Moore's predilection and habitual material. Herself of the modernist generation of Stevens, Williams, Pound, and Eliot, she knew Williams, Pound, and H. D. in her days at Bryn Mawr College; and in the 1920's she was associated with the New York magazine *The Dial,* becoming its editor from 1926 to 1929. Like Williams, she was a naturalist in her subject-matter, and would not have disagreed with Pound's programme for Imagism. Many of the American modernist poets learned to purge their beams at her empirical eye. Yet Eliot, who could not have accepted William's *dictum* "No ideas but in things," also admired Marianne Moore's poetry for the distinction of its language. In his preface to her *Selected Poems,* he judged that she was "one of those few who have done the language some service in my lifetime."

Marianne Moore appears at first an idiosyncratic writer. She chooses odd subjects and sees them from odd angles; she is miscellaneous in her subject-matter and unpredictable in her reflections; she writes in a chopped prose in lines of spectacular irregularity, but with metrical distinctness and, surprisingly often, rhyme. Yet her style, for all its asymmetry, is rapid, clear, unself-concerned, flexible, and accurate, and her work gradually discloses her exceptional sanity, intelligence, and imaginative depth. Unmistakably modern, she has no modernist formlessness; curious and precise, she is too brave in her vision to be an old maid. Some of these paradoxical qualities appear in her openings, which demand attention by their directness, as in "The Steeple-Jack":

> Dürer would have seen a reason for living
>   in a town like this, with eight stranded whales
> to look at; with the sweet sea air coming into your house
> on a fine day, from water etched
>   with waves as formal as the scales
>   on a fish.

or "Silence":

My father used to say,
"Superior people never make long visits,
have to be shown Longfellow's grave
or the glass flowers at Harvard.
Self-reliant like the cat –
that takes its prey to privacy,
the mouse's limp tail hanging like a shoelace from its mouth –
they sometimes enjoy solitude…"

or "To a Snail":

If "compression is the first grace of style,"
you have it. Contractility is a virtue
as modesty is a virtue.

or "Poetry":

I, too, dislike it.
   Reading it, however, with a perfect contempt for it, one discovers in
it, after all, a place for the genuine.

This last is a complete poem, and unusually brief, although most of her poems are meditations of this characteristic briskness. "The Steeple-Jack" is a classic among her longer poems, as is "A Grave," which begins:

Man looking into the sea,
taking the view from those who have as much right to it as you have to it yourself,
it is human nature to stand in the middle of a thing,
but you cannot stand in the middle of this;
the sea has nothing to give but a well excavated grave.

The resonance of that last line states openly, with "an elegance of which the source is not bravado," the essential seriousness which Marianne Moore often took pains to bury deep in her bright-eyed concern with the external world, of which she was such a connoisseur. Like La Fontaine, whose *Fables* she translated, she was fundamentally a humane moralist, however passionate and fine her observation of animals, baseball-players, and nature's remoter aspects; and she was fundamentally serious despite her turn for the smacking epigram.

Her career illuminated the American scene for an exceptionally long time, and to increasing recognition. Her powers did not diminish, but her idiosyncrasy and allusiveness intensified. Thoroughly American and modern, she demonstrated the possibility of a highly civilised and eclectic mind operating with discrimination and unsentimental enjoyment on the premise basic to so much modern American poetry, that everything that is human is material for poetry: "Whatever it is, let it be without/affectation" ("Love in America").

—M. J. Alexander

MORLEY, Christopher (Darlington). American. Born in Haverford, Pennsylvania, 5 May 1890. Educated at Haverford College, 1906–10; New College, Oxford (Rhodes Scholar), 1910–13. Married Helen Booth Fairchild in 1914; one son and three daughters. Member of the staff of Doubleday, Page and Company, publishers, New York, 1913–17, *Ladies Home Journal*, New York, 1917–18, *Evening Public Ledger*, Philadelphia, 1918–20, and the *New York Evening Post*, 1920–24; a Founder, 1920, and Columnist ("The Bowling Green"), 1924–39, *The Saturday Review of Literature*, New York. D.Litt.: Haverford College, 1933. Member, National Institute of Arts and Letters. *Died 28 March 1957.*

PUBLICATIONS

Collections

   Bright Cages (verse), edited by John Bracker.   1965.

Fiction

   Parnassus on Wheels. 1917.
   In the Sweet Dry and Dry, with Bert Haley.   1919.
   The Haunted Bookshop. 1919.
   Kathleen. 1920.
   Tales from a Rolltop Desk. 1921.
   Where the Blue Begins. 1922.
   Pandora Lifts the Lid, with Don Marquis.   1924.
   Thunder on the Left. 1925.
   Pleased to Meet You. 1927.
   The Arrow. 1927.
   Rudolph and Amina; or, The Black Crook. 1930.
   Human Being. 1932.
   Swiss Family Manhattan. 1932.
   The Trojan Horse. 1937.
   Kitty Foyle. 1939.
   Thorofare. 1942.
   The Man Who Made Friends with Himself. 1949.

Plays

   Thursday Evening (produced 1921).   1922.
   Rehearsal. 1922.
   One Act Plays (includes *Thursday Evening, Rehearsal, Bedroom Suite, On the Shelf, Walt, East of Eden*).   1924.
   Where the Blue Begins, with E. S. Colling.   1925.
   Good Theatre. 1926.
   Really, My Dear.... 1928.
   In Modern Dress. 1929.
   The Blue and the Gray; or, War Is Hell, from the play *Allatoona* by Judson Kilpatrick and J. Owen Moore.   1930.
   The Rag-Picker of Paris; or, The Modest Modiste, from the play by Edward Stirling.   1937.

Soft Shoulders (produced 1940).

Verse

The Eighth Sin.   1912.
Songs for a Little House.   1917.
The Rocking Horse.   1919.
Hide and Seek.   1920.
Chimneysmoke.   1921.
Translations from the Chinese.   1922.
Parson's Pleasure.   1923.
Toulemonde.   1928.
Poems.   1929.
Mandarin in Manhattan: Further Translations from the Chinese.   1933.
The Apologia of the Ampersand.   1936.
Footnotes for a Centennial.   1936.
The Middle Kingdom: Poems 1929–1944.   1944.
The Old Mandarin: More Translations from the Chinese.   1947.
Spirit Levels and Other Poems.   1946.
Poetry Package, with William Rose Benét.   1949.
The Ballad of New York, New York, and Other Poems, 1930–1950.   1950.
A Pride of Sonnets.   1951.
Gentlemen's Relish.   1955.

Other

Shandygaff.   1918.
Mince Pie: Adventures on the Sunny Side of Grub Street.   1919.
Travels in Philadelphia.   1920.
Pipefuls (essays).   1920.
Plum Pudding.   1921.
An Apology for Boccaccio.   1923.
Conrad and the Reporters.   1923.
Inward Ho!   1923.
The Powder of Sympathy.   1923.
Outward Bound.   1924.
Religio Journalistici.   1924.
Hostages to Fortune (miscellany).   1925.
Forty-four Essays.   1925; as *Safety Pins and Other Essays*, 1925.
Paumanok.   1926.
The Romany Stain.   1926.
I Know a Secret (juvenile).   1927.
The Case of Bouck White.   1927.
(Works).   12 vols., 1927.
The Tree That Didn't Get Trimmed.   1927.
Essays.   1928.
A Letter to Leonora.   1928.
Off the Deep End.   1928.
A Ride in the Cab of the Twentieth Century Limited.   1928.
The House of Dooner, with T. A. Daly.   1928.
The Worst Christmas Story.   1928.
Seacoast of Bohemia.   1929.

The Goldfish under the Ice (juvenile).   1930.
Apologia pro Sua Preoccupatione.   1930.
Born in a Beer Garden; or, She Troupes to Conquer: Sundry Ejaculations, with Ogden Nash and Cleon Throckmorton.   1930.
On the Nose.   1930.
Blythe Mountain, Vermont.   1931.
When We Speak of a Tenth –.   1931.
John Mistletoe (reminiscences).   1931.
Notes on Bermuda.   1931.
Ex Libris Carissimis (lectures).   1932.
Fifth Avenue Bus (miscellany).   1933.
Shakespeare and Hawaii (lectures).   1933.
Internal Revenue (essays).   1933.
"Effendi," Frank Nelson Doubleday, 1862–1934.   1934.
Hasta la Vista; or, A Postcard from Peru.   1935.
Old Loopy: A Love Letter for Chicago.   1935.
Rare Books: An Essay.   1935.
Streamlines (essays).   1936.
Morley's Briefcase.   1936.
Morley's Magnum.   1938.
History of an Autumn.   1938.
No Crabb, No Christmas.   1938.
Letters of Askance.   1939.
Another Letter to Lord Chesterfield.   1945.
The Ironing Board (essays).   1949.
Barometers and Bookshops.   1952.

Editor, *Record of the Class of 1910 of Haverford College.*   1910.
Editor, *American Rhodes Scholars, Oxford 1910–1913.*   1913.
Editor, *The Booksellers' Blue Book.*   2 vols., 1914.
Editor, *Making Books and Magazines.*   1916.
Editor, *Modern Essays.*   2 vols., 1921–24.
Editor, *The Bowling Green: An Anthology of Verse.*   1924.
Editor, *A Book of Days.*   1930.
Editor, *Ex Libris.*   1936.
Editor, with Louella D. Everett, *Bartlett's Familiar Quotations,* 11th edition.   1937; 12th edition, 1948.
Editor, *Walt Whitman in Camden: A Selection of Prose from Specimen Days.*   1938.
Editor, *The Best of Don Marquis.*   1939.
Editor, *Leaves of Grass,* by Walt Whitman.   1940.
Editor, *Sherlock Holmes and Dr. Watson: A Textbook of Friendship.*   1944.

Translator, *Two Fables,* by Alfred de Musset and Wilhelm Hauff.   1925.
Translator, *Max and Moritz,* by Wilhelm Busch.   1932.

Reading List: *Morley* by Mark I. Wallach, 1976; *Three Hours for Lunch: The Life and Times of Morley* by Helen McK. Oakley, 1976.

*   *   *

Christopher Morley was a distinguished and popular novelist, essayist, and poet, whose intense literary passions and promotions, such as his sponsorship of the writings of Joseph

Conrad and his organization (with his brothers) of the Baker Street Irregulars, combine with his writings to make him one of the few genuine American "men of letters."

Morley's earliest novels, *Parnassus on Wheels* and *The Haunted Bookshop*, are brief, simple stories of booksellers in World War I America, yet they set the tone for the more sophisticated works to follow, many of which also revolve around characters involved in the literary world. *Where the Blue Begins*, an allegory about the human quest for meaning in life, is written as a dog story and enjoyed considerable success in a children's edition, but is actually a profoundly and successfully serious book. *Thunder on the Left*, which followed, is a thoughtful and controversial fantasy about the problems of children trying to come to terms with adulthood.

Kitty Foyle, Morley's best-selling novel, is an ambitious interior monologue told by a working-class girl from Philadelphia. Kitty is an atypical Morley protagonist, neither intellectual nor literary, yet *Kitty Foyle* represents Morley at the peak of his style. Derived from Morley's experiences with the "new generation" of New York career girls in the 1920's and 1930's, Kitty nonetheless displays a striking degree of individuality. Although *Kitty Foyle* largely abandons Morley's usual "mission" of bringing literature to the common man, it paradoxically comes closest of all of Morley's works to being great literature itself.

Morley's last novel, *The Man Who Made Friends with Himself*, embodies much of what is weakest and strongest in Morley's novels: it is intensely personal, extravagantly allusive, and rich with quotation. Somewhat autobiographical, it is a complex and demanding book to read, but worth the effort for lovers of English style.

While Morley is best remembered as a novelist, his frequent and polished essays in *The Saturday Review*, which he helped found in 1920, were perhaps as important in establishing his distinctive reputation among his contemporaries as a "man of letters." Collected into published volumes, such as *Streamlines* and *The Ironing Board*, many of these discuss people, places, and events with literary ties. While most are meant to be informative, Morley's essays always undertake the additional task of entertaining the reader, and are among his most enjoyable works.

Much of Morley's poetry reflects his predominant concern with literature. His earliest poems, however, following his marriage in 1914, are both domestic in subject and sentimental in tone, a blend Morley (with the concurrence of his critics) coined "dishpantheism." Perhaps his most important poetry is an original genre he called "Translations from the Chinese," which Morley first conceived as a burlesque of free verse, but later developed into a shrewd, ironic vehicle for social commentary. These "Translations" are among the most readable works of a writer who, while not of the first rank, was one of his era's most versatile and interesting literary figures.

—Mark I. Wallach

MORRIS, Wright (Marion). American. Born in Central City, Nebraska, 6 January 1910. Educated at Lakeview High School, Chicago; Crane College, Chicago; Pomona College, Claremont, California, 1930–33. Married 1) Mary Ellen Finfrock in 1934 (divorced, 1961); 2) Josephine Kantor in 1961. Has lectured at Haverford College, Pennsylvania, Sarah Lawrence College, Bronxville, New York, and Swarthmore College, Pennsylvania; Professor of English, California State University, San Francisco, 1962–75. Also a photographer. Recipient: Guggenheim Fellowship, 1942, 1946, 1954; National Book Award, 1957; National Institute of Arts and Letters grant, 1960; Rockefeller grant, 1967. Honorary degrees: Westminster College, Fulton, Missouri, 1968; University of Nebraska, Lincoln,

1968; Pomona College, Claremont, California, 1973. Member, National Institute of Arts and Letters, 1970. Lives in Mill Valley, California.

PUBLICATIONS

Fiction

My Uncle Dudley.   1942.
The Man Who Was There.   1945.
The World in the Attic.   1949.
Man and Boy.   1951.
The Works of Love.   1952.
The Deep Sleep.   1953.
The Huge Season.   1954.
The Field of Vision.   1956.
Love among the Cannibals.   1957.
Ceremony in Lone Tree.   1960.
What a Way to Go.   1962.
Cause for Wonder.   1963.
One Day.   1965.
In Orbit.   1967.
Green Grass, Blue Sky, White House (stories).   1970.
Fire Sermon.   1971.
War Games.   1972.
Here Is Einbaum (stories).   1973.
A Life.   1973.
Real Losses, Imaginary Gains.   1976.
The Fork River Space Project.   1977.

Other

The Inhabitants (photo-text).   1946.
The Home Place (photo-text).   1948.
The Territory Ahead (essays).   1958.
A Bill of Rites, A Bill of Wrongs, A Bill of Goods (essays).   1967.
God's Country and My People (photo-text).   1968.
Morris: A Reader.   1970.
Love Affair: A Venetian Journal (photo-text).   1972.
About Fiction: Reverent Reflections on the Nature of Fiction with Irreverent Observations on Writers, Readers, and Other Abuses.   1975.
Structures and Artifacts: Photographs 1933–1954.   1976.
Conversations with Morris: Critical Views and Responses, edited by Robert E. Knoll.   1977.

Editor, The Mississippi River Reader.   1962.

Reading List: Morris by David Madden, 1964; Morris by Leon Howard, 1968; The Novels of Morris: A Critical Interpretation by G.B. Crump, 1978.

*   *   *

Wright Morris, who has been called "the most major minor novelist in America," has had greater success with the critics than with the novel-reading public. He is also an important photographer: his four "photo-text" books are interspersed among the many novels he has published since 1942. In addition, Morris's critical essays on the art of fiction, and its relation to life and the modern reader, are unusually candid and stimulating. In all of his fiction the characters are vivid Americans, their talk salty and often funny; but these people also struggle with the issues and problems that beset the modern world. Morris recognizes his estrangement from other novelists and novel readers, and the reasons for it: "In my use of language there is an element that the narrative novelist has no interest in, might even find obstructive. He would say, 'One of the things that is wrong with this novel is that it holds the reader up. He has to read too carefully.' I would agree."

The Nebraska plains of Morris's first nine years haunt his imagination, and his first five books (novels and photo-texts) all take him "home" again. Then in his novels of the early 1950's, Morris portrays people cut off from the past (and often from love): they are monsters (like Mrs. Ormsby of *Man and Boy*), or suicidal (like Will Brady of *The Works of Love*). In *The Deep Sleep* the Porter house in suburban Philadelphia becomes a symbol of America, and the events in the novel become American experience in miniature. In the three "major" Morris novels that followed – *The Huge Season*, *The Field of Vision*, and *Ceremony in Lone Tree* – past and present are transformed through heroism, love, and the creative imagination.

In most of his fiction Morris contrasts old and young, and the revolution of the 1960's gave him exciting new matter. New frontiers of sex are explored in *Love among the Cannibals* and *What a Way to Go*: in both erotic love is overtly important. Although the action is focused upon the animal pound in a small California town in *One Day*, the day is November 22, 1963: Morris suggests, as he also does elsewhere, that nature might well abandon human civilization and make a new start with an animal (like the chipmunk in *The Huge Season*). In typical Morris fashion, too, the intellectual pessimism is leavened by his fascination with life, revealed most clearly through the hundreds of grotesque but vital characters that crowd his novels. *In Orbit* reveals age looking at youth: age sees the horrible but hopeful, living new day, envies and even admires. The prototypical motorcycle hoodlum rapes and pillages, albeit in a sometimes burlesque way; the victims, who are "upright citizens" of a small town, are unable – apparently unwilling – to identify the culprit. Then a tornado sweeps through the village, and the townspeople have no more hope of stopping the marauding youth than of halting the devastating wind storm. Both seem awful natural forces.

In *Fire Sermon* Morris returns to the picaresque auto trip of his first novel, *My Uncle Dudley*; the journey is still from California to the midwest, but the time has moved forward from the 1920's to the 1960's. Using a familiar Morris pair-up, *Fire Sermon* takes an old man and a boy back to Nebraska, plus two hitch-hikers picked up on the way. This young hippie couple, totally free, inspire admiration in both the man and the boy; though it means the end of his day for the old man, he accepts the inevitable, natural succession of youth. *A Life* completes the story of the old man, who now seeks and achieves death at the hands of an Indian and thus fulfills a ritual requirement of nature.

Characters recur in Morris novels, sometimes (but not always) retaining the same names. Thus, Tom Scanlon first appears in *The World in the Attic*, is one of the central figures in *The Field of Vision*, and survives as the remaining inhabitant of Lone Tree, Nebraska, in *Ceremony in Lone Tree*. Taken together, Morris's works are intent on seeking out a usable past and its impact on the present, asserting the continuity of the American character, and positing the creative and vital forces in nature.

—Clarence A. Glasrud

MOTLEY, Willard (Francis). American. Born in Chicago, Illinois, 14 July 1912. Educated at elementary and high schools in Chicago. Married; two sons. Worked as a transient laborer, waiter, cook, ranch hand, etc., throughout the United States during the 1930's: served jail sentence for vagrancy, Cheyenne, Wyoming; writer from 1939; worked as a photographer, an interviewer for the Chicago Housing Authority, and as a writer for the Office of Civilian Defense, in Chicago, in the 1940's; moved to Mexico. 1951. *Died 5 March 1965.*

PUBLICATIONS

Fiction

> *Knock on Any Door.* 1947.
> *We Fished All Night.* 1951.
> *Let No Man Write My Epitaph.* 1958.
> *Let Noon Be Fair.* 1966.

Reading List: "Motley and the Sociological Novel" by Alfred Weissgärber, in *Studi Americani 7*, 1961.

* * *

A middle-class Black writer, Willard Motley refused to confine his work to racial subjects, deliberately moving into the Chicago slums in order to live in an amalgam of the backgrounds, religions, and races that later appear in his books. Sometimes called superior to Drieser's novels or Terkel's non-fiction studies, his novels are naturalist panoramas of slum conditions. He orchestrates a dozen lives together in the same appalling career from idealistic youth to death in defeat as "cop-killer," "junkie," "whore," society's labels for its weakest victims, Motley's protagonists. There are many echoes of Zola in Motley's Chicago, the devouring Beast. Few American social realists have written with Motley's angry brilliance on ghetto immigrants, drug addiction, jack-rolling, racketeering. In his finest novel, *We Fished All Night*, Motley widens his focus on social and economic conditions in the slum – the cycle of poverty and oppression that slowly transforms his gentle adolescent heroes into "punks" – to include corporate and political structures, indeed the gangsterism at the root of World War II which leaves the slum depopulated, its few "heroes" mutilated or insane. Motley's youths (Italian, Polish, Mexican, Black) are driven from home by brutality and squalor onto the streets for companionship and understanding; if they stay on the streets (in "the leer of the neon night") they end as hunted criminals; and if they try to move on, they claw their way among bribe-taking police and vote-buying politicians, ending just as hunted by their political enemies and just as criminal.

Every reader notes the flaws in Motley's work, the simplistic thesis of determinant slum environment, and the flaccidity of the last two novels where the artistic rigor relaxes and the vibrant anger often dissolves into bathos. But no reader denies Motley's astonishing ability to depict the pained squalor of life in the tenement, the poolroom, the bookie joint, the bar, the death-row cell, the addict's gibbered revery. Traditional in form, using flashback and narrated monologue within a tight chronological frame, the novels inter-relate through recurring characters, including successive generations, underscoring the sameness, the suffocating immutability of their world.

—Jan Hokenson

NABOKOV, Vladimir. Pseudonym: V. Sirin (for Russian works). American. Born in St. Petersburg, now Leningrad, Russia, 23 April 1899; left Russia in 1919, and lived in Berlin, 1922–37, and France, 1937–40; settled in the United States, 1940; naturalized, 1945. Educated at the Prince Tenishev School, St. Petersburg, 1910–17; Trinity College, Cambridge, B.A. 1922. Married Véra Slonim in 1925; one son. Instructor in Russian Literature and Creative Writing, Stanford University, California, Summer 1941; Lecturer in Russian, Wellesley College, Massachusetts, 1941–48; Research Fellow, Museum of Comparative Zoology, Harvard University, Cambridge, Massachusetts, 1942–48; Professor of Russian Literature, Cornell University, Ithaca, New York, 1948–59; Visiting Lecturer, Harvard University, Spring 1955. Lived in later life in Switzerland. Recipient: Guggenheim Fellowship, 1943, 1953; National Institute of Arts and Letters grant, 1951; Brandeis University Creative Arts Award, 1963; American Academy of Arts and Letters Award of Merit Medal, 1969; National Medal for Literature, 1973. *Died 2 July 1977.*

PUBLICATIONS

Fiction

Mashen'ka. 1926; translated by the author and Michael Glenny as *Mary*, 1970.
Korol', Dama, Valet. 1928; translated by the author and Dmitri Nabakov as *King, Queen, Knave*, 1968.
Zashchita Luzhina (The Luzhin Defense). 1930; translated by the author and Michael Scammell as *The Defense,*1964.
Vozrashchenie Chorba (The Return of Chorb)(story). 1930.
Podvig' (The Exploit). 1932; translated by the author and Dmitri Nabokov as *Glory*, 1971.
Kamera Obskura. 1933; translated by W. Roy as *Camera Obscura*, 1937; revised and translated by the author as *Laughter in the Dark*, 1938.
Otchayanie. 1936; translated by the author as *Despair*, 1937; revised edition, 1966.
Soglyadatay (The Spy). 1938; translated by the author and Dmitri Nabokov as *The Eye*, 1965.
Priglashenie na Kazn'. 1938; translated by the author and Dmitri Nabokov as *Invitation to a Beheading*, 1959.
The Real Life of Sebastian Knight. 1941.
Bend Sinister. 1947.
Nine Stories. 1947.
Dar. 1952; translated by the author and Michael Scammell as *The Gift*, 1963.
Lolita. 1955; translated by the author into Russian, 1967.
Vesna v Fial'te i Drugie Rasskazi (Spring in Fialta and Other Stories). 1956.
Pnin. 1957.
Nabokov's Dozen: A Collection of 13 Stories. 1958.
Pale Fire. 1962.
Nabokov's Quartet (stories). 1966.
Ada; or Ardor: A Family Chronicle. 1969.
Transparent Things. 1973.
A Russian Beauty and Other Stories, translated by Dmitri Nabokov. 1973.
Look at the Harlequins! 1974.
Tyrants Destroyed and Other Stories, translated by the author and Dmitri Nabokov. 1975.
Details of a Sunset and Other Stories. 1976.

Plays

Smertj (Death), *Deduschka* (Grandfather), *Poljus* (The Pole), *Tragediya gospodina Morna* (The Tragedy of Mr. Morn), and *Chelovek iz SSSR* (The Man from the USSR), in *Rul*, 1923–27.
Izobretenie Val'sa (produced 1968).   In *Russkiya Zapiski*, 1938; translated as *The Waltz Invention* (produced 1968), 1966.
Sobytie (The Event) (produced 1938).   In *Russkiya Zapiski*, 1938.
Lolita: A Screenplay.   1974.

Screenplay: *Lolita*,   1962.

Verse

(Poems).   1916.
(Two Paths).   1918.
Gorniy Put' (The Empyrean Path).   1923.
Grozd' (The Cluster).   1923.
Stikhotvoreniya, 1920–1951 (Poems).   1952.
Poems.   1959.
Poems and Problems.   1971.

Other

Nikolai Gogol.   1944.
Conclusive Evidence: A Memoir.   1951; as *Speak, Memory: A Memoir*, 1952; revised edition, as *Speak, Memory: An Autobiography Revisited*, 1966.
Nabokov's Congeries: An Anthology.   1968.
Strong Opinions (essays).   1973.

Editor and Translator, *Eugene Onegin*, by Aleksandr Pushkin.   4 vols., 1964; revised edition, 4 vols., 1976.

Translator, *Nikolka Persik* (Colas Breugnon), by Romain Rolland.   1922.
Translator, *Anya v Strane Chudes* (Alice in Wonderland), by Lewis Carroll.   1923.
Translator, *Three Russian Poets: Verse Translations from Pushkin, Lermontov and Tyutchev*.   1945; as *Poems by Pushkin, Lermontov and Tyutchev*, 1948.
Translator, with Dmitri Nabokov, *A Hero of Our Times*, by Mikhail Lermontov.   1958.
Translator, *The Song of Igor's Campaign: An Epic of the Twelfth Century*.   1960.

Bibliography: *Nabokov: Bibliographie des Gesantwerks* by Dieter E. Zimmer, 1963, revised edition, 1964; *Nabokov: A Bibliography* by Andrew Field, 1974.

Reading List: *Escape into Aesthetics: The Art of Nabokov* by Page Stegner, 1966; *Nabokov: His Life in Art*, 1967, and *Nabokov: A Biography*, 1975, both by Andrew Field; *Nabokov: The Man and His Work* edited by L. S. Dembo, 1967; *Nabokov* by Julian Moynahan, 1971; *Nabokov's Deceptive World* by W. Woodlin Rowe, 1971; *Nabokov* by Donald E. Morton, 1974; *Nabokov's Dark Cinema* by Alfred Appel, Jr., 1974; *Reading Nabokov* by Douglas Fowler, 1974; *Nabokov* by L. L. Lee, 1976; *The Real Life of Nabokov* by Alex de Jonge, 1976.

*   *   *

The most fruitful way to approach the extensive and varied Nabokov canon (verse, plays, short stories, autobiography, translations, critical articles, and works on chess and lepidoptery) is undoubtedly through the novels, particularly the earlier Russian ones which are frequently overlooked but which contain the fundamental themes and devices of the later works. For what is striking about Nabokov's art is the consistency with which it develops, structurally and thematically, from the initial exploration of nostalgia and émigré life of Berlin in *Mary* to the celebration of language and artifice and the treatment of time in *Ada*.

Nabokov's second novel, *King, Queen, Knave*, is the first to juxtapose crime and art for parodic purposes and leaves its hero, Franz, a myopic character (literally and figuratively), stranded outside the bliss of his criminal fictions. *The Eye*, a novella whose émigré narrator is beset with split perceptions of his self, is, according to Nabokov, the first work where he develops that "involute abode" of his later fiction. Of the other novels of this Berlin/Paris period, *Despair* is the most important, since Herman Karlovich is a recognizable (though very different) predecessor to *Lolita*'s Humbert Humbert. Herman is a wily, self-conscious villain who devises a complex crime involving the murder of his double, who, however, does not resemble Herman at all. Herman's "perfect crime," and his journal which records that crime, are flawed by the same misconception; he fails to realize that contingent reality cannot be manipulated and that "the invention of art contains far more truth than life's reality."

The Gift is important for its exploration of biography as a fictional form, an exploration which is also prominent in his first English novel, *The Real Life of Sebastian Knight*. V., the narrator, attempts to write the biography of his brother, Sebastian Knight, but is foiled at every turn since Knight's life moves with that same obliqueness as the chess piece after which he is named. Ultimately, however, V.'s narrative approximates Sebastian's life by virtue of the dynamic character of the unfulfilled quest which utilizes parody as "a kind of springboard for leaping into the highest region of serious emotion."

Pnin is a warmly witty but sad portrait of Professor Timofey Pnin, an aging Russian exile attempting to master American language and culture at a New England university; the professorial politicking finally defeats him. Besides its preoccupation with cultural exile, the novel shows a self-consciousness of language, though never to the extent that we find in Nabokov's best-known novel, *Lolita*. In fact, given that Humbert Humbert, the narrator and hero, writes about his nympholeptic escapades with the twelve-year old Lolita in prison where he has "only words to play with," language frames the entire novel and is the vehicle through which Humbert and Lolita are finally relegated to the "bliss of fiction." Humbert's sexual desire becomes a metaphor for the artistic desire to create, though not until Humbert learns the hard lesson that it is desire and not possession which is the transcendent reality. So when Humbert possesses Lolita in part I of the novel (the crime), he is forced to protect her jealously in a motel trek across America in part II (the getaway). He has violated the "intangible island of entranced time" which is established early in the novel with his childhood love, Annabel Lee. It is Annabel Lee in her "kingdom by the sea" who establishes the initial rift between desire and possession. Ultimately, Lolita is abducted from Humbert by Quilty, Humbert's double, and the final chase scene culminates in Quilty's murder, a comic, grotesque exorcism that allows Humbert some measure of grace in the "bliss of fiction."

Pale Fire is the most experimental and enigmatic of Nabokov's novels, since its structure entails a 999-line poem by John Shade and a foreword, commentary with footnotes, and index by Charles Kinbote, the poet's homosexual neighbour who is really an exile from the distant northern land of Zembla (Russia). Beyond the obvious parody of pedantic scholarship, the novel explores the interdependencies of multi-layered worlds, each reflecting and refracting the other: Shade tells his story in verse; Kinbote uses Shade's poem to reveal his Zemblan past; Gradus, a secret agent intent on killing Kinbote, murders Shade by mistake; and of course, stalking through the work there is Nabokov, the arch-inventor of them all. Because the narrative of each layer is invented and sustained by the other, the final effect is a spiral of artifice.

Ada, Nabokov's most ambitious fiction (although its status among critics remains uncertain), fuses the novelist's earlier themes and techniques with greater scope and linguistic dexterity. The opening three chapters present a baroque invocation, a fanfare of language for the core of the novel which chronicles the incestuous love affair of the precocious hero, Van Veen, and his sister, Ada. Van's obsession with the past and the novel's eroticism culminate in part IV in a long lecture on time and space. Here the past becomes an inseparable link to the present, making a "glittering 'now' that is the only reality of Time's texture." Erotic desire, the art of inventing, and the butterfly's life cycle are metaphors for the constant metamorphosis of the present, while the future is relegated to an unknowable realm of space. The narrative moves across an imaginary geography of overlapping Russian, European, and American landscapes, with an equally overlaid texture of language. All the familiar Nabokovian motifs and devices are heaped against the aristocratic setting of the "ardors and arbors of Ardis Hall": butterflies and botany, dreams and doubles, puns, word games, nostalgia, false leads, and eroticism. It is undoubtedly Nabokov's most festive celebration of language, artifice, and, what should not be overlooked, love.

Transparent Things is a novella bordering on the metaphysical as it deals with the transparency of objects in the present, and finally of life itself, as death, abetted by chance, brings Hugh Person to a characteristic Nabokovian ending. *Look at the Harlequins!* is a first-person memoir of a writer whose life and works have disguised parallels with Nabokov's own. It is a fiction created out of fiction, a deepening of the labyrinth of inventing. And while these two works never surpass *Ada*, they do illustrate what has been evident in Nabokov from the start, namely, that fiction becomes the only sustained reality beyond contingent existence – even, no doubt, the sustenance of self.

—Brent MacLaine

NASH, (Frederick) Ogden. American. Born in Rye, New York, 19 August 1902. Educated at St. George's School, Newport, Rhode Island, 1917–20; Harvard University, Cambridge, Massachusetts, 1920–21. Married Frances Rider Leonard in 1931; two daughters. Taught for one year at St. George's School, Newport; worked briefly as a bond salesman on Wall Street, 1924; worked in the editorial and publicity departments of Doubleday Doran, publishers, New York, 1925, and joined John Farrar and Stanley Rinehart when they left the firm to set up their own publishing house; Member, Editorial Staff, *The New Yorker* magazine; later retired from publishing to devote himself to his own writing. Recipient: Sarah Josepha Hale Award, 1964. Member, National Institute of Arts and Letters. *Died 19 May 1971.*

PUBLICATIONS

Collections

I Wouldn't Have Missed It: Selected Poems, edited by Linell Smith and Isabel Eberstadt. 1975.

Verse

Free Wheeling. 1931.
Hard Lines. 1931.
Hard Lines and Others. 1932.
Happy Days. 1933.
Four Prominent So and So's, music by Robert Armbruster. 1934; as *Four Prominent Bastards Are We,* 1934.
The Primrose Path. 1935.
The Bad Parents' Garden of Verse. 1936.
Bon Voyage. 1936.
I'm a Stranger Here Myself. 1938.
The Face Is Familiar: Selected Verse. 1940; revised edition, 1954.
Good Intentions. 1942.
The Nash Pocket Book. 1944.
Many Long Years Ago. 1945.
Selected Verse. 1946.
Nash's Musical Zoo. 1947.
Versus. 1949.
Family Reunion. 1950.
The Private Dining Room and Other New Verses. 1953.
You Can't Get There from Here. 1957.
Verses from 1929 On. 1959; as *Collected Verse from 1929 On,* 1961.
Scrooge Rides Again. 1960.
Everyone But Thee and Me. 1962.
Marriage Lines: Notes of a Student Husband. 1964.
The Mysterious Ouphe. 1965.
A Nash Omnibook. 1967.
Santa Go Home: A Case History for Parents. 1967.
There's Always Another Windmill. 1968.
Funniest Verses, edited by Dorothy Price. 1968.
Bed Riddance: A Posy for the Indisposed. 1970.
The Old Dog Barks Backwards. 1972.

Plays

One Touch of Venus, with S. J. Perelman, music by Kurt Weill, from *The Tinted Venus* by F. Anstey (produced 1943). 1944.
Sweet Bye and Bye (lyrics only), book by S. J. Perelman and Al Hirschfield, music by Vernon Duke (produced 1946).
Two's Company (lyrics only; revue) (produced 1952).
The Littlest Revue, with others (produced 1956).
The Beauty Part, with S. J. Perelman (produced 1961). 1963.

Screenplays: *The Firefly,* with Frances Goodrich and Albert Hackett, 1937; *The Shining Hour,* with Jane Murfin, 1938; *The Feminine Touch,* with George Oppenheimer and Edmund L. Hartmann, 1941.

Other

The Cricket of Carador (juvenile), with Joseph Alger. 1925.

Born in a Beer Garden; or, She Troupes to Conquer, with Christopher Morley and Cleon Throckmorton. 1930.
Parents Keep Out: Elderly Poems for Youngerly Readers (juvenile). 1951.
The Christmas That Almost Wasn't (juvenile). 1957.
The Boy Who Laughed at Santa Claus (juvenile). 1957.
Custard the Dragon (juvenile). 1959.
A Boy Is a Boy: The Fun of Being a Boy (juvenile). 1960.
Custard the Dragon and the Wicked Knight (juvenile). 1961.
The New Nutcracker Suite and Other Innocent Verses (juvenile). 1962.
Girls Are Silly (juvenile). 1962.
The Adventures of Isabel (juvenile). 1963.
A Boy and His Room (juvenile). 1963.
The Untold Adventures of Santa Claus (juvenile). 1964.
The Animal Garden (juvenile). 1965.
The Cruise of the Aardvark (juvenile). 1967.
The Scroobious Pip (juvenile), by Edward Lear (completed by Nash). 1968.

Editor, *Nothing But Wodehouse.* 1932.
Editor, *The Moon Is Shining Bright as Day: An Anthology of Good Humored Verse.* 1953.
Editor, *I Couldn't Help Laughing: Stories* (juvenile). 1957.
Editor, *Everybody Ought to Know: Verses Selected and Introduced.* 1961.

*   *   *

Ogden Nash's career as a writer of light verse began in the 1930's when he accepted defeat as a poet. Realizing that his serious verses were tongue-tied and sentimental, he began constructing a peculiar form of doggerel which broke all rules of symmetry and harmony in poetry. Lines grew as long as subway trains, capped by rhymes as outrageous as cocktail party chatter; philosophical questions were mocked by horse-sensical conclusions: "What is life? Life is stepping down a step or sitting on a chair,/And it isn't there." Though it wasn't great poetry, it made Nash America's most popular comic poet.

With these techniques, Nash was able to express poetically the plain-spoken American's frustration with poetic complication, as well as the conviction that, really, poetry is just prose that rhymes. (Or should be, Nash hints: "One thing that literature would be greatly the better for/Would be a more restricted use of simile and metaphor.") In the Introduction to the 1975 Nash collection *I Wouldn't Have Missed It,* Archibald MacLeish gave away the secret: "Nothing ... suggests the structure of verse but the rhymes" which are used baldly to shoehorn sentences into what looked like verse. Basing his poems not on the poetic line, but on the sentence, Nash became (in his work) a "wersifier" painting men, women, and society from their poetic backsides.

Like his wersification, Nash's subjects come straight out of everyday life: summer colds and Monday mornings, leaky faucets and crashing bores. He is assailed by the mundane torments of living, perplexed by the oddities and failings of human nature, and mystified by women, just as they are by men. Yet no matter how disastrous life may be, Nash reassures us that perhaps it isn't so bad after all: "When I consider how my life is spent,/I hardly ever repent."

—Walter Bode

NEMEROV, Howard.   American.   Born in New York City, 1 March 1920. Educated at Fieldston School, New York; Harvard University, Cambridge, Massachusetts, A.B. 1941. Served in the Royal Canadian Air Force, and the United States Air Force, 1941–45: First Lieutenant. Married Margaret Russell in 1944; three children. Instructor in English, Hamilton College, Clinton, New York, 1946–48; Member of the Literature Faculty, Bennington College, Vermont, 1948–66; Professor of English, Brandeis University, Waltham, Massachusetts, 1966–69. Since 1969, Professor of English, Washington University, St. Louis. Visiting Lecturer, University of Minnesota, Minneapolis, 1958–59; Writer-in-Residence, Hollins College, Virginia, 1962–64; Consultant in Poetry, Library of Congress, Washington, D.C., 1963–64. Associate Editor, *Furioso*, Madison, Connecticut, later Northfield, Minnesota, 1946–51. Recipient: National Institute of Arts and Letters grant, 1961; New England Poetry Club Golden Rose, 1962; Brandeis University Creative Arts Award, 1962; National Endowment for the Arts grant, 1966; Theodore Roethke Award, 1968; Guggenheim Fellowship, 1968; St. Botolph's Club Prize, 1968; Academy of American Poets Fellowship, 1970. D.L.: Lawrence University, Appleton, Wisconsin, 1964; Tufts University, Medford, Massachusetts, 1969. Fellow, American Academy of Arts and Sciences, 1966. Member, American Academy of Arts and Letters, 1976. Lives in St. Louis.

PUBLICATIONS

Verse

The Image and the Law.   1947.
Guide to the Ruins.   1950.
The Salt Garden.   1955.
Mirrors and Windows.   1958.
New and Selected Poems.   1960.
The Next Room of the Dream: Poems and Two Plays.   1962.
Five American Poets, with others, edited by Ted Hughes and Thom Gunn.   1963.
The Blue Swallows.   1967.
The Winter Lightning: Selected Poems.   1968.
The Painter Dreaming in the Scholar's House.   1968.
Gnomes and Occasions: Poems.   1972.
The Western Approaches: Poems 1973–1975.   1975.
Collected Poems.   1977.

Fiction

The Melodramatists.   1949.
Federigo; or, The Power of Love.   1954.
The Homecoming Game.   1957.
A Commodity of Dreams and Other Stories.   1959.
Stories, Fables, and Other Diversions.   1971.

Other

Poetry and Fiction: Essays.   1963.
Journal of the Fictive Life.   1965.
Reflexions on Poetry and Poetics.   1972.

Figures of Thought: Speculations on the Meaning of Poetry and Other Essays. 1978.

Editor, *Poets on Poetry.* 1965.

Reading List: *Nemerov* by Peter Meinke, 1968; *The Critical Reception of Nemerov: A Selection of Essays and a Bibliography* edited by Bowie Duncan, 1971; *The Shield of Perseus* by Julia Bartholomay, 1972.

*   *   *

Although Howard Nemerov has written a journal, two collections of short stories, three novels, and much fine criticism (including exceptionally perceptive essays on Wallace Stevens, Dylan Thomas, and Vladimir Nabokov), his primary importance is as a poet. He is a superior craftsman, particularly skilled at blank verse. Moreover, the content of his poetry is penetrating. Perhaps the foremost reason for this richness in content is that Nemerov believes that a major function of the poet is to scrutinize and describe reality precisely as it is. "The Private Eye" makes it clear that the artist should strip himself of preconceptions. In "Vermeer," Nemerov praises this painter for taking "what is, and seeing it as it is."

Despite the fact that reality contains patterns, Nemerov finds that, fundamentally, reality is primitive and chaotic. "The Town Dump" and "The Quarry" stress the relentless chaotic decay occurring in our world, while raw primitiveness is emphasized in "Lobsters." "Nightmare" shows that the primitive also exists within the human being. Nor is any Dionysian oneness fusing man and nature possible. Instead, nature is apt to paralyze man's will, as it does the speaker's in "Death and the Maiden."

Man, then, is a very limited creature, a main point in both of his verse plays, *Endor* and *Cain*, as well as in "Runes." For Nemerov the other major function of the artist is to create some kind of comforting order, even though this order is only temporary. Nemerov stresses this point again and again in such poems as "Elegy for a Nature Poet" and "Lines and Circularities." The artist can also remind us that nature can be lovely and exhilarating. However, we must not think that human creations can "replace" reality – the warning given in "Projection."

Because nature is ceaselessly changing, Nemerov suggests that man, too, should be flexible. "Lot Later" dramatizes this point. Inflexibility will trap man, for even sanctified history can later be proven false, the theme in "To Clio, Muse of History." Nevertheless, man should not let himself be crippled by cynicism, as is the Minister in *Endor*.

Nemerov's poetry is valuable because it incisively presents us with a no-nonsense view of the world, a view that is stark, but not entirely negative. In "The View from an Attic Window," he declares that we live amid chaos, that our individual lives are short, and that, as a result, "life is hopeless," yet "beautiful" – and we should try to endure and to grow. "Small Moment" states that if we do fully accept reality, we will also embody vibrant love.

—Robert K. Johnson

NIN, Anaïs. American. Born in Paris in February 1903; emigrated to the United States in 1914; later naturalized. Educated in elementary school in New York; thereafter self-taught.

Married Hugh Guiler (also called Ian Hugo) in 1920. Worked as a fashion and artist's model, 1918–20; studied psychoanalysis, then practised under Otto Rank in Europe, and briefly in New York; lived in Paris, 1930–40; writer from 1932; established Siana Editions, Paris, 1935; returned to New York, 1940. Member of the Advisory Board, Feminist Book Club, Los Angeles. Recipient: Prix Sévigne, 1971. Member, National Institute of Arts and Letters. *Died 14 January 1977.*

PUBLICATIONS

Fiction

House of Incest. 1936.
Winter of Artifice. 1939.
Under a Glass Bell. 1944; as *Under a Glass Bell and Other Stories,* 1947.
This Hunger. 1945.
Ladders to Fire. 1946.
Children of the Albatross. 1947.
Four Chambered Heart. 1950.
A Spy in the House of Love. 1954.
Solar Barque. 1958.
Cities of the Interior. 1959.
Seduction of the Minotaur. 1961.
Collages. 1964.
Cities of the Interior (collection). 1974.
Waste of Timelessness and Other Early Stories. 1977.
Delta of Venus: Erotica. 1977.

Other

D. H. Lawrence: An Unprofessional Study. 1932.
Realism and Reality. 1946.
On Writing. 1947.
The Diary, edited by Gunther Stuhlmann. 6 vols., 1966–76; as *The Journals,* 6 vols., 1966–77.
The Novel of the Future. 1968.
Unpublished Selections from the Diary. 1968.
Nuances. 1970.
An Interview with Nin, by Duane Schneider. 1970.
The Nin Reader. 1973.
A Photographic Supplement to the Diary. 1975.
A Woman Speaks: The Lectures, Seminars, and Interviews of Nin, edited by Evelyn Hinz. 1975.
In Favor of the Sensitive Man and Other Essays. 1976.
Aphrodisiac, with John Boyce. 1978.
Linotte: The Early Diary 1914–1920, translated by Jean Sherman. 1978.

Bibliography: *Nin: A Bibliography* by Benjamin Franklin, 1973.

Reading List: *Nin* by Oliver Evans, 1968; *The Mirror and the Garden: Realism and Reality in* the Writings of Nin by Evelyn Hinz, 1973; A Casebook on Nin edited by Robert Zaller, 1974; Collage of Dreams: The Writings of Nin by Sharon Spencer, 1977.

*   *   *

Anaïs Nin's fiction may best be described as symphonic tone poems in prose, with their programmatic intermingling of similar themes and characters from one novel to another. Her characters are dancers, actresses, artists, musicians, and writers, all impelled by inner visions, illusions, or frustrations, who play their solo parts contrapuntally and always return as in the rondo form to the central female protagonist, with whom they all interact. Also characteristic of tone poems, Nin's style is psychologically discursive and impressionistic, with dreams and interior monologues substituting for the realism, dialogue, and clearly delineated plots of more traditional narratives. And her language is rhythmic, rich in sensuous imagery, and symbolic.

Nin's interests and opinions weave in and out of her novels like leitmotifs as contrapuntally as her characters do. Haunting all her fiction are evocations of music – jazz, opera, symphony – which Nin views as the inevitable preserver of memory and thus a barrier to all efforts to escape the past. Her faith in psychoanalysis as a tool for plumbing that past for constructive creative resources pervades all the novels, as does her belief in the permanency of art in contrast to the ephemerality of politics. Her fiction is totally apolitical; it focuses instead on the intricacies of intense physical and emotional relationships. Through these relationships, Nin also manifests her strong conviction in the fundamentally different sensibilities of men and women. Her men are usually unable to accept emotional responsibilities, are frustrated by their inability to act, and are drawn to the vision and sensitivity of nurturing women. Her women are seductive, submissive, and vulnerable because of their need for men; at the same time, they struggle to overcome this dependency on authority figures and to develop into independent human beings. Nin's depiction of women's search for a synthesis of these contrary facets of their personality along with her explicit rendering of female responses to sexual and emotional encounters – traditionally described from the male perspective – have made her novels attractive to a wide audience.

While her fiction need not be read in any particular order, there is a gradual evolution of control over the structure and language of her novels during the thirty years of their composition. Her craft developed from the earliest, House of Incest, a random collection of poetic impressions, to later ones like Collages which are more complex in characterization and more ambitious in structure, artistically shaped cycles of portraits radiating from a central figure. If Nin's fiction is read chronologically and concurrently with her diaries of the same period, the essential function of the latter to her fictional mode becomes strikingly evident. It was from her experiences and the portraits delineated in her diaries that Nin drew the material for all her novels, sometimes rewritten, often lifted intact into them. And the characteristics of her diaries parallel those in her fiction: musically counterpointed themes and characters; mystical, sensual, and poetic prose; and an enduring faith in the artistic life, psychoanalysis, and the differing sensibilities of the male and the female.

—Estelle C. Jelinek

O'CONNOR, (Mary) Flannery.   American.   Born in Savannah, Georgia, 25 March 1925. Educated at the Women's College of Georgia, now Georgia College at Milledgeville, A.B. 1945; University of Iowa, Iowa City, M.F.A. 1947. Recipient: National Institute of Arts and

Letters grant, 1957; O. Henry Award, 1957, 1963, 1965; Ford Foundation grant, 1959; Henry H. Bellaman Foundation award, 1964; National Catholic Book Award, 1966; National Book Award, 1972. D.Litt.: St. Mary's College, Kentucky, 1962; Smith College, Northampton, Massachusetts, 1963. *Died 3 August 1964.*

PUBLICATIONS

Collections

The Complete Stories. 1971.
The Habit of Being: Letters, edited by Sally Fitzgerald. 1978

Fiction

Wise Blood. 1952.
A Good Man Is Hard to Find and Other Stories. 1955; as *The Artificial Nigger and Other Tales,* 1957.
The Violent Bear It Away. 1960.
Everything That Rises Must Converge. 1965.

Other

Mystery and Manners: Occasional Prose, edited by Sally and Robert Fitzgerald. 1969.

Editor, *Death of a Child.* 1961.

Bibliography: *O'Connor and Caroline Gordon: A Reference Guide* by Robert E. Golden and Mary C. Sullivan, 1977.

Reading List: *O'Connor* by Stanley Edgar Hyman, 1966; *The Added Dimension: The Art and Mind of O'Connor* edited by Melvin J. Friedman and Lewis A. Lawson, 1966 (includes bibliography by Lawson); *The True Country: Themes in the Fiction of O'Connor* by Carter W. Martin, 1969; *The World of O'Connor* by Josephine Hendin, 1970; *Invisible Parade: The Fiction of O'Connor* by Miles Orvell, 1972; *O'Connor* by Preston M. Browning, Jr., 1974; *O'Connor* by Dorothy Tuck McFarland, 1976; *The Pruning Word: The Parables of O'Connor* by John R. May, 1976.

*   *   *

Flannery O'Connor belongs to a small group of twentieth-century writers whose work is profoundly religious, not through direct statement or preachment but because its informing theme and structure are theological. Flannery O'Connor was raised as a Roman Catholic in the Protestant southern United States, and she found in the "Christ-haunted" fundamentalist religious beliefs of that region much that awoke responsive chords in her, despite her basic theological differences with the Protestant faith. She brought to the portrayal of the people of her region a clear, hard, witty style, an unblinking eye, and a sense of both the divine and the ridiculous; and she used her violent portrayals of grotesque people to express a deep and unsentimental religious faith. Fairly early in her career, she developed lupus, an incurable disease that progressed inexorably to its conclusion in her death at the age of 39. Much of her work was produced after this disease had initially struck, and a great deal of her best fiction is concerned with death, and often with death as a release or means of salvation. Although this is a limited theme, and the range of her work often seems distressingly narrow, Flannery O'Connor worked within the limits of her art with great commitment, artistic integrity, high technical skill, and frequent success.

She is primarily a writer of short stories. The collection *A Good Man Is Hard to Find* and the posthumous *Everything That Rises Must Converge* contained nineteen examples of her best work in this form. *The Complete Stories* added twelve more. Her first novel, *Wise Blood*, is a weaving together of material originally written in short story form. Her only other novel was *The Violent Bear It Away*. (She was working on a third novel at the time of her death but apparently without the expectation of ever completing it.) Despite excellent elements in both her novels, O'Connor will survive as a master of the short story form. Her stories were based on what she called "anagogical vision ... the kind of vision that is able to see different levels of reality in one image or one situation." It is this anagogical element which has led to very extensive examination of levels of meaning in her stories by many critics.

Wise Blood is the story of the preacher Hazel Motes, called, he believed, to preach "the Church without Christ," a man who is driven by acts of violent grace finally to accept the Jesus whom he had denied, to blind himself, and to die, and in his death to achieve a kind of salvation. *The Violent Bear It Away* is the record of the efforts of a boy, Francis Marion Tarwater, to escape the prophetic calling bequeathed for him by his dead great-uncle. A much more tightly organized work than *Wise Blood*, *The Violent Bear It Away* is really the harrowing chronicle of the struggle of cosmic forces, represented by the religious great-uncle and a very modern uncle, for the soul of Francis Tarwater. The great-uncle ultimately triumphs.

O'Connor's short stories deal with simple Georgia people, hungry with a passionate desire for a spiritual dimension which the nature of their lives and their beliefs deny them. The usual pattern in these stories is that of a desperate search through extreme, violent, and grotesque actions that usually culminate in the entry of divine grace through some instrumentality that bestows salvation in the moment of death. The frantic and misdirected struggles of these human beings result in a violent but comic representation that seems in many ways to reflect the long tradition of American southwestern humor, with its extreme portrayals of grotesque people in violent and unusual situations. Her work is most like that of Erskine Caldwell in terms of the grotesqueness of her characters, the extravagance of her actions, the sharp and vigorous starkness of her prose, and her kind of pervasive comic sense. However, where Caldwell presents his characters as people distorted as a result of economic deprivation, Flannery O'Connor's world is the world of people rendered grotesque by their inability to satisfy their spiritual hungers. All of her characters can be explained in one sense in St. Augustine's phrase, "Our souls are restless till they find rest in Thee." Among her short stories of particular distinction are "A Good Man Is Hard to Find," "Good Country People," "The Artificial Nigger," "The Lame Shall Enter First," "Revelation," "Greenleaf," and the short novel "The Displaced Person."

In her short life Flannery O'Connor accomplished much in her intense art. Narrow though her range and subjects are, they are pursued with great distinction and great force. Ultimately she will remain a minor figure in American letters, but a minor figure of enormous challenge, subtlety, and accomplishment.

—C. Hugh Holman

ODETS, Clifford.   American.   Born in Philadelphia, Pennsylvania, 18 July 1906; grew up in the Bronx, New York. Educated at Morris High School, New York, 1921–23. Married 1) the actress Luise Rainer in 1937 (divorced, 1941); 2) Betty Grayson in 1943 (died, 1954), one son and one daughter. Actor on radio and on Broadway, 1923–28, and with Theatre Guild Productions, New York, 1928–30; Co-Founder, Group Theatre, New York, 1930; wrote for the stage from 1933; film writer and director. Recipient: New Theatre League prize, 1935; Yale drama prize, 1935; American Academy of Arts and Letters Award of Merit Medal, 1961. *Died 15 August 1963.*

PUBLICATIONS

Plays

> *Waiting for Lefty* (produced 1935).   In *Three Plays*, 1935.
> *Awake and Sing!* (produced 1935).   In *Three Plays*, 1935.
> *Till the Day I Die* (produced 1935).   In *Three Plays*, 1935.
> *I Can't Sleep: A Monologue* (produced 1935).   1936.
> *Paradise Lost* (produced 1935).   1936.
> *Golden Boy* (produced 1937).   1937.
> *Rocket to the Moon* (produced 1938).   1939.
> *Night Music* (produced 1940).   1940.
> *Clash by Night* (produced 1941).   1942.
> *The Russian People*, from a play by Konstantin Simonov (produced 1942).
> *None But the Lonely Heart* (screenplay), in *Best Film Plays 1945*, edited by John Gassner
>   and Dudley Nichols.   1946.
> *The Big Knife* (produced 1949).   1949.
> *The Country Girl* (produced 1950).   1951; as *Winter Journey* (produced 1952), 1953.
> *The Flowering Peach* (produced 1954).   1954.
> *The Silent Partner* (produced 1972).

> Screenplays: *The General Died at Dawn*, 1936; *Black Sea Fighters*, 1943; *None But the Lonely Heart*, 1944; *Deadline at Dawn*, 1946; *Humoresque* with Zachery Gold, 1946; *Sweet Smell of Success*, with Ernest Lehman, 1957; *The Story on Page One*, 1960; *Wild in the Country*, 1961.

> Television Plays: *Big Mitch*, 1963; *The Mafia Man*, 1964.

Other

> *Rifle Rule in Cuba*, with Carleton Beals.   1935.

Reading List: *Odets* by R. Baird Shuman, 1963; *Odets: The Thirties and After* by Edward Murray, 1968; *Odets, Humane Dramatist* by Michael J. Mendelsohn, 1969; *Odets* by Gerald Weales, 1971; *Odets, Playwright-Poet* by Harold Cantor, 1978.

*   *   *

Clifford Odets's first produced play was *Waiting for Lefty*, a one-act agitprop drama based on the New York City taxi strike of 1934. It is uncharacteristic Odets in both form and intention. A group of naturalistic dramatic sketches set within a union meeting, still visible while the more intimate scenes are being played, *Waiting for Lefty* is non-realistic theater that breaks the conventional frame to invite the audience to join in the final call for a strike. Aside from this play, Odets remained within the American realistic tradition even when he attempted to open the form with cinematic techniques (*Golden Boy*), visual and musical devices (*Night Music*) and Yiddish-Biblical fantasy (*The Flowering Peach*). Although most of his plays, particularly the early ones like *Awake and Sing!* and *Paradise Lost*, have the mandatory optimistic ending decreed by the American Left in the 1930's, *Waiting for Lefty* is the only overt propaganda play Odets wrote, except for *Till the Day I Die*, an ineffective anti-fascist piece hastily written to fill out the bill when *Lefty* moved to Broadway. He did do a few sketches, like "I Can't Sleep," for benefit performances and he worked at two political plays, *The Cuban Play* and *The Silent Partner*, which he never got into final form. If *Waiting for Lefty* is uncharacteristic in some ways, it is also unmistakable Odets. Scenes like "Joe and Edna" and "The Young Hack and His Girl" show that Odets's political and social concerns look their best transformed into domestic conflict, and the language of those scenes set the tone for the Odets work to come. When Edna says "Get out of here!" meaning "I love you" and Sid, in affectionate exasperation, calls his brother, "that dumb basketball player," we get a first taste of the Odets obliquity – the wisecrack as lament, slang as lyricism – that, trailing its Yiddish and urban roots, enriches *Awake and Sing!* and *Paradise Lost* before it peters out in the self-parody of some of the lines in the screenplay *Sweet Smell of Success*.

Although *Waiting for Lefty* introduced Odets to audiences and critics, it was not his first play. *Awake and Sing!* was already written and about to open when *Lefty* was produced. *Awake and Sing!*, Odets's most enduring work, is *the* American depression play, a still vital example of the 1930's conviction that, however terrible the situation, it could be rectified by an infusion of idealistic rhetoric administered at the final curtain. Although Odets was a Communist when he wrote it (and the play carries a few verbal indications of that fact), its optimism is more generalized, tied into the historical American penchant for possibility which, battered by the first years of the depression, had begun to revive with the election of Franklin D. Roosevelt in 1932. Not only is Odets hooked into the American ideational mainstream in *Awake and Sing!* but he recalls earlier American drama in his choice of a family setting for his play and in his willing employment of melodramatic commonplaces – the suicide of Jacob, the pregnancy of Hennie. He transcends the structural weaknesses in the play with the creation of a milieu so real that an audience feels it can be touched; this texture – partly verbal, partly emotional – is probably a product not simply of Odets's talent but of the context in which the play was written. Odets was a member of the Group Theatre, an acting company that was a family of sorts, and his Bergers are an echo of the loving, quarreling Group company which was a home for Odets, one that – reacting like Ralph and Hennie to Bessie Berger's Bronx – he sometimes saw as a trap. All of his plays through *Night Music* were written for the Group actors, but *Paradise Lost*, which Odets once correctly described as "a beautiful play, velvety ... gloomy and rich," and *Rocket to the Moon* come closest in texture to *Awake and Sing!*

When the success of *Awake and Sing!* was followed by the failure of *Paradise Lost*, Odets went to Hollywood to work on *The General Died at Dawn*. After that, he vacillated between Hollywood and New York, commerce and art, guilt and regeneration. These terms suit his view of the matter as reflected in *The Big Knife*, in which the Odets surrogate, the actor Charlie Castle, is destroyed as man and artist by the movie business. Despite this gloomy view of Hollywood Odets constantly returned to a suspicion that the movies too were an art, all the more attractive for the size of the audience. Ironically, the movies he worked on were conventional Hollywood products; even the two he directed as well as wrote, *None But the Lonely Heart* and *The Story on Page One*, are interesting primarily for their attempt at poetic verisimilitude, the visual equivalent of the sense of milieu created by other means in *Awake and Sing!* and *Paradise Lost*.

Odets's greatest commercial successes were *Golden Boy*, a parable in boxing gloves about the destructiveness of the American success ethic, and *The Country Girl*, an effective sentimental melodrama about an alcoholic actor's attempt to recover his career and his life. Both plays show Odets's theatrical skill, but his most attractive failures, *Paradise Lost* and *Night Music*, display a bumbling sweetness that is as important a part of Odets's talent as his technical proficiency. Both the staccato dialogue of *Golden Boy* and the rambling non sequiturs of *Paradise Lost* are aspects of the authentic Odets voice which can still be heard at its purest in *Awake and Sing!*

—Gerald Weales

O'HARA, Frank (Francis Russell O'Hara). American. Born in Baltimore, Maryland, 27 June 1926. Educated privately in piano and musical composition, 1933–43; at New England Conservatory of Music, Boston, 1946–50; Harvard University, Cambridge, Massachusetts, 1946–50, B.A. in English 1950; University of Michigan, Ann Arbor (Hopwood Award, 1951), M.A. in English 1951. Served in the United States Navy 1944–46. Staff Member, 1951–54, Fellowship Curator, 1955–64, Associate Curator, 1965, and Curator of the International Program, 1966, Museum of Modern Art, New York. Editorial Associate, *Art News* magazine, New York, 1954–56; Art Editor, *Kulchur Magazine*, New York, 1962–64. Collaborated in several poem-painting and poem-lithograph projects. Recipient: Ford Foundation Fellowship, for drama, 1956. *Died 25 July 1966.*

PUBLICATIONS

Collections

    Collected Poems, edited by Donald Allen. 1971.
    Selected Poems, edited by Donald Allen. 1974.

Verse

    A City Winter and Other Poems. 1952.
    Oranges. 1953.
    Meditations in an Emergency. 1956.
    Hartigan and Rivers with O'Hara: An Exhibition of Pictures, with Poems. 1959.
    Second Avenue. 1960.
    Odes. 1960.
    Featuring O'Hara. 1964.
    Lunch Poems. 1964.
    Love Poems: Tentative Title. 1965.
    Five Poems. 1967.
    Two Pieces. 1969.
    Odes. 1969.

Hymns of St. Bridget, with Bill Berkson.   1974.
Poems Retrieved, 1951–1966, edited by Donald Allen.   1975.
Early Poems, 1946–1951, edited by Donald Allen.   1976.

Plays

Try! Try! (produced 1951; revised version, produced 1952).   In *Artists' Theatre,* edited
  by Herbert Machiz, 1960.
Change Your Bedding (produced 1952).
Love's Labor: An Eclogue (produced 1959).   1964.
Awake in Spain (produced 1960).   1960.
The General Returns from One Place to Another (produced 1964).

Screenplay: *The Last Clean Shirt.*

Other

Jackson Pollock.   1959.
A Frank O'Hara Miscellany.   1974.
Art Chronicles 1954–1966.   1974.
Standing Still and Walking in New York, edited by Donald Allen.   1975.
Early Writings, edited by Donald Allen.   1977.

Editor, *Robert Motherwell: A Catalogue with Selections from the Artist's
  Writings.*   1966.

Reading List: *O'Hara, Poet among Painters* by Marjorie Perloff, 1977.

*   *   *

Frank O'Hara's status as an important poet of the post-World War II era has only recently
been established. During his lifetime he was known only to a circle of friends, many of them
painters in New York whom he knew from his work as an Associate Curator of the Museum
of Modern Art. But his canon is large and runs to more than five hundred pages of text in
Donald Allen's edition of *The Collected Poems.*

O'Hara was cavalier about his reputation as a poet and reluctant to have his poetry in print.
As a result, his work largely went unnoticed in the review columns; when his name did
surface, he was taken lightly. Only very recently has his work received serious critical
attention; Marjorie Perloff's book vigorously argues his major status as an innovator of
lyrical poetry. Perloff and others consider O'Hara to have had an influence on younger poets
comparable to Charles Olson, Robert Creeley, and Allen Ginsberg.

O'Hara's poetry from 1951 to 1954 shows the influence of Pound, William Carlos
Williams, and Auden. His early poems, collected in *A City Winter and Other Poems,* are
lyrical and strive very deliberately for surprising effects. His friend, the poet John Ashbery,
once commented that this was O'Hara's "French Zen period," which is an astute observation
of the lushly surrealistic language of these poems. As he commented in an early poem,
"Poetry":

The only way to be quiet
is to be quick, so I scare
you clumsily, or surprise
you with a stab. A praying
mantis knows time more
intimately than I and is
more casual.

Auden once wrote to caution O'Hara against tiring the reader with an excess of surreal statements, and he appears to have heeded his counsel, for in the poetry of the later 1950's, gathered in *Meditations in an Emergency* and *Lunch Poems*, he exerted greater control over the structure of his poems and gave himself more intense freedom in brief, dazzling displays of lyrical exuberance.

In *Second Avenue* and other longer poems – "Easter," "In Memory of My Feelings," "Ode to Michael Goldberg('s Birth and Other Births)" and the late "Biotherm (for Bill Berkson)" – O'Hara, like Pushkin and Byron before him, created perhaps the essential hero of urban cultural life, a sophisticated romantic who thrives on the city's alien and exotic elements. His many shorter poems are briefer expressions of this same captivating persona.

O'Hara also succeeds in rendering consciousness and its fringe states with intense accuracy and daring in a style partly influenced by the methods and experiments of the Abstract Expressionist painters. O'Hara wrote several plays, and essays on contemporary painting collected in *Standing Still and Walking in New York* and *Art Chronicles 1954–1966*. Although not a theorist or trained critic of painting, his eye was sensitive to technique and his instinct sharp in discerning the great works of his time.

—Paul Christensen

O'HARA, John (Henry).   American.   Born in Pottsville, Pennsylvania, 31 January 1905. Educated at Fordham Preparatory School; Keystone State Normal School; Niagara Preparatory School, Niagara Falls, New York, 1923–24. Married 1) Helen Petit in 1931 (divorced, 1933); 2) Belle Mulford Wylie in 1937 (died, 1954), one daughter; 3) Katherine Barnes Bryan in 1955. Reporter for the *Pottsville Journal*, 1924–26 and for the *Tamaqua Courier*, Pennsylvania, 1927; Reporter for the *New York Herald-Tribune*, and for *Time* magazine, New York, 1928; rewrite man for the *New York Daily Mirror*, radio columnist (as Franey Delaney) for the *New York Morning Telegraph*, and Managing Editor of the *Bulletin Index* magazine, Pittsburgh, 1928–33; full-time writer from 1933; film writer, for Paramount and other studios, from 1934; Columnist ("Entertainment Week"), *Newsweek*, New York, 1940–42; Pacific War Correspondent for *Liberty* magazine, New York, 1944; Columnist ("Sweet and Sour"), *Trenton Sunday Times-Adviser*, New Jersey, 1953–54; lived in Princeton, New Jersey, from 1954; Columnist ("Appointment with O'Hara"), *Collier's*, New York, 1954–56, ("My Turn"), *Newsday*, Long Island, New York, 1964–65, and ("The Whistle Stop"), *Holiday*, New York, 1966–67. Recipient: New York Drama Critics Circle Award, 1952; Donaldson Award, 1952; National Book Award, 1956; American Academy of Arts and Letters Award of Merit Medal, 1964. Member, National Institute of Arts and Letters, 1957. *Died 11 April 1970.*

PUBLICATIONS

Collections

Selected Letters, edited by Matthew J. Bruccoli.   1978.

Fiction

Appointment in Samarra.   1934.
BUtterfield 8.   1935.
The Doctor's Son and Other Stories.   1935.
Hope of Heaven.   1938.
Files on Parade (stories).   1939.
Pal Joey (stories).   1940.
Pipe Night (stories).   1945.
Here's O'Hara (omnibus).   1946.
Hellbox (stories).   1947.
All the Girls He Wanted (stories).   1949.
A Rage to Live.   1949.
The Farmers Hotel.   1951.
Ten North Frederick.   1955.
A Family Party.   1956.
The Great Short Stories of O'Hara.   1956.
Selected Short Stories.   1956.
From the Terrace.   1958.
Ourselves to Know.   1960.
Sermons and Soda Water (includes *The Girl on the Baggage Truck, Imagine Kissing Pete, We're Friends Again*).   3 vols., 1960.
Assembly (stories).   1961.
The Cape Cod Lighter (stories).   1962.
The Big Laugh.   1962.
Elizabeth Appleton.   1963.
49 Stories.   1963.
The Hat on the Bed (stories).   1963.
The Horse Knows the Way (stories).   1964.
The Lockwood Concern.   1965.
Waiting for Winter (stories).   1966.
The Instrument.   1967.
And Other Stories.   1968.
Lovey Childs: A Philadelphian's Story.   1969.
The O'Hara Generation (stories).   1969.
The Ewings.   1972.
The Time Element and Other Stories, and *Good Samaritan and Other Stories,* edited by Albert Erskine.   2 vols., 1972–74.
The Second Ewings.   1977.

Plays

Pal Joey, music by Richard Rodgers, lyrics by Lorenz Hart, from the stories by O'Hara (produced 1940).   1952.

Five Plays (includes *The Farmers Hotel, The Searching Sun, The Champagne Pool, Veronique, The Way It Was*). 1961.

Screenplays: *I Was an Adventuress,* with Karl Tunberg and Don Ettlinger, 1940; *He Married His Wife,* with others, 1940; *Moontide,* 1942; *On Our Merry Way* (episode), 1948; *The Best Things in Life Are Free,* with William Bowers and Phoebe Ephron, 1956.

Other

Sweet and Sour (essays). 1954.
My Turn (newspaper columns). 1966.
A Cub Tells His Story. 1974.
An Artist Is His Own Fault: O'Hara On Writers and Writings, edited by Matthew J. Bruccoli. 1977.

Bibliography: *O'Hara: A Checklist,* 1972, and *O'Hara: A Descriptive Bibliography,* 1978, both by Matthew J. Bruccoli.

Reading List: *The Fiction of O'Hara* by Russell E. Carson, 1961; *O'Hara* by Sheldon Norman Grebstein, 1966; *O'Hara* by Charles C. Walcutt, 1969; *O'Hara* (biography) by Finis Farr, 1973; *The O'Hara Concern: A Biography* by Matthew J. Bruccoli, 1975.

*   *   *

John O'Hara's 374 short stories and 18 novels record the changing habits and values of the United States from World War I to the Viet Nam conflict. O'Hara began writing as a reporter, editor, press agent and script writer; he worked first in his native Eastern Pennsylvania coal region (Pottsville – his fictional Gibbsville), and later in New York and Hollywood. His short stories began appearing in the *New Yorker* in 1928, and his first novel, *Appointment in Samarra,* identified him as a first-rate writer. His short stories range from short monologues, reminiscent of Ring Lardner (whose influence he acknowledged), to hundred-page novellas that may be his finest work: O'Hara has been called America's best short-story writer. Through his involvement with the New York theatrical world – plus an acknowledged mastery of dialogue – he tried to write for the stage. Even though his *Pal Joey* became a hit Rodgers and Hart musical, O'Hara's *Five Plays* are a testament to his lack of success as a playwright.

As O'Hara's fame grew, it was often asserted that his first novel, *Appointment in Samarra,* was also his best. The fast pace and shifting point of view held the reader until the suicide of Julian English at the end, which is still being debated: did Gibbsville drive him to it (just after the Great Crash in 1929), or did the compulsion come from within him? Nearly all of O'Hara's stories hold the reader's interest in the same way: how will the characters develop and what will happen to them? O'Hara said he was picturing, as honestly as he could, how twentieth-century Americans were driven by money, sex, and a struggle for status – often to their own destruction. In 1935 O'Hara published *BUtterfield 8,* his only *roman à clef.* The heroine, Gloria Wandrous, is much like the Jazz Age celebrity Starr Faithfull, whose body was washed up on a Long Island beach in 1931. The novel was a popular success and extended O'Hara's fictional domain from Pennsylvania to New York City. *Hope of Heaven* pushed his range much farther, to Hollywood. But there is a link between all three of the first novels: the protagonist-narrator (and Hollywood scriptwriter) of *Hope of Heaven* is Jimmy Malloy, a former Gibbsville reporter who has covered the Gloria Wandrous murder/suicide/accident.

More than a hundred short stories and sketches were published in *The Doctor's Son and Other Stories*, *Files on Parade*, and *Pipe Night*. These tightly written stories present character and situation satirically, but O'Hara is not callous about the loneliness, misery, and degradation he reveals – on Broadway or in Gibbsville. The best-known of these stories are the heavily ironic monologues (in the form of letters) of Joey Evans, a night club master of ceremonies. *Pal Joey*, a collection of fourteen stories, became a Rodgers and Hart musical. Joey is a heel, an anti-hero, and the sexual innuendo was shocking in 1940; but *Pal Joey* also had a strong plot line and has been called the first realistic American musical.

A Rage to Live is the first of O'Hara's long and elaborately documented novels. The time period is 1900 to 1920 and the locale Fort Penn (Harrisburg, Pennsylvania), but the serious social history was obscured for many readers by his heroine's lack of sexual control. In *Ten North Frederick* O'Hara moved the setting back to Gibbsville, where Joe Chapin earns great wealth and prestige with the help of his family name, a Yale law degree, and considerable intelligence. But Chapin aspires to be President of the United States: he attempts to buy the lieutenant governorship, is duped by an Irish politician, and drinks himself to death in "the quiet, gentlemanly, gradual way in which he had lived his life," in Sheldon Norman Grebstein's words. *From the Terrace* is an even larger and more ambitious work: O'Hara tells the story of Alfred Eaton, a small-town Pennsylvania boy who goes to New York and Washington, becomes a great financier and government official, and finally discovers that his life is empty and meaningless. O'Hara regarded it as his masterpiece.

O'Hara wrote prodigiously in the last 15 years of his life. *Ourselves to Know*, a big novel set in Eastern Pennsylvania, uses a circular technique and shifting perspective in trying to understand and explain Robert Millhouser, who killed his wife and was acquitted in a murder trial. In the Foreword to *Sermons and Soda Water*, three novellas all filtered through the consciousness of Jimmy Malloy, O'Hara explains why he used this unpopular and unprofitable form instead of expanding each of the stories into a 350-page novel:

> I want to get it all down on paper while I can. I am now fifty-five years old and I have lived with as well as in the Twentieth Century from its earliest days. The United States in this Century is what I know, and it is my business to write about it to the best of my ability, with the sometimes special knowledge I have. The Twenties, the Thirties, and the Forties are already history, but I cannot be content to leave their story in the hands of the historians and the editors of picture books. I want to record the way people talked and thought and felt, and to do it with complete honesty and variety.

The Big Laugh is O'Hara's second Hollywood novel: his monologues of classic Hollywood types are bawdy, funny, and authentic. *Elizabeth Appleton* is an academic novel, focused on a weekend when the dean's wife sees her husband passed over for the presidency of a small Pennsylvania college. *The Lockwood Concern*, O'Hara's last major novel, is "a condensed big book" (400 pages): four generations of the family have lived in a small town near Gibbsville since 1840, but third-generation George Lockwood compulsively destroys the dynasty by driving his only son to a criminal career in California. Critics charged that O'Hara's protagonists often destroy themselves and their social fabric without explicable motivation.

There were three more novels to come. *The Instrument* explores the parasitism of playwright Yank Lucas: he deserts the star actress on opening night, writes a new play on their relationship, and she commits suicide. *Lovey Childs: A Philadelphian's Story* deals with a Main Line heiress and her playboy husband (Sky Childs), who became Twenties celebrities; after divorce she achieves a stable marriage with her proper Philadelphia cousin. This is O'Hara's weakest novel, but it aroused speculation about his interest in lesbianism. At his death in 1970 O'Hara had completed *The Ewings* and was at work on a sequel; better than the two previous novels, it is the story of a young Cleveland lawyer and his wife in the booming economy of World War I. Six short story collections appeared in the 1960's, and two more after O'Hara's death.

Before World War II an "official" review of O'Hara had been established. John Peale Bishop (1937) found him skillful but cynical, a post-Jazz Age follower of Hemingway and Fitzgerald. Edmund Wilson (1940) recognized that O'Hara was a social commentator and that his writing was "of an entirely different kind from Hemingway's." O'Hara resembles Fitzgerald more than any writer, and their friendship – O'Hara proof-read Fitzgerald's *Tender Is the Night* – was renewed during Fitzgerald's last bitter days in Hollywood. O'Hara was a staunch Fitzgerald champion when that was not a popular cause, and wrote the introduction to the *Viking Portable Fitzgerald* (1945). When the big O'Hara novels became best sellers in the 1950's and 1960's, critics objected to the "mere accuracy" of his dialogue and detail, to the "surface reality" of his American scenes, and to the social climbing and sexual conduct of his characters. But, even when they found him "a hack writer," critics continued to review his books, and John Steinbeck called O'Hara the most underrated writer in America. His work lives, no matter how unfashionably. Though some critics object that his characters are not worth writing about, O'Hara's readers do not agree; and they admire the clarity of his style even though the critics would like more complexity and ambiguity. The academic world objects to O'Hara's view of life and literature, but if future generations seek an American Balzac to lay bare life in the United States from 1900 to 1970, they will find John O'Hara the most complete, the most accurate, and the most readable chronicler.

—Clarence A. Glasrud

OLSON, Charles (John).   American.   Born in Worcester, Massachusetts, 27 December 1910. Educated at Wesleyan University, Middletown, Connecticut, B.A. 1932, M.A. 1933; Yale University, New Haven, Connecticut; Harvard University, Cambridge, Massachusetts. Taught at Clark University, Worcester, and Harvard University, 1936–39; Instructor and Rector, Black Mountain College, North Carolina, 1951–56; taught at the State University of New York at Buffalo, 1963–65, and the University of Connecticut, Storrs, 1969. Recipient: Guggenheim grant (twice); Wenner-Gren Foundation grant, to study Mayan hieroglyphics, 1952; National Endowment for the Arts grant, 1966, 1968. *Died 10 January 1970.*

PUBLICATIONS

Verse

Corrado Cagli March 31 Through April 19 1947.   1947.
Y & X.   1948.
Letter for Melville 1951.   1951.
This.   1952.
In Cold Hell, in Thicket.   1953.
The Maximus Poems 1–10.   1953.
Ferrini and Others, with others.   1955.
Anecdotes of the Late War.   1955.
The Maximus Poems 11–22.   1956.
O'Ryan 2 4 6 8 10.   1958; expanded edition, as *O'Ryan 12345678910,* 1965.

Projective Verse. 1959.
The Maximus Poems. 1960.
The Distances: Poems. 1960.
Maximus, From Dogtown I. 1961.
Signature to Petition on Ten Pound Island Asked of Me by Mr. Vincent Ferrini. 1964.
West. 1966.
Charles Olson Reading at Berkeley, edited by Zoe Brown. 1966.
Before Your Very Eyes!, with others. 1967.
The Maximus Poems, IV, V, VI. 1968.
Reading about My World. 1968.
Added to Making a Republic. 1968.
Clear Shifting Water. 1968.
That There Was a Woman in Gloucester, Massachusetts. 1968.
Wholly Absorbed into My Own Conduits. 1968.
Causal Mythology. 1969.
Archaeologist of Morning: The Collected Poems Outside the Maximus Series. 1970.
The Maximus Poems, Volume Three, edited by Charles Boer and George F. Butterick. 1975.

Plays

The Fiery Hunt and Other Plays. 1977.

Fiction

Stocking Cap: A Story. 1966.

Other

Call Me Ishmael: A Study of Melville. 1947.
Apollonius of Tyana: A Dance, with Some Words, for Two Actors. 1951.
Mayan Letters, edited by Robert Creeley. 1953.
A Bibliography on America for Ed Dorn. 1964.
Pleistocene Man: Letters from Olson to John Clarke during October, 1965. 1968.
Human Universe and Others Essays, edited by Donald Allen. 1965.
Proprioception. 1965.
Selected Writings, edited by Robert Creeley. 1966.
Letters for "Origin," 1950–1956, edited by Albert Glover. 1969.
The Special View of History, edited by Ann Charters. 1970.
Poetry and Truth: The Beloit Lectures and Poems, edited by George F. Butterick. 1971.
Additional Prose: A Bibliography on America, Proprioception, and Other Notes and Essays, edited by George F. Butterick. 1974.
The Post Office: A Memoir of His Father. 1975.
Olson and Ezra Pound: An Encounter at St. Elizabeth's, edited by Catherine Seelye. 1975.
Muthologos: The Collected Lectures and Interviews, edited by George F. Butterick. 1976.

Bibliography: *A Bibliography of the Works of Olson* by George F. Butterick and Albert Glover. 1967.

Reading List: *Olson/Melville: A Study in Affinity* by Ann Charters, 1968; *A Guide to the Maximus Poems of Olson* by George F. Butterick, 1978; *Olson: Call Him Ishmael* by Paul Christensen, 1978.

*   *   *

Although any final judgment regarding the work and influence of the poet Charles Olson remains controversial, he must nevertheless be regarded as a seminal force in the reshaping of American poetry written since World War II. Olson showed little inclination to be a poet until his mid-thirties. Shortly after the death of Roosevelt, however, Olson left government and committed himself to a literary career. By then he had written only the draft of a short book on Melville, *Call Me Ishmael*, and several conventional poems published in popular magazines. From these unpromising beginnings, Olson began writing in earnest in the late 1940's. With the help of Edward Dahlberg, a completely revised *Call Me Ishmael* was published in 1947; two years later, Olson composed "The Kingfishers," among the most innovative poems to have emerged since World War II. And in 1950, largely from the example of the techniques employed in "The Kingfishers," and ideas taken from a variety of sources, including William Carlos Williams, Pound, Dahlberg and his close friend Robert Creeley, Olson synthesized the provocative and highly influential manifesto, "Projective Verse."

This essay established a new set of conventions for the short poem. In place of the old rules of repetitive measure, rhyme, and fixed stanza, Olson introduced the principle that "form is an extension of content," or that form is the result of allowing content to assume its own partly accidental shape during composition. Around this main principle are certain technical corollaries: for example, the poet, rather than treating his theme in an orderly progression of ideas, should instead rush from "perception to perception" until his argument is exhausted. The poet should allow the rhythm of his breath during composition to determine the length of each line, so that he has scored it for the reading voice. And in fitting words together in the line itself, the poet should let sound, rather than sense, determine syntax. A logic of the ear should take precedence over intellect in the fashioning of language.

Olson suggested that all of these new conventions were dependent on a new stance to experience, which he called Objectism. The poet should no longer consider his mind a clearing house of data, from which to select bits of information for his poems. Rather, the poet should include the rest of his organism in the act of perception and awareness, and should feel himself rush out of his private emotion into the realms of phenomena free of self-consciousness and inhibition. Objectism called for the poet to accept himself as merely another object inhabiting the phenomenal welter making up the world. The techniques advised in the first half of the essay, then, are all the means of making experience direct and unmediated for the poet who plunges fully into the phenomena around him.

"The Kingfishers" satisfies most of the conditions of composition set forth in the "Projective Verse" essay. Its form is the result of a rush of discourse on a series of loosely related topics, of experiments in combinations of sounds, and of the arrangement of words in clusters to show the changing shape of his thinking moment by moment. This striking poem creates the feeling of having kept pace with the random and shifting content of the poet's awareness.

Olson's projective methodology and the example of "The Kingfishers" are clearly efforts to explore and even to track the behavior of the imagination. More significant is the fact that Olson's poetic brings poetry into the general current of free-forming methods then being applied to the other arts: atonal, free-form jazz composition, abstract expressionism, improvisational theater, and kinetic sculpture.

Olson went on to refine the doctrine now known as Objectism in subsequent essays and lectures, but his several collections of short poems and the long, sequential work *The Maximus Poems* are the basis of his reputation and influence as a poet. In 1953, Robert Creeley published Olson's first full-length volume of poems, *In Cold Hell, in Thicket*, which contains not only "The Kingfishers" but many of Olson's boldest shorter poems. Many, but by no means all, of these shorter poems are composed in the projective mode; others are written in a more leisurely-paced free verse style. The whole work is concerned with the burdens of tradition and influence the poet must cast off to pursue his own direction. The poet argues, often petulantly, against Ezra Pound, whom Olson identifies as his spiritual father and arch rival.

Creeley later edited Olson's *Selected Writings*, further establishing Olson's reputation as a key figure of the new poetry. A more finished and elaborate poetry emerges in *The Distances*, but there is less bold experiment in these maturer lyrical poems. Olson had moved to less defined areas of awareness; many of the poems are startling reenactments of dreams, in which the supralogical narratives are skillfully and persuasively dramatized, and there is a greater interest in myth and the content and forms of consciousness.

But the primary text for judging Olson as poet rests with his central work, the long, epical *Maximus* sequence, begun in the late 1940's and sustained to the last months of his life. The work remains unfinished, although the final volume, found among the poet's papers, has been edited and published. The work in one way is a celebration of the seacoast town of Gloucester, Massachusetts, where communal spirit among the fishermen thrived before industry was established; in another, it is close scrutiny of life in America and a search for an alternative ideology rooted in new spiritual awareness.

In the first volume, *The Maximus Poems*, Olson's persona, Maximus, named after an itinerant Phoenician mystic of the fourth century A.D., surveys contemporary Gloucester and finds its citizenry in disarray and the local culture ugly and alien. This judgment prompts a systematic inquiry into the origins of Gloucester and of America, which takes up the remainder of the volume. In the second volume, *Maximus IV,V VI*, the speaker widens his interests to include mythological lore, the history of human migration, religious literature, and the finer details of Gloucester's past, which seem to Maximus to re-enact certain of the myths and fables of the ancient world. The final volume, more somber in mood and subject, continues Maximus's intense survey of Gloucester and himself. A vision of a new cosmos is summoned in these poems, in the hope of redeeming and possibly reconstituting the communal ethos of Gloucester's past. But that hope gives way to remorse and disparagement of the reckless present and its deadening commercial enterprises.

The poem is among the more ambitious experiments in sustained narrative in the post-war period; it ranks in conception and execution with other verse epics of the modern period, including Pound's *Cantos*, Williams's *Paterson*, and Hart Crane's *The Bridge*. Although Olson is less musical in his language, and at times a dry poet given to long quotation from historic documents, the sweep of his thought and the scope of his imaginative arguments distinguish him as a major American poet of the Whitman tradition.

—Paul Christensen

O'NEILL, Eugene (Gladstone). American. Born in New York City, 16 October 1888; son of the actor James O'Neill. Toured with his father as a child, and educated at Catholic boarding schools, and at Betts Academy, Stamford, Connecticut; attended Princeton University, New Jersey, 1906–07, and George Pierce Baker's "47 Workshop" at Harvard University, Cambridge, Massachusetts, 1914–15. Married 1) Kathleen Jenkins in 1909 (divorced, 1912), one son; 2) Agnes Boulton in 1918 (divorced, 1929), one son and one daughter; 3) the actress Carlotta Monterey in 1929. Worked in a mail order firm in New

York, 1908; gold prospector in Honduras, 1909; advance agent and box-office man for his father's company, and seaman on a Norwegian freighter to Buenos Aires, 1910–11; Reporter for the *New London Telegraph*, Connecticut, 1912; patient in a tuberculosis sanitarium, where he began to write, 1912–13; full-time writer from 1914; associated with the Provincetown Players, New York, and Provincetown, Massachusetts, as actor and writer, 1914–20; wrote for the Theatre Guild; Manager, with Kenneth Macgowan and Robert Edmond Jones, Greenwich Village Theatre, New York, 1923–27; a Founding Editor, *American Spectator*, 1934; in ill-health from 1934: in later years suffered from Parkinson's Disease. Recipient: Pulitzer Prize, 1920, 1922, 1928, 1957; American Academy of Arts and Letters Gold Medal, 1922; Nobel Prize for Literature, 1936; New York Drama Critics Circle Award, 1957. Litt.D.: Yale University, New Haven, Connecticut, 1926. Member, National Institute of Arts and Letters, and Irish Academy of Letters. *Died 27 November 1953.*

PUBLICATIONS

Plays

> *Thirst and Other One Act Plays* (includes *The Web, Warnings, Fog, Recklessness*).   1914.
> *Thirst* (produced 1916).   In *Thirst and Other Plays*, 1914.
> *Fog* (produced 1917).   In *Thirst and Other Plays*, 1914.
> *Bound East for Cardiff* (produced 1916).   In *The Moon of the Caribbees ...*, 1919.
> *Before Breakfast* (produced 1916).   1916.
> *The Sniper* (produced 1917).   In *Lost Plays*, 1950.
> *In the Zone* (produced 1917).   In *The Moon of the Caribbees ...*, 1919.
> *The Long Voyage Home* (produced 1917).   In *The Moon of the Caribbees ...*, 1919.
> *Ile* (produced 1917).   In *The Moon of the Caribbees ...*, 1919.
> *The Rope* (produced 1918).   In *The Moon of the Caribbees ...*, 1919.
> *Where The Cross Is Made* (produced 1918).   In *The Moon of the Caribbees ...*, 1919.
> *The Moon of the Caribbees* (produced 1918).   In *The Moon of the Caribbees...*, 1919.
> *The Moon of the Caribbees and Six Other Plays of the Sea.*   1919.
> *The Dreamy Kid* (produced 1919).   In *Complete Works 2*, 1924.
> *Beyond the Horizon* (produced 1920).   1920.
> *Anna Christie* (as *Chris*, produced 1920; revised version, as *Anna Christie*, produced 1921).   With *The Hairy Ape, The First Man*, 1922.
> *Exorcism* (produced 1920).
> *The Emperor Jones* (produced 1920).   With *Diff'rent, The Straw*, 1921.
> *Diff'rent* (produced 1920).   With *The Emperor Jones, The Straw*, 1921.
> *The Straw* (produced 1921).   With *The Emperor Jones, Diff'rent*, 1921.
> *Gold* (produced 1921).   1921.
> *The First Man* (produced 1922).   With *The Hairy Ape, Anna Christie*, 1922.
> *The Hairy Ape* (produced 1922).   With *The First Man, Anna Christie*, 1922.
> *Welded* (produced 1924).   With *All God's Chillun Got Wings*, 1924.
> *All God's Chillun Got Wings* (produced 1924).   With *Welded*, 1924.
> *Desire under the Elms* (produced 1924).   In *Complete Works 2*, 1924.
> *Complete Works.*   2 vols., 1924.
> *The Fountain* (produced 1925).   With *The Great God Brown, The Moon of the Caribbees*, 1926.
> *The Great God Brown* (produced 1926).   With *The Fountain, The Moon of the Caribbees*, 1926.
> *Marco Millions* (produced 1928).   1927.

Lazarus Laughed (produced 1928).   1927.
Strange Interlude (produced 1928).   1928.
Dynamo (produced 1929).   1929.
Mourning Becomes Electra: A Trilogy (produced 1931).   1931.
Ah, Wilderness! (produced 1933).   1933.
Days Without End (produced 1934).   1934.
The Iceman Cometh (produced 1946).   1946.
Lost Plays (includes *Abortion, The Movie Man, The Sniper, Servitude, Wife for a Life*), edited by Lawrence Gellert.   1950.
A Moon for the Misbegotten (produced 1957).   1952.
Long Day's Journey into Night (produced 1956).   1956.
A Touch of the Poet (produced 1957).   1957.
Hughie (produced 1958).   1959.
More Stately Mansions (produced 1962).   1964.
Ten "Lost" Plays.   1964.
Children of the Sea and Three Other Unpublished Plays (includes *Bread and Butter, Now I Ask You, Shell Shock*), edited by Jennifer McCabe Atkinson.   1972.

Other

Inscriptions: O'Neill to Carlotta Monterey O'Neill, edited by Donald Gallup.   1960.

Bibliography: *O'Neill and the American Critic: A Summary and Bibliographical Checklist* by Jordan Y. Miller, 1973; *O'Neill: A Descriptive Bibliography* by Jennifer McCabe Atkinson, 1974.

Reading List: *The Haunted Heroes of O'Neill* by Edwin A. Engel, 1955; *O'Neill and His Plays: Four Decades of Criticism* edited by Oscar Cargill and other, 1961; *O'Neill* (biography) by Arthur and Barbara Gelb, 1962, revised edition, 1973; *The Tempering of O'Neill* by Doris Alexander, 1962; *O'Neill* by Frederic I. Carpenter, 1964; *O'Neill: A Collection of Critical Essays* edited by John Gassner, 1964; *The Plays of O'Neill* by John Henry Raleigh, 1965; *Playwright's Progress: O'Neill and the Critics* by Jordan Y. Miller, 1965; *O'Neill* by John Gassner, 1965; *O'Neill's Scenic Images* by Timo Tiusanen, 1968; *O'Neill: Son and Playwright,* 1968, and *O'Neill: Son and Artist,* 1973, both by Louis Sheaffer; *A Drama of Souls: Studies in O'Neill's Super-Naturalistic Techniques* by Egil Törnqvist, 1969; *O'Neill* by H. Frenz, 1971; *Contour in Time* by T. M. Bogard, 1972; *O'Neill: A Collection of Criticism* edited by Ernest Griffin, 1976.

*   *   *

Eugene O'Neill, writing dramas comparable to the best available overseas models, brought the American Theater of his actor-father's *Monte Cristo* into the twentieth century. He acknowledged (1936) drawing from the Greeks, Strindberg, and Nietzsche. Nietzsche gave this romantic pessimist a usable theory of classical tragedy: the Apollonian mask with the Dionysian force behind it.

The stage sea caught the real and the poets' seas in 1916 in O'Neill's first production.

Bound East for Cardiff compresses the international crew of the *S.S. Glencairn* into the wedge of a forecastle. Around Yank's dying, a rusting freighter continues toward Wales, the sea-sounds adding density to the squalid realism. Yet somehow, for the attentive Driscoll and audience, something spacious has been shown through or behind the seaman-life image that contains it. The play opened the Provincetown Players' new Playwrights' Theater in New York that fall, and within the next year three new scripts completed the *S.S. Glencairn* series. In *The Long Voyage Home* deliberate and casual inhumanity (Fate?) allows a shipmate to be shanghaied. Theatricality builds mood in all four *Glencairn* plays, but their author found the tropical night and carousing seamen of *Moon of the Caribbees* more poetic than the war-hysteria of *In the Zone* for conveying "the compelling inscrutable forces behind life."

O'Neill aspired to be a poet – to catch unexpected "rhythms" and to show man's "glorious self-destructive struggle to make the Force express him." A too "acutely conscious," too articulate protagonist or heavy schematization undermines many of the heroic searches in O'Neill's plays during the 1920's. Though thematically prophetic, *Diff'rent* and *Gold* blare out the undeniability of Life and the power of "the hopeless hope." They share with many O'Neill one-acters of 1916–20 a hammering illustrativeness. Still, O'Neill's purposefulness salvages moments in faulty plays like *Lazarus Laughed* and justifies even his overblown experiments. Spectacle and comedy in *Marco Millions* cannot make delightful the overwritten dialectic, as in *Fog* earlier, between Eastern poetry and Western business; yet Marco's epilogue journey from puzzlement to complacency comments expressively on a new function of O'Neill's theater. He insisted on testing forms and tampering with his audience.

The Pulitzer Prizes for *Beyond the Horizon* and *Anna Christie* designated O'Neill the outstanding American dramatist. The former, alternating indoor–outdoor scenes for affecting "rhythm," wrings two brothers and a wife through ironic choices of farm or sea. Still challenging for top actresses, *Anna Christie* sets an ex-prostitute, her barge-skipper father, and a hesitant seaman awash together in the rhythms of that "ole davil sea." *Strange Interlude*, awarded his third Pulitzer Prize of the decade, alternates outer, realistic dialogue with inner monologues to portray the figure of (O'Neill's) Woman. A nostalgic comedy, *Ah, Wilderness!* celebrates the happier side of the autobiographical setting of *Long Day's Journey into Night*, the tragedy which would win O'Neill his fourth Pulitzer Prize, posthumously. With Aeschylus's *Oresteia* lending substance and stature, *Mourning Becomes Electra* is a modern psychological myth placed in New England after the Civil War. His drafts show masks and asides abandoned once they have helped raise the three-play drama to the desired level of formal realism. Though finally unsatisfying to O'Neill in its language and melodrama, it was the basis for his Nobel Prize.

O'Neill's socially angry 1919 portrayals of Black Americans in *The Dreamy Kid* suffer from the lurid extremities of their situation, at the terrifying juncture of religion and criminality in a New York flat. A shared "Lawd Jesus!" signals the approach of the dark God; the all-black cast was another breakthrough. *All God's Chillun Got Wings* welds black Jim and white Ella into a Strindberg marriage; their love-hate festers ever more privately upon the racial violence of their destructive self-images. That the protagonists have O'Neill's parents' names adds another dimension of identification and concern. Watching *The Emperor Jones*, an audience awaiting the irregular firing of the hero's six bullets shares his panic in the increasing pulse-rate of the incessant drums and his dread of his next night vision. The final scene returns the audience to its daily (theatrical) reality, but with emotional overtones making them more aware than those who have not undergone the stripping away of the hero.

The Hairy Ape further dislocates hero and audience in each of eight scenes. Below decks, Yank epitomizes power among the half-naked crew members and identifies himself with steel, coal, and speed. The stokers move with demonic rhythm. When a young lady descends to call Yank a hairy ape, the titanic figure falls out of the rhythm of his own life. Yank's displacements accelerate until his love-death embrace of the gorilla at the zoo satisfies the play's imagery and demand for tragic inevitability, but also looses upon the city another sinister, unthinking force.

When after tiresome grandiloquence the artist Dion(-ysus) dies three-fourths of the way through *The Great God Brown*, the play actually shifts the character beneath the protagonist's mask. Brown, a businessman, puts on Dion's mask, and accepts his wife Margaret and mother-mistress Cybel. Shot as Brown's murderer and unmasked, he speaks his last ecstatic vision in a pietà with Cybel. She croons the eternal recurrence of spring, while upstage Margaret hymns her love to Dion's mask. Reenter the cop with *"grimy notebook"* to ask, "Well, what's his name?" "Man!" answers Cybel. "How d'yuh spell it?" The accumulated rhythms press this joking question into brute fact and poetic theater. Its hard mask distances those who cannot see the tragedy behind, but also drops an audience abruptly back into everyday rhythms. *Desire under the Elms* sets the same pattern more grimly and solidly in the dialect and rock farms of the New England in the gold-fevered 1850's. Ephraim Cabot, 75, returns with "God's message t'me in the spring" – a new wife, Abbie. Finally prisoners for murdering their love-child, she and mother-haunted Eben pause, *"strangely aloof and devout,"* to repeat the play's first line: "Purty, hain't it?" Then, as in *The Great God Brown* and later *The Iceman Cometh* the cop comes in at the normal level of greedy imperception: "Wished I owned it." With an ironic chuckle of recognition, an audience rejects the tragic imperception.

"A Tale of Possessors Self-Dispossessed," O'Neill's name for his 11-play cycle, would have traced an American family from pre-Revolution to 1932. In the fifth (the only one finished), *A Touch of the Poet*, Major Cornelius Melody, an immigrant Irish tavern-keeper near Boston, 1828, remembers heroics, recites Byron, and resents the Irish. His cruel pretensions victimize his wife and embarrass his daughter Sara, who sees a "poet" only in the wealthy Harfords' son. Americanization destroys Con's special dignity and vitality. Historical details and Irish humour enrich the tragic shift of power to a less noble generation. A double-length manuscript intended for destruction, *More Stately Mansions* dandles Simon Harford between his mother's symbolic garden and the realistic world of his mistress-wife Sara, 1832–41. In the edited and produced versions, artistic styles clash more than characters do. Another projected series has left only *Hughie* and the pattern of a dead title character, a talkative central character (Erie Smith), and a listener (the new nightclerk). Night sounds press New York upon the 1928 dialogue with multimedia effect.

The autobiographical plays that interrupted his cycle work have climactic monologues. *The Iceman Cometh* gathered the political, social, and psychological dreams-deferred into a period piece of 1912. All the characters and pipedreams of Harry Hope's flophouse bar had been New York familiars of O'Neill's. Everyone awaits the salesman Theodore Hickman who cometh, like Dionysus, every spring with drinks for Hope's birthday binge. This spring Hickey pushes the inhabitants into testing and destroying their pipedreams. Hickey's own mask of delusion is that he has murdered his wife out of love. The cops lead Hickey away; life returns to the booze and a kind of peace to everyone but Larry Slade, the sensitive O'Neill type. He recognizes death in disillusion but cannot die. *A Moon for the Misbegotten* is an often comic, sometimes lyric tragedy of entropy. On a Connecticut pigfarm soaked in September moonlight and an alcoholic haze, James plays out his 1923 epilogue to the story told in *Long Day's Journey into Night* and receives from huge Josie Hogan an absolution and benediction. O'Neill wrote *Long Day's Journey into Night* with "deep pity and understanding and forgiveness for *all* the four haunted Tyrones." The characters' self-indulgences are objectified as though "the Force behind" had become the playwright's own perspective. An opium-addicted mother, miserly father, alcoholic and tubercular sons use humor and hurting wit to sustain their tragedy. Conventional artistry and deeply felt characters keep the relentless exposition moving for almost five hours. Dope-dreaming Mary Tyrone – behind her, her family – finishes it: "... so happy for a time." Her line is a delicate mask of glass, cracking.

O'Neill thought drama began "in the worship of Dionysus," and critics have generally granted his plays this big, dark, tragic vision along with stage-worthy melodrama. A wild Celtic humor couches the inevitable destruction in his last tragedies. A period-richness informs them with a sense of history, and a more quietly compassionate understanding cleanses the combatants. Excellent posthumous productions and revivals showed unexpected delicacy in feeling and expression. This secured for the plays, more excruciatingly and less ironically, that massive "Force behind" which a younger playwright had often sought too directly. Outside his grandest schemes, he worked his Apollonian images with a finer, richer sensitivity.

—John G. Kuhn

PARKER, Dorothy (née Rothschild). American. Born in West End, New Jersey, 22 August 1893. Educated at Miss Dana's School, Morristown, New Jersey, and Blessed Sacrament Convent, New York City. Married 1) Edwin Pond Parker II in 1917 (divorced, 1928); 2) the film actor Alan Campbell in 1933 (divorced, 1947; remarried, 1950; died, 1963). Member of the editorial staff of *Vogue*, New York, 1916–17; member of the editorial staff and Drama Critic, *Vanity Fair*, New York, 1917–20; Book Reviewer ("Constant Reader" column), *The New Yorker*, 1925–27; free-lance writer from 1927; book reviewer for *Esquire*, New York, 1957–62. Founder, with Robert Benchley and Robert E. Sherwood, Algonquin Hotel Round Table, New York, in the 1930's. Recipient: O. Henry Award, 1929; Marjorie Waite Peabody Award, 1958. *Died 7 June 1967.*

PUBLICATIONS

Fiction

> *Laments for the Living.* 1930.
> *After Such Pleasures.* 1933.
> *Here Lies: The Collected Stories.* 1939.
> *Collected Stories.* 1942.

Plays

> *Close Harmony; or, The Lady Next Door,* with Elmer Rice (produced 1924). 1929.
> *Round the Town* (lyrics only; revue) (produced 1924).
> Sketches, in *Shoot the Works* (revue) (produced 1931).
> *The Coast of Illyria,* with Ross Evans (produced 1949).
> *The Ladies of the Corridor,* with Arnaud d'Usseau (produced 1953). 1954.
> *Candide* (lyrics only, with others), book by Lillian Hellman, music by Leonard Bernstein, from the story by Voltaire (produced 1956). 1957.

Screenplays: *Business Is Business,* with George S. Kaufman, 1925; *The Moon's Our Home,* with others, 1936; *Lady Be Careful,* with others, 1936; *Three Married Men,* with Alan Campbell and Owen Davis, Sr., 1936; *Suzy,* with others, 1936; *A Star Is Born,* with others, 1937; *Sweethearts,* with Alan Campbell, 1938; *Trade Winds,* with others, 1938; *The Little Foxes,* with others, 1941; *Weekend for Three,* with Alan Campbell and Budd Schulberg, 1941; *Saboteur,* with Peter Viertel and Joan Harrison, 1942; *Smash*

Up – The Story of a Woman, with others, 1947; *The Fan,* with Walter Reisch and Ross Evans, 1949.

Verse

Enough Rope. 1926.
Sunset Gun. 1928.
Death and Taxes. 1931.
Collected Poetry. 1931.
Collected Poems: Not So Deep as a Well. 1936.

Other

High Society, with George S. Chappell and Frank Crowninshield. 1920.
Men I'm Not Married To, with *Women I'm Not Married To,* by Franklin P. Adams. 1922.
The Portable Dorothy Parker. 1944.
The Best of Dorothy Parker. 1952.

Editor, *The Portable F. Scott Fitzgerald.* 1945.
Editor, with Frederick B. Shroyer, *Short Story: A Thematic Anthology.* 1965.

Reading List: in *An Unfinished Woman: A Memoir* by Lillian Hellman, 1969; *You Might as Well Live* (biography) by John Keats, 1970.

*   *   *

Dorothy Parker's writings were aptly characterized by Alexander Woollcott as "a potent distillation of nectar and wormwood, of ambrosia and deadly nightshade." This assessment covers her perennially popular volumes of short stories, *Laments for the Living* and *After Such Pleasures.* It also encompasses her three best-selling volumes of wry, bittersweet verse (not serious "poetry," she claimed), *Enough Rope, Sunset Gun,* and *Death and Taxes* – mostly love lamentations. It could also apply to her crisp, tart book reviews for the *New Yorker*; she dismissed Milne's *House at Pooh Corner* with "'Tonstant Weader fwowed up."

Her book reviews for *Esquire* (1957–62) are skimpier and less successful. Her major play, *The Ladies of the Corridor* (with Arnaud d'Usseau), a slice-of-life portrayal of aging, pathetic women who have lost their central purpose for living (through departures of husbands, lovers, children) is better as dialogue than as drama.

Many of Parker's well-crafted short stories focus on upper class Manhattan women of the 1920's and 1930's. The economic comfort of these women, whether young, middle-aged, or old, is counteracted by their superficial, pointless lives, barren of goals, meaningful activities, and inner resources. Although they are often physically attractive and elegantly dressed ornaments at the parties they live for, without such external social props they collapse.

Other people in Parker's stories do the *real* work; the men earn the money, the maids rear the children. So these women are bored, neurotic, unhappy, pampered parasites. Their fate is the fate of those who live through others, excessive emotional dependency: "Please, God, let him telephone me now." This cripples their potentiality for gaiety and charm and transforms them into shrill, malicious shrews who drink too much, talk too much, think too shallowly, and do too little. These characters are their own most pathetic victims; they seldom deceive others as they delude themselves.

Dorothy Parker excels in economically incisive descriptions of personalities, settings, costumes: a honeymooning bride "looked as new as a peeled egg." Her dramatic monologues are devastating, ironic characterizations. Thus the hypocritical "Lady with a Lamp" offers cold comfort to her alleged friend, jilted and unhappily recuperating from a clandestine abortion: "I worry so about you, living in a little furnished apartment, with nothing that belongs to you, no roots, no nothing." Parker's dialogues capture the cadences of real speech and the subtle nuances of personality and values: "Good night, useless," says the spoiled mother to her firstborn infant.

The essence of such social satire is the author's implicit desire for reform of these empty lives into significant existences. Her best story, "Big Blonde," which won the O. Henry Prize in 1929, epitomizes Parker's mixture of love and anger, coalesced into an enduring work of art. Indeed, many of Dorothy Parker's stories are memorable cameos, etched in acid and polished to gemlike lustre.

—Lynn Z. Bloom

PATCHEN, Kenneth. American. Born in Niles, Ohio, 13 December 1911. Educated at Warren High School, Ohio; the Experimental College, University of Wisconsin, Madison, 1928–29. Married Miriam Oikemus in 1934. Also an artist: one-man show of books, graphics, and paintings, Corcoran Gallery, Washington, D.C., 1969. Recipient: Guggenheim Fellowship, 1936; Shelley Memorial Award, 1954; National Endowment for the Arts Distinguished Service Grant, 1967. *Died 8 January 1972.*

PUBLICATIONS

Verse

> *Before the Brave.*   1936.
> *First Will and Testament.*   1939.
> *The Teeth of the Lion.*   1942.
> *The Dark Kingdom.*   1942.
> *Cloth of the Tempest.*   1943.
> *An Astonished Eye Looks Out of the Air, Being Some Poems Old and New Against War and in Behalf of Life.*   1945.
> *Outlaw of the Lowest Planet,* edited by David Gascoyne.   1946.
> *Selected Poems.*   1946; revised edition, 1958, 1964.
> *Pictures of Life and of Death.*   1947.
> *They Keep Riding Down All the Time.*   1947.
> *Panels for the Walls of Heaven.*   1947.
> *Patchen: Man of Anger and Light, with A Letter to God by Kenneth Patchen,* with Henry Miller.   1947.
> *CCCLXXIV Poems.*   1948.
> *To Say If You Love Someone and Other Selected Love Poems.*   1948.

Red Wine and Yellow Hair. 1949.
Fables and Other Little Tales. 1953.
The Famous Boating Party and Other Poems in Prose. 1954.
Orchards, Thrones and Caravans. 1955.
Glory Never Guesses: Being a Collection of 18 Poems with Decorations and Drawings. 1956.
A Surprise for the Bagpipe Player: A Collection of 18 Poems with Decorations and Drawings. 1956.
When We Were Here Together. 1957.
Hurrah for Anything: Poems and Drawings. 1957
Two Poems for Christmas. 1958.
Poem-scapes. 1958.
Pomes Penyeach. 1959.
Poems of Humor and Protest. 1960.
Because It Is: Poems and Drawings. 1960.
A Poem for Christmas. 1960.
The Love Poems. 1960.
Patchen Drawing-Poem. 1962.
Picture Poems. 1962.
Doubleheader. 1966.
Hallelujah Anyway. 1966.
Where Are the Other Rowboats? 1966.
But Even So (includes drawings). 1968.
Love and War Poems, edited by Dennis Gould. 1968.
Selected Poems. 1968.
The Collected Poems. 1968.
Aflame and Afun of Walking Faces: Fables and Drawings. 1970.
There's Love All Day, edited by Dee Danner Barwick. 1970.
Wonderings. 1971.
In Quest of Candlelighters. 1972.

Plays

Now You See It (Don't Look Now) (produced 1966).
Lost Plays, edited by Richard Morgan. 1977.

Radio Play: *City Wears a Slouch Hat,* 1942.

Fiction

The Journal of Albion Moonlight. 1941.
The Memoirs of a Shy Pornographer: An Amusement. 1945.
Sleepers Awake. 1946.
See You in the Morning. 1948.

Other

Patchen: Painter of Poems (exhibition catalogue). 1969.
The Argument of Innocence: A Selection from the Pictureworks, edited by Peter Veres. 1975.

Bibliography: *Patchen · A First Bibliography* by Gail Eaton, 1948.

Reading List: *Patchen: A Collection of Essays* edited by Richard Morgan, 1977.

* * *

Kenneth Patchen is in the tradition of American poets that descends from Walt Whitman through William Carlos Williams to the Black Mountain poets, and beyond them to such younger writers as Galway Kinnell and Michael Waters. That is to say, Patchen is a "redskin" poet as opposed to a "paleface." His poems do not make use of European-inspired formal devices; his language is deliberately a "barbaric yawp" (Whitman's famous phrase from *Song of Myself*); and his subject-matter is drawn from his own very American experiences. He is a poet of the open air and the open road, a hunter after experience, claiming a kind of mystical connection with the animals he kills (in this he is very like Hemingway, James Dickey, and, perhaps, Robinson Jeffers); his style is free-ranging, colloquial, wise-cracking, but also unembarrassedly ready with the big word, the huge emotion. In short, he sounds very like Carl Sandburg.

Yet Patchen is a self-conscious poet. He may *play* the cracker-barrel philosopher, but as Thomas Hardy said of William Barnes, "He sings his native woodnotes wild with a great deal of art." Look, for example, at so small a poem as "In Memory of Kathleen":

> How pitiful is her sleep.
> Now her clear breath is still.
>
> There is nothing falling tonight,
> Bird or man,
> As dear as she.
>
> Nowhere that she should go
> Without me. None but my calling.
>
> O nothing but the cold cry of the snow.

It is a very finely written poem of grief, and a subtle one. The play on "pitiful" is perhaps obvious; but the way in which "falling" anticipates the cry of the snow is not so obvious, yet entirely just; as is the extraordinarily compacted "None but my calling." "None" comes from the earlier "nowhere," and it means that Patchen finds himself utterly alone: she has gone where he can't follow, there is only *his* calling, *his* voice to be heard. That, and the cry of the snow: whiteness, death, its falling reminding him that she, too, has fallen in death. Glanced casually over, this little poem may seem hopelessly slight; looked at more carefully, it emerges as the work of a considerable poet.

Patchen doesn't always write with this degree of tense urgency. It is, I think, characteristic of his kind of poetry that there should be a great deal of sprawl about it; and while one may salute the energy that has led him to produce so many volumes of verse – he must be one of the most unflaggingly fertile of twentieth-century American poets – it is also possible to wish that some of his work had been more intensively worked over. There is, for instance, a wonderful idea, partly spoiled, in *First Will and Testament* which has at its core a play for voices, featuring a Mr. Kek and his brothel, to which come, in turn, a group of famous poets, Donne, Marvell, Jonson, etc.; and then jazzmen Beiderbecke, Armstrong, Allen; gangsters, sportsmen – all outsiders, all seeking warmth and love and a good time, and trying to escape "the enemy." Much of this is obviously borrowed from Auden, but it has some fizzing wit and a great deal of hard-hitting panache that are Patchen's own. The trouble is that it degenerates into Cummings-like sentimentality: all picaros are better than all lawmen; to be an artist you have to be on the outside, a society reject, a bum. In other words the play is written out of cliché, so that although it has local life it is finally soggy.

This criticism applies to a good deal of his work. Yet nothing I say here is intended to detract from the vitality of his best writing, which can crop up anywhere, and is just as likely to show itself in a late volume, like *When We Were Here Together*, as in an early one, such as *Before the Brave*.

—John Lucas

PERCY, Walker. American. Born in Birmingham, Alabama, 28 May 1916. Educated at the University of North Carolina, Chapel Hill, B.A. 1937; Columbia University, New York, M.D. 1941; intern at Bellevue Hospital, New York, 1942. Married Mary Bernice Townsend in 1946; two daughters. Contracted tuberculosis, gave up medicine, and became a full-time writer, 1943. Recipient: National Book Award, 1962; National Institute of Arts and Letters grant, 1967. Fellow, American Academy of Arts and Sciences; Member, National Institute of Arts and Letters. Lives in Covington, Louisiana.

PUBLICATIONS

Fiction

The Moviegoer. 1961.
The Last Gentleman. 1966.
Love in the Ruins: The Adventures of a Bad Catholic at a Time Near the End of the World. 1971.
Lancelot. 1977.

Other

The Message in the Bottle: How Queer Man Is, How Queer Language Is, and What One Has to Do with the Other. 1975.

Reading List: *City of Words* by Tony Tanner, 1971.

*   *   *

Walker Percy belongs to the movement in modern Southern writing that derives from T. S. Eliot and includes, among others, Allen Tate, Caroline Gordon, Robert Penn Warren, and William Faulkner. Percy is a traditionalist in reaction against what is perceived as the decay of moral standards, the loss of a sense of community and of shared values. His ideas are given rather full intellectual scope in his work of non-fiction, *The Message in the Bottle*. In his novels the issue is focused on sexuality, and the problem, as expressed in his fiction, is how to square sexual desire with traditional ideas of love and responsibility, complicated by the modern confusion of love and sex. What used to be regarded as sin and perversion is now acceptable to, even sanctioned by, church and state. The traditional concept of love is too idealistic to provide Percy's protagonists with a satisfactory pattern of behavior. Inevitably his novels involve the setting up of the problem and the working out of a solution, the protagonist wrestling with his moral confusion, then, finally, creating for himself a synthesis in which love and lust – giving and taking – are appropriately balanced.

His first novel, *The Moviegoer*, concludes with the protagonist, a lusty bachelor, failing in his latest sexual escapade and marrying a young woman of his own class, partly out of affection, but also because they share a sense of experienced responsibility. In *The Last Gentleman*, the hero, who suffers emotional detachment (which Percy sees as the chief modern malady) cures himself through his personal devotion to a dying youth and in turn helps cure a confused young woman and her cynical older brother. *Love in the Ruins*, set in the future "at a time near the end of the world," deals with the collapse of modern technology and concludes with the responsible marriage of the protagonist who tries to save his doomed world but, failing that, gives himself over to whiskey and lust for three beautiful women. At the novel's close he marries the most responsible and moral of the three and begins to live a simple, natural, and properly lustful life in the shadow of the remnants of the old Catholic Church. In *Lancelot* the pessimism is deeper, the solution more tenuous. The hero, at first tolerant of his wife's sexual infidelity, finally kills her and her lover, is confined to a mental institution, is "cured" and then released into the world. For a time, he takes on the responsibility of a young woman raped and maimed by a gang of thugs, but is rebuffed by the young woman in language suggestive to radical feminist ideology. Percy's latest protagonist then stands alone against a world shown to be corrupt beyond redemption. Even the Church, it seems, has fallen into the modern abyss confusion. A slight ray of final hope is that the young woman may eventually join him in his exile.

Percy's rendering of characters and scenes is striking, vivid, and bitingly satirical. He is a moral and, ultimately, a religious writer, but a perceptive novelist of manners as well. His sensitive and poetic style elevates material that less subtly treated might appear contrived and moralistic.

—W. J. Stuckey

PERELMAN, S(idney) J(oseph).   American.   Born in Brooklyn, New York, 1 February 1904. Educated at Brown University, Providence, Rhode Island, 1921–25, B.A. 1925. Married Laura West in 1929 (died, 1970); one son and one daughter. Writer and artist for *Judge* magazine, 1925–29, and for *College Humor* magazine, 1929–30; full-time writer from 1930; contributor to *The New Yorker* from 1931; lived in London, 1970–72. Recipient: New York Film Critics Award, 1936; Academy Award, 1956. Member, National Institute of Arts and Letters. Lives in New York City.

PUBLICATIONS

Prose

Dawn Ginsbergh's Revenge.   1929.

Parlor, Bedlam and Bath, with Q. J. Reynolds.   1930.
Strictly from Hunger.   1937.
Look Who's Talking.   1940.
The Dream Department.   1943.
Crazy Like a Fox.   1944.
Keep It Crisp.   1946.
Acres and Pains.   1947.
The Best of Perelman.   1947.
Westward Ha! or, Around the World in Eighty Clichés.   1947.
Listen to the Mocking Bird.   1949.
The Swiss Family Perelman.   1950.
The Ill-Tempered Clavicord.   1952.
Perelman's Home Companion: A Collector's Item (the Collector Being S. J. Perelman) of
     36 Otherwise Unavailable Pieces by Himself.   1955.
The Road to Miltown; or, Under the Spreading Atrophy.   1957; as *Bite on the Bullet; or,*
     Under the Spreading Atrophy, 1957.
The Most of Perelman.   1958.
The Rising Gorge.   1961.
Chicken Inspector No. 23.   1966.
Baby, It's Cold Inside.   1970.
Monkey Business.   1973.
Vinegar Puss.   1975.
Eastward Ha!   1977.
The Most of Perelman (omnibus).   1978.

Plays

Sketches in *The Third Little Show* (produced 1931).
Sketches, with Robert MacGunigle, in *Walk a Little Faster* (produced 1932).
All Good Americans, with Laura Perelman (produced 1933).
Sketches in *Two Weeks with Pay* (produced 1940).
The Night Before Christmas, with Laura Perelman (produced 1941).   1942.
One Touch of Venus, with Ogden Nash, music by Kurt Weill, based on *The Tinted Venus*
     by F. Anstey (produced 1943).   1944.
Sweet Bye and Bye, with Al Hirschfield, music by Vernon Duke, lyrics by Ogden Nash
     (produced 1946).
The Beauty Part, with Ogden Nash (produced 1961).   1963.

Screenplays: *Horse Feathers,* with others, 1932; *The Miracle Man,* with others, 1932;
Florida Special, with others, 1936; *Boy Trouble,* with others, 1939; *Ambush,* with Laura
Perelman and Robert Ray, 1939; *The Golden Fleecing,* with others, 1940; *Around the
World in Eighty Days,* with James Poe and John Farrow, 1956.

*   *   *

As a screenwriter, a playwright, and, primarily, an essayist, S. J. Perelman has spent nearly
fifty years perfecting a unique and surrealistic sytle of humor marked by an uncontrollable
imagination and an enormous, arcane vocabulary. Perhaps best described as a mixture of
Groucho Marx (with whom he worked) and James Joyce (whom he called "the comic writer
of the century"), Perelman is a roman candle of language, firing off metaphors where the
untrained eye might see only an unloaded verb: "Carstairs exchanged a quizzical glance with
his manservant, fitted it into an ivory holder, and lit it abstractedly." At the extreme,
Perelman's sentences leap from pillar to post with a sheerly linguistic logic, sneering at

cliché: "On her dainty egg-shaped head was massed a crop of auburn curls; the cucumbers she had grown there the previous summer were forgotten in the pulsing rhythm of the moment." Perelman's distinguishing characteristic is his total imaginative control of the work, and consequently neither his film scripts nor his stage plays have the comic intensity of the meticulously crafted essays.

Perelman's distaste for the mediocrity of the everyday world has manifested itself in a complete disdain for broad political and social satire. A large number of his essays take aim at popular movies, magazines, and novels, at newspapers, at advertising – soft prose and soft thinking of all stripes. Increasingly, however, he has turned inward, spinning off exotic tales from the merest personal anecdotes. Perelman is pleased to call himself a *feuilletoniste*, a writer of lapidary prose, and a crank who only writes when sufficiently enraged. He once summed up his interest in humor with these words (*New York Times Magazine*, 26 January 1969): "For me, its chief merit is the use of the unexpected, the glancing allusion, the deflation of pomposity, and the constant repetition of one's helplessness in a majority of situations."

—Walter Bode

PHILLIPS, David Graham. American. Born in Madison, Indiana, 31 October 1867. Educated in local schools; Asbury University, later DePauw University, Greencastle, Indiana, 1883–85; College of New Jersey, later Princeton University, 1885–87, A.B. 1887. Reporter for the *Cincinnati Star Times*, 1888, and the *Cincinnati Commercial Gazette*, 1889–90; settled in New York City: member of the editorial staff of the *Sun*, 1890–93; London Correspondent, 1893, General Reporter, 1893–95, Feature Writer, 1895–97, and Member of the Editorial Department, 1897–1902, *New York World*; full-time writer from 1902; active contributor to various national magazines, especially the *Saturday Evening Post*, Philadelphia, and *Cosmopolitan*, New York. *Died* (murdered) *24 January 1911.*

PUBLICATIONS

Fiction

The Great God Success. 1901.
Her Serene Highness. 1902.
A Woman Ventures. 1902.
Golden Fleece: The American Adventures of a Fortune-Hunting Earl. 1903.
The Master-Rogue: The Confessions of a Croesus. 1903.
The Cost. 1904.
The Social Secretary. 1905.
The Deluge. 1905.
The Mother-Light. 1905.
The Plum Tree. 1905.
The Fortune Hunter. 1906.
Light-Fingered Gentry. 1907.
The Second Generation. 1907.

Old Wives for New. 1908.
The Fashionable Adventures of Joshua Craig. 1909.
The Hungry Heart. 1909.
White Magic. 1910.
The Husband's Story. 1911.
The Conflict. 1911.
The Grain of Dust. 1911.
George Helm. 1912.
The Price She Paid. 1912.
Degarmo's Wife and Other Stories. 1913.
Susan Lenox: Her Fall and Rise. 1917.

Play

The Worth of a Woman (produced 1908). 1908.

Other

The Reign of Gilt. 1905.
The Treason of the Senate (essays). 1953.

*   *   *

David Graham Phillips's first novel, *The Great God Success*, concerns a newspaperman who gains fortune and power by championing the cause of the people against "the interests," but who sells out when he begins to identify with the rich. In *The Deluge, Light-Fingered Gentry, The Master-Rogue,* and *The Grain of Dust* Phillips also dealt with the corrupting influence of capitalism on essentially good men.

While in college, Phillips roomed with Albert Beveridge, who was later to serve as Senator from Indiana. They remained good friends for the rest of their lives, and Phillips used Beveridge as a model for his paragon of political virtues, Hampden Scarborough. In *The Cost*, Scarborough's career is contrasted with his rival in love, an evil industrialist named Dumont. Scarborough's legislation ultimately triumphs over the capitalist's trusts. In *The Plum Tree*, Scarborough becomes a foil to a dishonest political power-broker. In these, as in his other political novels, *The Fashionable Adventures of Joshua Craig* and *George Helm*, Phillips recommends a vague populism and a return to honesty as the answer to the enormous social and economic problems facing America. His interest seems to be in exposing corruption, not in solving problems.

In his two "economic" novels, Phillips was somewhat bolder. Victor Dorn, the hero of *The Conflict*, is a revolutionary who contends that Marx will dominate the next two thousand years as Christ has dominated the last two thousand. In *The Second Generation*, Phillips seems to recommend the abolition of inherited property because of the harm done to both society and property-owners themselves.

Yet Phillips's greatest achievement was in his novels dealing with women's place in modern society. In *A Woman Ventures, Old Wives for New, The Price She Paid*, and in his only play, *The Worth of a Woman*, he ridiculed the stereotypical weak, soft home-bodies and extolled the virtues of women who competed on equal terms with men. In *The Hungry Heart* he defended the rights of neglected women to seek sexual satisfaction outside the bonds of matrimony. Phillips's most impressive novel, *Susan Lenox: Her Fall and Rise*, published posthumously, chronicles the life of a girl who is condemned by social forces beyond her control to a life of vice and crime. Nothing in Dreiser or Sinclair can match the brutality of Phillips's pictures of slum life and the horrors of white slavery. Through all her degradation,

Susan maintains her essential dignity. When she overcomes her poverty, she still rejects all offers of respectability and marriage.

When Roosevelt applied the term "Muckraker" to a certain kind of investigative reporting, he was specifically referring to Phillips and his *Treason of the Senate*, and it is for his reporting, not his literary work, that history will remember him. Yet his novels provide a valuable insight into the hopeful, optimistic America of his era.

—William Higgins

PLATH, Sylvia.   American.   Born in Boston, Massachusetts, 27 October 1932. Educated at Smith College, Northampton, Massachusetts, B.A. (summa cum laude) in English 1955; Harvard University, Cambridge, Massachusetts, Summer 1954; Newnham College, Cambridge (Fulbright Scholar), 1955–57, M.A. 1957. Married the poet Ted Hughes in 1956; one daughter and one son. Guest Editor, *Mademoiselle* magazine, New York, Summer 1953; Instructor in English, Smith College, 1957–58; moved to England, 1959. Recipient: Yaddo Fellowship, 1959; Cheltenham Festival Award, 1961; Saxon Fellowship, 1961. *Died* (by suicide) *11 February 1963*.

PUBLICATIONS

Verse

A Winter Ship.   1960.
The Colossus and Other Poems.   1960; as The Colossus, 1967.
Ariel.   1965.
Uncollected Poems.   1965.
Fiesta Melons.   1971.
Crossing the Water, edited by Ted Hughes.   1971; as Crossing the Water: Transitional
  Poems, 1971.
Crystal Gazer and Other Poems.   1971.
Lyonesse: Hitherto Uncollected Poems.   1971.
Winter Trees.   1971.
Pursuit.   1973.

Play

Three Women: A Monologue for Voices (broadcast 1962; produced 1973).

Radio Play: Three Women, 1962.

Fiction

The Bell Jar. 1961.

Other

Letters Home: Correspondence 1950–1963, edited by Aurelia Schober Plath. 1975.
The Bed Book (juvenile). 1976.
Plath: A Dramatic Portrait (miscellany), edited by Barry Kyle. 1976.
Johnny Panic and the Bible of Dreams, and Other Prose Writings. 1977.

Editor, *American Poetry Now: A Selection of the Best Poems by Modern American Writers.* 1961.

Bibliography: *A Chronological Checklist of the Periodical Publications of Plath* by Eric Homberger, 1970; *Plath and Anne Sexton: A Reference Guide* by Cameron Northouse and Thomas P. Walsh, 1975.

Reading List: *The Art of Plath: A Symposium* edited by Charles Newman, 1970 (includes bibliography); *Plath* by Eileen M. Aird, 1973; *Plath: Method and Madness* by Edward Butscher, 1976, and *Plath: The Woman and Her Work* edited by Butscher, 1977; *Plath: Poetry and Existence* by David Holbrook, 1976.

*   *   *

The adolescent heroine of Sylvia Plath's only novel, *The Bell Jar*, has looked into her grave and seen a sobering and a maddening truth. Her suicidal hysteria, like that which finally took her author, is the anguish of a being who has realized her own gratuitousness, "Factitious, artificial, sham." What she has called her "self," that unique and coddled ego, is no more than a nexus of donated being, a field of battle where the conflicting forces of her environment, her familial and social experience, clash, divide, and coalesce. Plath herself wrote of the poem "Daddy" as "spoken by a girl with an Electra complex. Her father died while she thought he was God. Her case is complicated by the fact that her father was also a Nazi and her mother very possibly Jewish. In the daughter the two strains marry and paralyze each other – she has to act out the awful little allegory before she is free of it." While the details hardly correspond accurately to Plath's own biography, their symbolic function in the emotional ecology of her work is clear. The title poem of *The Colossus* acknowledges such a condition: addressed to her dead father ("I shall never get you put together entirely") it is self-consciously post-Freudian and pre-Christian: "A blue sky out of the Oresteia/Arches above us"; if her father is now no more than a "Mouthpiece of the dead," this is equally true of all selves, whose "hours are married to shadow," the marionettes of an unconscious in whose formation they had no hand. "Poem for a Birthday" is a complex dramatic monologue in which a psyche struggles towards birth, in "the city of spare parts" which is the world. Its voice is a Cinderella or Snow-White princess in nightmare exile among incomprehensible and uncomprehending powers, feeling herself "Duchess of Nothing," "housekeep[ing] in Time's gut end" and "married [to] a cupboard of rubbish." It is a representative text.

The imagery of Plath's poems undergoes endless transformations, in which the links are often suppressed or arbitrary: sudden shifts of tack and emotion lead off in unexpected directions. Her poetic narratives fork and proliferate in this way because, in unfolding the implications of a sequence of images, she uncovers the complex and contradictory possibilities condensed within them, the infantile traumas lying treacherously beneath the surface of adult experience. The same image can be charged with quite contradictory emotional valencies. The bee, for example, a recurring motif (her father was an apiculturalist), stirs rich, ambiguous feelings. It is a female, a source of honey and creativity, but it has a male sting; the hive includes drudges and drones, but also that dark leonine queen at the core; in "The Swarm" and "The Arrival of the Bee-Box", bees are the collective "black, intractable mind" of a genocidal Europe and the "swarmy," "angrily clambering" impulsions of the individual unconscious. Such transitions express her own sense of the self, not as a hierarchically ordered pyramid, but as an ensemble of possibilities, in which none usurps precedence for long, and to which only a provisional coherence can be given, in the specifying of a name and image ("The Arrival of the Bee-Box," after toying with the starvation or release of the bees which threaten and fascinate, concludes, "The box is only temporary"). Self for Plath is either a rigid, false *persona* or an amorphous, uncongealed, and fluid congeries, like the bee-swarm itself, undergoing constant metamorphosis, continually dying and being reborn in the mutations of the imagery. In "Elm," the social self speaks as a tree, rooted in its context, wrenched violently by a wind that "will tolerate no bystanding." But such fixity is an illusion, for its roots reach down to the dissolute sea, its branches "break up in pieces that fly about like clubs," it is dragged by the moon (usually the image of a sterile maternal force), and it contains subversive lives which are part of itself yet frighteningly independent:

> I am inhabited by a cry.
> Nightly it flaps out
> Looking, with its hooks, for something to love.
>
> I am terrified by this dark thing
> That sleeps in me;
> All day I feel its soft, feathery turnings, its malignity.

Plath repeatedly sees relationships as predatory, exploitative, and destructive, yet desired and necessary, as in "The Rabbit-Catcher" ("And we too had a relationship,/Tight wires between us,/Pegs too deep to uproot, and a mind like a ring/Sliding shut on some quick thing,/The constriction killing me also"). In "Tulips," even the smiles of husband and children, in a photograph, "catch onto my skin, little smiling hooks," while identity itself, in "The Applicant," is seen as a collection of functions, answers to others' questions, a poultice for their wounds, apple for their eyes, "A living doll" which is the accretion of artificial limbs and artificial commitments.

This aspect of her verse has made her co-option by the women's movement inevitable. But it is also just. Plath is, in fact, a profoundly political poet, who has seen the generic nature of these private catastrophes of the self, their public origin in a civilization founded on mass-manipulation and collective trickery. Esther Greenwood, in *The Bell Jar*, links her electric shock treatment with the electrocution which is the Rosenbergs' punishment for rebellion against the American way of life: she fears most of all being consigned to the charity wards, "with hundreds of people like me, in a big cage in the basement. The more hopeless you were, the further away they hid you." In a century which has shut away millions, in hospitals, concentration camps, and graveyards, where the self can be "wiped out ... like chalk on a blackboard" by administrative *diktat*, Plath sees a deep correspondence between the paternal concern of the psychiatrist and the authority of the modern state, even in its most extreme variants: both presuppose the self as victim, passive and compliant, as *sine qua non* of any "final solution." For Plath, concerned that "personal experience shouldn't be a kind of shut box and mirror-looking narcissistic experience," but "should be generally relevant, to such things as Hiroshima and Dachau and so on," the refusal to collaborate was a profoundly positive act, the assertion not of the nihilism of which she has been accused but of a more exacting and scrupulous conscience. If, in poems such as "Daddy" and "Lady Lazarus," she veers close to disintegration, she also promises a breakthrough into a resurrection which sheds the constricting husks of the past, a vengeful return which is only justice:

So, so. Herr Doktor.
So, Herr Enemy.
I am your opus,
I am your valuable,
The pure gold baby

That melts to a shriek.
I turn and burn,
Do not think I underestimate your great concern....

Herr God, Herr Lucifer
Beware
Beware.

Out of the ash
I rise with my red hair
And I eat men like air.

—Stan Smith

PORTER, Katherine Anne. American. Born in Indian Creek, Texas, 15 May 1890. Educated in Louisiana and Texas: at home, aged 3 to 8; in private school, 8 to 12; in an Ursuline Convent, 12 to 16. Married 1) Eugene Dove Pressly in 1933 (divorced, 1938); 2) Albert Russel Erskine, Jr., in 1938 (divorced, 1942). Reporter and Arts Critic, *Rocky Mountain News*, Denver, 1919; lived in Mexico and Europe between the wars; taught at Olivet College, Michigan, 1940; Lecturer in Writing, Stanford University, California, 1948–49; Guest Lecturer in Literature, University of Chicago, Spring 1951; Visiting Lecturer in Contemporary Poetry, University of Michigan, Ann Arbor, 1953–54; Fulbright Lecturer, University of Liège, Belgium, 1954–55; Writer-in-Residence, University of Virginia, Charlottesville, Autumn 1958; Glasgow Professor, Washington and Lee University, Lexington, Virginia, Spring 1959; Lecturer in American Literature for the United States Department of State, in Mexico, 1960, 1964; Ewing Lecturer, University of California at Los Angeles, 1960; Regents' Lecturer, University of California at Riverside, 1961. Library of Congress Fellow in Regional American Literature, 1944; United States Delegate, International Festival of the Arts, Paris, 1952; Member, Commission on Presidential Scholars, 1964; consultant in Poetry, Library of Congress, 1965–70. Recipient: Guggenheim Fellowship, 1931, 1938; New York University Libraries Gold Medal, 1940; Ford Foundation grant, 1959, 1960; O. Henry Award, 1962; Emerson-Thoreau Bronze Medal, 1962; Pulitzer Prize, 1966; National Book Award, 1966; National Institute of Arts and Letters Gold Medal, 1967; Mystery Writers of America Edgar Allan Poe Award, 1972. D.Litt.: University of North Carolina Woman's College, Greensboro, 1949; Smith College, Northampton, Massachusetts, 1958; Maryville College, St. Louis, 1968; D.H.L.: University of Michigan, Ann Arbor, 1954; University of Maryland, College Park, 1966; Maryland Institute, 1974; D.F.A.: La Salle College, Philadelphia, 1962. Vice-President, National Institute of Arts and Letters, 1950–52; Member, American Academy of Arts and Letters, 1967. Lives in College Park, Maryland.

PUBLICATIONS

Fiction

Flowering Judas. 1930; augmented edition, as *Flowering Judas and Other Stories,*
    1935.
Hacienda: A Story of Mexico. 1934.
Noon Wine (story). 1937.
Pale Horse, Pale Rider: Three Short Novels. 1939.
The Leaning Tower and Other Stories. 1944.
Selected Short Stories. 1945.
The Old Order: Stories of the South. 1955.
A Christmas Story. 1958.
Ship of Fools. 1962.
The Collected Stories. 1964; augmented edition, 1967.

Other

My Chinese Marriage. 1921.
Outline of Mexican Popular Arts and Crafts. 1922.
What Price Marriage. 1927.
The Days Before: Collected Essays and Occasional Writings.   1952; augmented edition,
    as *The Collected Essays and Occasional Writings,* 1970.
A Defense of Circe. 1955.
The Never-Ending Wrong (on the Sacco-Vanzetti case). 1977.

Translator, *French Song Book.* 1933.
Translator, *The Itching Parrot,* by Fernandez de Lizárdi. 1942.

Bibliography: *A Bibliography of the Works of Porter* by Louise Waldrip and Shirley Ann
Bauer, 1969: *Porter and Carson McCullers: A Reference Guide* by Robert F. Kiernan, 1976.

Reading List: *The Fiction and Criticism of Porter* by Harry John Mooney, Jr., 1957, revised
edition, 1962; *Porter* by Ray B. West, Jr., 1963; *Porter and the Art of Rejection* by William L.
Nance, 1964; *Porter* by George Hendrick, 1965; *Porter: The Regional Sources* by Winifred S.
Emmons, 1967; *Porter: A Critical Symposium* edited by Lodwick Hartley and George Core,
1969; *Porter's Fiction* by M. M. Liberman, 1973.

*   *   *

Katherine Anne Porter was probably the finest writer of short stories and novellas of her
time in the United States. Her last work of fiction, *Ship of Fools*, suggests either that the novel
as such was not her form or that the hatred and contempt aroused in her by German
behaviour under the Nazis had robbed her both of her usual skill and of her usual sense that
life, in all its sadness and frustrations, is incurably poetic. Her collection of essays, *The Days
Before*, however, is fascinating both in the excellence of its criticism and in the light it throws
on her own work: "I am passionately involved with those individuals who populate all these
enormous migrations, calamities, who fight wars and furnish life for the future." We see
such an individual in Porter's own stories (in *The Leaning Tower*, for instance) as a quiet,
imaginative, sad girl of old Southern family, aware of the past because of her grandmother
and her old negro servant, aware of the grotesque because of a visit to a circus whose clowns

frighten her, and aware of death and horror because of a brother who kills a pregnant rabbit and shows her the baby rabbits, who will now never be born in its womb. We see Miranda (in *Pale Horse, Pale Rider*) as a young girl who has married to flee from her family and yet in some ways emotionally dried up. Other stories, like *Noon Wine*, evoke a sense of fatality, violence springing from heat and bewilderment.

Porter's great gift as a storyteller is to take material, particularly a wistfulness for the past, a sense of the strangeness, loneliness, cruelty, and treachery of life, the decay of love, or the failure to be able to love, and to avoid the twin temptations of treating this material with either sentimentality or a cheap cynicism. She evokes gravely and gracefully both the potential beauty and the bewildering lurking betrayal of life. Born in Texas in 1890, but maturing as a writer in the 1930's, she combined in an unusual way a solid sense of the past and the atmosphere of place with a fine sense of that ambivalence or complexity of attitude that we have in mind when we talk of "modernity" in fiction. Her proper readers will have the sense of reading in two ages at once, and of being presented with two possible standards of judgment, one the firm, exact, and unargued standard of the Old South, the other the modern standard which, more frighteningly, hands over the task of judgment to the reader.

—G. S. Fraser

PORTER, William Sydney.   See HENRY, O.

POUND, Ezra (Weston Loomis).   American.   Born in Hailey, Idaho, 30 October 1885. Educated at Hamilton College, Clinton, New York, Ph.B. 1905; University of Pennsylvania, Philadelphia, M.A. 1906. Married Dorothy Shakespear in 1914. Taught at Wabash College, Crawfordsville, Indiana, 1906; travelled in Spain, Italy, and France, 1906–07; lived in London, 1908–20, in Paris, 1920–24, and in Rapallo, Italy, 1924–45: one of the creators of the Imagist movement; English Editor of *Poetry*, Chicago, 1912–19; Founder, with Wyndham Lewis, of *Blast*, 1914; English Editor of *The Little Review*, Chicago, 1917–19; Paris Correspondent of *The Dial*, 1922; Founder and Editor of *The Exile*, 1927–28. Broadcast over Italian Radio to the United States after 1941, in support of fascism, and was arrested and jailed for these broadcasts by the United States Army in 1945; imprisoned near Pisa, found unfit to stand trial for treason, and committed to St. Elizabeth's Hospital, Washington, D.C.; released in 1958; returned to Italy. Recipient: Academy of American Poets Fellowship, 1963; National Endowment for the Arts grant, 1967. *Died 1 November 1972.*

"Noh" or Accomplishment: A Study of the Classical Stage of Japan, with Ernest
   Fenollosa. 1916; as *The Classical Noh Theatre of Japan,* 1959.
Gaudier-Brzeska: A Memoir. 1916; revised edition, 1959.
Pavannes and Divisions. 1918.
Instigations. 1920.
Indiscretions; or Une Revue de Deux Mondes. 1923.
Antheil and The Treatise on Harmony. 1924.
Imaginary Letters. 1930.
How to Read. 1931.
ABC of Economics. 1933.
ABC of Reading. 1934.
Make It New: Essays. 1934.
Social Credit: An Impact. 1935.
Jefferson and/or Mussolini. 1935; revised edition, as *Jefferson e Mussolini,* 1944.
Polite Essays. 1937.
Guide to Kulchur. 1938; as *Culture,* 1938.
What Is Money For? 1939.
Carta da Visita. 1942; translated by John Drummond, as *A Visiting Card,* 1952.
L'America, Roosevelt, e le Cause della Guerra Presente. 1944; translated by John
   Drummond, as *America, Roosevelt, and the Causes of the Present War,* 1951.
Oro e Lavoro. 1944; translated by John Drummond, as *Gold and Labour,* 1952.
Introduzione alla Natura Economica degli S.U.A. 1944; translated by Carmine Amore,
   as *An Introduction to the Economic Nature of the United States,* 1950.
Orientamenti. 1944.
If This Be Treason. 1948.
The Letters of Pound, 1907–1941, edited by D. D. Paige. 1950.
Patria Mia. 1950; as *Patria Mia and The Treatise on Harmony,* 1962.
The Translations of Ezra Pound, edited by Hugh Kenner. 1953; revised edition, 1970.
Secondo Biglietto da Visita. 1953.
Literary Essays, edited by T. S. Eliot. 1954.
Pavannes and Divagations. 1958.
Impact: Essays on Ignorance and the Decline of American Civilization, edited by Noel
   Stock. 1960.
EP to LU: Nine Letters Written to Louis Untermeyer by Ezra Pound, edited by J. Albert
   Robbins. 1963.
Pound/Joyce: The Letters of Ezra Pound to James Joyce, edited by Forrest Read. 1967.
Redondillas: or, Something of That Sort. 1967.
The Caged Panther: Ezra Pound at St. Elizabeth's (includes 53 letters), by Harry M.
   Meachum. 1967.
DK: Some Letters of Pound, edited by Louis Dudek. 1974.
Pound and Music: The Complete Criticism, edited by R. Murray Schafer. 1977.

Editor, *Des Imagistes: An Anthology.* 1914.
Editor, *Catholic Anthology, 1914–1915.* 1915.
Editor, *Poetical Works of Lionel Johnson.* 1915.
Editor, *Passages from the Letters of John Butler Yeats.* 1917.
Editor, *Profile: An Anthology.* 1932.
Editor, *Rime,* by Guido Cavalcanti. 1932.
Editor, *Active Anthology.* 1933.
Editor, *The Chinese Written Character as a Medium for Poetry: An Ars Poetica.* by
   Ernest Fenollosa. 1936.
Editor, *De Moribus Brachmanorum, Liber Sancto Ambrosio Falso Adscriptus.* 1956.
Editor, with Marcella Spann, *Confucius to Cummings: An Anthology of Poetry.* 1964.

Translator, *The Sonnets and Ballate of Guido Cavalcanti.*   1912; as *Pound's Cavalcanti Poems,* 1966.
Translator, *Cathay: Translations.*   1915.
Translator, with Ernest Fenollosa, *Certain Noble Plays of Japan.*   1916.
Translator, *Dialogues of Fontenelle.*   1917.
Translator, *The Natural Philosophy of Love,* by Rémy de Gourmont.   1922.
Translator, *The Call of the Road,* by Edouard Estaunié.   1923.
Translator, *Ta Hio: The Great Learning,* by Confucius.   1928.
Translator, *Digest of the Analects,* by Confucius.   1937.
Translator, *Italy's Policy of Social Economics 1939–1940,* by Odon Por.   1941.
Translator, with Alberto Luchini, *Ta S'en Dai Gaku, Studio Integrale,* by Confucius.   1942.
Translator, *Ciung Iung, l'Asse che non Vacilla,* by Confucius.   1945.
Translator, *The Unwobbling Pivot and The Great Digest,* by Confucius.   1947.
Translator, *Confucian Analects.*   1951.
Translator, *The Classic Anthology Defined by Confucius.*   1954.
Translator, *Women of Trachis,* by Sophocles.   1956.
Translator, *Moscardino,* by Enrico Pea.   1956.
Translator, *Rimbaud* (5 poems).   1957.
Translator, with Noel Stock, *Love Poems of Ancient Egypt.*   1962.

Bibliography: *A Bibliography of Pound* by Donald Gallup, 1963, revised edition, 1969.

Reading List: *Pound: His Metric and Poetry* by T. S. Eliot, 1917; *The Poetry of Pound,* 1951, and *The Pound Era,* 1971, both by Hugh Kenner; *A Primer of Pound* by M. L. Rosenthal, 1960; *Pound* by G. S. Fraser, 1960; *Pound, Poet as Sculptor,* 1964, and *Pound,* 1976, both by Donald Davie; *The Life of Pound* by Noel Stock, 1970: *Pound: The Critical Heritage* edited by Eric Homberger, 1972; *Pound, The Last Rower: A Political Profile* by C. David Heymann, 1976; *Time in Pound's Work* by William Harmon, 1977.

*   *   *

In his preface to his little book on popular music, *All What Jazz,* the poet Philip Larkin names the jazz musician Charlie Parker, Picasso, and Ezra Pound as standing for all that he most detests in "modernism" in the arts. Larkin is probably, without being among the startlingly great, the most distinguished poet we have in England at this moment. I am not competent to speak about Parker. But Cubism, invented by Picasso and Braque, is, in spite of its comparatively short life in its pure form, the greatest revolution in painting since the first adequate exploitation of perspective, anatomy, and the golden section at the Renaissance. Similarly, for good or evil, modern poetry would not be what it is (or have been what it was) without Pound. It may be true that what Pound had personally to say through the medium of verse was either not very interesting or, as in his praise of Fascism, positively dangerous. He remains the greatest technical inventor in poetry in his century, and the history of twentieth-century poetry would be quite different without him. As an observer of life, Larkin is in many ways a more complex and subtle man than Pound. Still, if Larkin had never existed, we should lack four slim volumes of carefully undertoned verse, but the history of poetry in our century would be much what it is already.

Yet the comparison of Picasso and Pound is critically apt. Both, the one in Spain, the other in the American mid-west, started out of the main stream. When Picasso came to Paris from Spain, he left a country that had not even caught up with Impressionism. When Pound came to England in 1908, with his first volume *A Lume Spento* privately printed in Venice, he was imitating the poets of the 1890's, including Yeats in his very early phase, Swinburne, and the Pre-Raphaelites: he was about thirty years behind the times. T. E. Hulme and other members of the Poets' Club, now forgotten, were already experimenting with what was to be called Imagism, and an Englishman, F. S. Flint, was to work out its theory; it was left to Pound, when he got round to it in 1912, only to give it a name. His own Imagist poems are among the best, but not perhaps so good as the very best of his American acquaintance, Hilda Doolittle. Of his poems before *The Cantos*, the best are two translations, "The Seafarer" (his Anglo-Saxon was self-taught, and some of the lines are sonorous but meaningless) and "Cathay" (adapted from the American scholar Ernest Fenollosa's attempts to translate classical Chinese poetry through a knowledge of the Chinese ideograms), and the two-part *Hugh Selwyn Mauberley*.

A study of cultural decay in England since the Pre-Raphaelites, *Mauberley* begins with a mock-epitaph for Pound and an ironic but affectionate picture of the tradition of the Pre-Raphaelites and Decadents from which he derives; its second half deals with an imaginary character, Hugh Selwyn Mauberley, who chooses to drift hedonistically to his death. Yet the final poem created by Pound at the end of his section is a seventeenth-century pastiche, the final poem created by Mauberley; transforming hair into metal and flesh into porcelain under the electric light is very startlingly "modern." There is a sense also that the Mauberley figure, for all his drifting, feels more deeply than the satirically observant Pound figure. Like *The Waste Land*, of which it is in some sense a forerunner, *Hugh Selwyn Mauberley* has still to be satisfactorily construed. (There is likewise no agreed judgment about whether the startling mistranslations in *Homage to Sextus Propertius* are blunders or are satirical, though some intention to satirise the British Empire is obvious.)

Pound then embarked on a poem of enormous length, *The Cantos*. This is, in a certain sense, a modern epic, except that the heroic role is played now by Odysseus and now by a Renaissance adventurer like Sigismundo de Malatesta, and the sage figure now by Confucius and now by one of the American founding fathers like Jefferson or John Adams. The poem throughout assumes a knowledge in the reader of Pound's raw material and a knowledge of the economics of Major Douglas ("Can't move them with a cold thing like economics") and of exactly what Pound means by usury. There are very dull patches in the middle, but the account of Pound's imprisonment by American troops in Pisa (*The Pisan Cantos*) at the time of the Allied invasion of Italy is vivid. The later cantos are more fragmentary and harder to understand. The poem is a failure as a whole, but an amazing manual of poetic techniques.

—G. S. Fraser

POWERS, J(ames) F(arl). American. Born in Jacksonville, Illinois, 8 July 1917. Educated at Quincy College Academy, Illinois; Northwestern University, Chicago campus, 1938–40. Married the writer Betty Wahl in 1946; three daughters and two sons. Worked in Chicago, 1935–41; Editor, Illinois Historical Records Survey, 1938; worked as a hospital orderly during World War II; writer from 1943; taught at St. John's University, Collegeville, Minnesota, 1947; Marquette University, Milwaukee, Wisconsin, 1949–51; University of Michigan, Ann Arbor, 1956–57; Writer-in-Residence, Smith College, Northampton, Massachusetts, 1965–66. Recipient: National Institute of Arts and Letters grant, 1948; Guggenheim Fellowship, 1948; Rockefeller Fellowship, 1954, 1957, 1967; National Book Award, 1963. Member, National Institute of Arts and Letters.

PUBLICATIONS

Fiction

Prince of Darkness and Other Stories.   1947.
The Presence of Grace (stories).   1956.
Morte D'Urban.   1962.
Look How the Fish Live.   1975.

Reading List: *Powers* by John V. Hagopian, 1968.

*   *   *

J. F. Powers was frustrated trying to find work in Chicago during the depression years 1935–41. In the early years of World War II he met many social rebels in Chicago – workers, Blacks, and European exiles – and became a pacifist: he was appalled equally by the destructive war and patriotic propaganda. Early in 1943 he was the only lay person to attend a priests' retreat at St. John's Abbey in Collegeville, Minnesota. Following a period of reading and introspection Powers wrote "Lions, Harts, Leaping Does," in which Father Didymus attains true holiness as he dies, holding to his faith along with a strong sense of unworthiness. Three Powers sketches appeared in *The Catholic Worker* in 1943: "the upholstery of Christianity has held up better than the idea and practice.... Anyone who is not a saint is spiritually undersized – the world is full of spiritual midgets."

In *Prince of Darkness and Other Stories*, the best pieces have priest protagonists: the title story, "The Forks," "The Valiant Woman," and "Lions, Harts, Leaping Does." Among the eleven stories are three bitter tales about the plight of Chicago Blacks; "Jamesie," a story of adolescence that is probably autobiographical; and "Renner," a story of anti-Semitism. The critical reception of Powers's stories – especially among his fellow writers – was impressive. *The Presence of Grace* has nine stories, all but two of them about priests. The prevailing mood is mellow in these stories, and some reviewers found his clerical scenes deplorably picturesque instead of astringent.

Except for the story of Father Didymus, Powers used both humor and irony to expose priestly venality in his earlier stories: they reveal the dark side of "the endless struggle between religious idealism and selfish, worldly interests." Wit and subtle irony are still at work on priestly foibles in the nine stories of *The Presence of Grace*, but the absurdities seem less vicious and more forgivable. "Zeal" is a fair example: obtuse and bungling Father Early provokes his sophisticated bishop into a redeeming examination of his own soul.

Powers has published only one novel, *Morte D'Urban*, which grew out of a short story he had begun 15 years earlier. In "The Devil Was the Joker," the Order of St. Clement is a central concern; and some minor figures in the novel – Father Udovic, Monsignor Renton, and their Bishop – are the chief characters in "Dawn." For his novel Powers sets up two Minnesota dioceses, Great Plains and Ostergothenburg. Powers's own words best describe his intention: "The story is about Father Urban being sent to this foundation of the Order (Clementines) in Minnesota. He had been a big-time speaker, a poor man's Fulton Sheen. He was suddenly sent up here to this white elephant ... as one of the boys.... That's my story ... how he tried to put the place on its feet.... I thought it would be a nice little nut-brown novel, all kinds of irony." Though the critics reviewed *Morte D'Urban* favorably, most of them missed some levels of irony and even misinterpreted the point. Perhaps because parts of the novel had appeared in journals and Powers had an impressive reputation as a writer of short stories, many reviewers found *Morte D'Urban* episodic and lacking in unity as novel. Powers's ironic unifying devices were possibly too subtle.

Look How the Fish Live is uneven: half of the stories are clearly below Powers's usual high quality. Several of these inferior pieces, including the title story and "Tinkers," are new in subject matter and technique; but they fall far short of five stories in this collection that match Powers's best. These are stories of young, emancipated curates devoted to their creature comforts and with callow notions of how the Church should modernize; middle-aged priestly operators who specialize in efficiency, PR, and good housekeeping; elderly priests and dying bishops who clearly belong to another era but survive preposterously and precariously in an alien world. Through the agency of such Roman Catholic clerics, Powers views the modern world humorously and seriously at the same time – but always ironically.

Powers has always been a painstaking writer, and critics often praised his "structural finesse and verbal sensitivity," his "remarkable ear for the dialects and idioms of midwestern speech," and "the perfect fluency, realism, and economy" of his dialogue. The brilliant satire and subtle humor of *Morte D'Urban* have been recognized – though not widely enough; and Powers's use of the Arthurian matter has been variously interpreted and assessed. But one aspect of this and other Powers fiction has not been properly appreciated, perhaps because his Roman Catholic matter is probed so deeply and detailed so accurately. He uses the dilemma of Roman Catholicism in the middle years of the twentieth century to dramatize the impact of rampant materialism on a society trying to save – or find – its soul and sanity.

—Clarence A. Glasrud

PURDY, James (Otis).   American.   Born near Fremont, Ohio, 14th July 1923. Educated at the University of Chicago, 1941, 1946; University of Puebla, Mexico. Worked as an interpreter in Latin America, France, and Spain; taught at Lawrence College, Appleton, Wisconsin, 1949–53; full-time writer from 1953; Visiting Professor, University of Tulsa, Oklahoma, 1977. Recipient: National Institute of Arts and Letters grant, 1958; Guggenheim Fellowship, 1958, 1962; Ford Fellowship, for drama, 1961. Lives in Brooklyn, New York.

PUBLICATIONS

Fiction

> *Don't Call Me by My Right Name and Other Stories.*   1956.
> *63: Dream Palace* (stories).   1956; as *63: Dream Stories,* 1957.
> *Color of Darkness: Eleven Stories and a Novella.*   1957.
> *Malcolm.*   1959.
> *The Nephew.*   1960.
> *Children Is All* (stories and plays).   1961.
> *Cabot Wright Begins.*   1964.
> *Eustace Chisholm and the Works.*   1967.
> *An Oyster Is a Wealthy Beast* (story and poems).   1967.
> *Mr. Evening: A Story and Nine Poems.*   1968.
> *On the Rebound: A Story and Nine Poems.*   1970.
> *Sleepers in Moon-Crowned Valleys·Jeremy's Version.*   1970; *The House of the Solitary Maggot,* 1974.
> *I Am Elijah Thrush.*   1972.

In a Shallow Grave.   1976.
A Day after the Fair (stories and play).   1977.
Narrow Rooms.   1978.

Plays

Mr. Cough Syrup and the Phantom Sex, in *December 8,* 1960.
Cracks (produced 1963).
Children Is All (produced 1965).   In *Children Is All,* 1961.
Wedding Finger, in *New Directions 28,* 1974.

Verse

The Running Sun.   1971.
Sunshine Is an Only Child.   1973.

Bibliography: "Purdy" by George E. Bush, in *Bulletin of Bibliography,* March 1971.

Reading List: *Purdy* by Henry Chupack, 1975; *Purdy* by Stephen D. Adams, 1976.

*   *   *

"We're all alike, inside, and we're all connected."

"You can't run away from yourself. You can run to the ends of the earth, but you'll
be waiting for yourself there."

   James Purdy is a much neglected writer who stands firm against the literary establishment
which, as he has said, rejects his unconventional and often scalding portrayals of American
society: "From the beginning my work has been greeted with a persistent and even
passionate hostility." "The theme of American commercial culture," he adds, is "that man
can be adjusted ... that to be 'in' is to exist. My work is the furthest from this definition of
reality." Despite the difficulties in gaining publication ("Had it not been for Dame Edith
Sitwell, who prevailed upon a British publisher," states Purdy, "I would never have been
published in America and never heard of"), when *Color of Darkness* and, later, *Malcolm*
appeared, Purdy was recognized as a writer of extraordinary imagination, a fantasist who,
while concerned with matters common to the beats and the dramatists of the absurd − the
isolation of youth from peers, parents, and society − brought to his form a unique style.
Purdy combined surrealism with a meticulously rhetoric-free prose. He mixed realism, fairy
tale, and allegory, and created an entirely new form; he transcribed and often poeticized
native American speech within brutal satiric forms; he illustrated the exquisite varieties of
suffering that society imposes upon the innocent, the nonconformist. In *63: Dream Palace,*
Color of Darkness, The Nephew, and, perhaps his best-known work, *Malcolm,* he portrayed
the inevitable and lethal possessiveness within both heterosexual and homosexual love; the
need and yet fear of human companionship; man's failure in his struggle toward identity.
Malcolm, typical of Purdy's orphaned heroes and prototype of all Purdy's men-children
longing to belong and embrace an identity, becomes instead an appendage, an object − to be
used, manipulated, brutalized, and ultimately discarded by the so-called caring people of his
world. In *Children Is All, Cabot Wright Begins,* and *Eustace Chisholm and the Works,* Purdy

remains for his readers frightening – indeed deeply troubling – as he treats in detail taboo subjects like homosexuality, abortion, rape, and incest, within ingenious frames. *Cabot Wright Begins*, which portrays an American automaton who can assert a human identity only through acts of rape, is one of America's most savage and grotesque comedies. Purdy's tone remains defiant. As one of his earliest critics, Warren French, later wrote of *Eustace Chisholm*, in *A Season of Promise*: "I was scarcely prepared for the violently compressed power, the exhausting vehemence, the almost superhuman exorcism of the wanton evil that destroys many innocents that sets Purdy's new effort far apart from the whining and cocktail chatter that often passes for serious fiction."

Jeremy's Version and *The House of the Solitary Maggot*, the first two parts of Purdy's trilogy, *Sleepers in Moon-Crowned Valleys*, combine Purdy's gift for realism with the erotic phantasmagorias of his more elliptical works. Again, scathing humor and caustic wit indict a society and its efforts to neuterize the human spirit. Purdy abandons the symbolic concretizations of the erotic, in order to draw more palpably flesh-and-blood characters, people with whom one identifies more immediately. Somewhat like Faulkner in *The Sound and the Fury*, Purdy here creates in a post-bellum family a parable of fallen America. He portrays in incredible and vivid detail a family whose growth and decline is underscored by excruciating pride and pain, where parents and children (in all combinations) visit upon one another an occasional kindness, but more often a persistent cruelty. Purdy's subject again is, on the one hand, man's struggle for love – specifically in the context of birthright and family – and on the other, the inevitable selfishness, violence, and destruction that are played out in parent (especially the mother) and child in payment for the bonds of incest.

In a Shallow Grave, about a war veteran whose incredibly disfigured body is both the grave from which he must daily survive and the world in which he must submit himself, was described by *The New York Times* reviewer as "a modern Book of Revelation," a gripping, imaginative, "powerful" novel "with prophecies, vision and demonic landscapes."

What has been called Purdy's unremitting bitterness and grotesqueness of vision is ultimately transcended by an exquisite poetic prose, and by the author's deep feeling for mankind. Purdy's style, based upon, as he has said, "the rhythms and accents of American speech," has about it, as the review just cited noted, "briers in his voice, as if he meant to tear at his readers with a kind of harsh music … [a] deliberate scratching of the reader's ear" enabling the author "to mix evil and naiveté without spilling over into melodrama and tedious morality plays." Remarkable, in addition, is Purdy's richly textured, compressed, seemingly simple and direct prose which weaves together level upon level of symbol – often from nature (especially birds, flowers, animals, and light and dark), as well as from classical and biblical sources.

Finally, one is left with the author's profound compassion towards people. One may often feel anger, horror, and even repulsion towards Purdy's sadistic, licentious, and greedy people, but at the same time, one is haunted and overwhelmed by their loneliness and innocence. Purdy touches his readers on the deepest level, as he portrays, in every thing he writes, man's courage, dignity, and ultimate victory in the act of mere survival.

—Lois Gordon

PYNCHON, Thomas.   American.   Born in Glen Cove, New York, 8 May 1937. Educated at Cornell University, Ithaca, New York, 1954–58, B.A. 1958. Served in the United States Navy. Worked as an editorial writer for the Boeing Aircraft Corporation, Seattle, Washington; now a full-time writer. Recipient: Faulkner Award, 1964; Rosenthal Memorial Award, 1967; National Book Award, 1974; Howells Medal (refused), 1975.

PUBLICATIONS

Fiction

V.   1963.
The Crying of Lot 49.   1966.
Gravity's Rainbow.   1973.
Mortality and Mercy in Vienna (story).   1976.

Bibliography: *Three Contemporary Novelists: An Annotated Bibliography* by Robert M. Scotto, 1977.

Reading List: *Mindful Pleasures: Essays on Pynchon* edited by George Levine and David Leverenz, 1976; *The Grim Phoenix: Reconstructing Pynchon* by William M. Plater, 1978.

*   *   *

Thomas Pynchon's novels *V.*, *The Crying of Lot 49*, and *Gravity's Rainbow* have in common qualities that attract some readers and repel others. Both companies of readers are, however, likely to agree on what it is that they respond to in the work of Pynchon. It is an unremitting brilliance of invention, accompanied by a wide range of knowledge. The knowledge embraces the major course of European history over the past century, and it often deviates into nooks and crannies of the entire course of Western experience. In this respect, Pynchon has a novelist's plenty that makes him the peer of John Barth, William Gaddis, and others of his time. The consequence is that one has the sense of reading not only a novel but of progressing through pages from the *Britannica*, torn out at random.

The phrase "at random" is not entirely just. The assorted slices of erudition – scientific as well as cultural – are linked with Pynchon's often mad narrative sequences in ways that lead a reader to think, at a certain turn of a Pynchon novel, that he has come to the beating heart of the narrative. For throughout the tales are scattered clues that seem to lead from the witch's house of a particular novel – a place of confinement à la Hansel and Gretel – back to comprehension and mastery. But the clues to meaning – to the intent and often the animus of the novels – are scattered so generously that each reader is likely to follow a solitary path from the witch's hut (the novel as experienced) to some safe edge of a forest (the act of personal judgment).

Yet certain judgments are not wholly solitary. Each novel has a strand of interest that threads through scenes of great comic and satiric effect. There is, in *V.*, a decades-long pursuit of a mysterious being; one can hardly call this being a woman since her eyes are glass, her dentures precious metal, and her feet detachable. And there is, in *The Crying of Lot 49*, the effort of Mrs. Oedipa Maas to discover whether an ancient European secret society for distributing mail is still alive and functioning in today's California. In *Gravity's Rainbow* events in England and Germany during the closing years of World War II are concerned with English efforts to frustrate buzz bombs and other missiles and with German efforts to launch those missiles. (A young American named Slothrop has a sexual activity that seems linked with the arrival of the bombs. But this is only a small part of a variegated story.)

Such strands are obviously purloined from popular and facile tales of intrigue. In Pynchon's novels the strands become enmeshed in displays of language brilliance and events both grotesque and, if one has missed a clue or so, gratuitous. The clues – if that is what certain passages come to – sometimes do point to the identity of V., or the workings of the society that competes with the public mail systems of the world in *The Crying of Lot 49*, or that crisis of world order in *Gravity's Rainbow*. At other times, the clues are – or seem to be – self-subsistent rather than centers about which one can gather the motley contents of a novel.

V., for example, ranges from the 1910's to about 1956. European-based characters are touched by V. and "her" progress from being a human person to an assemblage of inanimate elements wondrously animated. In contrast, the American characters are known only in an immediate present; this is "The Crew," a collection of people united by their drinking and whoring and also by an uneasy but quite intermittent questioning of all they do. What is the relation between these two strands? Is the V. experience an account of the decadence that reached its terminus in Pynchon's boozy crew of young "Nueva Yorkers"? Similarly, is the Trystero group that Oedipa Maas pursues, come weal come woe, one that allures the heroine because it speaks, unclearly, of firm purpose asserting itself in a world where there is none? And is the action of the German rocket chief in *Gravity's Rainbow* – the launching of the body of his young lover inside one of the last rockets – a scream of despair for civilization or just one more comic incident among many such?

Pynchon, satiric and ironic at most times, moralistic in rare but intense passages, creates textures of narrative that distort – but do not much misrepresent – the society they mirror. Back and forth over this texture Pynchon's mind darts. It sometimes expresses an intellect that is disembodied and uninvolved. At other times, there is acknowledgement of a link between the novelist and what he sets down. But such a link is no sooner noted than it is severed.

—Harold H. Watts

QUEEN, Ellery.   Pseudonym for the cousins Frederic Dannay and Manfred B. Lee; also used the pseudonym Barnaby Ross.   Americans.   **DANNAY, Frederic**: born in Brooklyn, New York, 20 October 1905. Educated at Boys' High School, Brooklyn. Married 1) Mary Beck in 1926 (died), two sons; 2) Hilda Wisenthal in 1947 (died, 1972), one son; 3) Rose Koppel in 1976. Writer and art director for a New York advertising agency prior to 1931; full-time writer, with Manfred B. Lee, 1931–71, and on his own from 1971. Visiting Professor, University of Texas, Austin, 1958–59. Lives in Larchmont, New York.   **LEE, Manfred B.**: born in Brooklyn, New York, 11 January 1905. Educated at New York University. Married Catherine Brinker in 1942; four daughters and four sons. Publicity writer in New York for film companies prior to 1931; full-time writer, with Frederic Dannay, 1931 until his death. Justice of the Peace, Roxbury, Connecticut, 1957–58. *Died 3 April 1971.* Dannay and Lee edited *Mystery League* magazine, 1933–34, and *Ellery Queen's Mystery Magazine*, from 1941; they wrote the "Adventures of Ellery Queen" radio series, 1939–48; they were co-founders and co-presidents of Mystery Writers of America, and received Mystery Writers of America awards in 1945, 1947, 1949, Special Book Award, 1951, and Grand Master Award, 1961.

PUBLICATIONS

Fiction

The Roman Hat Mystery.   1929.
The French Powder Mystery.   1930.
The Dutch Shoe Mystery.   1931.

The Egyptian Cross Mystery. 1932.
The Greek Coffin Mystery. 1932.
The Tragedy of X: A Drury Lane Mystery. 1932.
The Tragedy of Y: A Drury Lane Mystery. 1932.
The Tragedy of Z: A Drury Lane Mystery. 1933.
Drury Lane's Last Case: The Tragedy of 1599. 1933.
The Siamese Twin Mystery. 1933.
The American Gun Mystery: Death at the Rodeo. 1933.
The Chinese Orange Mystery. 1934.
The Adventures of Ellery Queen (stories). 1934.
The Spanish Cape Mystery. 1935.
Halfway House. 1936.
The Door Between. 1937.
The Four of Hearts. 1938.
The Devil to Pay. 1938.
The Dragon's Teeth. 1939; as *The Virgin Heiresses,* 1954.
The New Adventures of Ellery Queen (stories). 1940.
Calamity Town. 1942.
There Was an Old Woman. 1943; as *The Quick and the Dead,* 1956.
The Case Book of Ellery Queen. 1945.
The Murderer Is a Fox. 1945.
Ten Days' Wonder. 1948.
Cat of Many Tails. 1949.
Double Double: A New Novel of Wrightsville. 1950; as *The Case of the Seven Murderers,* 1958.
The Origin of Evil. 1951.
Calendar of Crime (stories). 1952.
The King Is Dead. 1952.
The Scarlet Letters. 1953.
The Golden Summer (by Dannay). 1953.
The Glass Village. 1954.
Q.B.I.: Queen's Bureau of Investigation. 1955.
Inspector Queen's Own Case: November Song. 1956.
The Finishing Stroke. 1958.
The Player on the Other Side. 1963.
And on the Eighth Day. 1964.
The Fourth Side of the Triangle. 1965.
Queens Full (stories). 1965.
A Study in Terror. 1966; as *Sherlock Holmes Versus Jack the Ripper,* 1967.
Face to Face. 1967.
The House of Brass. 1968.
Cop Out. 1969.
The Last Woman in His Life. 1970.
A Fine and Private Place. 1971.

Play

Screenplay (by Lee): *Closed Gates,* with Frances Guihan, 1927.

Other

The Detective Short Story: A Bibliography. 1942; revised edition, 1969.

Queen's Quorum: A History of the Detective-Crime Short Story as Revealed by the 100 Most Important Books Published in the Field since 1845.   1951; revised edition, 1969. *In the Queens' Parlor and Other Leaves from the Editors' Notebook.*   1957.

Editor, *Challenge to the Reader: An Anthology.*   1938.
Editor, *101 Years' Entertainment: The Great Detective Stories 1841–1941.*   1941.
Editor, *Sporting Blood: The Great Sports Detective Stories.*   1942; as *Sporting Detective Stories,* 1946.
Editor, *The Female of the Species: The Great Women Detectives and Criminals.*   1943; as *Ladies in Crime,* 1947.
Editor, *The Misadventures of Sherlock Holmes.*   1944.
Editor, *Best Stories from Ellery Queen's Mystery Magazine.*   1944.
Editor, *Rogues' Gallery: The Great Criminals of Modern Fiction.*   1945.
Editor, *To the Queen's Taste.*   1946.
Editor, *The Queen's Awards,* later *Mystery Annuals* and *Anthologies* (from *Ellery Queen's Mystery Magazine*).   29 vols., 1946–75.
Editor, *Murder by Experts.*   1947.
Editor, *20th Century Detective Stories.*   1948.
Editor, *The Literature of Crime: Stories by World-Famous Authors.*   1950.
Editor, *International Case Book.*   1964.
Editor, *The Woman in the Case.*   1966; as *Deadlier Than the Male,* 1967.
Editor, *Poetic Justice: 23 Stories of Crime, Mystery, and Detection by World-Famous Poets.*   1967.
Editor, *Minimysteries: 70 Short-Short Stories of Crime, Mystery, and Detection.*   1969.
Editor, *Japanese Golden Dozen: The Detective Story World in Japan.*   1978.

Also compiled volumes of stories by Dashiell Hammett and others, and other anthologies.

Reading List: *Royal Bloodline: Ellery Queen* by Francis M. Nevins, Jr., 1974 (includes bibliography).

*   *   *

Ellery Queen is both the pseudonym and the detective creation of two Brooklyn-born first cousins, Frederic Dannay and Manfred B. Lee. At the time they created Ellery Queen, Dannay was a copywriter and art director for a Manhattan advertising agency and Lee a publicity writer for the New York office of a film studio. The announcement of a $7500 prize contest for a detective novel catalyzed the cousins into literary action in 1928, and Ellery's first adventure was published the following year. Dannay's experience in advertising may have inspired the innovation of using the same name for the cousins' deductive protagonist and for their own joint byline – a device that, along with the excellence of the books themselves, turned Ellery Queen into a household name and his creators into wealthy men.

In the late 1920's the dominant figure in American detective fiction was S. S. Van Dine (Willard Huntington Wright), an erudite art critic whose novels about the impossibly intellectual aesthete-sleuth Philo Vance were consistent best-sellers. The early Ellery Queen novels, with their patterned titles and their scholarly dilettante detective forever dropping classical quotations, were heavily influenced by Van Dine, though superior in plotting, characterization, and style. Ellery is a professional mystery writer and amateur sleuth who assists his father, Inspector Richard Queen, whenever a murder puzzle becomes too complex for ordinary police methods. His first-period cases, from *The Roman Hat Mystery* (1929) through *The Spanish Cape Mystery* (1935), are richly plotted specimens of the Golden Age deductive puzzle at its zenith, full of bizarre circumstances, conflicting testimony, enigmatic clues, alternative solutions, fireworks displays of virtuoso reasoning, and a constant crackle of intellectual excitement. All the facts are presented, trickily but fairly, and the reader is formally challenged to solve the puzzle ahead of Ellery. Most of Queen's distinctive story motifs – the negative clue, the dying message, the murderer as Iagoesque manipulator, the patterned series of clues deliberately left at scenes of crimes, the false answer followed by the true and devastating solution – originated in these early novels. Perhaps the best works of the first period are *The Greek Coffin Mystery* and *The Egyptian Cross Mystery*, which both appeared in 1932, the same year in which, under the second pseudonym of Barnaby Ross, Dannay and Lee published the first and best two novels in the tetralogy dealing with actor-detective Drury Lane: *The Tragedy of X* and *The Tragedy of Y*.

By 1936 the Van Dine touches had left Queen's work and been replaced by the influence of the slick-paper magazines and the movies, to both of which the cousins had begun to sell. In second-period Queen the patterned titles vanish and Ellery gradually becomes less priggish and more human. In several stories of the period he is seen working as a Hollywood screenwriter, reflecting the cousins' brief stints at Columbia, Paramount, and MGM. Most of Queen's work in the late 1930's is thinly plotted, overburdened with "love interest," and too obviously written with film sales in mind, but the best book of the period, *The Four of Hearts*, is an excellent detective story as well as a many-faceted evocation of Hollywood in its peak years.

At the start of the new decade most of the cousins' energies went into writing a script a week for the long-running *Adventures of Ellery Queen* radio series (1939–48) and accumulating a vast library of detective short stories. Out of this collection came Queen's *101 Years' Entertainment*, the foremost anthology of the genre, and *Ellery Queen's Mystery Magazine*, which throughout its life from 1941 till today has been edited solely by Dannay. In 1942 the cousins returned to fiction with the superbly written and characterized *Calamity Town*, a semi-naturalistic detective novel in which Ellery solves a murder in the "typical small town" of Wrightsville, U.S.A. Their third and richest period as mystery writers lasted sixteen years and embraced twelve novels, two short story collections and Dannay's autobiographical novel *The Golden Summer* (1953), published as by Daniel Nathan. In third-period Queen the complex deductive puzzle is fused with in-depth character studies, magnificently detailed evocations of place and mood, occasional ventures into a topsy-turvy Alice in Wonderland otherworld reflecting Dannay's interest in Lewis Carroll, and explorations into historical, psychiatric, and religious dimensions. The best novels of this period are *Calamity Town* itself; *Ten Days' Wonder*, with its phantasmagoria of biblical symbolism; *Cat of Many Tails*, with its unforgettable images of New York City menaced by a heat wave, a mad strangler of what seem to be randomly chosen victims, and the threat of World War III; and *The Origin of Evil*, in which Darwinian motifs underlie the clues and deductions. Finally, in *The Finishing Stroke*, the cousins nostalgically recreated Ellery's young manhood in 1929, just after the publication of "his" first detective novel, *The Roman Hat Mystery*.

"In my end is my beginning," says Eliot; and the cousins apparently meant to retire as active writers after *The Finishing Stroke*. Five years later, however, they launched a fourth and final group of Ellery Queen novels, from *The Player on the Other Side* (1963), the best book of the period, to *A Fine and Private Place* (1971), published almost simultaneously with Manfred Lee's death of a heart attack. The novels and short stories of period four retreat from all semblance of naturalistic plausibility and rely on what Dannay has called "fun and games" – heavily stylized plots and characterizations and the repetition of dozens of motifs from the earlier periods.

No new novels have appeared since Lee's death and none is likely in the future, although Dannay remains active and perceptive as ever in his capacity as editor of the *Mystery Magazine*. But the reputation of Ellery Queen, author and detective, has long been assured. Of all America's mystery writers Queen is the supreme practitioner of that noble but now dying genre, the classic formal detective story.

—Francis M. Nevins, Jr.

RANSOM, John Crowe. American. Born in Pulaski, Tennessee, 30 April 1888. Educated at Vanderbilt University, Nashville, Tennessee, B.A. 1909 (Phi Beta Kappa); Christ Church, Oxford (Rhodes Scholar), 1910–13, B.A. 1913. Served in the United States Army, 1917–19. Married Robb Reavill in 1920; three children. Assistant in English, Harvard University, Cambridge, Massachusetts, 1914; Member of the Faculty, 1914–27, and Professor of English, 1927–37, Vanderbilt University; Carnegie Professor of Poetry, 1937–58, and Professor Emeritus, 1959–74, Kenyon College, Gambier, Ohio. Visiting Lecturer in English, Chattanooga University, Tennessee, 1938; Visiting Lecturer in Language and Criticism, University of Texas, Austin, 1956. Member of the Fugitive Group of Poets; Founding Editor, with Allen Tate, *The Fugitive*, Nashville, 1922–25; Editor, *Kenyon Review*, Gambier, Ohio, 1937–59. Formerly, Honorary Consultant in American Letters, Library of Congress, Washington, D.C. Recipient: Guggenheim Fellowship, 1931; Bollingen Prize, 1951; Russell Loines Award, 1951; Brandeis University Creative Arts Award, 1958; Academy of American Poets Fellowship, 1962; National Book Award, 1964; National Endowment for the Arts award, 1966; Emerson-Thoreau Medal, 1968; National Institute of Arts and Letters Gold Medal, 1973. Member, American Academy of Arts and Letters, and American Academy of Arts and Sciences. *Died 3 July 1974.*

PUBLICATIONS

Verse

Poems about God. 1919.
Armageddon, with *A Fragment* by William Alexander Percy and *Avalon* by Donald Davidson. 1923.
Chills and Fever. 1924.
Grace after Meat. 1924.
Two Gentlemen in Bonds. 1927.
Selected Poems. 1945; revised edition, 1963, 1969.

Other

God Without Thunder: An Unorthodox Defense of Orthodoxy. 1930.
Shall We Complete the Trade? A Proposal for the Settlement of Foreign Debts to the United States. 1933.

The World's Body.   1938; revised edition, 1968.
The New Criticism.   1941.
A College Primer of Writing.   1943.
Poems and Essays.   1955.
Beating the Bushes: Selected Essays 1941–1970.   1972.

Editor, *Topics for Freshman Writing: Twenty Topics for Writing, with Appropriate Material for Study.*   1935.
Editor, *The Kenyon Critics: Studies in Modern Literature from the "Kenyon Review."*   1951.
Editor, *Selected Poems,* by Thomas Hardy.   1961.

Bibliography: "Ransom: A Checklist, 1967–76" by T. D. Young, in *Mississippi Quarterly 30,* 1976–77.

Reading List: *Ransom* by John L. Stewart, 1962; *The Poetry of Ransom: A Study of Diction, Metaphor, and Symbol* by Karl F. Knight, 1964; *The Equilibrist: A Study of Ransom's Poems 1916–1963* by Robert Buffington, 1967; *Ransom: Critical Essays and a Bibliography* edited by T. D. Young, 1968, and *Gentleman in a Dustcoat: A Biography of Ransom* by Young, 1976; *Ransom* by Thornton H. Parsons, 1969; *Ransom: Critical Principles and Preoccupations* by James E. Morgan, 1971; *The Poetry of Ransom* by Miller Williams, 1972.

*   *   *

As poet, teacher, critic, and editor, John Crowe Ransom was one of the most influential men of his generation. Although scholars and critics have agreed that Ransom commands an eminent position, they have disagreed on the precise nature of his contribution. The priorities Ransom established for his literary career displeased some of his friends. He was, as Allen Tate once said, "one of the great elegiac poets of the English language," who produced ten or twelve almost perfect lyrics which will be read as long as poetry is regarded as a serious art. Yet the major portion of his creative energies were devoted to the writing of poetry only for a very brief period. During the remainder of a long and active literary career, much of his thought and most of his effort were expended on speculations on the nature and function of poetic discourse; on the significance of religious myth, the need for an inscrutable God; and on discussions of the proper relations that should exist between man, God, and nature.

Most of the poetry for which Ransom will be remembered was written between 1922 and 1925 and published in *Chills and Fever* and *Two Gentlemen in Bonds.* During the winter of 1922 Ransom read at one of the Fugitive meetings his poem "Necrological," which convinced Allen Tate that almost "overnight he had left behind him the style of his first book *[Poems about God]* and, without confusion, had mastered a new style." All of his best poems are written in this "new style," what critics have come to refer to as his "mature manner": the subtle irony, the nuanced ambiguities, the wit, and the cool detached tone. In these poems Ransom uses a simple little narrative as a means of presenting the "common actuals"; an innocent character is involved in a common situation and through this involvement he comes to have a fuller understanding of his own nature. Few poets of his generation have been able to represent with greater accuracy and precision the inexhaustible ambiguities, the paradoxes and tensions, the dichotomies and ironies that make up the life of modern man. His poetry reiterates a few themes: man's dual nature and the inevitable misery and disaster that accompany the failure to recognize and accept this basic truth; mortality and the fleetingness of youthful vigor and grace, the inevitable decay of feminine beauty; the disparity between the world as man would have it and as it actually is, between what people want and need emotionally and what is available for them, between what man desires and what he can get; the necessity of man's simultaneous apprehension of nature's indifference and mystery and his appreciation of her sensory beauties; the inability of modern man, in his incomplete and fragmentary state, to experience love.

Throughout his career Ransom maintained that human experience can be fully realized only through art. In many of his critical essays – some of which are collected in *The World's Body*, *The New Criticism*, and *Beating the Bushes* – Ransom tries to define the unique nature of poetic discourse, which functions to "induce the mode of thought that is imaginative rather than logical," to recover "the denser and more refractory original world which we know loosely through our perceptions and memories." That which we may learn from poetry is "ontologically distinct" because it is the "kind of knowledge by which we must know what we have arranged that we cannot know otherwise." Only through poetry, which is composed of a "loose logical structure with a good deal of local texture," can man recover the "body and solid substance of the world." The basic kind of data which science can collect reduces the "world to a scheme of abstract conveniences." Whereas science is interesting only in *knowing*, art has a double function; it wants both to *know* and to *make*.

In many of his later essays Ransom attempts to demonstrate how the critic should react in his efforts to define the nature of poetic discourse and to justify its existence in a society becoming more and more enamored of the quasi-knowledge and the false promises of science. In essay after essay he insists that the truths that poetry contains can be obtained only through a detailed analytical study of the poems themselves, and he repeats one theme: without poetry man's knowledge of himself and his world is fragmentary and incomplete.

—T. D. Young

RAWLINGS, Marjorie Kinnan.   American.   Born in Washington, D.C., 8 August 1896. Educated at Western High School, Washington, D.C.; University of Wisconsin, Madison, B.A. 1918 (Phi Beta Kappa). Married 1) Charles Rawlings in 1919 (divorced, 1933); 2) Norton Sanford Baskin in 1941. Editor, YWCA National Board, New York, 1918–19; Assistant Service Editor, *Home Sector* magazine, 1919; staff member, *Louisville Courier Journal*, Kentucky, and *Rochester Journal*, New York, 1920–28; syndicated verse writer ("Songs of a Housewife"), United Features, 1926–28; lived in Florida from 1928; thereafter a full-time writer. Recipient: O. Henry Award, 1933; Pulitzer Prize, 1939. LL.D.: Rollins College, Winter Park, Florida, 1939; L.H.D.: University of Florida, Gainesville, 1941. Member, National Institute of Arts and Letters, 1939. *Died 14 December 1953.*

PUBLICATIONS

Collections

The Rawlings Reader, edited by Julia Scribner Bigham.   1956.

Fiction

> *South Moon Under.*   1933.
> *Golden Apples.*   1935.
> *The Yearling.*   1938.
> *When the Whippoorwill* – (stories).   1940.
> *Jacob's Ladder.*   1950.
> *The Sojourner.*   1953.

Other

> *Cross Creek.*   1942.
> *Cross Creek Cookery.*   1942; as *The Rawlings Cookbook*, 1960.
> *The Secret River* (juvenile).   1955.

Reading List: *Frontier Eden: The Literary Career of Rawlings* by Gordon E. Bigelow, 1972; *Rawlings* by Samuel I. Bellman, 1974.

*   *   *

Marjorie Kinnan Rawlings is a regional writer. Her work is inhabited by the simple people and natural settings of the Florida backwoods which she adopted as her home. Often paramount in her novels is the struggle against the vicissitudes of an uncertain existence by the poor white – the Florida cracker – commonly epitomized in an archetypical young protagonist with frontier virtues. These patterns are evident in her first four novels and in much of her short fiction.

South Moon Under depicts the difficulties of a hunter scratching out a living as a moonshiner in the Florida scrub country. The novel combines vividly descriptive scenes of rural existence with strong characterizations and an eventful plot. *Golden Apples* recounts the efforts of an orphaned and impoverished brother and sister to survive in late 19th-century northern Florida. They "squat" on the estate of an exiled and embittered young Englishman whom they patiently regenerate. The resourceful protagonist is a more convincing figure than the vaguely sketched Englishman in this flawed but dramatically forceful novel. In the novella *Jacob's Ladder* a rootless and destitute young cracker couple encounter adversities in luckless attempts to wrest a living from a bounteous but treacherous environment. The pair's deep mutual reliance and indomitable spirit are a poignant and emotionally powerful testament.

The author's internationally acclaimed novel *The Yearling* represents her finest achievement. The hero is 12-year-old Jody Baxter who lives with his parents in the Florida hammock country of the 1870's. As his family undergoes severe economic setbacks, Jody tames a fawn which becomes his forest-roaming companion. When, however, his pet cannot be restrained from eating the precious crops, it must be killed. The anguished boy feels betrayed by his father and severs their close relationship. Eventually they are reconciled. Tragedy has made a man of him. Throughout the story weave such themes as man's need to belong to the land which, in turn, belongs to those who lovingly cultivate it, and the inevitability of unfair and unexpected betrayal by man and nature. Rawlings's compellingly truthful portrait of a boy and his tender relationships is universally appealing. Her striking description of nature's elemental forces and the simple but significant events in the lives of people close to the land enrich an absorbingly ingenuous story. This distinguished novel stands as a classic of both adult and children's literature.

When the Whippoorwill –, a collection of the author's major short fiction, is highlighted by three richly amusing cracker comedies often told in the vernacular ("Benny and the Bird

Dogs," "Cocks Must Crow," and "Varmints"), and also contains a serious portrayal of a wife exploited by a shiftless backwoods bootlegger ("Gal Young 'Un") as well as the novella "Jacob's Ladder." While the remaining stories are undistinguished, the overall collection displays the hand of an able story-teller. *The Sojourner*, an ambitious but imperfect novel, is a wooden family-chronicle centering on a Job-like farmer toiling on a New York state farm owned by an unloving mother reserving her affection for his wandering elder brother. Missed are the Florida locales of her earlier fiction, also detailed with verve and warmth in the autobiographical *Cross Creek*.

Marjorie Kinnan Rawlings is a pastoral writer of percipience and power whose blaze on the tree of American regional literature has been cut deep enough to last.

—Christian H. Moe

REXROTH, Kenneth. American. Born in South Bend, Indiana, 22 December 1905; moved to Chicago, 1917. Educated at the Art Institute, Chicago; New School for Social Research, New York; Art Students' League, New York. Conscientious objector during World War II. Married 1) Andree Dutcher in 1927 (died, 1940); 2) Marie Kass in 1940 (divorced, 1948); 3) Marthe Larsen in 1949 (divorced, 1961), two children; 4) Carol Tinker in 1974. Past occupations include farm worker, factory hand, and insane asylum attendant. Painter: one-man shows in Los Angeles, New York, Chicago, San Francisco, and Paris. Columnist, *San Francisco Examiner*, 1958–68. Since 1953, San Francisco Correspondent for *The Nation*, New York; since 1968, Columnist for *San Francisco Magazine* and the *San Francisco Bay Guardian*, and Lecturer, University of California at Santa Barbara. Co-Founder, San Francisco Poetry Center. Recipient: Guggenheim Fellowship, 1948; Shelley Memorial Award, 1958; Amy Lowell Fellowship, 1958; National Institute of Arts and Letters grant, 1964; Fulbright Senior Fellowship, 1974; Academy of American Poets Copernicus Award, 1975. Member, National Institute of Arts and Letters. Lives in Santa Barbara, California.

PUBLICATIONS

Verse

In What Hour. 1941.
The Phoenix and the Tortoise. 1944.
The Art of Wordly Wisdom. 1949.
The Signature of All Things: Poems, Songs, Elegies, Translations, and Epigrams. 1950.
The Dragon and the Unicorn. 1952.
In Defence of the Earth. 1956.
The Homestead Called Damascus. 1963.
Natural Numbers: New and Selected Poems. 1963.
The Complete Collected Shorter Poems. 1967.

The Collected Longer Poems. 1968.
The Heart's Garden, The Garden's Heart. 1967.
The Spark in the Tinder of Knowing. 1968.
Sky Sea Birds Trees Earth House Beasts Flowers. 1970.
New Poems. 1974.

Plays

Beyond the Mountains (includes *Phaedra, Iphigenia, Hermaios, Berenike*) (produced 1951). 1951.

Other

Bird in the Bush: Obvious Essays. 1959.
Assays (essays). 1961.
An Autobiographical Novel. 1966.
Classics Revisited. 1968.
The Alternative Society: Essays from the Other World. 1970.
With Eye and Ear (literary criticism). 1970.
American Poetry in the Twentieth Century. 1971.
The Rexroth Reader, edited by Eric Mottram. 1972.
The Elastic Retort: Essays in Literature and Ideas. 1973.
Communalism: From Its Origins to the 20th Century. 1975.

Editor, *Selected Poems,* by D. H. Lawrence. 1948.
Editor, *The New British Poets: An Anthology.* 1949.
Editor, *Four Young Women: Poems.* 1973.
Editor, *Tens: Selected Poems 1961–1971,* by David Meltzer. 1973.
Editor, *The Selected Poems of Czeslav Milosz.* 1973.
Editor, *Seasons of Sacred Lust,* by Kazuko Shiraishi. 1978.

Translator, *Fourteen Poems,* by O. V. de L.-Milosz. 1952.
Translator, *100 Poems from the Japanese.* 1955.
Translator, *100 Poems from the Chinese.* 1956.
Translator, *30 Spanish Poems of Love and Exile.* 1956.
Translator, *100 Poems from the Greek and Latin.* 1962.
Translator, *Poems from the Greek Anthology.* 1962.
Translator, *Selected Poems,* by Pierre Reverdy. 1969.
Translator, *Love and the Turning Earth: 100 More Classical Poems.* 1970.
Translator, *Love and the Turning Year: 100 More Chinese Poems.* 1970.
Translator, *100 Poems from the French.* 1970.
Translator, with Ling O. Chung, *The Orchid Boat: Women Poets of China.* 1972.
Translator, *100 More Poems from the Japanese.* 1976.

Readling List: *Rexroth* by Morgan Gibson, 1972.

*   *   *

Kenneth Rexroth is a man of letters in the tradition of Robert Graves, W. H. Auden, and Edmund Wilson, although he has chiefly been a consolidator and synthesizer of others' ideas; this is true of his verse as well as of his many polemical essays on American culture.

Rexroth came to literature with an amazing intelligence, so wide and retentive of the bewildering cross currents of thought in the twentieth century that his writings capture the essence of each decade in the broad span of his works, which cover the play *Beyond the Mountains*; *An Autobiographical Novel*; translations, encompassing poems in Japanese, Chinese, French, Greek, and Spanish; criticism; and his own vast collections of poetry. Without pedantry or empty imitation, Rexroth has tapped the spirit of each of the major figures that emerged in his lifetime and illuminated it in his own boldly assertive style. An early interest in Asian poetry followed from Pound, whom Rexroth praised and criticized in his critical study, *American Poetry in the Twentieth Century*.

Rexroth's longer poems resemble the casual, narrative style of Auden, although comparisons should not be taken too far. In his polemic essays, his style and approach to the basic issues of American culture, industrial economy, depersonality in the mass population, and commerciality, are reminiscent of the early essays of Edmund Wilson, Paul Goodman, and Edward Dahlberg. Rexroth's poems on nature anticipated by many years the accurate, sensitive naturalist poems of Gary Snyder, who has in turn influenced Rexroth in his most recent work.

It is therefore difficult to isolate Rexroth from the stream of literature and ideas in which he has fashioned his work. But an essential Rexroth is perceptible in his elegant love poems and landscape meditations, gathered in *The Collected Shorter Poems*. These reveries and amorous lyrics present an unguarded, visionary persona unlike any in American poetry, as in "Camargue":

> Green moon blaze
> Over violet dancers
> Shadow heads catch fire
> Forget forget
> Forget awake aware dropping in the well
> Where the nightingale sings
> In the blooming pomegranate
> You beside me
> Like a colt swimming slowly in kelp
> In the nude sea
> Where ten thousand birds
> Move like a waved scarf
> On the long surge of sleep

The shorter poetry is brief, lyrical, touching on love, travels, occasionally social comment. The strain of the didactic is strong in Rexroth's work, especially in the long travelogue poem, *The Dragon and the Unicorn*.

Rexroth's polemical criticism of American literature and idealogy is contained in a number of volumes, *With Eye and Ear*, *The Alternative Society*, *Communalism*, and *American Poetry in the Twentieth Century*, where he is intensely perceptive and iconoclastic. In the last, he argues persuasively that American poetry should be traced not from Europe but from Native Indian cultures. As a figure central to most of the major phases of American writing throughout the century, Rexroth is a watershed of literary ideas and principles, and a writer who has communicated a stubborn, wilful intellect in a century of increasing squeamishness and doubt.

—Paul Christensen

RICE, Elmer. American. Born Elmer Leopold Reizenstein in New York City, 28 September 1892. Educated at a high school in New York; studied law in night school, LL.B. (cum laude), New York Law School, 1912; admitted to the New York Bar, 1913, but never practiced. Married 1) Hazel Levy in 1915 (divorced, 1942), one son and one daughter; 2) the actress Betty Field in 1942 (divorced, 1956), two sons and one daughter; 3) Barbara A. Marshall in 1966. Claims Clerk, Samstag and Hilder Brothers, New York 1907; Law Clerk, 1908–12; began writing and producing for the theatre, 1914, as Dramatic Director, University Settlement, and Chairman, Inter-Settlement Dramatic Society, New York; Scenarist, Samuel Goldwyn Pictures Corporation, Hollywood, 1918–20; freelance writer for Famous Players, the Lasky Corporation, and Real Art Films, Hollywood, 1920; returned to New York and organized the Morningside Players, with Hatcher Hughes; purchased and operated the Belasco Theatre, New York, 1934–37; Regional Director, Works Progress Administration Federal Theatre Project, New York, 1935–36; Founder, with Robert E. Sherwood, Maxwell Anderson, S. N. Behrman, Sidney Howard, and John F. Wharton, Playwrights Company, 1938; Lecturer in English, University of Michigan, Ann Arbor, 1954; Adjunct Professor of English, New York University, 1957–58. President, Dramatists Guild, 1939–43; President, Author's League of America, 1945–46; International Vice-President, and Vice-President of the New York Center, P.E.N., 1945–46. Recipient: Pulitzer Prize, 1929. Litt.D.: University of Michigan, 1961. Member, National Institute of Arts and Letters. *Died 8 May 1967.*

PUBLICATIONS

Plays

On Trial (produced 1914). 1919.
The Iron Cross (produced 1917). 1965.
The Home of the Free (produced 1917). 1934.
For the Defense (produced 1919).
Wake Up, Jonathan, with Hatcher Hughes (produced 1921). 1928.
It Is the Law, from a novel by Hayden Talbot (produced 1922).
The Adding Machine (produced 1923). 1923.
The Mongrel, from a play by Hermann Bahr (produced 1924).
Close Harmony; or, The Lady Next Door, with Dorothy Parker (produced 1924). 1929.
The Blue Hawaii, from a play by Rudolph Lothar (produced 1927).
Cock Robin, with Philip Barry (produced 1928). 1929.
Street Scene (produced 1929). 1929; revised version, music by Kurt Weill, lyrics by
    Langston Hughes (produced 1947). 1948.
The Subway (produced 1929). 1929.
A Diadem of Snow, in One-Act Plays for Stage and Study 5. 1929.
See Naples and Die (produced 1929). 1930.
The Left Bank (produced 1931). 1931.
Counsellor-at-Law (produced 1931). 1931.
The House in Blind Alley. 1932.
Blacksheep (produced 1932). 1938.
We, The People (produced 1933). 1933.
The Gay White Way, in One-Act Plays for Stage and Study 8. 1934.
Judgment Day (produced 1934). 1934.
The Passing of Chow-Chow (produced 1934). 1934.
Three Plays Without Words (includes Landscape with Figures, Rus in Urbe,
    Exterior). 1934.

Between Two Worlds (produced 1934).   In *Two Plays*, 1935.
Two Plays: Not for Children, and Between Two Worlds.   1935.
Not for Children (as *Life Is Real*, produced 1937; revised version, as *Not for Children*,
   produced 1951).   In *Two Plays*, 1935.
American Language (produced 1938).   1939.
Two on an Island (produced 1940).   1940.
Flight to the West (produced 1940).   1941.
A New Life (produced 1943).   1944.
Dream Girl (produced 1945).   1946.
The Grand Tour (produced 1951).   1952.
The Winner (produced 1954).   1954.
Cue for Passion (produced 1958).   1959.
Love among the Ruins (produced 1963).   1963.

Screenplays: *Help Yourself*, with others, 1920; *Rent Free*, with Izola Forrester and
Mann Page, 1922; *Doubling for Romeo*, with Bernard McConville, 1922; *Street Scene*,
1931; *Counsellor-at-Law*, 1933; *Holiday Inn*, with Claude Binyon and Irving Berlin,
1942.

Fiction

A Voyage to Purilia.   1930.
Imperial City.   1937.
The Show Must Go On.   1949.

Other

The Supreme Freedom.   1949.
The Living Theatre.   1959.
Minority Report: An Autobiography.   1963.

Bibliography: "Rice: A Bibliography" by Robert Hogan, in *Modern Drama*, February 1966.

Reading List: *The Independence of Rice* by Robert Hogan, 1965; *Rice* by Frank Durham,
1970.

*   *   *

Elmer Rice was one of the most prolific and technically proficient of modern American
dramatists, as well as, in many of his plays, an eclectic experimenter and an outspoken social
spokesman. Although he graduated from law school *cum laude* and was admitted to the New
York Bar, he gave up law to write plays; and one of his early pieces, a deftly constructed
thriller entitled *On Trial*, achieved a rather spectacular success in 1914. For the next nine
years, Rice wrote two kinds of plays – commercial potboilers, some of which were produced,
and experimental plays with social themes, which were generally not produced. In 1923,
however, he had a critical success when the Theatre Guild staged his Expressionistic satire
about the automated modern world, *The Adding Machine*. This play is one of Rice's few to

retain its popularity and effectiveness over the years, and is considered one of the significant modern American plays. A companion piece, *The Subway*, did not receive a production until 1929; although somewhat dated, it has some remarkable strengths and has been unfairly neglected. Rice's other plays until 1929 were either adaptations or collaborations (one with Dorothy Parker and one with Philip Barry) of little importance.

In 1929, after much difficulty in finding a producer, Rice's *Street Scene* opened in New York, ran for 602 performances, and won the Pulitzer Prize. The play is a realistic depiction of life on a segment of a New York street, with something of a melodramatic plot to tie its many diverse strands together. Its powerful impact was that of a "shock of recognition"; and only a huge cast requirement (more than eighty characters) has prevented its more frequent revival. Rice also directed this play, and was thereafter to direct all of his New York productions, as well as some by Behrman and Sherwood. Also in 1929 Rice produced a trivial light comedy, *See Naples and Die*, and, in 1931, a somewhat more substantial study of American expatriates in Paris, *The Left Bank*. The same year saw one of Rice's most durable pieces, *Counsellor-at-Law*. Somewhat akin in tone and pace to *The Front Page*, the play is full of hectic activity and a vehicle for a strong actor.

Three other plays of the 1930's show Rice's pre-occupation with social issues. *We, The People* is a sprawling "panoramic presentation" of American life, specifically critical but generally affirmative. Its large cast and many issues make it thin in characterisation and rather more akin to a movie scenario than to a play. In novel form, such as his novels *Imperial City* and *The Show Must Go On*, Rice was able to be fuller and more effective. In 1934 Rice acquired the Belasco Theatre in New York, intending to produce a season of his own work. The first play, *Judgment Day*, a serious melodrama based somewhat on the Reichstag fire trial, was an indictment of Fascism; it was a failure in New York, but a distinct success in London. Rice's second play at the Belasco, *Between Two Worlds*, was even less successful with the New York critics, though a better play. It is a thickly drawn Chekhovian drama of ideas, containing some of the playwright's best work. Set on an ocean liner and with the usual large cast, the play contrasts the values of capitalistic and communistic societies, and suggests that the best of two worlds must somehow be welded together. Rice was to have produced a third play, *Not for Children*, at the Belasco, but, disheartened by the critical response to the first two plays, he announced his disenchantment with the commercial stage and turned to travel and to writing a novel. The unproduced play (done some years later in an inferior revised version) is a richly droll, technically dazzling attack on the inadequacies and superficialities of the drama as an artistic form. Successful really only in its Dublin production at the Gate Theatre, the play remains a seriously neglected tour de force.

In 1938 Rice returned to the theatre as a partner in the Playwrights Company. Most of the plays he wrote for the company were patriotic social commentaries, such as *American Landscape* and *Flight to the West*, and thin work compared to the Belasco plays. One comedy, *Dream Girl*, which starred his second wife, Betty Field, was successful theatre; and his panoramic paean to New York City, *Two on an Island*, contains some excellent satiric writing in a rather trite plot.

Rice's last commercially produced plays were less ambitious in scope, but more thoughtful in content. *The Grand Tour* and *The Winner* were about the relation of morality to money, and, although not his most memorable work and set on a much smaller scale, both were quite craftsmanlike. *Cue for Passion* was a psychoanalytic version of the Hamlet story, set in California, and is really too weak in characterization to be successful. *Love among the Ruins* is a thoughtful contemplation of the contemporary world, in which a group of American tourists in Lebanon look back on America. Rather more ambitious than *The Winner*, the play is also somewhat dull.

When Rice died in 1967, he had written over fifty plays (of which about forty were published or produced), two long novels, a satire on the early movies, a knowledgeable book about the professional theatre, and a long autobiography. He will, however, be remembered primarily as a playwright, as one of the men who transformed the American theatre from the gentility of Clyde Fitch and the entertainment of David Belasco into a form for the serious depiction of life, the critical social statement, and the broadening of technique. Not as powerful as Eugene O'Neill, sometimes deficient in character drawing, and often simplistic in statement, Rice nevertheless left a handful of plays which must be considered part of the permanent American repertory.

—Robert Hogan

RICH, Adrienne (Cecile). American. Born in Baltimore, Maryland, 16 May 1929. Educated at Roland Park Country School, Baltimore, 1938–47; Radcliffe College, Cambridge, Massachusetts, 1947–51, A.B. (cum laude) 1951 (Phi Beta Kappa). Married Alfred Conrad in 1953 (died, 1970); three sons. Lived in the Netherlands, 1961–62; taught at the YM-YWHA Poetry Center Workshop, New York, 1966–67; Visiting Poet, Swarthmore College, Pennsylvania, 1966–68; Adjunct Professor, Graduate Writing Division, Columbia University, New York, 1967–69; Lecturer, 1968–70, Instructor, 1970–71, and Assistant Professor of English, 1971–72, City College of New York; Fannie Hurst Visiting Professor of Creative Writing, Brandeis University, Waltham, Massachusetts, 1972–73; Lucy Martin Donnelly Fellow, Bryn Mawr College, Pennsylvania, 1975. Since 1976, Professor of English, Douglass College, Rutgers University, New Brunswick, New Jersey. Member, Advisory Board, Feminist Press, Westbury, New Jersey. Recipient: Guggenheim Fellowship, 1952, 1961; Ridgely Torrence Memorial Award, 1955; Friends of Literature Grace Thayer Bradley Award, 1956; National Institute of Arts and Letters award, 1960; Amy Lowell Traveling Scholarship, 1962; National Translation Center grant, 1968; National Endowment for the Arts grant, 1969; Shelley Memorial Award, 1971; Ingram Merrill Foundation grant, 1973; National Book Award, 1974. D.Litt.: Wheaton College, Norton, Massachusetts, 1967. Lives in New York City.

PUBLICATIONS

Verse

A Change of World. 1951.
(Poems). 1952.
The Diamond Cutters and Other Poems. 1955.
Snapshots of a Daughter-in-Law: Poems 1954–1962. 1963.
Necessities of Life: Poems 1962–1965. 1966.
Selected Poems. 1967.
Leaflets: Poems 1965–1968. 1969.
The Will to Change: Poems 1968–1970. 1971.
Diving into the Wreck: Poems 1971–1972. 1973.
Poems Selected and New 1950–1974. 1975.
The Dream of a Common Language: Poems 1974–1977. 1978.

Other

Of Woman Born: Motherhood as Experience and Institution. 1976.

Reading List: "Voice of the Survivor: The Poetry of Rich" by Willard Spiegelman, in *Southwest Review,* Autumn 1975; *Rich's Poetry* edited by Barbara Charlesworth Gelpi and Albert Gelpi, 1975.

*   *   *

Adrienne Rich's comments on her early poems offer the best insight into the shape of her career. In "When We Dead Awaken: Writing as Re-Vision" (1971) she notices that "Beneath the conscious craft are glimpses of the split I even then experienced between the girl who wrote poems, who defined herself in writing poems, and the girl who defined herself by her relationships with men." In other contexts Rich extends her use of the term "splits" to explain the structure of all contemporary problems – artistic, psychological, and social. Insofar as she defines her poetry in terms of a response to splits within and without, Rich accepts the modernist premise that the poet begins his or her work in a fragmented world.

Her early poems in *A Change of World* and *The Diamond Cutters* use their mastery of formal elements to control and order the splits. The poems in *Snapshots of a Daughter-in-Law* continue the intense examination of experience, but they no longer insist on bringing all tensions under control by the end of the poem and risk very dearly bought defenses in order to get closer to the actual dynamics of experience. With this change of stance, her poems begin to confront the tensions she finds in the world with an eye towards changing the world, or changing that part of herself which formerly had been intimidated by the tensions. Rather than protecting the self or the poet's voice from the tensions in the world, these poems begin the process of integrating the self in order to encounter the world in a full and direct attempt to overcome the limitations of experience, or of that intimidating experience of the early poems. So, while speakers in the early poems took comfort and defined success in closing shutters and other protective habits developed by experience, the speaker in "The Phenomenology of Anger" (1972) finds the simmering frustrations and tensions a source of energy, and enjoys speculating on the shape of future experiences when the force of the anger breaks out from its containment.

Having begun this intense exploration of self and world, she finds a sense of wholeness in poems such as "Planetarium" (1971) and "Diving into the Wreck" (1973) which develop images that respect the integrity of conflicts within and without and still enable a holistic view of self and world. In one of Rich's latest and longest poems, "From an Old House in America," she extends the possibilities of her sense of an integrated identity to social and political contexts. She finds not only a positive definition of self, as she had in "Diving into the Wreck," but she also finds a place in which the self can work and interact in a positive and effective fashion. The speaker in "From an Old House in America" begins with a positive and comfortable sense of self and then extends her social and political connections with other inhabitants of the house, with other American women, contemporaries and ancestors, and finally, with all women in all places. In this re-integration of poet and world Rich gets beyond the self-conscious impasse of modernist aesthetics and begins the process of changing the world with a public voice whose authority and promise grow out of its successful resolution of "splits" in the world.

—Richard C. Turner

RICHTER, Conrad (Michael).   American.   Born in Pine Grove, Pennsylvania, 13 October 1890. Educated at the Susquehanna Academy and High School, Pennsylvania, graduated 1906. Married Harvena Achenbach in 1915; one daughter. Worked as a teamster, farm laborer, bank clerk, and journalist, in Pennsylvania, 1906–08; Editor, *Weekly Courier*, Patton, Pennsylvania, 1909–10; Reporter for the *Leader*, Johnstown, Pennsylvania, and the *Pittsburgh Dispatch*, 1910–11; private secretary in Cleveland, 1911–13; free-lance writer, in Pennsylvania, from 1914; settled in New Mexico, 1928. Recipient: New York University Society of Libraries gold medal, 1942; Pulitzer Prize, 1951; National Institute of Arts and Letters grant, 1959; National Book Award, 1960. Litt.D.: Susquehanna University, Selinsgrove, Pennsylvania, 1944; University of New Mexico, Albuquerque, 1958; Lafayette College, Easton, Pennsylvania, 1966; LL.D.: Temple University, Philadelphia, 1966; L.H.D.: Lebanon Valley College, Annville, Pennsylvania, 1966. Member, National Institute of Arts and Letters. *Died 30 October 1968.*

PUBLICATIONS

Fiction

> *Brothers of No Kin and Other Stories.* 1924.
> *Early Americana* (stories). 1936
> *The Sea of Grass.* 1937.
> *The Trees.* 1940; *The Fields*, 1946; *The Town*, 1950; complete version, as *The Awakening Land*, 1966.
> *Tacey Cromwell.* 1942.
> *The Free Man.* 1943.
> *Smoke over the Prairies and Other Stories.* 1947.
> *Always Young and Fair.* 1947.
> *The Light in the Forest.* 1953.
> *The Lady.* 1957.
> *Dona Ellen.* 1959.
> *The Waters of Kronos.* 1960.
> *A Simple Honorable Man.* 1962.
> *The Grandfathers.* 1964.
> *A Country of Strangers.* 1966.
> *The Wanderer.* 1966.
> *Over the Blue Mountain* (juvenile). 1967.
> *The Aristocrat.* 1968.
> *The Rawhide Knot and Other Short Stories.* 1978.

Other

> *Human Vibration: The Mechanics of Life and Mind.* 1925.
> *Principles in Bio-Physics.* 1927.
> *The Mountain on the Desert: A Philosophical Journey.* 1955.
> *Individualists under the Shade Trees in a Vanishing America.* 1964.

Reading List: *Richter* by Edwin W. Gaston, 1965; *Richter* by Robert J. Barnes, 1968; *Richter's Ohio Trilogy: Its Ideas, Themes, and Relationship to Literary Tradition* by Clifford D. Edwards, 1970.

*   *   *

Conrad Richter is the latest and one of the best novelists of the American frontier, in the tradition of James Fenimore Cooper and Willa Cather. To this tradition he brings a deeper perspective and a more self-conscious artistry, as suggested by his choice of titles: his first novel was *The Sea of Grass*, and his second volume of short stories, *Early Americana*. But his best fiction, by far, is the trilogy *The Trees, The Fields*, and *The Town*. These three novels narrate the growth of an American family from its early struggle with the wilderness and the Indians, through its settlement and clearing of the fields, to the beginnings of an industrial America in the new town.

Perhaps the best and certainly the most original of these novels is *The Trees*, which follows the migration of Sayward Luckett and her family through the forests of Western Pennsylvania to the Ohio frontier. But more powerful than any human protagonist is the brooding presence of the primeval trees, which shadow the lives of all those beneath, until "the woodsies" adopt their dark and often savage ways in order to survive. In this world tragedy is inevitable: Sayward's mother dies of fever, her huntsman father deserts (or disappears), and she is left to bring up her younger siblings. There is no room in this world for romance, and the novel ends with Sayward's strange marriage to a drunken young lawyer, a fugitive from his New England past. The later two novels of the trilogy continue the story of the new family into the modern world.

After this Ohio trilogy Richter's most interesting novels are two which use autobiographical material to describe the conflict between a preacher father and his son. *The Waters of Kronos* tells of an early pioneer town which has been condemned to make way for a new reservoir, whose waters – like the waters of time – will drown the memory of its pioneer past. Underlying this is the ancient myth of Kronos, the titan father conquered by the son. A second novel, *A Simple Honorable Man*, describes the infinite complexity of the conflicts which create the "simple" character of the titular hero.

Richter's best early novel, *The Sea of Grass*, tells of the pioneer Southwest, as do many of his short stories. *The Light in the Forest* narrates the tragic conflict of a white boy, kidnapped and brought up by Indians, who tries to return to his own people. This same conflict informs *A Country of Strangers*, whose heroine had also been raised by Indians. Three novels, *Tacey Cromwell*, *Always Young and Fair*, and *The Lady*, describe heroines of different types who cope in different ways with the male-dominated society of the frontier. Finally, several volumes of non-fiction develop the philosophy which gives form to all Richter's creative writing. The best of these is *The Mountain on the Desert*.

—Frederic I. Carpenter

RIDING, Laura. American. Born Laura Reichenthal in New York City, 16 January 1901; adopted the surname Riding in 1926. Educated at Cornell University, Ithaca, New York. Married 1) Louis Gottschalk; 2) the poet and critic Schuyler B. Jackson in 1941 (died, 1968). Associated with the Fugitive group of poets; lived in Europe, 1926–39; associated with Robert Graves, in establishing the Seizen Press and *Epilogue* magazine; returned to America, 1939, renounced poetry, 1940, and has since devoted herself to the study of linguistics. Recipient: Guggenheim Fellowship, 1973. Lives in Florida.

PUBLICATIONS

Verse

The Close Chaplet.   1926.

Voltaire: A Biographical Fantasy. 1927.
Love as Love, Death as Death. 1928.
Poems: A Joking Word. 1930.
Twenty Poems Less. 1930.
Though Gently. 1930.
Laura and Francisca. 1931.
The Life of the Dead. 1933.
The First Leaf. 1933.
Poet: A Lying Word. 1933.
Americans. 1934.
The Second Leaf. 1935.
Collected Poems 1938.
Selected Poems: In Five Sets. 1970.

Fiction

Experts Are Puzzled (stories). 1930.
No Decency Left, with Robert Graves. 1932.
14A, with George Ellidge. 1934.
Progress of Stories. 1935.
Convalescent Conversations. 1936.
A Trojan Ending. 1937.
Lives of Wives (stories). 1939.

Other

A Survey of Modernist Poetry, with Robert Graves. 1927.
A Pamphlet Against Anthologies, with Robert Graves. 1928; as *Against Anthologies,*
    1928.
Contemporaries and Snobs. 1928.
Anarchism Is Not Enough. 1928.
Four Unposted Letters to Catherine. 1930.
The Telling. 1972.
It Has Taken Long (selected writings), in "Riding Issue" of *Chelsea 35.* 1976

Editor, *Everybody's Letters.* 1933.
Editor, *Epilogue 1–3.* 3 vols., 1935–37.
Editor, *The World and Ourselves: Letters about the World Situation from 65 People of
    Different Professions and Pursuits.* 1938.

Translator, *Anatole France at Home,* by Marcel Le Goff. 1926.
Translator, with Robert Graves, *Almost Forgotten Germany,* by Georg Schwarz. 1936.

Bibliography: by Alan Clark, in *Chelsea 35,* 1976.

Reading List: *Riding's Pursuit of Truth* by Joyce Piell Wexler, 1977.

*   *   *

Laura Riding is, according to Kenneth Rexroth in *American Poetry in the Twentieth Century,* "the greatest lost poet in American literature." The inaccessibility of her poetry, both in the literal and figurative sense, partially accounts for this lack of attention. Since the publication of her substantial *Collected Poems* in 1938, she has published no new poetry and has allowed the re-issue of only one slender volume selected from the earlier edition. Hence her poetry is hard to find, and, once found, hard to follow. Her brief poem, "Grace," illustrates her obscurity:

> This posture and this manner suit
> Not that I have an ease in them
> But that I have a horror
> And so stand well upright –
> Lest, should I sit and, flesh-conversing, eat,
> I choke upon a piece of my own tongue-meat.

Characteristic of other poems by Riding, this one is virtually unadorned, with the single concrete image withheld until the last two lines. The subject matter is, typically and paradoxically, an examination of an interior feeling, a topic that one does not expect to find treated with this austerity.

Riding's definition of a poem in the preface to the *Collected Poems* is "an uncovering of truth of so fundamental and general a kind that no other name besides poetry is adequate except truth." This definition, if tautological, is indicative of Riding's strong commitment to purity in the language. This strong belief impelled her eventually to abandon the writing of poetry, for she found that she could not reconcile the necessity to keep the language pure with the desirability of making the poems sensuously appealing to the readers.

Riding's undeservedly neglected fiction has received even less attention than her poetry. Her *Progress of Stories*, a collection marked by impressive variety and a somewhat flamboyant wit, is unlike her poetry in tone although it treats similar themes. The comic sketch, "Eve's Side of It," for instance, complements such feminist poems as "Divestment of Beauty" and "Auspice of Jewels." She has deliberately adopted a lighter vein for these stories, she explains in the preface, because she is tired of the accusation of obscurity and being made "a scape goat for the incapacity of people to understand what they only pretend to want to know."

Of her numerous theoretical studies, the two she wrote in collaboration with Robert Graves are best known. Compared to her other works, *A Survey of Modernist Poetry* is a model of lucidity. It suggests a method of textual scrutiny that possibly influenced William Empson's *Seven Types of Ambiguity*. While the work of E. E. Cummings most often provides examples for the book, Riding's poem "The Rugged Back of Anger" is examined. To apply Riding's critical method to her poetry is helpful in understanding this austere and significant poet.

—Nancy C. Joyner

RINEHART, Mary Roberts. American. Born in Pittsburgh, Pennsylvania, in 1876. Educated in elementary and high schools in Pittsburgh, and at Pittsburgh Training School for nurses, graduated 1896. Married Dr. Stanley Marshall Rinehart in 1896 (died, 1932); three sons. Full-time writer from 1903; lived in Pittsburgh until 1920, in Washington, D.C., 1920–32, and in New York City from 1932. Litt.D.: George Washington University, Washington, D.C., 1923. *Died 22 September 1958.*

PUBLICATIONS

Fiction

The Circular Staircase. 1908.
The Man in Lower Ten. 1909.
When a Man Marries. 1909.
The Window at the White Cat. 1910.
The Amazing Adventure of Letitia Carberry. 1911.
Where There's a Will. 1912.
The Case of Jennie Brice. 1913.
The After House. 1914.
The Street of Seven Stars. 1914.
K. 1915.
Tish. 1916.
Bab, A Sub-Deb. 1917.
Long Live the King! 1917.
The Altar of Freedom. 1917.
The Amazing Interlude. 1918.
Twenty-Three and a Half Hours' Leave. 1918.
Love Stories. 1919.
Dangerous Days. 1919.
A Poor Wise Man. 1920.
The Truce of God. 1920.
Affinities and Other Stories. 1920.
Isn't That Just Like a Man! 1920.
More Tish. 1921.
Sight Unseen, and The Confession. 1921.
The Breaking Point. 1922.
The Out Trail. 1923.
Temperamental People (stories). 1924.
The Red Lamp. 1925.
Tish Plays the Game. 1926.
Nomad's Land (stories). 1926.
The Bat. 1926.
Lost Ecstasy. 1927.
Two Flights Up. 1928.
This Strange Adventure. 1929.
The Romantics (stories). 1929.
The Door. 1930.
Miss Pinkerton. 1932; as *The Double Alibi*, 1932.
The Album. 1933.
Mr. Cohen Takes a Walk. 1934.
The State Versus Elinor Norton. 1934.
The Doctor. 1936.
Married People (stories). 1937.
Tish Marches On. 1937.
The Wall. 1938.
The Great Mistake. 1940.
Familiar Faces: Stories of People You Know. 1941.
Haunted Lady. 1942.
Alibi for Israel and Other Stories. 1944.
The Yellow Room. 1945.

A Light in the Window.   1948.
Episode of the Wandering Knife: Three Mystery Tales.   1950.
The Swimming Pool.   1952.
The Frightened Wife and Other Murder Stories.   1953.

Plays

Double Life (produced 1906).
Seven Days, with Avery Hopwood (produced 1909).   1931.
Cheer Up (produced 1912).
The Bat, with Avery Hopwood, from novel *The Circular Staircase* by Rinehart
    (produced 1920).   1932.

Screenplay: *Aflame in the Sky,* with Ewart Anderson, 1927.

Other

Kings, Queens, and Pawns: An American Woman at the Front.   1915.
Through Glacier Park: Seeing America First, with Howard Eaton.   1916.
*Tenting Tonight: A Chronicle of Sport and Adventure in Glacier Park and the Cascade
    Mountains.*   1918.
My Story (autobiography).   1931; revised edition, 1948.
Writing Is Work.   1939.

*   *   *

Mary Roberts Rinehart, a successful writer of thrillers and of comic novels about the
travels and adventures of a spinster, "Tish," modelled on herself and her friends, may be
considered one of the founder figures of the American novel of mystery and suspense. From
her first successful novel, *The Circular Staircase,* to a late work like *The Album,* she used the
same pattern. The setting is usually in a more-or-less enclosed house, often a lodging house or
block of houses deliberately shut off from the outer world. The heroine is usually either an
inexperienced but bright young woman or a shrewd but eccentric spinster. By overhearing
odd conversations or mysterious footsteps the heroine slowly tracks down a murderer, whose
identity comes as a shock to her. But then a real detective, a minor character (he may have
been posing as one of the lodgers), rescues her in time. Miss Rinehart's novels are still
popular, especially in America, and their period and oddly wholesome flavour (one never
really believes that the heroine will suffer the fate looming over her) make them agreeable
reading. They were jocularly christened novels of the "Had I but known ..." school (they
were always told in the first person), and Mignon C. Eberhart was her most distinguished
successor.

—G. S. Fraser

ROBERTS, Elizabeth Madox.   American.   Born in Perryville, Kentucky, 30 October
1881; lived part of her childhood in Colorado. Educated at Covington Institute, Springfield,

Kentucky; Covington High School, Kentucky, 1886–1900; University of Chicago (Fiske Prize, 1921), 1917–21, Ph.B. in English 1921 (Phi Beta Kappa). Private tutor and teacher in various public schools, 1900–10; writer from 1920. Recipient: O. Henry Prize, 1930. Member, National Institute of Arts and Letters, 1940. *Died 13 March 1941.*

PUBLICATIONS

Fiction

The Time of Man. 1926.
My Heart and My Flesh. 1927.
Jingling in the Wind. 1928.
The Great Meadow. 1930.
A Buried Treasure. 1931.
The Haunted Mirror: Stories. 1932.
He Sent Forth a Raven. 1935.
Black Is My Truelove's Hair. 1938.
Not by Strange Gods: Stories. 1941.

Verse

In the Great Steep's Garden. 1915.
Under the Tree (juvenile). 1922; revised edition, 1930.
Song in the Meadow. 1940.

Reading List: *Roberts: An Appraisal* by J. Donald Adams, 1938; *Roberts, American Novelist* by Harry Modean Campbell and Ruel E. Foster, 1956; *Herald to Chaos: The Novels of Roberts* by Earl Rovit, 1960; *Roberts* by Frederick P. W. McDowell, 1963 (includes bibliography).

*   *   *

The philosophic idealism of Bishop Berkeley, the realistic conventions of regional fiction, and a poetic talent for rendering sensuous impressions are the unlikely ingredients that conjoin in the making of Elizabeth Madox Roberts's novels. Her characteristic way of harmonizing these disparate materials is through the focus of an introspective female who serves as narrator-protagonist – a controlling consciousness that shapes the contours of her own growing personality and those of the outside world, interactively and simultaneously. Two of Roberts's novels, *The Time of Man* and *The Great Meadow*, attained considerable success when they were originally published. The first chronicles the sensibility of a Kentucky girl, Ellen Chesser, whose experience as a migrant farm-wife is measured by the eternal cycles of poverty, labor, and the universal portions of grief, pain, joy, and love. Deliberately conceived on the model of the *Odyssey*, *The Time of Man* aims at a kind of epic quality in its unsentimental depiction of the struggle between creative life-instincts and the implacable limitations of the human condition. *The Great Meadow* reworks this theme, but its heroine, Diony, is a more sophisticated consciousness; she is aware of herself and her role, and the journey-motif is not the twenty-year wanderings of an impoverished farm family, but the great Western trek from Virginia to the founding of Kentucky in the late 18th century. Both novels allowed Roberts to develop and display her strengths as a novelist: a supple, lyrical prose style, admirably suited to the particular feminine sensibility that she espoused; a sense of rhythmical narrative structure that moves in slow, undramatic accretions of episodic action; and an unforced, natural symbolism infusing the texture of events.

Although these two novels are regarded as Roberts's major achievements, *My Heart and My Flesh* and *He Sent Forth a Raven* are scarcely less accomplished. The first was meant to be an antithetical sequel to *The Time of Man*, the protagonist, in this case, being stripped of all buffers against adversity only to assert an indomitable will to live. The second is Roberts's most ambitious effort; *He Sent Forth a Raven* invokes the allegorical grandeur of the Biblical story of Noah and *Moby-Dick*, and, although the novel is not entirely able to control its materials, it is rich in meaning and strangely powerful. She also wrote three other novels, two collections of short stories, and three volumes of poetry. Her poems – fresh, vivid, and marked by their capacity to record a direct sensuous immediacy – are frequently anthologized in collections of verse for children.

—Earl Rovit

ROBERTS, Kenneth (Lewis).   American.   Born in Kennebunk, Maine, 8 December 1885. Educated in local schools and at Cornell University, Ithaca, New York (Editor, *Cornell Widow*), 1904–08, A.B. 1908. Served in the United States Army, in the Intelligence Section of the Siberian Expeditionary Force, 1918–19: Captain. Married Anna Seiberling Mosser in 1911. Reporter and Columnist, *Boston Globe*, 1909–17, and also member of the editorial staff of *Life* Magazine, New York, 1915–18; Correspondent, in Washington, D.C., and Europe, for the *Saturday Evening Post*, Philadelphia, 1919–28; thereafter a full-time writer; lived in Italy, 1928–37, then settled in Kennebunkport, Maine. Recipient: special Pulitzer Prize, 1957. Litt.D.: Dartmouth College, Hanover, New Hampshire, 1934; Colby College, Waterville, Maine, 1935; Bowdoin College, Brunswick, Maine, 1937; Middlebury College, Vermont, 1938; Northwestern University, Evanston, Illinois, 1945. Member, National Institute of Arts and Letters. *Died 21 July 1957.*

PUBLICATIONS

Fiction

> *Arundel.*   1930.
> *The Lively Lady.*   1931.
> *Rabble in Arms.*   1933.
> *Captain Caution: A Chronicle of Arundel.*   1934.
> *Northwest Passage.*   1937.
> *Oliver Wiswell.*   1940.
> *Lydia Bailey.*   1947.
> *Boon Island.*   1956.

Plays

> *Panatella,* with Romeyn Berry, music by T. J. Lindorff and others (produced 1907). 1907.

The Brotherhood of Man, with Robert Garland. 1934.

Other

Europe's Morning After. 1921.
Sun Hunting: Adventures and Observations among the Native and Migratory Tribes of Florida. 1922.
Why Europe Leaves Home. 1922.
The Collector's Whatnot, with Booth Tarkington and Hugh Kahler. 1923.
Black Magic. 1924.
Concentrated New England: A Sketch of Calvin Coolidge. 1924.
Florida Loafing. 1925.
Florida. 1926.
Antiquamania. 1928.
For Authors Only and Other Gloomy Essays. 1935.
It Must Be Your Tonsils. 1936.
Trending into Maine. 1938.
The Kenneth Roberts Reader. 1945.
I Wanted to Write. 1949.
Don't Say That about Maine! 1951.
Henry Gross and His Dowsing Rod. 1951.
The Seventh Sense. 1953.
Cowpens: The Great Morale-Builder. 1957; as *The Battle of Cowpens*, 1958.
Water Unlimited. 1957.

Editor, *March to Quebec: Journals of the Members of Arnold's Expedition.* 1938.

*   *   *

Kenneth Roberts's reputation rests on his historical novels dealing with American history from the time of the French and Indian War to the War of 1812. These are long, character-and-action-packed novels that succeed admirably in bringing history to life. Because Roberts brought to the writing of fiction two decades of newspaper and magazine journalism and a passion for accurate detail, his novels are noteworthy for their historical accuracy. His interest in historical fiction began with a curiosity about his own Maine ancestors who had been involved in the American Revolution.

Roberts went about his novels as though he were writing history. He borrowed trunkloads of books from the Library of Congress and historical societies and ransacked the shelves of antiquarian book dealers. When he could not find what he wanted in printed sources, he went to the archives. In researching *Northwest Passage*, for example, he found in the British Public Record Office a large collection of previously unused letters, petitions, and reports written by Major Robert Rogers himself, who was to be the protagonist of the novel. When he was writing *Lively Lady* at his winter home off the coast of Tuscany he spent hours with Bowditch's *Navigator* and binoculars watching sailing ships in the harbor in order to master the details of sailing a brig.

Without the help of Booth Tarkington, his summer neighbor in Kennebunkport, Maine, however, Roberts might not have become a novelist. In 1928 Tarkington persuaded him to drop his journalism and begin his first novel. For the next 15 years Tarkington talked over plans, encouraged him and then, when the novels were in rough draft, acted as advisor and editor. Night after night Roberts read aloud from manuscripts and gratefully accepted suggestions for deletions and revisions. Roberts's diary shows that in one three-month period in 1936 he spent 58 nights reading the first 51 chapters of *Northwest Passage*.

Arundel is the story of Benedict Arnold's disastrous expedition against Quebec in 1775, narrated by a Richard Nason from Arundel, Maine. Nason's son is the protagonist of Roberts's next novel, *Lively Lady*, which deals with the operations of a privateer in the war of 1812. *Rabble in Arms* is also about men from Arundel who fight with Arnold, the hero of the novel, and ends with the Battle of Saratoga. *Captain Caution* is another sea story laid at the time of the War of 1812. *Northwest Passage* is Roberts's most memorable work and depicts the fascinating career of Major Rogers, Indian fighter during the French and Indian War, who dreamed of finding the Northwest Passage to the Pacific, was governor of Michilimackinac and later court-martialed. *Oliver Wiswell* is a novel of particular interest because it tells the story of the American Revolution from the viewpoint of a loyalist.

—James Woodress

ROBINSON, Edwin Arlington.   American.   Born in Head Tide, Maine, 22 December 1869; grew up in Gardiner, Maine. Educated at Gardiner High School, graduated 1888; Harvard University, Cambridge, Massachusetts, 1891–93. Free-lance writer in Gardiner, 1893–96; settled in New York City, 1896; worked as Secretary to the President of Harvard University, 1897; returned to New York, settled in Greenwich Village, and held various jobs, including subway-construction inspector, 1903–04; through patronage of Theodore Roosevelt, who admired his poetry, became Clerk in the United States Customs House, New York, 1904–10; spent summers at the MacDowell Colony, Peterborough, New Hampshire, 1911–34. Recipient: Pulitzer Prize, 1922, 1925, 1928; National Institute of Arts and Letters Gold Medal, 1929. Honorary degrees: Yale University, New Haven, Connecticut, 1922, and Bowdoin College, Brunswick, Maine. Member, American Academy of Arts and Letters. *Died 6 April 1935.*

PUBLICATIONS

Collections

Collected Poems.   1937.
Selected Letters, edited by Ridgely Torrence and others.   1940.
Tilbury Town: Selected Poems, edited by Lawrance Thompson.   1953.
Selected Early Poems and Letters, edited by Charles T. Davis.   1960.
Selected Poems, edited by Morton Dauwen Zabel.   1965.

Verse

The Torrent and the Night Before.   1896; revised edition, as *The Children of the Night*, 1897.
Captain Craig.   1902; revised edition, 1915.
The Town Down the River.   1910.

The Man Against the Sky.   1916.
Merlin.   1917.
Lancelot.   1920.
The Three Taverns.   1920.
Avon's Harvest.   1921.
Collected Poems.   1921.
Roman Bartholow.   1923.
The Man Who Died Twice.   1924.
Dionysus in Doubt.   1925.
Tristram.   1927.
Collected Poems.   5 vols., 1927.
Sonnets 1889–1927.   1928.
Fortunatus.   1928.
Three Poems.   1928.
Modred: A Fragment.   1929.
The Prodigal Son.   1929.
Cavender's House.   1929.
The Glory of the Nightingales.   1930.
Matthias at the Door.   1931.
Poems, edited by Bliss Perry.   1931.
Nicodemus.   1932.
Talifer.   1933.
Amaranth.   1934.
King Jasper.   1935.
Hannibal Brown: Posthumous Poem.   1936.

Plays

Van Zorn.   1914.
The Porcupine.   1915.

Other

Letters to Howard George Schmitt, edited by Carl J. Weber.   1940.
Untriangulated Stars: Letters to Harry de Forest Smith 1890–1905, edited by Denham
    Sutcliffe.   1947.
Letters to Edith Brower, edited by Richard Cary.   1968.

Editor, *Selections from the Letters of Thomas Sergeant Perry.*   1929.

Bibliography: *A Bibliography of the Writings and Criticisms of Robinson* by Lillian Lippincott,
1937; supplements by William White, in *Colby Library Quarterly,* 1965, 1969.

Reading List: *Robinson: A Biography* by Hermann Hagedorn, 1938; *Robinson* by Yvor
Winters, 1946, revised edition, 1971; *Robinson: The Literary Background of a Traditional
Poet* by Edwin S. Fussell, 1954; *Where the Light Falls: A Portrait of Robinson* by Chard
Powers Smith, 1965; *Robinson: A Poetry of the Act* by W. R. Robinson, 1967; *Robinson: A
Critical Introduction* by Wallace L. Anderson, 1967; *Robinson: The Life of Poetry* by Louis O.
Coxe, 1968; *Robinson* by Hoyt C. Franchere, 1968; *Appreciation of Robinson* (essays) edited
by Richard Cary, 1969; *Robinson: Centenary Essays* edited by Ellsworth Barnard, 1969.

*   *   *

More than any other poet of his time, Edwin Arlington Robinson made poetry his career. He neither travelled nor taught, married nor made public appearances. Aside from a handful of prose pieces and two unsuccessful plays, he devoted himself exclusively to the writing of poetry, publishing many volumes of verse in a forty-year period. He suffered during the first half of his career from neglect and near impoverishment; he suffered during his last years from an excess of adulation. After his signal success of *Tristram*, for which he won his third Pulitzer Prize, he was hailed as America's foremost poet. Although his reputation has diminished since his death, he is nevertheless established as the most important poet writing in America at the turn of the century and has a firm place as one of the major modern poets.

He was, as Robert Frost noted in his preface to *King Jasper*, "content with the old way to be new." The old way was his unwavering insistence on traditional forms. His poems demonstrate his facility in an impressive variety of verse forms, from blank verse in most of the long narratives to Petracharan sonnets and villanelles in his shorter work, but he was positively reactionary in his dismissal of the then current *vers libre* movement. In a letter, he once placed free verse along with prohibition and moving pictures as "a triumvirate from hell, armed with the devil's instructions to abolish civilization."

Robinson was new in his attitudes in and toward his poetry. He may be called an impersonal romantic, breaking with the nineteenth-century tradition by objectifying and dramatizing emotional reactions while at the same time emphasizing sentiment and mystical awareness. His combination of compassion and irony has become a familiar stance in modern poetry, and his celebrated advocacy of triumphant forbearance in the face of adversity anticipates the existential movement. In a letter to *The Bookman* in 1897, responding to the charge that he was pessimistic, he wrote, "This world is not a 'prison house,' but a kind of spiritual kindergarten where millions of bewildered infants are trying to spell God with the wrong blocks." While he was reluctant to be classified as an exponent of any formal philosophical or theological stance, he was entirely willing, in and out of his poetry, to condemn materialistic attitudes. Robinson's use of humor within his serious poetry, such as in *Amaranth*, placed a new importance on the comic.

While Robinson frequently wrote poems on conventional topics, his subject matter was new in his heavy emphasis on people. Unlike other romantic poets, he generally avoided the celebration of natural phenomena, bragging to a friend about his first volume that one would not find "a single red-breasted robin in the whole collection." Many of his short poems are character sketches of individuals, anticipating Edgar Lee Masters's *Spoon River Anthology*. All of the long narratives deal with complicated human relationships. Frequently they explore psychological reactions to a prior event, such as *Avon's Harvest*, Robinson's "ghost story" about a man destroyed by his own hatred, and *Cavender's House*, a dialogue between a man and his dead wife which deals with questions of jealousy and guilt. The people inhabiting Robinson's books include imaginary individuals; characters modeled on actual acquaintances, such as Alfred H. Louis in *Captain Craig*; figures from history, such as "Ben Jonson Entertains a Gentleman from Stratford," "Rembrandt to Rembrandt," and "Ponce de Leon"; and mythic figures, notably characters from the Bible and Arthurian legend.

Edwin S. Fussell, in his book on Robinson, devotes separate chapters to the English Bible and the Greek and Roman classics as significant influences on Robinson's work. English poets of particular importance to him are Shakespeare, Wordsworth, Kipling, Tennyson, and Robert Browning, although Robinson objected to the inevitable comparison between his character analyses and those of Browning. Among American poets Robinson found Emerson to be his most significant precursor. Because of his narrative impulse, his work is also compared to the fiction of Hawthorne and Henry James.

Robinson is best known today for his earliest work, the short sketches of characters, chiefly failures, who reside in Tilbury Town, the name he uses for Gardiner, Maine. Partially because of the frequency of their being anthologized, "Richard Cory," "Miniver Cheevy," and "Mr. Flood's Party" are his most famous poems. "Eros Turannos" has been singled out by Louis O. Coxe as the most impressive Tilbury poem. Also highly regarded are a few of the poems of medium length, notably "Isaac and Archibald" and "Aunt Imogen."

Not all of Robinson's poems are narratives, and some of the symbolic lyrics have been highly praised, particularly "For a Dead Lady" and the poem about which Theodore Roosevelt wrote, "I am not sure I understand 'Luke Havergal,' but I am sure that I like it." "The Man Against the Sky," the title poem of the first volume that received pronounced critical approval, is an ironic meditation on possibilities of philosophical attitudes. It has received a great deal of critical attention from both admirers and detractors. Robinson said that the poem "comes as near as anything to representing my poetic vision."

Critics have tended to neglect Robinson's long narratives, those thirteen book-length poems that occupied most of his attention during the second half of his career. According to his earliest biographer, Hermann Hagedorn, the difficulty Robinson had with *Captain Craig*, first in getting a publisher and then in the adverse critical reaction, was a devastating experience for the young poet. Until he issued his first *Collected Poems* in 1921, Robinson alternated his long poems with volumes of shorter, more readily acceptable pieces. After he was thoroughly established, however, he concentrated on the long narratives. Though these poems sometimes lend themselves to verbosity and repetition, they nevertheless provided Robinson with his most congenial form, allowing him to combine his talents of narration, characterization, and symbolic discursiveness.

—Nancy C. Joyner

ROETHKE, Theodore (Huebner).   American.   Born in Saginaw, Michigan, 25 May 1908. Educated at John Moore School, Saginaw, 1913–21; Arthur Hill High School, Saginaw, 1921–25; University of Michigan, Ann Arbor, 1925–29, B.A. 1929 (Phi Beta Kappa), M.A. 1936; Harvard University, Cambridge, Massachusetts, 1930–31. Married Beatrice O'Connell in 1953. Instructor in English, 1931–35, Director of Public Relations, 1934, and Varsity Tennis Coach, 1934–35, Lafayette College, Easton, Pennsylvania; Instructor in English, Michigan State College, East Lansing, Fall 1935; Instructor, 1936–40, Assistant Professor, 1940–43, and Associate Professor of English Composition, 1947, Pennsylvania State University, College Park; Instructor, Bennington College, Vermont, 1943–46; Associate Professor, 1947–48, Professor of English, 1948–62, and Honorary Poet-in-Residence, 1962–63, University of Washington, Seattle. Recipient: Yaddo fellowship, 1945; Guggenheim grant, 1945, 1950; National Institute of Arts and Letters grant, 1952; Fund for the Advancement of Education Fellowship, 1952; Ford Foundation grant, 1952, 1959; Pulitzer Prize, 1954; Fulbright Fellowship, 1955; Borestone Mountain Award, 1958; National Book Award, 1959, 1965; Bollingen Prize, 1959; Poetry Society of America Prize, 1962; Shelley Memorial Award, 1962. D.H.L.: University of Michigan, 1962. *Died 1 August 1963.*

PUBLICATIONS

Collections

On the Poet and His Craft: Selected Prose, edited by Ralph J. Mills, Jr.   1965.
Collected Poems.   1966.

Selected Letters, edited by Ralph J. Mills., Jr. 1968.
Selected Poems, edited by Beatrice Roethke. 1969.

Verse

Open House. 1941.
The Lost Son and Other Poems. 1948.
Praise to the End! 1951.
The Waking: Poems 1933–1953. 1953.
Words for the Wind: The Collected Verse. 1957.
The Exorcism. 1957.
Sequence, Sometimes Metaphysical, Poems. 1963.
The Far Field. 1964.
Two Poems. 1965.

Other

I Am! Says the Lamb (juvenile). 1961.
Party at the Zoo (juvenile). 1963.
Straw for the Fire: From the Notebooks of Theodore Roethke, 1943–1963, edited by
   David Wagoner. 1972.
Dirty Dinky and Other Creatures: Poems for Children, edited by Beatrice Roethke and
   Stephen Lushington. 1973.

Bibliography: *Roethke: A Bibliography* by James R. McLeod, 1973.

Reading List: *Roethke* by Ralph J. Mills, Jr., 1963; *Roethke: Essays on His Poetry* by Arnold
S. Stein, 1965; *Roethke: An Introduction to His Poetry* by Karl Malkoff, 1966; *The Glass
House: The Life of Roethke* by Allan Seager, 1968; *Profile of Roethke* by William Heyen,
1971; *Roethke's Dynamic Vision* by Richard Allen Blessing, 1974; *Roethke: The Garden
Master* by Rosemary Sullivan, 1975; *The Echoing Wood of Roethke* by Jenijoy La Belle, 1976.

*   *   *

   Theodore Roethke's posthumous collection, *The Far Field,* is a résumé and retrospect of a
lifetime's preoccupations, acknowledging its debt to those poets who have confronted the
mystery of personal extinction – the later Eliot and Yeats and that "Whitman, maker of
catalogues" whose "terrible hunger for objects" is repeated in these writings of a man who
has "moved closer to death, lived with death." Roethke always felt "the separateness of all
things," the fragility of being. In "The Dream" he had written "Love is not love until love's
vulnerable"; "The Abyss" adds a new, desperate urgency to the theme, poised on a dark stair
that "goes nowhere," knowing the abyss is "right where you are – /A step down the stair."
Yet if this last volume broods over childhood initiations into mortality, it also celebrates the
spontaneous impulse towards life, light, growth in which he shares:

> Many arrivals make us live: the tree becoming
> Green, a bird tipping the topmost bough,
> A seed pushing itself beyond itself....

> What does what it should do needs nothing more.
> The body moves, though slowly, towards desire.
> We come to something without knowing why.

Summoned once more to the field's end, in old age Roethke returned to "the first heaven of knowing," that second-childhood of radical innocence which has always been the American visionary's home. If "Old men should be explorers," he replies to the Eliot of *Four Quartets*, "I'll be an Indian./Iroquois," thus unashamedly assuming the role of the noble savage in retreat, whose "journey into the interior," into the heart of the continent, is also a "long journey out of the self," into the unconscious and preconscious, the elemental life of the planet.

There is a paradoxical resolution of stasis and motion throughout Roethke's work. "The Sententious Man" claims to "know the motion of the deepest stone"; in "The Far Field," imagery of dwindling, darkening, and decline shifts into sudden surges and spurts of life, as not only air, fire, and water but even earth takes on the fluidity which leaves no ground secure: "the shale slides dangerously," dust blows, rubble falls, the arroyo cracks, the swamp is "alive with quicksand." Amid this movement the self floats unperturbed: "I rise and fall in the slow sea of a grassy plain" (the theological punning here recurs throughout his verse); "And all flows past.... I am not moving but they are," for the soul, preparing itself for death, has finally found that longed-for "imperishable quiet at the heart of form." Throughout his verse, the *field* is a complex metaphor: it is the green field of nature, the field of perception, and, at their intersection, a heraldic field in which matter blazons forth spirit, where "All finite things reveal infinitude," disclosing, in the words of one of his earliest poems, "skies of azure/The pageantry of wings the eyes' right treasure."

Movement from closure to openness, finitude to immensity, has been the characteristic rhythm of all his poetry. The title poem of *Open House* proclaims this:

> My secrets cry aloud....
> My heart keeps open house,
> My doors are widely swung....
> I'm naked to the bone
> With nakedness my shield.
> Myself is what I wear.

The Lost Son pokes around in origins, under stones, in drains and subsoil, to find the answer to his most basic question: "Where do the roots go?" Roethke felt himself at home amidst the abundant verminous life of a vegetable nature which (as in "Cuttings, *later*") strains like a saint to rise anew in "This urge, wrestle, resurrection of dry sticks" – a world to which he was introduced in his florist father's greenhouses, where he learnt to "study the lives on a leaf: the little/Sleepers, numb nudgers"; and not only to study, but to find in them, as in the "Shoots [which] dangled and drooped,/Lolling obscenely" in "Root Cellar," an imagery of his own instinctual life. He was impressed by the stubborn persistence of this residual realm: "Nothing would give up life:/Even the dirt kept breathing a small breath."

His poems are rites of passage, exits and entrances where "the body, delighting in thresholds,/Rocks in and out of itself." *Praise to the End* employs the bouncy rhythms and inconsequential surrealism of nursery rhyme and baby talk, used to such effect in his poems for children, to enact the birth or rebirth of the scattered psyche (Roethke suffered from periodic mental illness) out of a tangle of instinctual impulses – eating, touching, snuffling, sucking, licking – in all of which identity is constituted as *lack* ("I Need, I Need"), a fall from innocence into disenchantment which brings us to our proper selfhood, aware of time and consequence, and able to announce "I'm somebody else now." In "Give Way, Ye Gates," one line of six verbs charts the whole pilgrimage through need, mutuality, and loss into separated being: "Touch and arouse. Suck and sob. Curse and mourn." The technique of this volume is a riddling, exclamatory questioning, like that of an insistent child who neither expects nor receives an answer, wanting only confirmation of its own puzzling existence. Yet this catechism of the "happy asker" reveals a world of correspondences where everything *is* an answer to everything else, and the creatures sing their own richness and diversity: "A house for wisdom. A field for revelation./Speak to the stones and the stars answer."

In his love poems this most physical of poets assumes a metaphysical lightness and delicacy, a clarity of syntax and almost allegoric translucence of imagery which recall Renaissance neo-platonism and the courtly love of the troubadours. His women (even the "woman lovely in her bones") are the Beatrices of a rarefied sensuality, "know[ing] the speech of light" and "cry[ing] out loud the soul's own secret joy"; but even here Roethke's playfulness is preserved in sudden unexpected carnalities of language ("pure as a bride.../ And breathing hard, as that man rode/Between those lovely tits"). "The Renewal" shows love to be the force that moves the stars, reducing to a oneness knowing and motion, the dualities of his universe, just as "Words for the Wind," which provided the title for his *Collected Verse*, sees it as both the journey and the destination of the soul:

> I cherish what I have
> Had of the temporal:
>
> I am no longer young
> But the wind and waters are;
> What falls away will fall;
> All things bring me to love.

—Stan Smith

RØLVAAG, O(le) E(dvart).   American.   Born on Donna Island, Helgeland, Norway, 22 April 1876; emigrated to the United States, 1896; naturalized, 1908. Educated in Donna schools to age 14; Augustana College, Canton, South Dakota, 1899-1901; St. Olaf College, Northfield, Minnesota, 1901-05, B.A. 1905, M.A. 1910; University of Oslo, 1905-06. Married Jennie Marie Berdahl in 1908; three sons and one daughter. Worked on his uncle's farm in South Dakota, 1896-99; Professor of Norwegian Language and Literature, 1906-31, and Head of the Norwegian Department, 1916-31, St. Olaf College; writer from 1912. Secretary, Norwegian-American Historical Association, 1925-31. Honorary degree: University of Wisconsin, Madison, 1929. Knight of the Order of St. Olaf, Norway, 1926. *Died 5 November 1931.*

PUBLICATIONS

Fiction

Amerika-breve (Letters from America).   1912; translated by Ella Tweet and Solveig Zempel, as *The Third Life of Per Smevik*, 1971.

Paa Glemte Veie (On Forgotten Paths).   1914.
To Tullinger: Et Billede fra Idag (Two Fools: A Picture of Our Time).   1920; revised
   edition, translated by Sivert Erdahl and Rølvaag, as *Pure Gold,* 1930.
Laengselens Baat.   1921; translated by Nora O. Solum, as *The Boat of Longing,* 1933.
I de Dage: Fortaelling om Norske Nykommere i Amerika (In Those Days: A Story of
   Norwegian Pioneering in America).   1924; *Ricket Grundlaegges* (The Founding of
   the Kingdom), 1925; both books translated by Lincoln Colcord and Rølvaag, as
   Giants in the Earth, 1927.
Peder Seier.   1928; translated by Rølvaag and Nora O. Solum, as *Peder Victorious,*
   1929.
Den Signede Dag (The Blessed Day).   1931; translated by Trygve M. Ager, as *Their
   Fathers' God,* 1931.

Other

Ordforklaring til Nordahl Rolfsens Laesebok for Folkeskolen, II.   1909.
Haandbok i Norsk Retskrivning og uttale til Skolebruk og Selvstudium, with P. J.
   Eikeland.   1916.
Norsk Laesebok, with P. J. Eikeland.   3 vols., 1919–25.
Omkring Faedrearven (essays).   1922.

Editor, *Deklamationsboken.*   1918.

Reading List: *Rølvaag: A Biography* by Theodore Jorgenson and Nora O. Solum, 1939;
Rølvaag: His Life and Art by Paul Reigstad, 1972.

*   *   *

O. E. Rølvaag's great achievement is *Giants in the Earth,* first published in Norway in 1924 and 1925, then translated into English by Rølvaag and Lincoln Colcord in 1927. The result is remarkable: to a bi-lingual reader the characters seem to be thinking and speaking in Norwegian patterns and cadence, even though the words are English and few Norwegian expressions are left untranslated. By common agreement, *Giants in the Earth* is America's best immigrant story, its great pioneering novel, and a towering documentary of the Middle West.

The events Rølvaag describes in *Giants in the Earth* occurred twenty-five years before he arrived in America. But the setting is the South Dakota he came to in 1896 at the age of twenty, the characters his own kind of Norwegian immigrants, and the events a composite of many accounts he had heard from Dakota pioneers. Writing the book in the 1920's, Rølvaag relied especially on the memory of his father-in-law, Andrew Berdahl. Although the prairie he describes is a formidable adversary for his pioneers, Rølvaag's characters are even more remarkable, especially the hard-driving, inventive, and irrepressible Per Hansa: he is the very type of the ideal American pioneer, yet also very Norwegian. But critics usually have even higher praise for Per's wife, Berit, who is neurotic, backward-looking, and fanatically religious. Rølvaag's pioneer has a dual struggle: against the unbroken prairie and a wife who thinks she has sinned unforgivably in disobeying her parents, in mating with Per Hansa, and in leaving Norway.

Per Hansa's story is heroic and tragic, rare qualities in twentieth century fiction. Berit lives on through the two sequels Rølvaag wrote – *Peder Victorious* and *Their Fathers' God* – and achieves a greatness of her own. The struggle to retain her Norwegian heritage in the new American settlements was a cause Rølvaag supported whole-heartedly. But the essential themes of the two later novels – assimilation and cultural clashes – lack the power and drama of the pioneering struggle. Of more interest is *Pure Gold*, a reworking of Rølvaag's 1920 novel *To Tullinger* (Two Fools): it is the stark tale of a pioneering couple who become monsters of greed. Rølvaag's own favorite was *Laengselens Baat*, which appeared in English translation as *The Boat of Longing* after his death. The strong note of pathos (perhaps pessimism) in this novel has two sources: Nils, a sensitive, artistic, young immigrant, encounters a materialistic America; and his Norwegian parents wait in vain for letters from their son.

Even though the greatness of *Giants in the Earth* was recognised at once, scholars and critics have been uneasy about assigning Ole Rølvaag a place in American literature: he wrote in Norwegian, not English. His psychological realism might owe something to Sherwood Anderson, but a greater influence stemmed from Knut Hamsun and Arne Garborg. As his correspondence reveals, Rølvaag wrote as fluently in English as in Norwegian. Working with translators in turning his novels into English, he weighed and considered each word and phrase. But Rølvaag taught Norwegian language and literature during most of his life in America. Despite Conrad's achievement in the English novel, Rølvaag thought that giving up his native language would require "a remaking of soul." Such a "spiritual readjustment" he would not undertake.

—Clarence A. Glasrud

ROTH, Henry. American. Born in Tysmenica, Austria-Hungary, 8 February 1906. Educated at the City College of New York, B.S. 1928. Married Muriel Parker in 1939; two sons. Worked for the Works Progress Administration (WPA), 1939; teacher at Roosevelt High School, New York, 1939–41; precision metal grinder in New York, Providence, Rhode Island, and Boston, 1941–46; teacher in Montville, Maine, 1947–48; attendant at the Maine State Hospital, 1949–53; waterfowl farmer, 1953–62; private tutor, 1956–65. Recipient: National Institute of Arts and Letters grant, 1965; City College of New York's Townsend Harris Medal, 1965; D. H. Lawrence Fellowship, University of New Mexico, 1968. Lives in Albuquerque, New Mexico.

PUBLICATIONS

Fiction

Call It Sleep.   1934.

Reading List: *Roth* by Bonnie Lyons, 1975.

*   *   *

The author of a single novel of intense power, Henry Roth has a minor but vital position in twentieth-century American writing. *Call It Sleep*, published in 1934 but neglected until reprinted in 1960, concentrates immigrant life, childhood experience, and Freudian theory in a striking, stream-of-consciousness narrative. Although Henry Roth has never published another novel – some short stories have appeared in periodicals – *Call It Sleep* remains an important work for its blending of Jewish myth, psychological symbol, and urban reality. A writer of the depression and part of a group to emerge in the 1930's in New York and Chicago (Michael Gold, Daniel Fuchs, Meyer Levin), Henry Roth nonetheless remains unique in his creation of a young hero caught between the foulness of life and the purity of dreams.

Call It Sleep appeared in the same year as the first American edition of *Ulysses*, and Roth, who was influenced by Joyce, employed the techniques of interior monologue, free association, and stylistic experimentation. Developing the myths of redemption and rebirth, Roth enlarged his novel from an autobiographical account of Jewish immigrants in Brooklyn and the Lower East Side to a dramatic exploration of childhood, family conflict, and Oedipal aggression. Four symbols dominate the novel: a cellar connoting dark, sexual fears, a picture with overtones of illicit sex, a piece of coal that is the key to flaming redemption and a trolley rail that is the means to a blinding, almost mystical power.

Language in the novel becomes a fascinating interweaving of English narrative, Yiddish speech, and idioms of the street. Emulating the tale of Isaiah and the burning coal of redemption, the young hero, David Schearl, in the climactic scene of the book virtually kills himself by forcing a milk ladle into the third rail of a trolley track. This act is the symbolic culmination of the hero's desperate effort to redeem himself and his world. His act of purification achieves his need for transcending the sordidness of everyday life – the family quarrels, beatings by his father, poverty of his neighborhood, mistreatment of his mother – that has plagued him.

Call It Sleep, for all its accuracy in portraying immigrant life and economic injustice, cannot be labeled a proletarian or radical novel. It is, rather, a work of vivid, imaginative power that surpasses the stereotypes of such fiction. But why has Henry Roth written no other major work? He explains this failure as not having to mature: "In *Call It Sleep* I stuck with the child, so I didn't have to mature.... I think I just failed at maturity, at adulthood." Shunning the life of a writer, Henry Roth has been a laborer, teacher, psychiatric attendant, and waterfowl farmer. But his distaste for literary life and small output does not detract from the value of his novel, which remains one of the most affecting works of American prose fiction.

—I. B. Nadel

ROTH, Philip (Milton). American. Born in Newark, New Jersey, 19 March 1933. Educated at Newark College, Rutgers University, 1950–51; Bucknell University, Lewisburg, Pennsylvania, 1951–54, A.B. 1954; University of Chicago, 1954–55, M.A. 1955. Served in the United States Army, 1955–56. Married Margaret Martinson in 1958 (died, 1968). Instructor in English, University of Chicago, 1956–58; full-time writer from 1958; Visiting Writer, University of Iowa, Iowa City, 1960–62; Writer-in-Residence, Princeton University, New Jersey, 1962–64; Visiting Writer, State University of New York at Stony Brook, 1966, 1967, and the University of Pennsylvania, Philadelphia, 1967, 1968, 1970, 1971. Member of the Corporation of Yaddo, Saratoga Springs, New York. Recipient: Guggenheim Fellowship, 1959; National Book Award, 1960; Daroff Award, 1960; National Institute of Arts and Letters grant, 1960; O. Henry Award, 1960; Ford Foundation grant, for drama, 1965; Rockefeller Fellowship, 1966. Member, National Institute of Arts and Letters, 1970.

PUBLICATIONS

Fiction

    Goodbye, Columbus, and Five Short Stories.   1959.
    Letting Go.   1962.
    When She Was Good.   1967.
    Portnoy's Complaint.   1969.
    Our Gang (Starring Tricky and His Friends).   1971.
    The Breast.   1972.
    The Great American Novel.   1973.
    My Life As a Man.   1974.
    The Professor of Desire.   1977.

Plays

    Heard Melodies Are Sweet, in *Esquire,* August 1958.
    The President Addresses the Nation (sketch; produced 1973).

Other

    Reading Myself and Others.   1975.

Bibliography: *Roth: A Bibliography* by Bernard F. Rodgers, Jr., 1974.

Reading List: *Bernard Malamud and Roth: A Critical Essay* by Glenn Meeter, 1968; "The Journey of Roth" by Theodore Solotaroff, in *The Red Hot Vacuum,* 1970.

*   *   *

"Sheer Playfulness and Deadly Seriousness are my closest friends," Philip Roth has remarked in interview; "I am also on friendly terms with Deadly Playfulness, Serious Playfulness, Serious Seriousness, and Sheer Sheerness. From the last, however, I get nothing; he just wrings my heart and leaves me speechless." Roth's early work explored with a tense and exasperated earnestness "the whole range of human connections ... between clannish solidarity ... and exclusion or rejection," the struggle of what he has called "the determined self" (in a double sense) against its contingent identity and environment. *When She Was Good* surprised his critics by delineating the self-deception and hypocrisy of small-town Gentile America with the same acid sharpness he brought to the anxieties, pieties, and suppressed hysteria of middle-class and metropolitan Jewry in *Goodbye, Columbus* and *Letting Go.* Roth's characters are usually painfully alert to the insistent and insidious dialogue of conscience with the unconscious: beneath the innocent and upright text of conversation and event lurks a subtext of amoral impulsions, disclosed through Freudian slips and misprisions, by displacement, gesture, and "unintended" innuendo. With *Portnoy's Complaint* the libido came into its own, redefining the ironic, self-conscious wit which enlivened the earlier works as the evasive strategy of "people [who] wear the old unconscious on their *sleeves.*" Portnoy complains that he is "the son in the Jewish joke – *only it ain't no joke!*", and the book mischievously ends with a "punch line" ("So. Now vee may perhaps to begin. Yes?") which brackets the whole confessional text as a pre-analysis warm-up on Dr. Spielvogel's couch.

(This same psychoanalyst returns in *My Life as a Man* as representative of a grey, reassuring normalcy which frames the novelist-hero's outrageously self-dramatizing "life.")

Portnoy's compulsive onanism, fêted with Rabelaisian panache, provides a constant analogy for the art of fiction itself (a "complaint" is both physical disorder and literary device). Story-telling is also an autotelic act, a self-sufficient and finally inconsequential spilling of the beans; and the theme is extended in *The Breast*, where Kepesh wakes to find himself translated into the literary tradition he has been teaching, metamorphosed into a huge, almost self-enclosed mammary gland – "Beyond sublimation. I made the word flesh. I have outKafkaed Kafka." *The Great American Novel* (its very title self-reflexive) is a tissue of parody and pastiche which suggests that baseball is not only *a* theme but *the* supreme fiction of American culture (as Roth remarked in an essay, "the literature of my boyhood"). *My Life as a Man* has as its main text the "True Story" of the novelist Peter Tarnopol, preceded by two "Useful Fictions" which are his short-story variations on the crisis of marital breakdown and blocked creativity which dominates his in-any-case fictitious "Life." Roth plays further games with the reader, alluding to previous writings of Tarnopol's that inevitably and teasingly recall his own earlier work. But if here narcissism in "life" (i.e., "content") becomes reflected in the auto-referentiality of the "text" (i.e., "form"), the sheer exuberance of Roth's invention makes it clear that he is not fixated in the dead-end "Sheer Sheerness" of his fictive analogue. If Tarnopol is only tangentially affected by the great historic events of his era, Roth has written of them at length in *Our Gang* (settling accounts in advance with the Nixon mafia) and in the essays collected as *Reading Myself and Others*. For Roth the introversions of contemporary fiction reflect a wider, social dilemma: "Defying a multitude of bizarre projections, or submitting to them," he has said, "would seem to me at the heart of everyday living in America." Adapting Philip Rahv's division of American writers into "redskins" and "palefaces" – the one rumbustious and anarchic, the other stiff and priggish – he has proposed his own third category, a subversive synthesis of the two, the "redface." Roth's is the poetry of embarrassment and exposure; by making *unease* both theme and narrative technique, he has fused play and seriousness into a style inimitably his own, which is not easily rendered "speechless."

—Stan Smith

RUKEYSER, Muriel. American. Born in New York City, 15 December 1913. Educated at Fieldston School, New York, 1919–30; Vassar College, Poughkeepsie, New York; Columbia University, New York, 1930–32. Has one son. Vice-President, House of Photography, New York, 1946–60; taught at Sarah Lawrence College, Bronxville, New York, 1946, 1956–57. Since 1967, Member, Board of Directors, Teachers–Writers Collaborative, New York. President, P.E.N. American Center, 1975–76. Recipient: Harriet Monroe Award, 1941; National Institute of Arts and Letters Award, 1942; Guggenheim Fellowship, 1943; American Council of Learned Societies Fellowship, 1963; Swedish Academy translation award, 1967. D.Litt.: Rutgers University, New Brunswick, New Jersey, 1961. Member, National Institute of Arts and Letters. Lives in New York City.

PUBLICATIONS

Verse

Theory of Flight. 1935.
U.S. 1. 1938.
Mediterranean. 1938.
A Turning Wind. 1939.
The Soul and Body of John Brown. 1940.
Wake Island. 1942.
Beast in View. 1944.
The Children's Orchard. 1947.
The Green Wave. 1948.
Orpheus. 1949.
Elegies. 1949.
Selected Poems. 1951.
Body of Waking. 1958.
Waterlily Fire: Poems 1932–1962. 1962.
The Outer Banks. 1967.
The Speed of Darkness. 1968.
29 Poems. 1970.
Breaking Open. 1973.
The Gates. 1976.

Play

The Color of the Day (produced 1961).

Fiction

The Orgy. 1965.

Other

Willard Gibbs (biography). 1942.
The Life of Poetry. 1949.
Come Back Paul (juvenile). 1955.
One Life (biography of Wendell Willkie). 1957.
I Go Out (juvenile). 1961.
Bubbles (juvenile). 1967.
Poetry and Unverifiable Fact: The Clark Lectures. 1968.
The Traces of Thomas Hariot. 1971.

Translator, with others, *Selected Poems of Octavio Paz.* 1963; revised edition, 1973.
Translator, *Sun Stone,* by Octavio Paz. 1963.
Translator, with Leif Sjöberg, *Selected Poems of Gunnar Ekelöf.* 1967.
Translator, *Three Poems by Gunnar Ekelöf.* 1967.
Translator, with others, *Early Poems 1935–1955,* by Octavio Paz. 1973.

*　　*　　*

Much has been said about the feminine voice in poetry, usually by critics. No one seems to know exactly what the "true" feminine voice is, except that somewhere between the despair and the joy of woman's second-class existence, a kind of experience is finally being written. Sylvia Plath wrote from this sensibility and a number of new lady poets have missed the joy expressed between the lines, where Plath had made words that work together. The assumption that despair should somehow outweigh joy in serious feminine poetry results from the Dickinson (and now, Plath) tradition.

Reading the work of Muriel Rukeyser, one quickly learns that feminism is not so easily defined. Once again, the near-answer is revealed for what it is, and we are thrown back to the poem itself. Rukeyser's work can be despairing, but her responses have larger potential. Even in moments of sad recollection, as in "Effort at Speech Between Two People," Rukeyser's voice is not entirely despondent:

> When I was three, a little child read a story about a rabbit
> who died, in the story, and I crawled under a chair   :
> a pink rabbit   :   it was my birthday, and a candle
> burnt a sore spot on my finger, and I was told to be happy.

Here, Rukeyser has successfully combined the elements of mature narrative with a verbal sense of what it was like to live through that third birthday. The poem is not cute, in any of its aspects, and in spite of succeeding lines ("I am unhappy. I am lonely. Speak to me.") never indulges in outright despondency. It is the hope for communication that has initially caused the poem which survives, echoed by lively images, and imbuing the poem ultimately with a sense of optimism.

Rukeyser's work is always tough, however, and never assumes the false authority that is so often mistaken for wisdom. She investigates nearly every aspect of life, from the desperate haircutting of a boy who needs work to "The Power of Suicide," one of her tight, excellent four-line poems:

> The potflower on the windowsill says to me
> In words that are green-edged red leaves:
> Flower   flower   flower   flower
> Today for the sake of all the dead   Burst into flower.

The simplicity of such a poem makes explication impossible: what gimmicks of "style" has the poet employed? One knows only that the poem is bound by a natural rhythm, and seems to relate a part of the poet's experience.

Some of Rukeyser's long poems, in particular "The Speed of Darkness," are among the finest we'll have to carry with us into the next century. Her vocabulary is truly of our generation, but she's writing poems of a longer endurance:

> Whoever despises the clitoris despises the penis
> Whoever despises the penis despises the cunt
> Whoever despises the cunt despises the life of the child.
>
> Resurrection music,   silence,   and surf.

In "Waterlily Fire," she curiously mixes hard consonant sounds with a softer, feminine voice:

> We pray : we dive into each other's eyes
> Whatever can come to a woman can come to me.
> This the long body : into life from the beginning....

The toughness of these poems suggests that "feminine," with all its present connotations, is not the correct adjective for Miss Rukeyser's work. The frankness of her love poems (read "What I See") combined with her muted optimism also makes for memorable poetry.

For the moment, such "optimism" seems the only valid voice that any poet, regardless of sex, can bring to his work. Anything else is a lie, or why would the poet trouble to write at all?

Muriel Rukeyser's poetry *is* feminine, but only because the poet is a lady. It is enduring because the poet has retained all of her "seventeen senses," and utilizes every one of them in her work.

—Geof Hewitt

RUNYON, (Alfred) Damon.   American.   Born in Manhattan, Kansas, 4 October 1880; grew up in Pueblo, Colorado. Educated in Pueblo public schools. Served in the United States Army during the Spanish-American War, 1898–1900. Married 1) Ellen Egan in 1911 (died), one son and one daughter; 2) Patrice del Grande in 1932 (divorced, 1946). Reporter for, successively, the Pueblo *Chieftain*, Colorado Springs *Gazette*, Denver *News*, Denver *Post*, and San Francisco *Post*, 1900–10; Sportswriter for the New York *American*, 1911–18, and Correspondent for Hearst newspapers in Mexico, 1912, and in Europe during World War 1, 1917–18; columnist and feature writer for King Features/International News Service, from 1918; producer at RKO and 20th Century Fox, Hollywood, 1942–43; in later years lived in Florida. Recipient: National Headliners Club of New York Feature Writing Prize, 1939. Died of Cancer: Damon Runyon Memorial Fund for Cancer Research established shortly after his death. *Died 10 December 1946.*

PUBLICATIONS

Collections

   A Treasury of Runyon, edited by Clark Kinnaird.   1958.

Fiction (stories)

   Guys and Dolls.   1931.
   Blue Plate Special.   1934.
   Money From Home.   1935.
   More Than Somewhat.   1937.
   Furthermore.   1938.
   The Best of Damon Runyon, edited by E. C. Bentley.   1938.
   Take It Easy.   1938.
   My Old Man.   1939.

My Wife Ethel. 1940.
Damon Runyon Favorites. 1942.
Runyon à la Carte. 1944.
In Our Town. 1946.
Short Takes. 1946.
Trials and Other Tribulations. 1948.
Runyon First and Last. 1949; as *All This and That*, 1950.
The Turps. 1951.

Play

A Slight Case of Murder, with Howard Lindsay (produced 1935).   1940.

Verse

The Tents of Trouble. 1911.
Rhymes of the Firing Line. 1912.
Poems for Men. 1947.

Other

Captain Eddie Rickenbacker, with Walter Kiernan.   1942.

*   *   *

Damon Runyon belongs to that long line of American journalists who make copy out of the comic potentiality of life around them. Much of that comedy derives from the rich variety of speech patterns among the various immigrant communities spread across the U.S.: German, Dutch, Polish, Irish; and, in Runyon's case, the Jewish-Italian speech of the Bronx and related areas of New York. For what gives Runyon his special distinction is that he wrote about life in the big city, whereas previous journalist/fiction-writers in his mould had largely confined themselves to small-town midwestern communities.

Runyon's world is that of the seedy mafiosa, barflies, compulsive gamblers, womanisers, men who sport names such as "Society Max," "Harry the Horse," "Rusty Charlie," "Feet Samuels," "Dancing Dan." All the stories about these characters are written in the continuous present tense, as though Runyon himself is one of the barflies, spinning a yarn into his neighbour's ear, making a chuckly anecdote out of his friends' misfortunes and misadventures. For example: "This Heine Schmitz is a very influential citizen of Harlem, where he has large interests in beer, and it is by no means violating any confidence to tell you that Heine Schmitz will just as soon blow your brains out as look at you. In fact, I hear sooner."

Once he had discovered this raffishly, down-at-heels, yet defiantly stylish world (or sub-world), and had discovered a style of narrating its doings, there was really no reason why Runyon shouldn't go on and on recounting anecdotes about it (much as Wodehouse, having invented Wooster and Jeeves, could set them in motion time after time). Runyon was, in fact, a prolific author. Quite apart from volumes of light verse, there were numerous collections of his short stories and a play. The verse and play need not detain us. They are lightweight, the verse reminiscent of poets like James Whitcomb Riley and Eugene Field, in that they tell folksy tales of lovable low-life characters, although in Runyon's case the characters were often of the city rather than of the country.

Of the volumes of short stories, perhaps the pick are *More Than Somewhat, Take It Easy*,

Furthermore, and *My Old Man*. The best of the stories are hilariously funny, and Runyon manages effortlessly to capture a style of speech which, in its aping of "polite" or "standard" American English, tells one only too graphically of the difficulties immigrant communities had in learning a new tongue, while desperately – or naturally – keeping to modes of expression that belonged to their mother-tongue. Who can forget Nathan Detroit's anxious questioning of ever-loving Adelaide: "Would you say that some doll might fall for some guy which you would not think she would do so?" Or Joe the Joker's remark that "Only last night, Frankie Ferocious sends for Ropes and tells him he will appreciate it as a special favour if Ropes will bring me to him in a sack"?

One could, of course, object that the real world of the Mafia is so cynically immoral that laughter about it is indefensible. Perhaps. But against that it has to be said that Runyon's world is no more real than the world of the Woosters, or of Blandings. In its own way, however, it is just as funny.

—John Lucas

SALINGER, J(erome) D(avid).   American.   Born in New York City, 1 January 1919. Educated in New York City public schools; at Valley Forge Military Academy, Pennsylvania; New York University; Columbia University, New York. Served as a Staff Sergeant in the 4th Infantry Division of the United States Army, 1942–46. Married Claire Douglas in 1953 (divorced, 1967); one son and one daughter. Writer from 1940; contributed to *The New Yorker*, 1948–59. Lives in New Hampshire.

PUBLICATIONS

Fiction

The Catcher in the Rye.   1951.
Nine Stories.   1953; as *For Esmé – With Love and Squalor, and Other Stories*.   1953.
Franny and Zooey (stories).   1961.
Raise High the Roof Beam, Carpenters, and Seymour: An Introduction.   1963.

Reading List: *The Fiction of Salinger* by Frederick L. Gwynn and Joseph L. Blotner, 1960; *Salinger and the Critics* edited by William F. Belcher and James W. Lee, 1962; *Salinger* by Warren French, 1963; *Studies in Salinger* edited by Marvin Laser and Norman Fruman, 1963; *Salinger: A Critical and Personal Portrait* by Henry A. Grunwald, 1964; *Salinger* by James E. Miller, 1965.

*   *   *

Of his writings, J. D. Salinger has so far wished to preserve only a novel and thirteen short stories, all published between 1948 and 1959, mostly in *The New Yorker*. Despite this limited body of work, Salinger was, at least between 1951 and 1963, the most popular American fiction writer among serious young persons and many alienated adults because of the way in which he served as a spokesman for the feelings of his generation. Thus his work is of unique interest as evidence of the sensibility of those times.

Salinger had taken a short-story writing course under Whit Burnett, the influential editor of *Story*, which gave many important American fiction writers their start. Salinger's first published work, "The Young Folks," appeared there in 1940. Like much of his later work, this slight piece contrasted the behavior of, on one hand, shy, sensitive and, on the other, tough, flippant, unfeeling young upper-middle-class urbanites. During the 1940's, Salinger published (in *Story* and most of the popular slick magazines like *Collier's*) another nineteen stories that he has not allowed to be collected. Some of these, like "This Sandwich Has No Mayonnaise," are of interest for introducing a character named Holden Caulfield, who resembles the later protagonist of *The Catcher in the Rye*, but who dies during World War II. Most are very short, heavily ironic tales about troubled young people defeated by what Holden Caulfield would call "the phony world." The only one of great interest in the light of Salinger's later achievement is the longest, "The Inverted Forest," a cryptic tale about an artist's relationship to society. The lines quoted from the poetry of the central figure, Raymond Ford – "Not wasteland, but a great inverted forest/with all the foliage underground" – suggest that all beauties are internal, so that the artist is exempt from external responsibilities.

The question of the sensitive individual's responsibility to the world remains the focal question in all of Salinger's better known fiction. *The Catcher in the Rye* is the comically grotesque account of Holden Caulfield's two-and-a-half-day odyssey through the waste land of New York City at Christmas time after he decides to quit his fashionable prep school. Holden dreams of escaping the city and going out west where he could build "a little cabin somewhere ... and live there for the rest of my life ... near the woods, but not right in them" (a description that foreshadows almost exactly the New England retreat where Salinger himself has lived for the past twenty years). In the speech that gives the novel its title, he tells his little sister Phoebe that the one thing he would like to do is stand guard over "all these little kids playing some game in this big field of rye and all" and "catch everybody if they start to go over the cliff." But Holden learns, when he sees obscenities scratched on the walls of Phoebe's elementary school, that "You can't ever find a place that's nice and peaceful, because there isn't any." And watching Phoebe ride the Central Park carousel, he realizes, "The thing with kids is, if they want to grab for the gold ring, you have to let them do it, and not say anything." Wiser but sadder, he decides that he must return home rather than take the responsibility for leading Phoebe astray.

Although Salinger is most often identified as the author of this novel, Holden Caulfield, who finally compromises with his social responsibilities, is not the typical hero in Salinger's work. The stories that the author has chosen to preserve begin and end with accounts of the suicide of Seymour Glass, oldest son and spiritual guide to his six siblings of a New York Irish-Jewish theatrical family. In "A Perfect Day for Bananafish," the first of *Nine Stories*, we learn only the circumstances of Seymour's suicide in a Miami Beach hotel. In "Seymour: An Introduction," his brother and interpreter Buddy offers at last the explanation for the event: "The true artist-seer ... is mainly dazzled to death by his own scruples, the blinding shapes and colors of his own sacred human conscience."

The eleven stories published between these two carry us from the account of the suicide to the illumination of its significance, and reflect along the way Salinger's increasing absorption in oriental philosophies, especially Zen Buddhism. Four of *Nine Stories* – "Uncle Wiggily in Connecticut," "The Laughing Man," "Just Before the War with the Eskimos," and "Pretty Mouth and Green My Eyes" – offer, like *The Catcher in the Rye*, depressing pictures of people trapped in the "phony" world, but dreaming of a "nice" world. In four of the later stories, however, Salinger suggests that the grim situation might be ameliorated – "Down at the Dinghy" portrays Seymour's sister's reconciliation of her small son to a threatening world; "For Esmé – With Love and Squalor" is a triumphant epithalamion for a young girl who has done meaningful good in a warring world; "DeDaumier-Smith's Blue Period" is an amazingly successful description of a mystical experience that leads a young man to forsake aggressive ambitions; and the famous concluding story, "Teddy," presents a boy who has truly absorbed the Buddhist concept of the illusoriness of material life and is prepared to move serenely beyond it.

In the longer "Glass Saga" stories, Salinger focuses on Seymour's siblings and presents, in "Franny," the story of the youngest child's breakdown when confronted with the "ego" of the squalid world of college and theater. In "Zooey," her brother literally talks her out of her breakdown by assuming the voice of the departed Seymour, and counselling, "An artist's only concern is to shoot for some kind of perfection, and *on his own terms*, not anyone else's." "Raise High the Roof Beam, Carpenters" prefaces "Seymour: An Introduction" with Buddy's fond recollection of Seymour's violent responses to beauty and his supreme affront to the rituals of his urban caste when he persuades his intended to run off with him on their wedding day instead of submitting to a fancy ceremony.

Since these stories were collected in 1963, Salinger has published only "Hapworth 16, 1924," a labored account of seven-year-old Seymour's prodigious sexual and intellectual proclivities as revealed by a letter home from summer camp. In the one interview he has granted in recent years – to protest an unauthorized edition of his uncollected stories – Salinger protested that he is still writing constantly, but he denounced publication as "a terrible invasion" of his privacy.

—Warren French

SANDBURG, Carl. American. Born in Galesburg, Illinois, 6 January 1878. Educated at Lombard College, Galesburg, 1898–1902. Served as a Private in the 6th Illinois Volunteers during the Spanish American War, 1899. Married Lillian Steichen in 1908; three daughters, including the poet Helga Sandburg. Associate Editor, *The Lyceumite*, Chicago, 1907–08; District Organizer, Social-Democratic Party, Appleton, Wisconsin, 1908; City Hall Reporter for the *Milwaukee Journal*, 1909–10; Secretary to the Mayor of Milwaukee, 1910–12; worked for the *Milwaukee Leader* and *Chicago World*, 1912; worked for *Day Book*, Chicago, 1912–17, also Associate Editor, *System: The Magazine of Business*, Chicago, 1913; Stockholm Correspondent, 1918, and Manager of the Chicago Office, 1919, Newspaper Enterprise Association; Reporter, Editorial Writer, and Motion Picture Editor, 1917–30, and Syndicated Columnist, 1930–32, *Chicago Daily News*; Lecturer, University of Hawaii, Honolulu, 1934; Walgreen Foundation Lecturer, University of Chicago, 1940; weekly columnist, syndicated by the *Chicago Daily Times*, from 1941. Recipient: Poetry Society of America Award, 1919, 1921; Friends of Literature Award, 1934; Roosevelt Memorial Association prize, for biography, 1939; Pulitzer Prize, for history, 1940, and for poetry, 1951; American Academy of Arts and Letters Gold Medal, 1952; National Association for the Advancement of Colored People Award, 1965. Litt.D.: Lombard College, 1928; Knox College, Galesburg, Illinois, 1929; Northwestern University, Evanston, Illinois, 1931; Harvard University, 1940; Yale University, New Haven, Connecticut, 1940; New York University, 1940; Wesleyan University, Middletown, Connecticut, 1940; Lafayette College,

Easton, Pennsylvania, 1940; Syracuse University, New York, 1941; Dartmouth College, Hanover, New Hampshire, 1941; University of North Carolina, Chapel Hill, 1955; Uppsala College, New Jersey, 1959; LL.D.: Hollins College, Virginia, 1941; Augustana College, Rock Island, Illinois, 1948; University of Illinois, Urbana, 1953. Commander, Order of the North Star, Sweden, 1953. Member, American Academy of Arts and Letters, 1940. *Died 22 July 1967.*

PUBLICATIONS

Collections

The Letters, edited by Herbert Mitgang.　1968.

Verse

In Reckless Ecstasy.　1904.
The Plaint of the Rose.　1904(?).
Incidentals.　1904.
Joseffy.　1910.
Chicago Poems.　1916.
Cornhuskers.　1918.
Smoke and Steel.　1920.
Slabs of the Sunburnt West.　1922.
(Poems), edited by Hughes Mearns.　1926.
Selected Poems, edited by Rebecca West.　1926.
Good Morning, America.　1928.
The People, Yes.　1936.
Bronze Wood.　1941.
Complete Poems.　1950; revised edition, 1970.
Harvest Poems 1910–1960, edited by Mark Van Doren.　1960.
Six New Poems and a Parable.　1961.
Honey and Salt.　1963.
Breathing Tokens, edited by Margaret Sandburg.　1978.

Fiction

Remembrance Rock.　1948.

Other

You and Your Job.　1908.
The Chicago Race Riots, July 1919.　1919.
Rootabaga Stories (juvenile).　1922.
Rootabaga Pigeons (juvenile).　1923.
Abraham Lincoln: The Prairie Years.　2 vols., 1926 (selection, for children, as *Abe Lincoln Grows Up,* 1928); *Abraham Lincoln: The War Years,* 4 vols., 1939; revised abridgement, as *Storm over the Land,* 1942; one volume selection *The Prairie Years and War Years,* 1954.

Rootabaga Country (juvenile).   1929.
Steichen, The Photographer.   1929.
Early Moon (juvenile).   1930.
Potato Face (juvenile).   1930.
Mary Lincoln, Wife and Widow, with Paul M. Angle.   1932.
Home Front Memo.   1943.
The Photographs of Abraham Lincoln, with Frederick Hill Meserve.   1944.
Lincoln Collector: The Story of Oliver R. Barrett's Great Private Collection.   1949.
Always the Young Strangers (autobiography).   1953; selection, for children, as *Prairie-
    Town Boy,* 1955.
The Sandburg Range (miscellany).   1957.
Wind Song (juvenile).   1960.

Editor, *American Songbag.*   1927; *New American Songbag,* 1950.
Editor, *A Lincoln and Whitman Miscellany.*   1938.

Screen documentary: *Bomber* 1945.

Bibliography: *Sandburg: A Bibliography* by Thomas S. Shaw, 1948.

Reading List: *Sandburg: A Study in Personality and Background* by Karl W. Detzer, 1941;
Sandburg by Harry Golden, 1961; *Sandburg* by Richard H. Crowder, 1964; *Sandburg* by
Mark Van Doren, 1969 (includes bibliography); *Sandburg: Lincoln of Our Literature* by
North Callahan, 1970; *Sandburg, Yes* by W. G. Rogers, 1970; *Sandburg* by Gay Wilson
Allen, 1972.

*   *   *

Harriet Monroe's magazine *Poetry* in 1914 gave conspicuous position to Carl Sandburg's
early poems. Readers were drawn by his Whitman-like quality, now vigorous and rugged,
now gentle and compassionate. His books *Chicago Poems* and *Cornhuskers* set the pace and
established him as a leading American poet. His free-verse lines were, at their best, musical
and varied. His subject matter was generally quarried from the cities and countryside of the
Midwest. His themes were built on concern for the common man, concomitant with his
interest in Socialism. Out of the Great Depression came his book *The People, Yes,* consisting
of folk sayings cemented together by optimistic prophecies to the effect that the ordinary man
would eventually receive his due. Sandburg's last book of poems, *Honey and Salt,* continued
to substantiate his thesis that the life of "the family of man" is not all sweet, that it is tempered
by the sobering experience of everyday existence and even by tragedy. In this book the old
poet, through his reliance on a proliferation of color images unusual in a writer at the end of
his career, proved to be as vigorous as a tyro one-third his age.
    The People, Yes had been a product of Sandburg's interest in folklore. Two collections of
the songs of the people established him as something of an authority: *The American Songbag*
and the expanded *New American Songbag.* In fact, for the twenty years preceding World War
II Sandburg traveled widely singing these songs to large audiences, accompanying himself on
the guitar.
    In prose biography Sandburg showed a skillful hand. He wrote of his wife's brother in
Steichen,The Photographer and of the wife of his life-long hero in *Mary Lincoln, Wife and
Widow.* His most famous prose work remains his 6-volume biography of Lincoln. If in this
monumental work (without footnotes and index) he occasionally rearranged the chronology
and indeed embroidered the facts, he nevertheless produced a rich and sensitive portrait, filled
with incident, pointed up with insight, and made brilliant with poetic truth. His *Always the*

Young Strangers tells the story of his own growing-up with a remarkable analytical objectivity in an enchanting style as engrossing as a novel.

Remembrance Rock was something else again. Commissioned by Metro-Goldwyn-Mayer to write a "great American novel" later to be made into a scenario for a moving picture, Sandburg turned out a wooden, repetitive piece of fiction, not only very long, but very tiresome. Like *The People, Yes* the book is packed with songs, proverbs, anecdotes, folk customs. Effective in a Depression poem, this subject matter was ill suited to the novel form. In spite of the book's ineptness, however, Sandburg was continuing to show his integrity and generosity, his hatred of bigotry, his consuming love for his native country.

He was popular with children. His *Rootabaga Stories*, *Rootabaga Pigeons*, and *Potato Face* enjoyed wide readership. The fantasy, inventiveness, humor, and light-heartedness in these stories were similar to many of the traits in his poems, selections from which, indeed, were collected in anthologies intended for children.

Sandburg no doubt will long be remembered for his Lincoln biography and for many of his poems. The reader can recall the alternating robustiousness and pathos of "Chicago," the delicate imagism of "Fog," the loud anger of "To a Contemporary Bunkshooter," the wholesome aspiration of *The People, Yes*. Even though one cannot place him in the very top rank of American poets, it is possible to say that to have read Sandburg is to have been the companion of a deeply rooted and dedicated citizen of the United States and of a conscious craftsman skilled in communicating the basic emotions, especially as felt by the "ordinary" person. It must be emphasized that Sandburg was moved not just by the masses, what he lovingly called "the mob." True, he was sympathetic with his "people" as they struggled toward the stars (one of his early poems chanted, "I am the people, the mob"), but his many poems about individuals showed him to be actively aware of the inescapable fact that every man and woman experiences troubles and ecstasies (e.g., "The Hangman at Home," "Helga," "Ice Handler," "Mag"). Furthermore, though Sandburg is linked with Lindsay and Masters as an Illinois poet, he is seen to be, on careful study, a poet of universals. If his most frequent subjects are the little people of his home state, his themes are nonetheless the concerns of all people everywhere.

—Richard H. Crowder

SANTAYANA, George. Spanish. Born in Madrid, 16 December 1863; emigrated with his family to the United States, 1872, but retained Spanish nationality. Educated at the Brimmer School, Boston; Boston Latin School; Harvard University, Cambridge, Massachusetts, 1882–86, B.A. 1886; studied in Berlin, 1886–88, and at King's College, Cambridge, 1896–97. Taught philosophy at Harvard University, 1889–1912: Professor of Philosophy, 1907–12; writer from 1894; Hyde Lecturer, the Sorbonne, Paris, 1905–06; lived in Europe from 1912, in England, 1914–18, and in Rome from 1920; Spencer Lecturer, Oxford University, 1923; lived in the Convent of Santa Stefano Rotondo, Rome, from 1939. Recipient: Royal Society of Literature Benson Medal, 1928; Columbia University Butler Gold Medal, 1945. *Died 26 September 1952.*

PUBLICATIONS

Collections

The Letters, edited by Daniel Cory.   1955.
Complete Poems, edited by William G. Holzberger.   1978.

Fiction

The Last Puritan: A Memoir in the Form of a Novel.   1935.

Plays

Lucifer: A Theological Tragedy.   1899; revised edition, 1924.
The Marriage of Venus, and *Philosophers at Court*, in *The Poet's Testament.*   1953.

Verse

Sonnets and Other Verses.   1894.
A Hermit of Carmel and Other Poems.   1891.
Poems.   1922.
The Poet's Testament: Poems and Plays.   1953.

Other

Lotze's System of Philosophy.   1889; edited by Paul Grimley Kuntz, 1971.
Platonism in the Italian Poets.   1896.
The Sense of Beauty, Being the Outlines of Aesthetic Theory.   1896.
Interpretations of Poetry and Religion.   1900.
The Life of Reason; or, The Phases of Human Progress.   5 vols., 1905–06; revised
    edition, with Daniel Cory, 1954.
Three Philosophical Poets: Lucretius, Dante, and Goethe.   1910.
Winds of Doctrine: Studies in Continental Opinion.   1913.
Egotism in German Philosophy.   1916; as *The German Mind,* 1968.
Character and Opinion in the United States.   1920.
Little Essays, edited by Logan Pearsall Smith.   1920.
Soliloquies in England and Later Soliloquies.   1922.
Scepticism and Animal Faith.   1923.
Dialogues in Limbo.   1925; revised edition, 1948.
Platonism and the Spiritual Life.   1927.
The Realm of Essence.   1927; *The Realm of Matter,* 1930; *The Realm of Truth,* 1937;
    The Realm of Spirit, 1940; complete version, as *The Realms of Being,* 4 vols., 1942.
The Genteel Tradition at Bay.   1931.
Five Essays.   1933; as *Some Turns of Thought in Modern Philosophy,* 1933.
Obiter Scripter: Lectures, Essays, Reviews, edited by Justus Buchler and Benjamin
    Schwartz.   1936.
The Works.   14 vols., 1936–37.
The Philosophy of Santayana, edited by Irwin Edman.   1936.

The Background of My Life. 1944; *The Middle Span,* 1945; *My Host the World,* 1953; complete version, as *Persons and Places,* 1963.

The Idea of Christ in the Gospels; or, God in Man. 1946.

Atoms of Thought: An Anthology of Thoughts, edited by Ira D. Cardiff. 1950; as *The Wisdom of Santayana,* 1964.

Dominations and Powers: Reflections on Liberty, Society, and Government. 1951.

Essays in Literary Criticism, edited by Irving Singer. 1956.

The Idler and His Works, and Other Essays, edited by Daniel Cory. 1957.

Vagabond Scholar (letters and dialogues with Bruno Lind). 1962.

Animal Faith and Spiritual Faith (essays), edited by John Lachs. 1967.

The Genteel Tradition: Nine Essays, edited by Douglas L. Wilson. 1967.

Santayana's America: Essays on Literature and Culture, edited by James Ballowe. 1967.

Santayana on America, edited by Richard Carlton Lyon. 1968.

Selected Critical Writings, edited by Norman Henfrey. 2 vols., 1968.

The Birth of Reason and Other Essays, edited by Daniel Cory. 1968.

Physical Order and Moral Liberty: Previously Unpublished Essays, edited by John and Shirley Lachs. 1969.

Translator, with others, *The Writings of Alfred de Musset,* revised edition, vol. 2. 1907.

Reading List: *The Philosophy of Santayana* by Paul S. Schilpp, 1940 (includes bibliography by Shonig Terzian); *Santayana and the Sense of Beauty* by Richard Butler, 1956; *Santayana's Aesthetics: A Critical Introduction* by Irving Singer, 1957; *Santayana: The Laters Years* by Daniel Cory, 1963; *Santayana, Art, and Aesthetics* by Jerome Ashmore, 1966; *Santayana* by Willard E. Arnett, 1968.

* * *

Born in Spain of a Roman Catholic family, George Santayana was a philosopher, an atheist and a materialist, but retained a deep affection for the Roman Catholic Church, and died in his old age, as an invalid, cared for by nuns in a Convent hospital in Rome. His working life was spent as Harvard where his colleague, the optimistic pragmatist William James, disliked Santayana intensely and felt that his dry, cynical sadness was corrupting. Few philosophers of his time, if any (the possible rivals are F. H. Bradley and Henri Bergson) have written with more charm and elegance. The defect of such a style in a philosopher, however, is that it lulls the reader who should be alert for logical flaws; as a result, it would be hard to summarise Santayana's thought. He might be described, perhaps, as a Platonising materialist; only matter was eternal, man was mortal, but man could abstract from matter intellectual essences which (except that they were final products, not sources of being) resembled Plato's world of forms and ideas. Santayana is perhaps at his best as a thinker when he steps away from abstract thinking and applies his mind to literature, as in *Three Philosophical Poets,* or to a place that appealed to him, as in *Soliloquies in England.* In his novel, *The Last Puritan,* based on his knowledge of young Americans through his teaching at Harvard, he tries to do justice to the best sides of that American tradition which, with his innately hierarchical and conservative attitude, he on the whole rejected.

—G. S. Fraser

SAROYAN, William.   American.   Born in Fresno, California, 31 August 1908. Educated in Fresno public schools. Served in the United States Army, 1942–45. Married Carol Marcus in 1943 (divorced, 1949; remarried, 1951; divorced, 1952); one daughter and one son, the poet Aram Saroyan. Past occupations include grocery clerk, vineyard worker, post office employee; Clerk, Telegraph Operator, then Office Manager of the Postal Telegraph Company, San Francisco, 1926–28; Co-Founder, Conference Press, Los Angeles, 1936; Founder and Director, Saroyan Theatre, New York, 1942; Writer-in-Residence, Purdue University, Lafayette, Indiana, 1961. Recipient: New York Drama Critics Circle Award, 1940; Pulitzer Prize, 1940 (refused). Member, National Institute of Arts and Letters. Lives in Fresno, California.

PUBLICATIONS

Fiction

The Daring Young Man on the Flying Trapeze and Other Stories.   1934.
Inhale and Exhale (stories).   1936.
Three Times Three (stories).   1936.
Little Children (stories).   1937.
A Gay and Melancholy Flux: Short Stories.   1937.
Love, Here Is My Hat (stories).   1938.
A Native American (stories).   1938.
The Trouble with Tigers (stories).   1938.
Peace, It's Wonderful (stories).   1939.
3 Fragments and a Story.   1939.
My Name Is Aram (stories).   1940.
Saroyan's Fables.   1941.
The Insurance Salesman and Other Stories.   1941.
48 Saroyan Stories.   1942.
31 Selected Stories.   1943.
Some Day I'll Be a Millionaire: 34 More Great Stories.   1943.
The Human Comedy.   1943.
Dear Baby (stories).   1944.
The Adventures of Wesley Jackson.   1946.
The Saroyan Special: Selected Short Stories.   1948.
The Fiscal Hoboes (stories).   1949.
The Twin Adventures: The Adventures of Saroyan: A Diary; The Adventures of Wesley Jackson: A Novel.   1950.
The Assyrian and Other Stories.   1950.
Rock Wagram.   1951.
Tracy's Tiger.   1951.
The Laughing Matter.   1953; as *The Secret Story,* 1954.
The Whole Voyald and Other Stories.   1956.
Mama, I Love You.   1956.
Papa, You're Crazy.   1957.
Love (stories).   1959.
Boys and Girls Together.   1963.
One Day in the Afternoon of the World.   1964.
After Thirty Years: The Daring Young Man on the Flying Trapeze (includes essays).   1964.
Best Stories of Saroyan.   1964.

My Kind of Crazy Wonderful People: 17 Stories and a Play.   1966.

Plays

The Man with the Heart in the Highlands, in *Contemporary One-Act Plays,* edited by
  William Kozlenko.   1938; revised version, as *My Heart's in the Highlands* (produced
  1939), 1939.
The Time of Your Life (produced 1939).   1939.
The Hungerers (produced 1945).   1939.
A Special Announcement (broadcast 1940).   1940.
Love's Old Sweet Song (produced 1940).   In *Three Plays,* 1940.
*Three Plays: My Heart's in the Highlands, The Time of Your Life, Love's Old Sweet
  Song.*   1940.
Subway Circus.   1940.
Something about a Soldier (produced 1940).
Hero of the World (produced 1940).
The Great American Goof (ballet scenario; produced 1940).   In *Razzle Dazzle,* 1942.
Radio Play (broadcast 1940).   In *Razzle Dazzle,* 1942.
The Ping Pong Game (produced 1945).   1940.
Sweeney in the Trees (produced 1940).   In *Three Plays,* 1941.
The Beautiful People (produced 1941).   In *Three Plays,* 1941.
*Three Plays: The Beautiful People, Sweeney in the Trees, Across the Board on Tomorrow
  Morning.*   1941.
Across the Board on Tomorrow Morning (produced 1941).   In *Three Plays.* 1941.
The People with Light Coming Out of Them (broadcast 1941).   In *The Free Company
  Presents,* 1941.
There's Something I Got To Tell You (broadcast 1941).   In *Razzle Dazzle,* 1942.
Hello, Out There (produced 1941).   In *Razzle Dazzle,* 1942.
Jim Dandy (produced 1941).   1941; as *Jim Dandy: Fat Man in a Famine,* 1947.
Talking to You (produced 1942).   In *Razzle Dazzle,* 1942.
*Razzle Dazzle; or, The Human Opera, Ballet, and Circus; or, There's Something I Got to
  Tell You: Being Many Kinds of Short Plays As Well As the Story of the Writing of Them*
  (includes *Hello, Out There, Coming Through the Rye, Talking to You, The Great
  American Goof, The Poetic Situation in America, Opera, Opera, Bad Men in the West,
  The Agony of Little Nations, A Special Announcement, Radio Play, The People with
  Light Coming Out of Them, There's Something I Got to Tell You, The Hungerers,
  Elmer and Lily, Subway Circus, The Ping Pong Players*).   1942.
Opera, Opera (produced 1955).   In *Razzle Dazzle,* 1942.
Get Away Old Man (produced 1943).   1944.
Sam Ego's House (produced 1947–48?).   In *Don't Go Away Mad and Two Other Plays,*
  1949.
Don't Go Away Mad (produced 1949).   In *Don't Go Away Mad and Two Other
  Plays.*   1949.
*Don't Go Away Mad and Two Other Plays: Sam Ego's House; A Decent Birth, A Happy
  Funeral.*   1949.
The Son (produced 1950).
The Slaughter of the Innocents (produced 1957).   1952.
The Oyster and the Pearl: A Play for Television (televised 1953).   In *Perspectives USA,*
  Summer 1953.
Once Around the Block (produced 1956).   1959.
The Cave Dwellers (produced 1957).   1958.
Ever Been in Love with a Midget (produced 1957).
Cat, Mouse, Man, Woman; and The Accident, in *Contact 1,* 1958.

Settled Out of Court, with Henry Cecil, from the novel by Henry Cecil (produced
  1960). 1962.
The Dogs; or, The Paris Comedy (as *Lily Dafon*, produced 1960).   In *The Dogs; or, The
  Paris Comedy and Two Other Plays*, 1969.
Sam, The Highest Jumper of Them All; or, The London Comedy (produced
  1960). 1961.
High Time along the Wabash (produced 1961).
Ah Man, music by Peter Fricker (produced 1962).
*Four Plays: The Playwright and the Public, The Handshakers, The Doctor and the
  Patient, This I Believe*, in *Atlantic*, April 1963.
Dentist and Patient, and Husband and Wife, in *The Best Short Plays 1968*, edited by
  Stanley Richards. 1968.
*The Dogs; or, The Paris Comedy and Two Other Plays: Chris Sick; or, Happy New Year
  Anyway, Making Money, and Nineteen Other Very Short Plays*. 1969.
The New Play, in *The Best Short Plays 1970*, edited by Stanley Richards. 1970.
Armenians (produced 1974).
The Rebirth Celebration of the Human Race at Artie Zabala's Off-Broadway Theatre
  (produced 1975).

Screenplay: *The Good Job*, 1942.

Radio Plays: *Radio Play*, 1940; *A Special Announcement*, 1940; *There's Something I Got
to Tell You*, 1941; *The People with Light Coming Out of Them*, 1941.

Television Plays: *The Oyster and the Pearl*, 1953; *Ah Sweet Mystery of Mrs. Murphy*,
1959; *The Unstoppable Gray Fox*, 1962.

Ballet Scenario: *The Great American Goof*, 1940.

Other

The Time of Your Life (miscellany). 1939.
Harlem as Seen by Hirschfeld. 1941.
Hilltop Russians in San Francisco. 1941.
Why Abstract?, with Henry Miller and Hilaire Hiler. 1945.
The Bicycle Rider in Beverly Hills (autobiography). 1952.
Saroyan Reader. 1958.
Here Comes, There Goes, You Know Who (autobiography). 1961.
A Note on Hilaire Hiler. 1962.
Me (juvenile). 1963.
Not Dying (autobiography). 1963.
Short Drive, Sweet Chariot (autobiography). 1966.
*Look at Us: Let's See: Here We Are: Look Hard: Speak Soft: I See, You See, We all See;
  Stop, Look, Listen; Beholder's Eye; Don't Look Now But Isn't That You? (us?
  U.S.?)*. 1967.
Horsey Gorsey and the Frog (juvenile). 1968.
I Used to Believe I Had Forever; Now I'm Not So Sure. 1968.
*Letters from 74 rue Taitbout; or, Don't Go But if You Must Say Hello to
  Everybody*. 1969; as *Don't Go But If You Must Say Hello to Everybody*, 1970.
Days of Life and Death and Escape to the Moon. 1970.
Places Where I've Done Time. 1972.
The Tooth and My Father (juvenile). 1974.
Famous Faces and Other Friends: A Personal Memoir. 1976.

Morris Hirshfield.   1976.
Sons Come and Go, Mothers Hang In Forever (memoirs).   1976.
Chance Meetings.   1978.

Editor, *Hairenik 1934–1939: An Anthology of Short Stories and Poems.*   1939.

Bibliography: *A Bibliography of Saroyan 1934–1963* by David Kherdian, 1965.

Reading List: *Saroyan* by Howard R. Floan, 1966.

*   *   *

Hailed by some as the greatest writer to come out of San Francisco since Frank Norris, William Saroyan is one of the striking paradoxes in 20th-century literary writing in America. If he has been dismissed for being non-literary, a critic of the eminence of Edmund Wilson has lauded him for his uncanny gift for creating atmosphere in his books: "Saroyan takes you to the bar, and he creates for you there a world which is the way the world would be if it conformed to the feeling instilled by drinks. In a word, he achieves the feat of making and keeping us boozy without the use of alcohol and purely by the action of art."

Saroyan never went beyond high school and thus exemplifies the successful homespun writer. *The Daring Young Man on the Flying Trapeze and Other Stories* was his first collection of short fiction, and many still consider it to be among his finest writing. A breathtakingly prolific writer (he produced about five hundred stories between 1934 and 1940), Saroyan is a short story writer, playwright, and novelist, but his claim to greatness rests essentially on plays like *My Heart's in the Highlands* and *The Time of Your Life* and on his short stories. He has been criticized for his pervasive sentimentality, but his retort to the charge is that it is a very sentimental thing to be a human being. And to the charge that his style is careless and sloppy, he responded: "I do not know a great deal about what the words come to, but the presence says, Now don't get funny; just sit down and say something: it'll be all right. Say it wrong; It'll be all right anyway. Half the time I *do* say it wrong, but somehow or other, just as the presence says, it's right anyway. I am always pleased about this."

One of his best stories, "A Daring Young Man on the Flying Trapeze," is an interior monologue revealing the recollections of a poor writer who lives in the troubled present while achieving distance from it by reaching back into the past centuries. Unperturbed on the conscious level by his problems, occasionally the young writer is embittered by such experiences as the need to sell his books to buy food. Finally, on returning to his room in the afternoon from his wanderings he dies a sudden and painless death. Saroyan's identification with his young protagonist is evident, despite the author's disclaimers. The story is suffused with pathos, though there is clearly an attempt to hold the sentimentality in check. The story would also appear to be a plea for sympathy and support for deprived writers. Among his plays, *The Time of Your Life* is the one that probably most fully reflects Saroyan the artist. It received both the Drama Critics Circle Award and the Pulitzer Prize, but Saroyan refused the latter as an expression of his contempt for commercial patronage of art. Despite its melodramatic plot the play, as Howard R. Floan admirably sums up, is "about a state of mind, illusive but real, whose readily recognizable components are, first, an awareness of America's youth – its undisciplined swaggering, unregulated early life – and, secondly, a pervasive sense of America in crisis: an America of big business, of labor strife, of depersonalized government, and, above all, of imminent war."

At seventy, Saroyan's interest in the comedy-tragedy of life remains undiminished: "Living is the only thing. It is an awful pain most of the time, but this compels comedy and dignity." What makes Saroyan stand out in American literary writing is his optimism about life despite the evidence to the contrary in the world around, especially as perceived by most American writers; and his buoyancy seems to work with his considerable reading public. But the major appeal of his writing comes from his characters, who are common people like gas station attendants, and from his heavily romantic emphasis on the individuality of man. With charming candour Saroyan not too long ago declared that his main purpose was to earn as much money as possible – a confession that has been used by adverse criticism to exaggerate the casualness of his writing and to withhold due recognition from him.

—J. N. Sharma

SCHWARTZ, Delmore.   American.   Born in Brooklyn, New York, 8 December 1913. Educated at the University of Wisconsin, Madison, 1931; New York Unive:.ity (Editor, *Mosaic* magazine), 1933–35, B.A. in philosophy 1935; Harvard University, Cambridge, Massachusetts, 1935–37. Married 1) Gertrude Buckman (divorced); 2) Elizabeth Pollet in 1949. Briggs-Copeland Instructor in English Composition, 1940, Instructor in English, 1941–45, and Assistant Professor of English, 1946–47, Harvard University. Fellow, Kenyon School of English, Gambier, Ohio, Summer 1950; Visiti·'3 Professor at New York University, Indiana School of Letters, Bloomington, Princeton University, New Jersey, and University of Chicago. Editor, 1943–47, and Associate Editor, 1947–55, *Partisan Review*, New Brunswick, New Jersey; associated with *Perspectives* magazine, New York, 1952–53; Literary Consultant, New Directions, publishers, New York, 1952–53; Poetry Editor and Film Critic, *New Republic* magazine, Washington, D.C., 1955–57. Recipient: Guggenheim Fellowship, 1940; National Institute of Arts and Letters grant, 1953; Bollingen Prize, 1960; Shelley Memorial Award, 1960. *Died 11 July 1966.*

PUBLICATIONS

Collections

Selected Essays, edited by Donald A. Dike and David H. Zucker.   1970.
What Is to Be Given: Selected Poems, edited by Douglas Dunn.   1976.

Verse

In Dreams Begin Responsibilities (includes short story and play).   1938.
Genesis: Book One (includes prose).   1943.
Vaudeville for a Princess and Other Poems (includes prose).   1950.
Summer Knowledge: New and Selected Poems 1938–1958.   1959.

Play

Shenandoah; or, The Naming of the Child.   1941.

Fiction

The World Is a Wedding and Other Stories.   1949.
Successful Love and Other Stories.   1961.

Other

Editor, *Syracuse Poems 1964.*   1965.

Translator, *A Season in Hell* (bilingual edition), by Arthur Rimbaud.   1939.

Bibliography: in *Selected Essays,* 1970.

Reading List: *Schwartz* by Richard McDougall, 1974; *Schwartz: The Life of an American Poet* by James Atlas, 1977.

*   *   *

It is difficult, reading Delmore Schwartz, to disentangle the poetry from the legend. The darling of the group of American intellectuals associated with the *Partisan Review* in the 1930's and 1940's — to which he contributed as poet, critic, and short story writer, and eventually became co-editor — Schwartz had a career worthy of the last *poète maudit*. A precociously brilliant first book, *In Dreams Begin Responsibilities*, was followed by a tragic decline into alcohol, insanity, and an early death, alone, in a seedy Manhattan hotel. Posthumously, Schwartz has undergone a literary "canonisation" in one of the most heartbreaking sequences of John Berryman's *Dream Songs* and as the eponymous "hero" of Saul Bellow's *Humboldt's Gift*. The life is forbiddingly close to stereotyped, "romantic" conceptions of "the Poet."

And Schwartz almost certainly saw himself in something like this role. The titles alone of some of his best known poems — "Do Others Speak of Me Mockingly, Maliciously?," "All of Us Always Turning Away for Solace" — suggest his fundamental view of the poet as one isolated from his tribe, cut off, as in the marvellous "The Heavy Bear Who Goes with Me," from contact even with his own body. The characteristic Schwartzian stance is apparent in his "Sonnet: O City, City": we live

> Where the sliding auto's catastrophe
> Is a gust past the curb, where numb and high
> The office building rises to its tyranny,
> Is our anguished diminution until we die.

In the same poem, however, he longs for an alternative human sympathy, "the self articulate, affectionate and flowing." Between these terms the course of his poetry runs.

It is a poetry that rarely loses touch with political and historical realities: "The Ballad of the Children of the Czar" and the verse play *Shenandoah* poignantly express Schwartz's understanding of his family's experience as Jewish immigrants to the States. There is the larger feeling, in many poems, of human beings *imprisoned* in time, bearing the guilt of generations, and Schwartz probes at his guilts and anxieties in a way that occasionally, as in "Prothalamion," points forward to the "confessional" poetry to be written by his more famous contemporaries Berryman and Lowell. The guardian angels of these poems, figures which haunt Schwartz's imagination and are returned to with obsessive insistence, are the heroic solitaries — Faust, Socrates, "Tiger Christ," "Manic-depressive Lincoln," and, above all, Hamlet.

But there is also in Schwartz, if less insistently, an energetically vibrant language and feeling, a kind of robust dandyism, as in "Far Rockaway":

> The radiant soda of the seashore fashions
> Fun, foam, and freedom. The sea laves
> The shaven sand. And the light sways forward
> On the self-destroying waves.

Douglas Dunn, in his introduction to *What Is to Be Given*, has referred to Schwartz's "sometimes dispiriting ebullience," and it is this that many critics have objected to in the later work. A poem like "Seurat's Sunday Afternoon along the Seine" certainly needs to be read without the expectation of those judicious ironies on which most modern poetry thrives. But, *relaxed into*, the stretch and sweep, the sheer verbal intoxication of the poem, carry persuasive power.

Schwartz is a poet, and a critic, too little read and too little understood. Recent re-publications, however, suggest that his work will survive, along with the best of his generation.

—Neil Corcoran

SEXTON, Anne (Harvey).   Born in Newton, Massachusetts, 9 November 1928. Educated at Garland Junior College, Boston, 1947–48. Married Alfred M. Sexton in 1948 (divorced, 1974); two daughters. Fashion Model, Boston, 1950–51; Scholar, Radcliffe Institute for Independent Study, Cambridge, Massachusetts, 1961–63; Teacher, Wayland High School, Massachusetts, 1967–68; Lecturer in Creative Writing, 1970–71, and Professor of Creative Writing, 1972–74, Boston University. Crawshaw Professor of Literature, Colgate University, Hamilton, New York, 1972. Recipient: Bread Loaf Writers Conference Robert Frost Fellowship, 1959; American Academy of Arts and Letters Traveling Fellowship, 1963; Ford Foundation grant, 1964; Shelley Memorial Award, 1967; Pulitzer Prize, 1967; Guggenheim Fellowship, 1969. Litt.D.: Tufts University, Medford, Massachusetts, 1970; Regis College, Weston, Massachusetts, 1971; Fairfield University, Connecticut, 1971. Honorary Member, Phi Beta Kappa, 1968. *Died 4 October 1974.*

PUBLICATIONS

Verse

To Bedlam and Part Way Back.   1960.
All My Pretty Ones.   1962.
Selected Poems.   1964.
Live or Die.   1966.
Poems, with Douglas Livingstone and Thomas Kinsella.   1968.

Love Poems. 1969.
Transformations. 1971.
The Book of Folly. 1972.
O Ye Tongues. 1973.
The Death Notebooks. 1974.
The Awful Rowing Towards God. 1975.
45 Mercy Street, edited by Linda Gray Sexton. 1976.

Play

Mercy Street (produced 1969).

Other

Eggs of Things (juvenile), with Maxine Kumin. 1963.
More Eggs of Things (juvenile), with Maxine Kumin. 1964.
Joey and the Birthday Present (juvenile), with Maxine Kumin. 1971.
The Wizard's Tears (juvenile), with Maxine Kumin. 1975.
Sexton: A Self-Portrait in Letters, edited by Linda Gray Sexton and Lois Ames. 1977.

Bibliography: *Sylvia Plath and Sexton: A Reference Guide* by Cameron Northouse and Thomas P. Walsh, 1975.

Reading List: *Sexton: The Artist and Her Critics* edited by J. D. McClatchy, 1978.

*   *   *

Anne Sexton is known primarily for her remarkable imagery and apparent personal honesty in poems ranging from the formally structured early work (*To Bedlam and Part Way Back*) to the quasi-humorous prose poems of *Transformations* and the evocative free form poetry of *Love Poems.* Sexton had published much of her most mature work in the years immediately preceeding her evident suicide, and her critical reputation has yet to acknowledge that last productive period.

Sexton was a model who married, reared two daughters, and came to poetry through a workshop at Boston University conducted by Robert Lowell. Influenced by Lowell and the writing of W. D. Snodgrass to break the restraint and intellectualism common to American poetry during the 1950's, Sexton wrote such moving personal poems as "The Double Image." Her consideration here of the relationship among a mother, daughter, and grandchild is important not only for the technical prowess with which she handled a possibly sentimental subject, but for the genuine insight into the women's condition. Encouraged by her friendship with Sylvia Plath, who also was a student in the Lowell workshop, Sexton mined areas of theme and image that were virtually unknown to contemporary poetry. "Those Times" re-creates her own childhood as a time of torment; "Little Girl, My String Bean, My Lovely Woman" celebrates her joy in her daughter; "Flee on Your Donkey" plumbs the depths of personal despair; "Menstruation at Forty" questions the mortality image from a feminine view – most of Sexton's poems are adventurous in that she is writing not only about unconventional subjects, but her quick progression from image to image lends an almost surreal effect to the poetry.

Rather than simply describing Sexton's work as "confessional," the over-used label that attached itself to any writing that seemed autobiographical in origin (as what poetry is, finally, not?), readers should be aware that her work manages to distill the apparently autobiographical details into an imagistic whole which convinces any reader of its authenticity. The life in Sexton's poems is the life of the imagination, regardless of whether or not she has used the facts from her own existence in the re-creation of that life. Once the poems from the late collections have been assimilated with the earlier work, her continuous interest in religious themes and images will become as noticeable as her use of feminine psychology and concerns. Sexton's importance to American poetry will not rest simply on her mental stability or instability, her suicide, or her use of personal detail in her work; her importance will rest, finally, on her ability to craft poems that moved the reader to the act of understanding.

—Linda W. Wagner

SHAPIRO, Karl (Jay).   Born in Baltimore, Maryland, 10 November 1913. Educated at the University of Virginia, Charlottesville, 1932–33; Johns Hopkins University, Baltimore, 1937–39; Pratt Library School, Baltimore, 1940. Served in the United States Army, 1941–45. Married 1) Evalyn Katz in 1945 (divorced, 1967); 2) Teri Kovach in 1969; two daughters, and one son. Associate Professor of Writing, Johns Hopkins University, 1947–50; Visiting Professor, University of Wisconsin, Madison, 1948, and Loyola University, Chicago, 1951–52; Lecturer, Salzburg Seminar in American Studies, 1952; State Department Lecturer, India, 1955; Visiting Professor, University of California, Berkeley and Davis, 1955–56, and University of Indiana, Bloomington, 1956–57; Professor of English, University of Nebraska, Lincoln, 1956–66, and University of Illinois, Chicago Circle, 1966–68. Since 1968, Professor of English, University of California at Davis. Editor, *Poetry*, Chicago, 1950–56, *Newberry Library Bulletin*, Chicago, 1953–55, and *Prairie Schooner*, Lincoln, Nebraska, 1956–66. Consultant in Poetry, Library of Congress, Washington, D.C., 1946–47. Recipient: National Institute of Arts and Letters grant, 1944; Guggenheim Fellowship, 1944, 1953; Pulitzer Prize, 1945; Shelley Memorial Award, 1946; Kenyon School of Letters Fellowship, 1956, 1957; Bollingen Prize, 1969. D.H.L.: Wayne State University, Detroit, 1960; D.Litt.: Bucknell University, Lewisburg, Pennsylvania, 1972. Fellow in American Letters, Library of Congress; Member, American Academy of Arts and Sciences, and National Institute of Arts and Letters. Lives in Davis, California.

PUBLICATIONS

Verse

Poems.   1935.
Five Young American Poets, with others.   1941.
Person, Place, and Thing.   1942.
The Place of Love.   1942.
V-Letter and Other Poems.   1944.
Essay on Rime.   1945.
Trial of a Poet and Other Poems.   1947.
Poems 1940–1953.   1953.
The House.   1957.

Poems of a Jew. 1958.
The Bourgeois Poet. 1964.
Selected Poems. 1968.
White-Haired Lover. 1968.
Adult Bookstore. 1976.
Collected Poems 1940–1977. 1978.

Play

The Tenor, music by Hugo Weisgall. 1956.

Fiction

Edsel. 1970.

Other

Poets at Work: Essays Based on the Modern Poetry Collection at the Lockwood Memorial Library, University of Buffalo, with others, edited by Charles D. Abbot. 1948.
English Prosody and Modern Poetry. 1947.
A Bibliography of Modern Prosody. 1948.
Beyond Criticism. 1953; as *A Primer for Poets,* 1965.
In Defense of Ignorance (essays). 1960.
Start with the Sun: Studies in Cosmic Poetry, with James E. Miller, Jr., and Bernice Slote. 1960.
A Prosody Handbook, with Robert Beum. 1965.
Randall Jarrell. 1967.
To Abolish Children and Other Essays. 1968.
The Poetry Wreck: Selected Essays 1950–1970. 1975.

Editor, with W. H. Auden and Marianne Moore, *Riverside Poetry 1953: Poems by Students in Colleges and Universities in New York City.* 1953.
Editor, *American Poetry.* 1960.
Editor, *Prose Keys to Modern Poetry.* 1962.

Bibliography: *Shapiro: A Bibliography* by William White, 1960.

*   *   *

Karl Shapiro is a poet of great versatility who has a sophisticated command of prosody and a sharp ear for speech rhythms and verbal harmonies. He is a man of considerable erudition, though he never finished college, and a serious though good-humored social critic. Since his first volume of poems in 1935, he has published continuously. As poet and critic, he always has taken an iconoclastic stance. He attacks intellectual poetry, poseurs, stuffed shirts, and the establishment with great vigor, and as a result has been a controversial figure. As editor of *Poetry* and *The Prairie Schooner* for 16 years, he was a significant force in contemporary poetry, and as a professor he has taught two decades of aspiring writers.

When Shapiro published *Selected Poems,* he ignored his first volume, about which he writes in "Recapitulations":

> My first small book was nourished in the dark,
> Secretly written, published, and inscribed.
> Bound in wine-red, it made no brilliant mark.
> Rather impossible relatives subscribed.

His first recognition came in 1941 when he appeared in *Five Young American Poets*. His next volume, *Person, Place, and Thing*, contains excellent poems of social comment in traditional form. "The Dome of Sunday" comments in sharp, clear imagery cast in blank verse on urban "Row houses and row-lives"; "Drug Store" observes youth culture satirically in unrhymed stanzas; "University [of Virginia]" mounts a low-keyed attack: "To hurt the Negro and avoid the Jew/Is the curriculum."

V-Letter and Other Poems contains some of the best poems to come out of World War II, some of which are "V-Letter," "Elegy for a Dead Soldier," "Troop Train," "The Gun," "Sunday: New Guinea," and "Christmas Eve: Australia." The form usually is rhymed stanzas, even *terza rima*, and here Shapiro's social comment finds a wider context. There also begin to be foreshadowings of later preoccupations: religious themes and attacks on intellectualism. "The Jew" anticipates *Poems of a Jew*, and "The Intellectual" ("I'd rather be a barber and cut hair/Than walk with you in gilt museum halls") looks toward attacks on Pound and Eliot in *In Defense of Ignorance*.

Although Shapiro does not write long poems (the exception is *Essay on Rime*, a youthful treatise on the art of poetry in which "Everything was going to be straightened out"), *Poems 1940–1953* contains an evocative, seven-part sequence telling the story of Adam and Eve. (This interest in myth reasserts itself in *Adult Bookstore* in a poignant version in 260 lines of "The Rape of Philomel.") This volume also contains "Israel," occasioned by the founding of that country: "When I see the name of Israel high in print/The fences crumble in my flesh.... " As a boy Shapiro grew up in a Russian-Jewish family not particularly religious, and after his bar mitzvah "I lost all interest in what I had learned." But *Poems of a Jew* explores his Jewishness with pride, wit, and irony, beginning with "The Alphabet" ("letters ... strict as flames," "black and clean" and bristling "like barbed wire").

As early as 1942 Shapiro had published a prose-poem, "The Dirty Word," but in 1964 he turned to this form exclusively in *The Bourgeois Poet*, dropping the kind of verses he previously had thought best, "the poem with a beginning, a middle, and an end ... that used literary allusion and rhythmic structuring and intellectual argument." He wanted a medium in which he could say anything he pleased – ridiculous, nonsensical, obscene, autobiographical, pompous. The individual pieces cover a wide variety of topics and, as earlier, they comment on persons, places, things. The longest (14 pages), "I Am an Atheist Who Says His Prayers," which reminds one of Shapiro's enthusiasm for Whitman, could have been called "Song of Myself." These prose poems (or free verse set as prose paragraphs) had a mixed reception. But Adrienne Rich noted that in his new style Shapiro was going through a "constant revising and purifying of his speech," as all poets must, and she thought parts of this volume were "a stunning success."

In *White-Haired Lover*, a cycle of middle-aged love poems, Shapiro returned to traditional forms, often the sonnet. This also is true of *Adult Bookstore*, a collection that ranges widely in subject. "The Humanities Building," "A Parliament of Poets," and the title poem show that Shapiro has not lost the wit, irony, and technique that have always characterized his work. "The Heiligenstadt Testament" is a splendid dramatic monologue of Beethoven's deathbed delirium, and among the poems occasioned by his move to California are "Garage Sale" ("This situation .../Strikes one as a cultural masterpeice") and a perfect Petrarchan sonnet on freeways and California suburbia.

The Poetry Wreck, which contains Shapiro's most important critical statements, throws light on his poetry, his sources, his beliefs. The derogatory essays on Pound and Eliot are reprinted along with admiring appraisals of W. H. Auden ("Eliot and Pound had rid the poem of emotion completely ... Auden reversed the process"), William Carlos Williams, "whose entire literary career has been dedicated to the struggle to preserve spontaneity and immediacy of experience," Whitman, Dylan Thomas, Henry Miller, and Randall Jarrell. Jarrell, whose "poetry I admired and looked up to most after William Carlos Williams," once said in a passage Shapiro quotes: "Karl Shapiro's poems are fresh and young and rash and live; their hard clear outline, their flat bold colors create a world like that of a knowing and skillful neo-primitive painting, without any of the confusion or profundity of atmosphere, or aerial perspective, but with notable visual and satiric force."

—James Woodress

SHEPARD, Sam. American. Born in Fort Sheridan, Illinois, 5 November 1943. Educated at Duarte High School, California; Mount San Antonio Junior College, Walnut, California, 1961–62. Married O-Lan Johnson Dark in 1969; one son. Worked as a "hot walker" at Santa Anita Race Track, a stable hand, sheep shearer, herdsman and orange picker, all in California; car wrecker, Charlemont, Massachusetts; busboy at the Village Gate, a waiter at Marie's Crisis Cafe, and musician with the Holy Modal Rounders, all in New York. Recipient: Obie Award, 1967, 1977; Guggenheim Fellowship, 1968, 1971; National Institute of Arts and Letters award, 1974; Brandeis University Creative Arts Award, 1975.

PUBLICATIONS

Plays

    Cowboys (produced 1964).
    Rock Garden (produced 1964; excerpt produced in *Oh! Calcutta!*, 1969). In *The Unseen Hand and Other Plays*, 1971.
    Up to Thursday (produced 1964).
    Dog (produced 1964).
    Rocking Chair (produced 1964).
    Chicago (produced 1965). In *Five Plays*, 1967.
    Icarus's Mother (produced 1965). In *Five Plays*, 1967.
    4-H Club (produced 1965). In *Mad Dog Blues and Other Plays*, 1967.
    Fourteen Hundred Thousand (produced). In *Five Plays*, 1967.
    Red Cross (produced 1966). In *Five Plays*, 1967.
    La Turista (produced 1966). 1968.
    Forensic and the Navigators (produced 1967). In *The Unseen Hand and Other Plays*, 1971.
    Melodrama Play (produced 1967). In *Five Plays*, 1967.
    Five Plays. 1967.
    Cowboys No. 2 (produced 1967). In *Mad Dog Blues and Other Plays*, 1971.
    Shaved Splits (produced 1969). In *The Unseen Hand and Other Plays*, 1971.
    The Unseen Hand (produced 1970). In *The Unseen Hand and Other Plays*, 1971.

Operation Sidewinder (produced 1970).   1970.
Holy Ghostly (produced 1970).   In *The Unseen Hand and Other Plays*, 1971.
Back Bog Beast Bait (produced 1971).   In *The Unseen Hand and Other Plays*, 1971.
Mad Dog Blues (produced 1971).   In *Mad Dog Blues and and Other Plays*, 1971.
Cowboy Mouth (produced 1971).   In *Mad Dog Blues and Other Plays*, 1971.
The Unseen Hand and Other Plays.   1971.
Mad Dog Blues and Other Plays.   1971.
The Tooth of Crime (produced 1972).   In *The Tooth of Crime, and Geography of a Horse
    Dreamer*, 1974.
Nightwalk, with Megan Terry and Jean-Claude van Itallie (produced 1973).
Blue Bitch (produced 1973).
Little Ocean (produced 1974).
Geography of a Horse Dreamer (produced 1974).   In *The Tooth of Crime, and
    Geography of a Horse Dreamer*, 1974.
The Tooth of Crime, and Geography of a Horse Dreamer.   1974.
Action (produced 1974).   In *Action, and The Unseen Hand*, 1975.
Action, and The Unseen Hand.   1975.
Killer's Head (produced 1975).   In *Angel City ...*, 1976.
Angel City (produced 1976).   In *Angel City ...*, 1976.
Angel City, Curse of the Starving Class, and Other Plays (includes *Killer's Head, Action,
    Mad Dog Blues, Cowboy Mouth, Rock Garden, Cowboys No. 2).*   1976.
Curse of the Starving Class (produced 1977).   In *Angel City ...*, 1976.
Suicide in B-flat (produced 1976).

Screenplays: *Me and My Brother*, with Robert Frank, 1967; *Zabriskie Point*, with
others, 1970; *Ringaleevio*, with Murray Mednick, 1971.

Fiction

Hawk Moon (stories).   1972.

Other

Rolling Thunder Logbook.   1977.

*   *   *

Sam Shepard shapes the intellectual, physical, and temporal spaces where improvisational
chance must happen for actors and audience. *Action*'s two couples seek through standard
improvisations to re-create lost group or individual identities that would enable them to
combat fear and cold and perhaps to act. The dramatic event characteristically witholds any
genuine resolution and focuses on the procession of images within an occasioning action-
celebration.

Most of Shepard's over thirty tragi-comedies, like *Action*, are set on a down-slope, "highs"
during the decline of a revolution (*Shaved Splits*), a literacy-based civilization (*Fourteen
Hundred Thousand*), or even Fourth-of-July celebrations (*Icarus's Mother*). Haunting power
plays arise from striking theatrical exercises. Three characters demand attention as
relationships deteriorate in *Red Cross*. Jim uses role-playing to dominate, until each woman
glides off through her compelling sexual/death aria, down a ski-slope or undersea, to a
private place. Returning to everyday hysteria and complacency, they leave their parasitic
victim-tormentor bleeding and empty. Despite established orders of fundamentalism,
Mariology, and gunslingers in *Back Bog Beast Bait*, a new beast slouches toward the stage to

be born – with the aid of poisonous mushrooms, totem animals, and a bewitching Cajun fiddler.

Language is a probe, a veil, an incantation, a mystery of voices. Diction and syntax catch and flow directly from the styles of different contemporary subcultures. The verbal vitality of a young man in an electric chair (*Killer's Head*) ignores and postpones the inevitable with talk of trucks, rodeos, distances, racing, breeding. Disorganizing-discovering voices often surprise the speaker. The seventh son of "Holy Ghostly" leads his father through ancient-modern myths and shamanisms to embrace his own dying. Their languages slip one to another, and roles slide and erode identities.

In the brilliant, extended battle of words and musical movement of *The Tooth of Crime*, Hoss's original, characterizing virtuosity falls to the power-stealing dazzle of Crow's mimicry. The art-and-power theme – begun in *Cowboy Mouth* and *Melodrama Play*, toyed with in *Mad Dog Blues* – finally bleeds through its images. *Angel City* explores the same theme with movies, instead of pop-rock. Indian magic reinforces its artists' mystery (intuition-inspiration) until the ultimate disaster film engulfs the audience too: "Even chaos has a form!" *Geography of a Horse Dreamer* charts the broken flow of inspiration through race-track and criminal images, until brothers' shotguns save the dreamer's magic neckbone from falling into a medicine bundle. Primitive magic that decorates the matched panels of punning *La Turista* is the overwhelming ground of power in *Operation Sidewinder*, *Holy Ghostly*, and *Back Bog Beast*, but it becomes a dangerous net-below in these later, and better, plays. Rituals cannot prevent the sale and destruction of a California family and farm in *Curse of the Starving Class*. Man is caught but falls through the magic charts or totems. Keeping Shepard's special coherence, *Action* and *Curse* somehow make his notoriously bizarre images, arias, and rituals feel inevitable as Russian realism.

This prolific young playwright knowingly freshens the conventions, terror, and pleasure essential to theatre.

—John G. Kuhn

SHERWOOD, Robert E(mmet). American. Born in New Rochelle, New York, 4 April 1896. Educated at Milton Academy, Massachusetts, 1909–14; Harvard University, Cambridge, Massachusetts, 1914–17, B.A. 1918. Served in the Canadian Black Watch, 1917–19: wounded in action, 1918; served as Special Assistant to the Secretary of War, Washington, D.C., 1939–42; Director, Overseas Branch, Office of War Information, 1942–44; Special Assistant to the Secretary of the Navy, Washington, D.C., 1945. Married 1) Mary Brandon in 1922 (divorced, 1934), one daughter; 2) Madeline Hurlock Connelly in 1935. Dramatic Editor, *Vanity Fair*, New York, 1919–20; Film Reviewer and Associate Editor, 1920–24, and Editor, 1924–28, *Life* magazine, New York; Literary Editor of *Scribner's Magazine*, New York, 1928–30; full-time playwright from 1930; Founder, with Elmer Rice, Sidney Howard, Maxwell Anderson, S. N. Behrman, and John F. Wharton, Playwrights Company, 1938. Secretary, 1935, and President, 1937–40, Dramatists Guild;

President, American National Theatre and Academy, 1940. Recipient: Megrue Prize, 1932; Pulitzer Prize, 1936, 1939, 1941, and, for biography, 1949; American Academy of Arts and Letters Gold Medal, 1941; Academy Award, 1946; Bancroft Prize, for history, 1949; Gutenberg Award, 1949. D.Litt.: Dartmouth College, Hanover, New Hampshire, 1940; Yale University, New Haven, Connecticut, 1941; Harvard University, 1949; D.C.L.: Bishop's University, Lennoxville, Quebec, 1950. *Died 14 November 1955.*

PUBLICATIONS

Plays

    The Road to Rome (produced 1926). 1927.
    The Love Nest (produced 1927).
    The Queen's Husband (produced 1928). 1928.
    Waterloo Bridge (produced 1929). 1930.
    This Is New York (produced 1930). 1931.
    Reunion in Vienna (produced 1931). 1932.
    Acropolis (produced 1933).
    The Petrified Forest (produced 1935). 1935.
    Idiot's Delight (produced 1936). 1936.
    The Ghost Goes West (screenplay), with Geoffrey Kerr, in *Successful Film Writing* by Seton Margrave. 1936.
    Tovarich, from a play by Jacques Deval (produced 1936). 1937.
    The Adventures of Marco Polo (screenplay), in *How to Write and Sell Film Stories* by Frances Marion. 1937.
    Abe Lincoln in Illinois (produced 1938). 1939.
    There Shall Be No Night (produced 1940). 1940.
    An American Crusader (broadcast 1941). In *The Free Company Presents*, edited by James Boyd, 1941.
    Rebecca (screenplay), with others, in *Twenty Best Film Plays*, edited by John Gassner and Dudley Nichols. 1943.
    The Rugged Path (produced 1945). Shortened version in *The Best Plays of 1945–46*, edited by Burns Mantle, 1946.
    Miss Liberty, music by Irving Berlin (produced 1949). 1949.
    Second Threshold, from a play by Philip Barry (produced 1951).
    Small War on Murray Hill (produced 1957). 1957.

Screenplays: *The Lucky Lady,* with James T. O'Donohoe and Bertram Bloch, 1926; *Oh, What a Nurse!,* with Bertram Bloch and Daryl F. Zanuck, 1926; *Age for Love,* 1931; *Around the World in Eighty Minutes with Douglas Fairbanks,* 1931; *Cock of the Air,* with Charles Lederer, 1932; *Roman Scandal,* with George S. Kaufman, 1933; *The Scarlet Pimpernel,* with others, 1935; *The Ghost Goes West,* with Geoffrey Kerr, 1936; *Over the Moon,* with others, 1937; *Thunder in the City,* with others, 1937; *The Adventures of Marco Polo,* 1938; *The Divorce of Lady X,* with Lajos Biro, 1938; *Idiot's Delight,* 1939; *Abe Lincoln in Illinois,* 1940; *Rebecca,* with others, 1940; *The Best Years of Our Lives,* 1946; *The Bishop's Wife,* with Leonardo Bercovici, 1947; *Man on a Tightrope,* 1953; *Main Street to Broadway,* with Samson Raphaelson, 1953.

Radio Play: *An American Crusader,* 1941.

Television Writing: *The Backbone of America,* 1954.

Fiction

The Virtuous Knight.   1931; as *Unending Crusade,* 1932.

Other

Roosevelt and Hopkins: An Intimate History.   1948; revised edition, 1950; as *The White House Papers of Harry L. Hopkins,* 2 vols., 1948–49.

Editor, *The Best Moving Pictures of 1922–23.*   1923.

Reading List: *Sherwood* by R. Baird Shuman, 1964; *The Worlds of Sherwood: Mirror to His Times 1896–1939,* 1965, and *The Ordeal of a Playwright: Sherwood and the Challenge of War,* edited by Norman Cousins, 1970, both by John Mason Brown; *Sherwood: Reluctant Moralist* by Walter J. Meserve, 1970.

*   *   *

Though of a generation very often described as "rootless" and "lost," Robert Sherwood was a romantic idealist with a liberal outlook whose plays closely corroborated the assumptions underlying the political philosophy of the Roosevelt administration and gave them powerful artistic expression. Alive to the need of creating an art imbued with a social and moral fervour, he believed that the one determining consideration for the future of the theatre was "its ability to give its audiences something they can't obtain, more cheaply and conveniently, in the neighbouring cinema palaces." The artist's lack of social purpose, he pointed out in his address to the P.E.N. International Congress in 1950, gave him a guilty sense of inadequacy – the uneasy knowledge that reform, though needed, was not taking place. The supreme task of "all writers, young and old" was, therefore, to achieve a reconciliation of the "problems of the human heart with a world state of mind that appears to become increasingly inhuman."

Sherwood's anxious apprehension of the insidious threats posed by a world situation indifferent to finer human sentiments constitutes a dominant resonance of his dramatic art. His realistic problem plays – whether set in Finland under Russian attack (*There Shall Be No Night*), or in a hotel in the Alps (*Idiot's Delight*) or in a gasoline station and lunch room in the Arizona desert (*The Petrified Forest*) – often relied on an extreme situation, a background of war or violence, to highlight his protagonists' search for viable ethical values and their eventual affirmation of freedom and peace. Sherwood's pacifism, though closely attuned to the feeling of liberals during the Roosevelt era, was never parochial or chauvinistic and displayed dynamic, even militant, modulations of growth over the years. If his first play, *The Road to Rome,* dealing comically with Hannibal's decision to defer his march on Rome, represents a plea for absolute peace, his last important play, *There Shall Be No Night,* is characterised by the realisation that freedom has to be defended even at the cost of endangering peace temporarily. In fighting the Russians in Finland, the scientist-protagonist of *There Shall Be No Night,* therefore, fights for the emancipation of all men from oppression and unfreedom. Likewise, *The Rugged Path* can be read, at one level, as an idealist's resolve to join the war in defence of peace and human dignity.

Several of Sherwood's plays exemplify his belief that the ability to make personal sacrifice is an index of moral refinement. Sacrifice appears, in *The Petrified Forest,* as a necessary means of preventing Nature from "taking the world away from the intellectuals and giving it back to the apes." On the other hand, *Abe Lincoln in Illinois,* chronicling Lincoln's struggling years before his election to the presidency, sensitively focuses on the relationship between an individual's sacrifice and national interest. Returning to the same moral issue, *There Shall Be*

No Night implies through the fate of its protagonist that "There is no coming to consciousness without pain."

Sherwood's moral bias often made him vulnerable to the charge of overt didacticism – and not without some justification. As one who always had his fingertips on the pulse of his age and depended securely on its grammar of assent, Sherwood, in a literary career spanning nearly three decades, rarely suggested new and daring departures from the opinions current in his milieu. As a result, the moralistic intentions of his plays tended to be so static that their appeal rarely extended beyond their topical issues. But it must also be recognized that his didacticism very often went beyond direct statements to become an integral aspect of dramatic form. In *Abe Lincoln in Illinois*, for example, the curtain is meant to drop just as the farewell crowd, which has been singing "John Brown's Body," reaches the line "His soul goes marching on." Also, his frequent use of comedy, as in *The Road to Rome* and *The Queen's Husband*, helped substantially in relieving the solemnity of potentially moralistic themes. Moreover, one sign of "health" that critics always detected in Sherwood was that his ironic consciousness did not overlook the flaws in his own plays and made him record them with rare candour and precision. To cite one instance, he found *The Road to Rome* defective, because it employed "the cheapest sort of device – making historical characters use modern slang."

Sherwood also experimented with several other kinds of writing, achieving mixed results. *The Virtuous Knight*, his early historic novel about the Third Crusade, was generally regarded as a failure, though its perusal in retrospect does provide useful insights into his treatment of the themes and techniques of character-delineation that were to be employed later in his plays. His scenario *The Best Years of Our Lives* won an Academy Award in 1946, but his TV show, *The Backbone of America* , produced a year before his death, turned out to be a dismal flop. The crowning success of his non-dramatic writing was his biography *Roosevelt and Hopkins*, based on his experience as special assistant to the Secretary of War, director of the Overseas Branch of the Office of War Information, and, more important, as Roosevelt's favourite speechwriter and unofficial adviser. The book, ranked among the finest histories of World War II written in the United States, received several awards.

In spite of his immense popular appeal in his own lifetime, Sherwood does not belong to the same class of playwrights as Eugene O'Neill, Arthur Miller, and Tennessee Williams. For this reason, as time passes, his plays are unlikely to be received with the same immediacy they once elicited. Still, there can be no denying that his realistic problem plays, inspirited as they were by his passion for freedom and peace, faithfully reflected the urges and anxieties of the American people and, in the attempt, made a significant contribution to American drama in the 1920's and 1930's.

—Chirantan Kulshrestha

SIMPSON, Louis (Aston Marantz). American. Born in Jamaica, West Indies, 27 March 1923; became a U.S. citizen. Educated at Munro College, Jamaica, 1933–40, Cambridge Higher Schools Certificate 1940; Columbia University, New York, B.S. 1948, A.M. 1950, Ph.D. 1959. Served in the United States Army, 1943–45: Purple Heart and Bronze Star. Married 1) Jeanne Claire Rogers in 1949 (divorced, 1954), one son; 2) Dorothy Roochvarg in 1955, one son and one daughter. Editor, Bobbs-Merrill Publishing Company, New York, 1950–55; Instructor, Columbia University, 1955–59; Professor of English, University of California, Berkeley, 1959–67. Since 1967, Professor of English, State University of New York at Stony Brook. Recipient: American Academy in Rome Fellowship, 1957; Edna St. Vincent Millay Award, 1960; Guggenheim Fellowship, 1962, 1970; American Council of

Learned Societies Grant, 1963; Pulitzer Prize, 1964; Columbia University Medal for Excellence, 1965; American Academy of Arts and Letters award, 1976. Lives in Port Jefferson, New York.

PUBLICATIONS

Verse

The Arrivistes: Poems 1940–1949.   1949.
Good News of Death and Other Poems.   1955.
A Dream of Governors.   1959.
At the End of the Open Road.   1963.
Five American Poets, with others, edited by Thom Gunn and Ted Hughes.   1963.
Selected Poems.   1965.
Adventures of the Letter I.   1971.
Searching for the Ox: New Poems and a Preface.   1976.

Plays

The Father Out of the Machine: A Masque, in Chicago Review, Winter 1951.
Andromeda, in Hudson Review, Winter 1956.

Fiction

Riverside Drive.   1962.

Other

James Hogg: A Critical Study.   1962.
Air with Armed Men (autobiography).   1972; as North of Jamaica, 1972.
Three on the Tower: The Lives and Works of Ezra Pound, T. S. Eliot, and William Carlos Williams.   1975.

Editor, with Donald Hall and Robert Pack, New Poets of England and America.   1957.
Editor, An Introduction to Poetry.   1967.

Reading List: Simpson by Ronald Moran, 1972.

*   *   *

Always more of a "paleface" than a "redskin" (to adopt Philip Rahv's famous categorization of American writers), Louis Simpson took some time to find his own poetic voice. His early poetry is heavily dependent on John Crowe Ransom, and much of the work of his first two volumes, The Arrivistes and Good News of Death, seems to derive from art rather than life. The exception comes with a remarkable group of war poems, especially "Carentan O Carentan" and "The Battle," which, with the exception of Randall Jarrell's, seem to me the best poems to have come from American poets' confrontation with World War II.

A Dream of Governors is a tired, "literary" volume, full of echoes of such poets as Nemerov, Hecht, and Wilbur, all of them more polished performers than Simpson himself. Reading it, you feel that Simpson's talent is all but dead. But *At the End of the Open Road* achieves a remarkable break-through. Gone are the formal posturings, the conventional subjects, the making of poems out of poems, that featured so heavily in the earlier volumes. It is as though Simpson has suddenly found his true subject, and with it an answerable style. Instead of trying to be like other poets, he is now content to be himself: he lets his Jewishness into the poetry, his sense of being something of an outcast, but an outcast who nevertheless knows he belongs to America, and who therefore sets out to celebrate his country, whenever he can find it and whatever it may prove to be. As the title of the volume hints, Simpson turns, as so many American poets have found themselves turning, to Walt Whitman. The Whitman he responds most deeply to is the poet who could embrace multitudes, engage contradictions, responsibly accept irresponsibility: whose gigantic achievement was to perceive the noble folly of American dreams. "All the grave weight of America/Cancelled! Like Greece and Rome./The future in ruins." Those lines come from "Walt Whitman at Bear Mountain," one of Simpson's best poems.

Most of the poems of *At the End of the Open Road* are written in an informal, loose-limbed manner, which more powerfully and convincingly convey the sense of a personal voice than the earlier poems had managed to do. And where Simpson does return to a more formal mode, as in the extraordinarily fine, wittily melancholic "My Father in the Night Commanding No," he does it without leaning on any other poet. Some of the finest poems in this remarkable volume are ones where Simpson broods on the inescapable fact of his Jewishness. He prods at it like an aching tooth, fascinated by it, yet fearing the pain it causes. The best of these is undoubtedly "A Story about Chicken Soup."

In *Adventures of the Letter I*, Simpson attempted to make further use of the style he had discovered for himself: musing, wryly observant, quizzical, contemplative. I think of it as a volume in which Simpson is marking time. There are no poems in it as good as the best of the previous volume; and yet it is an utterly readable, enjoyable piece of work by a poet who, having found his own voice, can be relied on not to bore. Like Whitman, Simpson has become at the very least a good companion.

—John Lucas

SINCLAIR, Upton. American. Born in Baltimore, Maryland, 20 September 1878; moved with his family to New York City, 1888. Educated at the City College of New York, 1893–97, A.B. 1897; Columbia University, New York, 1897–1901. Married 1) Meta H. Fuller in 1900 (divorced, 1911); 2) Mary Craig Kimbrough in 1913 (died, 1961); 3) Mary Elizabeth Willis in 1961 (died, 1967). Writer from 1893, novelist from 1900; founded socialist community, Helicon Home Colony, Englewood, New Jersey, 1906–07; Socialist candidate for Congress, from New Jersey, 1906; settled in Pasadena, California, 1915; Socialist candidate for Congress, 1920, and for the United States Senate, 1922, from California, and for Governor of California, 1926, 1930; moved to Buckeye, Arizona, 1953. Recipient: Pulitzer Prize, 1943; American Newspaper Guild Award, 1962. *Died 25 November 1968.*

PUBLICATIONS

Fiction

Springtime and Harvest: A Romance. 1901; as *King Midas,* 1901.
The Journal of Arthur Stirling. 1903.
Prince Hagen. 1903.
Manassas: A Novel of the War. 1904; as *Theirs Be the Guilt,* 1959.
The Jungle. 1906.
A Captain of Industry. 1906.
The Metropolis. 1908.
The Moneychangers. 1908.
Samuel the Seeker. 1910.
Love's Pilgrimage. 1911.
Sylvia. 1913.
Damaged Goods. 1913.
Sylvia's Marriage. 1914.
King Coal. 1917.
Jimmie Higgins. 1918.
The Spy. 1919; as *100%: The Story of a Patriot,* 1920; excerpt, as *Peter Gudge Becomes a Secret Agent,* 1930.
They Call Me Carpenter. 1922.
Oil! 1927.
Boston. 1928; abridgement as *August 22nd,* 1965.
Mountain City. 1929.
Roman Holiday. 1931.
The Wet Parade. 1931.
Co-op: A Novel of Living Together. 1936.
The Gnomobile: A Gnice Gnew Gnarrative with Gnonsense but Gnothing Gnaughty. 1936.
Little Steel. 1938.
Marie Antoinette. 1939; as *Marie and Her Lover,* 1948.
World's End. 1940.
Between Two Worlds. 1941.
Dragon's Teeth. 1942.
Wide Is the Gate. 1943.
Presidential Agent. 1944.
Dragon Harvest. 1945.
A World to Win. 1946.
Presidential Mission. 1947.
One Clear Call. 1948.
O Shepherd, Speak! 1949.
Another Pamela; or, Virtue Still Rewarded. 1950.
The Return of Lanny Budd. 1953.
What Didymus Did. 1954; as *It Happened to Didymus,* 1958.
The Cup of Fury. 1956.
Affectionately Eve. 1961.
The Coal War: A Sequel to King Coal. 1977.

Plays

Prince Hagen, from his own novel (produced 1909). 1909.

Plays of Protest (includes *Prince Hagen, The Naturewoman, The Machine, The Second-Story Man*). 1912.
Hell: A Verse Drama and Photo-Play. 1923.
The Pot Boiler. 1924.
Singing Jailbirds (produced 1930). 1924.
Bill Porter. 1925.
Wally for Queen! The Private Life of Royalty. 1936.
A Giant's Strength (produced 1948). 1948.

Verse

Songs of Our Nation. 1941.

Other

The Toy and the Man. 1904.
Our Bourgeois Literature. 1905.
Colony Customs. 1906.
The Helicon Home Colony. 1906.
A Home Colony: A Prospectus. 1906.
What Life Means to Me. 1906.
The Industrial Republic. 1907.
The Overman. 1907.
Good Health and How We Won It. 1909; as *The Art of Health,* 1909; as *Strength and Health,* 1910.
War: A Manifesto Against It. 1909.
Four Letters about "Love's Pilgrimage." 1911.
The Fasting Cure. 1911.
The Sinclair-Astor Letters: Famous Correspondence Between Socialist and Millionaire. 1914.
The Social Problem as Seen from the Viewpoint of Trade Unionism, Capital, and Socialism, with others. 1914.
Sinclair: Biographical and Critical Opinions. 1917.
The Profits of Religion. 1918.
Russia: A Challenge. 1919.
The High Cost of Living (address), with *This Misery of Boots,* by H. G. Wells. 1919.
The Brass Check. 1919; section entitled *The Associated Press and Labor,* 1920.
Press-titution. 1920.
The Crimes of the "Times": A Test of Newspaper Decency. 1921.
The Book of Life: Mind and Body. 1921; revised edition, 4 vols., 1950; *Love and Society,* 1922; revised edition, 4 vols., n.d.
The McNeal-Sinclair Debate on Socialism. 1921.
The Goose-Step: A Study of American Education. 1922; revised edition, n.d.
Biographical Letter and Critical Opinions. 1922.
The Millennium: A Comedy of the Year 2000. 1924.
The Goslings. 1924; excerpt, as *The Schools of Los Angeles,* 1924.
Mammonart. 1925.
Letters to Judd. 1926; revised edition, as *This World of 1949 and What to Do about It,* 1949.
The Spokesman's Secretary. 1926.
Money Writes! 1927.
The Pulitzer Prize and "Special Pleading." 1929.

Mental Radio.   1930; revised edition, 1962.

Socialism and Culture.   1931.

Sinclair on "Comrade" Kautsky.   1931.

American Outpost.   1932; as *Candid Reminiscences: My First Thirty Years,* 1932.

I, Governor of California, and How I Ended Poverty.   1933.

Sinclair Presents William Fox.   1933.

The Way Out − What Lies Ahead for America?   1933; as *The Way Out: A Solution to Our Present Economic and Social Ills,* 1933; revised edition, as *Limbo on the Loose: A Midsummer Night's Dream,* 1948.

EPIC Plan for California.   1934.

EPIC Answers: How to End Poverty in California.   1934.

Immediate EPIC.   1934.

The Lie Factory Starts.   1934.

An Upton Sinclair Anthology, edited by I. O. Evans.   1934; revised edition, 1947.

Sinclair's Last Will and Testament.   1934.

We, People of America, and How We Ended Poverty: A True Story of the Future.   1934.

Depression Island.   1935.

I, Candidate for Governor, and How I Got Licked.   1935; as *How I Got Licked and Why,* 1935.

What God Means to Me: An Attempt at a Working Religion.   1936.

The Flivver King.   1937.

No Pasoran! (They Shall Not Pass).   1937.

Our Lady.   1938.

Terror in Russia? Two Views, with Eugene Lyons.   1938.

Sinclair on the Soviet Union.   1938.

Expect No Peace!   1939.

Telling the World.   1939.

What Can Be Done about America's Economic Troubles?   1939.

Your Million Dollars.   1939; as *Letters to a Millionaire,* 1939.

Is the American Form of Capitalism Essential to the American Form of Democracy?   1940.

Peace or War in America.   1940.

Index to the Lanny Budd Story, with others.   1943.

To Solve the German Problem − A Free State?   1943.

The Enemy Had It Too.   1950.

A Personal Jesus: Portrait and Interpretation.   1952; as *Secret Life of Jesus,* 1962.

Radio Liberation Speech to the Peoples of the Soviet Union.   1955.

My Lifetime in Letters.   1960.

The Autobiography of Sinclair.   1962.

Editor, *The Cry for Justice* (anthology).   1915.

Bibliography: *Sinclair: An Annotated Checklist* by Ronald Gottesman, 1973.

Reading List: *This Is Sinclair* by James Lambert Harte, 1938; *The Literary Manuscripts of Sinclair* by Ronald Gottesman and Charles L. P. Silet, 1972; *Sinclair* by Jon A. Yoder, 1975; *Sinclair: American Rebel* by Leon Harris, 1975.

*   *   *

No American author has produced more writing, had a greater influence on society, and received less serious critical attention than Upton Sinclair. The depository of Sinclair manuscripts, books, and letters at The Lilly Library, Indiana University, weighs more than eight tons. More than 250,000 letters are included in the collection, letters to Shaw, Gandhi, Trotsky, Roosevelt, Kennedy, and countless letters to readers and critics concerning his own work and that of others. The material is available for work that might lead to a reassessment of Sinclair just as the discovery of the Malahide papers caused a radical change in critical opinion concerning James Boswell.

Upton Sinclair wrote on more subjects than we can catalogue; he was interested in extrasensory perception, religion, economics, alcoholism, and much more. He wrote ninety books and many pamphlets, and without his work the social world in which we live would probably lack many of the benefits we take for granted. But of those books, only one, *The Jungle*, has survived as an American classic, and critics are divided as to whether it is a classic of imaginative literature or a classic work of propaganda. Even the once popular Lanny Budd series (eleven novels, 1940–53), one of which, *Dragon's Teeth*, won the Pulitzer Prize, is all but forgotten. The key critical issue apparent in the rather limited Sinclair scholarship is whether Upton Sinclair is a genuine novelist or a very skilled and effective propagandist for social and Socialist reform. Most critics think the latter.

Van Wyck Brooks, in *The Confident Years*, acknowledged *The Jungle* as an outstanding example of muckraking literature; however, muckraking literature operates only on a level of social effect and falls short of the serious novel. *The Jungle* tells of the Lithuanian emigrant family of Jurgis Rudkus. Seeking the realization of the American Dream, the family settles in the Chicago of the early twentieth century. Jurgis goes to work in the stockyards (which provides Sinclair the opportunity to describe the filthy practices of the meat-packing industry) and the family moves into a ramshackle house, deceptively painted by the agent to appear new. There follows a series of tragedies and horrors as members of the family are killed or debased by a social system that cares nothing for the helpless people it exploits. Jurgis's futile attempts to strike back are rewarded with prison sentences. Finally, he learns of the Socialist movement. He finds a job in a hotel managed by a Socialist, and recaptures a sense of hope.

Despite certain well-constructed scenes of genuinely human life, such as the Lithuanian wedding of Jurgis and Ona, it is evident to most readers that Jurgis's family exists primarily as an index to gauge the failures of the social system that destroys them. They are acted upon; they do not act. Indeed, all we learn about human nature from *The Jungle*'s characters is that human nature can be perverted and debased by society. On the other hand, we learn a very great deal about the society. Readers in 1906 learned more than they imagined, and the conditions in the meat-packing industry, so well described by Sinclair, attracted the attention of reformers and presidents. The world of *The Jungle* is a naturalistic world, a world in which only the economically fit survive. Here, human lives are manipulated by an indifferent, if not hostile, scheme of things. But Sinclair's message is that the scheme can change. We have created or at least permitted the existence of the thing that oppresses us, and if enough are made aware of the full horror of that thing, the few who control and profit from it will have to surrender.

In *Upton Sinclair: American Rebel*, Leon Harris observes that successful propaganda must disappear. It seeks to make its ideas commonplace; it causes us to accept its message as the product of our own clear perception of the way things are. Then the actual organ of the propaganda fades in the glow of our self-satisfaction. Most of Sinclair's literature was, and was intended to be, just this kind of successful propaganda. The alteration in our lives and thinking has been tremendous, and we cannot imagine that it could ever be other than that society should care about the people who comprise it. Only on a very rare occasion does a piece of propaganda strike us with such impact that the work itself becomes part of the history that we study and remember, for it is dangerous to forget history. The result, as in the case of *The Jungle*, is a puzzle for critics who know that propaganda should fade away and novels should concern themselves with character development. Paradoxically, then, Upton Sinclair at his best fails in both genres and creates a work that the literate world insists is a classic.

—William J. Heim

SINGER, Isaac Bashevis. American. Born in Radzymin, Poland, 14 July 1904; emigrated to the United States in 1935, naturalized, 1943. Educated at the Tachkemoni Rabbinical Seminary, Warsaw, 1920–22. Married Alma Haimann in 1940; one son. Proofreader and translator for *Literarishe Bleter*, Warsaw, 1923–33; journalist for the *Jewish Daily Forward*, New York, from 1935. Recipient: Louis Lamed Prize, 1950, 1956; National Institute of Arts and Letters grant, 1959; Daroff Memorial Award, 1963; two National Endowment for the Arts grants, 1966; Brandeis University Creative Arts Award, 1969; National Book Award, for children's literature, 1970, and for fiction, 1974; Nobel Prize for Literature, 1978. D.H.L.: Hebrew Union College, Los Angeles, 1963; D.Lit.: Colgate University, Hamilton, New York, 1972; Litt.D.: Bard College, Annandale-on-Hudson, New York, 1974. Member, National Institute of Arts and Letters, 1965; American Academy of Arts and Sciences, 1969; Jewish Academy of Arts and Sciences; Polish Institute of Arts and Sciences. Lives in New York City.

PUBLICATIONS

Fiction

> *The Family Moskat*, translated by A. H. Gross. 1950.
> *Satan in Goray*, translated by Jacob Sloan. 1955.
> *Gimpel the Fool and Other Stories*, translated by Saul Bellow and others. 1957.
> *The Magician of Lublin*, translated by Elaine Gottlieb and Joseph Singer. 1960.
> *The Spinoza of Market Street and Other Stories*, translated by Elaine Gottlieb and others. 1961.
> *The Slave*, translated by the author and Cecil Hemley. 1962.
> *Short Friday and Other Stories*, translated by Ruth Whitman and others. 1964.
> *Selected Short Stories*. 1966.
> *The Manor*, translated by Elaine Gottlieb and Joseph Singer. 1967.
> *The Séance and Other Stories*, translated by Ruth Whitman and others. 1968.
> *The Estate*, translated by Elaine Gottlieb, Joseph Singer, and Elizabeth Shub. 1970.
> *A Friend of Kafka and Other Stories*. 1970.
> *Enemies: A Love Story*, translated by Alizah Shevrin and Elizabeth Shub. 1972.
> *A Crown of Feathers and Other Stories*. 1973.
> *Passions and Other Stories*. 1975.
> *Shosha*. 1978.

Plays

> *The Mirror* (produced 1973).
> *Schlemiel the First* (produced 1974).
> *Yentl, The Yeshiva Boy*, with Leah Napolin, from a story by Singer (produced 1974).

Other

> *In My Father's Court* (autobiography), translated by Channah Kleinerman-Goldstein and others. 1966.
> *Zlateh the Goat and Other Stories* (juvenile), translated by the author and Elizabeth Shub. 1966.
> *Mazel and Schlimazel; or, The Milk of a Lioness* (juvenile), translated by the author and Elizabeth Shub. 1967.

The Fearsome Inn (juvenile), translated by the author and Elizabeth Shub.   1967.
When Schlemiel Went to Warsaw and Other Stories (juvenile), translated by the author
    and Elizabeth Shub.   1968.
A Day of Pleasure: Stories of a Boy Growing Up in Warsaw (juvenile), translated by the
    author and Elizabeth Shub.   1969.
Elijah the Slave (juvenile), translated by the author and Elizabeth Shub.   1970.
Joseph and Koza; or, The Sacrifice to the Vistula (juvenile), translated by the author and
    Elizabeth Shub.   1970.
Alone in the Wild Forest (juvenile), translated by the author and Elizabeth Shub.   1971.
The Topsy-Turvy Emperor of China (juvenile), translated by the author and Elizabeth
    Shub.   1971.
The Wicked City (juvenile), translated by the author and Elizabeth Shub.   1972.
The Fools of Chelm and Their History (juvenile), translated by the author and Elizabeth
    Shub.   1973.
The Hasidim: Paintings, Drawings and Etchings, with Ira Moskowitz.   1973.
Why Noah Chose the Dove (juvenile), translated by Elizabeth Shub.   1974.
A Tale of Three Wishes (juvenile).   1976.
A Little Boy in Search of God: Mysticism in a Personal Light, with Ira
    Moskowitz.   1976.
Naftali the Storyteller and His Horse, Sus, and Other Stories (juvenile).   1976.
A Young Man in Search of Love, translated by Joseph Singer.   1978.

Editor, with Elaine Gottlieb, *Prism 2*.   1965.

Translator, *Pan*, by Knut Hamsun.   1928.
Translator, *All Quiet on the Western Front*, by Erich Maria Remarque.   1930.
Translator, *The Magic Mountain*, by Thomas Mann.   4 vols., 1930.
Translator, *The Road Back*, by Erich Maria Remarque.   1930.
Translator, *From Moscow to Jerusalem*, by Leon S. Glaser.   1938.

Bibliography: in *Bulletin of Bibliography*, January–March 1969.

Reading List: *Singer and the Eternal Past* by Irving Buchen, 1968; *The Achievement of Singer*
edited by Marcia Allentuck, 1969; *Critical Views of Singer* edited by Irving Malin, 1969;
Singer by Ben Siegel, 1969; *Singer* by Irving Malin, 1972.

*   *   *

Isaac Bashevis Singer is an example of a strange phenomenon of American Jewish
literature – a Yiddish writer who in his later years gained international fame through the
English translation of his novels and short stories. The Yiddish audience for which Singer
wrote was never a very large one; he did not willingly ascribe to either the nostalgic
yearnings of one school of Yiddishists, or the socialistic diatribes of the other school of
Yiddishists.
    The divorce from the latter school was especially difficult for the young Singer, for it
implied a separation from his older brother, Israel Joshua, also an accomplished writer. This
older brother was the first to open the door to secular education and to the questions which
inevitably awakened Isaac to the narrowness of his father's world of Hasidism and the
inadequacy of his mother's more rational, but nevertheless medieval, normative Judaism.
Unlike his brother Israel Joshua, Isaac Bashevis was unwilling to discard his past altogether;
he was unwilling to choose between mysticism and rationality, between past and present, or
even between gothicism and realism. Singer's art is a marriage of these diverse elements in

his past; they are what afford his fiction such charm on the one hand and such sophistication on the other.

In his early years, Singer wrote solely for the Yiddish press, under several pseudonyms – for example, Varshavsky and Segal. Even his name Bashevis is a pseudonym in honor of his mother, Bathsheba. These early pieces included feuilletons, autobiographical sketches, short fiction, and novels. Some of these have been translated into English, but many remain unknown to the non-Yiddish reading public. By 1950, Singer had begun the process which was to give him such fame in the next twenty years; he began to publish in English translation as well as in the original Yiddish.

The first major venture in this double publication was his epic novel *The Family Moskat*, appearing simultaneously in English and Yiddish. The significant differences between the Yiddish original and the English translation reveal the problematic nature of Singer's existence as an English writer. In the English version, the main characters are left to their doom in Warsaw on the eve of the Nazi takeover. In the Yiddish version, a youthful remnant escapes to Israel. The symbolic significance of their escape and tenuous existence is not lost on the Yiddish writer Singer, nor the Yiddish reader.

As defined by Irving Malin, Singer's novels can be divided into two groups, open and closed. *The Family Moskat* is probably the best example of his open novels. It is an historical family chronicle; the scope of the tale is large and has significant sociological implication; the style is primarily realistic. For Singer, these chronicles are most often set in a time during which the confined *shtetl* life of the East European Jew is being questioned. Other novels in this manner include *The Manor* and *The Estate*.

Of the second (closed) type of Singer novel, *Satan in Goray* is probably the clearest example. It is short, condensed in time; there is an aura of mystery and irrationality; the style, the characters, the setting are all symbolic. Set in the distressing era of the anti-Semitic pogromist Chmielnicki and the false messiah Shabbatai Zevi, this novel relates the disintegration of personality and community that resulted from these horrors of the Jewish past. Other closed novels include *The Magician of Lublin* and *The Slave*. (*Enemies: A Love Story* does not fit well into either slot, but it is more closed than open.)

Singer's symbolism, which owes much to the structure and style of *kaballah*, is evident in many of his short stories as well as the closed novels. In the best of the stories, the author suggests the complex dichotomies, the multiple levels of human existence, and the ambivalent nature of life itself by the use of name symbolism, the supernatural, and multiple narrators. Before the reader can with assurance interpret a story, he must note who tells that story. The reader of "The Destruction of Kreshev" does a disservice to Singer's art if he overlooks the fact that the narrator is Satan, surely an untrustworthy narrator. If he reads the superstitious tale "Zeitl and Rickel," he must note that an uneducated old woman is speaking. The happenings of these tales are filtered through a perspective that colors subject, tone, and conclusion. Even in the masterpiece "Gimpel the Fool," we must recognize that Gimpel himself tells the tale; his naivety and good nature determine the conclusion.

Another important narrator type in Singer's fiction is the semi-autobiographical narrator. In the more belletristic of the tales, he uses this portrait of himself as a mirror reflecting another's story. In "A Friend of Kafka," Jacques Kohn tells the history of his peculiar life. But we do not hear the tale directly; rather we hear it from a man bearing many similarities to the young Isaac Singer. He knew Jacques; Jacques told him a story, and he tells us.

The more simply autobiographical pieces are collected in two books (*In My Father's Court*, *A Day of Pleasures*). These sketches give a clear impression of the life of the young Singer, of his awakening experiences in life, love, and education, and his movement away from his father's narrow past. However, it is the more recent *A Little Boy in Search of God* that most tellingly reveals the intellectual ferment that troubled the young Singer and led him to the development of his twentieth-century mysticism.

Singer is modern in his vision of humanity: his treatment of sexuality and insanity alienated him from many of his Yiddish readers while enhancing his stature in the modern American mind. This rift has caused many of the English critics to overemphasize the modernity of the writer. In so doing, they have overlooked the medieval method of symbolism which adds much of the depth and beauty to Singer's work. Such confusion is only a natural consequence of his position as a Jewish-American writer, a man born in Poland but writing in New York, a man writing in Yiddish but being read in English, and a man looking toward the past to tell of the future.

—Barbara Gitenstein

SNODGRASS, W(illiam) D(ewitt).   American.   Born in Wilkinsburg, Pennsylvania, 5 January 1926. Educated at Geneva College, Beaver Falls, Pennsylvania, 1943–44, 1946; University of Iowa, Iowa City, 1949–55, B.A. 1949, M.A. 1951, M.F.A. 1953. Served in the United States Navy, 1944–46. Married 1) Lila Jean Hank in 1946 (divorced, 1953), one daughter; 2) Janice Wilson in 1954 (divorced, 1966), one son and one step-daughter; 3) Camille Rykowski in 1967. Instructor in English, Cornell University, Ithaca, New York, 1955–57, University of Rochester, New York, 1957–58, and Wayne State University, Detroit, 1959–67. Since 1968, Professor of English and Speech, Syracuse University, New York. Visiting Teacher, Morehead Writers Conference, Kentucky, Summer 1955, and Antioch Writers Conference, Yellow Springs, Ohio, Summers 1958–59. Recipient: Ingram Merrill Foundation Award, 1958; Longview Award, 1959; Poetry Society of America Special Citation, 1960; Yaddo Resident Award, 1960, 1961, 1965; National Institute of Arts and Letters grant, 1960; Pulitzer Prize, 1960; Guinness Award, 1961; Ford Foundation Fellowship, for drama, 1963; Miles Award, 1966; National Endowment for the Arts grant, 1966; Academy of American Poets Fellowship, 1972; Guggenheim Fellowship, 1972. Member, National Institute of Arts and Letters, 1972; Fellow, Academy of American Poets, 1973. Lives in Erieville, New York.

PUBLICATIONS

Verse

Heart's Needle.   1959.
After Experience: Poems and Translations.   1968.
Remains.   1970.
The Führer Bunker: A Cycle of Poems in Progress.   1977.

Other

In Radical Pursuit: Critical Essays and Lectures.   1975.

Editor, Syracuse Poems 1969.   1969.

Translator, with Lore Segal, Gallows Songs, by Christian Morgenstern.   1967.

Bibliography: *Snodgrass: A Bibliography* by William White, 1960.

*   *   *

In his essay "A Poem's Becoming" (*In Radical Pursuit*), W. D. Snodgrass charts the evolution of his verse from the the densely composed, ambiguous lyrics of his early years at the University of Iowa to a style of "becoming," in which a dramatic action unfolds through the speaker's intimate disclosures and self-revelations. But throughout his transitions to a freer mode of lyric delivery, he has remained a technically conservative poet, writing most work in tightly rhymed patterns and in set metrical rhythms.

Although the craftsmanship of *Heart's Needle* and *After Experience* is at once lustrous and immaculate, Snodgrass is chiefly to be noted for having given voice to the inner life of the average middle-class American who came to maturity during World War II. Like Lowell, whom he studied under, Snodgrass bases the speaker in his poems on his own life, from service in the war to graduate student days in Iowa to teaching posts around the country. His poems, however, are a careful selection of experiences that capture the disappointments, vicissitudes, and angst of a whole generation of Americans. The most emphatic theme of *Heart's Needle* and *After Experience* is a sense of an increasingly depersonalized identity as social life grows more rationalized.

Heart's Needle begins with the disenchantments of returning veterans, who, in "Returned to Frisco, 1946," reenter civilian life

> free to prowl all night
> Down streets giddy with lights, to sleep all day,
>
> Pay our own way and make our own selections;
> Free to choose just what they meant we should....

With this hint at authoritarianism, Snodgrass chronicles the life of the post-war American who carries pent-up, even violent, emotions under a carefully trained surface. Some of these poems have their speaker worry that he has grown too fearful and timid, as in "Home Town," where he has pursued, then eluded a bold, young girl:

> Pale soul, consumed by fear
> of the living world you haunt,
> have you learned what habits lead you
> to hunt what you don't want;
> learned who does not need you;
> learned you are no one here?

The lovely, complex music of the final sequence, "Heart's Needle," captures this likeable, confused new Everyman as he struggles to remain parent to his young daughter. Snodgrass gives these ten poems his richest, most daringly metaphorical speech.

After Experience continues the Everyman chronicle of *Heart's Needle*, but this volume is less carefully structured and often less resonant in its language. Many of the poems take up themes of captivity, terror, potential violence, and disaster. Typical is "Lobsters in the Window," with its moving depiction of the near-frozen lobster seen through a restaurant window:

He's fallen back with the mass
Heaped in their common trench
Who stir, but do not look out
Through the rainstreaming glass,
Hear what the newsboys shout,
Or see the raincoats pass.

The closing section of the volume features skilful translations of a number of poets, particularly Rilke.

—Paul Christensen

SNYDER, Gary (Sherman).   American.   Born in San Francisco, California, 8 May 1930. Educated at Reed College, Portland, Oregon, B.A. in anthropology 1951; Indiana University, Bloomington, 1951–52; University of California, Berkeley, 1953–56; studied Buddhism in Japan, 1956, 1964, 1965–68. Married 1) Alison Gass in 1950 (divorced, 1951); 2) the poet Joanne Kyger in 1960 (divorced, 1964); 3) Masa Uehara in 1967; two children. Held various jobs, including seaman and forester, 1948–56; Lecturer in English, University of California, Berkeley, 1964–65. Recipient: Bollingen Foundation Research Grant for Buddhist Studies, 1965; National Institute of Arts and Letters prize, 1966; Frank O'Hara Prize, 1967; Guggenheim Fellowship, 1968; Pulitzer Prize, 1975. Lives in California.

PUBLICATIONS

Verse

> *Riprap.*   1959.
> *Myths and Texts.*   1960; revised edition, 1978.
> *Hop, Skip, and Jump.*   1964.
> *Nanoa Knows.*   1964.
> *Riprap and Cold Mountain Poems.*   1965.
> *Six Sections from Mountains and Rivers Without End.*   1965; augmented edition, 1970.
> *Three Worlds, Three Realms, Six Roads.*   1966.
> *A Range of Poems.*   1966.
> *The Back Country.*   1967.
> *The Blue Sky.*   1969.
> *Sours of the Hills.*   1969.
> *Regarding Wave.*   1970.
> *Manzanita.*   1971.
> *Anasazi.*   1971.
> *The Fudo Trilogy: Spell Against Demons, Smokey the Bear Trilogy, The California Water Plan.*   1973.
> *Turtle Island.*   1974.

Other

Four Changes. 1969.
Earth House Hold: Technical Notes and Queries to Fellow Dharma
    Revolutionaries. 1969.
On Bread and Poetry: A Panel Discussion, with Lew Welch and Philip Whalen. 1976.
The Old Ways (essays). 1977.

Bibliography: in Schist 2, Summer 1974.

Reading List: "Snyder Issue" of In Transit, 1969.

*   *   *

Gary Snyder's writing is the chronicle of an itinerant visionary naturalist. His poetry contains few technical innovations, but consolidates the Imagist ideas of Pound and Williams and the free forms of Olson and the Beat poets. The poetry is wholly absorbed in the chronicle of the poet's wanderings, his religious training in Japan, and his mythic and cultural perception of nature and experience.

Snyder organizes most of his poetry according to experience rather than theme. In Riprap, the crisp, taciturn Imagist poems narrate his days as "look out" and "choker" in the remote reaches of the American northwest, and then his first trip to Japan on merchant tankers. The charm of these poems lies in the frank, modest, often tender lyric nature of the young observer, as in "Piute Creek":

> No one loves rock, yet we are here.
> Night chills. A flick
> In the moonlight
> Slips into Juniper shadow:
> Back there unseen
> Cold proud eyes
> Of cougar and Coyote
> Watch me rise and go.

Cold Mountain Poems contains translations of the Chinese poet, Han-Shan, in which Snyder shows skill as an interpreter and cunning in the choice of a poet like himself in vision and inclination. Han-Shan was a mountain recluse, whose regard for the mystery of nature is intense but not ponderous.

Myths and Texts, written before Riprap but not published until 1960, is the best orchestrated and developed of his works. By dividing the book into three parts, "Logging," "Hunting," and "Burning," Snyder creates an initiation ritual for his persona, who enters nature as a destroyer (working for logging companies), then as hunter, who must understand his prey to succeed, and who returns from these encounters awed by the power and will of nature. The themes of his early books establish the lines of development of his succeeding works. In The Back Country, he narrates experience from early years in Washington and Oregon, his departure for Japan in 1956, his later return to California. The volume has some notational lyrics, but the concision and intensity of most of the poems are deeply effective and dramatic.

Earth House Hold, a collection of prose, powerfully states the depth of his regard for the natural world and shows the maturing intellectual and spiritual subtlety of his mind over the twenty years it records. Snyder, now a cult figure of the ecology movement, carefully traces the evolution of his thought from jottings of natural phenomena to notes for the making of tribal culture in the post-industrial era. An able prose writer, Snyder is both factual and commanding as a theorist of a new pastoral ideology.

Regarding Wave and *Turtle Island* continue the chronicle of the poet through family life and residence in the United States, where environmental abuse has stirred him to a lyricism of greater and greater activism. The final passages of *Turtle Island* are a series of prose tracts on conservation addressed directly to the reader.

—Paul Christensen

STAFFORD, Jean. American. Born in Covina, California, 1 July 1915. Educated at the University of Colorado, Boulder, B.A. 1936, M.A. 1936; University of Heidelberg, 1936–37. Married 1) Robert Lowell, *q.v.*, in 1940 (divorced, 1948); 2) Oliver Jensen in 1950 (divorced, 1953); 3) the writer A. J. Liebling in 1959 (died, 1963). Instructor, Stephens College, Columbia, Missouri, 1937–38; Secretary, *Southern Review*, Baton Rouge, Louisiana, 1940–41; Lecturer, Queens College, Flushing, New York, Spring 1945; Fellow, Center for Advanced Studies, Wesleyan University, Middletown, Connecticut, 1964–65; Adjunct Professor, Columbia University, New York, 1967–69. Recipient: National Institute of Arts and Letters grant, 1945; Guggenheim Fellowship, 1945, 1948; National Press Club Award, 1948; O. Henry Award, 1955; Ingram-Merrill grant, 1969; Chapelbrook grant, 1969; Pulitzer Prize, 1970. Member, National Institute of Arts and Letters, 1970.

PUBLICATIONS

Fiction

Boston Adventure. 1944.
The Mountain Lion. 1947.
The Catherine Wheel. 1952.
Children Are Bored on Sunday (stories). 1953.
Bad Characters (stories). 1964.
Collected Stories. 1969.

Other

Elephi: The Cat with the High I.Q. (juvenile). 1962.
The Lion and the Carpenter and Other Tales from the Arabian Nights Retold (juvenile). 1962.
A Mother in History. 1966.

* * *

The art of Jean Stafford is the art of the miniaturist – the quickly realized short story, told with economy and control, is her ideal form. Many of her stories were published in *The New Yorker* and *The Saturday Evening Post*, and it is easy to detect the economy and tautness that come from the pressures of journalistic publication. "Miss Bellamy was old and cold," begins "The Hope Chest" (*Collected Stories*), "and she lay quaking under an eiderdown which her mother had given her when she was a girl of seventeen." In a sense, the half-dozen pages which follow merely expand the implications of that sentence. Typically, the story is rooted in the old woman's memories of her childhood and years as a young woman: most of Jean Stafford's writing deals with loneliness perceived by the child who suffers it or by the adult who was once the child.

Her own artistic eye, in fact, is that of the child poised on the brink of adult experience and seeing largely the concrete details of surrounding life. Her most successful writing enlarges its range by suggesting wider experience through symbols such as the mountain lion of her second novel, which represents the untamed, authentic power of the natural world into which the two young children of the story are plunged. The horrific violence which concludes the novel comes not from the lion but from man; like many of the stories, the work simmers with a brooding though suppressed sense of the brutality of experience.

Jean Stafford's other novels, *Boston Adventure* and *The Catherine Wheel*, are possibly less successful because they lack such a convincing controlling symbol. As usual, they are concerned with young people, but the world these young grow into suggests imprisonment and failure rather than fulfilment and enrichment. But although these are not her best works, the standard of their prose remains as high as in any of her stories.

—Patrick Evans

STAFFORD, William (Edgar). American. Born in Hutchinson, Kansas, 17 January 1914. Educated at the University of Kansas, Lawrence, B.A. 1936, M.A. 1947; University of Iowa, Iowa City, Ph.D. 1954. Conscientious Objector during World War II; active in Pacifist organizations, and since 1959 Member, Oregon Board, Fellowship of Reconciliation. Married Dorothy Hope Frantz in 1944; two daughters and two sons. Member of the English Department, 1948–54, 1957–60, and since 1960, Professor of English, Lewis and Clark College, Portland, Oregon. Assistant Professor of English, Manchester College, Indiana, 1955–56; Professor of English, San Jose State College, California, 1956–57. Consultant in Poetry, Library of Congress, Washington, D.C., 1970–71. United States Information Agency Lecturer in Egypt, Iran, Pakistan, India, Nepal, and Bangladesh, 1972. Recipient: Yaddo Foundation Fellowship, 1955; National Book Award, 1963; Shelley Memorial Award, 1964; National Endowment for the Arts grant, 1966; Guggenheim Fellowship, 1966; Melville Cane Award, 1974. D.Litt.: Ripon College, Wisconsin, 1965; Linfield College, McMinnville, Oregon, 1970. Lives in Portland, Oregon.

PUBLICATIONS

Verse

West of Your City. 1960.
Traveling Through the Dark. 1962.
Five American Poets, with others, edited by Thom Gunn and Ted Hughes. 1963.
Five Poets of the Pacific Northwest, with others, edited by Robin Skelton. 1964.
The Rescued Year. 1966.
Eleven Untitled Poems. 1968.
Weather. 1969.
Allegiances. 1970.
Temporary Facts. 1970.
Poems for Tennessee, with Robert Bly and William Matthews. 1971.
Someday, Maybe. 1973.
That Other Alone. 1973.
In the Clock of Reason. 1973.
Going Places. 1974.
Stories That Could Be True: New and Collected Poems. 1977.

Other

Down in My Heart (experience as a conscientious objector during World War II). 1947.
Friends to This Ground: A Statement for Readers, Teachers, and Writers of
    Literature. 1967.
Leftovers, A Care Package: Two Lectures. 1973.

Editor, with Frederick Candelaria, The Voices of Prose. 1966.
Editor, The Achievement of Brother Antoninus: A Comprehensive Selection of His
    Poems. 1967.
Editor, with Robert H. Ross, Poems and Perspectives. 1971.

Reading List: "Stafford Issue" of Northwest Review, Spring 1974, and of Modern Poetry
Studies, Spring 1975.

*   *   *

William Stafford's poetry exemplifies the best of what is left of American
transcendentalism. Like Emerson and Thoreau, he regards the human imagination as
"salvational," and many of his poems are about the capacity of the imagination to derive
meaning and awe from the world. Like the transcendentalists Stafford also regards the
natural world as a possible model for human behavior:

> The earth says every summer have a ranch
> that's minimum: one tree, one well, a landscape
> that proclaims a universe – sermon
> of the hills, hallelujah mountain,
> highway guided by the way the world is tilted.

But, although in Stafford's poems Nature ("the landscape of justice") evinces both a glimmer
of consciousness and a strict propriety of process, it contains few prescriptions definite

enough to be useful guides to human behavior. It provides only distant analogues. Nor is Nature a comforting maternal presence. If there be any one lesson which the human species might draw from natural process, it is humility, to know your place, to have local priorities. Stafford has an organic conception of poetry, which also recalls the transcendentalists. For him, poetry is a manifestation of the "deepest [truest] place we have":

> They call it regional, this relevance –
> the deepest place we have: in this pool forms
> the model of our land, a lonely one,
> responsive to the wind. Everything we own
> has brought us here: from here we speak.

Composition is thus, for Stafford, a means of bringing to light the dark processes of the self:

> I do tricks in order to know:
> Careless I dance,
> then turn to see
> the mark to turn God left for me.

The style of Stafford's poems is quiet and colloquial. Few of them are very long. Throughout his poetry, certain words recur with an intensionally symbolic meaning. The most prominent of these words are "dark," "deep," "cold," "far," "God," and "home." Many of his earlier poems are rhymed, some heavily, some with slant or touch rhyme. His earlier work shows a fondness for sprung rhythm rather than quantitative metric. Since 1960 his work has grown steadily more relaxed in form and more rhetorically inventive. Typical of such inventiveness is the poem "Important Things":

> Like Locate Knob out west
> of town where maybe the world
> began. Like the rusty wire
> sagged in the river for a harp
> when floods go by.
> Like a way of talking, the slur
> in hello to mean you and God
> still think about justice.
> Like being alone, and you are
> alone, like always.
> You always are.

—Jonathan Holden

STEELE, Wilbur Daniel. American. Born in Greensboro, North Carolina, 17 March 1886. Educated at kindergarten in Germany, 1889–92, and at schools in Colorado, 1892–1900; University of Denver Preparatory School, 1900–03; University of Denver, 1903–07, B.A. 1907; Boston Museum School of Fine Arts, 1907–08; Académie Julian, Paris, 1908. Married 1) Margaret Thurston in 1913 (died, 1931), two sons; 2) Norma Mitchell in 1932 (died, 1967). Free-lance writer; lived in Provincetown, Massachusetts, 1919–29; Co-

Founder, Provincetown Players, 1915; lived in Chapel Hill, North Carolina, 1929–32, Hamburg, Connecticut, 1932–56, and Old Lyme, Connecticut, 1956–64; in rest home and hospital after 1964. D.Litt.: University of Denver, 1932. *Died 26 May 1970.*

PUBLICATIONS

Fiction

> *Storm.* 1914.
> *Land's End and Other Stories.* 1918.
> *The Shame Dance and Other Stories.* 1923.
> *Isles of the Blest.* 1924.
> *Taboo.* 1925.
> *Urkey Island* (stories). 1926.
> *The Man Who Saw Through Heaven and Other Stories.* 1927.
> *Meat.* 1928; as *The Third Generation,* 1929.
> *Tower of Sand and Other Stories.* 1929.
> *Undertow.* 1930.
> *Diamond Wedding.* 1931.
> *Sound of Rowlocks.* 1938.
> *That Girl from Memphis.* 1945.
> *The Best Stories.* 1945.
> *Full Cargo: More Stories.* 1951.
> *Their Town.* 1952.
> *The Way to the Gold.* 1955.

Plays

> *Contemporaries* (produced 1915).
> *Not Smart* (produced 1916). In *The Terrible Woman* ... , 1925.
> *The Giants' Stair* (produced 1924). 1924.
> *Ropes,* in *The Terrible Woman* ... . 1925.
> *The Terrible Woman and Other One Act Plays.* 1925.
> *Post Road,* with Norma Mitchell (produced 1934). 1935.
> *How Beautiful with Shoes,* with Anthony Brown, from the story by Steele (produced 1935).
> *Luck,* in *One Hundred Nonroyalty Plays,* edited by William Kozlenko. 1941.

Reading List: *Steele* by Martin Bucco, 1972.

* * *

Between the Great War and the Great Depression Wilbur Daniel Steele was America's recognized master of the popular short story. Many of his nearly two hundred published stories (an unschematized history of certain values prevailing in America at the time) transcend the formulas and clichés of mass fiction. Steele submitted to his day's conventions, but, like Poe, created a medley of dazzling variations. By wedding the "New Psychology" to his tight plots, melodramatic adventures, jagged coincidences, and surprise endings, he achieved a particular and celebrated perfection. But as magazines turned increasingly to social realism, sensational confession, and quicksilver style, demand for Steele's intricate stories declined.

Through exotic detail and vivid suggestion, *The Best Stories of Wilbur Daniel Steele* evokes the atmospheres of Cape Cod, the South, the Caribbean, North Africa, and the Middle East. With remarkable purity of concentration Steele exploits the temporality of literature, subordinates part to whole, and makes each yarn a *Gestalt*. "Romantic" themes like suspected innocence, revenge and retribution, power of love and friendship, premonition, and return from the "dead" intertwine with such "realistic" ideas as heredity versus environment, law and conscience, divided self, quest for identity, and awakening. Sophoclean symmetry heightens the commonplace, but sometimes Steele's heavy-handed "chance" destroys his grim illusions. Still, his sinewy twists and shock endings (less meretricious then O. Henry's) force us to *re-see* life's awesome ironies and literature's delightful ones.

"The Man Who Saw Through Heaven," one of his most effective stories, dramatizes the physical and spiritual evolution of mankind in a *tour de force* of condensation. The classic "How Beautiful with Shoes" (also a Broadway play) renders the emotional awakening of a cloddish Appalachian girl abducted by a runaway psychotic. "When Hell Froze" is a memorable period piece. For sheer ingenuity and suspense "Footfalls," a tale of paternal revenge, has few equals. "Conjuh," "Blue Murder," "Bubbles," "The Body of the Crime," "For They Know Not What They Do" – these stories and many others have received high praise.

Steele's Euclidian logic, detective imagination, and knotty style suited the shorter form far better than the novel. His longer fiction, labored and wooden, displays feeble narrative line, thematic fuzziness, clotted exegesis, and trite detail. Perhaps *Meat*, an early novel which boldly indicts the perpetuation of weakness, is his best.

Today Wilbur Daniel Steele's radiant prize stories crop up in anthologies, and historians of the American short story acknowledge his uniqueness, but he attracts little serious critical attention. An important transitional writer who bridges the Poe-O. Henry and the Anderson-Hemingway traditions, Wilbur Daniel Steele was a marvelous technician who occasionally compelled his stories to the level of high art.

—Martin Bucco

STEIN, Gertrude.   American.   Born in Allegheny, Pennsylvania, 3 Feburary 1874; as a child lived in Vienna, Paris, and Oakland, California. Educated at schools in Oakland and San Francisco; Radcliffe College, Cambridge, Massachusetts, 1893–97; studied philosophy under William James; studied medicine at Johns Hopkins Medical School, Baltimore, 1897–1901. Writer from 1902; lived in Paris from 1903, with her friend Alice B. Toklas from 1908; center of a circle of artists, including Picasso, Matisse, and Braque, and of writers, including Hemingway and Fitzgerald. *Died 27 July 1946.*

PUBLICATIONS

Collections

Writings and Lectures 1911–1945 (selection), edited by Patricia Meyerowitz.   1967; as *Look at Me Now and Here I Am,* 1971.

Selected Operas and Plays, edited by John Malcolm Brinnin. 1970.

Fiction

Three Lives: Stories of the Good Anna, Melanctha, and the Gentle Lena. 1909.
The Making of Americans, Being a History of a Family's Progress. 1925.
A Book Concluding with As a Wife Has a Cow: A Love Story. 1926.
Lucy Church Amiably. 1931.
Ida: A Novel. 1941.
Brewsie and Willie. 1946.
Blood on the Dining Room Floor. 1948.
Things as They Are: A Novel in Three Parts. 1950.
Mrs. Reynolds, and Five Early Novelettes, edited by Carl Van Vechten. 1952.
A Novel of Thank You, edited by Carl Van Vechten. 1958.

Plays

Geography and Plays. 1922.
A Village: Are You Ready Yet Not Yet. 1928.
Operas and Plays. 1932.
Four Saints in Three Acts, music by Virgil Thomson (produced 1934). 1934.
A Wedding Bouquet: Ballet, music by Lord Berners (produced 1936). 1936.
In Savoy; or, Yes Is for a Very Young Man (produced 1946). 1946.
The Mother of Us All, music by Virgil Thomson (produced 1947). 1947.
Last Operas and Plays, edited by Carl Van Vechten. 1949.
In a Garden, music by Meyer Kupferman (produced 1951). 1951.
Lucretia Borgia. 1968.

Verse and Prose Poems

Tender Buttons: Objects, Food, Rooms. 1914.
Have They Attacked Mary. He Giggled. 1917.
Before the Flowers of Friendship Fade Friendship Faded. 1931.
Two (Hitherto Unpublished) Poems. 1948.
Stanzas in Meditation and Other Poems (1929–1933), edited by Carl Van Vechten. 1956.

Other

Portrait of Mabel Dodge. 1912.
Composition as Explanation. 1926.
Descriptions of Literature. 1926.
An Elucidation. 1927.
Useful Knowledge. 1928.
An Acquaintance with Description. 1929.
Dix Portraits. 1930.
How to Write. 1931.
The Autobiography of Alice B. Toklas. 1933.
Matisse, Picasso, and Gertrude Stein, with Two Shorter Stories. 1933.
Portraits and Prayers. 1934.

Chicago Inscriptions. 1934.
Lectures in America. 1935.
Narration: Four Lectures. 1935.
The Geographical History of America; or, The Relation of Human Nature to the Human Mind. 1936.
Everybody's Autobiography. 1937.
Picasso. 1938.
The World Is Round (juvenile). 1939.
Prothalamium. 1939.
Paris France. 1940.
What Are Masterpieces. 1940.
Wars I Have Seen. 1945.
    The Stein First Reader, and Three Plays (juvenile). 1946.
Selected Writings, edited by Carl Van Vechten. 1946.
Four in America. 1947.
Kisses Can. 1947.
Literally True. 1947.
Two: Gertrude Stein and Her Brother and Other Early Portraits (1908–1912), edited by Carl Van Vechten. 1951.
Bee Time Vine and Other Pieces (1913–1927), edited by Carl Van Vechten. 1953.
As Fine as Melanctha (1914–1930), edited by Carl Van Vechten. 1954.
Painted Lace and Other Pieces (1914–1937), edited by Carl Van Vechten. 1955.
Absolutely Bob Brown; or, Bobbed Brown. 1955.
To Bobchen Haas. 1957.
Alphabets and Birthdays, edited by Carl Van Vechten. 1957.
On Our Way (letters). 1959.
Cultivated Motor Automatism, with Leon M. Solomons. 1969.
Fernhurst, Q.E.D., and Other Early Writings, edited by Leon Katz. 1972.
A Primer for the Gradual Understanding of Stein, edited by Robert Bartlett Haas. 1972.
Reflections on the Atomic Bomb (unpublished writings), edited by Robert Bartlett Haas. 1974.
Dear Sammy: Letters from Stein and Alice B. Toklas, edited by Samuel M. Steward. 1977.

Bibliography: *Stein: A Bibliography* by Robert Wilson, 1974.

Reading List: *Stein: Form and Intelligibility* by Rosalind S. Miller, 1949; *Stein: A Biography of Her Work* by Donald Sutherland, 1951; *The Flowers of Friendship* (letters to Stein) edited by Donald Gallup, 1953; *Stein: Her Life and Work* by Elizabeth Sprigge, 1957; *The Third Rose: Stein and Her World* by John Malcolm Brinnin, 1959; *Stein* by Frederick J. Hoffman, 1961; *What Is Remembered* by Alice B. Toklas, 1963; *The Development of Abstractionism in the Writings of Stein,* 1965, and *Stein,* 1976, both by Michael J. Hoffman; *Stein and the Literature of Modern Consciousness* by Norman Weinstein, 1970; *Stein in Pieces* by Richard Bridgman, 1970; *Charmed Circle* by James Mellow, 1974; *Exact Resemblance to Exact Resemblance: The Literary Portraiture of Stein* by Wendy Steiner, 1978.

*   *   *

If Paul Cézanne, of whom Gertrude Stein wrote a "portrait" in 1911, broke with traditional forms (such as perspective) and traditional modes (such as pictorial replication), he did so by accenting the verticals, horizontals, and diagonals that he saw in nature. He moved painting towards geometric forms, towards the abstract, and developed new spatial patterns in which, by showing an object simultaneously from several viewpoints, planes and surfaces interacted visually on the canvas. His paintings are not of nature, but provide a visualisation of the formal parts of what he saw. Cézanne said that he did not paint pictures; he painted *paint*. Gertrude Stein does the same thing with words.

Her work is largely a systematic investigation of the formal elements of language (syntax, parts of speech, grammar, etymology, punctuation) or of the formal elements of literature (narrative, poetry, dialogue, fiction, drama), in which we see the skeleton of the writing or of the form rather than the burden it carries. Apparent nonsense, her work has been the subject of much ridicule (yet it has influenced three generations of writers). "Nobody knows what I am trying to do but I do and I know when I succeed," she said, in *As Fine as Melanctha*. William Carlos Williams (*Selected Essays*) praised her for "cleansing" the language, for "tackling the fracture of stupidities bound in thoughtless phrases, in our calcified grammatical constructions, and in the subtle brainlessness of our ... rhythms which compel words to follow certain others without precision of thought." Her concern is for writing (or reading) as movement; for literature, seen as something other than a body of reference work; for writing (reading) envisioned as the first concern of the immediate and attentive moment.

It is convenient to divide Gertrude Stein's work into three more-or-less distinct groups. The first consists of such well-known and comparatively straightforward narratives as *The Autobiography of Alice B. Toklas*, *Wars I Have Seen*, and *Three Lives*, which includes the much-anthologized "Melanctha," in which we see (or, more accurately, hear) Melanctha simultaneously from several angles, as in a Cubist painting. Some of the dialogue between Melanctha and Jeff has an effect much like that of Marcel Duchamp's painting *Nude Descending a Staircase*. Richard Wright records reading the story to "a group of semi-literate Negro stockyard workers" who "slapped their thighs, howled, laughed, stomped, and interrupted me constantly to comment on the characters" (*PM*, 11 March 1945). It is the language of speech.

The second group contains Stein's critical and exegetical work, such as *Composition as Explanation, Narration, What Are Masterpieces*, and the celebrated *Lectures in America*, in which she discusses her own writing, and, offering general reflections on the forms, genres, modes, and periods of English literature, explains the principles on which much of her own work is based. The fruit of protracted meditation on language, her exegeses are at times difficult to follow; as Thornton Wilder observed, "Miss Stein pays her listeners the high compliment of dispensing for the most part with that apparatus of illustrative simile and anecdote that is so often employed to recommend ideas." And when, in *Lectures in America*, she says "more and more one does not use nouns," she is pointing to the very plasticity of language one finds in the third group of her work, the overtly experimental and difficult writing.

Work in this group, such as *Tender Buttons, Stanzas in Meditation, An Acquaintance with Description*, or *How to Write*, may properly be thought of as "exemplary," since it demonstrates the principles enunciated in the exegetical work. While composing *How to Write* Stein called *Tender Buttons* "my first conscious struggle with the problem of correlating sight, sound and sense, and eliminating rhythm; – now I am trying grammar and eliminating sight and sound" (*Transition 14*, 1928), while in *Lectures in America* she said that in *Tender Buttons* "I struggled with the ridding of myself of nouns. I knew that nouns must go in poetry as they had gone in prose if anything that is everything was to go on meaning something." A noun is the name of a thing, and "if you feel what is inside that thing you do not call it by the name by which it is known"; instead, like Whitman, you "mean names without naming them." Breaking syntax, forcing words into multiple grammatical functions, in *Tender Buttons* or *Stanzas in Meditation* Stein seeks to write a poem which, taken as a whole, becomes itself a noun. For example, as Meredith Yearsley points out, under the title "A Box" the poem acts a box out linguistically by the quadruple repetition of a particular construction. The closedness of the box is caught by use of grammatical constructions which force the reader to rescan the sentence. Here, most clearly, Stein uses words the way Cézanne uses paint.

How to Write, originally entitled *Grammar, Paragraphs, Sentences, Vocabulary, Etcetera*, works similarly, through exploring the effect of semantic and syntactic anomalies in a prose which demands of the reader the expectation that words, the parts of speech, will hold their conventional position and function in the sentence. In a sentence like "It is very well a date which makes each separate in a leaf in a dismissal," the major source of difficulty is not in the lack of punctuation so much as in the ambiguous functions of words and phrases. In other sentences from "Arthur a Grammar" the reader need only supply punctuation to render the sentence wholly intelligible: "There is a difference between a grammar and a sentence this is grammar in a sentence I will agree to no map with which you may be dissatisfied and therefore beg you to point out what you regard as incorrect in the positions of the troops in my two sentences." In each case, the sentence acts out its meaning.

In such ways Stein's words remove themselves from the context in which they (may have) originated and acquire a new context in which they can assert their meaning by demonstrating it. The world of Gertrude Stein is one in which things are the cause rather than the content of language, and it is thus an interiorized world, where definitions are held in the process and in the moment of defining: Stein held that poetry is stasis, where the object, be it Melanctha or Roast Beef or Arthur a Grammar, fills all the available space, much as a Cubist object fills a crowded flat surface. The work is dense, and exuberant.

While the strength of Stein's personality might account for her influence on writers like Hemingway or Anderson, it does not account for her later influence, or for her friendship with painters like Picasso or Juan Gris. Later readers of her work, like Robert Duncan, George Bowering, or B. P. Nichol, find themselves, imitating her writing, turning to their own childhood. This is in part because Stein's language is devoid of allusion, seems to have no past, and things seem to speak directly, perceived in immediacy.

—Peter Quartermain

STEINBECK, John (Ernst). American. Born in Salinas, California, 27 February 1902. Educated at Salinas High School, graduated 1918; special student at Stanford University, California, 1919–25. Married 1) Carol Henning in 1930 (divorced, 1943); 2) Gwyn Conger in 1943 (divorced, 1949), two sons; 3) Elaine Scott in 1950. Worked at various jobs, including Reporter for the New York *American*, apprentice hod-carrier, apprentice painter, chemist, caretaker of an estate at Lake Tahoe, surveyor, and fruit picker, 1925–35; full-time writer from 1935; settled in Monterey, California, 1930, later moved to New York City; special writer for the United States Army Air Force during World War II; Correspondent in Europe for the New York *Herald Tribune*, 1943. Recipient: New York Drama Critics Circle Award, 1938; Pulitzer Prize, 1940; Nobel Prize for Literature, 1962. *Died 20 December 1968.*

PUBLICATIONS

Fiction

Cup of Gold: A Life of Henry Morgan, Buccaneer, with Occasional References to History. 1929.
The Pastures of Heaven. 1932.

To a God Unknown. 1933.
Tortilla Flat. 1935.
In Dubious Battle. 1936.
   Of Mice and Men. 1937.
   The Red Pony (stories). 1937.
   The Long Valley (stories). 1938.
   The Grapes of Wrath. 1938.
   The Moon Is Down. 1942.
Cannery Row. 1945.
The Wayward Bus. 1947.
The Pearl. 1947.
Burning Bright. 1950.
East of Eden. 1952.
Sweet Thursday. 1954.
The Short Reign of Pippin IV: A Fabrication. 1957.
The Winter of Our Discontent. 1961.

Plays

   Of Mice and Men (produced 1937). 1937.
   The Forgotten Village (screenplay). 1941.
   The Moon Is Down, from his own novel (produced 1942). 1943.
   Burning Bright, from his own novel (produced 1950). 1951.
   Viva Zapata! The Original Screenplay, edited by Robert E. Morsberger. 1974.

Screenplays: *The Forgotten Village,* 1941; *Lifeboat,* with Jo Swerling, 1944; *The Pearl,*
with Emilio Fernandez and Jack Wagner, 1947; *The Red Pony,* 1949; *Viva Zapata!,*
1952.

Other

Their Blood Is Strong. 1938.
Sea of Cortez: A Leisurely Journal of Travel and Research, with Edward F.
   Ricketts. 1941.
Bombs Away: The Story of a Bomber Team. 1942.
The Portable Steinbeck, edited by Pascal Covici. 1943; revised edition, 1946, 1958;
   revised edition, edited by Pascal Covici, Jr., 1971.
   Vanderbilt Clinic. 1947.
A Russian Journal, photographs by Robert Capa. 1948.
The Log from the Sea of Cortez. 1951.
Once There Was a War. 1958.
Travels with Charley in Search of America. 1962.
America and Americans. 1966.
The Journal of a Novel: The East of Eden Letters. 1969.
Steinbeck: A Life in Letters, edited by Elaine Steinbeck and Robert Wallsten. 1975.
The Acts of King Arthur and His Noble Knights, From the Winchester Manuscripts of
   Malory and Other Sources. 1977.

Bibliography: *A New Steinbeck Bibliography 1929–1971* by Tetsumaro Hayashi. 1973.

Reading List: *Steinbeck and His Critics* edited by E. W. Tedlock, Jr., and C. V. Wicker,

1957; *The Wide World of Steinbeck*, 1958, and *Steinbeck, Nature, and Myth*, 1978, both by Peter Lisca; *Steinbeck* by Warren French, 1961; *Steinbeck* by F. W. Watt, 1961; *Steinbeck* by Joseph Fontenrose, 1963; *Steinbeck and Edward F. Ricketts: The Shaping of a Novelist* by Richard Astro, 1973; *Steinbeck: The Errant Knight* by Nelson Valjean, 1975.

*   *   *

John Steinbeck often puzzled critics during his lifetime because early in his career his style and subject matter seemed to change with each new story, and after World War II there was a generally acknowledged but puzzling decline in his artistic prowess. Now, however, in a larger perspective we can see that underlying the apparent diversity of Steinbeck's work is a consistently developing vision of man's relation to his environment. This larger perspective is provided, in part, by the generally acknowledged end of the Age of Modernism, as described in Maurice Beebe's "What Modernism Was" (*Journal of Modern Literature*, July 1974). After offering a longer definition, Beebe approves Philip Stevick's observation that the modernist sensibility might almost be defined by "its irony, its implicit admiration for verbal precision and understatement." Marston LaFrance in *A Reading of Stephen Crane* (1971) traces this characteristic irony to Kierkegaard and describes its possessors as perceiving "a double realm of values where a different sort of mind would perceive only a single realm."

Steinbeck's varying works during the years of his greatest popularity and power in the 1930's were characterized by precisely this kind of irony. It is excellently illustrated by Sir Henry Morgan's speech at the end of Steinbeck's first novel, *Cup of Gold*, "Civilization will split up a character, and he who refuses to split goes under." Despite its importance in establishing Steinbeck's viewpoint, this apprentice work is strikingly different from his later books. A flamboyantly written historical costume drama about a Caribbean pirate who sacks the golden city of Panama to capture a legendary woman and then returns her to her husband for a ransom and sells out his piratical cohorts for high government position, *Cup of Gold* exudes the same disenchanted world-weariness as the abundant "Waste Land" literature of the 1920's.

A similar preoccupation with characters of mythical dimensions in a dying world colors one of Steinbeck's strangest novels, *To a God Unknown* (third published, it antedates the second). In this fantasy, Joseph Wayne – the leader among four brothers who allegorize lust, sanctimoniousness, animalism, and martyrdom – sacrifices himself to bring the needed rain to his parched valley. Here, as in the story-cycle called *The Pastures of Heaven*, Steinbeck discovers the beautiful, small valleys of his native California as the settings for his most powerful tales. But whereas *To a God Unknown* employs the same kind of baroque language and bizarre episodes as *Cup of Gold*, *The Pastures of Heaven* offers a lower-keyed, vernacular language and earthy tales of the defeat of good intentions in a Naturalistic manner that emphasizes the irony of man's sufferings in a paradisically beautiful setting.

Steinbeck continues to employ this Naturalistic viewpoint in his next works. *Tortilla Flat* seems at first glance much different from the others because of the archaic style arising from the effort to translate Malory's *Morte Darthur* into the language and actions of Mexican-American "paisanos" in Monterey, California; but beneath its surface of quaint humor, it, too, is an ironic fable of civilization "splitting up" a person: once the fabulous Danny abandons his "natural life" in the woods to become a property owner, he can never go back again and must die with a gesture of defiant despair. *In Dubious Battle*, which is often justifiably called the best American strike novel, deals realistically with tense labor problems among California apple growers and migrant pickers and ends as grimly as *Tortilla Flat*, with the disappearance of Doc Burton, the one man of objective good will in the story, and a murder that renders faceless a young labor organizer.

In *Of Mice and Men*, Steinbeck's first experiment in writing a play-novelette, Lennie, a tower of physical strength, must die because he has not the mentality to control his behavior and kills the soft things he loves to fondle. His death destroys also his protector George's dream of their some time finding security on a farm of their own. The stories collected in *The Long Valley* record similar helpless defeats – in the most familiar of them, "Chrysanthemums" and "Flight," we see first a love-starved woman exploited by a wily itinerant and then another young man whose mind is not strong enough to control his behavior driven to his death by shadowy pursuers. The collection concludes with one of Steinbeck's most popular and masterful works, *The Red Pony*. This four-story cycle depicts a sensitive boy's growing into maturity through his encounters on his father's ranch with the fallibility of man, the wearing out of man, the unreliability of nature, and the exhaustion of nature that leads to the extinguishing of man's dynamic urge for "Westering."

Steinbeck's next work after his success with *Of Mice and Men* was apparently planned as another ironic, defeatist tale entitled *L'Affaire Lettuceberg*, based on his observation of the outrageous plight of migrant workers who had fled the Midwestern Dust Bowl in hope of making a new start in California. During the writing, however, Steinbeck experienced a great change of heart, abandoned what he had written as "a smart-alec book," and, writing feverishly, recast his work as *The Grapes of Wrath*, his most popular and critically most highly acclaimed work.

The Grapes of Wrath alternates the story of the travails of the Joad family, share-croppers tractored out of Oklahoma who find only a hostile reception in the West, with inter-chapters that generalize this family history as a nation's tragedy. Through the inspiration of the martyred ex-preacher Jim Casy, the Joads at last learn the lesson of co-operation summed up by Ma's speech, "Use' ta be the fambly was fust. It ain't so now. It's anybody." Yet the novel is still modernist in sensibility, for the much discussed ending in which daughter Rosasharn offers breast milk intended for her own dead baby to a dying old man is ambiguous. The Joads have found temporary haven, but no security; the national tragedy can only be solved by the readers, not the writer. Steinbeck has, however, turned from characters who are helpless victims to those who learn to heighten their consciousnesses enough to transcend their afflictions.

After reshaping this key novel, Steinbeck would never revert completely to the ironical modernist point of view; but neither was he able consistently enough to contrive situations convincingly optimistic enough to provide an alternative. His two further play-novelettes, *The Moon Is Down* – written during World War II about the military occupation of a peaceful nation – and *Burning Bright* – a meditation on sterility that pleads that "the species must go staggering on" – suffered from "misplaced universalism." They were populated with two-dimensional allegorical figures from Medieval morality plays. Other works like the very popular *The Pearl, The Wayward Bus*, and the script for Elia Kazan's film *Viva Zapata!* – like the earlier short film *The Forgotten Village* – take Mexicans from underprivileged backgrounds and turn them into folk-Messiahs, "natural saints." (The driver of *The Wayward Bus* even has the initials J. C.) Kino's gesture in *The Pearl* of casting away the fabulous jewel that has brought only misery rather than promised fortune and the tribute at the end of Kazan's film to Zapata's indomitable spirit have heartened audiences, but they are theatricalized indications that Steinbeck, instead of looking ahead, seeks – as such later non-fiction works as *America and Americans* and the "Letters to Alicia" make clear – a return to simple, folk values of the past.

Only in *Cannery Row*, where Steinbeck again universalizes the comic story he tells through "inter-chapters," does he succeed in creating, through his portrait of Doc (based on his good friend Ed Ricketts), a remarkable figure who has both the selflessness and the sophistication to transcend the trials and temptations of the materialistic world through escape into "the cosmic Monterey" fragmentarily embodied in deathless art.

Steinbeck attempted to tell such a story of transcendence again in his most ambitious novel, *East of Eden*, by again alternating between two kinds of material, but this time they fail to fuse. The story of his own family returns to the lyrical Naturalism of his work of the 1930's, but the material is so heavily ironic that it fails to produce an affirmation; he seeks this through the labored fictional pursuit of the meaning of the Hebrew word "Timshel," which animates another allegorical fable – this one spiced up with much sensational material –

about a modern Adam, his errant wife, and his twin sons who re-enact the Biblical account of man's first family.

His subsequent fiction was trivial. *Sweet Thursday* brought back Doc and other characters from *Cannery Row*, but reduced Doc to a confused sentimentalist ministered to principally by kindly whores. *The Short Reign of Pippin IV* was a very funny, timely attack on French politics and art during the years of Charles de Gaulle, but its sketchiness makes it dated. Finally in *The Winter of Our Discontent*, Steinbeck tried to make a fresh start by writing about a small Long Island town. The novel developed from a very funny short story, "How Mr. Hogan Robbed a Bank," but the humor disappeared in this account of Ethan Allen Hawley's struggles with his conscience about having been betrayed by others and betraying others. While the novel does not quite become simply another revelation of modernist alienation (Hawley makes the affirmative gesture of rejecting suicide in order to help his daughter live) he really makes for less selfish reasons the same kind of compromise that Henry Morgan makes in Steinbeck's first novel. Thus Steinbeck's fiction returns at last almost full circle to the point where it had begun after achieving but falling away from the triumphant visions of *The Grapes of Wrath* and *Cannery Row*.

—Warren French

STEVENS, Wallace. American. Born in Reading, Pennsylvania, 2 October 1879. Educated at Harvard University, Cambridge, Massachusetts, 1897–1900; New York University Law School, 1901–03; admitted to the New York Bar, 1904. Married Elsie V. Kachel in 1909; one daughter, Holly. Worked as a Reporter for the New York *Herald Tribune*, 1900–01; practised law in New York, 1904–16; joined the Hartford Accident and Indemnity Company, Connecticut, 1916: Vice-President, 1934–55. Recipient: Harriet Monroe Poetry Award, 1946; Bollingen Prize, 1950; National Book Award, 1951, 1955; Pulitzer Prize, 1955. Member, National Institute of Arts and Letters, 1946. *Died 2 August 1955.*

PUBLICATIONS

Collections

Letters, edited by Holly Stevens. 1967.
The Palm at the End of the Mind: Selected Poems and a Play, edited by Holly Stevens. 1971.

Verse

Harmonium. 1923; revised edition, 1931.
Ideas of Order. 1935.
Owl's Clover. 1936.
The Man with the Blue Guitar and Other Poems. 1937.

Parts of a World. 1942.
Notes Toward a Supreme Fiction. 1942.
Esthetique du Mal. 1945.
Description Without Place. 1945.
Transport to Summer. 1947.
Three Academic Pieces: The Realm of Resemblance, Someone Puts a Pineapple Together, Of Ideal Time and Choice. 1947.
A Primitive Like an Orb. 1948.
The Auroras of Autumn. 1950.
Selected Poems, edited by Dennis Williamson. 1952.
Selected Poems. 1953.
Collected Poems. 1954.

Plays

Carlos among the Candles (produced 1917). In *Opus Posthumous,* 1957.
Three Travelers Watch a Sunrise (produced 1920). In *Opus Posthumous,* 1957.
Bowl, Cat, and Broomstick, in *Quarterly Review of Literature 16,* 1969.

Other

Two or Three Ideas. 1951.
The Relations Between Poetry and Painting. 1951.
The Necessary Angel: Essays on Reality and the Imagination. 1951.
Raoul Dufy: A Note. 1953.
Opus Posthumous (miscellany), edited by Samuel French Morse. 1957.

Bibliography: *Stevens: A Descriptive Bibliography* by J. M. Edelstein, 1973.

Reading List: *The Shaping Spirit: A Study of Stevens* by William Van O'Connor, 1950; *The Comic Spirit of Stevens* by Daniel Fuchs, 1963; *The Clairvoyant Eye: The Poetry and Poetics of Stevens* by Joseph N. Riddel, 1965; *The Act of the Mind: Essays on the Poetry of Stevens* edited by Roy Harvey Pearce and J. Hillis Miller, 1965; *On Extended Wings: Stevens' Longer Poems* by Helen H. Vendler, 1969; *Stevens: Poetry as Life* by Samuel French Morse, 1970; *Introspective Voyager: The Poetic Development of Stevens* by A. Walton Litz, 1972; *Stevens* by Lucy Beckett, 1974; *Stevens: The Poems of Our Climate* by Harold Bloom, 1977; *Souvenirs and Prophecies: The Young Stevens* by Holly Stevens, 1977.

Wallace Stevens is a poet who combined a long poetic career with another career, that of a business executive. The career that concerns us here – that of poet – produced a large body of work that circles around a lifelong consideration from which all his best poems radiate. Each poem is one testimony to an encompassing vision of what Stevens judges to be the prime obligation of a modern poet. That obligation leaves its mark on comparatively brief and early poems like "Peter Quince at the Clavier," "Sunday Morning," and "Thirteen Ways of Looking at a Blackbird" and continues in later and quite extensive works like *Transport to Summer* and *Ideas of Order.* Stevens is, early and late, concerned with a purification of the human intellect and sensibility – in the first place, the intellect and sensibility of the poet who is writing, and, in the second place, the intellect and the sensibility of the reader who responds to what the poet has written.

The purification takes place as service to a set of ideas – "ideas of order" in Stevens' phrase – that are ignored or, at best, served badly and intermittently in the culture to which Stevens belongs. Our sensibility has been corrupted by habits of thought that seduce the poet and his readers from a prime duty. Poet and reader have the chance, if they but respond rightly to the world which constantly surrounds them and indeed bombards them with endless impressions, to take in special sensations (the colors of light on the sea, the taste of cheese and pineapple, a musical cadence) and set them down in words. These sensations are most pure at a special time of the year (summer) and in southern climes where light and color are most intense. The sensations are adulterated by many things, by winter and northern climes, for example. Even more crucial in Stevens' account are the betrayals that are built into human culture, the dogmas and traditions and forms of artistic expression that are conventional and hackneyed. Stevens can speak bitterly of "statues" that dominate public squares and inhibit the innocent and intense sensory responses of the people who walk there.

Implied by this emphasis is a psychology – a theory of human perception – that is basically nominalistic. What is real and worthy of reverence – the poet's reverence and his readers' – is, for example, the contact the eye makes with a certain slant of light which is never the equivalent of some past contact with a slant of light. It is a mistake to move from several such special moments to any general conception about "shades of light." Each moment of perception must be preserved in its uniqueness, and the poet must, ideally, move no farther from that moment than the carefully selected set of words that allow him to make a verbal record. Stevens – a poet quite well-informed in such matters – is aware of the traps into which other poets and other human beings have fallen. In *Harmonium*, there is an "Invective Against Swans." Stevens writes: "The soul, o ganders, flies beyond the parks/And far beyond the discords of the wind." Here the "soul" has a vertigo that takes it beyond "parks" (and their clusters of rare and unique sensations) and beyond the manifestly rich "discords of the wind." The "soul" treacherously detaches the human sensibility from its proper and health-giving ground: the never-ending moments of intense sensation. The "soul" carries the human sensibility into a context of religious and social ideas that have at best a tenuous connection with "parks" and "discords of the wind."

The positive aspect of Stevens' reiterated warning appears in such lines as the following from "Credences of Summer" in *Transport to Summer*. Here, Stevens suggests, is sound belief: "The rock cannot be broken. It is the truth./It rises from land and sea and covers them." That is, the rock is – and remains – the source of acute physical perception. It is a natural object, far removed from any piece of stone that human hands have chipped at and made into a "statue" – is a memorial of some past event or an expression of human dogmas. A few more lines refine this particular statement, one that resembles countless others in Stevens' work. The "rock of summer" (a "rock of winter" is apparently inferior) is not "A hermit's truth nor symbol in hermitage." A "hermit's truth" is what the gander soul flutters toward. Stevens continues:

> It is the visible rock, the audible,
> The brilliant mercy of a sure repose,
> On this present ground, the vividest repose,
> Things certain sustaining us in certainty.

Brief annotation – and all of Stevens' work stimulates such effort – would indicate that it is the actual rock that is esteemed, not the idea, Platonic or otherwise, of "rock." From the visible rock the errant "soul" gains a sure and not a treacherous "repose." And the rock is a "present ground" and, as such, the source of the only certainty that a poet and his reader can have confidence in.

Such lines indicate a perspective that extends throughout Stevens' work like a prairie landscape, insistent and unaltering. The lines, elegant in expression and charged with authority, invite each person to be a "center" into which are gathered separate moments of "vividest repose." Not the ersatz "repose" of some religious or political certainty. Not, even, the "repose" that some poets, retreating from politics and dogma, try to discover in personal relations, intense and unshakable. For the fierce outcry which is Matthew Arnold's only comfort on the "darkling plain" of "Dover Beach" – "Ah, love, let us be true/To one another!" – Stevens would have scarcely more patience than he has for "statues." As he observes in *Parts of a World*:

> Words are not forms of a single word.
> In the sum of the parts, there are only the parts.
> The world must be measured by eye ...

To the villainous "gander soul," the whole is always greater than the sum of its parts and testimony to principle, to some inclusive order that lies in a divine mind or, at least, at the very roots of things. The "single word" (or Word, as Christians would say) is a delusion. Words serve the eye, and the eye takes in what aspect a "rock of summer" has at a particular moment.

As Stevens' large body of work indicates, such labor can be lifelong. It can exclude – and does – elements of existence that have counted for other poets and that, from Stevens' point of view, have corrupted them and those who read them. Stevens' "center" (the poet's awareness and perhaps his readers') is a clear crystal which sensation reaches – reaches and passes through with as little refraction as possible.

—Harold H. Watts

STICKNEY, Trumbull. American. Born in Geneva, Switzerland, 20 June 1874. Spent his childhood in Europe; tutored by his father. Educated at Walton Lodge, Clevedon, Somerset, 1886; Cutler's School, New York City, 1890; Harvard University, Cambridge, Massachusetts, 1891–95 (Editor, *Harvard Monthly*), B.A. (magna cum laude) 1895; the Sorbonne, Paris, Doctorat ès Lettres, 1903. Instructor in Greek, Harvard University, 1903–04. *Died 11 October 1904.*

PUBLICATIONS

Collections

> *Homage to Stickney* (selected verse), edited by James Reeves and Seán Haldane.   1968.
> *The Poems*, edited by Amberys R. Whittle.   1972.

Verse

> *Dramatic Verses.*   1902.
> *Poems*, edited by George Cabot Lodge, John Ellerton Lodge, and William Vaughn Moody.   1905.

Other

Les Sentences dans la Poésie Grecque d'Homère à Euripide. 1903.

Translator, with Sylvain Lévi, *Bhagavadgita.* 1938

Reading List: *The Fright of Time: Stickney* by Seán Haldane, 1970; *Stickney* by Amberys R. Whittle, 1973.

One of that group of gifted Americans who came to early maturity in the 1890's only to have their lives snuffed out before the first decade of the new century was completed, Trumbull Stickney is memorable on several counts. As an accomplished Greek and Sanskrit scholar and one of the first intellectual cosmopolitans to attempt a career in American letters, he exhibits a cultural impulse which is to be later followed more extensively by writers like Pound and Eliot. Further, along with William Vaughn Moody and George Cabot Lodge, he aimed at resuscitating verse-drama, and his work in this genre (*Prometheus Pyrphoros* and two fragments based on the lives of the Emperor Julian and the young Benvenuto Cellini) points forward to later efforts in the century. And, powerfully under the influence of Browning, he produced a number of "dramatic scenes" ("Kalypso," "Oneiropolos," "Lodovico Martelli," "Requiescam," etc.), although his instincts for dramatic conflict and psychological subtlety seem less vigorous than his evident delight in historical reconstruction.

It is perhaps the lyrical quality of his writing that suggests the most promise in his work. Almost suffocated in the cloying rhetoric of the *fin de siècle*, heavy with twilight and rose-dust and a fatigued embrace of futility, Stickney's lyrics frequently manage a new, if wistful, vitality to the clichés of Romantic decadence. In poems like "Chestnuts in November," "At Sainte-Marguerite," "Mt. Lykaion," and in isolated passages from "Eride," Stickney's tempered musicality sustains the conventional formal structures, raising these poems above the level of similar lamentations which the Mauve Decade manufactured in wholesale lots. And in poems like "With thy two eyes look on me once again," "Leave him now quiet by the way," and, especially, "Mnemosyne," a quiet strength joins with a precise sense of rhythmical phrasing to produce verse which possesses an autonomy of statement and genuine eloquence. It is futile to speculate on what might have been, but in half a dozen poems Stickney's success was authentic and undeniable. As graceful as Santayana's verse but more concretely sensual, with an intellectual structure as sturdy as the early Robinson's but more personal and direct in tone, Stickney's achievement illustrates the highest ambitions of his generation, while implying a technique that may compensate for the weaknesses of its gentility.

—Earl Rovit

STOUT, Rex (Todhunter). American. Born in Noblesville, Indiana, 1 December 1886. Educated at Topeka High School, Kansas; University of Kansas, Lawrence. Served in the United States Navy, 1906–08. Married 1) Fay Kennedy in 1916 (divorced, 1933); 2) Pola Hoffman in 1933; two daughters. Worked as an office boy, store clerk, bookkeeper, sailor, and hotel manager, 1916–27; full-time writer from 1927; Founding Director, Vanguard Press, New York; Master of Ceremonies, "Speaking of Liberty," "Voice of Freedom," and "Our Secret Weapon" radio programs, 1941–43. Chairman of the Writers' War Board, 1941–46, and the World Government Writers Board, 1949–75; President, Friends of Democracy, 1941–51, Authors' Guild, 1943–45, and Society for the Prevention of World War III, 1943–46; President, 1951–55, 1962–69, and Vice-President, 1956–61, Authors League of America; Treasurer, Freedom House, 1957–75; President, Mystery Writers of America, 1958. Recipient: Mystery Writers of America Grand Master Award, 1959. *Died 27 October 1975.*

PUBLICATIONS

Fiction

How Like a God. 1929.
Seed on the Wind. 1930.
Golden Remedy. 1931.
Forest Fire. 1933.
Fer-de-Lance. 1934.
The President Vanishes. 1934.
The League of Frightened Men. 1935.
O Careless Love! 1935.
The Rubber Band. 1936; as *To Kill Again*, 1960.
The Red Box. 1937.
The Hand in the Glove. 1937; as *Crime on Her Hands*, 1939.
Too Many Cooks. 1938.
Mr. Cinderella. 1938.
Some Buried Caesar. 1939.
Mountain Cat. 1939; as *The Mountain Cat Murders*, 1964.
Red Threads. 1939.
Double for Death. 1939.
Over My Dead Body. 1940.
Bad for Business. 1940.
Where There's a Will. 1940.
The Broken Vase. 1941.
Alphabet Hicks. 1941; as *Sounds of Murder*, 1965.
Black Orchids (stories). 1942.
Booby Trap (stories). 1944.
Not Quite Dead Enough (stories). 1944.
The Silent Speaker. 1946.
Too Many Women. 1947.
And Be a Villain. 1948; as *More Deaths Than One*, 1949.
The Second Confession. 1949.
Trouble in Triplicate (stories). 1949.
Three Doors to Death (stories). 1950.
In the Best Families. 1950; as *Even in the Best*, 1951.
Murder by the Book. 1951.
Curtains for Three (stories). 1951.
Triple Jeopardy (stories). 1952.
Prisoner's Base. 1952; as *Out Goes She*, 1953.
The Golden Spiders. 1954.

Three Men Out (stories). 1954.
The Black Mountain. 1954.
Before Midnight. 1955.
Might as Well Be Dead. 1956.
Three Witnesses (stories). 1956.
Three for the Chair (stories). 1957.
If Death Ever Slept. 1957.
Champagne for One. 1958.
And Four to Go (stories). 1958.
Plot It Yourself. 1959.
Crime and Again. 1959.
Murder in Style. 1960.
Three at Wolfe's Door (stories). 1960.
Too Many Clients. 1960.
The Final Deduction. 1961.
Gambit. 1962.
Homicide Trinity (stories). 1962.
The Mother Hunt. 1963.
Trio for Blunt Instruments (stories). 1964.
A Right To Die. 1964.
The Doorbell Rang. 1965.
Death of a Doxy. 1966.
The Father Hunt. 1968.
Death of a Dude. 1969.
Please Pass the Guilt. 1973.
Three Trumps (stories). 1973.
Triple Zeck (stories). 1974.
A Family Affair. 1975.
Justice Ends at Home and Other Stories. 1977.

Other

The Nero Wolfe Cookbook, with others. 1973.

Editor, *The Illustrious Dunderheads* (on American isolationists). 1942.
Editor, with Louis Greenfield, *Rue Morgue 1.* 1946.
Editor, *Eat, Drink, and Be Buried.* 1956; revised edition, as *For Tomorrow We Die*, 1958.

Reading List: *Stout: A Biography* by John McAleer, 1977.

*   *   *

At the beginning of a career undertaken after he had earned enough money in business to permit full devotion to writing, Rex Stout published four critically acceptable but unpopular "straight" novels. Then, in the decade after he had committed himself to the detective genre with the publication of *Fer-de-Lance*, he developed a variety of sleuths: "Dol" Bonner and Sally Colt in *The Hand in the Glove*, Tecumseh Fox who appeared in three novels, Alphabet Hicks in one novel bearing his name, Delia Brand in *Mountain Cat*, and Inspector Cramer of *Red Threads*. Stout is known, however, almost entirely because he was the creator of Nero Wolfe.

Like Sherlock Holmes, Stout's evident model for a Great Detective, Nero Wolfe so dominates the tales in which he appears that enthusiasts refer to them as though they were authorless – they are simply Nero Wolfe stories; and, again like his model and a small handful of other fictional detectives such as Charlie Chan or Sam Spade, Nero Wolfe – the enormously fat, eccentric genius-recluse – has achieved independence of the tales themselves. He is an autonomous figure in the popular imagination, familiar even to those with the slightest literary knowledge of his exploits.

There can be no doubt it was Stout's intention to create a mythic detective. The constellation of traits attributed to Wolfe coupled with his mental infallibility are the formula of a character who dominates as well as presides, and the narrative voice of Archie Goodwin, though it is quite unlike Dr. Watson's, provides for the distancing that surrounds the solver of mysteries with his own aura of mystery. Moreover, Archie's speech develops the illusion of a case's history with the attendant suspense necessary to deflect our awareness that the only subject of the fiction is the detective.

It would be incorrect, however, to describe Stout only as an imitator of formulas pioneered by Arthur Conan Doyle, because he artfully manages the genre of detection fiction in his own way. It is just that his way involves simplification of the genre rather than the transgression of conventions we usually associate with innovation. A striking example of Stout's simplification is in the setting of the stories. Wolfe's household is central to every tale. He never goes abroad to the classic country house or to walk the city's mean streets; thus, in one stroke we get both ambience (W. 35th St. equals Baker St.) and intensification of the detective's prominence, since clients and aides with the guilty and innocent suspects must all subject themselves to the force of his orbit, their thoughts and acts entirely subordinate to Wolfe's interpretations.

Fundamentally, the plot of every tale of detection is epistemological. It progresses through scenes of a detective's methodical expansion of his knowledge of the reality of some mysterious events until it is concluded by a celebration of rationality in which all the secondary characters witness the detective's literal creation of truth through summary analysis of events and motives. In plot, too, Stout has simplified. With Wolfe working on cases in his own study – the consummate armchair detective – each scene prefigures the classical denouement, maintaining a dominance by Wolfe's mind over events that matches the supremacy of his personality.

The result of Stout's simplification of the detection story is to invest the saga of Nero Wolfe with an Augustan formality. The incidents of the stories and novels vary, but each repeats invariable movements extolling the nature of a Great Detective.

—John M. Reilly

STRIBLING, T(heodore) S(igismund).   American.   Born in Clifton, Tennessee, 4 March 1881. Educated at Clifton public schools; Normal College, Florence, Alabama, graduated 1903; studied law at the University of Alabama, LL.B. 1904. Married Louella Kloss in 1930. Practiced law in Florence, 1906; member of the staff of the *Taylor-Trotwood Magazine*, Nashville, Tennessee, 1906–07; thereafter a full-time writer; wrote moral stories for Sunday School magazines, the income from which allowed him to travel and live in South America and Europe; later lived in Clifton; Instructor in Creative Writing, Columbia University, New York, 1936, 1940. Recipient: Pulitzer Prize, 1933. LL.D.: Oglethorpe University, Atlanta, Georgia, 1936. *Died 10 July 1965.*

PUBLICATIONS

Fiction

The Cruise of the Dry Dock. 1917.
Birthright. 1922.
Fombombo. 1923.
Red Sand. 1924.
Teeftallow. 1926.
Bright Metal. 1928.
East Is East. 1928.
Clues of the Caribbees, Being Certain Criminal Investigations of Henry Poggioli, Ph.D. 1929.
Strange Moon. 1929.
Backwater. 1930.
The Forge. 1931.
The Store. 1932.
Unfinished Cathedral. 1934.
The Sound Wagon. 1935.
These Bars of Flesh. 1938.

Reading List: *Stribling* by Wilton Eckley, 1975.

*

T. S. Stribling, who began as a writer of moral adventure tales for Sunday School magazines and then moved on to the pulps and finally to serious fiction, is remembered chiefly for *The Store*, which won him the Pulitzer prize in 1933. It is the second volume of his trilogy (*The Forge* and *Unfinished Cathedral* are the other two) dealing with the fortunes of the Vaiden family, particularly with the rise of Miltaides Vaiden from poor man to rich landowner and cotton planter in the ante-bellum South. In this trilogy, as in his other serious novels (*Birthright, Teeftallow, Bright Metal, Sound Wagon, These Bars of Flesh*), Stribling is a social satirist and local colorist. His strong point is his gift of observation, of setting down in credible language the look and feel of a natural landscape and the poor whites and blacks who inhabit it. His weaknesses are his themes (which tend to be simplistic), his plots (melodramatic), and his style (often crudely pretentious). Like Sinclair Lewis, Stribling is a social critic and debunker, his locale the middle South (Tennessee, Alabama), and his chief concern prejudice against blacks and the general narrow-mindedness of ingrown Southern communities. In *Birthright*, he deals with a Harvard-educated black from Tennessee forced to live the stereotyped role of an uneducated black laborer. But he has also debunked the American scene of lawyers and businessmen (*Sound Wagon*) and the American education college (*These Bars of Flesh*). Much of his fiction is hackwork, quickly turned out melodrama with a slight satirical edge. *Fombombo, Red Sand,* and *Strange Moon* mix satire, South American politics, business, and romance. Stribling also wrote detective stories (*Clues of the Caribbees*).

Stribling is an "objective" observer who sees history as a mechanical process, individuals as pawns in the grip of economic and social forces. His fiction is interesting to the literary historian for the way he blends popular stereotypes with old-fashioned liberal political and social ideas, and for the contrast offered between his mechanistic histories of the South and William Faulkner's mythical histories, a contrast that helps make clear not only Stribling's appeal to liberal critics in the 1930's but also the reason Faulkner was disliked and undervalued.

—W. J. Stuckey

STYRON, William. American. Born in Newport News, Virginia, 11 June 1925. Educated at Christchurch School, Virginia; Davidson College, North Carolina, 1942–43; Duke University, Durham, North Carolina, 1943–44, 1946–47, A.B. 1947. Served in the United States Marine Corps, 1944–45, 1951: 1st Lieutenant. Married Rose Burgunder in 1953; one son and three daughters. Associate Editor for McGraw Hill, publishers, New York, 1947; full-time writer from 1947; Advisory Editor, *Paris Review*, Paris and New York, since 1952; member of the Editorial Board of *The American Scholar*, Washington, D.C., since 1970. Fellow of Silliman College, Yale University, New Haven, Connecticut, since 1964. Recipient: American Academy of Arts and Letters Prix de Rome, 1952; Pulitzer Prize, 1968; Howells Medal, 1970. D.H.: Wilberforce University, Ohio, 1967: Litt.D.: Duke University, 1968; New School for Social Research, New York; Tufts University, Medford, Massachusetts. Member, National Institute of Arts and Letters, and American Academy of Arts and Sciences. Lives in Roxbury, Connecticut.

PUBLICATIONS

Fiction

    Lie Down in Darkness. 1951.
    The Long March. 1956.
    Set This House on Fire. 1960.
    The Confessions of Nat Turner. 1967.
    Sophie's Choice. 1979.

Play

    In the Clap Shack (produced 1972). 1973.

Other

    Editor, *Best Short Stories from "The Paris Review."* 1959.

Reading List: *Styron* by Robert H. Fossum, 1968; *Styron* by Cooper R. Mackin, 1969; *Styron's "The Confessions of Nat Turner": A Critical Handbook* edited by Melvin J. Friedman and Irving Malin, 1970 (includes bibliography); *Styron* by Richard Pearce, 1971; *Styron* by Marc L. Ratner, 1972; *The Achievement of Styron* edited by Irving Malin and Robert K. Morris, 1974.

*   *   *

With the publication of *The Confessions of Nat Turner*, William Styron fulfilled – unwittingly and with great reluctance – early predictions that he would prove worthy of great national attention. The novel, based on the extracted confession of an insurrectionary leader of the Southampton, Virginia, slave revolt of 1803, was published in the midst of profound racial turmoil in the late 1960's of the United States. The considerable literary strengths of the book – Styron's talents as a story teller, stylist, dreamer of the interior psyche – were submerged under a torrent of larger sociological and cultural questions. Black and white historians, sociologists, psychologists debated a morass of questions, especially (1) the propriety of a Southern white liberal's depicting a black slave hero; (2) the psychic image of Nat Turner as a sexually tormented and driven figure; (3) the complex vision on black-white race relations offered in the novel. Black scholar John E. Clarke collected a major body of the criticism in *William Styron's "Nat Turner": Ten Black Writers Respond* (1968).

Styron's first novel, *Lie Down in Darkness*, was exceptionally well-reviewed (although the inescapable debts to Faulkner and Wolfe were acknowledged), and Maxwell Geismar led the way in hailing it as "maybe the best novel since World War II." As a writer of the American South, Styron owes a debt to a strong literary and cultural stream. Louis D. Rubin, Jr., sums it up: "It involved ... a reliance upon the resources of a sounding rhetoric rather than understatement, a dependence upon the old religious universals ('love and honor and pity and pride and sacrifice,' as Faulkner once termed them) rather than a suspicion of all such external moral formulations, and a profound belief in the reality of the past as importantly affecting present behavior – an 'historical sense,' as contrasted with the dismissal of history as irrelevant and meaningless."

Throughout Styron's three novels, and in his shorter works as well, there is a consistent and abiding interest in the press of human social, political, and allied institutions and mores on the individual consciousness, and in the human consequences thereof. Styron's work is heavily reliant on the figures of the mind – on dream and nightmare, on interior monologue and fantasy, on the densities of memory and reflection. The Loftis family of his first novel – Milton and Helen and especially their daughter Peyton – is a moving group portrait of a family dismembered by the bankruptcy and collapse of Old Southern ways of being. In Peyton Loftis's flight to the North and finally New York, we see particularly the psychic devastation resultant from the demands of a shadow world of "old religious universals," but one no longer able to offer the place and fixity and comfort that once justified it.

Styron's interest in the individual psyche's response to the demands of a culture are nowhere more apparent than in his portrait of Nat Turner. While his novel does offer a vivid and moving image of slave life, Styron's clear interest is in the psychology of this unlikely slave leader. Under Styron's pen – to the great anger of certain black hagiographers – Turner emerges as a religious visionary and repressed polymorph, yearning for sexual contact with his white masters and mistresses and loathing himself for doing so.

Styron's most consistent fictional interest has been in the individual psychic results of the emergence of the South into the modern world, but he has also manifested a second concern in his work: in the tensions between the private conscience and mature sensibility and the incessant demands of the modern military establishment, seen in its most extreme American form in the United States Marine Corps. An early novella, *The Long March*, demonstrates this interest, as do his most recently published excerpt from a novel-on-progress, "Marriott, The Marine" (part of a novel entitled *The Way of the Warrior*), and the play *In the Clap Shack*.

Styron works slowly and painfully, and no doubt the turmoil around *The Confessions of Nat Turner* interrupted and threatened his work. But, based on recent excerpts, particularly the strongly autobiographical "Marriott, The Marine," his most absorbing and least mannered work in a long time, I would judge that his best work — and it would be considerable to top *Lie Down in Darkness* — is yet to be written.

—Jack Hicks

SUCKOW, Ruth. American. Born in Hawarden, Iowa, 6 August 1892; grew up in various Iowa towns. Educated at Grinnell College, Iowa, 1910–13; Curry Dramatic School, Boston, 1914–15; University of Denver, 1915–18, B.A. 1917, M.A. 1918. Married the writer Ferner Nuhn in 1929. Writer from 1918; Editorial Assistant on *The Midland*, Iowa City, 1921–22; owner and manager of the Orchard Apiary, Earlsville, Iowa, in the 1920's; spent winters in New York City, 1924–34; lived in Cedar Falls, Iowa, 1934–52, and Claremont, California, from 1952. M.A.: Grinnell College, 1931. *Died 23 January 1960.*

PUBLICATIONS

Fiction

 Country People. 1924.
 The Odyssey of a Nice Girl. 1925.
 Iowa Interiors (stories). 1926; as *People and Houses*, 1927.
 The Bonney Family. 1928.
 Cora. 1929.
 The Kramer Girls. 1930.
 Children and Older People (stories). 1931.
 The Folks. 1934.
 Carry-Over. 1936.
 New Hope. 1942.
 Some Others and Myself: Seven Stories and a Memoir. 1952.
 The John Wood Case. 1959.

Reading List: *Suckow* by Leedice McAnnelly Kissane, 1969; *Suckow: A Critical Study of Her Fiction* by Margaret Stewart Omrcanin, 1972.

*   *   *

In the 1920's Ruth Suckow was considered a major talent, destined to write novels and short stories of distinction, possibly a great American writer. H. L. Mencken published her short fiction in his *Smart Set* and *American Mercury*, and praised her extravagantly. Suckow's stories seemed to fit somewhere between Willa Cather and Sinclair Lewis, but to many she was more honest and straightforward than either. Fifty years later Ruth Suckow is considered a minor figure: a good Iowa regionalist, an uncompromising, unsentimental realist who wrote about the ordinary, middle-class people of the American heartland at the beginning of the automotive age.

After the 1920's the literary standing of Cather and Lewis was eclipsed by Hemingway, Dos Passos, Steinbeck, Fitzgerald, and Faulkner. Literary fashion turned against Ruth Suckow, but more important factors were responsible for her decline in stature. Her quiet, uneventful accounts worked best in short stories, but novels were more profitable and more prestigious. Her most ambitious novel, *The Folks* (727 pages), was a Literary Guild selection in 1934. More than twenty years elapse in this account of an Iowa small-town banker and his wife, and the start in life of their four children. The action extends to New York and San Diego, but the point of view is always Iowa small-town. Departing from her earlier practice, in this novel Suckow interprets and comments on the actions and motivations of her characters. But though people, places, and events ring true, there is too little drama, conflict, or interest in the people to sustain the long story. Two later novels – *New Hope* and *The John Wood Case* – drew little critical attention.

The Folks reveals Ruth Suckow's shortcomings. The same weaknesses are found in her earlier novels: *Country People*, *The Odyssey of a Nice Girl*, *The Bonney Family*, *Cora*, and *The Kramer Girls*. The last two of this group reveal her new interest in feminism; the earlier novels reveal the texture of small-town life in Iowa seen through the eyes of a young girl.

The short stories of *Iowa Interiors* and *Children and Older People* are Suckow's best work. The stories in a third volume, *Some Others and Myself*, are admittedly inferior – more reflective and contemplative, less objective. As in her longer fiction, the point of view in these stories is restricted and revealing: as the daughter of a small-town clergyman, Suckow saw many lonely, elderly couples and frustrated spinsters. She describes the countless family gatherings and church affairs she had been a part of, not social, political, and economic machinations. There is no explicit sex, no violence, no drama or suspense.

In his *Midwestern Farm Novel* Roy Meyer finds Suckow unsatisfactory because she sees Iowa farms – their people and problems – from the point of view of a small-town preacher's daughter who occasionally came out to those farms. A fellow-Iowan, the socialist Josephine Herbst, objected to Suckow's blindness to social implications. A comparison with her slightly older contemporary, Sherwood Anderson, is revealing: like Suckow's, Anderson's short stories are far better than his novels, but the psychological insights in Anderson's stories contrast sharply with the flatness and simplicity of her honest realism.

—Clarence A. Glasrud

TARKINGTON, (Newton) Booth. American. Born in Indianapolis, Indiana, 29 July 1869, and lived there for most of his life. Educated at Phillips Exeter Academy, New Hampshire; Purdue University, Lafayette, Indiana, 1888–89; Princeton University, 1889–93; did not graduate. Married 1) Laurel Louisa Fletcher in 1902 (divorced, 1911), one daughter; 2) Susannah Robinson in 1912. Writer from 1893; also an artist: illustrated *Character Sketches* by Riley and other works; member of the Indiana House of

Representatives, 1902–03; in later life also lived in Kennebunkport, Maine. Recipient: Pulitzer Prize, 1919, 1922; National Institute of Arts and Letters Gold Medal, 1933; Boy Scouts of America Silver Buffalo, 1935; Roosevelt Distinguished Service Medal, 1942; Howells Medal, 1945. A.M.: Princeton University, 1899; Litt.D.: Princeton University, 1918; De Pauw University, Greencastle, Indiana, 1923; Columbia University, New York, 1924; L.H.D.: Purdue University, 1939. Member, American Academy of Arts and Letters. *Died 19 May 1946.*

PUBLICATIONS

Collections

>   *The Gentleman from Indianapolis: A Treasury of Tarkington,* edited by John Beecroft. 1957.

Fiction

>   *The Gentleman from Indiana.* 1899.
>   *Monsieur Beaucaire.* 1900.
>   *The Two Vanrevels.* 1902.
>   *Cherry.* 1903.
>   *In the Arena: Stories of Political Life.* 1905.
>   *The Beautiful Lady.* 1905.
>   *The Conquest of Canaan.* 1905.
>   *His Own People.* 1907.
>   *The Guest of Quesnay.* 1908.
>   *Beasley's Christmas Party.* 1909.
>   *The Flirt.* 1913.
>   *Penrod.* 1914; *Penrod and Sam,* 1916; *Penrod Jashber,* 1929; complete revised version, as *Penrod: His Complete Story,* 1931.
>   *The Turmoil.* 1915; *The Magnificent Ambersons,* 1918; *The Midlander,* 1923; complete version, as *Growth,* 1927.
>   *Seventeen.* 1916.
>   *The Spring Concert* (story). 1916.
>   *Harlequin and Columbine and Other Stories.* 1918.
>   *Ramsey Milholland.* 1919.
>   *Alice Adams.* 1921.
>   *Gentle Julia.* 1922.
>   *The Fascinating Stranger and Other Stories.* 1923.
>   *Women.* 1925.
>   *Selections from Tarkington's Stories,* edited by Lilian Holmes Strack. 1926.
>   *The Plutocrat.* 1927.
>   *Claire Ambler.* 1928.
>   *Young Mrs. Greeley.* 1929.
>   *Mirthful Haven.* 1930.
>   *Mary's Neck.* 1932.
>   *Wanton Mally.* 1932.
>   *Presenting Lily Mars.* 1933.
>   *Little Orvie.* 1934.
>   *Mr. White, The Red Barn, Hell, and Bridewater.* 1935.

The Lorenzo Bunch. 1936.
Rumbin Galleries. 1937.
The Heritage of Hatcher Ide. 1941.
The Fighting Littles. 1941.
Kate Fennigate. 1943.
Image of Josephine. 1945.
The Show Piece (unfinished). 1947.
Three Selected Short Novels (includes *Walterson, Uncertain Molly Collicut,* and *Rennie Peddigoe*). 1947.

Plays

The Guardian, with Harry Leon Wilson. 1907; as *The Man from Home* (produced 1908), 1908; revised version, 1934.
Cameo Kirby, with Harry Leon Wilson (produced 1908).
Foreign Exchange (produced 1909).
If I Had Money (produced 1909).
Springtime (produced 1909).
Your Humble Servant, with Harry Leon Wilson (produced 1909).
Beauty and the Jacobin: An Interlude of the French Revolution (produced 1912). 1912.
The Man on Horseback (produced 1912).
The Ohio Lady, with Julian Street. 1916; as *The Country Cousin* (produced 1921), 1921.
Mister Antonio (produced 1916). 1935.
The Gibson Upright, with Harry Leon Wilson (produced 1919). 1919.
Up from Nowhere, with Harry Leon Wilson (produced 1919).
Poldekin (produced 1920). In *McClure's,* March–July 1920.
Clarence (produced 1921). 1921.
The Intimate Strangers (produced 1921). 1921.
The Wren (produced 1922). 1922.
The Ghost Story (juvenile) (produced 1922). 1922.
Rose Briar (produced 1922).
The Trysting Place (produced 1923). 1923.
Magnolia (produced 1923).
Tweedles, with Harry Leon Wilson (produced 1924). 1924.
Bimbo, The Pirate (produced 1926). 1926.
The Travelers (produced 1927). 1927.
Station YYYY (produced 1927). 1927.
How's Your Health?, with Harry Leon Wilson (produced 1930). 1930.
Colonel Satan (produced 1932).
The Help Each Other Club (produced 1933). 1934.
Lady Hamilton and Her Nelson (produced 1945). 1945.

Screenplays: *Edgar and the Teacher's Pet,* 1920; *Edgar's Hamlet,* 1920; *Edgar's Little Saw,* 1920; *Edgar, The Explorer,* 1921; *Get Rich Quick Edgar,* 1921; *Pied Piper Malone,* with Tom Geraghty, 1924; *The Man Who Found Himself,* with Tom Geraghty, 1925.

Radio Plays: *Maud and Cousin Bill* series, 1932–33 (75 episodes).

Other

Works. 21 vols., 1918–28.

The Works.   27 vols., 1922–32.
The Collector's Whatnot, with Hugh Kahler and Kenneth Roberts.   1923.
Looking Forward and Others (essays).   1926.
The World Does Move (reminiscences).   1928.
Some Old Portraits: A Book about Art and Human Beings.   1939.
Your Amiable Uncle: Letters to His Nephews.   1949.
On Plays, Playwrights, and Playgoers: Selections from the Letters of Tarkington to George C. Tyler and John Peter Tooley 1918–1925, edited by Alan S. Downer.   1959.

Translator, *Samuel Brohl and Company,* by Victor Cherbuliez.   1902.

Bibliography: *A Bibliography of Tarkington* by Dorothy Ritter Russo and Thelma L. Sullivan, 1949, supplement in *Princeton University Library Chronicle 16,* 1955.

Reading List: *Tarkington: Gentleman from Indiana* by James Woodress, 1955; *Tarkington* by Keith J. Fennimore, 1974.

*   *   *

Although Booth Tarkington was a very popular author during his lifetime, his reputation has dimmed since his death, and today few of his works are read. Yet he was an excellent fictional craftsman and a first-rate story teller, and his best novels are absorbing. Though there are no sexual titillation and little tragedy in his books, he has a sense of humor and observes and records the human comedy with a clear eye. His significance lies in his depiction of urban, midwestern, middle-class America during the decades of intensely rapid growth in the late 19th and early 20th centuries, and in his stories of children. He writes in the tradition of commonplace realism as pioneered by Howells.

His trilogy published under the collective title *Growth* is important. These novels study the social and economic life of a medium-sized midwestern city that may be identified as Indianapolis. *The Turmoil,* which contains a very contemporary-sounding indictment of air pollution and civic neglect in the pursuit of the dollar, is the story of an ascending family, the first-generation makers of the new industrial wealth. *The Magnificent Ambersons,* winner of a Pulitzer Prize, deals with an old family whose money was made in the Gilded Age. The family is engulfed by the encroaching industrialism of the 20th Century, and the wealth is dissipated by the second and third generations. *The Midlander,* which comes as close as Tarkington ever came to tragedy, is the unhappy story of a promoter-developer of the urban growth. Similar in subject and theme to the *Growth* trilogy is *Alice Adams,* perhaps Tarkington's best novel. This story, which deserves to be better known, is a poignant comedy of manners that details the unsuccessful efforts of a girl of modest circumstances to catch a socially prominent husband. Character, plot, and the theme of social mobility all are skillfully blended in this novel that won Tarkington a second Pulitzer Prize.

Tarkington's second major accomplishment lies in his boy stories, *Penrod, Penrod and Sam,* and *Penrod Jashber.* These distinguished tales in the tradition of the realistic boy-story begun by Mark Twain in *Tom Sawyer* appeal both to children and adults, are rich in authentic detail and dialogue, and may turn out to be the author's most enduring work. Tarkington also was adroit in depicting adolescents, but the vast change in teen-age mores since *Seventeen* appeared in 1916 makes this once-popular novel a period piece rather than a story of perennial interest.

Tarkington was a playwright as well as a novelist, and any history of American drama must accord him a niche for some of his two dozen plays. *The Man from Home*, which he wrote with Harry Leon Wilson, enjoyed a long run on Broadway, and his play *Clarence*, which starred Alfred Lunt and Helen Hayes at the beginning of their careers, was a memorable success. Few American novelists have mastered the play form as well as Tarkington.

—James Woodress

TATE, Allen. American. Born in Winchester, Kentucky, 19 November 1899. Educated at Georgetown Preparatory School, Washington, D.C.; Vanderbilt University, Nashville, Tennessee, B.A. 1922. Married 1) Caroline Gordon, *q.v.*, in 1924; 2) the poet Isabella Stewart Gardner in 1959; 3) Helen Heinz in 1966; has three children. Member of the Fugitive Group of Poets: Founding Editor, with John Crowe Ransom, *The Fugitive*, Nashville, 1922–25; Editor, *Sewanee Review*, Tennessee, 1944–46; Editor, Belles Lettres series, Henry Holt and Company, New York, 1946–48. Lecturer in English, Southwestern College, Memphis, Tennessee, 1934–36; Professor of English, The Woman's College, Greensboro, North Carolina, 1938–39; Poet-in-Residence, Princeton University, New Jersey 1939–42; Lecturer in the Humanities, New York University, 1947–51. Since 1951, Professor of English, University of Minnesota, Minneapolis: Regents' Professor, 1966; Professor Emeritus, 1968. Visiting Professor in the Humanities, University of Chicago, 1949; Fulbright Lecturer, Oxford University, 1953, University of Rome, 1953–54, and Oxford and Leeds universities, 1958–59; Department of State Lecturer at the universities of Liège and Louvain, 1954, Delhi and Bombay, 1956, the Sorbonne, Paris, 1956, Nottingham, 1956, and Urbino and Florence, 1961; Visiting Professor of English, University of North Carolina, Greensboro, 1966, and Vanderbilt University, 1967. Member, Phi Beta Kappa Senate, 1951–53. Since 1948 Fellow, and since 1956 Senior Fellow, Kenyon School of English (now School of Letters, Indiana University, Bloomington). Constutant in Poetry, Library of Congress, Washington, D.C., 1943–44. Recipient: Guggenheim Fellowship, 1928, 1929; National Institute of Arts and Letters grant, 1948; Bollingen Prize, 1957; Brandeis University Creative Arts Award, 1960; Gold Medal of the Dante Society, Florence, 1962; Academy of American Poets Fellowship, 1963; Oscar Williams-Gene Derwood Award, 1975; National Medal for Literature, 1976. Litt.D.: University of Louisville, Kentucky, 1948; Coe College, Cedar Rapids, Iowa, 1955; Colgate University, Hamilton, New York, 1956; University of Kentucky, Lexington, 1960; Carleton College, Northfield, Minnesota, 1963; University of the South, Sewanee, Tennessee, 1970. Member, American Academy of Arts and Letters; President, National Institute of Arts and Letters, 1968. Since 1964, Member, Board of Chancellors, Academy of American Poets. Lives in Sewanee, Tennessee.

PUBLICATIONS

Verse

The Golden Mean and Other Poems, with Ridley Wills. 1923.
Mr. Pope and Other Poems. 1928.

*Ode to the Confederate Dead, Being the Revised and Final Version of a Poem Previously
    Published on Several Occasions: To Which Are Added Message from Abroad and The
    Cross.*   1930.
Three Poems.   1930.
Robert E. Lee.   1932.
Poems 1928–1931.   1932.
The Mediterranean and Other Poems.   1936.
Selected Poems.   1937.
Sonnets at Christmas.   1941.
The Winter Sea: A Book of Poems.   1944.
Poems 1920–1945: A Selection.   1947.
Poems 1922–1947.   1948.
Two Conceits for the Eye to Sing, If Possible.   1950.
Poems.   1960.
The Swimmers and Other Selected Poems.   1970.
Collected Poems 1919–1976.   1977.

Play

The Governess, with Anne Goodwin Winslow (produced 1962).

Fiction

The Fathers.   1938; revised edition, 1960.
The Fathers and Other Fiction.   1976.

Other

Stonewall Jackson: The Good Soldier: A Narrative.   1928.
Jefferson Davis: His Rise and Fall: A Biographical Narrative.   1929.
Reactionary Essays on Poetry and Ideas.   1936.
Reason in Madness: Critical Essays.   1941.
Invitation to Learning, with Huntington Cairns and Mark Van Doren.   1941.
Sixty American Poets, 1896–1944: A Preliminary Checklist.   1945.
On the Limits of Poetry: Selected Essays, 1928–1948.   1948.
The Hovering Fly and Other Essays.   1949.
The Forlorn Demon: Didactic and Critical Essays.   1953.
The Man of Letters in the Modern World: Selected Essays, 1928–1955.   1955.
Collected Essays.   1959.
Essays of Four Decades.   1968.
Modern Literature and the Lost Traveller.   1969.
The Translation of Poetry.   1972.
The Literary Correspondence of Donald Davidson and Tate, edited by John T. Fain and
    T. D. Young.   1974.
Memoirs and Opinions 1926–1974.   1975.

Editor, with others, *Fugitives: An Anthology of Verse.*   1928.
Editor, with Herbert Agar, *Who Owns America? A New Declaration of
    Independence.*   1936.
Editor, with A. Theodore Johnson, *America Through the Essay: An Anthology for
    English Courses.*   1938.

Editor, *The Language of Poetry*.   1942.

Editor, *Princeton Verse Between Two Wars: An Anthology*.   1942.

Editor, with John Peale Bishop, *American Harvest: Twenty Years of Creative Writing in the United States*.   1942.

Editor, *Recent American Poetry and Poetic Criticism: A Selected List of References*.   1943.

Editor, *A Southern Vanguard* (the John Peale Bishop memorial anthology).   1947.

Editor, *The Collected Poems of John Peale Bishop*.   1948.

Editor, with Caroline Gordon, *The House of Fiction: An Anthology of the Short Story*.   1950; revised edition, 1960.

Editor, with Lord David Cecil, *Modern Verse in English, 1900–1950*.   1958.

Editor, with John Berryman and Ralph Ross, *The Arts of Learning*.   1960.

Editor, *Selected Poems of John Peale Bishop*.   1960.

Editor, with Robert Penn Warren, *Selected Poems*, by Denis Devlin.   1963.

Editor, *T. S. ELiot: The Man and His Work: A Critical Evaluation by Twenty-Six Distinguished Critics*.   1966.

Editor, *The Complete Poems and Selected Criticism of Edgar Allan Poe*.   1968.

Editor, *Six American Poets: From Emily Dickinson to the Present: An Introduction*.   1972.

Translator, *The Vigil of Venus*.   1943.

Bibliography: *Tate: A Bibliography* by Marshall Fallwell, Jr., 1969.

Reading List: *The Last Alternatives: A Study of the Works of Tate* by M. K. Meiners, 1963; *Tate* by George Hemphill, 1964; *Tate* by Ferman Bishop, 1967; *Rumors of Morality: An Introduction to Tate* by M. E. Bradford, 1969; *Tate: A Literary Biography* by Radcliffe Squires, 1971, and *Tate and His Works: Critical Evaluations* edited by Squires, 1972.

*   *   *

  Allen Tate is always associated with the Fugitives, the small group of Southern poets who were led by John Crowe Ransom of Vanderbilt University of Nashville during the early 1920's. But Tate was always his own man, and as a young Fugitive he found it necessary to reject much in the South; by 1924 he was living in New York City. Certainly Southern literary culture offered nothing that he could imitate directly, though his sense of the age led him to the French symbolists and hence back to Poe, about whom he was to write three of his most important essays. His best poem before 1925 is his version of Baudelaire's "Correspondences." This seems as important as his friendship with his first master, Ransom, because it allowed him access to the mainstream of modern poetry.

  In New York City, married to the novelist Caroline Gordon, Tate was on close terms with many writers of his generation, especially Hart Crane, and he could easily be put among the second generation of modernists (if we put Eliot, Pound, and Joyce in the first generation). It may well be that his regional sense was sharpened by his residence in the East and then Paris for six years. At any rate, by 1926 he was writing the first version of his most ambitious early poem, "Ode to the Confederate Dead." The recently published correspondence between Tate and his Fugitive friend Donald Davidson shows him at that time occupying a kind of intermediary position between Davidson, who was writing *The Tall Men*, a long poem about Tennessee, and Crane, who was working on *The Bridge*, a visionary poem about America. Almost by instinct Tate shunned the "epical" treatment of experience. Where his Southern quality emerges most convincingly is in the elevation of tone that was characteristic of the rhetoricians of this region. In a sense the Old South was organized by the voices of the preacher and the politician, and this legacy of public speaking descended to many of the writers of the modern Southern Renascence.

The 1930's was the Agrarian period for the old Fugitive group, and Tate was frequently involved in the controversies that grew out of this movement, which coincided with an extraordinary outburst of literary achievement in the South. But his main energy went into his poetry, and his *Selected Poems* is one of the best collections of poetry in the decade. This volume contains the final version of the "Ode to the Confederate Dead," a distinguished meditative poem called "The Mediterranean," and a dozen shorter poems of great power and considerable range, such as "Emblems," "The Cross," and "The Wolves."

Meanwhile he was becoming one of the most important American critics; his first volume, *Reactionary Essays on Poetry and Ideas*, fully established his position. As critic he has always taken a large view of literary culture, but many of his influential early essays were written about such contemporaries as Crane, Archibald MacLeish, and John Peale Bishop. Certain theoretical essays have become classics of modern criticism: "Tension in Poetry," "Techniques of Fiction," "The Hovering Fly," and "A Southern Mode of the Imagination." These have generated as much discussion as anything written during the last generation in the United States. Perhaps the finest essays are two on Poe and Dante, "The Angelic Imagination" and "The Symbolic Imagination," published in 1951 at a time when he was writing some outstanding poems. Tate's criticism, in fact, is very much the work of a poet and often provides the setting for his verse.

Another work in prose that is closely related to Tate's verse of the 1930's is his novel *The Fathers*, which has been even more admired in recent years than it was when it was first published. Influenced in its technique by Ford Madox Ford's *The Good Soldier* ("the masterpiece of British fiction in this century"), the novel dramatizes with a great poetic intelligence the destruction of a Virginia family at the beginning of the Civil War. The critic Radcliffe Squires has shown the extent to which Allen Tate drew on the history of his own family for the subject.

The last phase of Tate's poetry started during the early 1940's, though it was long anticipated. It includes the splendid satire "Ode to Our Young Pro-Consuls of the Air," an attack on the modern religion of the state; his very title proposes an analogy between America and Rome. This in a sense was preparatory for the long poem "Seasons of the Soul" and a later group of poems in *terza rima*, including "The Swimmers" and "The Buried Lake," his most impressive work of all. In these late poems Tate has set his experience (his own, his family's, his region's) against a background of Christian experience represented most fully by Dante, and has "imitated" Dante's verse more closely than any other American poet has done. Brilliant and sometimes restless, Allen Tate has been more than a fine poet: he has helped to set the standards for the literary community in the United States.

—Ashley Brown

TEASDALE, Sara. American. Born in St. Louis, Missouri, 8 August 1884. Educated privately. Married Ernst B. Filsinger in 1914 (divorced, 1929). Lived in Europe and the Middle East, 1905–07; settled in New York City, 1916. Recipient: Pulitzer Prize, 1917; Poetry Society of American Annual Prize, 1917. *Died 29 January 1933.*

PUBLICATIONS

Collections

Collected Poems. 1937.

Verse

Sonnets to Duse and Other Poems.   1907.
Helen of Troy and Other Poems.   1911; revised edition, 1922.
Rivers to the Sea.   1915.
Love Songs.   1917.
Vignettes of Italy: A Cycle of Nine Songs for High Voice.   1919.
Flame and Shadow.   1920; revised edition, 1924.
Dark of the Moon.   1926.
Stars To-Night: Verses New and Old for Boys and Girls.   1930.
A Country House.   1932.
Strange Victory.   1933.

Other

Editor, *The Answering Voice · One Hundred Love Lyrics by Women.*   1917; revised edition, 1928.
Editor, *Rainbow Gold: Poems for Boys and Girls.*   1922.

Bibliography: by Vivian Buchan, in *Bulletin of Bibliography 25,* 1967.

Reading List: *Teasdale: A Biography* by Margaret Haley Carpenter, 1960.

*   *   *

Sara Teasdale, whose verse suggests, in her own phrase, "a delicate fabric of bird song," is one of America's most charming lyrists. Well-received and popular for some fifteen years after *Love Songs* (1917) took the Pulitzer Prize for poetry, she was posthumously, and unjustly, somewhat underrated by the time *Collected Poems* appeared in 1937.

Miss Teasdale's first book of consequence was her third, *Rivers to the Sea,* in which signs of the mature poet became clearly evident. Happily, the best of her early work was incorporated into the body of *Love Songs,* whose seemingly artless musicality informs a most lucid lyricism. *Flame and Shadow* marks, if anything, an advance in emotional depth and "natural falterings"; but *Dark of the Moon,* while gracefully competent, appears somewhat anticlimactic in its minor accents: the book of a "woman seemingly poured empty." The first posthumous collection, *Strange Victory,* has, however, some of its author's most memorable pieces – in "All That Was Mortal," "Grace Before Sleep," "Advice to a Girl," and others.

Miss Teasdale's verse, repeatedly concerned with the stars, often reflective of her travels, always simple in technique and verse form and natural in statement, dewlike and fragile in quality, and gentle in its acceptance of sorrow (though never bathetic), poses no intellectual problems. Constantly preoccupied with beauty, as idea and as evocation, it offers instead quietly ironic, but joyful, acceptance of life, exquisiteness of feminine perception, and most delicate artistry. All of which does not deny that Miss Teasdale has occasionally "reached into the black waters whose chill brings wisdom," poems like "Wood Song" and numerous others being the memorable evidence.

—George Brandon Saul

THURBER, James (Grover). American. Born in Columbus, Ohio, 8 December 1894. Educated at Ohio State University, Columbus. Married 1) Althea Adams in 1922 (divorced, 1935), one daughter; 2) Helen Wismer in 1935. Code Clerk, American Embassy, Paris, 1918–20; Reporter, *Columbus Dispatch*, 1920–24, Paris edition of the *Chicago Tribune*, 1924–26, and the *New York Evening Post*, 1926–27; Editor, then writer, 1927–38, then freelance contributor, *The New Yorker* magazine; also an illustrator from 1929. Litt.D.: Kenyon College, Gambier, Ohio, 1950; Yale University, New Haven, Connecticut, 1953; L.H.D.: Williams College, Williamstown, Massachusetts, 1951. *Died 2 November 1961.*

PUBLICATIONS

Collections

Vintage Thurber: A Collection of the Best Writings and Drawings.   2 vols., 1963.

Short Stories and Sketches (illustrated by the author)

The Owl in the Attic and Other Perplexities.   1931.
The Seal in the Bedroom and Other Predicaments.   1932.
My Life and Hard Times.   1933.
The Middle-Aged Man on the Flying Trapeze: A Collection of Short Pieces.   1935.
Let Your Mind Alone! and Other More or Less Inspirational Pieces.   1937.
Cream of Thurber.   1939.
The Last Flower: A Parable in Pictures.   1939.
Fables for Our Time and Famous Poems Illustrated.   1940.
My World – and Welcome to It.   1942.
Men, Women, and Dogs: A Book of Drawings.   1943.
The Thurber Carnival.   1945.
The Beast in Me, and Other Animals: A New Collection of Pieces and Drawings about Human Beings and Less Alarming Creatures.   1948.
The Thurber Album: A New Collection of Pieces about People.   1952.
Thurber Country: A New Collection of Pieces about Males and Females, Mainly of Our Own Species.   1953.
Thurber's Dogs: A Collection of the Master's Dogs, Written and Drawn, Real and Imaginary, Living and Long Ago.   1955.
A Thurber Garland.   1955.
Further Fables for Our Time.   1956.
Alarms and Diversions.   1957.
Lanterns and Lances.   1961.
Credos and Curios.   1962.
Thurber and Company.   1966.

Plays

The Male Animal, with Elliott Nugent (produced 1940).   1940.
A Thurber Carnival, from his own stories (produced 1960).   1962.

Wrote the books for the following college musical comedies: *Oh My, Omar*, with Hayward M. Anderson, 1921; *Psychomania*, 1922; *Many Moons*, 1922; *A Twin Fix,* with Hayward M. Anderson, 1923; *The Cat and the Riddle*, 1924; *Nightingale*, 1924; *Tell Me Not*, 1924.

Other

Is Sex Necessary? or, Why You Feel the Way You Do, with E. B. White.   1929.
Many Moons (juvenile).   1943.
The Great Quillow (juvenile).   1944.
The White Deer (juvenile).   1945.
The 13 Clocks (juvenile).   1950.
Thurber on Humor.   1953(?).
The Wonderful O (juvenile).   1955.
The Years with Ross.   1959.

Bibliography: *Thurber: A Bibliography* by Edwin T. Bowden, 1968.

Reading List: *Thurber* by Robert E. Morsberger, 1964; *The Art of Thurber* by Richard C. Tobias, 1969; *Thurber, His Masquerades: A Critical Study* by Stephen A. Black, 1970; *The Clocks of Columbus: The Literary Career of Thurber* by Charles S. Holmes, 1973, and *Thurber: A Collection of Essays* edited by Holmes, 1974; *Thurber: A Biography* by Burton Bernstein, 1975.

*   *   *

James Thurber, who was not destined to be one of America's celebrated poets, first turned up in the pages of *The New Yorker* on 26 February 1927 with two forgettable bits of verse. His third contribution (5 March 1927) was more indicative of what was to come. Called "An American Romance," it is the account of a "little man in an overcoat that fitted him badly," who stations himself in a revolving door, defying a number of authority figures, and stays there until he is rewarded with instant celebrity. An ur-Walter Mitty, then, caught in an American landscape which Thurber would eventually view more sardonically, almost a fable for our time.

Thurber had been a newspaperman on the Columbus *Dispatch* and the Paris edition of the Chicago *Tribune* and a free-lance contributor to a number of publications before he arrived at *The New Yorker*, but it was with that magazine that his reputation both as writer and cartoonist was made, a reputation that he sometimes saw as limiting to his artistic aspirations. He served on the staff until 1938 and remained a contributor until 1961; eventually he tried to define the quality of the place and his own ambiguous attachment to it in *The Years with Ross*, which E. B. White called "a sly exercise in denigration, beautifully concealed in words of sweetness and love."

Thurber's first book was a collaboration with White, the parody volume *Is Sex Necessary?* His second, *The Owl in the Attic*, initiated the practice of collecting his magazine pieces which he would follow for the rest of his writing life. Sometimes – *My Life and Hard Times*, *Let Your Mind Alone!*, *The Years with Ross* – the group of essays was obviously conceived as a book; in most cases, the mixture is fortuitous, although occasionally, as in *Thurber's Dogs*, held together by a common subject matter. Of his early books, *My Life and Hard Times*, a marvelously funny mock biography, is the most impressive, the more so when one considers that Thurber returned to the same Ohio home ground to do the completely different and equally successful *The Thurber Album*.

There are many Thurbers: the playwright (*The Male Animal*, *A Thurber Carnival*); the author of children's books, of which *The White Deer* and *The 13 Clocks* are the happiest inventions; the adult fabulist of *Fables for Our Time* and *Further Fables*; the canine celebrant

(*Thurber's Dogs*); the social observer who could write so well about soap opera ("Soapland" in *The Beast in Me, and Other Animals*); the perceptive critic who could work through parody or direct comment and the concerned artist who defended humor from outside attack and inside timidity in the repressive atmosphere of the 1950's. Through all these, there is a persistent Thurber, the dark humorist who, one way or another, kept asking, as the moral of one of the *Further Fables* puts it, "Oh, why should the shattermyth have to be a crumplehope and a dampenglee?"

—Gerald Weales

TOLSON, Melvin B(eaunorus). American. Born in Moberly, Missouri, 6 February 1898. Educated at Lincoln High School, Kansas City, Missouri, graduated 1918; Fisk University, Nashville, Tennessee, 1918–20; Lincoln University, Oxford, Pennsylvania, 1920–23, B.A. 1923; Columbia University, New York, M.A. 1940. Married Ruth Southall in 1922. Teacher at Wiley College, Marshall, Texas, 1924–47; Professor of English and Drama, Langston University, Oklahoma, 1947–66. Poet-in-Residence, Tuskegee Institute, 1965. Mayor of Langston after 1954. Recipient: Omega Psi Phi Award in Creative Literature, 1945; National Institute of Arts and Letters award, 1966. D.L.: Lincoln University, 1954; D.H.L.: Lincoln University, 1965. Poet Laureate of Liberia, 1947; appointed permanent Breadloaf Fellow in Poetry, 1954. *Died 29 August 1966.*

PUBLICATIONS

Verse

Rendezvous with America. 1944.
Libretto for the Republic of Liberia. 1953.
Harlem Gallery: Book I, The Curator. 1965.

Play

The Fire in the Flint, from a work by Walter White (produced 1952).

Reading List: Introduction by Karl Shapiro to *Harlem Gallery*, 1965; *Tolson* by Joy Flasch, 1972.

*   *   *

On the basis of his first volume of poetry, *Rendezvous with America*, it would hardly have been possible to predict the kind of poet Melvin Tolson was to be a decade later. A poet who writes "I gaze upon her silken loveliness/She is a passion-flower of joy and pain/On the golden bed I came back to possess" does not show particular promise. Likewise the lines "America is the Black Man's country/The Red Man's, the Yellow Man's/The Brown Man's, the White Man's" are not suggestive of the great lines yet to come.

There are, however, certain characteristics of the earlier poetry which were to be developed in such a way as to become hallmarks of the later poetry, more its essence than ornament. The second stanza, for example, of "An Ex-Judge at the Bar" is in style and content very much like a good deal of Tolson's later poetry and untypical of the rather commonplace character of much of the first volume. That stanza, "I know, Bartender, yes, I know when the Law/Should wag its tail or rip with fang and claw./When Pilate washed his hands, that neat event/Set for us judges a Caesarean precedent," is in tone typically Tolsonian. The juxtaposition of the formal and the informal, the classical and the contemporary, the familiar and the unusual accounts in large measure for the unique character of Tolson's best poetry.

Such juxtapositions are more pronounced in *Libretto for the Republic of Liberia*, where, in addition, the "gift for language" noted in Allen Tate's introduction to the volume, becomes apparent. The effect of the juxtaposition of the learned encyclopedic references and the most abstruse vocabulary with commonplace references, vocabulary, and rhyme, managed within a highly traditional form, is pyrotechnic. The occurrence in the same context of French, German, Latin, Hebrew, Swahili, Arabic, Spanish, and Sanskrit references with commonplace activities, occupations, facts, and events created a system of tensions not unlike the dynamic of forces holding an atom or a galaxy together. Each element threatens to go off on its own; yet as long as the balance of forces remains constant, the system functions. Tolson, by virtue of an extraordinary mind and intelligence, keeps a vast array of disparate elements in constant relationship. His poetry is, therefore, coherent, and the primary effect it arouses is of the containment and control of vast reserves of energy.

This bears on Karl Shapiro's controversial statement in his introduction to *Harlem Gallery*, Tolson's final volume, that "Tolson writes in Negro." It is not at bottom the language which prompted Shapiro's observation. Rather, it is the intellectual disposition of the tension between two worlds that finds its manifestation in the language. Tolson belongs (and this distinguishes him from Eliot, Pound, and Hart Crane, whom he read avidly) to an Afro-American world and an American-European world, and he knows these worlds in intricate detail. The balance he sustains between them is the source of his power. Few understand him because few know both worlds as well, and few are as totally committed as he to such a high universal standard of values.

—D. B. Gibson

TOOMER, Jean (Nathan Eugene Toomer).   American.   Born in Washington, D.C., 26 December 1894. Educated at high schools in Brooklyn, New York, and Washington, D.C.; University of Wisconsin, Madison, 1914; American College of Physical Training, Chicago, 1916; New York University, summer 1917; City College of New York, 1917. Married 1) Margery Latimer in 1931 (died, 1932), one daughter; 2) Marjorie Content, 1934. Taught physical education in a school near Milwaukee, 1918; clerk in Acker, Merrall, and Conduit grocery company, New York, 1918; shipyard worker, New York; worked at Howard Theatre, Washington, D.C., 1920. Writer after 1922. Studied at Gurdjieff's Institute in Fontainebleau, France, 1924, 1926. *Died 30 March 1967.*

PUBLICATIONS

Fiction

Cane (includes verse).   1923.

Play

Balo, in *Plays of Negro Life,* edited by Alain Locke and Gregory Montgomery.   1927.

Other

Essentials (aphorisms).   1931.

Bibliography: "Toomer: An Annotated Checklist of Criticism" by John M. Reilly, in *Resources for American Literary Study,* Spring 1974.

Reading List: *In a Minor Chord* (on Toomer, Cullen, and Hurston) by Darwin T. Turner, 1971; *The Merrill Studies in Cane* edited by Frank Durham, 1971; *The Grotesque in American Negro Fiction: Toomer, Wright, and Ellison* by Fritz Gysin, 1975.

*   *   *

In a startling image of fulfillment Jean Toomer likened the descendants of slaves among whom he sought poetic motive to "purple ripened plums," the seed of one becoming "An everlasting song, a singing tree,/Caroling softly souls of slavery,/What they were, and what they are to me." The lyric containing this image, "Song of the Son," serves as one of the impressionistic epigraphs uniting *Cane* into a symbolic account of Toomer's effort to reconcile the technical sophistication of Harlem Renaissance art with folk life. His assertion that black rural life in Georgia provided him with the soil for a living literature ratified the cultural nationalism of the Renaissance, while the experimental form of this book demonstrated its kinship with literary modernism. For contemporaries, then, *Cane* promised a vitally new art.

Each of the stories, sketches, and poems making up *Cane* examines the possibility of intutive self-fulfillment. In the first part of the book, set in the South, a series of female characters achieve momentary redemption through expression of spontaneous feelings. The second part, set in Washington, D.C. variously represents characters whose feelings are blocked by social artifice. The whole concludes with a story-play in which the central figure, Kabnis, has internalized the violence and repression of caste relations so effectively that he is terrified of opening his senses at all. The complex intermingling of impressionism, expressionism, and generic forms in *Cane,* therefore, constitutes an argument for the spontaneity associated with "primitivism."

The tension between sophistication and spontaneity remained a dynamic source for

Renaissance writers, but not for Toomer. Shortly after *Cane* was published he met Gurdjieff, had a mystical experience, and turned his life-long need for meaning toward a search for a transcendent principle of unity. One consequence was denial of the significance of racial identity. Another was production of writing increasingly distant from the sensual style of *Cane.* Toomer, once a harbinger of new art, became a enigmatic historical figure.

Only a small portion of his later writings was published. For critics the most notable piece has been "Blue Meridian," a long, visionary poem about a new American race, which at its best resonates with the inspiration of Whitman. One must conclude that in Toomer biographical experience overwhelmed creative imagination. A search for identity became so compelling that he could no longer gain the distance needed to convert the motive of his life into the substance of successful literature.

—John M. Reilly

TRAVEN, B.   Pseudonym for a writer about whom very little is known. Most frequently identified with an American, Berwick Traven Torsvan: probably born in Chicago in 1890; lived in Germany during World War I; writer from 1926; lived in Mexico from the 1920's or 1930's until his death: Mexican citizen, 1951; married Rosa Elena Lujan in 1957. *Died 26 March 1969.*

Fiction

Das Totenschiff.   1926(?); as *The Death Ship,* 1934.
Der Wobbly.   1926; as *Die Baumwollpflücker,* 1929; as *The Cotton-Pickers,* 1956.
Der Schatz der Sierra Madre.   1927; as *The Treasure of the Sierra Madre,* 1934.
Der Busch (stories).   1928.
Die Brücke im Dschungel.   1929; as *The Bridge in the Jungle,* 1938.
Die Weisse Rose.   1929; as *The White Rose,* 1965.
Der Karren.   1930; as *The Carreta,* 1935.
Regierung.   1931; as *Government,* 1935.
Der Marsch ins Reich de Caoba: Ein Kriegsmarsch.   1933; as *March to Caobaland,*
    1961; as *March to the Monteria,* 1963.
Die Rebellion der Gehenkten.   1936; as *The Rebellion of the Hanged,* 1952.
Die Troza.   1936.
Ein General Kommt aus dem Dschungel.   1940; as *The General from the Jungle,* 1954.
Macario (in German).   1950.
Aslan Norval (in German).   1960.
Stories by the Man Nobody Knows: Nine Tales.   1961.
The Night Visitor and Other Stories.   1966.
Maze of Love.   1967.
The Kidnapped Saint and Other Stories, edited by Rosa Elena Lujan and Mina C. and H.
    Arthur Klein.   1977.

Other

Land der Frühlings (on Mexico).   1928.

Sonnen-Schöpfung: Indianische Legende.   1936; as *The Creation of the Sun and the Moon,* 1968.

Bibliography: "A Checklist of the Work of Traven and the Critical Estimates and Biographical Essays on Him" by E. R. Hagemann, in *Papers of the Bibliographical Society of America 53,* 1959.

Reading List: *Anonymity and Death: The Fiction of Traven* by Donald O. Chankin, 1975; *Traven: An Introduction* by Michael L. Baumann, 1976.

*   *   *

B. Traven kept his identity a closely guarded secret and never gave interviews to the press. He was probably born in Chicago of American Scandinavian parents; he had Marxist leanings, wrote usually in German, and died in Mexico City. His novel *The General from the Jungle* tells the story of a rebellion of Indians against a Mexican dictator. Among adventure writers he deserves a high place – on the same level as Jack London – while some of his themes bring to mind Conrad.

In all his fiction Traven is concerned with the problem of Mammon. "Gold is the devil," says one of the characters in *The Treasure of Sierra Madre* – a book on which John Huston based a successful film. Traven's most famous novel, and his finest, is *The Death Ship.* When it first came out in the mid-1930's in Germany, it sold over 200,000 copies before it was banned. Sub-titled "The Story of an American Sailor," it might be better described as the story of a hero without a name, for the author regards the sailor on a death ship as a gladiatorial hero whose Emperor is Mammon. Death ships are those which carry contraband, with ammunition and rifles hidden in crates labelled "Toys" or "Cocoa" or "Corned Beef." The crews are enlisted from men on the run – no names, no questions – or from seamen who have lost their papers and so have no status. This is what happens to Traven's hero, who is informed by the American consul in Paris: "I doubt your birth as long as you have no certificate of birth. The fact that you are sitting in front of me is no proof of your birth."

Later, Traven's hero, after a series of adventures with the Belgian and Dutch police and a short spell in a prison in Toulouse, finds himself aboard the *Yorikke,* a death ship that has put into Barcelona. Taken on as a fireman, he is made to work as a coal-shoveller. In a ship as old and patched up as the *Yorikke,* there is a constant danger that he may be burnt by the darts of scalding steam which continually escape from the pipes. He has to learn to slither from point to point like a snake. "Only the best snake dancers survived.... Others who had tried and failed were no longer alive." (In another novel, *March to Caobaland,* Traven writes: "Indian mahogany workers can be fed as royally as the stokers and oilers of a death ship where, as a rule, the food is of the lowest quality possible.")

The Nazis banned *The Death Ship* because they thought it Communist; some critics have made the same charge about Traven's other books. But this is to misinterpret them. Traven's fiction is as much an attack on bureaucrats, whatever their political creed, as it is a protest against the dictatorial power which money can invest in one man over another. Labour camps, no less than sweated labour, are both a part of the world of Mammon.

—Neville Braybrooke

TRILLING, Lionel.   American.   Born in New York City, 4 July 1905. Educated at Columbia University, New York, B.A. 1925, M.A. 1926, Ph.D. 1938. Married the writer

Diana Rubin in 1929; one child. Instructor in English, University of Wisconsin, Madison, 1926–27, and Hunter College, New York, 1927–32; Instructor, 1932–39, Assistant Professor, 1939–45, Associate Professor, 1945–48, Professor of English, 1948–70, Woodberry Professor of Literature and Criticism, 1965–70, University Professor, 1970–74, and University Professor Emeritus, 1974–75, Columbia University. George Eastman Visiting Professor, Oxford University, 1964–65; Norton Visiting Professor of Poetry, Harvard University, Cambridge, Massachusetts, 1969–70; Visiting Fellow, All Souls College, Oxford, 1972–73. Founder, with John Crowe Ransom and F. O. Matthiessen, and Senior Fellow, Kenyon School of Letters, Kenyon College, Gambier, Ohio, later the Indiana University School of Letters, Bloomington. Recipient: Brandeis University Creative Arts Award, 1968. D.Litt.: Trinity College, Hartford, Connecticut, 1955; Harvard University, 1962; Case-Western Reserve University, Cleveland, 1968; University of Durham, 1973; University of Leicester, 1973; L.H.D.: Northwestern University, Evanston, Illinois, 1963; Brandeis University, Waltham, Massachusetts, 1974; Yale University, New Haven, Connecticut, 1974. Member, National Institute of Arts and Letters, 1951; American Academy of Arts and Sciences, 1952. *Died 5 November 1975.*

PUBLICATIONS

Fiction

The Middle of the Journey.   1947.

Other

Matthew Arnold.   1939; revised edition, 1949.
E. M. Forster.   1943; revised edition, 1965.
The Liberal Imagination: Essays on Literature and Society.   1950.
The Opposing Self: Nine Essays in Criticism.   1955.
Freud and the Crisis of Our Culture.   1956.
A Gathering of Fugitives.   1956.
Beyond Culture: Essays on Literature and Learning.   1965.
Sincerity and Authenticity.   1972.
Mind in the Modern World.   1973.

Editor, *The Portable Matthew Arnold.*   1949; as *The Essential Matthew Arnold,* 1969.
Editor, *Selected Letters of John Keats.*   1951.
Editor, *Selected Short Stories of John O'Hara.*   1956.
Editor, with Steven Marcus, *The Life and Works of Sigmund Freud,* by Ernest Jones.   1961.
Editor, *The Experience of Literature: A Reader with Commentaries.*   1967.
Editor, *Literary Criticism: An Introductory Reader.*   1970.
Editor, with others, *The Oxford Anthology of English Literature.*   1972.

Reading List: *Three American Moralists: Mailer, Bellow, Trilling* by Nathan A. Scott, Jr., 1973; *Trilling: Negative Capability and the Wisdom of Avoidance* by Robert Boyers, 1977.

*   *   *

Lionel Trilling was one of America's most distinguished literary critics. His first two books were on Matthew Arnold and E. M. Forster, and these were followed by a number of essays in which, like Arnold and Forster, he tried to show how liberal cultural values fostered by the study of literature could help civilization. In some of his later works, especially perhaps in *Beyond Culture*, this liberal stance, though aggressively stated, is maintained with a good deal of pessimism.

An equal pessimism is found in some of Trilling's short stories and his one novel, *The Middle of the Journey*. The hero of this novel, John Laskell, recovering from a serious illness, visits his friends the Crooms in a Connecticut village. He finds himself involved with a woman in the village, Emily Caldwell, whose husband, Duck, works for the Crooms. A fleeting affair with Emily has little chance of success as her daughter Susan dies, attacked by the drunken Duck, though she has a weak heart and her death is accidental. The Crooms, who are presented unsympathetically, maintain that it is society, not Duck, who is responsible, whereas another friend of Laskell's, Gifford Maxim, a renegade communist who has adopted a Christian stance and whose defection is bitterly resented by the Crooms, thinks that Duck is guilty. Laskell takes up an indeterminate position, but does not feel that the rejection of the dogmatism of his friends is particularly effective, any more than his gesture of paying for Susan's funeral achieves anything. Written before the McCarthy witchhunts had brought the issue of communism in America into the limelight, *The Middle of the Journey* may seem a confusing novel at a time when McCarthy himself is virtually forgotten. But *The Middle of the Journey* is not just a novel about communism versus Christianity, as it might seem to be at first sight; it is, perhaps a little too obviously, a novel which strives to assert the liberal values of E. M. Forster and Matthew Arnold in an unsympathetic world, and as such, should take its place with Trilling's critical works.

—T. J. Winnifrith

UPDIKE, John (Hoyer).   American.   Born in Shillington, Pennsylvania, 18 March 1932. Educated in Shillington public schools; Harvard University, Cambridge, Massachusetts, A.B. (summa cum laude) 1954; Ruskin School of Drawing and Fine Arts, Oxford, 1954–55. Married Mary Pennington in 1953; two sons and two daughters. Staff Reporter, *The New Yorker*, 1955–57; full-time writer from 1957. Recipient: Guggenheim Fellowship, 1959; Rosenthal Award, 1960; National Association of Independent Schools Award, 1963; National Book Award, 1964; O. Henry Award, 1966. Member, National Institute of Arts and Letters. Lives in Ipswich, Massachusetts.

PUBLICATIONS

Fiction

The Poorhouse Fair.   1959.
The Same Door (stories).   1959.
Rabbit, Run.   1960.

Pigeon Feathers (stories).   1962.
The Centaur.   1963.
Of the Farm.   1965.
The Music School (stories).   1966.
Couples.   1968.
Bech: A Book (stories).   1970.
Rabbit Redux.   1971.
Museums and Women and Other Stories.   1972.
Warm Wine: An Idyll (story).   1973.
A Month of Sundays.   1975.
Picked-Up Pieces (stories).   1975.
Marry Me: A Romance.   1976.
The Coup.   1978.

Plays

Three Texts from Early Ipswich: A Pageant.   1968.
Buchanan Dying.   1974.

Verse

The Carpentered Hen and Other Tame Creature.   1958; as *Hoping for a Hoopoe,* 1959.
Telephone Poles and Other Poems.   1963.
Bath after Sailing.   1968.
Midpoint and Other Poems.   1969.
Seventy Poems.   1972.
Six Poems.   1973.
Tossing and Turning.   1977.

Other

The Magic Flute (juvenile), with Warren Chappell.   1962.
The Ring (juvenile), with Warren Chappell.   1964.
Assorted Prose.   1965.
A Child's Calendar.   1966.
Bottom's Dream: Adapted from Shakespeare's "A Midsummer Night's Dream."   1969.
A Good Place.   1973.

Editor, *Pens and Needles,* by David Levine.   1970.

Bibliography: *Updike: A Comprehensive Bibliography* by B. A. Sokoloff and Mark E. Posner, 1973.

Reading List: *Updike* by Charles Thomas Samuels, 1969; *The Elements of Updike* by Alice and Kenneth Hamilton, 1970; *Pastoral and Anti-Pastoral Elements in Updike's Fiction* by Laura E. Taylor, 1971; *Updike: Yea Sayings* by Rachael C. Burchard, 1971; *Updike* by Robert Detweiler, 1972; *Rainstorms and Fire: Ritual in the Novels of Updike* by Edward P. Vargo, 1973; *Fighters and Lovers: Theme in the Novels of Updike* by Joyce B. Markle, 1974.

*   *   *

The successes of John Updike are linked with *The New Yorker*, a magazine for which he was once a staff member and for which he has remained a frequent contributor. But many of his novels go beyond the limits of interest that are frequently attributed to the journal: a well-bred scepticism as to what is possible for human sensibility in our time. It is true that Updike's novels and, even more, his short stories sometimes conform to these limits which see all human effort as subject to the ironies of cross-purpose. But Updike's sensibility, particularly as it unfolds in his longer works, is not that of a writer who has fully acquiesced in the general decay and uncertainty of an era. Rather Updike takes shape as a writer who keeps circling around the modern detritus with a sharp eye for some fragmented persistence of meaning and order. He is a moralist out of season. The season for confident reading of meaning may be completed, but the desire for such activity persists in much of Updike's work.

This may not be immediately apparent to some readers who can doubt that there is any link between a continuing moral curiosity and the many passages in the novels which give explicit accounts of sexual success and sexual impotence. Yet the sexual adventures of the minister in *A Month of Sundays* are no more exactly set down than are the "spiritual" aspirations that lead the minister to compose discourses that link the presence of sexuality with the advent of Grace. For Updike is not the kind of Stoic moralist familiar to us in the eighteenth century and elsewhere who seeks to detect and defend a purely humanistic code of excellence. The code of excellence that reveals itself intermittently in the Updike novels is one that has its roots in the *O altitudos* that had their traditional expression in the transports of mystics and in the teaching of the New Testament itself. The minister of *A Month of Sundays* thinks of Barth and Tillich when he is not fornicating and sometimes when he is. Updike provides some of his novels with epigraphs from the New Testament and Pascal. And, in the midst of a reported life which seems quite discontinuous with these august phrases, Updike provides flickers of light and inchoate illuminations that direct attention beyond traditional common sense and the current doubt that there is any sense whatever to the lives that a novelist may at present describe.

There is, in several of the novels, a central figure that sums up the moral situation in which modern persons live and make their Updike-sponsored effort to enjoy their lives and understand them. In *The Centaur* Updike speaks of a sequence – priest, teacher, and artist – that links the present to the past. The central figure in *The Centaur* is a frustrated teacher of science in a high school; his prototype is the ancient centaur, Chiron, who tried to reveal to *his* recalcitrant pupils the wisdom that had come to the early Greek oracles and the priests of holy places. The ancient centaur was mocked and wounded by his pupils; so also is the high school teacher by *his* students. But the modern centaur's son, Peter, responds to the harassed and comic nobility of his father. And when that son becomes an artist – when he has left his father behind him – the son wonders whether his service of esthetic excellence continues or cancels the pursuits of his father. (Earlier, the father had wondered about the relation of his teaching activity to his father's career as a clergyman.) Is the artist son the last link in a chain that extends backwards in time and moral-religious experience? Or is he a link that is independent of the earlier ones, a servant of a good that has no contact with the earlier excellences that his father and grandfather were devoted to?

This is a question that much of Updike's work raises but does not answer. The question is not asked monotonously. In his first novel, *The Poorhouse Fair*, Updike contrasts the humanitarian Connor, the director of the poor house, with a ninety-year-old man who maintains touch with older sources of moral illumination. In *Rabbit Run* and *Rabbit Redux* the centre of awareness is Harry Angstrom, an ill-educated and adulterous printer who would, it seems, be singularly cut off from "priest" and "teacher." Yet Rabbit Angstrom is subject to malaises that have only a feeble source in his parents and that rather rise from his changes of partners, his ill-fulfilled obligations to his son, and his contact with a rebellious black. In the midst of a life that is badly broken up, Angstrom demands not only sexual gratification but moral illumination from persons who are as confused as he is. The illumination is transient and is usually lost in a subsequent catastrophic event. But the event that is more than event – that is illumination – has occurred. This is all that Updike can report in his *Rabbit* narratives and elsewhere. In *Marry Me* Updike leads his chief character, who is about to dissolve a "good" marriage, to observe that we are in the midst of "the twilight of the old morality, and there's just enough to torment us, and not enough to hold us in."

Such are most of Updike's novels: clever narratives that move from narrative to meditation. At first encounter, Updike's work seems to be devoted to the reproduction of textures that are self-evident: textures of the inconsecutive, textures composed by the crass indifference of most men to each other. All this is done with brilliance and is "right." But through this neatly comprehended terrain move "priestly" and academic ghosts, the shades of Updike's "centaur" and the "centaur's" father.

—Harold H. Watts

VAN DOREN, Mark (Albert). American.   Born in Hope, Illinois, 13 June 1894. Educated at the University of Illinois, Urbana, A.B. 1914, A.M. 1915; Columbia University, New York, Ph.D. 1920. Served in the Army during World War I. Married Dorothy Graffe in 1922; two sons. Instructor, 1920–24, Assistant Professor, 1924–35, Associate Professor, 1935–42, and Professor of English, 1942–59, Columbia University; also, Lecturer at St. John's College, Annapolis, Maryland, 1937–57. Literary Editor, 1924–28, and Film Critic, 1935–38, *The Nation*, New York; Participant in the radio program Invitation to Learning, CBS, 1940–42. Visiting Professor of English, Harvard University, Cambridge, Massachusetts, 1963. Recipient: Pulitzer Prize, 1940; Columbia University's Alexander Hamilton Medal, 1959; Hale Award, 1960; National Conference of Christians and Jews Brotherhood Award, 1960; Huntington Hartford Creative Award, 1962; Emerson-Thoreau Award, 1963. Litt.D.: Bowdoin College, Brunswick, Maine, 1944; University of Illinois, Urbana, 1958; Columbia University, 1960; Knox College, Galesburg, Illinois, 1966; Harvard University, 1966; Jewish Theological Seminary of America, New York, 1970; L.H.D.: Adelphi University, Garden City, New York, 1957; Mount Mary College, Milwaukee, Wisconsin, 1965; Honorary Fellow: St. John's College, 1959; Honorary M.D.: Connecticut State Medical Society, 1966. Member, American Academy of Arts and Letters. *Died 10 December 1972.*

PUBLICATIONS

Verse

> *Spring Thunder and Other Poems.*   1924.
> *7 P.M. and Other Poems.*   1926.
> *Now the Sky and Other Poems.*   1928.
> *Jonathan Gentry.*   1931.
> *A Winter Diary and Other Poems.*   1935.
> *The Last Look and Other Poems.*   1937.
> *Collected Poems 1922–1938.*   1939.
> *The Mayfield Deer.*   1941.
> *Our Lady Peace and Other War Poems.*   1942.

The Seven Sleepers and Other Poems.   1944.
The Country Year.   1946.
The Careless Clock: Poems about Children in the Family.   1947.
New Poems.   1948.
Humanity Unlimited: Twelve Sonnets.   1950.
In That Far Land.   1951.
Mortal Summer.   1953.
Spring Birth and Other Poems.   1953.
Selected Poems.   1954.
Morning Worship.   1960.
Collected and New Poems 1924–1963.   1963.
The Narrative Poems.   1964.
That Shining Place: New Poems.   1969.
Good Morning: Last Poems.   1973.

Plays

The Last Days of Lincoln (produced 1961).   1959.
Never, Never Ask His Name (produced 1965).   In *Three Plays*, 1966.
Three Plays (includes *Never, Never Ask His Name, A Little Night Music, The Weekend That Was*).   1966.

Fiction

The Transients.   1935.
Windless Cabins.   1940.
Tilda.   1943.
The Short Stories.   1950.
The Witch of Ramoth and Other Tales.   1950.
Nobody Says a Word and Other Stories.   1953.
Home with Hazel.   1957.
Collected Stories.   3 vols., 1962–68.

Other

Henry David Thoreau: A Critical Study.   1916.
The Poetry of John Dryden.   1920; revised edition, 1931; as *John Dryden: A Study of His Poetry,* 1946.
American and British Literature since 1890, with Carl Van Doren.   1925; revised edition, 1939.
Edwin Arlington Robinson.   1927.
Dick and Tom: Tales of Two Ponies (juvenile).   1931.
Dick and Tom in Town (juvenile).   1932.
Shakespeare.   1939.
Studies in Metaphysical Poetry: Two Essays and a Bibliography, with Theodore Spencer.   1939.
The Transparent Tree (juvenile).   1940.
Invitation to Learning, with Huntington Cairns and Allen Tate.   1941.
The New Invitation to Learning.   1942.
The Private Reader: Selected Articles and Reviews.   1942.
Liberal Education.   1943.

The Noble Voice: A Study of Ten Great Poems.   1946; as *Great Poems of Western Literature,* 1966.
Nathaniel Hawthorne.   1949.
Introduction to Poetry.   1951.
Don Quixote's Profession.   1958.
The Autobiography.   1958.
The Happy Critic and Other Essays.   1961.
The Dialogues of Archibald MacLeish and Van Doren, edited by Warren V. Busch.   1964.
In the Beginning, Love: Dialogues on the Bible, with Maurice Samuel, edited by Edith Samuel.   1973.
The Book of Praise: Dialogues on the Psalms, with Maurice Samuel, edited by Edith Samuel.   1975.

Editor, *Samuel Sewall's Diary.*   1927.
Editor, *A History of the Life and Death, Virtues and Exploits of General George Washington,* by Mason Locke Weems.   1927.
Editor, *An Anthology of World Poetry.*   1928; selection, as *An Anthology of English and American Poetry,* 1936.
Editor, *The Travels of William Bartram.*   1928.
Editor, *Nick of the Woods; or, The Jibbenainosay: A Tale of Kentucky,* by Robert Montgomery Bird.   1928.
Editor, *A Journey to the Land of Eden and Other Papers,* by William Byrd.   1928.
Editor, *An Autobiography of America.*   1929.
Editor, *Correspondence of Aaron Burr and His Daughter Theodosia.*   1929.
Editor, with Garibaldi M. Lapolla, *A Junior Anthology of World Poetry.*   1929.
Editor, *The Life of Sir William Phips,* by Cotton Mather.   1929.
Editor, with Garibaldi M. Lapolla, *The World's Best Poems.*   1932.
Editor, *American Poets, 1630–1930.*   1932; as *Masterpieces of American Poets,* 1936.
Editor, *The Oxford Book of American Prose.*   1932.
Editor, with John W. Cunliffe and Karl Young, *Century Readings in English Literature,* 5th edition.   1940.
Editor, *A Listener's Guide to Invitation to Learning, 1940–41, 1941–42.*   2 vols., 1940–42.
Editor, *The Night of the Summer Solstice and Other Stories of the Russian War.*   1943.
Editor, *Walt Whitman.*   1945.
Editor, *The Portable Emerson.*   1946.
Editor, *Selected Poetry,* by William Wordsworth.   1950.
Editor, *Introduction to Poetry.*   1951; as *Enjoying Poetry,* 1951.
Editor, with others, *Riverside Poetry: 48 New Poems by 27 Poets.*   1956.
Editor, *100 Poems.*   1967.

*   *   *

Mark Van Doren's poetry, which consists of over a thousand poems in *Collected and New Poems* and other volumes, including a posthumous collection, *Good Morning,* constitutes one of the more prolific and accomplished bodies of work by an American poet in the 20th century. While the sheer bulk has often astonished and sometimes dismayed critics, it represents, as Richard Howard has observed, "not so much an embarrassment as an embodiment of riches."

Van Doren was originally hailed by T. S. Eliot and others as a master of rural verse and conveniently placed in the tradition of Robert Frost. He soon demonstrated, however, a distinctive voice that deepened through a sustained middle period culminating in his first *Collected Poems* (1939) and which grew in variety of subject matter and range for over three more decades after he received the Pulitzer Prize in 1940. Influenced by John Dryden as a young scholar, Van Doren belongs in a group that might include Hardy, early Yeats, Graves and, in specifically American ways, Emily Dickinson, Edwin Arlington Robinson, and Frost. Allen Tate once wisely concluded, after also suggesting "a trace of William Browne (epigrams and *Britannia's Pastorals*, 1613), traces of Ben Jonson, more than a trace of Robert Herrick" that all of them might "add up to Mark Van Doren who is like nobody else."

Singularly devoid of the common French influences in modern verse, Van Doren also eschewed confessional or analytic tendencies. He treated his principal subjects, the cosmos, love, finality, family matters, and particularly children, animals, paradox, and knowledge in a lucid manner that transcends simplistic notions of modernity and personal sensibilities. There is a passionate intelligence lurking behind many of the poems that somehow never intrudes. Indeed, it is a subtle presence that calls forth different interpretations on subsequent readings, though there is never intentional obscurity.

His poetic corpus, apart from substantial accomplishments in other literary fields, contains an intricate world of pleasures, observations, and intellectual insights. As a master craftsman, Van Doren would make an excellent case study for the continuity of English lyric and narrative verse. He also personifies a humanistic and metaphysical approach that is American at its core, a kind of Emersonian individualism with contemporary concerns. Taken together, his work over a half-century illustrates the American literary presence at its best with a poetry that, as one critic observed, never having been in fashion, will never go out of fashion.

—William Claire

---

van DRUTEN, John (William). American. Born in London, England, 1 June 1901; emigrated to the United States, 1926; naturalized, 1944. Educated at University College School, London, 1911–17; subsequently studied law: awarded LL.B., University of London, 1922; Solicitor of the Supreme Court of Judicature, 1923. Special Lecturer in English Law and Legal History, University College of Wales, Aberystwyth, 1923–26; full-time writer from 1928. Recipient: American Academy of Arts and Letters Award of Merit Medal, 1946; New York Drama Critics Circle Award, 1952. *Died 19 December 1957.*

PUBLICATIONS

Plays

The Return Half (produced 1924).
Chance Acquaintance (produced 1927).
Diversion (produced 1928). 1928.
Young Woodley (produced 1928). 1928.
The Return of the Soldier, from the novel by Rebecca West (produced 1928). 1928.
After All (produced 1929). 1929.
London Wall (produced 1931). 1931.
Sea Fever, with Auriol Lee, from a play by Marcel Pagnol (produced 1931).

There's Always Juliet (produced 1931).   1931.
Hollywood Holiday, with Benn Levy (produced 1931).   1931.
Somebody Knows (produced 1932).   1932.
Behold We Live (produced 1932).   1932.
The Distaff Side (produced 1933).   1933.
Flowers of the Forest (produced 1934).   1934.
Most of the Game (produced 1935).   1936.
Gertie Maude (produced 1937).   1937.
Leave Her to Heaven (produced 1940).   1941.
Old Acquaintance (produced 1940).   1941.
Solitaire, from the novel by E. Corle (produced 1942).
The Damask Cheek, with Lloyd R. Morris (produced 1942).   1943.
The Voice of the Turtle (produced 1943).   1944.
I Remember Mama, from the novel *Mama's Bank Account* by Kathryn Forbes (produced 1944).   1945.
The Mermaids Singing (produced 1945).   1946.
The Druid Circle (produced 1947).   1948.
Make Way for Lucia, from novels by E. F. Benson (produced 1948).   1949.
Bell, Book, and Candle (produced 1950).   1951.
I Am a Camera, from *The Berlin Stories* by Christopher Isherwood (produced 1951).   1954.
I've Got Sixpence (produced 1952).   1953.
Dancing in the Chequered Shade (produced 1955).

Screenplays: *Young Woodley*, with Victor Kendall, 1930; *I Loved a Soldier*, 1936; *Parnell*, with S. N. Behrman, 1937; *Night Must Fall*, 1937; *The Citadel*, with others, 1938; *Raffles*, with Sidney Howard, 1939; *Lucky Partner*, with Allen Scott, 1940; *My Life with Caroline*, with Arnold Belgard, 1941; *Johnny Come Lately*, 1943; *Old Acquaintance*, with Lenore Coffee, 1943; *Forever and a Day*, with others, 1944; *Gaslight*, with Walter Reisch and John L. Balderston, 1944; *The Voice of the Turtle*, 1948.

Fiction

Young Woodley.   1929.
A Woman on Her Way.   1930.
And Then You Wish.   1936.
The Vicarious Years.   1955.

Other

The Way to the Present: A Personal Record.   1938.
Playwright at Work.   1953.
Widening Circle (autobiography).   1957.

*   *   *

A prolific writer – best known for his plays but also recognized as a novelist, screenwriter, and autobiographer – John van Druten delighted audiences for more than thirty years with his polished, urbane comedies. The persistent tone in his works is warm and gentle; his style has been praised for its convincing naturalness and controlled simplicity.

Van Druten's plots are often loosely structured, imitative, and readily forgettable. *I*

Remember Mama, one of his most popular works, for example, is structured as a series of vignettes linked together by tone and characters, but scarcely more unified than the collection of Kathryn Forbes's short stories on which it was based.

When there is a developed plot in either his original works or his adaptations, it is usually one of two variations on the same basic action: two people meet, have or contemplate having an affair, discover that they love each other, and then joyfully renounce wantonness and move toward a thoroughly conventional marriage (as in *There's Always Juliet*; *The Distaff Side*; *Bell, Book, and Candle*; *The Damask Cheek*; and *The Voice of the Turtle*); or, sadly, discover that their age, circumstance, or character prevents such a marriage (as in *Young Woodley*, *Old Acquaintance*, *The Mermaids Singing*, and *I Am a Camera*). In developing these plots, van Druten moves perilously close to the brink of sentimentality and heavy-handed moralism; but his wit and determination to master "the difficult art of sincerity" keep him, with rare exceptions, from plunging headlong into the abyss.

Indeed, van Druten's plays were consistently praised for their fresh dialogue, their unforced cleverness, and their sophisticated repartée. His fiction and autobiographies, too, are natural and eminently readable.

His awareness of the importance of style and his concern that his works be well-written are reflected both in his commentary on his own works and in his evaluation of the works of others. For example, he criticizes bad writing, which he describes as that which is filled with bathos, facetiousness, and an endless flow of shop-worn phrases that "produce no effect save that of total weariness." He states that only the immature taste can appreciate great sweetness or a "mustard and vinegar sharpness," which the experienced palate would disdain. And in his own works, from the beginning, he attempted to avoid these excesses.

Van Druten's artistry in writing dialogue brings his characters to life. They are unforgettable. Sally Bowles, the complex, misguided, comical, pathetic American ex-patriate in *I Am a Camera*, who leads the life of the grasshopper as the deadly threat of the Third Reich moves forward; Marta, the warm, clever, protective, stable foundation of her family in *I Remember Mama*; Gillian Holroyd, the thoroughly human witch in *Bell, Book, and Candle* – these are only three who clearly rise above the ordinary to the distinctive.

This ability to create memorable characters, and thus major roles, was early recognized by Hollywood, where van Druten wrote dialogue, adapted his own works and those of others, and collaborated on screen plays for major actors from virtually every important studio. He was largely responsible, for instance, for creating the role of Paula Alquist in *Gaslight*, a role for which Ingrid Bergman won the Academy Award in 1944. It is on such success that his reputation rests.

—Helen Houser Popovich

VAN VECHTEN, Carl. American. Born in Cedar Rapids, Iowa, 17 June 1880. Educated at Cedar Rapids High School; University of Chicago, Ph.B. 1903. Married 1) Anna Elizabeth Snyder in 1907 (divorced, 1912); 2) the Russian actress Fania Marinoff in 1914. Composer and journalist: Reporter, *Chicago American*, 1903–05; Assistant Music Critic, 1906–07, Paris Correspondent, 1908–09, *New York Times*; author of the program notes for the Symphony Society of New York, 1910–11; Drama Critic, *New York Press*, 1913–14. Member of the Board of the Cosmopolitan Symphony Orchestra, and the W. C. Handy Foundation for the Blind; Founder, 1941, and Honorary Curator, 1946, James Weldon Johnson Memorial Collection of Negro Arts and Letters, Yale University Library, New Haven, Connecticut. D.Litt.: Fisk University, Nashville, Tennessee, 1955. Member, National Institute of Arts and Letters, 1961. *Died 21 December 1964.*

PUBLICATIONS

Fiction

>*Peter Whiffle, His Life and Works.*   1922.
>*The Blind Bow-Boy.*   1923.
>*The Tattooed Countess.*   1924.
>*Firecrackers.*   1925.
>*Nigger Heaven.*   1926.
>*Spider Boy: A Scenario for a Moving Picture.*   1928.
>*Parties: Scenes from Contemporary New York Life.*   1930.

Other

>*Music after the Great War and Other Studies.*   1915.
>*Music and Bad Manners.*   1916.
>*Interpreters and Interpretations.*   1917; revised edition, as *Interpreters,* 1920.
>*The Merry-Go-Round.*   1918.
>*The Music of Spain.*   1918.
>*In the Garret.*   1920.
>*The Tiger in the House.*   1920.
>*Red: Papers on Musical Subjects.*   1925.
>*Excavations: A Book of Advocacies.*   1926.
>*Feathers.*   1930.
>*Sacred and Profane Memories* (essays).   1932.
>*Ex Libris,* in *Dance Index* (triple issue).   1942.
>*Fragments from an Unwritten Autobiography.*   2 vols., 1955.
>*With Formality and Elegance* (on photography).   1977.

>Editor, *Lords of the Housetops: Thirteen Cat Tales.*   1921.
>Editor, *My Musical Life,* by Nikolay Rimsky-Korsakoff, translated by Judah A. Joffe.
>   1923; revised edition, 1942.
>Editor, *Gertrude Stein: Selected Writings.*   1946.
>Editor, *Last Operas and Plays,* by Gertrude Stein.   1949.
>Editor, *Unpublished Writings of Gertrude Stein.*   8 vols., 1951–58.

Bibliography: *Van Vechten: A Bibliography* by Klaus W. Jonas, 1955.

Reading List: *Van Vechten and the Twenties,* 1955, and *Van Vechten,* 1965, both by Edward Leuders; *Van Vechten and the Irreverent Decades* by Bruce Kellner, 1968.

*   *   *

Carl Van Vechten's personal flamboyance in manner and dress, as well as his frequent enthusiasm for both the *avant garde* and the patently old-fashioned, labelled him a dilettante in his own time. The range and foresight in several distinct careers, however, mark him a unique and underestimated American writer.

A partial list of his discoveries is staggering. As a newspaper critic he endorsed the first performances in America of Isadora Duncan, Anna Pavlova, Mary Garden, Feodor Chaliapin, and Sergei Rachmaninoff, and he was the earliest American admirer of the music of Erik Satie, Richard Strauss, and Igor Stravinsky. In a series of volumes of musical and literary criticism – *Interpreters* and *Excavations* are particularly rewarding – his perceptions are startlingly fresh. He advocated musical scores for films by serious composers, the value of popular music and ragtime, ballet, Spanish music – all far in advance of other writers. He was one of the first to rediscover Herman Melville, and Ronald Firbank and Arthur Machen owe their American reputations to him. Van Vechten's tireless efforts on behalf of Gertrude Stein are well known; he was instrumental in placing the first books of Wallace Stevens and Langston Hughes; he fostered the careers of George Gershwin, Ethel Waters, Paul Robeson among musicians, and James Purdy among writers. His book about cats, *The Tiger in the House*, is seminal. He was largely responsible for the popular recognition of the Negro as a creative artist during the Harlem Renaissance.

Van Vechten is probably too analytical and discursive, too involved with amassing and cataloging outré material, to have written fiction of the first order, although all seven of his novels are variously engaging. Few books catch the charm of New York and Paris before the First World War so well as *Peter Whiffle*. None serves as such a good introduction to Harlem during the 1920's as *Nigger Heaven*. *The Tattooed Countess* criticizes small-town life at the turn of the century with a gently cheerful malice denied more resolute realists. Three novels document Van Vechten's "splendid drunken Twenties," as he called the period: *The Blind Bow-Boy*, *Firecrackers*, and *Parties* form a serious social trilogy in the disguise of buffoonery and farce, written with slinky elegance and wit.

Van Vechten gave up writing in favor of photography to document the century's celebrities for various collections he established: The James Weldon Johnson Memorial Collection of Negro Arts and Letters, at Yale, and The George Gershwin Memorial Collection of Music and Musical Literature, at Fisk, among others.

His work has dated very little; writing from the perspective of middle age, Van Vechten's evaluations of the 1920's are perhaps more solidly grounded than those of several more celebrated younger writers of the period.

—Bruce Kellner

VIDAL, Gore. American. Born in West Point, New York, 3 October 1925. Educated at Phillips Exeter Academy, New Hampshire, graduated 1943. Served in the United States Army, 1943–46. Full-time writer from 1944; Drama Critic, *Reporter* magazine, 1959; Democratic-Liberal Candidate for Congress, from New York, 1960. Member, Advisory Board, *Partisan Review*, New Brunswick, New Jersey, 1960–61; Member, President Kennedy's Advisory Committee on the Arts, 1961–63; Co-Chairman, The New Party, 1968–71. Lives in Rome.

PUBLICATIONS

Fiction

Williwaw. 1946.
In a Yellow Wood. 1947.
The City and the Pillar. 1948; revised edition, 1965.
The Season of Comfort. 1949.

1962).   1962.
Weekend (produced 1968).   1968.
An Evening with Richard Nixon and ... (produced 1972).   1972.

Screenplays: *The Catered Affair*, 1956; *I Accuse*, 1958; *The Scapegoat*, with Robert Hamer, 1959; *Suddenly Last Summer*, with Tennessee Williams, 1960; *The Best Man*, 1964; *Is Paris Burning?*, with Francis Ford Coppola, 1966; *Last of the Mobile Hot-Shots*, 1970.

Television Plays: *Barn Burning*, 1954; *Dark Possession*, 1954; *Smoke*, 1954; *Visit to a Small Planet*, 1955; *The Death of Billy the Kid*, 1955; *A Sense of Justice*, 1955; *Summer Pavilion*, 1955; *The Turn of the Screw*, 1955; *Honor*, 1956; *The Indestructible Mr. Gore*, 1960.

Other

Rocking the Boat (essays).   1962.
Reflections upon a Sinking Ship (essays).   1969.
A Search for the King: A Twelfth Century Legend.   1950.
Dark Green, Bright Red.   1950.
The Judgment of Paris.   1952.
Messiah.   1954; revised edition, 1965.
A Thirsty Evil: 7 Short Stories.   1956.
Julian.   1964.
Washington, D.C.   1967.
Myra Breckinridge.   1968.
Two Sisters: A Novel in the Form of a Memoir.   1970.
Burr.   1974.
Myron.   1975.
1876.   1976.
Kalki.   1978.

Fiction (as Edgar Box)

Death in the Fifth Position.   1952.
Death Before Bedtime.   1953.
Death Likes It Hot.   1954.

Plays

Visit to a Small Planet (televised, 1955).   In *Visit to a Small Planet and Other Television Plays*, 1957; revised version (produced 1957), 1957.
Honor (televised, 1956).   In *Television Plays for Writers: Eight Television Plays*, edited by A. S. Burack, 1957; revised version as *On the March to the Sea: A Southron Comedy* (produced 1962), in *Three Plays*, 1962.
Visit to a Small Planet and Other Television Plays (includes *Barn Burning, Dark Possession, The Death of Billy the Kid, A Sense of Justice, Smoke, Summer Pavilion, The Turn of the Screw*).   1957.
The Best Man: A Play of Politics (produced 1960).   1960.
Three Plays (Visit to a Small Planet, The Best Man, On the March to the Sea).   1962.
Romulus: A New Comedy, from the play by Friedrich Dürrenmatt (produced

Homage to Daniel Shays: Collected Essays 1952–1972. 1972; as Collected Essays
   1952–1972, 1974.
Great American Families, with others. 1977.
Matters of Fact and Fiction: Essays 1973–1976. 1977.

Editor, Best Television Plays. 1956.

Reading List: Vidal by Ray Lewis White, 1968; The Apostate Angel: A Critical Study of Vidal
by Bernard F. Dick, 1974.

*   *   *

Of all the critical overviews of the wide-ranging work of the American writer Gore Vidal,
his own appraisal may be as straightforward as one could hope for. In a foreword to a 1956
collection of his TV plays (Visit to a Small Planet and Other Television Plays), he says: "I am
at heart a propagandist, a tremendous hater, a tiresome nag, complacently positive that there
is no human problem which could not be solved if people would simply do as I advise."
There is a determined strain of social criticism – always articulate, often vituperative, and
sometimes just bitchy – at the center of most of his fiction, drama, and film scripts, especially
in his most recent work. Consumed by American political history, Vidal has fashioned
characters and situations that often serve as frontispieces for his heretical suspicions about the
past and his unrelieved cynicism with regard to the future. Fortunately, there is almost
always evidence of his considerable literary skill as well.
   Since the publication of Williwaw in the author's twenty-first year, Vidal has prompted
enthusiasm from critics lauding his early "promise." Whether that promise has been satisfied
after thirty years of work in popular American literature is still the central question in most
Gore Vidal reviews. But it is certain that the writer has managed to keep his name in
contention the whole time. He has found popular and critical success in fiction – first with
Williwaw, then with bestsellers like The City and the Pillar, Julian, Washington, D.C., Myra
Breckinridge, Burr, and 1876. He turned to television in its formative years, in the era of live
tele-drama, and produced well-received plays for Omnibus, Studio One, and the Philco
Television Playhouse (including the highly praised "Visit to a Small Planet"). His The Best
Man, written for the Broadway stage in 1960, was a major success, encouraging an
adaptation for film in 1964, followed by other film adaptations (including "Suddenly Last
Summer," co-written with Tennessee Williams) and original screenplays.
   But critics familiar with Gore Vidal's style and prolific outpourings seem to think that the
writer's talent lies with the perfection of the essay. Indeed, the 1977 publication of a
collection of his recent essays – Matters of Fact and Fiction – was greeted with all-around
good notices, even if some reviewers had reservations. Vidal's skill with the essay form is
hardly surprising in view of the usual criticisms of his other work as too polemical. It may
well be, as Vidal himself has suggested informally, that at the heart of his dramatic and
fictional efforts there is an essay, not only beating at the core of the work, but sometimes
overwhelming the conventions of the form that seeks to contain it.
   The elements of Vidal's creative polemic seem to be characterized by his gift for language,
his "wit" (in the classical sense), and his strong reactionary instincts. This last tendency,
Vidal's reactionary bent, seems puzzling at first, given his documented liberalism in social
and political affairs (television networks have used him as a representative "liberal
intellectual," and he actually ran for one of New York's Congressional seats on a suicidally
liberal platform). But the contradiction might be a natural consequence of being Gore Vidal,
grandson the T. P. Gore, respected Senator from Oklahoma, and son of a much admired
college athlete who was an instructor at West Point when Vidal was born. The reactionary
strain might be a case of his natural predispositions – based upon his aristocratic origins, his

attraction to money and power and his unshakeable suspicions about the stupidity of the American public – overwhelming whatever ideological hopes he claims.

What emerges, in the words of P. N. Furbank (in a 1974 piece in *The Listener*), is "a sort of patriotic gloom." Rooted as he was in the school-book traditions of American history and its institutions, Vidal seems to have been particularly embittered by the unflattering lessons of his historical scholarship and his personal experience. He is stuck with the residue of his expectations about American innocence and morality, confounded by what he knows about political history. So to do justice to both the dream and the informed reality, he has developed an articulate, even lyrical, cynicism about the direction of modern letters and the final collision of the Republic with the world it has, in part, created.

—Lawrence R. Broer

VONNEGUT, Kurt, Jr. American. Born in Indianapolis, Indiana, 11 November 1922. Educated at Cornell University, Ithaca, New York, 1940–42; University of Chicago, 1945–47. Served in the United States Army Infantry, 1942–45: Purple Heart. Married Jane Marie Cox in 1945; two daughters and one son. Police Reporter, City News Bureau, Chicago, 1946; worked in public relations for the General Electric Company, Schenectady, New York, 1947–50; free-lance writer from 1950; teacher at the Hopefield School, Sandwich, Massachusetts, from 1965; Visiting Lecturer, Writers Workshop, University of Iowa, Iowa City, 1965–67, and Harvard University, Cambridge, Massachusetts, 1970–71. Recipient: Guggenheim Fellowship, 1967; National Institute of Arts and Letters grant, 1970. Litt.D.: Hobart and William Smith Colleges, Geneva, New York, 1974. Member, National Institute of Arts and Letters, 1973. Lives in West Barnstable, Massachusetts.

PUBLICATIONS

Fiction

Player Piano. 1952.
The Sirens of Titan. 1959.
Canary in a Cathouse (stories). 1961.
Mother Night. 1961.
Cat's Cradle. 1963.
God Bless You, Mrs. Rosewater; or, Pearls Before Swine. 1965.
Welcome to the Monkey House: A Collection of Short Works. 1968.
Slaughterhouse-Five; or, The Children's Crusade. 1969.
Breakfast of Champions; or, Goodbye, Blue Monday. 1973.
Slapstick; or, Lonesome No More. 1976.

Plays

The Very First Christmas Morning, in *Better Homes and Gardens,* December 1962.
Fortitude, in *Playboy,* September 1968.
Happy Birthday, Wanda June (produced 1970). 1971.

Between Time and Timbuktu; or, Prometheus-5: A Space Fantasy (televised, 1972; produced 1975). 1972.

Television Play: *Between Time and Timbuktu*, 1972.

Other

Wampeters, Foma, and Granfalloons: Opinions. 1974.

Bibliography: *Vonnegut: A Descriptive Bibliography and Annotated Secondary Checklist* by Asa B. Pieratt, Jr., and Jerome Klinkowitz, 1974.

Reading List: *Vonnegut: Fantasist of Fire and Ice* by David H. Goldsmith, 1972; *The Vonnegut Statement*, edited by Jerome Klinkowitz and John Somer, 1973; *Vonnegut in America: An Introduction to the Life and Work of Vonnegut* by Jerome Klinkowitz and Donald L. Lawler, 1977; *Vonnegut* by James Lundquist, 1977; *Vonnegut* by Clark Mayo, 1977; *Vonnegut* by Richard Giannone, 1977.

*   *   *

In *Slaughterhouse-Five*, Vonnegut summarizes a science fiction novel by Kilgore Trout in which a time traveler goes back to the crucifixion and, with a stethoscope, listens to Christ's heart. The Savior, alas, is dead, stone dead. Trout is a character in several of Vonnegut's books, but his novel might well have been written by Vonnegut, for, like it, Vonnegut's novels portray a world in which there is no hope, no purpose, no salvation for the universe. Vonnegut is a moralist, but one who begins with the premise that morality, like civilization, merely expresses wishful thinking and chance. In this universe, divine intention is only imagined; it does not really exist.

Vonnegut's novels describe a deterministic, mechanistic world – a world of cause and effect with no overriding purpose or goal. The major novels and other works center on innocents like Billy Pilgrim (in *Slaughterhouse-Five*) and Dwayne Hoover (in *Breakfast of Champions*) who are victims both of other people and, more particularly, of an inability meaningfully to affect their own lives. For Vonnegut, civilization's problem is not that people don't, strictly speaking, take responsibility for their lives, but that they can't. *Breakfast of Champions* suggests that art offers at least temporary salvation, but it is more characteristic of Vonnegut's books to suggest that if there is any salvation for men, it lies in their innocence or their stupidity – and consequently their inability to understand how totally they are the product of circumstance, not free will.

Vonnegut's early reputation was largely among readers of science fiction. His books emphasize the obvious, if often overlooked, fact that the elaborate theoretical structures devised by modern technology and science have important moral implications. Since these structures tend to be entirely deterministic, they suggest that objective views of the universe have no room for chance or inspiration: everything has its immediate, ascertainable cause. True moral choice is, therefore, impossible.

In *Slapstick*, the most recent of his novels, Vonnegut argues that, at the least, "common decency" should characterize human relations. This conclusion may make his bleak moral view palatable to some readers, but it is also deeply sentimental. Vonnegut can appear sentimental even in his best work, but it may be this, together with his comic sense, that allows his work to escape the bitterness, if not the resignation, that his bleak view of experience would encourage.

—Edward Halsey Foster

WALLANT, Edward Lewis. American. Born in New Haven, Connecticut, 19 October 1926. Educated at the Pratt Institute, New York, 1947–50; New School for Social Research, New York, 1954–55. Served as a gunner's mate in the United States Navy, 1944–46. Married Joyce Fromkin in 1948; two daughters and one son. Worked as a graphic designer for various advertising agencies, New York, 1950–62. Recipient: Bread Loaf Writers' Conference Fellowship, 1960; Daroff Memorial Award, 1961; Guggenheim Fellowship, 1962. *Died 5 December 1962.*

PUBLICATIONS

Fiction

The Human Season. 1960.
The Pawnbroker. 1961.
The Tenants of Moonbloom. 1963.
The Children at the Gate. 1964.

Reading List: *The Landscape of Nightmare: Studies in the Contemporary American Novel* by Jonathan Baumbach, 1965.

*   *   *

Edward Lewis Wallant died at thirty-six, just as he was becoming known as a promising novelist. The four novels of this brief career center around two dominant motifs: the quest for family connections and the search for a viable religious-philosophical position. In *The Tenants of Moonbloom*, a spokesman comments, "There is a Trinity of survival, and it consists of Courage, Dream, and Love ... he who possesses all three, or two, or at least one of these things wins whatever there is to win. ..." All four of Wallant's protagonists become winners, in these terms, but first they must go through painful rebirths or births.

Joe Berman, a middle-aged plumber whose wife has just died in *The Human Season*, Wallant's first novel, curses his Jewish God for a time but then loses his belief in an anthropomorphic deity. In place of this, he comes to insist on the importance of the human capacity for wonder and love and to accept his own failings in family relationships. Thus he lays the ghosts of his god-like father, whom he loved too well, and his son, whom he feels he did not love enough. *The Pawnbroker*, Wallant's second novel, presents Sol Nazerman, whose wife and children died in a Nazi concentration camp, and where he was a subject of experimental surgery. Nazerman affects total cynicism and a harshness comparable to that of his Nazi tormentors, but his protective shell is broken by his young assistant in the pawnshop, Jesus Ortiz, who, with three other black men, plans to rob Sol. During the attempted robbery, Jesus, who has developed a confused filial love for Sol, takes the bullet intended for the pawnbroker, and Sol is spiritually reborn. This is not, however, an easy or sentimental resolution. Nazerman's rebirth is into "the crowding filth" of humanity, wherein he feels "hopeless, wretched, strangely proud."

Though published last due to an arrangement Wallant made before he died, *The Children at the Gate* was written third and is transitional. Here the protagonist, Angelo DeMarco, at eighteen, has never been emotionally alive. The agent of his awakening is a Jewish hospital orderly, a benevolent drug pusher and comic Christ figure whose symbol is the bedpan rather than the cross. The characters in this novel tend to be overdrawn, and the humor is sometimes forced, but the book provides a bridge to *The Tenants of Moonbloom*. Norman Moonbloom is another character in the process of becoming. After a protracted, cocoon-like education, his first job is as rental agent for his brother, owner of four tenement houses. Norman begins to empathize with the miserable tenants, and, though knowing it will do no real good, he sets out to repair everything in the tenements, as an act of personal affirmation. Norman's labors are preparatory to birth, and, as is the case in the other novels, coming to life includes recognition of death's inevitability, but for Norman this is not important. Through ritual initiation he has become identified with humanity and has thus achieved a kind of immortality.

In these novels, Wallant progressed from family concerns and questions of Jewish belief to Moonbloom's identification with the human family and an affirmation of the worldly value of the most inclusive religious ritual, the initiation rite. He progressed, also, from the rather grim acceptance of the first novel through reluctant affirmation in the second and third to joyful and comic belonging in the last, in which Moonbloom, at thirty-three, loses his virginity and learns to laugh. Near that last novel's end, Norman Moonbloom, covered with filth from a bathroom wall he is repairing, shouts, "I'M BORN!"

—James Angle

WARREN, Robert Penn. American. Born in Guthrie, Kentucky, 24 April 1905. Educated at Guthrie High School; Vanderbilt University, Nashville, Tennessee, B.A. (summa cum laude) 1925; University of California, Berkeley, M.A. 1927; Yale University, New Haven, Connecticut, 1927–28; Oxford University (Rhodes Scholar), B.Litt. 1930. Married 1) Emma Brescia in 1930 (divorced, 1950); 2) the writer Eleanor Clark in 1952, one son and one daughter. Member of the Fugitive Group of poets: Co-Founding Editor, *The Fugitive*, Nashville, 1922–25; Assistant Professor, Southwestern College, Memphis, Tennessee, 1930–31, and Vanderbilt University, 1931–34; Assistant and Associate Professor, Louisiana State University, Baton Rouge, 1934–42, and Founding Editor, *Southern Review*, Baton Rouge, 1935–42; Professor of English, University of Minnesota, Minneapolis, 1942–50; Professor of Playwriting, 1950–56, and Professor of English, 1962–73, Yale University; now Professor Emeritus. Consultant in Poetry, Library of Congress, Washington, D.C., 1944–45; Jefferson Lecturer, National Endowment for the Arts, 1974. Recipient: Caroline Sinkler Award, 1936, 1937, 1938; Houghton Mifflin Literary Fellowship, 1939; Guggenheim Fellowship, 1939, 1947; Shelley Memorial Award, 1943; Pulitzer Prize, for fiction, 1947, for poetry, 1958; Screenwriters Guild Robert Meltzer Award, 1949; Sidney Hillman Prize, 1957; Edna St. Vincent Millay Memorial Prize, 1958; National Book Award, for poetry, 1958; Bollingen Prize, for poetry, 1967; National Endowment for the Arts grant, 1968; Henry A. Bellaman Prize, 1970; Van Wyck Brooks Award, for poetry, 1970; National Medal for Literature, 1970; Emerson-Thoreau Medal, 1975. D.Litt.: University of Louisville, Kentucky, 1949; Kenyon College, Gambier, Ohio, 1952; University of Kentucky, Lexington, 1955; Colby College, Waterville, Maine, 1956; Swarthmore College, Pennsylvania, 1958; Yale University, 1959; Fairfield University, Connecticut, 1969; Wesleyan University, Middletown, Connecticut, 1970; Harvard University, Cambridge, Massachusetts, 1973; LL.D.: University of Bridgeport, Connecticut, 1965. Member, American Academy of Arts and Letters; Chancellor, Academy of American Poets, 1972. Lives in Fairfield, Connecticut.

PUBLICATIONS

Verse

Thirty-Six Poems. 1935.
Eleven Poems on the Same Theme. 1942.
Selected Poems 1923–1943. 1944.
Brother to Dragons: A Tale in Verse and Voices. 1953.
Promises: Poems 1954–1956. 1957.
You, Emperors and Others: Poems 1957–1960. 1960.
Selected Poems: New and Old 1923–1966. 1966.
Incarnations: Poems 1966–1968. 1968.
Audubon: A Vision. 1969.
Or Else: Poem/Poems 1968–1974. 1974.
Selected Poems 1923–1975. 1977.

Plays

Proud Flesh (in verse, produced 1947; revised [prose] version, produced 1948).
All the King's Men (produced 1959). 1960.

Fiction

Night Rider. 1939.
At Heaven's Gate. 1943.
All the King's Men. 1946.
Blackberry Winter (stories). 1946.
The Circus in the Attic and Other Stories. 1947.
World Enough and Time: A Romantic Novel. 1950.
Band of Angels. 1955.
The Cave. 1959.
Wilderness: A Tale of the Civil War. 1961.
Flood: A Romance of Our Times. 1964.
Meet Me in the Green Glen. 1971.
A Place to Come To. 1977.

Other

John Brown: The Making of a Martyr. 1929.
I'll Take My Stand: The South and the Agrarian Tradition, with others. 1930.
Understanding Poetry: An Anthology for College Students, with Cleanth Brooks. 1938;
    revised edition, 1950, 1960.
Understanding Fiction, with Cleanth Brooks. 1943; revised edition, 1959.
A Poem of Pure Imagination: An Experiment in Reading, in *The Rime of the Ancient
    Mariner,* by Samuel Taylor Coleridge. 1946.
Modern Rhetoric: With Readings, with Cleanth Brooks. 1949; revised edition, 1958.
Fundamentals of Good Writing: A Handbook of Modern Rhetoric, with Cleanth
    Brooks. 1950; revised edition, 1956.
Segregation: The Inner Conflict in the South. 1956.
Remember the Alamo! 1958.

Selected Essays. 1958.
The Gods of Mount Olympus. 1959.
The Legacy of the Civil War: Meditations on the Centennial. 1961.
Who Speaks for the Negro? 1965.
A Plea in Mitigation: Modern Poetry and the End of an Era. 1966.
Homage to Theodore Dreiser. 1971.
John Greenleaf Whittier's Poetry: An Appraisal and a Selection. 1971.
A Conversation with Warren, edited by Frank Gado. 1972.
Democracy and Poetry. 1975.

Editor, with Cleanth Brooks and J. T. Purser, *An Approach to Literature: A Collection of Prose and Verse with Analyses and Discussions.* 1936; revised edition, 1939, 1952.
Editor, *A Southern Harvest: Short Stories by Southern Writers.* 1937.
Editor, with Cleanth Brooks, *An Anthology of Stories from the Southern Review.* 1953.
Editor, with Albert Erskine, *Short Story Masterpieces.* 1954.
Editor, with Albert Erskine, *Six Centuries of Great Poetry.* 1955.
Editor, with Albert Erskine, *A New Southern Harvest.* 1957.
Editor, with Allen Tate, *Selected Poems,* by Denis Devlin. 1963.
Editor, *Faulkner: A Collection of Critical Essays.* 1966.
Editor, with Robert Lowell and Peter Taylor, *Randall Jarrell 1914–1965.* 1967.
Editor, *Selected Poems of Herman Melville.* 1971.
Editor, with Cleanth Brooks and R. W. B. Lewis, *American Literature: The Makers and the Making.* 2 vols., 1974.

Bibliography: *Warren: A Bibliography* by Mary Nancy Huff, 1968.

Reading List: *Warren: The Dark and Bloody Ground* by Leonard Casper, 1960; *Warren* by Paul West, 1964; *Warren: A Collection of Critical Essays* edited by John Lewis Longley, Jr., 1965; *A Colder Fire: The Poetry of Warren,* 1965, and *The Poetic Vision of Warren,* 1977, both by Victor H. Strandberg; *Web of Being: The Novels of Warren* by Barnett Guttenberg, 1975.

*   *   *

Robert Penn Warren is a distinguished American writer in at least three genres: the novel, poetry, and the essay. Although he has lived outside the South since 1942, he has so consistently written novels, essays, and poetry on southern subjects, in southern settings, and about southern themes that he must be regarded still as a southern writer. Over much of his work there is a typically southern brooding sense of darkness, evil, and human failure, and he employs a Gothicism of form and an extravagance of language and technique of a sort often associated with writing in the southeastern United States. Warren is a profoundly philosophical writer in all aspects of his work. Writing of Joseph Conrad, he once said, "The philosophical novelist, or poet, is one for whom the documentation of the world is constantly striving to rise to the level of generalization about values ... for whom the urgency of experience ... is the urgency to know the meaning of experience." The description fits him well.

In Warren's principal work in the novel and poetry, there are a persistent obsession with time and with history, a sense of man's imperfection and failure, and an awareness that innocence is always lost in the acts of achieving maturity and growth. His characters are usually men who destroy themselves through seeking an absolute in a relative universe. From John Brown, the subject of his first book, a biography, to Percy Munn, the protagonist of *Night Rider,* to Willie Stark of *All the King's Men,* to Jeremiah Beaumont of *World Enough and Time,* to Lilburn Lewis in the poem-play *Brother to Dragons,* to Jed Tewksbury in *A*

Place to Come To – Warren's protagonists repeat this pattern of the obsessive and ultimately self-destructive search for the impossible ideal.

His work usually rests on actual events from history or at least on actual historical situations – *Night Rider* on the Kentucky tobacco wars, *At Heaven's Gate* on a Nashville political murder, *All the King's Men* on the career of Huey Long, *World Enough and Time* on an 1825 Kentucky murder, *Band of Angels* and *Wilderness* on the Civil War, *The Cave* on Floyd Collins's cave entombment, *Flood* on the inundating of towns by the Tennessee Valley Authority, *A Place to Come To* to at least some extent on his own experiences as a college teacher, although the story can hardly be considered autobiographical. The poem *Brother to Dragons* is based on an atrocious crime committed by Thomas Jefferson's nephews. This concern with history and the individual implications of social and political events is also present in his non-fiction, such as *Segregation: The Inner Conflict in the South, The Legacy of the Civil War*, and *Who Speaks for the Negro?* These works, too, deal with fundamental issues of southern history.

In order to present the philosophical meaning of his novels and poems, Warren uses highly individualized narrators, such as Jack Burden in *All the King's Men*; special techniques of narrative point of view, as in *World Enough and Time*; frequently a metaphysical style; the illumination of events through contrast with enclosed and frequently recollected narratives, as in *Night Rider* and *All the King's Men*; and highly melodramatic plots which become elaborate workings out of abstract statements, as in *Band of Angels*.

His poetry reiterates essentially the same view of man. He began as an undergraduate at Vanderbilt University writing poetry with the Fugitive poetry group – John Crowe Ransom, Allen Tate, and Donald Davidson – and he continued to write a relatively fixed form, tightly constructed, ironic lyric verse until about 1943. Between 1943 and 1953 he concentrated predominantly on the novel. With *Brother to Dragons* he returned to poetic expression, and since that time has written extensively in both poetic and novelistic forms. The verse forms that he has used since 1953 have been much looser, marked by broken rhythms, clusters of lines arranged in patterns dictated by emotion, and frequent alternations in the level of diction. Behind his poetry, as behind his fiction, there is usually an implied, if not explicit, narrative pattern. This narrative pattern is often historical, as in "The Ballad of Billy Potts," *Brother to Dragons*, or *Audubon*. In his recent verse, Warren contrasts man's weaknesses and imperfections with the enduring stars, with time, and with eternity.

As a critic and teacher, Warren has had a profound influence on the study and criticism of literature. His textbook *Understanding Poetry*, written with Cleanth Brooks, a presentation of poetry in New Critical terms emphasizing the poem as an independent work of art, went a long way toward creating a revolution in how literature was taught in American colleges. He has written many other textbooks and critical studies such as his *Homage to Theodore Dreiser, John Greenleaf Whittier's Poetry*, and *Democracy and Poetry*.

Warren is still very active; during his 72nd year he published *Selected Poems 1923–1975* and a distinctive and distinguished novel, *A Place to Come To*. Warren's work in all genres is marked by a high concern with language, a depth of philosophical statement, a firm and rigorous commitment to a moral-ethical view of man, and a willingness to experiment often beyond the limits of artistic safety with the forms in which he works. Warren is a peculiarly indigenous American writer of great intelligence and of significant accomplishment. He can, with justice, be called our most distinguished living man of letters.

—C. Hugh Holman

WELTY, Eudora. American. Born in Jackson, Mississippi, 13 April 1909. Educated at Mississippi State College for Women, Columbus, 1926–27; University of Wisconsin, Madison, B.A. 1929; Columbia University School of Advertising, New York, 1930–31. Staff member, *The New York Times Book Review*, during World War II. Honorary Consultant in American Letters, Library of Congress, Washington, D.C., 1958. Recipient: O. Henry Award, 1942, 1943, 1968; Guggenheim Fellowship, 1942, 1948; National Institute of Arts and Letters grant, 1944, Howells Medal, 1955, and Gold Medal, 1972; Ford Fellowship, for drama; Brandeis University Creative Arts Award, 1965; Edward MacDowell Medal, 1970; Pulitzer Prize, 1973. D.Litt.: Denison University, Granville, Ohio, 1971; Smith College, Northampton, Massachusetts; University of Wisconsin, Madison; University of the South, Sewanee, Tennessee; Washington and Lee University, Lexington, Virginia. Member, American Academy of Arts and Letters, 1971. Lives in Jackson, Mississippi.

PUBLICATIONS

Fiction

A Curtain of Green and Other Stories. 1941.
The Robber Bridegroom. 1942.
The Wide Net and Other Stories. 1943.
Delta Wedding. 1946.
The Golden Apples (stories). 1949.
Selected Stories. 1954.
The Ponder Heart. 1954.
The Bride of Innisfallen and Other Stories. 1955.
Thirteen Stories, edited by Ruth M. Vande Kieft. 1965.
Losing Battles. 1970.
The Optimist's Daughter. 1972.

Other

Music from Spain. 1948.
Short Stories. 1949.
Place in Fiction. 1957.
Three Papers on Fiction. 1962.
The Shoe Bird (juvenile). 1964.
A Sweet Devouring (essay). 1969.
One Time, One Place: Mississippi in the Depression: A Snapshot Album. 1971.
A Pageant of Birds. 1974.
The Eye of the Story: Selected Essays and Reviews. 1978.

Bibliography: *Welty: A Reference Guide* by Victor H. Thompson, 1976.

Reading List: *Welty* by Ruth M. Vande Kieft, 1962; *A Season of Dreams: The Fiction of Welty* by Alfred Appel, Jr., 1965; *Welty* by J. A. Bryant, Jr., 1968.

*   *   *

Eudora Welty is a party to the great outpouring of fiction that is often referred to as the southern Renaissance, the discovery of solid traditions and uneasy tensions that color the work of William Faulkner, Katherine Anne Porter, Caroline Gordon, William Styron, and others. Welty's terrain overlaps that of Faulkner – the State of Mississippi. But it offers a contrasting appearance – indeed, a predominantly sunny one despite the shadows of ancient pain, present injustice, and future uncertainty that both Faulkner and Welty discover in their part of the South. But Welty's imaginative world maintains its special rules: rules of civility and of affection that protect the continuance of human meaning and human dignity. It is a continuance that may well be a "losing battle" (*Losing Battles* is the title of one of her novels), but it is never really a lost battle. The majority of the writer's characters reel under blows that chance, inheritance, and environment deal them, but they rise to hope and love another day. The compulsions they face and partly master are less awesome than those many a Faulkner person meets. True, there is guilt, but the guilt is personal rather than one which several generations have piled up. There are also authoritative patterns of life. But these patterns, in contrast to those of Faulkner, are familiar and easily identifiable rather than occult and mysterious. There is no "bear" or any other symbol of aboriginal compulsion moving back and forth in the delta and the hill country which Welty recollects and recreates in her short stories and her novels. The minds of her characters – rednecks, cotton aristocrats, and the "just folks" of small county seats – are indeed challenged by the events that overtake them. But the contests between minds and events issues in a draw, and sometimes better than a draw.

This can be seen in the many short stories, simple of surface but calculating in their approach to a revelatory conclusion. The story "Keela, The Outcast Indian Maiden" (in *A Curtain of Green*) seems, for most of its course, to be a study of the guilt a young man feels for his share in the exploitation of a little black man who has been kidnapped and exhibited as a freak in a sideshow. But by the end of the story the young man has made a sort of expiation of his share of guilt; this is a draw. But suddenly attention shifts to the little black man; *he* is only amused by the antics of his visitor and sits down to supper with his children; out of abasement the black man has won a minor victory.

The reverses and complexities that Welty meditates on are the stuff of her many stories. Such reverses and complexities also furnish out the longer works, with the possible exception of the early tale, *The Robber Bridegroom*, which is a pious salute to the violent times when Mississippi land was being invaded by white men, farmers, riverboat men, and robbers who attacked travellers on the Natchez Trace. This narrative has the willed simplicity of folk tale, as indeed do many of the short stories. But it is a simplicity that appears only intermittently in the longer novels, where the writer's imagination engages itself with a more or less contemporary milieu and the sensibilities educated there. *Delta Wedding* is a salute to the "cotton aristocrats" and their experience of power and complacency in the twenties of this century. Some characters in the novel enjoy their privileges, and others try to measure them and test them. The careless "lose" their battle; the thoughtful attain to an uneasy survival: a comprehension of their situation. It is a comprehension that, unfortunately, has to be recast from day to day.

This recasting is, in *Delta Wedding*, complex and difficult to express in a phrase. So it continues to be in shorter novels like *The Ponder Heart* and *The Optimist's Daughter*, two tales of matrimonial misadventures which are observed and studied by women – centers of awareness – who are sufficient vehicles for Welty's own discriminations. A more difficult book is *Losing Battles*. In this long account of a family reunion up in the Mississippi hills, the novelist for the most part dispenses with the fairly refined and privileged observers of her other novels. She also gives up the comic discriminations of *Delta Wedding* and *The Ponder Heart*. *Losing Battles* is, in sheer event, not far removed from the farce of Li'l Abner's Dogpatch; there are mad car accidents, watermelon fights, and gargantuan feastings. Nor does Miss Welty allow her own prose to reproduce the thoughts of her mostly back-country characters. The interminable conversations, fashioned from rural clichés, nevertheless become transparent envelopes through which appear the "contents" of each red-neck existence with a range of sensitivity almost as complex as that which is represented in *Delta Wedding*.

In short, Miss Welty has a wide range of strategies. But these all serve a concern that is strict, narrow, and unwavering: how persons respond to their opportunity to live, what comment they are able to make, the deep interest that lies in almost any such comment when it is carefully reproduced and charitably understood.

—Harold H. Watts

WESCOTT, Glenway. American. Born in Kewaskum, Wisconsin, 11 April 1901. Educated at the University of Chicago (President of the Poetry Society), 1917–19. Lived briefly in New Mexico, New York City and State, England, and Germany, 1919–25; lived in France and Germany, 1925–33; full-time writer from 1921. D.Litt.: Rutgers University, New Brunswick, New Jersey, 1963. President, National Institute of Arts and Letters, 1959–62; Member, American Academy of Arts and Letters. Lives in Rosemont, New Jersey.

PUBLICATIONS

Fiction

> *The Apple of the Eye*.   1924.
> *... Like a Lover* (stories).   1926.
> *The Grandmothers: A Family Portrait*.   1927; as *A Family Portrait*, 1927.
> *Good-bye, Wisconsin* (stories).   1928.
> *The Babe's Bed* (story).   1930.
> *The Pilgrim Hawk: A Love Story*.   1940.
> *Apartment in Athens*.   1945; as *Household in Athens*, 1945.

Verse

> *The Bitterns: A Book of Twelve Poems*.   1920.
> *Native of Rock: XX Poems, 1921–1922*.   1925.

Other

> *Elizabeth Madox Roberts: A Personal Note*.   1930.
> *Fear and Trembling* (essays).   1932.
> *A Calendar of Saints for Unbelievers*.   1932.
> *12 Fables of Aesop, Newly Narrated*.   1954.
> *Images of Truth: Remembrances and Criticism*.   1962.

Editor, *The Maugham Reader.*   1950.
Editor, *Short Novels of Colette.*   1951.

Bibliography: "Wescott: A Bibliography" by Sy Myron Kahn, in *Bulletin of Bibliography 22*, 1956.

Reading List: *Classics and Commercials* by Edmund Wilson, 1950; *Wescott* by William Rueckert, 1965; *Wescott: The Paradox of Voice* by Ira Johnson, 1971.

*   *   *

Glenway Wescott, a classmate of Yvor Winters and Vincent Sheean, was president of the Poetry Society at the University of Chicago. His Imagist lyrics appeared in *Poetry* and were later printed privately in two small volumes. He turned away from poetry after he came of age, and because of ill health left the university in 1919; for six restless years he lived briefly in New Mexico, the Berkshires, New York City, England, and Germany, usually with his lifelong friend Monroe Wheeler. Wescott's precocity, striking appearance (tall, blond), and cultivated British accent marked him during his expatriate years from 1925 to 1933, when he lived in Paris, at Villefrance-sur-Mer, and in Germany. In *The Autobiography of Alice B. Toklas*, Gertrude Stein records his first visit: "Glenway impressed us with his English accent. Hemingway explained. He said, when you matriculate at the University of Chicago, you write down just what accent you will have and they give it to you when you graduate." In the 1920's Wescott published impressive critical reviews (chiefly in *The Dial* and *The New Republic*), two novels, and a collection of short stories, though he has published very little in the succeeding 50 years.

Wescott was 23 when *The Apple of the Eye* was published. The story of Hannah Madoc, a Wisconsin farm woman, is told from various perspectives. It is a novel of initiation and of revolt against the hostile environment of farm and town – especially against repressive Puritanism. *The Grandmothers* was Wescott's greatest popular success. Alwyn Tower, reliving in France his Wisconsin childhood, is "a participating narrator, identical to the author's second (artistic) self" (Ira Johnson). His curiosity aroused by an old family album, the young man pieces together the story of his three grandmothers (one grandfather married twice). Cadenced prose and high sensitivity present the pioneer experience, always focused on Wescott's major themes of love and the self.

An introductory essay lent its title to *Good-bye Wisconsin*, a short story collection. The ten stories, and *The Babe's Bed*, a slightly longer short story published in a limited Paris edition, show Wisconsin as hostile to the realization of the self. Wescott published only five more short stories, from 1932 to 1942, none of them noteworthy. He is often classified as a midwestern realist and regionalist, and these stories obviously connect him with the "Revolt from the Village" writing of Edgar Lee Masters, Sherwood Anderson, and Sinclair Lewis. But Wescott's fiction also demonstrates his abandonment of realism, regionalism, and the provincial midwest for a European aesthetic existence and artistic ideal. Among his friends were Ford Madox Ford, Jean Cocteau, Elly Ney, and Rebecca West.

Wescott's current reputation as a stylist is based primarily on *The Pilgrim Hawk: A Love Story*, which first appeared in two issues of *Harper's Magazine* and has been reprinted and anthologized. Alwyn Tower, now in America, recounts a day's incident in France in 1940 which involves Irish and American expatriates and their servants. Tower's nostalgic reminiscence is heavily ironic, and the falcon is central to the love story Tower narrates. In addition to the two physical love triangles, a third appears to perceptive readers, a subtle examination of the conflict between appetite and control; as James Korges puts it (in *Contemporary Novelists*, 1976), "The reader is not told about the conflict of love and art; instead he receives it, as a powerful undercurrent in the story of an Irish couple and a hawk, which is also a story about love and art, freedom and captivity."

Wescott considered *Apartment in Athens* his contribution to the war effort. A German officer is billeted in the apartment of a Greek middle class intellectual. "The cramped physical and moral conditions, the readjustments in the relationships of the family, the whole distortion of the social organism by the unassimilable presence of the foreigner – all this is most successfully created" (Edmund Wilson). The novel, however, is marred by its ending, a long letter smuggled out of the prison cell of the condemned Greek father, and the anti-Nazi editorializing violates the fictional illusion.

Images of Truth collects the critical essays Wescott had published since 1939. His long essays on Katherine Anne Porter, Elizabeth Madox Roberts, Mann, Colette, Maugham, and Wilder are highly personal expressions of Wescott's own idiosyncratic views on life and literature. Wescott's Imagist poetry, which he abandoned early, has been long forgotten. His essentially lyric talent finds expression in his prose.

—Clarence A. Glasrud

WEST, Nathanael.   Pseudonym for Nathan Wallenstein Weinstein.   American.   Born in New York City, 17 October 1906. Educated at Brown University, Providence, Rhode Island, Ph.B. 1924. Married Eileen McKenney in 1940. Writer from 1930; managed a residential club hotel in Sutton Place, New York, in the early 1930's; assistant to William Carlos Williams in editing *Contact*, 1932; writer, in Hollywood, for Columbia Pictures, 1933, 1938, Republic Pictures, 1936–38, RKO Pictures, 1938, 1939, and Universal Pictures, 1938. *Died (in an auto accident) 22 December 1940.*

PUBLICATIONS

Collections

The Collected Works.   1957.

Fiction

The Dream Life of Balso Snell.   1931.
Miss Lonelyhearts.   1933.
A Cool Million: The Dismantling of Lemuel Pitkin.   1934.
The Day of the Locust.   1939.

Plays

Good Hunting: A Satire, with Joseph Shrank (produced 1938).

Screenplays: *The President's Mystery,* with Lester Cole, 1936; *Follow Your Heart,* with others, 1936; *Ticket to Paradise,* with others, 1936; *It Could Happen to You,* with Samuel Ornitz, 1937; *Rhythm in the Clouds,* with others, 1937; *Gangs of New York* (uncredited), 1938; *Orphans of the Street* (uncredited), 1938; *Born to Be Wild*, 1938; *Five Came Back*, with others, 1939; *I Stole a Million*, with Lester Cole, 1939; *The Spirit of Culver*, with others, 1939; *Men Against the Sky*, with John Twist, 1940; *Let's Make Music*, 1940.

Bibliography: *West: A Comprehensive Bibliography* by William White, 1975.

Reading List: *West: An Interpretive Study* by James F. Light, 1961; *West* by Stanley Edgar Hyman, 1962; *West: The Ironic Prophet* by Victor Comerchero, 1964; *The Fiction of West* by Randall Reid, 1967; *West: The Art of His Life* by Jay Martin, 1970, and *West: A Collection of Critical Essays* edited by Martin, 1971; *West: A Critical Essay* by Nathan A. Scott, 1971; *West's Novels* by Irving Malin, 1972.

*   *   *

While many of the writers of the 1930's found in the naturalistic tradition a form which would directly express their protest at what seemed to be the collapse or corruption of the American Dream, Nathanael West developed an oblique vision that may prove more lasting than the products of many of his contemporaries. A statement by his painter-protagonist, Tod Hackett (*The Day of the Locust*), provides a reasonable thematic definition of West's artistic intentions: "It is hard to laugh at the need for beauty and romance, no matter how tasteless, even horrible, the results of that are. But it is easy to sigh. Few things are sadder than the truly monstrous." Focusing relentlessly on the radical disparity between the romantic expectations pandered to by the mass-media and the actual limited portion which is the human lot, West's talent is to delineate "the truly monstrous" in a grotesque world that hovers ambiguously between the hilarious and the heartbreaking. Accepting more or less the same premises that underlie Eliot's *The Waste Land*, West's work is equally hallucinatory and probably more pessimistic, as well as more comic. It is partly indebted to the techniques of Surrealism that West absorbed in a brief post-college sojourn in Paris where he wrote his first novel (*The Dream Life of Balso Snell*), and its energy, I think, derives from a deep moral exasperation that could be a result of his youthful training in Judaism. Relatively overlooked when it was published, West's fiction brought the sub-genre of "Black Humor" into prominence after World War II when it served as a model of encouragement for such writers as Carson McCullers, James Purdy, Flannery O'Connor, and John Hawkes.

Although West wrote four novels in his abruptly ended career, he is remembered primarily for *Miss Lonelyhearts* and *The Day of the Locust*. In both novels West cultivates a stripped cinematic style, advancing his narrative in a spastic sequence of intense and fragmented scenes. As a Hollywood screenwriter for the last years of his life, West clearly found the discipline of the film compatible with his own penchant for constructing stories out of dominantly visual images, and *The Day of the Locust* is generally regarded as the premiere "Hollywood novel" in American fiction.

In *Miss Lonelyhearts*, the un-named protagonist is a bachelor newspaper columnist assigned to the job of giving advice to the lovelorn. Worn down by the barrage of unabated and insoluble misery that pours in on him and bedeviled by the savage nihilism of his city editor, Shrike, he finds himself unable even to imagine palliative possibilities for those who write to him. Further, his defensive cynicism and detachment erode as he begins to recognize his own condition in the broken human beings who are his suppliants. Killed finally in a ludicrous comedy of errors, he becomes a futile immolated Christ whose death is merely another addition to the crumpled heap of frustrated hopes that the novel assembles. West's dark mockery is pointed in all directions. The manipulators are as crippled and impotent as are the manipulated; nor does the novel permit any socio-political resolution of the problems it presents. Lacking a sane religious option for satisfying "the need for beauty and romance," the frenetic improvisations of the spiritually dispossessed can only be freakishly monstrous and sad.

The Day of the Locust displaces a greater imaginative volume, just as its setting – Hollywood at the time when it was dream-factory to the world – is a larger milieu than the newspaper office and bars of *Miss Lonelyhearts*. Here West places his artist-protagonist on the margins of the action and structures the novel on what might be termed the principle of "an image within an image." Tod Hackett is engaged in painting "The Burning of Los Angeles," a giant canvas that he intends to be prophetic in the Old Testament sense; and the novel as a whole duplicates on a greatly magnified screen his apocalyptic vision of a holocaust. Unlike the multitude of victims in *Miss Lonelyhearts*, the grotesques of *The Day of the Locust*, mindless as lemmings, purposeless as falling rain, seek vengeance for the rootlessness, disappointment, and excruciating boredom of their lives in random unprovoked destruction. If the keynote of *Miss Lonelyhearts* is a profound sadness wrested out of grotesque comedy, *The Day of the Locust* re-orchestrates that sadness with chords of terror. And the bitter humor of the earlier novel takes on accents of insane laughter in the later one.

—Earl Rovit

WHARTON, Edith (Newbold, née Jones). American. Born in New York City, 24 January 1862. Travelled in Italy, Spain, and France as a child; educated privately. Married Edward Wharton in 1885 (divorced, 1913). Lived in Newport, Rhode Island, after her marriage, and in Europe from 1907; a close frind of Henry James; helped organize the American Hostel for Refugees, and the Children of Flanders Rescue Committee, during World War I. Recipient: Pulitzer Prize, 1921; National Institute of Art and Letters Gold Medal, 1924. Litt.D.: Yale University, New Haven, Connecticut, 1923. Chevalier, Legion of Honour, 1916, and Order of Leopold, 1919. Member, American Academy of Arts and Letters, 1930. *Died 11 August 1937.*

PUBLICATIONS

Collections

A Wharton Reader, edited by Louis Auchincloss.   1965.
The Collected Short Stories, edited by R. W. B. Lewis.   1968.

Fiction

The Greater Inclination (stories).   1899.
The Touchstone.   1900; as *A Gift from the Grave*, 1900.
Crucial Instances (stories).   1901.
The Valley of Decision.   1902.
Sanctuary.   1903.
The Descent of Man and Other Stories.   1904.
The House of Mirth.   1905; edited by R. W. B. Lewis, 1963.

Madame de Treymes.   1907.
The Fruit of the Tree.   1907.
The Hermit and the Wild Woman, and Other Stories.   1908.
Tales of Men and Ghosts.   1910.
Ethan Frome.   1911; edited by Blake Nevius, 1968.
The Reef.   1912.
The Custom of the Country.   1913.
Xingu and Other Stories.   1916.
Summer.   1917.
The Marne.   1918.
The Age of Innocence.   1920.
The Glimpses of the Moon.   1922.
A Son at the Front.   1923.
Old New York: False Dawn (The 'forties), The Old Maid (The 'fifties), The Spark (The 'sixties), New Year's Day (The 'seventies).   1924.
The Mother's Recompense.   1925.
Here and Beyond (stories).   1926.
Twilight Sleep.   1927.
The Children.   1928.
Hudson River Bracketed.   1929.
Certain People (stories).   1930.
The Gods Arrive.   1932.
Human Nature (stories).   1933.
The World Over (stories).   1936.
Ghosts (stories).   1937.
The Buccaneers.   1938.

Plays

The Joy of Living, from a play by Hermann Sudermann (produced 1902).   1902.
The House of Mirth, with Clyde Fitch, from the novel by Wharton (produced 1906).

Verse

Verses.   1878.
Artemis to Actaeon and Other Verse.   1909.
Twelve Poems.   1926.

Other

The Decoration of Houses, with Ogden Codman, Jr.   1897.
Italian Villas and Their Gardens.   1904.
Italian Backgrounds.   1905.
A Motor Flight Through France.   1908.
Fighting France: From Dunkerque to Belfort.   1915.
Wharton's War Charities in France.   1918.
L'Amérique en Guerre.   1918.
French Ways and Their Meaning.   1919.
In Morocco.   1920.
The Writing of Fiction.   1925.
A Backward Glance (autobiography).   1934.

Editor, *The Book of the Homeless: Original Articles in Verse and Prose.*   1916.
Editor, with Robert Norton, *Eternal Passion in English Poetry.*   1939.

Bibliography: *Wharton: A Bibliography* by Vito J. Brenni, 1966; *Wharton and Kate Chopin: A Reference Guide* by Marlene Springer, 1976.

Reading List: *Wharton: A Study of Her Fiction* by Blake Nevius, 1953; *Wharton: Convention and Morality in the Work of a Novelist* by Marilyn Jones Lyde, 1959; *Wharton* by Louis Auchincloss, 1961; *Wharton: A Collection of Critical Essays* edited by Irving Howe, 1962; *Wharton and James: The Story of Their Friendship* by Millicent Bell, 1965; *Wharton: A Biography* by R. W. B. Lewis, 1975; *Wharton* by Richard H. Lawson, 1977; *A Feast of Words: The Triumph of Wharton* by Cynthia Griffin Wolff, 1978.

*   *   *

Edith Wharton was a versatile as well as a prolific writer. During her lifetime, she published over forty books, including some twenty novels, ten collections of short stories, books of verse, a pioneer work in interior design (with Ogden Codman, Jr.) *The Decoration of Houses,* several books of travel, an autobiography, and books on Italian villas, France, and fictional theory. It is by her fiction, however, that her importance as a writer must be judged. Mrs. Wharton was an admirer and close friend of Henry James. Because of that friendship and because of certain parallels between their lives (both New Yorkers, both expatriates) and between their fictions (both with an interest in the manners of the rich, and in Americans living abroad), as well as aesthetic principles Mrs. Wharton appears to have got from "the master," she has been called a disciple of James, an allegation that has obscured significant differences between them. James was a metaphysical writer, Mrs. Wharton a novelist of manners. James's method was to remove his characters from the effects of social forces and to locate his story in the minds of his characters, Mrs. Wharton's was to deal with the impact of social and moral forces on the lives of her protagonists. Conflict in James is usually internal. In Mrs. Wharton, it is almost always external, involving a superior individual in a struggle with the representatives of a social world with which the individual is fundamentally at odds.

The grand exception is *The Reef,* Mrs. Wharton's most Jamesian novel. Here the action is confined almost exclusively to a chateau in France and the issue narrowed to a psychological struggle in the mind of the heroine, Anna Leath, who discovers that the man she has agreed to marry has had an affair with the young woman who is about to marry her step-son. Despite the economy, the tightness, the remoteness from the usual social forces that move through Mrs. Wharton's pages, the conflict is much like that to be found in other Wharton novels, except that here it is treated as a psychological problem rather than a social and moral struggle. Anna Leath, the protagonist, cannot accept her fiancé's promiscuity nor can she give him up; and so, at the end of the novel, she is reduced to a state of tormented indecision.

In the first of her major novels, *The House of Mirth,* Lily Bart, a young woman from an old New York family ruined by financial reverses and extravagance, is caught between her love of beauty and luxury and her moral fastidiousness. If she should marry the man she loves she would live in what to her would be physical squalor; if she marries a man she does not love in order to get the material things essential to her sense of well being, she would violate her deepest nature. She manages to salvage her moral integrity but slides into poverty and, then, death, and a pathetic moral triumph.

Ethan Frome, a short novel that differs in some ways (a New England setting, impoverished rural characters) from Mrs. Wharton's typical fiction, nonetheless deals with an issue similar to the one that confronts Lily Bart: the conflict between social and moral conventions and the deep desires of the individual. Ethan Frome, married to a homely neuresthenic woman several years older than himself, falls in love with his wife's pretty cousin. Although he contemplates eloping with the girl, Mattie Wills, social pressures win out. Ethan and Mattie's attempt to escape their fate through suicide ends with them maimed for life and left in the care of the grim woman they had tried to foil.

Both *Ethan Frome* and *Summer*, Mrs. Wharton's other short New England novel, give fuller rein to sexual passion than other Wharton novels. Ethan and Mattie have to pay for their passion in a cruelly ironic way; Charity Royal, protagonist of *Summer*, is allowed a kind of idyllic bliss in the arms of her lover before the score is reckoned and she is obliged to marry her elderly guardian, a good, solid man who will give her a respectable place in the town of North Dormer and a name for her unborn child, but a passionless marriage.

In *The Age of Innocence*, the last of Edith Wharton's important novels, the same issue is dealt with in a lightly ironic way. Newland Archer has two choices: he can marry the conventional young woman to whom he is engaged or he can break with her and live with Ellen Olenska, a Europeanized American shown to be emotionally and aesthetically more attractive to Archer. The choice is between what is socially acceptable to old New York society and what most engages Archer's deepest feelings. Again, convention triumphs. Archer marries May. Ellen returns to Europe. Years later, in a kind of wistful epilogue, Archer visits Europe and, with his wife dead, might re-establish his relationship with Ellen. Archer fails to visit Ellen, however, and takes comfort from the knowledge that his life with May has had its compensations. Thus, it seems, Mrs. Wharton has made a kind of peace with the vexing conflict between personal desire and social obligation.

Custom of the Country, which appeared in 1913, strikes a note that was to be echoed increasingly after 1920. It is Mrs. Wharton's major satire on American life and its lays out in a manner that anticipates the cruder satires of Sinclair Lewis the rise of vulgar Americans from the West. Undine Sprague is the feminine version, Elmer Moffat the male. With neither taste nor moral scruple, they assail the old monied New York aristocracy, conquer it, and move on to Europe and repeat their triumph. Undine marries and divorces Ralph Marvel of New York, marries and divorces a French aristocrat and, then, marries Elmer Moffat who is now a multi-millionaire settled in Europe and buying up rare antique art. In this novel Mrs. Wharton's usual theme – the impingement of social and economic forces on the lives of sensitive individuals – is relegated to a minor role. Ralph Marvel's suicide (precipitated by Undine's greed) is but one of the brutal blows inflicted by Undine during her upward scramble.

After 1920 the satirical note predominated in novels such as *Twilight Sleep*, *The Children*, *Hudson River Bracketed*, and *The Gods Arrive*. In all of these novels there was a decided falling off both of artistic integrity and of imaginative energy. The brilliant, lucid style of the early work was scarcely visible now, except in *The Mother's Recompense* and in the non-satirical parts of *The Children*. *Glimpses of the Moon* was not much above the level of soap opera, and *Twilight Sleep* was a broader and less convincing satire on current representatives of American women than *Custom of the Country*. *Hudson River Bracketed* and *The Gods Arrive* deal with the career of an American novelist, Vance Weston, tracing his rise from obscurity in Euphoria, Illinois, to international fame in London and Paris, but they fail to bring his story into significant focus. In *The Buccaneers* Mrs. Wharton returned once more to the scene of her earlier and best triumphs, old New York before the turn of the century, but the novel remained unfinished at her death.

Among the seventy or so published short stories at least a dozen appear to have enduring quality, including "The Other Two," "Xingu," "Kerfol," "The Bunner Sisters," "The Triumph of Night," "Bewitched," "A Bottle of Perrier," "After Holbein," "Mr. Jones," "Pomegranate Seed," "Roman Fever," and "Joy in the House," and "The Eyes."

In 1934 Mrs. Wharton published her autobiography, an engaging though carefully selective account of her life, which referred only briefly to her disastrous marriage and dealt humorously and ironically with her eminent friend Henry James. Even before her death in 1937 Edith Wharton's literary reputation had begun to decline. It is only recently that interest in her work has revived, partly as the result of the new feminine consciousness. Still, even now, her novels and stories are not so highly regarded as they once were nor as seriously

treated by literary critics as they deserve to be. What were once regarded as her strengths –
her firm grasp of the social realities of her time and place, and her ready accessibility – now
appear to be her chief limitations. However, her two novels about New England life, *Ethan
Frome* and *Summer*, along with *The House of Mirth*, *The Reef* and *The Age of Innocence* are
among the best novels of their time and constitute an impressive body of work.

—W. J. Stuckey

WHEELWRIGHT, John (Brooks).   American.   Born in Boston, Massachusetts, in 1897.
Educated at Harvard University, Cambridge, Massachusetts; Massachusetts Institute of
Technology, Cambridge: studied architecture. Practised as an architect in Boston. Editor,
Poems for a Dime magazine. Official of the New England Poetry Society. *Died 15 September
1940.*

PUBLICATIONS

Collections

   Collected Poems, edited by Alvin H. Rosenfeld.   1972.

Verse

   Rock and Shell: Poems 1923–1933.   1933.
   Mirrors of Venus: A Novel in Sonnets, 1914–1938.   1938.
   Political Self-Portrait.   1940.
   Selected Poems.   1941.

Other

   Editor, *A History of the New England Poetry Club.*   1932.

*   *   *

John Wheelwright published three books during his lifetime, but none received sufficient
notice to give him reputation while alive. Wheelwright was not the average Socialist scribbler
of the Depression era, but a "proper Bostonian" of impeccable ancestry: on his father's side,
he claimed his radical blood from the first Wheelwright, an emigré from England in 1636,
who preached religious tolerance until he was banished from the Bay Colony. On his
mother's side, he descended from John Brooks, an early governor of Massachusetts.
   The contradictions explicit in such ancestry, radicalism, and political authority, were
manifest in Wheelwright's own character and poetry. He taunted Boston Brahmins with his
eccentric behavior in public and declared his allegiance to the proletariat, whose Depression

plight he championed in many poems. All the while he accepted his upper-class status and remained much of his life an official of the doughty New England Poetry Society.

Wheelwright was an erratic craftsman in his poems, even though he emphasized his technique in long prose commentaries that accompanied his three published books. Many poems are long-winded, prosaic, and loosely framed. But occasionally his poems spring out with unanticipated lyric genius, as in "Train Ride" (*Political Self-Portrait*). His "sonnet novel" *Mirrors of Venus*, generally over-wrought, includes his masterful elegy "Father":

> Come home. Wire a wire of warning without words.
> Come home and talk to me again, my first friend. Father,
> come home, dead man, who made your mind my home.

Wheelwright's work often takes the form of rambling poetic tracts, where he is an interpreter of what he felt to be the reshaping of America. As he wrote at the end of *Political Self-Portrait*, "The main point is not what noise poetry makes, but how it makes you think and act, – not what you make of it; but what it makes of you." Although this is unfair to the musical grace of much of his language, it is pointed and correct essentially about his intentions for his poetry.

His first book, *Rock and Shell*, shows the poet searching for some premise of unity in his experience, especially in the powerful opening poem, "North Atlantic Passage," which joins prose and poetry together. Spiritual loneliness is followed by sexual loneliness in this carefully plotted book. *Mirrors of Venus* is, as one critic described it, his *In Memoriam* to his friend Ned Couch, but sags generally from its weight of technical embellishments.

Political Self-Portrait is his best book; here he has found a balance between the wrought textures of language and loosely plotted ideological arguments. The poems are longer, more discursive, but intensely dramatic as they register a diffident, sensitive conscience faced with social unheaval and coming war. The poems are rich in imagery, raw in angry, direct language, but dignified overall by the depth of the speaker's convictions. Some of these poems have lost their edge now, but many, including "Collective Collect," "Bread-Word Giver," and "Train Ride" are lasting expressions of faith in humanity. "Dusk to Dusk," included in the recent *Collected Poems*, has an even shriller tone of indignation than *Political Self-Portrait*, and its structure seems driven to fragments by the unleashed energies of this unusual poet.

—Paul Christensen

WHITE, E(lwyn) B(rooks). American. Born in Mt. Vernon, New York, 11 July 1899. Educated at Mt. Vernon High School; Cornell University, Ithaca, New York, A.B. 1921. Served as a private in the United States Army, 1918. Married Katharine Sergeant Angell in 1929 (died, 1977); one son. Reporter, *Seattle Times*, 1922–23; advertising copywriter, 1924–25; Contributing Editor, *The New Yorker*, from 1927; Columnist ("One Man's Meat"), *Harper's*, New York, 1937–43. Recipient: National Association of Independent Schools Award, 1955; American Academy of Arts and Letters Gold Medal, 1960; Presidential Medal of Freedom, 1963; American Library Association Laura Ingalls Wilder Award, 1970; George G. Stone Center for Children's Books Award, 1970; National Medal for Literature, 1971. Litt.D.: Dartmouth College, Hanover, New Hampshire, 1948; University of Maine, Orono, 1948; Yale University, New Haven, Connecticut, 1948; Bowdoin College,

Brunswick, Maine, 1950; Hamilton College, Clinton, New York 1952; Harvard University, Cambridge, Massachusetts, 1954; L.H.D.: Colby College, Waterville, Maine, 1954. Fellow, American Academy of Arts and Sciences; Member, American Academy of Arts and Letters, 1974. Lives in North Brooklin, Maine.

PUBLICATIONS

Sketches and Prose

Is Sex Necessary? or, Why You Feel the Way You Do, with James Thurber.   1929.
Ho Hum.   1931.
Another Ho Hum.   1932.
Alice Through the Cellophane.   1933.
Every Day Is Saturday.   1934.
Farewell to Model T.   1936.
Quo Vadimus? or, The Case for the Bicycle.   1939.
One Man's Meat.   1942; augmented edition, 1944.
The Wild Flag: Editorials from the New Yorker on Federal World Government and Other Matters.   1946.
Here Is New York.   1949.
The Second Tree from the Corner.   1954.
The Points of My Compass: Letters from the East, The West, The North, The South.   1962.
A White Reader, edited by William W. Watt and Robert W. Bradford.   1966.
Essays.   1977.

Verse

The Lady Is Cold.   1929.
The Fox of Peapack and Other Poems.   1938.

Other

Stuart Little (juvenile).   1945.
Charlotte's Web (juvenile).   1952.
The Trumpet of the Swan (juvenile).   1970.
Letters, edited by Dorothy Lobrano Guth.   1976.

Editor, with Katharine S. White, *A Subtreasury of American Humor.*   1941.

Reading List: *White* by Edward C. Sampson, 1974.

*   *   *

In an editorial headnote in *Letters,* E. B. White refers to the "squibs and poems" that he began submitting to *The New Yorker* shortly after it was founded in 1925. He joined the staff of the magazine two years later and retained a real, if sometimes tenuous, connection with it for the rest of his writing life. His poems are conventional light verse, rather weak examples of a genre that tends toward wry sentiment, easy irony, and even easier rhyme. His important literary work is the care and feeding of the "squib," its transformation from fragile sketch to full-bodied essay. One of the tools in effecting that change was the discipline involved in writing the unsigned editorials, the "Notes and Comments" that he once called "my weekly sermon," samples of which have been collected in *Every Day Is Saturday* and *The Wild Flag*. It was the signed pieces, the "casuals" to use the *New Yorker* term, for which White became best known. As with most of the *New Yorker* humorists, he worked in a variety of styles (including the parody volume *Is Sex Necessary?* that he wrote with James Thurber), but he is at his most characteristic sketching ordinary incidents with affection and mild surprise, colored occasionally by outright fantasy. Most of his early work never escaped the pages of the magazine for which it was written, but the best of these pieces can be found in *Quo Vadimus?*

As early as 1929, in a letter to his brother, he wrote, "I discovered a long time ago that writing of the small things of the day, the trivial matters of the heart, the inconsequential but near things of this living, was the only kind of creative work which I could accomplish with any sincerity or grace." Although he never ceased to be concerned with "the small occasions," as he once called them, he came to know that the trivial and the inconsequential are inextricably bound with the vital, to write about everyday life with the awareness that it involved everyday death. The deepening tone in White's work began with "One Man's Meat," the monthly essay he started contributing to *Harper's* in 1937; it can be heard in later volumes like *The Second Tree from the Corner* and *The Points of My Compass*. In *Essays*, a retrospective gathering of more than forty years, White can be found at his saddest, his richest, his finest.

There is another White, but the author of the books for children is simply a gentler variation on the man who wrote *Essays*, as can be seen in the death of Charlotte and the rebirth made explicit in the arrival of all those baby spiders. *Charlotte's Web* is the most complex of White's children's books, placing a fantasy rescue in a realistic setting, using artifice to celebrate natural processes. Both *Stuart Little* and *The Trumpet of the Swan* are quest stories, but the first of these is probably White's most enduring book for children, not simply for the charm of its hero, but because it has an ending that does not end, a close that leaves Stuart – like White, like any good writer – still in search of beauty.

—Gerald Weales

WILBUR, Richard (Purdy). American. Born in New York City, 1 March 1921. Educated at Amherst College, Massachusetts, B.A. 1942; Harvard University, Cambridge, Massachusetts, M.A. 1947. Served in the United States Army, 1943–45. Married Charlotte Ward in 1942; one daughter and three sons. Member of the Society of Fellows, 1947–50, and Assistant Professor of English, 1950–54, Harvard University; Associate Professor of English, Wellesley College, Massachusetts, 1955–57. Since 1957, Professor of English, Wesleyan University, Middletown, Connecticut. General Editor, Laurel Poets series, Dell Publishing Company, New York. State Department Cultural Exchange Representative to the U.S.S.R., 1961. Recipient: Guggenheim Fellowship, 1952, 1963; American Academy in Rome Fellowship, 1954; Pulitzer Prize, 1957; National Book Award 1957; Edna St. Vincent Millay Memorial Award, 1957; Ford Foundation Fellowship, for drama, 1960; Melville Cane Award, 1962; Bollingen Prize, for translation, 1963, and for verse, 1971; Sarah Josepha Hale Award, 1968; Brandeis University Creative Arts Award, 1970; Prix Henri Desfeuilles, 1971;

Shelley Memorial Award, 1973. L.H.D.: Lawrence College, Appleton, Wisconsin, 1960; Washington University, St. Louis, 1964; D.Litt.: Amherst College, 1967. Member, American Academy of Arts and Sciences; since 1974, President, American Academy of Arts and Letters; Chancellor, Academy of American Poets. Lives in Cummington, Massachusetts.

PUBLICATIONS

Verse

The Beautiful Changes and Other Poems.   1947.
Ceremony and Other Poems.   1950.
Things of This World.   1956; one section reprinted as *Digging to China*, 1970.
Poems 1943–1956.   1957.
Advice to a Prophet and Other Poems.   1961.
The Poems.   1963.
Prince Souvanna Phouma: An Exchange Between Richard Wilbur and William Jay Smith.   1963.
Complaint.   1968.
Walking to Sleep: New Poems and Translations.   1969.
Seed Leaves: Homage to R. F.   1974.
The Mind-Reader: New Poems.   1976.

Plays

The Misanthrope, from the play by Molière (produced 1955).   1955; revised version, music by Margaret Pine (produced 1977).
Candide (lyrics only, with John LaTouche and Dorothy Parker), book by Lillian Hellman, music by Leonard Bernstein, from the novel by Voltaire (produced 1956).   1957.
Tartuffe. from the play by Molière (produced 1964).   1963.
School for Wives, from a play by Molière (produced 1971).   1971.
The Learned Ladies, from a play by Molière.   1978.

Other

Loudmouse (juvenile).   1963.
Opposites (juvenile), illustrated by the author.   1973.
Responses: Prose Pieces 1948–1976.   1976.

Editor, *A Bestiary* (anthology).   1955.
Editor, *Complete Poems of Poe.*   1959.
Editor, with Alfred Harbage, *Poems of Shakespeare.*   1966; revised edition, as *The Narrative Poems, and Poems of Doubtful Authenticity,*   1974.
Editor, *Selected Poems,* by Witter Bynner.   1978.

Translator, *The Funeral of Bobo,* by Joseph Brodsky.   1974.

Bibliography: *Wilbur: A Bibliographical Checklist* by John P. Field,   1971.

Reading List: *Wilbur* by Donald L. Hill, 1967; *Wilbur: A Critical Essay* by Paul F. Cummins, 1971.

*   *   *

Richard Wilbur's first volume of poems surprised its early readers in 1947: there was none of the standard theorizing about history or large "modern" issues and only occasional reflections of the poet's experiences in the war; instead, the poet of *The Beautiful Changes* spoke openly of beauty, unabashedly expressing his delight in the sights and sounds and movements of the world and demonstrating a dazzling virtuosity at recreating them in his verse. He also revealed his delight in wit, imaginative play, and even games. One of the poems was entitled simply "&," and his delights are joined in some lines from "Grace":

> One is tickled again, by the dining-car waiter's absurd
> Acrobacy – tipfingered tray like a wind-besting bird
> Plumblines his swinging shoes, the sole things sure
> In the shaken train.

In addition to the high spirits, the poems often almost exemplified elegance, poise, and good manners.

A number of those qualities and subjects came to seem even more startling in the years which followed. From the beginning up to *The Mind-Reader*, Wilbur's poetry has shown notable continuities. He has remarked that in his later poems he tends to move towards "a plainer and more straightforward" way of writing and, also, from poems that use a "single meditative voice balancing argument and counter-argument, feeling and counter-feeling" to more "dramatic" ones (such as "Two Voices in a Meadow" or "The Aspen and the Stream") that may use two opposing voices. Readers may also detect a general deepening of feeling and a clearer personal voice as well as some unpredictable developments. But most of the earlier qualities remain, and there continue to be signal exclusions: no confessional poetry and no free verse (Wilbur wrote that in the fairy story about the genie which could be summoned out of a bottle, he had always assumed that the genie gained his strength from being *in* the bottle).

It is unlikely that anyone could have predicted, however, that the poet who showed an almost Keatsian responsiveness to the sensuous should become the translator of Molière into extraordinary English couplets. In retrospect, it is clearer that Molière represents part of what Wilbur is, as well as what he admires: a humane voice of uncommonly rational common-sense; a user of language that is both familiar and chaste; a witty enemy of the pompous, the gross, and the fanatic; and a juggler, a master of poise and point. Nor could one have anticipated "Junk," the liveliest recreation of Anglo-Saxon meters and feeling since Pound, or the scathing Miltonic sonnet to Lyndon Johnson, or the tenderness of the translations from Charles d'Orléans, Voltaire, and Francis Jammes, or the effectiveness of "A Christmas Hymn," or the moving elegy for Dudley Fitts.

Neither could one have quite anticipated "Walking to Sleep," an extraordinary exploration of the paths, strategems, surprises, and terrors that lie between waking and sleep, nor "The Mind-Reader," although both long poems extend one of Wilbur's most persistent themes in his more obviously personal lyrics: the processes, reflections, and creations of the mind. Wilbur once remarked, "A good part of my work could, I suppose, be understood as a public quarrel with the aesthetics of Edgar Allan Poe." His continuous concern is evidenced by his edition of Poe's poems and a number of substantial essays on both the prose and the verse: three of the sixteen provocative and lucid essays in *Responses: Prose Pieces, 1948–1976* concern Poe. He once wrote, "There has never been a grander conception of poetry [than Poe's], nor a more impoverished one." As that sentence suggests, the quarrel continues because Wilbur finds it so difficult to make a decision once for all. His ambivalence (at the simplest level, his fascination with the intellectual, the perfectly beautiful and purely harmonious, and his almost simultaneous reaction away from such an ideal in an acceptance and love for the imperfect human and material reality that we can know here and now) is the theme of a number of his best poems. "A World Without Objects Is a Sensible Emptiness" is one of many that balances the soul's longing for purity and perfection with, almost simultaneously with the moment of ascension towards the empyrean, a counter movement as it accepts and rejoices in the body and its world. Wilbur's poetry often seems that of a natural Platonist who keeps learning to accept the Incarnation. "The Writer" movingly recognizes that the literary "flight" has its origins as well as final resting place in human suffering and love.

If Robert Frost has an authentic living heir, it is probably Wilbur – particularly as the poet of the short lyric in strict and familiar meters who speaks in the middle voice, wittily and movingly, to a wide audience. There are, however, important differences: Wilbur's voice is usually more obviously that of an urban man in contrast to the characteristic voice of the countryman which Frost so carefully crafted; and Frost never devoted such care to the attempt to translate, self-effacedly, the poetry of others, nor did he write for the public theater. But the most important difference is probably in their spirits. Frost did not share with anything like Wilbur's conviction the notion that "Love Calls Us to the Things of This World." It may have been, in part at least, that conviction which enabled Wilbur to make imaginatively convincing his "Advice to a Prophet" concerning how we might be persuaded not to destroy our earth.

—Joseph H. Summers

WILDER, Thornton (Niven). American. Born in Madison, Wisconsin, 17 April 1897. Educated at Oberlin College, Ohio, 1915–17; Yale University, New Haven, Connecticut, A.B. 1920; American Academy in Rome, 1920–21; Princeton University, New Jersey, A.M. 1926. Served in the United States Coast Artillery Corps, 1918–19; in the United States Army Air Intelligence, rising to the rank of Lieutenant-Colonel, 1942–45: honorary M.B.E. (Member, Order of the British Empire), 1945. Teacher, 1921–28, and House Master, 1927–28, Lawrenceville School, New Jersey. Full-time writer from 1928. Lecturer in Comparative Literature, University of Chicago, 1930–36; Visiting Professor, University of Hawaii, Honolulu, 1935; Charles Eliot Norton Professor of Poetry, Harvard University, Cambridge, Massachusetts, 1950–51. United States Delegate: Institut de Cooperation Intellectuelle, Paris, 1937; with John Dos Passos, International P.E.N. Club Congress, England, 1941; UNESCO Conference of the Arts, Venice, 1952. Recipient: Pulitzer Prize, for fiction, 1928, for drama, 1938, 1943; National Institute of Arts and Letters Gold Medal, 1952; Friedenpreis des Deutschen Buchhandels, 1957; Austrian Ehrenmedaille, 1959; Goethe-Plakette, 1959; Brandeis University Creative Arts Award, 1959: Edward MacDowell Medal, 1960; Presidential Medal of Freedom, 1963; National Book Committee's National Medal for Literature, 1965; Century Association Art Medal; National Book Award, for fiction, 1968. D. Litt.: New York University, 1930; Yale University, 1947; Kenyon College, Gambier, Ohio, 1948; College of Wooster, Ohio, 1950; Northeastern University, Boston, 1951; Oberlin College, 1952; University of New Hampshire, Durham, 1953; Goethe University, Frankfurt, 1957; University of Zurich, 1961; LL.D.: Harvard University, 1951. Chevalier, Legion of Honor, 1951; Member, Order of Merit, Peru; Order of Merit, Bonn, 1957; Honorary Member, Bavarian Academy of Fine Arts; Mainz Academy of Science and Literature. Member, American Academy of Arts and Letters. *Died 7 December 1975.*

Fiction

> *The Cabala.* 1926.
> *The Bridge of San Luis Rey.* 1927.
> *The Woman of Andros.* 1930.
> *Heaven's My Destination.* 1934.
> *The Ides of March.* 1948.
> *The Eighth Day.* 1967.
> *Theophilus North.* 1973.

Plays

> *The Trumpet Shall Sound* (produced 1927).
> *The Angel That Troubled the Waters and Other Plays* (includes *Nascuntur Poetae, Proserpina and the Devil, Fanny Otcott, Brother Fire, The Penny That Beauty Spent, The Angel on the Ship, The Message and Jehanne, Childe Roland to the Dark Tower Came, Centaurs, Leviathan, And the Sea Shall Give Up Its Dead, Now the Servant's Name Was Malchus, Mozart and the Gray Steward, Hast Thou Considered My Servant Job?, The Flight into Egypt*). 1928.
> *The Long Christmas Dinner* (produced 1931).   In *The Long Christmas Dinner and Other Plays,* 1931; libretto, music by Paul Hindemith (produced 1961), libretto published, 1961.
> *The Happy Journey to Trenton and Camden* (produced 1931).   In *The Long Christmas Dinner and Other Plays,* 1931; revised version, as *The Happy Journey,* 1934.
> *Such Things Only Happen in Books* (produced 1931).   In *The Long Christmas Dinner and Other Plays,* 1931.
> *Love and How to Cure It* (produced 1931).   In *The Long Christmas Dinner and Other Plays,* 1931.
> *The Long Christmas Dinner and Other Plays in One Act.*   1931.
> *Queens of France* (produced 1932).   In *The Long Christmas Dinner and Other Plays,* 1931.
> *Pullman Car Hiawatha* (produced 1962).   In *The Long Christmas Dinner and Other Plays,* 1931.
> *Lucrece,* from a play by André Obey (produced 1932).   1933.
> *A Doll's House,* from a play by Ibsen (produced 1937).
> *Our Town* (produced 1938).   1938.
> *The Merchant of Yonkers,* from a play by Johann Nostroy, based on *A Well-Spent Day* by John Oxenford (produced 1938).   1939; revised version, as *The Matchmaker* (produced 1954), 1955.
> *The Skin of Our Teeth* (produced 1942).   1942.
> *Our Century.*   1947.
> *The Victors,* from a play by Sartre (produced 1949).
> *A Life in the Sun* (produced 1955); as *The Alcestiad,* music by L. Talma (produced 1962).   Published as *Die Alkestiade,* 1958; as *The Alcestiad: or, A Life in the Sun, and The Drunken Sisters: A Satyr Play,* 1977.
> *The Drunken Sisters.*   1957.
> *Bernice* (produced 1957).
> *The Wreck of the 5:25* (produced 1957).
> *Plays for Bleecker Street* (includes *Infancy, Childhood,* and *Someone from Assisi*) (produced 1962).   3 vols., 1960–61.

Screenplays: *Our Town*, 1940; *Shadow of a Doubt*, 1943.

Other

The Intent of the Artist, with others. 1941.
Kultur in einer Demokratie. 1957.
Goethe und die Weltliteratur. 1958.

Bibliography: *A Bibliographical Checklist of the Writings of Wilder* by J. M Edelstein, 1959.

Reading List: *Wilder* by Rex Burbank, 1961; *Wilder* by Helmut Papajewski, 1961, translated by John Conway, 1968; *Wilder* by Bernard Grebanier, 1964; *The Art of Wilder* by Malcolm Goldstein, 1965; *The Plays of Wilder: A Critical Study* by Donald Haberman, 1967.

*   *   *

Many recent American writers have written both plays and fiction, but no other has achieved such a distinguished reputation for both as Thornton Wilder. He is distinguished also for the uniqueness of his works: each is a fresh formal experiment that contributes to his persistent conception of the artist's re-inventing the world by revivifying our preceptions of the universal elements of human experience.

Wilder's earliest published works in *The Angel That Troubled the Waters and Other Plays* are short pieces presenting usually fantastic situations in an arch, cryptic style employed by such favored writers of the 1920's as Elinor Wylie. A number of the plays deal with the special burden that falls upon persons who discover that they possess artistic gifts, and most of them demand staging too complex for actual performance.

Before he became a successful playwright, Wilder was a novelist. His first novel *The Cabala*, displays much the same preciosity as the early plays. It describes through loosely linked episodes the effort of an aspiring young American writer to be accepted by the Cabala, "members of a circle so powerful and exclusive that ... Romans refer to them with bated breath." These elegant figures turn out to be contemporary embodiments of the ancient Roman gods, and the veiled point of the work is that the United States is to succeed a decaying Rome as the next abiding place of these gods.

This fantasy did not attract many readers, but Wilder achieved an astonishing success with his next short novel, *The Bridge of San Luis Rey*, which became a surprise best seller. This episodic story about the perishability of material things and the endurance of love is exquisitely structured. It tells the stories of the five persons who die in the collapse of a famous Peruvian bridge with a framework provided by the narrative of a Brother Juniper, who investigates the accident to learn whether "we live by accident and die by accident, or live by plan and die by plan." For his efforts, both he and his book are publicly burned. The last sentence stresses that the only bridge that survives is love.

Wilder's third novel, *The Woman of Andros*, was attacked by socially-minded critics of the 1930's for evading present realities and retreating to the classical world; but this subtle fictionalization of Terence's *Andria* actually relates closely to Wilder's own seemingly dying world through its presentation of the death of the Greek world at the time of the coming of Christ because its commercial and artistic communities had become alienated. With his next novel, *Heaven's My Destination*, Wilder returned to contemporary America to create one of his most beguiling characters, George Brush, a high-school textbook salesman in the midwest, who fails comically and pathetically in his constant efforts to uplift other people and who recovers his faith only when he realizes that he must remain an isolated wanderer, happy only in the world that he makes for himself.

The world that we make for ourselves is the subject again of one of Wilder's most admired works and one of his major contributions to a myth of American community, the play *Our Town*. Wilder explained in *The Intent of the Artist* that he turned from the novel to the stage in the 1930's because "the theater carries the art of narration to a higher power than the novel or the epic poem." He was impatient, however, with the elaborate stage settings of the naturalistic theater, and he had already sought in short plays like *The Long Christmas Dinner* to tell a fundamental human story with only the simplest of props. His culminating experiment with this technique was *Our Town*, a chronicle of the value of "the smallest events in our daily life" in a traditional New England village.

Wilder next experimented with updating a nineteenth-century farce that had been popular in both English and German versions as *The Merchant of Yonkers*. Unsuccessful when first ponderously presented by Max Reinhardt, the play in a revised version entitled *The Matchmaker* was a popular success that subsequently provided the basis for the enormously popular musical comedy, *Hello, Dolly!* Wilder did enjoy enormous immediate success with his third major play. *The Skin of Our Teeth*, an expressionist fantasy about man's struggles for survival through the Ice Age, the Flood, and the Napoleonic Wars as symbolized by the travails of the Antrobus family. Again Wilder's timing was superb. A world reduced to doubt and despair by World War II responded enthusiastically to this affirmative vision of man's possible survival despite his destructive propensities.

Wilder served with American Intelligence units in Italy during World War II, and for his first post-war work returned to the novel and to a classical Roman setting for *The Ides of March*. This pseudo-history, which Malcolm Goldstein compares to "a set of bowls placed one within another," centers on the assassination of Julius Caesar, but traces through four overlapping sections an ever widening circle of events in order to present "the tragic difference between Caesar's idealistic visions and the sordid events for which they are finally responsible" – a subject fraught with implications for the mid-twentieth century.

After the comparatively cool reception of this work, Wilder published little for twenty years. Although his plays remained popular, he was generally too lightly regarded after World War II when existential *angst* dominated literary criticism. His writings were felt to be too affirmative and optimistic, and his long silence caused him to be regarded as an artist whose time had passed. Literary mandarins were startled, therefore, by the appearance in 1967 of his longest and most complex work, *The Eighth Day*. This novel jumps back and forth in time as it resurrects the events relating to a murder in a southern Illinois coal town early in the twentieth century, the false conviction of a man who escapes, and the eventual solution of the cunning crime. This mystery plot, however, provided only a backdrop for Wilder's observation that all history is one "enormous tapestry" and that "there are no Golden Ages and no Dark Ages. There is the oceanlike monotony of the generations of men under the alternations of fair and foul weather." At the center of the work stands the falsely accused John Ashley, who avoids succumbing to despair over this inescapable cycle by "inventing" afresh such fossilized institutions as marriage and fatherhood as he also invents small practical objects to make man's work easier. An old woman whom he meets sums up the sensibility that informs the novel, "The human race gets no better. Mankind is vicious, slothful, quarrelsome, and self-centered. ...[But] you and I have a certain quality that is rare as teeth in a hen. We work. And we forget ourselves in our work."

The Eighth Day triumphantly capped Wilder's "re-invention" of mankind, but he had one final delight for readers. Perhaps to complement James Joyce's and others' portraits of the artist as a young man *by* a young man, Wilder presented in his last published work, *Theophilus North*, an episodic novel about the artist as a young man *by* an old man. The seemingly loosely connected tales are actually – as in his other works – parts of an intricate mosaic that discloses against a background of the "nine cities" of Newport, Rhode Island, the nine career possibilities that a young man explores before discovering that being a writer will encompass all of them.

—Warren French

WILLIAMS, Tennessee (Thomas Lanier Williams).   American.   Born in Columbus, Mississippi, 26 March 1911. Educated at the University of Missouri, Columbia, 1930–32; Washington University, St. Louis, 1936–37; University of Iowa, Iowa City, 1938, A.B. 1938. Clerical Worker and Manual Laborer, International Shoe Company, St. Louis, 1934–36; held various jobs, including waiter and elevator operator, New Orleans, 1939; teletype operator, Jacksonville, Florida, 1940; worked at odd jobs, New York, 1942, and as a screenwriter for MGM, 1943. Full-time writer since 1944. Recipient: Rockefeller Fellowship, 1940; National Institute of Arts and Letters grant, 1944, and Gold Medal, 1969; New York Drama Critics Circle Award, 1945, 1948, 1955, 1962; Pulitzer Prize, 1948, 1955; *Evening Standard* award, 1958; Brandeis University Creative Arts Award, 1964. Member, American Academy of Arts and Letters, 1976. Lives in Key West, Florida, and New York City.

PUBLICATIONS

Plays

Cairo! Shanghai! Bombay! (produced 1936).
The Magic Tower (produced 1936).
Headlines (produced 1936).
Candles in the Sun (produced 1936).
Fugitive Kind (produced 1937).
Spring Song (produced 1938).
The Long Goodbye (produced 1940).   In *27 Wagons Full of Cotton*, 1946.
Battle of Angels (produced 1940).   1945; revised version, as *Orpheus Descending* (produced 1957), published as *Orpheus Descending, with Battle of Angels*, 1958.
At Liberty (produced 1968).   In *American Scenes*, edited by William Kozlenko, 1941.
Stairs to the Roof (produced 1944).
You Touched Me, with Donald Windham, suggested by the story by D. H. Lawrnece (produced 1944).   1947.
The Glass Menagerie (produced 1944).   1945.
27 Wagons Full of Cotton and Other One-Act Plays (includes *The Purification, The Lady of Larkspur Lotion, The Last of My Solid Gold Watches, Portrait of a Madonna, Auto-da-Fé, Lord Byron's Love Letter, The Strangest Kind of Romance, The Long Goodbye, Hello from Bertha*, and *This Property Is Condemned*).   1946; augmented edition (includes *Talk to Me Like the Rain and Let Me Listen* and *Something Unspoken*), 1953.
This Property Is Condemned (produced 1946).   In *27 Wagons Full of Cotton*, 1946.
Portrait of a Madonna (produced 1946).   In *27 Wagons Full of Cotton*, 1946.
The Last of My Solid Gold Watches (produced 1946).   In *27 Wagons Full of Cotton*, 1946.
Lord Byron's Love Letter (produced 1947).   In *27 Wagons Full of Cotton*, 1946; revised version, music by Raffaello de Banfield (produced 1964); libretto published, 1955.
Auto-da-Fé (produced 1947).   In *27 Wagons Full of Cotton*, 1946.
The Lady of Larkspur Lotion (produced 1947).   In *27 Wagons Full of Cotton*, 1946.
The Purification (produced 1954).   In *27 Wagons Full of Cotton*, 1946.
27 Wagons Full of Cotton (produced 1955).   In *27 Wagons Full of Cotton*, 1946.
Hello from Bertha (produced 1961).   In *27 Wagons Full of Cotton*, 1946.
The Strangest Kind of Romance (produced 1969).   In *27 Wagons Full of Cotton*, 1946.
Mooney's Kid Don't Cry (produced 1946).   In *American Blues*, 1948.
A Streetcar Named Desire (produced 1947).   1947.
Summer and Smoke (produced 1947).   1948; revised version, as *The Eccentricities of a Nightingale* (produced 1964), published as *The Eccentricities of a Nightingale, and Summer and Smoke*, 1965; revised version (produced 1976).

American Blues: Five Short Plays. 1948.

Ten Blocks on the Camino Real, in *American Blues.* 1948; revised version, as *Camino Real* (produced 1953), 1953.

The Case of the Crushed Petunias (produced 1957). In *American Blues,* 1948.

The Dark Room (produced 1966). In *American Blues,* 1948.

The Long Stay Cut Short; or, The Unsatisfactory Supper (produced 1971). In *American Blues,* 1948.

The Rose Tattoo (produced 1951). 1951.

I Rise in Flame, Cried the Phoenix: A Play about D. H. Lawrence (produced 1953). 1951.

Talk to Me Like the Rain and Let Me Listen (produced 1958). In *27 Wagons Full of Cotton,* 1953.

Something Unspoken (produced 1958). In *27 Wagons Full of Cotton,* 1953.

Cat on a Hot Tin Roof (produced 1955). 1955; revised version (produced 1973), 1975.

Three Players of a Summer Game (produced 1955).

Sweet Bird of Youth (produced 1956). 1959.

Baby Doll: The Script for the Film, Incorporating the Two One-Act Plays Which Suggested It: 27 Wagons Full of Cotton and The Long Stay Cut Short; or, The Unsatisfactory Supper. 1956.

Garden District: Something Unspoken, Suddenly Last Summer (produced 1958). 1958.

The Fugitive Kind: Original Play Title: Orpheus Descending (screenplay). 1958.

A Perfect Analysis Given by a Parrot (produced 1976). 1958.

The Enemy: Time, in *Theatre,* March 1959.

The Night of the Iguana (produced 1959; revised version, produced 1961). 1962.

Period of Adjustment: High Point over a Cavern: A Serious Comedy (produced 1959). 1960.

To Heaven in a Golden Coach (produced 1961).

The Milk Train Doesn't Stop Here Anymore (produced 1962; revised versions, produced 1962, 1963, 1964, 1968). 1964.

Slapstick Tragedy (The Mutilated and *The Gnädiges Fräulein)* (produced 1966). 2 vols., 1967; revised version of *The Gnädiges Fräulein,* as *The Latter Days of a Celebrated Soubrette* (produced 1974).

Kingdom of Earth, in *Esquire,* February 1967; revised version, as *Kingdom of Earth: The Seven Descents of Myrtle* (produced 1968). 1968.

The Two Character Play (produced 1967; revised version, produced 1969). 1969; revised version, as *Out Cry* (produced 1971), 1973; revised version (produced 1974).

In the Bar of a Tokyo Hotel (produced 1969). 1969.

I Can't Imagine Tomorrow (televised 1970; produced 1976). In *Dragon Country,* 1970.

Dragon Country: A Book of Plays (includes *In the Bar of a Tokyo Hotel, I Rise in Flame, Cried the Phoenix, The Mutilated, I Can't Imagine Tomorrow, Confessional, The Frosted Glass Coffin, The Gnädiges Fräulein, A Perfect Analysis Given by a Parrot*). 1970.

Senso, with Paul Bowles, in *Two Screenplays,* by Luigi Visconti. 1970.

A Streetcar Named Desire (screenplay), in *Film Scripts One,* edited by George P. Garrett, O. B. Harrison, Jr., and Jane Gelfann. 1971.

Small Craft Warnings (produced 1972). 1972.

The Theatre of Williams I–V. 5 vols., 1972–76.

The Red Devil Battery Sign (produced 1974; revised version, produced 1976; revised version, produced 1977).

Demolition Downtown: Count Ten in Arabic – Then Run (produced 1976).

This Is an Entertainment (produced 1976).

Vieux Carré (produced 1977).

Screenplays: *Senso (The Wanton Countess,* English dialogue, with Paul Bowles), 1949;

The Glass Menagerie, with Peter Berneis, 1950; *A Streetcar Named Desire,* with Oscar Saul, 1951; *The Rose Tattoo,* with Hal Kanter, 1955; *Baby Doll,* 1956; *Suddenly Last Summer,* with Gore Vidal, 1960; *The Fugitive Kind,* with Meade Roberts, 1960; *Boom,* 1968.

Television Play: *I Can't Imagine Tomorrow,* 1970.

Fiction

One Arm and Other Stories. 1948.
The Roman Spring of Mrs. Stone. 1950.
Hard Candy: A Book of Stories. 1954.
Three Players of a Summer Game and Other Stories. 1960.
Grand (stories). 1964.
The Knightly Quest: A Novella and Four Short Stories. 1967; augmented edition, as *The Knightly Quest: A Novella and Twelve Short Stories,* 1968.
Eight Mortal Ladies Possessed: A Book of Stories. 1974.
Moise and the World of Reason. 1975.

Verse

Five Young American Poets, with others. 1944.
In the Winter of Cities: Poems. 1956.
Androgyne, Mon Amour. 1977.

Other

Memoirs. 1975.
Letters to Donald Windham 1940–1965, edited by Windham. 1976.
Where I Live (essays). 1978.

Reading List: *Williams* by Signi Lenea Falk, 1961 (includes bibliography); *Williams: Rebellious Puritan* by Nancy M. Tischler, 1961; *Williams: The Man and His Work* by Benjamin Nelson, 1961; *The Dramatic World of Williams* by Francis Donahue, 1964; *The Broken World of Williams* by Esther M. Jackson, 1965; *Williams* by Gerald Weales, 1965; *Williams: A Tribute* edited by Jac Tharpe, 1977; *Williams: A Collection of Critical Essays* edited by Stephen S. Stanton, 1977; *The World of Williams* by Richard Freeman Leavitt, 1978.

*   *   *

Shortly before *Vieux Carré* opened on Broadway in 1977, Tennessee Williams wrote an article for the New York *Times* which began, "Of course no one is more acutely aware than I that I am widely regarded as the ghost of a writer." So he is. The name Tennessee Williams still conjures up the flamboyant plays of the 1940's and 1950's – *A Streetcar Named Desire, Cat on a Hot Tin Roof, Suddenly Last Summer.* Except for a period in the mid-sixties when he suffered mental and physical collapse, Williams has been a remarkably busy ghost. Since 1974, he has seen new plays staged in London, San Francisco, and New York, and he has published a novel (*Moise and the World of Reason*), a book of short stories (*Eight Mortal Ladies Possessed*), a book of poems (*Androgyne, Mon Amour*) and *Memoirs.* Artistically and personally, he has become an advertisement for the theme that has obsessed him since Amanda Wingfield tried to hold her disintegrating family together in *The Glass Menagerie* – survival.

When *Vieux Carré* opened, the critics did treat it as a ghost play, a nostalgic look at the New Orleans of Williams's youth, full of echoes of characters, situations, themes relentlessly familiar to Williams admirers. In the *Times* article, in *Memoirs*, in any number of interviews, Williams has attempted to explain how he was transformed from America's most popular serious playwright into an historical figure, inexplicably still active in the real world. His plays through *The Night of the Iguana*, he suggests, shared a similarity of style – "poetic naturalism" he calls it – which became so identified with him that when he made a shift into new styles, his audiences could not or would not follow him. It is true that there are great stylistic similarities among the Williams plays through *Iguana* and it is also true that he has lost the large audiences that once flocked to his work, but the new styles have their roots in his earlier work.

He has never been a realistic playwright, which may be what the phrase *poetic naturalism* is supposed to suggest, but he has always been capable of writing a psychologically valid scene in the American realistic tradition – the breakfast scene in *The Glass Menagerie*, for instance, or the birthday dinner in *A Streetcar Named Desire*. His characters are able to claim the allegiance of audiences who continue to identify with them even after they become larger than life (Big Daddy in *Cat on a Hot Tin Roof*, Alexandra Del Lago in *Sweet Bird of Youth*) or when the use of significant names (Val Xavier in *Orpheus Descending*, Alma in *Summer and Smoke*) turn them into myth or symbol. However grounded in realistic surface, the events in Williams's plays, particularly the violent events, take on meaning that transcends psychological realism ("Here is your God, Mr. Shannon," says Hannah when the storm breaks in *Night of the Iguana*), and when the violence moves off stage – the cannibalism in *Suddenly Last Summer*, the castration in *Sweet Bird of Youth* – the nonrealistic implications of event are heightened by its transformation into narrative (*Summer and Smoke*) or promise (*Sweet Bird of Youth*). From the glass menagerie through the dressmaker's dummies in *The Rose Tattoo* to the costumes, ritually donned by Shannon and Hannah in *Night of the Iguana*, Williams has always used sets, props, dress as devices whose significance runs deeper than the verisimilitude required by realism. When Williams deserted old forms – or thought he did – he brought two decades of nonrealistic theater with him. *Slapstick Tragedy* may have suggested absurdist drama to some of its viewers, but Polly and Molly, the grotesque comedy team whose voices sustain *The Gnädiges Fräulein*, are variations on Dolly and Beulah, who introduce *Orpheus Descending*, and Flora and Bessie, the "female clowns" of *The Rose Tattoo* and *A Perfect Analysis Given by a Parrot*. When each of the characters in *Small Craft Warnings* takes his place in the spotlight to sound his sorrow – a mechanism which suggests that the title of an earlier version of the play, *Confessional*, is more apt – we have at most an intensification of the device Williams used extensively in his earlier plays, most notably in Maggie's opening speech in *Cat on a Hot Tin Roof* and the soliloquies of Chance and Alexandra in *Sweet Bird of Youth*.

Stylistically, then, the later Williams plays grow out of the early ones. Nor are there surprising shifts in theme. The similarities between the pre- and post-*Night of the Iguana* plays can best be seen in the recurrence of characters. The Blanche of *Streetcar Named Desire*, whose variants people *Summer and Smoke*, *Camino Real*, *Sweet Bird of Youth*, and *Night of the Iguana*, is still visible in Isabel in *Period of Adjustment*, Miriam in *In the Bar of a Tokyo Hotel*, and, bizarrely, in the fish-trapping heroine of *The Gnädiges Fräulein*. Amanda – or at least her comic toughness – is apparent in Flora Goforth in *The Milk Train Doesn't Stop Here Anymore*, Myrtle in *Kingdom of Earth*, and Leona in *Small Craft Warnings*, and Laura, the frightened daughter of *The Glass Menagerie*, is present in characters as different as One in *I Can't Imagine Tomorrow* and Clare in *Out Cry*. Blanche, Amanda, Laura, three aspects of the perennial Williams character, the fugitive kind, who, male and female, has been the playwright's concern from his very early one-act plays to *Vieux Carré*. At first, his characters were simply outsiders, set off from the rest of society by a recognizable difference of one kind or another – Laura's limp, Blanche's defensive sexuality, Alma's pseudo-artistic sensitivity. It became increasingly clear – even as the forces that opposed his protagonists became more violent – that all men are outsiders. The murderous Jabe in *Orpheus Descending* is set apart by the disease that is killing him as obviously as Val is by his priapic aura, his guitar, and his snakeskin jacket, as Lady is by being Italian, as Carol Cutrere is by her unconsoling wealth and self-lacerating sex, as Vee Talbot is by her painting and her religious visions. Chance calls Alexandra "nice monster" in *Sweet Bird of Youth*, and she calls him "pitiful monster," and both are "Lost in the beanstalk country ... the country of the flesh-hungry, blood-thirsty ogre," but the play's ogre, Boss Finley, is supposed to be monster-ridden too and Williams keeps revising the play in the hopes that that point will emerge. The enemy is no longer the ugly other, but a surrogate self, or time (note all those age-obsessed Williams characters, like Mrs. Stone who wanted a Roman spring), or a godless universe. This last is presented most clearly in two plays, *Suddenly Last Summer* and *Night of the Iguana*, which come closest to making specific theological statements. Man, as Tennessee Williams sees him – as Tennessee Williams embodies him – is a temporary resident in a frightening world in an indifferent universe. The best he can hope is the transitory consolation of touching and the best he can do is hang on for dear (and only) life.

In the *Times* article quoted above Williams mentions his "private panic," his dreams "full of alarm and wild suspicion" that he wants to "cry ... out to all who will listen," and his continued revision of *Out Cry* emphasized his urgency. But that cry has always echoed through his work – his novels, his short stories, his poetry, his autobiography and all his plays. In the hope that the cry will come through more clearly, he has always revised and rewritten, turning short stories into plays, short plays into long ones, full-length plays into other full-length plays, as *Battle of Angels* became *Orpheus Descending*, and *Summer and Smoke* became *The Eccentricities of a Nightingale*. Audiences have withdrawn from Williams, I suspect, not because his style has changed or his concerns altered, but because in his desperate need to cry out he has turned away from the sturdy dramatic containers which once gave the cry resonance and has settled for pale imitations of familiar stage images; he has built on the direct address of the early soliloquies and the discursiveness of plays like *Night of the Iguana* and substituted lyric argument for dramatic language. It is a measure of his stature as a playwright and the importance of his central theme that each new play bears the promise of old vigor in new disguise. The promise has not been fulfilled for some years now, but while we wait, we can always turn back to those other Williams plays, elevated now to contemporary classics, which remind us that this ghost just may produce something worth waiting for.

—Gerald Weales

WILLIAMS, William Carlos. American. Born in Rutherford, New Jersey, 17 September 1883. Educated at a school in Rutherford, 1889–96; Chateau de Lancy, near Geneva, Switzerland, and Lycée Condorcet, Paris, 1897–99; Horace Mann High School, New York, 1899–1902; University of Pennsylvania, Philadelphia, 1902–06, M.D. 1906; did two years internship at hospitals in New York City, 1906–08, and post-graduate work in paediatrics at the University of Leipzig, 1908–09. Married Florence Herman in 1912; two sons. Practised medicine in Rutherford, 1910 until he retired in the mid 1950's. Editor, *Others*, 1919; Editor, with Robert McAlmon, *Contact*, 1920–23; Editor, with Nathanael

West, *Contact*, 1932. Appointed Consultant in Poetry, Library of Congress, Washington, D.C., 1952, but did not serve. Recipient: Loines Award, 1948; National Book Award, 1950; Bollingen Prize, 1952; Academy of American Poets Fellowship, 1956; Brandeis University Creative Arts Award, 1958; National Institute of Arts and Letters Gold Medal, 1963; Pulitzer Prize, 1963. LL.D.: State University of New York at Buffalo, 1956; Fairleigh Dickinson University, Teaneck, New Jersey, 1959; Litt.D.: Rutgers University, New Brunswick, New Jersey, 1948; Bard College, Annandale-on-Hudson, New York, 1948; University of Pennsylvania, 1952. Member, National Institute of Arts and Letters. *Died 4 March 1963.*

PUBLICATIONS

Collections

The Williams Reader, edited by M. L. Rosenthal.   1966.

Verse

Poems.   1909.
The Tempers.   1913.
Al Que Quiere!   1917.
Kora in Hell: Improvisations.   1920.
Sour Grapes.   1921.
Spring and All.   1923.
Go Go.   1923.
The Cod Head.   1932.
Collected Poems, 1921–1931.   1934.
An Early Martyr and Other Poems.   1935.
Adam & Eve & the City.   1936.
The Complete Collected Poems 1906–1938.   1938.
The Broken Span.   1941.
The Wedge.   1944.
Paterson, Book One.   1946; *Book Two,* 1948; *Book Three,* 1949; *Book Four,* 1951; *Book Five,* 1958; *Books I–V,* 1963.
The Clouds.   1948.
The Pink Church.   1949.
Selected Poems.   1949.
The Collected Later Poems.   1950; revised edition, 1963.
The Collected Earlier Poems.   1951.
The Desert Music and Other Poems.   1954.
Journey to Love.   1955.
Pictures from Brueghel and Other Poems.   1962.

Plays

Betty Putnam (produced 1910).
A Dream of Love (produced 1949).   1948.
Many Loves (produced 1958).   In *Many Loves and Other Plays,* 1961.
Many Loves and Other Plays: The Collected Plays (includes *A Dream of Love; Tituba's Children; The First President,* music by Theodore Harris; *The Cure*).   1961.

Fiction

A Voyage to Pagany.   1928.
A Novelette and Other Prose 1921–1931.   1932.
The Knife of the Times and Other Stories.   1932.
White Mule.   1937; *In the Money: White Mule, Part II*,1940; *The Build-Up*, 1952.
Life along the Passaic River (stories).   1938.
Make Light of It: Collected Stories.   1950.
The Farmers' Daughters: The Collected Stories.   1961.

Other

The Great American Novel.   1923.
In the American Grain.   1925.
The Autobiography.   1951.
Williams' Poetry Talked About, with Eli Siegel.   1952; revised edition, edited by
    Martha Baird and Ellen Reiss, as *The Williams-Siegel Documentary*, 1970, 1974.
Selected Essays.   1954.
John Marin, with others.   1956.
Selected Letters, edited by John C. Thirlwall.   1957.
I Wanted to Write a Poem: The Autobiography of the Works of a Poet, edited by Edith
    Heal.   1958.
Yes, Mrs. Williams: A Personal Record of My Mother.   1959.
Imaginations: Collected Early Prose, edited by Webster Schott.   1970.
The Embodiment of Knowledge, edited by Ron Loewinsohn.   1974.
Interviews with Williams: Speaking Straight Ahead, edited by Linda W.
    Wagner.   1976.

Translator, *Last Nights of Paris*, by Philippe Soupault.   1929.
Translator, with Raquel Hélène Williams, *The Dog and the Fever*, by Francisco de
    Quevedo.   1954.

Bibliography: *Bibliography of Williams* by Emily Mitchell Wallace, 1968.

Reading List: *Williams* by Vivienne Koch, 1950; *Williams: A Critical Study* by John
Malcolm Brinnin, 1963; *The Poems of Williams*, 1964, and *The Prose of Williams*, 1970, both
by Linda W. Wagner; *The Poetic World of Williams* by Alan Ostrom, 1966; *Williams: A
Collection of Critical Essays* edited by J. Hillis Miller, 1966; *An Approach to Paterson* by
Walter Peter Scott, 1967; *The Music of Survival* by Sherman Paul, 1968; *Williams: The
American Background* by Mike Weaver, 1971; *The Inverted Bell: Modernism and the
Counterpoetics of Williams* by Joseph N. Riddell, 1974; *Williams: The Knack of Survival in
America* by Robert Coles, 1975; *Williams: Poet from Jersey* by Reed Whittemore, 1975.

*   *   *

William Carlos Williams is one of the leading figures of American modernist poetry
whose recent recognition critically supports the impact his poems and fiction had throughout
the modern and contemporary periods. Williams was a writer's writer in that his reputation
existed chiefly among other writers – Ezra Pound, H. D., Marianne Moore, Hart Crane,
Wallace Stevens, John Dos Passos, Ernest Hemingway – at least until New Directions began
publishing his work in the late 1930's. Most of Williams's first dozen books were privately
printed or subsidized. Some were collections of poems; others were an innovative mixture of

poetry and prose, or of prose-poem form. Regardless of apparent genre, Williams wrote consistently in a mode based on the rhythms of the speaking voice, complete with idiomatic language, colloquial word choice, organic form and structure, and an intense interest in locale as both setting and subject.

This most American of poets was born of mixed parentage, and part of his fascination with the identification of – even the definition of – the American character may have stemmed from his own feeling of dislocation. His short early poems as well as his collection of essays on American historical figures, *In the American Grain*, present personae and scenes germane to the United States: "a young horse with a green bed-quilt/on his withers shaking his head," "A big young bareheaded woman/in an apron," "Flowers through the window/lavender and yellow//changed by white curtains." The fact that these scenes and characters are presented with neither apology nor psychological justification emphasized the aesthetic position that the thing was its own justification. Whether echoing James Dewey, Henri Bergson, or William James, Williams's innate pragmatism led him to a concentration on the unadorned image (as a means to universal understanding, truth) that opened many new directions in modern poetry. Williams did not use the image as symbol, a substitute for a larger idea; he was content to rest with the assumption that the reader could duplicate his own sense of importance for the red wheelbarrows and green glass between hospital walls, and thereby dismiss the equivocation of symbolism. As he said so succinctly in *Paterson*, "no ideas but in things."

Allied with the notion of presentation was the corollary that the author was to be as invisible as possible, so as not to dilute the effect of the concrete object or character. Not until his later poems did Williams change that tenet, but the strikingly personal "The Desert Music" and "Asphodel, That Greeny Flower" benefit from his use of a more personal stance toward the materials. Through the writing of his five-book epic poem, *Paterson*, through the 1940's to 1958, Williams was moving toward a kind of self-revelation, albeit unevenly. The epic concerns a poet-doctor-city persona named Paterson, tracing some events of the poet-doctor's life through an intense juxtaposition of scene, image, and memory. The technique of placing one image or scene against another, often without verbal transition, resembled the montage effect in the art contemporary with Williams; troubling as it was to his readers thirty years ago, it became the *modus operandi* for many contemporary writers, a way of increasing speed, of covering more images and sources of imagery, in the context of a rapidly-moving poem.

Williams established many new principles in the writing of his poetry – his confidence that the common American was an apt source of character, his joy in re-creating natural speech, his experimentation with a structure and line that would allow the flexible and fluid pace of speech to be presented – but his prose was also influential. From the 1923 *Spring and All*, when he combined aesthetic theory with such famous poems as "The Red Wheelbarrow," "To Elsie," and "At the Ballgame," to the trilogy of a family establishing itself in American business culture (the Stetchers in *White Mule, In the Money*, and *The Build-Up*), Williams turned away from the established conventions in order to present sharply, idiomatically, the gist of his drama. Much of his prose is carried through dialogue that makes Hemingway's seem contrived and redundant; most of his fiction has no ostensible plot. Moving as far from artifice as possible, his prose was criticized repeatedly for being artless; but contemporary readers have found the organic emphasis on language-structure-character an important direction for their own writing. "The Burden of Loveliness," "Jean Beicke," "The Use of Force" are stories often anthologized, provocative in their presentation of convincing characters whose human conditions proceed without drama, but – in Williams's handling – always with sympathy.

That Williams was a practicing physician until the mid 1950's adds some interest to his use of apparently real people in his fiction and poetry. The authenticity of his knowledge about people is undeniable, and he speaks movingly in his autobiography about the reciprocity between being a doctor (a pediatrician by specialization, but a general practitioner for all intents) and a writer. Working from insights that a more reclusive person might not have had, Williams was able to portray accurately many elements of the American culture that had not been treated in the literature of the twentieth century (Eliot's Prufrock would not have come to Williams's New Jersey office). Disturbed as he often was about his lack of time to write, he nevertheless acknowledged that his busy life was a rich one; and his writing after his retirement (a condition which occurred chiefly because of a severe stroke) frequently returned to subjects and characters from that more active life. The stories about Williams's writing during his rushed days as physician are apocryphal: pulling his car off the road while on his way to make a house call so that he could scribble a poem on a prescription blank; equipping his office desk with a hidden typewriter so that he could flip the machine in place between patients. His production as writer in the midst of his full days as doctor is amazing, but what made that production possible was his personal intent: he considered himself primarily a poet; his aim and direction in life were toward success in writing. No hurried schedule could prevent his implementing that dream.

Williams's poems are not all affirmative pictures of American character and scene; in fact, much of his writing during the 1930's and 1940's is bleak and despairing, and the early books of *Paterson* reflect that disillusionment with what had earlier appeared to be inexhaustible American promise. The late books of *Paterson*, however, supply Williams's own hard-won answers: love, even if foolhardy; virtue; knowing oneself; doing what one can; creating. These are hardly new answers, but their lack of innovation does not lessen their impact. Like Dante traveling through the Inferno, Paterson-Williams takes us into blind alleys (his poems are realistic because we see wrong answers as well as right ones, and sometimes no answers at all), only to move up through Limbo to a kind of modern-day heaven, a place with the answers at least implied in passages like :

> Through this hole
> at the bottom of the cavern
> of death, the imagination
> escapes intact.
> It is the imagination
> which cannot be fathomed.
> It is through this hole
> we escape....

From this resolution, it is only a step to the gentle poise of the last poems. One of the most striking poems of his Pulitzer prize-winning book, *Pictures from Brueghel*, is "Asphodel," the love poem to his wife of nearly fifty years, which speaks of "love, abiding love." "Death/is not the end of it," Williams writes, comparing love to "a garden which expands ... a love engendering/gentleness and goodness." Williams contrasts the quiet assurance of this love with "Waste, waste!/dominates the world. It is the bomb's work." And his love is broadened to include his total response to life, as he declares proudly toward the end of the poem:

> Only the imagination is real!
>   I have declared it
>   time without end.
> If a man die
>   it is because death
>   has first
> possessed his imagination....
>
> But love and the imagination
>   are of a piece
>   swift as the light
> to avoid destruction....

Williams's impact on modern American poetics might appear to have been largely technical, for all the discussion of his use of the local, the triadic line, the idiom; but in the last analysis readers and fellow writers probably respond as well to the pervasive optimism of the doctor-poet's view, and to the openness with which he shared his life and his reactions with his readers. One may forget the rationale for Williams's triadic line division; but one does not forget his candor and his affirmation.

—Linda W. Wagner

WILSON, Edmund. American. Born in Red Bank, New Jersey, 8 May 1895. Educated at Hill School, Pottstown, Pennsylvania, 1909–12; Princeton University, New Jersey, 1912–16, A.B. 1916. Served in the United States Army, in the Intelligence Corps, 1917–19. Married 1) Mary Blair in 1923; 2) Margaret Candy in 1930; 3) Mary McCarthy, *q.v.*, in 1938; 4) Elena Thornton in 1946; three children. Reporter, *New York Evening Sun*, 1916–17; Managing Editor, *Vanity Fair*, New York, 1920–21; Associate Editor, *New Republic*, New York, 1926–31; Book Reviewer, *The New Yorker*, 1944–48, and occasionally thereafter. Recipient: Guggenheim Fellowship, 1935; National Institute of Arts and Letters Gold Medal, for non-fiction, 1955; Presidential Medal of Freedom, 1963; Edward MacDowell Medal, 1964; Emerson-Thoreau Medal, 1966; National Book Committee's National Medal for Literature, 1966; Aspen Award, 1968. *Died 12 June 1972.*

PUBLICATIONS

Collections

Letters on Literature and Politics 1912–1972, edited by Elena Wilson. 1977.
A Wilson Celebration, edited by John Wain. 1978.

Fiction

I Thought of Daisy. 1929; revised edition, with *Galahad*, 1957.
Memoirs of Hecate County (stories). 1946; revised edition, 1958.
Galahad, with I Thought of Daisy. 1957.

Plays

The Evil Eye: A Musical Comedy, lyrics by F. Scott Fitzgerald (produced 1915).
The Crime in the Whistler Room (produced 1924). In *This Room and This Gin and These Sandwiches*, 1937.
Discordant Encounters: Plays and Dialogues. 1926.

This Room and This Gin and These Sandwiches: Three Plays (includes *The Crime in the Whistler Room, A Winter in Beech Street,* and *Beppo and Beth*).   1937.

The Little Blue Light (produced 1950).   1950.

Five Plays: Cyprian's Prayer, The Crime in the Whistler Room, This Room and This Gin and These Sandwiches, Beppo and Beth, The Little Blue Light.   1954.

The Duke of Palermo and Other Plays, with an Open Letter to Mike Nichols (includes *Dr. McGrath* and *Osbert's Career; or, The Poet's Progress*).   1969.

Verse

The Undertaker's Garland, with John Peale Bishop.   1922.

Poets, Farewell! (poems and essays).   1929.

Note-Books of Night (poems, essays and stories).   1942.

Three Reliques of Ancient Western Poetry Collected by Wilson from the Ruins.   1951.

Wilson's Christmas Stocking: Fun for Young and Old.   1953.

A Christmas Delerium.   1955.

Night Thoughts.   1961.

Holiday Greetings 1966.   1966.

Other

Axel's Castle: A Study in the Imaginative Literature of 1870–1930.   1931.

The American Jitters: A Year of the Slump (essays).   1932; as *Devil Take the Hindmost,* 1932.

Travels in Two Democracies (dialogues, essays, and story).   1936.

The Triple Thinkers: Ten Essays on Literature.   1938; augmented edition, as *The Triple Thinkers: Twelve Essays on Literary Subjects,* 1948.

To the Finland Station: A Study in the Writing and Acting of History.   1940.

The Boys in the Back Room: Notes on California Novelists.   1941.

The Wound and the Bow: Seven Studies in Literature.   1941.

Europe Without Baedeker: Sketches among the Ruins of Italy, Greece, and England.   1947; revised edition, 1966.

Classics and Commercials: A Literary Chronicle of the Forties.   1950.

The Shores of Light: A Literary Chronicle of the Twenties and Thirties.   1952.

The Scrolls from the Dead Sea.   1955; revised edition, as *The Dead Sea Scrolls 1947–1969,* 1969.

Red, Black, Blond, and Olive: Studies in Four Civilizations: Zuñi, Haiti, Soviet Russia, Israel.   1956.

A Piece of My Mind: Reflections at Sixty.   1956.

The American Earthquake: A Documentary of the Twenties and Thirties.   1958.

Apologies to the Iroquois.   1960.

Patriotic Gore: Studies in the Literature of the American Civil War.   1962.

The Cold War and the Income Tax: A Protest.   1963.

The Bit Between My Teeth: A Literary Chronicle of 1950–1965.   1965.

O Canada: An American's Notes on Canadian Culture.   1965.

A Prelude: Landscapes, Characters and Conversations from the Earlier Years of My Life.   1967.

The Fruits of the MLA.   1968.

Upstate: Records and Recollections of Northern New York.   1971.

A Window on Russia for the Use of Foreign Readers.   1972.

The Devils and Canon Barham: Ten Essays on Poets, Novelists, and Monsters.   1973.

The Twenties: From Notebooks and Diaries of the Period, edited by Leon Edel.   1975.

Israel, and The Dead Sea Scrolls.   1978.

Editor, *The Last Tycoon: An Unfinished Novel by F. Scott Fitzgerald, Together with The Great Gatsby and Selected Stories.*   1941.
Editor, *The Shock of Recognition: The Development of Literature in the United States Recorded by the Men Who Made It.*   1943; enlarged edition, 1955.
Editor, *The Crack-Up: With Other Uncollected Pieces, Note-Books and Unpublished Letters,* by F. Scott Fitzgerald.   1945.
Editor, *The Collected Essays of John Peale Bishop.*   1948.
Editor, *Peasants and Other Stories,* by Chekhov.   1956.

Bibliography: *Wilson: A Bibliography* by Richard David Ramsey, 1971.

Reading List: *Wilson: A Study of the Literary Vocation in Our Time* by Sherman Paul, 1965; *Wilson* by Warner Berthoff, 1968; *Wilson* by Charles P. Frank, 1970; *Wilson* by Leonard Kriegel, 1971.

*   *   *

Edmund Wilson is a kind of American equivalent to Cyril Connolly, a critic who is learned (Wilson was influenced at Princeton, by his French Professor, Christian Gauss) but prefers high journalism to academic teaching as his medium, and whose deliberately easy, witty, and colloquial style disguises his learning. He was the critic to whom writers of his time turned for both advice and friendship, and his correspondence shows both his frankness and his generosity with his advice and his time. Occasionally, perhaps, his friendship with other writers – as with Edna St. Vincent Millay, with whom in his youth he was in love – may have a little softened his critical judgment, but only very rarely. Of his many books of critical essays, *Axel's Castle* (the first clear introduction in the title essay to French Symbolism and its influence on great modern poets), *The Triple Thinkers*, and *The Wound and the Bow* are the deepest and most distinguished, but collections of his shorter pieces, largely written for *The New Yorker*, like *Classics and Commercials*, make perhaps even racier reading. His excellent book on the origins of the Russian Revolution, *To the Finland Station*, reflects an interest in Marxism that did not last.

He wrote minor but sometimes witty verses, and one of his two works of fiction, *I Thought of Daisy*, has a wit, a warmth, and an evocation both of the character of the heroine and of the older Bohemian world of New York that make it a novel one frequently re-reads. An anthology of responses to great American writers by their great contemporaries, *The Shock of Recognition*, is indispensable to any student of American literature. What one remembers most, however, of Wilson (whose interests stretched to the Dead Sea Scrolls, to read which he learned Hebrew in middle age, and the plight of the American Indian) is less any single book than a personality which combined a startling honesty, a rather frightening tartness, and a great generosity of spirit.

—G. S. Fraser

WINTERS, (Arthur) Yvor. American. Born in Chicago, Illinois, 17 October 1900. Educated at the University of Chicago, 1917–18; University of Colorado, Boulder, B.A., M.A. 1925; Stanford University, California, Ph.D. 1935. Married the writer Janet Lewis in 1926; one son and one daughter. Instructor in French and Spanish, University of Idaho, Pocatello, 1925–27; Instructor, 1928–37, Assistant Professor, 1937–41, Associate Professor, 1941–49, Professor of English, 1949–51, and Albert Guerard Professor of Literature, 1961–66, Stanford University. Founding Editor, *The Gyroscope*, Los Altos, California, 1929–30; Western Editor, *Hound and Horn*, 1932–34. Fellow, Kenyon School of English, Gambier, Ohio, 1948–50. Recipient: National Institute of Arts and Letters grant, 1952; Brandeis University Creative Arts Award, for poetry, 1959; Harriet Monroe Poetry Award, 1960; Guggenheim Fellowhip, 1961; Bollingen Award, 1961; National Endowment for the Arts grant, 1967. Member, American Academy of Arts and Sciences. *Died 25 January 1968.*

PUBLICATIONS

Verse

> *The Immobile Wind.* 1921.
> *The Magpie's Shadow.* 1922.
> *The Bare Hills.* 1927.
> *The Proof.* 1930.
> *The Journey and Other Poems.* 1931.
> *Before Disaster.* 1934.
> *Poems.* 1940.
> *The Giant Weapon.* 1943.
> *Three Poems.* N.d.
> *To the Holy Spirit.* 1947.
> *Collected Poems.* 1952; revised edition, 1960.
> *The Early Poems.* 1966.

Fiction

> *The Brink of Darkness.* 1932.

Other

> *Notes on the Mechanics of the Poetic Image: The Testament of a Stone.* 1924.
> *The Case of David Lamson: A Summary,* with Frances Theresa Russell. 1934.
> *Primitivism and Decadence: A Study of American Experimental Poetry.* 1937.
> *Maule's Curse: Seven Studies in the History of American Obscurantism.* 1938.
> *The Anatomy of Nonsense.* 1943.
> *Edwin Arlington Robinson.* 1946; revised edition, 1971.
> *In Defense of Reason.* 1947; revised edition, 1960.
> *The Function of Criticism: Problems and Exercises.* 1957.
> *On Modern Poets.* 1959.
> *The Poetry of W. B. Yeats.* 1960.
> *The Poetry of J. V. Cunningham.* 1961.
> *Forms of Discovery: Critical and Historical Essays on the Forms of the Short Poem in English.* 1967.

Uncollected Essays and Reviews, edited by Francis Murphy. 1976.
Hart Crane and Winters: Their Literary Correspondence, edited by Thomas Parkinson. 1978.

Editor, *Twelve Poets of the Pacific.* 1937.
Editor, *Selected Poems,* by Elizabeth Daryush. 1948.
Editor, *Poets of the Pacific, Second Series.* 1949.
Editor, with Kenneth Fields, *Quest for Reality: An Anthology of Short Poems in English.* 1969.

Bibliography: *Winters: A Bibliography* by Kenneth A. Lohf and Eugene P. Sheehy, 1959.

Reading List: *The Complex of Winters' Criticism* by Richard Sexton, 1974; "Winters Rehearsed and Reconsidered" by René Wellek, in *Denver Quarterly 10,* 1975.

*   *   *

The poetry of Yvor Winters falls into two phases, the Imagist phase (1920–28), and the Post-Symbolist phase (1929–68). During the first period Winters was writing markedly cadenced, imagistic free verse under the influence of William Carlos Williams, Ezra Pound, Glenway Wescott, H.D., and American Indian poetry. The influence was technical: that is, Winters learned to write his free verse by studying carefully selected poems he admired by these authors, but his own poems were not merely imitative. He developed a style of his own of great emotional intensity, brilliantly perceptive and even hypersensitive to the point of being hallucinative. The literary and autobiographical background of these early years is described by Winters in his Introduction to *The Early Poems,* in which he states that his philosophical position at that time was solipsistic and deterministic, a position which he later rejected. Some of the most remarkable of these verses are evocative of the life and landscape of New Mexico where Winters was recuperating from tuberculosis. At the same time, Winters was studying the mechanics of the image and how it was most effectively employed not only by the Imagists but by Coleridge, Browning, Hopkins, Robinson, Stevens, Emerson, and the French Symbolists.

In his late twenties Winters became impatient with the limitations of so-called free verse; he began to suspect that he could gain a greater emotional and intellectual range by the employment of the conventional iambic line as it occurs in the heroic couplet, the sonnet, in tetrameter and pentameter quatrains, and in other forms. *The Proof,* though it opens with poems written in the imagist manner, contains in the closing pages a number of verses in traditional iambic meters. The eight poems in *The Journey* are all in heroic couplets which show the influence not only of Dryden and Pope but also of the freely run-over couplets of Charles Churchill. One of the best of these, "On a View of Pasadena from the Hills," was directly influenced by Robert Bridges's 1899 poem in iambic pentameter couplets, "Elegy: The Summer-House on the Mound."

In his early thirties Winters was re-reading the poetry of Bridges, Hardy, Robinson, Stevens, Paul Valéry, and T. Sturge Moore with increasing admiration. All these poets (including Stevens in his best poem, "Sunday Morning") wrote in conventional prosody, a fact which strengthened Winters's conviction that free verse and imagism were temporary aberrations from the main tradition of Anglo-American verse. At this time he was forming the tastes and principles to be found in his critical essays, which were to attract considerably more attention than his poetry. In *Primitivism and Decadence* he analyzed the technical innovations of the "new poetry," and, although he admired a few free verse poems by H.D., Williams, Stevens, and Marianne Moore, he concluded that on the whole the experimentalist movement had been a failure. By the time he was writing the poetry that appeared in *The Giant Weapon* and in the *Collected Poems* of 1952 he had developed his critical theory concerning the nature of poetry, applied in a series of essays eventually published under the titles *In Defense of Reason*, *The Function of Criticism*, and *Forms of Discovery*. The gist of his theory is that a successful poem is a statement in words about human experience which communicates by means of verse – as distinct from prose, which is less precisely rhythmical than verse and therefore less effective in expressing emotion – appropriate feeling motivated by an understanding of the experience. In this kind of poetry full use is made of both the denotative and connotative significance of words. This theory is obviously operating in all the poetry of Winters's mature years.

Late in his career Winters began referring to what he called the post-symbolist style of the best American poetry of the twentieth century. In his essay "Poetic Styles Old and New" (1959), after a discussion of the two major styles of the Renaissance, the plain and the ornamental, he said in describing post-symbolism, "It ought to be possible to embody our sensory experience in our poetry in an efficient way, not as ornament, and with no sacrifice of rational intelligence." Sensory experience communicated by fresh and original imagery charged with rational significance occurs in Winters's best poems from about 1930 on, including "The Slow Pacific Swell" (1931), "Sir Gawaine and the Green Knight" (1937), and "A Summer Commentary" (1938).

A few dominant and closely related themes, explored in Winters's verse from the beginning of his career until the end, give to his work a remarkable coherence and unity. Among these are a recurrent examination of the relationship between the rational mind and the poetic sensibility which may enrich it or destroy it, a theme which derives from his own experience and also from the poetry of T. Sturge Moore. In his earliest verse the sensibility is dominant to the point of rational disintegration, and even as late as 1955 Winters was writing in his "At the San Francisco Airport": "The rain of matter upon sense/Destroys me momently." Achievement of balance between intellect and sensibility is the subject of "A Summer Commentary" and "Sir Gawaine and the Green Knight"; it is implicit in his allegorical poems on Greek subjects such as "Heracles," "Theseus," "Orpheus," and others. His concern with threats to the preservation of one's identity motivated a number of poems on death and the ravages of time, the most powerful of which are "For My Father's Grave," "To the Holy Spirit," "The Cremation," "A Leave-Taking," and "Prayer for My Son."

Winters is considered one of the most intellectual of all American poets. Yet he was keenly alive to the beauties of the sensory world as well as to its dangers. His purpose was "To steep the mind in sense/Yet never lose the aim." Consequently much of his poetry is remarkable for its freshly perceived descriptive detail of the natural world as in "The California Oaks" and "Time and the Garden." Finally it should be noted that Winters is the only twentieth-century poet of consequence who mastered the technique of free verse as practised by the Imagists and then abandoned it for conventional prosody, although he did not abandon what he had learned about the effective use of imagery. His poetry and his criticism present a significant case history of revolution and counter-revolution in modern poetry.

—Donald E. Stanford

WOLFE, Thomas (Clayton).   American.   Born in Asheville, North Carolina, 3 October 1900. Educated at the Orange Street grade school, Asheville, to age 11; North State Fitting School, Asheville, 1912–16; University of North Carolina, Chapel Hill (editor of the college magazine), 1916–20, B.A. 1920; Harvard University, Cambridge, Massachusetts, where he studied playwriting in George Pierce Baker's "47 Workshop", 1920–22, M.A. in English 1922. Instructor in English, Washington Square College, New York University, 1924–30; full-time writer from 1930; made several trips to Europe and lived briefly in London; travelled in the Pacific Northwest, 1938: contracted pneumonia. Recipient: Guggenheim Fellowship, 1930. Member, National Institute of Arts and Letters. *Died 15 September 1938.*

PUBLICATIONS

Collections

The Letters, edited by Elizabeth Nowell.   1956; selection, 1958.
The Wolfe Reader, edited by C. Hugh Holman.   1962.

Fiction

Look Homeward, Angel: A Story of the Buried Life.   1929.
Of Time and the River: A Legend of Man's Hunger in His Youth.   1935.
From Death to Morning (stories).   1935.
The Web and the Rock, edited by Edward C. Aswell.   1939.
You Can't Go Home Again, edited by Edward C. Aswell.   1940.
The Hills Beyond (stories), edited by Edward C. Aswell.   1941.
The Short Novels, edited by C. Hugh Holman.   1961.

Plays

The Return of Buck Gavin (produced 1919).   In *Carolina Folk-Plays,* second series, 1924.
The Third Night (produced 1919).   In *The Carolina Play Book,* September 1938.
Welcome to Our City (produced 1923).
Gentlemen of the Press (produced 1928).   1942.
Mannerhouse.   1948.

Verse

A Stone, A Leaf, A Door: Poems, edited by John S. Barnes.   1945.

Other

The Crisis in Industry.   1919.
The Story of a Novel.   1936.
A Note on Experts: Dexter Vespasian Joyner.   1939.
Letters to His Mother, Julia Elizabeth Wolfe, edited by John S. Terry.   1943.
The Years of Wandering in Many Lands and Cities.   1949.
A Western Journal: A Daily Log of the Great Parks Trip, June 20–July 2, 1938.   1951.
Wolfe's Purdue Speech, "Writing and Living," edited by William Braswell and Leslie A. Field.   1964.

The Letters to His Mother, Newly Edited from the Original Manuscripts, edited by C.
   Hugh Holman and Sue Fields Ross.   1968.
The Notebooks, edited by Richard S. Kennedy and Paschal Reeves.   2 vols., 1970.
The Mountains, edited by Pat M. Ryan.   1970.

Bibliography: *Of Time and Thomas Wolfe: A Bibliography with a Character Index*, 1959, and
Wolfe: A Checklist, 1970, both by Elmer D. Johnson.

Reading List: *Wolfe: A Critical Study* by Pamela Hansford Johnson, 1947, as *Hungry
Gulliver: An English Critical Appraisal of Wolfe*, 1948; *Wolfe: The Weather of His Youth* by
Louis D. Rubin, Jr., 1955, and *Wolfe: A Collection of Critical Essays* edited by Rubin, 1973;
Wolfe by Elizabeth Nowell, 1960; *Wolfe*, 1960, and *The Loneliness at the Core: Studies in
Wolfe*, 1975, both by C. Hugh Holman, and *The World of Wolfe* edited by Holman, 1962;
The Window of Memory: The Literary Career of Wolfe by Richard S. Kennedy, 1962; *Wolfe's
Albatross: Race and Nationality in America* by Paschal Reeves, 1969.

*   *   *

With the publication in 1929 of *Look Homeward, Angel*, American fiction was invested
with a fresh talent quite unlike that of any writer of the past. On its narrative level, it was a
story of maturation, covering the first twenty years in the life of a youth in conflict with his
family and his small North Carolina town, but it was no novel in the usual sense, but a loose
chronicle held together with an assemblage of some of the most memorable characters in
fiction. Noticeable throughout were vestiges of thwarted careers in playwriting and poetry
which Wolfe would have preferred. Availing himself of the titanism then permitted in
American fiction, and gifted with a Proustian power of nearly total recall of sights and
sounds, Wolfe lacquered the narrative of *Look Homeward, Angel* with dithyrambic
luxuriance and a sensuous Whitmanian prose, twisting easily from the rhetorical to the
dramatic. At his command, too, was a bent for caricature, even burlesque, and satire. His
comic exaggeration in depicting characters was never understood by those acquainted with
the models on whom they were based. Symbols – the angel, the ghost, trains, mountains, and
those images in the haunting refrain "a stone, a leaf, an unfound door" – underscored
Wolfe's intent in characterization and meaning.

   Its sequel, *Of Time and the River*, took Wolfe's autobiographical hero, Eugene Gant, to
Harvard, New York, and Europe. For his thesis, Wolfe appropriated the Joycean wanderer's
search for the father, and imposed an epic framework upon the narrative by intoning names
from famous Greek legends. In such a novel as this, Wolfe became, according to one ecstatic
comment, "our closest approach to Homer." Allied with the search for the father was an
attempt to discover America's greatness through the intensity of one man's experience, and to
reveal to Americans as totally as possible the loneliness and transiency of their lives. In order
to accomplish this, the hero was provided with a Faustian hunger, an obsessive and
unquenchable desire for achievement and knowledge. There must be, he proclaimed, "*never*
an end to curiosity! ... I must think. I must mix it all with myself and with America." *The
Story of a Novel*, Wolfe's confessional monograph of how *Of Time and the River* was written,
tells of a "great black cloud" within him which poured forth "a torrential and ungovernable
flood" about "night and darkness in America." The result was a novel of apparent
formlessness, but it was an intentional formlessness, symbolically parallel to the formlessness
of life itself and of his native land.

   Though Wolfe's second book was a great success, so sensitive was he to charges of
excessive emotional energy and lyricism that for his third, *The Web and the Rock*, he
promised to write an "objective" account of his hero, now named George Webber. Webber
was given a somewhat different background and young manhood, but in midstream Webber
took on the familiar traits of Eugene Gant – that is to say, Thomas Wolfe himself. A love*

affair with a woman much older than Webber led directly into *You Can't Go Home Again*, by the end of which Wolfe's promise of objectivity was realized, his understanding of social problems effected, and his transformation completed: from romantic egocentricity to a clearer vision of the realities of life, from chaos to order, from uncertainty to assurance, from self, in short, to mankind. In the development of a social consciousness, Wolfe's hero was propelled into a rejection of a number of youthful ambitions. No longer sufficient were success and fame and romantic love; of ultimate primacy was one's belief "that America and the people in it are deathless, undiscovered, and immortal, and must live."

After the publication of his first novel, Wolfe had only nine years to finish his writing. Since he was resolved on a one-man vision of life, everything was part of the "single" book, including his early plays, two volumes of *Letters*, his *Notebooks*, two collections of short stories, the excerpts and essays, and *A Western Journal*. That he produced such an abundance in so short a time was due to a compulsion to write almost continuously. He rarely took vacations, was annoyed by intrusions, and was committed wholly to his "work," as he called it. It has been argued that Wolfe should be read in isolated segments, as tone poems perhaps, or as short novels where his control can easily be observed. His books, according to another view, were rather a "fictional thesaurus," composed of many diverse elements – theatrical dialogue, choral ode, essay, travelogue, biography, oratory, lyric poetry, dramatic episode. Though his four major books were no more autobiographical than many single works by Melville and Twain, Fitzgerald and Hemingway, his persistent chronological continuum affronted some readers and critics in a way the practices of other novelists had not.

As an American writer – and he may turn out to be the most American writer – Wolfe was in the tradition of Emerson, Thoreau, Melville, Twain, Dreiser, Sandburg, and Sherwood Anderson. He shared the idealism of Jefferson and Whitman, especially in their projection of the American Dream in which lay the hopes of young men and women everywhere to do the best that was within them to do. His pages were often a sheer symbolic poetry of time and the river, of the web and the rock. Yet his greatest attainment was a fiction of scenes and characters remarkably vital, bountiful, and rich.

—Richard Walser

WRIGHT, Richard (Nathaniel).   American.   Born near Natchez, Mississippi, 4 September 1908; brought up in an orphanage. Educated in local schools through junior high school. Married 1) Rose Dhima Meadman in 1938; 2) Ellen Poplar; two daughters. Worked in the post office in Memphis, Tennessee, at age 15; later moved to New York; worked for the Federal Writers Project, and the Federal Negro Theatre Project; member of the Communist Party, 1932–44; Harlem Editor, *Daily Worker*, New York; lived in Paris from 1947. Recipient: Guggenheim Fellowship, 1939; Spingarn Medal, 1941. *Died 28 November 1960.*

PUBLICATIONS

Collections

The Wright Reader, edited by Ellen Wright and Michel Fabre.   1978.

Fiction

Uncle Tom's Children: Four Novellas.   1938; augmented edition, 1940.
Native Son.   1940.
The Outsider.   1953.
Savage Holiday.   1954.
The Long Dream.   1958.
Eight Men (stories).   1961.
Lawd Today.   1963.
The Man Who Lived Underground (story; bilingual edition), translated by Claude
    Edmonde Magny, edited by Michel Fabre.   1971.

Plays

Native Son (The Biography of a Young American), with Paul Green, from the novel by
    Wright (produced 1941).   1941.
Daddy Goodness, from a play by Louis Sapin (produced 1968).

Screenplay: Native Son, 1951.

Other

How Bigger Was Born: The Story of "Native Son."   1940.
The Negro and Parkway Community House.   1941.
Black Boy: A Record of Childhood and Youth.   1945.
12 Million Black Voices: A Folk History of the Negro in the United States.   1941.
Black Power: A Record of Reactions in a Land of Pathos.   1954.
Bandoeng: 1.500.000.000 Hommes, translated by Helene Claireau.   1955; as The Color
    Curtain: A Report on the Bandung Conference, 1956.
Pagan Spain.   1956.
White Man, Listen!   1957.
Letters to Joe C. Brown, edited by Thomas Knipp.   1968.
American Hunger (autobiography).   1977.

Bibliography: "A Bibliography of Wright's Words" by Michel Fabre and Edward Margolies,
in New Letters 38, Winter 1971; "Wright: An Essay in Bibliography" by John M. Reilly, in
Resources for American Literary Study, Autumn 1971.

Reading List: Wright by Constance Webb, 1968; The Art of Wright by Edward Margolies,
1969; The Most Native of Sons (biography) by John A. Williams, 1970; The Emergence of
Wright: A Study of Literature and Society by Keneth Kinnamon, 1972; Wright by David
Bakish, 1973; The Unfinished Quest of Wright by Michel Fabre, translated by Isabel Barzun,
1973 (includes bibliography); Wright: Impressions and Perspectives edited by David Ray and
R. M. Farnsworth, 1973.

*   *   *

Richard Wright's career can be described in terms of three reputations he has earned: the
realist protesting racial oppression, the typifier of the experience of entry into modern history,
and the author who makes his themes seem inevitable by the power of artistic craft. In the
best recent criticism these three reputations coalesce, appearing as the figure of different levels

of significance to be found in his writing; but while he was alive the fact of his race and his dissent from the culture of his native land, first as radical, then as expatriate, concentrated attention upon the thematic burden of his works.

Wright served a literary apprenticeship made harsh because of his poverty and the restrictions of Jim Crow but otherwise similar to other American authors'; yet he seemed to leap into literary prominence when his collection of stories, *Uncle Tom's Children*, won first prize in a contest sponsored by *Story* magazine for writers on the Federal Writers Project. The four novellas in that volume are arranged to depict the struggles of Southern black peasants in resistance to a caste system dependent upon lynch violence for its sanction and efficacy. For most reviewers the book was a shocking rendition of the facts of racial conflict in affecting narrative, its distinction not so much that the author was black, though reviews made as much of that as they did of the prize the book had won, but rather that *Uncle Tom's Children* told its stories from within the black experience. The book brought news that blacks could effectively articulate their victimization.

As though to match horror with horror, Wright's first published novel, *Native Son*, carried the story of racial conflict to the North where Bigger Thomas, Chicago-born and bred, acts out his role in the American racial drama by his murder of a white woman. At the risk of fulfilling racist expectations in his portrayal of Bigger, Wright completed his inversion of the stereotype of the black victim by showing violence as the necessary prelude to self-realization for his protagonist. Again Wright had written a book that brought news to its audience; *Native Son* was a cautionary tale for whites.

With the popular success of *Native Son* Wright became a public figure called upon to lecture and write as a spokesman for the American Negro. He was qualified for the role not only by literary success but also by a childhood in Mississippi and an adulthood in northern cities similar in pattern to the life of thousands of other black migrants, so it was appropriate that he organize that experience in literature: first with *12 Million Black Voices*, a documentary history of black peasants transplanted into urban life told in the poetic prose of a collective first person narration, and then with his own autobiography, *Black Boy*.

It is unusual for a person not yet forty to write an autobiography and to end the story even before he had established himself in adulthood, but Wright justifies his book by presenting it as at once his own and his people's story. For many other blacks this latter point was dubious. They charged that he had been extremely selective by omitting any positive portrayal of black cultural and family life. The point has merit, but *Black Boy* enhanced Wright's reputation as the realist who showed more profoundly than anyone before him the human waste that is the heritage of North American slavery.

There can be no doubt Wright felt personally threatened by racism in a way that literary success could not ameliorate. It was the motive for his move to Paris in 1947. Though objectively different, Wright's experience in the Communist Party (described in a portion of the original manuscript of *Black Boy*, cut from the book on advice of editors, published separately in 1944, and issued in the excised section of autobiography titled *American Hunger* in 1977) seems to have been psychologically as problematic as racism, so that when he exiled himself from America he was also without the political committment that had informed his work until 1944.

The first book he wrote in exile augmented Wright's second reputation. *The Outsider* portentously invites reading as philosophical fiction. Cross Damon seizes upon the accident of a false report of his death to embark upon a life free of contingency, where action is self-sanctioned and alienation grants perception of mankind in a world of dead myths. Cross, however, can neither escape anguish nor achieve disalienation in his version of freedom. In that respect his problem reflects the author's. Wright described himself in publicity for the novel as a man without ideological burdens for the first time in his life, but his own characteristic feeling of alienation produced an interesting novel undermined by its nihilism.

Wright needed new premises for his writing and found them in the Third World. The four non-fictional books he published from 1954 to 1957 derive from Wright's belief that his own experience was being repeated in the history of Africans and Asians moving from a preindustrial, traditional society into a modern, mass world. On the assumption of this congruity he wrote the accounts of Ghana, the Bandung Conference, Spain – which represented the world not yet touched by modernism – and the lectures published as *White Man, Listen!* All blend reportage and subjective response to show Richard Wright looking at, feeling with the world in change, and defining himself again as typical, though this time on a world-wide stage.

Wright's exile has sometimes been described as though it were the fag end of his career. In fact, it was a creative period twice as long as he had in the United States. Besides his non-fictional reports, he published three novels and compiled a collection of short stories, issued posthumously. *Savage Holiday* extends Wright's interest in extreme narrative situations to the plight of a white man trapped by psychosis and an accidental death for which he feels responsible. *The Long Dream*, meant to open a trilogy tracing the movement of a young man from Mississippi into life in Europe, is a tightly written *bildungsroman* neatly synthesizing Wright's conception of the psychological trauma of social experience in the person of "Fish" Tucker.

None of Wright's exile writings, however, received the critical or popular acclaim of his first works. There may be a variety of explanations for this, besides the possibility of their lesser quality, but a leading reason for the slump in his popular reputation must be that he no longer wrote as the realistic bringer of news about America and that his performance in the role of typifier of modern life had less authority than the writing by acknowledged "experts." Nevertheless, the exile works alert us to the importance of Wright as an artist.

Examining *The Outsider* and *Savage Holiday*, for instance, we find that their structures are inversions and parodies of the thriller genre, that the expressionistic parable "The Man Who Lived Underground," as well as the stories in *Eight Men*, include experiments in narrative stripped down to bare dialogue. Intrigued by these findings, we return to the early writings and find that they, too, are constructed so that transgression of the conventions of genre constitute meaning, with imagery and controlled narrative voice accounting for the impact of such stories as *Native Son* which we read at first without awareness of literary craft, and that the mediations of ideology in *Uncle Tom's Children* and the portrait of the artist in *Black Boy* are masterfully subordinated in character and plot. In short, we complete the survey of Wright's career by recognizing that the themes which won him fame as a realist and attention as an intellectual are the products of art. So, now we are ready to study Richard Wright in earnest.

—John M. Reilly

WYLIE, Elinor (Hoyt).   American.   Born in Somerville, New Jersey, 7 September 1885; brought up in Philadelphia and Washington, D.C. Educated at Miss Baldwin's School, Bryn Mawr, and Holton Arms School, Washington, D.C. Married Philip Hichborn in 1905 (died, 1911), one son; left her husband to elope with Horace Wylie, 1910, and moved to England with him as Mr. and Mrs. Waring; returned to the United States after Wylie's divorce, 1915, and married him, 1916 (divorced, 1923); moved to New York in 1921, and became a prominent figure in New York literary circles; married the poet William Rose Benét, *q.v.*, in 1923; thereafter lived in New York and London; Poetry Editor of *Vanity Fair*, New York, 1923–25; Editor, Literary Guild, New York, 1926–28. Recipient: Julia Ellsworth Ford Prize, 1921. *Died 16 December 1928.*

PUBLICATIONS

Collections

Collected Poems, Collected Prose, edited by William Rose Benét.   2 vols., 1932–33.

Verse

Incidental Numbers.   1912.
Nets to Catch the Wind.   1921.
Black Armour.   1923.
(Poems), edited by Laurence Jordan.   1926.
Trivial Breath.   1928.
Angels and Earthly Creatures: A Sequence of Sonnets.   1928.
Angels and Earthly Creatures (collection).   1929.
Nadir.   1937.
Last Poems, edited by Jane D. Wise.   1943.

Fiction

Jennifer Lorn: A Sedate Extravaganza.   1923.
The Venetian Glass Nephew.   1925.
The Orphan Angel.   1926; as *Mortal Image,* 1927.
Mr. Hodge and Mr. Hazard.   1928.

Reading List: *Wylie: The Portrait of an Unknown Lady* by Nancy Hoyt, 1935; *Wylie* by Thomas A. Gray, 1969.

*   *   *

Elinor Wylie's prestigious social background, striking personality, beauty, elegance, and conversational gifts, with the romantic aura of her daring break with conventional society when she eloped with Horace Wylie, made her a symbolic figure to many persons caught up in the "American poetic renaissance." Consequently, judgments of her writings were for some years infused with feelings about the writer. Thomas Gray's monograph of 1969 discusses widely differing views of her achievement.

In the essay "Jewelled Bindings" (1923), Wylie saw herself and a few other contemporary lyric poets as "enchanted by a midas-touch or a colder silver madness into workers in metal and glass ... in crisp and sharp-edged forms." They choose "short lines, clear small stanzas, brilliant and compact." Such standards produced her most widely known poems: the 3-quatrain "Let No Charitable Hope" that climaxes with "In masks outrageous and austere/ The years go by in single file;/But none has merited my fear,/And none has quite escaped my smile"; "The Eagle and the Mole," with its fastidious trimeter: "Avoid the reeking herd ..."; the art-for-art's-sake poem "Say not of Beauty she is good,/Or aught but beautiful"; and the exquisite "Velvet Shoes": "Let us walk in the white snow/In a soundless space...."

This preference for the delicately sensuous or even impalpable characterized many of her poems – "I love the look, austere, immaculate,/Of landscapes drawn in pearly monotones" – and her first two "novels." *Jennifer Lorn: A Sedate Extravaganza* appealed to a public that was seeking relief from the ugly realities. Set in the late 18th century in the realms of aristocracy and wealth in England and India, it is a long catalogue of lovely, delicate objects;

what plot it has concerns the fragile, fainting Jennifer and – the spine of the story – her husband Gerald, the exact, cool aesthete. It has been compared to a tapestry, and among the *mille fleurs* are many phrases and lines from 18th-century literature. Wylie's wide reading in this period showed itself also in the amusing *Venetian Glass Nephew*. Her long and perhaps abnormal admiration for Shelley brought about *The Orphan Angel*, in which the libertarian poet is rescued from drowning and accompanies a Yankee sailor to America and across the continent. This trend toward more realistic treatment continued in *Mr. Hodge and Mr. Hazard*, a satirical allegory on the stifling of the late romantics by the Victorians.

Mary Colum, who ranks Wylie as "one of the few important women poets in any literature," observes, "She seemed to write little out of a mood or out of a passing emotion ... but nearly always out of complex thought...." (*Life and the Dream*, 1947). Many found her poems cold; the fastidious speaker seeks isolation and death. A last group of sonnets, however, shows a capacity for love: "And so forget to weep, forget to grieve,/ And wake, and touch each other's hands, and turn/Upon a bed of juniper and fern." H. Lüdecke (in *English Studies 20*, December 1938) finds her not a "great" poet but a "rare" poet: "Refinement is her essential characteristic as an artist."

—Alice R. Bensen

YERBY, Frank (Garvin). American. Born in Augusta, Georgia, 5 September 1916. Educated at Paine College, Augusta, A.B. 1937; Fisk University, Nashville, Tennessee, M.A. 1938; University of Chicago, 1939. Married 1) Flora Helen Claire Williams in 1941 (divorced), two sons and two daughters; 2) Blanca Calle Perez in 1956. Instructor, Florida Agricultural and Mechanical College, Tallahassee, 1938–39, and Southern University and A. and M. College, Baton Rouge, Louisiana, 1939–41; Laboratory Technician, Ford Motor Company, Dearborn, Michigan, 1941–44; Magnaflux Inspector, Ranger (Fairchild) Aircraft, Jamaica, New York, 1944–45; full-time writer from 1945; settled in Madrid, 1954. Recipient: O. Henry Award, 1944.

PUBLICATIONS

Fiction

The Foxes of Harrow.   1946.
The Vixens.   1947.
The Golden Hawk.   1948.
Pride's Castle.   1949.
Floodtide.   1950.
A Woman Called Fancy.   1951.
The Saracen Blade.   1952.
The Devil's Laughter.   1953.
Benton's Row.   1954.

Bride of Liberty. 1954.
The Treasure of Pleasant Valley. 1955.
Captain Rebel. 1956.
Fairoaks. 1957.
The Serpent and the Staff. 1958.
Jarrett's Jade. 1959.
Gillian. 1960.
The Garfield Honor. 1961.
Griffin's Way. 1962.
The Old Gods Laugh: A Modern Romance. 1964.
An Odor of Sanctity. 1965.
Goat Song: A Novel of Ancient Greece. 1968.
Judas, My Brother: The Story of the Thirteenth Disciple. 1968.
Speak Now. 1969.
The Dahomean. 1971; as *The Man from Dahomey,* 1971.
The Girl from Storyville: A Victorian Novel. 1972.
The Voyage Unplanned. 1974.
Tobias and the Angel. 1975.
A Rose for Ana María. 1976.
Hail the Conquering Hero. 1977.

Reading List: *The Unembarrassed Muse* by Russel B. Nye, 1970.

*   *   *

Readers of his many best-selling romances are still amazed to discover that Frank Yerby began his career as a militant writer of black protest fiction. Perhaps a more surprising activity of his early years was his poetry writing. The careful and painstaking construction of sonnets does not seem a practice this supposedly inartistic teller of racy, swashbuckling tales would spend much time on. But Yerby is a writer and a person filled with curious complexities, and the more one studies his career the more one observes a fascinating and paradoxical phenomenon.

His first published short stories in the forties were outspoken and bitter works about the predicament of contemporary black Americans. "Homecoming" (*Common Ground,* 1946) ironically portrays the return to his home in the rural South of a young black veteran who has lost a leg defending democracy. His white neighbors view him as just another uppity nigger too big for his britches, and instead of receiving a hero's welcome he is almost lynched. "Health Card" (*Harper's,* May 1944), another early story, won an O. Henry Award. The work relates the humiliation a black soldier and his wife are forced to face in the South during World War II: it is assumed in the camp town where the protagonist is stationed that any black woman seen with a black man is probably a whore needing a "health card."

Around the time World War II ended, Yerby's life as a writer took a totally unpredictable turn. He had written an apparently realistic novel about black life but no publisher was interested in printing it. And so, according to a very cynical article he wrote for *Harper's* in 1959, he set out quite coolly and rationally to become a popular author. He studied those novels that had high sales over a period of years, and derived from them what almost amounts to a formula to ensure popularity. He would create escapist costume novels containing no dominating social problems. He would construct relatively tightly plotted stories about strong sexy men and vivacious sexy women.

Obviously, few writers who attempt to write racy adventurous novels become best sellers. But Yerby succeeded in an unprecedented fashion. Since his first published novel and first smash popular success, *The Foxes of Harrow,* Yerby has written hit after hit, many of which have been made into films. Around the mid-1950's his very high popularity began to decline, but it is still claimed that he has been on the best-seller lists more times since 1900 than any other American novelist, except for Mary Roberts Rinehart. This achievement seems even more remarkable when it is considered that since the 1960's his novels have rarely been reviewed in the major mass-circulation magazines. The audience he has built up apparently needs no stimulation beyond his books themselves.

The few critics who have taken his work seriously point out that he writes something closer to anti-romance than romance. Both his heroes and heroines are more apt to be cunning opportunists than virtuous aristocrats. The fantasy worlds his characters operate in – the Spanish Main, the Holy Land, the reconstruction South – are rather dirty and unglamorous places as he describes them. Moreover, the frequently restated charge that he has turned his back on his race (in *Anger and Beyond*, for example, Saunders Redding claimed that in ignoring his racial heritage Yerby was revealing "pathological overtones" in his fiction) is absolutely false. In many of his most popular novels, such as *Griffin's Way*, or *A Woman Called Fancy*, Yerby deals quite accurately with the treatment of blacks in the South. Yerby now distinguishes between his serious works (such as *Speak Now*) and his entertainments (practically any of his hits) and claims that in the future he is going to concentrate on the serious work. His distinction seems something of an apologetic defense, however, and perhaps an unnecessary one. For several decades he has been the most popular novelist in America addressing the racial theme.

—Jack B. Moore

ZUKOFSKY, Louis.   American.   Born in New York City, 23 January 1904. Educated at Columbia University, New York, M.A. in English 1924. Married Celia Thaew in 1939; one son. Teacher of English and Comparative Literature, University of Wisconsin, Madison, 1930–31; Visiting Assistant Professor, Colgate University, Hamilton, New York, 1947; Member of the Faculty, 1947–55, and Associate Professor, 1955–66, Polytechnic Institute of Brooklyn, New York. Poet-in-Residence, San Francisco State College, 1958; Guest Professor, Graduate School, University of Connecticut, Storrs, Fall 1971. Recipient: National Endowment for the Arts grant, 1966, 1968. *Died 12 May 1978.*

PUBLICATIONS

Verse

First Half of "A" – 9.   1940.
55 Poems.   1941.
Anew.   1946.
Some Time/Short Poems.   1956.
Barely and Widely.   1958.
"A" 1–12.   1959.

16 Once Published. 1962.
I's, Pronounced "Eyes". 1963.
After I's. 1964.
Found Objects 1962–1926. 1964.
Iyyob. 1965.
All: The Collected Short Poems, 1923–1958. 1965.
"A" Libretto. 1965.
All: The Collected Short Poems, 1956–1964. 1966.
Little: A Fragment for Careenagers. 1967.
"A" – *14.* 1967.
"A" 13–21. 1969.
All: The Collected Shorter Poems, 1923–1964. 1971.
"A" – *24.* 1972.
"A" 22 and 23. 1975.
"A." 1979.

Play

Arise, Arise. 1973.

Fiction

It Was. 1961.
Ferdinand, Including It Was. 1968.
Little. 1970.

Other

Le Style Apollinaire, translated by René Taupin. 1934.
5 Statements for Poetry. 1958.
Bottom: On Shakespeare. 1963.
Prepositions: The Collected Critical Essays. 1967.
Autobiography. 1970.

Editor, *An "Objectivists" Anthology.* 1932.
Editor, *A Test of Poetry.* 1948.

Translator, *Albert Einstein,* by Anton Reiser. 1930.
Translator, with Celia Zukofsky, *Catullus: Fragmenta,* music by Paul Zukofsky. 1969.
Translator, with Celia Zukofsky, *Catullus.* 1969.

Bibliography: *A Bibliography of Zukofsky* by Celia Zukofsky, 1969.

Reading List: *At: Bottom* by Cid Corman, 1966; "Zukofsky Issue" of *Grosseteste Review,* Winter 1970, and of *Maps 5,* 1974; by Peter Quartermain, in *Open Letter Second Series,* Fall 1973; by Barry Ahearn, in *Journal of English Literary History,* Spring 1978.

*   *   *

If William Carlos Williams, by writing about roses as though no-one had written about them before, freed the American language from its heavy dependence on English antecedents and associations, Louis Zukofsky, by stripping words of their meaning or by overloading them so that no single meaning comes through, showed writers like Robert Creeley and Robert Duncan (and others) how to let the movement of words generate a play and discovery of meaning by paying attention to their music so that the language might *sing*. It is a trick he learned from Apollinaire (about whom he wrote a book in 1932) and from Spinoza, who insisted that a thing is said to be free if it "exists by the mere necessity of its own nature and is determined in its actions by itself alone." For Zukofsky, the poem is an object.

Here is one of his poems:

FOR
Four tubas
or
two-by-four's.

Zukofsky's Brooklyn accent emphasises the palindromic echoes of "four tubas" and "tuba-fours"; the aural rhyme of "or" with "four" and the visual rhyme of "or" with the title, and the ambiguity of the apostrophe, all reflect a mind which not only delights in puns but also takes absolutely literally Pound's dictum that poetry is made up of sight, sound, intellection, and rhythm. The complexities of meaning are established through tentative possibilities of relationship which are never fully realised in the poem: the romantic, lyric implications of the title, the mundane quality of the last line, the echoing of the final "by" back to the meaning of the "ba" of the first line, the ambiguity of the prepositions, all of whose meanings have relevance to the structure of a poem which, highly comic yet at the same time moving, draws attention to the neglected minutiae of the language: prepositions, conjunctions, articles. The poetry is in the words, rather than in the ideas.

Thus, in "A," his long poem in 24 movements which explore most traditional verse forms ("A"-7 is a sonnet-cycle, "A"-9 is a double canzone, "A"-21 is a Roman comedy), Zukofsky plays on the possibilities of the indefinite article (as, earlier – in 1926 – he had written "Poem Beginning 'The'") while interweaving personal, political and aesthetic themes round two central figures: Bach and Shakespeare (music and poetry). If themes are stated, they are stated so that they may play against one another ("Words rangeless, melody forced by writing," in "A"-6), and much of the poem's complex play occurs as the result of pitting one specialised vocabulary or context against another – as, in "A"-9, modern physics is pitted against Marx, Cavalcanti, and Spinoza. Similarly, Zukofsky may pit one language against another, as in the opening of "A"-15 (English echoing the Hebrew sound of passages from the Book of Job), or in his "translation" of *Catullus*, where the English, repeating the sound of the Latin, comes to be seen, in its knotted turbulence, from "outside itself." Such work, innovative, difficult, often bewildering, and controversial, has nevertheless been influential: some readers, many of them poets, consider Zukofsky to rank with Pound and Joyce among twentieth-century writers.

—Peter Quartermain

NOTES ON CONTRIBUTORS

ALEXANDER, M. J. Lecturer in English, University of Stirling, Scotland. Author of *The Earliest English Poems*, 1966, and *Beowulf*, 1973. **Essay:** Marianne Moore.

ALLEN, Walter. Novelist and Literary Critic. Author of six novels (the most recent being *All in a Lifetime*, 1959); several critical works, including *Arnold Bennett*, 1948; *Reading a Novel*, 1949 (revised, 1956); *Joyce Cary*, 1953 (revised, 1971); *The English Novel*, 1954; *Six Great Novelists*, 1955; *The Novel Today*, 1955 (revised, 1966); *George Eliot*, 1964; *The Modern Novel in Britain and the United States*, 1964; and travel books, social history, and books for children. Editor of *Writers on Writing*, 1948, and *The Roaring Queen* by Wyndham Lewis, 1973. Has taught at several universities in Britain, the United States, and Canada; past editor of the *New Statesman*. **Essay:** Ring Lardner.

ANDERSON, David D. Professor of American Thought and Language, Michigan State University, East Lansing; Editor of *University College Quarterly* and *Midamerica*. Author of *Louis Bromfield*, 1964; *Critical Studies in American Literature*, 1964; *Sherwood Anderson*, 1967; *Anderson's "Winesburg, Ohio,"* 1967; *Brand Whitlock*, 1968; *Abraham Lincoln*, 1970; *Robert Ingersoll*, 1972; *Woodrow Wilson*, 1975. Editor or Co-Editor of *The Black Experience*, 1969; *The Literary Works of Lincoln*, 1970; *The Dark and Tangled Path*, 1971; *Sunshine and Smoke*, 1971. **Essay:** Louis Bromfield.

ANGLE, James. Assistant Professor of English, Eastern Michigan University, Ypsilanti. Author of verse and fiction in periodicals, and of an article on Edgar Lewis Wallant in *Kansas Quarterly*, Fall 1975. **Essay:** Edward Lewis Wallant.

ASHLEY, Leonard R. N. Professor of English, Brooklyn College, City University of New York. Author of *Colley Cibber*, 1965; *19th-Century British Drama*, 1967; *Authorship and Evidence: A Study of Attribution and the Renaissance Drama*, 1968; *History of the Short Story*, 1968; *George Peele: The Man and His Work*, 1970. Editor of the *Enriched Classics* series, several anthologies of fiction and drama, and a number of facsimile editions. **Essays:** S. N. Behrman; Ludwig Bemelmans; Paddy Chayefsky; George M. Cohan; Moss Hart; George S. Kaufman; George Kelly; Sidney Kingsley; Arthur Laurents; John Howard Lawson; Charles MacArthur.

AUBERT, Alvin. Associate Professor of English, State University of New York, Fredonia; Publisher and Editor of *Obsidian: Black Literature in Review. Author of Against the Blues* (verse), 1972. **Essay:** James Weldon Johnson.

BENSEN, Alice R. Professor Emerita of English, Eastern Michigan University, Ypsilanti. Author of *Rose Macaulay*, 1969. **Essay:** Elinor Wylie.

BLOOM, Lynn Z. Associate Professor of English, University of New Mexico, Albuquerque. Author of *Doctor Spock: Biography of a Conservative Radical*, 1972; *The New Assertive Woman* (with K. Coburn and J. Pearlman), 1975; *Strategies for Composition*, 1979; and of articles, reviews, and poetry in periodicals. Editor, with others, of *Bear, Man, and God: Approaches to Faulkner's The Bear*, 1964 (revised, 1971), and *Symposium*, 1969. **Essay:** Dorothy Parker.

BLOTNER, Joseph. Professor of English, University of Michigan, Ann Arbor. Author of *The Political Novel*, 1955; *The Fiction of J. D. Salinger* (with F. L. Gwynn), 1959; *The Modern American Political Novel, 1900–1960*, 1966; *Faulkner: A Biography*, 2 vols., 1974. Editor of *Faulkner in the University* (with F. L. Gwynn), 1959, and *Faulkner's Library: A Catalogue*, 1964. **Essay:** William Faulkner.

BODE, Walter. Editor in the Chemistry Department, University of California, Berkeley; Assistant Editor of *San Francisco Theatre Magazine*, and free-lance theatre and film critic. **Essays:** Roark Bradford; Ogden Nash; S. J. Perelman.

BRAYBROOKE, Neville. Writer and Editor; contributor to *The Times, T.L.S., Guardian, Saturday Review*, and *Sunday Telegraph*. Editor of the quarterly *The Wind and the Rain*, 1941–51. Author of *This Is London*, 1953; *London Green*, 1959; *London*, 1961; the novel *The Idler*, 1961; the play *The Delicate Investigation*, 1969. Editor of *T. S. Eliot: A Symposium*, 1958; *A Partridge in a Pear Tree: A Celebration for Christmas*, 1960; *Pilgrim of the Future: A Teilhard de Chardin Symposium*, 1966; *The Letters of J. R. Ackerley*, 1975. **Essays:** Djuna Barnes; B. Traven.

BROER, Lawrence R. Associate Professor of English, University of South Florida, Tampa. Author of *Hemingway's Spanish Tragedy*, 1973, and of many essays and reviews in journals. Editor of *Counter Currents*, 1973, and *The Great Escape of the '20's*, 1977, and Co-Editor of *The First Time: Initial Sexual Experiences in Fiction*, 1974. **Essays:** Stephen Vincent Benét; William Rose Benét; Gore Vidal.

BROWN, Ashley. Professor of English, University of South Carolina, Columbia; Contributor to *Sewanee Review, Shenandoah, Southern Review, Spectator*, and other periodicals. Editor of *The Achievement of Wallace Stevens* (with R. S. Haller), 1962, *Modes of Literature* (with John L. Kimmey), 1968, and *Satire: An Anthology* (with Kimmey), 1977. **Essays:** John Peale Bishop; Andrew Lytle; Allen Tate.

BUCCO, Martin. Professor of English, Colorado State University, Fort Collins. Former Assistant Editor, *Western American Literature*. Author of *The Voluntary Tongue* (verse), 1957, *Frank Waters*, 1969, *Wilbur Daniel Steele*, 1972, and of verse, fiction, and criticism in *Colorado State Review, Occident, Studies in the Novel*, and other periodicals. **Essay:** Wilbur Daniel Steele.

CALHOUN, Richard J. Alumni Professor of English, Clemson University, South Carolina; Co-Editor, *South Carolina Review*. Editor of *A Tricentennial Anthology of South Carolina Literature* (with John C. Guilds), 1971, *James Dickey: The Expansive Imagination*, 1973, and *Two Decades of Change* (with E. M. Lander, Jr.), 1975. **Essay:** James Dickey.

CARPENTER, Frederic I. Author of *Emerson and Asia*, 1930; *Emerson Handbook*, 1953; *American Literature and the Dream*, 1955; *Robinson Jeffers*, 1962; *Eugene O'Neill*, 1964; *Laurens van der Post*, 1969. Has taught at the University of Chicago, Harvard University, and the University of California, Berkeley. **Essays:** Robinson Jeffers; Conrad Richter.

CHRISTENSEN, Paul. Assistant Professor of Modern Literature, Texas A. & M. University, College Station. Author of *Old and Lost Rivers* (verse), and *Charles Olson: Call Him Ishmael*, 1978. **Essays:** A. R. Ammons; John Ashbery; John Berryman; Robert Bly; Louise Bogan; Robert Creeley; E. E. Cummings; Stanley Kunitz; Denise Levertov; James Merrill; W. S. Merwin; Frank O'Hara; Charles Olson; Kenneth Rexroth; W. D. Snodgrass; Gary Snyder; John Wheelwright.

CLAIRE, William.   Director of the Washington Office, State University of New York. Founding Editor and Publisher, *Voyages: A National Literary Magazine*, 1967–73. Author of *Publishing in the West: Alan Swallow*, and of two books of verse, *Strange Coherence of Our Dreams* and *From a Southern France Notebook*. Contributor to many periodicals, including *Antioch Review, American Scholar, The Nation, New Republic*, and the *New York Times*. **Essay:** Mark Van Doren.

COHN, Ruby.   Professor of Comparative Drama, University of California, Davis; Editor of *Modern Drama*, and Associate Editor of *Educational Theatre Journal*. Author of *Samuel Beckett: The Comic Gamut*, 1962; *Currents in Contemporary Drama*, 1969; *Edward Albee*, 1970; *Dialogue in American Drama*, 1971; *Back to Beckett*, 1973; *Modern Shakespeare Offshoots*, 1976. **Essays:** Edward Albee; Ed Bullins.

COLMER, John.   Professor of English, University of Adelaide, Australia; General Editor of Studies in Australian Culture. Author of *Coleridge: Critic of Society*, 1959; *Approaches to the Novel*, 1967; *E. M. Forster: "A Passage to India,"* 1967; *Forster: The Personal Voice*, 1975; *Patrick White: "Riders in the Chariot,"* 1977; *Coleridge to "Catch-22": Images of Society*, 1978. **Essay:** Joseph Heller.

CORCORAN, Neil.   Member of the Department of English, University of Sheffield. **Essays:** Conrad Aiken; Robert Lowell; Delmore Schwartz.

COX, Martha Heasley.   Professor of English and Director of the Steinbeck Research Center, San Jose State University, California. Author of *Maxwell Anderson Bibliography*, 1958; *A Reading Approach to College Writing*, 1959 (and later editions); *Writing: Form, Process, Purpose*, 1962; *Image and Value: An Invitation to Literature*, 1966; *Nelson Algren* (with Wayne Chatterton), 1975; and articles on Algren, Anderson, and John Steinbeck. Editor of *Classic American Short Stories*, 1969; Guest Editor of *Steinbeck Quarterly*, Summer 1971, and *San Jose Studies*, November 1975. **Essay:** Nelson Algren.

CROWDER, Richard H.   Professor Emeritus of English, Purdue University, Lafayette, Indiana. Fulbright Lecturer, University of Bordeaux, 1963–65. Author of *Those Innocent Years* (on James Whitcomb Riley), 1957, *No Featherbed to Heaven: Michael Wigglesworth*, 1962, and *Carl Sandburg*, 1964. Joint Editor, *Frontiers of American Culture*, 1968. **Essay:** Carl Sandburg.

DACE, Tish.   Associate Professor of Speech, Drama, and English, John Jay College of Criminal Justice, City University of New York. Theatre Critic, *Soho Weekly News*, and contributor to the *Village Voice*, the *New York Times*, and other newspapers. Author of *LeRoi Jones (Imamu Amiri Baraka): A Checklist of Works by and about Him*, 1971, *The Theatre Student: Modern Theatre and Drama*, 1973, and the article on Baraka in *Black American Writers*, 1978. **Essay:** LeRoi Jones.

EISINGER, Chester E.   Professor of English, Purdue University, Lafayette, Indiana. Author of *Fiction of the Forties*, 1963, and of articles in *Proletarian Writers of the Thirties*, 1968, and the *Saturday Review*. Editor of *The 1940's: Profile of a Nation in Crisis*, 1969. **Essay:** Louis Auchincloss.

EVANS, Patrick.   Lecturer in English and American Studies, University of Canterbury, Christchurch, New Zealand. **Essays:** Paul Bowles; Jean Stafford.

FANNING, Charles.   Assistant Professor of English, Bridgewater State College, Massachusetts. Author of *Finley Peter Dunne and Mr. Dooley: The Chicago Years*, 1978, and of articles on Dunne, the Chicago Irish, and Robert Lowell. Editor of *Mr. Dooley and the Chicago Irish: An Anthology*, 1976. **Essays:** George Ade; James T. Farrell.

FARMER, Philip José.   Free-lance writer. Author of more than 20 novels, the most recent being *The Dark Design*, 1977, and of *Tarzan Alive: A Definitive Biography of Lord Greystoke*, 1972. **Essays:** L. Frank Baum; Edgar Rice Burroughs.

FLORA, Joseph M.   Professor of English, University of North Carolina, Chapel Hill. Author of *Vardis Fisher*, 1965, *William Ernest Henley*, 1974, and *Frederick Manfred*, 1974. Editor of *The Cream of the Jest* by James Branch Cabell, 1975, and *A Biographical Guide to Southern Literature* (with R. A. Bain and Louis D. Rubin, Jr.), 1978. **Essays:** James Branch Cabell; Marc Connelly; Vardis Fisher; Zane Grey.

FOSTER, Edward Halsey.   Associate Professor and Director of the American Studies Program, Stevens Institute of Technology, Hoboken, New Jersey. Author of *Catharine Maria Sedgwick*, 1974; *The Civilized Wilderness*, 1975; *Josiah Gregg and Lewis Hector Garrard*, 1977; *Susan and Anna Warner*, 1978; and of articles on American literature and American studies. Editor of *Hoboken: A Collection of Essays* (with Geoffrey W. Clark), 1976. **Essay:** Kurt Vonnegut, Jr.

FRASER, G. S.   Reader in Modern English Literature, University of Leicester. Author of several books of verse, the most recent being *Conditions*, 1969; travel books; critical studies of Yeats, Dylan Thomas, Pound, Durrell and Pope; and of *The Modern Writer and His World*, 1953, *Vision and Rhetoric*, 1959, and *Metre, Rhythm, and Free Verse*, 1970. Editor of works by Keith Douglas and Robert Burns, and of verse anthologies. **Essays:** Carson McCullers; Katherine Anne Porter; Ezra Pound; Mary Roberts Rinehart; George Santayana; Edmund Wilson.

FRENCH, Warren.   Professor of English and Director of the Center for American Studies, Indiana University-Purdue University, Indianapolis; Member of the Editorial Board, *American Literature* and *Twentieth-Century Literature;* series editor for Twayne publishers. Author of *John Steinbeck*, 1961; *Frank Norris*, 1962; *J. D. Salinger*, 1963; *A Companion to "The Grapes of Wrath,"* 1963; *The Social Novel at the End of an Era*, 1967; and a series on American fiction, poetry, and drama, *The Thirties*, 1967, *The Forties*, 1968, *The Fifties*, 1971, and *The Twenties*, 1975. **Essays:** H. P. Lovecraft; J. D. Salinger; John Steinbeck; Thornton Wilder.

GABIN, Jane S.   Teaching Assistant in English, University of North Carolina, Chapel Hill. Author of an article on Dudley Buck; has directed a recital of the music and poetry of Sidney Lanier. **Essay:** John Gould Fletcher.

GIBSON, D. B.   Professor of English, Rutgers University, New Brunswick, New Jersey. Author of *The Fiction of Stephen Crane*, 1968. Editor of *Five Black Writers*, 1970, *Black and White: Stories of American Life*, 1971 and *Modern Black Poets*, 1973. **Essay:** Melvin Tolson.

GITENSTEIN, Barbara.   Assistant Professor of English, Central Missouri State University, Warrensburg. Author of articles on Nathaniel Hawthorne and Isaac Bashevis Singer in *The Comparatist* and *Yiddish*. **Essays:** Saul Bellow; Bernard Malamud; Isaac Bashevis Singer.

GLASRUD, Clarence A.   Professor of English Emeritus, Moorhead State University, Minnesota; Advisory Editor, *Studies in American Fiction;* Member of the Board of Publications, Norwegian-American Historical Association. Author of *Hjalmar Hjorth Boyesen: A Biographical and Critical Study*, 1963. Editor of *The Age of Anxiety*, 1960. **Essays:** Wright Morris; John O'Hara; J. F. Powers; O. E. Rølvaag; Ruth Suckow; Glenway Wescott.

GORDON, Lois.   Professor of English and Comparative Literature, Fairleigh Dickinson University, Teaneck, New Jersey. Author of *Strategems to Uncover Nakedness: The Dramas of Harold Pinter*, 1969, and of articles on Richard Eberhart, Randall Jarrell, Faulkner, T. S. Eliot, and Philip Roth. **Essays:** Richard Eberhart; Randall Jarrell; James Purdy.

HEATH-STUBBS, John.   Writer and Lecturer. Author of several books of verse, the most recent being *The Watchman's Flute*, 1978, a book of plays, and of *The Darkling Plain: A Study of the Later Fortunes of Romanticism*, 1950, *Charles Williams*, 1955, and studies of the verse satire, the ode, and the pastoral. Editor of anthologies and works by Shelley, Tennyson, Swift, and Pope; translator of works by Giacomo Leopardi, Alfred de Vigny, and others. **Essay:** Hart Crane.

HEIM, William J.   Associate Professor and Associate Chairperson of the Department of English, University of South Florida, Tampa; Assistant to the Editor, *Florida English Journal.* Author of "More Gold in Them Hills," in *Freshman English News*, Fall 1973, and "Letters from Young Dreiser," in *American Literary Realism*, 1975. **Essay:** Upton Sinclair.

HEWITT, Geof.   Poet and Editor; Contributing Editor, *New Letters*, Kansas City, Missouri. His most recent book of verse is *Stone Soup*, 1974. Editor of the poems of Alfred Starr Hamilton and of verse anthologies. **Essay:** Muriel Rukeyser.

HICKS, Jack.   Assistant Professor of English, University of California, Davis. Fulbright-Hays Lecturer, University of Paris XII, 1977–78; past editor of *Carolina Quarterly* and *California Quarterly.* Author of *Cutting Edges: Young American Fiction for the 1970's*, 1973. **Essays:** Donald Barthelme; William S. Burroughs; Jack Kerouac; William Styron.

HIGGINS, William.   Member of the Department of English, Western Carolina University, Cullowhee, North Carolina. **Essays:** Winston Churchill; David Graham Phillips.

HOEFER, Jacqueline.   Free-lance Writer. Author of essays on Beckett and other modern writers. **Essay:** Kay Boyle.

HOGAN, Robert.   Free-lance Writer. Former Professor of English, University of Delaware, Newark. Author of *The Experiments of Sean O'Casey*, 1960; *Arthur Miller*, 1964; *The Independence of Elmer Rice*, 1965; *The Plain Style* (with H. Bogart), 1967; *After the Irish Renaissance*, 1967; *Dion Boucicault*, 1969; *The Fan Club*, 1969; *Lost Plays of the Irish Renaissance* (with James Kilroy), 1970; *Eimar O'Duffy*, 1972; *Mervyn Wall*, 1972; *Conor Cruise O'Brien* (with E. Young-Bruehl), 1974; *The Irish Literary Theatre* (vol. 1 of *A History of the Modern Irish Drama*, with James Kilroy), 1975. Editor of several collections of plays and of anthologies of drama criticism. **Essay:** Elmer Rice.

HOKENSON, Jan.   Lecturer in Comparative Literature, University of California, Davis. Author of articles on Beckett, Céline, and Proust, in *James Joyce Quarterly*, *L'Esprit Créateur*, *Far-Western Forum*, and *Samuel Beckett: An Anthology of Criticism*, edited by Ruby Cohn, 1975. **Essays:** Ross Lockridge; Norman Mailer; Willard Motley.

HOLDEN, Jonathan.   Member of the English Department, Stephens College, Columbia, Missouri. Author of *Design for a House* (verse), 1972, and of poetry for *Antioch Review*, *North American Review*, and other periodicals. **Essay:** William Stafford.

INGE, M. Thomas.   Professor and Chairman of the Department of English, Virginia Commonwealth University, Richmond; Founding Editor of *Resources for American Literary Study* and *American Humor.* Author of *Donald Davidson: An Essay and a Bibliography*, 1965, and *Davidson*, 1971 (both with T. D. Young). Editor of works by George Washington Harris and William Faulkner, and of *Agrarianism in American Literature*, 1969; *The Black Experience*, 1969; *Studies in Light in August*, 1971; *Ellen Glasgow: Centennial Essays*, 1975. **Essay:** F. Scott Fitzgerald.

HOLMAN, C. Hugh. Kenan Professor of English, Chairman of the Division of Humanities, and Special Assistant to the Chancellor, University of North Carolina, Chapel Hill; Editor of *Southern Literary Journal*. Author or co-author of several books, including five detective novels; *The Development of American Criticism*, 1955; *The Southerner as American*, 1960; *Thomas Wolfe*, 1960; *Seven Modern American Novelists*, 1964; *The American Novel Through Henry James: A Bibliography*, 1966; *Three Modes of Modern Southern Fiction*, 1966; *Roots of Southern Writing*, 1972; *The Loneliness at the Core*, 1975. Editor of works by Thomas Wolfe, William Gilmore Simms, and others. **Essays:** Ellen Glasgow; Sinclair Lewis; John P. Marquand; Flannery O'Connor; Robert Penn Warren.

JELINEK, Estelle C. Instructor in English, San Francisco State University. Author of "Teaching Women's Autobiographies," in *College English*, September 1976, and "Anaïs Nin: A Critical Evaluation," in *Feminist Criticism: Essays on Theory, Poetry, and Prose* edited by Karen Olson and Cheryl L. Brown, 1978. **Essay:** Anaïs Nin.

JOHNSON, Robert K. Professor of English, Suffolk University, Boston. Author of articles on Richard Wilbur, Wallace Stevens, T. S. Eliot, and William Carlos Williams. **Essays:** Robert Frost; Archibald MacLeish; Howard Nemerov.

JOYNER, Nancy C. Member of the Department of English, Western Carolina University, Cullowhee, North Carolina. **Essays:** Laura Riding; Edwin Arlington Robinson.

KAPLAN, Zoë Coralnik. Adjunct Assistant Professor of Speech and Theatre, John Jay College of Criminal Justice, City University of New York. **Essay:** Rachel Crothers.

KELLNER, Bruce. Associate Professor of English, Millersville State College, Pennsylvania. Author of *Carl Van Vechten and the Irreverent Decades*, 1968; *The Wormwood Poems of Thomas Kinsella*, 1972; *The Poet as Translator*, 1973; *Alfred Kazin's Exquisites: An Excavation*, 1975. Editor of *Selected Writings of Van Vechten about Negro Arts and Letters*, 1978. **Essays:** Hortense Calisher; Joseph Hergesheimer; Carl Van Vechten.

KING, Kimball. Member of the Department of English, University of North Carolina, Chapel Hill. **Essay:** Lillian Hellman.

KINNAMON, Keneth. Professor and Associate Head of the English Department, University of Illinois, Champaign-Urbana. Author of *The Emergence of Richard Wright*, 1972, and of articles on Wright. Editor of *Black Writers on America: A Comprehensive Anthology* (with Richard K. Barksdale), 1972, and of *James Baldwin: A Collection of Critical Essays*, 1974. **Essays:** James Baldwin; Ralph Ellison; Langston Hughes.

KUHN, John G. Professor of English and Director of Theatre, Rosemont College, Pennsylvania. Author of an article in *Walt Whitman Review*, 1962, poems in *Denver Quarterly*, 1973, and a play, *Statu(t)es Like Cartoons*, produced 1976. **Essays:** Eugene O'Neill; Sam Shepard.

KULSHRESTHA, Chirantan. Reader in English, University of Hyderabad, India. Author of *The Saul Bellow Estate*, 1976; *Bellow: The Problem of Affirmation*, 1978; chapters in *Considerations*, edited by Meenakshi Mukherjee, 1977, and *Through the Eyes of the World: International Essays in American Literature*, edited by Bruce A. Lohof, 1978; and articles in *Chicago Review, American Review, Quest, Indian Literature*, and other periodicals. Editor of *Not by Politics Alone!* (with V. V. John), 1978. **Essays:** Michael Gold; DuBose Heyward; Robert E. Sherwood.

LEVERNIER, James A.   Assistant Professor of English, University of Arkansas, Little Rock. Contributor to *ESO: A Journal of the American Renaissance, Research Studies, The Markham Review, Explicator,* and other periodicals. Editor of *An Essay for the Recording of Illustrious Providences* by Increase Mather, 1977, and *The Indians and Their Captives* (with Hennig Cohen), 1977. **Essay:** Kenneth Fearing.

LOHOF, Bruce A.   Associate Professor and Chairman of the Department of History, University of Miami; Joint Editor of the *Indian Journal of American Studies,* and member of the editorial board of *Journal of Popular Culture.* Former Senior Fulbright-Hays Scholar and Director of the American Studies Research Centre, Hyderabad, India. Author of articles for *Social Studies Bulletin, Industrial Archaeology, Centennial Review,* and other periodicals, and of papers for the American Studies Association and the Popular Culture Association. **Essays:** James Agee; Zona Gale; H. L. Mencken.

LONGEST, George C.   Associate Professor and Assistant to the Chairman of the Department of English, Virginia Commonwealth University, Richmond. Author of *Three Virginia Writers: Mary Johnston, Thomas Nelson Page, and Amélie Rives Troubetzkoy,* 1978, and of many articles and reviews. **Essays:** Erskine Caldwell; Truman Capote.

LUCAS, John.   Professor of English and Drama, Loughborough University, Leicestershire; Advisory Editor of *Victorian Studies, Literature and History,* and *Journal of European Studies.* Author of *Tradition and Tolerance in 19th-Century Fiction,* 1966; *The Melancholy Man: A Study of Dickens,* 1970; *Arnold Bennett,* 1975; *Egilssaga: The Poems,* 1975; *The Literature of Change,* 1977; *The 1930's: Challenge to Orthodoxy,* 1978. Editor of *Literature and Politics in the 19th Century,* 1971, and of works by George Crabbe and Jane Austen. **Essays:** Paul Goodman; Kenneth Patchen; Damon Runyon; Louis Simpson.

LUDINGTON, Townsend.   Associate Professor of English, and Director of the Curriculum in Peace, War, and Defense, University of North Carolina, Chapel Hill. Editor of *The Fourteenth Chronicle: Letters and Diaries of John Dos Passos,* 1973. **Essays:** John Dos Passos; Jack London.

MacLAINE, Brent.   Graduate Student in the Department of English, University of British Columbia, Vancouver. **Essay:** Vladimir Nabokov.

MacSHANE, Frank.   Professor and Chairman of the Writing Division, School of the Arts, Columbia University, New York; Co-Editor of *Translation.* Author of *Many Golden Ages,* 1963; *The Life and Work of Ford Madox Ford,* 1965; *The Life of Raymond Chandler,* 1976. Editor of works by Ford Madox Ford and translator of several books by Miguel Serrano and works by Jorge Luis Borges. **Essays:** Raymond Chandler; Edward Dahlberg.

MADDEN, David.   Writer-in-Residence, Louisiana State University, Baton Rouge. Author of novels (the most recent being *Bijou,* 1974), short stories, plays, and critical works, including *Wright Morris,* 1964; *The Poetic Image in Six Genres,* 1969; *James M. Cain,* 1970; *Harlequin's Stick, Charlie's Cane,* 1975. Editor of works by Nathanael West and James Agee, and of several collections and anthologies. **Essay:** James M. Cain.

McNAUGHTON, Howard.   Senior Lecturer in English, University of Canterbury, Christchurch, New Zealand; Theatre Critic, *The Press* since 1968; Advisory Editor, *Act* since 1976. Author of *New Zealand Drama: A Bibliographical Guide,* 1974, and *Bruce Mason,* 1976. Editor of *Contemporary New Zealand Plays,* 1976. **Essay:** Ben Hecht.

MESERVE, Walter J.   Professor of Theatre and Drama, Indiana University, Bloomington. Author of *An Outline of American Drama*, 1965, *Robert Sherwood: Reluctant Moralist*, 1970, and *An Emerging Entertainment: The Drama of the American People to 1828*, 1977. Editor of *The Complete Plays of W. D. Howells*, 1960; *Discussions of Modern American Drama*, 1966; *American Satiric Comedies*, 1969; *Modern Dramas from Communist China*, 1970; *The Rise of Silas Lapham* by W. D. Howells, 1971; *Studies in "Death of a Salesman,"* 1972; *Modern Literature from China*, 1974. **Essays:** Susan Glaspell; Sidney Howard; Percy MacKaye.

MILLER, Jordan Y.   Chairman of the Department of English, University of Rhode Island, Kingston. Exchange Professor, University of East Anglia, Norwich, 1977. Author of *Eugene O'Neill and the American Critic*, 1962; *Maxwell Anderson: Gifted Technician*, 1967; *Eugene O'Neill*, 1968; *The War Play Comes of Age*, 1969; *Expressionism: The Wasteland Enacted*, 1974; *The Other O'Neill*, 1974. Editor of *American Dramatic Literature*, 1961, *Playwright's Progress*, 1965, and *Twentieth-Century Interpretations of "A Streetcar Named Desire,"* 1971. **Essays:** Lorraine Hansberry; William Inge.

MOE, Christian H.   Professor of Theatre, Southern Illinois University, Carbondale; Member of the Advisory Board, Institute of Outdoor Drama; Bibliographer, American Theatre Association. Author of *Creating Historical Drama* (with George McCalmon), 1965, an essay on D. H. Lawrence as playwright, and of several plays for children. **Essay:** Marjorie Kinnan Rawlings.

MOORE, Jack B.   Professor of English, University of South Florida, Tampa. Author of *The Literature of Early America*, 1968; *The Literature of the American Renaissance*, 1969; *Guide to "Idylls of the King,"* 1969; *Maxwell Bodenheim*, 1970; *The Literature of the American Realistic Period*, 1971; *Guide to "Last of the Mohicans,"* 1971. **Essay:** Maxwell Bodenheim; Frank Yerby.

NADEL, I. B.   Associate Professor of English, University of British Columbia, Vancouver. Author of articles on Victorian writing and Jewish fiction in *University of Toronto Quarterly, Criticism, Mosaic, Midstream, Event*, and other periodicals. **Essay:** Henry Roth.

NEVINS, Francis M., Jr.   Assistant Professor of Law, St. Louis University Law School, Missouri. Author of *The Mystery Writer's Art*, 1970, *Royal Bloodline: Ellery Queen, Author and Detective*, 1974, a novel *Publish or Perish*, 1975, and articles in *Detectionary, Journal of Popular Culture, Armchair Detective*, and other collections and periodicals. Editor of *Nightwebs: A Collection of Stories* by Cornell Woolrich, 1974. **Essays:** Erle Stanley Gardner; Ellery Queen.

NORDLAND, Brady.   Free-lance Writer and Researcher. **Essay:** Mary McCarthy.

PEDEN, William.   Professor of English, University of Missouri, Columbia. Author of *Nights in Funland and Other Stories*, 1968; *Twilight at Monticello* (novel), 1973; *The American Short Story: Continuity and Change 1940–1975*, 1975. **Essay:** O. Henry.

PERKINS, Barbara M.   Director of Writing Improvement, Humanities Program, Eastern Michigan University, Ypsilanti. **Essay:** Maxwell Anderson.

PERRY, Margaret.   Assistant Director for Reader Services, University of Rochester Libraries, New York; Contributing Editor, *Afro-American in New York Life and History*. Author of *A Bio-Bibliography of Countée P. Cullen*, 1971, *Silence to the Drums: A Survey of the Literature of the Harlem Renaissance*, 1976, and of several short stories published in periodicals. **Essay:** Countée Cullen.

POPOVICH, Helen Houser.   Associate Dean of the College of Arts and Sciences and Associate Professor of English, University of South Florida, Tampa. Author of articles on Samuel Beckett in *South Atlantic Bulletin 37,* 1972, and composition in *College Composition and Communication 27,* 1976. **Essays:** Arthur Kopit; John van Druten.

QUARTERMAIN, Peter.   Associate Professor of English, University of British Columbia, Vancouver. Author of "Louis Zukofsky: Re Location" in *Open Letter,* 1973; and "Romantic Offensive: *Tish*" in *Canadian Literature,* 1977. **Essays:** Robert Duncan; Allen Ginsberg; Gertrude Stein; Louis Zukofsky.

RAY, David.   Professor of English, University of Missouri, Kansas City; Editor of *New Letters,* Kansas City. His most recent book of verse is *Gathering Firewood: New Poems and Selected,* 1974. Editor of *The Chicago Review Anthology,* 1959, *Richard Wright: Impressions and Perspectives* (with Robert M. Farnsworth), and of verse anthologies. **Essay:** Horace Gregory.

REILLY, John M.   Associate Professor of English, State University of New York, Albany; Advisory Editor, *Obsidian: Black Literature in Review,* and *Melus.* Author of the bibliographical essay on Richard Wright in *Black American Writers* and of articles on Wright and other Afro-American writers, and on detective fiction, in *Colorado Quarterly, Phylon, CLA Journal, Journal of Black Studies, Armchair Detective, Journal of Popular Culture,* and other periodicals. Editor of *Twentieth-Century Interpretations of "Invisible Man,"* 1970, *Richard Wright: The Critical Reception,* 1978, and of the reference book *Detective and Crime Writers,* 1980. **Essays:** W. E. B. Du Bois; Dashiell Hammett; Zora Neale Hurston; Rex Stout; Jean Toomer; Richard Wright.

RICHARDS, Robert F.   Associate Professor of English, University of Denver, Colorado. Author of articles on Ralph Hodgson and Thomas Hornsby Ferril, and the introduction to *Words for Denver and Other Poems* by Ferril, 1966. Editor of *Concise Dictionary of American Literature,* 1969. **Essays:** Waldo Frank; Oliver La Farge; Don Marquis.

ROVIT, Earl.   Professor of English, City College of New York. Author of *Herald to Chaos: The Novels of Elizabeth Madox Roberts,* 1960; *Ernest Hemingway,* 1963; *The Player King,* 1965; *Saul Bellow,* 1967; *A Far Cry,* 1967; *Crossings,* 1973. **Essays:** John Barth; Theodore Dreiser; John Hawkes; O. Henry; James Jones; Elizabeth Madox Roberts; Nathanael West.

RUIHLEY, Glenn Richard.   Member of the Department of English, Eastern Michigan University, Ypsilanti. Author of *The Thorn of a Rose: Amy Lowell Reconsidered,* 1975. Editor of *A Shard of Silence: Selected Poems* by Lowell, 1957. **Essays:** Amy Lowell; Edgar Lee Masters; Edna St. Vincent Millay.

SAFFIOTI, Carol Lee.   Assistant Professor of English, University of Wisconsin-Parkside, Kenosha. **Essay:** Sterling Brown.

SANDERSON, Stewart F.   Director of the Institute of Dialect and Folk Life Studies, University of Leeds. Author of *Hemingway,* 1961 (revised, 1970), and of many articles on British and comparative folklore and ethnology, and on modern literature. Editor of *The Secret Common-Wealth* by Robert Kirk, 1970, and *The Linguistic Atlas of England* (with others), 1978. **Essay:** Ernest Hemingway.

SAUL, George Brandon.   Professor Emeritus of English, University of Connecticut, Storrs; Contributing Editor, *Journal of Irish Literature.* Author of fiction (*The Wild Queen,* 1967), verse (*Hound and Unicorn,* 1969, and *Adam Unregenerate,* 1977), and of critical works, including *Prolegomena to the Study of Yeats's Poems* (1957) and *Plays* (1958), *Traditional Irish Literature and Its Backgrounds,* 1970, and *In Praise of the Half-Forgotten: Essays,* 1976. Also a composer. **Essay:** Sara Teasdale.

SCHWAB, Arnold T.   Professor of English, California State University, Long Beach. Author of *James Gibbons Huneker: Critic of the Seven Arts,* 1963, *The Sound of Huneker* (forthcoming), and articles on Huneker, George Moore, and Joseph Conrad, in *American Literature, Nineteenth-Century Fiction,* and *Modern Philology.* **Essay:** James Huneker.

SEELYE, Catherine.   Free-lance writer. **Essay:** Vachel Lindsay.

SHARMA, J. N.   Academic Associate, American Studies Research Centre, Hyderabad. **Essay:** William Saroyan.

SHUCARD, Alan R.   Associate Professor of English, University of Wisconsin-Parkside, Kenosha. Author of two books of verse – *The Gorgon Bog,* 1970, and *The Louse on the Head of the Lord,* 1972. **Essays:** Gwendolyn Brooks; Walter Van Tilburg Clark; Robert Hayden.

SINGH, Amritjit.   Academic Associate, American Studies Research Centre, Hyderabad, India; Joint Editor of *The Indian Journal of American Studies.* Author of *The Novels of the Harlem Renaissance: Twelve Black Writers,* 1976, and of articles for Indian and American periodicals. Co-Editor of the bibliographies *Indian Literature in English,* 1977, and *Afro-American Poetry and Drama,* 1977. **Essay:** Claude McKay.

SMITH, Esther Marian Greenwell.   Professor of Language Arts, Polk Community College, Winter Haven, Florida. Author of *William Godwin* (with Elton E. Smith), 1965, articles on Melville and Hawthorne, and youth fiction for religious publishers. **Essay:** Pearl S. Buck.

SMITH, Stan.   Lecturer in English, University of Dundee, Scotland. Author of the forthcoming book *A Superfluous Man* (on Edward Thomas), and of articles on modern literature for *Critical Quarterly, Literature and History, Irish University Review, Scottish International Review,* and other periodicals. **Essays:** Sylvia Plath; Theodore Roethke; Philip Roth.

STANFORD, Donald E.   Professor of English, Louisiana State University, Baton Rouge; Editor of *The Southern Review.* Author of *New England Earth,* 1941; and *The Traveler,* 1955. Editor of *The Poems of Edward Taylor,* 1960; *Nine Essays in Modern Literature,* 1965; *Selected Poems of Robert Bridges,* 1974; *Selected Poems of S. Foster Damon,* 1974. **Essay:** Yvor Winters.

STEDMAN, Jane W.   Professor of English, Roosevelt University, Chicago. Author of *Gilbert Before Sullivan,* 1967, and of articles on Gilbert, Dickens, and the Brontës. Regular contributor to *Opera News.* **Essay:** David Belasco.

STOUCK, David.   Associate Professor of English, Simon Fraser University, Burnaby, British Columbia. Author of *Willa Cather's Imagination,* 1975, and of articles in *American Literary Scholarship.* **Essay:** Sherwood Anderson.

STUCKEY, W. J.   Associate Professor of English, Purdue University, Lafayette, Indiana; Founding Editor, *Minnesota Review;* Fiction Editor for *Quartet,* and Reader for *Modern Fiction Studies. Author of Pulitzer Prize Novels,* 1966, and *Caroline Gordon,* 1972. **Essays:** Edna Ferber; Caroline Gordon; Margaret Mitchell; Walker Percy; T. S. Stribling; Edith Wharton.

SUMMERS, Joseph H.   Professor of English, University of Rochester, New York. Author of *George Herbert: Religion and Art,* 1954, *The Muse's Method: An Introduction to Paradise Lost,* 1962, and *The Heirs of Donne and Jonson,* 1970. Editor of *Selected Poems* by Andrew Marvell, 1961, *The Lyric and Dramatic Milton,* 1965, and *Selected Poetry* by George Herbert, 1967. **Essays:** Elizabeth Bishop; Richard Wilbur.

TANSELLE, G. T. Professor of English, University of Wisconsin, Madison; Bibliographical Editor of *The Writings of Herman Melville* since 1968 (6 vols. so far published). Author of *Royall Tyler*, 1967; *Guide to the Study of United States Imprints*, 2 vols., 1971; *The Editing of Historical Documents*, 1978; and two series of articles on descriptive bibliography and scholarly editing in *Studies in Bibliography, The Library, Papers of the Bibliographical Society of America*, and *Book Collector*. **Essay:** Floyd Dell.

TRAVERSI, Derek A. Professor of English Literature, Swarthmore College, Pennsylvania. Author of *An Approach to Shakespeare*, 1938 (revised, 1968); *Shakespeare: The Last Phase*, 1954; *Shakespeare: From Richard II to Henry V*, 1957; *Shakespeare: The Roman Plays*, 1963; *T. S. Eliot: The Longer Poems*, 1976. **Essay:** T. S. Eliot.

TURNER, Richard C. Assistant Professor of English, Indiana University-Purdue University, Indianapolis. **Essay:** Adrienne Rich.

WAGNER, Linda W. Professor of English, Michigan State University, East Lansing. Author of *The Poems* (1964) and *Prose* (1970) *of William Carlos Williams; Denise Levertov*, 1967; *Hemingway and Faulkner: Inventors, Masters*, 1975; *Introducing Poems*, 1976; *John Dos Passos*, 1978. **Essays:** Anne Sexton; William Carlos Williams.

WALLACH, Mark I. Associate Attorney, Baker, Hostetler and Patterson, Cleveland, Ohio. Author of *Christopher Morley*, 1976, and of articles on Morley in *Markham Review*, February 1972, and cable television in *Case Western Reserve Law Review*, Winter 1975. **Essay:** Christopher Morley.

WALSER, Richard. Professor Emeritus of English, North Carolina State University, Raleigh. Author of *North Carolina Drama*, 1956; *Thomas Wolfe: An Introduction and Interpretation*, 1961; *Literary North Carolina*, 1970; *Thomas Wolfe, Undergraduate*, 1977. **Essays:** James Boyd: Paul Green; Thomas Wolfe.

WARNER, Val. Free-lance Writer. Author of *Under the Penthouse* (verse), 1973. Editor of *Centenary Corbière*, 1974. **Essay:** Shirley Jackson.

WATTS, Harold H. Professor of English, Purdue University, Lafayette, Indiana. Author of *The Modern Reader's Guide to the Bible*, 1949; *Ezra Pound and the Cantos*, 1951; *Hound and Quarry*, 1953; *The Modern Reader's Guide to Religions*, 1964; *Aldous Huxley*, 1969. **Essays:** John Cheever; James Gould Cozzens; Hilda Doolittle; William Gaddis; Jerzy Kosinski: Thomas Pynchon; Wallace Stevens; John Updike; Eudora Welty.

WEALES, Gerald. Professor of English, University of Pennsylvania, Philadelphia; Drama Critic for *The Reporter* and *Commonweal*. Author of *Religion in Modern English Drama*, 1961; *American Drama Since World War II*, 1962; *A Play and Its Parts*, 1964; *The Jumping-Off Place: American Drama in the 1960's*, 1969; *Clifford Odets*, 1971. Editor of *The Complete Plays of William Wycherley*, 1966, and, with Robert J. Nelson, of the collections *Enclosure*, 1975, and *Revolution*, 1975. **Essays:** Philip Barry; Robert Benchley; Arthur Miller; Clifford Odets; James Thurber; E. B. White; Tennessee Williams.

WEIR, Sybil B. Professor of English and American Studies, San Jose State University, California. Author of articles on Theodore Dreiser, Gertrude Atherton, Constance Fenimore Woolson, and Elizabeth Drew Stoddard. **Essay:** Gertrude Atherton.

WINNIFRITH, T. J. Member of the Department of English, University of Warwick, Coventry. Author of *The Brontës and Their Background: Romance and Reality*, 1973. **Essay:** Lionel Trilling.

WOODRESS, James. Professor of English, University of California, Davis; Editor of *American Literary Scholarship*. Author of *Howells and Italy, 1952; Booth Tarkington, 1955; A Yankee's Odyssey: The Life of Joel Barlow, 1958; Willa Cather: Her Life and Art, 1970; American Fiction 1900–1950, 1974*. Editor of *Voices from America's Past* (with Richard Morris), 1961, and *Eight American Authors*, 1971. **Essays:** Willa Cather; Kenneth Roberts; Karl Shapiro; Booth Tarkington.

YOUNG, Kenneth. Literary and Political Adviser, Beaverbrook Newspapers. Author of *John Dryden, 1954; A. J. Balfour, 1963; Churchill and Beaverbrook, 1966; The Greek Passion, 1969; Stanley Baldwin, 1976*; and other biographies and works on political and social history. Editor of the diaries of Sir R. Bruce Lochart. **Essay:** Henry Miller.

YOUNG, T. D. Gertrude Conaway Vanderbilt Professor of English, Vanderbilt University, Nashville. Author of *Jack London and the Era of Social Protest, 1950; The Literature of the South, 1952* (revised, 1968); *Donald Davidson: An Essay and a Bibliography* (with M. Thomas Inge), 1965; *American Literature: A Critical Survey, 1968; John Crowe Ransom: Critical Essays and a Bibliography, 1968; Ransom, 1970; Davidson* (with Inge), 1971. Editor of *The Literary Correspondence of Davidson and Tate* (with John T. Fain), 1974. **Essays:** Donald Davidson; John Crowe Ransom.